Public Choice III

This book represents a considerable revision and expansion of *Public Choice II* (1989). Six new chapters have been added, and several chapters from the previous edition have been extensively revised. The discussion of empirical work in public choice has been greatly expanded. As in the previous editions, all the major topics of public choice are covered. These include why the state exists, voting rules, federalism, the theory of clubs, two-party and multiparty electoral systems, rent seeking, bureaucracy, interest groups, dictatorship, the size of government, voter participation, and political business cycles. Normative issues in public choice are also examined, including a normative analysis of the simple majority rule, Bergson–Samuelson social welfare functions, the Arrow and Sen impossibility theorems, Rawls's social contract theory, and the constitutional political economy of Buchanan and Tullock.

Dennis C. Mueller is Professor of Economics at the University of Vienna. He previously taught for many years at the University of Maryland. Professor Mueller is the author of *Public Choice II, Profits in the Long Run, Constitutional Democracy*, and four other books, in addition to numerous articles in leading refereed journals. He is also the editor of the two-volume *The Economics of Politics* (2001), *Perspectives on Public Choice* (Cambridge University Press, 1997), and *The Dynamics of Company Profits* (Cambridge University Press, 1990), as well as six other titles. Professor Mueller is a past president of the Public Choice Society, the Southern Economic Association, the Industrial Organization Society, and EARIE. His main research interests continue to be in public choice and industrial economics.

Public Choice III

DENNIS C. MUELLER
University of Vienna

PUBLISHED BY THE PRESS SYNDICATE OF THE UNIVERSITY OF CAMBRIDGE
The Pitt Building, Trumpington Street, Cambridge, United Kingdom

CAMBRIDGE UNIVERSITY PRESS
The Edinburgh Building, Cambridge CB2 2RU, UK
40 West 20th Street, New York, NY 10011-4211, USA
477 Williamstown Road, Port Melbourne, VIC 3207, Australia
Ruiz de Alarcón 13, 28014 Madrid, Spain
Dock House, The Waterfront, Cape Town 8001, South Africa

http://www.cambridge.org

First published 2003

Printed in the United States of America

Typeface Times New Roman PS 11/13 pt.   *System* LaTeX 2_ε [TB]

A catalog record for this book is available from the British Library.

Library of Congress Cataloging in Publication Data
Public choice III / Dennis C. Mueller.
    p.   cm.
    Includes bibliographical references and index.
    ISBN 0-521-81546-0 – ISBN 0-521-89475-1 (pbk.)
    1. Elections.   2. Democracy.   3. Social choice.   4. Welfare economics.
5. State, The.
    JF1001 .M78   2002
    320 – dc21   2002022287

ISBN 0 521 81546 0 hardback
ISBN 0 521 89475 1 paperback

To Adrienne, Holly, Jacob, and Laurence

Contents

Contents xiii

Contents

Preface

This book is a revision of *Public Choice II*. In revising the book, I have largely retained the structure of *Public Choice II* – most of the material contained in that volume reappears in this one. In some cases, this has resulted in very modest changes in a chapter and in quite substantial changes in others. Several new chapters have been written to cover topics that have cropped up or increased in importance since the previous edition was written. I have also attempted to retain the same level of difficulty as the previous version. Because the literature has become continuously more theoretical and mathematical, more mathematics appears in the new material than in the previous text, and the distinction between "easy" and "difficult" sections denoted by a * has become more arbitrary. Some may question my decision not to drop more material from the previous text, where little new work has appeared, to leave more space for new material. I have chosen not to go this route because I still think of the book as a survey of *all* of the major topics in public choice. That little new has appeared concerning Arrow impossibility theorems in recent years does not imply that the issues raised by this work are any less important, or that they should be omitted in a basic course in public choice – or so I believe.

Public Choice III represents a substantial expansion of its predecessor, just as *Public Choice II* was a substantial expansion of its forerunner. Nevertheless, the fraction of the literature covered adequately by *Public Choice III* is far smaller than that of the earlier versions of the text. I fear that many readers will feel that I have done an inadequate job of covering this or that topic, or that I have unfairly neglected some important contributions. I apologize for such omissions. To keep the book within reasonable bounds, I have had to shortchange some questions and authors.

Those familiar with *Public Choice II* may find the following summary of changes helpful.

Chapter in PC III	Relationship to PC II
1	Modest revision of Ch. 1
2	Revised version of Ch. 2
3	Substantial revision of Chs. 3 and 23
4	Revised version of Ch. 4
5	Revised version of Ch. 5
6	Modest revision of Ch. 6
7	Modest revision of Ch. 7
8	Modest revision of Ch. 8
9	Modest revision of Ch. 9
10	New chapter
11	Revised version of Ch. 10
12	Revised version of Ch. 11
13	Substantial revision of Ch. 12
14	Revised version of Ch. 18
15	Substantial revision of Ch. 13
16	Revised version of Ch. 14
17	New chapter
18	New chapter
19	Substantial revision of Ch. 15
20	Substantial revision of Ch. 16 with additional material from Ch. 11
21	Revised version of Ch. 17
22	New chapter
23	Modest revision of Ch. 19
24	Modest revision of Ch. 20
25	Revised version of Ch. 21
26	Substantial revision of Ch. 22, almost a new chapter
27	New chapter that expands the material from Sec. C of old Ch. 20
28	New chapter
29	Modest revision of Ch. 24

I would like to thank several authors and publishers who have been kind enough to allow me to reproduce a figure or table from one of their publications.

1. Material from tables 1 and 3 in Avinash Dixit and Mancur Olson. 2000. "Does Voluntary Participation Undermine the Coase Theorem?" *Journal of Public Economics,* 76 (June): 309–35. Elsevier Science.
2. Material from tables 1 and 3 in Åsa Hansson and Charles Stuart. Forthcoming. "Peaking of Fiscal Sizes of Government," *European Journal of Political Economy*. Elsevier Science.
3. Figures 5.7b, 5.13, and 5.20b from Richard D. McKelvey and Peter C. Ordeshook. 1987. "A Decade of Experimental Research of Spatial Models of Elections and Committees," in J. M. Enelow and M. J. Hinich, eds. *Advances in the Spatial Theory of Voting*. Cambridge: Cambridge University Press, pp. 99–144.
4. Material from table in Norman Schofield. 1993. "Political Competition in Multiparty Coalition Governments," *European Journal of Political Research,* 23: 1–3. Kluwer Academic Publishers.

5. Material from table on page 91 of Ulrich Koester and Stefan Tangermann. 1990. "The European Community," in F. H. Sanderson, ed. *Agricultural Protection in the Industrial World.* Washington, D.C.: Resources for the Future, pp. 64–111.

6. Material from tables 10.1 and 10.3 in Dennis C. Mueller. 1996. *Constitutional Democracy.* Oxford: Oxford University Press.

7. Substantial portions of Dennis C. Mueller. 2001. "The Importance of Uncertainty in a Two-Stage Theory of Constitutions," *Public Choice,* 108, (Sept.): 223–58. Kluwer Academic Publishers.

8. Material from table 3.3.2 in Friedrich Schneider and Dominik H. Enste. 1998. "Increasing Shadow Economies All over the World – Fiction or Reality?" Mimeo. University of Linz.

9. Figure 6.1 in Michael Laver and Kenneth Shepsle. 1996. *Making and Breaking Governments.* Cambridge: Cambridge University Press.

10. Material from table 15.13 in Wolfgang C. Müller and Kaare Strøm, eds. 2000. *Coalition Governments in Western Europe.* Oxford: Oxford University Press.

11. Material from table C of the appendix to Gary W. Cox. 1997. *Making Votes Count.* Cambridge: Cambridge University Press.

12. Material from figure 4.1 in Alberto Alesina and Howard Rosenthal. 1995. *Partisan Politics, Divided Government, and the Economy.* Cambridge: Cambridge University Press.

Several colleagues were kind enough to read portions of the text and offer comments or point out mistakes in *Public Choice II*, and I would like to thank them for their kind help: Bernard Grofman, Douglas Hibbs, Arye Hillman, Wolfgang Müller, Shmuel Nitzan, Hans Pitlik, Thomas Stratmann, Rein Taagepera, and Ronald Wintrobe. Special mention must be made of the conscientious efforts of a student at the University of Vienna, Daniel T. Dickler, who scrutinized every line of *Public Choice II* and made numerous suggestions for improvement.

Putting together a manuscript of this size and scope involves a tremendous amount of effort to keep track of references, draw figures, construct and check tables, and the like. I have been extremely fortunate both at the University of Maryland and now here in Vienna to have been able to work with two excellent secretaries. My heartfelt thanks goes to Heide Wurm for all that she has done to help bring this book to fruition.

Dennis C. Mueller
Vienna, February 2002

CHAPTER 1

Introduction

Man is by nature a political animal.

Aristotle

This division of labour ... is the necessary, though very slow and gradual, consequence of a certain propensity in human nature which has in view no such extensive
utility; the propensity to truck, barter, and exchange one thing for another.

Whether this propensity be one of those original principles in human nature ...
or whether, as seems more probable, it be the necessary consequence of the faculties
of reason and speech, it belongs not to our present subject to enquire. It is common
to all men and to be found in no other race of animals, which seem to know neither
this nor any other species of contracts.

Adam Smith

Aristotle, observing the Greeks in the fourth century B.C., thought that man's natural
proclivities were toward discourse and political activity. Adam Smith, observing the
Scots in the eighteenth century A.D., saw instead a propensity to engage in economic
exchange. From the observations of these two intellectual giants, two separate fields
in the social sciences have developed: the science of politics and the science of
economics.

Traditionally, these two fields have been separated by the types of questions they
ask, the assumptions they make about individual motivation, and the methodologies they employ. Political science has studied man's behavior in the public arena;
economics has studied man in the marketplace. Political science has often assumed
that political man pursues the public interest. Economics has assumed that all men
pursue their private interests, and has modeled this behavior with a logic unique
among the social sciences.

But is this dichotomy valid? Could both Aristotle and Smith have been right?
Could political man and economic man be one and the same? In the field of public
choice, it is assumed that they are.

Public choice can be defined as the economic study of nonmarket decision making, or simply the application of economics to political science. The subject matter
of public choice is the same as that of political science: the theory of the state,
voting rules, voter behavior, party politics, the bureaucracy, and so on. The methodology of public choice is that of economics, however. The basic behavioral postulate of public choice, as for economics, is that man is an egoistic, rational, utility

1

maximizer.[1] This places public choice within the stream of political philosophy extending at least from Thomas Hobbes and Benedict Spinoza, and within political science from James Madison and Alexis de Tocqueville. Although there is much that is useful and important in these earlier contributions, and much that anticipates later developments, no effort is made here to relate these earlier works to the modern public choice literature, for they are separated from the modern literature by a second salient characteristic. The modern public choice literature employs the analytic tools of economics. To try to review the older literature using the analytic tools of its descendants would take us too far afield.[2]

Public choice has developed as a separate field largely since 1948. During the thirties, disenchantment with market processes was widespread, and models of "market socialism" depicting how governments could supplant the price system and allocate goods as efficiently as markets do, if not more so, came into vogue. Abram Bergson's (1938) seminal analysis of social welfare functions (SWFs) appeared to indicate how the economist's individualistic, utilitarian ethics could be incorporated into the government planner's objective function and help him to achieve a social welfare maximum as he managed the state.

Arrow's 1951 book was a direct follow-up to both Bergson's (1938) article and Paul Samuelson's parallel discussion of SWFs in *Foundations of Economic Analysis* (1947, ch. 8). Arrow's concern was to characterize the process, whether market or political, through which the SWF Bergson and Samuelson had described was achieved (rev. ed. 1963, pp. 1–6). Since Arrow's book, a large literature has grown up exploring the properties of social welfare or social choice functions.[3] It focuses on the problems of aggregating individual preferences to *maximize* an SWF, or to satisfy some set of normative criteria, that is, on the problem of which social state *ought* to be chosen, given the preferences of the individual voters. This research on optimal methods of aggregation naturally has spurred interest in the properties of *actual* procedures for aggregating preferences via voting rules, that is, on the question of which outcome will be chosen for a given set of preferences under different voting rules. The problem of finding a social choice function that satisfies certain

---

[1] For a detailed justification of this postulate in the study of voting, see Downs (1957, pp. 3–20), Buchanan and Tullock (1962, pp. 17–39), and Riker and Ordeshook (1973, pp. 8–37). Schumpeter's (1950) early use of the postulate also should be mentioned. One of the curiosities of the public choice literature is the slight *direct* influence that Schumpeter's work appears to have had. Downs claims that "Schumpeter's profound analysis of democracy forms the inspiration and foundation for our whole thesis" (1957, p. 27, n. 11), but cites only one page of the book (twice), and this in support of the "economic man" assumption. Most other work in the field makes no reference to Schumpeter at all.

  Tullock has made, in correspondence, the following observation on Schumpeter's influence on his work: "In my case, he undeniably had immense impact on me, although it was rather delayed. Further, although I read the book originally in 1942, I didn't reexamine it when I wrote *The Politics of Bureaucracy* (1965). In a sense, it gave me a general idea of the type of thing that we could expect in government, but there weren't any detailed things that could be specifically cited." I suspect that Schumpeter's work has had a similar impact on others working in the public choice field.

  For an interesting discussion of the public choice content of Schumpeter's work, see Mitchell (1984a,b).

[2] See, however, Black (1958, pp. 156–213), Buchanan and Tullock (1962, pp. 307–22), Haefele (1971), Ostrom (1971), Hardin (1997), Mueller (1997b), and Young (1997).

[3] For surveys, see Sen (1970a, 1977a,b), Fishburn (1973), Plott (1976), Kelly (1978), Riker (1982b), and Pattanaik (1997).

normative criteria turns out to be quite analogous to establishing an equilibrium under different voting rules. Thus, both Arrow's study (1963) of SWFs and Black's (1948a,b) seminal work on committee voting procedures build on the works of de Borda (1781), de Condorcet (1785), and C.L. Dodgson (Lewis Carroll) (1876). We discuss the most directly relevant topics of the SWF literature as part of normative public choice in Part V.

Part I also contains a normative analysis of collective action. The models of market socialism developed in the thirties and forties envisioned the state as largely an allocator of private goods. State intervention was needed to avoid the inefficient shortfalls in private investment, which Keynesian economics claimed were the cause of unemployment, and to avoid the distributional inequities created by the market. The immediate prosperity of the post–World War II years reduced the concern about unemployment and distributional issues. But concern about the efficiency of the market remained high among academic economists. The seminal works of the forties and fifties gave rise to a large literature on the conditions for efficient allocation in the presence of public goods, externalities, and economies of scale. When these conditions were unmet, the market failed to achieve a Pareto-optimal allocation of goods and resources. The existence of these forms of market failures provides a natural explanation for why government ought to exist, and thus for a theory of the origins of the state. It forms the starting point of our analysis of the state and is reviewed in Chapter 2. Chapter 3 takes up models of collective action that see redistribution as its main objective. Together these two activities – improving allocative efficiency and redistribution – constitute the only possible *normative* justifications for collective action.

If the state exists in part as a sort of analogue to the market to provide public goods and eliminate externalities, then it must accomplish the same preference revelation task for these public goods as the market achieves for private goods. The public choice approach to nonmarket decision making has been (1) to make the same behavioral assumptions as general economics (rational, utilitarian individuals), (2) often to depict the preference revelation process as analogous to the market (voters engage in exchange, individuals reveal their demand schedules via voting, citizens exit and enter clubs), and (3) to ask the same questions as traditional price theory (Do equilibria exist? Are they stable? Pareto efficient? How are they obtained?).

One part of the public choice literature studies nonmarket decision making, voting, as if it took place in a direct democracy. The government is treated as a black box or voting rule into which individual preferences (votes) are placed and out of which collective choices emerge. This segment of the literature is reviewed in Part II. Chapter 4 examines criteria for choosing a voting rule when the collective choice is restricted to a potential improvement in allocative efficiency. Chapters 5 and 6 explore the properties of the most popular voting rule, the simple majority rule. Chapters 7 and 8 present a variety of alternatives to the majority rule – some equally simple, others more complex. Part II closes with a discussion of how individuals can reveal their preferences for public goods not through the voice mechanism of voting, but by choosing to join different polities or public good clubs (Chapter 9).

Just as Arrow's book was stimulated in part by Bergson's essay, Downs's 1957 classic was obviously stimulated by the works of both Bergson and Arrow (pp. 17–19). To some extent, Downs sought to fill the void Arrow's impossibility theorem had left by demonstrating that competition among parties to win votes could have the same desirable effects on the outcomes of the political process as competition among firms for customers has on the outcomes of the market process. Of all the works in public choice, Downs's book has had perhaps the greatest influence on political scientists.

In the Downsian model, the government appears not merely as a voting rule or black box into which information on voter preferences is fed, but as an institution made up of real people – representatives, bureaucrats, as well as voters – each with their own set of objectives and constraints. The Downsian perspective on government underlies Parts III and IV of this book. Part III begins with a discussion of the implications of having multiple levels of government as in a federalist system. Chapters 11 and 12 examine the properties of two-party representative democracies. Although Chapter 11 reveals that Downs's original formulation of a model of two-party competition did not succeed in resolving the "Arrow paradox" of aggregating individual preferences to maximize an SWF, Chapter 12 discusses more recent models of two-party competition that do appear to achieve this goal.

All of the "founding fathers" of the public choice field were either American or British. Not surprisingly, therefore, most of the early literature in the field focused on two-party systems. In the last two decades, however, the study of multiparty systems by public choice analysts has expanded greatly. This work is reviewed in Chapter 13.

Although Downs's goal was to resolve the Arrow paradox, ironically one of the most important contributions of his book was to put forward a paradox of its own – namely, the paradox of why rational, self-interested people bother to vote at all. Downs's original model of the rational voter and the many extensions and modifications to it that have been made form the subject matter of Chapter 14.

The redistributive potential of representative government – which is generally treated under the heading of "rent seeking" – is the subject matter of Chapter 15. Part III closes with three chapters that review several theories of the state in which the state itself – in the form of the bureaucracy, the legislature, or an autocratic leadership – dictates outcomes with the citizenry relegated to playing a more passive role.

In arguing that government intervention is needed to correct the failures of the market when public goods, externalities, and other sorts of impure private goods are present, the economics literature has often made the implicit assumptions that these failures could be corrected at zero cost. The government is seen as an omniscient and benevolent institution dictating taxes, subsidies, and quantities so as to achieve a Pareto-optimal allocation of resources. In the sixties, a large segment of the public choice literature began to challenge this "nirvana model" of government. This literature examines not how governments may or ought to behave, but how they do behave. It reveals that governments, too, can fail in certain ways. This largely empirical literature on how governments do perform is reviewed in Chapters 19 through 22.

One of the major justifications for an increasing role for government in the economy during the first couple of decades following World War II was the Keynesian prescription that government policies are required to stabilize and improve the macroeconomic performance of a country. The evidence that governments' macroeconomic policies are affected by their efforts to win votes is examined in Chapter 19, which also looks at the impact of electoral politics on macroeconomic performance.

One of the early classics in the public choice literature is Olson's (1965) *The Logic of Collective Action*. In this book Olson applied public choice reasoning to the analysis of various collective action problems involving interest groups. Interest groups have been a focal point within the public choice literature ever since. Although their activities are discussed at several junctures in the book, Chapter 20 is devoted exclusively to the literature that models and measures the impact of interest groups on political outcomes.

One of the most remarkable developments over the half century following World War II has been the growth in size of governments around the world. Is this growth a response to the demands of citizens for greater government services because of rising incomes, changes in the relative price of government services, or a change in "tastes"? Does it reflect the successful efforts of some groups to redistribute wealth from others by means of the government? Or is it an unwanted burden placed on the backs of citizens by a powerful government bureaucracy? These and other explanations for the growth of government are discussed in Chapter 21.

Where Chapter 21 treats the size of government as the dependent variable in political/economic models of the state, Chapter 22 treats it as an explanatory variable. It reviews the literature that has tried to measure the impact of the growth of the government sector in the industrial democracies of the world on various measures of economic performance, like the growth of income per capita and the distribution of income in each country.

The Bergson-Samuelson SWF, which helped spark interest in preference aggregation procedures, is discussed along with other derivations of an SWF in Chapter 23. The Arrowian SWF literature is reviewed in Chapter 24. Although both of these approaches build their aggregate welfare indexes on individual preferences, both tend to shift attention from the preferences of the individual to the aggregate. Moreover, in both cases, the aggregate (society) is expected to behave like a rational individual, in the one case by maximizing an objective function, and in the other by ordering social outcomes as a rational individual would do. Therefore, the SWF literature bears more than a passing resemblance to organic views of the state in which the state has a persona of its own.

Buchanan's first article (1949) appearing before Arrow's essay was an attack upon this organic view of the state; Buchanan (1954a) renewed this attack following the publication of Arrow's book. In place of the analogy between the state and a person, Buchanan offered the analogy between the state and a market. He suggested that one think of the state as an institution through which individuals interact for their mutual benefit – that one think of government, as Wicksell (1896) did, as a quid pro quo process of exchange among citizens (Buchanan, 1986, pp. 19–27). The view of government as an institution for reaching agreements that benefit all citizens leads naturally to the perspective that the agreements are *contracts* binding all individuals. The contractarian approach to public choice is developed in Buchanan and Tullock's *The Calculus of Consent* (1962) and Buchanan's *The Limits of Liberty* (1975a). The approach taken in the former work also has a strong affinity to Rawls's (1971) influential contribution to the contractarian theory. Chapter 25 takes up Rawls's theory, while Chapter 26 reviews and integrates the models of collective choice which – following Buchanan and Tullock – have viewed politics as a two-stage process in which the "rules of the political game" are written in the first stage and the game is played in the second stage.

One indication of the significance of public/social choice's intellectual impact is the fact that three of the major figures in this field have been awarded Nobel prizes – Kenneth Arrow, James Buchanan, and Amartya Sen.[4] Although Sen's contributions to social choice go far beyond the topic of "the liberal paradox," this contribution of his has stimulated such a vast amount of work that it warrants separate treatment, which it gets in Chapter 27.

Although most of this book focuses on the accomplishments of public choice in extending our positive and normative understanding of politics, some criticisms that have been leveled against the public choice approach to politics are taken up in Chapter 28. A reader who is skeptical about whether rational actor models can offer anything to the study of politics might wish to glance ahead at Chapter 28 before plunging into the next 26 chapters. But I do not think that the reader can obtain a full appreciation for the advantages – and limitations – of the public choice approach without submerging him- or herself into its subject matter.[5] Thus, my recommendation is to save Chapter 28 and the critiques of public choice until after the reader has absorbed its lessons.

One of Wicksell's important insights concerning collective action was that a fundamental distinction exists between allocative efficiency and redistribution and that these two issues must be treated separately, with separate voting rules.[6] This insight reappears in Buchanan's work in which the constitutional and legislative or parliamentary stages of government are separated, and in Musgrave's *The Theory of Public Finance* (1959) in which the work of government is divided into allocative and redistributive branches. The distinction is also featured in this book and constitutes the theme of its closing chapter.

---

[4] One might arguably claim that *four* economists working in the field have won Nobel prizes, since William Vickrey's prize was awarded for his research on incentive systems, which anticipated the development of the family of "demand-revealing" voting mechanisms reviewed in Chapter 8.

[5] Rather than continually write "his or her," I shall sometimes make voters (politicians, bureaucrats, dictators, and so forth) men and sometimes women. I have tried to treat the two sexes evenhandedly in this regard.

[6] Wicksell's 1896 essay is part of the contribution of the "continental" writers on public economics. Besides Wicksell's work, the most important papers in this group are those of Lindahl (1919). Of the two, Lindahl has had greater influence on public goods theory, and Wicksell on public choice and public finance. Their works, along with the other major contributions of the continental writers, are in Musgrave and Peacock (1967).

PART I

Origins of the state

CHAPTER 2

The reason for collective choice – allocative efficiency

Had every man sufficient *sagacity* to perceive at all times, the strong interest which binds him to the observance of justice and equity, and *strength of mind* sufficient to persevere in a steady adherence to a general and a distant interest, in opposition to the allurements of present pleasure and advantage, there had never, in that case, been any such thing as government or political society; but each man, following his natural liberty, had lived in entire peace and harmony with all others. (Italics in original)

David Hume

Government is a contrivance of human wisdom to provide for human *wants*. Men have a right that these wants should be provided for by this wisdom. (Italics in original)

Edmund Burke

2.1   Public goods and prisoners' dilemmas

Probably the most important accomplishment of economics is the demonstration that individuals with purely selfish motives can mutually benefit from exchange. If A raises cattle and B corn, both may improve their welfare by exchanging cattle for corn. With the help of the price system, the process can be extended to accommodate a wide variety of goods and services.

Although often depicted as the perfect example of the beneficial outcome of purely private, individualistic activity in the absence of government, the invisible hand theorem presumes a system of collective choice comparable in sophistication and complexity to the market system it governs. For the choices facing A and B are not merely to trade or not, as implicitly suggested. A can choose to steal B's corn, rather than give up his cattle for it; B may do likewise. Unlike trading, which is a positive-sum game benefiting both participants in an exchange, stealing is at best a zero-sum game. What A gains, B loses. If stealing, and guarding against it, detract from A and B's ability to produce corn and cattle, it becomes a negative-sum game. Although with trading each seeks to improve his position and both end up better off, with stealing the selfish pursuits of each leave them both worse off.

The example can be illustrated with strategy Matrix 2.1. To simplify the discussion, let us ignore the trading option and assume that each individual grows only corn. Square 1 gives the allocation when A and B both refrain from stealing (A's

Matrix 2.1. *Stealing as prisoners' dilemma*

A \ B	Does not steal	Steals
Does not steal	1 (10, 9)	4 (7, 11)
Steals	2 (12, 6)	3 (8, 8)

allocation precedes *B*'s in each box). Both are better off when they both refrain from stealing, but each is still better off if he alone steals (cells 2 and 4). In Matrix 2.1, stealing is a dominant strategy for both players, so defined because it dominates all other strategy options by promising a higher payoff for the chooser than any other strategy, given any choice of strategy by the other player. In an anarchic environment, the independent choices of both individuals can be expected to lead both to adopt the dominant stealing strategy with the outcome cell 3. The distribution of corn in cell 3 represents a "natural distribution" of goods (so named by Bush [1972]), namely, the distribution that would emerge in an Hobbesian state of nature.

From this "natural" state, both individuals become better off by tacitly or formally agreeing not to steal, provided that the enforcement of such an agreement costs less than they jointly gain from it. The movement from cell 3 to cell 1 is a Pareto move that lifts the individuals out of a Hobbesian state of nature (Bush, 1972; Bush and Mayer, 1974; Buchanan, 1975a; Schotter, 1981). An agreement to make such a move is a form of "constitutional contract" establishing the property rights and behavioral constraints of each individual. The existence of these rights is undoubtedly a necessary precondition for the creation of the "postconstitutional contracts," which make up a system of voluntary exchange (Buchanan, 1975a). Problems of collective choice arise with the departure from Hobbesian anarchy, and are coterminous with the existence of recognizable groups and communities.

A system of property rights and the procedures to enforce them are a Samuelsonian public good in that "each individual's consumption leads to no subtraction from any other individual's consumption of that good."[1] Alternatively, a pure public good can be defined as one that *must* be provided in equal quantities to all members of the community. Familiar examples of pure public goods are national defense and police and fire protection. National defense is the collective provision against external threats; laws and their enforcement safeguard against internal threats; fire departments against fires. Nearly all public goods whose provision requires an expenditure of resources, time, or moral restraint can be depicted with a strategy box analogous to Matrix 2.1. Replace stealing with paying for an army, or a police force,

---

[1] Samuelson (1954, p. 386). The extent to which individuals can be excluded from the benefits of a public good varies. One man's house cannot be defended from foreign invasion without defending another's, but a house may be allowed to burn down without endangering another. Tullock (1971c) has suggested that voluntary payment schemes for excludable public goods could introduce cases resembling the latter.

or a fire department, and the same strategy choices emerge. <u>Each individual is better off if all contribute to the provision of the public good than if all do not, and each is still better off if only he does not pay for the good.</u>

A pure public good has two salient characteristics: jointness of supply and the impossibility or inefficiency of excluding others from its consumption, once it has been supplied to some members of the community (Musgrave, 1959, pp. 9–12, 86; Head, 1962). Jointness of supply is a property of the production or cost function of the public good. The extreme case of jointness of supply is a good whose production costs are all fixed, and thus whose marginal production costs are zero (e.g., a public monument). For such a good, the addition of more consumers (viewers) does not detract from the benefits enjoyed by others. Even a good with falling average costs, although positive marginal costs, has elements of jointness that raise collective provision issues.

The joint supply characteristic creates the potential gain from a cooperative move from cell 3 to 1. Given jointness of supply, a cooperative consumption decision is necessary to provide the good efficiently. If it took twice as many resources to protect A and B from one another as it does to protect only one of them, collective action would be unnecessary in the absence of nonexclusion. Each could choose independently whether or not to provide his own protection.

People can be excluded from the benefits from viewing a statue placed within a private gallery if they do not pay to see it. But people cannot be prevented from viewing a statue or monument placed in the central city square. For many public goods, the exclusion of some members of the community from their consumption is impossible or impractical. Failure of the exclusion principle to apply provides an incentive for noncooperative, individualistic behavior, a gain from moving from cell 1 to either cell 2 or cell 4. The impossibility of exclusion raises the likelihood that purely voluntary schemes for providing a public good will break down. Thus, together, the properties of public goods provide the raison d'être for collective choice. Jointness of supply is the carrot, making cooperative-collective decisions beneficial to all; absence of the exclusion principle is the apple tempting individuals into independent, noncooperative behavior.

Although the purest of pure public goods is characterized by both jointness of supply and the impossibility of exclusion, preference revelation problems arise even if only the first of these two properties is present. That is, an alternative definition of a public good is that it *may* be provided in equal quantities to all members of the community at zero marginal cost. The substitution of "may" for "must" in the definition implies that exclusion may be possible. A classic example of a public good fitting this second definition is a bridge. In the absence of crowding, the services of the bridge can be supplied to all members of the community, but they need not be. Exclusion is possible. As long as the marginal cost of someone's crossing the bridge remains zero, however, excluding anyone who would experience a marginal benefit from crossing violates the Pareto principle. Jointness of supply alone can create the need for collective action to achieve Pareto optimality.

Matrix 2.1 depicts the familiar and extensively analyzed prisoners' dilemma. The salient feature of this game is that the row player ranks the four possible outcomes

$2 > 1 > 3 > 4$, while the column player has the ranking $4 > 1 > 3 > 2$.[2] The non-cooperative strategy is dominant for both players. It is the best strategy for each player in a single play of the game regardless of the other player's strategy choice. The outcome, square 3, is a Cournot-Nash equilibrium.[3] It has the unfortunate property of being the only outcome of the prisoners' dilemma game that is not Pareto optimal. From each of the other three squares a move must make at least one player worse off, but from 3 a move to 1 makes both better off.

Despite the obvious superiority of the cooperative nonstealing outcome to the joint stealing outcome, the dominance of the stealing strategies ensures that the nonstealing strategies do not constitute an equilibrium pair, at least for a single play of the game. The cooperative solution may emerge, however, as the outcome of a "supergame" of prisoners' dilemma games repeated over and over by the same players. The cooperative solution can arise, even in the absence of direct communication between the players, if each player chooses a supergame strategy that effectively links his choice of the cooperative strategy in a single game to the other player's choice of this strategy. One such supergame strategy is for a player to play the same strategy in the present game as the other player(s) played in the previous game. If both (all) players adopt this strategy, *and* all begin by playing the cooperation strategy, the cooperative outcome emerges in every play of the game. This "tit-for-tat" strategy beat all others proposed by a panel of game theory experts in a computer tournament conducted by Axelrod (1984).

An alternative strategy, which achieves the same outcome, is for each player to play the cooperative strategy as long as the other player(s) does, and then to *punish* the other player(s) for defecting by playing the noncooperative strategy for a series of plays following any defection before returning to the cooperative strategy. Again, if all players begin by playing cooperatively, this outcome continues throughout the game (Taylor, 1987, ch. 3). In both of these cooperative strategies, equilibrium solutions to the prisoners' dilemma supergame, the equilibrium comes about through the *punishment* (or threat thereof) of the noncooperative behavior of any player, in this case by the noncooperation of the other player(s). This idea that noncooperative (antisocial, immoral) behavior must be punished to bring about conformity with group mores is to be found in most, if not all, moral philosophies, and forms a direct linkage between this large literature and the modern theory.[4]

When the number of players in a prisoners' dilemma game is small, it is obviously easier to learn their behavior and predict whether they will respond to cooperative strategy choices in a like manner. It is also easier to detect noncooperative behavior and, if this is possible, single it out for punishment, thereby further encouraging the

---

[2] An additional assumption that row player's payoff in box 2 and column's in box 4 add up to less than their two payoffs in box 1 is needed to ensure that they do not take turns jointly defecting and cooperating; that is, not stealing from one another for two periods yields higher payoffs than taking turns stealing from one another.

[3] A set of strategies $S = (s_1, s_2, \ldots, s_i, \ldots, s_n)$ constitutes a Nash equilibrium, if for any player i, s_i is his optimal strategy, when all other players $j \neq i$ play their optimal strategies s_j, $s_j \in S$.

[4] For classical discussions of moral behavior and punishment, which are most modern and in line with the prisoners' dilemma discussion, see Hobbes, *Leviathan* (1651, chs. 14, 15, 17, 18), and Hume (1751, pp. 120–7).

cooperative strategies. When numbers are large, it is easy for one or a few players to adopt the noncooperative strategy and either not be detected, since the impact on the rest is small, or not be punished, since they cannot be discovered or it is too costly to the cooperating players to punish them. Thus, voluntary compliance with behavioral sanctions or provision of public goods is more likely in small communities than in large (Coase, 1960; Buchanan, 1965b). Reliance on voluntary compliance in large communities or groups leads to free riding and the under- or nonprovision of the public good (Olson, 1965).

In the large, mobile, heterogeneous community, a formal statement of what behavior is mutually beneficial (e.g., how much each must contribute for a public good) may be needed even for individuals to know what behavior is consistent with the public interest. Given the incentives to free ride, compliance may require the implementation of individualized rewards or sanctions. Olson (1965, pp. 50–1, 132–67) found that individual participation in large, voluntary organizations like labor unions, professional lobbies, and other special interest groups was dependent not on the collective benefits these organizations provided for all of their members, but on the individualized incentives they provided in the form of selective benefits for participation and attendance, or penalties in the form of fines, and other individualized sanctions.

Thus, democracy, with its formal voting procedures for making and enforcing collective choices, is an institution that is needed by communities of only a certain size and impersonality. The family makes an array of collective decisions without ever voting; a tribe votes only occasionally. A metropolis or nation state may have to make a great number of decisions by collective choice processes, although many of them may not correspond to what we have defined here as a democratic process.[5] Similarly, small, stable communities may be able to elicit voluntary compliance with group mores and contributions for the provision of local public goods by the use of informal communication channels and peer group pressure. Larger, more impersonal communities must typically establish formal penalties against asocial behavior (like stealing), levy taxes to provide for public goods, and employ a police force to ensure compliance.

The size of the community, its reliance on formal sanctions and police enforcement, and the breakdown of the prisoners' dilemma may all be dynamically related. Detection of violators of the prisoners' dilemma takes time. An increase in the number of violations can be expected to lead to a further increase in violations but only with a time lag. If, because of an increase in community size or for some other reason, the frequency of violations were to increase, the frequency of violations in later periods could be expected to increase; the frequency of violations in still later periods would increase even further, and with these the need for and reliance on police enforcement of the laws. Buchanan (1975a, pp. 123–9) has described such a process as the erosion of a community's legal (that is, rule-abiding) capital.[6] Today, this form of capital is typically referred to as *social capital*. Putnam (2000) provides

---

[5] One must also keep in mind that democracy is but one *potential* means for providing public goods. Autocracies and oligarchies also provide public goods to "their" communities. Autocracies are discussed in Chapter 18.

[6] See Buchanan (1965b).

evidence of a dramatic decline in the stock of social capital in the United States over the recent generation.

Taylor (1987, pp. 168–79) relates the breakdown of the cooperative solution to the prisoners' dilemma not to the size of the community, however, but to the level of government intervention itself.[7] Intervention of the state in the provision of a community want or in the enforcement of social mores psychologically "frees" an individual from responsibility for providing for community wants and preserving its mores. State intervention leads to increased asocial behavior requiring more state intervention, and so on. Frey (1997b) makes an analogous argument. State-initiated bribes and sanctions designed to elicit cooperative behavior may "crowd it out" by destroying the intrinsic motivation of individuals to behave morally and as good citizens. These theories might constitute one explanation for the rising government expenditures that have occurred in this century. The increasing mobility and urbanization that have occurred during the century induce less voluntary cooperation by citizens and cause more state intervention. State intervention in turn reduces the internally motivated propensity for citizens to cooperate, necessitating still more state intervention.

This scenario of an unraveling of the social fabric mirrors to a remarkable degree the description by Rawls (1971, pp. 496–504) of the evolution of a just society, in which the moral (just, cooperative) behavior of one individual leads to increasingly moral behavior by others, reinforcing the cooperative behavior of the first and encouraging still more. The dynamic process in these two scenarios is the same, only the direction of change is reversed.

2.2   Coordination games

The prisoners' dilemma is a dilemma because cheating on the cooperative solution to the game is rewarded and, thus, individually rational. All situations in which one person's utility depends on the action of another do not reward "cheating," and thus do not give rise to the kind of collective action problem that characterizes the prisoners' dilemma. One such situation involves a *coordination* game.

Matrix 2.2 depicts one such game. If Row and Column both play strategy *A* they both receive the positive payoff *a*. If they coordinate on strategy *B*, they both receive a positive *b*, and if they fail to coordinate, they both receive a payoff of zero. Now suppose that each player knows all of the payoffs in Matrix 2.2 and must choose a strategy independently from the other player and in ignorance of the other player's strategy choice. Which strategy should a rational individual choose? Both players know that the other would like to choose the same strategy but, without knowledge of the other player's choice, there is obviously no unequivocal choice that a player can make.

---

[7] Indeed, "the main point [Taylor] set out to establish" was that "Cooperation can arise in the Prisoners' Dilemma supergame, no matter how many players there are" (1987, p. 104). On the next page he concedes, however, that "it is pretty clear that Cooperation amongst a relatively large number of players is 'less likely' to occur than Cooperation amongst a small number" (p. 105).

Matrix 2.2. *A coordination game*

G \ D	Strategy A	Strategy B
Strategy A	1 (a, a)	4 $(0, 0)$
Strategy B	2 $(0, 0)$	3 (b, b)

Suppose, however, that $b > a$. Clearly, both players now have a preference for coordinating on strategy B. Strategy B becomes a form of *Schelling point*, and both can be expected to choose this strategy (Schelling, 1960). But what if $b = a$? Now it would appear that our two players have little choice other than resorting to a coin flip – unless, of course, they were allowed to communicate with one another. With $b = a$, the two players are indifferent between coordinating on strategy A or B. If one of them were to propose that they coordinate on strategy B, the other would have no reason to object, *and he would have no reason to defect once the agreement had been reached*. Coordination games thus have an inherent stability to them that is absent in many other social-dilemma games, like the prisoners' dilemma.

Indeed, because of this inherent stability, Pareto-optimal sets of strategies can be expected to emerge when coordination games are repeated, under far less demanding behavioral assumptions than are needed to sustain Pareto-optimal outcomes in prisoners' dilemma supergames. Assume, for example, that all individuals are ignorant of the payoffs from the different combinations of strategies, the choices that the other player has made in the past, and the current choice of the other player. The only information a player has is what *her own* strategy choices were over a finite number of past plays of the game, and the payoffs she received. Given this limited knowledge she chooses to play the strategy that was most highly rewarded in the recent past.

For example, suppose that she can only recall the outcomes of the last five plays of the game, when she played A three times and B twice. Two of the three times that she played A, she got a; one of the two times that she played B, she was rewarded with b. She opts to increase the frequency with which she plays strategy A. If the other player adopts the same rule of thumb, the two players coordinate over time on strategy A and remain locked in on it so long as the payoff structure does not change.

Recent contributions to evolutionary game theory have modeled individual action as *adaptive learning*, wherein an individual's strategy choice today depends on the payoffs she, or those she can observe, have received in the recent past. These models demonstrate how coordinated strategy choices can emerge in games like that in Matrix 2.2.[8] These results are of great significance because they are based on far more realistic assumptions about the capacities of individuals to engage in rational

---

[8] See, for example, Sugden (1986); Warneryd (1990); Kandori, Mailath, and Rob (1993); and Young (1993).

Matrix 2.3. *Fence building as a game of chicken*

G \ D	Contributes to building fence	Does not contribute
Contributes to building fence	1 (3, 3)	4 (2, 3.5)
Does not contribute	2 (3.5, 2)	3 (1, 1)

action and about the ways in which learning takes place. They show how social conventions might evolve to solve coordination problems *without the need for the state*.[9]

Examples of coordination games include various conventions about driving: drive on the right, pass on the left, yield to cars approaching from the right, and so on. If all problems caused by social interaction were as simple as deciding on which side of the road everyone should drive, one might well imagine that it would be possible to do away with the state. But, alas, this is not the case, as our discussion of the prisoners' dilemma has already shown and the game of chicken further illustrates.

2.3   Public goods and chickens

The prisoners' dilemma is the most frequently used characterization of the situations to which public goods give rise. But the technology of public goods provision can be such as to generate other kinds of strategic interactions. Consider the following example.

The properties of two individuals share a common boundary. G owns a goat that occasionally wanders into D's garden and eats the vegetables and flowers. D has a dog that sometimes crosses into G's property, chasing and frightening the goat so that it does not give milk. A fence separating the two properties could stop both from happening.

Matrix 2.3 depicts the situation. With no fence, both D and G experience utility levels on one. The fence costs \$1,000 and each would be willing to pay the full cost if necessary to get the benefits of the fence. The utility levels of each (2) are higher with the fence than without it, even when they must pay the full cost alone. This assumption ensures that the utility levels of both individuals are still higher if each must pay only half the cost of the fence (square 1). Last of all, each is, of course, best off if the fence is built and he pays nothing (payoffs of 3.5 to G and D, respectively, in squares 2 and 4). Matrix 2.3 depicts the game of "chicken." It differs from the prisoners' dilemma in that the outcome in which no one contributes (cell 3), which is Pareto inferior to the outcome that both contribute (cell 1), is not an equilibrium. Since each individual is better off even if he must pay for the fence alone, each would be willing to move to square 2 or 4, as the case may be, rather than see the outcome remain at cell 3. Cells 2 and 4 are both equilibria in this game, and they

---

[9] It is possible that a society would lock in on a strategy A equilibrium, even though $b > a$, so that a limited role for the state in announcing which strategy citizens should coordinate on might still be desirable.

are the only two. The ordering of payoffs in a game of chicken for the row player is cell 2 > 1 > 4 > 3, whereas in a prisoners' dilemma it is 2 > 1 > 3 > 4. The interchange of the last two cells for both players causes the shift in the equilibrium.

In cells 4, 1, and 2, the fence is built. These cells differ only in who pays for the fence and the resulting utility payoffs. In cell 4, G pays the full $1,000 cost of the fence and experiences a utility level of 2. In cell 1, G pays $500 and receives a utility level of 3, while in cell 2 G pays nothing for a utility level of 3.5. The lower increment in utility in going from a $500 fall in income to no change in income, compared with going from a $1,000 fall in income to a $500 fall, reflects an assumption of the declining marginal utility of income. If both G and D have declining marginal utilities of income, as assumed in the figures in Matrix 2.3, then the solution that they share the cost of the fence is welfare maximizing as well as equitable. Under alternative assumptions, a stronger, higher fence may be built when the cost is shared, and the result may be an efficiency gain from the cost-sharing solution in cell 1. But the outcome in cell 1 is not an equilibrium. Both D and G will be better off if they can convince the other to pay the full cost of the fence. One way to do this is to precommit oneself not to build the fence, or at least to convince one's neighbor that one has made such a commitment so that the neighbor, say, D, believes that her choice is between cells 2 and 3, and thus naturally chooses cell 2.

The chicken game is often used to depict the interactions of nations (Schelling, 1966, ch. 2). Let D be a superpower, which favors having other countries install democratic institutions, and C a country favoring communist institutions. A civil war rages in small country S between one group seeking to install a communist regime and another group wishing to install a democratic constitution. The situation could easily take on the characteristics of a game of chicken. Each superpower wants to support the group favoring its ideology in S, and wants the other superpower to back down. But if the other superpower, say, C, is supporting its group in S, then D is better off backing off than supporting its group in S and thereby being led into a direct confrontation with the other superpower. Both powers are clearly better off if they both back off than if the confrontation occurs.

Given this game-of-chicken configuration of payoffs, each superpower may try to get the other to back off by precommiting itself to defending democracy (communism) wherever it is threatened around the world. Such a precommitment combined with a reputation for "toughness" could force the other superpower to back down each time a clash between communist and noncommunist forces occurs in a small country.

The danger in this situation, however, is that both superpowers become so committed to their strategy of supporting groups of their ideology, and so committed to preserving their reputations for toughness, that neither side backs down. The confrontation of the superpowers is precipitated by the civil war in S.

As in prisoners' dilemmas, the joint cooperation solution to the chicken game can emerge from a chicken supergame, if each player recognizes the long-run advantages to cooperation and adopts the tit-for-tat supergame strategy or an analogous one (Taylor and Ward, 1982; Ward, 1987). Alternatively, the two superpowers (neighbors) may recognize the dangers inherent in the noncooperative, precommitment strategy and directly approach one another and agree to follow the cooperative strategy. Thus, although the structure of the chicken game differs from that of the prisoners' dilemma, the optimal solutions of the game are similar, requiring some sort of formal or tacit agreement to cooperate. As the number of players increases, the likelihood that a formal agreement is required increases (Taylor and Ward, 1982; Ward, 1987). Thus, for the chicken game, as for the prisoners' dilemma, the need for democratic institutions to achieve the efficient, cooperative solution to the game increases as the number of players rises.

2.4*   Voluntary provision of public goods with constant returns to scale

In this section we explore more formally the problems that arise in the voluntary provision of a public good. Consider as the pure public good a levy or dike built of bags of sand. Each member of the community voluntarily supplies as many bags of sand as she chooses. The total number of bags supplied is the summation of the individual contributions of each member. The more bags supplied, the higher and stronger the dike, and the better off are all members of the community. Letting G_i be the contribution to the public good of individual i, then the total quantity of public good supplied is

$$G = G_1 + G_2 + G_3 + \cdots G_n. \tag{2.1}$$

Let each individual's utility function be given as $U_i(X_i, G)$, where X_i is the quantity of private good i consumes.

Now consider the decision of i as to how much of the public good to supply, that is, the optimal G_i, given her budget constraint $Y_i = P_x X_i + P_g G_i$, where Y_i is her income and P_x and P_g are prices of the private and public goods, respectively. In the absence of an institution for coordinating the quantities of public good supplied, each individual must decide independently of the other individuals how much of the public good to supply. In making this decision, it is reasonable to assume that the individual takes the supply of the public good by the rest of the community as fixed. Each i chooses the G_i that maximizes U_i, given the values of G_j chosen by all other individuals j. Individual i's objective function is thus

$$O_i = U_i(X_i, G) + \lambda_i(Y_i - P_x X_i - P_g G_i). \tag{2.2}$$

Maximizing (2.2) with respect to G_i and X_i yields

$$\frac{\partial U_i}{\partial G} - \lambda_i P_g = 0 \tag{2.3}$$

$$\frac{\partial U_i}{\partial X_i} - \lambda_i P_x = 0 \tag{2.4}$$

from which we obtain

$$\frac{\partial U_i/\partial G}{\partial U_i/\partial X_i} = \frac{P_g}{P_x} \tag{2.5}$$

as the condition for utility maximization. Each individual purchases the public good as if it were a private good, taking the purchases of the other members of the community as given. This equilibrium is often referred to as a Cournot or Nash equilibrium, as it resembles the behavioral assumption Cournot made concerning the supply of a homogeneous private good in an oligopolistic market.

Now let us contrast (2.5) with the condition for Pareto optimality. To obtain this, we maximize the following welfare function:

$$W = \gamma_1 U_1 + \gamma_2 U_2 + \cdots + \gamma_n U_n, \tag{2.6}$$

where all $\gamma_i > 0$. Given the positive weights on all individual utilities, any allocation that is not Pareto optimal – that is, from which one person's utility can be increased without lowering anyone else's – cannot be at a maximum for W. Thus, choosing X_i and G_i to maximize W gives us a Pareto-optimal allocation.

Maximizing (2.6) subject to the aggregate budget constraint

$$\sum_{i=1}^{n} Y_i = P_x \sum_{i=1}^{n} X_i + P_g G, \tag{2.7}$$

we obtain the first-order conditions

$$\sum_{i=1}^{n} \gamma_i \frac{\partial U_i}{\partial G} - \lambda P_g = 0 \tag{2.8}$$

and

$$\gamma_i \frac{\partial U_i}{\partial X_i} - \lambda P_x = 0, \qquad i = 1, n, \tag{2.9}$$

where λ is the Lagrangian multiplier on the budget constraint. Using the n equations in (2.9) to eliminate the γ_i in (2.8), we obtain

$$\sum_i \frac{\lambda P_x}{\partial U_i / \partial X_i} \cdot \partial U_i / \partial G = \lambda P_g, \tag{2.10}$$

from which we obtain

$$\sum_i \frac{\partial U_i / \partial G}{\partial U_i / \partial X_i} = \frac{P_g}{P_x}. \tag{2.11}$$

Equation (2.11) is the familiar Samuelsonian (1954) condition for the Pareto-optimal provision of a public good. Independent utility maximization decisions lead each individual to equate her marginal rate of substitution of the public for the private good to their price ratio, as if the public good were a private good (2.5). Pareto optimality, however, requires that the summation of the marginal rates of substitution over all members of the community be equated to this price ratio (2.11).

That the quantity of public good provided under the Cournot-Nash equilibrium (2.5) is less than the Pareto-optimal quantity can be seen by rewriting (2.11) as

$$\frac{\partial U_i/\partial G}{\partial U_i/\partial X_i} = \frac{P_g}{P_x} - \sum_{j \neq i} \frac{\partial U_j/\partial G}{\partial U_j/\partial X_j}. \tag{2.12}$$

If G and X are normal goods in each individual's utility function, then

$$\sum_{j \neq i} \frac{\partial U_j/\partial G}{\partial U_j/\partial X_j} > 0$$

and the marginal rate of substitution of public for private good for individual i defined by (2.12) is less than that defined by (2.5), which implies that a greater quantity of G and a smaller quantity of X_i are being consumed when (2.12) is satisfied than when (2.5) is.

To gain a feel for the quantitative significance of the differences, consider the special case where U_i is a Cobb-Douglas utility function, that is, $U_i = X_i^\alpha G^\beta$, $0 < \alpha < 1$, and $0 < \beta < 1$. Under this assumption (2.5) becomes

$$\frac{\beta X_i^\alpha G^{\beta-1}}{\alpha X_i^{\alpha-1} G^\beta} = \frac{P_g}{P_x}, \tag{2.13}$$

from which it follows that

$$G = \frac{P_x}{P_g} \frac{\beta}{\alpha} X_i. \tag{2.14}$$

Substituting from (2.1) and the budget constraint yields

$$\sum_i G_i = \frac{P_x}{P_g} \frac{\beta}{\alpha} \left(\frac{Y_i}{P_x} - \frac{P_g}{P_x} G_i \right), \tag{2.15}$$

from which we obtain

$$\left(1 + \frac{\beta}{\alpha} \right) G_i = -\sum_{j \neq i} G_j + \frac{\beta}{\alpha} \frac{Y_i}{P_g} \tag{2.16}$$

or

$$G_i = -\frac{\alpha}{\alpha + \beta} \sum_{j \neq i} G_j + \frac{\beta}{\alpha + \beta} \frac{Y_i}{P_g}. \tag{2.17}$$

Equation (2.17) implies that individual i voluntarily chooses to supply a smaller amount of the public good, the larger she believes the amount of public good provided by the other citizens to be. With only two individuals in the community, (2.17) defines the familiar reaction curve from duopoly theory. In this situation, it is a negativity-sloped straight line.

If all members of the community have identical incomes, Y, then all will choose the same levels of G_i, and (2.17) can be used to find the contribution in equilibrium of a single individual:

$$G_i = -\frac{\alpha}{\alpha + \beta}(n - 1)G_i + \frac{\beta}{\alpha + \beta}\frac{Y}{P_g}, \tag{2.18}$$

from which we obtain

$$G_i = \frac{\beta}{\alpha n + \beta}\frac{Y}{P_g}. \tag{2.19}$$

The amount of the public good provided by the community through independent contributions then becomes

$$G = nG_i = \frac{n\beta}{\alpha n + \beta}\frac{Y}{P_g}. \tag{2.20}$$

These quantities can be compared to the Pareto-optimal quantities. With all individual incomes equal, all individuals contribute the same G_i and have the same X_i left over, so that (2.11) becomes

$$n\frac{\beta X_i^\alpha G^{\beta - 1}}{\alpha X_i^{\alpha - 1}G^\beta} = \frac{P_g}{P_x}. \tag{2.21}$$

Using the budget constraint to eliminate the X_i and rearranging yields for the Pareto-optimal contribution of a single individual,

$$G_i = \frac{\beta}{\alpha + \beta}\frac{Y}{P_g} \tag{2.22}$$

and

$$G = nG_i = \frac{n\beta}{\alpha + \beta}\frac{Y}{P_g}. \tag{2.23}$$

Let us call the Pareto-optimal quantity of public good defined by (2.23) G_{PO}, and the quantity under the Cournot-Nash equilibrium (2.20), G_{CN}. Their ratio is then

$$\frac{G_{CN}}{G_{PO}} = \frac{\dfrac{n\beta}{\alpha n + \beta}\dfrac{Y}{P_g}}{\dfrac{n\beta}{\alpha + \beta}\dfrac{Y}{P_g}} = \frac{\alpha + \beta}{\alpha n + \beta}. \tag{2.24}$$

This ratio is less than one, if $n > 1$, and tends toward zero as n becomes increasingly large. Thus, for all communities greater than a solitary individual, voluntary, independent supply of the public good leads to less than the Pareto-optimal quantity being supplied, and the relative gap between the two quantities grows as community size increases.

The extent of underprovision of the public good at a Cournot-Nash equilibrium depends on the nature of the individual utility functions (Cornes and Sandler, 1986, ch. 5). For the Cobb-Douglas utility function, the greater the ratio of β to α, the *smaller* the extent of underprovision. With $\alpha = 0$ – that is, when the marginal utility of the private good is zero – $G_{CN} = G_{PO}$. This equality also holds with right-angled indifference curves, where again the marginal utility of the private good, holding the quantity of the public good fixed, is zero (Cornes and Sandler, 1986, p. 81). But with the familiar, smooth, convex-to-the-origin indifference curves, one can expect an underprovision of a voluntarily provided public good, and an underprovision whose relative size grows with the size of the community. To achieve the Pareto-optimal allocation, some institution for coordinating the contributions of all individuals is needed.

2.5*   Voluntary provision of public goods with varying supply technologies

Many public goods might be depicted using the summation technology of the previous section. Public goods of a prisoners' dilemma type – for example, community order, environmental quality – are provided by each individual contributing to the "production" of the public good by not stealing or not polluting. For the typical public good of this kind, the quantity supplied is to some degree additive with respect to each individual's contribution. The more people there are who refrain from stealing, the more secure is the community, and the greater is the welfare of its members.

There are other public goods, however, for which the participation of *all* members is necessary to secure *any* benefits. The crew of a small sailboat, two-man rowboats, and bobsleds are examples. For the rowboat to go in a straight line each rower must pull the oar with equal force. Under- or overcontributions are penalized by the boat's moving in a circle. Only the equal contribution of both rowers is rewarded by the boat's moving forward. With such goods, cells 2, 4, and 3 of Matrix 2.1 collapse into one and cooperative behavior is voluntarily forthcoming.

Goods such as these are produced by what Hirshleifer (1983, 1984) named the "weakest-link" technology. The amount of public good provided is equal to the smallest quantity provided by any member of the community. At the other pole from weakest-link technology one can conceive of a best-shot technology for which the amount of public good provided is equal to the largest quantity provided by any one member of the community. As an example of the best-shot technology, one can think of a community first having each member design a boat (bridge) for crossing a given body of water, and then the best design selected and constructed.

The weakest-link technology is like a fixed coefficient production function for public goods. Individual i's marginal contribution to public good supply, $\partial G / \partial G_i$, is zero, if his contribution exceeds that of any other member of the community ($G_i > G_j$ for some j). But $\partial G / \partial G_i$ equals the community supply function when $G_i < G_j$ for all j. The summation technology assumes an additive and separable production function, whereas the best-shot technology assumes a form of discontinuously increasing returns. The latter seems the least plausible of the three, so we consider only the cases falling in the range between the weakest-link and summation production technologies.

Consider a community of two Australian farmers whose fields are adjacent to another and border on a segment of the bush. Each night the kangaroos come out of the bush and destroy the farmers' crops. The farmers can protect their crops, however, by erecting fences along the border between their property and the bush.

Each farmer is responsible for buying fence for his own segment of the border. The following technologies can be envisaged:

> *Weakest link*: Kangaroos adapt quickly to changes in their environment and discover the lowest point in the fence. The number of kangaroos entering both farmers' fields is determined by the height of the fence at its lowest point.
>
> *Unweighted summation*: Kangaroos are very dumb and probe the fence at random. The number of kangaroos entering the two fields varies inversely with the average height of the two fences.
>
> *Diminishing returns*: If one farmer's fence is lower than the other's, some, but not all, kangaroos learn to probe only the lower fence, and the higher fence stops some kangaroos from going over.

Now consider the following general formulation of public good supply: Let G be the number of units of public good provided, defined in this case as the number of kangaroos prevented from entering the fields. Let the units of fence purchased at price P_f be defined so that

$$G = F_1 + w F_2, \qquad 0 \leq F_1 \leq F_2, \qquad 0 \leq w \leq 1, \tag{2.25}$$

where F_i is farmer i's purchase of fence. If $w = 0$, we have the weakest-link case, and $G = F_1$, the smaller of the two contributions. The larger w is, the more 2's contribution beyond 1's contributes to the supply of G, until with $w = 1$, we reach the unweighted summation supply function examined above. To simplify the problem, assume that both farmers have identical utility functions and both G and the private good X are noninferior. Then the farmer with the lower income will always choose to purchase the smaller quantity of fence, so that farmer 1 is the farmer with the smaller income of the two. He maximizes his utility $U_1(X, G)$ by choosing a level of private good consumption X_1 and contribution to the public good F_1 satisfying his budget constraint, $Y_1 = P_x X_1 + P_f F_1$. The solution is again (2.5), with the price of the public good now P_f.

The solution to the utility maximization problem for farmer 2 is, however,

$$\frac{\partial U_2 / \partial G}{\partial U_2 / \partial X} = \frac{P_f}{w P_x} \tag{2.26}$$

as long as $F_2 > F_1$. In effect, farmer 2 faces a higher relative price for the public good F, since his purchases do not contribute as much on the margin as 1's, owing to the technology defined by (2.25). The smaller w is, the less fence 2 buys (the smaller his optimal contribution to the public good). With small enough w, the solution to (2.26) would require $F_2 < F_1$. But then 2 would be the smaller contributor and his optimal contribution would be defined by (2.5). Since 2 favors a greater contribution than 1, he simply matches 1's contribution if satisfying (2.26) violates $F_2 > F_1$.

To determine the condition for the Pareto-optimal level of G, we choose levels of X_1, X_2, and G to maximize 1's utility, holding 2's utility constant, and satisfying (2.25) and the individual budget constraints; that is, we maximize

$$L = U_1(X_1, G) + \gamma [\bar{U}_2 - U_2(X_2, G)] + \lambda [G - F_1 - w F_2], \tag{2.27}$$

from which it follows that

$$\frac{\partial U_1/\partial G}{\partial U_1/\partial X} + w\frac{\partial U_2/\partial G}{\partial U_2/\partial X} = \frac{P_f}{P_x}. \tag{2.28}$$

Only in the extreme weakest-link case, where $w = 0$, is the condition for Pareto optimality for the community (2.28) satisfied by the two individuals acting independently, for then (2.28) collapses to (2.5), and both farmers purchase the amounts of fence satisfying (2.5).[10] With $w = 1$, on the other hand, we have the unweighted summation supply of public good, and (2.28) becomes (2.11), the Samuelsonian (1954) condition for Pareto optimality, and too little public good is being supplied.

Moreover, the difference between the quantity of public good supplied voluntarily when each farmer acts independently and the Pareto-optimal quantity increases with w. To illustrate this, again let both individuals have identical incomes Y, and identical utility functions $U = X^{\alpha} G^{\beta}$. Both then purchase the same quantity of fence F and private good X. From (2.5) and (2.25) we obtain the Cournot-Nash equilibrium quantity of public good supplied through the independent utility-maximizing decisions of the two farmers:

$$G_{CN} = \frac{\beta Y(1+w)}{P_f[\alpha(1+w)+\beta]}. \tag{2.29}$$

In the same way, (2.28) can be used to obtain Pareto-optimal G:

$$G_{PO} = \frac{\beta}{\alpha+\beta}\frac{Y}{P_f}(1+w). \tag{2.30}$$

Dividing (2.29) by (2.30) we obtain the ratio of independently supplied to Pareto-optimal quantities of public good:

$$\frac{G_{CN}}{G_{PO}} = \frac{\alpha+\beta}{\alpha(1+w)+\beta}. \tag{2.31}$$

With $w = 0$, the ratio is one, but it falls as w increases.

With n individuals, (2.28) generalizes to

$$\frac{\partial U_1/\partial G}{\partial U_1/\partial X} + w_2\frac{\partial U_2/\partial G}{\partial U_2/\partial X} + w_3\frac{\partial U_3/\partial G}{\partial U_3/\partial X} + \cdots + w_n\frac{\partial U_n/\partial G}{\partial U_n/\partial X} = \frac{P_f}{P_x} \tag{2.32}$$

and (2.31) generalizes to

$$\frac{G_{CN}}{G_{PO}} = \frac{\alpha+\beta}{\alpha(1+w_2+w_3+\cdots+w_n)+\beta}. \tag{2.33}$$

The gap between the independently provided and Pareto-optimal quantities of public good increases as the number of members of the community increases, and the weights on the additional contributions increase.

---

[10] This conclusion is contingent on the initial incomes of the two farmers and the implicit constraint that farmer 2 cannot transfer money to 1 or purchase fence for him. With w low enough or Y_2/Y_1 high enough, unconstrained Pareto optimality may require that 2 subsidize 1's purchase of fence. See Hirshleifer (1984).

Experiments by Harrison and Hirshleifer (1986) with two players indicate that individuals will voluntarily provide nearly the Pareto-optimal quantity of public good in weakest-link ($w = 0$) situations, but underprovide in summation and best-shot situations. Experimental results by van de Kragt, Orbell, and Dawes (1983) with small groups also indicate that efficient public good provision is forthcoming in situations resembling the weakest-link technology. Thus, voluntary provision of public goods without coordination or coercion at Pareto-optimal levels is possible when the technology of public good provision conforms to the weakest-link condition. Unfortunately, with large communities it is difficult to think of many public goods for which voluntary provision is feasible, and all w_i for contributions greater than the minimum are zero or close to it. In large communities, therefore, some institutional mechanism for coordinating and coercing individual contributions to the supply of public goods seems likely to be needed.

2.6   Externalities

Public goods are a classic example of the kinds of market failures economists cite as justification for government intervention. Externalities are the second primary category of market failure. An externality occurs when the consumption or production activity of one individual or firm has an *unintended* impact on the utility or production function of another individual or firm. Individual A plants a tree to provide herself shade, but inadvertently blocks her neighbors' view of the valley. The pulp mill discharges waste into the river and inadvertently raises the costs of production for the brewery downstream. These activities may be contrasted with normal market transactions in which A's action, say, buying the tree, has an impact on B, the seller of the tree, but the impact is fully accounted for through the operation of the price system. There is no market for the view of the valley or the quality of water in the river, and thus no price mechanism for coordinating individual actions. Given the existence of externalities, a non-Pareto-optimal allocation of resources often results.

To see the problem more clearly, let us consider a situation in which two individuals each consume private good X, and A consumes externality creating good E. Individual A then purchases X and E so as to maximize her utility subject to the budget constraint, $Y_A = X_A P_x + E_A P_e$; that is, A maximizes

$$L = U_A(X_A, E_A) + \lambda(Y_A - X_A P_x - E_A P_e). \tag{2.34}$$

Maximization of (2.34) with respect to X and E yields the familiar first-order condition for individual utility maximization when there are two private goods:

$$\frac{\partial U_A/\partial E}{\partial U_A/\partial X} = \frac{P_e}{P_x}. \tag{2.35}$$

But E is an activity that produces an externality and thus enters B's utility function also, even though B does not buy or sell E. We can solve for the Pareto-optimal allocation of X and E by maximizing one individual's utility, subject to the constraints that the other individual's utility is held constant, and the combined budget of the two individuals is not exceeded.

$$L_{PO} = U_A(X_A, E_A) + \lambda(\bar{U}_B - U_B(X_B, E_A))$$
$$+ \gamma(Y_A + Y_B - P_x X_A - P_x X_B - P_e E_A). \tag{2.36}$$

The presence of A's consumption of E, E_A, in B's utility function represents the externality nature of the E activity. Maximizing (2.36) with respect to X_A, X_B, and E_A yields

$$\frac{\partial L_{PO}}{\partial X_A} = \frac{\partial U_A}{\partial X} - \gamma P_x = 0, \tag{2.37}$$

$$\frac{\partial L_{PO}}{\partial X_B} = \lambda\left(-\frac{\partial U_B}{\partial X}\right) - \gamma P_x = 0, \tag{2.38}$$

$$\frac{\partial L_{PO}}{\partial E_A} = \frac{\partial U_A}{\partial E} - \lambda\frac{\partial U_B}{\partial E} - \gamma P_e = 0. \tag{2.39}$$

Using (2.37) and (2.38) to eliminate λ and γ from (2.39), we obtain as the condition for Pareto optimality

$$\frac{\partial U_A/\partial E}{\partial U_A/\partial X} + \frac{\partial U_B/\partial E}{\partial U_B/\partial X} = \frac{P_e}{P_x} \tag{2.40}$$

or

$$\frac{\partial U_A/\partial E}{\partial U_A/\partial X} = \frac{P_e}{P_x} - \frac{\partial U_B/\partial E}{\partial U_B/\partial X}. \tag{2.41}$$

Equation (2.41) gives the condition for Pareto optimality; (2.35), the condition for individual A's optimal allocation of her budget. Equation (2.35) governs the determination of the level of E, since only A decides how much E is purchased. If activity E creates a positive externality,

$$\frac{\partial U_B/\partial E}{\partial U_B/\partial X} > 0,$$

then

$$\frac{\partial U_A/\partial E}{\partial U_A/\partial X}$$

is larger than is required for Pareto optimality. A purchases too little E (and too much X) when E produces a positive external economy. Conversely, when E generates a negative externality,

$$\frac{\partial U_B/\partial E}{\partial U_B/\partial X} < 0,$$

and A buys too much of E.

Although seemingly a separate category of market failure, the Pareto-optimality condition for an externality is identical to that for a pure public good, as a comparison of (2.40) and (2.11) reveals (Buchanan and Stubblebine, 1962). The difference between a pure public good and an externality is that in the case of a public good all members of the community consume the *same* good, whereas for an externality the good (bad) consumed by the second parties may differ from that consumed by the direct purchaser. When A contributes to the purchase of flowers for the town square, she helps finance a public good. When A plants flowers in her backyard, she creates a positive externality for those neighbors who can see and enjoy them. If some of A's neighbors are allergic to pollen from the flowers in her backyard, A's plantings create a negative externality. What is crucial to the issue of Pareto optimality is not that A and B consume precisely the same good, but that A's consumption alters B's utility in a manner not accounted for through the price system. B is not excluded from the side effects of A's consumption, and it is this nonexcludability condition that joins public goods and externalities by one and the same Pareto-optimality condition. It is this nonexcludability condition that necessitates some coordination of A and B's activities to achieve Pareto optimality.

One way to adjust A's consumption of E to bring about Pareto optimality is for the government to levy a tax or offer a subsidy to the E activity. If, for example, E generates a negative externality, a tax on E equal to

$$-\frac{\partial U_B/\partial E}{\partial U_B/\partial X}$$

raises the price of E relative to X by precisely the amount necessary to achieve Pareto optimality. Alternatively, a subsidy to A for each unit of E she consumes, less than the amount implied by (2.35), achieves the same effect. The existence of a government to correct for externalities by levying taxes and offering subsidies is a traditional explanation for government intervention most frequently associated with the name of Pigou (1920).

In most discussions of Pigouvian taxes, the government is assumed to "know" the marginal rates of substitution of the different parties generating and affected by the externalities. Often the government is referred to as an individual, the policymaker, who possesses all of the information relevant to determine the Pareto-optimal allocation of resources and who then announces the optimal taxes and subsidies. But where does the policymaker obtain this information? In some situations – for example, when one factory's activities affect the costs of another – one might think of the government policymaker as gathering engineering data and using these to make a decision. But when individual utilities are affected, the engineer's information-gathering problem is greatly complicated. Much of this book is concerned with describing how democratic institutions reveal information concerning individual preferences on externality-type decisions. The next section discusses a more direct approach to the question.

2.7 The Coase theorem

Ronald Coase, in a classic article published in 1960, challenged the conventional wisdom in economics regarding externalities, taxes, and subsidies. Coase argued that the existence of an external effect associated with a given activity did not inevitably require government intervention in the form of taxes and subsidies. Pareto-optimal resolutions of externality situations could be and often were worked out between the affected parties without the help of the government. Moreover, the nature of the outcome was independent of the assignment of property rights, that is, in the case of a negative externality associated with E whether the law granted the purchaser of E the right to purchase E in unlimited quantities, or the law granted B the right to be protected from any adverse effects from A's consumption of E.

Although Coase develops his argument by example, and neither states nor proves any theorems, the main results of the paper are commonly referred to as the Coase theorem. The theorem can be expressed as follows:

The Coase theorem: *In the absence of transaction and bargaining costs, affected parties to an externality will agree on an allocation of resources that is both Pareto optimal and independent of any prior assignment of property rights.*

Pigou was wrong; government intervention is not needed to resolve externality issues.

Consider first a discrete case of the theorem. Let A be a factory producing widgets with a by-product of smoke. Let C be a laundry whose costs are raised by A's emissions of smoke. Given that A is in business, C's profits are $24,000, but if A were to cease production altogether, C's profits would rise to $31,000. A's profits are $3,000. Assuming A's factors of production can be costlessly redeployed, society is better off if A ceases production. C then earns a net surplus over costs of $31,000, while the combined surplus when both A and C operate is only $27,000.

But suppose that there are no laws prohibiting smoke emissions. A is then free to produce, and the socially inferior outcome would appear to ensue. It would, however, pay C to bribe the owners of A to cease production by promising to pay them $3,000 per annum. Alternatively, C could acquire A and close it down. If i is the cost of capital, and the market expects A to earn $3,000 profits per year in perpetuity, then the market value of A is $3,000/i$. The present discounted value to C of shutting down A is $7,000/i$, however. The owners of C realize an increase in wealth of $4,000/i$ by acquiring and closing A.

To see that the socially efficient outcome arises regardless of the assignment of property rights, assume that A's annual profit is $10,000 and the figures for C are as before. Now the efficient solution requires that A continue to operate. Suppose, however, that the property rights lie with C. Strict air pollution laws exist and C can file a complaint against A and force it to cease production. However, the profits of A are now such that A can offer C a bribe of $7,000 + \alpha, 0 \le \alpha \le$ $3,000, not to file a complaint. The owners of both firms are as well or better off under this alternative than they are if A closes, and the socially efficient outcome can again be expected to occur.

Note that under the conditions of the first example, where A's profits were only $3,000, it would not pay A to bribe C to allow it to continue to produce, and the socially efficient outcome would again occur.

When the externality-producing activity has a variable effect on the second party as the level of the activity changes, the Coase theorem still holds. If A's marginal rate of substitution of E for X (MRS_{EX}^A) falls as E increases, then $MRS_{EX}^A - P_e/P_x$ is negative sloped, as in Figure 2.1. The point where $MRS_{EX}^A - P_e/P_x$ crosses the

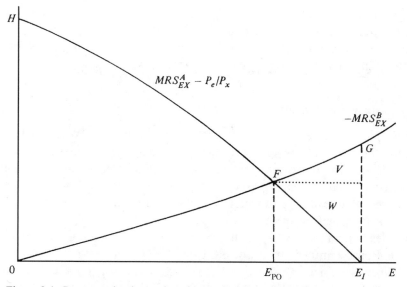

Figure 2.1. Pareto-optimal quantity of a good with external effects.

horizontal axis, E_1, is the level of E that A chooses when she acts independently of B. It is the level of E satisfying (2.35).

If E creates a negative externality on B, then $-MRS^B_{EX}$ is positive. In Figure 2.1, $-MRS^B_{EX}$ is drawn under the reasonable assumption that B is willing to give up an increasing amount of X to prevent A from consuming another unit of E, the higher E is. E_{PO} is the Pareto-optimal level of E, the level satisfying (2.41).

The area $E_{PO}FGE_1$ measures the utility loss to B from A's consumption of E_1 instead of E_{PO}. $E_{PO}FE_1$ measures A's utility gain from these extra units of E. Both B and A are made better off if A accepts a bribe of Z from B to consume E_{PO} rather than E_1, where $E_{PO}FE_1 < Z < E_{PO}FGE_1$. In particular, if B were to offer A a bribe of $E_{PO}F$ for each unit of E she refrained from consuming, A would choose to consume exactly E_{PO} units of E, and A would be better off by the area W and B by the area V as against the independent action outcome at E_1.

With the property rights reversed, B could forbid A from consuming E and force the outcome at 0. But then A would be foregoing $OHFE_{PO}$ benefits, while B gains only OFE_{PO}, as opposed to the Pareto-optimal allocation E_{PO}. Self-interest would lead A to propose and B to accept a bribe Z', to allow A to consume E_{PO}, where $OFE_{PO} < Z' < OHFE_{PO}$.[11]

Coase demonstrated his theorem with four examples drawn from actual cases. Several experiments have been run in which student subjects are given payoff tables that resemble those one would observe in an externality situation. Pareto-optimal

---

[11] For the quantity of E bought to be the same, whether A receives or pays the bribe, no income effects must be present. When they exist, precise solutions require the use of compensated demand functions (Buchanan and Stubblebine, 1962).

    I also abstract from the difficulty of people moving close to a negative externality to receive a bribe, as discussed by Baumol (1972).

outcomes are observed in well over 90 percent of the experiments.[12] The Coase theorem offers a logical and empirically relevant alternative to government action in externality situations. But does it hold up as the number of parties involved in the externality increases? We now address this question.

2.8   Coase and the core

The examples presented by Coase and those discussed above involve but two parties. Does the theorem hold when more than two parties are involved? Hoffman and Spitzer (1986) present experimental results in which Pareto-optimal allocations are achieved in Coasian bargains among as many as 38 parties. But Aivazian and Callen (1981) present an example in which the theorem breaks down with only 3 parties. Let us consider their example.

They deal with a factory, A, producing smoke and a laundry, C, as in our previous example. Representing company profits using the characteristic function notation of game theory, we can restate the previous example as having the following attributes: $V(A) = \$3,000$, $V(C) = \$24,000$, and $V(A, C) = \$31,000$, where $V(A, C)$ is a coalition between A and C, that is, a merger of A and C that results in A's ceasing production.

Now assume the existence of a second factory, B, producing smoke. Let the characteristic functions for this problem be defined as follows:

$$V(A) = \$3,000 \qquad V(B) = \$8,000 \qquad V(C) = \$24,000$$
$$V(A, B) = \$15,000 \qquad V(A, C) = \$31,000 \qquad V(B, C) = \$36,000$$
$$V(A, B, C) = \$40,000$$

The Pareto-optimal outcome is the grand coalition $V(A, B, C)$; that is, A and B cease production. If the property right lies with C, the Pareto outcome occurs, C forbids A and B to produce, and neither a coalition between A and B ($V[A, B] = \$15,000$) nor the two firms independently ($\$3,000 + \$8,000$) can offer C a large-enough bribe to offset its $\$16,000$ gain from going from $V(C)$ to $V(A, B, C)$.

Suppose, however, that A and B have the right to emit smoke. C offers A and B $\$3,000$ and $\$8,000$, respectively, to cease production. Such a proposal can be blocked by A offering to form a coalition with B and share $V(A, B) = \$15,000$ with allocations, say, of $X_A = \$6,500$, $X_B = \$8,500$. But C in turn can block a coalition between A and B by proposing a coalition between itself and B, with, say, $X_B = \$9,000$ and $X_C = \$27,000$. But this allocation can also be blocked.

To prove generally that the grand coalition is unstable, we show that it is not within the *core*. Basically, a grand coalition is within the core if no subset of the coalition can form, including an individual acting independently, and provide its members higher payoffs than they can obtain in the grand coalition. If (X_A, X_B, X_C) is an

---

[12] See Hoffman and Spitzer (1982, 1986); Harrison and McKee (1985); and Coursey, Hoffman, and Spitzer (1987).

allocation in the core, then it must satisfy conditions (2.42), (2.43), and (2.44):

$$X_A + X_B + X_C = V(A, B, C) \qquad (2.42)$$

$$X_A \geq V(A), X_B \geq V(B), X_C \geq V(C) \qquad (2.43)$$

$$X_A + X_B \geq V(A, B), X_A + X_C \geq V(A, C), X_B + X_C \geq V(B, C). \qquad (2.44)$$

Condition (2.44) implies that

$$X_A + X_B + X_C \geq \frac{1}{2}[V(A, B) + V(A, C) + V(B, C)], \qquad (2.45)$$

which from (2.42) implies that

$$V(A, B, C) \geq \frac{1}{2}[V(A, B) + V(A, C) + V(B, C)]. \qquad (2.46)$$

But the numbers of the example contradict (2.46):

$$\$40,000 < \frac{1}{2}(\$15,000 + \$31,000 + \$36,000) = \$41,000.$$

The grand coalition is not in the core.

The primary issue in the present example is the externality of smoke caused by factories A and B imposed upon the laundry C. That there are gains from internalizing this externality is represented by the assumptions that

$$V(A, C) > V(A) + V(C) \qquad (2.47)$$

$$V(B, C) > V(B) + V(C) \qquad (2.48)$$

$$V(A, B, C) > V(A) + V(B, C) \qquad (2.49)$$

$$V(A, B, C) > V(B) + V(A, C). \qquad (2.50)$$

In their example, Aivazian and Callen also make the assumption that an externality exists between the two smoking factories; that is, there are gains to their forming a coalition independent of the laundry C:

$$V(A, B) > V(A) + V(B). \qquad (2.51)$$

Now this is clearly a separate externality from that involving C and either or both of the two factories. Aivazian and Callen (p. 177) assume the existence of an economy of scale between A and B. But the existence of this second externality is crucial to the proof that no core exists. Combining (2.49) and (2.50) we obtain

$$V(A, B, C) > \frac{1}{2}[V(A) + V(B) + V(B, C) + V(A, C)]. \qquad (2.52)$$

If now $V(A, B) \leq V(A) + V(B)$ – that is, there are no economies to forming the A, B coalition – then

$$V(A, B, C) > \frac{1}{2}[V(A, B) + V(B, C) + V(A, C)] \qquad (2.53)$$

and condition (2.46) is satisfied. The grand coalition is now in the core. Aivazian and Callen's demonstration that no core exists when property rights are assigned to the factories comes about not simply because a third player has been added to the game, but because a second externality has also been added, namely, the gain from combining A and B. Moreover, the absence of the core hinges on the requirement that both externalities be eliminated simultaneously with the help of but one liability rule.

To what extent does this example weaken Coase's theorem? As long as we are concerned with eliminating the inefficiency caused by a single externality, I do not think that the example has much relevance. Suppose, for example, that the property rights are with A and B, but that the law allows C to close them if it pays just compensation. C offers the owners of A and B \$3,000 and \$8,000 per annum in perpetuity if they cease to operate. They refuse, demanding \$15,000. If the matter were to go to court, should the court consider an argument for awarding \$15,000 on the grounds that A and B could earn that much if they continued to operate *and if they decided to merge*? I doubt that any court would entertain such an argument. Nevertheless, by including the value of the coalition between A and B in the examination of the existence of the core, we have given legitimacy to a threat by A and B to merge and eliminate one externality as a hindrance to the formation of a coalition among C, A, and B to eliminate another. Conceptually, it seems preferable to assume that either A and B definitely will merge, absent agreement with C, or they will not. If they will, negotiation is between C and the coalition A, B and the Coase theorem holds, since $V(A, B, C) > V(C) + V(A, B)$. If A and B will not merge, (2.52) is the relevant condition for determining the existence of the core, and the theorem again holds.[13]

2.9   A generalization of the Coase theorem

The Coase theorem breaks down in Aivazian and Callen's example, because no stable coalition can form among the three actors. If firm C approaches A and proposes that they form a coalition that would increase both firms' profits, B steps forward and makes A a better offer. But this coalition is also vulnerable to a counteroffer from C. This form of *cycling* from one possible outcome to another will pop up throughout the book. It arises because each actor can *unilaterally* break any "agreement" and accept a better offer.

Bernholz (1997a, 1998) has proposed to rescue the Coase theorem, therefore, by restricting an individual's freedom to break a contract once made. Specifically, Bernholz requires that all *external* contracts and all *internal* contracts be *binding*, meaning that a contract, once made, can only be broken if *all* parties agree to break it. An example of an external contract would be an agreement between firms A and

---

[13] The combined market values of A and B must lie between \$11,000$/i$, the value the market places on the firms if it assigns a zero probability to their merging (\$3,000$/i$ + \$8,000$/i$), and \$15,000$/i$, the value of a merged firm. Thus, the option of C buying A and B and forming the grand coalition through merger must exist if ownership claims to A and B are for sale. Thus, in the spirit of the Coase theorem, individual actions and the market for firms can optimally eliminate the externality without government intervention.

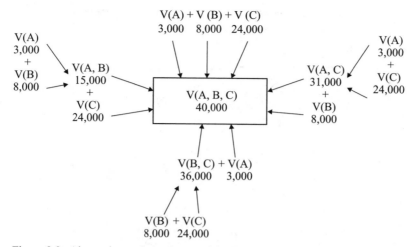

Figure 2.2. Alternative paths to the grand coalition.

C to merge and form a new firm. Once this contract has been signed, the requirement that all internal contracts be binding implies that *A* could accept an offer to merge with *B* only if *C* agreed. Since *C* is worse off playing the game alone, *C* would only agree to let *A* break and join with *B* if *A* and *B* offered *C* a compensating bribe. But the gain to *A* and *B* from forming a coalition is not sufficient to compensate *C* for its loss if *C* breaks with *A*, and thus *C* will never agree to allow *A* to merge with *B*. Once *A* and *C* have agreed to merge, the only new agreement possible is one to form the grand coalition, and it will be forthcoming, since it can lead to an improvement in the positions of all parties. Thus, when all internal and external contracts are binding, one of the four sequences of moves depicted in Figure 2.2 must take place. Either the three firms form the grand coalition immediately, or a pair of them merge, and then this pair goes on to merge with the remaining third company.

Given the presence of well-defined property rights and the absence of transaction costs, Bernholz (1997a, 1998) proves that the existence of binding internal and external contracts suffices to ensure that the Pareto frontier is reached. Starting from a state of anarchy, rational self-interested individuals could and would join a series of contracts that would carry them out to the Pareto frontier. No cycling problems of the type posed by Aivazian and Callen would arise, nor of the types discussed later in this book.[14] In a world of zero transaction costs, the state's only role would be to define the initial set of property rights and enforce all contracts to ensure that they are, indeed, binding. Coase's initial insight – that two rational individuals would, in the absence of transaction costs, contract to resolve a conflict over an externality in a way that achieves Pareto optimality – can be generalized to *all* individuals contracting to resolve *all* collective action problems optimally. (Bernholz's theorem does not, of course, overturn the demonstration that no core exists in the example of three factories, as well as in a much broader set of examples.

---

[14] Bernholz makes some additional assumptions, but the key assumptions for the proof are those of zero transaction costs and binding contracts.

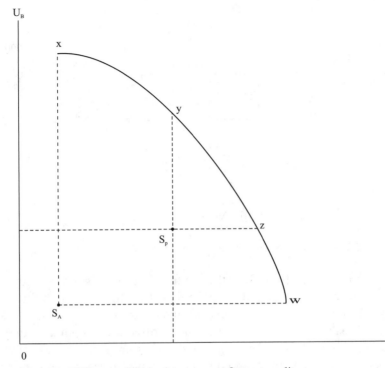

Figure 2.3. Utility possibilities in presence of an externality.

Thus, the possibility cannot be ruled out that a Pareto-optimal set of contracts is never achieved. Just as Buridan's ass stood paralyzed unable to choose between two equidistant stacks of hay, individuals faced with several contractual options, each of which would improve their welfare, may be unable to choose any one, and thus fail to join any. Although a logical possibility, for individuals who are more rational than Buridan's ass, one expects that they would eventually join one advantageous contract and then move on to others as they march toward the Pareto frontier.)

2.10   Does the Coase theorem hold without predefined property rights?

In our statement of the Coase theorem, the Pareto-optimal allocation is reached *independent of any initial assignment of property rights*. What happens, however, if there is no initial assignment of property rights? Does the Coase theorem still hold?

To see what is involved, consider Figure 2.3. A undertakes activity E which creates an externality that harms B, as discussed in the example involving Figure 2.1. The initial assignment of property rights favors A. S_P represents the levels of utility that A and B experience when A purchases E without regard for B (E_I in Figure 2.1). The minimum bribe that A will accept to achieve the Pareto-optimal outcome equals the triangular area under her demand schedule between E_I and E_{PO}.

If B pays only this minimum bribe his utility increases by the equivalent of $W + V$ in Figure 2.1, and the outcome shifts from S_P to y. If, on the other hand, all of the gains from reducing the level of E go to A, the outcome shifts from S_P to z. The curve connecting points y and z represents all of the combinations of utility that A and B can attain by reducing A's consumption of E to its Pareto-optimal level. The Coase theorem states that in the absence of transaction costs some point between y and z is attained.

What happens, however, if there are no assigned property rights? Presumably A will want to consume E_I. B will want to prevent A from consuming any E. To do so, B might buy a gun or hire a thug to intimidate A. Violence might ensue. Without assigned property rights A and B are thrust back into anarchy and additional resources might be wasted in the struggle to determine how much E, if any, A will be able to consume. The status quo under anarchy shifts back from S_P to S_A.

But if there are zero transaction costs, A and B will not stay at S_A; they will agree to move costlessly to some point on $y - z$. If by zero transaction costs we mean zero *bargaining costs*, then rational self-interested individuals will never expend resources to resolve conflicts, since these conflicts can always be resolved at no cost to both parties' advantage. A and B move instantaneously from S_A to $y - z$.

Such an interpretation of the zero transaction costs assumption both trivializes it and converts the Coase theorem into a tautology, which merely states that rational people will never pass up opportunities to make themselves better off at zero cost.[15]

At the same time, however, the argument helps illustrate just how important are the assumptions that we make about transaction costs, and it gives additional insight as to why property rights are valuable. The range of utility combinations that make both A and B better off is much greater when they are bargaining from point S_A than from point S_P. Thus, the stakes involved in the bargaining are much greater at S_A than at S_P. In the real world, where bargains are not costlessly consummated, it might be easier for A and B to strike a bargain if they start from point S_P, since the stakes are much smaller there. This in turn explains why individuals might choose from a state of anarchy like that represented by S_A to define property rights. Such rights may reduce future transaction and bargaining costs.[16]

2.11   Externalities with large numbers of individuals

The Coase theorem implies that when transaction costs are zero, all collective choices that promise a Pareto improvement are made. No public good with benefits greater than costs goes unprovided; no Pareto-relevant external effect is left unaltered; no firm that would make a profit fails to get started, no matter how large the number of participants needed to bring about the optimal collective choice.

In the next section, we shall indicate why the zero transaction costs assumption becomes increasingly implausible as the number of participants in a collective action increases. Now, however, we consider an argument that the Coase theorem is

[15] See Mueller (1991) and Usher (1998).
[16] See, again, Mueller (1991). We return to the issue of why rights might be defined in Chapters 26 and 27.

"undermined" by increasing numbers of participants, *even* when transaction costs remain zero.[17]

We have already demonstrated this proposition in Sections 2.4 and 2.5 for the case of voluntary individual contributions to a public good taking the contributions of all other individuals as given. Except in the case of the most extreme weakest-link technology, the quantity of the public good provided as a percentage of the Pareto-optimal amount becomes vanishingly small as the number of contributors increases.

Consider now a slightly different example involving a discrete public good that would seem to make the attainment of Pareto optimality through voluntary action more likely.[18] A dike that will forever protect a community from flooding can be built at a cost of C. Each of the N members of the community has identical tastes and income and would experience a utility gain of V if the dike were built. Obviously, the dike should be built if $NV > C$. But a collective decision must be made to provide this public good. A meeting is called to which all N members of the community are invited. Each person is free to attend or not. Those attending can decide whether to provide the public good and share its costs amongst themselves, or not. Absent an institution like the state that can *compel* contributions, however, those who do not attend the meeting cannot be forced to contribute to the public good's costs.

Given the zero transaction (bargaining) costs assumption, we can assume that the n individuals who show up at the meeting choose to build the dike, if $nV > C$, and, let us say, they decide to share its costs equally. Knowing this, each individual must decide whether to attend the meeting. With all individuals identical, it is reasonable to confine our attention to symmetric strategy choices. There are only two *pure* strategy choices – to participate or to abstain – and thus only two possible, symmetric Nash equilibria in pure strategies – one where all participate and one where all abstain. Let M be the minimum number of participants that suffices for the dike to be built, $(M - 1)V < C < MV$. Then participation is a symmetric, Nash equilibrium if and only if $M = N$. With $M < N$ and all other persons participating, an individual is better off abstaining and free-riding on the provision of the public good by the rest of the community. The case $M = N$ corresponds to the extreme form of weakest-link technology described in Section 2.4, and again produces the Pareto-optimal quantity of the public good with voluntary participation.

Abstention is a symmetric Nash equilibrium for any M above one. If two or more individuals must participate for the dike to be built, and all other $(N - 1)$ individuals

[17] We follow the development of the argument by Dixit and Olson (2000). See also, however, Palfrey and Rosenthal (1984).

[18] Voluntary contributions should be more likely with discrete public goods, because *no* public good is provided at all unless the total amount contributed exceeds the lump sum cost of the public good – referred to in the experimental literature as the "provision point." Although the existence of a provision point by itself does not seem to mitigate free-rider behavior in public goods experiments (Isaac, Schmidtz, and Walker, 1989; Asch, Gigliotti, and Polito, 1993), Isaac, Schmidtz, and Walker (1989) and Bagnoli and McKee (1991) do find significantly higher voluntary contributions in experiments that include both provision points and a give-back option. In these experiments an individual only "loses his contribution" if the provision point is reached and the public good is provided. This combination of a provision point and a give-back option characterizes the following example, and thus we would expect from these experiments that the participants at the meetings would decide whether the public good is provided would contribute the required amount.

are abstaining, there is no reason for the Nth individual not to abstain also. With even modestly large Ns, the number of situations in which $M \geq 2$ is likely to be far greater than the number satisfying $M = N$. Thus, if pure strategy equilibria were to emerge, they would most likely involve all members of the community abstaining.

Recognizing this, our sophisticated resident might choose to adopt a *mixed* strategy, that is, to participate with probability $P, 0 < P < 1$, and to abstain with probability $(1 - P)$. This way, if all persons choose the same P, there is at least a positive probability that the public good is provided. Of course, there must then also be a positive probability that the public good is *not* provided, and this alone undermines the Coase theorem to a degree.

Consider now the decision of Tip, a typical member of the community. If Tip participates, and the public good is provided, his net benefits are $(V - C/n)$ with n participants. His expected benefits if he participates are then the probability that the public good is provided, that is, the probability that $n \geq M \times (V - C/n)$.

$$\sum_{n=M}^{N} \frac{(N-1)!}{(n-1)!((N-1)-(n-1))!} P^{n-1}(1-P)^{(N-1)-(n-1)} \left[V - \frac{C}{n} \right]. \qquad (2.54)$$

The expected benefit from abstention is V times the probability that the public good is provided even when he abstains:

$$\sum_{n=M}^{N-1} \frac{(N-1)!}{n!(N-1-n)!} P^{n}(1-P)^{N-1-n} V. \qquad (2.55)$$

Whenever $n > M$, the public good would have been provided without Tip's participation, and he loses C/n. He experiences a *net* gain by participating only when his participation raises n to equality with M, an invent whose probability falls as N increases, holding M/N constant. Dixit and Olson (2000) calculate P, and the cumulative probability that enough people participate so that the public good is provided, π, for various values of C, M, and N, holding V fixed at 1.0. A few of their calculations are reproduced in Table 2.1.

When one person's participation is decisive, $C/M < V < C/(M + 1)$. The size of the gain from this person's participation $(V - C/M)$ is then the crucial number to induce participation. Thus, seemingly small changes in C can have big effects on P and π. With $M = 10$ and $N = 20$, the probability of an individual's participating falls from 0.091 to 0.011 as C goes from 9.1 to 9.9. But even in the case where $P = 0.091$, the probability that 10 or more people choose to participate is a mere 0.0000032. Even this probability looks large compared to the other entries in the table. Only for very small communities are the probabilities of participation, and that the public good is provided, reasonably high. (If $V = 1.0, C = 1.5, M = 2$, and $N = 6$, then $P = 0.176$ and $\pi = 0.285$.)

What would happen if someone called a meeting to provide a pure public good and no one came? Obviously, the public good would not be provided. But equally as obvious – if there are zero transaction costs – it would pay to call another meeting. Surely, if the public good failed to be provided at the first meeting, individuals would

Table 2.1. *Optimal participation probabilities, P, and public good provision probabilities, π, when participation is voluntary*

| | | | | $V = 1.0$ | | | |
| | $C = 9.1$ | | $C = 9.5$ | | $C = 9.9$ | |
N	P	π	P	π	P	π
			$M = 10$			
20	.091	$.32 \times 10^{-5}$	.053	$.18 \times 10^{-7}$	.011	$.40 \times 10^{-14}$
30	.048	$.76 \times 10^{-6}$	.027	$.37 \times 10^{-8}$	.005	$.66 \times 10^{-15}$
40	.032	$.43 \times 10^{-6}$	.018	$.20 \times 10^{-8}$	.004	$.33 \times 10^{-15}$
80	.014	$.20 \times 10^{-6}$	.008	$.87 \times 10^{-9}$	.002	$.14 \times 10^{-15}$
160	.007	$.15 \times 10^{-6}$	.004	$.61 \times 10^{-9}$	.001	$.94 \times 10^{-16}$
			$M = 50$			
60	.084	$.60 \times 10^{-43}$	.049	$.97 \times 10^{-55}$	.010	$.11 \times 10^{-88}$
100	.018	$.27 \times 10^{-58}$	.010	$.10 \times 10^{-70}$	.002	$.26 \times 10^{-105}$
150	.009	$.74 \times 10^{-62}$	.005	$.23 \times 10^{-74}$	$.001^a$	$.48 \times 10^{-109}$
200	.006	$.30 \times 10^{-63}$	$.003^a$	$.88 \times 10^{-76}$	$.001^a$	$.17 \times 10^{-110}$
250	.005	$.56 \times 10^{-64}$	$.003^a$	$.16 \times 10^{-76}$	$.001^a$	$.29 \times 10^{-111}$

[a] These numbers differ from the identical numbers in this column when written to four decimal places.

Source: Dixit and Olson (2000, Tables 1 and 3).

reevaluate their decisions to abstain, and show up at the second meeting, or the third, or the fourth. Alas, quite to the contrary. If more meetings were held, a rational, self-interested individual would be encouraged to *lower* his P and take a chance that enough people to provide the good show up at a meeting before he does.[19]

To ensure that the public good is provided in a reasonable amount of time, it is necessary to both call a meeting *and announce* that the public good will be provided only in the event that all N members of the community participate. The "threat" of not providing the public good if $M \leq n < N$ is credible, so long as there are no costs to calling another meeting, since in a meeting where $n < N$, all participants gain by adjourning and waiting until $n = N$. Knowing that the public good will only be provided when everyone attends the meeting, each person might as well attend the first meeting called. The Coase theorem is reconfirmed under the proviso that some agent (the state?) both calls a meeting of all community members and announces that the community will only reach a positive decision if all members participate.

We are thus forced to qualify the implications of the generalized Coase theorem discussed in Section 2.9. The requirement of binding external and internal contracts may not suffice to ensure that all Pareto-preferred contracts actually are written. When a nonexcludable public good is involved, it may be necessary to require that

[19] Of course, $\pi > 0$ if $P > 0$. Thus, as long as P does not go to zero, the possibility remains that the public good is provided, even if π becomes infinitesimal. If the zero transaction costs assumption is interpreted as implying that an infinitely large number of meetings could be called in an infinitely short period of time, then the Coase theorem is reconfirmed.

all members of the community participate in the writing of the binding contract to provide it.[20]

2.12 Externalities with large numbers of individuals – a second time

Several years ago residents of the community of Shangrila unanimously voted to tax themselves to pay for a dike that would protect them from floods. At that time they formed the Preservation of Shangrila from Floods Club (PSFC). The PSFC meets once a year to decide on the taxes needed to maintain the dike.

As Shangrila has grown and prospered, a second problem has arisen. The number of autos has grown so large that the air of Shangrila has become polluted. Jane, a jogger who owns a bike but no car, surmises that there are many like herself who would be willing to tax themselves to offer all automobile drivers a bribe to reduce the pollution from their cars. She decides to form a club – the Preservation of Shangrila from Pollution Club (PSPC). Consider now the task confronting Jane. She must first approach all of those who, like herself, desire cleaner air, and ask them to attend a meeting to form the PSPC. If they have read the previous section, some may choose not to attend this meeting in the hope that the meeting will agree to offer motorists the bribe and succeed in reducing pollution without their having to contribute anything. But even if all potential contributors attend, the meeting faces the task of deciding how much to collect from each participant and how much to offer as bribes. Should the PSPC form and overcome this obstacle, it still faces the formidable task of contacting all motorists and getting them to agree to undertake the measures necessary to improve air quality in exchange for the bribes. The zero transaction costs assumption is clearly untenable. The transaction costs of organizing these two groups of individuals are mind-boggling.

In desolation Jane is about to abandon her idea, when she remembers that she is already a member of a club that includes all of the relevant parties – the PSFC. She can make a tax/bribe proposal at the next meeting of the PSFC. If a Pareto-optimal reduction in pollution is possible, there must exist a combination of taxes and subsidies that will win the unanimous support of all citizens of Shangrila. Having resolved this issue, the meeting might go on to consider other issues, like protecting the community from fires and theft, lighting the streets, and so on.

We have discovered another possible reason for the state's existence: to economize on the transaction costs of making collective decisions. Although a separate, voluntary, contractual agreement might be relied upon to correct every market failure in a world of zero transaction costs, in the real world the costs of forming each separate club and writing each contract would be enormous. Once a club that includes all members of the community has been formed to resolve one market

---

[20] Dixit and Olson show, however, that this result is not robust to the introduction of a modest transaction cost in the form of a cost of attending the meeting. Given such a cost, each individual has an incentive to abstain to avoid it. Should enough persons attend a meeting to provide the public good ($n \geq M$), they now have the incentive to do so, even if $n < N$, so as to avoid incurring the cost of attending the meeting another time.

failure, considerable savings can be made in the costs of bringing together the different groups involved, if this same club is used to resolve other market failures. Thus, the state can be defined as a kind of involuntary membership club that exists to economize on transaction costs when resolving the many market failures that a community faces.[21]

2.13   Experimental results in the voluntary provision of public goods

The assumption of rational, self-interested behavior leads to the following two predictions:

1. In a two-person prisoners' dilemma game that is played only once, both players select the noncooperative strategy.
2. If a two-person prisoners' dilemma game is repeated indefinitely, both players *may* at some point begin to select the cooperative strategy at each new play of the game.

Neither of these predictions has been well supported in laboratory experiments in which subjects, typically university students, play prisoners' dilemma games or, what amounts to the same thing, decide how much to contribute voluntarily to the provision of a public good. Roughly half the participants in one-shot, two-person prisoners' dilemma games cooperate; voluntary contributions to pure public goods average roughly half of the cooperative strategy contribution in one-shot games and in the first round of repeated games. Contributions *fall* if the game is repeated with the same players, reaching the level consistent with the optimal noncooperative strategy after a half dozen or so plays of the game. Both sets of findings contradict the assumption that the subjects in these experiments would behave as rational egoists.[22]

Somewhat more reassuring for the prisoners' dilemma supergame predictions are results from oligopoly experiments, which show first a decline in cooperation as in prisoners' dilemma experiments, and then a continual increase in cooperation until the perfect-collusion/cooperative outcome is reestablished. This cooperative solution does not reemerge, however, until the oligopoly game has been replicated some 35 or more times (Alger, 1987; Benson and Faminow, 1988).

A behavioral assumption that is consistent with the results in these various experiments is that the subjects are *adaptive* egoists. Their current behaviors reflect their past conditioning. Most people since their childhoods have been rewarded for cooperating in prisoners' dilemma situations (being honest, helpful, generous)

---

[21] When one uses the government to correct for more than one externality and to determine public goods levels *simultaneously*, one confronts head on the problem raised by Aivazian and Callen (1981). One might then anticipate that the absence of a core – that is, the absence of an equilibrium – will be a problem with respect to government decisions on public goods and externalities. This anticipation is correct. See, also, Aivazian and Callen (2000).

[22] The number of experiments of this type is immense. The findings have been surveyed by Davis and Holt (1993, ch. 6), Roth (1995, pp. 26–35), Ledyard (1995), Ostrom and Walker (1997), and Hoffman (1997).

and punished for not cooperating. When they first view the payoffs in a typical voluntary-contribution-public-good experiment, they recognize this as a situation in which cooperation is expected and in the past has been rewarded. Their conditioned reaction is to cooperate, at least to a degree. Such cooperative behavior can quickly be extinguished, however, by the noncooperative or half-cooperative behavior of the other player(s). Indeed, the tit-for-tat strategy, which has fared so well in computer-simulated prisoners' dilemma games, is nothing more than a strategy for conditioning cooperation through the play of the game by rewarding past cooperation and punishing noncooperation.[23]

Evidence of the importance of prior conditioning for determining an individual's behavior in game situations has recently been provided by Glaeser, Laibson, Scheinkman, and Soutter (GLSS, 2000). Their experiments involved individuals' propensity to *trust* other individuals rather than to contribute to a public good; but if background variables are important in one context they are likely to be important in the other. GLSS found that people who disagreed with the statement "you can't trust strangers anymore" were more trusting in the experiments in which they later participated. Both whites and nonwhites tended to be more trusting of members of their own race than of members of a different race. This behavior seems likely to have been conditioned by the individuals' past experiences with strangers and members of other social groups.[24]

There are two reasons to expect the amount of cooperation in a prisoners' dilemma game, or contributions in a voluntary-contribution-public-good game to fall as the number of players increases: (1) the marginal gain from contributing falls as the number of players increases, and (2) it becomes more difficult to identify and punish defectors. The first explanation is the basis for the increasing inefficiency outcome of the voluntary contribution examples discussed in Sections 2.4, 2.5, and 2.11. This prediction has been well supported in the experimental literature. Although individuals do not free-ride to the degree predicted by the rational actor model, they do respond to marginal incentives and contribute more when there are greater marginal gains from doing so.[25]

In a two-person prisoners' dilemma game, defection by the other player can be easily detected and punished. With three or more players, it may be difficult to determine which other player defects, and it is certainly impossible to punish a player who has defected without also punishing all others. This important difference between

[23] Ahn, Ostrom, Schmidt, Shupp, and Walker (2001) and Clark and Sefton (2001) provide experimental evidence of this sort of conditioning of players in repeated game situations.

[24] We shall discuss the potential explanatory power of the adaptive egoism postulate at greater length in Chapter 14, when we attempt to explain another paradox for the rational actor model – why people vote.

[25] See Ledyard (1995, pp. 149–51). An exception to this finding is reported by Isaac, Walker, and Williams (1994), who find that increasing the marginal reward from a contribution while holding the number of players constant has either no effect, or perversely *reduces* the level of contributions, when the number of players is held constant. They do find, however, that when the marginal reward is reduced and the number of players is simultaneously increased, contributions fall. Fisher, Isaac, Schatzenberg, and Walker (1995) find that differences in marginal rewards from contributions within a group are associated with significant differences in contributions with higher marginal incentives associated with higher contributions. See also the discussion in Ostrom and Walker (1997, pp. 49–69).

two-person and *n*-person ($n > 2$) prisoners' dilemmas may explain why coopera-tion, in the form of perfect collusion, is often observed in duopoly games, where Cournot and other noncooperative equilibria dominate in all oligopoly games with three or more players (Holt, 1995, pp. 406–9). Although this conclusion is not with-out controversy, the results from voluntary-contribution-public-good experiments seem to imply that a player's contribution either remains constant or *increases* as the number of players increases, when the marginal gain from an individual con-tribution is held constant (Ledyard, 1995, pp. 151–8; Ostrom and Walker, 1997, pp. 49–69).

None of these experimental findings offers unqualified support for the predictions of the rational actor models regarding human behavior in prisoners' dilemma-type situations. These findings should not be viewed as undermining the explanation for the existence of the state that rests on prisoners' dilemma/market failure/free-rider behavior, however. In an experimental setting, cooperators and defectors can only be rewarded and punished through the play of the game, or perhaps if communication is allowed, through the verbal rewards and reprimands of the other players. In the real world, a much richer set of rewards and punishments is available, from the slap on the hand or a pat on the head given to a child, to chopping off a hand or a head, in the case of an adult. In real-world settings, individuals do not need to *discover* what their behavior should be and what the other "players" are likely to do, as often is the case in experiments; they are usually told directly. In many real-world settings, communication among the players is possible, and, in this regard, the consistent finding in experiments that cooperation increases when communication is allowed is reassuring.[26]

Thus, if anything, the results from the many prisoners' dilemma and voluntary-contribution-public-good experiments underline the need for an institution like the state that announces what behavior is expected of all individuals in these situations, and helps ensure that this behavior is forthcoming.

Bibliographical notes

Several studies have chosen the state of anarchy as a starting point and shown how property rights, or private protection agencies or the state might emerge as institutional solutions to the social dilemma presented by anarchy. See Skaperdas (1992), Usher (1992), and Sutter (1995).

The best, short introduction to the prisoners' dilemma game is probably by Luce and Raiffa (1957, pp. 94–113). Rapoport and Chammah (1965) have a book on the subject. Taylor (1987, pp. 60–108) presents in a collective choice context an exhaustive discussion of the possibilities of the cooperative solution emerging as an equilibrium in a prisoners' dilemma supergame. Hardin (1982, 1997) also discusses the prisoners' dilemma in a public choice context. Axelrod (1984) explores in depth

---

[26] See Davis and Holt (1993, pp. 334–8) and Ledyard (1995). Of particular interest in this regard are experiments by Gächter and Fehr (1997), who find that even a minimal opportunity to discuss contributions before and after the experiments serves as a sufficient degree of social sanctioning to induce students to contribute significantly more to the provision of a public good.

the tit-for-tat solution to the prisoners' dilemma supergame and its relevance to the achievement of cooperative outcomes in real-world situations.

Other works that link the prisoners' dilemma to public goods include Runciman and Sen (1965), Hardin (1971, 1982, 1997), Riker and Ordeshook (1973, pp. 296–300), and Taylor (1987, ch. 1). In his excellent survey of the public choice field, Inman (1987, pp. 649–72) discusses several additional explanations of a prisoner's dilemma and why government intervention may improve allocative efficiency.

The experimental literature on prisoners' dilemmas and voluntary contributions to public goods is surveyed by Davis and Holt (1993), Roth (1995), Ledyard (1995), Ostrom and Walker (1997), and Hoffman (1997).

Hamlin (1986) reviews the normative issues surrounding a rational choice theory of the state, placing heavy emphasis on prisoners' dilemma-type rationales for collective action.

Some interesting examples of real-world situations that take on the characteristics of the chicken game, as well as an analysis of solutions to the game, are given by Taylor and Ward (1982).

Classic discussions of externalities include the essays by Meade (1952) and Scitovsky (1954), as well as Buchanan and Stubblebine's (1962) paper and Baumol's book (1967b). Mishan (1971) surveys the literature and Ng (1980, ch. 7) has an interesting discussion of both externalities and the Coase theorem. Cornes and Sandler (1986) provide an integrated analysis of externalities and of both pure and quasi-public goods.

The core is discussed and defined by Luce and Raiffa (1957, pp. 192–6).

Dahlman (1979) links transaction costs and government intervention to the Coase theorem. Frohlich and Oppenheimer (1970) show that more than individual rationality and self-interest (e.g., transaction costs) are needed to conclude that the extent of free-riding increases with group size.

CHAPTER 3

The reason for collective choice – redistribution

Political organization is to be understood as that part of social organization which constantly carries on directive restraining functions for public ends. . . .

That the cooperation into which men have gradually risen secures to them benefits which could not be secured while, in their primitive state, they acted singly, and that, as an indispensable means to this cooperation political organization has been, and is, advantageous, we shall see on contrasting the states of men who are not politically organized with the states of men who are politically organized in less or greater degrees.

Herbert Spencer

As the state arose from the need to keep class antagonisms in check, but also arose in the thick of the fight between the classes, it is normally the state of the most powerful, economically dominant, class which by its means becomes also the politically dominant class and so acquires new means of holding down and exploiting the oppressed class. The ancient state was, above all, the state of the slave owners for holding down the slaves.

Friedrich Engels

When there is no middle class, and the poor greatly exceed in number, troubles arise, and the state soon becomes to an end.

Aristotle

A decent provision for the poor is the true test of civilization.

Samuel Johnson

It is easy to envisage government arising out of pristine anarchy to fulfill a collective need of the community (say, protection from a predator) or to coordinate hunting or other food-gathering activity. But it is just as easy to envisage a distributional motivation behind the origin of the state. The best hunter or warrior becomes the chief of the tribe and eventually acquires sufficient authority to extract tribute from his fellow tribesmen. War and police activity begin as the primary activities of "government" but gains from these activities are claimed by the authoritarian leader(s) of the tribe.

Thus, the state can be envisaged as coming into existence either to satisfy the collective needs of *all* members of the community, or to help gratify the wants of only a part of it. The first explanation corresponds to the achievement of allocative efficiency; the second to redistribution.[1]

The distinction between allocative efficiency and redistribution is fundamental in economics and public choice. In the allocation of private goods, market exchange can guide society "as if by an invisible hand" from points inside the Pareto-possibility frontier to a point upon it. However, this point is chosen blindly. How the gains from trade are distributed is determined arbitrarily, but since this distributional issue is resolved as a by-product of a process benefiting all parties, it need not become a bone of contention.

To obtain Pareto efficiency in the allocation of public goods, a collective choice process that is less anarchic than the market is required. A conscious choice of the quantities of each public good to be produced must be made and along with it the choice of means for paying for them. The issue of the distribution of the gains from collective action is more clearly visible in the allocation of public goods by a political process than it is in the allocation of private goods by a market exchange process. And the possibility arises that this and *other* distributional issues become dominant in the political process.

In this chapter we examine several hypotheses as to why redistribution occurs, after which we shall examine some statistics regarding the actual distribution activities of governments. We begin with four hypotheses of *voluntary* redistribution, hypotheses that predict that collective decisions to redistribute income – like collective decisions to improve allocative efficiency – could in principle be made *unanimously*.

3.1 Redistribution as insurance

At the time individuals emerge from the state of anarchy and form civil society, considerable uncertainty over the consequences of this step is likely. Some people may take great advantage of the secure property rights established in the new constitution and become rich. Others may be less successful. Buchanan and Tullock (1962, ch. 8) argue that this sort of uncertainty at the constitutional stage can lead individuals to include provisions for redistribution into the constitution.

To see what is involved, assume that there will be two income classes in the post-constitutional society, with every member of a given class having the same income, Y_i and $Y_2 > Y_1$. Let r be the number of rich in class 2 and p the number of poor in class 1. An individual uncertain of her future position chooses a tax of T on the rich and a benefit subsidy B to the poor so as to maximize the following objective function:

$$O = \pi_2 U_2(Y_2 - T) + \pi_1 U_1(Y_1 + B), \tag{3.1}$$

where π_2 and π_1 are the probabilities that she will be in classes 2 and 1, respectively

---

[1] For discussions of how exploitative dictatorship might emerge out of anarchy, see Skaperdas (1992), Usher (1992, ch. 4), Olson (1993), and Chapter 18. It is interesting to note that political anthropologists have engaged in the same debate regarding the origins of the state as modern public choice scholars have regarding its current activities. For an excellent review of the debate in political anthropology, see Haas (1982).

$(\pi_2 = r/(r + p), \pi_1 = p/(r + p))$. Assuming zero transaction costs in transferring income,

$$rT = pB. \tag{3.2}$$

Substituting for π_1, π_2, and T into (3.1) and maximizing with respect to B, we obtain

$$\frac{dO}{dB} = \frac{r}{r + p} \frac{dU_2}{dY} \left(-\frac{p}{r}\right) + \frac{p}{r + p} \frac{dU_1}{dY} = 0, \tag{3.3}$$

from which it follows that

$$\frac{dU_2}{dY} = \frac{dU_1}{dY}. \tag{3.4}$$

An individual who maximizes her expected utility given that she is uncertain over whether she will be rich or poor will support redistributive taxes that equate the marginal utilities of representative members of each group. If all individuals have the same utility functions, she chooses taxes and subsidies to equate incomes across all individuals.[2]

In creating institutions to redistribute from the rich to the poor, the uncertain individual insures herself against the possibility that she will be one of the poor. Uncertainty over future position *could* lead to unanimous agreement to include institutions for redistribution in the constitution. In this case the constitution becomes a kind of insurance contract.

The potential benefits from joining insurance contracts are obvious, indeed so obvious that people routinely enter into private contractual relationships to pool risks. To justify state provision of insurance against risks over private contracting, we need some sort of transaction cost or market failure reason to expect that market provision of insurance will be inferior to state provision. Two main reasons have been given.

The amount of risk borne by any single member of an insurance pool declines as the membership of the pool grows. When the risks associated with new members are the same as those attached to existing members, the optimal size of the membership in the pool is infinity. Insurance becomes a sort of "natural monopoly" with the optimal size of the "insurance club" being all members of society (Arrow and Lind, 1970).

The risks of being poor are not the same across all individuals, however. Those who are of below average intelligence or ambition have higher probabilities of being poor than the average person; higher intelligence, more ambitious people have lower probabilities. If it is possible for an individual to determine his own probability of being poor, but it is not possible for a private insurance company to make this determination, the sale of insurance by a private company could lead to an *adverse selection* problem.

To see what is involved consider the decision to purchase disability insurance. Assume now that all healthy individuals have identical incomes and utility functions.

---

[2] Lerner (1944, pp. 23–40) was the first to demonstrate that an equal distribution of income maximizes the expected utility of an individual uncertain of future position. See also Sen (1973) and Olson (1987).

Let Y_H be the income of a healthy person, and Y_D the income of a disabled person; $Y_D < Y_H$. Everyone is healthy in period 1 and can buy insurance against being disabled in period 2. For the entire population the probability of being disabled is π_D. Ignoring administrative and other transaction costs, a private insurance company would have to charge a premium (tax) of T to offer a benefit to the disabled of B such that $B = T/\pi_D$. Now consider the decision of individual i who is considering buying insurance against becoming disabled, and who has a subjective probability of being disabled of π_i. He wishes to maximize his expected utility over the two periods. Ignoring discounting this implies that he maximizes

$$E(U) = U(Y_H - T) + \pi_i U(Y_D + B) + (1 - \pi_i)U(Y_H). \tag{3.5}$$

Substituting for B and maximizing with respect to T we get

$$\frac{dE(U)}{dT} = -\frac{dU(Y_H - T)}{dY} + \frac{\pi_i}{\pi_D}\frac{dU(Y_D + B)}{dY} = 0 \tag{3.6}$$

or

$$\frac{dU(Y_H - T)}{dY} = \frac{\pi_i}{\pi_D}\frac{dU(Y_D + B)}{dY}. \tag{3.7}$$

When i's subjective probability of becoming disabled equals the population's probability, $\pi_i = \pi_D$, we obtain the same outcome as with (3.4). Individual i purchases an amount of insurance T, such that his marginal utility in the first period when his income is high equals his marginal utility in period 2 if he is disabled. An individual who *knows* or *thinks* he has a smaller chance of becoming disabled than the average person buys an amount such that

$$\frac{dU(Y_H - T)}{dY} < \frac{dU(Y_D + B)}{dY}, \tag{3.8}$$

which implies a smaller purchase of insurance. Individuals with $\pi_i > \pi_D$ buy larger than average amounts. This in turn implies that the average π_i for the insurance pool is greater than π_D. If individuals on average can accurately judge their own π_i, the private insurance company goes bankrupt. The existence of accurate private information about risks induces adverse selection in insurance markets, thereby leading to the disappearance of these markets.[3] Forcing everyone in society to join an insurance program can be a Pareto improvement over this situation.[4]

3.2   Redistribution as a public good

Under the second hypothesis,[5] the rich are seen as transferring income to the poor, not because they are uncertain about whether they might become poor, but out of empathy or similar altruistic motivation. This behavior can be analyzed using a

[3] It may be possible to separate high and low risk individuals and offer separate insurance contracts to each. Such separating equilibria may not exist, however, and when they do, they may promise lower expected utilities than one where all individuals are compelled to buy insurance at the same premium. See Arrow (1963), Akerlof (1970), Pauly (1974), and Rothschild and Stiglitz (1976).

[4] For further discussion see Overbye (1995b).

[5] This hypothesis was first developed by Hochman and Rodgers (1969).

similar framework to that just employed. Each member of the highest income group is envisaged as gaining some satisfaction from the utility gains of members of the lower classes. The highest income group acts as a sort of club that unanimously agrees to transfer income from itself to members of the lower group(s). Assuming three groups, with $Y_3 > Y_2 > Y_1$, then each member of group 3, when voting, can be seen as maximizing an objective function consisting of a weighted sum of the utilities of its own members and those of members of lower-income groups:

$$O = n_3 U_3(Y_3 - T) + \alpha_2 n_2 U_2(Y_2 + B_2) + \alpha_1 n_1 U_1(Y_1 + B_1), \qquad (3.9)$$

where n_3, n_2, and n_1 are the numbers of individuals in groups 3, 2, and 1, respectively; T is the tax imposed on the richest group, and B_1 and B_2 are the per capita subsidies to the other two groups. Each member of the richest group places full weight on the utility of each member of its own group, and partial weights ($\alpha_1 \leq 1, \alpha_2 \leq 1$) on the utilities of members of other groups. Substituting from the budget constraint

$$n_3 T = n_2 B_2 + n_1 B_1 \qquad (3.10)$$

and maximizing with respect to B_1 and B_2 yields

$$\frac{dO}{dB_1} = -n_3 U_3' \left(\frac{n_1}{n_3}\right) + \alpha_1 n_1 U_1' = 0 \qquad (3.11)$$

$$-n_3 U_3' \left(\frac{n_2}{n_3}\right) + \alpha_2 n_2 U_2' = 0, \qquad (3.12)$$

from which it follows that

$$U_3' = \alpha_2 U_2' = \alpha_1 U_1'. \qquad (3.13)$$

If a member of the richest class places the same weight on the utilities of members of classes 1 and 2 ($\alpha_1 = \alpha_2$) and assumes that each derives the same utility from income, then (3.13) implies subsidies to members of classes 1 and 2 so as to equate their marginal utilities of income. Since $Y_1 < Y_2$, if the marginal utility of income falls with increasing income, then the incomes of the lowest class must be raised to equality with those of class 2 before any transfers are made to class 2 (von Furstenberg and Mueller, 1971).

A saintly altruist who placed equal weight on her own utility as on that of others ($\alpha_1 = \alpha_2 = 1$) would vote to equate everyone's income. Everyday altruists who place more weight on their own utility than on the utilities of others ($0 < \alpha < 1$) will not favor transfers so large as to bring their own incomes into equality with those to whom they make transfers.

Equation (3.13) could be used to predict the voting behavior of a member of the highest-income group on redistribution or the charitable contributions of such a person. Since charity is a purely voluntary act, whereas government redistribution programs are not, one wonders why, if all the members of group 3 do favor redistribution, reliance is not made on private charities (clubs) for redistribution.

An argument for government intervention relies again on the free-rider problem. If a member of group 3 wishes to see the welfare of all individuals in group 1 raised, and not just a few whom she knows personally, she cannot achieve her goal alone. If all members of group 3 feel likewise, they can achieve their goal by joint-collective action. But if a voluntary association is employed, free-riding may ensue, and less than the Pareto-optimal amount of redistribution may occur. The Pareto-optimal approach to redistribution sees redistribution through the government occurring as if only the rich voted, and when they did they used the unanimity rule.

3.3   Redistribution to satisfy fairness norms

Under the first two hypotheses to explain redistribution, it is the utility gain to the giver that drives her decision to give. When 2 buys insurance because she is uncertain whether she will become sick at some future date, she effectively agrees to give money to 1, conditional upon 1 becoming sick and she, 2, remaining healthy. Her motive is to avoid her own utility loss should she become sick without having insurance. The fact that 2 is better off, because of the insurance as a result of 1 redistributing some of her income to 2, is incidental to 1's decision to purchase insurance.

Similarly, under Pareto-optimal redistribution it is the utility gain to the giver that accounts for the decision to redistribute. This motivation is most apparent when someone gives money to a beggar out of fear that if she does not, the beggar may harm her.

A third form of voluntary redistribution does not seem to fit either of these first two explanations. This third type has been perhaps most vividly revealed in experiments like the dictator game. In one set of these experiments, Eichenberger and Oberholzer-Gee (1997) selected students to be dictators on the basis of their having scored well on a short test. Dictators were each given seven Swiss francs and instructed that they had been paired with another student who had not been chosen as a dictator. Neither student knew who the other one was, nor would their identities be revealed after the experiment. Dictators were told that they could voluntarily decide to give some or all of their seven francs to the anonymous other student. The choice most consistent with advancing narrow self-interest would be to give nothing, yet on average dictators gave about one third of the seven francs to the unknown students.[6]

These experimental findings cannot be explained as a form of insurance, since the dictator knows she has and can keep the seven francs. There is no risk of her becoming the other student. Since she does not know who the other student is, it is also not clear why she would get utility out of making the other student better off. Note that the explanation put forward originally by Hochman and Rodgers is inapplicable to this situation. There is no reason for the dictator to believe that the anonymous other student is worse off than the dictator – other than by the seven francs.

---

[6] Similarly, in "gangster" experiments in which students without money were allowed to take up to seven francs from anonymous students who had been awarded this money for their performance on a test, the gangster students took away "only" about three-fourths of the seven francs. Similar outcomes have been reported in other studies (Kahneman, Knetsch, and Thaler, 1986; Davis and Holt, 1993, pp. 263–68).

Eichenberger and Oberholzer-Gee (1997) postulate that the student-givers in the dictator games are following a *fairness norm* when they choose to give some of "their" seven francs to the paired student. They recognize that there was an element of chance in who was chosen dictator and who was not, and thus feel that *fairness dictates* that they share the seven francs.

Eichenberger and Oberholzer-Gee also hypothesize that dictators will be more generous when it "costs them less," and thus that they will *vote* to give away a larger fraction of seven francs when the action is a collective decision, than when they decide the amount unilaterally. When the redistribution choice is made collectively, it is cheaper *to express* a willingness to give, since one's vote has only a probabilistic impact on the outcome.[7] Eichenberger and Oberholzer-Gee predict the most generosity on the part of dictators when it costs them nothing – for example, when they merely respond to a survey question asking what amount dictators ought to give. *Some* of Eichenberger and Oberholzer-Gee's experiments support these predictions.

Notions of fairness seem to figure prominently in many sorts of experiments. One class of experiments that comes very close to the dictator game is the ultimatum game. A single play analogue to the experiment just described would have the first student *propose* a distribution of the seven francs with the second student having the option to reject the proposal. If he does, neither student gets anything. If player 1 proposes $7 - e$ for herself and e for player 2, selfish behavior on the part of 2 would have her accept the proposal so long as $e > 0$. Selfish behavior on the part of player 1 would have her choose a very small e. But ultimatum game experiments typically involve the first players proposing es of 30 percent or so of the sum to be distributed, *and* player 2s *rejecting* es > 0, when they fall substantially below this sort of division. The explanation most frequently given for this seemingly irrational behavior is again the idea of a fairness norm. The offers of many player 1s are constrained by his norm, and when an e is chosen which is so low as to violate a 2's fairness norm, he punishes this player 1 by rejecting her proposal.[8] Given these and other experimental results that document the importance of notions of fairness, these notions cannot be ruled out as an explanation for voluntary redistribution.

Discussion

On the surface, our first three explanations for redistribution seem rather different. Each would seem to be a potential explanation for the state to engage in redistribution once it existed, or perhaps to come into existence in the first place. When one pushes beneath the surface, however, the differences between the three forms of redistribution begin to blur.

Although the existence of true uncertainty over future positions might lead purely self-interested individuals to join insurance contracts that redistribute income once

---

[7] This argument is a special case of the *expressive voting* hypothesis discussed in Chapter 14.

[8] See Güth, Schmittberger, and Schwarze (1982); Kahneman, Knetsch, and Thaler (1986); and Güth and Tietz (1988, 1990).

Kirchsteiger (1994) demonstrates, however, that envy may also play a role in ultimatum games.

the true states of the world have been revealed, both Harsanyi (1955) and Rawls (1971) develop *normative* theories in which individuals *assume for ethical reasons* that they are uncertain over future positions. Rawls even names his theory *justice as fairness*, and one can think of his depiction of the social contract as a kind insurance contract as just one way of articulating a fairness norm. We shall take up Harsanyi's theory in Chapter 23 and Rawls's theory in Chapter 25.

Perhaps sight of the beggar triggers not fear, but compassion, and one whispers to oneself "there but for the grace of God go I" as one drops the coins into the beggar's palm. This altruistic act of giving now begins to resemble Rawls's normative theory of justice, which in turn is rooted in our intuitive notions of fairness. Although a Swiss university student may not be moved to thank God for being selected the dictator in the dictator game, some recognition of the chance nature of her selection may help explain her generosity.

Short of psychoanalyzing each giver, it may be difficult to determine which of these three explanations for voluntary redistribution is really at work. Indeed, if we wish to go beyond merely accounting for the existence of voluntary redistribution, but wish to try and predict *which persons* are likely to give and how generous they will be, we shall probably want to introduce the kind of psychological-behavioral theories that we discussed in the previous chapter, which can help us to explain cooperation in prisoners' dilemma games, for the two sorts of "irrational behavior" have much in common.[9]

3.4 Redistribution to improve allocative efficiency

The first three theories of redistribution rest on particular assumptions about people's preferences: they are risk averse, altruistic, or conform to certain norms of fairness. The fourth theory makes no special assumption about individual preferences, but instead assumes that there are differences in the productivities of individuals. Under this assumption redistributions of incomes and productive resources can lead to improvements in allocative efficiency that make all members of society better off. The argument is again easiest to see if we start from a state of anarchy.[10]

P and U live in a community that contains a fixed amount of land that can be used to grow corn. P is a productive farmer and if she works all of the land she can grow 100 units of corn. U is a relatively unproductive farmer and if he works all of the land he can grow only 50 units. Figure 3.1 depicts the community's production possibility frontier.

The distribution of land in anarchy is such that P and U could obtain the allocation A if both devoted all of their energy to growing corn. But each can unilaterally obtain still more corn by stealing from the other, and can be expected to devote some time to stealing. Both engage in the unproductive activity of stealing and they wind up at point A' instead of A. As discussed in the previous chapter, one

---

[9] Wilson (1993) argues, however, that a "moral sense," of which a sense of fairness is a part, is at least in part inherited. Assuming Wilson is correct, then we would expect all people to give voluntarily to a degree, but we would still need other factors to predict which people give more or less.

[10] The following discussion is based on Bös and Kolmar (forthcoming).

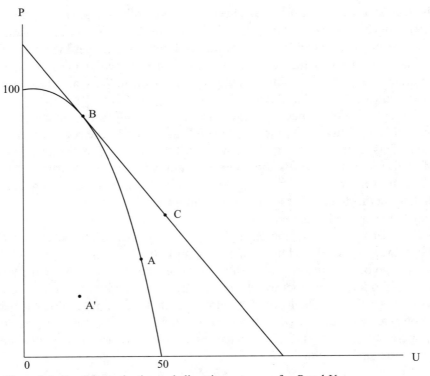

Figure 3.1. Possible production and allocation outcomes for P and U.

rationale for the existence of the state is that this institution can prevent P and U from engaging in predatory activities and allow them to reach point A.

Because of P's greater productivity, the total product of the community would be increased if land were transferred from U to P. U would never agree to such a transfer, however, if predatory actions are prohibited, because any movement to the left along the production-possibilities curve makes U worse off. Such a transfer might be brought about, however, *if* P agreed to share her corn with U. The maximum total production of corn occurs at B. An agreement between P and U that initially transferred land to P and subsequently transferred corn from P to U could allow the community to obtain a point like B, where both parties are better off than they were with the original distribution of land.

If the state already existed and it enforced property rights and contracts while prohibiting theft, the move from A to C could, of course, be achieved through private contracting. P merely *buys* the land from U. Such transfers of resources from less productive to more productive owners is an everyday occurrence in a market economy. If, however, we assume that the state does *not* exist, then such an exchange is impossible. U would never voluntarily transfer land to P, even if P promised to share her corn with him, for in the absence of an institution to enforce this promise, it is not *credible*. Once P was in possession of the land, she would have no incentive to share its fruits with U. The Pareto-improving exchange of land for corn might be brought about by a constitutional agreement between P and U that both made the more productive P rich in land, and guaranteed that she subsequently shares the product of her labor with the poorer U.

Land is not as important a factor of production today as it once was, and so this example may not seem very relevant as an explanation for redistribution policies today. It can be modified, however, to rationalize other sorts of transfers. For example, Us might be uneducated children of the poor who would, if educated, become highly productive members of the community. State programs that taxed the wealthy and provided free education for the poor could then sufficiently increase the total income of the community so that all of its members are better off.

3.5   Redistribution as taking

All four of the motives for redistribution described so far could in principle lead to government redistribution programs even under the unanimity rule.

Almost no democratic system makes its collective decisions using the unanimity rule.[11] Once government action can be taken despite the opposition of some citizens, redistribution can take on the form of pure involuntary transfers from the losers to the winners under the political process.

Before we can fully understand why and how redistribution takes place, we need to understand how government works. Most of this book is concerned with this question and we shall be discussing redistribution as taking at several places. For now we shall be content with a simple model that largely abstracts from the mechanics of the political process.

Let us assume again two groups, whose members obtain utility from income, and that own *political* resources that they can spend to obtain additional income in the form of government subsidies. Of course, only one group can obtain positive subsidies, so that the other group must use its political resources to reduce its taxes. Let Y_i be the income of a member of the ith group, U_i her utility, and R_i her political resources, $i = 1, 2$. All members of group 1 have the same utility functions $U_1 = U_1(Y_1 + B, R_1)$, where $(\partial U_1/\partial Y_1) > 0$, $(\partial^2 U_1/\partial Y_1^2) < 0$, and $(\partial U_1/\partial R_1) < 0$, and $(\partial^2 U_1/\partial R_1^2) < 0$. Having to utilize political resources to obtain benefits B lowers a group 1 member's utility. For group 2 we have $U_2 = U_2(Y_2 - T, R_2)$, $(\partial U_2/\partial Y_2) > 0$, $(\partial^2 U_2/\partial Y_2^2) < 0$, $(\partial U_2/\partial R_2) < 0$, and $(\partial^2 U_2/\partial R_2^2) < 0$, where T is the per capita tax needed to provide B.

To understand the problem fully we need to know more about the nature of its institutions, the goals of those who are a part of government, and the constraints on their pursuit of these goals. Abstracting from these we can simply define political resources in such a way that $B = B(R_1, R_2)$, $(\partial B/\partial R_1) > 0$, $(\partial^2 B/\partial R_1^2) < 0$, $(\partial B/\partial R_2) < 0$, and $(\partial^2 B/\partial R_2^2) < 0$.

A member of group 1 chooses R_1 so as to maximize

$$O_1 = U_1(Y_1 + B_1, R_1) = U_1(Y_1 + B(R_1, R_2), R_1), \tag{3.14}$$

[11] The "almost" could be dropped were it not for various associations of nations, like the European Union, that employ the unanimity rule for some or all of their collective decisions.

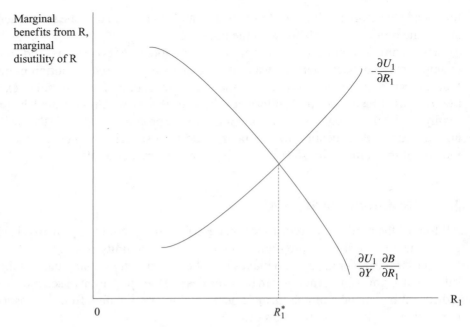

Figure 3.2. The optimal expenditure of political resources.

which yields

$$\frac{\partial O_1}{\partial R_1} = \frac{\partial U_1}{\partial Y}\frac{\partial B}{\partial R_1} + \frac{\partial U_1}{\partial R_1} = 0 \tag{3.15}$$

or

$$\frac{\partial U_1}{\partial Y}\frac{\partial B}{\partial R_1} = -\frac{\partial U_1}{\partial R_1}. \tag{3.16}$$

This condition is illustrated in Figure 3.2. A member of group 1 expends her political resources until the marginal disutility from their loss $[-(\partial U_1/\partial R_1)]$ just equals the marginal utility from the extra subsidy this expenditure yields $[(\partial U_1/\partial Y)(\partial B/\partial R_1)]$. An analogous relationship holds for a member of group 2, with the only difference being that his marginal gain comes from reduced tax payments.

Since B is a function of both R_1 and R_2, one's optimal R_1^* depends on R_2, and the two groups are only in full equilibrium when each has chosen its optimal R^* conditional upon the other group j being at its optimal R_j^*.[12]

Political resources can take many forms. In a democracy there might be effort exerted by a group for one party (handing out leaflets, stuffing envelops, telephoning) to bring about its victory. Here one might expect groups with low opportunity costs of time (unemployed, retired) to do well at winning subsidies.

[12] This is a Nash equilibrium. If we specified functional forms for U_1 and B, then (3.16) could be used to solve for optimal R_1^* as a function of R_2 and the parameters in the U_1 and B functions. This equation would constitute a *reaction function* for a member of group 1. Substituting the reaction function of a member of group 2 into this equation would allow us to solve for R_2^* and R_1^* at the Nash equilibrium.

An aristocratic class may be able to win favors from the government by inviting certain members of the government to become part of the aristocracy. The aristocracy's political resource in this situation is its right to define its membership. The cost of adding members of government to the aristocracy is that it loses some of its exclusivity, and the value of being a member declines.

During the Middle Ages, the Church was able to obtain wealth from the state by using its special relationship to God, and selling places in Heaven and other favors to royalty (Ekelund et al., 1996).

The simplest form of political resource is, of course, money itself. It can be used to win favors by bribing those in government, lobbying them, contributing to their campaigns, and so on. When R_1 is money, then U_1 becomes $U_1(Y_1 + B - R_1)$, and (3.16) becomes

$$\frac{\partial B}{\partial R_1} = 1. \tag{3.17}$$

The optimal expenditure of the political resource money occurs when the last dollar spent to obtain a government benefit yields one dollar in benefit.

Involuntary redistribution must make someone worse off, and can make everyone worse off. We usually think of involuntary redistribution as money flowing from one group to the government and out again to a second group, with the first group being made worse off and the second better off. Such a situation would definitely occur through a pure tax/subsidy scheme if only one group expended resources to win the subsidy. The fact that it was willing to spend its resources would imply that its gross benefits exceed the resources spent.

If both groups expend resources to win subsidies, the end result may be that they are both worse off than they would have been had they each not attempted to obtain a subsidy. To see this assume that both groups spend money lobbying for a subsidy and that their efforts perfectly offset one another. Neither group obtains any benefits from their lobbying, and both are worse off by the amount of resources spent on lobbying. The production-possibility frontier shifts inward by the amount of resources spent on lobbying, and the new equilibrium is at a point interior to that obtainable if the groups did not engage in efforts to bring about involuntary redistribution. (Of course, the lobbyist receives income from the two groups. If we assume that lobbying is a perfectly competitive industry, however, each lobbyist's income just equals her opportunity costs – the income she could earn in another occupation. If we assume that these alternative occupations are, unlike lobbying, socially productive, then society's loss from the efforts by the two groups to get subsidies is the marginal product of the lobbyists in these socially valuable activities.)

The situation becomes worse when we recognize that the taxes and subsidies cannot be levied costlessly. The benefits to group 1 are the total taxes levied on group 2 *less* the transaction costs, c, of bringing the transfer about:

$$n_1 B = n_2 T - c\,^{13}. \tag{3.18}$$

---

[13] n_1 and n_2 are the numbers of members in groups 1 and 2.

Included in c are the costs of printing tax and subsidy forms and mailing them out, monitoring to see that all members of group 2 pay their taxes and only bonified group 1 members get subsidies, prosecuting cheaters, and so on. To the social loss from diverting people into unproductive lobbying must be added the social loss from creating a bureaucracy whose only function is to arrange involuntary transfers. Also, to be added to c are the *deadweight losses* that arise because of the adverse incentive effects of the taxes and subsidies. For example, if I is raised by taxing the income of members of group 2, they may work and save less thereby contracting the production possibility frontier still further. Subsidies to group 1 may reduce their work effort. Browning (1987, 1989) calculated that the sum of all of these transaction costs of transferring income can come to *nine times* the value of the income transferred.

To whom do these transfers go? The poor, the rich, the middle class; capitalists, big business, organized labor, the landed aristocracy, the "power elite," "special interests" of all sorts – the number of beneficiaries of government redistribution proposed at one time or another is almost countless. We shall not examine every "theory" about redistribution that has ever been proposed, but we shall take up in later chapters several that have been put forward within the public choice literature. For now, we satisfy ourselves with a look at the patterns of redistribution that exist and how they line up against the hypotheses discussed so far, and at a few tests of specific hypotheses.

3.6   Income transfers in the United States

Our first explanation for redistribution considers it as a form of insurance. The citizen is uncertain about whether he will become unemployed, become ill, grow old, and so on and votes for social insurance to protect against these uncertainties. It is interesting in this regard to recall that the major social insurance programs in the United States were created during the Great Depression, a time when both the actualities and the probabilities of being unemployed or in poverty soared. Although the economic uncertainties of the Great Depression would lead many to favor government-provided insurance programs, they might also have impressed upon individuals the nature and magnitude of the general uncertainties we all face.

The same thing may have happened during World War II. Dryzek and Goodin (1986) remark upon the common risks all Britons experienced during the bombings of Britain in World War II. They argue that these common risks made the British more aware of their ties with their fellow countrymen. The mental experiment of putting oneself in the position of one's neighbor became easier. "Partiality and impartiality [were] fused" and the British voted for expansions in social insurance programs covering not only damages from the war, but also all of the common risks that a society faces. Dryzek and Goodin (1986) present evidence linking the expansion of social insurance programs in Britain to World War II events. They also present cross-national evidence that the social insurance programs in other countries expanded in proportion to the war-related uncertainties a country endured.

Whatever the underlying motivations, social insurance programs constitute the largest fraction of direct transfers in the United States. In 1995 90.4 percent of all

Table 3.1. *Federal, state, and local transfer payments in the United States, 1995 (millions of dollars)*

	A. Federal government		
	Expenditures	As a percent of all transfers	As a percent of total budget
1. Insurance-like programs, total	630,316	90.4	38.7
a. Retirement	357,286	51.2	
b. Disability	49,430	7.9	
c. Unemployment	21,576	3.1	
d. Medicare	180,214	25.8	
e. Veterans insurance programs	21,810	3.1	
2. Noninsurance transfers	67,271	9.6	4.1
a. Welfare and social services	47,120	6.8	
b. Other	17,981	2.6	
c. Veterans	1,412		
d. Housing	87	<0.1	
e. Agriculture	90	<0.1	
f. Labor training	581	0.1	
3. Total transfers net of interest payments	697,587	100.0	42.8
4. Total federal budget	1,628,419		100.0
	B. State and Local		
	Expenditures	As a percent of all transfers	As a percent of total budget
1. Insurance-like programs, total	7,369	3.7	
a. Workers' compensation and temporary disability insurance	7,369	3.7	
2. Noninsurance-like programs, total	191,586	96.3	
a. Medicaid	155,017	77.9	
b. Welfare and social services	37,785	19.0	
c. Other	6,153	3.1	
3. Total transfers net of interest payments	198,955	100.0	20.1
4. Total state and local budget	991,271		100.0

Source: Survey of Current Business, October 1998, Tables 3.16 and 3.17.

direct transfers at the federal level were in insurance-like programs that were not means-tested (see Table 3.1A). Most of the redistribution at the state and local level is, on the other hand, means-tested (Table 3.1B). This form of redistribution might be broadly consistent with the insurance motive for redistribution if its support were due to uncertainty on the part of the rich that they would some day become poor. The spread of insurance during the Great Depression and following World War II would be consistent with this interpretation. But means-tested redistribution to the poor might also be an example of Pareto-optimal redistribution. As noted above the different types of motives behind redistribution are difficult to disentangle.

One area that seems particularly well suited to explanation by the Pareto-optimal approach to redistribution is in-kind transfers like housing, food, and medical care. Since recipients value in-kind transfers at less than their nominal value, a redistribution program that was based only on the giver's utility from seeing recipients have higher utility levels would consist of cash transfers (Aaron and von Furstenberg, 1971; Giertz, 1982). That some individuals are willing to contribute to the poor in the form of specific consumption items implies that it is the poor's level of housing, food consumption, and medical care that is of interest to the taxpayers. But more direct evidence supporting the Pareto-optimal approach over competing hypotheses is lacking.

3.7   Redistribution and the distribution of income

When most people think of "redistribution" they think of taking money from the rich and transferring it to the poor. But social insurance programs and other governmental redistribution do not necessarily take that form. When Bill Gates retires, he will be entitled to add a monthly social security check from the government to the millions in income he will continue to earn as the founder and former CEO of Microsoft. How much governmental redistribution does go to the poor, and what is its impact on the distribution of income?

Unfortunately these simple and basic questions are very difficult to answer. A full answer would need to consider the incidence of both taxes and transfers, and also the incidence of other government expenditures and regulations. The distributional impact of taxes is easier to gauge than the impact of expenditures, but even here substantial disagreement often exists regarding the incidence of some taxes.[14] For expenditures, things are much worse. Are the benefits that the rich receive from police protection and national defense proportional to their tax payments? Should expenditures on police and defense be thought of as providing any final-consumption social benefits at all, or are they intermediate goods to be netted out when determining the final distribution of benefits and costs from government action (Meerman, 1980)? The distributional effects of governmental regulations are even more difficult to gauge, and to my knowledge have never been estimated. How much income do the shareholders and employees in liquor companies lose as a result of a ban on advertising their products on television? How much money does the taxi driver lose from having to charge a regulated fare set on a meter (or perhaps the taxi's passenger loses)?

The simplest calculations of redistribution take into account only taxes and cash or near-cash transfers. In the United States, these result in a slight rich-to-poor redistribution.[15] Table 3.2 presents estimates for the United States for 1984. Comparing the first and last lines of the table, we see that government policies reduce the share of income received by the highest-income quintile by roughly 15 percent, and raise

---

[14] See, for example, the survey by Mieszkowski (1969).

[15] A similar conclusion has been reached in several studies that have tried to take into account the benefits from government expenditures. See Gillespie (1965, 1976), Dodge (1975), Reynolds and Smolensky (1977), and Musgrave and Musgrave (1980, p. 276).

Table 3.2. *Corrected family income distribution, 1984 (percent)*

	Share of income received by each quintile of families				
	1st (poorest)	2nd	3rd	4th	5th (richest)
Current population survey definition (pretax, cash only)	4.7	11.0	17.0	24.4	42.9
Current population survey definition less taxes	5.8	12.3	17.8	24.1	40.0
Current population survey definition less taxes plus Medicare, Medicaid, and food stamps	7.2	12.2	17.7	24.3	38.7
Current population survey definition less taxes plus Medicare, Medicaid, food stamps, and employer fringe benefits	6.7	12.3	17.6	24.3	39.1
Line above adjusted for differences in family sizes across quintiles	7.3	13.4	18.1	24.4	36.8

Note: When 1984 census income statistics are corrected for taxes, in-kind government and private benefits, and family size, the family income distribution becomes moderately more equal.
Source: Levy (1987, p. 195).

the share of the lowest quintile by roughly 50 percent. Nevertheless, families in the highest-income quintile receive five times the average income of those in the lowest quintile, even after adjustments for the impact of government.

Table 3.3 compares the primary income distribution for all households in 14 OECD countries to the disposable incomes per adult, where disposable income is obtained from primary income by adding transfers and subtracting taxes. Levy's figure of 4.7 percent of pretax income for the lowest quintile in the United States in 1984 can be compared with the OECD's figure of 4.0 percent in 1986. Levy's net of transfer figure of 7.3 percent can be compared with the OECD's 5.7 percent. (No figures on the primary distribution of income were given for Norway and New Zealand.)

Several things stand out in this table. First, disparities in primary income across countries are dramatic. In Ireland, for example, the bottom 10 percent of the income distribution has virtually no income, and thus the ratio of the income of the top decile to the bottom decile (D90/D10) is a whopping 138 in Ireland when one looks at primary incomes. The distribution of primary income will be largely a function of the earning structure in a country, its level of unemployment, its age distribution, and of course government policies that may affect these variables – like minimum wage laws that affect both the structure of earnings and the level of unemployment.

Tax and transfer policies do flatten the distribution of income and, as in the United States, they do so mainly by raising the incomes of the bottom two deciles. Indeed, in some countries like Belgium and Italy, the top decile's share of disposable income is identical or nearly so to its share of primary income.

Using the ratio of the top to bottom deciles of disposable income shares as an index of distribution, Austria (4.6), Belgium (4.7), and Finland (4.0) come out to be the most egalitarian countries; Switzerland (9.8), Ireland (10.0), and the United States (12.5), the least egalitarian.

Table 3.3. *Primary and disposable income distributions in 16 OECD countries*

Country	Year	Income type	Cumulative decile shares											
			10%	20%	30%	40%	50%	60%	70%	80%	90%	95%	Top 10%	D90/D10
Austria[a]	1987	Disposable	4.1	10.1	17.2	25.4	34.4	44.2	54.8	67.2	81.1	91.8	18.9	4.6
Australia	1985	Primary	1.6	6.1	12.1	19.3	27.8	37.6	48.8	61.6	77.0	–	23.0	14.4
		Disposable	2.9	7.7	13.7	21.0	29.4	39.0	50.2	63.0	78.3	87.3	21.7	7.5
Belgium	1988	Primary	3.7	9.1	15.5	23.0	31.8	41.8	53.0	65.5	80.1	–	19.9	5.4
		Disposable	4.2	10.2	17.1	25.0	33.8	43.5	54.3	66.4	80.3	88.4	19.7	4.7
Canada	1987	Primary	1.2	4.7	10.1	17.0	25.4	35.2	46.7	60.0	76.0	–	24.0	20.0
		Disposable	2.8	7.8	14.1	21.5	30.1	39.8	50.7	63.3	78.4	87.5	21.6	7.7
France	1984	Primary	1.7	5.6	10.7	16.9	24.5	33.5	44.1	56.7	72.4	–	27.6	16.2
		Disposable	3.0	8.3	14.6	21.8	29.9	39.1	49.5	61.6	76.3	85.5	23.7	7.9
Germany	1984	Primary	2.2	7.3	13.6	20.9	29.4	39.1	50.1	62.7	77.9	–	22.1	10.0
		Disposable	4.0	9.8	16.6	24.2	32.9	42.5	53.2	65.3	79.4	87.8	21.6	5.4
Ireland	1987	Primary	0.2	3.2	8.0	14.2	21.8	30.8	41.8	55.2	72.4	–	27.6	138.0
		Disposable	2.5	7.1	12.6	19.3	27.1	36.3	47.0	59.6	75.1	84.7	24.9	10.0
Italy	1986	Primary	2.5	7.4	13.5	20.4	28.4	37.6	48.5	61.1	76.2	–	23.8	9.5
		Disposable	3.1	8.0	13.9	20.7	28.7	38.0	48.7	61.2	76.2	85.4	23.8	7.7
Luxembourg	1985	Primary	3.8	9.5	16.1	23.5	32.0	41.5	52.3	64.6	79.5	–	20.5	5.4
		Disposable	4.3	10.2	17.1	24.8	33.5	43.1	53.9	66.0	80.4	88.8	19.6	4.6
Norway	1986	Disposable	3.9	9.8	16.9	24.9	33.9	43.7	54.6	66.7	80.6	88.7	19.4	5.0
Sweden	1987	Primary	0.5	3.3	8.5	15.3	23.8	34.2	46.5	60.5	76.8	–	23.2	46.4
		Disposable	3.3	9.5	16.9	25.3	34.6	44.8	55.9	68.2	81.9	89.7	18.1	5.5
Switzerland	1982	Primary	1.7	6.3	12.4	19.4	27.2	36.1	46.1	57.8	71.9	–	28.1	16.5
		Disposable	2.8	8.0	14.1	21.0	29.0	37.8	47.7	58.9	72.5	81.3	27.5	9.8
United Kingdom	1986	Primary	1.6	5.5	11.2	18.1	26.4	36.1	47.2	60.3	76.4	–	23.6	14.8
		Disposable	2.5	7.5	13.5	20.5	28.7	38.2	49.1	61.8	77.1	86.4	22.9	9.2
United States	1986	Primary	1.0	4.0	8.9	15.3	23.3	32.7	43.8	57.2	74.0	–	26.0	26.0
		Disposable	1.9	5.7	11.2	18.0	26.2	35.7	46.9	60.2	76.3	86.2	23.7	12.5
Finland	1987	Primary	0.6	3.3	8.4	15.1	23.7	33.8	45.6	59.3	75.8	–	24.2	40.3
		Disposable	4.5	10.8	18.1	26.4	35.6	45.6	56.6	68.6	82.2	90.0	17.8	4.0
Netherlands	1987	Primary	2.8	8.1	14.4	21.6	29.7	38.8	49.5	61.9	76.7	–	23.3	8.3
		Disposable	4.1	10.1	16.9	24.5	33.0	42.5	53.2	65.3	79.4	87.8	20.6	5.0
New Zealand	1988	Disposable	3.2	8.5	14.7	21.9	30.2	39.9	51.0	63.9	79.1	–	20.9	6.5

Note: [a] Excludes self-employment income.

Disposable income is per adult equivalent; primary income is for households.

Definitions for three countries at bottom of table differ slightly from those for other countries. See definitions in Atkinson, Rainwater, and Smeeding (1995); data are from Table 4.3, p. 44 and Table 6.6, p. 87.

3.8   Redistribution to special interests

The pattern of income transfers in the United States at the federal level consists mostly of insurance-like redistributions, transfers at state and local levels go mostly to the poor. The net effect of taxes and transfers in major industrialized countries raises the incomes of the lowest deciles of the income distribution relative to the highest. These patterns are broadly consistent with those predicted by the voluntary redistribution hypotheses and it is tempting to conclude that one or more of them must explain these patterns. Such an inference is difficult to confirm, however, and some parts of the pattern directly contradict it.

If government-run pension schemes were true insurance programs, all participants would pay certain fractions of their income during their working lives into a fund. Those who survived to retirement would be paid out of this fund. Redistribution would partly take the form of an *intrapersonal*, intergenerational transfer of income from Ms.X, the worker at time t, to Ms.X, the retiree at the $t + n$, and in part an interpersonal transfer from Ms.Y at time t to Ms.X at $t + n$, resulting from Y's departure prior to $t + n$.

This is *not* how government-run pension schemes in the major developed countries are run, however. Ms.X's pension checks at time $t + n$ are covered directly out of taxes paid by all of the Ys working at $t + n$. The transfers are from the present generation of workers to past generations of workers. This feature of government-pension systems implies that the levels of taxes and transfers that they involve may reflect *involuntary redistribution*. Under a true insurance-pension program, Ms.X and Ms.Y would decide the level of transfers to be made at time $t + n$ and thus the taxes they would pay at t, uncertain of whether they would survive to $t + n$. Under the pay-as-you-go pension systems that actually operate Ms.X *knows* when she votes for higher pension payments at $t + n$ that she will directly benefit from them and that someone else will pay for them. Her motivation for voting for higher pension transfers is fully consistent with the rational egoism postulate, and a theory of redistribution as taking.

The same can be said of other forms of redistribution. When farmer X votes for a candidate who promises higher price supports for farm products and higher transfers to farmers, X knows that he will be a direct beneficiary of these policies. The urban bank clerk must consider the probability of her becoming a farmer as negligible, and if she supports such programs because she has the farmer's welfare in her utility function, she is probably voting for redistribution to someone with a *higher* income than hers. In 1985 two thirds of the $7.7 billion in cash subsidies went to farms with over $100,000 in annual sales – a mere 13.8 percent of all farms. Roughly, one-third of all subsidies went to farms with more than $1 billion in net worth.[16] Agricultural protection policies in Japan helped raise farm household incomes from a rough equality with those of urban workers in 1955 to 32 percent higher than urban worker incomes in 1984.[17]

[16] Gardner (1990, pp. 27–29); Schultze (1972) reports similar figures for the late 1960s.
[17] Adjusting for differences in household size one observes a rise from 77 percent below urban incomes in 1955 to 14 percent above in 1984. See Hayami (1990, p. 206).

Table 3.4. *Costs and benefits of the EU's common agricultural policy in comparison with a free market outcome, 1980 (millions of U.S. dollars)*

Country	Producers	Consumers	Government	Net
EC-9	−30,686	34,580	11,494	15,388
West Germany	−9,045	12,555	3,769	7,279
France	−7,237	7,482	2,836	3,081
Italy	−3,539	5,379	1,253	3,093
Netherlands	−3,081	1,597	697	−787
Belgium/Luxembourg	−1,624	1,440	544	320
United Kingdom	−3,461	5,174	1,995	3,708
Ireland	−965	320	99	−546
Denmark	−1,736	635	302	−799

Note: Negative numbers indicate costs; positive numbers indicate benefits.
Source: Buckwell, A., David R. Harvey, Kenneth J. Thomson, and Kenn A. Parton (1982, pp. 90–134), as presented in Koester and Tangermann (1990, p. 97).

Many of the benefits to farmers from governmental agriculture policies do not come in the form of direct cash subsidies, but rather through price floors and other policies that raise agricultural prices. This means that the costs to the citizen/ consumer from this form of redistribution are greater than the budget transfer figures. Table 3.4 presents estimates of the benefits to consumers and taxpayers (positive numbers in nine European Union countries) from abandoning the EU's Common Agricultural Policy (CAP) in favor of a free market in agricultural products. The aggregate costs to farmers from shifting to free markets and dropping all subsidies ($30,686 million) are roughly two thirds of the benefits that consumers ($34,580 million) and taxpayers ($11,494 million) would receive. Each euro added to a European farmer's pocket by the CAP takes €1.50 out of a consumer/taxpayer's pocket.

There are many forms of redistribution in the industrial democracies that benefit middle and upper income groups, and are difficult to reconcile with the various voluntary-redistribution hypotheses discussed at the beginning of this chapter, so many in fact that some scholars regard *all* government activity as selfishly and redistributively motivated (Meltzer and Richard, 1978, 1981, 1983; Peltzman, 1980; Aranson and Ordeshook, 1981). Table 3.5 presents the distribution of governmental transfers across 15 OECD countries. The pattern of transfers for Australia is perhaps what one might expect if redistribution were driven by altruistic-insurance motives. In 1984 40.1 percent of all government transfers went to those in the bottom quintile of the income distribution, while only 8 percent went to the highest quintile. But these figures imply that over 50 percent of all transfers in Australia go to the three middle quintiles, and this holds true for every other country in the table except Switzerland and Norway in 1986. Individuals at all levels of the income distribution receive substantial transfers, with those in the highest quintile receiving a *larger* fraction of transfers in France, Italy, Luxembourg, and Sweden than those in the lowest quintile. In France and Italy the highest quintile of the population actually received a greater share of governmental transfers *than any other quintile*. These patterns of

Table 3.5. *Distribution of transfers by quintile and average transfers as a percent of median equivalent income*

		Bottom	2	3	4	Top	Total	Average transfers as a percent of median equivalent income
Australia	1981	42.8	22.2	13.3	12.5	9.2	100.0	10.8
	1985	40.1	24.6	14.4	12.9	8.0	100.0	11.3
Belgium	1985	22.9	22.5	21.9	16.6	16.1	100.0	33.3
	1988	21.5	23.6	20.1	16.1	18.7	100.0	34.9
Switzerland	1982	38.5	19.2	15.6	13.3	13.3	100.0	7.3
Canada	1981	33.0	22.9	17.9	14.1	12.1	100.0	10.1
	1987	29.5	24.2	19.2	15.0	12.1	100.0	12.4
France	1979	19.7	21.2	18.8	17.7	22.6	100.0	22.2
	1984	17.5	21.8	18.4	17.7	24.7	100.0	25.0
Germany	1984	21.8	22.2	16.7	21.0	18.3	100.0	19.8
Ireland	1987	32.0	21.9	21.3	15.2	9.6	100.0	20.5
Italy	1986	15.6	16.4	19.7	20.7	27.6	100.0	21.4
Luxembourg	1985	17.3	18.3	19.5	22.5	22.4	100.0	23.7
Netherlands	1983	21.8	21.8	18.4	20.4	17.6	100.0	28.5
	1987	24.9	21.3	16.9	17.7	19.2	100.0	28.3
Norway	1979	34.0	20.9	16.4	13.6	15.1	100.0	13.5
	1986	21.5	16.6	14.2	12.2	11.0	100.0	15.1
Sweden	1981	18.0	23.9	19.8	19.5	18.7	100.0	35.0
	1987	15.2	25.8	21.7	19.9	17.4	100.0	35.5
United Kingdom	1979	30.6	20.0	17.4	17.0	15.0	100.0	18.5
	1986	26.7	25.9	19.4	16.1	11.9	100.0	24.3
United States	1979	29.7	21.1	17.4	14.7	17.1	100.0	8.9
	1986	29.2	21.2	17.1	17.5	15.1	100.0	9.4
Finland	1987	25.9	22.6	18.2	15.8	17.6	100.0	27.7

Source: Atkinson, Rainwater, and Smeeding (1995), Table 7.5, p. 107.

redistribution can only be explained by assuming that at least some redistribution is involuntary. Throughout this book, we shall consider several theories that explain how this redistribution can come about.

Bibliographical notes

This chapter benefitted from the surveys of Rodgers (1974) and Oppenheimer (1979).

Levy (1987) has written an interesting account of the changes in income distributional patterns that have occurred in the United States since World War II without focusing on the public choice process, however.

Rae (1981) and associates have pulled together an interesting assortment of the different definitions of equality that underlie discussions of redistribution.

Goodin (1988) analyzes and defends redistribution policies from a normative perspective.

Public choice in a direct democracy

CHAPTER 4

The choice of voting rule

Decision by majorities is as much an expedient as lighting by gas.

William Gladstone

There are two general rules. First, the more grave and important the questions discussed, the nearer should the opinion that is to prevail approach to unanimity. Second, the more the matter in hand calls for speed, the smaller the prescribed difference in the number of votes may be allowed to become: when an immediate decision has to be reached, a majority of one should suffice.

Jean-Jacques Rousseau

This and the next four chapters explore the properties of various voting rules. These rules can be thought of as governing the polity itself, as when decisions are made in a town meeting or by referendum, or an assembly, or a committee of representatives of the citizenry. Following Black (1958), we shall often refer to "committee decisions" as being the outcomes of the voting process. It should be kept in mind, however, that the word "committee" is employed in this wider sense, and can imply a committee of the entire polity voting, as in a referendum. When a committee of representatives is implied, the results can be strictly related only to the preferences of the representatives themselves. The relationship between citizen and representative preferences is taken up later.

4.1   The unanimity rule

Since all can benefit from the provision of a public good, the obvious voting rule for providing it would seem to be unanimous consent. Wicksell (1896) was the first to link the potential for all to benefit from collective action to the unanimity rule. The unanimity rule, coupled with the proposal that each public good be financed by a separate tax, constituted Wicksell's "new principle" of taxation. To see how the procedure might work, consider a world with two persons and one public good. Each person has a given initial income, Y_A and Y_B, and a utility function defined over the public and private goods, $U_A(X_A, G)$ and $U_B(X_B, G)$, where X is the private good and G the public good. The public good is to be financed by a tax of t on individual A, and $(1 - t)$ on individual B. Figure 4.1 depicts individual A's indifference curves between the private and public good. Let the prices of the private and public good be such that if A had to pay for all of the public good ($t = 1$), A's budget constraint

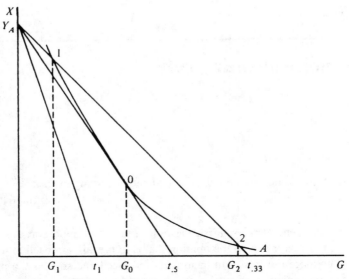

Figure 4.1. Optimal quantities for a voter at different tax prices.

line would be $Y_A t_1$. If A must pay only half of the cost of the public good, his budget constraint line would be $Y_A t_{.5}$, and so on. With a tax share of 0.5 A's optimal choice for a quantity of public good would be G_0. Note, however, that the tax–public good combinations $(t_{.33}, G_1)$ and $(t_{.33}, G_2)$ are on the same indifference curve as $(t_{.5}, G_0)$, and that one could calculate an infinite number of tax–public good quantity combinations from Figure 4.1 that lie upon indifference curve A. It is thus possible to map indifference curve A into a public good–tax space (Johansen, 1963).

Figure 4.2 depicts such a mapping. Points 0, 1, and 2 in Figure 4.2 correspond to points 0, 1, and 2 in Figure 4.1. Indifference curve A in Figure 4.2 is a mapping from the corresponding curve of Figure 4.1.

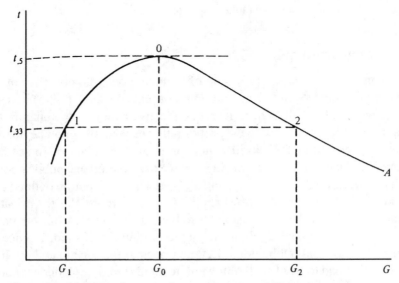

Figure 4.2. Mapping of voter preferences into tax–public good space.

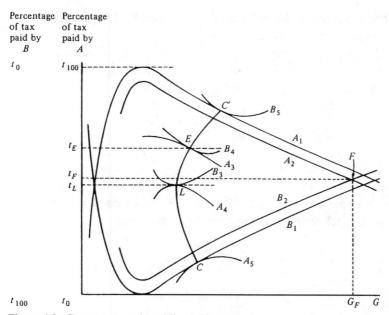

Figure 4.3. Contract curve in public good–tax space.

To map all points from Figure 4.1 into public good–tax space, we redefine each individual's utility function in terms of G and t alone. From the budget constraint, we obtain

$$X_A = Y_A - tG$$
$$X_B = Y_B - (1 - t)G. \tag{4.1}$$

Substituting from (4.1) into each individual's utility function, we obtain the desired utility functions for A and B defined over G and t:

$$U_A = U_A(Y_A - tG, G)$$
$$U_B = U_B(Y_B - (1 - t)G, G). \tag{4.2}$$

Figure 4.3 depicts a mapping of selected indifference curves for A and B from public good–private good space into public good–tax space. A's share of the cost of the public good runs from 0, at the bottom of the vertical scale, to 1.0 at the top. B's tax share runs in the opposite direction. Thus, each point in Figure 4.3 represents a set of tax shares sufficient to cover the full cost of the quantity of public good at that point. Each point is on an indifference curve for A, and one for B. Embedded in each point is a quantity of private goods that each individual consumes as implied by his budget constraint (4.1), the quantity of the public good, and his tax share. A_1 and B_1 are the levels of utility, respectively, if each individual acted alone in purchasing the public good, and thus bore 100 percent of its cost.[1] Lower curves for A (higher for B) represent higher utilities. The set of tangency points between A's and B's indifference

---

[1] To simplify the discussion, we ignore spillovers from one individual's unilateral provision of the public good on the other's utility. One might think of the public good as a bridge across a stream. A_1 and B_1 represent the utilities that each individual can obtain if each builds his own bridge. Within A_1 and B_1 are points of higher utility for both that can be obtained by cooperating and building but one bridge.

curves, CC', represents a contract curve mapping the Pareto-possibility frontier into the public good–tax share space.

To see that each point on CC' is a Pareto-efficient allocation, take the total differentials of each individual's utility function with respect to t and G, holding the initial incomes (Y_A, Y_B) constant:

$$\triangle U_A = \frac{\partial U_A}{\partial X}(-t)dG + \frac{\partial U_A}{\partial G}dG + \frac{\partial U_A}{\partial X}(-G)dt$$

$$\triangle U_B = \frac{\partial U_B}{\partial X}(-1+t)dG + \frac{\partial U_B}{\partial G}dG + \frac{\partial U_B}{\partial X}(G)dt. \tag{4.3}$$

Setting the total change in utility for each individual equal to zero, we can solve for the slope of each individual's indifference curve:

$$\left(\frac{dt}{dG}\right)^A = \frac{\partial U_A/\partial G - t\partial U_A/\partial X}{G(\partial U_A/\partial X)}$$

$$\left(\frac{dt}{dG}\right)^B = -\frac{\partial U_B/\partial G - (1-t)\partial U_B/\partial X}{G(\partial U_B/\partial X)}. \tag{4.4}$$

Equating the slopes of the two indifference curves, we obtain the Samuelsonian condition for Pareto efficiency (1954):

$$\frac{\partial U_A/\partial G}{\partial U_A/\partial X} + \frac{\partial U_B/\partial G}{\partial U_B/\partial X} = 1. \tag{4.5}$$

Now consider the following public choice process. An impartial observer proposes both a pair of tax shares, t_F and $(1 - t_F)$, and a quantity of the public good, G_F. If the combination falls within the eye formed by A_1 and B_1, both individuals prefer this proposal to share the cost of the public good to having to provide all of the public good themselves. Both will vote for it, if they vote sincerely. F now becomes the status quo decision and new tax share–quantity pairs are proposed.[2] When a combination falling within the eye formed by A_2 and B_2 is hit upon, it is unanimously preferred to F. It now becomes the status quo and the process is continued until a point on CC', like E, is obtained. Once this occurs, no new proposal will be unanimously preferred, that is, can make both individuals better off, and the social choice has been, unanimously, made.

Note that for the tax shares inherent in the allocation E, each individual's optimal quantity of public good differs from the quantity of the public good selected. A prefers less of the public good, B prefers more. Given the tax shares t_E and $(1 - t_E)$, therefore, each is being "coerced" into consuming a quantity of the public good that differs from his most preferred quantity (Breton, 1974, pp. 56–66). This form of coercion can be avoided under a slightly different variant of the voting procedure

---

[2] Of course, the rule for selecting a new tax share or a new public good–tax share combination in the procedure described above must be carefully specified to ensure convergence to the Pareto frontier. For specifics on the characteristics of these rules, the reader is referred to the literature on Walrasian-type processes for revealing preferences on public goods as reviewed by Tulkens (1978).

(Escarraz, 1967; Slutsky, 1979). Suppose, for an initially chosen set of tax shares t and $(1 - t)$, that voters must compare all pairs of public good quantities, and a given quantity is chosen only if it is unanimously preferred to all others. This will occur only if the two individuals' indifference curves are tangent to the tax line from t at the same point. If no such quantity of public good is found for this initially chosen t, a new t is chosen and the process repeated. This continues until a t is found at which all individuals vote for the same quantity of public good against all others. In Figure 4.3, this occurs at L for tax shares t_L and $(1 - t_L)$. L is the Lindahl equilibrium.

The outcomes of the two voting procedures just described (E and L) differ in several respects.[3] At L, the marginal rate of substitution of public for private goods for each individual is equal to his tax price:

$$\frac{\partial U_A/\partial G}{\partial U_A/\partial X} = t \qquad \frac{\partial U_B/\partial G}{\partial U_B/\partial X} = (1 - t). \tag{4.6}$$

L is an equilibrium then, in that *all* individuals prefer this quantity of public good to any other, *given each individual's assigned tax price*. E (or any other point reached via the first procedure) is an equilibrium in that at least one individual is worse off by a movement in any direction from this point. Thus, L is preserved as the collective decision through the unanimous *agreement* of all committee members on the quantity of public good to be consumed, *at the given tax prices*; E is preserved via the *veto power* of each individual under the unanimity rule. How compelling these differences are depends on the merits of constraining one's search for the optimum public good quantity to a given set of tax shares (search along a given horizontal line in Figure 4.3). The distribution of utilities at L arrived at under the second process depends only on the initial endowments and individual preferences, and has the (possible) advantage of being independent of the sequence of tax shares proposed, assuming L is unique. The outcome under the first procedure is dependent on the initial endowments, individual utility functions, *and* the specific set and sequence of proposed tax–public good combinations. Although this "path dependence" of the first procedure might be thought undesirable, it has the (possible) advantage of leaving the entire contract curve CC' open to selection. As demonstrated above, all points along CC' are Pareto efficient, and thus cannot be compared without additional criteria. It should be noted in this regard that if a point on CC', say, E, could be selected as most preferred under some set of normative criteria, it could always be reached via the second voting procedure by first redistributing the initial endowments in such a way that L was obtained at the utility levels implied by E (McGuire and Aaron, 1969). However, the informational requirements for such a task are obviously considerable.

We have sketched here only two possible *voting* procedures for reaching the Pareto frontier. Several papers have described Walrasian/tâtonnement procedures for reaching it when public goods are present. These all have a "central planner" or "auctioneer" who gathers information of a certain type from the citizen-voter,

---

[3] For a detailed discussion of these differences, see Slutsky (1979).

processes the information by a given rule, and then passes a message back to the voters to begin a new round of voting. These procedures can be broadly grouped into those in which the planner calls out tax prices (the ts in the preceeding example), and the citizens respond with quantity information – the process originally described by Erik Lindahl (1919) (see also Malinvaud, 1970–1, sec. 5); and those in which the planner–auctioneer calls out quantities of public goods and the citizens respond with price (marginal rate of substitution) information, as in Malinvaud (1970–1, secs. 3 and 4) and Drèze and de la Vallée Poussin (1971). A crucial part of all of these procedures is the computational rule used to aggregate the messages provided by voters and generate a new set of signals. It is this rule that determines if, and when, and where on the Pareto frontier the process leads. Although there are obviously distributional implications to these rules, they are in general not designed to achieve any specific normative goal. The planner–auctioneer's single end is to achieve a Pareto-efficient allocation of resources. These procedures are all subject to the same important distinction as to whether they allow the entire Pareto frontier to be reached or always lead to an outcome with a given set of conditions, like the Lindahl equilibrium. As such, they also share the other general properties of the unanimity rule.

4.2   Criticisms of the unanimity rule

The unanimity rule is the *only* voting rule certain to lead to Pareto-preferred public good quantities and tax shares, a feature that led Wicksell (1896) and later Buchanan and Tullock (1962) to endorse it. Two main criticisms have been made against it. First, a groping search for a point on the contract curve might take considerable time, particularly in a large community of heterogeneous tastes (Black, 1958, pp. 146–7; Buchanan and Tullock, 1962, ch. 6). The loss in time by members of the community in discovering a set of Pareto-optimal tax shares might outweigh the gains to those who are saved from paying a tax exceeding their benefits from the public good. An individual who was uncertain over whether he would be so "exploited" under a less than unanimity rule might easily prefer such a rule rather than spend the time required to attain full unanimity. The second objection against a unanimity rule is that it encourages strategic behavior.[4] If A knows the maximum share of taxes that B will assume rather than go without the public good, A can force B to point C on the contract curve, by voting against all tax shares greater than t_C. All gains from providing the public good then accrue to A. If B behaves the same, the final outcome is dependent on the bargaining strengths of the two individuals. The same is true of the other equilibria along the contract curve (Musgrave, 1959, pp. 78–80). Bargaining can further delay the attainment of the agreement as each player has to "test" the other's willingness to make concessions.

The "bargaining problem" under the unanimity rule is the mirror image of the "incentive problem" in the voluntary provision of a public good. The latter is a direct consequence of the joint supply–nonexclusion properties of a public good. Given

---

[4]   See Black (1958, p. 147), Buchanan and Tullock (1962, ch. 8), Barry (1965, pp. 242–50), and Samuelson (1969).

these properties, each individual has an incentive to understate his preferences and free-ride, since the quantity of public good provided is largely independent of his single message. The literature on voluntary preference revelation procedures has by and large sidestepped this problem by assuming honest preference revelation in spite of the incentives to be dishonest. The strongest analytic result to justify this assumption has been that sincere message transmittal is a minimax strategy; that is, sincere revelation of preferences maximizes the minimum payoff that an individual can obtain (Drèze and de la Vallée Poussin, 1971). But a higher payoff might be obtained through a misrepresentation of preferences, and some individuals can be expected to pursue this more daring option. If to remove this incentive one compels all citizens to vote in favor of a public good quantity–tax share proposal before it is provided, the free-rider problem disappears. Each individual's vote is now essential to the public good's provision. This reversal in the individual's position in the collective decision alters his strategic options. Where an individual might, under a voluntary revelation scheme, gamble on the rest of the group providing an acceptable quantity of the public good without his contributing, under the unanimity rule he might gamble on the group's reducing the size of his contribution rather than risk his continual blocking of the collective outcome. Although the strategy options differ, both solutions to the public good problem are potentially vulnerable to strategic behavior.

Experimental results of Hoffman and Spitzer (1986) and Smith (1977, 1979a,b, 1980) indicate that strategic bargaining on the part of individuals in unanimity rule situations may not be much of a problem. The Hoffman-Spitzer experiments were designed to see whether the ability of individuals to achieve Pareto-optimal allocations in Coase-type externality situations deteriorates as the number of affected parties increases. Since all affected parties had to agree to a bargain before it could be implemented, the experiments essentially tested whether strategic bargaining by individuals would overturn Pareto-optimal allocation proposals under the unanimity rule. Hoffman and Spitzer (1986, p. 151) found that "if anything, efficiency improved with larger groups" (with groups as large as 20 on a side).

Even if strategic behavior does not thwart or indefinitely delay the achievement of a unanimous decision, one might object to the unanimity rule on the grounds that the outcome obtained depends on the bargaining abilities and risk preferences of the individuals (Barry, 1965, p. 249; Samuelson, 1969). Such a criticism implicitly contains the *normative* judgment that the proper distribution of the gains from cooperation *should not* be distributed according to the willingness to bear risks. One can easily counter that they *should*. An individual who votes *against* a given tax share to secure a lower one risks, under a unanimity rule, not having the good provided at all, or if so in a less than optimum quantity. Voting in this manner expresses a low preference for the public good, in much the same way as voting against the tax share does, because it is "truly" greater than the expected benefits. Someone not willing to vote strategically might be said to value the public good higher, and therefore perhaps ought to be charged a higher price for it.

We are clearly in the realm of normative economics here, as we were in comparing points E and L, and need criteria as to how the gains from cooperation *ought* to be shared.[5] Indeed, in a full evaluation of the unanimity rule its normative properties must be considered. Wicksell's advocacy of the unanimity rule was based on its normative properties. The unanimity rule would protect individuals from being coerced by other members of the community, he argued. Wicksell used "coerced" not in the sense employed by Breton, who took it to mean having a different evaluation of the public good *at the margin* from one's tax price, but in the sense of being coerced through a collective decision to pay more for a public good than its benefits are in toto. This argument for the unanimity rule stems directly from Wicksell's view of the collective choice process as one of mutually beneficial voluntary exchange among individuals, as is Buchanan and Tullock's (1962) (see also Buchanan, 1975b). This emphasis on the "voluntary exchange" nature of collective choice underlies the classic essays by both Wicksell and Lindahl and forms an intellectual bond between them, leading in Wicksell's case to the unanimity principle, and in Lindahl's to a set of tax prices equal to each individual's marginal evaluation of the public good. It also explains the reference to "just" taxation in the titles of each of their essays. We shall return to these issues in Chapter 6.

4.3   The optimal majority

When a less than unanimous majority is sufficient to pass an issue, the possibility exists that some individuals will be made worse off via the committee's decision; Wicksell's coercion of the minority can take place. If the issue is of the public good–prisoners' dilemma variety, and there exist reformulations of the issue that could secure unanimous approval, the use of a less-than-unanimity rule can be said to impose a cost on those made worse off by the issue's passage, a cost that could be avoided through the expenditure of the additional time and effort required to redefine the issue so that its passage benefits all. This cost is the difference in utility levels actually secured and those that would have been secured under a full unanimity rule. Buchanan and Tullock were the first to discuss these costs and refer to them as the "external costs" of the decision rule (1962, pp. 63–91; see also Breton, 1974, pp. 145–8).

Were there no costs associated with the unanimity rule itself, it would obviously be the optimal rule, since it minimizes these external decision costs. But the time required to define an issue in such a way as to benefit all may be considerable. In addition to attempting to find a formulation of the proposal benefiting all, time may be required to explain the nature of the benefits of the proposal to some citizens unfamiliar with its merits. On top of these costs must be added the time lost through the strategic maneuvering that might take place as individuals jockey for more favorable positions along the contract curve, as described earlier.

Most observers, including those most favorably disposed toward the unanimity rule like Wicksell and Buchanan and Tullock, have considered these latter costs sufficiently large to warrant abandoning this rule. If all need not agree to a committee decision, what percentage should agree? The preceeding considerations suggest a trade-off between the external costs of having an issue pass against which the

---

[5] At least two normative proposals for sharing these gains are dependent on the bargaining or risk preferences of the individuals (Nash, 1950; Braithwaite, 1955).

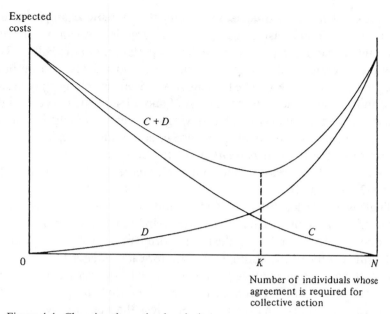

Figure 4.4. Choosing the optimal majority.

individual is opposed, and the costs of time lost through decision making. At the one pole stands unanimity, under which any individual can block any agreement until he has one with which he is satisfied, or which he feels is the best he can obtain. The external decision costs under this rule are zero, but the decision time costs may be infinite. At the other extreme, each individual decides the issue alone. No delays may occur, as with a pure private good decision, but the external costs of allowing each individual to decide unilaterally for the community are again potentially infinitely large.

These various possibilities are depicted in Figure 4.4, which is taken from Buchanan and Tullock (1962, pp. 63–91). The costs of a particular collective decision are presented along the vertical axis; the number of people 0 up to N, the committee size, required to pass the issue are presented along the horizontal axis. Curve C is the external cost function representing the expected loss of utility from the victory of a decision to which an individual is opposed under the committee decision rule. Curve D depicts the decision-time costs of achieving the required majority to pass the issue as a function of the size of the required majority. The optimal majority is the percentage of the committee at which these two sets of costs are together minimized. This occurs at K, where the vertical addition of the two curves reaches a minimum. The optimal majority to pass the issue, given these cost curves, is K/N. At this percentage, the expected gain in utility from redefining a bill to gain one more supporter just equals the expected loss in time from doing so.

Since these costs are likely to differ from issue to issue, one does not expect one voting rule to be optimal for all issues. The external costs will vary depending on both the nature of the issues to be decided and the characteristics of the community deciding them. Ceteris paribus, when opinions differ widely or information is scarce, lengthy periods of time may be required to reach a consensus, and if the likely costs to opposing citizens are not too high, relatively small percentages of the community might be required to make a decision. Again, the extreme example here is the pure private good. In contrast, issues for which large losses can occur are likely to require higher majorities (for example, issues pertaining to the Bill of Rights).[6] The larger the community, the greater the number of individuals with similar tastes and, thus, the easier it is likely to be to achieve a consensus among a given *absolute* number of individuals. Thus, an increase in N should shift the curve D rightward and downward. But the fall in costs of achieving a consensus among a given number is unlikely to be fully proportional to the rise in community size. Thus, for issues of a similar type, the optimal *percentage* of the community required to pass an issue K/N is likely to decrease as the community increases in size (Buchanan and Tullock, 1962, pp. 111–16).

Individuals whose tastes differ widely from most others in the community can be expected to favor more inclusive majority rules. Individuals with high opportunity costs of time should favor less inclusive majority rules. Buchanan and Tullock assume that the choice of the optimal majority for each category of issues is made in a constitutional setting in which each individual is uncertain over his future position, tastes, and so on. Therefore, each views the problem in the same way, and a unanimous agreement is achieved as to which less-than-unanimity rule to use for each set of issues. When such a consensus does not exist, the knotty question that must be faced is what majority should be required to decide what majorities are required on all other issues? Having now faced this question, we shall move on.

4.4   A simple majority as the optimal majority

The method of majority rule requires that at least the first whole integer above $N/2$ support an issue before it becomes the committee decision. Nothing we have said so far indicates why $K/N = N/2$ should be the optimal majority for the bulk of a committee's decisions; and yet it is the voting rule of choice across the world from parliamentary assemblies down to the local meeting of the Parent-Teacher Association. As Buchanan and Tullock (1962, p. 81) note, for any one rule, such as the majority rule, to be the optimal majority for a wide class of decisions, there must exist some sort of a kink in one of the cost functions at the point $N/2$, causing the sum of two curves to obtain a minimum in a substantial proportion of the cases at this point.

A possible explanation for a kink in the decision-making cost curve, D, at $N/2$ can be obtained by considering further the internal dynamics of the committee decision process. When less than half of a committee's membership is sufficient to pass an issue, the possibility exists for both the issue A and the issue's converse ($\sim A$) to pass. Thus, a proposal to increase school expenditures by 10 percent might first achieve a winning majority (of, say, 40 percent) and a counterproposal to cut expenditures by 5 percent may also receive a winning majority. The committee could, when less than half of the voters suffice to carry an issue, become deadlocked in an endless series of offsetting proposals absorbing the time and patience of its members. The method of simple majority rule has the smallest possible required majority to pass

---

[6] In Chapter 26 a more formal and general analysis of the constitutional choice of a voting rule is presented.

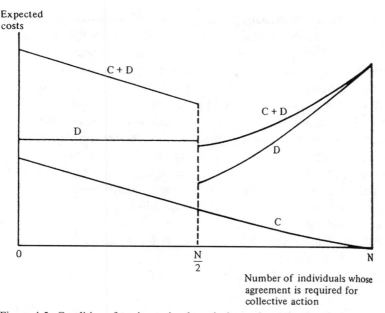

Figure 4.5. Conditions favoring a simple majority as the optimal majority.

an issue, which avoids the possibility of self-contradictory issues simultaneously passing (Reimer, 1951).

In Figure 4.5, decision cost and external cost curves have been drawn such that their minimum would lie to the left of $N/2$ were D to continue to decline as it moves leftward from $N/2$. But the D curve is higher to the left of $N/2$ owing to the extra decision costs of having conflicting issues pass. This portion of the D curve has been drawn as a straight line, but it could conceivably be U- or inverted U-shaped to the left of $N/2$. The discontinuity at $N/2$ makes this majority the optimal majority for this committee.[7]

---

[7] Tullock (1998, pp. 16–17, 93–94) has objected to my rationalization of the universal popularity of the simple majority rule by positing a discontinuity in the decision-costs curve. He cites presidential elections in the United States and parliamentary elections in the United Kingdom as examples of the application of less than majority rules, because U.S. presidents are occasionally elected without receiving a majority of the popular vote, and the party that wins a majority of seats in the British House of Commons almost never receives a majority of the votes cast. But these are examples of *electoral* rules that can convert less than a majority of the popular vote into the victory of a candidate or party. We are concerned here with the choice of a *committee voting rule*. Neither the House of Commons nor either of the two houses of the U.S. Legislature employ a less than 50 percent majority rule, nor am I aware of any committee that does so, nor does Tullock give an example of such a committee. Indeed, if the British Parliament employed, say, a 40 percent majority to pass legislation, then a party that failed to win a majority of the seats in an election would not necessarily "lose" the election. As long as it got more than 40 percent of the seats, it, along with the "winning" party, could pass legislation.

More fundamentally, however, Tullock misses the whole point of the argument. *If* constitutional conventions choose parliamentary voting rules by weighing the external and decision-making costs of each rule, as Buchanan and Tullock first posited, *then* there is *no way* to explain the ubiquitous use of the simple majority rule *without* the existence of a kink or discontinuity in one of the two curves at $K/N = N/2$. If the discontinuity is not in D, then it must be in E.

An alternative way to explain the popularity of the simple majority rule would, of course, be to abandon the kind of cost calculus that Buchanan and Tullock introduced. We shall examine other criteria for choosing the simple majority rule in Chapter 6. In Chapter 26 we integrate the two approaches.

Absent a discontinuity in D, a minimum for $C + D$ only occurs to the left of $N/2$ when the D curve rises more rapidly as it moves to the right than C does moving to the left; that is, decision costs vary much more over the range of committee sizes than do the external costs of collective decision making. $N/2$ is the optimal majority for the committee because of the discontinuity in the D curve. Thus, the choice of $N/2$ as the optimal majority is driven by the shape of the D curve. The method of simple majority rule will be selected as *the* committee decision rule by a committee whose members place a relatively high value on the opportunity costs of time. Were it not for the loss of time involved in having conflicting proposals like A and $\sim A$ pass, the minimal cost majority for the committee would be less than 0.50. The simple majority is optimal because it is the smallest majority one can select and still avoid having conflicting proposals both obtain winning majorities.

Speed is not the majority rule's only property, however. So important is the simple majority rule as a voting procedure that we shall devote most of the next two chapters to discussing its other properties.

Bibliographical notes

Tulkens (1978) presents an excellent review of the literature on tâtonnement procedures for revealing preferences on public goods. Milleron (1972) reviews the literature on public goods more generally.

The seminal discussions of the "voluntary exchange" approaches of Lindahl and Wicksell are by Musgrave (1939) and Buchanan (1949). See also Head (1964).

The relationship between Wicksell's voting theory and the Lindahl equilibrium is taken up by Escarraz (1967), who first described a way in which the Lindahl equilibrium could be reached under a unanimity voting rule. Escarraz argues that the unanimity rule was a necessary assumption underlying Lindahl's belief that the equilibrium would be reached and might have been implied in Lindahl's concept of an "even distribution of political power." Under this interpretation, Lindahl's even distribution of political power, Wicksell's freedom from coercion, the unanimity rule, and a set of tax prices equal to the marginal rates of utility for the public good all become nicely integrated.

CHAPTER 5

Majority rule – positive properties

> But as unanimity is impossible, and common consent means the vote of the majority, it is self-evident that the few are at the mercy of the many.
>
> John Adams

5.1   Majority rule and redistribution

As Chapter 4 indicated, a committee concerned only with providing public goods and correcting for externalities might nevertheless choose as its voting rule the simple majority rule, if it placed enough weight on saving time. But speed is not the only property that majority rule possesses. Indeed, once issues can pass with less than unanimous agreement, the distinction between allocative efficiency and redistribution becomes blurred. Some individuals are inevitably worse off under the chosen outcome than they would be were some other outcome selected, and there is in effect a redistribution from those who are worse off because the issue has passed to those who are better off.

To see this point more clearly, consider Figure 5.1. The ordinal utilities of two groups of voters, the rich and the poor, are depicted on the vertical and horizontal axes. All of the members of both groups are assumed to have identical preference functions. In the absence of the provision of any public good, representative individuals from each group experience utility levels represented by S and T. The point of initial endowment on the Pareto-possibility frontier with only private good production is E. The provision of the public good can by assumption improve the utilities of both individuals. Its provision thus expands the Pareto-possibility frontier out to the curve $XYZW$. The segment YZ corresponds to the contract curve in Figure 4.3, CC'. Under the unanimity rule, both groups of individuals must be better off with the provision of the public good for them to vote for it. So the outcome under the unanimity rule must be a quantity of public good and tax share combination, leaving both groups somewhere in the YZ segment along the Pareto-possibility frontier.

But there is no reason to expect the outcome to fall in this range under majority rule. A coalition of the committee's members can benefit by redefining the issue to increase their benefits at the expense of the noncoalition members, say, by shifting the tax shares to favor the coalition. If the rich were in the majority, they could be expected to couple the public good proposal with a sufficiently regressive tax package so that the outcome wound up in the XY segment. If the poor were in the majority, the taxes would be sufficiently progressive to produce an outcome in ZW.

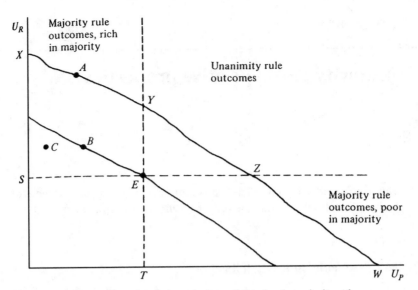

Figure 5.1. Outcomes under the unanimity and the simple majority rule.

Given the opportunity to redefine the issue proposed through the alteration of either the quantity of the public good provided, the tax shares, or both, one can expect with certainty that the outcome of the collective choice process *will* fall outside of the Pareto-preferred segment *YZ* (Davis, 1970). As long as the issue could be continually redefined in such a way that a majority still benefited, it would pass, and a stable majority coalition could, in principle, push a minority back as far along the Pareto-possibility frontier as their consciences or the constitution allowed.

The process of transforming a proposal unanimously supported into one supported by only a simple majority resembles that described by Riker (1962), in which "grand" coalitions are transformed into minimum winning coalitions. In developing his theory of coalitions, Riker makes two key assumptions: (1) decisions are made by majority rule and (2) politics is a zero-sum game. He assumes that the allocational efficiency decisions (quantities of public goods) are all optimally resolved as a matter of course, and that the political process is left with the distributional issue of choosing from among the Pareto-efficient set (pp. 58–61). Thus, Riker (1962, pp. 29–31) takes the extreme position that politics involves *only* redistribution questions, and is a pure zero-sum game. Given that the game is to take from the losers, the winners can obviously be better off by increasing the size of the losing side, as long as it remains the losing side. Under majority rule, this implies that the losing coalition will be increased until it is almost as large as the winning coalition, until the proposal passes by a "bare" majority. In Riker's description, the committee is made up of several factions or parties of different sizes, rather than two "natural" coalitions, as depicted earlier, and the process of forming a minimum winning coalition consists of adding and deleting parties or factions until two "grand" coalitions of almost equal size are formed. In regular committee voting, the process would consist of adding and deleting riders to each proposal, increasing the number of losers, and increasing the benefits to the remaining winners.

Several writers have described ways in which majority rule can lead to redistribution other than via the obvious route of direct cash transfers. The pioneering effort in this area was by Tullock (1959). Tullock described a community of 100 farmers in which access to the main highway is via small trunk roads, each of which serves only 4 or 5 farmers. The issue comes up as to whether the entire community of 100 should finance the repair of all of the trunk roads out of a tax on the entire community. Obviously one can envisage a level of repairs and set of taxes on the individual farmers under which such a proposal would be unanimously adopted. But under majority rule it is to the greater advantage of some to propose that only one half of the roads are repaired out of a tax falling on the entire population. Thus, one can envisage a coalition of 51 of the farmers forming and proposing that only the roads serving them are repaired out of the community's general tax revenue (Tullock discusses other possible outcomes, which we take up shortly). Such a proposal would pass under majority rule, and obviously involves a redistribution from the 49 farmers who pay taxes and receive no road repairs to the 51 farmers whose taxes cover only slightly more than one half of the cost of the road repair.

In the Tullock example, redistribution to the 51 farmers in the majority coalition takes place through the inclusion in the entire community's budget of a good that benefits only a subset of the community. Each access road benefits only 4 or 5 farmers and is a public good with respect to only theses farmers. The optimal size of jurisdiction for deciding each of these "local" public goods would seem to be the 4 or 5 farmers on each access road. The inclusion of private goods in the public budget as a means of bringing about redistribution was first discussed by Buchanan (1970, 1971) and has been analyzed by several other writers. Building on Buchanan's papers, Spann demonstrated that the collective provision of a private good financed via a set of Lindahl tax prices leads to a redistribution from the rich to the poor (Spann, 1974). To see this, consider Figure 5.2. Let D_P be the demand schedule for the poor and D_R for the rich. Let X be a pure private good with price = marginal social cost = P_X. If the good is supplied to the market privately, the poor purchase X_P at price P_X; the rich purchase X_R. Assume next that the good is collectively purchased and supplied to the community in equal quantities per person, as if it were a public good. The optimal quantity of X is then given by the intersection of the community demand schedule, obtained by vertically summing the individual demand schedules. (We ignore here income effect considerations. The argument is not substantively affected by this omission.)

The supply schedule under collective provision is obtained by multiplying the market price of the good by the number of members of the community. If we assume for simplicity an equal number of rich and poor, the community will purchase X_C units of the good for each individual. At this quantity, a poor individual places a marginal evaluation on the good of X_CH, and his Lindahl tax is t_P. A member of the rich group pays t_R. In effect, the poor receive a subsidy of $ACHt_P$, the difference between the price they pay for the good and its social cost multiplied by the quantity they consume. But their consumer surplus gain from the collective provision of the private good is only $ABHt_P$. Thus, there is a deadweight loss of BCH through the collective provision of X. In addition to the direct transfer of income from R

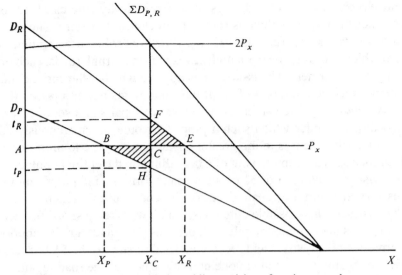

Figure 5.2. Redistribution with the public provision of a private good.

to P ($t_P HCA$) via the subsidization of P's purchase of X, R is worse off by being forced to consume a less than optimal amount of X. R loses the consumer surplus triangle FCE.

This loss in efficiency comes about through the constraint placed on each individual's behavior, when all are forced to consume the same quantity of the private good. Given the costs of producing the private good, all could be made better off by being allowed to maximize their individual utilities at the set of market prices for this and the other goods. The additional constraint that all consume the same quantity lowers the set of attainable utilities. But the poor are better off receiving the redistribution in this form than not at all, and if it is not feasible for them to obtain direct cash subsidies via lump-sum transfers, and it is possible to obtain them through the collectivization of private good supply, then the latter is worth pursuing.

The inefficiency brought about by constraining the rich to consume less than their most preferred quantity of X can be removed by allowing them to purchase additional units in the market. Most governments that publicly provide housing, medical care, education, and similar goods that could be provided by the market do allow individuals to supplement what they receive from the state, or to opt out of the system entirely. When upper income groups pay to send their children to private schools as they do in the United States and the United Kingdom, or obtain health care from private physicians rather than from the free National Health Service in the United Kingdom, an additional form of redistribution from rich to poor occurs as the well-to-do pay part of the costs of the publicly provided good, but consume none of it. Although allowing the rich to purchase the private good on the market reduces the efficiency loss from providing this private good publicly, it does not eliminate it entirely, as those remaining in the program continue to be forced to purchase the private good under the artificially imposed constraint of an equal quantity and/or uniform quality (Besley and Coate, 1991).

The inefficiency also remains when the upper income groups continue to use the publicly provided service, but supplement their purchases on the market. If the quantity (quality) of the public service is chosen using the simple majority rule, the chosen quantity or quality may be greater than that which both the rich and the poor prefer. The poor oppose the collective choice because they are forced to consume more of the publicly provided good than they wish, given their tax price; and the rich too would prefer to pay less in taxes, consume less of the publicly provided service, and purchase more in the market.[1]

Where publicly provided education at the elementary school level redistributes income from the highest to the lowest income groups, publicly provided higher education redistributes from the lowest to the middle income groups, and where professional education in law, medicine, and business is freely provided by the state – as it is throughout most of Europe – redistribution is from the average taxpayer to those who will soon join the highest income groups in society.[2]

As the pattern of governmental transfers depicted in Table 3.5 of Chapter 3 reveals, all redistribution is not from rich to poor, nor even predicated on differences in incomes. Occupation, sex, race, geographic location, recreational preferences, and political affiliation can all be used to delineate the targets of redistribution. What is required for redistribution to take place under majority rule is that the members of the winning coalition be clearly identifiable, so that the winning proposal can discriminate in their favor, either on the basis of the distribution of the benefits it provides (for example, Tullock's unequal distribution of roads at equal taxes) or the taxes it charges (for example, Buchanan and Spann's equal quantities of private good X at unequal taxes).

Regardless of what form it takes, and regardless of whether political choice under majority rule is a pure zero-sum game, as Riker assumes, or involves allocational efficiency changes *plus* redistribution, the fact remains that the redistributional characteristics of any proposal will figure in its passage, and that majority rule creates the incentive to form coalitions and redefine issues to achieve these redistributional gains. Indeed, from the mere knowledge that an issue passed with some individuals in favor and others opposed, one cannot discern whether it really was a public good shifting the Pareto-possibility frontier out to $XYZW$ in Figure 5.1 coupled to a tax unfavorable to the poor, say, resulting in an outcome at A; a pure redistribution along the private-good Pareto-efficiency frontier resulting in B; or an inefficient redistribution from the poor to the rich via the collective provision of a private good resulting in, say, C. All one can say with much confidence is that the rich appear to believe that they will be better off, and the poor that they will be worse off from passage of the proposal; that is, the move is into the region $SEYX$.

Thus, even if the emergence of states is better explained as cooperative efforts undertaken to benefit all members of the community rather than as a power move by one group in society to exploit the rest, it is now clear that the use of the majority rule to make collective decisions must transform the state at least in part into a

---

[1] Gouveia (1997). This result relies on the median voter theorem introduced in Section 5.3* of this chapter.

[2] The allocational (in)efficiency and redistribution properties of education are discussed by Barzel (1973) and Barzel and Deacon (1975).

redistributive state. Since all modern democracies use the majority rule to a considerable degree to make collective decisions – indeed the use of the majority rule is often regarded as the mark of a democratic form of government – all modern democratic states must be redistributive states in part, if not in toto.

5.2   Cycling

Given that majority rule must induce some element of redistribution into the collective decision process, we take up next an attribute of majority rule when a pure redistribution decision is to be made. Consider a three-person committee that must decide how to divide a gift of $100 among them using majority rule. This is a pure distributional issue, a simple zero-sum game. Suppose that V_2 and V_3 first vote to divide the $100 between themselves, 60/40. V_1 now has much to gain from forming a winning coalition. He might propose to V_3 that they split the $100, 50/50. This is more attractive to V_3, and we can expect this coalition to form. But now V_2 has much to gain from trying to form a winning coalition. He might now offer V_1 a 55/45 split forming a new coalition, and so on. When the issues proposed involve redistribution of income and wealth, members of a losing coalition always have a large incentive to attempt to become members of the winning coalition, even at the cost of a less-than-equal share.

The outcome of a 50/50 split of the $100 between a pair of voters is a von Neumann-Morgenstern solution to this particular game (Luce and Raiffa, 1957, pp. 199–209). This game has three such solutions, however, and there is no way to predict which of these three, if any, would occur. Thus, the potential for cycles, when issues involve redistribution, seems quite large. It is always possible to redefine an issue to benefit one or more members and harm some others. New winning coalitions containing some members of the previously losing coalition and excluding members of the previously winning coalition are always feasible. But, as we have seen from the discussion of majority rule, when issues can be amended in the committee, any pure allocative efficiency decision can be converted into a combination of a redistribution and an allocative efficiency change via amendment. Thus it would seem that when committees are free to amend the issues proposed, cycles must be an ever-present danger.

The possibility that majority rule can lead to cycles across issues was recognized over two hundred years ago by the Marquis de Condorcet (1785). Dodgson (1876) analyzed the problem anew one hundred years later, and it has been a major concern of the modern public choice literature beginning with Black (1948b) and Arrow (1951, rev. ed. 1963).[3] Consider the following three voters with preferences over three issues, as in Table 5.1 (> implies preferred). X can defeat Y, Y can defeat Z, and Z can defeat X. Pairwise voting can lead to an endless cycle. The majority rule can select no winner nonarbitrarily.[4]

If we define Z as a payoff to voters V_2 and V_3 of 60/40, Y as the payoff (50, 0, 50), and X as (55, 45, 0), the ordinal rankings of issues in Figure 5.3 correspond

---

[3] For a discussion of these and other early contributions, see Black (1958), Riker (1961), and Young (1997).
[4] See A.K. Sen's discussion (1970a, pp. 68–77).

Table 5.1. *Voter preferences that induce a cycle*

	Issues			
Voters	X	Y	Z	X
1	>	>	<	
2	>	<	>	
3	<	>	>	
Community	>	>	>	

to the zero-sum pure distribution game. But it is also possible to get orderings as in Table 5.1 and Figure 5.3 for issues involving allocational efficiency. If X, Y, and Z are sequentially higher expenditures on a public good, then the preferences of Voters 1 and 3 can be said to be single-peaked in the public good–utility space (see Figure 5.3). Voter 2's preferences are double-peaked, however, and herein are a cause of the cycle. Change 2's preferences so that they are single-peaked, and the cycle disappears.

One of the early important theorems in public choice was Black's (1948a) proof that majority rule produces an equilibrium outcome when voter preferences are single-peaked. If voter preferences can be depicted along a single dimension, as with an expenditure issue, this equilibrium lies at the peak preference for the median voter. Figure 5.4 depicts the single-peaked preferences for five voters. Voters 3, 4, and 5 favor m over any proposal to supply less. Voters 3, 2, and 1 favor it over proposals to supply more. The preference of the median voter decides.

5.3*   The median voter theorem – one-dimensional issues

The proof follows Enelow and Hinich (1984, ch. 2). The two key assumptions for the median voter theorem are (1) that issues are defined along a single dimensional

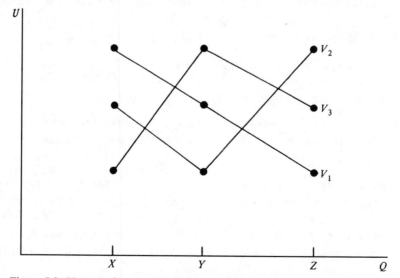

Figure 5.3. Voter preferences that induce a cycle.

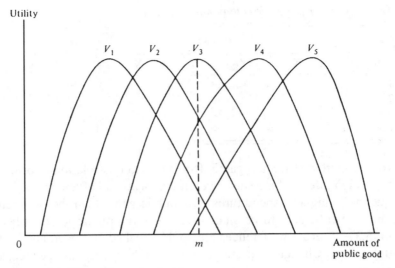

Figure 5.4. The median voter decides.

vector x and (2) that each voter's preferences are single-peaked in that one dimension. Let voter i's preferences be represented by a utility function $U_i()$ defined over x, $U_i(x)$. Let x_i^* be voter i's most preferred point along the x vector. Call x_i^* i's ideal point.

Definition: x_i^* is i's ideal point if and only if (iff) $U_i(x_i^*) > U_i(x)$ for all $x \neq x_i^*$.

Definition: *Let y and z be two points along the x dimension, such that either y, z $\geq x_i^*$ or $y, z \leq x_i^*$. Then voter i's preferences are single-peaked iff $[U_i(y) > U_i(z)] \leftrightarrow [|y - x_i^*| < |z - x_i^*|]$.*

In other words, the definition of single-peaked preferences says that if y and z are two points on the same side of x_i^*, then i prefers y to z if and only if y is closer to x_i^* than z is. If all preferences are single-peaked, then preferences like those of Voter 2 in Figure 5.3 cannot occur (note z is 2's ideal point in this figure).

Definition: *Let $\{x_1^*, x_2*, \ldots, x_n^*\}$ be the n ideal points for a committee of n individuals. Let N_R be the number of $x_i^* \geq x_m$, and N_L be the number of $x_i^* \leq x_m$. Then x_m is a median position iff $N_R \geq n/2$ and $N_L \geq n/2$.*

Theorem: *If x is a single-dimensional issue, and all voters have single-peaked preferences defined over x, then x_m, the median position, cannot lose under majority rule.*

Proof: Consider any $z \neq x_m$, say, $z < x_m$. Let R_m be the number of ideal points to the right of x_m. By definition of single-peaked preferences, all R_m voters with ideal points to the right of x_m prefer x_m to z. By definition of median position, $R_m \geq n/2$. Thus, the number of voters preferring x_m to z is at least $R_m \geq n/2$. x_m cannot lose to z under majority rule. Similarity, one can show that x_m cannot lose to any $z > x_m$. □

5.4   Majority rule and multidimensional issues

Single-peakedness is a form of homogeneity property of preference orderings (Riker, 1961, p. 908). People who have single-peaked preferences on an issue *agree* that the issue is one for which there is an optimum amount of the public good, and that the farther one is away from the optimum, the worse off one is. If quantities of defense expenditures were measured along the horizontal axis, then a preference ordering like the ordering in Figure 5.4 would obviously imply that Voter 1 is somewhat of a dove and Voter 5 a hawk, but a consensus of values would still exist with respect to the way in which the quantities of defense expenditures were ordered. The median voter theorem states that a consensus of this type (on a single-dimensional issue) is sufficient to ensure the existence of a majority rule equilibrium. During the Vietnam War, it was often said that some people favored *either* an immediate pullout or a massive expansion of effort to achieve total victory. Preferences of this type resemble Voter 2's preferences in Figure 5.3. Preference orderings such as these can lead to cycles. Note that the problem here may not be a lack of consensus on the way of viewing a single dimension of an issue, but on the dimensionality of the issue itself. The Vietnam War, for example, raised issues regarding both the U.S. military posture abroad and humanitarian concern for the death and destruction it wrought. One might have favored high expenditures to achieve the first, and a complete pullout to stop the second. These considerations raise, in turn, the question of the extent to which any issue can be viewed in a single dimension.

If all issues were unidimensional, multipeaked preferences of the type depicted in Figure 5.3 might be sufficiently unlikely so that cycling would not be much of a problem. In a multidimensional world, however, preferences of the type depicted in Table 5.1 seem quite plausible. Issues X, Y, and Z might, for example, be votes on whether to use a piece of land for a swimming pool, tennis courts, or a baseball diamond. Each voter could have single-peaked preferences on the amount to be spent on each activity, and a cycle would still appear over the issue of how the land should be used. The introduction of distributional considerations into a set of issues can, as already illustrated, also produce cycles.

A great deal of effort has been devoted to defining conditions under which majority rule does yield an equilibrium. Returning to Figure 5.4 we can see, somewhat trivially, that m emerges as an equilibrium because the other four voters are evenly "paired off" against one another regarding any move from m. This condition has been generalized by Plott (1967), who proved that a majority rule equilibrium exists if it is a maximum for one (and only one) individual, and the remaining even number of individuals can be divided into pairs whose interests are diametrically opposed; that is, whenever a proposal is altered so as to benefit a given individual A, a given individual B must be made worse off.

To see the intuition behind Plott's important result, consider first Figure 5.5. Let x_1 and x_2 be two issues, or two dimensions of a single issue. Let individual preferences be defined over x_1 and x_2, with point A the ideal point, the most preferred point in the x_1x_2 quadrant for individual A. If one envisages a third dimension, perpendicular

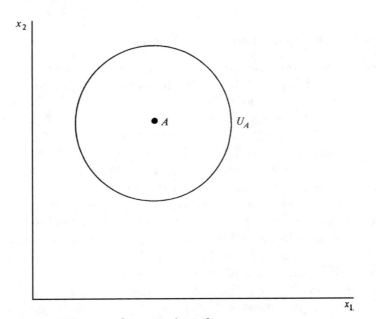

Figure 5.5. Outcome for a committee of one.

to the x_1x_2 plane, with utility measured in this third dimension, then point A is a projection of the peak of individual A's utility "mountain" onto the x_1x_2 plane. Pass a second plane through the mountain between its peak and floor and it will intersect the mountain in curves representing equal levels of utility. One such curve, drawn as a circle, is presented in Figure 5.5.

If we thought of individual A as a committee of one making choices using majority rule, then rather obviously and trivially she would choose point A. For her it is the dominant point in the x_1x_2 quadrant; that is, *it is a point that cannot lose to any other point.* What we seek to determine are the conditions for the existence of a dominant point under majority rule for committees larger than one.

Let B join A to form a committee of two. Under majority rule, any point that is off the contract curve, like D in Figure 5.6, can be defeated by a point on the contract curve, like E, using majority rule. Thus, no point off the contract curve can be a dominant point. At the same time, points like E on the contract curve cannot lose to other points on the contract curve like A and B. In a choice between A and E, voter A chooses A, B chooses E, and the result is a draw under majority rule. For a committee of two, the set of dominant points under majority rule is the contract curve. With circular indifference curves, the contract curve is the straight line segment joining A and B.

It should be clear from this example that dominance and Pareto optimality are closely related. Indeed, for E to be a dominant point, it must be in the Pareto set of every majority coalition one can construct, for were it not, there would exist some other point Z in the Pareto set for a majority coalition, which is Pareto preferred to E. This coalition will form and vote for Z over E.

Now consider a committee of three. Let C's ideal point be at C in Figure 5.7. The Pareto sets for each majority coalition are again the straight line segments joining

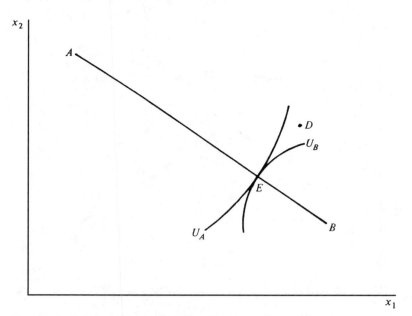

Figure 5.6. Outcomes for a committee of two.

each pair of ideal points, AC, BC, and AB. There is no point common to all three line segments, and thus no point is contained in all three Pareto sets. By the logic of the previous paragraph, there is no dominant point under majority rule. A point like D in $A - C$'s Pareto set lies outside of $A-B$'s Pareto set. There thus exist points on AB, like Z, that can defeat D.

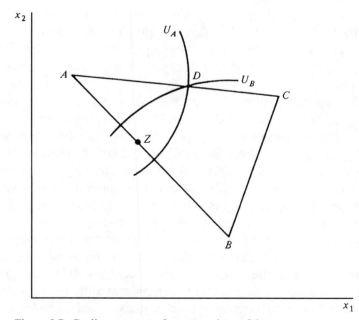

Figure 5.7. Cycling outcomes for a committee of three.

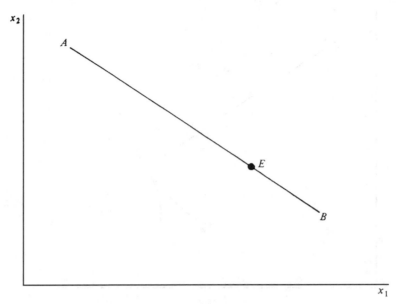

Figure 5.8. Equilibrium outcome for a committee of three.

The triangle ABC inclusive of its borders constitutes the Pareto set for the committee of three. Were the unanimity rule employed, the committee would be led to some point within ABC or on its boundary. Once there, the committee would be stuck, unable to move unanimously to another point. All points in and on ABC are potential equilibria. Under the majority rule, however, only the Pareto sets for the majority coalitions are relevant. There are three of them, but with no common point among them, no equilibrium exists.

The situation would be different if the third committee member's ideal point fell on the segment AB or its extension, say, at E (Figure 5.8). The three majority coalition Pareto sets are again the segments joining the three ideal points, AB, AE, and EB. However, now they have a point in common, E, and it is the dominant point under majority rule.

When the third committee member's ideal point falls on the ray connecting the other two members' ideal points, what was a multidimensional choice problem collapses into a single-dimensional choice problem. The committee must select a combination of x_1 and x_2 from along the ray through A and B. The conditions for the median voter theorem are applicable, and the committee choice is at the ideal point for the median voter, point E. Note also that the interests of the remaining committee members, A and B, are both diametrically opposed and "balanced" against one another as Plott's theorem requires for an equilibrium.

Now consider adding two more members to the committee. Obviously, if their ideal points were to fall along the ray through AB, an equilibrium would still exist. If one point were above and to the left of E and the other below and to the right, then E would remain the single dominant point under majority rule. But if both points fell outside of AB but were still on its extension, say, above and to the left of A, an equilibrium would still exist. In this case, it would be at A.

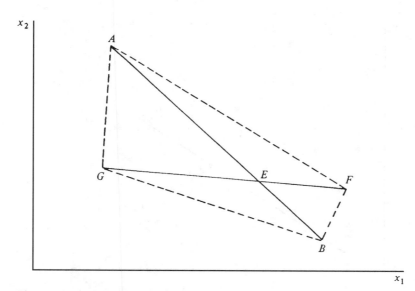

Figure 5.9. Outcome for a committee of five.

But the ideal points of the new members do not have to fall along *AB* extended for a dominant point to continue to exist. Suppose the two new committee members had ideal points falling on a line segment passing through *E*, but not coinciding with *AB*, say, like *F* and *G* in Figure 5.9. With a committee of five, three are needed to form a majority coalition. The Pareto sets for the majority coalitions are the triangles *AEF*, *AEG*, *GEB*, and *BEF*, and the line segments *AEB* and *GEF* (see Figure 5.9). These six Pareto sets have but one point in common, *E*, and it is the dominant point under majority rule. *E* remains the equilibrium because the two new members' interests are symmetrically positioned on opposite sides of *E*, and thus one's interests are balanced against the other's. As long as new committee members would continue to be added in pairs with ideal points on line segments passing through *E*, and on opposite sides of it, this balance would not be upset and *E* would remain the committee's equilibrium choice under majority rule.

The dominance of *E* in Figure 5.9 does not follow as it did in Figure 5.8 from a direct application of the median voter theorem. The issue space cannot be collapsed to a single-dimensional representation in Figure 5.9. But *E* is a median point in a more general sense. Pass any line through *E*, like *WW* in Figure 5.10, and there are three points on or to the left of (above) this line, as well as three points on or to the right of (below) it. A movement from *E* to the left will be opposed by a majority of the committee (*EBF*) as will a movement to the right (*EAG*). Since this is true for all possible lines that one can draw through *E*, all possible moves from *E* are blocked – hence its equilibrium nature. *E* satisfies the definition of a median point presented in Section 5.3*, with respect to the areas left and right of the line *WW* through *E*. The number of ideal points at or to the left of *E* is greater than $n/2$, as is the number at or to the right, where *n*, the committee size, in this case is 5. Since this property holds for every *WW* one can draw through *E*, *E* is a median point *in*

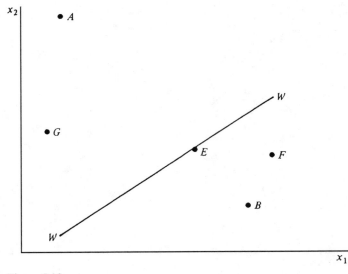

Figure 5.10.

all directions. The theorem – that the necessary and sufficient condition for E to be a dominant point under majority rule is that it be a median in all directions – is proved in the next section.

5.5*   Proof of the median voter theorem – multidimensional case

This theorem was first proved by Davis, DeGroot, and Hinich (1972); we again follow Enelow and Hinich (1984, ch. 3).

We begin by generalizing the definitions of N_R and N_L. N_R is the number of ideal points to the right of (below) any line passing through E; N_L is the number of ideal points to the left of (above) this line. Continue to assume circular indifference curves.

Theorem: *E is a dominant point under majority rule iff $N_R \geq n/2$ and $N_L \geq n/2$ for all possible lines passing through E.*

Proof:
Sufficiency: Pick any point $Z \neq E$ (see Figure 5.11), and inquire whether Z might nevertheless defeat E under the simple majority rule. Draw ZE. Draw WW perpendicular to ZE. Given that all indifference curves are circles, E is closer to any ideal point to the right of (below) WW than is Z. N_R voters prefer E to Z. By assumption, $N_R \geq n/2$. E cannot lose to Z.

Necessity: We must show that if Z is a point not satisfying the $N_R \geq n/2$ and $N_L \geq n/2$ condition for some WW line drawn through it, then it cannot be a dominant point. Let Z and WW in Figure 5.12 be such that $N_R < n/2$. Then $N_L > n/2$. Now move WW parallel to its original position until it reaches some point Z' on the perpendicular to WW such that N_L' just satisfies the

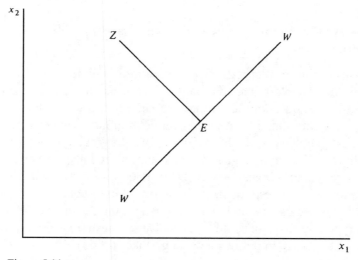

Figure 5.11.

condition $N'_L \leq n/2$ for the line $W'W'$ through Z'. Clearly, some point Z' satisfying this condition must eventually be reached. Now choose Z'' between Z and Z' on the line segment ZZ'. N''_L defined with respect to the line through Z'' parallel to WW must satisfy $N''_L > n/2$. But the N''_L voters with ideal points to the left of $W''W''$ must all prefer Z'' to Z. Thus Z cannot be a dominant point. $\qquad\square$

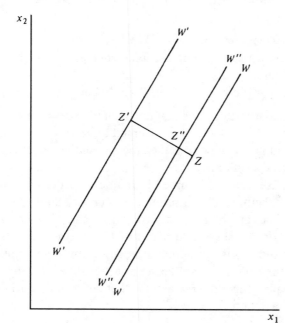

Figure 5.12.

5.6   Majority rule equilibria when preferences are not defined in spatial terms

So far, the results of this chapter regarding an equilibrium under majority rule have been derived in the context of a spatial model of choice. This is perhaps a natural way to approach choice questions for economists since they often analyze individual choices assuming utility functions defined over continuous variables and illustrate their results using geometry. But whether one views the results so far in a positive light (an equilibrium does exist under majority rule) or in a negative one (but only under very stringent assumptions), one might wonder how sensitive the results are to the formulation of the questions in spatial terms. Might better or worse results ensue if one abandoned the spatial context for examining majority rule? After all, voters do not typically think in spatial terms. These questions echo an attack on the public choice approach to politics levied by Stokes (1963), when public choice spatial models first began to intrude into the political science literature.

All of the major results concerning consumer behavior can be derived without the help of geometry or calculus, if one assumes that individual preferences satisfy certain basic rationality axioms (Newman, 1965). Since the theorems regarding consumer behavior derived from these axioms closely resemble those derived using calculus, one might suspect that the same will be true regarding collective decision functions like majority rule. And this suspicion is borne out.

The concept of an ideal point for an individual carries over directly into the axiomatic approach, if we assume that individual preferences satisfy the three axioms of reflexivity, completeness, and transitivity. Using R to denote the relationship "at least as good as," that is, either strict preference P or indifference I, then the axioms are

> *Reflexivity:* For every element x in the set S, $x R x$.
> *Completeness:* For every pair of elements x and y in the set S, $x \neq y$, either $x R y$, or $y R x$, or both.
> *Transitivity:* For every triple x, y, and z in S, $(x R y$ and $y R z) \rightarrow (x R z)$.

If individual preferences satisfy these three axioms, then they define an *ordering* over the set of alternatives, S. The individual is assumed to be capable of ranking all of the alternatives in S, and the ideal point is then the alternative ranked highest, that is, the alternative preferred to all others.

Given that individual preferences are assumed to define an ordering, a natural way to approach the issue of whether an equilibrium exists under majority rule is to ask whether majority rule defines an ordering, in particular, to ask whether majority rule satisfies transitivity. If it does, then an alternative that beats (or at least ties) all others must exist in any set, and this is our dominant (equilibrium) outcome.

Majority rule does define an ordering over the set of alternatives S if individual preferences, in addition to satisfying the three axioms that define an ordering, also satisfy the extremal restriction axiom.[5]

---

[5] Sen and Pattanaik (1969). Other variants on this axiom (all equally restrictive) and on the basic theorem are discussed by Sen (1966, 1970a, chs. 10, 10*).

> *Extremal restriction:* If for any ordered triple (x, y, z) there exists an individual i with preference ordering $x P_i y$ and $y P_i z$, then every individual j who prefers z to x $(z P_j x)$ must have preferences $z P_j y$ and $y P_j x$.

There are several things to observe about this axiom. First, although it does not require a spatial positioning of alternatives, it does require that individuals view alternatives in a particular way. Individuals must order issues x, y, z or z, y, x; they cannot order them y, x, z, for example.

Second, the condition does not require that all individuals have either the $x P_i y P_i z$ ordering or the $z P_j y P_j x$ ordering. The second part of the condition is only triggered if some individual prefers z to x. But no one may prefer z to x. All may either prefer x to z or be indifferent between them. If they are, then the theorem states that no cycle can occur.

Third, if one wants to think of the issues as ordered in a left-to-right way (x, y, z), then the condition resembles single-peakedness but is not equivalent to it. In particular, the condition allows for the preferences $x I_j z P_j y$ when the preferences $x P_i y P_i z$ are present. If y is the middle issue, then the preference ordering $x I_j z P_j y$ implies twin peaks at x and z. The condition does mandate, however, that the two peaks at x and z must be of equal altitude.

Although the extremal restriction avoids defining the issues in spatial terms, it is in other respects a severe constraint on the types of preference ordering people can have if majority rule is to satisfy transitivity. If a committee must decide whether a vacant lot is to be used to build a football field (x), tennis court (y), or a swimming pool (z), then some individuals may reasonably prefer football to tennis to swimming. But equally reasonably, others may prefer tennis to swimming to football. If both types of individuals are on the committee, however, the extremal restriction is violated and a voting cycle under majority rule may ensue. This theorem is proved in the next section.

5.7* Proof of extremal restriction – majority rule theorem

Theorem: *Majority rule defines an ordering over any triple (x, y, z) iff all possible sets of individual preferences satisfy extremal restriction.*

The proof follows Sen (1970a, pp. 179–81).

Sufficiency: The most interesting cases involve those in which at least one voter has preferences:

1. $x P_i y P_i z$.

In addition to voters of type 1, the extremal restriction allows there to be voters with the following four sets of preference orderings:[6]

2. $z P_j y P_j x$
3. $y P_j z I_j x$

---

[6] In fact, it allows for more than these four, but the others are eliminated once there is one voter for whom $z P x$.

4. zI_jxP_jy
5. zI_jxI_jy.

Voters of type 5 can be assumed to abstain, and shall be ignored hereafter. Now assume that the theorem does not hold; that is, assume the existence of a forward cycle

$$xRy, \ yRz, \text{ and } zRx,$$

where the unsubscripted R implies the social ordering under majority rule. Call $N(zP_ix)$ the number of individuals who prefer z to x:

$$(zRx) \rightarrow [N(zP_ix) \geq N(xP_iz)]. \tag{5.1}$$

By assumption, at least one individual has the ordering xP_iyP_iz. Thus,

$$N(xP_iz) \geq 1 \tag{5.2}$$

and from (5.1)

$$N(zP_ix) \geq 1.^7 \tag{5.3}$$

Call N_1 the number of individuals with preferences as given in (1) above, N_2 as in (2), and so on.

$$(xRy) \rightarrow (N_1 + N_4 \geq N_2 + N_3) \rightarrow [N_4 \geq (N_2 - N_1) + N_3] \tag{5.4}$$

$$(yRz) \rightarrow (N_1 + N_3 \geq N_2 + N_4) \rightarrow [N_3 \geq (N_2 - N_1) + N_4] \tag{5.5}$$

$$(zRx) \rightarrow (N_2 \geq N_1). \tag{5.6}$$

For both (5.4) and (5.5) to hold,

$$N_2 = N_1 \tag{5.7}$$

and thus

$$N_3 = N_4. \tag{5.8}$$

But then

$$(N_2 + N_3 \geq N_1 + N_4) \rightarrow (yRx) \tag{5.9}$$

$$(N_2 + N_4 \geq N_1 + N_3) \rightarrow (zRy) \tag{5.10}$$

$$(N_1 \geq N_2) \rightarrow (xRz). \tag{5.11}$$

However, (5.9) through (5.11) imply a backward cycle. Thus, if extremal restriction is satisfied, a forward cycle can exist only in the special case when a backward cycle does. A cycle ensues because society is indifferent among all three issues. The number of voters preferring x to y equals the number preferring y to x, the number preferring y to z equals the number preferring z to y, and the number preferring x to z equals the number preferring z to x.

---

[7] Conditions (5.2) and (5.3) ensure that the only preference orderings in the committee that can satisfy the extremal restriction axiom are among the five types given above.

If one assumes the theorem is violated by a backward cycle, an analogous argument demonstrates that extremal restriction also implies a forward cycle.

Necessity: We must show that violation of the extremal restriction axiom can lead to intransitive social preferences under the majority rule.

Assume one i with

$$x P_i y P_i z. \tag{5.12}$$

Extremal restriction is violated if one j has the ordering

$$z P_j x \text{ and } z P_j y \text{ and } x R_j y \tag{5.13}$$

or the ordering

$$z P_j x \text{ and } y P_j x \text{ and } y R_j z. \tag{5.14}$$

Assume (5.12) and (5.13) hold. Then under majority rule

$$x P y I z I x,$$

which violates transitivity.

Next assume (5.12) and (5.14) hold. Then under majority rule

$$x I y P z I x,$$

which is again in violation of the transitivity axiom. When the extremal condition is not satisfied, majority rule may be incapable of producing a complete ordering over all alternatives.

5.8 Restrictions on preferences, on the nature and number of issues, and on the choice of voting rule that can induce equilibria

5.8.1 *Preference homogeneity*

For the reader who is unfamiliar with the public choice literature, the results on majority rule equilibrium must seem both surprising and disconcerting. Can the most frequently employed voting rule really produce the kind of inconsistency implied by its violation of the transitivity property? Are the types of preferences needed to bring about an equilibrium under majority rule really as unlikely to arise naturally as the preceeding theorems suggest?

Unfortunately, the answers to these questions appear to be "yes." This is nicely illustrated in Kramer's (1973) generalization of the single-peakedness condition to more than one dimension. Kramer's theorem is particularly revealing to economists because he explores voter choices in the familiar environment of budget constraint lines and convex indifference curves.

In Figure 5.13, let x_1 and x_2 represent the quantities of two public goods, or two attributes of a single public good. BB is the budget constraint line for the committee. All points on or within BB are feasible alternatives. Let U_1^A and U_2^A be two indifference curves for individual A. A's preferences over the triple (x, y, z)

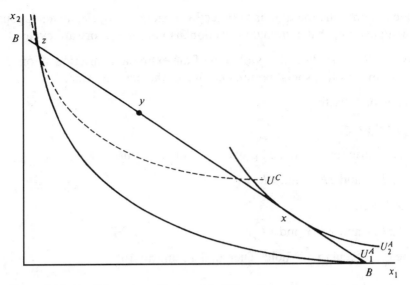

Figure 5.13. Possible cycles with normal indifference curves.

are $x P_A y P_A z$. Let C have the dotted indifference curve U^C. C's preferences over (x, y, z) are $y P_C z P_C x$. The extremal restriction defined in Section 5.6 is violated. With individuals like A and C on the committee, majority rule may produce a cycle over triples like (x, y, z) selected from the feasible set. But there is nothing unusual about A and C's indifference curves other than that they intersect. When can we be certain that we avoid all preference orderings that violate extremal restriction over the feasible set? Only when all individuals have identical indifference maps, or as Kramer (1973, p. 295) puts it, when there is "complete unanimity of individual preference orderings."[8]

And so we return to a unanimity condition. If what we seek is a voting rule to reveal individual preferences on public goods, the options would appear to be as follows. A unanimity rule might be selected that possibly requires an infinite number of redefinitions of the issue until one that benefited all citizens was reached. Although each redefinition might, in turn, be defeated until a point on the Pareto-possibility frontier had been reached, once attained, no other proposal could command a unanimous vote against it, and the process would come to a halt. The number of times an issue must be redefined before a passing majority is reached can be reduced by reducing the size of the majority required to pass an issue. Although this "speeds up" the process of obtaining the *first* passing majority, it slows down, perhaps indefinitely, the process of reaching the *last* passing majority, that is, the one that beats all others. For under a less-than-unanimity rule, some voters are made worse off. This is equivalent to a redistribution from the opponents of a measure to its proponents. As with any redistribution measure, it is generally possible to redefine an issue transferring the benefits among a few individuals and to obtain a new winning coalition. The Plott "perfect balance" condition ensures an equilibrium under majority rule by imposing

---

[8] Were we to allow pairwise comparisons among all points along BB and exclude all points within BB from consideration, then convex utility functions would imply single-peaked preferences along the one dimension BB defines, and the median voter theorem would apply. Allow points interior to BB to be chosen under majority rule, or add a third dimension to the issue set and this escape hatch is closed, however.

a form of severe symmetry assumption on the distribution of preferences that ensures that any redefinition of an issue always involves symmetric and offsetting redistributions of the benefits. The same counterbalancing of interests is contained in the median-in-all-directions condition, while extremal restriction also tends to limit the contest to those with strictly opposing interests (for example, $x P_i y P_i z$ types against $z P_j y P_j x$ types). The Kramer "identical utility functions" condition removes all conflict, and thereby eliminates all questions of redistribution.

The redistributive characteristics of less-than-unanimity rules explain the similarities between the proofs and conditions for a majority rule equilibrium, and those establishing a social welfare function (or the impossibilities thereof). Both flounder on their inability to choose among Pareto-preferred points, that is, to handle the question of redistribution (see Sen, 1970a, chs. 5 and 5*).

These theorems all establish the *possibility* of a cycle when their restrictive conditions are not met. They do not establish the inevitability of a cycle. As Kramer (1973) notes, the existence of a majority with identical preferences is sufficient to ensure a majority rule equilibrium regardless of the preferences of all other voters (see also Buchanan, 1954a). More generally, we might wish to inquire as to how often in practice a set of preferences arises that leads to a cycle.

A large number of studies have computed the probabilities of cycles using simulation techniques. When no special restrictions are placed on the types of preference orderings individuals may have, the probability of a cycle is high, and approaches one as the number of alternatives increases.[9] We have noted that a cycle cannot occur if a majority of voters have identical preferences. Thus, we might expect that as various homogeneity assumptions are made about voter preferences, the probability of a cycle decreases. And this is so. Niemi (1969) and Tullock and Campbell (1970) found that the probability of a cycle declines as the number of single-peaked preferences increases. Williamson and Sargent (1967), and Gehrlein and Fishburn (1976a) found that the probability of cycles declines with the proportion of the population having the same preferences,[10] and similarly Kuga and Nagatani (1974) have discovered that it increases with the number of pairs of voters whose interests are in conflict. These results suggest that the probability of a cycle under majority rule would be low if the collective choice process were restricted to movements from off the contract curve to points on it – that is, the kinds of decisions the unanimity rule might be able to handle – where voter interests tend to coincide.

5.8.2 *Homogeneous preferences and qualified majority rules*

The results reviewed in Section 5.8.1 indicate that the probability of cycles under the simple majority rule falls as voter preferences become more homogeneous. The probability of a cycle can also be reduced by increasing the majority required to defeat the status quo.

To see this, consider Figure 5.14a. A community must decide the quantities of two public goods, x_1 and x_2, as before. The citizens' ideal points are uniformly

---

[9] Garman and Kamien (1968), Niemi and Weisberg (1968), DeMeyer and Plott (1970), Gehrlein and Fishburn (1976b). This literature is reviewed in Niemi (1969), Riker and Ordeshook (1973, pp. 94–7), and Plott (1976).
[10] See also Abrams (1976) and Fishburn and Gehrlein (1980).

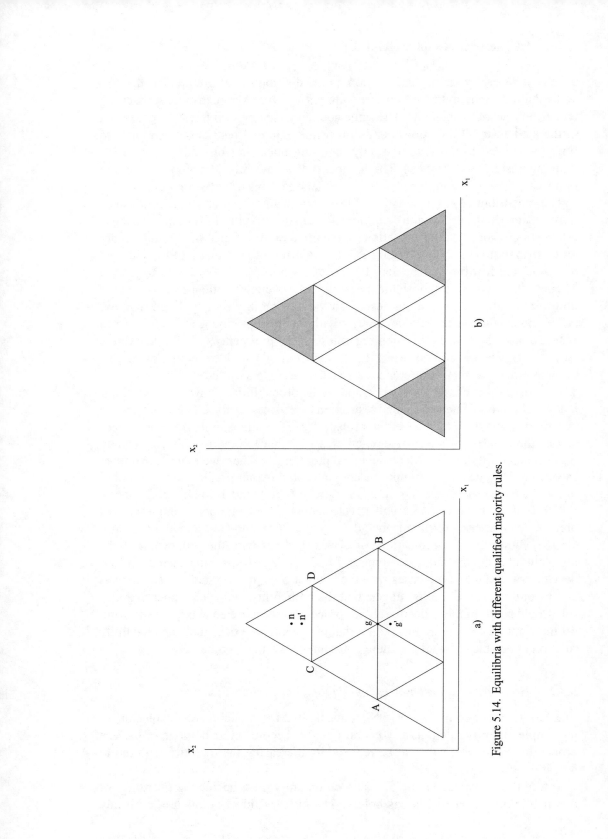

Figure 5.14. Equilibria with different qualified majority rules.

distributed over an area that forms an equilateral triangle. Each point in the triangle represents one voter's ideal point. The lines through the triangle divide it into nine smaller triangles of equal areas. No point in the large triangle satisfies Plott's perfect balance condition, and thus there is no equilibrium under the simple majority rule. For example, point g, the center of gravity of the large triangle, would lose to a point slightly below it like g'. There are five small triangles below the horizontal line $\overline{AB}$ through g, and only four above it. Thus, five ninths of the citizens prefer points below g to it, and some point like g' can win a majority against g.

On the other hand, *every* point in the large triangle is an equilibrium under the unanimity rule. The large triangle constitutes the Pareto set and once a proposal in the Pareto set has been accepted as the status quo, any attempt to move from it will be vetoed. Intuitively one expects that the set of points that are possible equilibria shrinks as the majority required to displace the status quo is reduced until it becomes the null set. And this intuition is correct. Under an 89 percent required majority, for example, point n will lose against any point slightly below it like n', since 89 percent of the ideal points lie below line $\overline{CD}$, and thus more than 89 percent of the community prefers n' to n. None of the points in the three shaded triangles in Figure 5.14b is an equilibrium under an 89 percent required majority, since for each such point another can be found within the unshaded region that can defeat it. None of the points in the six unshaded triangles can lose to any other point under an 89 percent majority rule.

The smallest majority that produces an equilibrium outcome in this situation is a five-ninths majority. There are five small triangles on one side of each line drawn through g, and four on the other. If more than five ninths of the population must vote for a proposal for it to defeat g, then the citizens with ideal points located in the four triangles can block any proposal by the other citizens to replace g with a point in the five-triangle space. Any other line drawn through g as, say, a vertical line, divides the large triangle into two areas, each containing less than five-ninths of the population. Thus no point can defeat g under a five-ninths majority rule. It is the unique stable equilibrium in this situation.

This example raises the question of whether it is possible to determine for different situations the minimum qualified majority that guarantees the existence of an equilibrium. This question was first addressed by Black (1948b). Under the assumption that all individuals have convex preferences defined over an n-dimensional issue space, Greenberg (1979) proved that m^*, the required majority to guarantee the existence of at least one equilibrium point in the issue space, must satisfy the following condition:

$$m^* \geq \frac{n}{(n+1)}. \tag{5.15}$$

With $n = 1$, $m^* = 0.5$ and (5.15) merely restates the median voter theorem. With convex preferences defined over a single-dimensional issue space, requiring one vote more than a 50 percent majority suffices to guarantee the existence of an equilibrium outcome. Equation (5.15) implies, however, that m^* continues to rise and approaches unanimity as the number of dimensions in the issues space rises.

In an important further development, Caplin and Nalebuff (1988) have shown that m^* can be significantly lowered by placing restrictions on *both* the preferences of members of the community and the distribution of their ideal points. With a two-dimensional issue space each individual's utility is as depicted in Figure 5.5, namely, she has a most preferred combination of x_1 and x_2, and her utility falls off as the chosen combination moves away from this ideal point. If utility were depicted along a third axis perpendicular to the page, it would take the shape of a cone or mountain with its peak at the ideal point A. Now imagine placing each member of the committee's utility mountain on Figure 5.5, and that the aggregation of all of these mountains is itself a mountain with a single peak somewhere within the $x_1 x_2$ quadrant. Given these assumptions about individual preferences and the distribution of their ideal points, Caplin and Nalebuff prove that m^* must satisfy the following condition:

$$m^* \geq 1 - \left(\frac{n}{n+1}\right)^n. \tag{5.16}$$

Once again when $n = 1$, $m^* = 0.5$. When $n = 2$, $m^* = 5/9$ as in the example above, and m^* continues to increase with n, reaching a maximum of less than 64 percent, since the limit of $(n/(n+1))^n$ as n approaches infinity is $1/e$, and $1/e < 0.368$. A 64 percent majority suffices to ensure the existence of at least one point in any n-dimensional issue space that cannot lose to any other point, even when n is infinitely large. Preferences of the type needed to establish (5.16) seem quite reasonable *if* voting is on quantities of public goods, and the tax formulas for financing the public goods are predetermined.[11] The assumption that the density function of the voters' ideal points be concave is much stronger, and imposes a degree of *social consensus* on the community (the community is not divided into clusters of different voters each favoring combinations of public good quantities that differ radically from one another). Assuming a generalized single-peakedness in more than one direction plus a degree of social consensus suffices to eliminate the possibility of cycles, if we are willing to abandon the simple majority rule for a 64 percent qualified majority.[12]

This result of Caplin and Nalebuff requires that we reconsider the question of the optimal majority for a voting rule discussed in Chapter 4. In Figures 4.4 and 4.5, we depicted decision-making costs rising continuously from a required majority of 0.5. Such an assumption might be reasonable, if we thought of the process as a search for new tax/quantity combinations that allow us to add one person at a time to an ever-growing coalition that favored each new proposal. If, however, we think of the community's task as that of choosing a combination of several public good quantities or attributes, a more reasonable assumption may be that each new proposal drops some members from the previous winning coalition and adds new

---

[11] Individual preferences do not have to yield circular indifference curves as in Figure 5.5; the preferences need only be single-peaked in the n-dimensional issue space. The reader is referred to Caplin and Nalebuff (1988, pp. 790–2) for a full statement of the assumptions needed for the proof.

[12] The assumption that the distribution of voter ideal points is concave is relaxed to allow for log-concavity in Caplin and Nalebuff (1991), where a *mean* voter theorem in an n-dimensional issue space is proved.

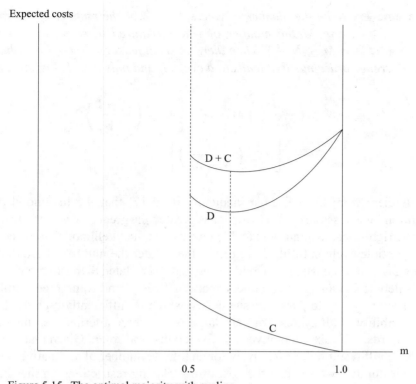

Figure 5.15. The optimal majority with cycling.

ones. We have seen how such changes in coalition composition can generate cycles. Caplin and Nalebuff's theorem suggests that in this sort of environment, decision-making costs may actually *fall* as the majority required to pass an issue rises from 0.5 until cycles are no longer possible. The D-curve would now have a U-shape, and whether it is discontinuous at an m of 0.5 would be irrelevant, as the D-curve would reach a minimum to the right of 0.5. With the bottom of the U somewhere around a majority of 0.64, the combined $C + D$ costs would then reach a minimum slightly to the right of the bottom of the U in D, and something like a two-thirds qualified majority would minimize the sum of decision-making costs and the external costs of collective decisions (see Figure 5.15).[13]

5.8.3 *The relationship between numbers of issues and alternatives and the required majority*

In a spatial world where one chooses different combinations of public goods quantities, the set of possible alternatives is infinite. One way to eliminate the possibility of cycles beyond raising the majority required to choose an alternative is to limit the number of alternatives in the issue set. This result is nicely illustrated in a theorem of James Weber (1993).

---

[13] Coggins and Perali (1998) suggest that the Venetians understood the advantage of using a 64 percent majority rule already in the thirteenth century as is revealed by their choice of rules for choosing the Doge.

Theorem: *Let N be the number of voters, $N \geq 2$, A the number of alternatives, $A \geq 2$, and M the number of voters required to select an alternative, $(N/2) < M \leq N - 1$. Then there exists at least one set of individual preference orderings that leads to a cycle, if and only if (5.17) is satisfied:*

$$\left[N \geq \left(\frac{A}{A-1} \right) M \right] \longleftrightarrow \left[M \leq \left(\frac{A-1}{A} \right) N \right]$$

$$\longleftrightarrow \left[A \geq \left(\frac{N}{N-M} \right) \right]. \tag{5.17}$$

It is clear from the left-most inequality in (5.17) that the likelihood that the condition for a possible cycle is satisfied is greater, the greater N is for a given A and M. The right-most inequality in (5.17) reveals that the likelihood that the condition for a possible cycle is fulfilled is greater, the greater the number of alternatives is holding N and M constant. The middle inequality is related to the theorem of Caplin and Nalebuff. For any given numbers of alternatives A, and committee members N, a required majority to pass an issue exists, which is sufficiently high to eliminate the possibility of all cycles. For very large N and three alternatives, this majority is two-thirds; with six alternatives it is five-sixths; and so on. Given that the Caplin and Nalebuff result holds effectively for an infinite number of alternatives and very large electorates, we see that the cost of not placing restrictions on the shapes of committee members' preferences and their distribution, as Weber's theorem does not, is to require very high majorities to eliminate cycles, even with fairly small numbers of issue alternatives.

5.9   Logrolling

When faced with a simple binary choice between X and $\sim X$ under majority rule, an individual's obvious best (dominant) strategy is to state honestly his preference for X or $\sim X$. Majority rule records only these ordinal preferences for each individual on the issue pair. The condition for the Pareto optimality of the supply of public goods requires information on the relative intensity of individual preferences; however, the marginal rates of substitution of public for private goods must sum to the ratio of their prices. Since this information is not directly gathered under majority rule, it is not particularly surprising that the outcomes under majority rule may not satisfy the Pareto-optimality condition.

The Pareto-optimal allocation of private goods also requires information on individual preference intensities, but this information is elicited by the "voting" process for private goods as individuals selfishly engage in the exchange of goods and services to maximize their own utilities. But with voting on public issues, each individual is constrained to cast but one vote for or against a given issue – unless, of course, one allows individuals to exchange votes.

The buying and selling of votes by individual citizens is outlawed in all democratic countries. That such laws exist and are occasionally violated suggests that individual

Table 5.2. *Vote trading example*

Voters	Issues	
	X	Y
A	−2	−2
B	5	−2
C	−2	5

intensities of preference regarding the value of a vote do differ. Although buying and selling votes is also prohibited in parliamentary bodies, the more informal process – "you vote for my pet issue and I'll vote for yours" – is difficult to police. Exchanges of this sort have occurred in the U.S. Congress for as long as it has been in existence. That they do exist, in spite of a certain moral stigma to their use, has two implications. Intensities of preference on issues must differ across congressmen. The assumption that congressmen's actions can be explained as the pursuit of self-interest is buttressed. The natural inclination to engage in trade, "to truck and barter," as Adam Smith called it, seems to carry over to the parliamentary behavior of elected representatives.

To understand the process, consider Table 5.2. Each column gives the utility changes to three voters from an issue's passage; defeat produces no change. If each is decided separately by majority rule, both fail. Voters B and C have much to gain from X and Y's passage, however, and can achieve this if B votes for Y in exchange for C's vote for X. Both issues now pass to B and C's mutual benefit.

The existence of beneficial trades requires a nonuniform distribution of intensities. Change the two 5s to 2s and B and C gain nothing by trading. This equal intensity condition is often invoked in arguments in favor of simple (without trading) majority rule, and are taken up in Chapter 6 when we consider the normative case for majority rule.

The trade between B and C can be said to have improved the welfare of the community of three voters if the numbers in Table 5.2 are treated as cardinal, interpersonally comparable utilities. Without trading, the majority tyrannizes over the relatively more intense minority on each issue. Through vote trading, these minorities express the intensity of their preferences, just as trading in private goods does, and improve the total welfare change of the community. With trading there is a net gain of 2 for the community.

An obvious condition for an improvement in community welfare through the changes in outcomes that vote trading brings about is that the cumulative potential utility changes for the (losing) minority members exceed the cumulative potential utility changes for the winning majority members on the issues involved. Change the 5s to 3s or the −2s of A to −4s, and the same trades emerge as before, since the pattern of trades depends only on the *relative* intensities of preferences of the voters. The sum of utilities for the community with trading is then negative, however. An exchange of votes increases the likelihood of the participants winning on their relatively more important issues. It *tends*, therefore, to increase their realized gains.

Table 5.3. *Trading possibilities*

			Utilities		
Winning pair	Losing pair	Trading voters	A	B	C
X, Y	~X, ~Y	B and C	−4	3	3
X, ~Y	X, Y	A and B	−2	5	−2
~X, ~Y	X, ~Y	A and C	0	0	0

These increases *can* increase the utility gain for the entire community. However, trading also imposes externalities (utility losses) on the nontraders who would have been better off in the absence of trading,[14] and, if these are large, they can outweigh the gains to the traders, lowering the community's net welfare. Critics of logrolling have typically envisaged situations such as these. They assume that the cumulative potential gains of the majority exceed those of the minority. Vote trading that reverses some of the outcomes of simple majority rule lowers collective welfare when this is true.

Tullock's (1959) argument that majority rule *with trading* can lead to too much government spending is of this type. Let *A*, *B*, and *C* be three farmers; and *X* be a road of use to only farmer *B*, and *Y* a road of use to only *C*. If the gross gains to a farmer from the access road are 7 and the cost is 6, which is shared equally, we have the figures of Table 5.3. With these costs and benefits, total welfare is improved by logrolling. But a bill promising a gross gain of 5 at a cost of 6, equally shared, also passes. Such a bill lowers community welfare by excessively constructing new roads, roads whose total benefits are less than their total costs. Again, the problem arises because majority rule can involve allocation and redistribution at the same time. The two bills involve both the construction of roads with gross benefits of 5 and costs of 6, and the redistribution of wealth from *A* to *B* and *C*; the latter can be sufficient to pass the bills.

An important difference separating logrolling's critics and proponents is their views as to whether voting is a positive- or negative- (at best zero-) sum game. If the latter, the game is obviously bad to begin with, and anything that improves its efficiency can only worsen the final outcome. The numerical examples that Riker and Brams (1973) present in their attack on logrolling are all examples of this type, and the examples they cite of tariff bills, tax loopholes, and pork barrel public works are all illustrations of bills for which a minority benefits, largely from the redistributive aspects of the bill, and the accumulative losses of the majority can be expected to be large.[15] The worst examples of logrolling cited in the literature are always issues of this type in which private or local public goods are added to the agenda for redistribution purposes to be financed out of public budgets at a higher level of aggregation than is appropriate (Schwartz, 1975). The best the community can hope for is the defeat of all of these issues. Riker and Brams (1973) logically recommend reforms to eliminate logrolling opportunities.

---

[14] See Taylor (1971, p. 344) and Riker and Brams (1973).
[15] See also Schattschneider (1935), McConnell (1966), and Lowi (1969).

A private good or a very local public good of course will be of great interest to a few and of little interest to the majority. The conditions necessary for logrolling are likely to be satisfied, therefore, through the incorporation of these goods into the community's agenda. But preference intensities can also vary considerably across individuals on what are truly pure public goods – for example, defense, education, and the environment. On issues such as these, vote trading can be a superior way for revealing individual preference intensities over the public goods.

One of the most positive and influential discussions of vote trading's potential was presented by Coleman (1966b). He depicted the members of the committee or legislature as entering into logrolling agreements on all public good issues. Each voter forms agreements to swap votes with other voters of the type described above. Each voter increases his ability to *control* those *events* (issues) about which he feels most intense in exchange for a loss of control over those events about which he cares little. A form of ex ante Pareto optimum is reached in which no voter feels he can increase his expected utility by agreeing to exchange another vote. This equilibrium is the optimum of Coleman's social welfare function.

Unfortunately, whatever potential a vote trading process has for revealing relative intensities of preference, and thereby improving the allocation of public goods, may go unrealized, because the trading process may not produce stable coalitions nor be free from strategic misrepresentation of preferences. When vote trades are parts of only informal agreements and take place in sequence, voters are motivated both to misstate their preferences at the time an agreement is formed and to violate the agreement after it is made. A voter who would benefit from X might pretend to oppose it and secure support for some other issues he favors in "exchange" for his positive vote for X. If successful, he wins on both X and the other issue. But the other "trader" might be bluffing, too, and the end results of trading become indeterminate (Mueller, 1967).

Even when bluffing is not a problem, cheating may be. When issues are taken up seriatim, there is an obvious and strong incentive for the second trader to renege on his part of the bargain. This incentive must be present, since the same preference orderings that produce a logrolling situation imply a potential voting cycle. Consider again the example in Table 5.3. In addition to X and Y with payoffs as in Table 5.3, we have the issues $\sim X$ and $\sim Y$ that "win" if X and Y fail. Both have payoffs for the three voters (O, O, O). Thus, four combinations of issues might result from the voting process: (X, Y), $(\sim X, Y)$, $(X, \sim Y)$, and $(\sim X, \sim Y)$. The committee must choose one of these four combinations. If we envisage voting as taking place on the issue pairs, then a cycle exists over the three pairs $(\sim X, \sim Y)$, (X, Y), $(X, \sim Y)$. In terms of the vote-trading process, the existence of this cycle implies that no stable trading agreements may be possible. We have seen that a trade between B and C to produce (X, Y) would make them both better off than the no-trade outcome $(\sim X, \sim Y)$ (see Table 5.3). But A can improve her position by offering to vote for X if B refrains from voting for Y. Thus, (X, Y) can be beaten (blocked) by $(X, \sim Y)$. But C can then offer A the option of no loss of utility if they both agree to vote sincerely and reestablish the victory of $(\sim X, \sim Y)$. From here the trading cycle can begin again. Moreover, the only condition under which a potential logrolling situation is certain not to create the potential for a cycle is when a unanimity rule is imposed (Bernholz, 1973). Allowing for individual intensity differences as in a logrolling process does not allow us to escape the cycling problem. On the contrary, the existence of the one implies the presence of the other, as we shall now demonstrate.

5.10*   Logrolling and cycling

We illustrate the theorem following Bernholz (1973) with the simple example of the previous section. The key assumption is that each voter i has a well-defined preference ordering, which satisfies the following independence condition over the relevant issues.

Independent issues: If $XP_i \sim X$, then $(XY)P_i(\sim XY)$.
All voters vote sincerely at each juncture.

Definition: *A logrolling situation exists if*

$$\sim XRX \tag{5.18}$$

$$\sim YRY \tag{5.19}$$

$$XYP \sim X \sim Y, \tag{5.20}$$

where R and P are the social preference orderings defined by whatever voting rule is being used. In a pairwise vote, $\sim X$ defeats X and $\sim Y$ defeats Y. But the pair XY can defeat $\sim X \sim Y$.

Theorem: *The existence of a logrolling situation implies intransitive social preferences. The existence of a transitive social preference ordering implies the absence of a logrolling situation.*

Proof of First Proposition: Assume a logrolling situation exists [i.e., (5.18), (5.19), and (5.20) hold]. Then winning coalitions h must exist (i.e., majority coalitions under majority rule) for which

$$\sim XR_h X \tag{5.21}$$

$$\sim YR_h Y \tag{5.22}$$

$$XYP_h \sim X \sim Y. \tag{5.23}$$

From (5.21) and (5.22) and the independent issues assumption,

$$\sim X \sim YR_h X \sim Y \tag{5.24}$$

$$X \sim YR_h XY. \tag{5.25}$$

Since each respective h is a winning coalition,

$$\sim X \sim YRX \sim Y \tag{5.26}$$

$$X \sim YRXY. \tag{5.27}$$

Combining (5.20), (5.26), and (5.27), we have

$$\sim X \sim Y R X \sim Y R X Y P \sim X \sim Y. \tag{5.28}$$

The existence of a logrolling situation implies intransitive social preferences.   □

Proof of Second Proposition: We assume the first part of a logrolling situation exists and demonstrate that transitive social preferences imply the absence of the second part (5.20); that is, assume

$$\sim X R X \tag{5.18}$$

$$\sim Y R Y. \tag{5.19}$$

This implies

$$\sim X R_h X \tag{5.29}$$

$$\sim Y R_h Y. \tag{5.30}$$

By the independent issue assumption,

$$\sim X Y R_h X Y \tag{5.31}$$

$$\sim X \sim Y R_h \sim X Y. \tag{5.32}$$

Since each h is a winning coalition,

$$\sim X Y R X Y \tag{5.33}$$

$$\sim X \sim Y R \sim X Y. \tag{5.34}$$

But then

$$\sim X \sim Y R \sim X Y R X Y. \tag{5.35}$$

If the social preferences are transititve, then $\sim X \sim Y R X Y$, and the last part of the definition of a logrolling situation is not satisfied. The existence of transitive social preferences implies the absence of a logrolling situation.   □

5.11   Testing for logrolling

Claims of "horse trading" to create majority coalitions and select cabinets in Europe, and to pass legislation in the United States are as old as democracy in these countries.[16] But because vote trading takes place in "smoke filled rooms" out of the public's eye, it is often difficult to verify that it has in fact taken place and to identify the traders. Does vote trading occur on all legislation in the U.S. Congress, some, or none? If it occurs only some of the time can we identify the issues upon

---

[16] For examples and discussion, see Mayhew (1966) and Ferejohn (1974).

which it takes place? By providing a rigorous definition of logrolling, public choice allows us to answer these questions.

If issues d and s are involved in a logroll, then we know from logrolling's definition that both must pass with the traded votes and fail without them. A supporter of s who trades her vote on d for votes on s votes against her own and/or her constituents' preferences on d. This vote costs her something and she will trade it only if she gets something more valuable in return – enough votes to secure s's victory. It follows that she would not trade her vote on d if s loses even with the trade, and thus we should observe no trading on losing issues. Furthermore, she should not trade her vote on d if s can win without the trade, and thus we should observe no trading on issues that win by substantial margins. The votes on issues involved in logrolling should be close and successful, and the margin of success should be provided by the traded votes.

Stratmann (1992b) has tested these implications of logrolling with data on various votes on the 1985 Farm Bill in the U.S. House of Representatives. It is common practice to explain how a congressman votes by sets of variables that measure the characteristics of the *district* from which he comes, x_D, and characteristics of the *candidate* (for example, ideology), x_C. Thus, in trying to explain voting on three farm bill amendments that would affect peanut farmers (p), dairy farmers (d), and sugar farmers (s) without taking into account the effects of logrolling, one might estimate the following system of equations:

$$p = a_p + b_p x_D + c_p x_C + u_p$$
$$d = a_d + b_d x_D + c_d x_C + u_d \qquad (5.36)$$
$$s = a_s + b_s x_D + c_s x_C + u_s.$$

If logrolling occurred on these three amendments, however, then the probability that someone who supports farm interests on sugar voting for farm interests on dairies should be higher than that predicted simply by his personal and his district's characteristics. This implication of logrolling can be tested by adding the predicted votes on the other two bills to each equation in (5.36) to obtain (5.37).

$$p = a_p + \beta_p \hat{d} + \gamma_p \hat{s} + b_p x_D + c_p x_C + u_p$$
$$d = a_p + \alpha_d \hat{p} + \gamma_d \hat{s} + b_d x_D + c_d x_C + u_d \qquad (5.37)$$
$$s = a_s + \alpha_s \hat{p} + \beta_s \hat{d} + b_s x_D + c_s x_C + u_s$$

where $\hat{p}$, $\hat{d}$, and $\hat{s}$ are the predicted votes on each amendment from (5.36).[17] Table 5.4 presents some of Stratmann's results.

As measures of district and congressman's characteristics Stratmann used the amount of campaign contributions each candidate received from the respective farm group's political action committee (PAC), the fraction of the district's population that is engaged in peanut (respectively, dairy and sugar) farming (Farmer), and the

---

[17] Kau and Rubin (1979) suggest adding the actual votes on the other issues, but this approach gives biased estimates of the coefficients on the logrolling variables.

Table 5.4. *Econometric evidence of the presence of logrolling*

Dependent variable	$\hat{p}$	$\hat{d}$	$\hat{s}$	Const	PAC	Farmer	Party
				\multicolumn{4}{c}{Explanatory variables}
p		.36*	.53*	−.15	−1.04	71*	−.84*
d	.01		.21*	.14	.18*	.67*	−.72*
s	.45*	.30*		−.33*	1.37*	6.6	.23

Source: Stratmann (1992b, Table 1).

party affiliation of the representative (Republican = 1, Democrat = 0).[18] *Const* is the constant or intercept. An asterisk indicates that the coefficient was significant at the 5 percent level or better. The dependent variable was a one if the representative voted with the farm interests, a zero if he voted against them.

Focusing first on the significant exogenous variables, we see that the probability that a congressman voted in favor of a farm group's interests rises with the amount of contributions that he receives from its PAC (dairies and sugar), and the fraction of his district engaged in this sort of farming (peanuts and dairies). Republicans voted against farmer interests on the peanuts and dairy amendments with a high probability.

Turning to the key logrolling-hypothesis variables, we see that five of the six predicted votes on the other two farm amendments are significant in the three equations. Also, the coefficients are quite large. The probability that someone who was predicted to vote for the sugar amendment also voted for the peanut amendment was 0.53 over and above that predicted on the basis of the candidate and district characteristics included in the model. As one might expect, the congressmen who are predicted to have switched their votes as a result of the trades had estimated probabilities of voting for the respective amendments that fell in the 0.3 to 0.5 range without the trades. These congressmen would, presumably, have to be offered less to switch their vote than would congressmen who were predicted to have only a 0.0 to 0.3 probability of voting for the respective amendments without the trades (Stratmann, 1992b, p. 1171).

Stratmann did not report the $\hat{p}$, $\hat{d}$, and $\hat{s}$ values, but the coefficients in Table 5.4 and the *actual* votes in the three bills can be used to obtain estimates of these variables: $\hat{p} = 61$, $\hat{d} = 207$, and $\hat{s} = 176$. Based only on the votes generated by the district and congressmen's characteristics, farm interests would have lost on both the peanut and sugar amendments, and would have squeaked through on the dairy amendment by a 207 to 205 margin. It is interesting that the only insignificant codetermined variable in the three equations was for $\hat{p}$ in the dairy equation. Votes from supporters of peanut farmers' interests were not needed by the dairy interests, and they do not appear to have demanded them. Votes from the sugar interests converted a narrow 207 to 205 victory into a 245 to 167 victory by our rough calculations, and logrolling spelled the difference between victory and defeat on the other two amendments.

---

[18] A congressman's ACLU rating was also included to measure his ideology, but it was insignificant in the equations reported here and is ignored.

Stratmann also tests for the presence of logrolling on a dairy amendment that the dairy interests won by a 351 to 36 margin, and on a wheat amendment, on which the farm interests suffered a 251 to 174 defeat. As the theory predicts, no evidence of vote trading is found on these two issues.

"Logrolling" is a distinctly American expression and, as we have just seen, does appear to take place in the U.S. Congress. It does not appear to be unique to that legislative body, however. Elvik (1995), for example, claims that it can explain the distribution of highway expenditures across Norway, a distribution that benefit-cost ratios and the like fail to account for.[19]

5.12   Agenda manipulation

5.12.1   *Agenda control in a spatial environment*

Surely by now the patient reader has grown weary of cycling theorems. Yet we have but scratched the surface of a vast literature establishing cycling and instability results of one form or another. That majority rule leads to cycles has been a (some would say *the*) major theme of the public choice literature. Yet is the problem that serious? Do committees really spin their wheels endlessly as the cycling results seem to suggest? Probably not, and we shall consider several reasons why committees avoid endless cycles in the next section. But before we do let us examine some results that illustrate the potential significance of the cycling phenomenon.

In an important paper, McKelvey (1976) first established that when individual preferences are such as to produce the potential for a cycle with sincere voting under majority rule, then an individual who can control the agenda of pairwise votes can lead the committee to any outcome in the issue space he chooses. The theorem is developed in two parts. First, it is established that with a voting cycle it is possible to move the committee from any starting point S an arbitrarily large distance d from S. In Figure 5.16, let A, B, and C be the ideal points for three voters and S the starting point. If each individual votes sincerely on each issue pair, the committee can be led from S to Z to Z' to Z'' in just three steps. The farther one moves away from S, the larger the voter indifference circles and the larger the steps will become. The process can continue until one is any d one chooses from S.

Now let r be the radius of a circle around S such that (1) the target point of the agenda setter is within the circle (say, ideal point A) and (2) at least $n/2$ ideal points for the committee (in this case two) are within the circle of radius r. Now choose d such that $d > 3r$ and one is certain that a majority of the committee favors A over the last Z^n obtained in the cycle, the $Z^n d$ distance from S. The last pairwise choice offered the committee is then Z^n versus A, and A wins. The agenda setter then either calls a halt to the voting or picks new proposals that will lose to A. Thus, a member of a committee with the power to set the agenda can bring about the victory of his most preferred outcome.

McKelvey's theorem has two important implications. First, and most obviously, the power of the agenda setter may be substantial. If this power is vested in a given

---

[19] See also Fridstøm and Elvik (1997).

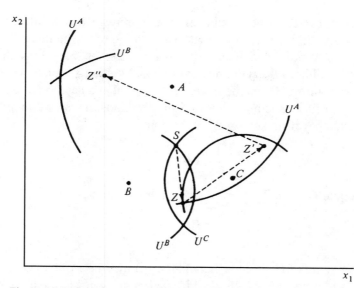

Figure 5.16. Agenda manipulation possibilities.

individual or subcommittee, then one must take precautions lest those with agenda-setting power secure a disproportionate share of the gains from collective action. Second, the existence of a voting cycle introduces a degree of unpredictability to the voting outcomes that may provide an incentive for some to manipulate the process to their advantage. The fact that a committee has reached a decision may in itself not have much normative significance until one learns by what route it got there.

5.12.2 *Agenda control in a divide-the-cake game*

Harrington (1990) has demonstrated the potential power of an agenda setter under quite different conditions than those assumed in Section 5.12.1. Imagine that a committee is offered a gift of G dollars to be divided among its n members. The procedure for selecting a division of G is as follows: one member is selected at random to propose a division of G. If m or more members of the committee, $1 \leq m \leq n$, vote for this proposal it is implemented and the game is over. If the proposal fails to receive at least m votes, another committee member is chosen at random to make a new proposal, and the process continues until some proposal secures the required m votes. To simplify the discussion, let us assume that all members have identical preferences.

Consider first the strategy of a person selected to propose a division of G. She can expect that each member of the committee has some reservation price, that is, some minimum amount x, that he will vote for rather than wait for the outcome of another round. Because all members have identical preferences, whatever one person accepts, all accept. Thus, the proposer maximizes her payoff as the agenda setter by proposing x for $m - 1$ members, $G - (m - 1)x$ for herself, and nothing for the remaining $n - m$ committee members, assuming that her share of G is greater than the common reservation price x.

Now consider the calculus of a member of the committee when deciding what his reservation price should be. He knows that in any round of the game he has a $1/n$ chance of being the proposer and obtaining $G - (m - 1)x$, an $(m - 1)/n$ chance of being any other member of the winning coalition and getting x, and an $(n - m)/n$ chance of getting nothing. If a member were risk neutral and had no preference for present income over future income, he would simply choose a reservation price that equals his expected payoff in any round of the game,

$$x = \frac{1}{n}[G - (m - 1)x] + \frac{m - 1}{n}x + \frac{m - n}{n} \cdot 0. \tag{5.38}$$

Then x would equal G/n, and the proposer's payoff would be

$$\left(\frac{n - m + 1}{n}\right) G. \tag{5.39}$$

The proposer's share of G exceeds that of all other members of the committee so long as $m < n$, and grows as m falls until it reaches one-*half* of the amount to be distributed under the simple majority rule.

If members of the committee are risk averse or have positive time preferences, they will accept some positive x less than G/n in any round rather than run the risk and incur the delay of waiting for another round of the procedure. Thus, the expression in (5.39) constitutes a *lower bound* for the proposer's payoff. The more risk averse and impatient the committee members are, the greater the advantage of the agenda setter.

Harrington is also able to demonstrate the same sort of advantage for an agenda setter under alternative assumptions about how the division game is played. These results are important in that they do not depend on the agenda setter's having an entrenched position due to seniority or the like. Even a randomly selected agenda setter can have a significant advantage over the other committee members. The results do depend crucially on the use of a qualified majority rule that falls short of requiring full unanimity, and thus again illustrate the potential of the unanimity rule to protect the interests of all members of a committee, this time against a selfish agenda setter.[20]

5.13   Why so much stability?

If cycling problems are as pervasive as the public choice literature implies, then why do committee outcomes in Congress and in state legislatures seem to be so stable, both in the sense that the committees do reach decisions and that these outcomes do not gyrate from one meeting of the committee to the next, and from one session of the legislature to the next? This challenging question was put forward by Tullock (1981) and we shall take it up on more than one occasion in this book.

---

[20] Additional constraints could be imposed, of course. Buchanan and Congleton's (1998) generality principle would require equal treatment of all members, and thus an equal division. Even adding the requirement that a proposal be seconded reduces the agenda setter's power somewhat. See also Baron and Ferejohn (1987).

In Section 5.12 we already encountered one answer to this question, and not a comforting one. An agenda setter may lead the committee to an outcome particularly pleasing to the agenda setter, and keep it there. This solution to the cycling problem is one of several possible answers to Tullock's question that rely on a particular institution like the agenda setter to structure the voting sequence so as to avoid cycles. Robert's Rules of Order and other similar committee procedures are probably the most familiar examples of institutional constraints on a committee that by restricting the possibility of defeated proposals reappearing on the agenda, limit the scope for cycles. We discuss two additional examples of structure-induced equilibria later in this section. But we first consider the simplest of all explanations for the absence of cycles – the nature of the issues themselves precludes them.

5.13.1 *Issues are indeed of one dimension*

As one contemplates the sorts of issues that typically come up in a legislative assembly, the number of potential dimensions of the issue space seems almost unbounded. Defense appropriations involve considerations of national security; a tax on carbon dioxide emissions involves trade-offs between economic growth and environmental protection; a ban on smoking in public places involves considerations of national health and individual liberties. Despite the seemingly boundless range of concerns these sorts of issues raise, an individual's views on these issues often seem to be highly correlated. Once one knows that a representative has voted for a substantial increase in defense spending and against the tax on carbon dioxide emissions, one can predict that this representative will vote against the smoking ban. To the extent this is true, this suggests that the number of dimensions of the "issue" space is much smaller than it first appears. There are but a few underlying "ideological" dimensions, like the familiar liberal–conservative dichotomy, that will allow us to explain and predict how congressmen vote.

Poole and Rosenthal (1985, 1991) have developed a procedure that they call NOMINATE, that allows them to apply factor analysis techniques to data on congressional voting to uncover the underlying "ideological" dimensions of the issue space. They succeeded in correctly classifying some 81 percent of the votes in the U.S. Senate and 83 percent of the votes in the House between 1789 and 1985 with a single dimension.[21]

Poole and Smith (1994) use NOMINATE to identify the most salient dimension of the issue space, and then present evidence that supports both the median voter theorem and the usefulness of concentrating upon a single dimension of the issue space. Their results can be illustrated with the help of Figure 5.17. Suppose a representative's ideal point on a given issue has been identified as lying at point R, where M has been identified as the median position in this dimension and S is the status quo. Then this representative knows that if she proposes her ideal point, it will lose to the status quo. A representative who seeks to make a winning proposal will thus propose a *compromise* like C that is not at her ideal point, and is closer to

---

[21] See also Hinich and Pollard (1981), Poole and Romer (1985), Laver and Schofield (1990), Enelow and Hinich (1994), and Hinich and Munger (1994).

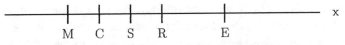

Figure 5.17. Issue proposals along a single-dimensional issue space.

M than S is. In contrast, a representative who seeks merely to make an "ideological statement" of her principles proposes her ideal point R and suffers defeat. Poole and Smith report evidence consistent with these predictions. Eighty-one percent winning proposals in the Senate were closer to the median position on the issue up for a vote than was the status quo; 62 percent of the losing proposals were farther away. Sponsors who "wanted to win" offered compromises that were closer to the median than their ideal points. Poole and Smith's ability to collapse the diverse issues that come up in the Senate using NOMINATE into a single dimension and accurately predict how senators will vote using this single-dimensional issue space demonstrates the saliency of this one dimension. The fact that senators make proposals and vote in this single-dimensional issue space as the median voter theorem predicts suggests that its equilibrium prediction may hold in the Congress.

Ladha (1994) also employs NOMINATE to identify representative positions, and confirms the predictions of the single-dimensional, medial-voter model. Ladha finds that a series of amendments to a proposal that moves it from E to R to C results in a narrowing of opposition to the amendments with voters on the far right and left not changing their votes, while those toward the center do switch as the amended proposals pass over their identified ideal points.

These results help to establish the predictive content of the median-voter model, and our trust in the usefulness of assuming that the relevant issue space is single-dimensional. Nevertheless, virtually all studies that have tested for the presence of more than one underlying dimension to the issue space have found more than one.[22] The potential for cycles cannot be dismissed completely on the grounds that all issues involve essentially a division along a single, left–right ideological line.

5.13.2 *Voting one dimension at a time*

The median voter theorem requires both a single-dimensional issue space and single-peaked preferences. If the issue space were known to be, or constrained to be, of one dimension – expenditures on space exploration – the single-peaked preferences assumption would not seem to be a major concern. What is implausible is the assumption that the issue space is one-dimensional.

Suppose, therefore, that we have a two-dimensional issue space, but that we limit voting to but one dimension at a time. Consider Figure 5.18, where x_1 and x_2 are two public goods vectors. Tax rates to finance the public goods are assumed given, so that A, B, and C are again the ideal points of our three voters. With each voter free to propose any point in the positive orthant, a cycle can ensue. But let the committee

---

[22] See, again, Poole and Rosenthal (1985, 1991), Poole and Romer (1985), Laver and Schofield (1990), and Hinich and Munger (1994); and for a direct critique of the NOMINATE procedure regarding its implied underlying dimensionality, Koford (1989, 1990).

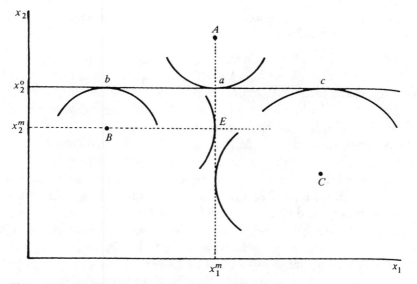

Figure 5.18. Equilibrium outcomes with sequential votes.

rule be that voting must take place one dimension at a time. Take x_2° as initially given and have the committee vote on the level of x_1, given x_2°. With circular (or ellipsoid) indifference contours, each voter has single-peaked preferences along the horizontal line x_2°. B favors point b, A favors a, and C favors c. A is the median voter in the x_1 dimension and x_1^m is the quantity of x_1 chosen under majority rule. Now fix x_1 at x_1^m and allow the committee to decide the quantity of x_2. B is now the median voter and x_2^m is the quantity of x_2 chosen. Point E is an equilibrium under majority rule given the constraints that x_1 and x_2 must be voted upon one dimension at a time.[23]

With tax shares fixed, the Pareto set is the triangle with apexes at A, B, and C. E falls inside this triangle and is Pareto optimal under the constraint that tax shares are fixed. But taxes are one of the important variables a committee must decide. If the choice of tax rate can be formulated as a one-dimensional issue – say, the degree of progressivity of an income tax – then tax progressivity can be voted on as a separate issue, holding x_1 and x_2 constant, and an equilibrium outcome chosen in these three dimensions. But this equilibrium outcome need not be Pareto optimal (Slutsky, 1977b). To find the Pareto-optimal quantities of x_1 and x_2, one chooses x_1, x_2 and the individual tax shares so as to maximize the sum of the utilities of the committee. The resulting solution must satisfy the Samuelsonian condition for the Pareto-optimal allocation of a public good. Choosing quantities of each public good and tax rates one dimension at a time in effect adds further constraints to the maximization problem. There is no reason to suspect that this constrained committee choice will coincide with what the unconstrained solution would be, and in general it will not. The price of an equilibrium under majority rule can be high.

[23] E is a median in two directions. To be an unconstrained equilibrium, it must be a median in all directions, which it is not. Allow the committee to vote on combinations of x_1 and x_2 along a ray through E running in a northeast direction, and E will not be the chosen point.

5.13.3 *Logrolling equilibria*

The theorems that logrolling situations imply voting cycles and that agenda setters can achieve their ideal points in cyclic situations assume that every voter at each step of a voting sequence votes sincerely. Voters, like the children of Hamlin, follow the agenda setter blindly wherever he goes. These theorems assume a seemingly unrealistic degree of myopia on the part of voters.

Consider again the trading cycle illustrated with the help of Tables 5.2 and 5.3. B first agrees to trade votes with C, then deserts her for A, who in turn jilts B for C. For a true cycle to enfold, B and C, not having learned their lessons, must again agree to swap votes and we repeat the cycle. But surely rational individuals should not allow themselves to be dragged through too many revolutions of this cycle before they begin to foresee the short-run nature of each trade. Once each trader realizes that an apparently advantageous trade is likely to be overturned, he might try to stick to a *relatively* advantageous pair of trades once made, or never allow himself to be talked into a trade to begin with. Note, in this regard, the inherent instability of the outcome pairs $(X, \sim Y)$ and $(\sim X, Y)$. Under each of these two outcomes one individual (B or C) gets her maximum potential gain. Thus, were the coalition $A-B$ to form to produce $(X, \sim Y)$ as the outcome pair, A can threaten to leave B, since both A and C are better off when they form a coalition than when A stays with B. But B's only alternative to A is a coalition with C, which makes B worse off. Thus, B prefers preserving the $A-B$ coalition, but if A is rational, B will be incapable of doing so. Now consider the $B-C$ coalition to produce (X, Y). Either B or C could become better off by joining A to produce $(X, \sim Y)$ or $(\sim X, Y)$, respectively. Both have the identical threats to make against the $B-C$ coalition. Thus, if one individual begins to waver in her support for the $B-C$ coalition, the other can issue the counterthreat to bolt and joint with A. Since both are confronted by the same threats and counterthreats, each may decide that it is better to remain in the $B-C$ coalition.

Considerations such as these lead one to predict a coalition between B and C with outcomes (X, Y), even though no core exists. This outcome is contained in the main solution concepts, which have been proposed to solve simple bargaining games (e.g., the von Neumann-Morgenstern solution, the bargaining set, the kernel, and the competitive solution). If vote trading in parliamentary committees resembles the kinds of bargaining deliberations that underlie these different solution concepts, then stable, predictable outcomes from a logrolling process can be expected even though no core exists and myopic trading would produce a cycle. Oppenheimer (1979) has argued in favor of the bargaining set as predictor of outcomes from logrolling, whereas McKelvey and Ordeshook (1980) have found that outcomes from vote-trading experiments conform to the competitive solution.

In the game depicted in Tables 5.2 and 5.3, either voter B or C could ensure the outcome $(\sim X, \sim Y)$ that arises when each voter sincerely states her true preferences by voting against both issues. If B, say, votes against X and Y, A can achieve her most preferred outcome $(\sim X, \sim Y)$ by voting sincerely. C can make her no better

Matrix 5.1. *Logrolling options*

		Voter C	
		Vote for X and Y	Vote for Y and against X
Voter B	Vote for X and Y	1 (+3, +3)	2 (−2, +5)
	Vote for X and against Y	3 (+5, −2)	4 (0, 0)

proposal and $(\sim X, \sim Y)$ will be the committee choice. Thus, if B or C were fearful that trading would produce an outcome that left them worse off than the sincere voting outcome $(\sim X, \sim Y)$, they could make sure that this outcome comes about by following the *sophisticated* strategy of voting against both issues.[24] Enelow and Koehler (1979) show that the majority, which produces the sincere voting outcome, always can preserve this outcome by the appropriate sophisticated voting strategy, even when logrolling with sincere voting would overturn it.

Thus, there is reason to suspect that either (X, Y) or $(\sim X, \sim Y)$ would emerge as the committee outcome in the example from Tables 5.2 and 5.3. Although either B or C can preserve $(\sim X, \sim Y)$ by sophisticated voting, the temptation to join with one another to produce (X, Y) must be strong. What might prevent them from ever doing so is the fear that once the $B−C$ coalition has formed, the other trading partner will fail to deliver on her part of the trade (or join with A). This danger is particularly likely when issues X and Y are decided sequentially. We have here another example of a prisoners' dilemma (Bernholz, 1977). Matrix 5.1 depicts the strategic options for voters B and C when issues X and Y must be decided as before. Both voters are better off with the trade (square 1) than without it (square 4), but the incentive to cheat is present. If issue X is decided before issue Y and voter C lives up to her part of the bargain by voting for X, the outcomes in column 2 become infeasible. Voter B must choose between squares 1 and 3, and her choice is obvious if there is no possibility for voter C to retaliate.

As we have seen in Chapter 2, the cooperative solution to the prisoners' dilemma emerges only if each player thinks that her choice of the cooperative strategy is likely to induce the corresponding strategy choice of the other player. If the strategy options are played in sequence and the game is played but once, the first player has no means by which to influence the second player's decision at the time the latter is made. Thus, one would not expect vote trading to take place over issues decided sequentially among coalitions that form but a single time. A stable, cooperative

---

[24] The distinction between sincere and sophisticated voting was introduced by Farquharson (1969). In a sequence of pairwise votes, an individual votes *sincerely* if at each step in the sequence she votes for the element of the issue pair that she prefers. An individual votes *sophisticatedly* at each step if she determines the optimal strategy by considering all future steps in the sequence and the future behavior of the other players. Sophisticated voting requires the individual to engage in backward induction and to eliminate all weakly dominated strategies from consideration.

vote-trading game can be expected only when the issues on which votes are traded are all decided simultaneously, say, as part of an omnibus highway bill; or when the same constellations of issues come up time and time again, and a prisoners' dilemma supergame emerges. Bernholz (1978) has discussed the latter possibility. Under the assumptions that the same types of issues do arise again and again, he shows that the likelihood of a stable prisoners' dilemma supergame emerging is positively related to both the net potential gains from cooperation and the probability that the same players reappear in each successive game. As Bernholz notes, the depiction of logrolling situations as single plays of a prisoners' dilemma supergame is plausible for a legislative assembly, whose members continually represent the same interest and have reasonably long tenure.

In Section 5.11 we discussed evidence indicating that vote trading had in fact taken place across three amendments to a farm bill despite our proof in Section 5.10 that the existence of these very trades demonstrates the presence of an underlying set of preferences that would produce a cycle under the majority rule. What or who prevented the cycle from destroying the set of trades that transpired? The "what" might be the procedures through which bills are brought to a floor vote. The "who" is almost certainly the two parties' leadership. Arranging vote trades and ensuring that bargains are kept is the job of party leaders and their whips. These "agenda setters" are elected to their posts by their fellow party members presumably in part on the basis of how capable they are at avoiding cycles and satisfying the goals of all party members, not just the leaders. Both Haefele (1971) and Koford (1982) see party leadership as effectively guiding the legislature to outcomes that maximize the welfare of the party membership. Their rather optimistic description of how the legislative process functions stands in sharp contrast to most of the logrolling-majority rule-cycling literature.[25]

5.13.4 *Empirical evidence of cycling*

We have reviewed theorems that imply that cycling is almost inevitable, and arguments why it might not occur at all. Which are correct? Is cycling truly rare, as Tullock's rhetorical question (why so much stability?) assumes, or can it in fact be observed? We close this chapter by examining two sets of evidence pertaining to the presence of cycles. In this subsection we look at some evidence from the U.S. Congress; in the next we look at evidence from the experimental laboratory.

A cycle exists when y defeats x, z defeats y, and x in turn defeats z. Few committees are likely to be so dense as to propose precisely the same x that was defeated in an earlier vote against y. Cycling is more likely to manifest itself by a proposal that comes close to x defeating z, which then loses to a proposal that resembles y. Detecting cycles by examining the content of individual proposals is likely to be a long and tedious task.

---

[25] The same can be said of the model of vote trading recently developed by Philipson and Snyder (1996), who assume the existence of an auctioneer/party leader who arranges trades between high- and low-intensity voters on a single-dimensional issue to achieve an equilibrium at which the summed utilities of the voters are maximized. Mueller, Philpotts, and Vanek (1972) established a similar result by simulating Walrasian vote markets.

Table 5.5. *Predicted payoffs and variances of payoffs with and without cycling*

| | *A. With Cycling* | | | |
Issues	Voter 1	Voter 2	Voter 3	Variance
1	0.75	0.25	0	0.097
2	0	0.75	0.25	0.097
3	0.25	0	0.75	0.097
Sum	1	1	1	0

Sum of individual variances $(3 \times (0.097)) = 0.292$

	B. With Stable Coalition			
1	0.5	0.5	0	0.055
2	0.5	0.5	0	0.055
3	0.5	0.5	0	0.055
Sum	1.5	1.5	0	0.5

Sum of individual variances $(3 \times (0.055)) = 0.167$

A cycle can leave evidence of itself of another form, however. The identities of members of the winning coalition should change over time, as well as the distribution of the payoffs to the committee. Consider again the simple three-person-divide-the-dollar game discussed earlier. Part A of Table 5.5 presents payoffs that we might expect to see in the presence of a majority rule cycle. Players 1 and 3 form a winning coalition on the first issue, 1 and 2 on the second, and so on. The outcome of a vote on any single issue involves a quite asymmetric distribution of the dollar, with one player receiving at least one-half and another nothing. Thus, the variance in the payoffs from the vote on any issue could be large and the sum of the variances should grow over time. When a cycle is present, however, a player who loses in one round of voting should win in a subsequent round, and thus the aggregate payoffs in the presence of a cycle should be much more evenly divided than the payoffs in any round, and the variance of the sum of payoffs should be much less than the sum of the variances from the individual rounds.

Part B of Table 5.5 presents the pattern of payoffs one might expect in the absence of a cycle, when a stable coalition exists. We again expect an uneven distribution of the dollar in any single round, and thus a positive variance in the payoffs in this round, but now we expect the same distribution of payoffs to persist over time. The variance of the sum of the payoffs will, therefore, not be less than the sum of the variances from the individual rounds as predicted when a cycle exists, but much greater.

Stratmann (1996a) has used these implications of cycling to test for its presence in the pattern of federal grants to congressional districts in the United States between 1985 and 1990. These federal programs contain the major categories of pork-barrel legislation, and thus can be regarded as largely redistributive in nature, and thus likely to exhibit cycling if it exists in the Congress. Table 5.6 presents some of his findings. The first thing to note is that the payoffs to congressional districts are quite unevenly distributed. In every year a *minority* of districts benefits from a given grant

Table 5.6. *Characteristics of federal grants to congressional districts, 1985–90*

Year 1	Number of programs 2	Programs benefiting a minority of districts 3	Benefiting programs benefiting a minority of districts (%) 4	Variance of sums 5	Sum of variances 6
1985	592	543	91.7	5.6 E16	7.1 E15
1986	624	571	91.5	2.7 E16	5.5 E15
1987	637	575	90.3	2.2 E16	5.6 E15
1988	679	616	90.7	2.4 E16	6.4 E15
1989	706	646	91.5	2.7 E16	6.6 E15
1990	791	724	91.5	4.1 E16	7.2 E15

Source: Stratmann (1996a, Tables 5 and 6).

program for more than 90 percent of the programs. In 1989 the mean federal grant to the ten districts that benefited the most from these programs was $968 million – *over 75 times more than* the 10 districts benefiting least from the program averaged. Columns 5 and 6 in Table 5.6 reveal that the variance of the sums of the payoffs in any year are from four to nine times the sum of the variances in that year, contradicting a prediction that cycling occurred across these grant programs in any given year. The correlations across payoffs over time are 0.9 or better, suggesting that cycling did not occur over time (Stratmann, 1996a, p. 25).[26] Stratmann's findings strongly imply that a stable coalition existed in the U.S. Congress between 1985 and 1990 when it came to the disbursement of federal grants.

Although these results suggest a "tyranny of the majority" in the U.S. Congress, they still present some puzzles. Why, for example, would a district whose representative was left out of the winning coalition receive any grants at all? Why are so many of the votes on these pork-barrel programs so lopsided?[27] Several authors have answered these questions by arguing that a norm of *universalism* exists in the Congress.[28] Rather than encourage cycles and run the risks of losing out by forming majority coalitions that pass redistributive legislation by narrow majorities, a coalition of the whole forms and everyone is allowed a share of the funds that flow from Washington.

Although "universalism" is an appealing way out of the paradox of near-unanimous support for redistributive programs, it too is not without its problems. One does not usually expect universal norms to dictate that one person's share *ought* to be 75 times greater than that of the next person. Indeed, when one factors in the taxes each district pays to finance these programs, many districts – quite possibly a majority – are *net losers*. Why are congressional norms both universal and so unegalitarian?

---

[26] Van Deemen and Vergunst (1998) also fail to find evidence of cyclic preferences in the data on Dutch national elections for the years 1982, 1986, 1989, and 1994. Kurrild-Klitgaard (2001) did detect the potential for a cycle *if* Danish voters had been allowed to choose their prime minister directly in the 1994 election.

[27] See Ferejohn (1974) and Mayhew (1974, pp. 88–113).

[28] See Weingast (1979); Weingast, Shepsle, and Johnsen (1981); Shepsle and Weingast (1981); and Niou and Ordeshook (1985). This explanation was also part of Tullock's (1981) answer to the stability question.

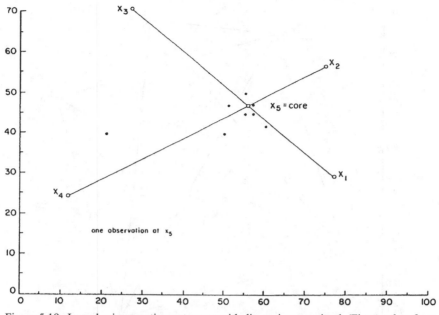

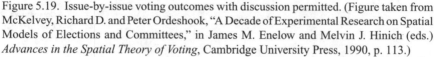

Figure 5.19. Issue-by-issue voting outcomes with discussion permitted. (Figure taken from McKelvey, Richard D. and Peter Ordeshook, "A Decade of Experimental Research on Spatial Models of Elections and Committees," in James M. Enelow and Melvin J. Hinich (eds.) *Advances in the Spatial Theory of Voting*, Cambridge University Press, 1990, p. 113.)

A possible answer to this question is that the relevant coalitions to consider are not one set of congressmen against another, but all congressmen against the citizens. Because the taxes that pay for these redistributive programs are general and diffuse, the citizens are unaware of the costs of these federal grants and consider only the concentrated benefits that they receive. Each congressman is evaluated on the basis of his marginal contribution to the district's welfare and any grants it receives are counted as part of these marginal contributions. Although a congressman whose district receives only $10 million in grants has not won as much as the congressman whose district got $750 million, he has still "won" something. It is only the taxpayer-citizen who loses under this interpretation.[29]

5.13.5 *Experimental evidence of cycling*

The most controlled environment to test for the presence of cycling is within the experimental laboratory, and a variety of experiments have been conducted which bear on this question. Many of these have defined the issue set spatially, as we have throughout much of this chapter. A set of preferences is induced in these experiments by giving participant i a reward of D dollars if the committee chooses a particular point x_i in the two-dimensional issue space, with successively lower payoffs awarded to i the farther the committee's choice is from x_i. Although most studies have induced circular indifference curves, some have induced ellipses and even more exotic shapes.

---

[29] For a formal modeling of this way around the "universalism paradox" see Schwartz (1994).

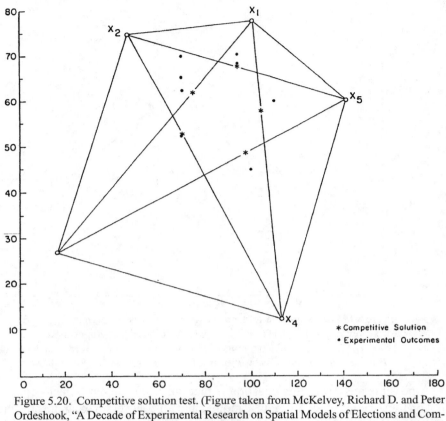

Figure 5.20. Competitive solution test. (Figure taken from McKelvey, Richard D. and Peter Ordeshook, "A Decade of Experimental Research on Spatial Models of Elections and Committees," in James M. Enelow and Melvin J. Hinich (eds.) *Advances in the Spatial Theory of Voting*, Cambridge University Press, 1990, p. 113.)

The earliest experimental results for committee voting test to see whether the committee chooses a Condorcet winner, when one exists. By Plott's (1967) theorem, an equilibrium will only exist in a spatial voting game if there is an odd number of players, and pairs of players are perfectly lined up on opposite sides of one player's ideal point, as in Figure 5.9 where each letter is a voter's ideal point and the unique winning point is at E. Fiorina and Plott (1978) were the first to run experiments of this type and they found that the committee's choices did tend to cluster around this equilibrium (core) outcome, even though they seldom coincided with it. Many subsequent experiments have confirmed Fiorina and Plott's findings. One such set of outcomes by McKelvey and Ordeshook (1987) is presented in Figure 5.19. Each point is an experiment's outcome. The core is at player 5's ideal point, x_5, and most of the points chosen in the experiments are clustered around this point with one falling precisely on top of it. Note, however, that one committee managed to wander off quite a ways to the left.

Thus, it appears that committees do gravitate toward a Condorcet winner when one exists. Where do they locate when one does not exist? One answer, which underlies McKelvey's (1976) agenda setter theorem, is that the committee might wind up anywhere on the page, or several miles from it. But such predictions strain one's credibility. More reasonable would be a prediction that the committee chooses

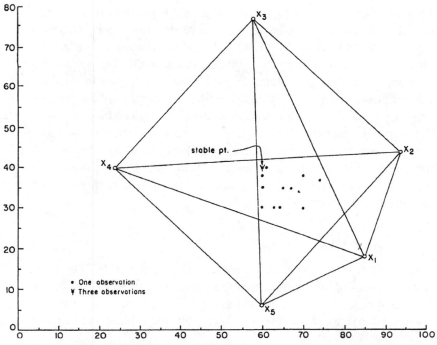

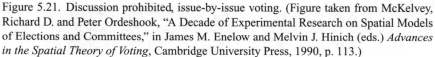

Figure 5.21. Discussion prohibited, issue-by-issue voting. (Figure taken from McKelvey, Richard D. and Peter Ordeshook, "A Decade of Experimental Research on Spatial Models of Elections and Committees," in James M. Enelow and Melvin J. Hinich (eds.) *Advances in the Spatial Theory of Voting*, Cambridge University Press, 1990, p. 113.)

a point somewhere inside the Pareto set, or even somewhere in the middle of this set. Game theory has generated several solution concepts – like the bargaining, uncovered and Banks sets – to predict where this outcome might be. (We shall discuss some of these concepts in Chapter 11, where the issue of cycling will again arise in the context of two-candidate competition.) Figure 5.20 presents the outcomes from a set of experiments by McKelvey, Ordeshook, and Winer (1978) designed to test the predictive power of one of these solution concepts – the competitive solution. All experiments resulted in a point being chosen within the Pareto set, which is the area contained within the large pentagon formed by the outside lines connecting the five ideal points. Each asterisk represents an outcome predicted by the competitive solution. All of the committees' chosen points come close to the predicted outcomes, with a few falling right on them. The McKelvey, Ordeshook, and Winer experiments and many others conducted to test different hypotheses about committee choices when no core exists reveal that the majority rule selects outcomes that are both within the Pareto set, and which tend to cluster near one another, although not as closely together as when a core exists.[30]

In Section 5.13.2 we illustrated how a majority rule equilibrium can be induced with a multidimensional issues space if the issues are voted on one dimension at a time. Figure 5.21 presents the results from yet another set of experiments by

---

[30] These and other results from the experimental literature on spatial voting are surveyed by McKelvey and Ordeshook (1990).

McKelvey and Ordeshook (1984) that tests this prediction. The "stable point" is at the intersection of the two horizontal and vertical lines that pass through the median ideal points in the two directions. The points chosen in the experiments do not cluster as closely to this stable point as they did to the core point in Figure 5.19, but they are more closely clustered than in Figure 5.20, even though no core exists in each of these experiments, *if* the committees were free to offer new proposals in any way they wished. By constraining the committees to change only one dimension of the proposals at a time, this last set of experiments produced a concentrated cluster of outcomes. Indeed, all of the points chosen fall within the pentagon formed by the intersection of the diagonal contract curves. Even adding a modest amount of structure to a committee's procedures can make a noticeable difference in the stability of its outcomes.

Bibliographical notes

The literature on majority rule is reviewed by Enelow (1997) and Young (1997). A rigorous proof of the median voter theorem is presented by Kramer (1972). Kramer and Klevorick (1974) established a similar result for local optima, and Kats and Nitzan (1976) have shown that a local equilibrium is likely to be a global equilibrium under fairly mild conditions.

Following Plott (1967), the major papers on stability conditions in multidimensional models have been Kadane (1972), Sloss (1973), Slutsky (1977a), Schofield (1978), and Cohen (1979).

Hoyer and Mayer (1974) prove the median-in-all-directions theorem using elliptical indifference curves.

The literature on axiomatic restrictions on preference orderings to produce majority rule equilibria is reviewed in Inada (1969), Sen (1970a), Plott (1971), Taylor (1971), and Pattanaik (1997).

In addition to the papers cited, Simpson (1969) and Kramer (1977) have made important contributions specifying the conditions under which a particular majority, m^*, suffices to ensure an equilibrium.

The seminal discussions of logrolling in public choice are by Downs (1957), Tullock (1959), and most extensively by Buchanan and Tullock (1962). In political science, the classic reference is Bentley (1907).

Arguments that logrolling can, in the proper structural setting, improve on the outcomes from simple, sincere majority voting have been presented by Coleman (1966a,b, 1970); Mueller (1967, 1971, 1973); Wilson (1969, 1971a,b); Mueller, Philpotts, and Vanek (1972); Koford (1982); and Philipson and Snyder (1996).

The negative side of logrolling has figured more prominently in the political science literature (Schattschneider, 1935; McConnell, 1966; Lowi, 1969; Riker and Brams, 1973; Schwartz, 1975).

The theorem relating logrolling to cycling appears in various forms in Park (1967), Kadane (1972), Oppenheimer (1972, 1975), Bernholz (1973, 1974a, 1975), Riker and Brams (1973), Koehler (1975), and Schwartz (1981). A very useful review of this literature with additional proofs is given by Miller (1977). A less technical review of the logrolling literature is given by Stratmann (1997).

Shepsle and Weingast (1981) discuss several possible institutions to bring about "structure-induced" equilibria. Niemi (1983) emphasizes the potential importance of limiting the issue set to a few choices and presents a weakened version of the single-peakedness condition.

Bernholz (1974b) was the first to propose limiting consideration to a single dimension at a time to induce equilibria. Both Slutsky (1977b) and Shepsle (1979) offer proofs of the result.

Coleman (1983) emphasizes the importance of the long-run context in which logrolling takes place in bringing about stability, and Bernholz proves some relevant theorems (1977, 1978, 1997).

The experimental literature on spatial voting is surveyed by McKelvey and Ordeshook (1990).

CHAPTER 6

Majority rule – normative properties

Unanimity is impossible; the rule of a minority, as a permanent arrangement, is wholly inadmissible; so that, rejecting the majority principle, anarchy or despotism in some form is all that is left.

Abraham Lincoln

... unless the king has been elected by unanimous vote, what, failing a prior agreement, is the source of the minority's obligation to submit to the choice of the majority? Whence the right of the hundred who do wish a master to speak for the ten who do not? The majority principle is itself a product of agreement, and presupposes unanimity on at least one occasion.

Jean-Jacques Rousseau

In Chapter 4 we argued that the ubiquitous popularity of majority rule might be attributable to the speed with which committees can make decisions using it. This quickness defense was undermined considerably in Chapter 5 by the results on cycling. A committee caught in a voting cycle may not be able to reach a decision quickly, and the outcome at which it eventually does arrive may be arbitrarily determined by institutional details, or nonarbitrarily determined by a cunning agenda setter. Is this all one can say in majority rule's behalf? Does the case for the majority rule rest on the promise that quasi-omniscient party leaders can arrange stable trades to maximize the aggregate welfare of the legislature discussed in Section 5.13.3?

When asked to explain majority rule's popularity, students unfamiliar with the vast public choice literature on the topic usually mention justness, fairness, egalitarian, and similar normative attributes that they feel characterize majority rule. Thus, to understand why majority rule is so often the committee rule, one must examine its normative as well as its positive properties. In this chapter we offer three sets of normative arguments in favor of the simple majority rule. The second two, although seemingly different, will prove to be quite closely related. The first will be seen to rest on a radically different conception of the nature of democratic choice from the other two.

6.1 Condorcet's jury theorem

Let us assume that after hearing all of the evidence in a case that the probability of a judge reaching the correct verdict regarding the accused's innocence is 0.6.

Obviously in trials presided over by one judge, the correct verdict will be reached 60 percent of the time. A tribunal that employed the unanimity rule would make the correct decision only 21.6 percent of the time. On the other occasions it would either fail to reach a unanimous verdict or would unanimously reach the wrong verdict. If, however, the tribunal used the simple majority rule, it would *always* reach a verdict, and would reach the correct verdict 64.8 percent of the time. Moreover, the probability that a panel of judges reaches the correct verdict grows continuously as its size increases – provided that it employs the simple majority rule.

This property of the simple majority rule was first discussed by the Marquis de Condorcet (1785) over 200 years ago. Condorcet's famous theorem reads as follows:

Condorcet Jury Theorem: *Let n voters (n odd) choose between two alternatives that have equal likelihood of being correct a priori. Assume that voters make their judgments independently and that each has the same probability p of being correct* $(1/2 < p < 1)$*. Then the probability that the group makes the correct judgment using the simple majority rule is*

$$P_n = \sum_{h=(n+1)/2}^{n} [n!/h!(n-h)!]p^h(1-p)^{n-h},$$

which approaches one as n becomes large.[1]

This theorem can be used to justify having both large juries and their use of the simple majority rule. The Athenian practice of having the assembly of all citizens serve as a jury in some cases and its use of the simple majority rule put Condorcet's theorem into practice more than two millennia before he proved it.

The theorem can also be used to justify direct democracy as, say, in the form of referenda. Suppose, for example, that all members of society wish to see the crime and suffering associated with the illegal sale and use of drugs eliminated. A proposal is made to legalize and regulate the sale of drugs in the belief that this measure would eliminate the profits and crime associated with drugs, just as the repeal of Prohibition in the United States in 1933 put an end to bootlegging. Other people argue, however, that legalizing drugs would increase their use and lead to even more crime and misery. The Condorcet jury theorem states that a national referendum on this issue would make the *correct* judgment of the facts with a near-one probability, if the probability of any single individual making the correct judgment is greater than 0.5, and all citizens make their judgments independently of one another.

The theorem can also serve as a normative defense of two-party representative government, of a majoritarian/plurality rule for electing representatives, if it is legitimate to assume that all citizens want the same things from their government or representative. If all citizens in the United States, for example, want the president to be a person of high integrity, a good administrator, a person who balances the

---

[1] Statement of theorem taken from Young (1997, p. 183). See also Young (1988).

budget and produces low inflation and unemployment, and so on, then the contest for the presidency will be to select "the best person for the job," where all citizens agree on the criteria for "best." If each citizen is able to determine with a probability greater than 0.5 the candidate who comes closest to fulfilling these criteria, then the popular election of the president will select the *best* person with a near-one probability.

The jury theorem rests on several assumptions, which might be questioned: (1) a common probability of being correct across all individuals, (2) each individual's choice is independent of all others, and (3) each individual votes sincerely (honestly) taking into account only his own judgment as to the correct outcome.

Allowing each individual i to have his own probability p_i does not fundamentally alter the theorem. For example, if the distribution of the p_is is symmetric, then the theorem still holds if the mean of the distribution is greater than one half.[2]

A potentially more serious problem arises when the second condition is relaxed. Imagine, for example, that when the jury meets to decide the fate of the accused, they begin by going around the table with each juror stating her opinion. In such an environment, where no one knows for sure if the accused is guilty, it is possible that those speaking late in the sequence are influenced by the opinions stated earlier. The more jurors who have already said "guilty," the more likely it is that the next juror says guilty. Clearly, in this situation the information content from the aggregation of all votes is less than if the jurors secretly wrote their opinions on pieces of paper. In the limit, if all jurors merely repeat the opinion of the first juror to speak, the probability of their then unanimous verdict being correct is no greater than that of any single juror's being correct. Fortunately, if the correlation between any two jurors' votes is not too high, the "truth revealing" property of majority rule is not overturned. Ladha (1992) computed the following expression for the upper bound for the correlation between any two votes that still allows the jury theorem to hold:

$$\hat{p} = p - \frac{n}{n-1}\frac{1-p}{p}(p - 0.25). \tag{6.1}$$

As the size of the electorate, n, grows, the *lowest* possible value for the upper bound approaches 0.25.[3]

This last example indirectly raises the question of the source of information from which voters make their decisions, and whether it is indeed optimal for them to vote sincerely ignoring how other citizens vote. Austen-Smith and Banks (1996) have presented a "model [in which] sincere behavior by all individuals is not rational even when individuals have . . . a common preference, [and] sincere voting does not constitute a Nash equilibrium" (p. 34). To see the logic behind their arguments, consider the following game.

There are two urns. One contains 60 white balls and 40 black balls, the other 1 black ball. This information is common knowledge to all n players. A ball will be

---

[2] See Grofman, Owen, and Feld (1983) and Shapley and Grofman (1984). Shapley, Grofman, Nitzan, and Paroush (1982) proved early generalizations of the theorem in which weighted voting is optimal, where each voter i's weight is $w_i = \ln(p_i/1 - p_i)$.

[3] See also Shapley and Grofman (1984), Ladha (1993, 1995), Berg (1993), and Ben-Yashar and Nitzan (1997).

drawn from one of these two urns, and the n players must decide using the simple majority rule what the color of this ball is (n is odd). If they decide correctly, they each receive a cash prize. A neutral game master first flips a coin to determine the urn from which this ball will be taken. He then picks a ball from this urn and shows it to the first player. He returns this ball to the urn and picks another ball from it and shows it to the second player. This continues until all n players have been shown one ball from this urn. The game master then picks another ball from the urn and the players vote on its color. At the time that they vote, each player is unaware of the outcome of the coin flip and knows only the color of the one ball that she has been shown.

Now consider the strategy choices of a single player, Alice. If she has been shown a black ball, she knows that it could have come from either urn, and she calculates the probability of the winning ball's being black as $0.7 \ (0.5(1) + 0.5(0.4))$. Her optimal strategy based solely on her private information is to vote black. This vote reveals her private information as the jury theorem requires. But voting for black is not her optimal strategy, once she takes into account that the other voters are making similar calculations and the collective choice will be made using the majority rule.

Under the majority rule two possibilities exist: one of the other colors has gotten a clear majority of the votes of the other $n - 1$ players, or they are divided evenly between the two colors. Since $n - 1$ is an even number, if one color has a clear majority it must win by at least two votes not counting Alice's vote. Her vote cannot change the outcome, and she can forget about this possibility. When the other $n - 1$ players are evenly divided over the color, however, Alice's vote is pivotal. But in this case half of the other players have voted white. If even one of those voting white does so because he has been shown a white ball, Alice knows that the winning ball comes from the urn containing 60 white balls. The probability that it is a black ball is not 0.7 as her private information would lead her to believe, but 0.4. If she ignores the fact that some other voters must be shown a white ball when the votes of the other players are evenly split, and simply votes on the basis of her private information, she will tilt the committee's choice in favor of the lower probability event. She and all other members of the committee are better off if Alice ignores her private information and votes taking into account only the common knowledge about the game, and the fact that her vote is only decisive when the other players are evenly split.

What is true for Alice is, of course, true for all other players. The individually optimal strategy for everyone is to vote white, and everyone voting white is a Nash equilibrium. Once everyone understands the structure of the game and adopts the sophisticated strategy that this structure dictates, all will vote white even though the overall probability of drawing a white ball is only 0.3. Moreover, all vote white even in the event that every player has been shown a black ball. In this game sincere voting is irrational, and rational (sophisticated) voting on the part of everyone produces worse outcomes than sincere voting. Austen-Smith and Banks (1996) prove that these pathological results can be produced under a variety of assumptions that do not violate the basic spirit of the Condorcet jury theorem.

Unfortunately, there are many Nash equilibria in these sorts of games. Fortunately, on the other hand, not all of them involve the degree of pathology of the previous example in which everyone votes white. Indeed, in this example when $n = 3$, two persons voting sincerely and one voting strategically (always white) is also a Nash equilibrium, and it yields higher expected payoffs to the committee than would *all three* voting sincerely.[4] Ladha, Miller, and Oppenheimer (1995) have run experiments with games of the type just described, and found that when the games are repeated and the players can verify how the other players voted in earlier rounds, as well as their private information, that the players can lock in on combinations in which some vote sincerely and some vote following the sophisticated strategy of assuming that they are the pivotal player.

What should we conclude from this discussion? Is it most plausible to assume that people vote sincerely taking into account their private information (in which case the jury theorem may be a reasonable defense of majority rule), that they vote strategically assuming that they are a pivotal voter, or some combination of the two? In contemplating this question, perhaps it is useful to return to the example of a referendum on legalizing drugs. If such a referendum were held today in the United States, each citizen would place a probability of, say, 0.6 on the status quo being the best option, and 0.4 on legalization being better, given the common knowledge about the two options that exists today. But the referendum is announced for one year from today. Thus, each citizen has time to gather information and cast an informed vote. Some read about life under Prohibition in the United States and changes following its repeal. Others read about Holland's experience with the de facto legalization of the "softer" drugs. Some even travel to Holland to witness the effects first hand. When the day of the referendum comes, the sophisticated voter recognizes that his vote will only "count" if the other 80 million voters split evenly on both sides of the issue. But this would imply that all of the information gathering of the other voters has led to as many people in favor of the status quo as the number in favor of legalization. The aggregate effects of the private information on the vote are a wash. The sophisticated voter now recognizes that the information he has gathered is no more likely to have led him to the correct judgment than a flip of a coin would. The sophisticated voter recognizes that his vote will be pivotal only in the event that his private information is worthless, and thus he rationally ignores his private information and bases his vote on the common knowledge that he and his fellow citizens shared one year ago.

Indeed, if he were truly rational, he would not vote at all, since the probability of 80 million voters splitting precisely evenly on any issue is infinitesimal. Any costs of gathering information and voting will outweigh the expected gain from casting the pivotal vote, given the low probability of this event. More paradoxical than why a rational voter would reveal his private information and vote sincerely is why he would vote at all.

---

[4] More generally, Ladha, Miller, and Oppenheimer (1995) prove that there exists some minority $m < n/2$ for any committee of size n, n being odd, such that the probability that the committee votes correctly (and thus its expected payoff) is *higher* than that predicted by the Condorcet jury theorem, when the minority votes strategically ignoring its private information, and the majority votes *informatively* using its private information.

This "voting paradox" strikes at the very normative foundations of democracy, just as the Condorcet jury theorem purports to provide a normative foundation for majoritarian democracy. Many attempts have been made to resolve this paradox, and we shall examine some of them in Chapter 14. One hypothesis as to why people vote sees them voting out of a sense of civic duty, in step with a social norm. If this hypothesis does resolve the paradox of *why* people vote, it may also provide an explanation for *how* they vote on issues like those assumed in the Condorcet jury theorem. If the good citizen knows that the efficacy of the use of majority rule as a means for determining the *correct* policy depends on his honestly revealing what his private views are on this policy, perhaps he will vote sincerely – if he votes at all.

The assumptions underlying the Condorcet jury theorem depict politics as a cooperative, positive sum game. All citizens have the same objective – to convict the guilty and acquit the innocent, to choose the best person to fill the office. Many observers of politics do not view it in such a favorable light, however. Many view politics as a noncooperative, zero-sum game. The issue to be decided in the national referendum is whether to ban all abortions. People do not disagree about the *facts* involved, but rather over the ethical issues. A national referendum on this issue would simply determine which side is allowed to impose its judgment on the other. Can the use of the simple majority rule be given a normative justification in these situations? We turn to two sets of arguments that say it can.

6.2 May's theorem on majority rule

A most important theorem concerning majority rule was proved a half century ago by May (1952). May begins by defining a *group decision* function:

$$D = f(D_1, D_2, \ldots, D_n),$$

where n is the number of individuals in the community. Each D_i takes on the value $1, 0, -1$ as voter i's preferences for a pair of issues are $x P_i y$, $x I_i y$, and $y P_i x$, where P represents the strict preference relationship and I indifference. Thus, the D_i serve as ballots, and $f(\cdot)$ is an aggregation rule for determining the winning issue. Depending on the nature of the voting rule, $f(\cdot)$ takes on different functional forms. Under the simple majority rule, $f(\cdot)$ sums the D_i and assigns D a value according to the following rule:

$$\left(\sum_{i=1}^{n} D_i > 0 \right) \rightarrow D = 1$$

$$\left(\sum_{i=1}^{n} D_i = 0 \right) \rightarrow D = 0$$

$$\left(\sum_{i=1}^{n} D_i < 0 \right) \rightarrow D - 1.$$

May defines the following four conditions:[5]

> *Decisiveness*: The group decision function is defined and single valued for any given set of preference orderings.
>
> *Anonymity*: D is determined only by the values of D_i, and is independent of how they are assigned. Any permutation of these ballots leaves D unchanged.
>
> *Neutrality*: If x defeats (ties) y for one set of individual preferences, and all individuals have the same *ordinal* rankings for z and w as for x and y (i.e., $x R_i y \rightarrow z R_i w$, and so on), then z defeats (ties) w.
>
> *Positive responsiveness*: If D equals 0 or 1, and one individual changes his vote from -1 to 0 or 1, or from 0 to 1, and all other votes remain unchanged, then $D = 1$.

The theorem states that a group decision function is the simple majority rule *if and only if* it satisfies these four conditions. It is a most remarkable result. If we start from the set of all possible voting rules one can conceive of, and then begin imposing conditions we wish our voting rule to satisfy, we shall obviously reduce the number of viable candidates for our chosen voting rule as we add more and more conditions. May's theorem tells us that once we add these four conditions, we have reduced the possible set of voting rules to but one, the simple majority rule. All other voting rules violate one or more of these four axioms.

This result is both surprising and ominous. It forebodes that if we were to demand more of a voting rule than that it satisfy only these four axioms, that is, were we to demand a fifth axiom, then even majority rule might not qualify and we would have no voting rule satisfying the proposed conditions. Chapter 5 also gives us a strong hint as to what that fifth condition might be – transitivity. But for the moment we are concerned with the choice between just two issues, and we need not concern ourselves with transitivity. The foreboding can be suppressed until Chapter 24.

The equivalence between majority rule and these four conditions means that all of the normative properties majority rule possesses, whatever justness or egalitarian attributes it has, are somewhere captured in these four axioms, as are its negative attributes. We must examine these conditions more closely.

Decisiveness seems at first uncontroversial. If we have a *decision* function, we want it to be able to decide at least when confronted with only two issues. But this axiom does eliminate all probabilistic procedures in which the probability of an issue's winning depends on voter preferences. Positive responsiveness is also a reasonable property. If the decision process is to reflect each voter's preference, then a switch by one voter from opposition to support ought to break a tie.

The other two axioms are less innocent than they look or their names connote. The neutrality axiom introduces an issue-independence property.[6] In deciding a pair of issues, only the ordinal preferences of each voter over this issue pair are

---

[5] The names and definitions have been changed somewhat to reflect subsequent developments in the literature and to simplify the discussion. In particular, the definition of neutrality follows Sen (1970a, p. 72).

[6] Sen (1970a, p. 72) and Guha (1972).

considered. Information concerning voter preferences on other issue pairs is ruled out, and thereby one means for weighing intensities is eliminated. The neutrality axiom eliminates voting rules like the Borda count and point voting described in the next two chapters. It requires that the voting rule treat each issue pair alike regardless of the nature of the issues involved. Thus, the issue of whether the lights on this year's community Christmas tree are red or blue is decided by the same kind of weighing of individual preference orderings as the issue of whether John Doe's property should be confiscated and redistributed among the rest of the community.

Where the neutrality axiom guarantees that the voting procedure treats each *issue* alike, anonymity assures that each *voter* is treated alike. On many issues this is probably a desirable property. On the issue of the color of the Christmas lights, a change of one voter's preferences from red to blue and another from blue to red probably should not affect the outcome. Implicit here is a judgment that the color of the tree's lights is about as important to one voter as to the next. This equal intensity assumption is introduced into the voting procedure by recording each voter's expression of preference, no matter how strong, as a plus or minus one.

But consider now the issue of whether John Doe's property should be confiscated and distributed to the rest of the community. Suppose John is a generous fellow and votes for the issue and the issue in fact passes. Suppose now that John changes his vote to negative, and that his worst enemy, who always votes the opposite of John, switches to a positive vote. By the anonymity condition, the issue still should pass. A voting procedure satisfying this procedure is blind as to whether it is John Doe or his worst enemy who is voting for the confiscation of John Doe's property. In some situations this may obviously be an undesirable feature.

6.3*   Proof of May's theorem on majority rule

Theorem: *A group decision function is the simple majority rule iff it satisfies the four conditions stated in Section 6.2.*

That majority rule implies the four conditions is rather obvious.

1. It always adds to an integer, which by the decision function is transformed into -1 or 0 or $+1$, and thus is decisive.
2. Change any $+1$ to -1, and any -1 to $+1$, and the sum is left unchanged.
3. If the rankings are the same on any two pairs of issues, then so too will be the vote summations.
4. If $\sum D_i = 0$, increasing any D_i will make $\sum D_i > 0$, and decide the contest in favor of x. If $\sum D_i > 0$, increasing any D_i will leave $\sum D_i > 0$ and will not change the outcome.

Now we must show that the four conditions imply the majority rule. We first show that the first three conditions imply

$$[N(-1) = N(1)] \rightarrow D = 0, \tag{6.2}$$

where $N(-1)$ is the number of votes for y and $N(1)$ is the number for x.

Assume that (6.2) does not hold – for example, that

$$[N(-1) = N(1)] \rightarrow D = 1. \tag{6.3}$$

When the number of votes for y equals the number of votes for x, the outcome is x.

Now relabel y to z and x to w, where a vote for z is now recorded as a -1 and a vote for w as a $+1$. Reverse all $+1$s to -1s, and -1s to $+1$s. By anonymity, this latter change should not affect the group decision. All individuals who originally regarded x at least as good as $y(x R_i y)$ will now regard z as at least as good as w. By the neutrality axiom, the collective outcome must be z if it was originally x. But z is equivalent to y, not x. The decisiveness axiom is violated.

Thus, (6.3) is inconsistent with the first three axioms. By an analogous argument one can show that (6.4) is inconsistent with the first three axioms:

$$[N(-1) = N(1)] \rightarrow D = -1. \tag{6.4}$$

Thus, (6.2) must be valid. From (6.2) and positive responsiveness, we have

$$[N(1) = N(-1) + 1] \rightarrow D = +1. \tag{6.5}$$

When the number of votes for x is one greater than the number for y, then x must win. Now assume that when the number of votes for x is $m - 1$ greater than the number for y, x wins. A change in preferences of one voter so that the number preferring x to y is now m greater than the number preferring y to x cannot reverse the outcome by positive responsiveness. By finite induction, the four conditions imply the method of simple majority rule.

6.4   The Rae-Taylor theorem on majority rule

Although on the surface they seem quite different, May's theorem on majority rule is quite similar in its underlying assumptions to a theorem presented by Rae (1969) and Taylor (1969).

Rae (1969, pp. 43–4) sets up the problem as one of the choice of an optimal voting rule by an individual who is uncertain over his future position under the voting rule. Thus, the discussion is set in the context of constitutional choice of a voting rule as introduced by Buchanan and Tullock (1962, pp. 3–15).[7] Politics, as Rae and Taylor depict it, is a game of conflict. Some individuals gain from an issue's passage; some inevitably lose. The representative individual in the constitutional stage seeks to avoid having issues he opposes imposed upon him, and to impose issues he favors on others. He presumes that the gains he will experience from a favorable issue's passage will equal the loss from an unfavorable issue's passage, that is, that all voters experience equal intensities on each issue.[8] Issues are impartially proposed so that each voter has the same probability of favoring or opposing

---

[7] See also Buchanan (1966).

[8] Rae (1969, p. 41, n. 6). The importance of this equal intensity assumption has been recognized by several writers. Additional references for each assumption are presented in the notes to Table 6.1, where the assumptions are summarized.

any issue proposed. Under these assumptions, it is reasonable to assume that the representative voter selects a rule that minimizes the probability of his supporting an issue that is defeated, or opposing an issue that wins. Rae (1969) illustrates and Taylor (1969) proves that majority rule is the only rule that satisfies this criterion.[9]

The full flavor of the theorem can best be obtained by considering an example of Brian Barry (1965, p. 312). Five people occupy a railroad car that contains no sign either prohibiting or permitting smoking. A decision must be made as to whether those occupants of the car who wish to smoke are to be allowed to do so. If an individual placed himself in the position of one who was uncertain as to whether he would be a smoker or nonsmoker, the natural assumption is that nonsmokers suffer as much from the smoking of others as smokers suffer from being stopped from smoking.[10] The equal intensity assumption seems defensible in this case. With this assumption, and uncertainty over whether one is a smoker or nonsmoker, majority rule is the best decision rule. It maximizes the expected utility of a constitutional decision maker.

This example illustrates both the explicit and implicit assumptions underlying the Rae-Taylor theorem on majority rule. First, the situation is obviously one of conflict. The smoker's gain comes at the nonsmoker's expense, or vice versa. Second, the conflictual situation cannot be avoided. The solution to the problem provided by the exit of one category of passenger from the wagon is implicitly denied.[11] Nor does a possibility exist to redefine the issue to remove the conflict and obtain a consensus. Each issue must be voted up or down as is. Fourth, the issue has been randomly or impartially selected. In this particular example, randomness is effectively introduced through the chance assemblage of individuals in the car. No apparent bias in favor of one outcome has been introduced via the random gathering of individuals in the car. The last assumption contained in the example is the equal intensity assumption.

The importance of each of these assumptions to the argument for majority rule can perhaps best be seen by contrasting them with the assumptions that typically have been made in support of its antithesis, the unanimity rule.

6.5   Assumptions underlying the unanimity rule

As depicted by Wicksell (1896) and Buchanan and Tullock (1962), politics is a cooperative, positive-sum game. The committee's business is the collective satisfaction of needs common to all members. The committee (or community) is a voluntary association of individuals brought together for the purpose of satisfying these common needs.[12] Since the association is voluntary, each member is guaranteed the right to preserve his own interests against those of the other members. This right

---

[9] The "only" must be qualified when the committee size, n, is even. With n even, majority rule and the rule $n/2$ share this property. See Taylor (1969). Chapter 26 contains a proof of the simple majority rule's optimality under assumptions similar to those made by Rae and Taylor.

[10] This assumption would seem less "natural" to many in the United States today than it did 35 years ago.

[11] Rae (1975) stresses this assumption in the implicit defense of majority rule contained in his critique of unanimity.

[12] See also Buchanan (1949).

is preserved by the power contained in the unanimity rule to veto any proposal that runs counter to an individual's interest, or through the option to exit from the community, or both.

Given that the purpose of the committee is the satisfaction of the wants of the committee members, the natural way for issues to come before it is from the individuals themselves. Each individual has the right to propose issues that will benefit him and that he thinks might benefit all. Should an initial proposal fail to command a unanimous majority, it is redefined until it does, or until it is removed from the agenda. Thus, the political *process* implicit in a defense of the unanimity rule is one of discussion, compromise, and amendment, continuing until a formulation of the issue is reached benefiting all. The key assumptions underlying this view of politics are both that the game is cooperative and positive sum, that is, that a formulation of the issue benefiting all exists, *and* that the process can be completed in a reasonable amount of time, so that the transaction costs of decision making are not prohibitive.[13]

Let us also illustrate the type of voting process that the proponents of unanimity envisage through the example of fire protection in a small community. A citizen at a town meeting proposes that a truck be purchased and a station built to provide fire protection, and couples his proposal, in Wicksellian fashion, with a tax proposal to finance it. Suppose that this initial tax proposal calls upon each property owner to pay the same fraction of the costs. The citizens with the lowest-valued property complain. The expected value of the fire protection (the value of the property times the reduction in the risk of fire) to some property owners is less than their share of the costs under the lump-sum tax formula. Enactment of the proposal would make the poor subsidize the protection of the property of the rich. As an alternative proposal, a proportional tax on property values is offered. The expected benefits to all citizens now exceed their share of its cost. The proposal passes unanimously.

6.6   Assumptions underlying the two rules contrasted

Fire protection, the elimination of smoke from factories, and similar examples used to describe the mutual benefits from collective action all pertain to public goods and externalities – activities in which the market fails to provide a solution beneficial to all. The provision of these public goods is an improvement in allocative efficiency, a movement from a position off the Pareto frontier to a point on it. Proponents of unanimity have assumed that collective action involves collective decisions of this type.

---

[13] Both Wicksell (1896) and Buchanan and Tullock (1962) recognize that decision time costs may be sufficiently high to require abandonment of a full unanimity rule in favor of a near unanimity rule (Wicksell) or some even lower fractional rule. Indeed, much of Buchanan and Tullock's book is devoted to the choice of the optimal "nonunanimity" rule, as discussed in Chapter 4. Thus, one might question whether they can legitimately be characterized as champions of unanimity. I have chosen them as such because I think their arguments can be fairly characterized as stating that *were it not for these transaction costs*, unanimity would be the best rule, and, therefore, that some rule approaching unanimity, or at least greater than a simple majority, is likely to be the best in many situations. In contrast, Rae (1975) and Barry (1965) both argue that their critique of unanimity is not based solely on the decision cost criterion.

In contrast, many advocates of majority rule envisage conflictual choices in which no mutually beneficial opportunities are available, as occurs when a community is forced to choose from among a set of Pareto-efficient opportunities. In the fire protection example, there might be a large number of tax share proposals that would cover the cost of fire protection and leave all better off. All might receive unanimous approval when placed against the alternative of no fire protection. Once one of these proposals has achieved a unanimous majority no other proposal from the Pareto-efficient set can achieve unanimity when placed against it. Any other proposal must make one voter worse off (by raising his tax share), causing him to vote against it.

Criticisms of unanimity and defenses of majority rule often involve distributional or property rights issues of this type. In Barry's example, the train car's occupants are in conflict over the right to clean air and the right to smoke; Rae (1975, pp. 1287–97) uses the similar example of the smoking factory and the rights of the nearby citizens to clean air in criticizing the unanimity rule. In both cases, a property rights decision must be made with distributional consequences. If the smokers are given the right to smoke, the seekers of clean air are made worse off. Even in situations in which the latter can be made better off by bribing the smokers to reduce the level of smoke, the nonsmokers are worse off by having to pay the bribe than they would be if the property right had been reversed and the smokers had to offer the bribe (Rae, 1975). Buchanan and Tullock (1962, p. 91) discuss this same example, but they assume that the initial property rights issue has already been fairly resolved at the constitutional stage. This illustrates another difference between the proponents of unanimity and majority rule. The former typically assume decision making takes place *within* a set of predefined property rights; the latter, like Barry and Rae, assume that it is the property rights decision itself that must be made. In Barry's example it is the only decision to be made. Rae's argument is more complicated. He argues that the constitution cannot resolve all property rights issues for all time, so that technological and economic changes cause some property rights issues to *drift* into the resolution of public goods and externalities. In either case, however, unanimous agreement on the property rights issue of who has the initial claim on the air is obviously unlikely under the egoistic-man assumptions that all writers have made in this discussion. A less than unanimity rule *seems* necessary for resolving these initial property rights-distributional issues.

The last statement is qualified because it requires the other assumptions introduced in the discussion of majority rule: exit is impossible (or expensive); the issue cannot be redefined to make all better off. The need for the first assumption is obvious. If the occupants of the railroad car can move to another car in which smoking is explicitly allowed or prohibited, the conflict disappears, as it does if either the factory or the nearby residents can move costlessly. The importance of the second assumption requires a little elaboration.

Consider again the example of smoking in the railway car. Suppose the train is not allowed to proceed unless the occupants of this car can decide whether smoking is to be allowed or not. If the unanimity rule were employed, the potential would exist for the type of situation critics of unanimity seem to fear the most – a costly impasse. Out of this impasse, the minority might even be able to force the majority to capitulate, if the benefits to the majority from the train's continuation were high enough. Under these assumptions, majority rule is an attractive alternative to unanimity.

Now change the situation slightly. Suppose that *all passengers of the entire train* must decide the rules regarding smoking before the train may proceed. Since there is undoubtedly some advantage in having the entire train from which to choose a seat rather than only part of it, a rational egoist can be expected to prefer that the entire train be declared an area that accords with his preferences regarding smoking. If majority rule were used to decide the issue, then smoking would be either allowed or prohibited throughout the train. But if a unanimity rule were employed, the train's occupants would be forced to explore other alternatives to having the entire train governed by the same rule. The proposal of allowing smoking in some sections and prohibiting it in others might easily emerge as a "compromise" and win unanimous approval over having the train remain halted. Members of the majority would be somewhat worse off under this compromise than they would have been had the entire train been designated according to their preferences, but members of the minority would be much better off. An impartial observer might easily prefer the compromise forced on the group by the unanimity rule to the outcome forthcoming under majority rule.

The arguments in favor of majority rule implicitly assume that such compromise proposals are not possible. The committee is faced with mutually exclusive alternatives.[14] Mutually beneficial alternatives are assumed to be technologically infeasible or the voting process is somehow constrained so that these issues cannot come before the committee.

Table 6.1 summarizes the assumptions that have been made in support of the majority and unanimity decision rules. They are not intended to be necessary and sufficient conditions, but are more in the nature of the most favorable conditions under which each decision rule is expected to operate. It is immediately apparent from Table 6.1 that the assumptions supporting each decision rule are totally opposed to the assumptions made in support of the alternative rule. The importance of these assumptions in determining the normative properties of each rule can be seen easily by considering the consequences of applying each rule to the "wrong" type of issue.

6.7   The consequences of applying the rules to the "wrong" issues

6.7.1   *Deciding improvements in allocative efficiency via majority rule*

On an issue that all favor, nearly one-half of the votes are "wasted" under majority rule. A coalition of the committee's members could benefit from this by redefining the issues to increase their benefits at the expense of noncoalition members. In the town meeting example, one could easily envisage a reverse scenario. An initial proposal to finance fire protection via a proportional property tax is made.

---

[14] Buchanan and Tullock (1962, p. 253) and Rae (1969, pp. 52–3).

Table 6.1. *Assumptions favoring the majority and unanimity rules*

Assumption	Majority rule	Unanimity rule
1. Nature of the game[a]	Conflict, zero sum	Cooperative, positive sum
2. Nature of issues	Redistributions, property rights (some benefit, some lose)	Allocative efficiency improvements (public goods, externality elimination)
	Mutually exclusive issues of a single dimension[b]	Issues with potentially several dimensions and from which all can benefit[c]
3. Intensity	Equal on all issues[d]	No assumption made
4. Method of forming committee	Involuntary; members are exogenously or randomly brought together[e]	Voluntary; individuals of common interests and like preferences join[f]
5. Conditions of exit	Blocked, expensive[g]	Free
6. Choice of issues	Exogenously or impartially proposed[h]	Proposed by committee members[i]
7. Amendment of issues	Excluded, or constrained to avoid cycles[j]	Endogenous to committee process[i]

[a] Buchanan and Tullock (1962, p. 253); Buchanan (1966, pp. 32–3).
[b] Barry (1965, pp. 312–14); Rae (1975, pp. 1286–91).
[c] Buchanan and Tullock (1962, p. 80); Wicksell (1896, pp. 87–96).
[d] Rae (1969, p. 41, n. 6); Kendall (1941, p. 117); Buchanan and Tullock (1962, pp. 128–30).
[e] Rae (1975, pp. 1277–8).
[f] Wicksell (1896, pp. 87–96); Buchanan (1949). This assumption is common to all contractarian theories of the state, of course.
[g] Rae (1975, p. 1293).
[h] This assumption is implicit in the impartiality assumed by Rae (1969) and Taylor (1969) in their proofs, and in Barry's example (1965, in particular on p. 313).
[i] Wicksell (1896); Kendall (1941, p. 109).
[j] Implicit.

All favor the proposal and it would pass under the unanimity rule. But the town meeting now makes decisions under majority rule. The town's wealthiest citizens caucus and propose a lump-sum tax on all property owners. This proposal is opposed as being regressive by the less well-to-do members of the community, but it manages to secure a majority in its favor when placed against the proportional tax proposal. A majority coalition of the rich has succeeded in combining the provision of fire protection with a regressive tax on the poor. Wicksell's (1896, p. 95) belief that the unanimity rule would favor the poor was probably based on similar considerations.

But there are other ways in which de facto redistribution can take place under majority rule. A coalition of the residents of the north side of the town might form and propose that the provision of fire protection for the entire town be combined with the construction of a park on the north side, both to be financed out of a proportional tax on the entire community.[15] On the assumption that the southsiders do not benefit

[15] This example resembles Tullock's (1959) example in his demonstration that majority rule can lead to *over*expenditure in government, as discussed earlier.

from the park, this proposal would redistribute income from the southsiders to the northsiders just as clearly as a proposal to lower the taxes of the northsiders and raise the taxes of the southsiders would.

Thus, under majority rule, a process of issue proposal and amendment internal to the committee can be expected to convert purely positive-sum games of achieving allocational efficiency into games that are a combination of an allocational change and a redistribution. As Buchanan and Tullock (1962, pp. 190–2) have shown, when logrolling games allow side payments, the redistribution of wealth for and against any proposal will balance out. In logrolling games where direct side payments are not allowed, the exact values of the net income transfers are more difficult to measure. Nevertheless, when stable coalitions cannot be formed, the dynamic process of issue redefinition under majority rule to produce winning and losing coalitions of nearly equal size and differing composition can be expected to result in essentially zero *net* redistribution in the long run. Riker's assumption that all politics is a zero-sum game of pure redistribution might characterize *the long-run redistributive aspects of the outcomes* of the political process under majority rule.

This potential of majority rule must be stressed. The redistributive properties of majority rule can have a dynamic such that the winning majority only barely defeats the losing majority, thus justifying Rae's assumption that the probability that one favors the winning issue equals the probability that one favors the losing issue. Add to that the equal intensity assumption that Rae makes, and May's axioms build in, and we have the expected utility gains for the winners on any issue equaling the expected utility losses of the losers. Thus, the assumptions underlying the normative properties of majority rule imply that there are no *net* expected utility gains from the passage of any issue. The game is zero sum in expected utilities as well as dollar payoffs. But then why play the game? The normative assumptions building a case for majority rule when applied to any issue pair undermine its use in the long run. This feature of majority rule may help explain why some observers like Brittan (1975) are frustrated with the long-run benefits to society from majority rule democracy.

We have seen that the redistributive characteristics of majority rule can make stable winning coalitions difficult to maintain and can lead to cycles. If a stable, winning coalition can form, however, the transaction costs of cycling and of forming and destroying coalitions can be greatly reduced or eliminated. If committee members are free to propose and amend issues, a stable majority coalition can engage in continual redistribution from the losing committee members. This "tyranny of the majority" outcome may be even more undesirable than a futile, but more or less impartial, redistribution emerging under a perpetual cycle (Buchanan, 1954a). Stratmann's (1996) tests for the presence of cycling in the U.S. Congress, discussed in the previous chapter, suggest that such a stable, tyrannous majority exists there, at least on federal grants.

Thus, implicit in the arguments supporting majority rule we see the assumption that no stable majority coalition forms to tyrannize over the minority, and a zero-transaction-costs assumption, analogous to the zero-decision-time assumption supporting the unanimity rule. The issue proposal process is to be established so that cycles either cannot form or, if they do, they add a purely redistributive component to a set of allocational efficiency decisions that are predetermined or somehow unaffected by the cycling-redistribution process. Whether this process of issue redefinition, coalition formation, and cycling results in any net welfare gains remains an open question.

6.7.2   *Deciding redistribution by unanimity*

Any issue over which there is unavoidable conflict is defeated under a unanimity rule. Redistribution of income and wealth, other than of the voluntary sort described in Chapter 3, and redefinitions of property rights are all blocked by this rule.

Critics of unanimity have found two consequences of this outcome particularly disturbing. First is the possibility that all progress halts.[16] The train cannot proceed until the five occupants of the car have reached a consensus on the smoking issue. Most technological progress leaves some people worse off. Indeed, almost any change in the economic or physical environment may make someone worse off. Even if the legalization of drugs would eliminate all associated crime and suffering, the few drug barons who profit from their illicit sale would be made worse off and would vote to block legalization.[17] Although in principle each proposed change, down to the choice of color of my tie, could be collectively decided with appropriate compensation paid to those injured, the decision costs of deciding these changes under a unanimity rule are obviously prohibitive. The decision costs objection to the unanimity rule reappears. In addition, as an implicit defense of majority rule, this criticism seems to involve the assumption that technological change, or those changes involving de facto redistributions of income and property rights, are impartial. The utility gain to any individual favoring a change equals the utility loss to an opponent. And, over time, these gains and losses are impartially distributed among the population. Behind this assumption is another, that the process by which issues come before the committee is such that it is impossible to amend them so they will benefit one group systematically at the expense of the others. Time and the environment impartially cast up issues involving changing property rights and redistribution, and the committee votes these issues up or down as they appear, using majority rule. All benefit in the long run from the efficiency gains inherent in allowing technological progress to continue unencumbered by deadlocks in the collective decision process.

The second concern about using the unanimity rule to decide redistribution and property rights is that the veto power this rule gives a minority benefits one particular minority, violating a generally held ethical norm. The abolition of slavery is blocked by the slave owners, the redistribution of income by the rich. If one group achieves a larger than average share of the community's income or wealth via luck, skill,

---

[16] See Reimer (1951), Barry (1965, p. 315), and Rae (1975, pp. 1274, 1282, 1286, 1292–3).

[17] This conservatism inherent in the unanimity rule would appear to be one of Rae's main arguments against it, as in his discussion of property rights drift in the smoking chimney example (1975, pp. 1287–93). As Tullock (1975) points out, however, these criticisms do not suffice as a justification for majority rule to decide this issue. The other assumptions we have discussed are needed.

or cunning, the unanimity rule ensures that this distribution cannot be upset by collective action of the community. Under the unanimity rule, those who gain from the maintenance of the status quo always succeed in preserving it.[18]

6.8   Conclusions

A follower of the debate over majority and unanimity rule could easily be forgiven for concluding that there is but one type of issue to be decided collectively, and one best rule for making collective decisions. Thus Wicksell (1896, p. 89) argues:

> If any public expenditure is to be approved . . . it must generally be assumed that this expenditure . . . is intended for an activity useful to the whole of society and so recognized by all classes without exception. If this were not so . . . I, for one, fail to see how the latter can be considered as satisfying a collective need in the proper sense of the word.

A similar position is inherent in all contractarian positions, as in John Locke (1939, p. 455, § 131).

> Men . . . enter into society . . . only with an intention in everyone the better to preserve himself, his liberty and property (for no rational creature can be supposed to change his condition with an intention to be worse), the power of the society, or legislative constituted by them, can never be supposed to extend farther than the common good, but is obliged to secure everyone's property.[19]

On the other extreme, we have Brian Barry (1965, p. 313):

> But a *political* situation is precisely one that arises when the parties are arguing not about mutually useful trades but about the legitimacy of one another's initial position. (Italics in original)

And in a similar vein William Riker (1962, p. 174):

> Most economic activity is viewed as a non-zero-sum game while the most important political activity is often viewed as zero-sum.

But, it should now be clear that the collective choice process is confronted with two fundamentally different types of collective decisions to resolve, corresponding to the distinction between allocation and redistribution decisions (Mueller, 1977). Some important political decisions involve potentially positive-sum game decisions to provide defense, police and fire protection, roads, environmental protection, and

---

[18]   Barry (1965, pp. 243–9); Rae (1975, pp. 1273–6, 1286).

[19]   Kendall (1941) depicted Locke as a strong defender of majority rule. The only explicit reason Locke (p. 422, § 98) gives for using the majority rule in place of unanimity is a sort of transaction cost problem of assembling everyone, analogous to the Wicksell-Buchanan-Tullock decisions cost rule for choosing some less-than-unanimity rule. In this sense, Locke is a consistent unanimitarian.

so on. These decisions are made neither automatically nor easily. It is similarly obvious that part of political decision making must and should concern itself with the basic questions of distribution and property. The inherent differences between the underlying characteristics of these two types of decisions suggest both that they should be treated separately conceptually and, as a practical matter, that they should be resolved by separate and different collective decision processes.

In some ways, it is an injustice to Wicksell to have quoted him in the present context, for it was one of Wicksell's important insights, and the most influential contribution to the subsequent development of the literature, to have recognized the distinction between allocation and redistribution decisions, and the need to treat these decisions with separate collective decision processes. Indeed, in some ways he was ahead of his modern critics, for he recognized not only that the distribution and allocation issues would have to be decided separately, but also that unanimity would have to give way to majority rule to resolve the distribution issues (1896, p. 109, note m). But Wicksell did not elaborate on how the majority rule would be used to settle distribution issues, and the entire normative argument for the use of the unanimity rule to decide allocation decisions is left to rest on the *assumption* that a just distribution has been determined prior to the start of collective decision making on allocation issues.

Unfortunately, none of the proponents of majority rule has elaborated on how the conditions required to achieve its desirable properties are established. Somewhat ironically, perhaps, the normative case for using majority rule to settle property rights and distributional issues rests as much on decisions taken *prior to* its application, as the normative case for using the unanimity rule for allocation decisions rests on an already determined just income distribution. The Rae-Taylor theorem presupposes a process that is impartial, in that each voter has an equal chance of winning on any issue and an equal expected gain (or loss) from a decision's outcome. Similar assumptions are needed to make a compelling normative case for May's neutrality and anonymity conditions. But what guarantees that these conditions will be met? Certainly they are not met in the parliaments of today, where issue proposals and amendments are offered by the parliamentary members, and the outcomes are some blend of cycles, manipulated agendas, and tyrannous majorities. To realize majority rule's potential for resolving property rights and redistribution issues, some new form of parliamentary committee is needed that satisfies the conditions that majority rule's proponents have assumed in its defense. A constitutional decision is required.

But what rule is used to establish this new committee? If unanimity is used, those favored by the status quo can potentially block the formation of this new committee, whose outcomes, although fair, would run counter to the status quo's interest. But if the majority rule is employed, a minority may dispute both the outcomes of the distribution process and the procedure by which it was established. What argument does one use to defend the justness of a redistribution decision emerging from a parliamentary committee to a minority that feels the procedure by which the committee was established was unfair and voted against it at that time? This question seems as legitimate when raised against a majority rule decision, whose justification rests on the fairness of the issue proposal process as it does when raised against a unanimity rule that rests its justification on some distant, unanimous agreement on property rights. At some point, the issue of how fairness is introduced into the decision process, and how it is agreed upon, must be faced.

We have run up against the infinite regress problem. The only satisfactory way out of this maze is to assume that at some point unanimous agreement on a set of rules and procedures was attained.[20] If this agreement established a parliamentary committee to function under the majority rule, then the outcomes from this committee could be defended on the grounds that all at one time must have agreed that this would be a fair way of resolving those types of issues that are allowed to come before the committee. This interpretation places the majority rule in a secondary position to the unanimity rule at this stage of the analysis and reopens the question of how unanimous agreement, now limited perhaps to establishing the parliamentary procedures to decide both distributional and allocation efficiency issues, is reached. We take up this question in Part V.

Bibliographical notes

The normative issues and literature regarding the simple majority rule are reviewed by Rae and Schickler (1997) and Young (1997). The most general generalization of the Condorcet jury theorem has been proved by Ben-Yashar and Nitzan (1997) who also reference much of the earlier literature. Sen (1970a, pp. 71–3) offers another proof of May's (1952) theorem, and Campbell (1982) presents a related result.

---

[20] See Buchanan and Tullock (1962, pp. 6–8).

CHAPTER 7

Simple alternatives to majority rule

My scheme is intended only for honest men.

Jean-Charles de Borda

Several alternatives to the majority rule have been proposed down through the years. Three of the newest and most complicated of these are presented in Chapter 8. Here we discuss some of the simpler proposals.

These voting procedures are usually not considered a means of revealing preferences on a public good issue, but a means of choosing a candidate for a given office. All issues cannot be chosen simultaneously. Only one of them can be. Although such choices are perhaps most easily envisaged in terms of a list of candidates for a vacant public office, the procedures might be thought of as being applied to a choice from among any set of mutually exclusive alternatives – such as points along the Pareto-possibility frontier.

7.1   The alternative voting procedures defined

Majority rule: Choose the candidate who is ranked first by more than half of the voters.

Majority rule, runoff election: If one of the m candidates receives a majority of first-place votes, this candidate is the winner. If not, a second election is held between the two candidates receiving the most first-place votes on the first ballot. The candidate receiving the most votes on the second ballot is the winner.

Plurality rule: Choose the candidate who is ranked first by the largest number of voters.

Condorcet criterion: Choose the candidate who defeats all others in pairwise elections using majority rule.

The Hare system: Each voter indicates the candidate he ranks *highest* of the m candidates. Remove from the list of candidates the one ranked highest by the fewest voters. Repeat the procedure for the remaining $m - 1$ candidates. Continue until only one candidate remains. Declare this candidate the winner.

The Coombs system: Each voter indicates the candidate he ranks *lowest* of the m candidates. Remove from the list of candidates the one ranked lowest by the most voters. Repeat the procedure for the remaining $m - 1$

147

candidates. Continue until only one candidate remains. Declare this candidate the winner.

Approval voting: Each voter votes for the k candidates ($1 \leq k \leq m$) he ranks highest of the m candidates, where k can vary from voter to voter. The candidate with the most votes is the winner.

The Borda count: Give each of the m candidates a score of 1 to m based on the candidate's ranking in a voter's preference ordering; that is, the candidate ranked first receives m points, the second one $m - 1, \ldots$, the lowest-ranked candidate one point. The candidate with the highest number of points is declared the winner.

7.2   The procedures compared – Condorcet efficiency

This array of procedures is already lengthy and we could easily add to the list, although these cover the most frequently discussed procedures. Each has a certain intuitive appeal. How can one decide which is best?

There are several criteria for defining "best." First, we might define the axiomatic equivalents to each procedure, as we did with majority rule in Chapter 6, and compare the procedures on the basis of their axiomatic properties. These axioms are often rather abstract, however, and thus it may be somewhat difficult to declare procedure A superior to B just by looking at its axiomatic properties. We might declare one property most important, and compare the procedures on the basis of their ability to realize this property. The literature has proceeded in both ways, and we shall discuss the procedures in both ways.

The first of the axioms May (1952) requires of a voting procedure is that it is *decisive*; that is, it must pick a winner. Majority rule satisfies this criterion when there are but two candidates, a restriction May imposed on the problem. Choosing from a pair of alternatives is, however, the simplest *choice* one can conceptualize, and all of the above procedures select the same winner when $m = 2$. Interesting cases involve $m \geq 3$. With $m > 2$ no candidate may receive a majority of first-place votes, and no candidate may defeat all others in pairwise contests. Thus, when $m > 2$, both majority rule and the Condorcet criterion may declare no candidate a winner. Each of the other procedures will pick a winner.[1] Thus, for those who, on the basis of the arguments of Chapter 6, feel the majority rule ought to be the community's decision rule, interest in the other procedures arises only when $m > 2$.

Although the other procedures always pick a winner, even when a Condorcet winner does not exist, they do not always choose the Condorcet winner when one does exist. Table 7.1 presents a set of preference orderings for five voters in which X is the winner under the plurality rule, although Y is a Condorcet winner. Since a single vote for one's most preferred candidate is a possible strategy choice for voters under approval voting, X might also win under this procedure with the preference orderings of Table 7.1.

---

[1] We ignore ties. With large numbers of voters, ties are unlikely. The Borda count can easily be changed to accommodate ties in rankings (Black, 1958, pp. 61–4).

Table 7.1.

V_1	V_2	V_3	V_4	V_5
X	X	Y	Z	W
Y	Y	Z	Y	Y
Z	Z	W	W	Z
W	W	X	X	X

In Table 7.2, X is the Condorcet winner, while Y would be the winner by the Borda count. In Table 7.3, X is again the Condorcet winner, while issue W wins under the Hare system. Under each of the procedures other than majority rule, a winner may be chosen which is not the Condorcet winner even when the latter exists.

If one finds the properties of majority rule most attractive, then failure to select the Condorcet winner when one exists may be regarded as a serious deficiency of a procedure. One way to evaluate the different procedures is to compute the percentages of the time that a Condorcet winner exists and is selected by a given procedure. Merrill (1984, 1985) has made these percentage calculations and named them Condorcet efficiencies, that is, the efficiency of a procedure in actually selecting the Condorcet winner when one exists. Table 7.4 reports the results from simulations of an electorate of 25 voters with randomly allocated utility functions and various numbers of candidates.[2]

The first six rows report the Condorcet efficiencies for six of the procedures defined in Section 7.1. Voters are assumed to maximize expected utility under approval voting by voting for all candidates whose utilities exceed the mean of the candidates for that voter (Merrill, 1981). With two candidates, all procedures choose the Condorcet winner with efficiency of 100. The efficiency of all procedures is under 100 percent with three candidates. The biggest declines in efficiency in going from two to three candidates are for the plurality and approval voting procedures. When the number of candidates is as large as ten, the six procedures divide into three groups based on their Condorcet efficiency indexes: the Hare, Coombs, and Borda procedures all achieve about 80 percent efficiency; majority rule with one runoff and approval voting achieve about 60 percent efficiency; and the plurality rule selects the Condorcet winner only 42.6 percent of the time.

Table 7.2.

V_1	V_2	V_3	V_4	V_5
X	X	X	Y	Y
Y	Y	Y	Z	Z
Z	Z	Z	X	X

---

[2] Merrill (1984, p. 28, n. 4) reports that Condorcet efficiency is not very sensitive to the number of voters.

Table 7.3.

V_1	V_2	V_3	V_4	V_5
Y	W	X	Y	W
X	Z	Z	Z	X
Z	X	W	X	Z
W	Y	Y	W	Y

It is implausible to assume that an electorate would go to the polls nine separate times, as would be required under either the Hare or Coombs systems with 10 candidates. Therefore if either of these procedures were actually used, as a practical matter one would undoubtedly simply ask voters to write down their complete rankings of the candidates, and use a computer to determine a winner following the prescribed rule. Thus, the informational requirements of the Hare, Coombs, and Borda procedures are identical; they differ only in how they process this information. Given that they rely on the same information sets, it is perhaps not surprising that they perform about the same.

Of the six procedures listed in Table 7.4, the runoff and plurality procedures are the only ones in common use today. Thus, another way to look at the results of Table 7.4 is to calculate the gains in Condorcet efficiency in abandoning the plurality or runoff rule in favor of one of the other four procedures. The biggest gains obviously come in going to the Hare, Coombs, or Borda procedures, particularly if the number of candidates exceeds five. But much more information is demanded of the voter at the election. Approval voting might then be compared with the runoff and plurality system as a relatively simple procedure with Condorcet efficiency properties that exceed those of the plurality rule and approach those of the runoff system as the number of candidates expands. An important advantage of approval voting over the majority rule–runoff procedure is that approval voting requires that voters go to the polls only once (Fishburn and Brams, 1981a,b).

Table 7.4. *Condorcet efficiency for a random society (25 voters)*

Voting system	Number of candidates				
	3	4	5	7	10
Runoff	96.2	90.1	83.6	73.5	61.3
Plurality	79.1	69.4	62.1	52.0	42.6
Hare	96.2	92.7	89.1	84.8	77.9
Coombs	96.3	93.4	90.2	86.1	81.1
Approval	76.0	69.8	67.1	63.7	61.3
Borda	90.8	87.3	86.2	85.3	84.3
Social utility maximizer	84.6	80.2	77.9	77.2	77.8

Source: Merrill (1984, p. 28).

Table 7.5. *Utilitarian efficiency for a random society (25 voters)*

Voting system	Number of candidates				
	3	4	5	7	10
Runoff	89.5	83.8	80.5	75.6	67.6
Plurality	83.0	75.0	69.2	62.8	53.3
Hare	89.5	84.7	82.4	80.5	74.9
Coombs	89.7	86.7	85.1	83.1	82.4
Approval	95.4	91.1	89.1	87.8	87.0
Borda	94.8	94.1	94.4	95.4	95.9
Condorcet	93.1	91.9	92.0	93.1	94.3

Source: Merrill (1984, p. 39).

7.3 The procedures compared – utilitarian efficiency

Although the relative achievement of Condorcet efficiency may be an important property for those who favor majority rule as the voting procedure, for others it may not be the decisive factor in choosing a rule. Consider again Table 7.2. Issue X is the Condorcet winner. But this voting situation is clearly one that has some characteristics of a "tyranny of the majority." Under majority rule, the first three voters are able to impose their candidate on the other two, who rank him last. Y, on the other hand, is more of a "compromise" candidate, who ranks *relatively* high on all preference scales, and for this reason Y might be the "best" choice from among the three candidates. Y would be chosen under the Borda procedure, and under approval voting if any two of the voters (V_1, V_2, V_3) thought highly enough of Y to vote for both X and Y under approval voting, and not just for X. The closer Y stands to X, and the farther it stands from Z, the more likely it is that one of these voters will vote (X, Y) under approval voting and not just X.

An alternative normative criterion to that of Condorcet efficiency for a voting procedure is that it should maximize a utilitarian welfare function of, say, the form

$$W = \sum_i U_i, \tag{7.1}$$

where the U_is are cardinal interpersonally comparable utility indexes for each voter i defined over the issue set. The bottom row of Table 7.4 reveals that the candidate whose choice would maximize (7.1) is the Condorcet winner only about 80 percent of the time. How, then, do the six procedures measure up against this utilitarian yardstick?

Table 7.5 presents further simulation results for a 25-person electorate. Note first that the Condorcet winner measures up rather well against the utilitarian maximum W criterion. But so, too, does the Borda count. It achieves a higher aggregate utility level for any number of candidates greater than two than the Condorcet winner would, if the Condorcet winner could always be found, or greater than any of the other five procedures would. Bordley (1983) presents analogous results. Although not providing full cardinal utility information, as is needed to achieve

100 percent efficiency in maximizing W, the Borda count, by providing a much richer informational base, is able to come fairly close to this objective.

Of additional interest in Table 7.5 is the performance of approval voting relative to the informationally more demanding Coombs and Hare systems. Given its performance by this utilitarian yardstick and its greater simplicity, we confine further attention to the Borda and approval voting procedures.

7.4   The Borda count

7.4.1   *Axiomatic properties*

Judged by the simulation results of Section 7.3, the Borda count would appear to be a potentially attractive voting procedure. What are its other normative properties?

Suppose we were to proceed as May (1952) did and seek an axiomatic representation of the Borda count. The first axiom May imposed was decisiveness – the procedure must be able to pick a winner from a binary pair. Some property like decisiveness is obviously attractive for any voting procedure. We can do this more formally by saying that we want the voting procedure to define a set of best elements, which we shall define as a choice set (Sen, 1970a, p. 10).

Definition of choice set: *An element x in S is a best element of S with respect to the binary relation R if and only if for every y in S, $x R y$. The set of best elements in S is called its choice set $C(S, R)$.*

Thus, we wish to have a voting rule that defines a choice set. Young (1974) proved that the Borda count was the only voting rule that defines a choice set and satisfies the four properties of neutrality, cancellation, faithfulness, and consistency.

As in May's theorem, the neutrality property is a form of impartiality with respect to issues or candidates. The names of the candidates or the nature of the issues do not matter.

The cancellation property, like anonymity in May's theorem, is a form of impartiality toward voters. Any voter i's statement "x is preferred to y" is balanced or canceled by any other voter j's statement "y is preferred to x"(Young, 1974, p. 45). What determines the social ordering of x and y is the number of voters who prefer x to y versus the number preferring y to x. The identities of the voters do not matter.

The faithfulness property is the totally innocuous condition that the voting procedure, when applied to a society consisting of only one individual, chooses as a best element that voter's most preferred element, that is, is faithful to that voter's preferences.

The above properties seem inherently reasonable. Indeed, they are all satisfied by majority rule. The more novel property is consistency.

Consistency: Let N_1 and N_2 be two groups of voters who are to select an alternative from the set S. Let C_1 and C_2 be the respective sets of alternatives

Table 7.6.

	N_1			N_2		
V_1	V_2	V_3	V_4	V_5	V_6	V_7
z	x	y	z	z	x	x
x	y	z	x	x	y	z
y	z	x	y	y	z	y

that the two groups select using voting procedure B. Then if C_1 and C_2 have any elements in common (i.e., $C_1 \cap C_2$ is not empty), then the winning issue under procedure B when these two subgroups are brought together ($N_T = N_1 \cup N_2$) is contained in this common set of elements ($C_T = C_1 \cap C_2$).

This consistency property has obvious intuitive appeal. If two groups of voters agree on an alternative when choosing separately from a set of alternatives, they should agree on the same alternative when they are combined.

Majority rule also satisfies the consistency condition when the issue space and voter preferences are such as to ensure that a Condorcet winner always exists (Young, 1974, p. 44). Suppose, for example, that all issues were single dimensional and all voter preferences single peaked. Let m_1 be the median voter outcome for a committee of size N_1, where N_1 is odd. Let the interval $m_2 - m_2'$ be the choice set under majority rule for another committee of size N_2, where N_2 is even. If m_1 falls in the interval $m_2 - m_2'$, then m_1 will be the majority rule winner if the two committees combine, since one voter from N_1 has m_1 as a most preferred point, and $[(N_1 - 1)/2 + N_2/2]$ voters have preference peaks to the left of m_1 and the same number have peaks to the right of m_1. In this situation, majority rule satisfies the consistency property.

But we cannot always be sure that the conditions guaranteeing a Condorcet winner are satisfied. When they are not, then a cycle can arise of the form $x R y R z R x$. If in such situations we define the choice set as (x, y, z), the majority rule violates the consistency property, as the following example from Plott (1976, pp. 562–3) illustrates.

Let N_1 and N_2 be groups of voters with preference orderings as in Table 7.6. For N_1, a cycle over x, y, and z exists and we define the choice set as (x, y, z). For N_2, x and z tie and both beat y so its choice set is (x, z). The intersection of these two choice sets is (x, z) and the consistency criterion requires that x and z tie under majority rule when N_1 and N_2 are combined. But they will not tie. The committee $N_1 + N_2$ selects z as the unique winner using majority rule, thus violating the consistency condition.

An alternative way to look at the problem is to note that those versions of majority rule that do satisfy the consistency criterion, like the Condorcet principle, do not always define a nonempty choice set. Thus, if in going from two to three or more elements in our issue set, we wish the voting rule to continue to be capable of

Table 7.7.

V_1	V_2	V_3	V_4	V_5
X	X	X	Z	Z
Y	Y	Y	X	X
Z	Z	Z	W	W
W	W	W	Y	Y

picking a winner, and we wish to have the properties of neutrality, cancellation, faithfulness, and consistency, more information is required than is provided under the simple majority rule. Young's theorem demonstrates that the information needed is the complete preference ordering of every voter over the full issue set.[3]

7.4.2 *The Borda count and the "tyranny of the majority"*

In Section 7.3 we illustrated how the simple majority and plurality rules can lead to a "tyranny of the majority" in that a majority coalition gets its first choice over an alternative ranked relatively high by all voters. This sort of tyranny of the majority can be generalized.

Consider the set of voter preferences in Table 7.7. A coalition of the first three voters can impose its preferences on the community under the simple majority rule regardless of how the issues are presented to the voters. If the voters must choose from all four issues, the coalition imposes its first choice X. If the collective choice is restricted to the issues Y, Z, and W, the coalition imposes its first choice, Y, from among these three issues. Regardless of which combination of issues is presented to the voters, the coalition of the first three voters always gets its most preferred outcome.

X would also win under the Borda count if it were among the issues presented to the voters, but if for some reason X were an infeasible option and the voters had to choose among Y, Z, and W, Z would win under the Borda count. By taking into account more information about voter preferences, the Borda count can break a majority coalition's power to impose its will on the community over all possible sets of choices. Baharad and Nitzan (2001) prove that scoring rules like the Borda count, which take into account the preferences of voters over the full set of issues, are

---

[3] Nitzan and Rubinstein (1981) have replaced Young's faithfulness property with a monotonicity condition and proved an equivalence between these four axioms and the Borda count, where the Borda count now provides a complete ranking of all of the alternatives. The monotonicity condition can be stated as follows:

> **Monotonicity:** Let x and y be two distinct alternatives, and U and U' two sets of profiles of voter preferences. Suppose that the voting rule ranks x at least as good as y, $x R y$, under both sets of profiles U and U'. Let z be a third alternative such that for voter i, z is preferred to x ($z P_i x$) in U, but $x P_i z$ in U'. Then the voting rule must designate x as strictly preferred to y ($x P y$) in U'.

This monotonicity condition demands that an alternative's relationship relative to a second alternative be strengthened if its status improves against some other third alternative.

superior to rules like the plurality and simple majority rules with respect to avoiding this sort of tyranny of the majority.[4]

7.4.3 *The Borda count and strategic manipulation*

Although the Borda count has axiomatic properties that seem at least the equal of majority rule, and it performs well when measured by the yardsticks of the utilitarian welfare function or of avoiding tyrannous majorities, its Achilles' heel is commonly felt to be its vulnerability to strategic behavior (Pattanaik, 1974; M. Sen, 1984). Consider again Table 7.2. Issue Y wins using the Borda count when all voters vote sincerely. If the first three voters were to state their rankings of the issues as XP_iZP_iY, however, the Borda count would select X as the winning issue. Thus, an incentive exists for voters 1 to 3 to misstate their preferences, *if they know the preferences of other voters and expect the other voters to vote sincerely.*

With three or more issues *all* voting procedures can be manipulated by one voter's misstating her preferences, however, so the relevant question to ask of a voting procedure is whether it is *more* susceptible to manipulation than other procedures.[5] Saari (1990) has attempted to answer this question by examining all possible preference orderings with committees of three or more members, and three or more issues. Saari constructs a measure of *micro*manipulability, which is the percentage of the situations in which one person or a small coalition could make themselves better off by misstating their preferences under a given voting rule. He finds that among the most popular choices of voting rules, like those examined in this chapter, the Borda count performs the best, either minimizing or coming close to minimizing the likelihood of successful manipulation.

If one group of voters can behave strategically, so can another. If voters 4 and 5 in Table 7.2 suspect that the other voters are trying to manipulate X's victory, they can try to avoid having their worst alternative, X, win by misstating their preferences as $Z P Y P X$. With both groups of voters now misstating their preferences, Z wins under the Borda rule. Thus, voters 1 to 3 take a chance when they raise Z above Y in their stated preference orderings of bringing about not X's victory, but Z's. The Borda count satisfies a nonnegativity or monotonicity condition (J.H. Smith, 1973). Lifting Y above Z in a voter's stated preference, ordering either raises or leaves unchanged Y's position in the social ordering, while having the reverse effect on Z. A risk-averse voter, uncertain of the relative chances of X, Y, and Z winning, either due to ignorance of other voter preferences or uncertainty about their possible strategic behavior, maximizes her expected utility under the Borda procedure by honestly stating her true ranking of the three issues.

As the electorate grows large the likelihood of a voter's knowing the preferences of the others grows small, and thus so do the chances of successfully manipulating

---

[4] The properties of another scoring rule – point voting – are addressed in the next chapter.

[5] The main theorems about the potential for strategic manipulation of all voting procedures were first proved by Gibbard (1973) and Satterthwaite (1975). Their results are discussed in Chapter 24.

the outcome. Moreover, the probability of any one voter's vote being decisive also declines, of course. Thus, the likelihood of successful strategic manipulation of the outcomes under the Borda count will decline as the number of voters increases.[6]

7.5   Approval voting

With large numbers of alternatives, the Borda procedure has the possible disadvantage of complexity. The voter must list her complete ranking of the set of alternatives, which with fairly large issue sets could discourage individuals from voting.

In contrast, approval voting asks voters only to draw a line through their preference ordering so as to separate the candidates into those they approve of and those they do not. If the candidates are relatively evenly spaced from one another in terms of expected utility payoffs, then this line will divide the set of candidates roughly into two equal-sized groups (Merrill, 1981). Voters need not concern themselves with how the two sets of candidates stack up against one another within the approval and disapproval sets.

When the number of candidates is few, or voters are indifferent between various pairs of candidates, approval voting also has some advantages over other procedures in discouraging strategic behavior. Brams and Fishburn (1978) have proven that when voter preferences are dichotomous in the sense that it is possible for every voter i to divide the set of all candidates S into two subsets, S_{i1} and S_{i2}, such that i is indifferent among all candidates in S_{i1}, and among all in S_{i2}, then under approval voting there is a single undominated strategy – vote for all candidates in the subset S_{ij} who are ranked higher than those in the other subset. Approval voting is the only voting procedure to have a unique, undominated strategy for all possible dichotomous preference relationships.

When voter preferences are trichotomous – that is, candidates are divided into three indifference groups, S_{i1}, S_{i2}, S_{i3} – then the only undominated strategies under approval voting are to vote sincerely for either (1) all candidates in the most preferred group or (2) all candidates in the two most preferred groups. Approval voting is the only voting system that is sincere in this sense for every possible trichotomous preference relationship.

When voter preferences are multichotomous – that is, four or more indifference groups are required – no voting procedure is sincere or strategy-proof for all possible multichotomous preference relationships.

Since all procedures discussed in this chapter are identical to majority rule when there are only two candidates, the importance of the results for dichotomous candidates rests on the plausibility of assuming voter indifference between various pairs of candidates in a multicandidate race. On this issue opinions differ (Niemi, 1984). Approval voting proved to be more susceptible to micromanipulation than the Borda count in Saari's (1990) comparisons.

---

[6] Holding the number of alternatives fixed. Conversely, the potential for manipulation rises as the number of alternatives increases (Nitzan, 1985).

Table 7.8. *Delegate totals under various decision rules*

Candidate	Plurality rule	Double election	Condorcet choice	Borda count	Adjusted[a] Borda count
McGovern	1,307	766	766	766	584
Muskie	271	788	869	869	869

[a] Adjusted Borda count is modified to allow for ties. See Black (1958, pp. 61–4).
Source: Joslyn (1976, Table 5, p. 12).

Beyond whatever advantages it possesses in discouraging strategic behavior, however, approval voting deserves serious attention as a possible substitute for the plurality and majority rule–runoff rules because of its superior performance, as judged by the Condorcet or utilitarian efficiency criteria, and greater simplicity than the Hare, Coombs, Borda, and to some extent majority rule–runoff procedures.

7.6 Implications for electoral reform

State presidential nominating elections and elections of representatives to the House and Senate in the United States are based on a first-past-the-post criterion, that is, the plurality rule. Yet the plurality rule scores worst by the Condorcet and utilitarian efficiency criteria. This observation has led to recommendations that an alternative rule be introduced, particularly in presidential primaries where the number of candidates may be large (Kellett and Mott, 1977).

The possible significance of such a reform is revealed in Joslyn's (1976) study of the 1972 Democratic presidential primaries. Joslyn argued that the plurality rule favored extremist candidate George McGovern, who was the first choice of a plurality of voters in many states but was ranked relatively low by many other voters, over "middle-of-the-road" Edmund Muskie, who was ranked relatively high by a large number of voters. Joslyn's most striking result is his recalculation of final delegate counts under the various voting rules presented in Table 7.8 (double election is a two-step runoff procedure). The interesting feature of this table is the dramatic increase in Muskie's delegate strength under *any* of the voting procedures other than the plurality rule.[7]

One might argue that Muskie *should* have been the Democratic party's nominee in 1972 and that, therefore, one of the other voting procedures is preferable to the plurality rule. Muskie would have had a better chance to defeat Nixon than McGovern, and McGovern's supporters would probably have preferred a Muskie victory to a McGovern defeat in the final runoff against Nixon. And, with the infinite wisdom of hindsight, one can argue that "the country" would have been better off with a Muskie victory over Nixon.

The rules of the game do matter.

---

[7] Muskie would undoubtedly also have faired much better against McGovern had approval voting been used. See Kellett and Mott (1977) and Brams and Fishburn (1978, pp. 840–2).

Bibliographical notes

The seminal discussion of the various voting rules is by Black (1958, pp. 55–75). Black also presents biographical discussions of the work of the Marquis de Condorcet (pp. 159–80) and Jean-Charles de Borda (pp. 156–9, 178–90). See also Young's 1988 article and his 1997 survey.

The Borda count is also discussed by Plott (1976, pp. 560–3), Sen (1982, pp. 187–7, 239–40, 376–7), and Schwartz (1986, pp. 179–81). Saari (1994) develops a new geometric methodology to examine the properties of voting rules. In addition to reestablishing many of the known properties of the various voting rules, like cycling under the majority rule, Saari uncovers several attractive features of the Borda count with his new methodology.

The properties of approval voting were first discussed by Brams (1975, ch. 3) with important extensions presented by Brams and Fishburn (1978) and Fishburn and Brams (1981a,b). The major results on approval voting are pulled together in their book (Brams and Fishburn, 1983).

CHAPTER 8

Complicated alternatives to majority rule

In this Method [the Method of Marks], a certain number of marks is fixed, which each elector shall have at his disposal; he may assign them all to one candidate, or divide them among several candidates, in proportion to their eligibility; and the candidate who gets the greatest total of marks is the winner.

This method would, I think, be absolutely perfect, if only each elector wished to do all in his power to secure the election of *that candidate who should be the most generally acceptable*, even if that candidate should *not* be the one of his own choice: in this case he would be careful to make the marks exactly represent his estimate of the relative eligibility of *all* the candidates, even of those he *least* desired to see elected; and the desired result would be secured.

But we are not sufficiently unselfish and public-spirited to give any hope of this result being attained. Each elector would feel that it was *possible* for each other elector to assign the entire number of marks to his favorite candidate, giving to all the other candidates zero: and he would conclude that, in order to give his *own* favorite candidate any chance of success, he must do the same for him.

Charles Dodgson (Lewis Carroll)

In 1954, in what has become the classic paper on public goods, Paul Samuelson both defined the necessary conditions for Pareto optimality in the presence of public goods and cast a pall over the field of public economics by asserting that no procedure could be constructed to reveal the information on preferences required to determine the quantities of public goods that would satisfy the Pareto-optimality condition. In a section entitled "Impossibility of Decentralized Spontaneous Solution," Samuelson (1954, p. 182) stated that *"no decentralized pricing system can serve to determine optimally these levels of collective consumption"* (italics in original).

So influential was this article, that for a generation economists merely repeated Samuelson's words and lamented the absence of a satisfactory procedure for revealing individual preferences. And with good reason. Traditional voting schemes seemed vulnerable to the transaction costs and strategic incentives inherent in the unanimity rule, or the paucity of information and onus of compulsion characterizing less-than-unanimity rules, most notably the majority rule.

But then in the seventies, a revolution suddenly erupted. New procedures began to appear one after the other, which claimed to have solved the preference revelation problem. As so often happens in the mechanical arts, once one scientist demonstrated that the impossible might be possible, others were moved to follow, and a wave of developments ensued. In this chapter we review this literature, focusing upon three

Table 8.1.

Voter	Issue		
	P	S	Tax
A	30		20
B		40	0
C	20		10
Total	50	40	30

rather different types of procedures. We begin with the procedure that has attracted the greatest attention.

8.1   The demand-revealing process

8.1.1   *The mechanics of the process*

This procedure was first described by Vickrey in 1961, although he attributed the idea to "an interesting suggestion" Lerner threw out in *Economics of Control* (1944). Consequently, the procedure might be said to antedate Samuelson's paper by 10 years. But neither Lerner nor Vickrey applied the procedure to the problem of revealing preferences for public goods, and its potential importance was not recognized until the appearance of papers by Clarke (1971, 1972) and Groves (1973).

To understand how the procedure works, consider the collective choice between the two issues P and S. Assume a committee of three with preferences as given in Table 8.1. Voter A expects to be the equivalent of $30 better off from the victory of P, voter C $20, and voter B prefers S by the equivalent of $40. The procedure for selecting a winner is to first ask all three voters to state in dollars the amount of benefits they expect from the victory of their preferred issue, and then add these figures, declaring the issue with the most expected benefits the winner. In the present example this is P, since it promises gains of 50 to voters A and C, whereas S benefits B by only 40.

The voters are induced to declare their true preferences for the issues by announcing that they will be charged a certain tax, depending on the responses they make and their impact on the final outcome. This tax is calculated in the following way: the dollar votes of all other voters are added up and the outcome determined. The voter-in-question's dollar votes are now added in to see if the outcome is changed. If it is not, he pays no tax. If it is, he pays a tax equal to the *net* gains expected from the victory of the other issue in the absence of his vote. Thus, a voter pays a tax only when his vote is decisive in changing the outcome, and then pays not the amount he has declared, but the amount needed to balance the declared benefits of the other voters on the two issues. The last column of Table 8.1 presents the taxes on the three voters. Without A, there are 40 dollar votes for S and 20 for P. A's vote is decisive in determining the outcome, and imposes a net cost of 20 on the other two voters, and that is A's tax. B's vote does not affect the outcome, and he pays no

Table 8.2.

Voter	Issue P	Issue S	Tax
A	30		10
B		40	0
C	20		0
A'	30		10
B'		40	0
C'	20		0
Total	100	80	20

tax. Without C's vote, S would again win, so C pays a tax equal to the net benefits the other voters would have received had he not voted ($40 - 30 = 10$).

Under the tax each voter has an incentive to reveal his true preferences for the two issues. Any amount of benefits from P that voter A declared equal to or greater than 21 would leave the collective decision, *and his tax*, unchanged. If he declared net benefits of less than 20, S would win, and A's tax would fall from 20 to 0, but his benefits of 30 would also disappear. A voter pays a tax only if his vote is decisive, and the tax he pays is always equal to or less than the benefits he receives. Thus, there is no incentive to understate one's gains, for then one risks foregoing a chance to cast the deciding vote at a cost less than the benefits. And there is no incentive to overstate one's preferences, since this incurs the risk of casting the decisive vote and receiving a tax above one's actual benefits, albeit less than one's declared benefits. The optimal strategy is honest revelation of preferences.

To maintain this desirable incentive property, the tax revenue raised to induce honest revelation of preferences cannot be returned to the voters in such a way as to affect their voting decision. The safest thing to do with the money to avoid distorting incentives is to waste it. But this implies that the outcome from the procedure will not be Pareto optimal (Groves and Ledyard, 1977a,b; Loeb, 1977). The amount by which the procedure falls short of Pareto optimality can be stated explicitly: it is the amount of revenue raised by the incentive tax. In the example above, this amount is substantial, equaling three times the net gains from collective action.

Fortunately, the amount of taxes raised under the demand-revealing procedure should decline as the number of voters increases (Tideman and Tullock, 1976, 1977). To see why this is so, consider Table 8.2, in which the preferences of three other voters, A', B', and C', identical to those of A, B, and C, have been included. The issue P still wins, of course, now by a surplus of 20. Voter C's tax has fallen from 10 to 0, however, and A's from 20 to 10. Without voter C, the net benefits on the two issues over the other voters are 0 (80 for P and 80 for S). Although his vote tips the outcome in favor of P, his gain of 20 does not come at the *net* expense of the other voters. So C pays no tax. A still pays a positive tax, but the amount has been reduced, since the net cost of his vote on all other voters has fallen. With the addition of three more voters (A'', B'', C'') with preferences identical to A, B, and C, the outcome would again not change, and the taxes on all voters would now be zero.

Thus, the collective decision of this committee of nine would be Pareto optimal. Although the procedure does allow for a weighing of intensities in determining the outcome, the effect of any one voter's preferences on the final outcome will dwindle, as with other voting procedures, as the number of voters increases. Since a voter's tax equals his impact on the other voters, it too dwindles as the size of the group increases.

Groves and Ledyard (1977c, p. 140) claim to be able to construct counterexamples in which the incentive tax surplus is arbitrarily large, and Kormendi (1979, 1980) has pressed the same point. But such examples rely on expanding the committee by adding equal numbers of voters who favor P and S. If the committee were equally divided between voters favoring P and voters favoring S, every vote might be decisive and the amount of tax revenue raised would be large, whereas the *net* social benefit would be very small. However, we would then have essentially a distributional issue, the Ps versus the Ss. For a pure public good that all favor, the incentive-tax revenue should vanish as n increases. For a rigorous demonstration, see Rob (1982).

The procedure can reveal individual demand schedules for a public good, from whence its name arises. We follow here the exposition of Tideman and Tullock (1976). Each individual is asked to report his complete demand schedule for the public good. These schedules are then vertically added to obtain the aggregate demand for the public good. The intersection of this schedule and the supply schedule for the good determines the quantity provided. If each individual has honestly reported his demand schedule, the procedure determines the Pareto-optimal quantity of public good, as defined by Samuelson (1954) and Bowen (1943).

Individuals are again induced to reveal their true preferences via a special tax imposed upon them. In fact, there are two taxes imposed upon the individual, one designed to cover the full costs of producing the public good and the other to ensure honest revelation of preferences. In our first example, the first of these two taxes was implicitly assumed to be part of the proposals P and S. Let us assume that the public good can be supplied at constant unit costs C, and that each voter is assigned a share of these costs, T_j, such that $\sum_{j=1}^{n} T_j = C$. These T_js are the first components of each individual's tax. The other component is computed in a way analogous to that used to assign each individual a tax in the preceding example. Namely, one first determines the quantity of public good that would be demanded in the absence of individual i's demand schedule and contribution to the public good's total costs. The quantity with his demand schedule and contribution is determined next. The difference represents the impact of this individual's preferences on the collective outcome. The cost to the other voters of the shift in quantity that recording his preferences brings about is the absolute value of the difference between the costs of producing these extra units and the sum of the individual demand schedules over these units. Thus, if i forces the community to consume more than it would have without his demand-schedule vote, the costs of the extra output will exceed their willingness to pay for it, and i is charged the difference. Conversely, if voter i causes the community to consume less than they would have, their aggregate demand for the extra units of public good will exceed the good's costs, and the

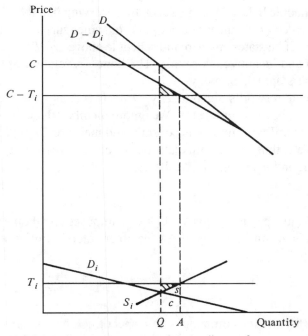

Figure 8.1. Some new processes for revealing preferences.

difference, the loss in consumers' surplus to the other voters, is charged to the ith voter.

The latter possibility is illustrated with the help of Figure 8.1. Omitting i's demand schedule, aggregate demand for the public good is $D - D_i$. Subtracting his preassigned tax share, the cost of the public good is $C - T_i$. With i's preferences removed, the community would purchase A. With i's preferences included, the community purchases Q, the quantity at which aggregate demand and supply are equal. The cost imposed on the other voters of this shift in outcomes is the difference between the amount that the other voters would be willing to pay for the extra units $(A - Q)$ and the taxes they would have to pay $(C - T_i)(A - Q)$ for these units, which is the cross-hatched triangle above the line $C - T_i$. This triangle represents the additional tax, apart from $T_i Q$, that the ith voter must pay.

That the ith voter's optimal strategy is to reveal his true demand schedule in the presence of this incentive tax becomes clear when we construct an effective supply schedule of the public good, S_i, to the ith voter, by subtracting the $D - D_i$ schedule from C. The intersection of the individual voter's demand for the public good, D_i, and this S_i schedule is for him the optimal quantity of public good, which, of course, is Q. By stating his demand schedule as D_i, voter i forces the community to consume Q instead of A, and thereby saves himself the rectangle $T_i(QA)$ in taxes. He must pay the incentive tax represented by the cross-hatched triangle below T_i, which equals the cross-hatched triangle above $C - T_i$, and loses the consumers' surplus represented by the quadrilateral, c. His net gain from forcing the community to Q rather than leaving it at A is thus the triangle s. That there is nothing to be gained by stating a demand schedule below D_i can be seen by observing that the triangle s vanishes at Q. To the left of Q, i's incentive tax plus consumer surplus loss would exceed his tax saving T_i. If he states any demand schedule above D_i, T_i exceeds his consumer surplus gain and incentive tax saving. The honest revelation of his true demand schedule D_i is i's optimal strategy.

To see how the procedure works algebraically, write $U_i(G)$ as voter i's utility from consuming G. Let t_i be i's incentive tax. We ignore income effects, so we can assume that the marginal utility of money is constant and measure $U_i(G)$ in dollar units. Voter i's objective is thus to maximize utility, U_i, net of i's share of the cost of the public good, T_iG, and incentive tax, t_i; that is,

$$O_i = U_i(G) - T_iG - t_i. \tag{8.1}$$

The incentive tax that i must pay is the cost that i's vote imposes on all other voters by bringing about G; it is the difference between the other voters' utilities at G and their cost shares:

$$t_i = \sum_{j \neq i}(T_jG - U_j(G)). \tag{8.2}$$

Substituting (8.2) into (8.1) and maximizing with respect to G, one obtains

$$dO_i/dG = U_i'(G) - T_i - \sum_{j \neq i}(T_j - U_j'(G)). \tag{8.3}$$

Setting (8.3) equal to zero, we can solve for the optimal G for i to state, given i's tax share T_i and the incentive tax t_i. Rearranging this first-order condition, we obtain the Samuelsonian condition for the Pareto-optimal provision of G:

$$\sum_i U_i'(G) = \sum_i T_i = C. \tag{8.4}$$

Note that although the quantity of the public good selected is Pareto optimal, it is also generally true that $U_i'(G) \neq T_i, i = 1, n$, as can also be seen in Figure 8.1. An important element of the procedure is that an individual's share of the cost of a public good is independent of his stated demand schedule. This independence is necessary to ensure the honest revelation of preferences. Only the (probably rather small) incentive tax, represented by the cross-hatched triangle in Figure 8.1, is directly related to the individual's reported demand schedule, and the funds raised here are to be wasted, or at least not returned in any systematic way to the payer.

The idea of a two-part tariff to ensure an efficient allocation of resources in industries characterized by economies of scale, or large fixed costs, has been around for some time. The most obvious examples are probably the electric and gas industries (see, e.g., Kahn, 1970, pp. 95–100). The principles underlying these pricing schemes are analogous to those of the demand-revealing process. A proportional charge is made to each customer for his use of the service, and an extra charge is made for the costs on other buyers that a customer's demand imposes at the peak (margin) of the system's capacity. Public goods are also characterized by high fixed costs, the joint supply property; and the demand-revealing process is thus a perhaps not-too-surprising, if somewhat long-awaited, extension of the idea of the two-part tariff into the public good area.

Green and Laffont (1977a) have demonstrated that the class of demand-revealing processes first developed by Groves (1973) in effect defines the full set of procedures of this type, of which the preceeding examples concern but one variant, for which honest revelation of preferences is the dominant strategy. That is, regardless of what message the other voters supply to the message-gathering agent, it is always an individual's optimal strategy to reveal his true preferences. This property of the procedure is dependent on an absence of interaction between an individual's fixed tax share, revealed demand schedule, and the revealed demand schedules of the other individuals. There is no way, direct or indirect, by which individuals can influence the taxes that they pay other than through the immediate effect of their revealed demand schedules. Thus, the procedure is a purely partial equilibrium approach that abstracts from any interactions among voters via income effects or other means.

Although honest preference revelations and the Samuelson efficiency conditions are ensured under the partial equilibrium variants of the demand-revealing process, budget balance is not, and so Pareto efficiency cannot be presumed. As already noted, the size of the total tax intake from the incentive tax is a matter of some controversy, and so, too, therefore the significance of the Pareto-inefficiency property. Groves and Ledyard (1977a) developed a general equilibrium version of the demand-revealing process in which budget balance is achieved. Each individual reports a quadratic approximation to his true demand function of the following form:

$$m_i = \beta_i G - \frac{\gamma}{2n} G^2, \tag{8.5}$$

where γ is a constant across all individuals, G is the quantity of public goods, and n is the number of consumers. The individual's tax is given as

$$T_i = a_i G^*(m) + \frac{\gamma}{2} \left[\left(\frac{n-1}{n} \right) (m_i - \mu_i)^2 - \sigma_i^2 \right], \tag{8.6}$$

where a_i is a preassigned tax share, $G^*(m)$ is the quantity of public good chosen as a result of the aggregation of all individual messages, μ_i is the mean of all of the *other* voters' messages, and σ_i is the standard error of all of the other voters' messages. Each individual pays a fixed tax share, a_i, and variable tax that increases with the size of the difference between his proposed quantity and the proposed quantity of all other voters, and decreases in proportion to the amount of dispersion among the other proposals. Thus a voter is again penalized to the extent that his proposed public good quantity differs from that of all other voters, but his penalty is smaller, the more disagreement there is among the other voters over the desired quantity of public good. To supply his optimal message, a voter must know his preassigned tax share, the fixed constant, and the mean and standard error of all other voters' messages. Thus, a sequential adjustment procedure is required in which each voter is supplied with the computed mean and standard error of the other voters' messages on the preceding round of calculations to make a calculation in the present one. The present messages then become the data for making new mean and standard error statistics for each voter. The process continues until equilibrium is obtained.[1]

Under the Groves-Ledyard procedure, the tax on each individual can be designed to ensure budget balance, and if each voter treats the messages of the others as given, each has the incentive to reveal his own preferences honestly, and a Pareto-optimal equilibrium can be established (1977a, pp. 794–806). But it may not be in each voter's best interests to treat the messages of all other voters as given. The achievement of budget balance and individual equilibrium via a multistep adjustment process makes each individual's message at one step of the process dependent on the other individuals' messages at the preceding stage. A voter who could deduce the effect of his message on the messages of other voters in subsequent rounds of voting might have an incentive to manipulate their messages in later rounds via dishonest indication of his own demand schedule in earlier rounds. The proofs of Pareto optimality that Groves and Ledyard offer assume essentially Cournot-type behavior: each voter treats the messages of the other voters as fixed at each stage of the adjustment process. Once voters begin to take the reactions of other voters into account, Stackelberg-type behavior may be individually optimal, and both the honest-revelation and Pareto-efficiency properties of the mechanism may be lost (Groves and Ledyard, 1977b, pp. 118–20; Groves, 1979; Margolis, 1983).

Although honest revelation of individual preferences is not the dominant strategy under the Groves-Ledyard balanced budget variant of the demand-revealing procedure, it is a Nash equilibrium. That is, given that all other individuals honestly reveal their preferences at each step in the process, it is in each voter's best interest to do so. The significance of this property of the procedure rests heavily on whether it is reasonable to expect voters to adopt a Cournot-type frame of mind when sending messages, at least when the number of voters is fairly large. This issue cannot be settled on the basis of *a priori argument*.[2]

Many criticisms were levied against the family of demand-revelation processes when they were first proposed. One set of these concerns the revenue raised by the incentive tax. To preserve the incentive properties of the procedure, the revenue collected through the incentive tax paid by individual i cannot be returned to her. This problem could easily be circumvented without having to burn the money raised by the incentive tax. If, for example, two communities of roughly equal size were to use the procedure, they might simply agree to swap incentive tax revenue each year and return the funds on a pro rata basis to the citizens. Bailey (1997) proposed giving each person an equal portion of the incentive tax revenues paid by the other $n - 1$ citizens in the community.

Potentially more serious is the problem raised when the incentive tax revenue is large enough to induce significant income effects. Once income effects are allowed,

---

[1] Groves and Loeb (1975) first discussed the possibility of achieving budget balance when the consumer's, in this case a firm's, demand schedule is a quadratic function of the form previously given.

[2] The basic result is established by Groves and Ledyard (1977a). For a discussion of its significance, see Greenberg, Mackay, and Tideman (1977), and Groves and Ledyard (1977c).

however, we move into the general equilibrium framework first explored by Groves and Ledyard (1977a). To handle income effects adequately, one needs even stronger assumptions and a more complicated voting procedure than Groves-Ledyard (Conn, 1983),[3] and the dominance property of preference revelation vanishes.[4]

The remaining difficulties of the process are shared by most, if not all, other voting processes:

Information incentives: To the extent that the size of the incentive tax levied on any individual falls as the number of voters increases, the incentive to provide information conscientiously dwindles.[5] Thus, the one-step demand-revealing process is caught in a form of numerical dilemma. If the numbers involved are small, the incentive taxes may be large, but then, so too is the potential problem arising from significant income effects. If the numbers are large, the Pareto inefficiency may be relatively small, but so too is the incentive to supply the needed information. Much of the information coming from the process could be inaccurate, although not systematically dishonest. Clarke (1977), Green and Laffont (1977b), Tullock (1977a), and Brubaker (1986) have discussed ways to circumvent this problem by relying on representative systems or sampling techniques.

Coalitions: A coalition of voters who felt they would be 100 better off from the victory of P could increase the chances of P's winning significantly by all agreeing to claim that they were 200 better off under P's victory. As long as P won by more than 200, they would be better off under the coalition than acting independently. If P won by less than 100 or lost, they would be no worse off. Only if P won by between 100 and 200, an unlikely event if the coalition is very large, would a voter be worse off under the outcome with the coalition than without it. Thus, incentives to form coalitions to manipulate outcomes exist under the demand-revealing process (Bennett and Conn, 1977; Riker, 1979).

Tullock (1977c) is undoubtedly correct in arguing that the problem of coalition formation is unlikely to be serious if the number of voters is large and voting is by secret ballot. For then incentives to free-ride will exist within the coalition. A single voter's optimal strategy is to urge the formation of a 200-vote coalition and then vote 100 himself. If all voters follow this strategy, we are left with honest preference revelation.[6]

But with small numbers of voters and publicly recorded votes, as in a representative body, the conditions for coalition formation are more favorable. This is particularly true because we usually elect representatives

---

[3] For further discussion of the problems raised by income effects or nonseparable utility functions, see Groves and Ledyard (1977b), Green and Laffont (1977a, 1979), and Laffont and Maskin (1980). For a defense of the assumption, see Tideman and Tullock (1977).

[4] For the most general discussion of this problem, see Hurwicz (1979).

[5] See Clarke (1971, 1977), Tideman and Tullock (1976), Tullock (1977a, 1982), Margolis (1982a), and Brubaker (1983).

[6] For further discussion, see Tideman and Tullock (1981).

as members of parties, which are natural coalition partners. Again we find ourselves confronted by a numerical dilemma: in a direct democracy with a large number of voters, no one has an incentive to gather information *or* join a coalition; in small committees of representatives, incentives exist to gather information about not only one's own preferences, but also those of others who may be potential coalition members.

Bankruptcy: Under the demand-revealing process it is possible for an outcome to emerge in which the entire private wealth of an individual is confiscated (Groves and Ledyard, 1977b, pp. 116–18). This is true of almost any voting procedure other than the unanimity rule, however, and is probably not a serious, practical problem. It does point out the need to view the process as taking place within some sort of system of constitutional guarantees and constraints upon the types of issues that come before the committee, however.[7]

Thus, the demand-revealing process is very much in the spirit of the Wicksellian approach to collective choice. Collective decision making is *within* a system of prescribed property rights, and *upon* a just distribution of income. The goal of collective action is to improve allocative efficiency, not to achieve distributive justice. Such redistribution as will take place is of the Pareto-optimal variety and is more appropriately viewed as part of the "allocation branch" of the public weal than of the "distribution branch."[8]

8.1.2   *Vernon Smith's auction mechanism*

Vernon Smith (1977, 1979a,b) was the first to examine experimentally a simplified version of the demand-revelation process. In his experiments, each individual i announces both a bid, b_i, which is the share of the public good's cost that i is willing to cover, and a proposed quantity of the public good, G_i. The tax price actually charged i is the difference between the public good's costs, c, and the aggregate bids of the other $n - 1$ voters, B_i; that is,

$$t_i G = (c - B_i)G, \tag{8.7}$$

where $B_i = \sum_{j \neq i} b_j$, and $G = \sum_{k=1}^{n} G_k/n$. The procedure selects a quantity of public good only when each voter's bid matches his tax price and each voter's proposed public good quantity equals the mean:

$$b_i = t_i \text{ and } G_i = G, \text{ for all } i. \tag{8.8}$$

After each iteration of the procedure, voters are told what their tax prices and the public good quantity would have been had (8.8) been achieved at that iteration. If a voter's bid falls short of his tax price he can adjust either his bid or proposed public

---

[7] For further discussion of the bankruptcy issue, see Tullock (1977a), Tideman and Tullock (1977), and Groves and Ledyard (1977b,c).

[8] Tullock (1977d) has explored the redistributive potential of the process and claims somewhat more for it. On the distinction between Pareto-optimal redistribution and other kinds, see Hochman and Rodgers (1969, 1970).

good quantity to try to bring about an equilibrium. Only when all unanimously agree to both their tax prices and the public good quantity does the procedure stop.

At an equilibrium (8.8) is satisfied, and i's utility can be written as

$$V_i = U_i(G) - T_i G, \tag{8.9}$$

where the utility from consuming G is expressed in money units. Maximizing (8.9) with respect to G_i we obtain the condition for i's optimal proposed quantity for the public good,

$$dV_i/dG_i = U_i'/n - t_i/n = 0$$
$$U_i' = t_i. \tag{8.10}$$

Each voter equates his marginal utility from the public good to his tax price. Summing (8.10) over all voters, we obtain

$$\sum_{i=1}^{n} U_i' = \sum_{i=1}^{n} t_i = \sum_{i=1}^{n}(c - B_i) = c. \tag{8.11}$$

Equations (8.10) and (8.11) define the conditions for the Lindahl equilibrium.

The auction mechanism induces individuals to reveal their preferences for the public good by charging each voter a tax based not on his stated preference for the public good, but on the aggregate of all other stated preferences (bids). Each voter must be willing to make up the difference between the public good's costs at the aggregate bids of the other voters for the good to be provided. The ultimative incentive to state one's preferences honestly is provided by the knowledge that the good will not be provided unless all unanimously agree to a single quantity and set of tax prices.

Experiments by Smith (1977, 1979a,b, 1980) using this variant of the demand-revealing process indicated a fairly fast convergence on the Lindahl equilibrium. Harstad and Marrese (1982) also reported convergence to efficient outcomes in nine experiments with the Groves-Ledyard procedure. Thus, the vulnerability to individual strategizing of processes requiring sequential adjustment mechanisms may not be serious. The Public Broadcasting System has successfully employed another form of preference revelation procedure to allocate program space (Ferejohn, Forsythe, and Noll, 1979), and Tideman (1983) obtained some success with fraternity students using the demand-revealing process. These real-world experiments with demand-revealing procedures further buttress our confidence that its theoretical liabilities can be overcome in practice.

8.2 Point voting

We seek from a voting process two pieces of information: the quantity of the public good that satisfies the Pareto-optimality condition, and the set of tax shares that finances the purchase of this quantity. The demand-revealing process sidesteps the second question by starting with a preassigned set of tax shares that suffice to cover the cost of supplying the public good. It induces honest preference revelation to determine the Pareto-optimal quantity of public good by means of the special incentive tax.

The need to charge a tax to induce honest preference revelation creates the problem of disposing of the revenue raised by the incentive tax under the one-step demand-revealing process, and makes the normative properties of the process dependent on the normative properties of the initial income distribution. These disadvantages can be avoided by giving each voter a stock of vote money that can be used to reveal preferences for public goods and has no other monetary value. No problem of disposing of the money collected exists, and the initial distribution of vote money can be made to satisfy any normative criterion one wishes. Hylland and Zeckhauser (1979) have proposed such a procedure.

The idea of giving citizens stocks of vote points and allowing them to allocate these points across the issue set in accordance with their preference intensities is not new.[9] The difficulty with point voting has always been that it does not provide the proper incentives for honest preference revelation, as Dodgson was well aware in the passage quoted at the beginning of this chapter. Individuals can better their realized outcomes by overstating their preferences on their most intense issues (Philpotts, 1972; Nitzan, Paroush, and Lampert, 1980; Nitzan, 1985). The important innovation of Hylland and Zeckhauser is their vote-point aggregation rule that provides voters with the proper incentive for honest preference revelation. They are able to show that with the appropriate determination of the vote points assigned to each citizen, voters reveal their true preferences for public goods when the government aggregates the *square roots* of the points of each voter. The main steps in this demonstration are outlined in the next section.

8.3*   An explication of the Hylland-Zeckhauser point-voting procedure

We again assume the existence of preassigned tax shares for each citizen for each public good. Each citizen can calculate her total tax bill for each quantity of public good, and thus can determine the optimal quantities of each public good given her tax shares. This point-voting procedure, like the demand-revealing process, does not address the question of what the tax shares for each citizen should be. Its objective is to reveal preference intensities to determine the Pareto-optimal quantities of the public goods.

There are K public goods whose quantities must be determined. Each voter i is given a stock of vote points, A_i, to be allocated across the K public goods issues according to the voter's preference intensities. If voters wish to increase the quantity of the public good, they allocate a positive number of vote points to it; if they wish to decrease the quantity, they allocate a negative number of vote points. If $| a_{ik} |$ is the absolute number of vote points that voter i allocates to issue k, then the a_{ik}s

---

[9] Dodgson's comment at the beginning of this chapter suggests that he did not invent the procedure, so it is probably over 100 years old. See more recent discussions by Musgrave (1959, pp. 130–1), Coleman (1970), Mueller (1971, 1973), Intriligator (1973), and Nitzan (1975).

must satisfy

$$\sum_{k=1}^{K} |a_{ik}| \le A_i. \tag{8.12}$$

The government converts an individual's vote points into increments or decrements in the proposed quantity of public good using the rule

$$b_{ik} = f(a_{ik}), \tag{8.13}$$

where b_{ik} takes on the sign of a_{ik} and $(b_{ik} = 0) \leftrightarrow (a_{ik} = 0)$. The most straightforward rule is, of course, $b_{ik} = a_{ik}$, but, as we shall see, this rule does not provide the proper incentive for honest preference revelation. The quantities of public goods are determined through an iterative procedure. The government-auctioneer announces an initial proposal of public good quantities, perhaps the levels provided last year.

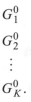

$$G_1^0$$

$$G_2^0$$

$$\vdots$$

$$G_K^0.$$

Each voter responds by stating an allocation of vote points across the K issues, which satisfies (8.12). If a voter wants a larger quantity of G_k than G_k^0, she allocates positive vote points to issue k, that is, $a_{ik} > 0$, and vice versa. The government determines a new vector of proposed public good quantities using (8.13); that is,

$$G_1^1 = G_1^0 + \sum_{i=1}^{n} b_{i1}$$

$$G_2^1 = G_2^0 + \sum_{i=1}^{n} b_{i2}$$

$$\vdots$$

$$G_K^1 = G_K^0 + \sum_{i=1}^{n} b_{iK}.$$

The process is repeated until a vector of public good quantities is obtained such that the aggregated votes for changing each public good quantity all sum to zero; that is,

$$\sum_{i=1}^{n} b_{ik} = 0, \qquad k = 1, K. \tag{8.14}$$

There are three questions of interest concerning the procedure:

1. Does it converge?
2. What are the normative properties of the bundle of public goods quantities it selects?
3. What form does $f()$ take?

Demonstrating that an iterative procedure converges is never an easy task. Hylland and Zeckhauser (1979) make a reasonable case for the convergence of this procedure, and we leave this issue aside.

The normative property we seek is Pareto optimality. This property is assured if we can choose a vector of public good quantities $G = (G_1, G_2, \ldots, G_K)$, which maximizes

$$W(G) = \sum_{i=1}^{n} \lambda_i U_i(G), \tag{8.15}$$

where $U_i(G)$ is voter i's utility defined over the public good quantity vector G (see Chapter 2, Section 2.4*). For $W(G)$ to be at its maximum, the following first-order condition must be satisfied for each of the K public goods:

$$\sum_{i=1}^{n} \lambda_i \frac{\partial U_i}{\partial G_k} = 0, \qquad k = 1, K. \tag{8.16}$$

The appropriately weighted marginal utilities must just balance, so that any change in G_k results in offsetting changes in weighted $\partial U_i / \partial G_k$s. We now have two conditions that our equilibrium vector of public goods must satisfy, (8.16) and (8.14). Clearly, we could ensure the Pareto optimality of any equilibrium vector to which the procedure converged, if

$$b_{ik} = \lambda_i \frac{\partial U_i}{\partial G_k}. \tag{8.17}$$

Then whenever convergence was achieved, that is,

$$\sum_{i=1}^{n} b_{ik} = 0, \qquad k = 1, K,$$

(8.16) would also be satisfied, and Pareto optimality would be ensured. We now have a clue as to the form $f()$ should take. It must be chosen to satisfy (8.17).

Now consider i's decision for allocating her stock of vote points, A_i, at any step in the iterative procedure. She wishes to maximize her utility defined over the vector of public goods, given her vote-point budget constraint as given in (8.12); that is, she must at the $t + 1$th iteration maximize

$$O_i = U_i \left(G_1^t + \sum_{j \neq i} b_{j1} + b_{i1}, \ldots, G_k^t \sum_{j \neq i} b_{jk} + b_{ik} \cdots \right.$$
$$\left. G_K^t + \sum_{j \neq i} b_{jK} + b_{iK} \right) + \mu_i \left(A_i - \sum_{k=1}^{K} |a_{ik}| \right). \tag{8.18}$$

The G_k^t are the announced quantities of public goods from the previous iteration and are fixed. The $\sum_{j \neq i} b_{jk}$ are the aggregated vote points of the other voters on this iteration and are not subject to i's control. Thus, i can change only the b_{ik}. Equation

(8.18) obtains a maximum when the following K equations are satisfied:

$$\frac{\partial U_i}{\partial G_k} f'(a_{ik}) = \mu_i, \qquad k = 1, K \tag{8.19a}$$

when $a_{ik} > 0$, or

$$\frac{\partial U_i}{\partial G_k} f'(a_{ik}) = -\mu_i, \qquad k = 1, K \tag{8.19b}$$

when $a_{ik} < 0$. Substituting for $\partial U_i / \partial G_k$ in (8.17), we obtain

$$b_{ik} = f(a_{ik}) = \frac{\lambda_i \mu_i}{f'(a_i k)} \tag{8.20}$$

when $a_{ik} > 0$. Now λ_i is the weight i gets in W, and μ_i is the Lagrangian multiplier from (8.18). Thus, $\lambda_i \mu_i = C$, a constant. The function $f(\ )$ must be such that

$$f(a_{ik}) f'(a_{ik}) = C. \tag{8.21}$$

From the observation that

$$\frac{d f(a_{ik})^2}{d a_{ik}} = 2 f(a_{ik}) f'(a_{ik}) \tag{8.22}$$

we obtain

$$\frac{d f(a_{ik})^2}{d a_{ik}} = 2C. \tag{8.23}$$

If we integrate (8.23), we obtain

$$f(a_{ik})^2 = 2C a_{ik} + H, \tag{8.24}$$

where H is an arbitrary constant of integration. Setting $H = 0$, we obtain

$$f(a_{ik}) = \sqrt{2C a_{ik}} = \sqrt{2\lambda_i \mu_i a_{ik}}. \tag{8.25}$$

Since μ_i represents the marginal utility of a vote point to i, μ_i can be changed by changing i's stock of vote points, A_i. In particular, if A_i is chosen such that

$$\mu_i = 1/(2\lambda_i), \tag{8.26}$$

then $f(a_{ik})$ takes on the simple form

$$f(a_{ik}) = \sqrt{a_{ik}}. \tag{8.27}$$

The utility-maximizing vote-point allocations of each voter will be such as to maximize the weighted welfare function W, (8.15), for appropriately chosen A_is, if the government-auctioneer determines the quantities of public goods by aggregating the square roots of each citizen's vote-point allocations. Taking the square root of vote-point allocations provides a sufficient penalty to overallocating vote points to more intense issues to offset the tendency to misrepresent preferences under naive point voting $[f(a_{ik}) = a_{ik}]$ mentioned earlier.

Note that an egalitarian assignment of vote points, $A_i = A$ for all i, is consistent with giving each individual equal weight in the social welfare function, W, if and only if the marginal utility of a vote point is the same for all voters. This condition can, in turn, be interpreted as being equivalent to assuming that all voters have an equal stake, that is, an equal expected utility gain from collective action (Mueller, 1971, 1973; Mueller, Tollison, and Willett, 1975). Alternatively, an egalitarian assignment of vote points can be interpreted as an implicit decision to give lower weights (λ_is) in the social welfare function to those with more intense preferences (higher μ_is).

The equilibrium obtained in the Hylland-Zeckhauser point-voting scheme is a Nash equilibrium, and strategizing on intermediary steps or coalitions could overturn the results. On the other hand, strategies for "beating the system" are not readily apparent.

8.4   Voting by veto

The demand-revealing and point-voting procedures call to mind analogies with market mechanisms in that real money or vote money is used to express preferences, and equilibrium is achieved through a tâtonnement process. The welfare properties of the procedures depend in part on the implicit interpersonal, cardinal utility comparisons that arise from aggregating dollar or point votes. In contrast, voting by veto (hereafter VV) utilizes only ordinal utility information.[10] Pareto optimality is achieved, as with the unanimity rule, through the rejection of Pareto-inferior outcomes. The procedure also resembles majority rule in important respects.

VV differs from the two procedures discussed earlier in this chapter in that it allows one to determine both the quantities of public goods and the tax shares to finance them. It differs from all voting procedures, as typically analyzed, in formally including the issue proposal process in the procedure, rather than assuming that voting takes place on a predetermined issue set.

The procedure has two steps. In the first, each member of the committee makes a proposal for the outcome of the committee process. These proposals could be the quantity of a single public good and the tax formula to finance it, or a whole vector of quantities of public goods with accompanying tax formulas. At the end of step 1, an $n + 1$ proposal set exists consisting of the proposals of the n committee members and a status quo issue s (what was done last year, zero levels of all public goods, ...). A random process is then used to determine an order of VV. The order of VV is announced to all members of the committee. The individual placed first in the veto sequence by the random process begins by eliminating (vetoing) one proposal from the $n + 1$ element proposal set. The second veto-voter eliminates one proposal from the remaining n proposals. VV continues until all n members of the committee have vetoed one proposal. The one unvetoed proposal remaining in the issue set is declared the winner.

---

[10] This procedure was first discussed by Mueller (1978), with further development by Moulin (1979, 1981a,b, 1982) and Mueller (1984).

Table 8.3. *Rankings of issues in voting by veto example*

	Voters		
Issues	A	B	C
a	1	2	3(2)
b	3	1	2(3)
c	2	3	1
s	4	4	4

To see the properties of VV consider the following example for a committee of three. The voters, A, B, and C, propose issues a, b, and c, which together with s form the issue set. Let the individual preference orderings be as in Table 8.3, ignoring the two entries in parentheses.

Assume that each individual knows the other voters' preference orderings. Suppose that the randomly determined order of VV is A, then B, then C. A can make his proposal a winner by vetoing b. If B then vetoes either a or s, C will veto the other issue in this pair (s or a), and c wins. Because B prefers a to c, B's best strategy is to veto c, leaving C to veto s, making a the winner.

Now suppose that the randomly determined voting order is ACB. A no longer can get his proposal to win. If A vetoes c, C vetoes a or s, and b wins. If A vetoes b, C vetoes a, and c wins. Because A prefers c to b, he will veto b, leaving c to become the winner. The winners for the six possible permutations of voting sequences are as follows:

$$ABC \rightarrow a \qquad BCA \rightarrow b$$
$$ACB \rightarrow c \qquad CAB \rightarrow d$$
$$BAC \rightarrow a \qquad CBA \rightarrow b.$$

Each issue proposed by a committee member has a one-in-three chance of winning.

The preferences in Table 8.3 produce a cycle over a, b, and c in pairwise voting under majority rule. Thus, in this opening example, the parallel between majority rule and VV seems close. Where the former produces a cycle over three issues, VV selects a winner at random with equal probability.

Now replace the two entries for C in Table 8.3 by those in parentheses; that is, assume that C now prefers a to b, all other rankings remaining the same. With this one change, the probability of a's winning jumps to 5/6. The only order of VV that selects a different issue than a is CAB, which leads to c's victory.

This example illustrates an important incentive property of VV. A increases the probability of his proposal winning by advancing it in the preference ordering of another voter. Thus, the procedure establishes incentives to make proposals that, although perhaps favoring oneself, stand relatively high in the other voters' preferences. Of course, the same incentive exists for all voters, and a competition ensues to make the proposal standing relatively highest in all voters' preferences.

Table 8.4. *The elimination of proposals and voting by veto: example 2*

Voter	Rejects, r_i	Sets of possible winning proposals
V_1	p_3 or p_2 or p_1	$\{p_1\}$ or $\{p_2\}$
V_2	p_4 or p_3 or p_2	$\{p_1, p_2\}$ or $\{p_1, p_3\}$
$\vdots$		
V_{n-3}	p_{n-1} or p_{n-2} or p_{n-3}	$\{p_1, \ldots, p_{n-4}, p_{n-3}\}$ or $\{p_1, \ldots, p_{n-4}, p_{n-2}\}$
V_{n-2}	p_n or p_{n-1} or p_{n-2}	$\{p_1, \ldots, p_{n-3}, p_{n-2}\}$ or $\{p_1, \ldots, p_{n-3}, p_{n-1}\}$
V_{n-1}	p_n or p_{n-1}	$\{p_1, \ldots, p_{n-2}, p_{n-1}\}$ or $\{p_1, \ldots, p_{n-2}, p_n\}$
V_n	s	$\{p_1, p_2, \ldots, p_n\}$

The procedure can be shown to select a unique winning proposal out of any $n + 1$ element proposal set, given the randomly determined VV sequence (Mueller, 1978, 1984). Moreover, the chances that an issue will win vary directly with its position in each voter's ranking of the $n + 1$ proposals. The lower a proposal is ranked by a voter, the lower are its chances of winning.

To see the latter point and further illustrate the properties of the procedure, consider the following example. A committee of n is offered a gift of G dollars if they can agree on a distribution of the gift. If they cannot agree, they retain the status quo distribution of nothing. Although the issue here is basically how to distribute G, the example resembles a public good decision under the unanimity rule in that all are better off only if they can all agree on a single proposal. The issue is one for which majority rule would produce a cycle. Let us examine the outcome under VV.

The initial, selfish instinct of a voter might be to propose that all of G go to himself and nothing to the other $n - 1$ committee members. But this would make his proposal no better than the status quo and almost surely result in its defeat. He must offer some of G to the other voters.

What defeats a proposal is a low rank in another voter's preference ordering. Thus, whatever amount of G a voter sets aside for the other committee members should be divided equally, since to discriminate against any one voter greatly increases the probability that this voter vetoes the proposal. Assuming that i selfishly desires a bit more of G for himself than he sets aside for others, i's proposal will look like the following:

$$\left(\frac{G}{n} - \frac{e_i}{n-1}, \frac{G}{n} - \frac{e_i}{n-1}, \ldots, \frac{G}{n} + e_i, \ldots, \frac{G}{n} - \frac{e_i}{n-1} \right). \tag{8.28}$$

Voter i proposes an egalitarian distribution of G with something extra for himself, $G/n + e_i$, and divides the remainder equally among the other $n - 1$ voters, giving each $G/n - e_i/(n - 1)$. Assume that all proposals other than s take this form. We can now designate the proposals according to their degree of egalitarianism. Call p_1 the proposal with the smallest e_i (that is, the most egalitarian), p_2 the proposal with the second smallest e_i, and so forth. Assume no two proposals have the same e_i.

Now let the order of VV be determined as in Table 8.4. V_1 is the first to vote, V_2 the second, and so on. Once the VV sequence is determined, it is announced to all voters. Given the nature of the proposals, any voter can easily determine the complete rankings of the $n + 1$ proposals for all other voters. All voters rank the status quo proposal s last. All know that the last to go in the VV sequence, V_n, ranks s last. Given a choice between s and any other proposal, V_n rejects s. Thus, none of the voters will waste their veto on s, and s is left for V_n to veto. We can designate s with V_n as the proposal he definitely rejects. Considering V_n we can determine the set of possible winning issues as $\{p_1, p_2, \ldots, p_n\}$. Voter V_{n-1} receives three proposals, one of which is s, and rejects the lower ranked of the two other proposals. Of the possible winning proposals, $\{p_1, p_2, \ldots, p_n\}$, V_{n-1} would veto the proposal ranked lowest by him in this set against any other proposal. Call this proposal r_{n-1}. If any voter who precedes V_{n-1} were to reject r_{n-1}, he would waste his veto. All will leave r_{n-1} for V_{n-1} to reject. Given the nature of the proposals, we can narrow the list of possible candidates for r_{n-1}. V_{n-1} ranks the least egalitarian of the proposals, p_n, lowest since it promises him the lowest payoff, unless p_n is his proposal. If V_{n-1} proposed p_n, he did not propose p_{n-1}, and ranks it lowest. Thus, V_{n-1} must reject either p_n or p_{n-1}.

Proceeding thus we can work our way up the list of voters, associating with each an issue to be rejected. If V_{n-1} proposed p_n, then V_{n-2} did not, and V_{n-2} rejects p_n. Considering both V_{n-1} and V_{n-2}, one or both did not propose p_n, and p_n is definitely rejected by one of the last three voters. Considering the last three voters, s and p_n are definitely eliminated as possible winning issues. As we work our way up the VV sequence, we discover that all proposals are eliminated as possible winners except p_1 and p_2, the two most egalitarian proposals!

The most egalitarian proposal, p_1, wins most of the time because all voters other than its proposer rank it second to their own proposal. If the proposer of p_2 happens to come first in the voting sequence (is V_1), he can make his proposal the most egalitarian of the proposals by rejecting p_1; p_2 can win only if its proposer is V_1.[11] The probability that a given individual comes first in the voting sequence approaches zero as n increases, and thus the probability that any proposal other than the most egalitarian proposal wins approaches zero as the committee grows.

More generally, VV selects proposals ranked relatively high on all preference orderings. When the issue space is single-dimensional, and voter preferences single-peaked, VV assigns nonzero probabilities of winning to only the middle one-third proposals, with the highest probability going to the median proposal. This tendency to pick proposals "in the middle" is reinforced by the incentives facing voters at the proposal stage.

Let x and y be quantities of two public goods, or quality dimensions of a single public good to be decided by the committee. Let $U_i(x, y)$ be i's utility function reaching a maximum at some point I in the positive orthant. Assume circular indifference curves around I. Proposals take the form of combinations of x and y, $p_i(x_i, y_i)$. The probability that any other voter j will reject p_i is higher the farther p_i is from j's utility maximum, J; call this probability $\pi_j^i(x_i, y_i)$. The probability

---

[11] Note that p_2 does not always win when its proposer votes first. When he is followed by the proposer of p_3, p_2's proposer will not veto p_1, because then p_3's proposer would veto p_2. Thus, p_1 wins even when the proposer of p_2 vetoes first, if this person is followed by the proposer of p_3.

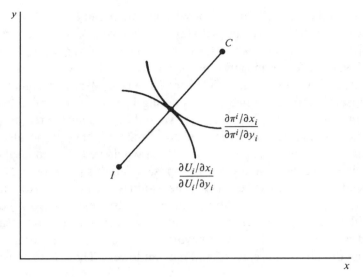

Figure 8.2. Determination of voter i's proposal.

that any of the other $n - 1$ voters will reject p_i is

$$\pi^i = \sum_{j \neq i} \pi^i_j. \tag{8.29}$$

Although π^i is not continuous, it is reasonable to assume that it approaches a continuous function with a minimum at C, the center of the distribution of peak utilities of the other $n - 1$ voters, as n grows large. Let $\bar{U}_i$ be i's expected utility if his proposal does not win. His task is to propose a pair of characteristics (x_i, y_i) to maximize his expected utility, $E(U_i)$.

$$E(U_i) = (1 - \pi^i)U_i(x_i, y_i) + \pi^i \bar{U}_i. \tag{8.30}$$

Maximizing (8.30) with respect to x_i and y_i and setting each equation equal to zero, we derive

$$\frac{\partial U_i}{\partial x_i}(1 - \pi^i) - U_i \frac{\partial \pi^i}{\partial x_i} + \frac{\partial \pi^i}{\partial x_i} \bar{U}_i = 0$$

$$\frac{\partial U_i}{\partial y_i}(1 - \pi^i) - U_i \frac{\partial \pi^i}{\partial y_i} + \frac{\partial \pi^i}{\partial y_i} \bar{U}_i = 0 \tag{8.31}$$

from which we obtain

$$\frac{\partial U_i / \partial x_i}{\partial U_i / \partial y_i} = \frac{\partial \pi^i / \partial x_i}{\partial \pi^i / \partial y_j}. \tag{8.32}$$

Equation (8.32) defines a point of tangency between an indifference curve of i and an isoprobability of rejection locus around C (see Figure 8.2), a point on a pseudocontract curve running from i's optimum point, I, to the center of the density function defined over the other voters' optima. In making a proposal, i is pulled along this contract curve in the direction of C by the knowledge that the probability of his proposal's rejection is higher, the farther it lies from C. Application of VV will lop off the proposals lying farthest from the center of the density function defined over all optima, leaving as possible winners only a subset of proposals clustered around the center.

VV suffers from some of the same shortcomings as other procedures. As the number of participants grows, the incentive to participate declines. The process is also vulnerable to coalitions. If two of the three committee members in the preceeding example could agree to discriminate against the third, they could combine redistributive elements into their proposals, making themselves better off, and the third person even worse off than under the status quo. The excluded member could veto but one of the proposals, and the other would win. As with other voting rules, however, the coalition problem is less important the larger the number of voters.

8.5   A comparison of the procedures

When Samuelson (1954, p. 182) proclaimed the task of revealing individual preferences for public goods impossible, he was assuming that a form of benefit tax would be used to finance the purchase of the public good. An individual's share of the costs of the public good would be tied to his stated preference for it. The demand-revealing process and point voting solve the preference-revelation problem by severing the link between stated preference and share of cost, as do other related processes like Smith's (1977) auction process.

Although these processes do not make a voter's share of the costs of a public good directly related to his stated preferences for it, they do impose a cost upon the voter for moving the committee outcome in a given direction. As Groves (1979, p. 227) observed, "The idea of a 'quid pro quo' is fundamental to an economic theory of exchange." With the exception of the logrolling models, the idea of a quid pro quo has not been part of either theoretical or real-world democratic processes; perhaps this explains their limited success at achieving Wicksell's goal of a *voluntary* exchange process of government. In most democratic procedures, votes are distributed as essentially free goods, with the only real constraint on their use being the ticking of the clock.

The procedures discussed in this chapter all break with this tradition in a fundamental way. The demand-revealing and point-voting schemes require that the voter be prepared to spend real money or fungible vote money to change the committee outcome. Under VV, vetoes are no longer free goods as they would be under the unanimity rule. Each individual has but one proposal to make, and one veto to cast.

Each of the procedures is also in the Wicksellian tradition in that the key equity issues are assumed to have been resolved prior to the application of the procedures.[12] For both the demand-revealing and point-voting procedures, the individual shares of the costs of the public good are predetermined. With demand revelation, the outcomes are further dependent on the initial distribution of income; with point

---

[12] For a discussion of this in the context of the demand-revealing process, see Tideman (1977).

voting, on the distribution of vote points. VV leaves aside the issue of initial income distribution.

Given a just starting point, the goal of collective action is to increase the welfare of all, and the task of the collective decision process is to indicate those situations where that is possible. The proposals differ, however, in the way that the gains from collective action are distributed. The demand-revealing process moves individuals out along their demand or offer curves to maximize the sum of consumer surpluses across individuals. The gains from collective action are distributed to those with the lowest shares of the public good costs and the highest initial incomes.[13] With point voting, the gains go to those with the lowest initial tax shares and highest initial stocks of vote points. With VV, the analogy is to the cake-cutting exercise, as brought about by the random determination of an order of VV. The gains from collective action will tend to be equal across individuals, and the normative characteristic of the process is set by this egalitarian property.

The Wicksellian voluntary exchange approach is ineluctably tied to philosophical individualism (Buchanan, 1949). Each individual enters the collective choice process to improve his own welfare, and the process is established so that all may benefit. Implicit here are a set of constitutional guarantees or constraints upon the collective decision process and, I believe, an assumption that coalitions of one group *against* another do not form. Each man strives *for* himself, but, as in the market, does not strive, collectively at least, *against* any other. The three proposals here all assume some form of constitutional constraints on the issues coming before the committee, and explicitly rule out coalitions. Under the demand-revealing process, the tax charged an individual is exactly equal to the cost that his participation in the process imposes on all others. Under VV, an individual can protect himself against a discriminatory threat to his well-being by any other voter's proposal through the veto he possesses.

In addition to the inherently individualistic orientation of these three proposals, they also resemble one another in the demands they place upon the individual who participates in the process. A simple yes or no will not do. The individual must evaluate in dollars his benefits under various possible alternatives, and, in the case of VV, also the benefits for other voters. This task is made easier by another Wicksellian characteristic of the procedures; each assumes that an expenditure issue and the tax to finance it are tied together. Although this latter feature might actually make the voter's decision task easier, the kind of information required of him under the three procedures is far more sophisticated than that obtained under present voting systems. It is also more sophisticated than one might expect "the average voter" to be capable of supplying, at least if one accepts the image of him gleaned from the typical survey data regarding his knowledge of candidates and issues. To many, the information required of voters will constitute a significant shortcoming of these processes. To me it does not. If we have learned one thing from the sea of work that has emerged following the classic contributions on public goods and democratic choice by Samuelson and Arrow, it is that the task of preference revelation in

---

[13] Tullock (1977b) has elaborated on the normative properties of the demand-revealing process.

collective decisions is not an easy one. If we must further assume that the individuals whose preferences we seek to reveal are only capable of yes or no responses, the task is hopeless from the start.

Much of the discussion of these procedures, pro and con, has been in the context of their use by the citizens themselves, as in a direct democracy. A more plausible application of them would appear to be by a committee of representatives, as in a parliament. Here the charge that the procedures are "too complicated" for the voters would carry less weight. Viewed as parliamentary procedures, both point voting and VV would appear to have an advantage over demand revelation, since they do not depend on the use of real money incentives. (Who pays the incentive tax, the citizens or the representatives?) The allocation of a representative's vote points or the characteristics of his proposals under VV would also be useful information for voters when evaluating their representatives. Only the assumption that there are no coalitions would appear to constitute a problem, at least within a two-party system. With only two parties, for example, VV would yield the same outcomes as the simple majority rule. Both point voting and VV can be adapted for use in a multiparty parliamentary system, on the other hand, and both would have the advantage of allowing all parties to influence the outcomes rather than only those of the majority coalition, which forms "the government."[14]

Although each has its weak points, these three procedures suggest that the knotty problem of preference revelation in collective choice can be resolved as both a theoretical and practical matter. Whether the optimal solution will be a variant on one of these processes or on a process yet to be discovered cannot at this point be ascertained. But the basic similarities running across these three processes are so strong, despite the inherently different procedural mechanics by which they operate, that one is led to suspect that these same characteristics will be a part of any "ultimate" solution to the preference revelation problem. And, if this is true, it further highlights Wicksell's fundamental insight into the collective choice process.

Bibliographical notes

In addition to the procedures discussed in this chapter, mention should be made of those proposed by Thompson (1966), Drèze and de la Vallée Poussin (1971), and Bohm (1972).

---

[14] Mueller, 1996a, ch. 11.

CHAPTER 9

Exit, voice, and disloyalty

Among the laws that rule human societies there is one which seems to be more precise and clear than all others. If men are to remain civilized or to become so, the art of associating together must grow and improve in the same ratio in which the equality of conditions is increased.

Alexis de Tocqueville

In his book *Exit, Voice, and Loyalty* (1970), Albert Hirschman developed the useful distinction between processes in which individuals express their preferences via entry or exit decisions, and those in which some form of written, verbal, or voice communication is employed. An example of the first would be a market for a private good in which buyers indicate their attitudes toward the price-quality characteristics of a good by increasing or decreasing (entry or exit) their purchases. An example of the exercise of voice to influence a price-cost nexus would be a complaint or commendation of the product delivered to the manufacturer. A necessary condition for the effective use of exit is obviously that the potential users of this option be mobile: and full mobility of both buyers and sellers (free entry and exit) is an assumption underlying all demonstrations of market efficiency. In contrast, the literature focusing on voting processes, public choice and political science, has almost exclusively assumed (most often implicitly) that exit is not an option. The boundaries of the polity are predefined and inclusive; the citizenry is fixed. A citizen is at most allowed to abstain from participating in the political process, but he cannot leave the polity to avoid the consequences of its decisions.

Given the assumption of fixed boundaries and citizenry, the characteristics of a pure public good, nonexcludability and jointness of supply, require that a collective *voice* or nonmarket decision process be used to reveal individual preferences and achieve Pareto efficiency, as Samuelson (1954) emphasized. But many goods are "pure" public goods in a limited sense only. For these goods, the nonexclusion principle and/or the jointness of supply property may not be applicable over the full range of possible distribution and production alternatives. For these quasi- or local public goods, the possibility may exist for employing *exit* as an alternative or complement to the *voice* process. These possibilities are reviewed in the present chapter.

9.1   The theory of clubs

Consider the effect of retaining only the joint supply property of public goods. Exclusion is possible, but the addition of a new member lowers the average cost of the good to all other members; that is, there are economies of scale. If average costs fall indefinitely, the optimal size of the consumption group is the entire population, and the traditional public good problem exists. If they eventually stop falling or rise, either because scale economies are exhausted or because of the additional costs of crowding, the optimal size of the consumption group may be smaller than the population. When those who do not contribute to the costs of providing the public good can be excluded from its consumption, the potential exists for a group of individuals to agree voluntarily to provide the public good only to themselves. We shall define such a voluntary association established to provide excludable public goods as a *club*. Although we shall generally assume that the provision of the public good to club members involves at least some fixed costs, and perhaps some falling variable costs, it should be noted that the public good provided by some *social* clubs consists entirely of the presence of the other members of the club. A bridge club is an example. Here there may be no costs, other than time, to providing the public good, and no benefits other than those arising from the association with the other bridge-playing members. But exclusion is possible, and the analysis of these clubs parallels that of the more general case of interest here. Voluntary associations to provide (or to influence the provision of) nonexcludable public goods do not meet the definition of a club employed here, although these associations sometimes call themselves clubs (for example, the Sierra Club). These associations typically attempt to influence the provision of the public good by some other body, such as a state or national legislature, and are treated here as interest groups rather than clubs (see Chapters 15, 20, and 21).

Buchanan (1965a) was the first to explore the efficiency properties of voluntary clubs using a model in which individuals have identical tastes for both public and private goods. To see what is involved, consider the example Buchanan first employed, the formation of a swimming club. Assume first that the size of the pool, and thus its total cost (F), is fixed and the only issue to be decided is the size of the club. Figure 9.1 depicts the marginal benefits and marginal costs from an additional member as seen by any other member. Given identical tastes and incomes, it is reasonable to assume equal sharing of the costs. The marginal benefit to the first member from adding the second member to the club is the saving of one half the cost of the pool, that is, $MB = F/2$. The marginal benefit of a third member to the first two is the additional saving of one third of the cost of the pool ($F/3$). The additional benefits from adding new members, the savings to the other members from further spreading the fixed costs, continue to fall as the club size (N) increases, as depicted by MB in Figure 9.1. The marginal costs of a new member are given by MC. These are psychic costs. If individuals prefer to swim alone, these will be positive over the entire range. If individuals enjoy the company of others in small-enough numbers, the marginal costs of additional members will be negative over an initial range of

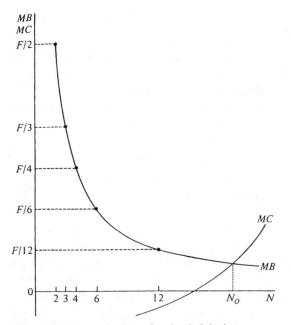

Figure 9.1. Determination of optimal club size.

club sizes. Eventually, the positive costs of crowding will dominate, however, and the optimal club size, N_0, is determined where the marginal cost of an additional member from enhanced crowding just equals the reduction in the other members' dues from spreading the fixed costs over one more club member.[1]

Figure 9.1 can also be used to depict the polar cases of pure private and pure public goods. For a pure public good, the addition of one more member to the club never detracts from the enjoyment of the benefits of club membership to the other members. The marginal cost schedule is zero everywhere and coincides with the horizontal axis. The optimal club size is infinity. For a pure private good, say, an apple, crowding begins to take place on the first unit. If a consumer experiences any consumer surplus from the apple, the foregone utility from giving up half of his apple exceeds the gains from sharing its costs and optimal club size is one. Even with such seemingly private goods as apples, however, cooperative consumption may be optimal. If, for example, the unit price of apples is lower when sold by the bushel, the distribution of apples exhibits joint supply characteristics and might dictate optimal-sized buying clubs of more than one.

The theory of clubs can be extended to take into account the choice of quantity and other characteristics of the collective consumption good. This extension is, perhaps, most easily undertaken algebraically. Let a representative individual's utility be defined over private good X, public good G, and club size N, $U = U(X, G, N)$. Let the cost of providing the public good to the club include a fixed cost, F, and a unit cost (price) of P_g. Assume that each individual has not only the same utility function U, but the same income Y, and that each pays the same fee, t, for membership in the club. In deciding what level of public good to provide and what size of club to

---

[1] See McGuire (1972, pp. 94–7) and Fisch (1975).

establish, we assume that the utility of a representative club member is maximized. This objective might arise as the conscious choice of the founding club members, or be imposed by a competitive market for club memberships. When competition for membership exists, any club that did not provide maximum utility to its members, given the technology of providing the excludable public good, would not survive. Taking into account the budget constraint of a representative member, we obtain the following Lagrangian function to be maximized:

$$L = U(X, G, N) + \lambda(Y - P_x X - t). \tag{9.1}$$

If the club must operate under a balanced budget constraint, then t must satisfy $tN = F + P_g G$. Using this equation to replace t in (9.1), we obtain

$$L = U(X, G, N) + \lambda(Y - P_x X - F/N - P_g G/N). \tag{9.2}$$

Maximizing (9.2) with respect to X, G, and N yields first-order conditions

$$\frac{\partial L}{\partial X} = \frac{\partial U}{\partial X} - \lambda P_x = 0 \tag{9.3}$$

$$\frac{\partial L}{\partial G} = \frac{\partial U}{\partial G} - \lambda P_g/N = 0 \tag{9.4}$$

$$\frac{\partial L}{\partial N} = \frac{\partial U}{\partial N} + \frac{\lambda(F + P_g G)}{N^2} = 0. \tag{9.5}$$

From (9.3) and (9.4) we obtain

$$N \frac{\partial U/\partial G}{\partial U/\partial X} = \frac{P_g}{P_x}. \tag{9.6}$$

The quantity of public good provided to club members must be chosen so that the Samuelsonian condition for Pareto-optimal provision is satisfied; that is, the summation of the marginal rates of substitution of public for private goods over all club members must equal the ratio of their prices.

From (9.4) and (9.5) we obtain

$$N = -\frac{\partial U/\partial G}{\partial U/\partial N} \cdot \frac{F + P_g G}{P_g}. \tag{9.7}$$

If an expansion of club size induces unwanted crowding, $\partial U/\partial N < 0$, and (9.7) implies an $N > 0$. The larger the disutility from crowding relative to the marginal utility of the public good, the smaller the optimal club size. The greater the fixed costs of providing the public good to club members, the larger the optimal size of the club, owing to the advantages of spreading these fixed costs over a larger club membership.

The assumption that individuals have identical tastes and incomes is more than just an analytic convenience. It is often inefficient to have individuals of different tastes in the same club if this can be avoided. If all individuals are identical, except that some prefer rectangular pools and others oval ones, then the optimal constellation of clubs sorts individuals into oval and rectangular pool clubs.[2] Some differences in tastes for the public good can be accommodated efficiently in a single club, however. For example, if some individuals wish to swim every day and others only once a week, this heterogeneity of preferences can be efficiently handled by charging the different members different fees for the club service. If the only costs from increasing club size come from crowding, the optimal fees to finance the club will include a charge per visit. A similar user fee is needed to obtain the optimal allocation and use of the club good, if the costs of providing it (maintenance, for example) are positively related to use (Berglas, 1976; Sandler and Tschirhart, 1984, 1997, pp. 342–3; Cornes and Sandler, 1986, pp. 179–84).

If the constellation of preferences and technologies for providing excludable public goods is such that the number of optimally constituted clubs, which can be formed in a society of a given size, is large, then an efficient allocation of these excludable public goods through the voluntary association of individuals into clubs can be envisaged. Pauly (1967, p. 317) compares the rules or charter of the club to a social contract unanimously accepted by all members, and the theory of clubs, under these assumptions, is obviously much in the spirit of the contractarian and voluntary exchange approaches to public choice and public finance. With large numbers of alternative clubs available, each individual can guarantee himself the equal benefits for an equal share of the costs assumed earlier, since any effort to discriminate against him will induce his exit into a competing club, or the initiation of a new one. If optimal club sizes are large relative to the population, however, discrimination is possible and stable equilibria may not exist. With an optimal club size of two-thirds of the population, for example, only one such club can exist. If it forms, those not in it are motivated to lure members away by offering disproportionate shares of the benefits gained from expanding the smaller club. But the remaining members of the larger club are motivated to maintain club size, and can attract new members by offering the full benefits of membership in the big club; and so on. No stable distribution of club sizes and benefits need exist (Pauly, 1967, 1970). Analytically, the problem is identical to the emptiness of the core in the presence of externalities discussed in Chapter 2, or more generally the cycling problem (see Section 9.4*).

Even when a stable constellation of clubs exists, when optimal club sizes are large relative to the population's size, not all individuals may be part of an optimally constituted club. Although the voluntary association of individuals to form clubs increases their utilities, it may not maximize the aggregate utility of the entire population, defined to include those not a part of optimally sized clubs (Ng, 1974; Cornes and Sandler, 1986, pp. 179–84). We illustrate this point in Section 9.3 with a slightly different form of club.

9.2   Voting-with-the-feet

In the theory of clubs, exclusion from the consumption of the public good is assumed to be possible through some institutional device. A fence is built around the swimming pool and only club members are allowed inside the fence. Even when

---

[2] Buchanan (1965a) and McGuire (1974).

there is no fence around the swimming pool, however, those individuals who live a great distance from the pool are effectively excluded from its use by the costs of getting to it. When the consumption of a public good requires that one be at a certain location, distance can serve as an exclusionary device. If different bundles of public goods of this type are offered at different locations, a spatial division of the population into "clubs" of homogeneous tastes would arise from individuals choosing to reside in that local polity, which offered them their ideal constellation of public goods. No ballots would have to be cast. All preferences would be revealed through the silent voting-with-the-feet of individuals exiting and entering communities, a possibility first noted by Tiebout (1956).

In contrast to the disappointing promise of majority rule, the utopian quality of the unanimity rule, and the imposing complexity of the newer, more sophisticated procedures, Buchanan's clubs and Tiebout's voting-with-the-feet seem to accomplish the task of revealing individual preferences by the surprisingly simple device of allowing people to sort themselves out into groups of like tastes. The efficiency and mutual gain Wicksell sought from the unanimity rule in his voluntary exchange approach to collective action arise through the voluntary association of individuals in clubs or local polities.

Buchanan described the properties of a single club, and the optimality conditions [(9.6) and (9.7)] for membership in a single, isolated club. Tiebout described the process of voting-with-the-feet as one that could achieve Pareto optimality with respect to the entire population. But a local polity is a form of club, and clubs are a type of polity. Thus, conditions (9.6) and (9.7) must also hold for a single local polity, and a world of clubs must in principle offer the same potential as the Tiebout model does for achieving Pareto efficiency defined over the entire population. Moreover, any problems of stability or Pareto inefficiency that one can show exist with respect to one model, probably hold for the other.

The following conditions to ensure the global optimality of excludable public goods provision thus apply to both the clubs and voting-with-the-feet models:[3]

1. Full mobility of all citizens
2. Full knowledge of the characteristics of all communities (clubs)
3. Availability of a range of community (club) options spanning the full range of public good possibilities desired by citizens
4. Absence of scale economies in producing the public good and/or smallness of the optimum scale of production relative to the population size
5. Absence of spillovers across communities (clubs)
6. Absence of geographical constraints on individuals with respect to their earnings

Assumptions 1 and 6 are peculiar to the voting-with-the-feet model, but some sort of freedom-of-association assumption is certainly implicit in the clubs model if it is to produce global optimality. Some special difficulties with respect to assumption 6 are discussed below. Assumptions 1 and 5 tend to work at cross-purposes. The larger

---

[3] See Tiebout (1956), Buchanan and Wagner (1970), Buchanan and Goetz (1972), McGuire (1972), Oates (1972), and Pestieau (1977).

the community, the more costly it is to leave it, and the lower mobility is. Thus, exit is a more reasonable alternative from small than from large communities. On the other band, the smaller the community, the more likely it is that the benefits from the provision of any specific public good will spill over onto other communities and cause externalities across communities and non-Pareto allocations.

Assumptions 2 and 3 raise complementary issues. The basic argument assumes a full range of possible baskets of public goods available at the start. But how is this spectrum of opportunities established? Two possibilities come to mind: some central authority or auctioneer could set up different local communities and clubs with different baskets of public goods and inform all potential citizens of the characteristics of each community club. There are two obvious difficulties to this resolution of the problem, however. First, assuming a central authority knows what baskets of public goods must be supplied disposes of a large portion of the preference revelation problem, which the model is supposed to solve. If the central authority knew which people had which preferences, it could simply assign individuals to the appropriate club or local polity. Second, even if it is to some extent feasible, this solution to the preference-revelation problem violates the decentralized spirit of the Buchanan and Tiebout models.[4]

More appropriate is the assumption that entrepreneurs exist who create clubs and polities, where needed, for a share of the "profits" generated from providing a desired quantity or package of public goods. These clubs and polities could be set up on a not-for-profit basis, in which case the rewards to the entrepreneurial founders would, presumably, come in a nonpecuniary form, for example, the power and prestige associated with founding an organization. Tiebout uses the term "city managers" rather than mayors for the local polities' leadership, presumably in recognition of their entrepreneurial role. Frey and Eichenberger (1995, 1999) have recently emphasized the creation of public goods clubs, which they name functional, overlapping, and competing jurisdictions (FOJC) as a way of better matching public good supply and citizen preferences.

It must also be stressed that many goods with significant joint supply characteristics, but for which exclusion is practicable, are provided by profit-seeking entrepreneurs. Television program production and broadcasting are good examples of an activity with significant joint supply properties, but for which exclusion is possible with the help of scrambling devices and coaxial cables. Thus, one finds private firms offering packages of television programs for fees alongside publicly provided program packages. The former are basically consumption clubs formed to consume a particular bundle of television programs, while the publicly broadcast programs are available to citizens only near the points of transmission. Land developers receive an entrepreneurial return for the particular constellation of public and private good characteristics that they combine in the communities they create.

As always with a market-provided good or service, full Pareto optimality cannot be assumed unless the good is provided competitively. Moreover, the provision of excludable public goods by a monopoly raises efficiency issues that go beyond those

---

[4] See Pauly (1970) and McGuire (1972).

that exist for a private good monopoly (Brennan and Walsh, 1981; Burns and Walsh, 1981). Nevertheless, the presence of many profit-making firms in competition with nonprofit clubs and local polities in providing excludable public goods (television, recreation and sports, education, travel, health care) attests to the importance of the entrepreneurial function in providing excludable public goods.

Although clubs can be single (swimming) or multiple (tennis, golf, and swimming) goods providers, local polities inevitably supply a number of goods and services and possess the potential for supplying many more. As the number of public good dimensions increases, the plausibility of assumption 3 declines. With one public good issue to decide, such as the proportion of tulips in the public square, 101 communities suffice to allow each individual to consume his optimal fraction of tulips to the nearest percentile. With two issues, the proportions of oaks and tulips, the number of communities needed to ensure Pareto optimality leaps to 101 squared. Each additional public good raises the number of polities required to a higher exponent. If the number of public goods is very large, one reaches a solution in which the number of communities equals the size of the population. Each community/individual becomes a polity with a basket of public–private goods (garden, woods) tailored to his own tastes, a possible consequence of the model that Tiebout himself recognized.[5]

9.3 Global optimality via voting-with-the-feet

Pareto optimality in a global sense requires that the incremental change in net benefits to the community that an individual joins equal the incremental loss to the community he leaves:

$$\sum_{i=1}^{n} \Delta U_A^i = -\sum_{i=1}^{m} \Delta U_B^i. \tag{9.8}$$

The change in utility of the nth individual to join community A is his total utility from being in $A(U_A^n)$, just as his loss from leaving B is his total utility in B, U_B^m. Equation (9.8) can thus be rewritten as

$$U_A^n + \sum_{i=1}^{n-1} \Delta U_A^i = U_B^m + \sum_{i=1}^{m-1} \Delta U_B^i. \tag{9.9}$$

In a world of pure competition, each factor owner's marginal product is the same in all industries and areas. If externalities and other market failures are not present, the welfare of others is unaffected by one's location. All ΔU^i are zero except for the moving individual, and he naturally locates in his most favored community. With public goods present, the ΔU^i for individuals in a community are positive for an additional entrant, as the total costs of the public good become spread over a larger number of individuals. A new entrant thus confers positive externalities for a community producing a pure public good. Alternatively, a new entrant can produce

---

[5] See also Pestieau (1977).

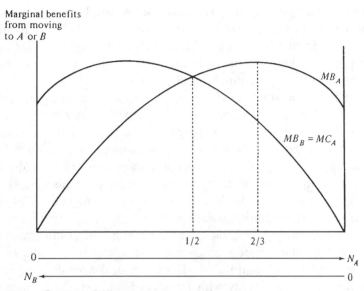

Figure 9.2. Marginal benefit from migration curves.

congestion costs, negative externalities, to a community that has grown beyond the optimal size for its locally provided public goods. In either case, since the moving individual compares only his utility levels in the two communities and ignores the marginal effects of his move on the others (the ΔU^is in A and B), voting-with-the-feet in general will not produce Pareto optimality in the presence of public goods and externalities.[6]

To see how a non-Pareto-efficient equilibrium can emerge, assume that there exist only two communities in which an individual can live, A and B. Each community is identical as are all of the residents. Each community provides a public good, which is optimally provided when two-thirds of the potential residents of the two communities consume it. Thus, there are enough individuals for only one optimally sized community. The situation is depicted in Figure 9.2. Curve MB_A represents the *average* benefits to a member of community A from membership in the community as a function of community size. These first rise as a result of the economies of scale property of the public good, and then begin to fall as crowding costs begin to outweigh the benefits from cost sharing. The curve MB_A also represents the *marginal* benefits to a member of community B from migrating to A. MB_B is the mirror image of MB_A defined with respect to the population of B.

The population of B is read from right to left along the horizontal axis. MB_B is also the marginal cost (MC_A) to a citizen of B from migrating to A. As usual, individual equilibrium occurs where marginal cost intersects marginal benefits *from below*. No such intersection exists in the figure. The intersection at an equal division of population is a local minimum. At any distribution in which one community has a higher population than the other, benefits are higher from membership in

[6] See Buchanan and Wagner (1970); Buchanan and Goetz (1972); Flatters, Henderson, and Mieszkowski (1974); and Pestieau (1977).

the larger community. Migration is from the smaller to the larger community, and this continues until all of the population enters into one of the communities. If congestion costs rise significantly, MB_A might decline fast enough following its peak to intersect MC_A. This would yield an equilibrium for the larger of the two cities at a size above its optimum, but below that of the entire population. In either case, however, the equilibrium city sizes achieved via voluntary migration are not those that maximize the average utility level of all individuals in the two communities. The latter would occur in this example when the population is equally divided between the two communities. This distribution of population maximizes the *average* benefits from *being* in either community. But, once this point is left, the *marginal* benefits from switching to the larger community exceed those of staying, and population redistributes itself until the stable but inefficient equilibrium is obtained (Buchanan and Wagner, 1970).

Although the assumption that the optimal-sized community is more than half the total population may seem unrealistic when one thinks of an area and population as large as the United States, often the potential migrant may not be considering such a wide spectrum of options. The relevant choice may be staying in small town B or moving to nearby large city A. Within this circumscribed range of choice, the optimal-sized community may be more than half the combined populations of the two communities, and the tendency for overpopulating the central city may become evident.

If the optimal-sized polity is less than half the population, the marginal benefits and cost schedules intersect and yield a stable equilibrium with the population evenly divided between the two communities. This equilibrium does result in a maximization of the potential benefits to each citizen, given the constraint that there should be but two communities. When addditional communities can be created, and the optimal-sized community is small relative to the total population, we return to a Tieboutian world in which free migration and the creation of new fiscal clubs can result in a set of communities, each of optimal size.

Additional complications are introduced into the Tieboutian world, however, if individuals earn part of their incomes outside the community. Assume again two communities with identical production possibilities, and individuals of identical tastes. Within any community, each individual receives the same wage, w, from supplying his services to the local production process, and a differential income, $r_i \geq 0$, that is tied to him and not to his location. This income can be thought of as coming from dividends, as in Tiebout's example, or as rents on assets peculiar to the individual, such as the income of a recording star. We shall refer to this income as simply rental income, covering all nonlocation-specific sources. Now consider two communities with equal numbers of workers, identical production possibility frontiers, and identical tax structures. In equilibrium the total private and public good production in community A must equal the sum of its rental and wage income:

$$\sum_{i}^{N_A} Y_i + G = N_A w_A + \sum_{i}^{N_A} r_i. \tag{9.10}$$

The utility of a resident of A is given by

$$U_i(Y_i, G, N_A), \tag{9.11}$$

as before. Substituting for G from (9.10) into (9.11), we have

$$U_i(Y_i, N_A w_A + \sum r_i - \sum Y_i, N_A). \tag{9.12}$$

The assumption of identical tax structures implies that the individual can purchase the same bundles of private goods, Y_i, in both communities. With equal populations and production possibilities, N_A and w_A equal N_B and w_B, respectively. Assuming the public good is not an inferior good, some of any additional rental income in A will go to increased public good production. Thus, $\sum r_i - \sum Y_i$ is larger in A than in B if $\sum r_i$ is larger in A than in B. Since public goods enter an individual's utility function with a positive sign, an individual is better off joining the community with the higher rents, assuming all other community characteristics are the same.

If the communities have different rental incomes, the same set of tax structures may not be optimal in both communities. Nevertheless, if tastes are the same, an individual always receives a more attractive tax–public good package from the community with higher rental income.

Higher rental incomes thus play the same role in attracting individuals from the other community as does a larger population in the presence of joint supply characteristics. Indeed, from (9.12) it can be seen that rental income, the wage rate, and the population size all enter the utility function in the same way through the public good term. Thus, any increase in population, the wage rate, or rental income, ceteris paribus, increases an individual's utility by increasing the quantity of public goods available. An increase in population also enters the utility function negatively, however, through the congestion effect represented by the third argument in the utility function. Increasing population can also be expected to drive the wage rate down, reducing an individual's command over private goods, and thereby his welfare. In contrast, higher rental income has an unambiguous positive impact.

Just as an individual's welfare is higher if he enters the community with the higher rental income, the community's welfare is higher, the higher the rental income of any new entrant. The depressing effects on wages and costs in terms of increased congestion from a new member are identical, but the benefits from increased tax revenue to finance public good provision are obviously greater, the greater the newcomer's rental income.[7] If the community has expanded to the point where the marginal gain from spreading the public good's costs over another taxpayer just equals the marginal cost in terms of reduced wages and congestion, adding another individual who is just a wage earner makes the community worse off. But if he has a high-enough rental income, the additional gains from financing an expansion of public good supply out of this rental income outweigh these costs. Regardless of what the community's size is, an additional member can always increase the welfare of all existing members if he brings with him a high-enough rental income.

---

[7] This effect is particularly apparent in the Flatters et al. (1974, pp. 101–2) model in which a golden rule is obtained where all rents go to public good production and all wages to private good production. This model is based on different assumptions from those of the discussion here, however.

In the same way that full mobility between communities may not bring about a Pareto-optimal distribution of the population, where economies of scale in public good production are large, full mobility is unlikely to bring about a Pareto-optimal distribution of the population in the presence of rents. In the preceeding example, the socially optimal distribution of the population is that which equates the marginal product of a worker in each community. This occurs at equal community sizes. But if the distribution of rents differs between the two communities, migration toward the community with the higher rents will occur. This migration will continue until the fall in marginal product and rise in congestion costs are large enough to offset the advantage that this community has from higher rents, and average utility levels in the two communities are equal.

To achieve the socially optimal distribution of population, taxes and subsidies must he levied on either residence in or movement in and out of a given community. One possibility is to grant a central authority the right to make transfers across communities. Such an authority would then determine what the socially optimum distribution of population was, and levy taxes and subsidies to achieve this optimum distribution. In the general case, the central authority would attempt to achieve the equilibrium condition given in (9.9). This requires a tax equal to $\sum_{i=1}^{n} \Delta U_A^i$ on community A if A is the community that is, or would become, too large, and a subsidy equal to $\sum_{i=1}^{m} \Delta U_B^i$ to community B if it would lose population. If the only difference between the two communities were the level of rental income, the policy would be simple to implement. The central authority would levy a tax on rental income in the community with higher initial rental income and offer a subsidy to the community with lower rental income to bring about equal rental incomes and populations in both communities.[8]

Alternatively, Pareto optimality can be achieved in a decentralized way, by granting each community the right to tax immigration and emigration. If the externalities for community A from immigration were positive, it could offer a subsidy to newcomers equal to $\sum \Delta U_A^i$ and levy an identical tax on emigration. If B did the same, all individuals would be forced to internalize the external costs their moving entailed, and Pareto efficiency would be obtained.[9]

Although these alternatives have identical efficiency outcomes, they differ both in spirit and in their equity properties. The latter weds Tiebout's decentralized voting-with-the-feet with the theory of exclusive clubs to produce a decentralized solution to the population allocation problem. The enactment of such a system of taxes and subsidies by local communities immediately provides communities favored by natural characteristics, population size, income, and so on with a valuable property right, which they exercise by taxing members outside their community (i.e., those who would have entered in the absence of the tax-subsidy scheme). The centralized solution vests the entire population with a property right in both communities and achieves allocational efficiency by taxing *all* members of the favored community to subsidize the disfavored community.

---

[8] Flatters et al. (1974) and McMillan (1975).
[9] Buchanan (1971) and Buchanan and Goetz (1972).

The difference in policies can be most easily seen by considering again our rent example but assuming that individual rents are not tied to given individuals, but are locational rents accruing to all residents of a given community. Granting the right to tax migration into the community with higher rents to its residents would allow them to achieve permanently higher utility levels than would be achieved in the less-favored community. Those who were lucky enough or quick enough to be born or move into a geographically more desirable area would forever be better off than those left in the less desirable areas. In contrast, the centralized solution would equate utility levels across communities by taxing the higher rent areas and subsidizing the low-rent ones.

Even when rental incomes are tied to individuals rather than locations, Tieboutian revelation of preferences coupled with local taxes and subsidies can raise equity issues. As noted earlier, a community can always be made better off by admitting someone whose rental income is high enough. Once a community has reached its optimal size for sharing the costs of public goods, it might adopt a policy of, say, admitting only new members who bring with them a rental income above the average. This can be accomplished by establishing zoning requirements on lot sizes and apartment dwellings that effectively screen out those with incomes below a given level. The mobile individual, on the other hand, is better off joining a community with greater rental income than he receives. The intersection of these two strategies could be a sorting out of individuals into communities of equal rental incomes. The identical incomes and preferences assumption that Buchanan assumed for convenience in initiating the study of clubs is a plausible outcome to a Tieboutian search for optimum communities (Buchanan and Goetz, 1972; Epple and Romer, 1991).

9.4*   Clubs and the core

The preceeding discussion raises three issues with regard to the global properties of a world of clubs and voting-with-the-feet preference revelation: (1) whether an equilibrium distribution of the population among the clubs (communities) exists, (2) whether any equilibrium that occurs is Pareto efficient, and (3) what the redistributive-equity properties of the outcomes are. To further illustrate these issues we consider a simple example first presented by Ellickson (1973).

Assume that each individual i has the hyperbolic utility function $u_i = x_i g$ defined over private good x and public good g. Each individual in a club consumes the same quantity of g. Since $\partial u_i / \partial x_i = g$, the marginal utility of the private good is the same for all individuals within a club. We are working with transferable utility in x.

The unit costs of providing the good g to clubs of size 1, 2, and 3 are, respectively, a, b, and c. If $a = b = c$, we have a pure public good. If $a = 1/2b = 1/3c$ we have a pure private good. If the good is a pure public good, the optimal club size is the population. If it is a pure private good, optimal club size is one. We assume a public good with congestion costs so that

$$a < b < 2a$$

$$b < c < (3/2)b.$$

Consider first the quantity of g chosen and utility level obtained when an individual acts alone. Let w_i be i's wealth. We maximize u_i subject to the budget constraint $w_i = x_i + ag$; that is,

$$L_i = x_i g + \lambda(w_i - x_i - ag). \tag{9.13}$$

Maximizing with respect to g and x_i,

$$\partial L_i/\partial g = x_i - \lambda a = 0 \tag{9.14}$$

$$\partial L_i/\partial x_i = g - \lambda = 0. \tag{9.15}$$

Solving for x_i,

$$x_i = ag. \tag{9.16}$$

From the budget constraint and (9.16)

$$w_i = x_i + ag = 2ag, \tag{9.17}$$

from which

$$ag = \frac{w_i}{2} \tag{9.18}$$

and

$$u_i = x_i g = ag^2 = \frac{w_i^2}{4a}. \tag{9.19}$$

Equation (9.19) gives the security level of utility for any individual i, the level of utility i can achieve acting alone. No individual joins a club or community unless she can secure a utility of at least $w_i^2/4a$.

Let us now derive the conditions under which a club of two forms. The Samuelsonian condition for Pareto optimality requires that the sum of the marginal rates of substitution (MRS) for the two club members equals the marginal cost of the public good; that is,

$$MRS_i + MRS_j = b. \tag{9.20}$$

Now

$$MRS_i = \frac{\partial u_i/\partial g}{\partial u_i/\partial x} = \frac{x_i}{g}, \tag{9.21}$$

so that

$$\frac{x_i}{g} + \frac{x_j}{g} = b \tag{9.22}$$

or

$$x_i + x_j = bg. \tag{9.23}$$

The combined budget constraint for the club is

$$w_i + w_j = x_i + x_j + bg. \tag{9.24}$$

From (9.23) and (9.24) we obtain the Pareto-optimal quantity of the public good for a club of two.

$$g = \frac{w_i + w_j}{2b}. \tag{9.25}$$

To be induced to join a club of two, each individual must achieve a utility level of at least what she can achieve acting alone. From (9.24) we can write i's utility as

$$u_i = x_i g = (w_i + w_j - x_j - bg)g = (w_i + w_j)g - bg^2 - x_j g. \tag{9.26}$$

Now $x_j g$ is j's utility. If we set that at $w_j^2/4a$, the minimum level j is willing to accept and be in the club, then whether a club of two forms can be determined by seeing whether i's utility in the club exceeds her security level, that is, whether

$$u_i = (w_i + w_j)g - bg^2 - \frac{w_j^2}{4a} \geq \frac{w_i^2}{4a}. \tag{9.27}$$

Using (9.25) to replace g and some algebra yields

$$\frac{(w_i + w_j)^2}{b} \geq \frac{w_i^2 + w_j^2}{a} \tag{9.28}$$

as the necessary condition for a club of two to form. Whether a club forms depends on the respective wealth of i and j and the relative costs of supplying g in the two contexts. To see what is involved, assume that $w_j = \alpha w_i$, where $0 \leq \alpha \leq 1$. Then for (9.28) to hold the following condition must be satisfied:

$$\frac{1 + 2\alpha + \alpha^2}{1 + \alpha^2} \geq \frac{b}{a}. \tag{9.29}$$

Both sides of (9.29) lie in the range between 1 and 2, but the lower α is, the lower the left-hand side of (9.29) is. For a club of two to form, j's income must be sufficiently high relative to i's to allow her share of the costs of g to be large enough to compensate i for the crowding effect j's joining the club has (i.e., b's being greater than a).

The condition for the Pareto-optimal provision of the public good to a club of three requires that

$$g = \frac{w_i + w_j + w_k}{2c}. \tag{9.30}$$

In a manner analogous to the above demonstrations, one can show that the value of a coalition of three, $V(ijk)$, is $(w_i + w_j + w_k)^2/4c$. For the grand coalition to form, (9.31) and (9.32) must be satisfied:

$$V(ijk) \geq V(i) + V(j) + V(k)$$
$$V(ijk) \geq V(ij) + V(k) \tag{9.31}$$

$$V(ijk) \geq V(jk) + V(i)$$
$$V(ijk) \geq V(ik) + V(j) \tag{9.32}$$

where $V(i) = w_i 2/4a$, and $V(ij) = (w_i + w_j)^2/4b$. Suppose now that i and j have the same incomes, and k's income is α fraction of i's; that is,

$$w_i = w_j = w$$

$$w_k = \alpha w.$$

Consider just the implications of (9.32). Note first that an outcome in which i and j form a club dominates an outcome in which either i or j plays alone and the other forms a club with k:

$$V(ij) + V(k) \geq V(jk) + V(i) = V(ik) + V(j) \tag{9.33}$$

since

$$\frac{(2w)^2}{4b} + \frac{\alpha^2 w^2}{4a} > \frac{(1+\alpha)^2 w^2}{4b} + \frac{w^2}{4a} \tag{9.34}$$

if $b/a < 2$ and $\alpha < 1$. Thus, if only a club of two forms, it will be the wealthier two individuals that form the club. For the poorer k to be admitted, (9.35) must hold:

$$\frac{(2+\alpha)^2 w^2}{4c} > \frac{4w^2}{4b} + \frac{\alpha^2 w^2}{4a}. \tag{9.35}$$

The smaller c is relative to b and a, and the larger α is, the more likely (9.35) is to be satisfied. The poorer k will be invited to join the club by i and j if her income is high enough.

Now assume that $\alpha = 1/3$, $a = 1$, $b = 3/2$, and $c = 2$. Given these parameter values, (9.35) does not hold and a club of three does not form. A club of the two wealthier individuals will form, however, since $4w^2/4b > 2w^2/4a$ with $b = 3/2$ and $a = 1$. If the two wealthier individuals can both form a club and keep k out, they will. If, however, it is not possible to prevent individuals from moving into the community, k may choose to do so. Whether she chooses to join the community will depend on her assigned tax share once there. If, for example, the community were required to finance g by charging all members the Lindahl tax price for g, k would be better off in the community than if she remained outside and provided g for herself. Her Lindahl tax price is her MRS, which is x_k/g. Thus, from the budget constraint,

$$w_k = x_k + \frac{x_k}{g} \cdot g \tag{9.36}$$

or

$$x_k = w_k/2. \tag{9.37}$$

Half of k's income goes to pay for g, and half is left for private good consumption. Given her Lindahl tax share, her utility in the community of three is

$$u_k = x_k g = \frac{\alpha w}{2} \frac{(2+\alpha)w}{2c} = \frac{7}{72} w^2, \tag{9.38}$$

while playing the game alone she has only

$$u_k = \frac{\alpha^2 w^2}{4a} = \frac{w^2}{36}. \tag{9.39}$$

Thus, k will choose to join the community if she can, even though the aggregate utility of the community is lower with her in it than it is when she is outside it. It should also be obvious that k could choose to move to the richer community even if she left behind other k's who were made worse off by her departure from their community.

Even though the club of three provides lower aggregate utility than the club of two plus k playing the game alone, the effective redistribution from the richer two members to the poorer one when g is provided to all three members and financed at Lindahl tax prices makes her entry into the community to her advantage. We witness here exactly the same kind of Pareto-inefficient redistribution that we observed in Chapter 5 when a pure private good was provided to a community at equal quantities as *if* it were a public good and financed at Lindahl tax prices.

The Pareto inferiority of the club-of-three solution in this example implies that i and j would be better off bribing k to stay out of the community if her entry requires that she be charged only the Lindahl tax price for g. They even would be better off, of course, if they could prevent her from entering by forcing her to pay more than her Lindahl price, by charging her an entrance fee, or by some other institutional device (e.g., a zoning requirement).

Finally, we show that when the grand coalition is not in the core, no core may exist, even though a coalition of two can provide its members with higher utilities than when they play alone. Assume $w_i = w_j = w_k = w$. Let $a, b,$ and c be such that

$$V(ijk) = \frac{(3w)^2}{4c} < \frac{4w^2}{4b} + \frac{w^2}{4a} = V(ij) + V(k) > \frac{3w^2}{4a}$$

$$\frac{3w^2}{4a} = V(i) + V(j) + V(k). \tag{9.40}$$

At least one member of the $i - j$ coalition must pay at most her Lindahl tax price so that this individual's utility is at least

$$u_i = \frac{w}{2} \cdot \frac{2w}{2b} = \frac{2w^2}{4b}. \tag{9.41}$$

But (9.40) implies that

$$\frac{4w^2}{4b} > \frac{2w^2}{4a} = 2V(k). \tag{9.42}$$

Thus, a member of the $i - j$ coalition who pays at most her Lindahl tax price must have higher utility than the individual left outside of the coalition. The outside individual k must be able to offer the member of $i - j$ paying at least the Lindahl tax price a more attractive proposal to form a two-person coalition and $i - j$ cannot be sustained. We have here precisely the same kind of instability we confronted in Chapter 2 in the presence of multiple externalities (Aivazian and Callen, 1981).

9.5   Voting-with-the-feet: empirical evidence

In the Tiebout model rational individuals exit communities offering less attractive public goods–tax packages in favor of those providing more attractive packages. Three sets of testable implications follow from this assumption: (1) individuals do move in response to local government expenditure–tax offerings, (2) this migration process sorts people into groups of homogeneous tastes consuming the bundles of public goods of their choice, and therefore (3) individuals are more satisfied with their local public goods–tax packages where Tiebout sorting takes place.[10]

With respect to the first implication, numerous studies have found that both the levels of local public services and tax rates influence *whether* a family moves, and the choice of community into which it moves.[11] For example, an examination of responses to survey questions in the Columbus, Ohio, area in 1966 indicated a significant correlation between individual perceptions that there were problems facing the neighborhood and intentions to move (Orbell and Uno, 1972). Moreover, there was a greater tendency in urban areas to resort to exit instead of voice than there was in the suburbs. Individuals appeared to feel that voice is a more effective option in suburbs than it is in the city. John, Dowding, and Biggs (1995) report that a fifth of those who changed jurisdictions in the London area gave tax rates as an important factor in their decision to move.[12]

While the wealthy move away from high taxes, the poor move toward high welfare payments (Gramlich and Laren; 1984; Blank, 1988; Cebula and Koch, 1989; Cebula, 1991). So systematic is this migration, that state governments take it into account when setting welfare payment levels. A state that has large numbers of poor people living in its neighboring states sets a lower level of welfare payments (Smith, 1991).[13]

A particularly well-suited group for testing the Tiebout hypothesis is the elderly, since their incomes are typically from nonwage sources and thus their choice of residence is not likely to be dependent on characteristics of the job market. Cebula (1990) found that the elderly were significantly more likely to move to states that did not have an income tax. Results of Conway and Houtenville (1998), however, paint a much more complicated picture. They attempt to account for both the tax incentives that the elderly have to move from one state to another, and for the government expenditure incentives. Their results for out-migration generally support the predictions of the Tiebout model. Elderly citizens are more likely to leave states with high tax shares and high prices for public services. High property taxes appear

[10] A fourth possible implication, that housing values are bid up in high expenditure/tax communities (Oates, 1969) is more problematic and is not reviewed here. See, however, Edel and Sclar (1974); Hamilton (1976); and Epple, Zelenitz, and Visscher (1978).

[11] For a review of the literature up to 1979, see Cebula (1979). For updates, see Cebula and Kafoglis (1986) and Dowding, John, and Biggs (1994).

[12] See also the additional evidence presented by Dowding and John (1996).

[13] For a review of this literature with additional references see Brueckner (2000).

Table 9.1. *Frequency distribution of income homogeneity indexes, Los Angeles county municipalities, 1950, 1970*

	0.333–0.339	0.340–0.349	0.350–0.369	0.370–0.379	0.400+	Total
1950	25	5	5	3	4	42
	(0.60)	(0.12)	(0.12)	(0.07)	(0.010)	(100)
1970 (old cities)	9	13	11	4	5	42
	(0.21)	(0.31)	(0.26)	(0.10)	(0.12)	(100)
1970 (new cities)	1	9	12	1	7	30
	(0.03)	(0.30)	(0.40)	(0.03)	(0.23)	(100)
1970 (all cities including 3 old 1950 cities for which 1950 data were missing)	12 (0.16)	22 (0.29)	23 (0.31)	5 (0.07)	13 (0.17)	75 (100)

Note: Percentages in parentheses.
Source: Miller, *Cities by Contract*, Cambridge, MA: MIT Press, 1981, p. 134.

to be a particularly strong stimulus to exit a state. Conway and Houtenville's results for in-migration do not support the Tiebout hypothesis, however. The elderly tend to move into states that have much the same characteristics as the ones that they leave. Factors other than the composition and efficiency of the public sector across states appear to determine the elderly's choice of a new home, once they choose to move.[14]

As in so many areas, California has led the world in the increasing trend toward greater mobility, with Los Angeles being the archetypical late-twentieth-century city. If the Tiebout process succeeds at sorting people into more homogeneous local communities, then the effects of the process should be apparent in Los Angeles. They are.

Gary Miller (1981, chs. 6 and 7) computed Herfindahl-like indices of income inequality (the sum of the squares of the percentages of the population in different income strata) for municipalities in Los Angeles County in 1950 and 1970. Since he used only three income strata, complete income heterogeneity would imply an index of 0.333, while complete homogeneity (all residents in the same income strata) would imply an index of 1.0. In 1950, 60 percent of the 42 cities for which data were available were virtually indistinguishable from the maximum degree of heterogeneity, and from Los Angeles County as a whole (index = 0.335) (see Table 9.1). Only 10 percent of 1950 municipalities fell into the most homogeneous category (0.400+).

The distribution of indices in 1970 shifted distinctly toward greater homogeneity, with only 16 percent of the municipalities in the most heterogeneous category and 17 percent in the most homogeneous category, even though Los Angeles County

---

[14] Part of the explanation for the inconsistency between Conway and Houtenville's results and the Tiebout hypothesis may be due to the level of aggregation of their analysis. States with high property taxes and levels of public services may on average attract individuals who make desirable neighbors. The local communities in which the elderly locate in these states may, however, have low education expenditures and property taxes. The elderly's choice of a new home may also simply be dominated by nonpublic-sector factors like the desire to be near children or grandchildren.

as a whole remained heterogeneous in income in 1970 (index = 0.334), as it was in 1950. Perhaps the strongest evidence that the Tiebout process does result in increased income homogeneity comes from the 30 newly created municipalities. To the extent that new municipalities come into existence to satisfy demands unmet by existing communities, their composition should accord most closely, in an age of high mobility, with the Tiebout hypothesis. Only 1 of the 30 newly created municipalities had income heterogeneity comparable to that of the entire county; almost one-fourth of the new municipalities fell into the most homogeneous category. In Miller's study, it appears to be largely a common preference for lower taxes and the avoidance of the redistributive outlays of the larger, older cities that drives the formation of new, suburban communities. Miller also presents evidence of increasing racial homogeneity within, and increasing heterogeneity across Los Angeles municipalities between 1950 and 1970.

Grubb (1982) also documents Tiebout sorting in the Boston metropolitan area, and Hamilton, Mills, and Puryear (1975) find less inequality of income within Standard Metropolitan Statistical Areas (SMSAs), the greater the number of school districts from which citizens can choose, and in general a better fit to Tiebout-model variables for suburban than for central city observations. Similar results have been reported by Eberts and Gronberg (1981). The Tiebout process is again found to work as predicted, and in so doing to produce less dispersion of incomes within the local polity.

Using a much longer time span than all the other studies, Rhode and Strumpf (2000), however, have found evidence of *decreasing* heterogeneity *across* communities using several measures of heterogeneity. Their work suggests that additional factors beyond mobility affect intra- and intercommunity heterogeneity over the very long run.[15]

Corroborative evidence of a different kind has been presented by Munley (1982) and Gramlich and Rubinfeld (1982a). Tiebout sorting should be more complete the greater the number of different political jurisdictions in which a mobile citizen can choose to live. Consistent with this prediction is Munley's finding that the dispersion of voter demands for education in Long Island, New York, decreased as the number of school jurisdictions in a geographic area increased. Similarly, Gramlich and Rubinfeld find a smaller residual variance in expenditure demands in the Detroit metropolitan area than in other parts of Michigan where a smaller number of local communities are available to the citizen.

Implicit in the Tiebout process is the assumption that when citizens with homogeneous preferences form a community, the community supplies the level of expenditures that these citizens demand, and thus that the citizens are more satisfied with the bundles of local public goods, which they consume. This part of the Tiebout model is supported by Gramlich and Rubinfeld's (1982a, p. 556) finding that two-thirds of Detroit metropolitan area voters surveyed wished to see no change in government expenditures, and the average desired change was only −1 percent. Although the percentage of voters desiring no change in expenditures (60 percent)

---

[15] Stein (1987) also offers equivocal evidence regarding Tiebout sorting.

was high throughout the rest of Michigan, that this percentage is lower than for Detroit suggests that the greater number of communities in which Detroit metropolitan area residents can choose to reside allows them to locate in communities that better provide them with the level of expenditures they demand.

Gramlich and Rubinfeld's findings are corroborated by Ostrom (1983) and Mouritzen (1989), who both report that citizens express greater satisfaction with local public services in urban areas with larger numbers of local jurisdictions. Brueckner's (1982) evidence that property values in 54 Massachusetts communities suggested neither an over- nor underprovision of local public goods provides still further support for the Tiebout hypothesis.

9.6   Voluntary association, allocational efficiency, and distributional equity

Wicksell's voluntary exchange approach achieves allocational efficiency by imposing a unanimity rule on the polity so that each collective decision must benefit all before it can pass. The approach assumes from the beginning that a predefined polity and citizenry exist.

The theory of clubs and voting-with-the-feet seek to determine a Pareto-optimal distribution of public goods through the voluntary association of individuals of like tastes. Here the dimensions of the polity and citizenship are outcomes of the "voting" process. These processes generally achieve Pareto optimality by grouping individuals into clubs and polities of homogeneous tastes. In the extreme, they satisfy Kramer's (1973) severe condition for consistent majority rule decisions, that all individuals have identical indifference maps, through the imposition of a silent unanimity rule.[16] These processes can realistically be assumed to come close to satisfying this goal, when, relative to the size of the population, (1) the number of public goods is small and/or (2) the number of distinct preferences for combinations of public goods is small. Since *the* task of public choice is the revelation of (differing) individual preferences for public goods, club formation and voting-with-the-feet, in part, solve the public choice problem by limiting its scope.

Despite these qualifications, the ability to exclude some individuals from the benefits of a public good remains a potentially powerful mechanism for revealing individual preferences. If A seeks the construction of tennis courts and B a golf course, then in a community in which all must consume the same bundle of public goods, and preferences are revealed by voting, regardless of what the eventual outcome is, it is likely to involve nonoptimal quantities of at least one good for one of the voters. This voter, say, A, is then worse off than she would have been had B also preferred tennis to golf and was willing to bear a larger share of this sport's costs. If A were incumbent to the community and B outside, A would clearly prefer that others with preferences closer to hers join the community, and, if it were in her power might discriminate in their favor over B.

---

[16] See also McGuire (1974), and on the relationship between voting-with-the-feet and the unanimity rule, see Pauly (1967, p. 317).

   In Frey and Eichenberger's (1995, 1999) proposal it is not citizen mobility that drives competition across communities, but the entry and exit of political units in a federalist system.

None of this is very troubling if the public goods are tennis and golf, and the polities private clubs. No one objects too strenuously to a tennis club's restricting membership to those who want to play tennis. But the implications are less comforting for more general definitions of public goods. As we have seen, when individuals have positive income elasticities of demand for public goods, they can benefit from being in a community with incomes higher on average than their own from the additional units of the public good it provides. Even when each individual is taxed her marginal evaluation of the public good – that is, the Lindahl price – an effective redistribution from rich to poor occurs through the egalitarian distribution of the public good that of necessity occurs when rich and poor consume it together. But one's income elasticity of demand can be regarded as a sort of "taste" for a public good. If the incumbent membership of a local polity is free to exclude new members, then one can expect a sorting out of individuals into local polities of identical tastes *and* incomes, thus thwarting the possibility for this type of redistribution.

Wicksell assumed that voting on allocational issues took place following the determination of a just distribution of income. The same assumption could be made to support a voluntary association solution to the public good problem. But here it must be recognized that the voluntary association approach is likely to affect the distribution of income, while revealing preferences for public goods. A given distribution of private incomes might be considered just when individuals reside in communities of heterogeneous income strata, so that the relatively poor benefit from the higher demands for public goods by the relatively well-to-do. The same distribution of income might be considered unjust if individuals were distributed into communities of similar income and the relatively poor could consume only those quantities of public goods which they themselves could afford to provide.

The latter is the logical outcome of the voting-with-the-feet process, and one that is coming to pass. If the resulting distribution from this process were thought to be unjust, one could correct it by making transfers across communities, but here one runs directly into the issue of the proper bounds of the polity and the rights of citizenship.

In a federalist system there are two possible ways to view citizenship. Primary citizenship can reside with the local polity, and the central polity can be thought of as a mere union or confederation of the local polities with certain powers delegated to it. Conversely, primary citizenship can reside with the central state, with the local polities being merely administrative branches of the central government and having powers delegated from above. Under the first view of the polity, it would seem that the rights of the local polity to define its own citizenship and to pick and choose entrants would dominate the right of citizens in the larger confederation to migrate, free of hindrances, to any local polity. Here we see a direct clash between two of the conditions for achieving a decentralized, efficient allocation of public goods: the full mobility assumption, and the right of the local polity to tax and subsidize migration. If primary citizenship lies with the central state, then presumably individuals would be free to enter and exit local communities without incurring locally imposed penalties. Equity issues would be viewed from the perspective of the central polity, and it would be free to engage in intergovernmental transfers.

The same distinction exists with respect to clubs. The freedom to form voluntary associations can be regarded as one of the basic rights of the individual. To exercise this right in an optimal way, club members must be free to determine the quality and quantity characteristics of the excludable public good supplied to themselves *and* the size of the club's membership. When the supply functions for excludable public goods and the size of the population allow for the formation of many, individually optimally sized clubs, voluntary club formation can achieve a Pareto-optimal allocation of resources across the whole community. The outcome is entirely analogous to the Pareto-optimal allocation of resources that voluntary actions in the market achieve when large numbers of buyers and sellers exist. Indeed, firms are merely clubs of factor owners formed to achieve economies of joint supply in production, where the clubs discussed in this chapter arise to achieve economies from joint supply in consumption. Once again as in the market, however, when technology and population size combine to yield but a small number of optimally sized clubs, the independent utility-maximizing decisions of individuals may not achieve an outcome that is optimal from the perspective of the entire community.

In Chapter 2 we argued that the state emerges as a low-transaction-cost institution for achieving the cooperative agreements necessary for Pareto optimality in the presence of public goods and externalities. By extension, clubs, local polities, and the whole federalist institutional structure of the state might be formed to minimize the transaction costs of making collective decisions (Tullock, 1969; Breton and Scott, 1978).[17] But the discussion of this chapter reveals that the creation of new political jurisdictions within the state, the assignment of functions and revenue sources to different units, and the definition of citizen rights within a federated state raise issues that go beyond transaction costs savings and allocative efficiency. They go to the heart of the normative characteristics of the polity.

9.7   The theory of revolution

When neither the ballot nor the feet constitute adequate modes of expression, there is still Chairman Mao's barrel of the gun. One might expect to find more said about revolutions than has been the case, given their role in real-world politics. For the public choice analyst, the puzzle of revolutions is why individuals participate in them, and thus why they ever occur.

Consider the decision of individual i as to whether to participate in a revolution in her country, and if so how much time to contribute. She is unhappy with the present regime and anticipates benefits of β_i should the revolution succeed and a new order be imposed. The probability of this occurring is a function of the time i contributes to the revolution, t_{ir}, and the time all other citizens contribute, $O_{ir} = \sum_{j \neq i} t_{jr}$. Call this probability $\pi(t_{ir}, O_{ir})$. In addition to the gains, should the revolution succeed, i may receive personal pleasure from participating in the revolutionary movement, whether it succeeds or not, $P_i(t_{ir}, O_{ir})$.

---

[17] By further analogy, clubs of factor owners (firms) arise to minimize transaction costs in production (Coase, 1937).

Against these benefits the costs of participation must be weighed. Should i be caught and punished, she faces a fine or imprisonment promising a utility loss F_i. The probability that she will be caught, C_i, is a function of the time she devotes to the revolution, t_{ir}, the time others devote, O_i, and the resources expended by the regime to crush the revolution, R, that is, $C_i(t_{ir}, O_i, R)$ with expected partial derivatives

$$\frac{\partial C_i}{\partial t_{ir}} > 0, \qquad \frac{\partial C_i}{\partial O_i} < 0, \qquad \frac{\partial C_i}{\partial R} > 0.$$

In addition, by devoting time to the revolution, i foregoes income. If w is the market wage, then this opportunity cost is $w t_{ir}$.

The expected benefits from participating in the revolution are then

$$E_i = \beta_i \pi_i(t_{ir}, O_{ir}) + P_i(t_{ir}, O_{ir}) - F_i C_i(t_{ir}, O_i, R) - w t_{ir}. \tag{9.43}$$

Maximizing (9.42) with respect to t_{ir}, we obtain

$$\beta_i \frac{\partial \pi_i}{\partial t_{ir}} + \frac{\partial P_i}{\partial t_{ir}} = F_i \frac{\partial C_i}{\partial t_{ir}} + w \tag{9.44}$$

as the condition i must satisfy when determining her optimal level of revolutionary activity. The marginal expected gain in public good benefits (β_i) from an extra hour of participation plus the marginal personal enjoyment must equal the added risk of being caught when spending another hour in the revolution plus the foregone wage from not having worked that hour.

With O_i large, the change in both π_i and C_i from an additional hour of participation for the average person will be negligible. Whether someone participates or not, and if so to what degree, thus depends almost solely on the purely personal satisfaction from participation in the revolutionary movement weighed against the foregone income from taking time away from market activity (Tullock, 1971a, 1974), a result resembling that in the voting literature.

For the average citizen, the benefits from the revolution's success are the pure public good benefits from living under one regime rather than under another. But for a few, β_i represents the benefits from a position in the new government formed after the revolution. For these leaders, both β_i and $\partial \pi / \partial t_{ir}$ may be much larger than for the average individual. Thus, it is easier to explain the participation of the leaders of a revolutionary movement using a rational choice model than the participation of the rank and file (Silver, 1974; Tullock, 1974). Note, however, that for the leaders, F_i and $\partial C_i / \partial t_{ir}$ may also be higher. Under a rational choice theory, leaders of a revolution are like entrepreneurs in the theory of the firm, risktakers with extreme optimism regarding their ability to beat the odds.

The marginal effect of an average individual's contribution to the revolution's success should fall with the aggregate contributions of others, O_i. This free-rider effect will lower t_{ir} (Olson, 1965; Austen-Smith, 1981a). But there is also safety in numbers. The marginal risk of being caught, $\partial C_i / \partial t_{ir}$, may also shift downward with an increase in the revolutionary activity of others, thereby encouraging more revolutionary participation (Gunning, 1972; DeNardo, 1985). The personal rewards from participating in the revolution may also be characterized by a bandwagon effect and rise as others join the movement. Thus, participation levels could be characterized by increasing or diminishing returns to scale.

An increase in the resources devoted to crushing the revolution should lead to an increase in the marginal probability of getting caught, and thus discourage participation. Participation should be lower the higher the pecuniary costs, w.

Although the rational behavior approach to revolutionary activity gives some insights into why revolutions occur, it does not generate a rich harvest of testable implications. It does appear, however, that a revolution's success is greatly affected by the resources that the regime devotes to stopping it and thereby to curbing participation (Silver, 1974; DeNardo, 1985).

Perhaps the most distinctive implication of the theory is the prediction that participation declines with the wage rate. Austen-Smith (1981a) also has shown that it declines with a reduction in uncertainty about the wage if participants are risk averse. Tests of these implications by Finney (1987) indicate that the number of deaths from political violence in a country is negatively related to both the level and growth in national income, and is positively related to the standard deviation of the growth rate (a measure of uncertainty).

Although results such as Finney's are encouraging, it is yet to be seen how far a rational behavior model can go in explaining such extreme behavior as occurs in revolutions. Just as with the voluntary provision of a public good, the optimal choice for most rational individuals, when a meeting is called to stage a revolution, is to stay home (Olson, 1965; Dixit and Olson, 2000). Nevertheless, these models fill an analytical gap in the public choice literature. In a closed polity, an individual is always in danger of being "exploited" or "tyrannized" by a majority or minority of her fellow citizens. Her choices in such situations are to continue to rely on voice in the hope that the outcomes will change, to seek a new polity by migration, or to create a new one by revolution. The goal of public choice theory must be to explain all three choices.

Bibliographical notes

The discussion of efficiency and equity in a federalist system predates the public choice–Tiebout literature. See, for example, Buchanan (1950, 1952), Scott (1950, 1952a,b), and Musgrave (1961).

Ng (1985b) shows that one cannot have efficiency with club formation without violating *either* equity as argued earlier *or* freedom (voluntary association).

The clubs–Tiebout literatures have been surveyed by Henderson (1979); Sandler and Tschirhart (1980, 1997); Dowding, John, and Biggs (1994); and Inman and Rubinfeld (1997). Ostrom and Walker (1997) discuss the properties of a variety of club- and polity-like organizations.

The properties of markets in price-excludable public goods are analyzed by Oakland (1974), Burns and Walsh (1981), Brennan and Walsh (1981), and Walsh (1986).

PART III

Public choice in a representative democracy

CHAPTER 10

Federalism

Everyone knows that a great proportion of the errors committed by the State legislatures proceeds from the disposition of the members to sacrifice the comprehensive and permanent interest of the State, to the particular and separate views of the counties or districts in which they reside. And if they do not sufficiently enlarge their policy to embrace the collective welfare of their particular state, how can it be imagined that they will make the aggregate prosperity of the Union, and the dignity and respectability of its government, the objects of their affections and considerations? For the same reason that the members of the State legislatures will be unlikely to attach themselves sufficiently to national objects, the members of the federal legislature will be likely to attach themselves too much to local objects. The States will be to the latter what towns and counties are to the former. Measures will be too often decided according to their probable effect, not on the national prosperity and happiness, but on the prejudices, interests, and pursuits of the governments and people of the individual States.

The Federalist (James Madison)

In Part III we examine the properties of the different institutions of representative government that have been devised to supplement or replace direct democracy as a means of representing individual preferences. We begin with the United States's contribution to the evolution of representative government – *federalism* – because it is in some ways related to the theory of clubs reviewed in the preceding chapter.

10.1 The logic of federalism

10.1.1 *The assignment problem*

Imagine a polity of nine persons divided into three local communities with three persons each. There are two public goods to be provided, G_L and G_F, where G_F is a public good like national defense, which when supplied to one community benefits all, and G_L is a public good with localized *spillovers*, like police protection. Let G_L and G_F be single-dimensional public goods, and the nine members of the polity have single-peaked preferences with ideal points as depicted in Figure 10.1. All

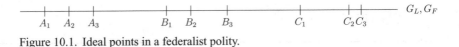

Figure 10.1. Ideal points in a federalist polity.

nine consume G_F in equal quantities. Individuals A_1, A_2, and A_3 belong to local community A, and they consume only the amount G_L supplied to their community. The same is true for the three individuals belonging to B and the three belonging to C.

Suppose now that the amounts of both G_L and G_F are decided by the larger community of nine using the simple majority rule, and that the quantity of G_L chosen by the larger polity is provided to each of the three smaller ones. With single-peaked preferences and single-dimensional issue spaces, the logic of the median voter theorem applies, and the quantities of both G_L and G_F provided correspond to the ideal point of the median voter in the polity of nine, B_2. Because G_F has the properties of a pure public good for the larger community of nine, any quantity of G_L and G_F chosen *must* be consumed by all nine citizens and, given that the simple majority is used to select this quantity, the amount B_2 can be regarded as the optimum. But the public good properties of G_L allow different quantities of it to be provided to each of the three local communities. It is obvious from the location of the ideal points in Figure 10.1 and the assumption of single-peaked preferences that the members of community A can all be made better off if a smaller quantity of G_L than B_2 is supplied, and the members of C will be better off with a larger quantity. Such quantities will be chosen if each local community can choose its own quantity of G_L using the simple majority rule. Thus, a superior institutional arrangement to having the quantities of both G_L and G_F decided by the larger community is to *assign* the authority to decide G_F to the larger community, and the authority to decide G_L to the three smaller ones. Having done so, one has created a *federalist* state.

A federalist state has two salient properties: (1) separate and overlapping levels of government exist and (2) different responsibilities are attached to the different levels of government. The polar case of a federalist system would have specific authorities for different activities assigned to each level of government, with each level able to determine both the expenditure levels for the activities assigned to it, and the taxes to cover these expenditures. No federalist country fits this polar case, however. In the United States, for example, primary responsibility for law enforcement lies with state and local levels of government, but Congress has passed laws governing certain criminal offenses, and federal police – like the FBI – often duplicate or assist the activities of state and local police. In many countries commonly thought of as federalist states, like the Federal Republic of Germany, regional and local levels of government have very limited authority to levy their own taxes, and thus are limited to allocating funds raised by and transferred to them by the central government. Nevertheless, all countries that are generally regarded as federalist in structure exhibit these two salient features to some degree.

A normative justification for the state is to provide public goods and resolve market failures and social dilemmas. The extension of this logic to a political community composed of states within states would determine the bounds of each governmental component on the basis of the extent of the spillovers from the public goods it was assigned, or the size of the community that was caught in a prisoners' dilemma. If the dimensions of the spillovers from two public goods were identical, both could be assigned to the same level of government. If, however, no two public goods had exactly the same geographic spillovers, the optimal federalist structure would see each public good provided by a different government, each law determined and enforced by a different government. An individual could easily be a citizen in thousands of different, overlapping governments.

Quite obviously such a situation could *not* be optimal. We have run into our old friend "transaction costs," and just as the existence of transaction costs ultimately explains the existence of the state, the existence of transaction costs explains why a federalist state is optimally composed of a few levels of government with multiple functions assigned to each level rather than thousands of levels of government with one task each. Even in a direct democracy, each citizen must incur the costs of participating in the meetings that decide what actions are warranted. He then must monitor those who carry out the tasks he has authorized. Replacing direct democracy with representative democracy lifts the burden of actually deciding budgets and taxes from the citizen to his representatives, but adds the burdens of having to participate in the process that selects the representatives, and extends the citizens monitoring duties to both the representatives he has chosen and the bureaucrats who execute the collective decisions. If citizens are mobile across communities, we must add in the costs of their having to decide which community to live in, and then of moving to it. When those who design a federalist system address the assignment problem, they must balance all of these transaction costs of having multiple levels of government against the informational efficiencies that arise from having the dimensions of a governmental unit match the benefits this government can provide to its citizens.

Why then not have a single level of government that decides all issues? The nonoptimality of this assignment in our example is contingent upon our constraining the upper level of government to choose the *same* levels of x for each community. But there is no reason to impose such a constraint. With freedom to select different G_Ls, a proposal to supply A_2 of G_L to community A, B_2 to B, and C_2 to C defeats a proposal to provide B_2 of G_L to all three communities. The three citizens of B are indifferent between these two proposals, while the six voters from A and C favor separate levels of G_L. Thus, a single assembly of all citizens assigned responsibility for determining the levels of both local and national public goods could, in principle, duplicate the outcomes arising when the public goods are assigned to local communities. The explanation for why the levels of *all* public goods are not decided in a single assembly of all citizens (or of their representatives) is again a matter of transaction costs. Once we expand the list of public goods to include all local, regional, and national goods, the task that a single assembly would face deciding the levels of each bundle of goods for each community would become mind-boggling.[1]

10.1.2 *Federalism with geographic representation*

The discussion so far has assumed that direct democracy is employed at both levels of government. Let us now assume that representative government is employed at the higher level of government. Each local community elects one representative to an assembly of the higher level of government. (The remainder of Part III deals with representative government, and so we shall not go into the details of how it functions here, but rather consider simplified versions of it.)

Assume first that the authority to decide the level of G_F has been assigned to the representative assembly of the higher level of government, and that the levels of G_L continue to be decided using direct democracy and the simple majority rule. Under these assumptions, the quantities of G_L chosen in the three communities will continue to correspond to the ideal points of the median voter in each community, and can be regarded as optimal, given the constraint of using the simple majority rule.[2]

Let us assume that representatives are elected using the plurality or first-past-the-post system. The candidate receiving the most votes wins. If the only issue that the representative assembly decides is the quantity of G_F, then the candidates can be expected to compete for votes by promising to vote for certain levels of G_F, if elected to the assembly. The issue to be decided is which position along the G_F line the winning representative occupies. The median voter theorem again applies, and the three elected representatives favor the quantities of G_F corresponding to points A_2, B_2, and C_2. If the representative assembly decides the quantity of G_F using the simple majority rule, B_2 is chosen and this system of federalism and representative government selects the same outcomes as would be chosen under direct democracy at each level.

Assume now that the representative assembly is also authorized to decide the quantities of G_L. If we again assume that the same quantity of G_L must be supplied to each local community, then the outcome under this form of geographic representation is the same as under direct democracy. Representative A_2 favors B_2 over any point to its right, representative C_2 favors B_2 to any point to its left, and representative B_2 favors B_2 over all other points, so B_2 wins. Geographic representation in this case produces the same outcome as direct democracy would, and the same is also true if we allow the quantities of G_L supplied to each community to vary.

[1] The classic economic studies linking the characteristics of public goods and transaction costs to the assignment of tasks are by Tullock (1969), Oates (1972), and Breton and Scott (1978). This literature is reviewed by Inman and Rubinfeld (1997).

[2] The chosen quantities will not in general maximize the sum of the utilities of the communities' members or the sum of their consumer surpluses. Thus, by these normative criteria, the chosen outcomes are inferior to, say, those that would be chosen using the demand-revelation process. The proposition that the outcome corresponding to the ideal point of the median voter does not maximize the sum of utilities is demonstrated in Chapter 20. The different normative criteria that one might apply to the collective decision process are the subject matter of Part V.

The situation changes, however, once we expand the dimensionality of the issue set and introduce taxes.

10.2 Why the size of government may be "too large" under federalism

10.2.1 *Logrolling*

Assume that we continue to have a single-dimensional issue space as depicted in Figure 10.1 with the same nine voters as before. A representative assembly has been elected consisting of three representatives who favor the positions A_2, B_2, and C_2. The assembly is now free, however, to determine both the spending on the local public good and the taxes to pay for it. One possible outcome would be to supply the amounts A_2, B_2, and C_2 of G_L to the three communities with tax rates chosen so that each community's tax payments just covered its own consumption of G_L. But this outcome would be inferior from the point of the Bs and Cs, say, to one in which a tax was levied on the As but no G_L was supplied to them, and this revenue was used to pay for G_L in B and C. Such an outcome would lower the effective tax rates that the Bs and Cs would have to pay for G_L and G_F, and thus would shift the ideal point of each member of community B and C to the right in Figure 10.1. Thus, their representatives would favor higher levels of G_L in both communities. A coalition between the representatives of B and C would favor this outcome, therefore, to one in which each community chooses its own level of G_L and pays for it out of its own taxes. If a coalition between the representatives of B and C could form, it could impose this outcome, and there would be "too much" G_L provided in these communities relative to the levels that would arise if the provision of G_L were the responsibility of each local government.

This example resembles Tullock's (1959) example of the overprovision of roads among a community of 100 farmers, where each farmer is served by one road. Tullock does not assume the existence of representative government, and the over-provision outcome might well occur in a direct democracy. The individual citizens in B and C have just as great of an incentive to discriminate against A as do their representatives. This sort of discrimination and potential inefficiency is not per se a product of their being a federalist system and geographic representation; it is due solely to the use of the simple majority rule. What federalism and geographic representation are likely to affect is the *form* that discrimination and redistribution take, *not* their existence.

To see this, consider what might occur under the polar alternative to this form of geographic representation – *at-large* representation. All voters no matter where they live must choose from the same list of candidates. Of course, nations consist of more than nine persons, and their national legislatures have hundreds of seats. Citizens do not choose among *individuals* to fill these seats, but among *parties*. In an at-large representation system, citizens choose from a list of parties, and several parties can be expected to win seats in the legislature.[3] Let us, therefore, think of

---

[3] The characteristics of multiparty systems are the subject of Chapter 13.

the citizens as being represented by parties, but continue for simplicity to assume that there are only nine citizens in the entire polity with preferences for G_L and G_F as in Figure 10.1. If we continue to assume that these citizens are separated geographically into three smaller communities containing the three As and so on, then it would be reasonable to expect an at-large election to produce three parties – the A, B, and C parties – with equal numbers of seats in the national assembly. This allocation of seats can be expected to produce *exactly* the same outcomes as under a geographic system of representation. With a geographic distribution of preferences over the set of collective decisions to be decided, as just described, there is no reason to expect great differences in the outcomes under at-large representation.

Consider now, however, a different geographic distribution of preferences. Instead of communities A, B, and C, we have three communities 1, 2, and 3, with citizens A_1, B_1, and C_1 in community 1; A_2, B_2, and C_2 in community 2; and so on. The high, medium, and low demanders are dispersed evenly across the country. With this geographic distribution of preferences over the set of collective decisions to be decided, geographic representation will lead to the three communities being represented by individuals who hold the positions B_1, B_2, and B_3. B_2 will again be the quantity of G_F chosen. If the quantities of G_L are selected in the higher level of government's assembly, a coalition between the representatives of two of the local communities can again be expected to discriminate against the third by, say, taxing it for G_L but not providing it, and instead providing more G_L to themselves.

The situation is likely to be quite different under at-large representation, however. Here one could again expect A, B, and C parties to win seats by promising to represent the high, medium, and low demanders for G_L and G_F. A coalition between two of the parties would now be based on the levels of their demands for the public goods, and discrimination would likely be against either the high- or the low-demand groups, depending on which coalition formed. If the differences in the demands for the public goods were based on differences in incomes, with the Cs having the highest incomes, then the discrimination and redistribution that would result under the simple majority rule would be related to an individual's income and not her geographic location. Note that under at-large representation, if the levels of G_L in each local community were decided at the national level, a coalition between the A and B parties would ceteris paribus favor a uniform provision of G_L in all local communities that was between A_3 and B_1, and thus *less* than the outcome in two of the three communities, when they alone are responsible for this decision.[4] This is why the words "too large" are placed in quotation marks in the title of this section. In a federalist system, the discrimination and redistribution that result when higher levels of government provide local public goods are likely to result in greater quantities of local public goods being supplied to some communities than would occur if each local community chose its own quantity, and smaller quantities in others.

This latter conclusion depends on there being the kind of exploitation of the minority by the majority under the simply majority rule that Tullock described in

---

[4] Baron (1993) presents a model in which the provision of a local public good by the central government can have equally ambiguous results.

his farmers/roads example. Some have argued that this sort of discrimination does not in fact occur. We examine their arguments next.

10.2.2 *Universalism*

The results of the previous section presume that a winning coalition in the legislature of the central government exploits the potential inherent in the majority rule and provides the local public good to only its members and/or provides these goods using discriminatory tax formulas. This sort of "tyranny" by the majority coalition has obvious attractions for its members but, given the high probabilities of cycling, it also has its risks. The representative or party that finds itself in a winning coalition today may be on the losing side tomorrow. To avoid such risks, several authors have claimed that legislatures adopt a norm of *universalism*. Every local community is supplied any local public that the central government supplies.[5]

If the legislature of the higher level of government is to choose the levels of G_L for each local community using a norm of universalism, one might expect it to supply the amounts A_2, B_2, and C_2 if the citizens' preferences were as depicted in Figure 10.1. The empirical evidence in support of universalism suggests that the high demanders have greater influence in the legislature, however (Weingast and Marshall, 1988; Hall and Grofman, 1990). Thus, instead of the set of outputs A_2, B_2, and C_2 being provided, A_3, B_3, and C_3 are.

Often the effect of geographic representation seems not to be that a particular local public good is provided by the central government to each local community, but that different local public goods are provided. Each representative in the federal legislature proposes a "pet project" that her constituents would like to see the federal government finance. The application of the norm of universalism results in all of their wishes being fulfilled.

Schwartz (1994) presents a model to explain why this comes about. Each representative is concerned only about being reelected, and her constituents are only concerned about their pet projects being provided. The constituents ignore the costs of these projects, which are spread across the entire federal polity, and the outcome is that bundles of local public goods get provided by the central government that individually would have been turned down by their respective local communities. *Too much* of each local public good is provided.

10.3 Intergovernmental grants under federalism

One important feature of federalist systems is that one level of government may not actually provide a public good for another level, but merely transfers money to it. These intergovernmental grants are usually from the higher levels to the lower ones, but not always. The European Union's budget is made up of grants from the 15 national governments of the countries in it. In this section we explore the properties

---

[5] An explanation for universalism that is less dependent on the assumption of selfish utility maximization would be that members are moved out of a sense of fairness to apply legislation universally. See Weingast (1979), Niou and Ordeshook (1985), and Weingast and Marshall (1988).

of such grants. We first look at the normative argument for having such grants, and then at the empirical evidence relating to their effects.

10.3.1 *Intergovernmental grants to achieve Pareto optimality*

Intergovernmental grants can improve the allocation of resources when a locally provided public good has positive externalities. One example of such a public good is highways. In some federalist systems, like the United States, each regional government is responsible for building and maintaining the roads in its political jurisdiction. In addition to its own citizens using these roads, however, the citizens of other jurisdictions sometimes use them. To achieve Pareto optimality the demand for maintenance and construction of these roads should be measured by summing the demand schedules of all users, whether they are citizens of the jurisdiction or not. But the political system only records the demands for roads in a given jurisdiction of its own citizens. The demand for roads by all citizens in the country is underestimated, and the resulting quantity of road services provided is less than the Pareto-optimal quantity.

In this example, the provision of roads by one community leads to a *positive externality* with respect to other communities, and the problem can be investigated like that of any externality. The problem is exactly like that analyzed in Section 2.6 except that the externality is symmetric. In the case of two communities, A and B, the amount of the public good, G_A, that A consumes equals its own provision of roads, R_A, plus a fraction s_A of the amount of roads supplied by B, $0 < s_A < 1$; and the same is true for B:

$$G_A = R_A + s_a R_B, \qquad G_B = R_B + s_B R_A. \tag{10.1}$$

If all citizens in A have the same incomes, Y_A, and utility functions, $U_A(X_A, G_A)$, then they will unanimously agree to construct the amount of roads that maximizes the following Lagrangian:

$$L_I = U_A(x_A, G_A) + \lambda(Y_A - P_x x_A - P_r R_A), \tag{10.2}$$

where P_x and P_r are the prices of the private good X and roads, and G_A satisfies (10.1). Maximization of (10.2) leads to the familiar first-order condition

$$\frac{\partial U_A/\partial G_A}{\partial U_A/\partial X_A} = \frac{P_r}{P_x}. \tag{10.3}$$

An analogous condition could be derived for the representative citizen from B (all Bs also have identical utility functions).

To obtain the Pareto-optimal quantity of roads, we maximize the utility of a representative A with respect to the four decision variables X_A, X_B, R_A, and R_B, subject to the constraint that the utility of a representative B is held constant, and the aggregate budget constraint.

$$L_{PO} = U_A(X_A, G_A) + \lambda(\bar{U}_B - U_B(X_B, G_B))$$
$$+ \gamma(Y_A + Y_B - P_x X_A - P_x X_B - P_r R_A - P_r R_B). \tag{10.4}$$

This yields the four first-order conditions:

$$\frac{\partial L_{PO}}{\partial X_A} = \frac{\partial U_A}{\partial X_A} - \gamma P_x = 0$$

$$\frac{\partial L_{PO}}{\partial X_B} = \frac{\partial U_B}{\partial X_B} - \gamma P_x = 0$$

$$\frac{\partial L_{PO}}{\partial R_A} = \frac{\partial U_A}{\partial G_A}\frac{\partial G_A}{\partial R_A} - \lambda\frac{\partial U_B}{\partial G_B}\frac{\partial G_B}{\partial R_A} - \gamma P_r = 0$$

$$\frac{\partial L_{PO}}{\partial R_B} = \frac{\partial U_A}{\partial G_A}\frac{\partial G_A}{\partial R_B} - \lambda\frac{\partial U_B}{\partial G_B}\frac{\partial G_B}{\partial R_B} - \gamma P_r = 0.$$

(10.5)

From (10.1) we have

$$\frac{\partial G_A}{\partial R_A} = 1, \qquad \frac{\partial G_A}{\partial R_B} = s_B, \qquad \frac{\partial G_B}{\partial R_B} = 1, \qquad \frac{\partial G_B}{\partial R_A} = s_A. \qquad (10.6)$$

Substituting from (10.6) into (10.5) and rearranging yields (10.7):[6]

$$\frac{\partial U_A/\partial G_A}{\partial U_A/\partial X_A} = \frac{P_r}{P_x} - s_B\frac{\partial U_B/\partial G_B}{\partial U_B/\partial X_B}$$

$$\frac{\partial U_B/\partial G_B}{\partial U_B/\partial X_B} = \frac{P_r}{P_x} - s_A\frac{\partial U_A/\partial G_A}{\partial U_A/\partial X_A}.$$

(10.7)

Equation (10.3) states the condition that is fulfilled when the representative citizen from A maximizes her utility ignoring the consequences of this decision for B. An analogous condition holds for B. Substituting these into (10.7) gives us

$$\frac{\partial U_A/\partial G_A}{\partial U_A/\partial X_A} = (1 - s_B)\frac{P_r}{P_x}$$

$$\frac{\partial U_B/\partial G_B}{\partial U_B/\partial X_B} = (1 - s_A)\frac{P_r}{P_x}.$$

(10.8)

To achieve the Pareto-optimal supply of roads in the two communities a Pigouvian subsidy must be offered to a community per unit of roads purchased that equals the proportionate spillovers from its roads onto the other community.

One way to obtain this outcome is for the higher level of government to levy lump sum taxes on both communities and then offer each of them subsidies in the form of *matching grants*. The effects of a matching grant on a local community's purchases are illustrated in Figure 10.2. In the absence of any grant the community faces the budget constraint BB and purchases X_0 of the private good and G_0 of the public good. A 50 percent matching grant results in the federal government's purchasing one unit of G for every unit of G purchased by the local community and is equivalent

---

[6] Compare the analogous derivation for externalities in equations (2.34) through (2.41).

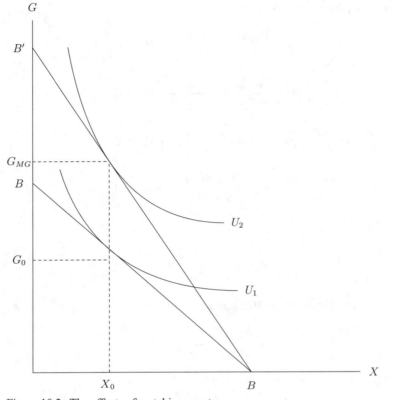

Figure 10.2. The effects of matching grants.

to a 50 percent reduction in the price of G to the local community. This shifts the community's budget constraint line out to BB', and it now purchases G_{MG} of the public good. If G is a normal good, both the substitution and the income effects of the matching grant cause the amount of G purchased to increase. These two effects work in opposite directions with respect to its consumption of the private good X, however, and the net effect could be a reduction in the amount of X purchased. Should this occur, the increase in the amount of G brought about by the matching grant would be *greater* than the amount of money actually transferred from the central to the local government. Thus, matching grants are a potentially powerful way to influence the patterns of spending by local communities.

A second form of intergovernmental grant often employed is an *unrestricted* or *general* grant. As its name implies such grants are unconditional and allow the local government the freedom to spend the money any way it chooses, including as a *tax expenditure*, that is by cutting its local taxes to some or all of its citizens and thereby allowing them to use some of the grant to increase their private consumption. The effects of an unrestricted grant are illustrated in Figure 10.3. In the absence of the grant the community's budget constraint is BB and it purchases X_0 and G_0 of the two goods. The unrestricted grant allows the community to increase its consumption of the private good by $B' - B$ if it offsets all of the grant by a tax cut, or to increase its consumption of public goods by this amount. The community's budget constraint

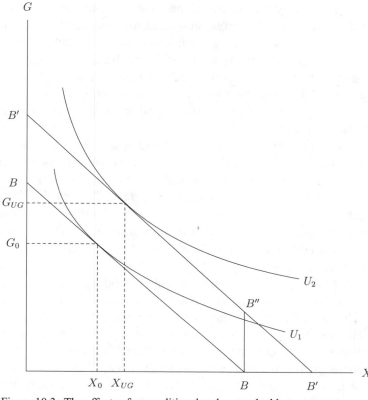

Figure 10.3. The effects of unconditional and earmarked lump-sum grants.

line shifts out to $B'B'$, and it now purchases G_{UG} of the public good and X_{UG} of the private good. If both G and X are normal goods, the amounts of each purchased increase. An unrestricted grant's only impact on the quantity of local public goods purchased comes through its income effect, and thus it can be expected to lead to a smaller increase in the local community's spending on public goods than a matching grant.

A third form of intergovernmental grant is an *earmarked* or *specific* grant. Earmarked grants can only be used to finance the programs for which they are earmarked, but they resemble unconditional grants in that they do not constrain the local government to spend any specific amounts of its own money on these programs. Thus, specific grants can also provide local governments with the freedom to reduce their taxes. An earmarked grant does not allow the community to reduce its consumption of the public good for which it is earmarked below the level of the grant. Thus, an earmarked grant of the same magnitude as the unrestricted grant just discussed would shift the community's budget constraint line out by $B' - B$ from point B on the X axis (see Figure 10.3). The new budget constraint becomes the kinked line $BB''B'$. If the quantity of the public good that the community would have purchased in the absence of the specific grant exceeds the amount of the grant, which is the case in Figure 10.3, then an earmarked grant's only impact on the quantities of the two goods purchased also comes entirely through its income effect, and the outcome is exactly the same as if there had been no conditions attached to the grant. If the quantity of the public good that the community would have purchased in the absence of the specific grant is less than the amount of the grant, then an earmarked grant increases the quantity of the public good purchased up to the level of the grant. Of the three grants discussed, clearly matching grants give the central government "the most bang for its buck" in affecting the direction of local government spending, and thus are most compatible with a "spillovers" rationale for intergovernmental grants.

An alternative justification for intergovernmental grants is to offset differences in fiscal capacities across communities. Consider again the example using Figure 10.1, and assume that the reason community A wishes to purchase less of the two public goods is that its citizens have lower incomes than in B and C. Following the argument for Pareto-optimal redistribution presented in Chapter 3, citizens in B and C may get utility out of transferring money to community A. A proportional or progressive federal income tax combined with a federal grant to A could thus be a form of Pareto-optimal redistribution.

If citizens in A prefer smaller quantities of public goods than those in B and C because they are poorer than the citizens of B and C, then consumption of private goods in A also will be lower than in the other two communities. If now citizens in B and C merely wish to raise the welfare of citizens in A through intergovernmental grants, then they will do so by voting for an *unrestricted* grant. Such a grant allows citizens in A to use the funds any way they choose, and thus to allocate these funds between public and private goods to maximize their utilities. It is the form of intergovernmental grant which is most compatible with citizen/consumer sovereignty. Thus, the logic underlying the optimal form of intergovernmental grant is completely reversed when the goal is to achieve Pareto optimality – where matching grants are to be preferred to correct inefficiencies arising from intergovernmental spillovers, unconditional grants are optimal to eliminate the "interpersonal externalities" that arise when the residents of wealthy communities contemplate the situation of people in poorer ones.

Sometimes it is argued that intergovernmental grants to poorer communities are needed, not simply to allow the citizens in these communities to increase their welfare as best they see fit by expanding their consumption of both private and public goods, but rather to allow (induce) them to increase their purchases of specific *governmentally provided* goods. Citizens in wealthy communities only get utility out of the additional consumption of certain public goods by a poor community. One example of such a good might be education. If A must provide education to its citizens out of its own tax revenues, the median voter favors A_2 of education. But citizens in B and C believe that no child should receive less of an education than is implied by, say, B_2 of education. If such were the case, matching or earmarked federal grants to local communities for education might be needed to achieve Pareto optimality.

There are other factors that affect the nature and size of intergovernmental grants, but many of these are hypotheses about why these grants *actually* exist, rather than hypotheses about why they *ought* to exist. We take them up in the next subsection, therefore.

10.3.2 *The empirical evidence on intergovernmental grants*

The analysis of intergovernmental grants leads to some very clear predictions as to their effects on local governments' spending. If a local government's budget is, say, 5 percent of the income of its residents, and the income elasticity of demand for local public goods is one, then 5 percent of any block grant to a local government should wind up as an increase in local government spending, and the rest be allocated to the private consumption and savings of its residents, since for such an unconditional grant, only its income effect is at work. This simple prediction has, however, been consistently disconfirmed in the empirical literature. Local government spending has been found to increase by anywhere from 25 percent of the size of the grant to over 200 percent, with the average estimate exceeding 50 percent.[7] Money from the central government transferred to a local government largely "sticks where it lands" – in the local government's budget. So consistent is this result that it has acquired its own name: the *flypaper effect.*

Such a consistent and dramatic refutation of the predictions of the simple governmental grants model has led to a huge literature, which has either reworked the model to try and get it to fit the data, or reworked the data to try and get them to fit the model.[8] The literature is too vast for us to wade very deeply into it. We content ourselves here, therefore, with an examination of two explanations for the flypaper effect that rely on public choice reasoning, and a brief look at the econometric criticisms.

One explanation for the flypaper effect is that it is due to *fiscal illusion* (Courant, Gramlich, and Rubinfeld, 1979; Oates, 1979) . Tanzi (1980) has traced the concept of fiscal illusion back to John Stuart Mill and also cites Pareto as a source. But it is to the Italian economist Puviani (1897, 1903) that credit must go for emphasizing the importance of fiscal illusion to a positive theory of government (see also the discussion in Buchanan, 1967, pp. 126–43). The general idea of fiscal illusion is that there are certain revenue sources of the government that are unobserved or not fully observed by the citizens. If money from these sources is spent, some or all citizens benefit from these expenditures, and support for the government increases. Because the citizens are unaware of the source of these expenditures, they do not perceive the pain of having either paid higher taxes or foregone a tax cut to bring about this increase in expenditures. Thus, spending revenue from sources that are hidden from the citizens' view by fiscal illusion should increase the popularity of the government and thus those in government who seek reelection have an obvious incentive to spend any revenue that is subject to fiscal illusion, and seek revenue that has this characteristic. With respect to intergovernmental grants the fiscal illusion argument is that voters do not perceive that these grants are implicitly to *them* and not to those in their local government, and thus that all of the money could be

---

[7] The 25 percent figure comes from Gramlich and Galper. Kurnow (1963), the earliest study that Gramlich (1977) lists in his survey of the empirical literature, estimated increases in local expenditures that were 245 percent of the size of the grant.

[8] For surveys of this literature, see Gramlich (1977), Inman (1979), Fisher (1982), Heyndels and Smolders (1994, 1995), Hines and Thaler (1995), Becker (1996), and Bailey and Connolly (1998).

given to the voters if those in government chose to do so. The citizens' ignorance of the economics of intergovernmental grants leads to fiscal illusion regarding these grants. This fiscal illusion *allows* those in the local government to spend a higher fraction of the grant money than would maximize the voters' utilities. The local government exploits this opportunity and the "paradox" of the flypaper effect is explained.

The preceeding explanation of the flypaper effect relies on the motivation of elected officers in local government to increase their popularity. A second explanation of the flypaper effect emphasizes the motivation of the unelected officers in local government who reside in its bureaucracies. Niskanen (1971) has hypothesized that government bureaucrats seek to maximize the size of their budgets. His theory also relies on information asymmetries, but now it is the elected members of government who lack information and are exploited by the appointed bureaucrats who have it.[9] An explanation for the flypaper effect based on this theory could run as follows: the central government provides a grant earmarked for education to a local government. The grant is less than the local government's current education budget, and thus is equivalent to an unconditional grant and should result in only a modest increase in local education expenditures. Members of the local education bureaucracy, however, are keen on spending the money and take advantage of the elected politicians' ignorance of the costs and benefits of education to convince them that this money "really is needed to improve the quality of local schooling." A large fraction of the grant winds up as an *addition* to the local education budget.[10]

The prediction of a modest budgetary impact of intergovernmental grants applies only to unconditional and (most) earmarked grants. The budgetary impact of matching grants could be large. It is not always easy to determine the nature of the grants made, however, and thus some matching grants have been included in the empirical studies that find a flypaper effect. This is one possible empirical explanation for it.

A related explanation is that an earmarked grant may, *implicitly*, be a matching grant (Chernick, 1979). When the central government decides to provide a local community with a grant earmarked for education, it presumably does so because it wants the local government to spend more on education. If the local government chooses to use most of the grant to cut taxes and not increase education outlays, the central government's objective has not been met. This outcome could significantly reduce the probability of a similar grant from the central government in the future. If members of the local government realize this – and if they do not, members of the central government are likely to make them aware of this danger – they will treat the earmarked grant as a matching grant and expand their education budget by more than the amount warranted from the income effect of the grant alone. It is better for the elected local politicians to obtain money from the central government, even if they must spend it on education, than not to obtain it at all.

---

[9] Niskanen's theory is discussed in Chapter 16 along with the related theory of Brennan and Buchanan (1980).

[10] Wilde's (1968, 1971) explanation for the flypaper effect anticipates Niskanen's model to some extent. Schneider and Ji (1987) provide empirical support for a bureaucratic power explanation by showing that the extent of competition between governments, which presumably reduces a bureaucracy's monopsony power, reduces the magnitude of the flypaper effect.

Several criticisms have been made of the econometrics employed in flypaper-effect estimations. But improving the econometrics alone does not seem capable of eliminating it.[11] Perhaps the simplest, and yet potentially most devastating attack on the empirical evidence for a flypaper effect is by Becker (1996). She is able to eliminate the flypaper effect simply by substituting a logarithmic functional form for the linear one commonly used. In much econometric work, such substitutions have only modest effects on the conclusions drawn. That it should have such a dramatic effect in this literature is noteworthy. Pending confirmation of Becker's findings with other data sets, however, one still must conclude that a significant fraction of federal grant money seems to stick where it lands at the local governmental level.[12]

10.4   Why the size of government may be "too large" *and* "too small" under federalism

Much of the public choice literature, as with that on the flypaper effect, argues in one way or another that government grows to be *too large*, too large in the sense of being larger than the size that would maximize the median voter's utility, or would maximize some welfare function defined over the utilities of members of the community. There are some reasons to believe that at least some parts of the government sector may be too small in a democracy, however. This danger is particularly likely in a federalist state with geographic representation.[13]

To illustrate how government expenditures can be too large and too small at the same time we assume a two-level federalist state. Instead of assuming that the preferences of the median or representative voter are decisive, as in the two earlier models presented in this chapter, we assume that the preferences of those in the government are decisive. The main goal of elected government officials is assumed to be reelection. The more the government spends, holding taxes constant, the happier voters are and the higher the probability of incumbent politicians being reelected. Assuming that this probability increases at a diminishing rate, we can depict the marginal valuation of expenditures by elected officers in the local and federal governments as MV_L and MV_F in Figures 10.4a and 10.4b. (If we were to assume that it is the preferences of those in the bureaucracy that are decisive, and that they are budget maximizers, then these curves represent the marginal utilities of bureaucrats in the local and federal governments.)

While spending money wins votes, ceteris paribus, raising taxes loses them. MC_L and MC_F in Figures 10.4a and b depict the marginal costs in reduced popularity from raising the revenue to pay for the expenditures at the two levels of government. If the constitution assigns local public goods to the local government, and national public goods to the federal level, then the local and federal governments choose to supply the quantities G_L^0 and G_F^0, where the marginal gain in the probability of

---

[11] See Wyckoff's (1991) review and tests.

[12] Worthington and Dellery (1999) have confirmed Becker's finding using grants data in Australia.

[13] Downs (1961) was one of the first to argue from a public choice perspective that government may be too small in a democracy.

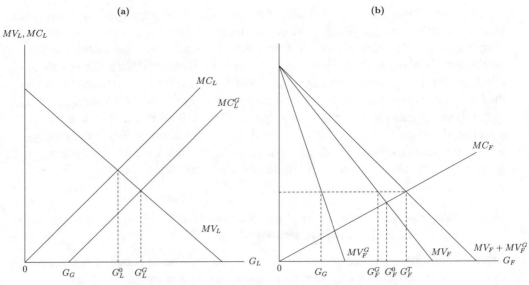

Figure 10.4. Effects of grants on government expenditures in a federalist system.

being reelected from an increase in expenditures just equals the reduction in the probability of being reelected from an increase in taxes.

Now assume that representatives to the national legislature are elected geographically, and that this legislature is free to provide local public goods directly, or to provide grants to the local government. These representatives can then increase their chances of being elected by both spending more on the national public goods and by spending more on the local ones. Let MV_F^G in Figure 10.4b represent the marginal valuation of those in the national legislature of increases in local expenditures for this reason. The marginal valuation of expenditures at the federal level on both national and local public goods is then $MV_F + MV_F^G$. The new level of total federal expenditures including grants to the local government or direct purchases of local public goods is G_F^T, which is made up of G_F^G in expenditures by the central government on national public goods, and G_G in grants or direct local expenditures ($G_G = G_F^T - G_F^G$). The central government's total outlays increase; its expenditures on national public goods decline from G_F^0 to G_F^G. Financing local public goods out of federal revenues has crowded some national public goods out of the federal budget. If G_F^0 were the optimal level of expenditures on national public goods, then the shift of funding of some of the local government's budget to the national level would have resulted in *too small* of a federal budget on national public goods.[14]

Turning to the local level of government in Figure 10.4b, we see that a grant of G_G shifts the local government's marginal cost schedule over to MC_L^G. The new level of local expenditures including the grant is G_L^G. Even though we have assumed

---

[14] A model in which political competition leads vote-maximizing politicians to choose Pareto-optimal quantities of public goods is discussed in Chapter 12. This model would predict a decline in welfare from allowing the central government to finance local public goods, and the resulting outcome as depicted in Figure 10.4b.

that the grant was a block grant rather than a matching grant, by allowing the local government to cut taxes somewhat, the grant lowers its marginal costs of purchasing local public goods and results in an increase in expenditures on local public goods of $G_L^G - G_L^0$, an amount that exceeds that which we would expect from the income effect alone.[15]

A comparison of Figures 10.4a and 10.4b reveals that the *net effect* of the intergovernmental transfers on the total size of the government sector is *positive*. The decline in spending on the national public goods, $G_F^0 - G_F^G$, is less than the increase in expenditures on local public goods, $G_L^G - G_L^0$. A federalist form of government with geographic representation and intergovernmental grants can result in less than the optimal expenditures at the national level and more than the optimal level at the local level.

Grossman (1989a) has tested the prediction that intergovernmental grants lead to a larger total government sector using both cross-sectional and time series data for the United States.[16] His cross-section estimates were for 1976–7 using data from the 48 continental states. One set of estimates is given in (10.9):

$$G = .036^{**} + 6 \times E^{-5**}\, TR + 4 \times E^{-6*}\, Y + 1 \times E^{-4**}\, FTR + 3 \times E^{-4}\, MFG$$

$$n = 48, \qquad \bar{R}^2 = .583 \qquad (10.9)$$

** = significant at 5 percent level, $\quad$ * = significant at 10 percent level.

In this equation, G is state and local taxes as a fraction of personal income; TR is state transfers to local communities divided by state population, FTR is federal transfers to the state divided by state population, and MFG is state population divided by the number of multiple function governments in the state (basically cities and counties). The third variable was insignificant, but the other two were significant. The positive coefficient on TR indicates an increase in the size of the total government sector in a state in proportion to the amount of funds passed from the state-level government to local ones. The positive coefficient on FTR is evidence of the flypaper effect. Grossman's estimate implies an elasticity of state expenditures out of federal grants of 31 percent. His time series estimates using federal, state, and local government expenditure data also confirm the hypothesis that intergovernmental transfers in a federalist system lead to an expansion of the total size of the government sector.[17]

A somewhat different form of governmental waste occurs when two governments compete to supply the same service. Here a form of "common pool" problem arises with both governments over exploiting the pool of tax payer resources.[18]

---

[15] The difference in the results from this model and the simple model of grants used in the previous section arises because that model implicitly assumed that the marginal costs of purchasing more public goods were constant in the absence of matching grants, where here we assume that the marginal costs *to the politicians* are increasing.

[16] The above model is a simplified version of Grossman's. For a much more elaborate model of intergovernmental transfers in a federalist system, see Renaud and van Winden (1991).

[17] Although Grossman did not test explicitly for the presence of crowding out, the fact that one of the predictions of his model was supported leads one to expect that its other implications are also likely to be present in the data.

[18] See models and evidence provided by Flowers (1988), Migué (1997), and Wrede (1999).

Table 10.1. *Distribution of European Union expenditures by budget category, 1985 and 1995 (percentages)*

		1985	1995
Redistribution	Agriculture and fisheries	72.9	53.6
	Regional policy	5.9	13.6
	Social policy	5.7	11.9
Allocative efficiency	Research, energy, transport	2.6	5.6
	External policies	.	6.2
	Administrative costs	4.6	5.1
	Miscellaneous	4.4	4.5

Source: Goodman, 1996, pp. 101, 105–6.

The possibility that under geographic representation local interests shift local projects to the national budget and thereby crowd out national interests has largely been discussed in the context of the United States.[19] However, the European Union (EU) in many ways provides a cleaner and more dramatic example of this phenomenon. The most important decision-making body of the EU is the *Council*, which meets in Brussels. Each member country is represented on the Council by delegates appointed by each country's government. Thus, in the EU's most important decision-making body, representation is geographically based, as in the United States.

The Council faces a very severe budget constraint. Its funds come from contributions from the member countries, which are already pressing up against the upperbound of the tax revenue that they can raise (see Chapter 22). The entire budget of the EU amounts to less than 3 percent of the EU's GDP. Thus, if any local – in this case *national* – public programs work their way into the EU's budget, the potential for crowding out European-wide public goods is large.

On the other hand, until 1991 the Council made decisions using the unanimity rule. Given our discussion of this rule in Chapter 4, one might have expected that its use would prevent local public goods and involuntary redistribution from entering the EU's budget, but this has not been the case. Instead, the Council seems to have practiced the same kind of universalism that many see in the U.S. Congress. Table 10.1 breaks the EU budgets in 1985 and 1995 down into various large categories. Outlays that were purely or largely redistributional made up almost 85 percent of the EU budget in 1985, and almost 80 percent in 1995. Activities that could be fairly clearly identified as having salient public good properties accounted for only 2.6 percent of the EU budget in 1985. Even if we categorize the EU's aid to non-EU countries (External Policies) as a "Pareto-optimal redistribution," and thus a form of allocative efficiency activity, outlays to improve allocative efficiency accounted for only 11.2 percent of the EU budget in 1995.

Today the biggest single item in the EU's budget is, as it has always been, subsidies to farmers. One might argue, at the national level, that these could constitute a

[19] See, for example, Ferejohn (1974) and Fiorina (1977a).

form of Pareto-optimal redistribution. French citizens get utility from seeing French farmers better off, and therefore are willing to pay higher prices for food and higher taxes to subsidize their farmers. It is hard to press this argument at the level of the EU, however. To do so one would have to argue that the average citizen in, say, Portugal, gets utility from seeing French farmers better off – *even though the average French farmer is richer than the average Portuguese citizen*. What explains the predominance of agricultural redistribution in the EU's budget is the same kind of pork-barrel politics that has led to large farm subsidies in America. Each European country's farmers can impose sufficient political costs on its government to induce it to lobby hard for high subsidies.

Given the scale of redistribution in the EU, and given the size of its budget, there is nothing left over to finance those European-wide public goods that ought to justify its existence – like foreign policy and defense. Assuming that there *are* some European-wide public goods, then the EU's redistribution policies, fostered by its *con*federalist political structure with geographic representation, has resulted in too small of government outlays in the one area that should justify the EU's existence – the provision of these public goods.

10.5 The problem of centralization under federalism

The 1949 Constitution of the Federal Republic of Germany did indeed create a *federal* republic. The constitution assigned specific sources of tax revenue, like the personal and corporate income taxes, and wealth and death taxes, to the Länder, the regional governments in Germany. In 1950 roughly 40 percent of all tax revenue in Germany was raised by the regional and local governments. By 1995 this figure had fallen to a mere 7 percent, as the federal government had taken over all major sources of tax revenue (Blankart, 2000).

In 1929 expenditures by the federal government in the United States were less than half of state and local governments' expenditures. Today they are more than 50 percent *greater* than state and local expenditures.[20]

This process of centralization of governmental finances has been repeated again and again in many countries. So common is it that some Europeans refer to it as *Popitz's law* in reference to the German scholar who discussed "the power of attraction of the central government" more than 70 years ago.[21]

In Blankart's (2000) account of the workings of Popitz's law in Germany over the second half of the twentieth century, elected members of the Länder were willing accomplices in the process which stripped their governments of their tax authority. They did so to free themselves of the necessity of having to compete with one another in setting tax rates. The central government effectively helped organize a cartel among the Länder governments to eliminate tax competition.

Grossman and West's (1994) description of the process of centralization in Canada over the same period is very similar to that of Blankart for Germany. A cartel among

---

[20] See Table 21.1.

[21] See discussion in Vaubel (1994) and Blankart (2000).

the Canadian provinces in conjunction with the central government has significantly reduced differences in tax rates across the provinces. To reduce the competitive pressure Tiebout migration places on the provinces, *equalization* grants from the federal to the provincial governments have been instituted.

Cartels among lower levels of government to eliminate tax competition and migration do not merely help centralize governmental activity; they increase its scale. The mechanics of this process are much the same as those described earlier with respect to the effects of intergovernmental grants on government size. Grossman and West provide econometric evidence that links the centralization of government activity in Canada to the growth in size of its total government sector. Blankart provides more indirect evidence for Germany in the form of a comparison between Germany and Switzerland. Whereas governmental revenue sources have become dramatically more centralized in Germany since World War II, in Switzerland they have become more *de*centralized. During the same time period, Germany's governmental sector has grown 20 percent faster than Switzerland's.[22]

Switzerland's example shows that Popitz's law can sometimes be repealed. Several features of Switzerland's political institutions help account for this achievement. Swiss citizens are able to petition for a referendum to reconsider any major action by their elected government. These referenda have often been used to repeal increases in expenditures and taxes. Some local communities continue to employ direct democracy, thereby eliminating the possibility of those in government substituting their preferences regarding government programs for those of the citizens. Most importantly, Swiss citizens have consistently resisted attempts to weaken their direct control over government as, for example, in their repeated rejection of entry into the EU.[23]

Potentially, the constitution can also help preserve a decentralized federalist structure by clearly assigning different functions and revenue sources to the different levels of government. Such an assignment was present in the 1949 German Constitution, however, and it was simply amended to accommodate the centralization process, as was Canada's (Blankart, 2000; Grossman and West, 1994, p. 22). Section 8 of the U.S. Constitution assigns a short and rather specific list of functions to the federal government, except for the first in the list – to "provide for the common Defense and general Welfare of the United States." This constitutional assignment of functions succeeded in preventing the central government from encroaching upon the activities of state and local governments for a century and a half, until the Constitution was "amended" by judicial reinterpretation in the 1930s. The lesson one draws from these examples is that a constitutional assignment of functions must be accompanied by procedures that make amendment of the constitution difficult, and that the judiciary must be steadfast in its interpretation

---

[22] See Table 21.2.

[23] For further discussion of the Swiss case, see Frey (1994). Vaubel (1996) also finds in a cross-national comparison that referenda on federal tax increases deter centralization. He identifies several other factors that deter centralization including, most importantly, the age of the constitutional court.

of the constitution for it to be effective in preventing the erosion of a federalist structure.[24]

Bibliographical notes

Classic studies of federalism in the economics and political science literatures, outside of *The Federalist* itself, include Riker (1964), Elazar (1966), Friedrich (1968), Oates (1972), and Breton and Scott (1978).

For a recent survey of the economics/public choice literature, see Inman and Rubinfeld (1997).

Gillette (1997) offers a general discussion of the assignment problem and the conflicts between governments that arise in a federalist system.

Strumpf and Oberholzer-Gee (2000) present evidence that the presence of geographically concentrated groups with intense preferences can influence the assignment of responsibility in a federalist system.

Filippov, Ordeshook, and Shvestova (2001) analyze the problem of avoiding political instability in federalist systems.

---

[24] Ackerman (1998) recounts the events of the 1930s that removed the constitutional barriers to the federal government's expansion of activities. Aranson (1992a,b) describes how the Supreme Court valiantly, but in the end unsuccessfully, tried to protect the country's federalism from attacks upon it by the Congress. See also Niskanen (1992).

Filippov, Ordeshook, and Shvestova (2001) are highly skeptical about the potential of jurisdictional assignments of governmental functions in the constitution to protect federalism.

CHAPTER 11

Two-party competition – deterministic voting

Politicians neither love nor hate. Interest, not sentiment, governs them.

Earl of Chesterfield

. . . a candidate for the Presidency, nominated for election by the whole people, will, as a rule, be a man selected because he is not open to obvious criticism, and will therefore in all probability be a mediocrity.

Sir Henry Sumner Maine

With large numbers of voters and issues, direct democracy is impossible. Even in polities sufficiently small so that all individuals can actually come together to debate and decide issues – say, a polity of 500 – it is impossible for all individuals to present their own views, even rather briefly, on every issue. Thus the "chairman's problem" is to select individuals to represent the various positions most members of the polity are likely to hold (de Jouvenal, 1961). When the polity is too large to assemble together, representatives must be selected by some means.

The public choice literature has focused on three aspects of representative democracy: the behavior of representatives both during the campaign to be elected and while in office; the behavior of voters in choosing representatives; and the characteristics of the outcomes under representative democracy. The public choice approach assumes that representatives, like voters, are rational economic actors bent on maximizing their utilities. Although it is natural to assume that voters' utilities are functions of the baskets of public goods and services they consume, the "natural assumption" concerning what maximizes a representative's utility is not as easily made. The fundamental hypothesis of Downs's (1957, p. 28) model is that "parties formulate policies in order to win elections, rather than win elections in order to formulate policies." His study was the first to explore systematically the implications of this assumption, and the literature has developed around the framework he laid.[1]

Much of the literature on public choice and political science has centered on representative democracy because it is the dominant mode of political expression. Although many of the issues discussed in this literature have been described here in the context of a model of direct democracy or committees, the committees in mind are often assemblies of representatives and the coalitions are parties. Many of the

---

[1] For a well-documented defense of the vote-maximizing assumption, see Mayhew (1974).

230

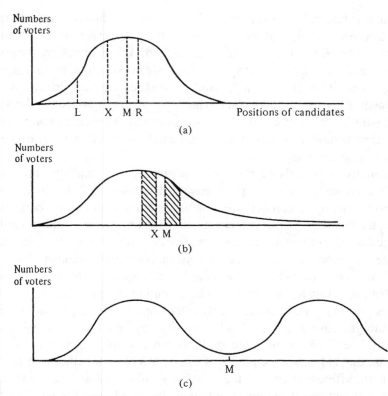

Figure 11.1. Median voter outcomes under two-party competition.

problems and results already discussed carry over almost directly into the area of representative democracy. Thus, the reader will perhaps not be surprised to find the median outcome, cycling, and logrolling all reappearing.

11.1 Outcomes under two-party democracy

Hotelling first presented the median voter theorem as an outcome of two-party representative democracy in 1929, and this paper is a clear intellectual antecedent to both Downs's and, more directly, Black's work. Indeed, it could be regarded as *the* pioneering paper in public choice, for it was the first direct attempt to use economics to analyze a political process.

In the Hotelling-Downs model, political opinion is depicted as lying along a single liberal–conservative (left-right) dimension. Each voter is assumed to have a most preferred position along the spectrum for his candidate or party[2] to take. The farther the candidate is from this position, the less desirable his election is for the voter; thus, the Hotelling-Downs model assumes single-peaked preferences. Figure 11.1 depicts a frequency distribution of most preferred candidate positions. We assume, first, that this frequency distribution is unimodal and symmetric.

---

[2] The words "candidate" or "party" can be used interchangeably here, for the implicit assumption when discussing parties is that they take a single position in the voter's eyes.

If every voter votes, and votes for the candidate closest to the voter's most preferred position, L receives all the votes of individuals lying to the left of X, the midpoint of the segment LR. R receives all votes to the right of X. If L and R are the positions that the two candidates take, R wins. L can increase his vote total by moving toward R, shifting X to the right, as can R. Both candidates are thus driven toward the position favored by the median voter. The logic of the argument is the same as that demonstrating the victory of the *issue* favored by the median voter, for in the Hotelling-Downs model there is only one issue to be decided: how far to the left or right the winning candidate will be.

The assumptions underlying this initial result are so unrealistic (one-issue dimension; a unimodal, symmetric preference distribution; all individuals vote; two candidates) that many researchers were naturally led to examine the consequences of relaxing them. As long as all voters vote, the median outcome holds regardless of the distribution of preferences. As long as all voters vote, the voters lying between a candidate's position and the farthest extreme on his side of the other candidate are "trapped" into voting for him. Thus, a candidate can "go after" the votes of the other candidate by "invading his territory" and both continue to move toward the median.

Smithies (1941) pointed out in an early extension of Hotelling's model, however, that voters might leave a candidate as he moved away from them to support another (third) candidate or simply not vote at all. Two reasonable assumptions about abstentions are that (1) candidate positions can be too close together to make voting worthwhile (indifference), and (2) the nearest candidate may still be too far away to make voting attractive (alienation). Letting P_j be the platform of candidate j, P_i^* the ideal point (platform) of voter i, and $U_i(P_j)$ voter i's utility from platform j; then we can formally define indifference and alienation as follows:

> **Indifference:** Voter i votes if and only if $|U_i(P_1) - U_i(P_2)| > e_i$ for some $e_i > 0$.
>
> **Alienation:** Voter i votes if and only if there exists some $\delta_i > 0$, such that $[U_i(P^*) - U_i(P_j)] < \delta_i$, for $j = 1$ or 2.
>
> The e_i and δ_i are voter specific constants that determine whether they vote or not.

If the probability that a voter does not vote is an increasing function of the closeness of two candidates' positions, a movement toward the center of a symmetric distribution of preferences has a symmetric effect on the two candidates' vote totals. The pull of the median remains, and the equilibrium is again at the median. Indifference does not affect this result. If the probability that a voter will abstain is an increasing function of a candidate's distance from him, the candidate is pulled toward the mode of the distribution. If the distribution is symmetric and unimodal, the median and mode coincide, however, and again the median voter result is not upset. Thus, neither indifference nor alienation, nor the two combined will affect the tendency of two candidates to converge on the position most favored by the median voter when the frequency distribution of voter preferences is symmetric and unimodal (Davis, Hinich, and Ordeshook, 1970).

The median voter result can be upset, however, if the distribution of voter preferences is either asymmetric or multimodal. If the distribution is asymmetric, but unimodal, the optimal position for each candidate is pulled toward the mode if voters become alienated as candidates move away from them (Comanor, 1976). This can be seen by considering Figure 11.1b. Suppose that both candidates are at M, the median of the distribution. A move of one to X decreases the probability that the voters in the cross-hatched region to the right of M will vote for him. The move also increases the probability by the same amount that the voters in the cross-hatched region to the left of X will vote for him (the two cross-hatched areas having equal bases). Since there are more voters in the region to the left of X than in the region to the right of M, the net effect of a move toward the mode taking into account only the effect of alienation must be to increase a candidate's expected vote. However, because M is the median, the same number of voters must lie to the left and right of this point, and the effect of alienation on the candidate's vote must dominate for small moves from M. As Comanor (1976) has shown, however, the distance between the median and mode is not likely to be great enough to cause a significant shift in candidate positions owing to alienation away from those predicted under the median voter hypothesis.

Figure 11.1c depicts a bimodal symmetric distribution. As one might expect, the presence of alienation *can*, via the logic just discussed, lead the candidates away from the median toward the two modes (Downs, 1957, pp. 118–22). But it need not. If weak, alienation can leave the median outcome unchanged or produce no stable set of strategies at all; such is the strength of the pull toward the middle in a two-party, winner-take-all system (Davis et al., 1970).

A spreading out of candidates may occur if elections consist of two steps: competition for nomination within parties, and competition among parties. To win the party's nomination, the candidate is pulled toward the *party* median; the need to win the election pulls him back toward the *population* median. If he treats the other candidate's position as fixed, a Cournot strategy game results, with equilibria generally falling between the party and population medians (Coleman, 1971, 1972; Aranson and Ordeshook, 1972; Calvert, 1985).

In Chapter 5 we noted that single-peakedness ensures a majority rule equilibrium in general only when issues are defined over a single dimension. When this occurs, single-peakedness ensures that Plott's perfect balance criterion is met for an outcome at the peak preference of the median voter. But the single-peakedness condition does not ensure the existence of an equilibrium when we move to more than one dimension. The reader will not be surprised to learn, therefore, that the results concerning the instability of majority rule equilibria in a multidimensional world carry over directly for the literature on representative democracy. The problem a candidate faces in choosing a multidimensional platform that defeats all other platforms is, under majority rule, the same as finding an issue in multidimensional space that defeats all other issues.

One can combine the assumptions of multimodal distributions and alienation and envisage a candidate presenting a platform of extreme positions on several issues and winning the support of a sufficient number of minorities to defeat another

Table 11.1

	Voter		
Issue	A	B	C
I	4	−2	−1
II	−2	−1	4
III	−1	4	−2

candidate taking median positions on all. When this happens, a minority, which supports a candidate for the position he takes on a couple of key issues, regardless of his position on others, is essentially trading away its votes on the other issues to those minorities feeling strongly about these other issues.[3]

Unfortunately, the possibility of logrolling producing cycles persists. Consider the voter preferences in Table 11.1. Suppose that two candidates vie for election on three issues. If the first takes a position in favor of all three, the outcome that maximizes the net utility gains for all voters, he can be defeated by a candidate favoring any two issues and opposing the third (say, PPF), since two of the three voters always benefit from the defeat of an issue. PPF can be defeated by PFF, however, and PFF by FFF. But all three voters favor PPP over FFF, and the cycle is complete. Every platform can be defeated.

In a single election, candidates cannot rotate through several platforms, and cycling is not likely to be evidenced. Over time it can be. To the extent that incumbents' actions in office commit them to the initial platform choice, challengers have the advantage of choosing the second, winning platform. Cycling in a two-party system should appear as the continual defeat of incumbents (Downs, 1957, pp. 54–62).[4]

Thus we confront again the political instability issue, appearing now as the danger of revolving-door political representation. Yet how well supported is this prediction? Although it is difficult to discern a cycle from a committee's actions, the predication that incumbent candidates are regularly defeated is rather easily tested. In Table 11.2 data are presented on the frequency with which the incumbent *party's* candidate is defeated in a gubernatorial election. To the extent that candidates of the party holding the governor's chair must run on the record of the previous governor, whether that is the same person now running for office or a new one, the cycling theorem predicts the defeat of the candidate whose party currently is represented in the governor's chair.

In addition to the cycling theorem's prediction that the probability of a change in control of the governorship is one, two other "naive" hypotheses can be put forward:

1. *Random hypothesis:* The elections are random events, perhaps because voters do not take the trouble to gather information about the candidates

---

[3] Downs (1957, pp. 132–7); Tullock (1967a, pp. 57–61); Breton (1974, pp. 153–5). Note that this form of logrolling is even easier to envisage when issues are arrayed in more than one dimension. When this occurs, one need not assume alienation to get a dominant logrolling strategy.

[4] Of course, one of the advantages of being an incumbent is that one can rewrite the election laws to favor incumbents.

Table 11.2. *Election outcomes and growth rates, 1775–1996*

Time period (1)	Number of elections (2)	Fraction of changes in party[a] (3)	Winning party's vote fraction (4)	Difference between 1st and 2nd parties (5)	Minority party totals (6)
1775–93	41	.273	.708[b]	.489[b]	.073[b]
1794–1807	85	.133[b]	.700[b]	.426[b]	.026
1808–19	95	.211	.637[b,c]	.297[c]	.022[b]
1820–34	163	.190[b]	.675[b]	.406[b,c]	.055[b]
1835–49	201	.292[c]	.551[b,c]	.142[b,c]	.039
1850–9	156	.296	.541[b]	.137[b]	.056[b]
1860–9	176	.260	.627[b,c]	.271[c]	.017[b,c]
1870–9	167	.259	.571[b,c]	.177[b,c]	.035
1880–9	160	.244	.580	.196	.036
1890–9	178	.299	.551[b,c]	.172[b]	.070[b,c]
1900–9	184	.143[b,c]	.588[c]	.218[c]	.043[c]
1910–19	185	.315[c]	.565[b]	.215	.085[b,c]
1920–9	187	.211[c]	.619[c]	.269[b]	.031[c]
1930–9	180	.320[c]	.608	.248	.032
1940–9	178	.243	.633[b]	.272	.010[b]
1950–9	173	.236	.612	.232	.009[c]
1960–9	156	.372[b,c]	.568[b,c]	.146[b,c]	.010[b]
1970–9	151	.391[b]	.596	.160[b]	.024[b]
1980–9	120	.325	.569	.160	.018[b]
1990–6	103	.379[b]	.565	.175[b]	.040
1775–1996	3,039	.273	.596	.226	.037

[a] Adjusted by removing first election in each state, since no party change is possible in this election.
[b] Significantly different (5 percent two-tail) from mean of remainder of sample.
[c] Significantly different (5 percent two-tail) from mean of preceding subsample.

Source: Glashan (1979); Mueller (1982); Election Research Center (1985); Scammon, Gillivary, and Cook (1998); and Congressional Quarterly (1998).

because the incentive to do so is low. This hypothesis leads to the prediction that the probability of a change in the party of the governor is 0.5 in the U.S. two-party system.[5]

2. *Conspiracy hypothesis:* The incumbents can manipulate the system or voter preferences so that they are never defeated. The probability of their defeat is zero.

Since the birth of the Republic, the party of the incumbent governor has failed to regain the governorship only slightly more than one-fourth of the time. Although the frequency of change in the party occupying the governor's chair has increased since the 1960s, in no decade has the challenging party won a gubernatorial election as much as 40 percent of the time. On average over the U.S.'s history gubernatorial elections have produced a turnover in the governor's chair falling about halfway between the elections being rigged for the incumbent party and a coin toss. The

[5] Some states have at times had more than two parties with candidates for the governorship, but then the appropriate probability figure is only slightly less than 0.5.

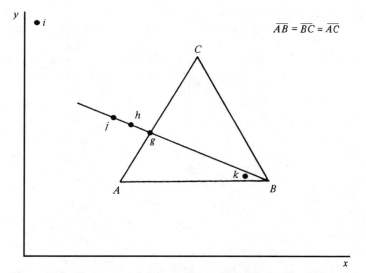

Figure 11.2. Three-voter electorate with equilateral triangle as Pareto set.

revolving-door hypothesis of cycling theory is resoundingly rejected.[6] As with the outcomes from committee voting, Tullock's question, "Why so much stability?" is appropriate.

11.2   Two-party competition in a constrained policy space

11.2.1   *The uncovered set*

One explanation for the apparent stability of electoral politics, at least as judged by the policy outcomes of the process, may be that candidates do not choose platforms from the entire feasible policy space, but restrict their choices to a particular subset of the policy space.

Consider Figure 11.2, where the ideal points of three voters are again depicted assuming a two-dimensional issue space. If voter indifference curves are concentric circles centered at the ideal points, then the lines $\overline{AB}$, $\overline{BC}$, and $\overline{AC}$ are contract curves for each respective pair of voters, and form the sides of the Pareto set.

As indicated in Chapter 5, no point in the $x - y$ orthant can defeat all other points under majority rule, and the cycling property of majority rule could lead to a sequence of pairwise votes that leads anywhere in the feasible policy space, for example, to point i. Moreover, some points like j lying outside of the Pareto set can defeat points like k inside it in a direct majority rule vote. But do we really expect candidates in a two-party election to pick platforms like i or even j? Will the

---

[6] Of course, in many state elections only one party has put forward a gubernatorial candidate. But this fact still seems more in keeping with the conspiratorial hypothesis than with the cycling hypothesis. Given the inherent vulnerability of the incumbent predicted by cycling theory, why is it that the Democrats in Vermont and Republicans in Alabama have been so ineffective in coming up with platforms and candidates to challenge the incumbents?

inherent attractiveness of platforms near the voter ideal points not manifest itself somehow?

Tullock (1967a,b) was one of the first to argue that cycling would be restricted to a fairly circumscribed space near the point where the voters' median lines intersect.[7] Theoretical justification for this prediction has been provided by Miller's work on the uncovered set.[8]

The uncovered set: The uncovered set is the set of all points y within the set of feasible alternatives S, such that for any other alternative z in S, either yPz or there exists some x in S such that $yPxPz$, where aPb means a beats b under majority rule.

Absent a Condorcet winner, no platform is unbeatable. But if a candidate chooses a platform from the uncovered set, she knows that she is at most "once removed" from defeating any platform her opponent chooses. At worst, her platform will be involved in a cycle of length three with any platform that defeats it. Conversely, if she chooses a platform that is covered, not only can this platform be defeated, but the platforms that defeat it include some that her platform cannot defeat. Thus, her platform can be contained in a transitive triple in which it is the least preferred of the three platforms.

To see this point more clearly, assume that there are but four distinct choices, x, y, z, and w, from which two candidates must choose one as a platform. Majority rule establishes the following binary relationships:

$$xPy \qquad yPz \qquad zPx$$
$$xPw \qquad yPw \qquad wPz.$$

Outcomes x, y, and z are all uncovered. For example, although z beats x, z is in turn beaten by y, which x can beat. Similarly, neither x nor z covers $w - z$ because it loses to w, and x because it is defeated by z. However, y does cover w, since it both beats w and is defeated by x, which w cannot beat; y defeats both z and w, and w defeats only z. The outcome that w defeats is a subset of the outcome that y defeats. Thus, y dominates w as a strategy choice; y defeats every outcome w can defeat, and y defeats w, also. The uncovered set, in this case (x, y, z), consists of the undominated set of platforms.[9]

Returning to Figure 11.2, we can easily see that j is covered by h, since h beats j and is in turn defeated by g, but j cannot defeat g. Every point that j defeats is also defeated by h, so that no candidate should choose j over h.

When there are three voters and the Pareto set is an equilateral triangle, as in Figure 11.2, the uncovered set is the Pareto set (Feld et al., 1987). But the uncovered

---

[7] A median line divides the issue space so that no more than half of the voter ideal points are on either side of it (see Chapter 5, Sections 5.4 and 5.5).

[8] The initial exposition is in Miller (1980), with a correction in Miller (1983). Further explication is given by Ordeshook (1986, pp. 184–7) and Feld et al. (1987).

Other papers that argue that observed outcomes under majority rule will fall in a circumscribed area within the policy space, although not necessarily one that is identical to the uncovered set, include McKelvey and Ordeshook (1976); Kramer (1977); McKelvey, Ordeshook, and Winer (1978); and Schofield (1996).

[9] This property holds in general; see Ordeshook (1986, pp. 184–6).

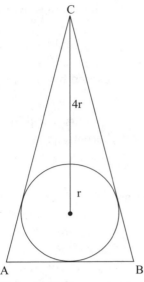

Figure 11.3. Three-voter electorate with isosceles triangle as Pareto set.

set can be much smaller than the Pareto set. McKelvey (1986) has proved that the uncovered set is always contained within a circle of radius $4r$, where r is the radius of the circle of minimum radius that intersects all median lines.[10] This latter circle has been defined as the yolk. With an equilateral triangle, the yolk is tangent to each side at its midpoint. But consider now the three voter ideal points, which form an isosceles triangle with a height of $6r$, where r is the radius of the circle, which is again tangent to the three median lines (see Figure 11.3). McKelvey's theorem implies that ideal point C, although still within the Pareto set, is now outside the uncovered set and thus is dominated by points near and along $\overline{AB}$.

In Figure 11.4, two more voters have been added with ideal points to either side of m, the median of $\overline{AB}$. The three median lines are now $\overline{CD}, \overline{CE}$, and $\overline{AB}$. The radius of the yolk shrinks to $e < r$, and so too the dimensions of the uncovered set. As more and more voters are added to either side of m along $\overline{AB}$, the uncovered set converges on m. The outcome under two-candidate competition, when candidates restrict their choices to the uncovered set, approaches in this case what one would expect from the median voter theorem, if voter C were not present, even though C's presence suffices to destroy Plott's (1967) perfect balance condition and the guarantee of an equilibrium it provides.

As a final example, consider Figure 11.5. Voter ideal points are all arrayed on the circumference of the circle with radius c centered at o. Plott's (1967) condition ensures an equilibrium at o only when voter ideal points occur in pairs at the opposite ends of lines of length $2c$, which pass through o, as for example A and B, *and* one voter's ideal point is at o. Even with no voter's ideal point at o, however, the uncovered set shrinks in toward o as more voter ideal points are added at random

---

[10] Feld et al. (1987) prove that the uncovered set is always within $3.7r$ of the center of the yolk, and conjecture that for three voters it is within $2.83r$ of the center.

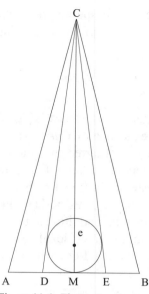

Figure 11.4. Five-voter electorate with isosceles triangle as Pareto set.

to the perimeter of this circle, yielding o or points very near it as the predicted outcomes under two-party competition when candidates choose their platforms from the uncovered set.

With voter ideal points as in Figures 11.4 and 11.5, one's intuition suggests that candidates will choose platforms at or near points m and o. But both m and o can be defeated under majority rule, as can every other point in the $x - y$ space. Most of the literature in public choice has been content to leave the discussion at that, the implication being that any and all outcomes in $x - y$ space are (equally) likely.

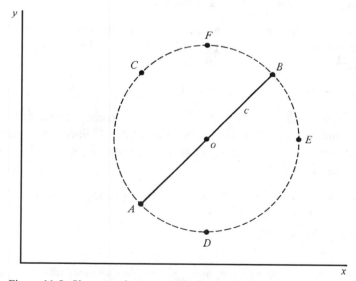

Figure 11.5. Six-voter electorate with circular Pareto set.

The dominance property of the uncovered set seems a compelling reason to choose points within it, however, and this in turn draws our attention back to points near m and o.[11]

11.2.2 *The uncovered set with high valence issues*

In one of the first critiques of the Downsian spatial model Stokes (1963) chastised Downs for, among other things, neglecting the existence of *valence* issues in his model. Valence issues are issues for which all voters agree that more is better than less. An example might be honesty. All voters prefer an honest candidate to a dishonest one, and the more honest a candidate is perceived to be, the higher she stands in every voter's estimation. Although Stokes was perhaps justified in criticizing Downs for ignoring valence issues, in fact their addition to the Downsian model can help to produce equilibria even with a multidimensional issue space.

To see this assume again that there are only three voters. Let voter i's utility from the platform of candidate j be given as follows:

$$U_i^j = K_i + \gamma V_j - |I_i - P_j|^2. \tag{11.1}$$

V_j is the value of the valence issue in each voter's utility function and γ is the weight this issue gets. $|I_i - P_j|$ is the Euclidean distance between voter i's ideal point, I_i, and the platform of candidate j, P_j. Assume now that the three voters' ideal points are located at the corners of an equilateral triangle as depicted in Figure 11.6, with the coordinates $A(1, 1)$, $B(3, 1)$, and $C(2, 1 + \sqrt{3})$. Assume further that all voters evaluate candidate 1 higher on the valence issue than candidate 2, $V_1 > V_2$. If candidate 1 chooses as a platform the point one-third of the way up the line from C bisecting line $\overline{AB}$, the utilities to each voter from 1's platform will be as follows:

$$U_i^j = K_i + \gamma V_1 - (2\sqrt{3}/3)^2 = K_i + \gamma V_1 - 4/3. \tag{11.2}$$

The best response of candidate 2 is to choose the midpoint of one of the lines between two voters' ideal points, that is, 2, 2′, or 2″. This platform promises each of these two voters

$$U_i^j = K_i + \gamma V_2 - (1)^2 = K_i + \gamma V_2 - 1. \tag{11.3}$$

Thus, if $\gamma(V_1 - V_2) > 1/3$, there is no platform that 2 can choose that will defeat 1.

Ansolabehere and Snyder (2000) have examined the conditions needed to generate equilibrium strategies in the presence of valence issues. Among the theorems that they prove is the following:

Theorem: *Suppose $V_1 > V_2$. Then an equilibrium pair of strategies (P_1, P_2) exists if and only if $r < \sqrt{\gamma(V_1 - V_2)}$,*

where r is the radius of the yolk.

---

[11] Goff and Grier (1993) argue that patterns of voting in Congress are more easily accounted for by assuming that outcomes are falling within the uncovered set.

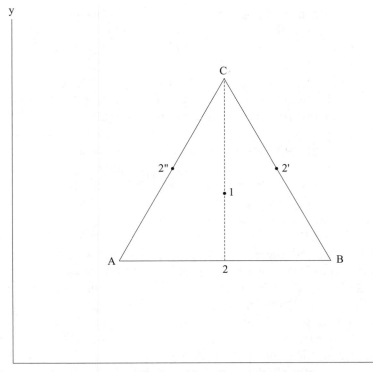

Figure 11.6. Three-voter electorate with equilateral triangle as Pareto set.

Thus, for any given distribution of voter ideal points, there exists a difference of the valence issue(s) between the two candidates sufficiently large to guarantee the leading candidate on this issue victory, if she selects a platform near the center of the yolk. The addition of valence issues both increases the likelihood that equilibria exist, and our expectation that the winning platform will lie near the center of the distribution of voter ideal points.

11.3   Relaxing the assumptions of the Downsian model

Several authors have questioned the plausibility of some of the assumptions that underlie Downs's model. By relaxing these assumptions, one can sometimes find another explanation for not observing the degree of instability expected from the model in a multidimensional context. One set of models relaxes the assumption that a voter votes with probability one for the candidate who takes a position closest to her ideal point. This class of models is treated in Chapter 12. Here we briefly discuss two additional modifications of the Downsian model.

11.3.1 *Candidates have preferences over policies*

Wittman (1973, 1977) was one of the first to question Downs' assumption that candidates were only interested in winning elections. If candidates are concerned about the *policy* outcomes of elections, as well as whether they are elected or not, they will be less quick to abandon certain policy positions to win votes. Wittman's suggestion has found considerable empirical support in *partisan* political cycle models (see Chapter 19).

Kollman, Miller, and Page (1992) allow candidates to give weight to their own ideologies when choosing positions, and to have imperfect information on voters' preferences. Simulations of two-candidate competitions lead to convergence on centralist positions.

Glazer and Lohman (1999) also model candidates as having personal preferences on policies, and allow them to precommit to certain policy positions. This action takes these issues out of the election, and thereby reduces the dimensionality of the issue space and the likelihood of cycling.

If the issue space can be reduced to a single dimension, the cycling problem disappears, of course, if we can invoke the single-peakedness assumption. Poole and Romer (1985) employed a least-squares multidimensional unfolding technique to map the ratings of members of the House of Representatives by 36 interest groups into a multidimensional policy space. They found that three dimensions suffice to obtain all of the predictive power inherent in the ratings, with a single liberal conservative dimension providing 94 percent of the explanatory power. In a follow-up study, Poole and Rosenthal (1997) analyzed *every roll call vote* in the House and Senate between 1789 and 1985. They too appear to be able to explain most of the voting behavior of individual members of Congress with a single ideological dimension.

If the issue space in presidential elections were similar to that in Congress, then the Poole-Romer-Rosenthal results would imply an issue space for these elections that conforms to that of the simple Hotelling-Downs model. Most observers of politics outside of the United States identify at least two salient dimensions to the political policy space.[12] Thus, dispensing with the potential for political instability by reducing the issue space to a single dimension does not seem possible for countries other than, perhaps, the United States.[13]

11.3.2 *Candidates can enter and exit the contests*

The Downsian model assumes that candidates are only concerned about winning the election and treats the number of candidates as a given. In addition to assuming that candidates are concerned about policy outcomes, a few papers have explored the implications of allowing candidates (citizens) to enter and exit an election.[14]

To see what is involved, let us assume that citizens are only concerned about policy outcomes. They obtain no personal rewards from being a candidate or winning an election other than that they can implement their most preferred policy. Becoming

---

[12] See, for example, Budge, Robertson, and Hearl (1987); Budge (1994); Laver and Schofield (1990); Schofield (1993a,b, 1995); and Schofield, Martin, Quinn, and Whitford (1998).

[13] Kenneth Koford (1989, 1990) has also challenged the result for the United States.

[14] See Palfrey (1984); Feddersen, Sened, and Wright (1990); Osborne and Slivinski (1996); Besley and Coate (1997); and Congleton and Steunenberg (1998). The following discussion relies on Besley and Coate.

a candidate implies incurring a fixed cost of C, however. Assume that all citizens vote for the candidate who promises them the highest utility. With entry and exit possible, an equilibrium must satisfy two conditions. No citizen who has chosen to be a candidate can increase her expected utility by changing her platform or withdrawing from the election. No citizen who is not a candidate can increase her expected utility by becoming one.

For an equilibrium to exist in which there is only one candidate, there must exist a platform choice that is a Condorcet winner. One citizen who's most preferred outcome is this platform chooses to become a candidate, and no one else bothers to incur the cost of entry, since no other platform can win. For an equilibrium to exist in which there are exactly two candidates, there must exist two issues that evenly divide the electorate, and no third issue favored by a larger number of voters. Since no one will choose to be a candidate unless he thinks he has a chance of winning, equilibria with higher numbers of candidates also require a number of separate issues equal to the number of candidates, which partition the population into groups of equal size.

One interesting result from the citizen-candidate model is that the equilibrium under the Downsian spatial model in which two candidates adopt the platform favored by the median voter is *not* an equilibrium. If one candidate has taken the position favored by the median voter, no second citizen would choose to be a candidate and take the same position, since she would incur the cost of being a candidate without obtaining any benefits from the victory of a preferred policy. With a single-dimensional issue space the only equilibrium involving two candidates has them taking positions on either side of the median position. Each of the two candidates must have an equal chance of winning, and the gain to each from victory must exceed the cost of becoming a candidate. The citizen-candidate model of elections thus gives an additional rationale for candidates in two-party elections not adopting identical platforms.

11.4 Testing the median voter hypothesis

Numerous studies have attempted to penetrate the "veil of representative democracy" by modeling government expenditure decisions *as if* they were made along a single, left-right dimension, and could essentially be treated as the private choices of the median voter.[15] A typical median voter model assumes that voters maximize utility subject to a budget constraint that includes their tax price for the public good, and derives the following demand equation for the median voter:

$$\ln G = a + \alpha \ln t_m + \beta \ln Y_m + \gamma \ln Z + \mu, \tag{11.4}$$

where G is government expenditures, t_m and Y_m are the tax price and income of the median voter, respectively, and Z is a vector of taste parameters (number of children, Catholic or non-Catholic, and so on). Equation (11.4) is then estimated using cross-sectional data on local expenditures of some kind.

---

[15] For surveys of this literature, see Deacon (1977a,b) and Inman (1979).

A large number of studies have tested some variant on the median voter hypothesis as given by (11.4). The overwhelming majority claim support for the median voter hypothesis on the basis of statistically significant coefficients on both Y_m and t_m of the correct sign. Denzau and Grier (1984) provide further evidence in support of the hypothesis by demonstrating that these coefficients vary over a narrow range when 12 "conditioning" (Z) variables gleaned from the literature are included in equations incorporating data on New York school districts.

The merits of the public choice approach can perhaps be best assessed by comparing its findings with those of the "traditional approach," which related government expenditures to urbanization, population size and density, mean community income, and perhaps several other socioeconomic variables, depending on the good in question.[16] Most of these variables might be included in the Z vector of taste or shift variables, and many have reappeared in public choice studies. The key innovations of the public choice approach have been to replace mean income with median income and to add the median voter's tax price. The inclusion of the tax price variable is a clear improvement over previous studies that did not include tax shares in the demand equation, because it indicates that the purchase of public goods is the outcome of some form of collective choice process in which the *cost* of the public good to the voter, as well as its value to him as reflected by socioeconomic characteristics, is important.

The good performance of median income in explaining local public expenditures cannot be interpreted as readily as lending support to the public choice approach. As already noted, most existing studies have assumed that local public good demand is related to *mean* incomes, and it would take a rather peculiar model of local public finance to obtain a prediction that income and expenditures were unrelated. Therefore, the contribution of the public choice approach must be to argue that it is *median* voter income that determines public good demand, not *mean* voter income. Most studies have not tested this hypothesis. Indeed, it is very difficult to test, given the other assumptions needed to test a median voter demand equation using cross-sectional data. As Bergstrom and Goodman (1973, pp. 286–7) point out, to estimate this equation on cross-sectional data one must assume a certain *proportionality* between the distributions of voters across local communities to ensure that the quantity demanded by the voter with the median income always equals the median quantity of public goods demanded in each community. However, if this proportionality holds, the means of the distributions will also be proportional, the correlation between mean and median income across communities will be perfect, and there will be no way to discriminate between the public-choice-approach demand equation and its rivals on the basis of this variable. The only way for the public choice approach to yield different predictions from other models is if the ratio of median to mean incomes differs across communities; that is, if there are different degrees of skewness across communities, and these differences in skewness are important in determining the demand for public goods.

---

[16] For a survey of this literature, see Gramlich (1970).

Pommerehne and Frey (1976) have tested this latter hypothesis. They found that the median income variable did work somewhat better at explaining local public expenditures than mean income did, although the superiority of median income as an explanatory variable was not particularly dramatic. More convincing support for the superiority of median income over mean income was obtained in a follow-up study by Pommerehne (1978), who used data on 111 Swiss municipalities to test the hypothesis. These data have the important and singular advantage of allowing one to ascertain the effect of having representative democracy, since the sample contains municipalities that make decisions via direct, town-meeting procedures and those that rely on representative assemblies. Pommerehne found that median income performed significantly better than mean income at explaining public expenditures in cities employing direct democracy. In the cities employing representative democratic procedures, median income led "to somewhat superior results," but its "explanatory power is not significantly better in any expenditure category."

Thus, the introduction of representatives into the democratic decision process does seem to introduce a sufficient amount of "white noise" to disguise or almost disguise the relationship between median voter preferences and final outcomes. This throws a cloud of doubt over the U.S.-based estimates, which rely entirely on representative election outcomes. Interestingly enough, Pommerehne found that even the existence of an optional or obligatory referendum on expenditure bills in cities governed by representative assemblies added enough of a constraint on the representatives' behavior to make the median voter model perform perceptibly better than for those cities in which representative democracy was able to function unchecked.

Turnbull and Mitias (1999) have conducted rigorous econometric tests of the performance of *median* voter income and tax price variables in an expenditure model versus *mean* values of these variables using county and state level data. Their tests tend to reject *both* specifications at both the state and county levels. The only level of government at which the median voter model is not rejected is at the municipal level – the lowest of the three levels of government examined.[17]

Gramlich and Rubinfeld (1982a) have gone even farther in suggesting that the performance of median voter income in most studies may merely be an artifact of aggregation in the cross-sectional data used to test the hypothesis. Using survey data for Michigan, they found that "higher-income individuals within a community . . . do not appear to have any greater taste for public spending" than lower-income individuals. The income elasticity of demand for expenditures "is very close to zero" when measured within communities (1982a, p. 544). The positive elasticities estimated in cross sections are due entirely to a positive association between community income and expenditures, precisely the relationship that the "traditional approach" estimated and the public choice approach sought to improve upon.

---

[17] Turnbull and Djoundourian (1994), and Turnbull and Mitias (1999). Further support for the median voter model using municipal data is provided by Deno and Mehay (1987), Wyckoff (1988), and Turnbull and Chan (1998).

A further cloud on the predictive power of the median voter model is provided by the *range* of estimates of the key parameters that have been reported. The income elasticities in the Bergstrom and Goodman (1973) study ranged from 0.16 to 1.73, while the tax price elasticities ranged from −0.01 to −0.50 (Romer and Rosenthal, 1979a, p. 159), although these estimates are for a single model applied to comparable bodies of data. Deno and Mehay's (1987) estimate of the income elasticity of demand for general government services at the municipal level in the states of Michigan and Ohio is 0.76, while Turnbull and Djoundourian's (1994) estimate for municipalities in the five Midwest states of Michigan, Ohio, Illinois, Indiana, and Wisconsin is 0.22. Turnbull and Djoundourian's estimate of the tax price elasticity for these five states (−0.88) comes close to Deno and Mehay's estimate of −0.72 for Michigan and Ohio, but both are far away from Deno and Mehay's estimate for the entire United States of −0.12.

All of this underlines the point that caution must be exhibited when interpreting the empirical results from public choice models. As in all areas of economics, the sophistication and elegance of the theoretical models of public choice far exceed the limits placed by the data on the empirical models that can be estimated. In going from the theoretical models to the empirical "verifications," additional assumptions and compromises must often be made that further hamper a clear interpretation of the results as constituting direct support for a hypothesis. What one is willing to conclude boldly on the basis of results analytically derived from *assumed* behavioral relationships, one must conclude circumspectly on the basis of estimated behavioral equations.

This same caution must be exercised in drawing the broader conclusion that a given set of results from a model based on public choice supports the public choice approach. It is common practice in economics to "test" a hypothesis by checking whether the results are "consistent" with it without exploring whether they are also consistent with other, conflicting hypotheses. Although it is perhaps unfair to hold public choice to higher standards than the other branches of economics, I do not think that this methodology suffices here. To demonstrate that public choice has something useful to contribute to the existing empirical literature on public finance and public policy, its models must be tested against the existing models, which ignore public choice considerations. Unless public choice–derived models can outperform the "traditional, ad hoc" models against which they compete, the practical relevance of public choice theories must remain somewhat in doubt. To date, few studies have attempted such comparisons. Three of those reviewed in this section that do make such comparisons (Pommerehne and Frey, 1976; Pommerehne, 1978; Turnbull and Chan, 1998) present evidence that is hardly encouraging as to the potential for predicting the outcomes of *representative government* with a model that treats the median voter as if he were dictator.

11.5   Are local public expenditures public or private goods?

In addition to estimating median income and tax price elasticities, several papers estimate a "degree-of-publicness" parameter based on the coefficients of the tax price and population variables. This parameter is defined in such a way that "if [it] were nearly zero, there would be substantial economies to large city size since in larger cities, more consumers could share in the costs of municipal commodities with only minor crowding effects. Where [it] is about one, the gains from sharing the cost of public commodities among persons are approximately balanced by the disutility of sharing the facility among more persons" (Bergstrom and Goodman, 1973, p. 282). All of the studies discussed here find that this parameter is close to one. Borcherding and Deacon (1972, p. 900) urge that "great care should be exercised in interpreting" this coefficient, and in particular note that "normative conclusions drawn from the finding that the goods appear better classified as private or quasi-private rather than public are highly conjectural." Nevertheless, the temptation to make these normative conjectures is obviously appealing to many, and more than one writer has succumbed to it.[18] Such conclusions are not warranted, however. The coefficients upon which this degree-of-publicness parameter is estimated are obtained from cross-sectional equations based on observations from communities of differing sizes, each of which supplies these services (assumed homogeneous across communities) collectively to all members. A parameter estimate of one for police protection implies that a citizen living in a city of two million is no better off after weighing the reduced costs of spreading additional police protection across more taxpayers against the additional costs (crime?) resulting from crowding than a citizen living in a city of one million. It does *not imply* that individuals in the larger city can contract for "private" police protection as efficiently as municipal police departments can supply it. Since no private-contract police service systems are included in the studies, nothing can be said about their costs relative to public police protection. Nor can one even say that citizens in a part of the city of two million can efficiently form a club and provide their own police protection. If there are heavy spillovers from one part of a city to another, there may be no efficient way to supply police protection to a city of two million other than to supply it to all collectively, even though the net benefits from police protection to a citizen in a city of two million may be no greater than those to a citizen of a city half as large. The conclusion that the results of these studies imply that police protection is a private good comes from a confusion of the joint supply and nonexclusion characteristics of public goods. The studies cited above show that the net joint supply benefits of public good provision have generally been exhausted for the range of community sizes considered. Whether subsets of these communities can efficiently be excluded from the benefits of providing these services to other subsets, so that they can be provided via private or local clubs, is another, as yet untested, hypothesis.

Bibliographical notes

The spatial voting and electoral competition literature has been surveyed by Taylor (1971), Riker and Ordeshook (1973, ch. 12), Borooah and van der Ploeg (1983), Enelow and Hinich (1984), Calvert (1986), and Ordeshook (1986, ch. 4; 1997).

---

[18] See, for example, Niskanen (1975, pp. 632–3); Borcherding, Bush, and Spann (1977).

Barr and Davis (1966) and Davis and Haines (1966) made the pioneering efforts to apply the median voter model, and their work has been followed up by more sophisticated attempts by Borcherding and Deacon (1972), Bergstrom and Goodman (1973), Peterson (1973, 1975), Clotfelter (1976), Pommerehne and Frey (1976), Deacon (1978), Inman (1978), Pommerehne (1978), Holcombe (1980), Congleton and Bennett (1995), and Ahmed and Greene (2000).

The critical remarks in Sections 11.4 and 11.5 parallel in many respects the review by Romer and Rosenthal (1979a).

For further discussion and critiques of the degree-of-publicness parameter, see Inman (1979, p. 296) and Oates (1988a).

CHAPTER 12

Two-party competition – probabilistic voting

It suffices for us, if the moral and physical condition of our own citizens qualifies them to select the able and good for the direction of their government, with a recurrence of elections at such short periods as will enable them to displace an unfaithful servant, before the mischief he mediates may be irremediable.

Thomas Jefferson

The social meaning or function of parliamentary activity is no doubt to turn out legislation and, in part, administrative measures. But in order to understand how democratic politics serve this social end, we must start from the competitive struggle for power and office and realize that the social function is fulfilled, as it were, incidentally – in the same sense as production is incidental to the making of profits.

Joseph Schumpeter

The cycling problem has haunted the public choice literature since its inception. Cycling introduces a degree of indeterminacy and inconsistency into the political process that hampers the observer's ability to predict outcomes, and clouds the normative properties of the outcomes achieved. The median voter theorem offers a way out of this morass of indeterminateness, a way out that numerous empirically minded researchers have seized. But the median voter equilibrium remains an "artifact" of the assumption that issue spaces have a single dimension (Hinich, 1977). If candidates can compete along two or more dimensions, the equilibrium disappears and with it the predictive power of the econometric models that rely on this equilibrium concept.

Not surprisingly, numerous efforts to avoid these dire implications of assuming multidimensional issue spaces have been made. Some of these were discussed in the previous chapter. Here we focus upon one set of models that makes a particularly plausible and powerful modification to the standard two-party spatial competition model and produces equilibrium outcomes. We begin by reexamining why the standard model fails to achieve an equilibrium.

12.1 Instability with deterministic voting

Consider again a situation in which there are three voters with ideal points at A, B, and C in the two-dimensional issue space, $x - y$ (Figure 12.1). With separable utility functions, voter indifference contours are concentric circles and the Pareto

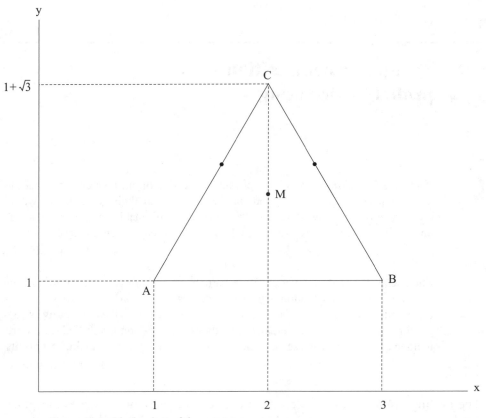

Figure 12.1. Ideal points of three voters.

set is the triangle with apexes at A, B, and C. The two candidates compete by choosing points in the $x - y$ positive quadrant.

Our intuition suggests that the candidates choose points inside ABC. Could a point outside the triangle win more votes than a point inside the triangle, given that the former must always provide lower utility to *all three* voters than some points inside the triangle? Intuition further suggests that competition between the candidates for the three votes drives the two candidates toward the middle of the triangle, to some point like M.

But we have seen in Chapter 5 that point M cannot be an equilibrium if candidates seek to maximize their votes and voters vote for the candidate who takes the closest position to a voter's ideal point. If candidate 1 is at M, then 2 can defeat 1 by taking any position within the three lenses formed by U_A and U_B, U_A and U_C, and U_B and U_C (see Figure 12.2). Note that these lenses include points like N outside the Pareto set. But any point that 2 chooses can be defeated by a countermove by 1, and so on, ad infinitum.

Let us consider again the assumption that each voter votes with certainty for the candidate whose platform is closest to the voter's ideal point. Candidate 1 has taken a position at P_1 in Figure 12.3, and candidate 2 is considering taking positions along the ray AZ. In deciding what point along AZ to choose, 2 contemplates the effect of

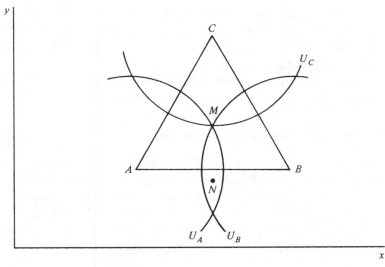

Figure 12.2. Cycling possibilities.

this choice on the probability of winning A's vote. Under the deterministic voting assumption that voter A votes for the candidate closest to point A, this probability remains zero as long as 2 remains outside U_A, and then jumps to one as 2 crosses the U_A contour. The probability of A's voting for 2 is a discontinuous step function equaling zero for all points outside U_A and one for all points inside.

That a candidate expects voters to respond to changes in her platform in such a jerky manner seems implausible for a variety of reasons. First of all, A is unlikely to be perfectly informed about the two candidates' positions, and thus A may not realize that 2 has moved closer to his ideal point. Second, other random events may impinge upon A's decision, which either change his preferences or change his vote

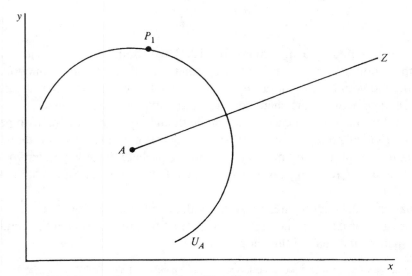

Figure 12.3. Voter A's response to candidate 2's moves.

in an unpredictable way. Third, 2 may not know with certainty where A's ideal point lies. Thus, a more realistic assumption about 2's expectation of the probability of winning A's vote is that it is a continuous function of the distance 2's position lies from A, increasing as 2 moves closer to A.[1]

With this plausible alternative to the deterministic voting assumption, two-party competition for votes can produce equilibrium outcomes.

12.2   Equilibria under probabilistic voting

Deterministic voting models assume that voter choices gyrate schizophrenically as candidates move about competing for votes. A slight movement to the left loses A's vote, but wins B's and C's. Candidates seek to maximize their expected number of votes, and these in turn are simply the sum of the probabilities that each voter will vote for the candidate. Define π_{1i} as the probability that voter i votes for candidate 1, and EV_1 1's expected vote. Then candidate 1 seeks to maximize

$$EV_1 = \sum_{i=1}^{n} \pi_{1i}. \tag{12.1}$$

Under deterministic voting, π_{1i} and π_{2i} take the following step-function form:

$$(\pi_{1i} = 1) \leftrightarrow U_{1i} > U_{2i}$$

$$(\pi_{1i} = 0) \leftrightarrow U_{1i} \leq U_{2i} \tag{12.2}$$

$$(\pi_{2i} = 1) \leftrightarrow U_{1i} < U_{2i},$$

where U_{1i} and U_{2i} are i's expected utilities under the platforms of 1 and 2, respectively.

Probabilistic voting models replace (12.2) with the assumption that the probability functions are continuous in U_{1i} and U_{2i}; that is,

$$\pi_{1i} = f_i(U_{1i}, U_{2i}), \qquad \frac{\partial f_i}{\partial U_{1i}} > 0, \qquad \frac{\partial f_i}{\partial U_{2i}} < 0. \tag{12.3}$$

The task of finding a maximum for (12.1) will be much easier if the π_{1i} are smooth, continuous concave functions, rather than discontinuous functions. The probabilistic voting assumption makes this substitution, and it lies at the heart of the difference between the characteristics of the two models.

The utility functions of each voter can be thought of as mountains with peaks at each voter's ideal point. The probabilistic voting assumption transforms these utility mountains into probability mountains, with the probability of any voter voting for a given candidate reaching a peak when the candidate takes a position at the voter's ideal point.

Equation (12.1) aggregates these individual probability mountains into a single aggregate probability mountain. The competition for votes between candidates drives them to the peak of this mountain.

---

[1] For further justification of the probabilistic voting assumption, see Hinich (1977); Coughlin, Mueller, and Murrell (1990); and Hinich and Munger (1994, pp. 166–76).

That the positioning of the candidates at the peak of this mountain is an equilibrium can be established in a variety of ways. For example, the zero-sum nature of competition for votes, combined with the continuity assumptions on the π_{1i} and π_{2i} (implying the continuity of EV_1 and EV_2), can be relied upon to establish a Nash equilibrium if the issue space over which the candidates compete is compact and convex (Coughlin and Nitzan, 1981a). If the probability functions are strictly concave, the equilibrium is unique, with both candidates offering the same platforms.

12.3   Normative characteristics of the equilibria

Let us examine the properties of the equilibria further by making some specific assumptions about the probability functions. First of all, we assume that all voters vote so that the probability that i votes for candidate 2 is one minus the probability that i votes for 1; that is,

$$\pi_{2i} = 1 - \pi_{1i}. \tag{12.4}$$

In addition to satisfying (12.3), the probability functions must be chosen so that

$$0 \leq f(\ ) \leq 1 \tag{12.5}$$

for all feasible arguments. As a first illustration, let us assume that $f_i(\cdot)$ is a continuous and concave function of the differences in utilities promised by the two candidates' platforms:

$$\pi_{1i} = f_i(U_{1i} - U_{2i}), \qquad \pi_{2i} = 1 - \pi_{1i}. \tag{12.6}$$

Consider now a competition for votes between the two candidates defined over a policy space that consists simply of the distribution of Y dollars among the n voters.[2] Each voter's utility is a function of his income, $U_i = U_i(y_i)$, $U_i' > 0, U_i'' < 0$. Candidate 1 chooses a vector of incomes $(y_{11}, y_{12}, \ldots, y_{1i},$ and so on) to maximize her expected vote, EV_1, subject to the total income constraint; that is, she maximizes

$$EV_1 = \sum_i \pi_{1i} = \sum_i f_i(U_i(y_{1i}) - U_i(y_{2i})) + \lambda \left(Y - \sum_i y_{1i} \right). \tag{12.7}$$

Candidate 2 chooses a vector of incomes that maximizes $1 - EV_1$, which is to say a vector that minimizes EV_1. If the $f(\cdot)$ and $U(\cdot)$ functions are continuous and strictly concave, both candidates will choose the same platforms. These platforms will in turn satisfy the following first-order conditions:

$$f_i' U_i' = \lambda = f_j' U_j', \qquad i, j = 1, n. \tag{12.8}$$

Each candidate equates the weighted marginal utilities of the voters with the weights (f_i'), depending on the sensitivity of a voter's voting for a candidate to differences in the utilities promised by the candidates. The greater the change in the probability of

---

[2] Coughlin (1984, 1986) has analyzed this problem.

voter i's voting for 1 in response to an increase in $U_{1i} - U_{2i}$, the higher the income promised to i by both candidates.

If the probabilistic response of all voters to differences in promised utilities were the same – that is, $f_i'(\ ) = f_j'(\ )$ for all i, j, – then (12.8) simplifies to

$$U_i' = U_j' \text{ for all } i, j = 1, n. \tag{12.9}$$

This condition is the same one that must be satisfied to maximize the Benthamite social welfare function (SWF)

$$W = U_1 + U_2 + \cdots + U_i + \cdots + U_n. \tag{12.10}$$

Thus, when the probabilistic response of all voters to differences in the expected utilities of candidate platforms is the same, the competition for votes between the candidates leads them to choose platforms that maximize the Benthamite SWF.[3] When the probabilistic responses of voters differ, candidate competition results in the maximization of a weighted Benthamite SWF.

A reasonable alternative to the assumption that voter decisions depend on the *differences* in expected utilities from the candidates' platforms is that they depend upon the ratios of utilities, that is, that π_{1i} is of the form

$$\pi_{1i} = f_i(U_{1i}/U_{2i}). \tag{12.11}$$

Substituting (12.11) into (12.7), and recalling that $U_{1i} = U_{2i}$ at the equilibrium, we obtain

$$f_i' \frac{U_i'}{U_i} = \lambda = f_j' \frac{U_j'}{U_j}, \qquad i, j = 1, n \tag{12.12}$$

as the first-order conditions for expected vote maximization for each of the candidates. When the marginal probabilistic responses are identical across all voters, this simplifies to

$$\frac{U_i'}{U_i} = \frac{U_j'}{U_j}, \qquad i, j = 1, n, \tag{12.13}$$

which is the first-order condition obtained by maximizing the Nash SWF

$$W = U_1 \cdot U_2 \cdot U_3 \cdots U_n. \tag{12.14}$$

Once again, candidate competition is seen to result in the implicit maximization of a familiar SWF.[4]

As a final example, consider again the spatial competition example with the three voters depicted in Figure 12.1. Let us assume that the probabilities of i supporting candidates 1 and 2 are defined by (12.6). Since we know this problem is equivalent to the maximization of (12.10), we can find the equilibrium platform that maximizes (12.10). We write the three voters' utility functions as $U_a = Z_a - (1-x)^2 - (1-y)^2$, $U_b = Z_b - (5-x)^2 - (1-y)^2$, $U_c = Z_c - (3-x)^2 - (5-y)^2$, where

---

[3] Ledyard (1984) obtains the Benthamite SWF using an assumption analogous to (12.6).
[4] Coughlin and Nitzan (1981a) obtain the Nash SWF from an assumption about the π_is analogous to (12.11).

the Z_is represent the utility levels achieved at each voter's respective ideal point. The two first-order conditions are

$$2(1-x) + 2(5-x) + 2(3-x) = 0$$
$$2(1-y) + 2(1-y) + 2(5-y) = 0,$$

(12.15)

from which we obtain the expected vote-maximizing platform for both candidates (3, 7/3), the point M in Figure 12.1. Competition for votes does drive the two candidates into the Pareto set to a point in the middle of the triangle.

When one assumes that the probabilities of voter support depend on differences in expected utility, competition drives candidates toward the (weighted) arithmetic mean of the voters' utilities. When the probabilities depend on ratios of utilities, the equilibrium is driven toward the geometric mean. Still other assumptions about the relationship between the probability of a voter's support and his expected utility under the competing platforms would produce equilibria at still other points. But as long as the probability of winning an individual's vote responds positively to increases in the voter's utility from a candidate's platform, then equilibria can be expected to be found within the Pareto set, and thus have desirable normative properties (Coughlin, 1982, 1992).

12.4 Equilibria with interest groups

The previous section describes a set of results under the probabilistic voting assumption that are indeed salutary. Political competition can produce equilibrium outcomes, and these outcomes can have potentially attractive normative properties. In this section we discuss an extension to the probabilistic voting model that sheds additional light on the nature of the outcomes obtained.

Coughlin, Mueller, and Murrell (1990) have extended the probabilistic voting model to allow for the impact of interest groups on political competition. Interest groups are defined as groups of individuals with identical tastes and incomes. If U_{ij} is the utility function of voter j who is a member of interest group i, then $U_{ij} = U_i$, for all $j = 1, n_i$, where n_i is the size of the ith interest group. Each individual is a member of one interest group.

The deterministic voting assumption (12.2) is replaced with the following assumption:

$$(\pi_{1ij} = 1) \leftrightarrow (U_{1i} > U_{2i} - b_{ij})$$
$$(\pi_{1ij} = 0) \leftrightarrow (U_{1i} \leq U_{2i} - b_{ij})$$
$$(\pi_{2ij} = 1) \leftrightarrow (U_{1i} < U_{2i} - b_{ij}).$$

(12.16)

The b_{ij} are "bias" terms. A $b_{ij} > 0$ implies a positive bias in favor of candidate 1 on the part of the jth voter in the ith interest group. The utility this voter expects from candidate 2's platform must exceed that expected from 1's platform by *more* than b_{ij}, before 1 loses this individual's vote to 2.

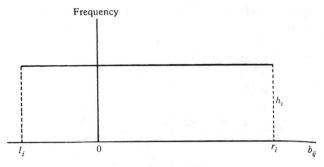

Figure 12.4. A uniform distribution of biases.

A probabilistic element is introduced into the model by assuming that the bias terms are random variables drawn from a probability distribution with parameters known to both candidates. Figure 12.4 depicts a uniform probability distribution for an individual in a given interest group. This group can be said to be biased in favor of candidate 1, since the bulk of the distribution lies to the right of the zero bias line. Nevertheless, some members of this group will be associated with negative bias terms. If candidate 1 matches 2's platform, she wins most but not all of the votes of interest group i.

The assumption that interest groups are biased toward or away from certain candidates or parties accords with observed voting patterns. Whites in the South and blacks everywhere in the United States tend to vote Democratic. Yankee farmers tend to vote Republican. On the other hand, not every Yankee farmer votes Republican.

The assumption that candidates know the distributions of bias terms, but not the individual bias term, implies that neither candidate can say with certainty how a given member of a particular interest group will vote. What they can predict is that they will pick up a greater fraction of an interest group's vote, the greater the difference in the utility their platform promises the representative interest group member over that of their opponent.

Assumption (12.16) makes the probability of i's supporting candidate 1 dependent on the difference between the utilities promised by the platforms of the two candidates. The first-order condition for expected vote maximization is thus of the form in (12.8). When the biases are drawn from the uniform distribution, however, f_i', the change in probability of winning the vote of a member of interest group i, is just the height of the uniform distribution, h_i, from which the b_{ij} are drawn, since the area of the uniform distribution equals one, $h_i = 1/(r_i - l_i)$. Thus, under the assumption that the bias terms are uniformly distributed, two-candidate competition for votes leads each candidate to offer platforms that maximize the following welfare function:

$$W = \alpha_1 n_1 U_1 + \alpha_2 n_2 U_2 + \cdots + \alpha_m n_m U_m, \qquad (12.17)$$

where the $\alpha_i = f_i' = 1/(r_i - l_i)$. The greater the difference between r_i and l_i, the boundaries on the uniform distribution for interest group i, the greater the range over which the b_{ij} are distributed. The greater this range, the more important the

b_{ij} become in determining how an interest group's membership votes, and the less important the promised utilities are. Given the latter, both candidates give less weight to this group's interests in choosing platforms.

The results from this probabilistic voting model with interest groups resemble those of the earlier models in that equilibria exist and are Pareto optimal. In fact, an additive welfare function is maximized, albeit one that assigns different weights to the different interest groups.

This latter property raises important normative issues about the equilibria obtained in the competitive struggle for votes. Although candidates are uncertain about how the members of different interest groups will vote, they are uncertain in different degrees about different groups. One way in which interest groups attempt to influence public policy is to make candidates aware of potential votes to be won from their interest group by taking certain positions in their platforms. Interest groups try to increase the welfare of their membership by reducing candidate uncertainty over how their membership votes.

But this in turn implies that different interest groups receive different weights in the candidates' objective functions and thus receive different weights in the social welfare function, which is implicitly maximized through candidate competition. When candidates are unsure of the votes of different groups, and these groups have different capabilities in approaching candidates, then one's benefits from political competition depend in part upon the interest group to which one belongs. The egalitarianism inherent in the slogan "one man, one vote" is distorted when interest groups act as intermediaries between candidates and citizens.

12.5 An application to taxation

12.5.1 *The logic*

Probabilistic voting models have become increasingly popular over the past 20 years for analyzing electoral politics. Much of the literature on interest groups has employed this model, for example, and we shall focus upon it in Chapter 20. Here we confine ourselves to a brief look at an application of the model to taxation.

Let us imagine a country with a two-party political system. The economy has one private good, X, and the government supplies one public good, G, which it finances with taxes on individual incomes. We shall assume that the government can levy a separate tax, t_i, on each individual i. Each individual's income, Y_i, is devoted entirely to her own personal consumption of X and her tax payment, $Y_i = (1 - t_i)X_i$. Under these assumptions, the expected vote function of party 1, as given in (12.7), is modified to become

$$EV_1 = \sum_1 \pi_{1i} = \sum_i f_i(U_i(G, X_{1i}) - U_i(G, X_{2i}))$$

$$+ \lambda \left(\sum_i Y_i - G - \sum_i X_i \right). \tag{12.18}$$

To balance its budget, the government must choose individual tax rates, t_i, such that $G = \sum_{i=1}^{n} t_i Y_i$. Party 1 maximizes its expected vote by choosing G and the t_i to maximize (12.18). Maximizing with respect to G yields the first-order condition

$$\sum_{i=1}^{n} f_i' \frac{\partial U_i}{\partial G} = \lambda. \tag{12.19}$$

Setting $G = \sum_{i=1}^{n} t_i Y_i$ in the budget constraint term of (12.18), substituting into each $U_i(G, X_i)$ from the individual budget constraints, and then maximizing with respect to t_i gives the following first-order conditions:

$$f_i' \frac{\partial U_i}{\partial X_i} = \lambda, \qquad i = 1, n. \tag{12.20}$$

A comparison of (12.19) and (12.20) with (2.8) and (2.9) from Chapter 2 reveals that they are the same except that we have now implicitly assumed that $P_G = P_X = 1$, and the γ_is from (2.8) and (2.9) have been replaced by f_i's. The γ_is in (2.8) and (2.9) were the positive weights placed on each individual's utility in the SWF (2.6) that was maximized to find the Pareto-optimal quantity of the public good. The f_i's are the weights that each party implicitly places on the utilities of each individual when it maximizes its expected vote. As was done in Chapter 2, each f_i' from (12.20) can be used to replace an f_i' in (12.19) to yield

$$\sum_i \frac{\partial U_i / \partial G}{\partial U_i / \partial X_i} = 1, \tag{12.21}$$

where (12.21) is again the Samuelsonian (1954) condition for Pareto optimality in the presence of public goods when $P_G = P_X$. Although each party is only interested in maximizing its expected votes, the competition for votes forces each to choose individual taxes and a public good quantity that satisfies the conditions for Pareto optimality.

Although the outcome of electoral politics from the probabilistic voting model satisfies the condition for Pareto optimality, the realized utility levels implied by (12.19) and (12.20) are possibly quite different from those that an impartial social planner might induce by selecting a set of γs for his SWF. Equation (12.19) implies that the political process produces a large quantity of the public good if the votes of those who favor large quantities of the public good are highly responsive to the announced platforms of the parties (their $f'(\cdot)$s are large). Equation (12.20) states that individuals whose votes are highly responsive to the announced platforms of the parties are left with command over larger quantities of the private good (are assigned low taxes).

This comparison of the first-order conditions that one obtains by maximizing an SWF, and the first-order conditions that are implicitly obtained through the process of electoral competition, reveals a perhaps surprising similarity between the predictions for tax policy that emerge from a *positive* analysis of taxation using the probabilistic voting model, and the *normative* prescriptions that one derives from optimal tax theory. Both imply, for example, the potential for a highly complex tax structure. When individual utility functions differ greatly and yet all must consume the same quantities of public goods, assigned tax prices may have to differ greatly to satisfy the first-order conditions for Pareto optimality. When individuals differ greatly in their access and responsiveness to politics, parties may be forced to offer individuals and groups greatly different tax prices if the parties wish to maximize their chances of getting elected.

These predictions from the positive analysis of taxation differ greatly from the normative prescriptions of scholars like Simons (1938) and most recently Buchanan and Congleton (1998), who argue that the equitable treatment of individuals requires that citizens in similar situations be taxed similarly.[5] Despite the many advocates of such forms of horizontal equity, and the many proposals for broad-based and "flat" taxes, the tax code in the United States and most other developed countries remains a thicket of exemptions and special privileges. Thus, this prediction of the positive theory seems, from casual observation, to be borne out. We turn now to some more systematic evidence regarding the determinants of tax structure.

12.5.2 *The evidence*

The probabilistic voting model predicts that tax policy is slanted in favor of persons and groups who are able to deliver votes to a party that offers them favorable tax treatment. To test the model one needs to identify the persons or groups with the greatest capacities for delivering votes, and test to see whether they receive favorable treatment in the tax structure. Since no indexes of political strength are readily available, the probabilistic voting model does not immediately lead to strong predictions as to which specific groups are going to receive favorable tax treatment.

A second difficulty in testing the implications of the probabilistic voting model arises because it makes some of the same predictions as its competitors. For example, a major result in the optimal tax literature is that tax policy should attempt to minimize deadweight losses. A vote-maximizing party will also be interested in containing deadweight losses, however, because they cause it to lose votes. Indeed, the optimal set of taxes from the point of view of a vote-maximizing party – as for the welfare function maximizing social planner – would be a set of lump-sum taxes. The two ideal policies would differ not in the *form* that the taxes would take, but rather in their magnitudes. Thus, evidence like that presented by Kenny and Toma (1997), that tax and seigniorage policy in the United States over time has tended to smooth income, as the optimal tax literature says it should, is also consistent with the hypothesis that these policies are introduced by parties seeking to maximize votes in elections.[6]

The most obvious alternative to the probabilistic voting model for explaining tax policy is the median voter model. But here, too, the two models may lead to similar predictions, if it is reasonable to assume that the middle class is an effective political group (has a high f' in (12.20)). Does the existence of tax deductions for children

---

[5] See the discussion by Hettich and Winer (1999, ch. 5).

[6] The same, of course, can be said for many of the other empirical studies that attempt to test propositions from optimal tax theory. See references in Kenny and Toma (1997) and Hettich and Winer (1999, ch. 8).

imply that parents are a politically effective interest group, that the median voter has children, or that the social planner has placed extra weight on the utility functions of people with children?

Despite these conundrums, in some cases it is possible to infer that an observed pattern of taxes is consistent with certain groups exercising greater influence in the determination of taxes. For example, owners of expensive houses are not likely to get extra weight in a reasonable social planner's welfare function nor to include the median voter in their group. Hunter and Nelson's (1989) finding that the share of total tax revenue in Louisiana parishes accounted for by property taxes is inversely related to the percent of the homeowners who own expensive houses, thus seems to confirm their hypothesis that these wealthy homeowners are an effective political group in Louisiana.[7]

Hettich and Winer (1984, 1999, ch. 9) employ the probabilistic voting model to motivate their study of the reliance on the income tax as a source of revenue across states. The clearest support for the probabilistic voting model actually comes from the second equation in their model, which predicts whether a state allows residents to credit their property tax payments against their state income tax obligations. Once again wealthy homeowners appear to exert significant political influence as do citizens over 65.[8]

Although the number of studies that directly test for the importance of political strength in determining tax structure is small, the results so far are encouraging.

12.6   Commentary

When Anthony Downs put forward his economic theory of democracy, he seemed to suggest that the outcomes from a political system in which candidates competed for the votes of the electorate would somehow avoid the nihilistic implications of the cycling literature, and more generally Arrow's impossibility theorem (see, e.g., Downs, 1957, pp. 17–19). Downs did not succeed in demonstrating any normative results concerning the outcomes from political competition, however, and the subsequent literature on spatial voting models proved in one paper after another that cycling is potentially just as big a problem when candidates compete for votes as it is for committee voting.

The literature on probabilistic voting appears to drive a giant wedge between the public choice literature on committee voting and that on electoral competition. Committee voting is inherently deterministic, and cycling problems will continue to confound the outcomes from committee voting under rules like the simple majority rule. But if voters reward a candidate who promises them a higher utility by increasing the likelihood of voting for the candidate, then competition for votes between candidates leads them "as if by an invisible hand" to platforms that maximize social welfare. The analogy between market competition and political competition does

---

[7] A parish in Louisiana is the local political unit corresponding to the county in other states. Farmers were also identified as an effective political group by Hunter and Nelson.

[8] Many additional variables, which Hettich and Winer hypothesize will be significant, prove to be so. But often these other variables might also be consistent with alternative models.

exist. Both result in Pareto-optimal allocations of resources. Downs's faith in the efficacy of political competition has at long last been vindicated.

Several writers have questioned the reasonableness of some of the assumptions upon which the main theorems in the probabilistic voting literature rest, namely, that the probability functions of a voter voting for a given candidate are monotonically increasing and concave in the utility promised to the voter by the candidate, and the issue set over which the candidates compete is compact and convex (Slutsky, 1975; Usher, 1994; Kirchgässner, 2000).

Kirchgässner, for example, questions the generality of the probabilistic voting models by constructing an example for three voters with ideal points located to form a triangle as in Figure 12.1. He then chooses probabilities such that candidate 2 can increase her chances of winning the votes of A and B by moving to the midpoint of $\overline{AB}$ by more than enough to offset the reduction in the probability of C voting for her, assuming candidate 1 is located at M. Thus Kirchgässner argues cycling can also arise with probabilistic voting.

Clearly, a three-voter electorate is a rather unusual assumption and it might be reasonable to assume that candidates hop about trying to win the votes of two of the three voters. With a large number of voters and a unimodal distribution of ideal points, such jumping around with probabilistic voting would seem much less reasonable. Even with a three-voter electorate, however, the theorems proving the existence of equilibria under probabilistic voting remain valid – if one maintains the assumptions of the theorems.

In their proofs of the existence of an equilibrium under probabilistic voting, Coughlin and Nitzan (1981a,b) assume that the probability of voter i voting for each of the two candidates is a concave function of the following form:

$$\pi_{1i} = \frac{U_{1i}}{U_{1i} + U_{2i}}, \qquad \pi_{2i} = \frac{U_{2i}}{U_{1i} + U_{2i}}. \tag{12.22}$$

Now assume that each voter i's utility from the platform of candidate j takes the following form:

$$U_i^j = K - \mid I_i - P_j \mid^2, \tag{12.23}$$

where I_i is voter i's ideal point, P_j is the platform of candidate j, and $\mid I_i - P_j \mid$ is the Euclidean distance between the two points. K is a positive constant that represents the utility each voter experiences from an $x - y$ combination located at his ideal point. K must be sufficiently large to make $U_i^j > 0$, if it makes sense to provide the public goods x and y at all.

If candidate 1 locates at M, equidistant from A, B, and C, and candidate 2 is halfway between A and B, then the probability of candidate 1 getting the vote of either A or B is

$$\pi_{1A} = \pi_{1B} = \frac{K - \left(\frac{2}{\sqrt{3}}\right)^2}{K - \left(\frac{2}{\sqrt{3}}\right)^2 + K - 1} = \frac{K - \frac{4}{3}}{2K - \frac{7}{3}}, \tag{12.24}$$

while the probability of getting C's vote is

$$\pi_{1C} = \frac{K - \frac{4}{3}}{K - \frac{4}{3} + K - 3} = \frac{K - \frac{4}{3}}{2K - \frac{13}{3}}. \tag{12.25}$$

The respective probabilities for candidate 2 are

$$\pi_{2A} = \pi_{2B} = \frac{K - 1}{2K - \frac{7}{3}}, \qquad \pi_{2C} = \frac{K - 3}{2K - \frac{13}{3}}. \tag{12.26}$$

Summing each probability function over the three voters we obtain π_1 and π_2, from which it is easy to show that

$$(\pi_1 > \pi_2) \longleftrightarrow \left(K > \frac{1}{2}\right). \tag{12.27}$$

Recalling that K must be sufficiently large to make the provision of x and y to the community worthwhile, it is easy to see that (12.27) is satisfied for each of the platforms of the two candidates. Candidate 2 does not increase her probability of winning by leaving point M.

If we think of the two candidates as promising different bundles of public goods, then the imposition of a budget constraint on the government or a resources constraint on the economy would suffice to make the issue set satisfy the compactness and convexity assumption. With two public goods, x and y, and a budget constraint, B, the condition is satisfied. Are these reasonable assumptions? Is there a finite probability that a given citizen will vote for candidate 1 for every possible platform this candidate might choose? Do these platforms range to infinity in some directions of the issue space? Ultimately, these are questions about the voter's psychology that cannot be resolved by logical argument.[9]

An alternative to testing the accuracy of the assumptions underlying the theorems is, of course, to test their implications. In a two-party system like that of the United States do the candidates seem to converge on the same (similar) positions on the full set of issues? Do the outcomes of the electoral process sometimes produce candidates who take extreme positions on one set of issues, and other times take them on a totally different set? If the reader thinks that this is the case, then she should be skeptical of the assumptions underlying the probabilistic voting models. If she does not, she can take some comfort in their implications.

Even if we accept the underlying assumptions of the probabilistic voting models and their implications about equilibria under two-party competition, they can raise additional normative issues of a less salutary nature. The probabilistic voting model

---

[9] Enelow and Hinich (1989) introduce a probabilistic element in a two-party electoral model as a random error term in a candidate's expectation of her share of the vote. Whether an equilibrium exists or not is shown to depend on "the variance of the random element ..., the size of the feasible set of candidate policy locations, the salience of policies among voters, the dimensionality of the policy space, and the degree of concavity in voter utility functions" (p. 110). Thus, Enelow and Hinich's probabilistic voting model illustrates some of the points Kirchgässner makes in his critique. The existence of an equilibrium is not guaranteed by the introduction of a random element in the two-party model. Once again, however, it is not easy to say whether the assumptions about the size of the feasible set, concavity of voter utility functions, and so on needed to ensure an equilibrium are reasonable or not.

with interest groups implies that different groups receive different weights in the welfare function, which candidate competition implicitly maximizes. The empirical literature on taxation discussed earlier and that reviewed in Chapter 20 underscore the importance of this issue by providing ample evidence of a two-way exchange relationship between candidates and interest groups. While it is comforting to know that political competition takes us to an equilibrium on the Pareto-possibility frontier, before we sing the praises of two-party democracy too loudly we might wish to inquire about where this point on the frontier lies. Before passing judgment on the merits of a two-party system, it also might be prudent to compare it to its alternatives – one-party and multiparty systems. We take up multiparty systems in the next chapter, and leave single-party systems for Chapter 18.

Bibliographical notes

The first articles to establish the existence of equilibria under probabilistic voting assumptions were by Davis et al. (1970) and Hinich, Ledyard, and Ordeshook (1972, 1973). Although the equilibrium result was clearly there, the significance of the result was not appreciated by this observer, because the probabilistic element in the models was assumed to be due to abstentions when candidates were too far from a voter's ideal point. Thus, equilibria appeared to emerge as a sort of accidental consequence of some voters refusing to vote. This seemed a shaky foundation upon which to build a strong normative case for the outcomes from electoral competition. As the literature has evolved, however, the emphasis has shifted from abstentions to uncertainty on the part of candidates and/or voters. Relevant papers in this evolution include Comanor (1976), Denzau and Kats (1977), Hinich (1977), Coughlin and Nitzan (1981a,b), Coughlin (1982, 1984, 1986), and Ledyard (1984). Enelow and Hinich (1984, ch. 5), Ordeshook (1986, pp. 177–80; 1997), and Coughlin (1992) provide overviews of this literature.

The normative significance of the results is brought out most clearly by Coughlin and Nitzan (1981a), Coughlin (1982, 1984, 1992), and Ledyard (1984) and stressed most forcefully by Wittman (1989, 1995).

Wittman (1984) extends the equilibrium results to competition among three or more candidates, Austen-Smith (1981b) to multiconstituency party competition.

Samuelson (1984) assumes that candidates begin at different starting points and are constrained in how far from these starting points they can move in any election. Equilibria occur with the candidates adopting different platforms and having different expected vote totals. Hansson and Stuart (1984) obtain similar results by assuming that candidates have utility functions defined over the strategy choices.

The public choice analysis of taxation was launched by Hettich and Winer (1984, 1988), who have also surveyed the major contributions to the literature (Hettich and Winer, 1997, 1999).

Finally, mention must be made of an important related work of Becker (1983). Becker does not model the process of political competition, but assumes that government is a form of market for equilibrating interest group demands for favors. At the assumed equilibrium, Pareto optimality holds as in the equilibria of the probabilistic voting models.

CHAPTER 13

Multiparty systems

There is a radical distinction between controlling the business of government and actually doing it.

John Stuart Mill

13.1 Two views of representation

Views are divided on the role and function of elections in the democratic process and, therefore, on one of the basic constitutive elements of democratic theory. In one view, elections serve primarily to choose a government – a cabinet, administration, or executive – and only secondarily, if at all, to reflect the preferences or opinions of citizens. In that view, a cabinet governs as long as it retains the confidence (reflects the preferences or opinions) of the elected parliament.... There is a tendency for those who opt for that view – which we should note provides the foundation for the theory of *responsible* government – to focus on questions and issues that pertain to cabinets more than on those related to parliament and to citizens.

According to a second view, elections are primarily instruments in the hands of the public to signal particular preferences or opinions to competing representatives and only secondarily to fulfill the function of choosing a government. The basis of that view, which provides the foundation for the theory of *representative* government, is the assumption that governments seek to meet the preferences of citizens for public policies which would otherwise be unavailable or available in suboptimal quantities.

(Breton and Galeotti, 1985, pp. 1–2)

The two-party or two-candidate competition model of Chapters 11 and 12 provides a theoretical foundation for the first view of government. As long as the two parties or candidates must from time to time compete for the votes of the citizens, they will remain responsive to citizens' preferences. Each citizen's preference receives a positive weight in the competing candidates' objective functions. But with a large electorate, that weight will be small, and the equilibrium at which the candidates arrive may be a great distance from the citizen's most preferred platform. Moreover, since the government governs for several years, the "issues" over which the candidates compete are not specific proposals for expenditures and programs, but more general ideological and policy positions. Thus, in voting for a particular candidate the citizen does not vote for someone who will closely and directly represent the citizen's preferences. The citizen votes for the candidate or party to whom he wishes to entrust the power to govern for the upcoming electoral period. This view of the process of government resembles somewhat Hobbes's selection of a sovereign, with the amendment that the sovereign must periodically stand for reelection.

The "ideal type" for the second view of government is Athenian democracy. Government outcomes should reflect the preferences of the people as in a direct democracy. One needs representative democracy only if the polity is too large for all citizens to assemble and decide issues directly. In choosing representatives, one seeks to select those whose voting duplicates that which would occur were all of the citizens to assemble and vote directly on the issues.

Ideal models of the first view of democracy were presented in Chapters 11 and 12. We sketch an ideal representation of the second model of democracy in the next section, and then go on to discuss proportional representation systems as they appear in the real world.

13.2 Selecting a representative body of legislators

We seek an assembly in which each citizen is represented by someone whose preferences are identical to those of the citizen.[1] Such a representative assembly cannot be formed, however, unless some citizens have preferences identical to others. Otherwise the only truly representative assembly would have to include all of the citizens. Assume, therefore, that the citizenry can be divided into s groups with all members of each group having perfectly homogeneous preferences on public issues. Let the number of citizens with preference of the ith type be n_i. Then a fully representative body can be formed by selecting s individuals, one from each group, giving each representative votes in the assembly proportional to the number of individuals represented, for example, the representative of the ith group has n_i votes. Such an assembly would have each citizen represented by someone whose preferences were identical to those of the citizen, and all citizens' preferences represented in proportion to their frequency in the polity.

The simplest way to form such an assembly would be to make the rewards for serving sufficiently attractive so that members of each group would be induced to run for office. Assuming citizens vote for representatives with preferences identical to their own, a fully representative assembly would be formed.

If s were so large as to make the assembly itself unwieldy, then its size could be limited by (1) fixing the number of seats at some figure m and allowing only the m candidates with the highest vote totals to take seats, or (2) setting a minimum on the number or percentage of votes a candidate must receive to be allowed to take a seat in the assembly. The first proposal guarantees that at most m seats are filled in the assembly. The second allows a variable number of seats to be filled, but a number less than s can be guaranteed by setting the number of votes required to be elected high enough.

---

[1] The model in this section resembles that discussed by Tullock (1967a, ch. 10); Mueller, Tollison, and Willett (1972, 1975); and Mueller (1996a, ch. 8).

The second two proposals would both result in some citizens having voted for candidates who did not win seats in the assembly. This feature could be avoided by having a second, runoff election among the winners on the first round to determine the number of votes each could cast in the assembly. Each citizen could then vote for the representative elected in the first round whose preferences came closest to those of the citizen. Although representation would then not be perfect, it would come much closer to the ideal than the outcome from a two-candidate winner-take-all contest.

Finally, if the feasible size of an assembly m were large relative to s, one could simply choose m citizens at random from the population and rely on the law of large numbers to ensure that the assembly formed consists of members whose preferences are in the same proportions as those of the polity at large (Mueller, Tollison, and Willett, 1972).

13.3   Proportional representation in practice

A large discrepancy exists between the ideal proportional representation (PR) system just described and its real-world counterparts. In only two countries, Israel and the Netherlands, do voters in all parts of the country face the same list of parties and candidates. In all other countries, the nation is divided into districts with each district electing several representatives. Thus, the mode of representation is typically a compromise between the extreme form of geographic representation in the first-past-the-post systems, and a fully at-large PR system.

In the typical PR system, the legislative and executive branches are combined. Following an election a head of government and her cabinet is either chosen directly by the legislature, or appointed by the head of state (the president, the queen) following the advice of the legislature. Thus, when a set of parties succeeds in putting together a majority coalition, it can effectively choose the chief executive and her fellow cabinet members – it can form "the government."[2]

In the remainder of this chapter, we discuss the properties of electoral politics in PR systems, and their consequences. We begin a review of the some of electoral rules that are found in PR systems.

13.4   Electoral rules

Our ideal PR system had but one district and as many persons elected from that district as there were seats in the legislature. Real-world PR systems differ in both the number of districts into which the nation is divided and the number of persons that can be elected from each district. The fewer the districts into which the polity is divided and the more persons elected per district, the more a geographically

---

[2] In the United States it is common to refer to "the government" when talking about the legislature, the executive branch and its accompanying bureaucracies, and even the judiciary. My use of the word "government" in this book generally follows this American convention. In parliamentary democracies, "the government" typically refers to the cabinet, that is, the executive authority concentrated in the parliament. In parliamentary democracies, the wider panoply of public sector activities are lumped under the heading of "the state."

based system resembles our ideal PR system. In any system in which more than one person is elected from a district, a formula must be chosen to translate votes in the district into seats in the parliament. These formulas can result in differences between the percentage of the national vote a party gets and its percentage of seats in the parliament. We shall first illustrate what is involved with five of the most often used formulas.

13.4.1 *The Hare, Droop, Imperiali, d'Hondt, and Sainte-Lagué formulas*

Consider Table 13.1.[3] A nation of 10,300,000 voters is divided into 10 districts. Seats in the parliament are apportioned to each district in proportion to population, for example, district 1 has twice the population of district 2 and therefore can fill twice as many seats. The population in each district is such as to make the allocation of seats exact. Every 100,000 voters elect one representative. (Usually, of course, even the fairest apportionment of seats results in some differences in voters per seat across districts.) Eight parties seek seats in the parliament, but all eight do not run candidates in each district. When a party fails to enter a list of candidates in a district, an NL (no list) is entered. A voter in any district votes for a single party. The seats assigned to that district are allocated in proportion to the votes cast in that district. We have assumed that the allocation rule is the largest remainder rule. Under this formula, one first calculates the Hare quotient

$$q = \frac{v}{s}, \tag{13.1}$$

where v is the total number of votes cast in a district, and s the number of seats it can fill. The number of seats won by each party is determined by dividing the number of votes won by the party, v_p, by q. This division gives a nonnegative integer I plus some fraction f, $0 \leq f < 1$; that is,

$$\frac{v_p}{q} = I + f. \tag{13.2}$$

The allocation of seats to parties proceeds by first giving each party a number of seats equal to its I. The remaining seats are assigned according to which parties have the largest remainders, f. For example, on the basis of the Is for each party, the allocation of seats in district 1 gave three seats to A, one to D, and two to G. The remaining two seats were given to A and H, since they had the highest remainders.

The second-to-last column of Table 13.1 gives the total votes won by each party (V) across the nation and the number of seats each would obtain if the formula in (13.2) were applied to the national totals rather than district by district. The last column cumulates the seats won across the ten districts. The correspondence between the seats won in the ten districts and what would have been won if the entire nation were a district is close, but not perfect. The largest remainder formula when

---

[3] This table and much of the discussion in this section are taken from Mueller (1996a, ch. 10).

Table 13.1. *Distribution of seats in a multirep-multidistrict system*

District	1		2		3		4		5		6		7		8		9		10		Totals		Actual seats
Party	v	s	v	s	v	s	v	s	v	s	v	s	v	s	v	s	v	s	v	s	v	s	
A	349,851	4	489,441	5	141,222	1	73,444	1	NL		111,422	1	141,383	1	268,317	3	NL		4,525		1,579,605	16	16
B	NL		69,617	1	92,856	1	101,867	1	17,642		71,683	1	155,363	2	182,741	2	81,646	1	115,922	1	889,337	9	10
C	41,442		NL		52,956	1	NL		66,817	1	NL		646,522	7	433,829	4	124,317	1	611,323	6	1,977,206	20	20
D	107,814	1	31,145		NL		32,496		75,323	1	NL		NL		110,009	1	111,666	1	224,103	2	692,556	7	6
E	NL		180,017	2	66,100	1	115,466	1	NL		88,238	1	333,661	3	101,842	1	NL		89,306	1	974,630	10	10
F	23,500		16,333		41,323		304,275	3	80,969	1	NL		141,682	1	NL		NL		79,221	1	687,303	7	6
G	227,275	2	490,376	5	480,727	5	170,631	2	59,249		192,349	2	NL		162,300	2	190,841	2	NL		1,973,748	19	20
H	50,118	1	323,071	3	224,816	2	101,821	1	NL		236,308	2	81,389	1	140,962	1	91,530	1	275,600	3	1,525,615	15	15
Totals	800,000	8	1,600,000	16	1,100,000	11	900,000	9	300,000	3	700,000	7	1,500,000	15	1,400,000	14	600,000	6	1,400,000	14	10,300,000	103	103

Notes: v, Popular vote for each party; *s*, number of seats in parliament assigned by largest remainders formula; NL = no list.

268

applied to the total votes cast in the nation would assign an extra seat to parties D and F, and one less seat to B and G.

Although the Hare quotient coupled with a largest-remainders rule for allocating leftover seats in a district is the most straightforward and easiest to apply, it is not the only one in use. Two variants on the Hare quotient are the Droop quota, d,

$$d = \frac{v}{s+1} \quad \text{or} \quad d = \frac{v}{s+1} + 1, \tag{13.3}$$

and the Imperiali

$$i = \frac{v}{s+2}, \tag{13.4}$$

with d as defined on the left side of (13.3) and i rounded up to the next integer. The d'Hondt method computes no quotient, but rather simply allocates the seats in a district by repeated application of the largest-remainders principle. The modified Sainte-Laguë formula uses $1.4, 3, 5, 7, \ldots$ as divisors instead of $1, 2, 3, 4, \ldots$ as under the d'Hondt. Still other variants on these are or have been used.[4] As we shall see, these differ in how well they match party seats to party votes, but all tend to achieve a reasonable correspondence between the two.

13.4.2 *The single-transferable vote (STV)*

In STV systems the citizen votes for a particular candidate, or more accurately candidates, rather than for a party per se. Namely, each voter ranks the candidates running in her district. Winners are determined using the second Droop quota defined above; that is,

$$d = \frac{v}{s+1} + 1, \tag{13.5}$$

where v and s are the total votes and seats in a district as before. One first determines the number of candidates with first-place votes in excess of d. These candidates are all elected. Any first-place votes for a given candidate above those required for him to reach d are then assigned to the voters' second choices. If with these transferred votes any candidate has more than d, the extra votes are assigned to the voters' third choices, and so on until the s seats are filled. STV is currently employed in the Republic of Ireland, Malta, Northern Ireland (to elect representatives to the European Parliament), Australia (to elect representatives to the Senate), and in some American cities.

When voters confine their ranking of candidates to those from a single party, STV results in the same party representation as under the largest-remainders formula (Lijphart, 1986, p. 175). The main difference between STV and a party list system

---

[4] The various formulas are illustrated and compared by Carstairs (1980, chs. 2 and 3), Balinsky and Young (1982), Lijphart (1986), and Amy (1993, pp. 225–38).

is that under the list system the party leadership gets to determine which persons fill the seats won by the party; under STV the voters make this determination. Under STV the voters may depose a party leader, for example, by giving her very low ranks, while under a list system she would be elected so long as her rank among the party leadership was higher than the number of seats her party won.

STV would seem to have all of the merits of a party list system – the voters can after all rank the candidates in the same order as that advocated by the party – plus the obvious advantage of allowing the voters to provide the additional input into the election process of their views on the relative merits of the party members. A particular advantage claimed for STV is that it allows ethnic, religious, and gender groups to single out party members from their group for election.[5]

13.4.3 *Limited voting*

Under limited vote systems each voter can cast c votes, $c \le s$, where s is the number of seats to be filled in the district. The s candidates receiving the most votes in a district assume its seats in the parliament. The votes are cast for persons rather than parties, and so limited voting resembles STV in a way since the voter can indicate which members of a party he wishes to see in the parliament. But the voter can also cast his votes for persons in different parties. The only country in which limited voting with $c > 1$ is used today is Spain to elect the upper house.[6]

Limited voting is a compromise between pure PR systems in which the parties or persons receive votes in the parliament in direct proportion to the votes cast for them, and plurality systems in which representatives are elected with greatly different numbers of votes. This latter characteristic creates strategic problems for both the voters and the parties' running candidates. Suppose, for example, four seats can be filled from a district and each voter can cast three votes, the typical case in Spain. A voter might like to see all four seats filled by representatives from his most preferred party, but can cast but three votes. If the party runs four candidates, the voter must choose one candidate of the four not to vote for. If all voters who support this party choose not to vote for the same person, only three members of the party will be elected. If the number of voters supporting this party is large, however, all four seats might have been filled by representatives of this party under an alternative pattern of voting. This may lead some voters to vote for their fourth choice from the party, say, and not for their first choice, under the expectation that their first choice will receive considerably more than the number of votes required to get elected. But if large numbers of voters act the same way, their first choice might fail to get elected, while their fourth choice is elected.

A symmetric problem faces the parties in choosing the number of candidates to run. A party that runs four candidates for four seats might spread its votes

---

[5] For further discussion of the merits and demerits of STV, see Hallett (1984), Katz (1984), Amy (1993, pp. 183–91, 193–7), and Bowler and Grofman (2000b).

[6] For a discussion of limited voting in general, and the Spanish experience in particular, see Lijphart, Lopez, and Sone (1986) and Cox (1997, pp. 115–17).

so thinly that it elects only two; when by running three it could have elected all three. If it runs only three, however, it passes up the chance of electing four. These strategic considerations suggest that limited voting systems are a less attractive means for eliciting information on voter preferences than PR party list or STV systems.

13.4.4 *Single-nontransferable-vote systems (SNTV)*

A special case of limited voting has $s > 1$ and $c = 1$. When both s and c equal 1, we have the plurality system, so that SNTV is clearly closer to a plurality system than limited voting systems with $c > 1$. Indeed, when $c = s > 1$, limited voting resembles STV, so that limited voting approximates PR or plurality systems as s and c are large or small. Japan, Korea, and Taiwan have used SNTV, but recent constitutional changes in Japan have replaced this system with a mixture of single-member districts that use the plurality rule and a PR system for the remaining seats.[7]

13.5 Electoral rules and the number of parties

What difference do the electoral rules make? Under the plurality rule, minority parties whose support is evenly distributed across the country do not win seats. Over time, the continual lack of success of these parties can be expected to dry up their financial support and discourage both their members and leaders. Thus, under the plurality rule one expects minority parties to disappear, unless their supporters are concentrated in particular geographic areas. One expects the plurality rule to produce two-party systems.

In 1954 Maurice Duverger claimed that this tendency under the plurality rule in fact "approaches most nearly perhaps to a true sociological law."[8] Duverger's law rests on the presumption that citizens vote strategically.

To see why consider the decision calculus of a voter under the plurality rule, when there are candidates from three parties competing for her vote. Based on preelection polls and the past performance of the three parties in her district, she judges the probabilities of the three candidates' victories to be $\pi_A > \pi_B > \pi_C$. For her vote to make a difference, the two candidates receiving the most votes must *tie* save for her vote, and she must cast the decisive vote for one of them. Unless π_B and π_C are very close, the probability of a tie between the candidates from parties A and C must be much smaller than the probability of a tie between A and B. If the voter wants to have a real chance of affecting the outcome of the election, she does not "waste" her vote on the candidate from party C, but rather

---

[7] For further discussion of SNTV systems, see Lijphart, Lopez, and Sone (1986); and Grofman, Lee, Winckler, and Woodall (1999).

[8] As quoted by William Riker (1982a, p. 754). Riker reviews both the intellectual history of the "law" and the evidence gathered on its behalf.

gives it to the candidate from either A or B whose victory she prefers. Under the plurality rule rational voters desert the minority parties in favor of the two leading parties.[9]

The logic of the voter's calculus that underpins Duverger's law can be generalized to electoral systems, which allow two or more representatives to be chosen from a district, and leads to the general prediction that there will be more than two parties competing for votes when more than one representative is elected from each district. This prediction is often referred to as *Duverger's hypothesis*.

Assume now that two representatives can be elected in a district and there are candidates from four parties competing for the two seats. The voter judges the probabilities of each party's winning a seat to be $\pi_A > \pi_B > \pi_C > \pi_D$. If the differences between each pair of probabilities are substantial, the voter will waste her vote by voting for *either* party A *or* for party D. The front running candidate is almost certain to win one of the two seats, and so the meaningful competition is for the second seat. The probability of a tie for second between the candidates of the parties expected to come in second and third is much greater than the probability of a tie for second between the fourth-ranked party and any of the other three. If the voter wants to have a chance of affecting the election's outcome, she chooses between the two candidates vying for the *marginal* seat in the district. If M representatives are chosen from the district, then the competition for the marginal seat is between the candidates ranked Mth and $M + 1$th in the preelection polls, and the rational voter concentrates on these two candidates.[10]

This line of reasoning leads to some fairly precise predictions. Not only should we expect to find only two major parties, where one representative is elected from each district (single-member districts), the number of major parties should increase with the average size of an electoral district. The logic linking district size and number of parties only applies at the district level, however. In a single-member district, one's vote is likely to be wasted if one votes for the fourth strongest party in the district, even if it is on average the strongest party across the country. Thus, both Duverger's law and hypothesis must be qualified in countries where party strengths differ greatly across regions.[11]

Before one can test whether there is a relationship between the number of representatives elected per district and the number of parties, one needs to consider what is meant by the "number of parties." In a country with five parties, each obtaining 20 percent of the popular vote, it seems reasonable to speak of there being five major parties. If the five parties received 60, 30, 7, 2, and 1 percent of the vote, respectively, however, it would seem more difficult to call this "a five-party system," as one would expect it to perform much more like a one-party or two-party system. To allow for differences in the relative sizes of parties, most scholars measure the

---

[9] If the number of voters in her district is large, the rational voter may realize that the probability of a tie for first between any two of the candidates is infinitesimal, and *not vote at all*. Thus, the hypothesis that rational voters vote strategically includes an assumption that they vote *as if* their votes had a meaningful chance of affecting the outcome. We take up the question of why rational individuals vote at all in the next chapter.

[10] See McKelvey and Ordeshook (1972), and Cox (1997, chs. 2, 4, and 5).

[11] Humes (1990) demonstrates that more than two parties may survive when $M = 1$, if the decisions of parties to exit are made simultaneously.

Table 13.2a. *Median numbers of representatives per district (M), effective numbers of parties (ENV, ENS), deviations from proportionality (Dev), and relative reduction in the number of parties (RRP)*

Single-member districts	Year	*M* (effective)	ENV	ENS	*Dev* (%)	RRP (%)
Australia	1984	1.0	2.79	2.38	11.5	18.7
Bahamas	1987	1.0	2.11	1.96	19.2	7.7
Barbados	1986	1.0	1.93	1.25	–	54.4
Belize	1984	1.0	2.06	1.60	22.0	28.8
Botswana	1984	1.0	1.96	1.35	17.2	45.2
Canada	1984	1.0	2.75	1.69	24.9	62.7
Dominica	1985	1.0	2.10	1.76	34.8	19.3
France	1981	1.0	4.13	2.68	20.6[a]	54.1
Grenada	1990	1.0	3.84	3.08	–	24.7
India	1984	1.0	3.98	1.69	31.8	135.5
Jamaica	1989	1.0	1.97	1.60	–	23.1
Korea (South)	1988	1.0	4.22	3.56	–	18.5
New Zealand	1984	1.0	2.99	1.98	19.0	51.0
St. Kitts and Nevis	1984	1.0	2.45	2.46	–	−0.4
St. Lucia	1987	1.0	2.32	1.99	26.0	16.6
St. Vincent and Grenadines	1984	1.0	2.28	1.74	17.8	31.0
Trinidad and Tobago	1986	1.0	1.84	1.18	–	55.9
United Kingdom	1983	1.0	3.12	2.09	23.4	49.3
United States	1984	1.0	2.03	1.95	6.7	4.1
Means		1.0	2.68	2.00	21.1	30.5

Sources: See Table 13.2b.

effective number of parties for a country. This statistic can be calculated based on the number of votes each party received across the country in the election (ENV), or based on its number of seats in the legislature (ENS). If v_p is the number of votes party p received in the election, and v is the total number of votes cast, then ENV is defined as follows

$$\text{ENV} = \frac{1}{\sum_{p=1}^{n}\left(\frac{v_p}{v}\right)^2} \tag{13.6}$$

with the analogous formula holding for party seats (s_p) in a legislature with s seats

$$\text{ENS} = \frac{1}{\sum_{p=1}^{n}\left(\frac{s_p}{s}\right)^2}. \tag{13.7}$$

In the preceeding two five-party examples, the ENV when each party gets 20 percent of the votes is 5, and in the second case it is 2.2.[12]

Table 13.2 presents ENV and ENS figures for 19 single-member-district (SMD) and 34 multimember-district democratic (MMD) countries. It is readily apparent that SMD systems produce lower numbers equivalents, regardless of whether these

[12] An analogous statistic – the "numbers equivalent" – is used in the industrial organization literature to measure the effective number of firms in an industry. It is simply one over the Herfindahl index of concentration. In political science it is often also called the Laakso-Taagepera index (Laakso and Taagepera, 1979).

Table 13.2b. *Median numbers of representatives per district (M), effective numbers of parties (ENV, ENS), deviations from proportionality (Dev), and relative reduction in the number of parties (RRP)*

Multimember districts	Year	R/D (effective)	ENV	ENS	*Dev* (%)	RRP (%)
Argentina	1985	9.0	3.37	2.37		42.2
Austria	1986	30.0 (20)	2.72	2.63	4.3	3.4
Belgium	1985	8.0 (12)	8.13	7.01	7.7	16.0
Bolivia	1985	17.5	4.58	4.32		5.6
Brazil	1990	30.0	9.68	8.69	5.9	11.4
Columbia	1986	8.0	2.68	2.45	3.4	9.4
Costa Rica	1986	10.0 (8)	2.49	2.21	1.2	12.7
Cyprus	1985	12.0	3.62	3.57		1.4
Denmark	1984	11.0 (25)	5.25	5.04	2.9	4.2
Dominican Republic	1986	5.0	3.19	2.53		26.1
Ecuador	1984	3.0	10.32	5.78	16.0	78.5
El Salvador	1985	4.0 (4)	2.68	2.10		27.6
Finland	1983	17.0 (13)	5.45	5.14	3.9	6.0
Germany	1983	1.0 (10)	3.21	3.16	0.8	1.6
Greece	1985	6.0 (3)	2.59	2.14	9.0	21.0
Honduras	1985	9.0	3.49	2.80	2.2	24.6
Iceland	1983	7.0 (60)	4.26	4.07	4.3	4.7
Ireland	1987	5.0 (4)	3.46	2.89	3.2	19.7
Israel	1984	120.0 (50)	4.28	3.86	5.8	10.9
Italy	1983	24.0 (20)	4.51	4.11	4.5	9.7
Japan	1986	4.0 (4)	3.35	2.57	6.9	30.4
Liechtenstein	1986	15.0	2.28	1.99		14.6
Luxembourg	1984	21.0 (16)	3.56	3.22	7.5	10.6
Malta	1987	5.0 (5)	2.01	2.00	2.6	0.5
Mauritius	1983	3.0	1.96	2.16		−9.3
Netherlands	1986	150.0 (75)	3.77	3.49		8.0
Norway	1985	10.0 (90)	3.63	3.09	8.7	17.5
Peru	1985	9.0	3.00	2.32		29.3
Portugal	1983	16.0 (12)	3.73	3.41	5.7	9.4
Spain	1986	7.0 (7)	3.59	2.81	17.5	27.8
Sweden	1985	12.0 (12)	3.52	3.39	2.0	3.8
Switzerland	1983	12.0 (8)	5.99	5.26	4.3	13.9
Uruguay	1989	11.0	3.38	3.35		0.9
Venezuela	1983	11.0 (27)	2.97	2.42	7.9	22.7
Means		19.2 (19.2)	4.10	3.48	5.8	14.9

[a] Based on first-round votes.

Sources: *Dev* figures are for 1985 and are from Taagepera and Shugart (1989, Table 10.1).

RRP (%) = (ENV/ENS-1)100. Effective *M* are for the early 1980s and are from Taagepera and Shugart (1989, Table 12.1).

All other figures are from Cox (1997, Appendix C).

statistics are based on seats won in the assembly or votes cast in the elections. It is also obvious that the formulas used to translate votes into seats tend to concentrate power on the larger parties in both types of systems, with the greater concentration taking place within the SMD countries.

The mean number of parties based on seats in the legislature of SMD countries turns out to be precisely 2.00, and thus offers rather dramatic support for Duverger's law. An examination of the figures for the individual countries, however, reveals several significant deviations from two-party systems with Barbados, Trinidad, and Tobago coming close to being single-party states, and France, Grenada, and South Korea all having ENSs above 3. Nevertheless, 13 ENSs for the 19 SMD countries lie between 1.5 and 2.5.

The larger-than-predicted number of parties for France has often been attributed to its use of a two-stage electoral rule. To be elected in the first round, a candidate must receive a majority of the votes cast. If no candidate obtains an absolute majority in the first round, candidates receiving less than 12.5 percent of the votes are eliminated from the ballot and a second round of voting takes place at which only a plurality is required to win. The logic underlying Duverger's law should hold at the second stage, however, and thus I find it difficult to see why one should not expect two dominant parties to emerge over time in France.[13]

The numbers in parentheses in the M column are Taagepera and Shugart's (1989) adjustments to the numbers of representatives per district specified in the electoral law. Their adjustments take into account whether there are second-tier adjustments in the number of seats each party gets based on its share of the vote at a higher level of aggregation as in Austria and Germany, the effects of threshold percentages of the national vote, and so on. Sometimes the effects of these adjustments are quite large as, for example, in effectively reducing the number of representatives elected per district in the Netherlands from 150 to 75, while *raising* the number for Norway from 10 to 90.[14]

The logic underlying the $(M + 1)/M$ hypothesis leads to the prediction not only that there are two parties when $M = 1.0$ and more than two parties when $M \geq 2$. It predicts that the number of parties should rise with M. The data in Table 13.2b are also consistent with this prediction. Table 13.3 presents the mean ENSs for different ranges of M. As more representatives are elected from each district in a country, the effective number of parties in the legislature increases.

Cox (1997, ch. 11) has undertaken a systematic analysis of the relationship between the size of electoral districts and the number of parties represented in the national assembly. Using data for the countries in Table 13.2, he estimated the

---

[13] Such a tendency is further strengthened by the propensity for coalition partners to withdraw in the runoff elections. See Tsebelis (1990).

[14] The Netherlands uses a party-list system at the national level, so the Dutch vote for parties, not persons. There are 150 seats in the Dutch Parliament, but the threshold for taking seats eliminates the possibility of their being 150 parties in the Parliament.

Cox lists Germany as an SMD country. Only half of the 496 seats are filled this way, however. The other half are filled based on the shares of votes each party receives in the (now) 16 Länder. I have categorized Germany with the MMD countries, therefore, based on the effective size of its electoral districts.

Table 13.3. *Effective numbers of parties in legislature, number of representatives elected per district, and deviations from proportionality*

M	Mean ENS	Mean *Dev* (Taagepera and Shugart, 1989)	Mean *Dev* (Lijphart, 1990)
1.0	2.00 (19)	21.1 (13)	12.9 (6)
2.0 ≤ 5.0	2.12 (8)	7.5 (5)	7.5 (4)
6.0 ≤ 10.0	3.34 (7)	4.9 (6)	5.6 (9)
11.0 ≤ 15.0	3.98 (7)	4.8 (4)	
> 15.0	4.09 (11)	5.8 (9)	3.5 (12)[a]

[a] Weighted average of figures for Ms of 1–25, and > 25.

Notes: Number of countries upon which calculations made are in parentheses.
Mean ENS and *Dev* for Taagepera and Shugart are taken from Table 13.2.

following equation:

$$\text{ENS} = 0.58 + 0.51\text{ENV} + 0.08\text{ENV} \times \ln(M) + 0.37\text{ENV} \times \text{UP}, \qquad R^2 = 0.921$$

where $\ln(M)$ is the natural log of the median number of representatives elected per district, and UP is an adjustment for the existence of upper tier allocation formulas as exist in Germany.[15] Countries in which the distribution of voter preferences is such as to give larger numbers of parties' votes tend to have larger numbers of parties represented in the legislature. The effect of having large numbers of parties win votes is enhanced by electoral rules that allow large numbers of representatives to be elected from each district.[16]

As noted above, when party strengths differ significantly across a country, Duverger's law and hypothesis are likely to break down. Significant geographic differences in party strengths are likely to be associated with ethnic and religious heterogeneity. Cox thus tries to explain the numbers equivalents based on votes across countries using an index of ethnic diversity and $\ln(M)$. He obtains the best fit when these two variables are interacted. Countries that elect large numbers of representatives from each electoral district *and* have large numbers of different ethnic groups tend to have larger numbers of parties winning votes.[17]

13.6 Electoral rules and the degree of proportionality

We saw in Table 13.1 that the seats allocated to each party in a PR representation system may not be strictly proportional to the votes each party gets across the country, when the country is divided into electoral districts for selecting representatives. The differences between votes won and seats allocated in the legislature can become quite dramatic, however, in electoral systems in which one representative is elected from each district.

---

[15] Thus, Cox records Germany's M as 1.0, and accounts for the fact that the *effective M* in Germany is much higher with the dummy UP. All coefficients are highly significant.

[16] See also Taagepera and Shugart (1989, ch. 13).

[17] Cox (1997, pp. 214–18); see also Ordeshook and Shvetsova (1994).

Table 13.4. *Distribution of votes across 10 electoral districts (numbers of votes in millions)*

Party	District 1	2	3	4	5	6	7	8	9	10
A	3	3	3	3	3	3	3	3	3	3
B	3	3	2	2	3	0	3	3	3	3
C	0	0	0	0	0	4	4	4	4	4
D	0	0	4	4	4	3	0	0	0	0
E	4	4	1	1	0	0	0	0	0	0
Total	10	10	10	10	10	10	10	10	10	10

To see this, consider Table 13.4. The distribution of voters by party in each of 10 districts is depicted for a polity of 100 million. Each district has 10 million voters. Under the plurality rule, the two largest parties nationally, A and B, would win no seats, although they account for 30 and 25 percent of the votes in the country. Party C would win half of the seats, 2.5 times its share of the national vote, and parties D and E would each win a fraction of seats that doubles their shares of the national vote. Although this example is contrived and is obviously extreme, when voters from each party are randomly distributed across electoral districts, even small percentage advantages in popular support for a given party can translate into large percentage advantages in seats held under the plurality rule (Segal and Spivak, 1986).

This example raises the question of just how closely different electoral rules match seats in the legislature to votes across the nation. The column labeled *Dev* in Table 13.2 provides an answer to this question. *Dev* is the deviation from strict proportionality between the vote shares for each party, v_p, and its share of the seats in the legislature, s_p, as calculated by Taagepera and Shugart (1989) using the following formula:

$$Dev = \frac{1}{2} \sum_{p=1}^{n} \|s_p - v_p\|. \tag{13.8}$$

The mean deviation from proportionality for the SMD countries is 21.1 percent, as compared to a mean *Dev* for the MMD countries of 5.8 percent.

The last column in Table 13.2 presents the percentage reduction in the effective number of parties that takes place under each system, when going from measuring number of parties in vote shares versus shares of seats in the legislature. Despite the 78.5 percent decline in number of parties recorded in Ecuador – which only elects three representatives per district on average – the relative reduction in parties in the MMD countries is only half of that in the SMD countries.

In Table 13.3, the middle column of numbers gives the mean deviation from proportionality for different ranges of M. There is a big drop in going from one representative per district to a range from 2 to 5, and another small drop in going from 2–5 to 6–10. The sample sizes are small, however, and the mean *Dev* actually rises a bit for the sample of countries with Ms > 15.

The third column in Table 13.3 gives comparable figures for deviations from proportionality as calculated by Lijphart (1990) for the period 1945 through 1985. Lijphart's observations are mean values of *Dev* for each country over the 40-year period. Lijphart uses a much smaller sample of SMR countries than do Taagepera and Shugart, and gets a much lower *Dev* than we obtain from the Taagepera and Shugart numbers. Nevertheless, the same general pattern can be observed with a big drop in the mean deviation from proportionality in going from SMR to MMR with two to five representatives per district, and still further small declines as district size expands.

Lijphart also compared the different methods for converting votes into seats. He found some differences here, also, but the differences were smaller than those related to the number of representatives per district. The smallest deviations from proportionality were observed in the five countries that use the largest-remainder (LR)-Hare and Sainte-Lague methods (mean *Dev* = 2.6 percent). The LR-Droop, LR-Imperiali, modified Sainte-Lague, and STV systems came in second (six countries with a mean *Dev* = 4.5 percent). The d'Hondt method was the least proportional of the PR formulas tried, with a mean *Dev* of 5.9 percent in the 14 countries where it is used.[18]

13.7   The goals of parties

One of the most frequently cited sentences of Downs is his assertion that: "Parties formulate policies in order to win elections rather than win elections in order to formulate policies" (1957, p. 28). Party policies play a purely instrumental role in politics, and parties are willing to shift policies any distance to win elections. This assumption of ideological flexibility underlies the Downsian assumption that parties maximize expected votes and the prediction that they converge on the ideal point of the median voter in a two-party system with a single-dimensional issues space. Indeed, it leads to the prediction that the party of the Left would readily leapfrog over the party of the Right should the party of the Right mistakenly take up a position to the left of the median voter's ideal point.

To apply Downs's assumption about party motivation to PR systems, one needs to think of it at two levels: the choice of a position along the ideological spectrum before an election, and the choice of whether or not to join a coalition to form a cabinet after the election. The first thing to note when trying to apply the assumption at the level of elections in a multiparty system is that "winning" has a different meaning than in a two-party system. Ignoring the possibility of a tie, with two parties, one must win a majority of the vote and can form the government. With more than two parties, no party may win an absolute majority, and thus one can often say that "*no* party has won the election." One can also say with equal accuracy that *every* party wins in a multiparty election, in that every party (generally) wins some seats,

---

[18] For further evidence on the consequences of electoral laws, see Rae (1971), Rose (1984), Grofman and Lijphart (1986), Taagepera and Shugart (1989), Lijphart (1994), and Powell (2000).

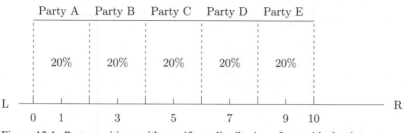

Figure 13.1. Party positions with a uniform distribution of voter ideal points.

and thus lives on to fight another election *and, most importantly,* to bargain for a position in the cabinet that forms after the election.

Theorems establishing an equilibrium set of policy positions with multiparty/multicandidate systems are very difficult to prove, and often imply rather complicated or implausible equilibrium conditions.[19] On the other hand, casual observation of European PR systems suggests that parties do settle into certain positions in ideological space and tend to stay there. Each European country has its socialist/red party, its Christian democratic/black party, its green party, and so on, and virtually every observer will place the Christian democrats to the right of the socialists and the greens to their left. Shifts in positions occur, but parties do not appear to leapfrog about the issue space in search of votes (Budge, Robertson, and Hearl, 1987); nor do they all converge on the same set of policies.

One way to account for these phenomena is to weaken or abandon Downs's vote-maximization assumption, and replace it with one that gives weight to a party's ideology.[20] Let us assume, therefore, that the sole goal of a party's leadership is to represent the ideological position of its supporters, and that it does so by adopting the median position *of its supporters*. If we assume as in the Downsian model a single-dimensional issue space with citizens voting for the party whose position is closest to their ideal point, then an equilibrium results with parties spread across the ideological spectrum.[21]

Figure 13.1 depicts the equilibrium with five parties and a uniform distribution of voter ideal points. Each party gets 20 percent of the votes, and the position occupied by the median party, party C, coincides with the ideal point of the median voter.

Figure 13.2 depicts a distribution of voter ideal points that is nonuniform. Although the median voter still supports party C, its position (5) no longer coincides with the median voter's ideal point (M = 5.67). Moreover, party D actually wins a greater share of the vote by occupying the space that contains the greatest density

---

[19] See, for example, Hinich and Ordeshook (1970, pp. 785–8); Lindeen (1970); Selten (1971); Wittman (1984); Greenberg and Weber (1985); Breyer (1987); de Palma, Hong, and Thisse (1990); Hermsen and Verbeek (1992); Lin, Enelow, and Dorussen (1999); and Hamlin and Hjortlund (2000).

[20] Downs's assumption that politicians single-mindedly maximize votes at the expense of ideological consistency was criticized early on in the context of the two-party model by Wittman (1973). In a detailed analysis of elections in the Netherlands and Germany, Schofield, Martin, Quinn, and Whitford (1998) show that parties may pass up the opportunity to increase their votes in an election, and thus their weight in the next parliament, because it would force them to bargain from an ideological position that lies farther from their ideal point in the negotiations to form a cabinet. See also Adams (1999, 2000).

[21] This is proved by McGann (2002) with the additional assumptions that the number of parties is fixed, and they are ordered left to right.

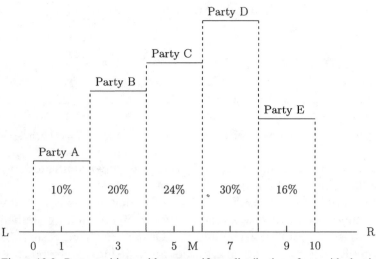

Figure 13.2. Party positions with a nonuniform distribution of voter ideal points.

of voters. Party A, on the other hand, is disfavored by the relatively small fraction of the electorate located in its ideological space.

McGann (2002) also examines the implications of assuming that party positions are chosen with one eye on the preferences of the party's supporters and the other on the potential gain in votes from shifting positions. As one might expect, such a change of goals tends to shift party positions toward the median of the distribution of voter ideal points, and reduces the shares of votes won by the centralist parties.

Party leaders must also consider whether they should compromise their party's ideological position at the second stage of the electoral process, when a cabinet is formed. If two or more parties form a cabinet, at least one of them must acquiesce to the implementation of a set of policies that does not correspond fully to its most preferred set. Compromise with a party's policy preferences is often the price of getting to influence what the actually implemented policies are. Thus, one might restate the first part of Downs's assumption for multiparty systems to read "parties change policies to join cabinets."

In the next subsection we examine several hypotheses that make different predictions regarding the formation of cabinets. Some assume that a party is willing to "move any distance" to join a cabinet; others assume that policy inertia persists at the cabinet formation stage, and use this assumption to predict which parties are likely to form cabinets.

13.7.1 *Coalition theories with a one-dimensional issue space*

Demokrastan has seven political parties holding seats. These parties compete for votes along a single-dimensional issue space. Each party has positioned itself along this left–right line as follows:

A	B	C	D	E	F	G
15	28	5	4	33	9	6

An election is held, and each citizen votes for the party that comes closest to her ideal point. The election results in a distribution of the 100 seats in the parliament according to the numbers under each party's letter. As often happens in multiparty systems, no single party holds a majority of the seats.

If Demokrastan's parliament, like most others, uses the simple majority rule, it is reasonable to assume that the goal of any parties that seek to form a coalition is to build one that controls at least 51 seats, so that it can decide all bills that come up during the parliamentary session. There are 61 possible coalitions that control at least 51 seats, the grand coalition of all seven parties; any six of the seven parties (six possibilities); B plus any four parties, E plus any four parties, and B and E plus any three parties (18 possibilities); 24 possible four-party coalitions; 10 possible three-party coalitions; and 1 possible two-party coalition between B and E. Which, if any, of these 61 coalitions will come together to select a cabinet?

Von Neumann and Morgenstern (1953) were arguably the first to have provided a hypothesis about which coalition might form. They proposed that a *minimal winning coalition* would form.

Definition: *A coalition is a minimal winning coalition if the removal of any one member results in its shifting from a majority to a minority coalition.*

The intuition behind von Neumann and Morgenstern's proposal is obvious. Any additions to a minimal winning coalition are going to take up cabinet positions that would otherwise go to the original members, and are likely to shift the outcomes from the coalition away from those favored by the original members. There are 11 possible minimal winning coalitions in Demokrastan's parliament (BE, ABF, ACE, ADE, AEF, AEG, $ABCD$, $ABCG$, $ABDG$, $CDEF$, and $DEFG$).

Riker (1962) extended the intuition underlying the minimal winning coalition as a solution concept one step further, and argued that it would be the *smallest* minimal winning coalition that would form. This hypothesis rests on modeling politics as a zero-sum game. The plausibility of this assumption is best appreciated by thinking of all political issues as involving zero-sum redistributions of wealth. In such a game, the optimal strategy is to allow the opposing coalition to be as large as possible, while remaining a losing–paying coalition. With respect to the formation of cabinets, the prize to be divided is the fixed number of positions in the cabinet. Each party wants to have as many cabinet posts as it can. The larger its relative size is in the coalition, the greater is its claim on cabinet positions. This argues for making the size of the minimal winning coalition, in terms of number of seats in the parliament, as small as possible. Riker thus proposed the *minimum* winning coalition as a solution concept.

Definition: *A minimum winning coalition contains the smallest number of seats of all minimal winning coalitions.*

There is one minimum winning coalition among the 11 minimal winning coalitions. $CDEF$ controls 51 seats and is the smallest possible majority coalition.

Forming a coalition entails bargaining among the potential coalition members, and bargaining takes time. It is reasonable to assume, therefore, that it is easier for three parties to form a coalition, than for four, and easier still for two parties to form a coalition. Thus, one might expect that the coalition containing the smallest number of parties is the most likely to form (Lieserson, 1966). This hypothesis also leads to a unique prediction in our example – a coalition between parties B and E.

The four hypotheses considered so far base their predictions solely on the *sizes* of the potential members of a winning coalition or their number. Their *positions* along the left/right issue dimension are ignored. These hypotheses thus incorporate Downs's assumption that policies have no intrinsic value to a party's leadership. Its only goal is to be part of the winning coalition. Party B is just as willing to join a coalition with E as with C or A.

If winning is not everything, however, party B should prefer a coalition with C to one with E, ceteris paribus, because the policy outcomes from such a coalition are likely to lie much closer to B's position along the left/right issue space. The next two hypotheses about the composition of a winning coalition assume that the positions of potential coalition members also affect their chances of joining the winning coalition.[22]

Axelrod (1970) proposed that the parties forming a winning coalition must be adjacent to one another along the single policy dimension. This *minimal-connected-winning* (MCW) hypothesis reduces the number of potential winning coalitions in our example to four – $ABCD$, $BCDE$, $CDEF$, and $DEFG$. Note that the requirement that the parties sit adjacent to one another along the ideological-issue dimension means that a coalition may be MCW without being minimal winning. $CDEF$ is such a coalition. Party D's seats are not needed to form a winning coalition, but to drop it would break the connection across the four parties. If C, E, and F form a minimal-winning coalition, it costs them nothing in terms of divergence from their policy positions to include D in the coalition.

It seems plausible that it is easier for two parties to agree on a common set of policies when they are situated close to one another along the policy line than when they are far away. Party F can reach an agreement with E more readily than with G. Extending this line of reasoning leads one to predict that the winning coalition will be the MCW coalition with the smallest range (de Swaan, 1973). Invoking this closed-minimal-range hypothesis leads to the unique prediction that coalition $CDEF$ forms.

Although these six hypotheses do not include all of those that have been proposed, they include the most widely cited and those that have garnered the most empirical support. To test the last two, we need to locate each party in a country along a left/right issue dimension. To do so scholars of European politics have relied on judgments by panels of experts, mass survey data, and content analysis

---

[22] For further discussion of the differences between theories that treat parties as purely office seekers or as office and policy oriented, see Laver and Schofield (1990, chs. 3–5) and Müller and Strøm (1999, pp. 5–9). Müller and Strøm (1999) contains case studies illustrating how party leaders act when the goals of pursuing votes, office and party, are in conflict. Our discussion in this section relies heavily on Laver and Schofield.

Table 13.5. *Frequency of coalition types, by country, 1945–1987*

Country	Majority situations	Minority situations					Total
		Surplus not MCW	MCW not MW	MCW and MW	MW not MCW	Minority	
Austria	6	–	–	5	1	1	13
Belgium	1	4	–	7	8	2	22
Denmark	–	–	–	2	–	18	20
Finland	–	17	–	4	1	10	32
Germany	2	–	–	9	1	–	12
Iceland	–	2	–	6	4	2	14
Ireland	4	–	–	–	3	5	12
Italy	4	8	6	–	3	14	35
Luxembourg	–	1	–	8	1	–	10
Netherlands	–	5	3	4	2	3	17
Norway	4	–	–	3	–	8	15
Sweden	1	–	–	5	–	10	16
Total	22	37	9	53	24	73	218

Source: Laver and Schofield (1990, p. 100).

of party manifestos.[23] Since scholars disagree to some extent on the positions of the various parties, and even sometimes on which parties are de facto members of the coalition that forms the government, it is not surprising to find some disagreement over how well the different theories predict the coalitions observed. Taylor and Laver (1973), de Swaan (1975), and de Swaan and Mokken (1980) all claim that the MCW hypothesis provides the best explanation for the observed data. But Warwick (1979, 1994) finds that the MCW hypothesis adds no explanatory power to the predictions given by the minimal-winning-coalition hypothesis (MW). Laver and Schofield's (1990) more recent comparison lends support to Warwick's position.

The first thing to note in Table 13.5 is that a third of the governments in Europe between 1945 and 1987 were minority governments. Since all of the theories are predicated on the assumption that parties wish to be part of a majority coalition, this substantial fraction of minority governments must be viewed as a contradiction to all of them.

The second striking fact to note is how rare it is in PR systems that one party wins a majority of the seats. This occurs barely 10 percent of the time.

Turning now to the success rates of the MCW and MW in predicting which coalitions form, we see that there were 123 instances when no single party received a majority of the seats in the parliament. Of these 62, just over 50 percent, were MCW coalitions, and 77 were MW (62.6 percent). Only 9 of the MCW governments were not also MW. Thus, the classifications of Laver and Schofield reconfirm the judgment of earlier observers that the MCW hypothesis adds little predictive power over the MW.

---

[23] For a discussion and comparison of these techniques, see Laver and Schofield (1990, pp. 245–65).

In our seven-party example, there were 61 possible coalitions, which could form and would control a majority of the seats in the parliament. Of these only 11 were MW. If our null hypothesis were that each of the 61 possible majority coalitions were equally likely, then we would expect to observe a MW about one sixth of the time. The numbers in our example should come fairly close to those for the average European parliament, and thus we should expect to see a MW about one-sixth of the time, *when a majority coalition succeeds in forming*. The prediction that the coalition that forms a government will be MW does far better than just assigning each possible majority coalition an equal probability of forming. The success rate for the MW goes up still further if we add in all of the governments that were formed by a single party with a majority of the seats, since these, too, are MW.

The four other single-dimensional coalition theories discussed earlier all select subsets of either the MCW or the MW sets of coalitions. They thus have even lower success rates at predicting which coalition forms than do the MW and MCW. All six theories predict that some majority coalition forms, and thus the large fraction of minority governments contradicts all six theories. One explanation for the existence of so many minority governments is that policy does matter a lot to parties, and affects their willingness to form coalitions.[24]

In our seven-country example, if no government forms and the parties merely vote on legislation, the one-dimensional nature of the issue space leads us to predict the victory of proposals at the median position. *All* of the proposals made by party *D* should win. Given its central position, *D* might thus try and form a government by itself. Although it is unlikely that a party with only 4 percent of the seats in parliament would try to form a minority government, if *D* had, say, 40 percent of the seats it might very well try.

Van Roozendaal (1990, 1992, 1993) defines a *central party* in exactly the same way as we defined a median position in Chapter 5. Including the votes of the central party, there are 50 percent or more of the votes in the parliament to both the right and the left of the central party's position. Extending the logic of the median voter theorem to cabinet formation, van Roozendaal predicts that central parties will be members of every government – majority or minority – that forms.

Of the 196 European governments examined by Laver and Schofield (1990, p. 113) 165 contained or were supported by a central party. Thus, van Roozendaal's theory of cabinet formation obtains considerable empirical support. Nearly 20 percent of the governments formed *did not* contain a central party, however; and so we still need some auxiliary assumptions or a more general theory. One possibility is that the issue space is not one dimensional as assumed by van Roozendaal and several of the other theories considered so far. If the issue space has a second dimension, then *D*, with only 4 percent of the seats in the parliament, might well find itself left out of the government. Although it is in a pivotal position in a single-dimensional issue space, it may not be so in a multidimensional space. We turn now to two theories of coalition formation that allow for more than one dimension in the issue space.

---

[24] For an analysis of why minority governments form so often, see Strøm (1984, 1996).

13.7.2 *Coalition theories with two- or more-dimensional issue spaces*

13.7.2.1 *The political heart.* Once the issue space has two or more dimensions, the possibility of cycles arises. Cycling in cabinet formation takes the form of unstable coalitions. A coalition among parties A, B, and E is preferred to one among A, B, and C, but the ABE coalition loses to BEF, and so on.

In Chapter 11 we argued that voting in a multidimensional issue space may not lead to cycles that span the entire space because some points dominate others. Winning proposals can reasonably be assumed to be confined to some central area of the issue space like the uncovered set or the yolk. Constructs like the uncovered set and the yolk cannot be easily generalized to predict winning grand coalitions, however, because the outcome is a joining of parties with different ideal points. The question to be answered is not which unique point in the issue space will be chosen, but rather which unique coalition of parties will form. Nevertheless, we might also expect that the parties in the winning coalition will be located in some central region of the issue space, and some concept analogous to the uncovered set will define this region. Schofield (1993a,b, 1996a) has proposed such a region, which he calls the *heart* of the polity.

To locate the heart we must first locate all median lines in a two-dimensional issue space, or median planes in a multidimensional space. All points along or to one side of a median line (plane) add up to a majority of votes in the legislature. In Figure 13.3 the parties in Israel's parliament, the Knesset, are placed in a two-dimensional issue space formed by party positions on national security issues and their secular/religious ideological position. The median lines are based on the number of seats (given beneath party) that each party won in the 1988 election. There are three such lines and they form a triangle. This triangle constitutes the political heart in this seating of the Knesset. The Pareto set is the area bounded by the ideal points of all parties, so we see that the heart lies within the Pareto set. (The heart always lies within or at worst coincides with the Pareto set.)

If we now consider a party like the Degel Hatora, labeled *DH* in the figure, we can see that it was at a disadvantage in trying to get its most favored position chosen, because a majority of the votes in the Knesset are held by parties on or to the left of the median line through *SHAS* and *LIK*, and thus all of these parties strictly prefer some points closer to this median line than *DH*'s ideal point. In contrast points within the heart can only lose to other points within the heart. Cycling is thus expected to be confined to within the heart, and one expects the coalition that eventually forms to contain one or more members of the heart. Two governments held office during the four years up to the next election: first a coalition led by Likud and including Labor (*LAB*), followed by a coalition that included Likud and *SHAS*.

Figure 13.4 illustrates the situation after the 1992 election in Israel. The three median lines now intersect at the Labor Party's ideal point, which constitutes the *core*. No point can command a majority over Labor's ideal point. The clear prediction is that Labor will be part of the winning coalition that forms the government – as it was.

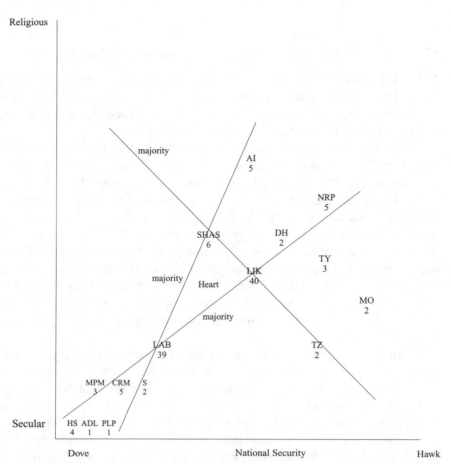

Figure 13.3. The Knesset in 1988. *Source*: Schofield (1997, p. 289)

When all median lines intersect at a single point, it constitutes the core. When they do not intersect at a single point, the area that they enclose is called the *cycle set*. The heart is the union of the cycle set and the core. Schofield's theory predicts that any coalition that forms a government contains at least one of the parties in the heart. The theory seems to have considerable predictive power (Schofield, 1993b).

13.7.2.2 *The dimension-by-dimension median.* We saw in Chapter 5 that an equilibrium could sometimes be "manufactured" in a multidimensional issue space by voting one dimension at a time.[25] Laver and Shepsle (1996) have extended this idea from voting on issues to the formation of cabinets. They note that cabinet formation is not simply about which parties form the government, but about which parties get which cabinet ministries. They assume that if party *A* gets the finance industry, it does not merely implement an economic policy *near* its ideal point along the economic policy dimension; it implements the policy, which *exactly corresponds* to its ideal point in this dimension. This assumption greatly reduces the number of

---

[25] See also Kadane (1972) and Slutsky (1977b).

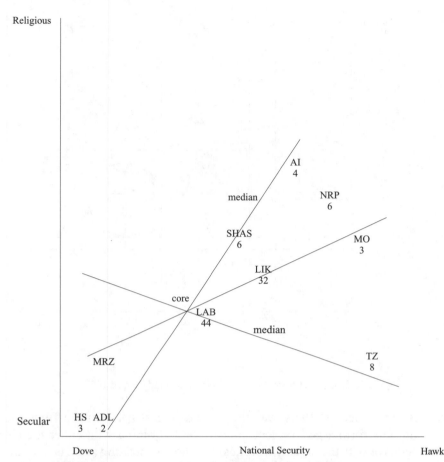

Figure 13.4. The Knesset in 1992. *Source*: Schofield (1997, p. 290)

possible outcomes from the coalition process, and thus increases the chances of an equilibrium outcome.

To see what is involved, consider Figure 13.5, which depicts the positions of the four major German parties in 1987. The two most important policy dimensions in Germany have been identified as economic and foreign policy. The ideal points of the four parties have been identified with dots. The two lines through the dot labeled *GG* represent the Green Party's position on economic and foreign policy. Each intersection of two lines represents a possible cabinet allocation of the ministries of finance and foreign policy. For example, the intersection labeled *GC* is an allocation of the finance ministry to the Green Party and the foreign affairs ministry to the Christian Democrats, whose ideal point is labeled *CC*. If the Christian Democrats were to form a government by themselves, they would fill both ministries and the cabinet outcome would be at *CC*. To avoid clutter, all possible cabinets have not been labeled. The points *FF* and *SS* represent the ideal points of the other two parties, the Free Democrats and the Socialists.

No party had a majority of the seats in the Bundestag. The Christian Democrats had enough seats to be able to form a majority coalition with any one of the other

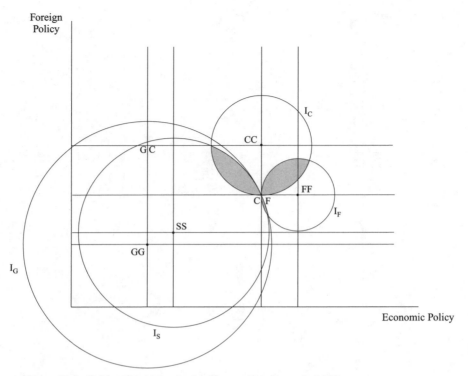

Figure 13.5. Cabinet formation in the German Bundestag in 1987.

parties. The Socialist Party was the second largest party in the Bundestag, but it could only form a government in coalition by joining with either the Christian Democrats or with the other two parties. The median position in the economic policy dimension was thus occupied by the Christian Democrats, while the median in the foreign policy dimension was occupied by the Free Democrats. The dimension-by-dimension median was at *CF*, therefore.

The Christian Democrats and the Free Democrats had formed the previous government, and had split these two key ministries with the Christian Democrats occupying the Finance Ministry and the Free Democrats having the Foreign Affairs ministry. The cabinet assignment *CF* was, therefore, the status quo. The question confronting the parties following the 1987 election was whether a new assignment of ministries and perhaps a new coalition of parties could defeat this status quo.

The circles labeled I_G, I_S, I_C, and I_F represent indifference curves for the four parties, which pass through the status quo point. Any point inside one of these circles is favored over the status quo cabinet by the party whose indifference curve is represented. The shaded, lens-shaped regions represent the *winsets* against the status quo, all of the points favored by a majority coalition over the status quo. The winsets are not empty, and thus the policies represented by the status quo allocation of ministries would lose to many other policy combinations in the legislature, *if the legislature were to vote on these policy combinations*. A central assumption of the Laver and Shepsle model is, however, that the legislature is not allowed to vote on combinations in these winsets, but is merely offered the policy favored by the party occupying the appropriate ministry. What is relevant, therefore, is not whether the winset is nonempty, but whether it contains any points where the lattice lines drawn in the figure intersect. If the winset does contain such a lattice point, there exists a cabinet allocation that can defeat the status quo, and the theory predicts that this new cabinet forms. No lattice points are contained in the winsets for point *CF*, and so the Laver-Shepsle theory predicts that the status quo is sustained. The theory makes the precise prediction that the Christian Democrats and Free Democrats will form the government, *and* that the finance ministry will go to the Christian Democrats and Foreign Policy to the Free Democrats, which is exactly what happened.

In this particular example, the dimension-by-dimension median involves a coalition of two parties. It could of course happen that a single party occupies this position. If one did and its winsets did not contain any lattice points, then there would be no allocation of cabinet posts that could defeat its filling both posts. Laver and Shepsle (1996, pp. 69–78) define such a party as being *very strong* and predict that it is in any equilibrium cabinet that can form.

They also define *merely strong* parties. A merely strong party's ideal point has a nonempty winset, but all lattice points in this winset imply cabinet allocations of which it is a part. Imagine, for example, that the Green Party's position on economic issues was shifted far enough to the right in Figure 13.5 so that its lattice line and the horizontal line through *CC* intersected in the (newly drawn) winset to *CF*. The Christian Democrats could then move closer to their ideal point by dropping the Free Democrats as coalition partners and joining with the Greens, and presumably would do so, if this new coalition would not lose to another, which left the Christian Democrats worse off. Thus, a merely strong party is strong because it can veto shifts away from its ideal point, and thereby tends to control "the making and breaking of governments." Both types of strong parties tend to be relatively large and centrally positioned in the issue space (Laver and Shepsle, 1996, pp. 184–5).

One of the important advantages of the Laver-Shepsle theory is that it can account for and indeed predicts minority governments, as, for example, when a party with less than a majority of the seats in the parliament is very strong. The theory can also account for surplus majority coalitions, when the issue space contains three or more dimensions (Laver and Shepsle, 1996, pp. 266–9). Thus, just as the existence of governments that exclude a median party in a one-dimensional issue space implies that the issue space may have more than one dimension, the existence of governments with surplus majorities implies that the issue space may have more than two dimensions, if one accepts the rest of the premises of the Laver and Shepsle theory.

Laver and Shepsle (1996, chs. 6–9) subject their theory to several empirical tests including thousands of simulations of coalition formation. In general, the theory obtains impressive support in both the simulations and when confronted with data on actual cabinet formations. It seems somewhat better at explaining the coalitions that form in countries like Sweden, which contain one large, centrally located party than in countries like Belgium and Denmark, which have numerous small- and medium-sized parties. But all in all the theory holds up quite well, particularly when one takes into account how specific its predictions are.

13.8   Cabinet stability

13.8.1 *The duration of governments*

In a parliamentary system, the government survives only as long as it can preserve its support from a majority of the members of the parliament. When there are but two parties this task is relatively easy, as the majority party's leadership must only maintain the support of the members of its own party. But when a coalition of parties forms the government, the task becomes more difficult. The different parties have different views as to what the government's program should be, and perhaps different views as to the costs, or benefits, from having a government fall and either a new coalition of parties take over or a new election called. Thus, one expects the life of a government to be shorter in multiparty systems.

The criticism that PR leads to unstable government is the most venerable, most frequent, and most forcefully leveled criticism against it (e.g., Hermens [1933, 1941, 1951], Schumpeter [1950, pp. 272–3], Black [1958, pp. 81–2]). Taylor

Table 13.6a. *Average duration of European governments by type: 1945–1987 (months)*

	AUS	GER	BEL	ICE	LUX	NOR	IRE	SWE	DEN	NET	FIN	ITA	Total
Single-party majority	46		46			48	49	24					45
Surplus coalition with majority party	24	49										16	26
Unconnected non-MW coalition			10	40						47	15	11	17
Connected (but non-MW) coalition			18	40	5					38	16	22	23
MCW but not MW coalition										25		20	22
Surplus coalition	24	49	12	40	5					34	15	17	21
MW and MCW coaliton	40	33	27	36	45	31		24	43	35	15		35
MW but not MCW coalition	39	33	24	44	61		42			23	33	17	31
Minimal coalition	40	33	25	39	47	37	42	24	43	31	19	17	33
Minority coalition with support	67		5	10		24	36	44	30		24	12	26
Minority coalition without support			2	5		25	27	21	16	4	7	6	15
Minority coalition	67		7	8		24	30	30	22	4	10	9	19
Total	41	37	22	34	45	32	39	28	26	27	15	13	26

Source: Schofield (1993b).

Table 13.6b. *Number and average duration of European governments by type: 1948–1998 (months)*

	AUS	GER	BEL	ICE	LUX	NOR	IRE	SWE	DEN	NET	FIN	ITA	Total
Number of cabinets	21	25	32		15	25	21	25	30	22	36	47	25.5[a]
Average duration[b]	28	23	17		39	25	30	26	21	27	16	12	23.4[a]

[a] Average includes France and Portugal. France has 22 cabinets with a mean duration of 21 months; Portugal 10 with a mean duration of 20 months.

[b] Müller and Strøm's figures are in days. I have converted to months by dividing by 30.

Source: Müller and Strøm (2000b, p. 585).

and Herman (1971) were among the first of many studies to test whether this criticism was well-founded. Using data for 196 governments from the post–World War II period, they found that government stability, measured as the duration of the government in days, was negatively correlated with both the number of parties in the parliament ($r = -0.39$) and the number in the coalition forming a government ($r = -0.307$). A Herfindahl-type index of party fractionalization ($F = 1 - \sum p_i^2 = 1 - $ ENS, $p_i = $ proportion of the seats held by the ith party) was negatively correlated with government stability both when measured for the full parliament ($r = -0.448$) and for the government ($r = -0.302$). One-party governments lasted on average 1107.9 days, almost twice as long as coalition governments (624.5 days).

Warwick (1979, 1994) focused upon the durability of *coalition* governments, and found that majority coalitions lasted longer than minority coalitions, and that MW coalitions lasted much longer than other types. Government durability was inversely related to the number of parties in the government. Several other studies have reconfirmed these findings in different ways.[26]

Table 13.6 presents a summary of the data on European government durations over the 1945–87 period as assembled by Schofield (1993b), and over 1948–98 by Müller and Strøm (2000b). First note that there is a great deal of variation in the lengths of governments' lives both across countries and across types of coalition structures. The average Italian government lasted barely 1 year, while governments in Luxembourg have lasted as long as 5 years with a mean of 45 months in Schofield's data and 39 months in that of Müller and Strøm.

Among the coalition types, single-party-majority governments have lasted the longest (mean of 45 months); minority governments have had the shortest lives (mean of 19 months). Minimal-winning coalitions last on average half again as long as surplus coalitions (33 versus 21 months). The dominance of single-party-majority governments over all other forms in terms of stability would be reinforced if data on the duration of governments in plurality-rule systems were included in the table.[27]

[26] See Powell (1981, 2000), Midlarsky (1984), Schofield (1987), and Taagepera and Shugart (1989, pp. 99–102); for additional discussion and references, Warwick (1979, 1994) and Laver and Schofield (1990).

[27] See also Lijphart (1984, 1999).

13.8.2 *The death of governments*

Where the early research measured government stability as the *length of a government's life*, the most recent work has focused on predicting the *probability of its death*.

In its simplest form this approach views government deaths as purely a function of random events.[28] The *Achille Lauro* sinks at sea, and the Italian government falls soon thereafter. Although the probability of a ship under the Italian flag sinking at sea is probably greater than for that of a ship under Luxembourg's flag, one expects that the dramatic differences in the lengths of government lives apparent in Table 13.6 are not all due to chance. Some underlying institutional differences exist that turn random events into government deaths in Italy more frequently than in Luxembourg.

In a seminal contribution, King, Alt, Burns, and Laver (1990) tried to determine what these underlying differences were. They modeled the *hazard rate* – the conditional probability that a government dies at time t – as an exponential function of a set of institutional and political variables drawn from the literature on government stability. Defining H as this hazard rate, we have

$$H = \exp(-\beta' x), \tag{13.9}$$

where x is a vector of the variables thought to affect cabinet deaths, and β' is a vector of the coefficients to be estimated.[29] Consistent with the previous literature, King et al. found that majority governments had lower hazard rates and cabinets with high degrees of fractionalization had higher rates.

Warwick (1994) has extended and retested the model of King et al. Table 13.7 presents the estimates for two of his equations. The six variables included in Equation 1 were the only ones that proved to be significant from a much larger set with which Warwick experimented. The different variables try to capture various aspects of the complexity of the bargaining situation and the costs to the parties should the government fall. For example, the larger the fraction of the members of one government who reappear in the next one (returnability), the smaller the expected cost to any one party from the government falling, and the more likely the government is to fall. The positive coefficient on polarization might be explained as follows: the more polarized a parliament is (that is, the stronger the parties on the far left and right are), the greater the likely loss in votes in the next election for any party that compromises on its policy position by moving toward the center. Since coalition formation and maintenance *depend* on compromise, coalition governments in polarized systems are more likely to die.

Of particular interest are the coefficients on majority status and the effective number of parties in the government. A government formed by a majority coalition has a significantly lower probability of collapsing than a minority government. The effective number of parties in the government is simply the ENS for the parties making up the cabinet. Consistent with the literature on government duration and

---

[28] The pioneering contribution here was Browne, Frendreis, and Gleiber (1986).
[29] For the derivation of this equation see King et al. (1990) and Warwick (1994, pp. 17–21).

Table 13.7. *Determinants of the hazard rate for government deaths*

	Equations	
Covariates	1	2
Majority status	−1.11 (0.16)	−1.37 (0.23)
Postelection status	−0.61 (0.15)	−0.51 (0.17)
Investiture	0.44 (0.15)	0.50 (0.19)
Effective number of parties in the government	0.20 (0.06)	0.11 (0.07)
Returnability	1.60 (0.47)	1.34 (0.51)
Polarization	3.54 (0.62)	2.62 (0.83)
Ideological diversity		0.34 (0.14)
Log-likelihood ratio	−1,120	−842
Number of cases	360	284

Standard errors in parentheses.
Variable definitions: See Warwick (1994, pp. 39–40, 53–62).
  Majority status. Is the government a majority coalition?
  Postelection status. Is the government the first after an election?
  Investiture. Is a formal vote of investiture required?
  Effective number of parties in the government. The ENS for the parties that make up the government.
  Returnability. Proportion of government parties represented in the next government following a
    collapse or early termination, calculated by system.
  Polarization. Proportion of seats held by extremist parties.
  Ideological diversity. An index of the ideological diversity of the parties in the government based on
    the parties' positions along a left–right ideological scale, a clerical–secular scale, and a regime-
    support–antipathy scale.
Source: Warwick (1994, Tables 3.3, 4.4).

King et al., Warwick finds that the probability of a government falling increases with the number of parties in the coalition that forms it.[30]

Equation 2 in Table 13.7 includes an index of the ideological diversity of the coalition of parties forming the government. This index is constructed from three other indexes – a normal left–right scaling, a clerical–secular scaling, and a scaling related to regime support. It has a positive and significant effect on the hazard rate. The greater the ideological diversity across the parties forming the government, the higher the probability that their coalition falls apart. Once ideological diversity is included in the model, the number of parties in the government loses its statistical significance. Warwick (pp. 64–7) interprets this result as implying that the effective number of parties proxies for ideological diversity, when the latter is omitted, and that it is really this ideological diversity that increases the likelihood that a multiparty government falls, not the number of parties in it per se.

This inference seems too strong. Although there may in fact be considerable ideological diversity within a single party, when an ideological index is created,

---

[30] For discussion of the other variables in Equation 1 see Warwick (1994, ch. 3).

  Strøm (1985) also found that majority status significantly lengthened the life of a cabinet. He also found that parties in minority governments tended to do better in elections than those in majority governments, and concluded from this that being in a minority government may be more advantageous for party leaders. Taagepera and Shugart (1989, pp. 99–102) found that ENS for the entire parliament is inversely linked to government duration.

each party is treated as an individual actor and given a single value along an ideological scale. Thus, a government formed by a single party with the majority of seats in the parliament has zero ideological diversity as measured by either the range or the variance of such an index. When two parties form a coalition, the index of their ideological diversity must be positive, unless they occupy exactly the same position in ideological space, and it is likely that a coalition of three parties will have a greater range or variance in its ideological indexes than a coalition of two. Thus, there is an inherent positive and possibly strong correlation between an index of the ideological diversity of a coalition and the number of parties that compose it. Since both of these variables are proxies for concepts that are difficult to measure precisely, one has to expect that different proxies might produce a different ordering of the statistical significance of the two variables.

We saw earlier that the degree of ethnic and social heterogeneity in a country was positively related to the effective number of parties in the country. The more parties there are in the parliament, the smaller the share of seats of any one party, and the more parties that are needed to form a majority coalition. If the ideological diversity in a country is reflected in the parties in its parliament, then again we can expect greater degrees of ideological diversity across the parties forming a government to be positively associated with their number. Thus, I am inclined to interpret Warwick's results for Equation 2 of Table 13.7 as implying that both the number of parties that make up a government and their ideological diversity are likely to be positively related to the probability of its demise.

Once ideological diversity is present in the model, Warwick finds that minimal-winning coalitions are no more likely to survive than other forms (pp. 67–72). The only characteristic of a coalition that proves to be significant and highly so in explaining the hazard rate is its majority status.

A large literature has now rather firmly established that good economic conditions increase the likelihood that a president or a government is reelected, and that presidents and parties take this into account when setting their economic policies (see Chapter 19). This literature has largely ignored the question of whether economic conditions also affect the life expectancy of a government. It seems quite plausible that they would. Bad economic times might lead parties to bolt a coalition for fear of being held responsible for the state of the economy at the next election; good economic times might keep coalitions in tact as all members want to take credit at the next election for the state of the economy. Warwick's data are consistent with these conjectures (ch. 5). The difficult economic environment of the 1980s and 1990s seems to have both increased hazard rates over all of Western Europe, and made them more sensitive to changes in unemployment and inflation, with inflation being given increasing weight by voters over time.[31]

---

[31] The poor state of the German economy in the early 1980s made it unlikely that the coalition between the Socialist party and the Free Democrats would return to power after the next election. This fact seems to have contributed to the Free Democrats' decision to form a new coalition with the Christian Democrats (Poguntke, 1999). The Austrian Socialist party's decision in 1966 not to renew the grand coalition with the People's party also was influenced by the deteriorating state of the economy at that time (Müller, 1999).

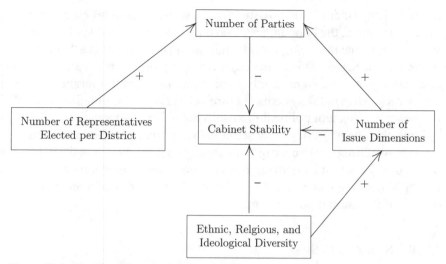

Figure 13.6. The determinants of cabinet stability.

13.8.3 *Summary*

The literature reviewed in this section with respect to cabinet stability, plus some of the findings from earlier sections can be summarized with the help of a diagram (Figure 13.6). The politics of a country with a single religious denomination is not likely to split along religious lines. Linguistic differences will not be a salient policy dimension in a country where everyone speaks the same language. The ethnic, religious, and ideological heterogeneity of a country determines the dimensionality of its issue space. The number of salient political issue dimensions in a country in turn affects the number of political parties it has. The number of political parties is also affected, however, by the electoral rules of the country. In particular the number of political parties will be positively related to the number of representatives that can be elected from each electoral district. Both the number of political parties and the degree of ideological heterogeneity are inversely related to cabinet stability.

One could add many more boxes to Figure 13.6, and perhaps additional arrows. At the constitutional level, for example, social diversity may explain the choice of electoral rules. Switzerland and Belgium both abandoned SMD representation toward the end of the nineteenth century as a response to violent protests by citizens who objected to being represented by someone from a different linguistic or religious group (Lakeman, 1974, pp. 192–99; Carstairs, 1980, chs. 6 and 13). Which brings us to the question of the relationship between electoral rules and social stability.

13.9 Social stability

Under the plurality rule nearly half of the citizens may be represented by someone they did not vote for; with three or more parties, quite often more than half are "represented" in this way (Buchanan and Tullock, 1962, p. 242). In the election that returned Tony Blair's Labour Party to office with a "landside" 60 percent of the seats in the Parliament, the Labour Party won only slightly above 44 percent of the popular vote – about what the *losing* presidential candidate receives in a "landslide" election in the United States. This characteristic of the plurality rule can lead to alienation and may explain the significantly lower voter turnouts in plurality rule, two-party democracies than in PR systems.[32] Powell (1982) has also found significantly higher frequencies of violent political protest in two-party democracies.

Thus, the advantage of greater stability that is often claimed for two-party political systems would appear to need qualification. The stability *within* the political process that is brought about by denying diverse minorities proportionate representation in the legislatures to some extent is offset by the decisions of alienated minorities to opt out of the normal political process.

13.10   Strategic voting

Strategic voting can occur for two reasons: (1) the voter does not want to vote for a candidate or party with a very small chance of winning a seat in his district; or (2) the voter does not want to vote for a party with a very small chance of joining the coalition that forms the government. In this section we discuss the evidence for both types of strategic voting, beginning with the plurality-rule countries.

13.10.1 *Strategic voting under the plurality rule*

As we have seen, Duverger's law rests on the premise that the first type of strategic voting takes place in single-member districts, which use the plurality rule. For strategic voting to lead to two dominant parties, however, voters must judge the chances of the third party's candidate winning a seat to be significantly lower than for the second-place candidate. If the parties expected to come in second or third are expected to obtain similar fractions of the vote, there is no reason to desert the third candidate for the second. Thus no strategic voting is expected when the second and third parties' candidates have similar probabilities of winning. If we then calculate the ratio of the third party's candidate's votes to the second party's candidate's votes, $3P/2P$, we should expect this ratio to exhibit a bimodal distribution across districts. Where the probabilities of the second and third candidates' winning differ greatly, $3P/2P$ should be close to zero; where these probabilities are close, they should be close to 1.0. The in-between ratios should fall out.

A significant difference between the second party's expected share of the vote and that of the third is a necessary but not a sufficient condition for strategic voting. If the leading party in a district is thought to be an almost certain winner, then there is no reason to desert the third party for the second, since both have too small of a chance of winning. One might as well cast one's vote for the party one most prefers,

---

[32] See Powell (1981), Jackman (1987), Blais and Carty (1990), Amy (1993, ch. 7), and Mueller and Stratmann (2002). Mudambi, Navarra, and Nicosia (1996) find evidence of more information gathering by Sicilian voters under PR electoral rules.

as the outcome of the election is a foregone conclusion. Thus, one does not predict a bimodal distribution of $3P/2P$ ratios in districts where the probabilities of the leading party's victory are high.

The Liberal Democrats'[33] emergence as a major third party in Great Britain in recent years makes it a good country to test these predictions. Cox (1997, pp. 85–9) has done so. In districts that were not closely contested, he found a unimodal distribution of $3P/2P$ ratios with a mode between 0.3 and 0.4. In very closely contested districts, on the other hand, a bimodal distribution of these ratios was observed as the strategic voting hypothesis predicts, with one mode between 0.1 and 0.2 and a second between 0.9 and 1.0.

Although Cox's results strongly suggest that strategic voting has occurred in Great Britain, they do not imply that large fractions of Britons vote strategically. The hypothesis predicts no strategic voting in districts where the leading party has a high probability of winning, nor where the differences in probabilities of victory between the second and third parties are small. Even where neither of these two conditions is met, all voters are not voting strategically. Survey studies that ask voters about their intentions seem to suggest that from 5 to 15 percent of the British vote strategically.[34] This evidence of strategic voting combined with that discussed above regarding the relationship between votes and seats implies that the Liberal Democrats in Great Britain have been doubly disadvantaged by the use of the plurality rule. Some voters desert it for the two major parties so as not to waste their votes with the result being that the actual number of votes that the Liberal Democrats receives is less than the fraction of voters who rank this party first, and the electoral system transforms the Liberal Democrats' share of votes cast into a significantly smaller share of the seats in the Parliament.

Cox (1997, pp. 81–3) also tested for the presence of strategic voting in Germany, and found evidence that it has also taken place. Survey results again confirm the statistical evidence that strategic voting has taken place.

13.10.2 *Strategic voting in multiparty systems*

The generalization of tests involving the distributions of the ratio $3P/2P$ to multi-member district systems requires that one looks at the ratio $(M + 1)/M$, where M is the number of representatives selected from a district. A brief glance at Table 13.2 suggests that the logic of this test will break down as M grows large. A simple-minded interpretation of the theory would imply 76 parties competing for votes in the Netherlands, but clearly the effective numbers for parties in this country are much lower. Cox (1997, ch. 5) found that the predictions regarding the ratios $(M + 1)/M$ do hold up, so long as M remains below five. Thus, strategic voting would appear not to affect the outcomes in PR systems, where district size is moderately high.[35]

---

[33] Formerly the Alliance.
[34] Cox (1997, pp. 85–9) cites and discusses several studies.
[35] Ordeshook and Zeng (1994) discuss the incentives to vote strategically under STV.

Voters typically have priors on not only the expected share of the vote each party will win in an election, but also which parties are likely to form coalitions. These priors can also induce strategic voting.

Consider again the example of Demokrastan, where the parties are positioned along a single-dimensional, left–right issue space. The numbers below the line now represent the *expected* number of seats for each party following the election.

A	B	C	D	E	F	G
15	28	5	4	33	9	6

The constitution of Demokrastan obligates the president to invite the party receiving the most votes in an election to form a government. If the election goes as expected, E will be invited to form a government, and either a *CDEF* or a *DEFG* coalition is anticipated. Supporters of party A now have a strong incentive to vote for B to lift its seat total above E's, since B should favor an *ABCD* coalition. Anticipating this, supporters of F and G might then switch their votes to E. Even such a simple convention of asking the largest party to form a government can lead to strategic voting and a flow of votes to the largest parties.

Strategic voting can also work to the advantage of smaller parties, however. Consider the following example adapted from Cox (1997, pp. 197–8). The positions of the German Social Democratic Party (S), Free Democrats (F), and Christian Democrats (C) are as follows:

S	F	C
49	4	47

The numbers below the line are again the expected share of the national vote for each party just prior to the election. The German Constitution imposes a threshold of 5 percent of the national vote for a party to obtain any seats in the Bundestag. If the preelection polls are correct, the Free Democrats will not make the threshold and the other two parties divide the seats proportionally. The Social Democratic Party can form the government alone. The ideology of the Free Democrats lies closer to that of the Christian Democrats than to the Socialists, and if they would manage to get over the threshold, they would form a majority coalition with the Christian Democrats. Knowing this Christian Democrats have an incentive to vote for the Free Democrats to ensure that they get at least 5 percent of the vote. Situations like this have been common in Germany since 1961, and the Free Democrats have attempted to take advantage of their position near the center of the ideological spectrum by openly encouraging German citizens to vote strategically.[36]

13.11   Commentary

We began this chapter with a quotation from Albert Breton and Gianluigi Galeotti (1985) regarding two views of representation. It should be clear from this chapter and the two preceding ones that both two-party, winner-take-all systems and PR

---

[36] For further discussion and citations, see Cox (1997, pp. 194–8) and Poguntke (1999, p. 232).

systems are representative in the sense that each citizen's preferences receive weight in the final outcomes of the political process. In two-party systems, the individual citizen's preferences influence the platforms upon which the candidates run and the outcomes to the extent that the necessity to stand for reelection forces the winners to implement the platforms upon which they run. In the PR systems, each citizen is represented by a party for which he has voted, or the party of the person for whom he has voted. The choice of parties is wider, and the citizen can vote for a party that represents his preferences more closely than in the two-party systems.

The two views on representation lead logically to alternative electoral rules for choosing representatives. Duverger's law predicts that the plurality rule will produce two dominant parties, and on average it does. But in many of the so-called two-party countries, like Canada and Great Britain, strong third and even fourth parties often exist. As a consequence, voters can have incentives to vote strategically, so that the votes cast for each party do not necessarily reflect the first-choice preferences of the citizens, and the party that wins a majority of the seats in the legislature often has done so without winning a majority of the popular vote. Indeed, it can happen that a majority of the voters would prefer another party to the one that "wins" an election.[37]

To produce more than two parties in the legislature, one needs to elect more than one party or person from each electoral district. The number of parties in the legislature tends to increase with the number of representatives elected per district (M), and when M exceeds five strategic voting seems to disappear. With M moderately large, PR systems also exhibit modest deviations from an allocation of seats in the parliament that is strictly proportional to the votes received. Thus, most real-world PR systems might be considered to be reasonable approximations to the "ideal system" described at the beginning of this chapter as far as their representation of different sets of voter preferences is concerned.

The logic underlying the ideal PR system is to represent the preferences of all citizens in the national assembly in proportion to their numbers in the population at large, and then to aggregate these preferences in an optimal way. For the reasons discussed in Chapters 4, 5, and 6, the simple majority rule is unlikely to achieve this optimal aggregation. In addition to a high qualified majority rule, some version of point voting or voting by veto might be used, so that *all* citizens' preferences have a chance to influence the outcome. Under an ideal PR system, the legislative and executive branches would be separated, and the executive branch's task would be to execute "the will of the people," as expressed through the votes taken in the fully representative legislature.[38]

---

[37] Both of these disadvantages of two-party systems that use the plurality rule to manufacture a parliamentary majority could be eliminated by adopting a two-round electoral rule to award parties seats, similar to the rule used to elect the president of France. All citizens across the country would face the same list of parties in each round, and votes would be tallied on a national basis. If no party received a majority of the votes cast in the first round, a second round of voting restricted to the two parties receiving the most votes in the first round would be held. The $(M + 1)/M$ logic should apply to this rule, and one expects a two-party system to evolve over time. For further discussion, see Mueller (1996a, chs. 9 and 10).

[38] For further discussion of the differences between the two types of systems and ways to create their ideal prototypes, see Mueller (1996a, chs. 8–10).

Real-world PR systems differ from this ideal in that they inevitably employ the simple majority rule for parliamentary decisions, and they merge the executive and legislative functions of government by requiring that the parliament chooses, or at least acquiesces to the choice of, the chief executive and her cabinet. This requirement under the cabinet form of PR changes the strategic options for the voter. If the legislature employed a voting rule that allowed the party for which she voted to influence the outcome, the citizen would have a strong incentive to vote for the party with the closest position on the issues to her own. However, if only *some* parties will join the cabinet, and the cabinet will decide all government policies, the rational citizen should consider the probability that each party will enter the cabinet, as well as its position on the issues, when deciding which party to vote for. Thus, under the cabinet form of PR, the distribution of votes across parties may also inaccurately reflect the distribution of citizens' preferences for the policy positions of each party.

Despite these important differences between real-world electoral systems and their theoretical counterparts, one might expect that the two come close enough to one another that we can use the results from the public choice literature to compare real-world electoral systems. In a pure two-party system, one party *always* wins a majority of the votes and seats in the parliament, and thus majority governments with their inherent stability can be expected. In real-world two-party systems, majority governments do not always form, but they form far more often than in PR systems, as one expects.[39]

With two parties and a single-dimensional issue space, both compete for the vote of the median voter and the winning platform coincides with her ideal point. The probabilistic voting model introduced in Chapter 12 leads us to expect equilibrium outcomes in two-party systems, even when there is more than one dimension to the issue space, with the winning party located at the mean of the distribution of voters' ideal points. Even when equilibria may not exist, theoretical constructs like the uncovered set and the yolk lead us to expect outcomes in two-party systems that lie near the center of the distribution of voters' ideal points (see Chapter 11).

The literature on multiparty systems leads – perhaps somewhat surprisingly – to very similar conclusions. When a single-dimensional issue space exists, the party occupying the ideal point of the median voter can be expected to join any coalition that forms, or to form the government by itself, even perhaps when it does not occupy a majority of the seats in the parliament. When the issue space has more than one dimension, the winning coalition that forms the government is likely to contain the party located at the dimension-by-dimension median, if such a party exists, or at least at the median of one of the dimensions of the issue space. Concepts like the uncovered set and the yolk are replaced by the heart to predict which parties join coalition governments, but again the implication is that they will be somewhere near the center of the distribution of voters' ideal points. In multiparty systems the median voter is replaced as the key actor by the "central" or "core" or "strong" party.

---

[39] Blais and Carty (1988) find that a single party wins an absolute majority of the seats in the parliament 72 percent of the time in two-party systems versus only 10 percent of the time under PR.

Powell (2000) has recently undertaken an extensive comparison between two-party and multiparty systems.

Strong parties are large and centrally located, while core parties are positioned at the intersection of median lines. The almost exclusive use of the simple majority rule in all two-party and multiparty systems instills a powerful centripetal tendency into them regardless of the particular electoral rule used to fill the seats in their legislatures.

The use of the Downsian spatial voting model by students of both two-party and multiparty systems results not surprisingly in a great concern over the *positions* of the candidates and parties in the two systems. The often implicit assumption in the literature is that the policies implied by the positions occupied in the issue space get adopted. The concern of observers like Breton and Galeotti about *responsible* government is often not over the nature of the policies promised, but over whether the promises are kept and the policies actually are enacted. When the government reneges on its promises in a two-party system, the voters have a clear strategy for punishing it by voting for the opposition party. In PR systems, the voter's best strategy is less clear, since "responsibility" for past policies is shared by all members of the coalition, and the voter does not obviously advance her own interests by weakening the party that most closely represents them. Not surprisingly, one finds that *changes* in government following an election are more likely to be observed in two-party than in multiparty systems.[40]

The vast literature on cycling leads one to expect cabinet instability to take the form of constantly changing policies. The most significant cost of cabinet instability may be the complete paralysis of the government. Schofield (1995) has shown, for example, that the Christian Democrats occupied a near-core position in the Italian issue space throughout the post–World War II period, and thus were members of every one of the 50 or so governments that formed up until the mid-1990s. At that time Italians voted *all* of the major parties in Italy out of office, and the Christian Democrats vanished as a party. One presumes that this occurred not because Italian voters were unhappy with the major parties' policy positions, but with their implementation of these policies. Thus, the most significant differences among electoral systems may not come in how well voters' preferences are represented in the legislature, or in how the legislature decides what ought to be done, but in whether the legislature decides anything at all, and in the implementation of its decisions. We return to these issues in Chapter 17.

Bibliographical notes

The standard format for articles on PR or multiparty systems is to begin with one or more lengthy quotations from classic works. I know of no other area in public choice in which the average age of a source quoted is so great. Whether this tendency reflects the brilliance of the first writers on the topic or the paucity of talent devoted to the topic since, I am not sure. Perhaps it merely reflects the lack of interest in the topic by Anglo-Saxon scholars. I defer in part to this tradition

---

[40] Blais (1991, p. 242) compares PR and two-party systems according to several additional performance criteria, as do Grofman and Reynolds (2001), and Powell (2000).

with my opening quotation from a relatively recent article by Breton and Galeotti (1985).

Among the classics, John Stuart Mill's *Considerations on Representative Government*, first published in 1861, is worth reading for its discussion of both PR and political theory more generally.

More recent discussions of the normative properties of PR include Pitkin (1967), Riker (1982a), Chamberlin and Courant (1983), Johnston (1984), Rose (1984), Sugden (1984), Blais (1991), Powell (2000), and Grofman and Reynolds (2001).

For a formal analysis of various rules for allocating seats in the legislature based on electoral votes, see Balinsky and Young (1978, 1982). Myerson and Weber (1993), Myerson (1999), and Persson and Tabellini (2000a, ch. 8) examine issues of stability and performance in different electoral systems.

Schofield (1997) surveys the spatial literature on multiparty systems and provides a simple introduction to the concept of the heart. Austen-Smith (1996) suggests some modifications of the heart to eliminate the possibility that it selects an outcome not in the uncovered set.

Grofman and van Roozendaal (1997) provide an excellent survey of the literature on cabinet stability. Müller and Strøm (2000a) contains 15 essays on coalition governments in Europe. Grofman, Lee, Winckler, and Woodall (1999) contains 18 essays on the single nontransferable vote as used in Japan, Korea, and Taiwan. Twelve essays on the single-transferable-vote procedure are included in Bowler and Grofman (2000a).

CHAPTER 14

The paradox of voting

When we move . . . away from the private concerns of the family and the business office into those regions of national and international affairs that lack a direct and unmistakable link with those private concerns, individual volition, command of facts and method of inference soon cease to fulfill the requirements of the classical doctrine. What strikes me most of all and seems to me to be the core of the trouble is the fact that the sense of reality is so completely lost. Normally, the great political questions take their place in the psychic economy of the typical citizen with those leisure-hour interests that have not attained the rank of hobbies, and with the subjects of irresponsible conversation. These things seem so far off; they are not at all like a business proposition; dangers may not materialize at all and if they should they may not prove so very serious; one feels oneself to be moving in a fictitious world.

The reduced sense of reality accounts not only for a reduced sense of responsibility but also for the absence of effective volition. One has one's phrases, of course, and one's wishes and daydreams and grumbles; especially, one has one's likes and dislikes. But ordinarily they do not amount to what we call a will – the psychic counterpart of purposeful responsible action. In fact, for the private citizen musing over national affairs there is no scope for such a will and no task at which it could develop. He is a member of an unworkable committee, the committee of the whole nation, and this is why he expends less disciplined effort on mastering a political problem than he expends on a game of bridge. . . .

Thus the typical citizen drops down to a lower level of mental performance as soon as he enters the political field. He argues and analyzes in a way which he would readily recognize as infantile within the sphere of his real interests. He becomes a primitive again. His thinking becomes associative and affective. And this entails two further consequences and ominous significance.

First, even if there were no political groups trying to influence him, the typical citizen would in political matters tend to yield to extra-rational or irrational prejudice and impulse. . . . Moreover, simply because he is not "all there," he will relax his usual moral standards as well and occasionally give in to dark urges which the conditions of private life help him to repress. But as to the wisdom or rationality of his inferences and conclusions, it may be just as bad if he gives in to a burst of generous indignation. This will make it still more difficult for him to see things in their correct proportions or even to see more than one aspect of one thing at a time. Hence, if for once he does emerge from his usual vagueness and does display the definite will postulated by the classical doctrine of democracy, he is as likely as not to become still more unintelligent and irresponsible than he usually is. At certain junctures, this may prove fatal to his nation.

Joseph Schumpeter

The Americans . . . are fond of explaining all the actions of their lives by the principle of self-interest rightly understood; they show with complacency how an enlightened regard for themselves constantly prompts them to assist one another and inclines them willingly to sacrifice a portion of their time and property to the welfare of the state. In this respect . . . they frequently fail to do themselves justice; for in the United States as well as elsewhere people are sometimes seen to give way to those disinterested and spontaneous impulses that are natural to man; but the Americans seldom admit that they yield to emotions of this kind; they are more anxious to do honor to their philosophy than to themselves.

Alexis de Tocqueville

The distinguishing characteristic of public choice is the assumption that individuals in the political arena as in the marketplace behave rationally and in their own self-interest. We have examined models of candidate competition based on this assumption, but as yet have said little about the key actor in the political drama, the individual voter. This chapter fills that void.

14.1   The rational voter hypothesis

14.1.1   *Expected utility maximization*

The rational voter hypothesis was first developed by Downs (1957, chs. 11–14) and later was elaborated by Tullock (1967a, pp. 110–14) and Riker and Ordeshook (1968, 1973). In deciding between two parties or candidates, the voter envisages the different "streams of utility" to be derived from the policies promised by each candidate. The voter calculates the expected utility from each candidate's victory, and naturally votes for the candidate whose policies promise the highest utility. Thus, voting is a purely instrumental act in the theory of rational voting. One votes to bring about the victory of one's preferred candidate. The benefit from voting is the difference in expected utilities from the policies of these two candidates. Call this difference B.

Of course, it is unlikely that one's vote decides the outcome of the election. One's vote has an impact on the outcome only when (1) the votes of all other voters are evenly split between the two candidates, or (2) one's preferred candidate would lose by one vote if one did not vote. Call the probabilities of these two events occurring P_1 and P_2, respectively. If one's preferred candidate has a 50/50 chance of eventually winning should the first election end in a draw, then the probability that a single individual's vote will be instrumental in bringing about the victory of the voter's preferred candidate is $P = P_1 + (1/2)P_2$. The expected benefits from voting are PB.

P has been calculated in several ways. Under one approach, each voter can be viewed as picking a ball out of a bag in which p fraction of the balls are labeled candidate 1 and $(1 - p)$ are labeled candidate 2. Each voter is assumed to have a prior as to what p is. If there are N voters and N is odd, then P_1 for any one voter is simply the probability that exactly one half of the remaining $(N - 1)$ voters would pick a ball labeled candidate 1 and the remaining one half would pick a ball labeled candidate 2, given this voter's prior p. P then becomes

$$P = \frac{3e^{-2(N-1)(p-\frac{1}{2})^2}}{2\sqrt{2\pi(N - 1)}}. \tag{14.1}$$

P declines as N increases, and as p diverts from $1/2$.[1] Even when $p = 1/2$, however, the probability that a single vote will decide the election is but 0.00006, when there are 100,000,000 voters.[2] If there were some cost, C, to voting, then the expected benefits from one's preferred candidate's victory would have to be large indeed to make the voter's calculus produce an expected utility gain from voting $(PB - C > 0)$.

The above approach can be criticized on the grounds that it implies that there is an infinitesimal probability that *all* voters would pick a ball labeled candidate 1 and candidate 2 would receive zero votes. Voters do not decide how to vote by picking balls out of hats. On election day, it is more reasonable to assume that *all* voters are committed to voting for either candidate 1 or candidate 2. Each voter has some prior, p, of the fraction of the population of potential voters who are committed to candidate 1, based perhaps on preelection polls. The rational voter knows, however, that this p is measured with error. Thus, in deciding whether to vote, a rational voter must calculate the probability that her vote will make or break a tie, given p, and the inaccuracy with which it is estimated. This probability is inversely related to $\sqrt{Np(1 - p)}$, the standard deviation of the estimated number of people voting for candidate 1, and thus also becomes infinitesimal as N becomes large.[3]

Several people have noted that the probability of being run over by a car going to or returning from the polls is similar to the probability of casting the decisive vote.[4] If being run over is worse than having one's preferred candidate lose, then this potential cost of voting alone would exceed the potential gain, and no rational self-interested individual would ever vote. But millions do, and thus the paradox.

---

[1] Owen and Grofman (1984) derive the following formula for the probability that a voter's vote breaks a tie when N is odd:

$$P_{OG} = \frac{2e^{-2(N-1)(p-1/2)^2}}{\sqrt{2\pi(N - 1)}}.$$

Now P_1 is simply the probability that N will be odd (0.5) times P_{OG}, and P_2 is the same. Thus, $P \approx (1/2)P_{OG} + (1/4)P_{OG}$, which is the formula in the text. See also Beck (1975), Margolis (1977), and Mayer and Good (1975).

[2] Peters (1998, p. 180) omits the 2 from the denominator of (14.1) and thus computes P as 0.00012.

[3] With $p = 0.51$ and $N = 100,000,000$, $P = 6 \times 10^{-6}$ (Fischer, 1999, p. 274).

The formula in (14.1) implies a very sharp fall in P, as p moves away from 0.5, while the sampling approach just described implies a much flatter, and more plausible relationship between P and p. See Mayer and Good (1975), Fischer (1999), and Shachar and Nalebuff (1999).

[4] Skinner (1948, p. 265) appears to be the first to have used the probability of an auto accident as a foil to puncture the rational voter hypothesis, writing some nine years before Downs, cited in Goodin and Roberts (1975). Meehl (1977) also uses it.

There are essentially three ways around the paradox: (1) redefine the rational voter's calculus so that the rational action is now to vote; (2) relax the rationality assumption; (3) relax the self-interest assumption. All three routes have been pursued. We begin with three attempts that continue to assume rational, self-interested behavior, as it has traditionally been depicted in public choice, and then consider more radical departures from this behavioral assumption.

14.1.2   *A taste for voting*

The simplest way to reconcile voter rationality with the act of voting is to posit the existence of benefits stemming from the act itself, but not dependent on the consequence of the act, that is, not depending on whether the vote is decisive. Individuals may have a patriotic or civic itch, and voting helps scratch that itch, yielding benefits (utility) D.[5] Thus, a person votes if $PB + D - C > 0$. With PB tiny, the act of voting is explained by the private gains (psychic income) from the act of voting itself, D, exceeding the personal costs of going to the polls, C. Voting is not undertaken as an instrumental act to determine the winning candidate, but as a private, or symbolic act from which satisfaction is derived independent of the outcome of the election.

This modification of the rational voter hypothesis does reconcile the act of voting with individual rationality, but does so by robbing the rational, self-interest hypothesis of its predictive power. Any hypothesis can be reconciled with any conflicting piece of evidence with the addition of the appropriate auxiliary hypothesis. If I find that the quantity of Mercedes autos demanded increases following an increase in their price, I need not reject the law of demand, I need only set it aside, in this case by assuming a taste for "snob appeal." But in so doing I weaken the law of demand, as a hypothesis let alone as a law, unless I have a tight logical argument for predicting this taste for snob appeal.

So it is with rescuing the rational, self-interested voter hypothesis by assuming a taste for civic duty. If this taste explains the act of voting, what else might it explain? If the voter is carried to the polls by a sense of civic duty, what motivation guides her actions once there? Does she vote for the candidate, whose policies advance the voter's narrow interests, or does her sense of civic duty lead her to vote for the candidate, whose victory is most beneficial to the general, public interest? If voters can be moved by civic duty, why not politicians and bureaucrats? Without a theory explaining the origin, strength, and extent of an individual's sense of civic duty, merely postulating a sense of civic duty "saves" rational egoism by destroying its predictive content.

14.1.3   *Voting as a game of cat and mouse*

If each rational voter were to decide not to vote because her vote has too small of a chance of affecting the outcome, and all voters were rational, no one would vote. But

---

[5] See Riker and Ordeshook (1968). Tullock (1967a, p. 110) described these personal, psychic gains from voting as a negative cost, C.

then any one voter could determine the outcome of the election by voting. Whether it is in fact rational for an individual to abstain depends on whether other voters are abstaining. The greater the number of other voters I expect will rationally abstain, the more rational it is for me to vote. The result is an n-person, noncooperative game, in which each person's strategy, to vote or to abstain, is dependent on her expectations with regard to the other voters' decisions. Under some assumptions, the solutions to this game involve positive numbers of individuals voting (Ledyard, 1981, 1984; Palfrey and Rosenthal, 1983). But when individuals are uncertain about the costs of voting of other citizens and the size of the electorate is large, a rational individual votes only if the psychic benefits from voting exceed the costs (Palfrey and Rosenthal, 1985). This effort to rescue the rational voter hypothesis by resorting to game theory does not succeed. Let us examine another.

14.1.4 *The rational voter as minimax-regret strategist*

In a much discussed article, Ferejohn and Fiorina (1974, p. 525) set out "to show one means of rescuing rational choice theorists from this embarrassing predicament" of the voting paradox. They recognize that the Achilles' heel of rationality is the tiny but positive probability that a vote will change the outcome of an election. They then posit that voters may be using a decision strategy that does not weigh each possible event by its probability, but rather gives all events equal weight, like the minimax-regret strategy. Under this decision rule, one calculates not the actual payoff for each strategy choice and state-of-the-world combination, but the regret, that is, the loss one would experience in choosing the given strategy should this state of the world occur, as opposed to the best alternative strategy under this state of the world. One then chooses the action that minimizes the regret. Voting for one's second choice is, not surprisingly, a dominated strategy. So the decision reduces to whether to vote for one's first choice or to abstain. There are essentially two relevant states of the world to consider: S_I, the outcome of the election, is independent of whether one votes; S_D, by voting the individual, produces the victory of one's preferred candidate by either breaking a tie or forcing a runoff, which the candidate wins. If one votes and the outcome is independent of one's vote, one regrets voting because one has incurred C to no avail (see Matrix 14.1, cell (a): entries are sizes of regrets). If the outcome is independent of one's vote and one abstains, one has no regrets (b); the same is true if one votes and casts the decisive vote (c). If the net gains from having one's candidate's victory (B) are at least double the costs of voting, C, then one's maximum regret occurs when one abstains and one's vote would have been decisive (d). The minimax-regret strategy is to vote.

The minimax-regret strategy is extremely conservative and leads to rather bizarre behavior when applied to other decisions or even when extended within the voting context, as several critics have stressed.[6] Suppose, for example, that a voter is indifferent between the Republican and Democratic candidates. His minimax-regret strategy is then to abstain. Suppose now that the Nazi Party enters a candidate. Now the minimax-regret criterion forces the voter to the polls to avoid the possible,

---

[6] Beck (1975), Goodin and Roberts (1975), Mayer and Good (1975), and Meehl (1977).

Matrix 14.1. *Minimax-regret options.*

		States	
		S_I	S_D
Strategies	Vote	(a) C	(c) 0
	Abstain	(b) 0	(d) B-C

although highly unlikely, event that the Nazi candidate will win, *and will do so by a single vote.*

Few situations in everyday life in which individuals routinely employ minimax-regret strategies come to mind. Indeed, it is easier to think of examples where people exhibit the reverse tendency. Losing one's home and possessions must be a disaster at least comparable to having one's second choice for president win, and probably occurs with no less probability than that one's vote decides an election. Yet most people do not protect themselves against losses from floods even when insurance is sold at rates below actuarial value (Kunreuther et al., 1978).[7] Is it reasonable to assume that the same person is a risktaker with respect to home and personal possessions, but becomes minimax-regret conservative when deciding whether or not to vote?

Ferejohn and Fiorina seem to think so. They cite Levine and Plott (1977) in support of the "possibility that individuals act as if they vary their decision rules in response to the decision context" (1975, p. 921). People also vote. The issue is not whether these things happen, but whether they can be explained and predicted using the rational egoism postulate. If individuals commonly switch from extremely risk-averse strategies to risk-taking strategies, how are we to predict their behavior? What theory tells us which situations elicit which strategy? To rationalize a given action ex post as possibly consistent with the use of a particular decision strategy in this situation does not suffice to justify the rational egoism postulate as the foundation of a *general* behavioral theory, unless one has a theory to predict which decision strategies are chosen in which situations.

14.2   The rational voter hypothesis: the evidence

Ferejohn and Fiorina's major defense of their thesis rests upon empirical evidence. The key determinant of voter turnout under the minimax-regret hypothesis is $B - C$. The costs of voting are difficult to define and measure, but data on the perceived differential between candidates are gathered in surveys like those conducted by the University of Michigan Survey Research Center (SRC). These may be used as a

---

[7] On the other hand, some people do buy flood insurance, even though the probability of such an event is very low. Peters (1998) uses behavior such as this and assumptions about risk aversion less extreme than that of Ferejohn and Fiorina to try to rehabilitate the rational Downsian voter who votes.

measure of B. B also figures prominently in the Downsian expected utility model, as does P. Ferejohn and Fiorina's test of the minimax-regret hypothesis is to see whether differences in B and P are significantly related to voter abstentions. Under minimax-regret, only B should be related to voter turnout; the probability of the voter being decisive does not matter. Under Downsian expected utility maximization, both B and P should be related. The choice between the hypotheses rests on whether P, the probability that a voter's vote will be decisive, is systematically related to abstentions.

Examining pre- and postelection survey results for 1952, 1956, 1960, and 1964, they find the minimax-regret hypothesis supported five times, the Downsian hypothesis only once (1975). A glance at Figure 14.1 reveals why one might not be surprised by the weak performance of P that Ferejohn and Fiorina observed. In this figure, T plots the percentage of the voting-age population that voted in each presidential election from 1932 to 2000. W plots the votes going to the winning presidential candidate as a percentage of the combined votes of the Republican and Democratic candidates. The Downsian model predicts that troughs in W should coincide with peaks in T. The Kennedy–Nixon election of 1960 matches the highest turnout during the 64-year period with the narrowest margin of victory, and thus conforms well to this prediction. But turnout declined only slightly from its 1960 peak at the 1964 Johnson landslide victory, and several other years – like 1948 and 1976 – seem out of line with the Downsian model's prediction.

About 90 percent of the respondents in Ferejohn and Fiorina's sample claimed to have voted. This is a much higher percentage than is typical of the United States and suggests a nonrandom sample or misrepresentation of voter behavior. More important, the variation in abstention rates is likely to be too small to allow one to run tests against other variables. A look at some additional evidence is warranted.

Kenny and Rice (1989) found that over a third of survey respondents sometimes "worried" that if they did not vote their preferred candidate would lose by only one vote. Consistent with the minimax explanation of voting, a higher percentage of these respondents voted in the 1985 election than for the remainder of those surveyed.

Blais et al. (1995) observed an even higher fraction of Canadian students who "would feel terrible if I didn't vote and my candidate lost by one vote," and these students also exhibited a higher proclivity to vote in the 1993 national election. In a regression explaining the decision to vote, however, the "minimax variable" proved to be statistically insignificant once other variables measuring the individual's sense of civic duty were included. "Those who believe it is the duty of every citizen to vote are prone to say they would feel really terrible if they did not vote and their candidate lost by one vote" (Blais, Young, Fleury, and Lapp, 1995, p. 833). Consequently, the minimax-regret explanation for voting cannot be distinguished empirically from the taste-for-voting explanation.

One of the first papers to present empirical evidence in support of the full rational voter hypothesis was by Riker and Ordeshook (1968), from which we have taken the $R = PB + D - C$ formulation of this hypothesis. Riker and Ordeshook examined 4,294 responses to the 1952, 1956, and 1960 prepresidential SRC questionnaires.

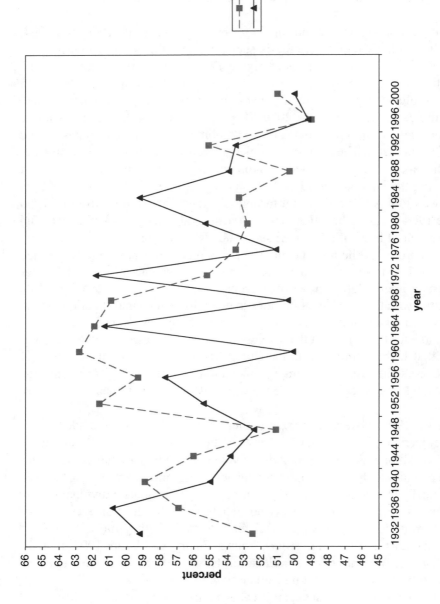

1932 1936 1940 1944 1948 1952 1956 1960 1964 1968 1972 1976 1980 1984 1988 1992 1996 2000

year

T is percentage of the voting age population that voted for a presidential candidate.
W is winning presidential candidate's percentage of the votes going to the Republican and Democratic candidates.

Figure 14.1. Winning percentages (W) and voter turnouts (T) in U.S. presidential elections, 1932–2000. *Source:* U.S. Department of Commerce, *Statistical Abstract of the United States*, various editions.

They cross-tabulated responses to see whether P, B, and D have a significant impact on the probability of an individual's voting. They found that when one holds the levels of the other two variables fixed, P, B, and D all tend to have a significant impact on the probability of voting in the way that the rational voter hypothesis predicts. Thus, the Riker-Ordeshook results support both the instrumental-vote portion of the rational voter hypothesis (PB matters), as well as the tastes (D) matter portion.

Although P, B, and D all seem related to voter behavior in the manner that the rational voter hypothesis predicts, the quantitative importance of D is much greater than that of either P or B. The difference in probability of voting between those with high P (that is, those who thought the election would be close) and those with low P, ignoring both B and D, is 78 versus 72 percent. Eighty-two percent of those with high values for B voted, as opposed to 66 percent of those with low Bs. However, 87 percent of those with high Ds voted against only 51 percent of those with low Ds. D was operationalized by Riker and Ordeshook through questions related to citizen duty. Thus, the difference between a high and a low sense of citizen duty has a much larger quantitative impact on voter turnout than do differences between high values of either P or B and low values of these variables. Both parts of the rational voter hypothesis are supported in the Riker-Ordeshook study, but the taste component has the greatest quantitative impact.

Among the most ambitious tests of the rational voter hypothesis in terms of both sample size and number of variables included was that of Ashenfelter and Kelley (1975). They examined the responses of 1,893 individuals surveyed by the SRC in connection with the 1960 and 1972 presidential elections. They related individual answers to the question, "Did you vote?" to a large set of variables grouped under the following headings:

1. Personal characteristics
2. Cost variables
3. Strategic value of voting
4. Interest in campaign
5. Obligation toward voting.

These variables can be related to the rational voter hypothesis

$$R = PB + D - C, \tag{14.2}$$

with C obviously related to group 2 variables, P and B both related to 3; B and possibly D related to 4; and D and 5 related. The personal characteristics of each individual (education, income, age, and so on) could be related to any one of the components of R and do not clearly discriminate among the hypotheses.

Ashenfelter and Kelley's results gave mixed support for the rational voter hypothesis. Several measures of the cost of voting were statistically significant and of the right sign. Most important among these were the existence of a poll tax and literacy tests, legal in 1960 but abolished by 1972. A six-dollar poll tax in 1960 reduced the probability of an individual voting by 42 percent (Ashenfelter and Kelley, 1975, p. 708). This result gives one a rough idea of what the distribution of $PB + D$ is for a large fraction of voters. Several of the other variables introduced as proxies for the costs of voting did not perform well, although multicollinearity among the cost variables was a problem.

Turning to proxies for P and B, Ashenfelter and Kelley (1975, p. 717) did not find that a voter's perception of whether the race is close or not had a statistically significant relationship to the probability of voting. On the other hand, this proxy for P was of the correct sign (t value of 1.4 in the pooled regression), and the difference in the percentage of voters who thought the 1972 Nixon landslide would be close and the percentage that thought the Nixon-Kennedy 1960 election would be close was so great (10 versus 60 percent) that the difference in the levels for this variable between 1960 and 1972 was enough to explain 40 percent of the change in turnout between 1960 and 1972 (pp. 720–1). Both of these findings are of considerable importance in explaining an otherwise perplexing inconsistency in the literature on voter participation, and we shall return to them.

Of the variables that might measure an individual's perception of the differences between the candidates, B, the answer to the question, "How do you think you will vote?" proved to have the most explanatory power. If, at the time of the survey, an individual was undecided as to how she would vote, there was a 40 percent lower probability that this individual would vote at all (p. 717). If an individual's indecision arises because of a small perceived difference between the two candidates, a small B, then this result offers considerable support for the rational voter hypothesis. But if indecision concerning how one will vote stems from indecision over whether one will vote – that is, one is not interested in the election – then the impact of the finding is less clear. Some people may simply prefer to remain aloof from the political process.

Individuals who felt a "strong obligation" to vote did so with a 30 percent higher probability; those with a "very strong obligation" voted 38 percent more often (pp. 719–20). These variables, measuring a sense of obligation to vote, had substantial explanatory power. Their impressive perfomance underlines the importance of the D term in the rational voter's calculus.

Ashenfelter and Kelley (1975, p. 724) concluded, "The theory of voting that is best supported by our results is that which posits a sense of duty or obligation as the primary motivation for voting. The variables with the greatest quantitative impact on voting are education, indecision, the dummy variables representing the sense of an obligation to vote, and certain cost variables." This study offers rather strong support for the Tullock-Riker-Ordeshook interpretation of rational voting, which sees the D and C terms in the $BP + D - C$ equation as dominating the voting decision. As noted earlier, indecision might arise from a small B term, but indecision might also detract from the D term, if the sense of obligation to vote is weakened by not knowing for whom to vote. Education should ceteris paribus reduce the importance of the BP term, since higher education levels should make one less susceptible to the misconception that one's vote makes a difference (that P is large). Education's positive impact on voting must then come through the D and C terms. We shall consider education's role in explaining voting again.

A very similar pattern of results appeared in Silver's (1973) analysis of 959 SRC questionnaires from the 1960 election survey. Several cost variables were significant, as were interest in the campaign, sense of citizen duty, and education. Whether the individual thinks the election will be close or not did not have a significant impact on the probability of voting. Thus, the only support for the BP portion of the rational voter hypothesis in Silver's results came through the "interest in the campaign" responses, if one assumes that these measure B, although Silver regarded them as an index of D.

The same general picture of the voter's decision reappeared in the analysis of survey results for some 2,500 voters in the 1968 presidential election using Opinion Research Corporation and SRC data by Brody and Page (1973). In explaining abstentions they focused upon the importance of indifference – the perceived difference between candidates, and alienation – the difference between a voter's position and her preferred candidate's position. Abstentions did increase with both indifference and alienation, but not by enough to confirm a purely instrumentalist interpretation of the act of voting. Forty-three percent of the 201 individuals who saw no difference between the candidates ($B = 0$) voted nonetheless. Forty-four percent of the 174, who were both alienated and indifferent, chose to vote (Brody and Page, 1973, p. 6). For these voters and probably for many others, the D and C terms of R must explain the decision to vote.

A fifth test of the rational voter hypothesis using SRC data, although explicitly built on Downs' formulation, is more difficult to interpret. Frohlich et al. (1978) constructed proxies for B, P, and D from the SRC questions by combining various questions using different weights. They then made various assumptions about the distribution of the unknown C variable, and used combinations of B, P, D, and C[8] to predict both turnout and choice of candidate for the 1964 presidential election. The assumption that C is lognormally distributed worked best, and with this assumption they could predict turnout with an R^2 of 0.847.[9] But Frohlich et al. did not report their results in such a way to allow one to gauge the relative importance of BP, D, and C in explaining turnout, although the assumption concerning the distribution of C was important. However, the individual's opinion as to the efficacy of her vote (the proxy for P) did appear to be important, suggesting that P played a bigger role in explaining turnout in the study by Frohlich et al. than it did in those of Ferejohn and Fiorina, and Ashenfelter and Kelley.

Matsusaka and Palda (1993) presented survey evidence on voting in the May 1979 and February 1980 general elections in Canada. They found that a voter's expectation of the closeness of the election did not have a statistically significant impact on the probability of someone's voting. No direct measures of B, C, or D were included.

The results from these six studies plus four more are summarized in Table 14.1. To the four key variables in the Downsian model – P, B, D, and C – have been added two of the sociological variables that come up most consistently with the same signs, education (E) and income (Y). Even here, however, some exceptions exist.

---

[8] They formulated the $R = BP + D - C$ equation slightly differently, but their formulation and the one used here are equivalent.

[9] As with the Ferejohn and Fiorina SRC sample, a gigantic 90.9 percent of the subjects reported having voted, raising issues of representativeness or misrepresentation.

Table 14.1. *Summary of studies testing the Downsian model (with extensions) using survey data*

Study	Sample and time period	P	B	D	C	E	Y
Riker and Ordeshook, 1968	4,294 questionnaires 1952, 1956, 1960 U.S. presidential elections	+	+	+			
Brody and Page, 1973	2,500 questionnaires 1968 presidential election		0			+	
Ashenfelter and Kelley, 1975	1,893 questionnaires 1960 + 1972 U.S. presidential elections	0	+	+	−	+	+
Silver, 1973	959 questionnaires 1960 U.S. presidential election	0	+?	+?	−	+	
Frohlich, Oppenheimer, Smith, and Young, 1978	1,067 questionnaires 1964 presidential election	+	+?	+?	−?		
Parry, Moyser, and Day, 1992	Nearly 1,600 questionnaires 1984 and 1985 U.K. national and local elections	+?	+?			−	0
Matsusaka and Palda, 1993	2,744 questionnaires 1979 and 1980 Canadian national elections	0				+	0
Knack, 1994	4,651 questionnaires 1984, 1986, 1988 U.S. national elections			+		+	+
Greene and Nikolaev, 1999	Nearly 21,000 questionnaires 1972–1993 U.S. elections	−				+	+
Thurner and Eymann, 2000	1,400 questionnaires 1990 German national election		+ (weak)[a]				

Notes: P, B, D, and C are proxies for the main components of the Downsian model, $R = PB + D − C$. E and Y stand for the education level and income of the voter.

"+" indicates a significant positive effect on the probability a survey respondent said that s/he voted, "−" a negative and significant coefficient, and a "0" an insignificant coefficient. Blank spaces imply that the variable was left out. A question mark implies uncertainty over whether the proxies used are related to the relevant variables.

[a] Thurner and Eymann test whether perceived differences in party positions on key issues increased the likelihood of the respondent's voting. For only one issue – immigration policy – was a significant effect found. I interpret this as weak support for the importance of B.

As noted above, respondents to voting surveys systematically overstate the frequency with which they vote. For example, 91 percent of the respondents to a survey in Canada stated that they voted in the 1979 Canadian general election for which the actual turnout was only 76 percent (Matsusaka and Palda, 1999). This degree of overstatement introduces an error in the measurement of the dependent variable that reduces the explanatory power of the model and explains why the typical model using survey data can explain only a small percentage of the variation in the dependent variable. Indeed, Matsusaka and Palda (1999) find that the estimates of a model with 36 explanatory variables do not allow them to classify correctly any more of the voters than they are able to classify simply by predicting that *everyone* votes.

This difficulty with survey data is avoided when one uses actual turnout data. In these studies the rational voter hypothesis is tested by relating aggregate figures on voter turnout at, say, the state level, to characteristics of the population of voters in that state. These studies have basically tested to see whether P, the probability that a vote changes the outcome, has a significant impact on voter turnouts. They have done so by regressing turnout figures on p, the percentage of the vote going to the leading candidate, and N, the size of the jurisdiction. Reference to the formulas used to calculate P, which were discussed in Section 14.1.1, indicates that P varies inversely with both N and the deviation of p from $1/2$. Table 14.2 summarizes the results from 26 studies, abstracting from the functional form used to introduce N and $(p - .5)$. Some use the expected (actual) percentage of the vote going to the winning candidate to proxy for $(p - .5)$; others use the winner's margin of victory. Each differs from the other with respect to choice of functional form and choice of other variables included. We focus here on $(p - .5)$ and N, but again report the results for education and income when these are included. A negative coefficient for $(p - .5)$ or N is interpreted as being consistent with what the rational voter hypothesis predicts. Only signs and significance levels are given in the table. Cebula and Murphy (1980) attempt an ex ante measure of $(p - .5)$ by limiting their sample to states with a Democratic majority in the lower house and estimating $(p - .5)$ as the fraction of the house that is Democratic. Foster's (1984) last set of results employs a similar ex ante measure of $(p - .5)$, but for both Republican and Democratic majorities. Shachar and Nalebuff (1999) estimate an equation to determine the expected vote. Most other studies assume rational expectations on the part of voters and measure $(p - .5)$ by the actual split in the vote between the candidates on election day.

The most ambitious of the studies – separated from the others by horizontal lines – is that of Foster (1984), who reestimates models from four studies, and estimates his own model using data for the 1968, 1972, 1976, and 1980 presidential elections. Instability in the coefficient estimates for cross sections precluded pooling the data to reestimate the Barzel-Silberberg and Kau-Rubin models, so the results for the individual cross sections are presented. In general, voter turnouts are not related to $(p - .5)$ or N in Foster's retesting of the rational voter hypothesis. Outside of the Nixon landslide in 1972, $(p - .5)$ does quite badly. N performs only moderately more consistently.

Foster (1984, p. 688) concludes "that the perceived probability of a tied election at the state level is not a powerful or reliable factor in explaining across-state variation in voter participation rates in presidential elections." This conclusion seems justified regarding his own estimates, and his reworking of the four other studies. But an examination of the other studies in Table 14.2 reveals that $(p - .5)$ and N have the predicted sign more often than not, and when their coefficients are significant they are, with but one exception, of the correct sign. Although closeness does not always "count" in elections, it does so more often than not.

Table 14.2. *Impact of the probability of a vote's being decisive on voter turnouts*

Study	Sample and time period	$(p - .5)$	N	E	Y
Barzel and Silberberg, 1973	122 gubernatorial elections, 1962, 1964, 1966, 1968	−(.01)	−INS		
Silberman and Durden, 1975	400 congressional districts, 1962	−(.01)	−(.01)		+(.01)
Tollison, Crain, and Paulter, 1975	29 gubernatorial elections, 1970	−(.10)	+INS		
Kau and Rubin, 1976	50 states, 1972 presidential	+INS	−(.01)		
Settle and Abrams, 1976	26 national presidential elections, 1868–1972, omitting 1944	−(.01)			
Crain and Deaton, 1977	50 states, 1972 presidential	−(.01)	−INS		+(.01)
Cebula and Murphy, 1980	35 states, 1976 presidential	−(.10)[a]			
Chapman and Palda, 1983	Electoral districts in 5 Canadian provinces, 1972–8	−(.05)[b]		+(.01)[c]	−(.01)[d]
Patterson and Caldeira, 1983	46 states, 1978, 1980 gubernatorial elections	−(.05)		+(.05)	INS
Foster, 1984 Barzel-Silberberg	50 states,				
	1968 presidential	+(.05)	+INS		
	1972 presidential	−(.01)	−INS		
	1976 presidential	−INS	−INS		
	1980 presidential	+INS	−INS		
Foster, 1984 Kau-Rubin	50 states,				
	1968 presidential	+(.05)	−INS		
	1972 presidential	−(.01)	−INS		
	1976 presidential	+INS	+INS		
	1980 presidential	−INS	−INS		
Foster, 1984 Silberman-Durden	200 states pooled, 1968, 1972, 1976, 1980 presidential	−INS	−(.10)		+(.01)
Foster, 1984 Crain-Deaton	200 states pooled, 1968, 1972, 1976, 1980 presidential	−INS	−(.01)		+(.01)
Foster, 1984 Wolfgram-Foster	200 states pooled, 1968, 1972, 1976, 1980 presidential	−(.10)[a]	−INS		
Tucker, 1986	362 contests for state legislature in Washington, 1976–82	−(.01)			
Hansen, Palfrey, and Rosenthal, 1987	1806 elections in Oregon school districts, 1970–3		−(.01)		
Durden and Gaynor, 1987	847 observations, 1970 and 1982 congressional elections	−(.01)	−(.01)		+(.01)

Study	Sample and time period	(p − .5)	N	E	Y
Capron and Kruseman, 1988	26 democratic countries, 1959–66		−(.01)		
Darvish and Rosenberg, 1988	108 municipalities in Israel, 1978, 1983		−(.01)		−(.01)
	Knesset, Israel, 1977, 1981		−INS		+(.10)
Cox and Munger, 1989	270 contest for U.S. House of Representatives, 1982	−(.01)		+(.01)	+(.01)
Filer, Kenny, and Morton, 1991, 1993	County level data, U.S. presidential elections 1948, 1960, 1980			+(.01)	+(.01)[e]
Kirchgässner and Schimmelpfennig, 1992	248 electoral districts, German national election of 1987	−(.01)	−(.05)		
	650 electoral districts, U.K. national election of 1987	−(.01)	INS		
Matsusaka, 1993	885 California ballot propositions, 1912–90	INS			
Fort, 1995	Nuclear power plant referenda in the U.S., 562 counties, 1976, 1980	−(.01)		+(.01)	
Grofman, Collet, and Griffin, 1998	Off-year House and Senate elections, 1952–92	−(.01)			
Shachar and Nalebuff, 1999	50 states, presidential elections 1948–88	−(.01)[f]	−(.01)	+(.01)	+(.01)

Notes: $(p − .5)$ = expected (actual) percentage of vote for leading candidate or the winner's margin of victory; N = size of jurisdiction.

[a] Proxy for ex ante measure of closeness used, proportion of Democrats in the lower house for all states with more than 50 percent Democratic representation.

[b] Significant in 6 of 10 provincial elections, of wrong sign and insignificant in 3 of 10.

[c] Coefficient on education generally positive, often significant.

[d] Coefficient on income always negative, sometimes significant.

[e] Nonlinear specification.

[f] Predicted closeness from a regression equation.

Skepticism about the importance of closeness is strengthened, on the other hand, when one considers some of the biases that arise when aggregate voting data are used to test the Downsian-rational-voter model. For example, candidates and interest groups have a greater incentive to mobilize their supporters when elections are expected to be close. Thus, voter turnout can arise in close elections not because voters have an enhanced opinion of the efficacy of their votes, but because more pressure has been placed on them to vote (Cox and Munger, 1989; Aldrich, 1993, 1995, 1997, pp. 387–9; Matsusaka and Palda, 1993; Shachar and Nalebuff, 1999).

Matsusaka and Palda (1993) test for the bias introduced by the "ecological fallacy" of substituting actual ex post election outcomes for the voters' expectations of the closeness of the election prior to voting. As reported earlier, they do not find that the anticipated closeness of the election significantly affected the probability of the survey respondents' voting. The aggregate, ex post data for the same election, on the other hand, revealed a significant negative coefficient on the margin of victory, as the Downsian model predicts. Matsusaka and Palda interpret this disparity in outcomes as confirmation of the ecological fallacy. In a separate study using California ballot propositions, Matsusaka (1993) again finds the closeness of the context to be unimportant in explaining the number of the votes cast.

Grofman, Collet, and Griffin (1998), on the other hand, claim to have uncovered an ecological fallacy that works against the Downsian voter model. "Because, on average, a higher proportion of Republican-leaning voters register, a higher proportion of the Republican (Republican-leaning) registrants come to the polls, and a higher proportion of the Republican-leaning voters who are at the polls cast a ballot for a full slate of offices . . . there is a possibility for an ecological confound in looking at the link between turnout and competition in cross-sectional terms. The ecological effect operates so that maximum turnout will not occur when Republican versus Democratic vote shares are nearly 50-50, . . . but rather will occur in more lopsided elections in which the Republican vote share is substantially above 50 percent" (p. 235, footnotes omitted). Although they do not uncover this ecological confound in all of their regressions, they do tend to find the margin of victory to be a significant determinant of turnout in Senate and House elections (see Table 14.2). [10] As is unfortunately so often the case in empirical tests of a controversial hypothesis, different researchers reach opposing conclusions concerning the quantitative and statistical significance of the key variables – in this case of $(p - 0.5)$ and N in the Downsian voter model.

Here the Ashenfelter-Kelley results with regard to voter perceptions of the closeness of an election should be recalled. They found that there was a statistically weak and quantitatively small positive effect on the chances of an individual voting if the individual thought that the election was close. Changes in voters' perceptions of the closeness of an election should vary considerably from one election to another. A preelection Gallup poll projection of a candidate's getting 60 percent of the vote makes the candidate's victory a virtual certainty. Few would bet against a candidate with preelection poll percentages in the 54 to 56 range. The difference in prior probabilities between an election that is "too close to call," like the 1960 Kennedy-Nixon or 2000 Bush-Gore contests and the 1972 Nixon landslide over McGovern, is the difference between a coin flip and a sure bet. With these shifts in odds, even if only some voters are weakly influenced by changes in their perception of the closeness of the contest, large changes in turnout may ensue. This consideration may explain why the closeness of the race in each state seems to have had a significant impact on voter turnouts in Nixon's 1972 landslide win (Crain and Deaton, 1977; Foster-Barzel-Silberberg and Foster-Kau-Rubin, 1984), and why efficacy affected voter turnouts in Johnson's 1964 landslide (Frohlich et al., 1978).

---

[10]   See also Grofman's (1993b) discussion of biases in testing the Downsian voter model, and Shachar and Nalebuff (1999).

In some ways a weak performance of P in explaining voter turnouts supports the overall view of the voter as a rational egoist more than it contradicts this image. Even when the probability of each voter's voting for one of the candidates is .5, the probability of a single vote being decisive in a polity of 100,000,000 is only 0.00006. As Riker and Ordeshook (1968) note regarding their finding that voter turnout is responsive to changes in P, this finding implies an unusually elastic response by voters to changes in probabilities. If drivers responded to changes in the probability of accidents to the same degree, heavy rain would find the roads abandoned. Riker and Ordeshook (1968, pp. 38–9) suggest that the highly elastic response of voters to changes in P may be due to the persuasive impact of television and radio announcements claiming that "your vote counts."[11] Consistent with Riker and Ordeshook's explanation of the importance of *perceived* closeness of the election are the results of Tollison, Crain, and Paulter (1975). They found an enhanced impact for the closeness variable in states with relatively large newspaper circulation. "Information concerning the expected outcome [tends] to make more people vote in close races" (p. 45). But if voters are so easily misled concerning the importance of their vote, one's confidence in the intelligence of the rational voter is weakened. Although naiveté and rationality are not strictly opposites, the existence of the former does undermine the importance of the rationality assumption somewhat.

The results reviewed here suggest that the relationship between changes in P and voter abstentions is weaker than Riker and Ordeshook concluded. If so, then voters are less naive about their ability to change the outcome of the election, and thus behave in what seems like a more sophisticatedly rational way. But in so doing they confirm the more cynical interpretation of voter rationality, that is, the noninstrumentalist view that voting is determined solely by its entertainment–psychic income value (D) and private costs (C). This interpretation raises the issue, in deriving a theory of voting, of the determinants of D and C.

Some components of C are easy to identify. Poll taxes, literacy tests, and other barriers erected in the southern states to prevent blacks from registering or voting have been found to have significant, negative effects (Ashenfelter and Kelley, 1975; Filer, Kenny, and Morton, 1991; and the case studies in Davidson and Grofman, 1994). Similarly, Jackman (1987) has found that voter turnouts tend to be higher in countries in which small fines are levied for not voting.

Several states in the United States construct jury lists from voter registration rolls. This practice raises the cost of registering to vote by increasing the likelihood if one does that one is called to jury duty. Knack (1993, 2000) found that selecting jurors from voter registration lists significantly lowers the likelihood of people registering to vote, as well as voter participation rates.

Heckelman (1995) found a seven-percentage-point decline in voting in U.S. gubernatorial elections following the introduction of secret ballots in the early 1890s.

---

[11] As noted earlier, the intensity with which citizens are told that their vote counts or the frequency with which they receive other messages and pressure to vote may increase in districts where a close vote is expected, giving rise to a spurious correlation between turnouts and closeness.

The incentive to bribe people to vote for a particular candidate declined dramatically once the briber could not verify that the bribe recipient had in fact voted for the "right candidate." When bribes for votes declined, so too did voting.[12]

One popularly held belief is that bad weather deters citizens from voting. Shachar and Nalebuff (1999) observed turnouts in U.S. presidential elections declined when it rained, but both Knack (1994) and Matsusaka and Palda (1999) found that the weather had no significant impact on turnouts in the United States and Canada. However, Knack (1994) did observe that bad weather caused a significant drop in the likelihood that those with a low sense of civic duty would vote, while it had no effect on the voting of those with a high sense of civic duty. Knack's findings underscore the joint importance of the D and C terms in the Downsian model.[13]

From whence springs a sense of civic duty, a taste for voting, and how does one predict its variability across individuals and over time? We now examine two answers to this question.

14.3   The expressive voter hypothesis

In trying to reconcile the act of voting with rational individual behavior, Fiorina (1976) offered the hypothesis that an individual voted not to bring about a particular election outcome, but to *express* an opinion as to what that outcome should be. The utility gain from voting comes from the act of voting itself and the opportunity for expression that this act affords, not from the expected payoff from the outcome of the election. This utility gain from expression becomes another candidate for inclusion in D to explain the act of voting.

Of course, this expressive voter hypothesis is just as tautological as the taste for voting hypothesis unless we can define what it is that some people what to express, and others do not, and thereby construct a refutable hypothesis. One possibility is that the voter wants to express a preference for the candidate who promises her the highest utility payoff after the election. We all like people "who are on our side" more than those who seek to harm us; people who are similar to ourselves over those who are radically different; and so on. If candidate X promises to do more for us – or less against us – than candidate Y, then we might choose to vote for X, not because we thought that in so doing we would bring about her victory, but as a way of expressing our support for her position, of thanking her for standing up for our interests, of cheering her on. This interpretation of the expressive voting hypothesis makes D a function of B, as, for example,

$$D = D' + B, \tag{14.3}$$

where D' captures other items in D, like a sense of civic duty. This interpretation implies that B alone and not P or PB should have the most explanatory power in the

---

[12] See also Heckelman (2000).
[13] See also Knack (1992).

Downsian model. This predition is identical to that of the minimax-regret hypothesis, and thus Ferejohn and Fiorina's (1975) evidence in favor of minimax-regret can also be interpreted as support for an expressive voting hypothesis. Studies finding P to be a significant factor and B of modest significance should be counted against it, on the other hand. This first interpretation of the expressive voter hypothesis leads to the same prediction as the Downsian model with respect to *how* an individual votes, if she votes. Its novelty comes entirely in explaining *why* an individual votes.

Several writers have offered a quite different interpretation of expressive voting. They claim that by uncoupling the act of voting from the outcome of the election, the existence of a low P with large electorates frees the voter to express preferences that deviate dramatically from those that she would reveal if she thought that her vote would be decisive. Brennan and Buchanan (1984) suggest, for example, that the noninstrumentalist nature of voting may lead to more irresponsible voting. The voter believes that X's victory would be a disaster for the country. But X is the only candidate who condemns the influx of immigrants and promises "to do something about them." The voter feels threatened by the increasing numbers of immigrants and gives vent to her anxiety by voting for X, an action she would never take if she thought that X's victory hinged on her vote.

Alternatively, knowledge that one's vote "does not count" may induce one to express more noble sentiments. Some people give to charities, stop to help someone whose car has broken down, cart used bottles and cans to recycling bins, and so on. One explanation for these seemingly unselfish actions is that the actor's behavior is governed by norms or moral convictions, like the "golden rule," that prescribe certain sorts of behavior toward others. Since voting involves collective decisions that affect all members of the community, norms that govern conduct toward others might be expected to be particularly likely to come into play when individuals vote. When individuals vote they express their views as to what is good for the community and which candidate's election is most in the public interest.[14]

This interpretation of expressive voting seems to be contradicted by the evidence that many individuals vote strategically, however (Cox, 1997). In a single-member district contest a voter will not vote for her first choice if this person is running third or fourth in the preelection polling. She chooses not to "throw away her vote" in this way, and instead votes for one of the two front-runners. If this voter only wished to express her views as to which candidate's victory would be best for the community, one would not expect her to give the polls any weight. Her desire not to "waste her vote" seems to suggest that she thinks her "vote counts," and thus that she views voting as an instrumental action.

Both Carter and Guerette (1992) and Fischer (1996) have run experiments to test a private interest/public interest form of the expressive voting hypothesis. They tested whether subjects were more likely to give money to a charity rather than claim

---

[14] Although Brennan and Lomasky (1993) and Brennan and Hamlin (2000) admit that expressive voting might take a vindictive form, their books place much more emphasis on the well-intentioned voter, and constitute a spirited defense of this version of the expressive voter hypothesis.

it for themselves when the probability of their vote counting declined. Both studies found weak evidence of expressive voting.[15]

This version of the expressive voter hypothesis has much in common with the ethical voter hypothesis.

14.4   The ethical voter hypothesis

All of the studies reviewed so far see the individual as maximizing his utility, and thus are broadly consistent with the behavioral postulate underlying all public choice. Even the last hypothesis considered posits that it is the utility that an individual gets from expressing his views about the public interest that leads him to vote. The interpretation of the act of voting discussed in this section goes a step farther.[16] It views the voter as having two sets of preferences, an ethical set and a selfish set. The latter includes only one's own utility; the former includes the utilities of others, or one's perception thereof. In some situations – for example, the consumer in the marketplace – only one's selfish preferences come into play. One maximizes one's utility as conventionally defined. In others, one employs one's ethical preferences. Voting is one of those situations in which one's ethical preferences govern.

This Jekyll-and-Hyde view of man's nature has a long and distinguished ancestry. The importance of "a sense of civic duty" in explaining voting resonates with this "ethical voter" hypothesis, as does the interpretation of expressive voting which sees it as an opportunity to express one's views about the public interest. But the ethical voter hypothesis suffers from the same deficiency as the "taste for participation" as an explanation for voting. Instead of providing us with a hypothesis with which we can develop a theory of voting and perhaps of other cooperative-social behavior, it provides an ex post rationalization for the act. It provides the end for a story about voting, not the beginning for a behavioral theory of voting.

The kind of ethical-selfish dichotomy presumed in the ethical theory of voting might be operationalized as a predictive theory by assuming that each individual i maximizes an objective function of the following form:[17]

$$O_i = U_i + \theta \sum_{j \neq i} U_j. \tag{14.4}$$

A purely selfish voter sets $\theta = 0$; a fully altruistic voter sets $\theta = 1$, as in Harsanyi (1955). In either case, the individual is behaving rationally in the sense of maximizing an objective function. In either case, the analyst benefits from the most important advantage of the rationality assumption, clear predictions about human behavior, in

---

[15] Fischer critiques Carter and Guerette's experimental design and claims to find much stronger support for expressive voting than they did. Of the 82 participants 42 voted selfishly in all eight of his experiments, however, with another 20 voting consistently altruistically. The remaining 20 did not vote consistently, as the expressive voting hypothesis predicted. Thus, the hypothesis accounted for the behavior of at best something less than a quarter of the participants in the experiment.

[16] See Goodin and Roberts (1975), Margolis (1982b), and Etzioni (1986). Harsanyi's (1955) approach is the same, although he does not discuss the act of voting. See also Arrow's (1963, pp. 81–91) discussion.

[17] This approach is elaborated in Mueller (1986).

this case in the form of first-order conditions to the maximization of (14.4) with θ equal to either zero or one.

Hudson and Jones (1994) have estimated θ, and thus have provided a direct test of this interpretation of the ethical voter hypothesis. They conducted two surveys in Bath, England in 1988 and 1992. Voters were asked to comment on different policy proposals regarding changes in taxes and expenditures on health, education, and social benefits. Voters first identified their preferred policy, and then stated (1) whether they thought that the policy would benefit themselves personally, and (2) whether they thought that the policy would be in the public's interest. From the answers to these questions Hudson and Jones inferred magnitudes of θ of 0.66 in 1988, and 0.73 in 1992.

In Hudson and Jones's survey voters were confronted with a choice between proposals that were in their self-interest and proposals in what they perceived to be the public's interest. In an analysis of voting in Oregon intermediate election districts by Jeffrey Smith (1975), voters were effectively confronted with a simple choice: did they favor higher taxes or not? Voting took place on whether tax burdens of the districts should be equalized or not, with equalization raising the tax rates of some districts and lowering those of others. A simple application of the self-interest hypothesis implied a vote for equalization if it lowered one's taxes – against it if it raised them. The percentage favoring equalization was positively related to whether one gained from equalization, and was larger for large gains (Smith, 1975, p. 64).

Percentage of large[18] gainers favoring equalization	60.7
Percentage of small gainers favoring equalization	52.9
Percentage of small losers favoring equalization	46.1
Percentage of large losers favoring equalization	32.7

Note that in this survey voters did not face a direct choice between their own private interest and the public interest (although one might argue that an ethical voter would vote for equalization out of a sense of fairness). While a majority voted consistently with their self-interest, over 40 percent of the population voted to raise their tax rates. Some factors beyond private interest must have influenced the voting of this substantial fraction of citizens.[19]

Tax limitation proposals raise private/public interest trade-offs more directly through the reductions in government spending implied, if the limitation proposal succeeds. Gramlich and Rubinfeld (1982b) found from an examination of the responses of 2,001 households to a telephone survey in Michigan that transfer recipients (the aged, unemployed, and those on welfare) had only a moderately higher tendency to vote against a tax limitation proposal than nonrecipients. A more significant difference occurred for public employees; yet even here, 42 percent of those voting voted to *restrict* expenditures. In general, self-interest voting models have not done well in explaining voting on Proposition 13 issues (Lowery and

---

[18] Large gainers (losers) had their tax rates lowered (raised) by equalization by more than $1 per $1,000 of assessed value.

[19] A similar interpretation lends itself to Bloom's (1979) analysis of voting on tax classification in Massachusetts.

Sigelman, 1981). Rather, votes for these proposals seem better treated as "symbolic acts" against "bad government" by citizens seeking improved government efficiency, the kinds of actions one might expect from a civic-minded (expressive) voter.

More direct comparisons with Hudson and Jones's test of the ethical voter hypothesis are obtained in studies of *economic voting*, which estimate the relative weights placed on *egotropic* and *sociotropic* variables. Egotropic variables measure voter expectations regarding the effect of the government's policies on the voter's own income, employment status, and so on. Sociotropic variables measure voter expectations regarding the effect of the government's policies on the economy at large, that is, on the welfare of all citizens. By linking voters' support for the government to their answers to these sorts of questions, researchers have been able to estimate equivalents to θ in (14.4), where $\theta = 1$ implies full weight on sociotropic variables, and $\theta = 0$ implies full weight on the egotropic variables. Estimates of θ falling between 0.5 and 1.0 have been made for the United States, the United Kingdom, France, and Germany.[20] Only Danish voters seem to conform largely to the egotropic economic man assumption in studies by Nannestad and Paldam (1996, 1997). They estimate a θ for Denmark of about 0.15.[21]

Findings in public goods experiments that individuals tend to contribute voluntarily about half of the difference between jointly optimal and the individually optimal amounts (Hoffman, 1997) are also consistent with a θ of about 0.5.

All of the preceding tests of the motivation of voters directly or indirectly assume that the voter behaves either ethically or selfishly. The voter is given a choice between a proposal that is the public interest and one in his narrow interest, $0 < \theta < 1$. No effort is made to test an *un*ethical voter hypothesis, and no allowance is made for the possibility that $\theta < 0$. However, Sears, Law, Tyler, and Allen (1980) found in their analysis of Center for Political Studies survey data for the 1976 presidential election that racial prejudice was one of the "symbolic attitudes [that] had strong effects" in explaining voting on four controversial policy areas, "while self-interest had almost none" (see also Sears, Hensler, and Speer, 1979). Mr. Hyde and Dr. Jekyll are joined by Simon Legree. On issues regarding the treatment of men and women sexist attitudes might well play a role. The set of different preferences that the individual might draw upon grows. Even if we assume that we can specify the arguments of the individual utility functions that go into (14.4) – income, public good quantities, and the like – we cannot estimate such a model unless we can also specify the determinants of θ. How can one predict when an individual will behave selfishly and when ethically, or the degree to which one's ethical preferences govern one's actions, when ethical behavior is not a simple either-or decision? What makes Danish voters more egotropic than their German neighbors? What makes economics students free-ride to a greater degree than students from other disciplines (Marwell and Ames, 1981)? To predict such differences one needs to do more than merely posit the existence of ethical preferences; one needs a theory of how ethical preferences

---

[20] Kinder and Kiewiet (1979), Markus (1988, 1990), and Lewis-Beck (1988). See also Fiorina (1978, 1981), Kiewiet (1981, 1983), Kirchgässner (1985), and Lewin (1991).

[21] Estimate inferred from Table 6 in Nannestad and Paldam (1996).

are formed, what determines their strength, and what triggers their use. One needs a theory of learning, which probably must be found in the areas of psychology or sociology.

14.5 Ethical preferences as selfish behavior

Behavioral psychology offers a relatively simple description of the learning process.[22] Actions followed by rewards increase in frequency. Actions followed by punishment decline in frequency. Man learns to avoid doing that which brings about pain, and to do that which produces pleasure. When one observes how man learns, it is difficult to reject the postulate that man is innately a selfish animal. The same principles appear to describe the learning processes of all animals. Man differs from other animals not in how he learns, but in what he learns. Man is capable of learning far more complex behavioral patterns than are other creatures.[23]

Ethical behavior is learned. Much of this learning takes place when we are children. When we commit acts that harm others we are punished by our parents, teachers, and other adult supervisors. Actions that benefit others are rewarded. Ethical behavior patterns learned as children can be maintained at high frequency levels through adulthood by only occasional positive and negative reinforcement.[24] What we normally describe as ethical behavior is inherently no more or less selfish than what we call selfish behavior. It is a conditioned response to certain stimuli governed by past reinforcement experience.

There are several advantages to using behavioral psychology or some version of cognitive psychology that subsumes its principles to explain ethical behavior. First, it allows us to work with a single conceptualization of man, a conceptualization consistent with the selfish-egoism postulate underlying both economics and public choice. Second, it allows us to develop a purely positive theory of behavior, free from the normative prescripts that often accompany the Jekyll-and-Hyde view of man. Third, it gives us some insight into what variables might explain why some individuals behave in what is commonly described as an ethical manner, and some do not. Home environment during childhood, educational experience, religion, community stability, and any other factors that might affect an individual's ethical learning experience become possible candidates as explanatory variables in a positive theory of ethical behavior. Thus, ethical behavior such as voting can be explained if one retains the self-interest assumption of public choice and drops, or at least relaxes, the rationality assumption.

Equation (14.4) can be used to describe behavior in situations involving ethical choices if one assumes that individuals act *as if* they were maximizing (14.4), with some θ not necessarily equal to zero or one. The argument is similar to Alchian's (1950) argument that competition eliminates less profitable firms, leaving only the

---

[22] For reviews of the basic principles of behavioral psychology, see Notterman (1970), and Schwartz and Lacey (1982, chs. 1–6).

[23] To explain complex behavior some variant of cognitive theory will most likely be required. But as the opening quotation from Schumpeter suggests, voting is probably best treated as a relatively simple, habitual action.

[24] See references in n. 22.

most profitable, whose actions resemble those they would have chosen had they consciously been maximizing profit even when they were not. It is in society's collective interest in certain contexts to establish institutions that condition people to behave as if they were maximizing (14.4) with $\theta = 1$. Although this degree of cooperative behavior is seldom achieved, the conditioning process is usually successful in eliciting some degree of cooperation. Observed behavior thus resembles what one would expect if individuals consciously maximized (14.4) with some $\theta > 0$, even though (because) individual behavior is governed by social conditioning.[25] Under this interpretation θ is a behavioral parameter to be explained by the individual's or group's conditioning history, not a choice variable set equal to zero or one depending on whether the individual has chosen today to be Hyde or Jekyll.[26]

14.6   The selfish voter

Normally, when we model individual behavior, an individual's past history plays no part in the analysis. Sunk costs are sunk, bygones are bygones, and all that matters are the future consequences of an individual's action. With respect to voting, this conceptualization of the voting act boils the number of relevant variables down to three: the benefits from the preferred candidate's victory, B; the probability that one's vote will bring about this victory, P; and the costs of getting to the polls, C.

Modeling individual behavior as conditioned by past learning shifts one's attention from the future payoffs from different actions to the past history of the individual. The list of potential explanatory variables is expanded considerably.

We have already made the point that years of education might, if voters were purely rational and egoistic, be expected to be negatively related to the probability of voting. The uneducated might be duped by television advertisements to believe their vote would count, but the more educated should remain rationally cynical regarding the efficacy of their vote.

One learns more than probability theory in school, however. One also learns to cooperate. Number of years of successfully completed schooling measures the

---

[25] Darwinian selection will play a role in determining which social institutions or even which social groups survive. If the collective gains from cooperation are large, those groups that are more successful at eliciting cooperative behavior (inducing individuals to behave as if $\theta = 1$) will have higher survival chances. Evolutionary forces may also select gene structures more conducive to the teaching and learning of cooperative behavior, when cooperation raises individual survival chances.

[26] Overbye (1995a) proposes an explanation for voting that leads to many similar predictions to the behavioral theory just discussed, except that his theory is fully consistent with the selfish, rational actor assumption. Building on Frank (1988), Overbye argues that people vote to develop a *reputation* as the kind of person who votes, just as charitable giving can be interpreted as an *investment* in developing a reputation for generosity. Such reputations serve as signals to others that the actor is the kind of person who will not cheat on a contract, cooperates in prisoners' dilemmas, and so on. In the long run such reputations lead to higher incomes, happier personal relationships, and the like. Thus developing such a reputation by voting is a rational action that is in the long-run selfish interest of the individual. Overbye's hypothesis leads to analogous predictions as the psychological explanation given above, because the value of such a reputation depends on an individual's peer group. Thus, many of the same sociological variables that one expects will be correlated with conditioned habits to cooperate are predicted to be important by Overbye.

Hudson (1995) and Uhlaner (1989a,b, 1993) come closer to the behavioral approach outlined here in hypothesizing a link between voting and group membership, and the rewards and approbation of one's peers.

amount and strength of conditioning in the numerous cooperative games played in a school environment. By the time one graduates one has been rewarded again and again for going by the rules and doing what is expected, and one has usually been punished on those occasions when one has broken the rules. One expects those with more education to behave more cooperatively, to break fewer rules, be they driving laws or social mores, and to do more of what is expected of them as a citizen. Years of education have proven to be positively and significantly related to voter turnout in virtually every study of voter participation.[27]

Income is another variable which invariably picks up the wrong sign in explaining voter turnout from what a straightforward application of the rational egoism postulate would imply. The higher one's income, the higher the opportunity cost of time, and ceteris paribus the lower the probability that one goes to the polls.[28] Yet income is consistently, positively correlated with the probability of voting.[29]

Income, like a graduation certificate, is a mark of success at playing by certain rules of the societal game. (Of course, some individuals accumulate income by successfully breaking the rules, but I doubt that many of these persons are part of the SRC panels.) Individuals with high income are more likely to go by the rules, and to live within the social mores. Moreover, their high incomes are evidence that they have been rewarded for doing so, since money is society's chief token reinforcer. High-income individuals, like the highly educated, can be expected to break fewer rules and to behave in other socially cooperative ways, like voting.

This interpretation of voting as a sort of conditioned "good habit" would seem to be consistent with Blais and Young's (1999) experimental results. They observed a significant drop in participation rates among Canadian university students after they had heard a 10-minute lecture explaining the logic of the Downsian voter model. It appeared that many "students generally do not think in terms of benefits and costs" when they vote, but rather for them voting "is an unreflective and habitual act, based primarily on a sense of duty" (pp. 52–3). When they heard the act characterized as a rational choice involving weighing benefits and costs, an additional 7 percent chose not to vote.

There are other explanations than the one given above for why income and education might be positively related to political participation, of course. For example, education may reduce the cost of gathering information about candidates and thus be positively related to voting as predicted by the rational voter model.[30] Without denying the possible relevance of these explanations, I nevertheless favor starting from

---

[27] Campbell et al. (1964, pp. 251–4); Milbrath (1965); Kelley, Ayres, and Bowen (1967); and Verba and Nie (1972, pp. 95–101). See also studies cited in Tables 14.1 and 14.2.

Education appears to have a strong, positive effect on voting in the Patterson and Caldeira (1983) study; also, when correlated separately with voting. Its failure to have a significant impact when income is included is probably due to multicollinearity, a problem observed in several studies.

[28] See discussion of Russell, Fraser, and Frey (1972); and Tollison and Willett (1973).

[29] Dahl (1961) and Lane (1966) as cited by Frey (1971); Milbrath (1965); Kelley, Ayres, and Bowen (1967); Dennis (1970); and Verba and Nie (1972, pp. 95–101). See also studies in Tables 14.1 and 14.2.

An important exception is Chapman and Palda (1983), who get a significant negative coefficient, as predicted by the rational voter hypothesis. See also Mueller and Stratmann (2002).

[30] See in particular Frey (1971), and ensuing interchange among Russell (1972), Fraser (1972), Frey (1972), Tollison and Willett (1973), and Chapman and Palda (1983).

a behavioralist view toward voting and other forms of cooperative behavior, both because this approach offers a more natural explanation for why these and other background characteristics of the voter matter, and because this approach offers greater potential for developing additional hypotheses about individual behavior in situations like voting, when narrowly self-interested behavior is inconsistent with the behavior that social conditioning dictates.

If education is positively related to voting because it reduces the costs of political participation, for example, one would expect a secular rise in participation rates since education levels have been rising. Yet since the early 1960s voter participation in the United States has declined steadily and dramatically (see Figure 14.1). Abramson and Aldrich (1982) attribute at least two-thirds of this decline to two factors: (1) weakening voter identification with the political parties, and (2) declining beliefs in the responsiveness of government. Both of these factors may in turn be explained as the result of negative rewards from voting in presidential elections since 1960. In a normal presidential election, over half of the voters are rewarded for going to the polls in that this action is followed by their preferred candidate's victory. In this way, majority rule tends to sustain political participation. Since 1960, however, three presidents have been elected whose performance in office must have been a great disappointment to their supporters: Johnson because of Vietnam, Nixon because of Watergate, and Carter because of an overall poor performance.[31] Thus, voting for the winning candidate was punished, and this punishment may explain the drop in the frequency with which individuals have gone to the polls after 1960. Figure 14.1 also reveals that the downward spiral in voting turnouts since 1960 has simply brought voter turnouts in the United States back to their level near the bottom of the Great Depression in 1932, where disillusionment with the government was again high.

This behavioral explanation of voting can also be interpreted as support for the expressive voter hypothesis. Brennan and Buchanan (1984) liken voting to cheering at a sporting event. In each case the actor obtains personal pleasure from the act; in each case the action has a negligible effect on the outcome of the contest. A fan's cheering is rewarded if his team wins; most fans cheer for the home team. Winning home teams provide more positive reinforcement for their supporters. Winning home teams tend to have higher attendance levels and more vocal fans than do losing teams.[32]

This positive-reinforcement interpretation of voting is also consistent with the overwhelming evidence of higher turnouts in countries with multiparty systems than in two-party democracies (Jackman, 1987). In a multiparty system, the actions of nearly all voters are reinforced in that the party for which they voted wins some

---

[31] To this list we may some day be able to add Clinton, because of his sexual escapades, but at this writing it is too soon to say.

[32] Matsusaka (1995) offers a somewhat different behavioral explanation for the decline in voting in U.S. presidential elections since 1960. He puts forward a variant of the expressive voter hypothesis in which voters obtain more utility from voting, the more confident they are about the superiority of their preferred candidate. Matsusaka speculates that Vietnam, Watergate, and the like increased uncertainty among Americans about what the "correct model of the world" is, and thus about which candidate to vote for. This enhanced uncertainty led to the decline in turnouts.

seats. In a two-party system, a substantial fraction of all voters are punished for voting by the defeat of their party.

14.7   Summary and implications

All of the public choice literature as it pertains to the outcomes of committee voting or elections assumes that voters vote, whether sincerely or strategically, to attain that outcome promising them the highest benefits. All of public choice is based on the assumption that it is the attainment of B in the equation $R = PB + D - C$ that determines the way in which an individual votes.

The logical foundation for this assumption is significantly undermined in elections or committees in which the number of voters is large. P is then infinitesimal, the PB term vanishes, and considerations other than the instrumental value of the vote determine whether or not an individual votes, or at least they ought to if the individual is both rational and sufficiently intelligent to make a reasonable guess as to the magnitude of P.

The empirical literature reviewed here is reassuring with respect to both the intelligence and the rationality of voters in that it indicates that P has a rather weak (statistically) and inconsistent relationship to the decision to vote. The primary explanation for why individuals vote comes from the D and C terms in R, as Downs (1957) and Tullock (1967a) first asserted.

The interpretation and specification of the components of C have been fairly uncontroversial, and considerable empirical evidence indicates that turnout falls as the costs of voting rise. Considerable disagreement exists, on the other hand, over the interpretation and modeling of D.

One interpretation is that some individuals get utility from expressing their preferences for a particular candidate through the act of voting. This interpretation provides an explanation for *why* a person votes, but not for how she votes. To use the expressive voter hypothesis to explain how people vote one needs to specify what it is exactly that people want to express by voting.

In contrast to the expressive voter hypothesis, the ethical voter hypothesis is an explanation for *how* a person votes. She votes as her ethical preferences tell her to vote. The fully ethical voter with a $\theta = 1$ votes for the proposal that maximizes the aggregate welfare of the community in which her utility has a negligible weight. The *rational*, ethical voter realizes, however, that the probability that her vote brings about this outcome is also negligible, and she thus abstains. To obtain an ethical theory of why people vote from the ethical theory of voting one must posit that voting improves the welfare of others by, say, improving the quality of the outcomes of the political process (better outcomes arise when all vote), or by helping to maintain democratic institutions. The D term in $R = PB + D - C$ is essentially the effect of one's vote on the welfare of all others.[33] Thus, the ethical voter hypothesis as an explanation for why people vote essentially subsumes the premise of the civic-duty rationale for voting in its set of givens.

---

[33] This is the way Frohlich et al. (1978) describe the term in their Downsian test.

While the expressive and ethical voter hypotheses offer rationales for why and how people vote, neither provides a set of testable propositions without further elaboration. To see why this is so consider again the voting/cheering analogy. Why do some fans cheer? – to express support for a team. Suppose now that we wish to go beyond merely rationalizing why some fans engage in the seemingly irrational act of cheering. Suppose that we wish to predict which fans cheer and which do not, which team they cheer for, how loudly they cheer, and so on. How would we proceed? One way would be to survey fans at a game. We might then find that those fans who cheer for the home team tend to come from the home team's area. Many of those cheering for the visiting team have traveled from its area. Going further and inquiring how they came to be fans, we might find that they grew up in the area, their parents took them to games when they were children, most of their school mates as children also rooted for the team, and so on. We would not be surprised to find that the backgrounds of people at the game who do not cheer are quite different. From this sort of information we could begin to construct a set of variables measuring the personal characteristics of sports fans, which would allow us to predict cheering behavior.

Such an approach would be similar to the survey studies used to study voter behavior. Behavioral psychology offers an explanation for why an individual's personal history is an important determinant of his current behavior, and a guide as to which variables are likely to be important in explaining voting. Applying the principles of behavioral psychology is a particularly attractive way for public choice to introduce "sociological variables" like education and family background into a model of voter behavior, because it is fully compatible with the *egoistic* portion of the rational-egoism postulate, and in certain contexts behavioral psychology predicts that individuals act *as if* they were maximizing a utility function.

Such a behavioralist theory of voting can be interpreted simply as an alternative to rational actor theories including the expressive and ethical voter variants. However, one can also view the different theories as complementary. Behavioral psychology provides a theory of preference formation that can guide the selection of variables in the preferences that an expressive voter wishes to express, for example. The evidence reviewed above indicates that individuals place considerable weight on the welfare of others when stating their preferences toward certain government policies. They respond to survey questions *as if* they were maximizing an objective function that places a positive weight on the welfare of others. An expressive-ethical voter hypothesis is consistent with these survey responses. Several implications follow.

First, if voting itself were a (conditioned) ethical action, then estimates of the weight placed on the utilities of others, the θ of (14.4), that are based on survey responses of *citizens* would *underestimate* the θs for *voters*, since citizens with high θs would vote in higher proportions than the average survey respondent. Experiments like those of Fischer (1996), where voting is effectively compelled by the nature of the experiment, overestimate the extent of purely self-interested behavior in the population.[34]

---

[34] Recall that slightly more than half of the participants voted selfishly in all eight of Fischer's experiments, with the remainder splitting equally between consistently altruistic and expressively altruistic voting.

This observation has an important implication for proposals to increase voter turnouts artificially by, say, fining people who do not vote (Lijphart, 1997). Such measures would increase the participation rates of "selfish voters" relative to "ethical voters," and thus might actually reduce the quality of the social outcomes.

This danger is increased if an important reason for voter abstentions is voter uncertainty over the choice of candidates, as Matsusaka (1995) argues and considerable survey evidence suggests.[35] Compelling more people to vote is thus likely to drive many people to the polls who are uncertain or undecided between the candidates. This hardly seems like a way to improve the outcomes of elections.[36]

The key normative question raised by the literature on why and how people vote is whether substituting a (conditioned) expressive-ethical voter for the rational, self-interested voter of the traditional public choice model will improve or worsen the outcomes from the process. Unfortunately, no simple "yes" or "no" answer can be given to this question.[37] Even when people place weights on the welfare of others, they may disagree in their rankings of various policy alternatives. Cycling is thus still possible, and with it comes the possibility of agenda manipulation and the like.

On the other hand, filtering issues through an ethical/ideological screen does tend to reduce the dimensionality of the issue space and thereby the likelihood of cycles (Hinich and Munger, 1994, chs. 6 and 7). Introducing ethical/ideological considerations can also increase their saliency, however, and make compromise more difficult. On issues like abortion, school busing, immigration policy, and the official status of languages, the middle of the ideological spectrum may be sparsely occupied. Even when the ethical/ideological framing of issues reduces the issue space to a single left/right dimension, political instability may ensue if ethical/ideological divisions in the polity lead to polarization (Sartori, 1976). The inability to compromise on an ethical issue helped lead the United States into a bloody civil war. Belgium and Canada have been driven to the brink of dissolution over language issues; Northern Ireland and Israel over religion.

The probabilistic voting model predicts equilibria in two-party electoral systems at which some form of social welfare function is maximized. With interest groups and campaign contributions added to the model, the weights each group implicitly receives in the social welfare function change, but the predicted outcomes remain Pareto optimal. These predictions are not affected by the substitution of expressive-ethical preferences of the sort implied by (14.4) for selfish ones. Only the weights assigned to the different groups change.

Such an amendment might greatly enhance the predictive power of these models. For example, farmers in developed countries have been extraordinarily successful at getting democratically elected governments to award them large subsidies and high price supports. Agricultural subsidies have made up more than half of the European

---

[35] Being undecided before an election and not voting in it tend to be significantly correlated. See, for example, Ashenfelter and Kelley (1975, p. 717).

[36] Very little work exits that tests for the effects of high voter participation on the outcomes of the political process. See, however, Husted and Kenny (1997), Lott and Kenny (1999), and Mueller and Stratmann (2002).

[37] For arguments for a qualified "yes" to this question, see Brennan and Lomasky (1993) and Brennan and Hamlin (2000).

Union's budget throughout its existence despite the fact that the European Council has operated under the unanimity rule for much of this period. Why have farmers been so much more successful at winning favors for democratic governments than, say, nurses or plumbers? One reason may be that every child in these countries grows up reading books and singing songs about the good life and the good people on the farm. Countless books and movies depict courageous farm families struggling against bad weather and nasty bankers to keep their farms operating. The citizens of all developed countries have been conditioned to think fondly of farmers and implicitly place heavy weights on their welfare when voting. Miners have also received particularly favorable treatment in literature, song, and film, and they too do very well at the public trough.

Do the outcomes of the democratic process *improve* with the reweighting of the utilites of different groups that occurs when citizens express their ethical preferences when voting instead of their narrow selfish ones? The answer to this question depends on how well the new set of weights matches those of the reader's own preferences.

Bibliographical notes

For a survey of the literature on why people vote, see Aldrich (1997). For a survey of how they vote, see Fiorina (1997).

Merrill and Grofman (1999) develop the Downsian spatial model to explain *how* citizens will vote. The empirical support for their predictions using data from France, Norway, and the United States can be interpreted as support for the rational, self-interested voter hypothesis – once one abstracts from the question of whether the act of voting is itself rational.

CHAPTER 15

Rent seeking

The *positive* evils and dangers of the representative, as of every other form of government, may be reduced to two heads: first, general ignorance and incapacity, or, to speak more moderately, insufficient mental qualifications, in the controlling body; secondly, the danger of its being under the influence of interests not identical with the general welfare of the community. (Italics in original)

John Stuart Mill

In Chapter 12 we discussed a model of political competition in which politicians provide policies or legislation to win votes, and citizens and interest groups provide votes. From the discussion up to this point, it seems reasonable to think that the legislation consists of either public goods with characteristics that appeal to given groups of voters or income transfers from one sector of the population to another. The latter might be a tax loophole benefiting a particular group coupled with a rise in the average tax rate to make up for the revenue lost through the loophole. Income can be transferred from one group to another by other, more subtle means, however.

The government can, for example, help create, increase, or protect a group's monopoly position. In so doing, the government increases the monopoly rents of the favored groups at the expense of the buyers of the groups' products or services. The monopoly rents that the government can help provide are a prize worth pursuing, and the pursuit of these rents has been given the name of rent seeking.

15.1 The theory of rent seeking

Rent seeking was first discussed systematically by Tullock (1967c). The term "rent seeking" was first used to describe the activity in question by Krueger (1974). Figure 15.1 depicts the demand schedule for a monopolized product. If the monopoly charges the monopoly price P_m instead of the competitive price P_c, the rectangle R of monopoly rent is created, as is the welfare triangle L of lost consumers' surplus on the output of the monopolized product, that would have been produced under perfect competition but is not provided by the monopolist.

In the traditional discussion of monopoly, it has been customary to treat L as a measure of the efficiency loss due to monopoly, and R as a pure redistribution of income from the consumers of the monopolized product or service to its producers. Suppose, however, that the monopoly has been created and is protected by an action of the government. For example, an airline might have been granted a monopoly

333

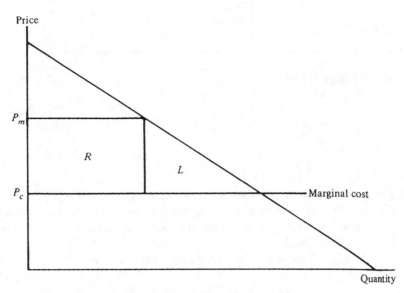

Figure 15.1. The social costs of monopoly with rent seeking.

over the routes between two or more cities. If there were more than one airline in the country that could service the routes, then R, or the present discounted value of R, would be a prize to be awarded to the airline that succeeds in inducing the government to grant it the monopoly over the routes. If the airlines could invest resources and increase the probability of obtaining the monopoly, they would do so. Tullock's (1967c) initial insight revealed that these invested resources may constitute a social cost of monopoly in addition to the welfare triangle L.

Buchanan (1980a, pp. 12–14) has identified three types of rent-seeking expenditures that may be socially wasteful:

1. The efforts and expenditures of the potential recipients of the monopoly
2. The efforts of the government officials to obtain or to react to the expenditures of the potential recipients
3. Third-party distortions induced by the monopoly itself or the government as a consequence of the rent-seeking activity

As examples of each of these, assume that the airlines employ lobbyists to bribe the government official who awards the routes. It becomes known that the income of this government official is supplemented by bribes, and thus lower-level government officials invest time studying the airlines industry to improve their chances of obtaining this position. Finally, assume that the government's additional tax revenue from creating the monopoly leads to a competition among other interest groups for subsidies or tax breaks. The lobbying effort of the airlines industry is an example of the first type of social waste. The extra efforts of the bureaucrats to be promoted is an example of the second category (assuming that they do not improve the route allocation process, which is a reasonable assumption if the awards are determined by the bribes). The expenditures induced by the other interest groups to capture the extra tax revenue generated are an example of the third category of social waste.

Note that the bribe itself is not regarded as a social waste. If an airline could win a monopoly position simply by offering a bribe, and this bribe could be costlessly transmitted to the government official awarding the routes, and this was all that the bribe brought about, then no social waste would be created by the bribe. It would simply be a further redistributional transfer from the passengers of the airline, through the airline to the government official. The social waste in passing the bribe comes in the transaction costs of making the bribe, the fee of the lobbyist, and the wasted time and money of the bureaucrats competing for the promotion that places them in the position to receive the bribes.[1]

Considerable attention has been devoted in the literature to the issue of whether the rents of monopoly are totally dissipated by socially wasteful expenditures to capture them. We shall explore this question with a series of models beginning with the basic rent-seeking model with a fixed number of players. We shall then consider the consequences of free entry, sequential plays of the game, and a number of extensions of the model that have been proposed.

15.1.1 *The basic rent-seeking model with a fixed number of players*

In the basic rent-seeking game n players each invest I to capture a rent of R. The probability that any individual rent seeker captures the rent is assumed to be proportional to her investment,

$$\pi_i(I_i) = \frac{f_i(I_i)}{\sum_{j=1}^{n} f_j(I_j)}, \tag{15.1}$$

where $\partial \pi_i / \partial I_i > 0$. Investments in rent seeking exhibit diminishing, constant, or increasing returns as $\partial^2 \pi_i / \partial I_i^2 < 0, = 0,$ or > 0. Tullock (1980) introduced this model under the assumption that $f_i(I_i) = I_i^r$, and much of the literature has explored this variant of the model. In this formulation, rent seeking has diminishing, constant, or increasing returns as $r < 1, = 1,$ or > 1.

Under the assumption that all rent seekers are risk neutral, each chooses the I that maximizes her expected gain $E(G)$,

$$E(G) = \left(\frac{I^r}{I^r + T} \right) R - I, \tag{15.2}$$

where T is the impact of the total outlays of the other $n - 1$ rent seekers, $T = \sum_{j \neq i} I_j^r$. Under the Cournot-Nash assumption that the other rent seekers' outlays remain fixed, the first-order condition from (15.2) is

$$\frac{r I^{r-1} R}{I^r + T} - \frac{r I^{r-1} I^r R}{(I^r + T)^2} - 1 = 0. \tag{15.3}$$

---

[1] That some expenditures to obtain rents may be transfers of one sort or another and not a pure social waste has been discussed by Brooks and Heijdra (1986). Congleton (1988) points out that the payment to the lobbyist is not simply a transfer, assuming that she could be employed doing something socially productive.

Assuming a symmetric equilibrium, we obtain from (15.3)

$$I = \frac{(n-1)}{n^2} r R. \tag{15.4}$$

A risk-neutral rent seeker invests the I given in (15.4), as long as this I when substituted into (15.2) yields a nonnegative expected gain. When the implied expected gain is negative, the potential rent seeker does not participate. Three sets of outcomes, depending on the value of r, are of special interest.

15.1.1.1 *Diminishing or constant returns, $r \le 1$.* Substituting (15.4) into (15.2) and rearranging, we obtain the following condition to ensure a nonnegative expected gain from participation:

$$\frac{n}{n-1} \ge r. \tag{15.5}$$

Since the minimum n of interest is two, $1 < n/(n-1) \le 2$, and (15.5) is satisfied for *all* $r \le 1$. With diminishing or constant returns to rent seeking, an equilibrium always exists with positive rent-seeking investments.

The total amount invested at this equilibrium is n times the I implied by (15.4),

$$nI = \frac{n(n-1)}{n^2} r R = \frac{(n-1)}{n} r R. \tag{15.6}$$

Dividing this number by R, we obtain the total amount invested in rent seeking as a fraction of the rents sought,

$$\frac{nI}{R} = \frac{(n-1)}{n} r. \tag{15.7}$$

With constant returns to scale an analogous result to that of the Cournot oligopoly model is obtained. The fraction of the total rent which is dissipated ranges from 1/2 for two rent seekers up to full dissipation as n approaches infinity.

With diminishing returns to rent seeking ($r < 1$), the fraction of the rent dissipated is *always* < 1. For example, with $r = 1/2$, the fraction of R dissipated must be between 1/4 and 1/2.

15.1.1.2 *Increasing returns with $1 < r \le 2$.* If $n \ge 2$, the upper bound of $n/(n-1)$ is 2, and (15.5) implies an upper bound for r of 2. With $r = 2$ and $n = 2$, each rent seeker invests $R/2$ and the total sum invested equals the total rent sought.

With smaller rs equilibria can exist with ns greater than 2. For example if $r = 1.5$, an equilibrium exists with $n = 3$ at which full dissipation occurs. If $n = 2$, only 3/4 of R is dissipated. The reason for the inverse relationship between r and the number of rent seekers who can exist in the rent-seeking game with $I > 0$ is easy to see from (15.4). Let I^* be the I that satisfies this optimality condition. Then $\partial I^*/\partial r = (n-1)R/n^2 > 0$. An increase in r holding n constant increases the optimal investment for each rent seeker, and thereby the likelihood that the sum of the investments exceeds R, at which point participation in the game becomes irrational. On the other hand, an increase in n reduces a rent seeker's optimal investment, $\partial I^*/\partial n < 0$, thus increasing the likelihood of an equilibrium with positive Is.

With $1 < r \leq 2$, full dissipation of R occurs for values of n and r, which satisfy (15.5) as an equality; for example, $n = 2$ and $r = 2$, $n = 3$ and $r = 1.5$, $n = 4$ and $r = 4/3$, and so on. For all other equilibria with $I > 0$, $nI < R$.

15.1.1.3 *Increasing returns with $r > 2$.* With $r > 2$, increasing returns are sufficiently strong that no pure strategy equilibria exist. The extreme form of increasing returns would resemble an auction with R going to the rent seeker making the highest I. Each rent seeker has an incentive to try to outbid the other rent seekers so long as $I < R$, and an escalation of bids can be anticipated that leads all I toward R. In a normal auction, as say for a painting, the highest bidder gets the painting and pays out the amount bid, while all other bidders return home absent the painting but still in possession of the money that they bid. The nature of rent seeking is such, however, that all rent seekers forfeit their investments. No politician gives back the campaign contributions and bribes he received from those who are not rewarded with tariffs, price supports, etc. In a rent-seeking, bidding contest nI would appear likely to approach nR (Tullock, 1980).

Before I reaches R, however, the expected gain to a rent seeker becomes negative, and a risk-neutral rent seeker drops out. After all rent seekers have dropped out, the competition can begin again. No Nash equilibrium in pure strategies exists for this game, but mixed-strategy equilibria do exist at which all rents are fully dissipated ex ante.[2]

A mixed strategy is one in which each rent seeker effectively pulls an I out of a hat containing an infinite number of different Is lying between zero and R. Since no rational, risk-neutral person will enter such a game if her expected gain is negative, it is not surprising to find that the expected payoffs from this game are zero. In an actual play of such a game, the Is each player draws will in general not sum to precisely equal R. Thus, overdissipation of R can be expected *on some occasions*, when there are significant increasing returns to rent seeking. Baye, Kovenock, and de Vries (1999) demonstrate that the probability of observing overdissipation declines with N, but only as far as 0.44, when $N = \infty$.

15.1.2 *The impact of free entry*

Whenever the expected gain to a rent seeker remains positive after the entry of additional rent seekers, n can be expected to increase if entry is unrestricted. We saw in Subsection 15.1.1 that an equilibrium always exists with $I > 0$, when $0 < r \leq 1$. Thus, entry can always be expected in this case with n approaching infinity. From (15.7) we obtain

$$\lim_{n \to \infty} \frac{nI}{R} = r. \tag{15.8}$$

[2] See Hillman and Samet (1987) and Baye, Kovenock, and de Vries (1994).

Thus, in the case of free entry and constant returns to scale ($r = 1$), we expect full dissipation of the rent. Following Posner (1975), most empirical studies that have tried to measure the losses from rent seeking have assumed constant returns and free entry, and thus have approximated the rent-seeking losses by the area of the monopoly rent rectangle.

With ($1 < r \leq 2$), some finite $n^* \geq 2$ exists, such that the expected gain from an I^* satisfying (15.4) is nonnegative, while for $n^* + 1$ the expected gain is negative. Free entry will thus produce an equilibrium at which $n = n^*$. R will be fully dissipated if this n^* is such that (15.5) is satisfied as an equality; less than fully dissipated if it is satisfied as an inequality. The smaller r is, the larger n^* is, and the greater is the expected fraction of R that is dissipated.

As noted in Subsection 15.1.1.3, with $r > 2$ the only equilibria to the game are mixed-strategy equilibria with the rents fully dissipated ex ante by the sum of rent-seeking investments. This result is independent of n.

15.1.3 *Rent seeking with sequential investments*

Up until this point we have assumed that all players choose the levels of their investments simultaneously. As already mentioned, this way of modeling rent seeking is analogous to the Cournot oligopoly model, *except* that the normative implications are reversed. Where increasing the number of sellers in an oligopoly increases output and thereby social welfare because price falls, increasing the number of players in a rent-seeking game *reduces* social welfare by increasing the total funds invested in rent seeking.

Sequential output choices in an oligopoly were first studied by the German mathematician von Stackelberg. In the von Stackelberg oligopoly model, the first player to select an output can take advantage of the negative-sloped reaction curves that characterize a quantity-setting game by selecting an output that is greater than the equilibrium output in the simultaneous-play, Cournot game. If two sellers have different costs of production, society is better off in a Stackelberg duopoly game if the lower cost seller goes first. Once again in a sequential-play, rent-seeking game the situation is exactly reversed. Less funds are invested and society is consequently better off if the more effective rent seeker goes second.

To see this, consider a simple two-player rent-seeking game in which the first player leads by choosing an investment I_L, and the second player follows with an investment I_F. The mathematics is somewhat simpler if we capture the relative effectiveness of each player's investments through a multiplicative factor α rather than through an exponential relationship. Thus, we write the probability that L wins the rent-seeking contest as

$$\pi_L(I_L) = \frac{I_L}{I_L + \alpha I_F}, \tag{15.9}$$

where $\alpha < 1$ implies that the first player's investments are more effective than those of the second, and $\alpha > 1$ implies the reverse. L's expected gain from playing the game can then be written as

$$E(G_L) = \left(\frac{I_L}{I_L + \alpha I_F}\right) R - I_L. \tag{15.10}$$

Maximizing (15.10) with respect to I_L produces

$$I_L = \sqrt{\alpha R I_F} - \alpha I_F. \tag{15.11}$$

The analogous exercise with respect to F's choice of I_F yields

$$I_F = \sqrt{\frac{R I_L}{\alpha}} - \frac{I_L}{\alpha}. \tag{15.12}$$

Equations (15.11) and (15.12) define the optimal choices of I_L and I_F, given the other player's investment. These two equations thus define the reaction functions for each player. L can exploit his first-mover advantage by substituting F's reaction function, (15.12), into L's gain function, (15.10), and choosing the I_L that maximizes this expression. Making this substitution we obtain

$$E(G_L) = \frac{I_L}{I_L + \alpha\left[\sqrt{\frac{I_L R}{\alpha}} - \frac{I_L}{\alpha}\right]} R - I_L. \tag{15.13}$$

which simplifies to

$$E(G_L) = \frac{I_L}{\sqrt{\alpha R I_L}} R - I_L. \tag{15.14}$$

Maximizing (15.14) with respect to I_L yields

$$I_L = \frac{R}{4\alpha}. \tag{15.15}$$

Substituting this value of I_L into (15.12) gives us follower F's optimal response to L:

$$I_F = \frac{R}{2\alpha}\left(1 - \frac{1}{2\alpha}\right). \tag{15.16}$$

It is easy to see from (15.15) and (15.16) that when the investments of both players are equally effective (that is, $\alpha = 1$), both invest the same amount, $R/4$, and the outcome is the same as under the simultaneous-play, Cournot game.

When $\alpha \neq 1$, the player whose investment is more effective earns a higher expected return by going *second*, while the weaker player earns a higher return by going first. This can be seen by using (15.15), (15.16), and (15.10) to obtain the expected gain from being the leader or follower:

$$E(G_L) = \frac{R}{4\alpha} \tag{15.17}$$

$$E(G_F) = R\left(1 - \frac{1}{2\alpha}\right)^2. \tag{15.18}$$

With $\alpha = 3/4$, the first player to choose an investment is the stronger player and his expected gain from (15.17) is $R/3$. Assuming the same relative strengths, but that the stronger play goes second, would imply $\alpha = 4/3$ and an expected gain for the now stronger, second player as given by (15.18) of $25R/64$, which is greater than $R/3$. If the players can choose both *when* to invest as well as how much, the stronger player will opt to go second, the weaker to go first, and society will be better off than under any alternative sequence, since the total amount invested will be minimized.

In this example we have assumed that the two players differ according to the relative effectiveness of their investments, as captured by α. An additional complication would be to assume that the two players value the rents differently. With $\alpha = 1$, the player who places the highest value on the rent will prefer to go second, and will make the highest investment. More generally, if α_1 measures the effectiveness of player 1's investments, α_2 the effectiveness of player 2's investments, and R_1 and R_2 are the values of the rents to the two players, then player 1 will invest more and opt to go second, if and only if $\alpha_1 R_1 > \alpha_2 R_2$.[3]

15.1.4 *Relaxing the assumptions*

The assumptions underlying the basic rent-seeking model have been relaxed in many ways. We shall not discuss every variant on this model that has been introduced. A few of the more important extensions warrant some attention, however.

15.1.4.1 *Risk-neutrality.* Consider first the effect of dropping the risk-neutrality assumption. Hillman and Katz (1984) illustrate the effects of risk aversion by rent seekers for the special case in which risk aversion is introduced by assuming that each individual has a logarithmic utility function. Table 15.1 is taken from their paper. The R/As are the rents to be gained relative to a rent seeker's initial wealth. The ns are the numbers of rent seekers. Note that when the rents to be won are small relative to the rent seeker's initial wealth (e.g., less than 20 percent), over 90 percent of the value of the rents is dissipated by the competition to obtain them. This result also holds when risk aversion is introduced by assuming other forms of utility functions (Hillman and Katz, 1984, pp. 105–7).

Much of the rent-seeking literature discusses the process as if rent seekers were individuals acting on their own behalf. In these cases, it is sometimes reasonable to assume that the value of the sort of rents sought is large relative to the initial assets of the rent seekers. But in most instances of rent seeking through the public sector, and probably in private sector rent seeking also, the size of the rents sought will be small relative to the assets of the rent seekers. If we assume that the stockholders of a corporation are the ultimate recipients of its profits, then the rents that the airline would earn by having a monopoly over an air route between two cities must be compared to the aggregate wealth of the stockholders of the airline. The rents that milk farmers earn from an increase in the price supports for milk must be divided

---

[3] Our exposition here has followed Leininger (1993). See also the more general results of Baik and Shogren (1992) who build on Dixit (1987), Hillman and Riley (1989), and Nitzan (1994a).

Table 15.1. *Competitive rent dissipation, logarithmic utility, A = 100*

R/A	n						
	2	3	5	10	50	100	1 000
0.10	98	97	96	96	95	95	95
0.20	95	94	93	92	91	91	91
0.50	88	85	83	82	81	81	81
1.00	76	74	72	70	70	69	69
5.00	32	34	35	36	36	36	36
10.00	18	21	22	23	24	24	24

Source: Hillman and Katz (1984).

by the assets of all milk farmers. In public sector rent seeking, the ratio of potential rents to initial assets of the relevant rent-seeking groups should be small, and the relevant rows of Table 15.1 are one and maybe two. Competitive rent seeking can be expected to result in nearly a full dissipation of the rents even when the rent seekers are risk-averse.[4]

The issue of the size of the rent seekers' assets becomes more complicated when we recognize the principal-agent problem in the joint stock company or the other forms of interest groups. The decision to invest airline revenues to win a monopoly on an air route is made by the airline's managers. To whose wealth should the investment be compared?

When the manager-agents of shareholders are the relevant actors in the rent-seeking game, the assumption that these actors are risk-averse is no longer very plausible. The bulk of the money that the airline's management is investing belongs to the company's shareholders, and this fact will induce managers to take greater risks (Jensen and Meckling, 1976). When rent seekers are agents investing the money of their principals, risk-taking behavior is more plausible than risk aversion, and an overdissipation of rents can be expected. Similar considerations probably apply to the rent-seeking actions of the agents of other interest groups (labor unions, farm associations).

Knight (1934) argued that the self-selection process for choosing entrepreneurs made entrepreneurs as a group risk takers. He thus predicted that aggregate profits would on average be negative owing to the overcompetition for profits by risk-taking entrepreneurs. Since profits and rents are one and the same to the individual entrepreneur, Knight's assumption would lead one to expect that entrepreneurial rent seeking under competitive conditions more than fully dissipates all potential rents. Moreover, this conclusion should hold whether the rents sought come from private market investments (e.g., advertising and patenting), or from political markets (campaign expenditures, lobbying). The principal-agent problem should, if anything, exaggerate this tendency.

---

[4] More generally, Konrad and Schlesinger (1997) show that an increase in the degree of risk aversion on the part of rent seekers has an *ambiguous* impact on the size of their investments.

15.1.4.2 *Rent seeking among groups.* When groups engage in rent seeking, there are two opposing effects on the levels of investment undertaken. First, by joining a group an individual effectively forms a cartel with all other members of the group. This increases the effectiveness of the group's rent-seeking efforts and increases the group's expected gain (Baik and Shogren, 1995). On the other hand, if the contributions of each group member are not specified with penalties imposed for underpayment, the usual free-rider problem arises and individuals tend to contribute less than the collectively optimal amounts – which of course from the point of view of society is good (Nitzan, 1991)!

Under the constant returns-to-scale assumption ($r = 1$ in (15.2)), the optimal payoff to each group member will be proportional to her contribution to the group's efforts, and the sum of all group investments will again tend to fully dissipate the rents sought (Lee, 1995).

15.1.4.3 *Rent seeking when the probability of winning is not defined logistically.* Using (15.1) to define the probabilities of each rent seeker's victory has the disadvantage of leaving these probabilities undefined when all investments are zero. A reasonable assumption to make in this case would be that each player has the same probability of winning, but then (15.1) would imply a discontinuous leap to one in the probability of victory for any player if she spends even a tiny sum to win the rent. Zero rent-seeking outlays is thus a very unstable equilibrium when the probabilities of success are defined logistically as in (15.1). This disadvantage can be avoided by assuming that the probabilities of winning the rent depend on the *differences* in the amounts spent on rent seeking rather than their ratios (Hirshleifer, 1989). This variant of the rent-seeking model also has some problematic implications, however. For example, with two rent seekers, A and B, the probability that A wins the rent takes the form $\pi_A = f(I_A - I_B)$. This probability will be the same whether A invests \$100 and B \$1, or A invests \$1,000,100 and B \$1,000,001.[5]

15.1.4.4 *Designing rent-seeking contests.* Much of the literature assumes that the value of the prize in a rent-seeking contest is the same for all players. The value of a license to import automobiles might well differ across potential importers, however. One airline may be able to make higher profits on a given route than another. When this is the case, the government may be able to increase the magnitude of the total rent-seeking outlays by appropriately structuring the rent-seeking contest.

Consider first a rent-seeking contest with two players who place the values R_1 and R_2 on the prize to be won – say, an import license. The prize will be awarded to the importer making the largest rent-seeking investment. No pure strategy equilibrium exists. When $R_1 = R_2 = R$, each player chooses an investment at random from the uniform distribution running from zero to R (Hillman and Samet, 1987). If $R_1 > R_2$, on the other hand, player 2 will realize that his optimal investment using this strategy is less than 1's, and thus that his chances of winning are less. This

---

[5] For an axiomatic characterization of the different types of rent-seeking contests, see Skaperdas (1996).

realization will induce 2 to invest still less than he would if $R_1 = R_2$. Thus, when one player places a much higher evaluation on the prize than do the other players, the other players are discouraged from investing, and the total rent-seeking outlays will be less than under a more equal distribution of payoffs to the rent seekers. Because of this, the government may actually increase its revenue from the rent-seeking contest by designing it in such a way that the player with the highest valuation is ineligible to compete for the prize.

To see this, consider a contest in which the prize is awarded to the player making the highest investment. The values of the prize to each player are $R_1 \geq R_2 > R_3 \geq \ldots R_n$. Baye, Kovenock, and de Vries (1993) have shown that in such a contest the maximum amount that the government can win, W, is given by the following expression:

$$ W = \left(1 + \frac{R_2}{R_1}\right) \frac{R_2}{2}. \tag{15.19} $$

Because of the decline in investments by players 2 through n as R_1 increases, W varies inversely with R_1. If now $R_1 = 100$, $R_2 = 50$, and $R_3 = 45$, (15.19) implies that W will be 37.5 with player 1 allowed to bid for the prize, and 42.75 with player 1 excluded from the game. Given the similar evaluations of the prize by players 2 and 3, the increase in their investments caused by player 1's exit from the game more than offsets the loss of 1's investment. One way for the government to exclude player 1 is to run the contest in two stages. The government first announces a "short list" of eligible bidders (importers) for the prize (license), and then allows those on the list to make investments (bribes, campaign contributions, and so on). Player 1 does not make it onto the short list.[6]

15.2   Rent seeking through regulation

The traditional economic rationale for regulation sees the regulated industry as a "natural monopoly" with falling long-run average costs. The classic bridge example is a polar case of the natural monopoly situation. A single bridge is needed and, once built, the marginal cost of allowing additional cars to cross it is zero (crowding aside). The optimal toll on the bridge is then zero. However, if a private firm operates the bridge, it sets the price at the revenue-maximizing level, and the result is a socially inefficient under-utilization of the bridge. Any industry with continuously falling long-run average costs is a "natural monopoly" in the sense that only one firm is needed to supply all of the industry's output. Regulation is said to be needed to restrain that one firm from taking advantage of its monopoly position. In terms of Figure 15.1, regulation is thought to be necessary to help consumers capture some fraction of the consumers' surplus triangle L.[7]

---

[6] For further discussion and additional examples of the optimal design of rent-seeking contests, see Nitzan (1994c) and Gradstein (1998).

[7] In practice, regulation in the United States has tended to resemble average cost pricing more than marginal cost pricing, so that some welfare triangle losses have occurred even when regulation has worked well (Kahn, 1970).

In the regulatory process, producer and consumer interests are opposed. The higher the price that the regulators set, the bigger the monopoly rent rectangle going to the producers. Since regulation is a political bureaucratic process, it is reasonable to assume that the sellers of a regulated product place some pressure on the regulators to raise price and increase the size of the rectangle. In a seminal contribution to the regulation debate, Stigler (1971) shifted attention away from largely normative discussions of what price should be to minimize L, to a positive analysis of how the struggle to secure R determines price. Although predating the rent-seeking literature, Stigler's paper draws attention to the rent-creating powers of regulators and the rent-seeking efforts of those regulated.

In an important extension of Stigler's argument, Peltzman (1976) integrated both consumers and producers into the rent-seeking struggle. He depicted regulation as being supplied by a vote-maximizing politician. Let V, the number of votes the politician receives, be a function of the utilities of both the regulated producers, U_R, and the consumers of the regulated product, U_C:

$$V = V(U_R, U_C), \qquad \frac{\partial V}{\partial U_R} > 0, \qquad \frac{\partial V}{\partial U_C} > 0. \tag{15.20}$$

For simplicity, assume consumer and regulator utilities are linear in R and L; that is,

$$U_R = R, \qquad U_C = K - R - L, \tag{15.21}$$

where K is an arbitrary constant. Then assuming that the proper second-order conditions hold to ensure an interior maximum, the vote-maximizing regulator sets price, P, to satisfy

$$\frac{dV}{dP} = \frac{\partial V}{\partial U_R}\frac{dR}{dP} - \frac{\partial V}{\partial U_C}\frac{dR}{dP} - \frac{\partial V}{\partial U_C}\frac{dL}{dP} = 0 \tag{15.22}$$

or

$$\frac{\partial V}{\partial U_R}\frac{dR}{dP} = \frac{\partial V}{\partial U_C}\left(\frac{dR}{dP} + \frac{dL}{dP}\right). \tag{15.23}$$

The vote-maximizing regulator sets a price such that the marginal gain in support from the producers for an increment in monopoly rents, R, is just offset by the loss in consumer votes from a combined rise in R and L.

Although most regulated industries are not monopolies, the number of sellers is generally small. It is certainly small relative to the number of consumers. The costs of organizing the producers and the concentration of the benefits, R, on each producer are likely to combine to make $\partial V/\partial U_R$ large relative to $\partial V/\partial U_C$, at least over an initial range of values for R (Olson, 1965; Stigler, 1971; Peltzman, 1976). Stigler (1971) stresses this point in arguing that the main beneficiaries of regulation are the regulated firms. Price will be raised until dR/dP falls sufficiently far, or $\partial V/\partial U_C$ becomes sufficiently large to bring (15.23) into equality. But note also that as long as $\partial V/\partial U_C > 0$ – that is, as long as there is some loss in votes from reducing consumer utility – (15.23) will not be satisfied at the rent-maximizing price, where $dR/dP = 0$. When $dR/dP = 0$, dL/dP is greater than zero, and that combined with $\partial V/\partial U_C > 0$ makes the right-hand side of (15.23) positive. The vote-maximizing politician may favor the regulated industry's producers, but stops short of setting price at the rent-maximizing level (Peltzman, 1976, pp. 222–41; Becker, 1976). Peltzman derives several interesting implications from his analysis. One is that "*either* naturally monopolistic or naturally competitive industries are more politically attractive to regulate than an oligopolistic hybrid" (1976, pp. 223–4, italics in original). Equation (15.23) implies that regulation brings price to a level somewhere between the pure monopoly and pure competition prices. Assuming oligopoly prices tend to lie intermediate between monopoly and competitive levels, then oligopolists and their consumers have less to gain from regulation than do the consumers of a natural monopoly product or the producers of a competitive product. By this argument, Peltzman helps to explain the ubiquitous regulation of agriculture around the world and other interventions in seemingly competitive industries like trucking and taxicabs in the United States.

Stigler (1971) emphasized the strength of the regulated groups in using the regulatory process to enhance their incomes, and several studies are supportive of this view of regulation (for example, Shepherd, 1978; Paul, 1982; Ulrich, Furtan, and Schmitz, 1987; Alexander, 1997). A classic example of the social costs of rent seeking through regulation was the commercial airline industry in the United States until it was deregulated in the late 1970s. The Civil Aeronautics Board (CAB) controlled price competition, but allowed airlines to compete for customers by offering non-price frills like free drinks, movies, and half-empty planes. The airlines competed away, through additional costs, the rents granted them by the prices that the CAB set (Douglas and Miller, 1974).

Posner (1975) assumed that the entire rectangle R is dissipated through rent-seeking outlays, and then used estimates of the rise in price brought about by regulation to calculate $R + L$ in several industries as a measure of the social costs of regulation. Posner's figures are reproduced in Table 15.2. The η_1 column presents demand elasticities calculated under the assumption that the industry sets price so as to maximize monopoly rents, $(P - MC)/P = 1/\eta$, using the independent estimates of the price rise under regulation. The estimates in the η_2 column are from econometric studies of demand elasticity for the industries. The C_1 and C_2 columns are measures of $R + L$ made using the η_1 and η_2 estimates, respectively. They are all fairly large, both in an absolute sense and relative to existing estimates of the social cost of monopoly in the private sector that rely only on measures of L.

Peltzman (1976) stressed the trade-off between consumer and regulator interests in the final vote-maximizing equilibrium. In trying to test the Peltzman generalization of the Stigler theory, scholars have generally tried to find variables that

Table 15.2. *Social costs of regulation*

	Regulatory price increase (%)	Demand elasticity		Costs (as % of industry sales)	
		η_1	η_2	C_1	C_2
Physician's services	0.40	3.500	0.575	0.42	0.31
Eyeglasses	0.34	0.394	0.450	0.39	0.24
Milk	0.11	10.00	0.339	0.15	0.10
Motor carriers	0.62	2.630	1.140	0.57	0.30
Oil	0.65	2.500	0.900	0.60	0.32
Airlines	0.66	2.500	2.360	0.60	0.19

Source: Posner (1975, p. 84). See original for references to sources for the various estimates.

measure both producer–seller and consumer interests. Leffler (1978), Keeler (1984), Primeaux, Filer, Herren, and Hollas (1984), and Becker (1986) all present evidence consistent with the view that both consumer and producer interests receive some weight in the final regulatory outcomes.

Paul and Schoening (1991) have extended the basic Peltzman model to include third-party rent seeking. They find evidence of third-party rent seeking, and support for the capture theory in their analysis of electricity price regulation. In particular, electricity prices are higher in states where the regulators are appointed than where they are elected. On the other hand, Teske (1991) found that elected commissioners were *more* willing to grant telephone rate changes in response to company requests. His case study of U.S. West does reveal that the firm was a very successful lobbyist, however.

Ippolito and Masson (1978) show that regulation in the milk industry redistributes rents from one group of producers to another, and from one group of consumers to another. Kamath's (1989) study of the regulation of the sugar market in India provides further evidence in support of the capture theory. Wise and Sandler (1994) also find that agricultural interests are able to influence legislation on pesticide regulation, while more diffuse, environmental interest groups were not successful. Salhofer, Hofreither, and Sinabell (2000) estimate the rectangle and triangle losses from rent seeking through agricultural protection in Austria. Although they find that Austrian farmers gain at the consumers' and taxpayers' expense, they find that up- and downstream producers in the food industry gain even more.

Two articles have employed the event-study approach to test for the presence of rent seeking. This approach examines changes in the stock prices of firms affected by regulations at the time that the regulations are announced. Schwert (1977) concluded from the declines in the market values of the major stock exchanges that consumers received substantial redistributive gains from the passage of legislation in the 1930s regulating the stock exchanges.

Beck and Connolly (1996), on the other hand, were not able to identify significant effects on the share prices of companies affected by government actions using a sample of 48 observations. Their explanation for the lack of any wealth effects from winning a rent-seeking contest is that kickbacks and other investments that the firms make fully offset the rents, which are eventually won. This explanation goes too far, however. Although we have seen that there are many assumptions under which the total outlays of *all* rent seekers may sum to the value of the prize sought, the outlays of the subset that actually wins the prize presumably fall short of it. If not, why would any rational person enter the contest? Beck and Connolly attempt to account for their findings by invoking the winner's curse. This, however, amounts to assuming that rent seekers are not rational.

15.3   Rent seeking and the political process

The Stigler-Peltzman theory of regulation begins with the conflict between the sellers and buyers over price, and analyzes how this conflict might be resolved by the state in response to political pressure from both sides. The two groups involved are easily identified, as are their interests. In other rent-seeking situations, both the identities of the rent-seeking groups and their interests may be more difficult to determine. A more general politico-economic model of the rent-seeking process is required.

Building on a paper by Stigler (1976), McCormick and Tollison (1981) attempt to develop such a model. They make the fundamental assumption that all legislation consists of wealth transfers. Legislatures are organized to transfer wealth efficiently. Each individual or interest group is a potential supplier of wealth transfers, and at the same time a potential demander. The legislature takes from those who are least capable of resisting the demands for wealth transfers and gives to those who are best organized for pressing their demands. Thus, like the Stigler-Peltzman theory of regulation, McCormick and Tollison's (1981, chs. 1–3) theory builds on Olson's (1965) theory of interest group formation.

To succeed in securing a wealth transfer, an interest group must win a majority of votes in both houses of a bicameral legislature. The more seats there are in each house, the more resources that must be devoted to winning legislator votes. Moreover, assuming that there are diminishing returns to securing votes in any house, holding the total number of seats constant, it is easier to win legislator votes the more evenly divided the total number of seats in the two houses is. McCormick and Tollison (1981, pp. 45–55) find that these two variables, number of seats and the ratio of seats in the two houses, are significantly related to the degree of economic and occupational regulation across the states, and to the total number of bills enacted. Campbell (1994) also argues that these two characteristics of New Hampshire's legislature explain its relatively low levels of taxes. McCormick and Tollison go on to analyze the determinants of legislator wages, gubernatorial salaries, and other issues (1981, chs. 4–7).

Complementing the McCormick-Tollison models of government is the theory of the independent judiciary put forward by Landes and Posner (1975). They too see legislators as selling legislation for "campaign contributions, votes, implicit promises of future favors, and sometimes outright bribes" (p. 877). In this setting, an independent judiciary can increase the value of the legislation sold today by making it somewhat immune from short-run political pressures that might try to thwart or overturn the intent of the legislation in the future. And this is apparently what the founding fathers had in mind when they established an independent judiciary in the Constitution. In the Landes-Posner theory, the first Amendment emerges "as a form of protective legislation extracted by an interest group consisting of publishers, journalists, pamphleteers, and others who derive pecuniary and non-pecuniary income from publication and advocacy of various sorts" (p. 893). By such fruit has the dismal science earned its reputation.

Less jaundiced implications emerge when interest groups are incorporated into the political process using one of the probabilistic voting models discussed in Chapter 12. In these models competition for votes leads each party to propose a platform, which maximizes some form of social welfare function in which all voters' utilities have positive weights. Although interest groups can be viewed as "buying legislation," once campaign contributions and lobbying are introduced into the models, they continue to imply that political outcomes are efficient insofar as they satisfy the Pareto-optimality condition.[8] These models have formed the logical foundation for much of the literature on endogenous trade policy to which we now turn.

15.4   Rent seeking through tariffs and quotas

15.4.1   *The economic effects of tariffs, quotas, and voluntary export restraints*

Few issues elicit greater agreement among economists than the proposition that society's welfare is maximized when there is free trade.[9] Yet tariffs, quotas, and other restrictions on international trade abound, and trade policy is a constant subject of political debate. As with regulation policies, one suspects that the allocative efficiency gains from free trade so obvious to the economist have been sacrificed to provide the equally obvious rents and redistributive gains that restrictions on trade engender.

To see what is involved, consider Figure 15.2. Let S_M be the supply of imports of product X, and S_D the supply of domestic production. S_T and D are the total supply and demand schedules in the domestic country. Under free trade, X_F is purchased at a price P_F, with output divided between domestic production, D_F, and imports, M_F. Now let a tariff be imposed on imports that shifts the import supply schedule including the tariff to S'_M. Total supply shifts to S'_T, and X_R divided into M_R and D_R is sold at a price P_R.

---

[8] See discussion in Chapter 20.
[9] For a review of the caveats, see Findlay and Wellisz (1986, pp. 221–2).

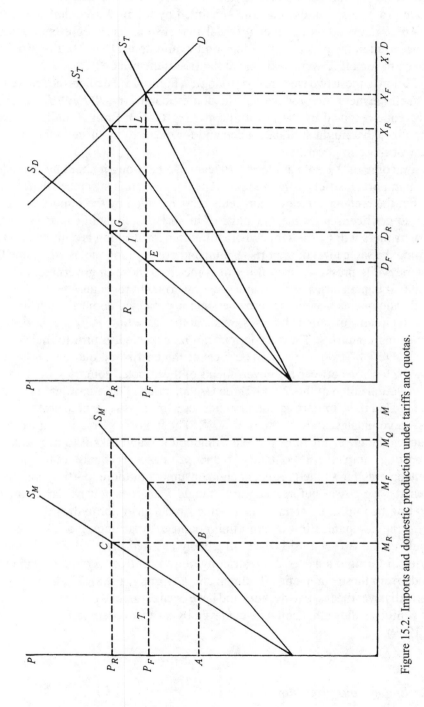

Figure 15.2. Imports and domestic production under tariffs and quotas.

349

The tariff brings about the welfare loss represented by the consumers' surplus triangle L on the foregone consumption $X_F - X_R$, and the triangle I under the domestic producers' supply schedule generated by the increased domestic output $D_R - D_F$. Triangle I constitutes a social loss insofar as it represents domestic resources used in the production of the additional output $D_R - D_F$ that would not have been needed if X were available at the free-trade price P_F.

In addition to these two welfare-loss triangles, Figure 15.2 depicts the rents earned by the factor owners and producers in the domestic industry, $R(P_R P_F E G)$, and the tariff revenue received by the government, $T(P_R C B A)$. Both R and T represent income flows that might stimulate a demand for the tariff by those in the protected industry or those in government.

The outcome of X_R sold at a price P_R can also be brought about by imposing a quota on imports restricting them to M_R. The domestic industry receives R in rents again, but the rectangle T now represents rents received by the importers "lucky" enough to get licenses for the M_R units of imports. Thus, political pressure from domestic sellers will be the same whether the trade restriction is a quota or a tariff (assuming the same level of imports results), but pressure for quotas will come from importers, while pressure for tariffs will come from those in government or from the eventual beneficiaries of the increase in government revenue.

Tariffs and quotas benefit factor owners in the protected domestic industries and perhaps recipients of import licenses, while at the same time harming producers in the exporting countries. These exporters can be expected to turn to their governments for "relief" from the adverse effects of the tariffs and quotas. The result is likely to be tension between the governments of the affected countries, or charges of treaty violations filed at the World Trade Organization. These unwanted outcomes can be avoided if the importing country chooses a third instrument to protect its producers – a voluntary export restriction, VER. The importing country's government approaches the government of the exporting country and asks it to negotiate with the exporting companies a "voluntary" reduction in exports equal, say, to $X_R - D_R$. The outcome as far as the producers and consumers in the importing country are concerned is exactly as before, but the rectangle T accrues now neither to the government of the importing country as revenue from a tariff nor to the importers, but rather to the companies in the exporting country. By arranging a VER the governments of the two countries have effectively assisted the producers in the two countries in forming a cartel and restricting output. Both governments can expect gratitude from these companies (Hillman and Ursprung, 1988). VERs have grown dramatically over the last two decades and have been estimated to result in protection levels as high as those that could be achieved by an ad valorem tariff of 40 percent (Tarr, 1989).

15.4.2 *Endogenous protection models*

Not all industries receive protection from import competition, and those that do receive it in varying degrees. How can one predict which industries will succeed at gaining protection? Several studies have sought to answer this question by treating protection as an endogenous variable in models, which try in some way to account for the influence of political factors.[10] In one such model Grossman and Helpman (1994) seek to explain the "sale of protection" with a model in which the government is assumed to maximize a weighted sum of the utilities of all citizens plus the political contributions of the lobbyists seeking protection. This objective function is very similar, of course, to the one that one obtains as a result of political competition in the probabilistic voting models. And it leads to similar results in terms of the implied efficiency of the protectionist outcomes. The welfare loss triangle L in Figure 15.2 will be smaller, the more inelastic the domestic demand for the product is, and thus their model predicts, ceteris paribus, higher tariffs on products with more inelastic demand schedules. Not surprisingly, it also predicts higher tariffs in industries in which interest groups are well organized.

Goldberg and Maggi (1999) found support for these and the other predictions of the model using 1983 data for 3-digit SIC industries in the United States. Their measure of protection is the level of nontariff trade barriers, while their measure of interest group strength is a dummy variable defined according to whether an industry's campaign contributions were above or below $100 million in 1981–2.

A study of protection that is somewhat more closely related to the rent-seeking literature is that of Lopez and Pagoulatos (1994). They first estimate the size of the rent-seeking rectangles, R and T in Figure 15.2, and then relate these to political action committee (PAC) contributions. They find a positive and highly significant relationship. The more industry PACs give to politicians, the larger are their rents from tariff protection.

Where Goldberg and Maggi (1999) and Lopez and Pagoulatos (1994) both relate measures of actual protection to PAC contributions, other studies have related the way congressmen vote on protectionist legislation to the levels and sources of their PAC contributions. Baldwin (1985, pp. 59–69) examined the effect of union contributions to congressmen on their vote on the Trade Act of 1974; Coughlin (1985) examined the effect of contributions from labor on congressional voting on the Automotive Products Act of 1982, a piece of domestic content legislation; and Tosini and Tower (1987) analyzed the effect of contributions by interest groups from the textile industry on congressional voting on the Textile Bill of 1985. All three studies found a positive and significant effect of the size of political contributions from the interest group, and the probability that a congressman voted in favor of the protective legislation. Other significant variables in these studies measure the importance of the industries that would be protected in the congressman's district or state, the unemployment rate in the state, and the congressman's party affiliation.[11]

Following earlier studies Lopez and Pagoulatos (1994) also include a measure of industry concentration in their model. This variable's inclusion can be justified

---

[10] See in particular Findlay and Wellisz (1982); Mayer (1984); Hillman (1982, 1989); Magee, Brock, and Young (1989); Vousden (1990); and Trefler (1993).

[11] See also the review of the effects of PAC contributions on congressmen's votes in Chapter 20.

on two grounds: first, the more highly concentrated an industry, the easier it is to organize and thus the more effective its lobbying may be (Olson, 1965). Second, the more concentrated an industry, the easier it is for its producers to raise prices and take advantage of a reduction in competition from foreign producers. In addition to Lopez and Pagoulatos, studies by Pincus (1975), Marvel and Ray (1983), Godek (1985), and Trefler (1993) have also found tariffs to be higher in concentrated industries. Caves (1976) and Finger, Hall, and Nelson (1982) found industry concentration to be negatively related to tariff protection, however.

The same logic that predicts a positive correlation between seller concentration ratios and trade protection leads one to expect a negative correlation between buyer concentration and protection, and this too has been observed (Pincus, 1975; Trefler, 1993).

The Olsonian argument about group size and effectiveness in organizing receives further support from the fact that farmers receive more protection in the developed countries where they are small in number than in the developing countries where their numbers are large (Balisacan and Roumasset, 1987). The generally higher levels of tariffs in consumer goods industries further support the Olsonian argument (Baack and Ray, 1983; Marvel and Ray, 1983; Ray, 1991).

While consumers generally tend to be poorly organized, workers are often very well organized, and thus it is not surprising to find that tariff protection tends to be higher for labor-intensive industries (Caves, 1976; Anderson, 1980; Saunders, 1980; Ray, 1981, 1991; Marvel and Ray, 1983; Dougan, 1984; Baldwin, 1985).

These studies reveal that the political process responds to interest group pressure by offering trade protection. They do not answer the question, however, of whether this protection "merely" results in transfers to the favored factor owners, or whether it induces investments that dissipate the transfers. In her pioneering article, Krueger (1974, pp. 52–4) enumerated the many forms of social waste that can arise when governments "sell protection": (1) construction of excess plant capacity, when licenses are awarded in proportion to firms' plant capacities; (2) excessive entry and therefore less than optimal-sized firms, when licenses are allocated pro rata to applicants; (3) lobbying efforts and bribes in the form of hiring relatives of customs officials who are less productive than their earnings, to obtain import licenses; and (4) the wasteful competition among those in the government to be in a position to receive bribes.

Krueger presented data on the rents generated from several categories of licenses in India, the largest of which was imports, indicating a potential loss from rent seeking in 1964 of 7.3 percent of national income. Figures for 1968 for import licenses in Turkey implied a waste of resources equivalent to 15 percent of GNP (Krueger, 1974, pp. 55–7). As with Posner's calculations, these estimates are rough, but nonetheless impressive.

In the rent-seeking model of a natural monopoly, we start with the monopoly already in existence, and the issue is simply how much of its monopoly position it exploits and whether the rents are fully dissipated. The natural starting point when thinking about rent seeking through trade protection is, however, perfectly free trade. From this starting point trade protection results in both Harberger-triangle losses and potential rent-dissipating investments. If the latter are sufficiently large to dissipate the full, potential rent, then the social costs from rent seeking through trade protection exceed the size of the rectangle.[12]

15.4.3 *Remaining puzzles*

The bulk of the endogenous trade policy literature begins with the assumption that governments use trade policy to redistribute income to certain groups, and then tries to explain which groups will be so favored and to what degree. In his excellent survey of this literature, Rodrik (1995) raises two troublesome questions. If the goal of trade policy is to redistribute rents and incomes, why do governments choose such an inefficient policy instrument to achieve this goal instead of relying, say, on direct income transfers and tax cuts, production subsidies, and the like, which generally have much smaller deadweight losses associated with them? Why do governmental interventions with free trade so overwhelmingly take the form of *restrictions* on trade like tariffs and quotas instead of stimuli to trade like export subsidies, given that the latter often dominate trade restrictions in terms of efficiency? Rodrik reviews the scant number of rational choice models that has addressed these two questions, but fails to come up with satisfactory answers.

The questions Rodrik raises with respect to trade policies are essentially the same questions public finance economists have raised for many years about the simultaneous popularity and inefficiency of in-kind transfers in comparison to cash transfers as a way to redistribute income. My personal hunch is that to answer these questions fully, one must step outside of the narrow bounds of rational choice models.

One might begin, for example, with the "irrational" asymmetry between the weights people place on a given loss in income relative to an equivalent gain in income (Kahneman and Tversky, 1979, 1984). This asymmetry would lead one to expect that people would lobby much more vigorously to reverse a loss of income caused by an expansion of imports than they would to obtain an increase income from an export subsidy. A related psychological factor is a sort of "Duesenberry effect" of subsidies. People become accustomed to a subsidy and lobby much more vigorously against its removal than they do for its introduction. These psychological regularities fit nicely with several of the "stylized facts" of trade policy: (1) trade protection is often a response to invents that adversely affect certain groups or industries like a sharp drop in the price of an imported good or a recession (Kurth, 1979; Takacs, 1981; McKeown, 1983; Ray, 1987; Magee, Brock, and Young, 1989, ch. 11; Hansen, 1990; Trefler, 1993; Rama, 1994; O'Halloran, 1994); (2) actual levels of trade protection or efforts to obtain relief are positively related to unemployment rates both over time and cross-sectionally (Takacs, 1981; Magee, 1982; Baldwin, 1985, pp. 142–80; Bohara and Kaempfer, 1991; Schuknecht, 1991; Trefler, 1993; Das and Das, 1994); and (3) the "path dependence" of trade protection. Once a trade

---

[12] It is possible, however, when one starts in a second-best situation, that rent seeking can sometimes improve welfare, as, for example, by eliminating a trade barrier (Bhagwati and Srinivasan, 1980; Bhagwati, 1982).

restriction is put into place, it tends to persist over time (Brainard and Verdier, 1997; Gardner and Kimbrough, 1989).

It should be noted that to the extent that irrational behavior is part of the explanation of the pervasive use of trade restrictions to redistribute income, it is only the behavior of those seeking compensation that is irrational in that they appear to *over*react to certain adverse events. The political response in catering to this lobbying effort may be perfectly rational – that is, vote-maximizing – on the part of the parties in government. Indeed, because of the difficulty of identifying and quantifying the losses to individual factor owners from events like a sharp drop in the price of an imported good, a tariff or quota may be the lowest cost way of channeling the redistribution to the "right" recipients (Feenstra and Lewis, 1991).

15.5   Rent seeking in other governmental activities

Regulation and trade restrictions are but two ways in which government alters the distribution of income. Direct transfers are a third, and they too can give rise to investments to change their size and the direction of their flow (Tullock, 1971d). More generally, Aranson and Ordeshook (1981, pp. 81–2) stress that even the production of a good with public good characteristics, like a highway, has distributional effects that may significantly influence the collective decision to provide the good:

> A larger view of production would embrace the idea that some contractor must build a road to the exclusion of other contractors. Some concrete manufacturer receives a subcontract while other manufacturers do not. Some bureaucrats must receive the wages for planning and overseeing construction, while another bureaucrat (or his agency) or even private sector taxpayers do not. And, those who speculate correctly on land in one area gain a windfall over those who speculate incorrectly elsewhere. In sum, a federally funded interstate highway system in production can be much like a private good; its supply is limited and subject to exclusion.

The entire federal budget can be viewed as a gigantic rent up for grabs for those who can exert the most political muscle.

The distributional consequences of government contracting can be expected to influence the flow of lobbying and campaign expenditures as in the rent-seeking models. Campaign expenditures should come from those seeking government contracts, and contracts should flow to those making contributions. Zardkoohi (1985) has found that the amount of campaign contributions a firm makes is positively and significantly related to the percentages of federal and state government outputs purchased by the firm's industry, and whether or not industry-specific regulation was applicable to the firm's industry. Wallis (1986) found that in the 1930s large states used their numerical advantages in the House to garner greater shares of federal relief programs than the Senate was willing to award them. Not surprisingly, those who work in the government also participate in the rent-seeking game. Waters and Moore (1990) have shown that the passage of state laws favoring public sector employees is positively related to measures of the strength of public employee

Table 15.3. *Estimates of the welfare losses from rent seeking*

Study	Economy	Year	Welfare loss
Krueger (1974)	India	1964	7% GNP
Krueger (1974)	Turkey	1968	15% GNP (trade sector)
Posner (1975)	United States	various years	3% GNP (regulation)
Cowling and Mueller (1978)	United States	1963–6	13% GCP[a] (private monopoly)
Cowling and Mueller (1978)	United Kingdom	1968–9	7% GCP[a] (private monopoly)
Ross (1984)	Kenya	1980	38% GDP (trade sector)
Mohammad and Whalley (1984)	India	1980–1	25–40% GNP
Laband and Sophocleus (1988)	United States	1985	50% GNP
Lopez and Pagoulatos (1994)	United States	1987	12.5% of domestic consumption

[a] GCP = gross corporate product.
Source: Adapted from Tollison (1997, Table 1, p. 514).

unions and inversely related to the strength of those interest groups which oppose them.

15.6   How large are the welfare losses from rent seeking?

Estimates of the welfare losses from rent seeking divide themselves into two categories. One set proxies the welfare losses by the areas of the profit rectangles and welfare triangles caused by tariffs or market power, or uses other proxies like increases in government spending. These estimates tend to be quite large ranging up to 50 percent of GDP. A few illustrative examples are given in Table 15.3.

A second group of studies uses the money actually spent on lobbying and the like. These studies have come up with estimates suggesting that the welfare losses are tiny fractions of the rents involved. For example, Dougan and Snyder (1993) calculate that federal oil regulation in the 1970s resulted in a net welfare-triangle loss of some $1.1 billion. The combined lobbying outlays of the interest groups affected by the regulation was estimated to be $125 million – 11 percent of the *triangle* loss.[13]

A similar conclusion can be drawn from Goldberg and Maggi's (1999) estimates for the Grossman/Helpman model. Recall that this model presumes that the government maximizes a weighted sum of the utilities of all citizens and the outlays of the interest groups. Goldberg and Maggi's estimates imply a weight of 0.98 on the welfare of the citizens, and 0.02 on that of the interest groups. These weights appear less surprising when one recognizes that impediments to international trade in the

---

[13] See also Tullock (1988).

United States are on average rather low. Although rent seeking through protectionist measures occurs and it has the predicted consequences, its effects do not appear to be very significant.

Before one removes rent-seeking costs entirely from one's list of social ineffi-ciencies, however, one must recall that the outlays of those who successfully obtain rents are only a part of the social waste from rent seeking. To the investments of the successful rent seekers in the petroleum industry, one must add the outlays of unsuccessful rent seekers in other industries who were encouraged to try their luck after observing government policies in this industry. Moreover, the wealth changes that government policies bring about induce additional investments by those who try to anticipate these changes and profit from this knowledge. When the defense department announces that General Dynamics has won the competition for a par-ticular weapons system and Boeing has lost, the typical stock market reaction is a rise in the price of General Dynamic's shares and a fall in the price of Boeing's shares. Anyone with knowledge of this contract decision before it is announced can earn a handsome profit on the stock market, even though she has no direct stake in the rents distributed by the government. The investments in information gathering to *anticipate* rent transfers must be added to the investments made to bring them about when calculating the full costs of rent seeking (Hirshleifer, 1971; Tollison, 1989.)

This latter example reminds us that rent seeking does not only occur in the public sector, and any attempt to estimate the total costs of rent seeking in the economy must include the costs of rent seeking in the private sector. An army of stockbrokers and analysts exists on Wall Street and elsewhere throughout the country. Billions of dollars are spent gathering information about companies so that investors can choose the "right companies" for their portfolios. Although an efficient capital market does lower the cost of capital to firms seeking capital on the equity market, only a small fraction of each year's annual investment by companies is financed through new issues of stock. Over 95 percent of the shares traded are not new issues. Any gain that a trader makes by buying shares in the "right company" is offset by a loss suffered by the person who sold the shares. The fact that some companies earn large rents and these rents fluctuate over time leads to tremendous investments in time and money by those who try and anticipate these changes and profit from them.

Cowling and Mueller (1978) included all corporate advertising in their estimates of the social costs of monopoly. Some advertising does inform buyers about cer-tain characteristics of a product and improves the allocation of resources; thus, all advertising cannot be regarded as a social waste. But a great deal of advertising is intended merely to redistribute the rents being earned by companies in a given market. Some nontrivial fraction of all corporate advertising must be regarded as rent-seeking investments.

The same can be said for some fraction of R&D expenditures, and for the patent lawyer fees that make R&D profitable. Indeed, a large fraction of the activities of *all* lawyers can be regarded as pure rent seeking. Rent seeking by lawyers has been linked to slow economic growth (Courbois, 1991). Rama (1994) has also shown that rent seeking via trade protection has had adverse effects on economic growth in Uruguay, albeit with a considerable lag. More generally, the evidence that the size of the government sector is inversely related to growth rates in the developed countries can be interpreted as evidence of the costs of rent seeking to the extent that rent seeking produces larger government sectors (see discussion in Chapter 22).

This observation suggests an alternative procedure for estimating the welfare losses from rent seeking in a society to those commonly employed. One could go through the national income accounts and identify all activities that are solely or primarily related to rent seeking. Such an exercise would produce a list that goes well beyond the lobbyists and people involved in political advertising. Although one cannot imagine a healthy capitalist economy without any stock analysts, lawyers, corporate advertising, and the like, it seems equally obvious that the tremendous rents generated by an economy like that of the United States have produced an equally impressive number of rent seekers.

In closing this chapter, it is interesting to compare the approach to measuring the social costs of rent seeking just described with the attempt by Phillips (1966) some time ago to measure "the social costs of monopoly capitalism." He too proceeded by adding different items from the national income accounts. His criterion was different, however; namely, activities that existed under monopoly capitalism that would not exist in an ideal socialist state. Thus, he included all defense expenditures, since in 1966 these were solely intended to protect American capitalism from Soviet communism. Although most public choice scholars would probably regard *some* of the defense budget as providing a pure public good, most would also probably agree with Aranson and Ordeshook (1981) that some fraction is also simply due to rent seeking.

Interestingly, Phillips (1966) included all the income of lawyers as part of the social cost of monopoly capitalism. This item would, as already noted, also figure prominently in any complete inventory of the social costs of rent seeking. Phillips also included all advertising. When he finished his list summed to 50 percent of GDP – a figure which matches the largest of those that have been estimated in the rent-seeking literature.

Bibliographical notes

The seminal contributions of Tullock (1967c) and Krueger (1974) along with several others have been brought together in a rent-seeking anthology by Buchanan, Tollison, and Tullock (1980).

Tollison (1982, 1997) and Nitzan (1994b) have surveyed the rent-seeking literature. The public choice literature concerning the determinants of protectionism has been reviewed by Frey (1984, chs. 2 and 3; 1985 in German; 1985, chs. 2 and 3); Nelson (1988); Hillman (1989); Magee, Brock, and Young (1989); Rodrik (1995); and Magee (1997). Bhagwati and Rosendorff (2001) collect some of the major contributions in this literature.

To the extent that bribes are pure transfers, they do not strictly belong to the wasteful rent-seeking category. But they do belong to the seamy tail of the distribution of activities rent seekers pursue. Hillman and Ursprung (2000) show how rent seeking in the form of bribes and corruption can lead to a nation's economic decline. Rose-Ackerman (1978, 1999) analyzes corruption from a public choice perspective. Her books are good complements to the rent-seeking literature.

CHAPTER 16

Bureaucracy

There can be no doubt, that if power is granted to a body of men, called representatives, they, like any other men, will use their power, not for the advantage of the community, but for their own advantage, if they can.

James Mill

Each official is evidently more active within the body to which he belongs than each citizen within that to which he belongs. The government's actions are accordingly influenced by the private wills *of its members* much more than the sovereign's [citizenry's] by those of its members – if only because the official is almost always individually responsible for any specific function of sovereignty. (Italics in original)

Jean-Jacques Rousseau

The preceding chapters have focused upon the demand side of public choice. The citizen voter's preferences determine outcomes in the public sector. Government, like the market in a pure exchange economy, is viewed simply as an institution for aggregating or balancing individual demands for public policies. Those in government, the candidates and representatives, have been depicted as single-mindedly seeking to be elected. To do so they must please voters, so that those in government are merely pawns of those outside in a competitive political system. Only in the rent-seeking literature just reviewed does one begin to obtain a glimpse of another side of government. Politicians may not live by votes alone. They, too, may seek wealth and leisure. Their preferences may impinge on the outcomes of the public sector.

In this chapter and the next we examine several models that give those in government a role in determining policies beyond that of simply carrying out the revealed demands of the citizens. These may be viewed as models of the supply of government policies.

In many cases government outputs are supplied by government controlled or regulated *bureaucracies*. The term "bureaucracy" was introduced by the French philosopher, Vincent de Gourmay, in 1765, and has had since its introduction a negative connotation (van Creveld, 1999, p. 137). While the term *laissez faire*, also introduced by de Gourmay, conjures up images of freedom of action and efficiency – at least to an economist – the term *bureaucracy* suggests routinized and constrained behavior, and inefficiency. The antithesis of the iconoclastic entrepreneur operating in free markets is the conformist bureaucraat seated behind his desk.

The bureaucrat, like everyone else, can be assumed to be a selfish utility maximizer. But what is it that he maximizes? Weber (1947) assumed that the bureaucrat's natural objective was *power*. "Power" is a concept frequently employed by political scientists and sociologists, and totally ignored by economists[1] and practitioners of public choice. Given Weber's stature as a social scientist, it seems prudent to pay some heed to his thinking on this matter. As we shall see in the following section, there is an interpretation of political power that not only is prominent in the political science and sociology literature, but also fits in well with the analysis of government and bureaucracy in public choice. We begin by developing this concept, and then turn to models that grant the government a degree of power over the citizens.

16.1   Uncertainty, information, and power

At the most intuitive level, the word "power" connotes the ability or capacity to do something (Wagner, 1969, pp. 3–4).[2] But "something" can stand for a variety of objects, each of which leads to a different kind of power. Physical power is the ability to apply force. Economic power is the capacity to purchase goods, and so on. Political power must be defined as the ability to achieve certain ends through a political process. To observe the exercise of political power, some actors must have conflicting goals. If all members of a committee, including A, favor x over y and x is chosen, we cannot say that A has exercised power. If only A favors x and x is chosen, A has political power.

Russell (1938) defined three ways in which an individual can exert influence in a political context: (1) by exercising direct physical power, for example, by imprisonment or death; (2) by offering rewards and punishments; and (3) by exerting influence on opinion through the use of education and propaganda. The first two are closely related to a more general type of political power, which we might call procedural power. A might achieve his choice of x because the rules of the committee make him dictator, or grant him the right to set an agenda by which the committee is led to choose x. The procedural power granted the agenda setter figures prominently in one of the models examined below. But it is the third source of influence Russell listed that is most closely related to a more general notion of political power. Education, propaganda, and persuasion are all forms of information. Information has value, or grants power, only in the presence of uncertainty. Uncertainty creates the potential to exercise power; information provides the capacity to do so.

Political power means inducing someone to do something that he did not want to do, as when A gets a committee to choose x when all but A favor feasible alternative y (Simon, 1953; Dahl, 1957, p. 80). In the agenda-setter example discussed in Chapter 5, it was not simply the authority A has to set the agenda that brought about this outcome. It was the *knowledge* A had of every other committee member's preferences, coupled with their *ignorance* of the sequence of votes that would be

---

[1] Market power, the ability to raise price, is a limited use of the term by economists.
[2] This section borrows heavily from Mueller (1980).

taken. Given this uncertainty on the part of all committee members save A, A could induce the committee to choose z over y, z' over z, and so on until x was reached. But if all committee members save A favor y over x, they could impose y by not voting for z against y. Their lack of information compared to A gave A the power to use his position as agenda setter to bring about x's victory.

Returning to Russell's list of sources of power, we can see that it is the uncertainty that surrounds a dictator's use of physical power or a supervisor's issuance of rewards and punishments that allows these people to control their subordinates. If B knows with certainty that A will give him a reward if B does X, as the rules require it, then B in carrying out X exercises as much power over A as A does over B. In a bureaucracy in which no uncertainty existed, lines of authority might exist, but no real power would accompany authority. All employees would know all of the possible events that might occur and all could predict the eventual outcomes or decisions that would follow each. Employee grievance procedures would be completely codified and both the supervisor's and the employee's reaction to any situation would be perfectly predictable. In a world of complete certainty, all individuals are essentially acting out a part, "going by the rules," and those at the top of the bureaucracies are as devoid of discretionary power as those at the bottom. All power is purely procedural (see Simon, 1953, p. 72).

This type of situation comes close to the conditions existing in the French monopoly that Crozier (1964) described in *The Bureaucratic Phenomenon*. As Crozier depicts it, the monopoly does operate in a world of certainty, with one exception: the machines sometimes break down. This places the women operating the machines completely under the power of the mechanics responsible for repairing them, since the women have a quota of output for each day and must work harder to make up for any downtime. More interesting, the supervisors who nominally have more authority also have less power than the mechanics. Since the mechanics know how to repair the machines, and the supervisors do not, the supervisors are unable to exert any real control over the mechanics (Crozier, 1964, pp. 98–111).

It is instructive to note the tactics used by the mechanics to preserve their power. The operators were severely scolded for "tinkering" with their machines in an effort to keep them going or to repair them. Only the mechanics knew how to repair the machines; each machine was different, and just how it needed to be fixed was known only to the mechanics. Repairing them was an art, not a science. When clashes arose between the mechanics and the supervisors, it was over whether the latter could, on occasion, work at repairing the machines. The supervisors were further hampered in this endeavor by the continual "mysterious" disappearance of machine blueprints from the factory. The mechanics always worked without the aid of blueprints.

One sees in the power exerted by the mechanics in Crozier's case study a modest form of the power of experts in a bureaucracy. Max Weber emphasized the power of expertise, and it will appear again in the models discussed next. More generally, we shall see that all incorporate assumptions in various ways regarding the power stemming from asymmetric possession of information in a world of uncertainty.

16.2   The budget-maximizing bureaucrat

Bureaucratic man pursues power. Economic man pursues profit. In Knight's (1921) theory of profit, profit exits because of uncertainty and is earned by those who possess the daring and *information* to allow them to make correct decisions under uncertainty. Thus, there is a close link between the economic theory of profit and the political theory of power. Both profit and power exist owing to uncertainty; both accrue to the possessors of information.

In the modern corporation, the information gatherers and processors of information are the managers. They are the possessors of power. A major difference between the business corporation and the public bureau is that the power of managers can be monetarized. The business of corporations is making profits, and managers as information gatherers are its main recipients.

Legally, however, corporations belong to the stockholders, and the custom persists that they are the rightful recipients of corporate profits. Thus, managers are unable to pay themselves all the profits they create. They are forced to claim corporate profits in less conspicuous ways than simply salaries and cash bonuses. Numerous substitute goals have been put forward: on-the-job consumption, excess staff and emoluments (Williamson, 1964), security (Fisher and Hall, 1969; Amihud and Lev, 1981), and a host of nonpecuniary goals that one can lump together under the heading of X-inefficiency (Leibenstein, 1966; Comanor and Leibenstein, 1969).

Many of the nonpecuniary goals of managers are likely to be correlated with the size or growth in size of the corporation (Baumol, 1959; Marris, 1964, ch. 2). Large size can also be used as a justification for higher compensation packages, and thus can allow managers to justify greater direct cash payments to themselves. The bigger and more complex the firm is, the more difficult it is for stockholders to monitor the activities of managers, and the more power managers have. Thus, size and growth in size are plausible goals, along with profits, of corporate managers.

The pursuit of profits is not the perceived legitimate goal of public bureaus, and thus it is even more difficult for public bureaucrats to convert the power they have into income. The nonpecuniary goals of management become the logical objectives of the public bureaucrat. Among these, size and risk aversion have received the most attention. The first systematic effort to study bureaucracies within a public choice framework was made by William Niskanen, and we turn now to his model of bureaucracy.[3]

16.2.1 *Environment and incentives*

One of the key characteristics of a government bureau is the nonmarket nature of its output (Downs, 1967, pp. 24–5). Indeed, a bureau does not typically supply a number of units of output as such, but levels of *activities* from which output levels

---

[3] Niskanen's book (1971) was preceded by two insightful looks at bureaucracy by Tullock (1965) and Downs (1967). Although written by two of the founding fathers of the public choice field, these earlier works do not attempt to develop a theory or model of bureaucracy from a public choice perspective. Instead, they use the economics methodology to examine various facets of bureaucratic organizations.

must be inferred (Niskanen, 1971, pp. 24–6). Thus, the Department of Defense maintains numbers of combat personnel and weapon systems, although it supplies various degrees (units) of defensive and offensive capabilities. Its budget is defined over the activities it maintains, even though the purchasers – the taxpayers and their representatives – are ultimately interested only in the "final outputs" of combat capabilities that these activities produce. The reason for this is obvious: it is easier to count soldiers and airplanes than it is units of protection. This "measurement problem," inherent in so many of the goods and services that public bureaus provide, creates a monitoring problem for the funding agency. Given the unmeasurable nature of a bureau's outputs, how can the purchaser monitor the efficiency of its production?

The monitoring problem is intensified by the bilateral monopoly nature of the bureau–sponsor relationship (Niskanen, 1971, p. 24). That the buyer of a bureau's output would be a monopsonist follows almost from the nature of the good sold. A public good is by definition consumed by all the people, and the agent of all the people is a monopsonist buyer on their behalf. Of course, we have seen that the government may not engage in the supply of only pure public goods, but, nevertheless, it remains the sole agent of whatever interest group it represents in dealing with public bureaucracies. Even if the government acts as the sole agent for the population, or an interest group, it does not necessarily have to buy from a single source, even though if often does. The usual reason for granting a bureau a monopoly on the provision of a given service is to avoid wasteful duplication. Although there is certainly some validity in this justification, the monopoly nature of most bureaus also frees them from competitive pressure to be efficient and denies the funding agency an alternative source of information by which to gauge the efficiency of the monopolist bureaus, thus compounding the monitoring problem inherent in the nature of the bureau's output.

Inefficient production of a bureau's services is further induced by the scheme of compensation of bureaucrats. While managers in a private corporation can usually claim a share of the savings (profits) generated by an increase in efficiency, public bureaucrats' salaries are either unrelated or indirectly, and perhaps inversely (Warren, 1975), related to improved efficiency. Thus, the public bureau is characterized by weak external control on efficiency and weak internal incentives.

If the bureaucrat has no financial incentive to pursue greater efficiency, what are his goals, and how are they related to efficiency? Niskanen (1971, p. 38) lists the following possible goals of a bureaucrat: "salary, perquisites of the office, public reputation, power, patronage, output of the bureau, ease of making changes, and ease in managing the bureau."[4] He then asserts that all but the last two are positively and monotonically related to the size of the budget.

16.2.2 *The model*

The bureau receives a budget from its funding agency (say, congress or the parliament), which is a function of the *perceived* output of the bureau's service:

$$B = B(Q), \qquad B' > 0, \qquad B'' < 0. \tag{16.1}$$

---

[4] Downs also devotes a good deal of space to the goals of bureaucrats (1967, pp. 81–111).

This function may be thought of as a public benefit or utility function. Public benefits are assumed to increase, but at a diminishing rate, with increasing output.

The bureau has a cost function for producing its output that, over the relevant range at least, increases at an increasing rate like a competitive firms's cost schedule:

$$C = C(Q), \qquad C' > 0, \qquad C'' > 0. \tag{16.2}$$

This cost schedule is known only to the bureau's members (or a subset thereof). This is how the monitoring problem arises. The funder knows its total benefit schedule (16.1), but sees only an activity budget from the bureau. Therefore it cannot determine whether this output is being supplied Pareto efficiently, that is, if, at the margin, public benefits equal public costs. The funder sees only the total output of the bureau and its total budget. This frees the bureau to maximize its budget subject to the constraint that its budget cover the costs of production. If we assume that the bureau does not turn money back to the funder, this constraint is satisfied as an equality and the bureau's objective function is

$$O_B = B(Q) + \lambda(B(Q) - C(Q)), \tag{16.3}$$

whose first-order condition yields

$$B'(Q) = \frac{\lambda}{1 + \lambda} C'(Q) \tag{16.4}$$

$$B(Q) = C(Q). \tag{16.5}$$

Optimality from the point of view of the funder requires that the marginal benefit of an extra unit of output to the funder equal its marginal cost to the bureau:

$$B'(Q) = C'(Q). \tag{16.6}$$

The Lagrangian multiplier represents the marginal utility of an expansion of the budget constraint to the bureau and is positive. Thus, (16.4) implies that $B' < C'$. The budget is expanded beyond the point where marginal public benefits equal marginal costs. If B and C are quadratic, B' and C' become straight lines and we have the situation depicted in Figure 16.1, taken from Niskanen (1971, p. 47). Instead of requesting a budget that would result in the output Q_0, and thereby maximize the net benefits of the funder, the bureau requests the larger budget consistent with the output Q^*. At Q^* triangle E equals triangle F. All of the consumer surplus gains from the production of the infra marginal units of output up to Q_0 are balanced out against the excess of marginal costs over marginal benefits on the units between Q_0 and Q^*.

Niskanen also discusses the possibility that the funder's demand schedule would be so far to the right, or inelastic, that the marginal benefit of Q to the funder would fall to zero before F grew as large as E. The constraint that total budget equals total cost would not be operative then, and the bureau would simply request the output level at which the funder is satiated. This situation is represented by the B'_S schedule and Q_S quantity in Figure 16.1.

The possibility that a funder might become satiated from a given public good before a bureau had exhausted all of the consumers' surplus it is capable of exploiting could lead a budget-maximizing bureaucrat to propose other outputs besides the one

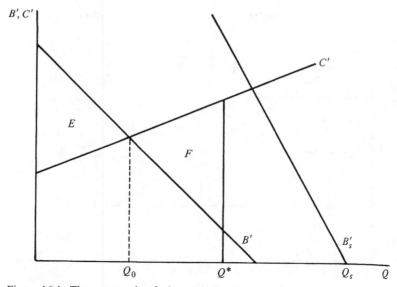

Figure 16.1. The oversupply of a bureau's output.

for which it is solely responsible. This could take the form of radical innovations, or more plausibly, infringements of one bureau onto another bureau's domain, or onto the domain of the private market.

16.3   Extensions of the model

The power of the bureaucracy to obtain budgets greater than those desired by the sponsor stems from three important characteristics of the bargaining situation assumed by Niskanen: (1) the bureau is a monopolist supplier, (2) it alone knows its true cost schedule, and (3) it is institutionally allowed to make take-it-or-leave-it budget proposals. Relaxing any of these assumptions weakens the bureau's position vis-à-vis the sponsoring agency.

16.3.1   *Alternative institutional assumptions*

The ability to make only take-it-or-leave-it budget proposals gives the bureau an extremely strong agenda-setting role, a fact that presumably occurs to the sponsor. The sponsor might reasonably request that the bureau state the costs of a range of outputs from which the sponsor then chooses. If the sponsor is still ignorant of the bureau's true costs and the bureau knows the sponsor's true demand, this new arrangement can leave the bureau in the same position as before, but it can alternatively force the bureau to announce its true marginal cost schedule.

Suppose that the bureau must announce a unit price P at which it will supply output Q, with the sponsor free to choose Q. The budget of the bureau is now

$$B = PQ, \tag{16.7}$$

with $Q = f(P)$ being the sponsor's demand schedule, which is known to the bureau. The bureau then chooses a P to maximize (16.7) subject to the constraint $B \geq C(Q)$.

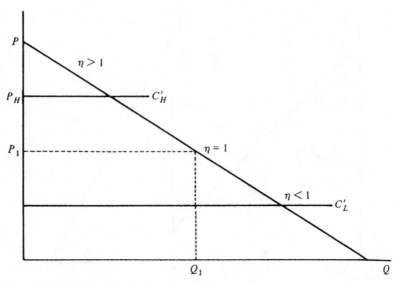

Figure 16.2. Options for a price-setting bureau.

The first-order condition for this problem is simply

$$\frac{dB}{dP} = Q + P\,\frac{dQ}{dP} = 0,\tag{16.8}$$

from which one obtains

$$\eta = \frac{P}{Q}\frac{dQ}{dP} = 1.\tag{16.9}$$

If the constraint $B \geq C(Q)$ is not binding, the bureau chooses the unit price at the point on the bureau's demand schedule where its demand elasticity, η, equals unity. If the constraint is binding, the bureau selects the *lowest* price for which the budget covers its total costs. The possibilities, assuming a straight-line demand schedule and constant marginal costs, are depicted in Figure 16.2. With the low marginal cost schedule C'_L, the bureau can announce the price P_1 at which revenue under the demand schedule is maximized. When marginal costs exceed P_1, however, the bureau is forced to reveal its true marginal costs to obtain the maximum budget possible, for example, $P_H = C'_H$. Thus, when the bureau must declare a unit price or price schedule, instead of a take-it-or-leave-it proposal, its ability to force a higher-than-optimal budget on the sponsor depends on the elasticity of the sponsor's demand. If marginal costs intersect demand in the elastic portion of the demand schedule, the bureau honestly declares true costs. Only when the demand for its services is inelastic can the bureau expand its budget beyond the sponsor's preferred level by announcing a higher price for its output than its true costs (Breton and Wintrobe, 1975; Bendor, Taylor, and van Gaalen, 1985).[5]

---

[5] Clarr (1998) gives the sponsor the authority to regulate both the price and output of the bureau, and derives second-best policies for the sponsor. In general, it still cannot obtain the first-best outcome because it lacks knowledge of the bureau's costs.

Considerable power resides with the bureau owing to its ability to conceal its costs. In practice, this too is limited. Monitoring agencies, like the U.S. General Accounting Office, may detect budget excesses and report them to the sponsor. Whistle-blowers within the bureau inform sponsors from time to time of budget excesses. Thus, in declaring a $P > C'(Q)$, the bureau runs the risk of incurring a penalty in the form of a future reduction in budget, or direct sanctions on personnel (curtailed discretionary budget items, lost promotions, dismissal).

Let the expected penalty from announcing a $P > C'$ be $\pi(P), \pi' > 0$. If π is defined in units comparable to B, then the bureau's objective can be written as the maximization of

$$O = B - \pi(P), \tag{16.10}$$

from which the condition

$$\eta = \frac{P}{Q}\frac{dQ}{dP} = 1 - \pi' \tag{16.11}$$

is obtained. If the constraint $B \geq C(Q)$ is not binding, the bureau announces a price lower than P_1, that is, a price in the inelastic portion of its demand schedule, to reduce the probability of incurring the penalty (Bendor, Taylor, and van Gaalen, 1985). Wherever the sponsor can partially monitor and penalize the bureau, the bureau is forced to declare a price closer to its true marginal costs.

This conclusion is strengthened if we assume, as is often done, that bureaucrats are risk-averse. If bureaucrats are risk-averse, each additional dollar of budget provides lower marginal utility while each additional increase in price raises the expected penalty from being caught, causing increasing marginal disutility. The risk-averse bureaucrat will thus declare a still lower price than the risk-neutral bureaucrat (Bendor, Taylor, and van Gaalen, 1985).

Allowing the sponsor to monitor the bureau and gather information shifts power from the bureau to the sponsor compared with the original situation in which the bureau knows the sponsor's demand but the sponsor is ignorant of the bureau's cost. The sponsor's position can be further strengthened if one assumes that the sponsor can conceal its demand from the bureau. Miller and Moe (1983) show how this assumption can also force the bureau to reveal its true costs.

Finally, the bureau's hand is weakened if it must compete for budget funding with other bureaus. If each bureau must announce prices at which it will supply output, then the sponsor can use the bids of other bureaus as information to gauge a bureau's true costs. In effect, the competing bureaus serve as monitors of a bureau's activity, forcing it to declare lower prices.[6]

---

[6] McGuire, Coiner, and Spancake (1979); Bendor, Taylor, and van Gaalen (1985). Niskanen (1971, chs. 18–20) emphasizes the potential for competition between bureaus as well as between bureaus and the private sector as a restraining force on a bureau's discretionary power.

Eighteen of the 38 Herfindahl indexes for government-provided goods and services that Carroll (1989) estimated for 1985 were less than 0.5, implying that in these cases the market structure was equivalent to no worse than a duopoly. She goes on in a subsequent paper to argue, however, that the competitive environments that bureaus find themselves in may actually lead to *larger* budgets and greater inefficiency, because public bureaucracies tend to favor nonprice over price competition (Carroll, 1990).

Thus, relaxing any of the assumptions of the original budget-maximizing-bureau model shifts the outcome away from the excessive budget result, and in several cases yields the optimally sized budget.

16.3.2 *Bargaining between sponsor and bureau*

Sponsors compete for votes on the basis of how well government programs have served the interests of voters. Bureaucrats compete for promotions, and bureaus compete for funds on the basis of how well they are judged to have supplied the outputs sponsors desire. The interests of the two main actors conflict, and the most general way to view the sponsor–bureau conflict over the size of the bureau's budget and other characteristics of its output mix is as a bargaining game between sponsor-demander and bureau-supplier (Breton and Wintrobe, 1975, 1982; Miller, 1977; Eavey and Miller, 1984). The bureau has monopoly power to some degree and information (expertise) on its side. But the sponsor controls the purse strings. It can offer rewards and punishments, gather information to an extent, and conceal its own hand. The most plausible outcome, as in most bargaining models, is a compromise. The bureau's budget falls short of the bureaucrat's target, but is greater than the sponsor would want.

16.4   Alternative behavioral assumptions

Migué and Bélanger (1974) pointed out that the relentless use of budget funds to expand the bureau's output would conflict with one of the presumed objectives for having larger bureau budgets – to pursue other goals. Weatherby (1971) suggested, à la Williamson (1964), that the expansion of personnel would be one of the additional goals pursued by bureaucrats. The pursuit of this goal would result in higher costs per unit of output, and might be regarded as a particular form of the more general goal of maximizing X-inefficiency or organizational slack.

Chant and Acheson have developed and tested a model of central bank behavior in which the central bankers pursue prestige and risk avoidance.[7] Consistent with our preceeding discussion of power, central bankers in the Chant/Acheson model are very secretive. Chant and Acheson develop and test their model with respect to the behavior of the Bank of Canada, but emphasis placed on secrecy would fit many other bureaucracies and central banks – most notably the new European Central Bank.

Although prestige is unlikely to be an important bureaucratic goal in many agencies (for example, sanitation and transportation departments), avoiding risks seems likely to characterize the behavior of many bureaucrats. We shall take a bit closer look, therefore, at the slack-maximizing and risk-avoiding models of bureaucratic behavior.

16.4.1 *The slack-maximizing bureaucrat*

In Figure 16.3, Q represents the output of a bureau and Y represents all of the other items in the sponsor's budget.[8] The sponsor has a total budget of B that it can divide

---

[7] See Chant and Acheson (1972, 1973) and Acheson and Chant (1973).
[8] The exposition here follows Wyckoff (1990).

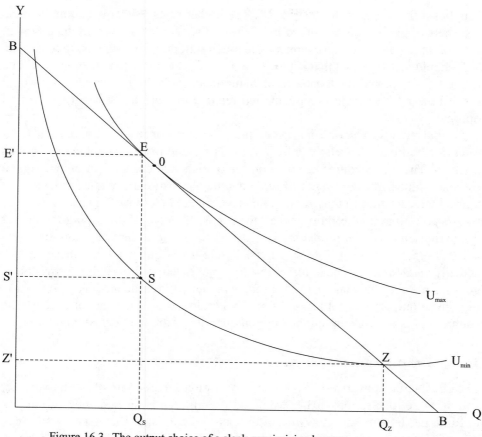

Figure 16.3. The output choice of a slack-maximizing bureau.

between the output of the bureau and the other items in its budget. *BB* is thus the budget constraint line of the sponsor.

U_{max} and U_{min} are two indifference curves of the sponsor, or if we think of the sponsor as an elected assembly that faithfully follows the wishes of the median voter, indifference curves for this voter. Given its budget constraint line, the optimal combination of Y and Q for the sponsor is at point O.

U_{min} is the minimum level of utility that the sponsor will tolerate before shifting to another source of supply and closing the bureau down. The only combinations of Q and budget that the bureau can possibly attain, therefore, lie on or above U_{min} and on or below *BB*.

A budget-maximizing bureau chooses to supply the output Q_Z, which yields its maximum possible budget, BZ'. Any points along U_{min} to the left of Z involve smaller total budgets, but include *slack*. Slack is measured by the distance between a point on U_{min} and a point directly above it on the *BB*-line. A slack-maximizing bureau would choose the point along U_{min} at which the vertical distance to the *BB*-line is maximized, that is, the slope of U_{min} and *BB* are the same. This occurs at point S in Figure 16.3.

The slack-maximizing bureau produces output Q_S. With zero slack, this output could be supplied to the sponsor at a total cost of BE' to the sponsor. The bureau supplies it, however, at the cost of BS'. The higher costs may come about because members of the bureau do not work as hard as they could have, or produce Q with a suboptimal combination of inputs – too much staff and emoluments, for example.

It should also be noted that if Q were a normal good for the sponsor, S would lie to the left of O, and the existence of X-inefficiency in the bureau actually would result in *too little* output being supplied relative to what the sponsor would find optimal.[9]

Several studies have used data envelopment analysis or similar econometric techniques to estimate the relative efficiency of state and private suppliers of various goods.[10] These procedures use data on the outputs and costs of different firms to estimate some sort of *efficiency frontier*, and then measure the relative efficiency of a firm by its distance to this frontier. Such a measure in terms of Figure 16.3 would be BE'/BS', that is, the ratio of the lowest possible cost of producing the output Q_S to the actual cost of producing it. Most of these studies find that state suppliers are *less efficient* than private suppliers. Figure 16.3 illustrates that these studies actually *understate* the social losses due to X-inefficiency in the public provision of goods, since they only take into account the higher costs associated with production of a given output, and not the additional social loss that comes about because the community is not consuming the optimal quantity of the publicly supplied good.

16.4.2   *The risk-avoiding bureaucrat*

The effects of risk aversion on a bureau's performance are more difficult to predict and measure. In Section 16.3.1, we noted that risk aversion may move a budget-maximizing bureau back toward the efficient bureau size. But risk aversion can induce bureaus to avoid projects that their sponsors would want them to undertake, if the sponsors could without cost monitor all bureau activities. Peltzman (1973) estimated that the Federal Drug Administration costs the United States more lives than it saves by excessively delaying the certification of new drugs. This behavior is attributed to the much greater risks the drug administrators perceive that they face if they approve a drug that turns out to be unsafe, than they face from delays in approval. Gist and Hill (1981) reported that officials of the Department of Housing and Urban Development allocated funds to cities with less risky investment projects to avoid the criticism that the projects were not successful, even though the purported goal of the program was to help "distressed" cities, that is, cities for which the risks in housing programs were high.

Lindsay (1976) gathered data indicating that risk-averse Veterans Administration hospital officials concentrate on providing outputs that are easily measured (hospital beds, patient days) at the cost of quality of service, an unmeasurable dimension of

---

[9] Since the slope of U_{min} at S is the same as that of BB, we could shift BB leftward until it becomes tangent to U_{min} at S. S would thus constitute the optimal combination of Y and Q for the sponsor at the lower budget implied by this displaced BB-line. If Q were a normal good for the sponsor, less of it would be bought when the sponsor's income declines.

[10] For recent examples see Hayes and Wood (1995); Duncombe, Miner, and Ruggiero (1997); Hayes, Razzolini, and Ross (1998); and Majumdar (1998).

output. Dávila, Pagán, and Grau (1999) make a similar argument with respect to the Immigration and Naturalization Service (INS). Because it is easier to measure the number of people caught illegally *entering* the country than it is to measure the number of illegal immigrants *in* the country, the INS devotes too much resources to preventing the entry of illegal immigrants, and not enough to capturing those already in the country. These examples further illustrate the importance of information in controlling a bureaucracy. The sponsor is not without some power to control the bureaucracy, since some dimensions of bureau performance can be measured. But if all dimensions cannot be monitored, then some power rests with those in the bureau who can use it to create slack and/or to secure their positions.

16.5 Empirical tests

All the models of bureaucracy reviewed so far suggest that bureau budgets will be too big in some sense because bureaucrats have the discretion to pursue their own goals at the sponsor's (citizen's) expense. Breton and Wintrobe (1982, pp. 96–7) have argued, on the other hand, that bureaucrats, like corporate managers, are not totally free to pursue their own goals; indeed, they may have less discretionary power than their private sector counterparts, because they operate in an environment in which considerable competition for promotions exists. If anything, public bureaucrats are more mobile than corporate managers; this suggests that the market for public bureaucrats is more competitive than the market for company managers. Bureau sponsors, the elected representatives of parliament, and the executive also function in a competitive environment. They must stand for periodic reelection. Thus, they are under continuous pressure to control bureaucratic excesses to the best of their ability.[11]

Thus, as so often is the case, whether and to what degree government bureaucracies oversupply goods or are inefficient remain empirical questions. In this section, we examine some of the evidence that has been accumulated on this issue.

16.5.1 *Power of the agenda setter*

The hypothesis that bureau budgets exceed the optimum levels of their parliamentary review committees is often difficult to test directly, since output is hard to measure and the optimum levels for the review committee cannot be established. In Oregon, however, school budgets are determined by a process that allows one to observe the budget-maximizing bureaucrat in action. Each school district has a budget maximum determined by law. School boards can increase the budget size, however, by proposing larger budgets at an annual referendum. If the newly proposed budget gets more than 50 percent of the votes cast, it replaces the legally set limit. If the school board's budget fails, the budget reverts back to the level set by the law.

This situation allows one to test hypotheses regarding school board officials' motivation, if one assumes that the optimum level of expenditures would be that

---

[11] For two vigorous defenses of governmental efficiency that emphasize the competitiveness of democratic institutions, see Wittman (1995) and Breton (1996).

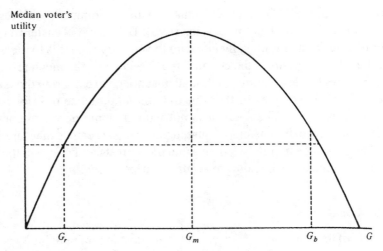

Figure 16.4. Options for the budget-maximizing agenda setter.

most preferred by the median voter, if voting were on all possible expenditure levels. Figure 16.4 depicts the utility function of the median voter defined over school expenditures G. Let G_r be the level of expenditures to which the school budget reverts if the referendum fails. While the median voter's most preferred expenditure is G_m, she would be willing to vote for G_b rather than see the budget revert to G_r. Thus, when the reversion level for the school budget is below the most favored budget of the median voter, the school board can force the median voter to vote for a larger budget than the one she prefers by forcing her to choose between this higher budget and the reversion level.

Romer and Rosenthal (1978, 1979b, 1982) have analyzed and tested a model of the Oregon school budget referenda process. They predict the budget expenditures that the median voter would demand using a standard median voter model and find that, where the reversion levels are below the levels necessary to keep the school system viable, referenda pass leading to school budgets anywhere from 16.5 to 43.6 percent higher than those most preferred by the median voter. Further corroboration for the budget-maximizing school bureau hypothesis is contained in the data for the 64 districts that either failed to hold a referendum or failed to pass one. When the reversion budget exceeds the level favored by the median voter, one expects that the school board does not call an election, and simply assesses the full 100 percent of its statutorily set base. The mean assessment for these 64 districts was over 99 percent of their bases.[12]

[12] See also Filimon (1982).

Additional evidence of the use of discretionary power by public officials is provided by Shapiro and Sonstelie (1982), who show that Proposition 13 in California took away discretionary funds from local officials and forced them to choose different budget expansion paths. Using data on community college budgets in California, Kress (1989) also found that Proposition 13 took away discretionary power from college bureaucrats.

Ruttan (1980) points to the agricultural research program of the U.S. Department of Agriculture (USDA) as an important counterexample to the budget-maximizing bureau story. The high rates of return on agricultural research estimated in numerous studies imply a significant underinvestment in agricultural research. This finding would be consistent with higher unit costs for the USDA if the demand for this service were highly elastic.

The Oregon school budgeting system provides school officials an unusually attractive opportunity to increase budget sizes by the power granted them to make take-it-or-leave-it referendum proposals. But, as noted earlier, most bureau budgets are the outcome of a bargaining process between the bureau and its sponsors. Using classroom experiments, Eavey and Miller (1984) have shown that merely granting the sponsor-demanders the right to confer and form coalitions increases their power vis-à-vis the agenda setter. The Eavey-Miller experiments produced outcomes falling in a bargaining range between the review committee's most preferred choice and that of the agenda setter. Fort (1988) found that for nonrepeated hospital bond issues, the outcomes did not differ from what one would expect from the median voter hypothesis.

16.5.2 *Cost differences between publicly and privately provided services*

In some cases, the nature of a bureau's services makes it difficult to expand its output beyond the level that the community demands. A school system cannot educate more children than are sent to school; the sanitation department cannot collect more garbage than the community puts out to be collected. In these situations, a bureau's members can only take advantage of the discretion that they have by introducing slack into their budget, that is, by providing the fixed output demanded by the community at a higher cost than necessary. The extra costs could reflect higher than competitive salaries, more personnel than are needed to provide the service, or general X-inefficiency. Numerous studies have compared the provision of similar services by public and private firms. Table 16.1 summarizes the findings for 71 studies. In only 5 were public firms found to be more efficient than their private counterparts. In another 10 there were no significant differences in the performances of the two types of companies, while in the remaining 56 studies state-owned companies were found to be significantly less efficient than privately owned firms supplying the same good or service. The provision of a good or service by a state bureaucracy or by a state-owned company generally leads to lower residual profits, and/or higher costs and lower productivity.[13]

In several of the studies comparing public and private provision of a good or service, the private firms are regulated to some degree. Differences between public and private company performance in these cases may be reduced or eliminated through the regulation process. For example, electricity rate regulation in the United States provides incentives for profit-maximizing suppliers to choose inefficiently large amounts of capital equipment.[14] For this reason, the most revealing comparisons in Table 16.1 may be the ones at the very end of the table between privately and state-owned companies operating in nonregulated sectors like manufacturing and mining.

---

[13] Vining and Boardman (1992, Table 2) present a much longer list of studies including many that are unpublished or difficult to locate. Roughly the same pattern of findings is revealed in their table.

[14] See Averch and Johnson (1962). The study of the West German insurance industry by Finsinger, Hammond, and Tapp (1985) is much more an indictment of the regulatory process in Germany and the inefficiencies that it causes than an example of state companies outperforming private ones.

Table 16.1. *Cost and productivity indices: alternative organizational forms*

Activity: author	Unit/organizational form	Findings
1. Airlines		
Davies (1971, 1977, 1981)	Australia/sole private domestic vs. its lone public counterpart	Efficiency indices of private 12–100% higher
Forsyth and Hocking[b] (1980)	Australia's one private and one publicly owned airlines (1964–76)	Similar performace
2. Banks		
Davies (1981)	Australia/one public vs. one private bank	Sign and magnitude in all indices of productivity, response to risk, and profitability favor private banks
Davies and Brucato (1987)		Government-owned banks hold less risky assets and are less profitable than private banks
3. Bus and transit service		
Oelert (1976)	Municipal vs. private bus service in selected West Germany cities	Cost public bus service 160% higher per km than private equivalents
Bails (1979)	School buses in six U.S. states (1976–7)	Costs are lower in school districts which contract with private sector than for state-owned systems
McGuire and Van Cott (1984)	School buses in 275 districts in Indiana (1979–80)	Privately owned bus services have 12% lower costs than state-owned
Pashigian (1976)	Transit systems in 117 U.S. cities (1971)	Publicly owned systems have lower profit margins and revenue per vehicle
4. Cleaning services		
Bundesrechnungshof (1972)	Public production vs. private contracting out in West Germany post office	Public service 40–60% more costly
Hamburger Senat (1974), Fischer-Menshausen (1975)	Public production vs. private contracting out in West Germany public building	Public service 50% more costly than private alternative
5. Debt collection		
Bennett and Johnson (1980a)	U.S. General Accounting Office study/federal government supplied service vs. privately contract-for equivalents	Government 200% more costly per dollar of debt pursued
6. Electric utilities		
Meyer[a] (1975)	Sample of 60–90 U.S. utilities/public vs. private firms	Very weak indication of higher costs of private production

Activity: author	Unit/organizational form	Findings
Moore (1970)	Sample of U.S. utilities/27 municipal vs. 49 private firms	Overcapitalization greater in public firms; total operating costs of public production higher
Spann[b] (1977b)	Four major U.S. cities/public (San Antonio, Los Angeles) vs. private (San Diego, Dallas) firms	Private firm adjusted for scale as efficient and probably more so with respect to operating cost and investment (per 1,000 kWh)
Wallace and Junk (1970)	By region in U.S./public vs. private firms	Operating costs 40–75% higher in public mode; investment (per kWh) 40% more in public mode
Atkinson and Halvorsen[b] (1986)	U.S. electric utilities (1970)	Privately and publicly owned are equally efficient
DiLorenzo and Robinson[b] (1982)	U.S. electric utilities	Privately and publicly owned are equally efficient
Peltzman (1971)	135 U.S. electric utilities (1966)	Privately owned are more efficient
7. Fire protection		
Ahlbrandt (1973)	Scottsdale, Arizona (private contract) vs. Seattle area (municipal) fire departments	Municipal fire departments 39–88% higher cost per capita
Pescatrice and Trapani[a] (1980)	56 electric utilities in the U.S. (1965, 1970)	Publicly owned have 24–33% lower costs
8. Forestry		
Bundesregierung Deutschland (1976)	Public vs. private forest harvesting in West Germany (1965–75)	Operating revenues 45 DM per hectare higher in private forests
Pfister (1976)	Private vs. public forests in state of Baden-Württemberg	Labor input twice as high per unit of output in public compared with private firms
9. Hospitals and nursing homes		
Clarkson (1972)	Sample of U.S. hospitals/ private nonprofit vs. for profit	"Red tape" more prevalent in nonprofits; greater variation in input ratios in nonprofits; both suggest higher cost of nonprofit outputs
Lindsay[a] (1976)	U.S. Veterans Administration vs. proprietary hospitals	Cost per patient day less in V.A. hospital unadjusted for type of care and quality; less "serious" cases and longer patient stays in V.A.; preference for minority group professionals compared with proprietary hospitals

(*continued*)

Table 16.1 (*continued*)

Activity: author	Unit/organizational form	Findings
Rushing (1974)	Sample of 91 short-stay hospitals in U.S. mid-South region/private nonprofits vs. for-profit	Substitution among inputs and outputs more sluggish in nonprofit hospitals
Wilson and Jadlow (1982)	1,200 U.S. hospitals producing nuclear medicine/government vs. proprietary hospitals	Deviation of proprietary hospitals from perfect efficiency index less than public hospitals
Becker and Sloan[b] (1985)	1979 data on 2,231 U.S. hospitals	Costs and profitability similar in private for profit, private nonprofit, and publicly owned hospitals
Frech (1985)	U.S. nursing homes	Private profit-seeking have 5–29% lower costs than nonprofit homes; 34–41% lower costs than state-owned homes
Tuckman and Chang[b] (1988)	Nursing homes in Tennessee	No significant cost differences between for-profit and nonprofit homes
10. Housing		
Muth (1973)	Construction costs in U.S. cities, private vs. public agencies	Public agencies 20% more costly per constant quality housing unit
Rechnungshof Rheinland-Pfalz (1972)	Public vs. private cost of supplying large public building projects in the West German state of Rheinland-Pfalz	Public agencies 20% more costly than private contracting
Schneider and Schuppener (1971)	Public vs. private firm construction costs in West Germany	Public firms significantly more expensive suppliers
11. Insurance sales and servicing		
Finsinger[a] (1981)	5 public vs. 77 private liability and life firms in West Germany	Same rate of return and no obvious cost differences between organizational forms
Kennedy and Mehr (1977)	Public car insurance in Manitoba vs. private insurance in Alberta	Quality and services of private insurances higher than those of the public one
Finsinger, Hammond, and Tapp[a] (1985)	96 German life insurance companies, 83 German automobile insurance companies (1979)	Public enterprises have lower costs than private stock companies
Frech (1976)	78 health insurance companies	Profit seeking companies have 15% lower costs than nonprofit

Activity: author	Unit/organizational form	Findings
12. Ocean tanker repair and maintenance		
Bennett and Johnson (1980a)	U.S. General Accounting Office/Navy vs. commercial tankers and oilers	U.S. Navy from 230 to 5,100% higher
13. Railroads		
Caves and Christensen[b] (1980)	Canadian National (public) vs. Canadian Pacific (private) railroads	No productivity differences recently, but CN less efficient before 1965, the highly regulated period
14. Refuse collection		
Collins and Downes[b] (1977)	53 cities and municipalities in the St. Louis County area, Missouri/public vs. private contracting-out modes	No significant cost differences
Columbia University Graduate School of Business Studies: Savas (1974, 1977a, 1977b, 1980), Stevens and Savas (1978)	Many sorts of U.S. cities/ municipal vs. private monopoly, franchise vs. private nonfranchise firms	Public supply 40–60% more expensive than private, but monopoly franchise only 5% higher than private nonfranchised collectors
Petrovic and Jaffee (1977)	83 cities in midwestern U.S./public vs. private contracting-out modes	Cost of city collection is 15% higher than the price of private contract collectors
Hirsch[b] (1965)	24 cities and municipalities in the St. Louis city-county area, Missouri/public vs. private firms	No significant cost differences
Kemper and Quigley (1976)	101 Connecticut cities/private monopoly contract vs. private nonfranchise vs. municipal firms	Municipal collections costs 14–43% higher than contract, but private nonfranchise 25–36% higher than municipal collection
Kitchen (1976)	48 Canadian cities/municipal vs. private firms	Municipal suppliers more costly than proprietary firms
Savas[b] (1977c)	50 private vs. 30 municipal firms in Minneapolis	No significant cost differences
Pier, Vernon, and Wicks[a] (1974)	26 cities in Montana/ municipal vs. private firms	Municipal suppliers more efficient
Pommerehne (1976)	102 Swiss municipalities/ public vs. private firms	Public firms 15% higher unit costs
Spann (1977b)	Survey of various U.S. cities/ municipal vs. private firms	Public firms 45% more costly
Bennett and Johnson (1979)	29 private firms vs. one public trash collection authority in Fairfax County, Virginia	Private firms more efficient

(continued)

Table 16.1 (*continued*)

Activity: author	Unit/organizational form	Findings
Edwards and Stevens (1978)	77 U.S. cities (1975)	Prices 41% lower when cities contract with private firms
Stevens (1978)	340 public and private U.S. collectors (1974–5)	Labor productivity lower in public monopolies than in private ones
15. Saving and loans		
Nicols (1967)	California Savings and Loans/ cooperative or mutuals vs. stock companies	Mutuals have 13–30% higher operating costs
16. Schools		
Chubb and Moe (1990)	Test scores for over 7,000 U.S. high school students (1982, 1984)	Students in private schools outperform students in public schools
17. Slaughterhouses		
Pausch (1976)	Private vs. public firms in 5 major West Germany cities	Public firms significantly more costly because of overcapacity and overstaffing
18. Water utilities		
Crain and Zardkoohi (1978)	112 U.S. firms/municipal vs. private suppliers; case study of two firms that each switched organizational form	Public firms 40% less productive with 65% higher capital-labor ratios than private equivalents; public firm that became private experienced an output per employee increase of 25%; private firm that became public experienced an output per employee decline of 40%
Mann and Mikesell (1976)	U.S. firms/municipal vs. private suppliers	Replicates Meyer's (1975) electricity model, but adjusts for input prices; found public modes more expensive by 20%
Morgan (1977)	143 firms in six U.S. states/ municipal vs. private suppliers	Costs 15% higher for public firms
Feigenbaum and Teeples[b] (1983)	57 private and 262 public water companies in U.S. (1970)	Two types of firms perform the same
19. Weather forecasting		
Bennett and Johnson (1980a)	U.S. General Accounting Office study/U.S. Weather Bureau vs. private contracted-for service	Government service 50% more costly

Activity: author	Unit/organizational form	Findings
20. Industrial companies in private sector		
Boardman and Vining (1989)	500 largest non-U.S. corporations in the world (1983): 419 private, 58 state-owned, 23 mixed ownership	Mixed and state-owned companies have lower profitability and productivity than private companies
Funkhouser and MacAvoy (1979)	100 Indonesian companies (1971)	Profit rates 14–15% lower for publicly owned companies; prices the same; costs higher
Majumdar (1998)	Used data envelopment analysis to measure the relative efficiency of a large sample of Indian companies (1973–89)	State-owned companies have average efficiency scores of .64–.66, where 1.0 is most efficient. Mixed ownership companies have mean scores of .91, privately owned average .975
Picot and Kaulmann (1989)	Sample of large companies drawn from 6 countries and 15 industries (1975–84)	Privately owned firms have higher profitability and productivity than state-owned companies
Gugler (1998)	94 Austrian companies (1975–94)	State-owned have lower profitability than bank-, family-, and foreign-owned companies
Vining and Boardman (1992)	370 large Canadian companies (1986)	Privately owned companies are significantly more profitable and efficient than state-owned; mixed ownership companies fall in-between

[a] Public sector less costly or more efficient.

[b] No significant difference in costs or efficiencies.

All studies without an [a] or [b] found the public sector firms to have higher costs or lower efficiency.

Source: Borchering, Pommerehne, and Schneider (1982, pp. 130–3) with additions.

As noted above, a large literature exists discussing the principal-agent problem in joint-stock companies and the various goals corporate managers pursue with the discretion that they have. State-owned companies have several tiers of principal-agent relationships, however. Rational ignorance leads citizens to be poor monitors of elected officials. Information asymmetries give the managers of state-owned companies considerable discretion vis-à-vis the elected members of the legislature. In situations where some state agency monitors the state-owned enterprises on behalf of the legislature, yet another principal-agent relationship is introduced with further scope for the appearance of slack and X-inefficiency. All six studies at the end of Table 16.1 found that the privately owned companies significantly outperformed the state-owned companies in the same sectors. Even partial ownership by the state substantially reduced performance. If companies that face competition can become so inefficient, what should we expect from bureaucracies that supply hard-to-measure outputs and face little or no competition?

16.6   The government as Leviathan

16.6.1   *Theory*

The family of bureaucracy models initiated by Niskanen depicts a bargaining situation between a bureau and a sponsor, like the U.S. Congress. In Niskanen's original model, the bureaucracy has all of the relevant information and power; the sponsor has only the money and the power to turn down the bureau's offer. Subsequent refinements of the Niskanen model have shifted power toward the sponsor and altered the bureau's objective function. In the next chapter, we consider a group of models that are almost the polar reverse of the Niskanen model – all of the power lies with the sponsor. Before turning to these, however, we examine a model more in the spirit of that of Niskanen.

In Brennan and Buchanan's (1980) Leviathan model, the sponsor – congress or a parliament – and the bureaucracy that supplies public goods and services are fused. This monolith monopolist then exploits its power over the citizenry à la Niskanen by maximizing the size of the public sector. Political competition is an ineffective constraint on government owing to the rational ignorance of voters, the uncertainties inherent in majority rule cycling, and outright collusion among elected officials (Brennan and Buchanan, 1980, pp. 17–24).

Although political competition cannot constrain the government's desire to expand, constitutional limitations on sources of tax revenue and on debt and money creation can. Brennan and Buchanan assume that the only truly effective constraints on government in the long run are contained in constitutional rules limiting government's power to tax, issue debt, and print money.

With the government viewed as a malevolent revenue maximizer rather than a benevolent public good provider, many of the traditional propositions of the public finance tax literature are stood on their heads (Brennan and Buchanan, 1980, p. 2). Traditional analysis assumes that the purpose of government is to raise a *given amount of revenue* subject to certain efficiency and equity constraints; Brennan and Buchanan assume that citizens seek to impose constraints on the government bureaucracy limiting its revenues to a given amount. To see the difference, consider the familiar problem of how to tax income without discriminating against leisure. Let *AB* in Figure 16.5 represent an individual's opportunity locus in the absence of any tax. An "ideal tax" would shift the individual's opportunity locus toward the origin without distorting his choice between income and leisure, say, to *CD*, by taxing an individual's *capacity* to earn income and not just the income actually earned. If the taxing authority is free to raise revenue only by means of a tax on earned income, however, it must raise the equivalent amount of revenue, *AC*, by imposing a much higher effective tax rate on earned income, as is implicit in the opportunity line, *EB*. If the amount of tax revenue to be raised were a fixed amount, as the normative literature on optimal taxation assumes, the tax on the more comprehensive tax base

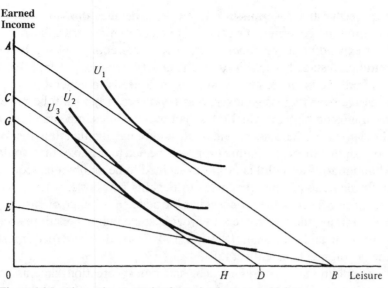

Figure 16.5. Alternative strategies for taxing income and leisure.

would be preferred, since $U_2 > U_3$. However, if the budget-maximizing bureaucrat were free to tax both earned income and leisure, there is no reason to assume he would stop with a tax revenue of AC. If the citizen would tolerate a reduction in utility by the taxing authority to U_3, then the budget-maximizing bureaucrat would push tax rates up sufficiently to raise AG. The difference between a comprehensive definition of income and a restricted definition is not the level of utility of the voter-taxpayer for a given tax revenue, but the amount of tax revenue taken at a given utility level under the grasping Leviathan view of government.

If the voter always finished up at the same utility level whatever the definition of the tax base, he would be indifferent to the resolution of this question. Brennan and Buchanan assume, however, that there are physical and institutional limits to how high nominal tax rates on a given revenue base can be raised. Given such limits, the bureaucracy's capacity to tax the citizenry is weaker under a narrow definition of the tax base than under a broad one. A citizen who expected bureaucrats to maximize their budgets would constrain their ability to do so by constitutionally restricting the kinds of income and wealth that could be taxed.

The Brennan-Buchanan model also turns the standard analysis of excess burden in taxation on its head. With the amount of revenue to be raised by taxation fixed, the optimal tax is the one that induces the minimum amount of distortion, which falls on the most inelastic sources of revenue. With the government maximizing the amount of revenue raised, the citizen seeks to limit it to more elastic tax bases and shelter parts of his income and wealth from taxation entirely.

When Brennan and Buchanan apply their analysis to other aspects of taxation, they sometimes reach conclusions analogous to those existing in the normative tax literature, but the underlying logic is quite different. Because a vote-maximizing government has the incentive to introduce special tax concessions favoring narrowly defined interest groups, a citizen writing a tax constitution to constrain Leviathan would require that the government impose tax schedules that are uniform across persons to limit the government's capacity to engage in tax price discrimination as a means of expanding its revenue. Thus, "horizontal equity" would be favored at the constitutional stage because it limits the government's degrees of freedom, and not for any other ethical reasons.[15] Similar logic leads in general to a preference for progressive over regressive taxes: less revenue can typically be raised by tax schedules imposing high marginal rates than by schedules imposing low ones.

The Leviathan model also provides an additional justification for Wicksell's (1896) prescription that expenditure proposals be tied to the taxes that would finance them. Although to Wicksell this proposal seemed to be an obvious requirement to ensure informed choices by citizens as to benefits and costs, when governments seek to maximize revenue the proposal has the added advantage of ensuring budget balance and forcing the government to provide some public benefit to secure more revenue (Brennan and Buchanan, 1980, pp. 154–5). Bridges and roads must be built before the government can collect tolls.

Although traditional analyses of debt and money creation have assumed that government's motivation is benign, in the hands of a Leviathan seeking ever new sources of revenue, both of these policy instruments become extremely dangerous. Balanced budget constitutional amendments follow naturally, as do restrictions on the government's capacity to print money (Brennan and Buchanan, 1980, chs. 5, 6, and 10), with the ultimate restriction – "denying government the power to create money under any circumstances at all" (Brennan and Buchanan, 1980, p. 130) – being possibly the best means to control the abuse of this power.

In the Brennan-Buchanan model of the state, the citizens have lost almost all control over government. They set government on its way, when they forge the constitutional constraints on government at its inception. The government's power to pursue its own objectives is greatly aided by the "rational ignorance" of voters of their true tax bills, the full impact of debt, and money creation. The information-power nexus reappears in the Leviathan model as fiscal illusion and rational ignorance. From time to time, citizens may perceive that the government Leviathan has gone too far in pursuing its own ends and may rise from their lethargy to reforge certain bonds on government, as in the tax and debt revolts of the seventies, and the brief triumph of fiscal conservatism in the United States during the early nineties. But between these surges of citizen control the government proceeds on its revenue-maximizing course within whatever constraints the constitution effectively allows.

16.6.2 *Empirical testing – government expenditures and taxes*

The central hypothesis of the Leviathan model is that only constitutional constraints on the sources of revenue or levels of expenditure can curb the appetite for growth by those in government. A revealing illustration of the importance of such constraints has been recounted by Campbell (1994). New Hampshire's constitution requires

---

[15] A similar line of argument, although with a more normative flavor to it, is developed by Buchanan and Congleton (1998).

that its tax rates be proportional. Its lower house also has an unusually large number of seats, and the ratio of its seats to the number of seats in the upper house is very large. Following the arguments of McCormick and Tollison (1981), these features of the New Hampshire constitution should make it difficult for interest groups to change it. The consequence is that New Hampshire has one of the narrowest tax bases of any of the 50 U.S. states – no sales taxes, and an income tax that is limited to interest and dividends. The consequence is that New Hampshire has much lower taxes and government expenditures than its neighboring states.

As evidence that New Hampshire residents approve of the outcomes from this constrained governmental sector, Campbell cites the much higher growth rates in population, which New Hampshire has experienced relative to its neighboring states. Citizens have voted for a constrained Leviathan with their feet by migrating into New Hampshire from neighboring states, and by exiting in smaller numbers.

Campbell's account of the importance of the tax base in determining government size has been supported in a broader study by Nelson (1986). He found that those states that tax personal income have significantly larger government sectors, and that the relative size of the government sector varied inversely with the number of local government units. If one assumes that having more local government units signifies a stronger federalist structure and more intensive constraints on government through intergovernmental competition, then this result also supports the Leviathan model. Campbell also noted that New Hampshire has a more decentralized governmental structure than neighboring Vermont, Maine, and Massachusetts. Further evidence for the importance of decentralization in explaining government size is provided by Deacon (1979), Mehay (1984), Mehay and Gonzales (1985), and Marlow (1988). Several cross-national studies have also found that federalist structures are inversely related to government size (Cameron, 1978; Saunders, 1986; Schneider, 1986; Mueller and Stratmann, 2002). Oates (1985), on the other hand, found no support for the Leviathan hypothesis using data on federalist constitutional structures and the degree of centralization of tax revenue. The same was observed by Nelson (1986) in his cross-sectional analysis of U.S. state data.

The beneficial effects of intergovernmental competition will not emerge, of course, if governments collude, which in the Leviathan model they have every reason to do. Intergovernmental grants are an attractive vehicle for making the side payments needed to cement collusive agreements among supposedly competing governments (Brennan and Buchanan, 1980, pp. 182–3). New Hampshire makes less use of intergovernmental grants than neighboring Vermont, Maine, and Massachusetts (Campbell, 1994, pp. 140–1). Grossman (1989a,b) and Grossman and West (1994) provide more systematic evidence for the United States and Canada.[16]

The ultimate constraints on Levithan in Brennan and Buchanan's schema are provided by the constitution. The success of Proposition 13-type movements in reducing government size offers further support for their thesis (Shapiro and Sonstelie, 1982; Kress, 1989).

---

[16] For further discussion and evidence, see Chapters 10 and 21.

16.7   Conclusions

Most of the public choice literature is in the citizen-over-the-state tradition. Just as the individual consumer is sovereign in the marketplace, ultimate authority is assumed to rest with the citizens.

But the word "sovereign" did not originate as a synonym for citizen. Historically, the word has referred to a single person ruling the people as head of a monarchy. The state was something separate from, indeed above, the people it ruled. Citizens are expected to serve the state; the state is not servant to the people.

This second view of the state appears most vividly in Brennan and Buchanan's Leviathan model, but elements of this view are also present in the bureaucracy models. Which model best explains the outcomes of the polity probably depends both on the outcomes that one wishes to explain and on the polity. The citizen-over-the-state model is probably more appropriate for describing the public policies of the Swiss canton of Appenzell; the Leviathan model is perhaps more appropriate for countries like France and Germany.

Both Brennan and Buchanan's Leviathan model and Niskanen's bureaucracy model assume that the actor's main goal is to maximize budget size. The sovereign and the bureaucrat are both empire builders of sorts. In the private sector such empire-building behavior is quite consistent with maximizing wealth, as managerial salaries tend to be highly correlated with company size. Civil service rules in most countries, however, do not link bureaucrats' salaries closely to the size of their bureaus (Johnson and Libecap, 1989). In the public sector, the bureaucrat typically exercises his discretion by creating and taking advantage of organizational slack. The public school system in America fails its citizens not by educating too many students, but by educating them poorly – poorly in comparison to students educated in more efficiently organized private schools (Chubb and Moe, 1990).

Although there is considerable evidence that public slack and inefficiency exist, there is also evidence that citizens are able to exercise some control over Leviathan. Hayes and Wood (1995), for example, found less evidence of bureaucratic slack in the provision of police service in those Illinois municipalities where citizens had stronger incentives to be informed. The average efficiency score of a municipal police department was 0.96 on a scale of 0 to 1.0. Hayes, Razzolini, and Ross (1998) came up with a similar finding for other government services supplied by Illinois municipalities. Duncombe, Miner, and Ruggiero (1997) found that public schools in New York State were closer to the efficiency frontier in school districts in which citizens had greater incentives to become informed. The Proposition 13 movement provides yet another example of citizens taking action to (re)take control over government.

Some scholars like Brennan, Buchanan, Niskanen, and Usher (1992) look at the state and see a grasping beast set upon exploiting its power over citizens to the maximum degree. Others, like Breton (1996) and Wittman (1995), when they gaze upon the state see an institutional equivalent to the market in which democratic competition produces efficiency levels comparable to those achieved by market competition. Which view is closer to reality? This is obviously an empirical question.

We have presented some of the relevant evidence in this chapter. We consider more later, particularly in Chapters 20, 21, and 22.

Bibliographical notes

Surveys of the bureaucracy literature include Orzechowski (1977), Moe (1997), and Wintrobe (1997).

The agenda control model of bureaucracy has been extended to more than one government activity by Mackay and Weaver (1981).

In Breton's (1974) theory of representative democracy, the government is modeled as a monopoly supplier of certain highly desired public goods like defense, police and fire protection, and highways. Auster and Silver (1979) also describe the history of the state as if it were a monopolist.

CHAPTER 17

Legislatures and bureaucracies

> To what expedient, then, shall we finally resort, for maintaining in practice the
> necessary partition of power among the several departments, as laid down in the
> Constitution? The only answer that can be given is, that as all these exterior provi-
> sions are found to be inadequate, the defect must be supplied, by so contriving the
> interior structure of the government as that its several constituent parts may, by
> their mutual relations, be the means of keeping each other in their proper places.
>
> The Federalist, No. 51

In the rent-seeking model of politics discussed in Chapter 15, politicians buy and
sell legislation to interest groups. The legislature is a marketplace at which rents are
bought and sold. Problems of bureaucratic discretion are ignored. The legislature
is in complete control. In stark contrast, in the first model of bureaucracy discussed
in the previous chapter, the legislature is at the complete mercy of an all-powerful
bureaucracy. Both types of models are, of course, polar cases derived to illustrate
certain features of the political process. In this chapter we take a further look at
the relationship between the legislature and the bureaucracies charged with implementing the policies initiated in the legislature. We also consider the separate role
played by the chief executive in presidential systems like that of the United States,
and the role of the judiciary. We begin with a model that completely reverses the
power relationship of the Niskanen bureaucracy model.

17.1 The Congressional-dominance model

17.1.1 *Congressional dominance through administrative structure*

Let us assume as in the rent-seeking model that each member of Congress seeks to
win reelection by supplying legislation to her constituents and the interest groups
that supply her with campaign funds. She alone cannot supply the legislation that
her constituents want, however. She must first induce a majority of her colleagues
in the legislature to vote for the legislation, and then she must make sure that the
bureaucracy charged with implementing the legislation does so in a way that corresponds to the wishes of her constituents. The first difficulty could be circumvented
if Congress were organized as a market in which each legislator could purchase the
votes she needed for the legislation she desired. But this is not the case. Instead of
literally buying or trading votes, members of Congress can only strike agreements

to trade, and these are potentially vulnerable to some members misrepresenting their preferences, reneging on promises, cycling, and so on.[1]

Weingast and Marshall (1988) argue that Congress has designed an organizational structure that solves both the problem of making sure that agreements do not come unstuck, and the problem of bureaucratic compliance. In particular, by establishing committees to both propose legislation and to monitor those entrusted with its implementation, and then filling these committees with representatives who have strong interests in the legislation assigned to each committee, Congress has created an institutional structure that vests rights to initiate and block legislation in those members of Congress who can most benefit from these rights. Moreover, the process by which differences between House and Senate versions of bills get resolved in joint committees gives key members of the original sponsoring committees the power to ensure that deals once made do not become unstuck.

> Instead of trading votes, legislators in the committee system institutionalize an exchange of influence over the relevant rights. Instead of bidding for votes, legislators bid for seats on committees associated with rights to policy areas valuable for their reelection. In contrast to policy choice under a market for votes, legislative bargains institutionalized through the committee system are significantly less plagued by problems of ex post enforceability.
>
> (Shepsle and Weingast, 1987, p. 148)

Congressional committees can use "the power of the purse" which they control to discipline the agencies that report to them. Because members of the committees have strong interests in the way the legislation is implemented, free-rider problems in gathering information and monitoring bureau behavior are mitigated. Moreover, committee members can often rely on their constituents to do the monitoring for them. If the Department of Agriculture is not treating the dairy farmers the way Congress wants them to be treated, the dairy farmers will know, and they have an incentive to set off a "fire alarm" that makes their grievances known to the congressional committees that draw up the department's budget.[2]

Empirical support for the Congressional-dominance model is provided by many studies that have found a significant relationship between a congressman's committee assignments and the federal monies flowing into his district. Pork-barrel legislation comes first to mind when one thinks of congressmen selling legislation, and membership on the House Public Works Committee does increase one's share of the federally funded pork (Ferejohn, 1974). But one can also benefit from being on the Ways and Means, Appropriations, Agriculture, Armed Services, Banking and Currency, and many more committees (Goss, 1972; Strom, 1975; Arnold, 1979; Holcombe and Zardkoohi, 1981; Rich, 1989; Cohen and Noll, 1991; Alvarez and Saving, 1997; Kroszner and Stratmann, 1998).[3] If one's constituents favor smaller

---

[1] See Mueller (1967), Park (1967), and the discussion of logrolling in Chapter 5.

[2] See McCubbins and Schwartz (1984). However, too many "false alarms" may destroy the efficacy of this means of control (Lupia and McCubbins, 1994).

[3] For counterarguments and evidence see, however, Rundquist and Griffith (1976), Rundquist (1978), and Krehbiel (1991).

federal spending, membership on oversight committees can also serve to rein in budget-maximizing bureaucrats.

Several studies have examined congressional influence over the regulatory policies of the Federal Trade Commission and the Justice Department. Here, too, members of the relevant "watch-dog" committees appear to be able to influence the kinds of cases brought by the government and *where* they are brought.[4] At least in some areas, Congress appears to be able to get the public bureaucracies to do its bidding.

17.1.2 *Congressional dominance through administrative procedure*

McCubbins, Noll, and Weingast (1987, 1989), often referred to as "McNollgast" in the subsequent literature, have developed a somewhat different variant of the Congressional-dominance model from that of Weingast, Moran, and Marshall. The basic structure of the model is again that of a principal–agent relationship, but the emphasis is now upon Congress' power to control government bureaucracies by defining the administrative procedures under which they must operate. By requiring that an agency announce a rule or policy change well in advance of implementing it, for example, Congress ensures that the affected interest groups have ample time to present arguments for and against it. By requiring that an agency hold public hearings on a policy change before implementing it, Congress ensures that interest groups have a legitimate venue in which to air their arguments. McNollgast also argue that the principal–agent problem Congress faces in providing legislation to its constituencies is to an important degree resolved by the constituents themselves monitoring the agencies that impact them, but McNollgast differs from the rest of the Congressional-dominance literature in stressing the potential Congress has to control governmental bureaucracies "up front" through its authority to define the administrative procedures under which the bureaucracies must operate. Congress, the principal, "writes the contract" that constrains its bureaucratic agents. This contract includes not only a broad statement of purpose and budget to accomplish this purpose, but detailed administrative procedures that ensure the bureaucracies will not be able to stray very far off course in pursuit of their own agenda.

17.2   The impact of uncertainty and transaction costs

Although the evidence and arguments marshaled for the Congressional-dominance model are sufficiently persuasive to lead one to abandon at least the strongest variants of the bureaucratic-power models of the last chapter, a few puzzles regarding the relationship between the legislature and the bureaucracies under its control remain. Why, for example, does the U.S. Congress sometimes adopt very broad legislation, as in the area of antitrust, which appears to give the regulatory agencies considerable scope for discretionary action, and in other cases, such as some environmental legislation, it specifies quite specific standards? Why are regulations sometimes

---

[4] See Faith, Leavens, and Tollison (1982); Weingast and Moran, 1983; Coate, Higgins, and McChesney (1990); Vachris (1996); and the collection of essays in Mackay, Miller, and Yandle (1987). Eisner and Meier (1990) dispute the importance of congressional influence, however.

monitored by governmental agencies like the Federal Drug Administration, and other times by the courts? In this section, we examine two sets of answers that have been given to these questions.

17.2.1 *Uncertainty and the locus of responsibility*

Fiorina (1982a) has emphasized the importance of uncertainty on the part of congressmen over the possible impacts of a piece of legislation as a key factor in determining the form that it takes. Suppose, for example, that representatives from cotton-growing states and those beholden to cotton interests for campaign contributions seek to repay their supporters with legislation. A tariff on imported cotton will have a direct and measurable effect on the wealth of cotton producers, and is an action that the representatives who pass the tariff can take immediate credit for. The preferred form of legislation is a tariff with the specific rate set by the Congress.

Consider, on the other hand, the 1887 legislation that created the Interstate Commerce Commission (ICC) to regulate the railroads, and the Sherman Antitrust Act passed in 1890. Both of these were in response to the rising populist tide at the end of the nineteenth century and had workers, farmers, small firms, and conceivably consumers as their targeted beneficiaries. But there must have been considerably more uncertainty on the part of congressmen over both the actual impacts of the legislation on intended targets and the future political costs from the likely losers from the legislation – the railroads and other large "trusts." Broadly written legislation administered by agencies directly under Congress' control provided Congress with the opportunity to "fine tune" the legislation over time through its control over the ICC and the Justice Department.[5]

17.2.2 *Uncertainty, transaction costs, and commitment*

The literature discussed so far from Niskanen through McNollgast contains models with essentially two actors: a legislature and a bureaucracy. Moe (1990a,b) and Horn (1995) add a third actor to the drama: future legislatures. Their work, like that of Fiorina, Weingast, and others, stresses both the uncertainty over the future that legislators face, and the transaction costs involved in getting the bureaucracies to implement it as intended. But Moe and Horn also call attention to the problem of *commitment* faced by the legislators at the time that they enact legislation. Even if they can reign in the bureaucracies as tightly as the Congressional-dominance models imply, how can they prevent future legislatures from undoing the deals done today?

In providing an answer to this question, Horn develops a model of legislature–bureaucratic interaction that incorporates all of the features of the models discussed so far. When writing a piece of legislation Congress must decide (1) whether to

---

[5] Libecap's (1992) analysis of the passage of the Sherman Act is consistent with the economic-interests-driven model of Fiorina. Poole and Rosenthal's (1993) analysis of voting on the Interstate Commerce Act of 1887 implies, however, that it was the *ideology* of a congressman that determined how he voted on the act and not the economic interests of his constituents.

write a broad, vague statute or a clear and specific one; (2) whether to implement the statute through the private sector, a governmental bureaucracy, or a state-owned enterprise; (3) if the private sector is chosen, whether to monitor the implementation through a regulatory agency or the courts; (4) what administrative procedures will govern the behavior of a regulatory agency or a public bureaucracy; (5) what civil service rules will govern the hiring, firing, and promotion of those who work in these agencies; and so on. Given the uncertainties involved and the underlying principal–agent relationships, Congress faces an extremely complex optimization problem whenever it introduces a major piece of legislation. On the other hand, as Horn describes it, Congress also has an arsenal of control mechanisms at its disposal that it can manipulate to achieve its desired outcome at minimal transaction costs.

To illustrate the richness of Horn's theory, consider the role he sees civil service rules playing in the drama. Imagine that a Congress is elected that is much less committed to environmental protection than previous Congresses that passed the Environmental Protection Act, created the Environmental Protection Agency (EPA), and so on. The new Congress would be tempted to try and achieve its goals by replacing many of the people in the EPA who are strongly committed to environmental protection with others who are less committed or even hostile to it. The elaborate protection civil service rules give to governmental employees eliminates this option from the current Congress' arsenal, however. Horn's explanation for the displacement of the spoils system of governmental patronage that existed in the United States in the nineteenth century with the independent civil service system that exists today is that Congress wished to increase the value of the legislation passed at any point in time by making it more immune to subsequent reversals.

Epstein and O'Halloran (1999) also rely on transaction costs theory to explore the question of congressional delegation. They extend the work of Horn and Moe, however, by drawing out the implications for delegation in the presence of divided government. When the presidency is controlled by one party and Congress by another, the principal–agent problem that arises when responsibility for policies is delegated increases the likelihood that Congress (1) does not delegate, (2) uses more specific language when it delegates, and (3) delegates to an independent agency rather than to a department within the Executive Branch.

Horn, Epstein, and O'Halloran provide considerable corroborative evidence for their theories. These theories pose, however, a puzzling question for the public choice literature. Why would a legislator enacting a bill today constrain the freedom of a legislator tomorrow, given that she is likely to be one and the same person? The answer Horn gives is that by imposing such a constraint a legislator greatly increases her ability to raise funds and reward constituents today, and this gain must presumably offset the opportunities to sell legislation that are closed off for her tomorrow. But this answer seems to presume a sophistication and far-sightedness on the part of constituents that are at odds with the picture of the myopic, rationally ignorant voter found throughout the public choice literature.[6] Can voters and

---

[6] Indeed, it seems at odds with Horn's (1995, p. 12) own assumption of rational ignorance on the part of constituents.

interest groups recognize that their long-run goals will be better served if a piece of legislation is vaguely formulated, delegated to a regulatory agency with such and such administrative rules, and so forth, rather than clearly written and monitored by the courts?

17.3   Congress and the president

In a presidential system of government, like that of the United States, many of the bureaucracies that deliver the programs created in the legislature are under the supervision of the president. In this situation, the issue of whether the legislature can succeed in getting the bureaucracy to carry out the legislature's goals has an added dimension – whether the president will accede to the wishes of the Legislative Branch. We explore this issue in this section.

17.3.1   *The legislature controls the president*

Consider Figure 17.1. The quantities of two public goods, x and y, must be decided. Both the president and the Congress are modeled as unitary actors with preferences defined over x and y. L is the ideal point of Congress (the legislature), and P is the president's ideal point. The curves U_{Li} and U_{Pi} represent indifference curves for the legislature and the president. S is the status quo combination of x and y.

The legislative game between the president and the legislature proceeds as follows: the legislature first chooses a combination C of x and y. The president then has the choice of vetoing this proposal or signing off on it. If he signs off, C becomes the new combination of x and y. If he vetoes, the legislature has the option of overriding the veto. In the United States this requires a two-thirds majority in both houses of Congress. If the legislature can override a presidential veto of L, it obviously proposes this point. The more interesting case arises when the legislature cannot override a presidential veto.

The legislature knows that the president will veto any proposal that makes him worse off than he is at the status quo S. His indifference curve through S, U_{P2}, this represents the boundary of the feasible combinations of x and y that the legislature can hope to achieve. Any proposal above and to the left of U_{P2} will be vetoed resulting in the victory of S. Given this veto constraint, the legislature's optimal proposal is C_L.

The strategic interaction between the president and the legislature can also be depicted with the help of the game tree in Figure 17.2. The legislature moves first and can propose $C = S$ or a different C. Assuming that some Cs exist that both offer the legislature a higher utility than S and will not be vetoed, it is in the interests of the legislature to propose one of these Cs, as, for example, C_L. The president is indifferent between this proposal and S and thus, let us assume, does not veto it; and therefore C wins.[7]

---

[7] For further discussion of these sorts of models, see Shepsle and Weingast (1981), Denzau and Mackay (1983), and Kiewiet and McCubbins (1988).

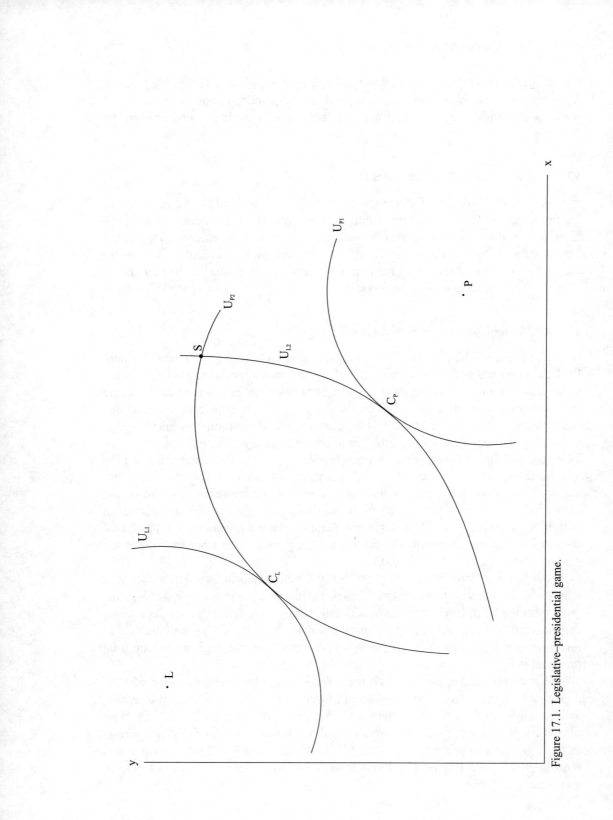

Figure 17.1. Legislative–presidential game.

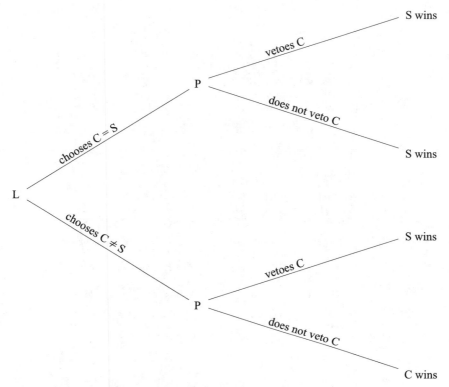

Figure 17.2. Game tree when legislature moves first.

17.3.2 *Presidential control over the legislature*

Ingberman and Yao (1991) have suggested that the president sometimes seizes the first-mover advantage in the legislative game by *committing* himself to certain policies before the legislature can make its proposals. The legislative game is now as in Figure 17.3. The president first decides whether or not to commit to a particular policy, C_P. If he does not commit, the legislature is free to propose whatever it wishes, and the game proceeds as in the previous subsection. If, on the other hand, the president commits to a combination C_P, as say depicted in Figure 17.1, the game proceeds along the bottom branch of the tree in Figure 17.3. The legislature is still free to propose C_L, of course, but if it does so and the president keeps his commitment to veto anything other than C_P, the status quo will result. Eliminating the weakly dominated strategies beyond the president's commitment stage reduces the game tree to that depicted in Figure 17.4. If there exist proposals like C_P that the legislature will accept over the status quo and that provide more utility for the president than C_L, it is in the president's interest to commit to these policies.

Of course, if the legislature were truly indifferent between the C to which the president was committed and the status quo, it might propose the status quo just to spite the president. To avoid this risk, and to avoid not obtaining his preferred outcome because he had misjudged the position of U_{L2}, the president is likely to

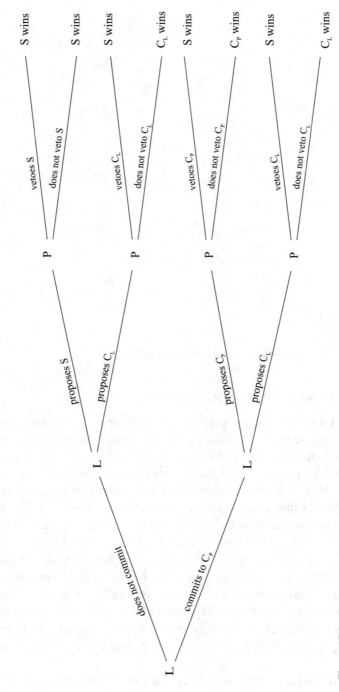

Figure 17.3. Game tree when president can commit.

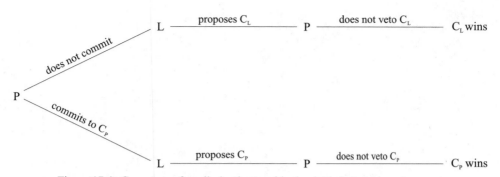

Figure 17.4. Game tree after eliminating weakly dominated strategies.

commit himself to proposals that promise some surplus in utility for the legislature over that provided by the status quo. Taking into account the uncertainties in the situation, for example, the president might commit to vetoing any proposals above and to the left of line CC in Figure 17.5. This line now becomes the boundary of the opportunity set for the legislature, and it will choose the point on it that provides it with the highest utility, for example, C_{LC}. When the president can precommit to certain policy combinations, the likely outcome of the legislative game is a compromise proposal providing gains over the status quo for both the president and the legislature.

As always with precommitment strategies, one must inquire whether they are credible. If the legislature's proposal is just inside of U_{P2}, the president's indifference curve through S, would he in fact veto it to keep his commitment? Obviously in a one-shot game this action would be irrational, and thus the commitment noncredible. But the legislative game between Congress and the president is repeated many times over an electoral cycle. Vetoing a bill that would provide the president with a small increment in utility can be a rational strategy in such repeated games if it makes the president's veto threats creditable and thus leads to future proposals from the legislature that promise large gains to the president.

In practice, of course, the president cannot observe the Congress' indifference map nor can it observe his. Uncertainty exists on both sides as to what the other will do. Cameron (2000) has recently modeled the bargaining strategies of both sets of actors, and used his model to interpret the use of the veto by American presidents.

17.3.3 *The problem of deadlocks*

Some of the commitments that a president makes occur during election campaigns. Congressmen must also stand for election, however, and they too may make commitments to their constituents. When both branches precommit to minimum or maximum expenditure policies, the result can be a set of precommitments that ensure the victory of the status quo.

To see this consider Figure 17.6. The president has promised to veto any proposal from Congress that does not promise combinations of x and y to the right of the $CP - CP$ line. The legislature has promised its constituents that it will *not* propose any combinations to the right of the $CL - CL$ line. There are no points within the

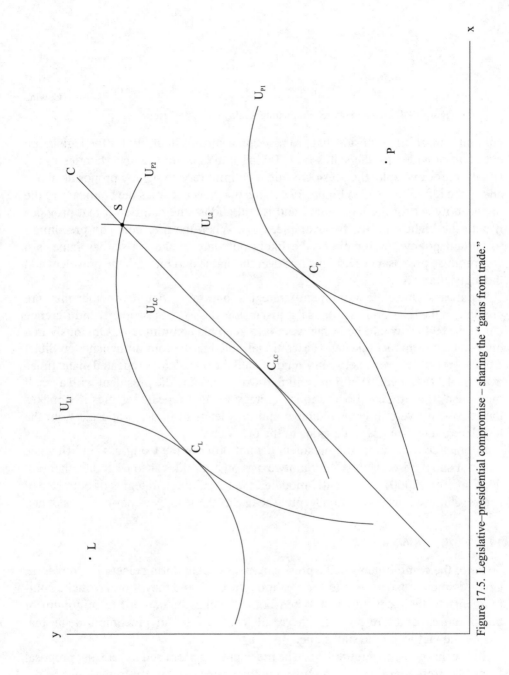

Figure 17.5. Legislative–presidential compromise – sharing the "gains from trade."

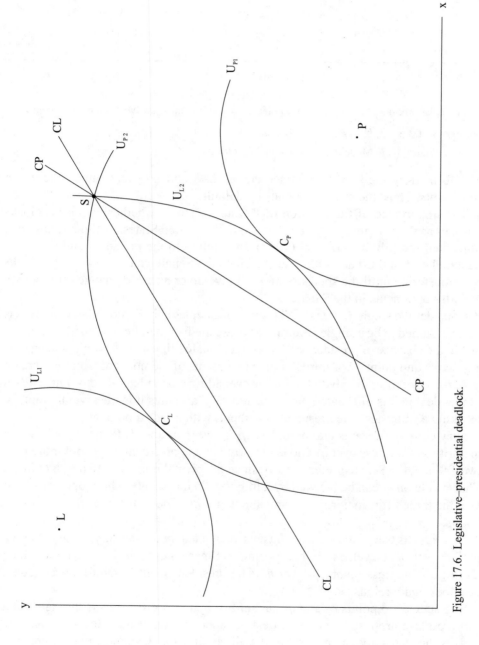

Figure 17.6. Legislative–presidential deadlock.

397

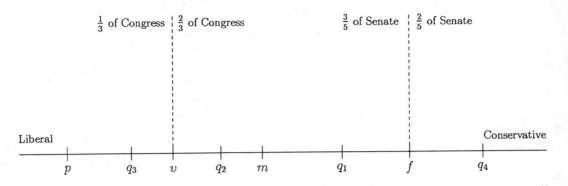

p = ideal point of president, v = veto pivotal point, m = ideal point of median member of Congress,

f = filibuster pivotal point, q_i = status quo points

Figure 17.7. Modeling congressional deadlocks.

lens formed by the two indifference curves U_{P2} and U_{L2} that satisfy these two constraints. Thus, the status quo wins by default.

The importance of the position of the status quo to whether or not deadlocks arise, or as they are more popularly called in the United States, gridlocks, has been illustrated recently by Krehbiel (1998). In addition to the president and Congress Krehbiel adds a third actor, the Senate, since the Senate can also cause deadlocks by filibustering until the sponsors of a bill give up or agree to change it to mollify the bill's opponents in the Senate.

Consider the single-dimensional issue space depicted in Figure 17.7. Congress is again assumed to be a single committee whose median member has an ideal point at m.[8] In the absence of presidential vetoes and Senate filibusters m would win against any status quo point. Two-thirds of the ideal points of members of Congress are on or to the right of v, the pivotal point for overriding a presidential veto. Three-fifths of the ideal points of senators lie to the left of f and thus it is the pivotal point for blocking a filibuster. The president is a liberal with an ideal point at p.

Now consider a status quo point like q_1 between m and f. Point m could win a majority in Congress over q_1 and is preferred by the president to q_1. But more than two-fifths of the Senate prefer q_1 to m, since the pivotal point f is to the right of q_1. Thus a vote on m can be blocked by a filibuster in the Senate. The proponents of m lack the three fifths majority to bring about cloture. The status quo wins; deadlock reigns.

The same is true if the status quo is between v and m as, say, at q_2. The president prefers q_2 to m and vetoes a bill proposing m. Since v lies to the left of q_2, more than a third of Congress favors q_2 over m. The president's veto cannot be overridden; deadlock again reigns.

The status quo points q_3 and q_4 cannot triumph, however. If q_3 is the status quo Congress can propose v and override a presidential veto if he bothers to cast one. If q_4 is the status quo, a proposal of f will obtain enough support in the Senate to

---

[8] The importance of differences between House and Senate preferences is illustrated by Morris and Munger (1998).

kill the filibuster. An interesting feature of Krehbiel's theory is that the existence of deadlocks in U.S. politics *does not* depend on the presidency and Congress being controlled by different parties. All that matters are the positions of the pivotal points and the status quo.

17.4 Congress, the president, and the judiciary

17.4.1 *Adding the judiciary to the model*

The third potential actor in the legislative drama is, of course, the judiciary. In many countries like the United States, the judiciary can intervene in the legislative game by declaring the compromise reached between the executive and legislative branches null and void. It does so by deciding that the legislation is inconsistent with the language or the intent behind the language in the Constitution.

The judiciary can be introduced into the model of the previous section by assuming that it, too, has preferences defined over x and y. If the judiciary's ideal point lies to the right and below point P in Figure 17.1, or to the left and above L, its addition to the game will not affect the outcome, since its set of outcomes preferred to the status quo will contain those of one of the other actors. The situation changes, however, if the judiciary's ideal point lies closer to the status quo than do the ideal points of the president and the legislature. An example is depicted in Figure 17.8. The judiciary's ideal point is J and it will veto any proposals that fall outside of its circular indifference curve, U_C, through S. The set of alternatives to the status quo that might be proposed by the legislature and not vetoed by either the president or the judiciary is now reduced from the lens falling between U_{P2} and U_{L2} to the darkened portion of the lens. This set would be reduced still further if we allow the president to precommit to certain combinations.

Very often the judiciary's ideal point coincides with the status quo. In this case the set of legislatively feasible alternatives to the status quo is empty, of course. A fairly recent example along these lines occurred in California. The governor wished to change policy to deny immigrants access to the public schools and healthcare system. The California Supreme Court preferred the status quo to this policy, and imposed it by declaring the governor's proposals unconstitutional.[9]

17.4.2 *The goals of the judiciary*

In modeling the legislative game, it is reasonable to assume that the "preferences" of the legislature and the president are a reflection of the preferences of the voters who elect them, and thus in principle testable hypotheses can be derived as to when a president will veto legislation, make a commitment to veto, and so on. In many countries and in all of the federal courts of the United States, judges are not elected,

---

[9] Many studies have analyzed the behavior of the judiciary from a public choice perspective. See, for example, Mashaw (1985, 1990), Ingberman and Yao (1991), Ferejohn and Weingast (1992a,b), Levy and Spiller (1994), and the papers collected in Stearns (1997). Stearns (1994) offers a critique of some applications of public choice to the analysis of the judiciary.

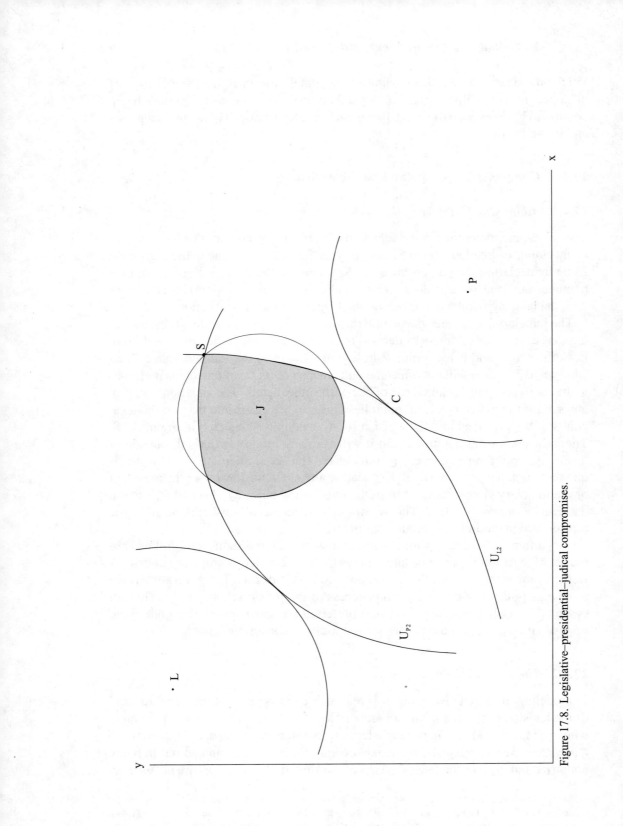

Figure 17.8. Legislative–presidential–judical compromises.

but rather appointed, and often their appointments are for life. What determines the "preferences" of a person who must neither stand for reelection nor fear loss of income and position as a result of the preferences that she reveals through her judicial decisions?

Landes and Posner (1975) offered one of the earliest answers to this question. They claimed that the framers of the U.S. Constitution wished to increase the value of the legislation sold to interest groups by increasing its permanence. This goal was accomplished through the creation of an independent judiciary that could use its independence to veto the "sale" of new legislation which would reduce the value of past sales.

Although this hypothesis has some intuitive appeal in countries in which a sitting legislature writes the constitution, it runs into some historical difficulties as an account of the judiciary's independence in the United States. First of all, the octogenarian Benjamin Franklin, future president James Madison, and several others who met in Philadelphia were neither members of the national legislature at that time, nor were likely to have contemplated becoming members of the legislature created in the Constitution. Second, the U.S. judiciary's independence arguably owes more to subsequent judicial interpretation of the Constitution – as, for example, in Chief Justice John Marshall's decision in *Marbury v. Ames* – than to its original language.

An independent judiciary would play an important role as an agent of the citizens in a *normative* theory of constitutions in which the constitution is written by the citizens to advance their own interests. Such an independent agent is needed to help mitigate the principal–agent problem between the citizens and their agents in the legislative and judicial branches. Even though in such a normative theory, the judiciary's independence only *allows* members of the judiciary to intervene on behalf of the citizens, it does not provide them with positive incentives to do so.[10]

The public choice literature's approach to the problem of defining the objectives of the judiciary has been to assume it away – that is, to assume an objective for the judiciary without defending this assumption, and then to proceed to analyze the consequences of this assumption for legislative outcomes. Although this approach can be defended as a first step in integrating the judiciary into models of legislative behavior, it obviously makes such models of limited use, unless we can determine more concretely what it is that judges maximize and why they do so. The question of the motivation of judges in an independent judiciary remains largely an empty black box in the public choice literature.[11]

17.5 Legislative decision making in the European Union

Although the literature on legislative/executive bargaining and compromise has been dominated by studies of the institutional structure of the United States, some additional work has been done on other countries. Although institutional structures differ, of course, in other countries, the analytical apparatus used to study the United

---

[10] For further discussion, see Mueller (1996a, ch. 19).

[11] See, however, Posner (1993). It is also possible that the preferences of judges do not really matter, because the law evolves in such a way that only "efficient laws" survive (Priest, 1977; Rubin, 1997).

States can easily be adapted to the institutions of other countries. We illustrate this point with a brief discussion of decision-making procedures in the European Union.

There are three main actors in the European Union: the Commission, the Council, and the Parliament. The Commission is the European Union's equivalent to the executive branch, and consists of a president and commissioners from each member country. The Council can be regarded as one "chamber" in the European Union's political system, with representatives appointed by each member country. The members are assigned votes according to the size of the country. The Parliament is the European Union's second chamber. Its members are elected from each member country, with countries again assigned seats in rough proportion to size.

Figure 17.9 presents a simplified schemata of the sequence of decision making under the so-called cooperation procedure of the European Union.[12] The Commission initiates the legislative process by making a proposal for new legislation. Its proposal goes to the European Parliament which can accept it as is, amend it, or reject it by a simple majority vote. If the proposal is not rejected, it goes to the Council. If the Council accepts it without amendment it becomes law. If the Council amends the proposal, it goes back to the Parliament for a final reading. The Parliament has three options at this juncture: (1) accept the proposal as is, (2) amend the proposal and send it back to the Council, or (3) reject the proposal. Rejection of the proposal at this stage requires an absolute majority of the total number of seats in the Parliament. If the Parliament either rejects or amends the proposal it received from the Council, it goes back to the Council. The Council can only override the Parliament's rejection by a unanimous vote. It can also amend the Parliament's amended proposal only through a unanimous vote.

The procedure sketched in Figure 17.9 gives the European Parliament an effective veto over any legislative proposals coming from the Council, *if the Parliament can get one member of the council to support its veto*. This veto provides the Parliament with agenda-setting power, which it might be able to use to obtain its most preferred outcome among the set of outcomes that the Council is willing to accept in place of the status quo. This point can be illustrated with the help of Figure 17.10, which is simply a relabeled version of Figure 17.1, where P now stands for the ideal point of the European Parliament, and C the ideal point of the Council. To simplify the discussion, the preferences of the Commission have not been included in the figure. It is assumed that a majority of the Commission will accept any proposal that emerges from this procedure as was also the case in Figure 17.9.

If C is the ideal point of a *qualified majority of the Council* sufficiently large to approve legislation, and U_{C1} and U_{C2} are indifference curves for this qualified majority, then the Parliament will be able to amend the Commission's proposal on its second reading so that it corresponds to point C_P and obtain its most preferred outcome from the set of proposals that both the Parliament and the Council prefer to the status quo (the points within the lens formed by U_{P2} and U_{C2}).[13] If, on the other hand, C is the ideal point of a Council in unanimous agreement, then it will

---

[12] My discussion follows Tsebelis (1994, 1997); see also Steunenberg (1994) and Crombez (1996, 1997).

[13] At the present time there are 15 member countries in the European Union, and a total of 87 weighted votes. A qualified majority consists of 62 or more votes.

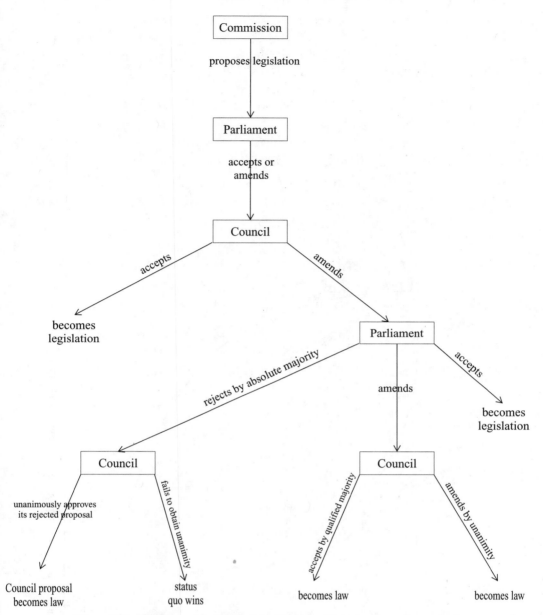

Figure 17.9. Sequence of decisions under European Union's cooperation procedure.

be able to impose this outcome if a majority of the Commission prefers this point to the status quo.

New procedures introduced in the Maastricht Treaty of 1992 add an additional step to the decision procedure just described. If the Council does not accept the proposal that emerges from a second reading in the Parliament the issue goes to a conciliation committee consisting of 15 representatives from the Council and 15 from the Parliament. Should this committee fail to reach an agreement, the Council is empowered to make a final proposal. Depending on the nature of the issue, this

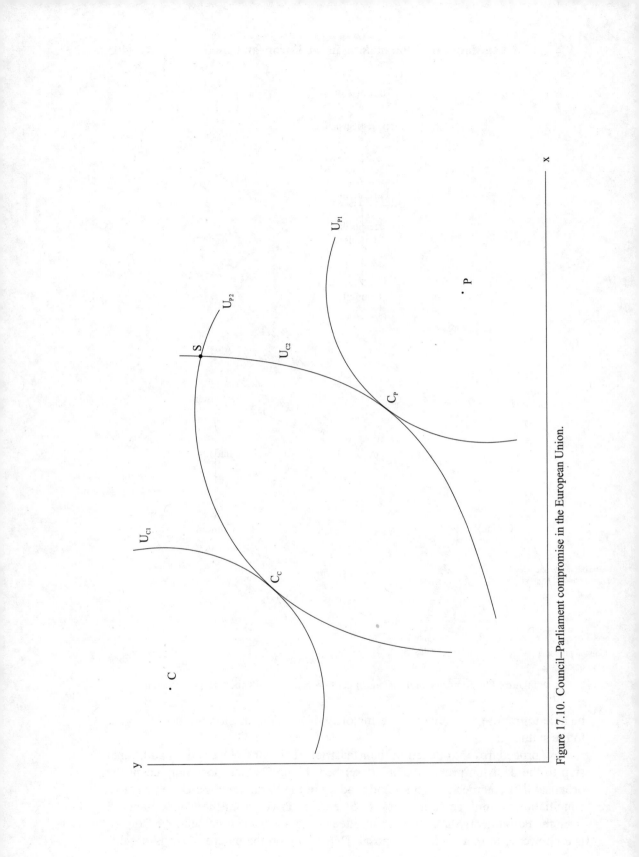

Figure 17.10. Council–Parliament compromise in the European Union.

proposal may require either a unanimous agreement by the Council or a qualified majority. The Council's proposal can only be voted down by an absolute majority of the Parliament. This new conciliation procedure puts the Council in the agenda-setting role at the end of the process, and increases the likelihood of proposal C_C winning instead of C_P.

Neither the Commission nor the Council nor the Parliament is a unitary actor with unique ideal points and indifference maps, of course; thus, a full analysis of decision making in the European Union requires a more elaborate structure and the use of concepts like the core, the uncovered set, and the tournament equilibrium set.[14] Such an analysis is beyond the scope of this chapter.

17.6   Conclusions

The literature on voting rules reviewed in Part I of this book assumes that voters choose outcomes directly. Whichever point in $x-y$ space a committee chooses gets implemented. The literature on representative democracy reviewed in the beginning chapters of Part II also assumes that the policies promised by candidates or parties in their efforts to win votes are implemented once the election is over. The discussions in the present and preceding chapters reveal, however, that these views of the political process are far too simplistic. The tabulation of ballots on election day constitutes the end of one sort of political struggle, the beginning of another – the latter being the struggle among those within the government, both elected and appointed, to shape the actual outcomes that emerge from the political process.

Bibliographical notes

Wintrobe (1997) and Moe (1997) have surveyed the literatures on bureaucracy and legislative/executive branch bargaining. Tsebelis and Money (1997) have described and analyzed bargaining and joint decision-making procedures in several countries as well as the European Union.

Bergman, Müller, and Strøm (2000) contain several papers analyzing delegation issues in European parliamentary democracies.

---

[14] The concept of the uncovered set was discussed in Chapter 11. The tournament equilibrium set was first discussed by Schwartz (1990). Applications of these analytic tools to bicameral decision making include Cox and McKelvey (1984), Hammond and Miller (1987), and Tsebelis and Money (1997).

CHAPTER 18

Dictatorship

> To sum up, for the Fascist everything is within the state and there exists nothing, human or spiritual, or even less has value, outside of the state. In this sense Fascism is totalitarian and the Fascist state interprets, develops and multiplies the whole life of the people as a synthesis and unity of each value.
>
> Benito Mussolini

The postulate of *methodological individualism* underlies all public choice analysis. In trying to explain governmental actions, we begin by analyzing the behavior of the individuals who make up the government. In a democracy these are the voters, their elected representatives, and appointed bureaucrats. The postulate of methodological individualism has a normative analogue. The actions of government *ought* to correspond, in some fundamental way, to the preferences of the individuals whom these actions affect – the citizens of the state. This postulate of *normative individualism* underlies much of the normative analysis in public choice. It is quite understandable, therefore, that virtually all research in public choice has concentrated on the analysis of democratic governments, first because virtually all public choice scholars have lived in democratic countries and thus this form of political system has the most intrinsic interest for them, and second because they feel that all governmental systems ought to be organized as democracies.

If one were to categorize every government that has existed anywhere on the earth from the beginning of recorded history as either a democracy or a dictatorship, and weigh each government by its duration, one would find that democratic governments have made up only a tiny fraction of all present and past governments – a fraction that corresponds to the amount of attention public choice scholars have devoted to *non*democratic governments in their research. Even today, at the beginning of the third millennium, when democratic governments are more prevalent around the world than at any other time in history, they do not make up a quarter of all governments.[1] Anyone seeking to know how actual governments function in different parts of the world must take up the study of dictatorship. In the last decade or so, public choice scholars have begun to work on this challenging topic. This chapter reviews some of their efforts.

The fourth edition of *The Concise Oxford Dictionary* defines a dictator as an "Absolute ruler, usually temporary or irregular, of a State, especially one who

---

[1] *Freedom House* (1997) classifies only 22 percent of all countries as having the set of political freedoms and civil liberties that we associate with full-fledged democracy.

suppresses or succeeds a democratic government; [a] person with absolute authority in any sphere." This definition aptly fits that archetype dictator, Adolph Hitler. He succeeded and suppressed a democracy, ruled with absolute authority, and, mercifully, his rule was temporary. Those who have lived under the rule of Fidel Castro or lived under Joseph Stalin might question the characterization of dictatorship as *temporary*, and neither of these rulers replaced democracies. Both did suppress whatever democratic tendencies existed in their countries, however, and both share with Hitler – and with all other dictators – the property that the authority of the dictator is to a degree *absolute*. This attribute of dictatorship suggests that the public choice analysis of dictatorship, grounded as it is on methodological individualism, might involve merely the analysis of the preferences and actions of one individual – the dictator. No dictator rules entirely alone, however. He is surrounded by a bureaucracy that must carry out his dictates, and thus confronts the same sorts of principal–agent problems that exist in all bureaucracies. And even the citizens he suppresses have options of whether to resist the government's actions or support them, and if resistance is chosen whether it is passive or active, and so on. Thus, we shall find that despite the significant differences that exist between dictatorships and democracies, the same basic methodological approach can be applied to the analysis of each. Indeed, we shall find that several concepts analyzed in previous chapters come into play again in the analysis of dictatorship. We begin at the beginning with an account of the origins of dictatorship out of anarchy.

18.1   The origins of dictatorship

We noted in Chapter 2 that cooperative solutions to prisoners' dilemmas and the provision of public goods might come about in small, stable communities without the erection of formal governmental institutions through the rational, self-interested behavior of individuals engaged in a series of prisoners' dilemma supergames. Such informal mechanisms to induce efficient cooperation break down, however, as the number of players increases and their identities change. One response to such breakdowns would be for all players to come together and design a set of democratic institutions for resolving these collective action problems that will be to the mutual advantage of all players. Such a response would be in the Wicksellian tradition that underlies much of the public choice literature, and is the focal point of Chapters 25 and 26. Such *collective* responses to collective action problems fall prey to the same free-riding behavior that gives rise to the problems in the first place, however (Dixit and Olson, 2000). One might expect, therefore, that real-world solutions to collective action problems more often involve the actions of single individuals or small groups. Recognizing the potential gains from providing some public goods and rules for resolving prisoners' dilemmas, certain entrepreneurial individuals step forward and establish the institutions for providing these goods and services.

Olson (1993, 2000) characterized the rise of dictatorships much in this way. A dictator is a wealth maximizer, who lives by transferring the wealth generated by those he rules to himself. One strategy such a wealth maximizer might follow in a world in which all individuals live in peaceful anarchy in small communities would be to create a military force and move from one community to the next expropriating any and all wealth each community has accumulated. In such a world, however, any individual who is not part of a roving army has no incentive to accumulate wealth, since she must live in expectation that a *roving bandit* and his army will appear and rob her of her accumulated wealth. A rational, wealth-maximizing bandit will wish to give individuals incentives to create wealth, therefore, so there is more wealth for him to take away. Such incentives can be provided if the bandit takes only a part of a community's wealth, and protects its remaining wealth from other roving bandits. Thus, a roving bandit can accumulate more wealth by becoming a *stationary* bandit and providing all of the public goods and services that will induce those he robs to produce wealth, including police protection and defense against external attacks. In this way dictatorship is born.[2]

Both the bandit and the community he preys upon are better off if the bandit becomes stationary and cultivates and protects *his* community. Although immobility on the part of the bandit aligns his interests with those of the community, it does not bring them into perfect alignment. The community's wealth falls short of the level it would obtain with a *benevolent* dictator who maximized the wealth of the community. To see what is involved, let us deal with income flows rather than wealth stocks. The dictator provides public goods like roads and bridges, a judicial system that enforces contracts and protects property, and so forth. Thus, national income, Y, increases with the amount of public goods, G, $Y = Y(G)$, with $\partial Y/\partial G > 0$, $\partial^2 Y/\partial G^2 < 0$. To finance the provision of the public goods, the dictator levels a proportional tax, t, on income. This tax has disincentive effects on effort, and thus higher taxes lead to falling national income. The simplest way to capture this effect is to assume a constant elasticity with respect to the tax rate, η, and write realized income as $Y_r = Y(1 - \eta t)$.

The dictator's consumption, C, must also come out of the tax revenue raised, and thus $tY_r = G + C$. The dictator wishes to maximize his consumption subject to this constraint. If we use this constraint to substitute for C, the dictator can be thought of as choosing G and t so as to maximize the objective function, $O_D = tY(G)(1 - \eta t) - G$. This leads to the following two first-order conditions:

$$t\frac{dY}{dG} - 1 = 0 \tag{18.1}$$

$$Y - 2\eta tY = 0, \tag{18.2}$$

and from these we obtain

$$\frac{dY}{dG} = \frac{1}{t} \tag{18.3}$$

$$t = \frac{1}{2\eta}. \tag{18.4}$$

Equation (18.4) defines the same optimal tax rate as obtained by Brennan and

---

[2] Volckart (2000) describes how the modern state arose in medieval Germany as an institution for providing protection and generating rents.

Buchanan (1980) in the Leviathan model, for in the present model the dictator is exploiting the population in exactly the same way as in the Leviathan model, with the exception that the money taken from the citizens goes to finance the dictator's own consumption rather than the expansion of the state.

If public goods provide no utility to the citizens of the community other than through their impact on income, the citizens would of course wish to maximize the income of the community net of the amount needed to pay for the public goods, $Y(1 - \eta t) - G$. If we maximize this societal objective function, O_S, with respect to G, we obtain

$$\frac{\partial O_S}{\partial G} = \frac{dY}{dG}(1 - t\eta) - Y\eta \frac{\partial t}{\partial G} - 1 = 0, \tag{18.5}$$

taking into account that t is a function of G through the budget constraint. The first term in (18.5), $(dY/dG)(1 - t\eta)$, is the marginal gain to the community from increasing the quantity of public goods. The second term, $Y\eta(\partial t/\partial G)$, is the marginal cost of increasing the amount of public goods owing to the fact that an increase in G requires an increase in t, and this increase reduces Y because of the disincentive effects of taxation. The third term in (18.5), -1, captures the marginal cost of increasing G that arises because G must be financed out of Y.

Despite the simplicity of the relationships assumed, solving for an explicit value of t leads to a quite complicated expression relating t to dY/dG. Fortunately, it is apparent from the objective functions of the dictator and the community, O_D and O_S, that the quantity of the public good provided by the dictator falls below the socially optimal quantity.

$$O_D = tY(G)(1 - \eta t) - G \tag{18.6}$$

$$O_S = Y(G)(1 - \eta t) - G. \tag{18.7}$$

These two objective functions are plotted in Figure 18.1. Owing to the concavity of $Y(G)$, and the fact that $(1 - \eta t)$ falls with t, O_S is concave in G, as is O_D. Owing to the need to finance the dictator's consumption out of tax revenue, t is higher under dictatorship for any level of G (and thus $(1 - \eta t)$ is lower). This, coupled with the fact that the first term in O_D is multiplied by $t < 1$, ensures that O_D reaches a maximum before O_S does. A dictatorship supplies a smaller level of G than would be socially optimal.

18.2 The goals of dictators

18.2.1 *The consumption of the dictator*

The Roman emperor Nero indulged himself in every possible consumption activity; France's Louis XIV, "the Sun King," built a palace at Versailles that would have turned Nero green with envy; England's Henry VIII indulged a voracious appetite for food, drink, and wives; when Imelda Marcos, wife of the Philippines' longtime dictator, hurriedly fled the country following her husband's death, among the many possessions that she left behind were 3,000 pairs of shoes. The list of autocrats who have taxed their subjects to support extravagant and exotic lifestyles is nearly

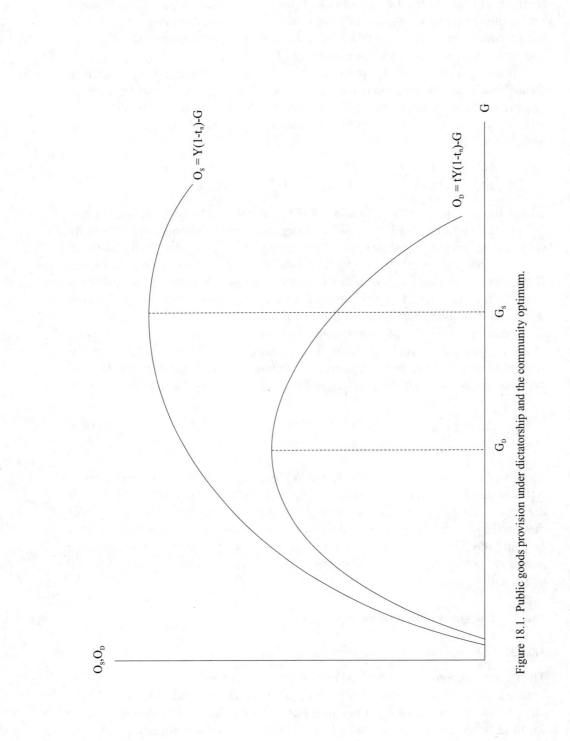

Figure 18.1. Public goods provision under dictatorship and the community optimum.

endless. The assumption of the previous section – that a dictator uses his authority to transfer income from his subjects to enhance his personal consumption – fits many a dictator.

18.2.2 *Power*

But not all dictators aspire to live "like Kings." Adolph Hitler lived rather modestly, despite the extent of his absolute power, as did Jean Calvin in the days when he and his followers imposed a religious autocracy on the citizens of Geneva. Some dictators seem to be driven by desires that go well beyond their personal consumption. In these and analogous cases, the dictator espouses a particular ideology that he wishes to inculcate in others. The dictator seeks power to maintain and spread a particular ideology. For Hitler it was Fascism; for Calvin a particular version of Protestantism that came to be called Calvinism. The dictator possessed by such an ideology seeks that his subjects espouse and live by the principles that underlie the ideology. He seeks *power* over his subjects, power to control what they think and what they do. Jean Calvin, for example, dictated what the Genevans would wear, where they could live, and the names they could give their children (Bernholz, 1997b, pp. 289–90). The goal of Fascism was to control every aspect of the subject's life, as the quotation from Mussolini at the beginning of this chapter reveals.[3] Any system like Fascism or Calvinism that seeks total control over individuals' lives we shall place under the category of *totalitarianism*.[4] Our second possible goal of a dictator is power – the power to control some, in the limit all, of the actions of those he governs.

18.2.3 *Security*

Since many may find the power and/or life-style of the dictator attractive, many may wish to replace him. If the dictator wishes to continue to exercise power and enjoy the perquisites of office, he must thwart the efforts of others to replace him. Remaining in office – job security – is the third and most obvious goal that a dictator is likely to pursue, and one of the most difficult to achieve (Tullock, 1987).

In this book we have examined the behavior of three actors in a democracy – the citizen-voter, the elected politician, and the appointed bureaucrat. A dictator combines all three roles, and thus not surprisingly his motivations are a combination of the assumed motives of the three different actors in a democracy. In a dictatorship it is the preferences of the dictator, not those of the citizen, that are paramount, and thus government taxes and expenditures are oriented at least in part toward satisfying his consumption wishes, just as in a democracy government taxes and expenditures are oriented, at least in part, toward maximizing citizens' benefits from private and public good consumption. As head of state the dictator is in command of the government bureaucracy and he must, at a minimum, exercise power over this

---

[3] This quotation is taken from Bernholz (1991, p. 431), where a definition and discussion of the properties of totalitarian movements can be found.

[4] For further discussion of the properties of totalitarianism and references to the non-public choice literature dealing with it, see Bernholz (1991, 1997b) and Wintrobe (1998, pp. 7–11, 58–68).

bureaucracy to achieve his other goals. If he wishes to impose a particular ideology on all his subjects, he must exercise power over all of them. Thus the dictator, like every other bureaucrat, seeks power. And finally, like every elected politician, he wants to remain in office. We now explore in some detail how the dictator goes about achieving these goals.

18.3   The functioning and survival of dictatorships

18.3.1   *The utility-maximizing dictator*

Given the discussion of the previous section we can now express the dictator's utility as a function of consumption, C, power, P, and security, S, $U(C, P, S)$. To obtain these objectives we shall assume, following Wintrobe (1990, 1998), that the dictator relies on two strategic instruments – the *loyalty* of his subjects and *repression* of them. Loyalty is won by making the citizens better off. We shall assume that the loyalty of the dictatorship's subjects increases with their after-tax incomes, $L = L(Y_T)$, $L' > 0$, $L'' < 0$. To repress certain actions of the citizens, the dictator must expend resources on police, jails, informers, and so on. Thus, the level of repression is a function of the amount of tax revenue devoted to it, $R = R(T_R)$, $R' > 0$, $R'' < 0$. Both the power of the dictator and his security in office can reasonably be assumed to increase with the loyalty of his subjects, and the amount of resources devoted to repression, $P = P(L, R)$, $\partial P/\partial L > 0$, $\partial^2 P/\partial L^2 < 0$, $\partial P/\partial R > 0$, $\partial^2 P/\partial R^2 < 0$; $S = S(L, R)$, $\partial S/\partial L > 0$, $\partial^2 S/\partial L^2 < 0$, $\partial S/\partial R > 0$, $\partial^2 S/\partial R^2 < 0$.

As before we assume that the dictator raises revenue through a tax on the population's income. We could assume that this income is a function of the level of public goods supplied as before, and solve for both this level and the tax rate. Since no new insights can be expected from this additional complexity, we shall simply assume that both the level of public goods, G, and gross national income, Y, are fixed. The dictator's task then reduces to that of choosing a level of consumption, C, and expenditures on repression, T_R, to maximize his utility. Given these values, the total amount to be raised in taxes is determined, and this in turn fixes the after-tax income of the population ($Y_T = Y - G - C - T_R$), and thereby the level of their loyalty. Maximizing U with respect to C and T_R yields

$$\frac{\partial U}{\partial C} = \frac{\partial U}{\partial C} - \frac{\partial U}{\partial P}\frac{\partial P}{\partial L} - \frac{\partial U}{\partial S}\frac{\partial S}{\partial L} = 0 \tag{18.8}$$

$$\frac{\partial U}{\partial T_R} = -\frac{\partial U}{\partial P}\frac{\partial P}{\partial L} + \frac{\partial U}{\partial P}\frac{\partial P}{\partial R}R' - \frac{\partial U}{\partial S}\frac{\partial S}{\partial L} + \frac{\partial U}{\partial S}\frac{\partial S}{\partial R}R' = 0. \tag{18.9}$$

Rearranging (18.8) we get

$$\frac{\partial U}{\partial C} = \frac{\partial U}{\partial P}\frac{\partial P}{\partial L} + \frac{\partial U}{\partial S}\frac{\partial S}{\partial L}. \tag{18.10}$$

The dictator chooses a level of consumption such that the marginal utility from the last tax talent[5] devoted to his consumption just equals the marginal utility from increased power and security he would receive if that talent were not raised in taxes, and thereby increasing the loyalty of the citizenry.

Rearranging (18.9) we get

$$\left(\frac{\partial U}{\partial P} \frac{\partial P}{\partial R} + \frac{\partial U}{\partial S} \frac{\partial S}{\partial R} \right) R' = \frac{\partial U}{\partial P} \frac{\partial P}{\partial L} + \frac{\partial U}{\partial S} \frac{\partial S}{\partial L}. \tag{18.11}$$

The dictator devotes tax revenue to repression up to the point where the marginal gain from an extra talent spent on repression just equals the marginal utility from increased loyalty that this talent would produce if it were not raised in taxes.

18.3.2 *Tinpots and totalitarians*

Wintrobe (1990, 1998) has examined the behavior of polar cases of dictators, who are only interested in either power or in their personal consumption. Those who pursue only power he calls "totalitarians," and those who maximize their own consumption he calls "tin pots." Equations (18.8) and (18.10) drop out for the totalitarian, and we are left with the condition (18.11) for optimally balancing the gains from increased loyalty and repression. For the tin pot dictator, all terms involving the $\partial U/\partial P$ drop out of (18.10) and (18.11), and we are left with

$$\frac{\partial U}{\partial C} = \frac{\partial U}{\partial S} \frac{\partial S}{\partial S} \tag{18.12}$$

$$\frac{\partial S}{\partial R} R' = \frac{\partial S}{\partial L}. \tag{18.13}$$

The tin pot balances the marginal gain in utility from an increase in consumption against the marginal gain from another dollar left to the people to increase his security, and divides money between building loyalty and increasing repression so that it is equally effective on the margin at increasing security.

A threat to a dictator's security can be interpreted as a rise in $\partial U/\partial S$. The reaction of the tin pot to such a challenge to his rule is unambiguous. He reduces consumption to increase loyalty and reequilibrate the two sides of (18.12). The reaction of the totalitarian is more ambiguous. The increase in $\partial U/\partial S$ increases both the right- and the left-hand sides of (18.11). Whether the totalitarian responds by cutting taxes to increase loyalty, or by raising them to increase repression depends on the relative effectiveness of these two strategies.

An exogenous increase in national income produces a windfall increase in the loyalty of the population, and thereby a fall in the marginal impact of reducing taxes on the population. The right-hand sides of both (18.12) and (18.13) fall and the tin pot responds by increasing taxes and spending more on repression to increase his

---

[5] So as not to suggest that any particular country is a dictatorship, I have chosen this ancient unit of money for our dictatorship.

security and more on his personal consumption.[6] An exogenous increase in national income decreases both terms on the right-hand side of (18.11) and thus leads the totalitarian to raise taxes and increase repression so as to increase both his power and his security.

18.3.3 *Selective strategies to survive*

We have until now assumed that loyalty and repression – although quite different in their causes – are similar in their effects. Both can enhance the power and security of the dictator if more resources are devoted to them. The preceding models do not specify, however, how these resources are spent; whether the actions of all citizens are monitored and repressed, or only those of some; whether the incomes of all citizens are increased to win their loyalty, or only those of some. Repressive policies – government informers, secret police, death squads – seem likely to breed distrust and fear, and in many cases to destroy the goodwill and loyalty that other government policies, like free education, subsidized housing and the arts, and sound economic policies might engender. Thus, it seems plausible that a dictator will make his investments in fostering loyalty and repression selectively. One strategy would be to cultivate the loyalty of those individuals or groups who can contribute the most to the success of the dictatorship, and repress those who are best able to harm it. Thus, the military's loyalty is enhanced by high salaries and fat budgets, while student groups and the press are censored and repressed.[7]

Up until now we have assumed that the dictator supplies public goods to increase the incomes of all members of society both to build the loyalty that contributes to the dictator's power and security, and to maximize his potential tax revenue. But a given group's loyalty can be won just as readily by *transferring* income to it from some other group as from creating income through the provision of pure public goods and sound economic policies. Thus, the rational dictator can be expected not only to transfer income from the community to himself to satisfy his personal consumption desires and his personal ambitions, but also to transfer income to segments of the community whose loyalty he most wants to strengthen. Those groups that see their incomes taken away to finance such transfers become the obvious targets of repression.

We might model this process by assuming that the success of the dictatorship, however measured, or more narrowly its security, S, is a function of the utility levels realized by each group in the country, which in turn are functions of the income earned by each member of a group and any subsidy/transfers it receives, $U_i = U_i(Y_i + s_i)$, where s_i is the subsidy to a member of group i, which if it is

---

[6] Wintrobe (1998, chs. 3 and 5) assumes that loyalty is an increasing function of repression at low levels of repression. Thus, an exogenous increase in loyalty caused by an increase in income allows the tin pot to reduce repression. I prefer to keep the concepts of loyalty and repression separate. Loyalty connotes the *voluntary* allegiance of citizens to the dictator out of gratitude or trust. Repression enhances the *involuntary* support for the dictator from fear and coercion.

[7] This reasoning explains why I separate loyalty and repression. If outlays to increase loyalty also benefited targets of repression, then it would be sensible to assume that $L = L(Y_T, R)$ with $\partial L / \partial R < 0$.

negative becomes a tax. As a group's income grows its loyalty to the regime and contribution to its success grow. Each group's contribution to the regime's success can be different, however. To simplify, we shall merely capture these differences with the group-specific parameter, α_i. In addition, the success of the dictatorship depends on the resources it devotes to repression. Once again we shall assume that the contributions to the regime's success from repression differ across groups, and simply measure these differential responses with the parameter, β_i. The security of the dictatorship can now most simply be written as additive in these two terms,

$$
\begin{aligned}
S = {} & n_1[\alpha_1 U_1(Y_1 + s_1) + \beta_1 R(T_{R1})] + n_2[\alpha_2 U_2(Y_2 + s_2) + \beta_2 R(T_{R2})] \\
& + \cdots + n_i[\alpha_i U_i(Y_i + s_i) + \beta_i R(T_{Ri})] + \cdots + n_m[\alpha_m U_m(Y_m + s_m) \\
& + \beta_m R(T_{Rm})]
\end{aligned}
\tag{18.14}
$$

where T_{Ri} is the amount of tax revenue devoted to repressing group i, and n_i is its size. The dictator's task is to maximize S subject to the constraint that the total amount of positive subsidies and tax revenue devoted to repression equals the amount of tax revenue raised (negative subsidies).[8]

$$
\sum_{i=1}^{m} n_i s_i + \sum_{i=1}^{m} n_i T_{Ri} = 0.
\tag{18.15}
$$

In addition to this budget constraint there are constraints that expenditures on repression cannot be negative, and that no tax on a group can exceed externally determined income, if $s_i < 0$, then $| -s_i | \le Y_i$, and $T_{Ri} \ge 0$, for all i. Maximizing (18.14) with respect to the s_i and T_{Ri} subject to these constraints yields first-order conditions of the following form for all groups for which the inequality constraints are not binding:

$$
\alpha_i U_i' = \alpha_j U_j' = \beta_k R' = \beta_h R'.
\tag{18.16}
$$

Income is redistributed across groups to equate the marginal impacts on the security of the government of increasing the income of a member of any group. Tax revenues are allocated to repressing each group to again equate the marginal impacts on security of repressing a member of any group. For groups with very low β_is the gains from repression are so low that no funds are devoted to this activity. Groups with very low αs have all of their incomes taxed away.

In reality, a more complicated functional form linking S and the utilities of the citizenry and the gains from repressing them seems plausible. For example, the gains from repressing a given group are likely to increase with the amount of income taxed away from it, that is, β_i is a function of s_i. But we need not explore these more complicated alternatives to see that the optimal set of policies of a dictator are likely to involve the selective use of rewards and punishments.[9] It is worth noting in this context that the task faced by the dictator of choosing tax/expenditure policies is

---

[8] We ignore once again the dictator's consumption and provision of public goods.
[9] For additional discussion of selective strategies by dictators, see Wintrobe (1998, chs. 6–8).

similar to that faced by the competing parties in a two-party electoral system under the assumptions of the probabilistic voting model (see Chapter 12). When interest groups make different contributions to the success of a party, it promises them differential benefits from governmental programs. Competition for votes between the two parties leads them to offer a set of policies that maximize some form of weighted social welfare function. The dictator does not have to compete against an organized opposition, but must live in constant fear that some general, or corporal, or alienated academician will set a train of events into motion that will result in the dictator's downfall. This uncertainty leads the dictator to maximize an objective function that is dependent on the utilities of the citizens. It differs most from that of a party in a democracy in that the weights it places on the utilities of some groups may effectively be negative.

18.3.4   *The dictator's dilemma*

Thus, we see that citizens will experience differential gains and losses from governmental policies under a dictatorship as in a democracy. Rent seeking will take place and different groups will compete for these rents. To achieve his goals, the dictator must determine who his true supporters and enemies are, whom to reward, and whom to punish, the αs and βs of the previous subsection. In a democracy this information is readily available. Interest groups offer visible support for a party in the form of votes and campaign contributions, and a politician can fairly easily determine which groups are most loyal to him – which groups deserve rewards. But in a dictatorship support for the government is much more passive. It takes the form of *not* actively opposing the government, not sabotaging its policies and starting a revolution to overthrow it, and so forth. All groups have an incentive to *fain* support for the dictatorship even if they are actively working to undermine it. The dictator faces the daunting task of determining which groups *truly* support him, which are merely pretending to do so, and which are actively but secretly plotting his overthrow.

Moreover, the incentive to conceal one's true intentions and opinions about the dictatorship increases with the level of repression and the dictator's willingness to exercise absolute power. Every citizen must wonder when she openly expresses an opinion about the dictator or his policies whether her views may be used not to improve her welfare, but to single her out for repression. Thus, the rational citizen in a dictatorship can be expected to conceal her true feelings about the dictator and his policies, and this is true from the average citizen on the street right up to the dictator's closest and most important advisors. Thus arises the dictator's dilemma.[10] The more absolute his power and the more ruthless his use of repression to stay in office, the poorer his sources of information are as to how to exercise his power most effectively. Paradoxically, the *effective* power of the dictator who uses fear and repression to remain in office may actually decline as he makes more and more use of these strategies.

---

[10]   The term comes from Wintrobe (1998, pp. 20–39); see also Elster (1993, pp. 66–9).

To build support for his regime the dictator needs a way of credibly signaling to those whose loyalty he seeks to win that he will not subsequently turn upon them. Those seeking rents and other rewards from the dictator need a way of signaling their willingness to trade their loyalty for rents. Most generally, the dictator needs criteria to determine who should be rewarded and who not, and who should be the target of repression. Here ideology can play a useful role. In a theocracy, for example, citizens can be distinguished on the basis of whether they are members of the religion of the state or not. Nonmembers become the obvious targets for repression and taxation. Support for the dictator is built among members of the religion through transfers and other measures to win loyalty. The ideology of the regime identifies the likely winners and losers from governmental policy, and commits the dictator to some degree not to employ repression against members of the state religion. The existence of a state religion helps to make the dictator's promises credible. Other criteria for differentiating among the citizenry have been by economic interest (Communism) and ethnic group (Fascism, Apartheid, Nationalism).[11]

18.3.5 *The limits of totalitarianism*

The discussion of the previous subsection reveals why few dictators have ever come close to achieving the ambitious goal set for fascism by Mussolini at the beginning of this chapter – certainly he did not realize it. One explanation is that the totalitarian is likely to lack the information needed to achieve his goals. A second reason is that he is likely to lack the necessary resources.

Returning to (18.14) we see that the dictator will want to tax some groups and transfer sources to others to win the latter's loyalty. Additional resources are needed to repress still other groups, probably including those heavily taxed. Over time the productivity of the groups targeted for heavy taxation and repression is likely to decline. To maintain tax revenues the regime must expand the list of targets for taxation and repression. As their productivity declines, the list of targeted groups must be expanded yet again, and so on. A second reason why a totalitarian regime may not be able to achieve its goal of complete ideological subjugation of the population is that it lacks the necessary economic resources.[12]

18.4   The rise and decline of dictatorships

In Section 18.1 we described how a dictatorship might arise out of a state of pure anarchy. Very often dictorial regimes come into being following a war or revolution, or the collapse of a different form of government. The Ottomans defeated in battle and then replaced a crumbling Byzantine theocracy. Napolean Bonaparte erected his dictatorial empire in a France torn by strife and conflict following the French Revolution. The Communist dictatorship that established and dominated the Soviet

---

[11] For further discussion, see Bernholz (1991, 1997b) and Wintrobe (1998, chs. 7 and 8).

[12] See Wintrobe (1998, chs. 3 and 5). The empirical evidence linking dictatorships and economic performance is discussed below.

Union throughout most of the twentieth century arose following a revolution that erupted in Russia during World War I. It replaced the monarchy of the Romanoffs. Hitler's Fascist dictatorship replaced a democratic system of government during the economic crisis in Germany in the 1930s. Fidel Castro led a revolutionary army that replaced an unpopular dictator in Cuba. In these and many other examples one could cite, the new regime replaces a corrupt or decaying regime at a time of great insecurity and unhappiness in the country. The new dictatorial regime thus often begins with considerable support from at least some sectors of the population. The successful dictator extends and strengthens his initial support. Rewards are meted out to build loyalty among some groups; repression is used to control the (possible) disloyalty of others. If the movement that led to the rise of the dictatorship had an ideology, the dictator may employ it to develop loyalty.

The victors in a revolutionary struggle, like the winners of any contest, are filled with joy and enthusiasm, a conviction that they and their ideology have been vindicated. This enthusiasm, bred from victory, can help to provide the energy needed to construct the many institutions that are needed to sustain the dictatorship over the long run. But with time such enthusiasm wanes, memories of victory fade, and the dictatorship goes into decline. The most recent and spectacular example of a decline and eventual collapse of a dictatorial system has been, of course, the collapse of the Communist regimes in the Soviet Union and Eastern Europe. Both Wintrobe (1998) and Olson (2000) have provided complementary explanations for this decline, focusing on the properties of the gigantic, bureaucratic systems of state planning in these countries.

In the classic depiction of a hierarchical organization, information relevant to the success of the organization (changes in the tastes of clients or customers, new technological options) is gathered at the bottom of the hierarchy and passes upward, and commands are given at the top and pass downward. Both types of information are subject to distortion and dissipation as they pass through the hierarchy. In addition to inadvertent losses of content as information passes through the hierarchy there are intentional distortions and destruction of information as members of a hierarchy opportunistically pursue their own goals. The task of each supervisor is to reduce such *control losses* so that the organization succeeds at achieving the goals laid down by the person(s) at the top.[13]

Wintrobe (1998, chs. 9 and 10), building on Breton and Wintrobe (1982), distinguishes between *vertical exchanges* in a hierarchical organization, and *horizontal exchanges*. Subordinates provide certain services for their supervisors who in turn offer them certain rewards. Trust is established between subordinates and supervisors in this way, and such vertical exchanges thereby lead to the organization's successfully satisfying its goals. The enthusiasm that characterizes the early years of a new dictatorial system combined with strong commitments to the ideology underlying the dictatorship can be expected to strengthen the levels of trust between vertically linked members of state bureacracies, and thus to contribute to

---

[13] Classic discussions of these properties of hierarchies are by Simon (1961) and Williamson (1964, 1975). See also Milgrom and Roberts (1992).

the dictatorship's efficiency. Wintrobe (ch. 9) argues that vertical trust was particularly strong in the Soviet state's bureaucracies during the first decades following the revolution, and that this helps explain the extraordinary and otherwise surprising success and apparent efficiency of Soviet central planning over much of the twentieth century.

In contrast to vertical exchanges, horizontal exchanges undermine the efficiency of hierarchical organizations. Horizontal exchanges take place between individuals at a given level of the hierarchy. Any interests that these individuals hold in common, other than the overarching goals of the organization, are likely to *conflict* with these overarching goals. For example, all scientists in a research laboratory are likely to have a common interest in expanding their freedom to define the research topics that they pursue. The success of the laboratory at answering the questions assigned to it may be undermined, however, if the research of its members ranges too far away from the assigned questions. Thus, as horizontal linkages develop in a bureaucracy its efficiency can be expected to fall. Trust relationships develop between people who occupy similar positions in the hierarchy, as they exchange favors for one another (you say that my research is good for the organization, and I'll say that yours is; you cover for me, and I'll cover for you).

Since vertical exchanges contribute to the success of the organization, they can be openly advertised and joined. Indeed, rewarding one subordinate for doing a good job is likely to have a bigger positive impact on the organization's success if her co-workers at the same level of the hierarchy are made aware of the reward than if it is kept secret. Vertical exchanges can be put in writing and easily verified. Horizontal exchanges that benefit the participants in the transaction, but damage the organization's efficiency, must be made and kept in secret. When several individuals are involved, these exchanges resemble cartel arrangements. In a market economy, horizontal cartel arrangements may need to be tacitly joined to avoid the scrutiny of the authorities charged with maintaining competition to promote the efficiency of the economy. Horizontal cartel arrangements among bureaucrats may also need to be joined tacitly to avoid the scrutiny of those standing higher in the hierarchy who stand to lose if the organization becomes less efficient.

All members of a horizontal cartel are caught in a prisoners' dilemma. The rents created by the cartel are a public good for it. All members of the cartel benefit if the collusive agreement is maintained, but each individual member can benefit still more from cheating on the cartel. In a horizontal price-fixing cartel such cheating takes the form of (usually secret) price reductions. In a horizontal cartel among bureaucrats, cheating may take the form of "blowing the whistle" on the other members, and thereby obtaining a handsome reward or promotion.

Such whistle-blowing is quite likely during the early days of a dictatorial regime, when many of its members remain "loyal to the cause" and committed to the regime's underlying ideology. As time passes, memories of the revolution fade, and ardor for its ideological principles cools. Whistle-blowing may become less prevalent. With time it is also easier to determine whom one can trust to remain loyal to the cartel, and who the likely whistle-blowers are. Thus, the horizontal exchanges and rent-seeking cartels that undermine a bureaucracy's efficiency only appear in mature bureaucracies. Just as the institutional sclerosis and rent-seeking that produce economic decline appear only in mature democracies, where sufficient time has elapsed since the revolution or war that launched them, so too institutional sclerosis and rent-seeking within the giant bureaucracies that manage a centrally planned economy become debilitating only as the years pass following the revolution or war that launched the underlying dictatorship. Both Wintrobe and Olson "credit" Stalin for postponing the onslaught of bureaucratic sclerosis, and thus for prolonging the Soviet Union's "economic miracle" by destroying the horizontal exchange and cartel patterns within the Soviet bureaucracies through his many and brutal purges. These purges both shuffled the potential membership of any horizontal cartel and raised the penalty on anyone for whom a whistle was blown. Bureaucratic sclerosis became inevitable once the purges ceased, and the Soviet bureaucracies were able to settle into a peaceful maturity.

18.5 Dictatorship and economic performance

Do democracies outperform dictatorships? Several writers have addressed this important question both theoretically and empirically. Unfortunately, neither literature gives an unequivocal answer. Let us begin with the theoretical approaches.

18.5.1 *The relative advantages of dictatorship and democracy*

In Section 18.1, we saw that a consumption-maximizing dictator would supply a smaller amount of public goods than would be optimal for the entire community. This result implies that in a democracy, *which makes its collective decisions using the unanimity rule*, both the level of public goods and national income will be higher than in a dictatorship in which the dictator chooses the level of public goods to maximize his personal consumption. No democracies make their collective decisions using the unanmity rule, however, and we know that in majoritarian democracies, the winning majority may act as a dictator transferring income from the minority to itself. Will its outcomes be worse or better than those under a dictatorship?

To see what is involved, let us assume as in Section 18.1 that national income is a function of the quantity of public goods supplied, and diminishes as the proportional tax on income rises, $Y = Y(G)(1 - \eta t)$, where again η is the elasticity of income with respect to the tax rate. The objective of the dictator was to maximize his consumption, which equaled total tax revenue less the amount spent on public goods,

$$O_D = tY(1 - \eta t) - G. \tag{18.17}$$

The full community, on the other hand, would wish to maximze the difference between total income and the cost of the public goods,

$$O_S = Y(1 - \eta t) - G. \tag{18.18}$$

One way to think of a majority coalition behaving is that it both selects an amount of public goods and, like the dictator, transfers some of the income from the community to itself in the form of a subsidy, S. Tax revenues must thus cover both public goods expenditures and the subsidy,

$$tY(1 - \eta t) = G + S. \tag{18.19}$$

Let m be the fraction of the community that is in the majority coalition. Its objective is then to maximize its share of national income net of taxes plus its subsidy,

$$O_M = m(1 - t)Y(1 - \eta t) + S. \tag{18.20}$$

Using (18.19) to replace S in (18.20) we obtain

$$O_M = m(1 - t)Y(1 - \eta t) + tY(1 - \eta t) - G. \tag{18.21}$$

With $m = 0$, (18.21) reduces to (18.17) and we have the objective function of the consumption-maximizing dictator. With $m = 1$, (18.21) reduces to (18.18) and we have the objective function of the community, which maximizes income net of public goods costs. Thus the objective function for a redistributive majority coalition falls between that of a pure dictatorship and a community functioning under the unanimity rule, and its chosen tax rates and public good quantities will also fall between these two values.[14]

Although it is instructive to think of a majority coalition merely paying itself a subsidy out of general tax revenue, given the disincentive effects of taxation a majority coalition would not both tax itself and offer itself a subsidy. An alternative strategy would be to tax itself, and the minority, at different rates. If we let t_m be the tax rate for the majority coalition, and t_n be the tax rate for the minority coalition, the objective function of the majority coalition becomes merely the maximization of its net of tax income, subject to the budget constraint:

$$O_M = m(1 - t_m)Y(1 - \eta t_m) + \lambda[G - mt_mY(1 - \eta t_m) \\ - (1 - m)t_nY(1 - \eta t_n)]. \tag{18.22}$$

Despite the simplicity of this formulation, the maximization of (18.22) does not yield values for t_m and dY/dG that allow easy, intuitive interpretations. It does for t_n, however. The tax rate imposed on the minority by the majority is exactly the same as that imposed on the community by the consumption-maximizing dictator.[15] Thus, although a majority coalition in a democracy can be expected to exploit the minority in much the same way as a dictator would, its choices with respect to itself will be less exploitative, and the outcomes for a majoritarian democracy will come closer to those that maximize the community's welfare than for a dictatorship.

These arguments abstract from the problems dictators might have keeping their jobs, and their possible interest in power and various ideological goals that may lower the community's welfare. Overland, Simons, and Spagat (2000) have recently explored the implications of introducing uncertainty over survival into a model of

---

[14] For further discussion using a more elaborate model, see McGuire and Olson (1996).

[15] Maximizing (18.22) with respect to t_n yields as a first-order condition
$$\lambda[-(1 - m)Y(1 - 2\eta t_n)] = 0.$$
Since $\lambda > 0$, the expression within the square brackets must equal zero, implying that $t_n = 1/2\eta$.

a consumption-maximizing dictator. They assume that the probability of a dictator being overthrown falls as the prosperity of the community increases. If the initial conditions – in their model the initial capital stock – are favorable enough to produce a standard of living above a critical threshold, the dictatorship has a sufficiently high probability of surviving that the dictator chooses policies to promote growth, since he knows that it is highly likely that he will be around to skim off his share of the national income. If the initial conditions are unfavorable, however, the probability of the dictatorship surviving is low and the dictator plunders the economy. Overland, Simons, and Spagat thus predict that dictatorships fall into two categories: one performing very well in terms of economic growth, the other performing disastrously.

In a quite different model, Robinson (2000) has shown that dictators may choose *not* to invest in public goods like education that would improve the welfare of the community, because a well-educated society is more capable of overthrowing the dictator.

These results make it difficult to predict whether dictatorships should perform well or poorly in terms of economic growth. And the same can of course be said for democracies, *once* we allow for various forms of rent seeking, cycling, budget-maximizing bureaucracies, and the like.[16] As is often the case, the issue must be settled empirically.

18.5.2   *The relative economic performance of dictatorships and democracies*

Levels of income or the growth of income per capita are often used as performance measures in international comparisons, and essentially all the comparative literature on democracy and dictatorship use these sorts of measures. These abstract, of course, from many of the attributes of democracy that most citizens would hold dear. For example, one might be much happier living in a country in which one is free to read whatever one chooses, than in one where this freedom is absent, even if income levels and growth rates in the two countries were the same. Nevertheless, it is interesting to ask whether these standard measures of economic performance are systematically related to the degree of freedom and democracy. A quite extensive literature has attempted to offer an answer.

Although there are problems in defining and measuring economic performance properly, these pale into insignificance alongside the problem of defining and measuring freedom and democracy. The standard approach now is to combine various indexes of civil, economic, and political freedoms into one or more grand indexes. In some cases, for example Scully and Slottje (1991) and de Haan and Siermann (1998), the emphasis is on *economic* freedoms; indexes of "freedom of the foreign exchange regime," "freedom from work permits," and the like are combined. In other studies, the focus is more on *democratic* freedoms.

---

[16] For further discussion of the different theoretical arguments and references to the literature, see Przeworski and Limongi (1993).

Most reassuringly for advocates of free market and capitalist systems, measures of economic freedom do seem to correlate positively with per capita growth rates in income. De Haan and Siermann (1998), for example, found that the coefficients on nine different measures of economic freedom all had the correct sign in regressions to explain per capita income growth, and at least some of these were statistically significant and passed a set of sensitivity tests. In a follow-up study, de Haan and Sturm (2000) report, however, that only *increases* in economic freedom have a significant impact on economic growth, not the levels.[17] Wu and Davis (1999), on the other hand, also found a positive relationship between growth of income and a composite index of economic freedom, and Knack and Keefer (1995) found that the protection of property rights was positively associated with economic performance across all forms of political systems.

Less reassuring for advocates of democracy has been the pattern of relationships between democratic/political freedoms and income growth rates. Although some studies have established a significant positive link between measures of political freedom and growth (e.g., Pourgerami, 1992), others have found that authoritarian regimes have better growth records (Adelman and Morris, 1973; Barro, 1996). Przeworski and Limongi (1993) reviewed 21 empirical studies that tested for a link between type of political system and economic growth and were unable to determine any consistent pattern in the results. One reason for these ambiguous findings is apparent from the discussion of the decline of bureaucratically run, centrally planned economies in the previous section. In Chapter 22 we shall discuss hypotheses and evidence that suggest that *democracies* can also go into economic decline. Both may go through "life cycles," so that their economic growth rates vary significantly depending on the age of the regime. Proper testing for the effects of democracy and dictatorship must differentiate between young and mature variants of these two systems.

A second difficulty that arises when measuring the impact of democracy on economic performance is that neither democracy nor dictatorship come in a single form. Among the European, Anglo-Saxon, and Latin American countries that fall fairly clearly under the heading of democracy, there are potentially important differences in electoral rules (two-party, multiparty, presidential), in the use of institutions of direct democracy like the referendum, federalist structures, and the like. Within the set of dictatorships, there are also important differences. Wintrobe (1998), for example, first distinguishes among totalitarian, tinpot, tyrannical, and timocratic dictatorships (chs. 1–5). Later he draws distinctions along economic lines among kleptocratic, capitalist authoritarian, command economy, and shadow economy dictatorial systems (chs. 6–10). Not only is there no reason to expect all of these different sorts of dictatorships to exhibit similar levels of economic performance, Wintrobe's analysis demonstrates why one should definitely expect that at least some of them will perform quite differently from one another. Indeed, the likelihood that different dictators would choose policies with dramatically different economic consequences for their subjects was apparent in the simple models analyzed in Sections 18.1 and 18.2.

---

[17] Berggren (1999) finds that increases in economic freedoms reduce income inequality.

The main empirical implication of the model of Overland, Simons, and Spagat (2000) described earlier is that there should be a larger *variance* in the growth rates of dictatorships than there is for democracies. They present evidence that this is the case.[18]

18.5.2.1 *A direct test of Wintrobe's model of dictatorship.* Schnytzer and Šušteršič (1997) use membership in the Communist Party in Yugoslavia over the period of 1953–88 as an index of support for the Communist regime, support which contributed to its stability over this period. Between 1953 and 1988 membership in Yugoslavia's Communist Party varied both over time and across the several republics that made up the Yugoslav Republic. One possible explanation for this variability is that membership in the party increases as the popularity of the party increases. This hypothesis would lead us to expect, in line with the political business cycle literature reviewed in Chapter 19, that membership would be inversely correlated with macroeconomic variables like unemployment and inflation rates. Membership in the Communist Party could, on the other hand, measure the degree of loyalty to the regime resulting from "political exchanges" between the government and the citizens as Wintrobe hypothesizes. Schnytzer and Šušteršič (1997, p. 121) "assume that jobs, or the likelihood of obtaining promotion, were a very important source of rents provided by the Party to its members. The relative value of this rent increased with unemployment. Therefore, we should expect LCY [League of Communists of Yugoslavia] membership to be positively related to unemployment" – exactly the opposite prediction from the political-business-cycle-popularity hypothesis. For analogous reasons they expect LCY membership to be inversely correlated with the level of real wages. Time series regressions yielded the strongest support for these predictions in the two provinces with largely Serbian populations, where the Communist government was most firmly established – Serbia and Montenegro. Little empirical support for the political exchange hypothesis was found in the non-Serb republics of Slovenia and Macedonia, where the Communist government was weakest. Empirical support for the political exchange hypothesis fell in between these two extremes in Bosnia/Herzegovina and Croatia, which have mixed Serbian populations and had Communist regimes with strengths that also fell between those of the four other republics. The findings of Schnytzer and Šušteršič are consistent with the hypothesis that governments in Serbia and Montenegro, and to a lesser extent in Bosnia/Herzegovina and Croatia, reinforced and sustained a mixed ideology of Serb-nationalism and Communism through political exchange as implied by Wintrobe's model of dictatorship.

18.6   Conclusions

The word "democracy" conjures up the the image of the sovereignty of the citizens. The citizens decide the policies of the state, and only their preferences count. In

---

[18] For further discussion of the conceptual and econometric problems in trying to *explain* differences in economic growth rates in terms of whether countries are classified as democracies or dictatorships, see Przeworski and Limongi (1993).

contrast, the word "dictatorship" connotes the antithesis of democracy. Only the dictator's preferences count. The collective choices of the citizens in a *direct* democracy arguably come reasonably close to meeting the ideal of citizens' sovereignty. Even here one must worry about the problem of rational ignorance on the part of voters, and cycling under some choices of voting rules. But these aside, one expects a fair correspondence between what the citizens want from the state and what they get.

This correspondence is expected to be decidedly weaker when an assembly of elected representatives of the citizens decides what governmental policy ought to be, and appointed bureaucrats implement it. This latter institutional structure introduces problems of aggregating citizen preferences to select representatives, principal–agent problems between the citizens and their representatives, between their representatives and the bureaucrats whom they appoint to carry out their policies, and principal–agent problems across the hierarchical levels of the governmental bureaucracies. Nevertheless, there still is a widespread belief that representative democracies – despite all of their faults – do a much better job of satisfying the preferences of their citizens than do dictatorships, since in representative democracies the citizen-principals continue to exercise *some* control over their politician-bureaucrat agents, while in a dictatorship, this control is absent.

The literature reviewed in this chapter casts doubts upon the validity of this stark contrast. The dictator faces principal–agent problems in getting the bureaucrats, whom he nominally controls, to advance the interests of the dictator and not their own. This forces the dictator to employ rewards and sanctions to induce bureaucratic compliance, in much the same way as in a democracy. The citizens can make the dictator feel more or less secure by granting or withholding their loyalty and support. This forces the dictator to weigh the impacts of his chosen policies on the welfare of the citizenry, in much the same way as elected party officials must weigh the impacts of their policies on the welfare of voters. Rent seeking can be expected in both kinds of political systems.

These similarities help explain why it has been difficult to identify empirically differences in performance indicators, like growth rates in income per capita, between dictatorships and democracies.

These observations do not imply, of course, that there are no significant differences between democracies and dictatorships. The scope for repressive policies to increase power and security of office is much greater under most dictatorships than in most democracies. The existence of a constitutionally defined set of individual rights and liberties, and an independent judiciary adds further protections for citizens in *some* democracies that are absent in most dictatorships. The greatest advantage of democracy over dictatorship may not be that democracies outperform dictatorships on average, but that democracies seldom sink to the depth of misery that one too often observes under dictators.

Bibliographical notes

The seminal contribution to the public choice literature on dictatorship was by Tullock (1987). Kurrild-Klitgaard (2000) has recently presented evidence in support of one of Tullock's key predictions about succession in dictatorships. Between 935 and 1849 there was considerably more stability when the monarch's successor was selected using hereditary rules that clearly identified the next monarch, than when there was ambiguity over his identity.

PART IV

Applications and testing

CHAPTER 19

Political competition and macroeconomic performance

All political history shows that the standing of the Government and its ability to hold the confidence of the electorate at a General Election depend on the success of its economic policy.

Harold Wilson (as quoted in Hibbs, 1982c)

In this part of the book we present four applications of the public choice approach to explaining real-world phenomena. The first application tries to explain the macroeconomic policies of governments. To what extent are these determined by the competitive struggle for votes? To what extent do voters take into account the macroeconomic performance of a government when deciding how to vote? These questions have elicited a variety of theoretical models to explain governmental macroeconomic policies and a gigantic number of empirical studies. Indeed, probably no other area of public choice has witnessed as much empirical testing of its propositions as this area of politico-macroeconomic models. Alas, as too often happens with empirical work, not all authors reach the same conclusions as to what "the data show," and the literature is therefore filled with often spirited exchanges. We shall not attempt to resolve all of the outstanding disagreements, but will try instead to give the reader a feel for the nature of the debate on various issues and the weight of the empirical support on each side of a question. We begin with the question that Harold Wilson obviously considered an established fact. Does the state of the economy affect how voters vote?

19.1   Macroeconomic performance and political success

19.1.1   *Vote and popularity functions*

The seminal study linking macroeconomic performance to political success was by Kramer (1971). He sought to explain the percentage of the vote going to Republican candidates for the House of Representatives between 1896 and 1964 by the state of the economy. Kramer found that the votes going to incumbent members of the House were inversely related to the rate of inflation and positively related to the growth in income.

Considerable evidence exists that confirms Kramer's initial findings in one way or another. Table 19.1 lists several studies that have tested whether unemployment (U), inflation (P), or real income affect the percentage of the vote that a candidate or party

429

Table 19.1. *The effect of macroeconomic conditions on votes for parties or presidents*

Country-dependent variable	Author(s)	Time period	Lagged dependent variable	Inflation rate (P)	Unemployment rate (U)	National income (Y)
U.S. House elections						
Republicans' vote shares	Kramer (1971)	1896–1964		$-0.41^{*}P_t$	$-0.001\Delta U_t$	$0.27^{*}Y_t$
Republicans' vote shares	Stigler (1973)	1896–1970		$-0.21^{**}(P_t - \bar{P})$		$0.17^{*}(Y_t - \bar{Y})$
Republicans' vote shares	Alesina and Rosenthal (1995)	1915–1988	0.89^{**}			$0.03\Delta Y_t$
Probability of an incumbent's reelection	Grier and McGarrity (1998)	1916–1994		$-0.43^{*}P_t$	$-0.40^{**}U_t$	$0.32^{*}Y_t$
Senate elections						
Incumbent party's share of vote	Peltzman (1990)	1950–1988		$-3.6^{**}\sum_{j=-48}^{-1}(P_{t+j} - \hat{P}_{t+j})^a$		$1.1^{**}\sum_{j=-48}^{-1}\Delta \ln Y_{t+j}$
Republicans	Bennett and Wiseman (1991)	1952–1986		ins[b]	ins[b]	ins[b]
Presidential elections						
Incumbent party's vote	Chressanthis and Shaffer (1993)	1976–1990	0.18^{**}	$0.05P_t^c$	$-0.08\dfrac{\Delta U_t^c}{U_t}$	$0.59^{**}\Delta Y_t^c$ $0.01\dfrac{\Delta Y_t^c}{Y_t}$
In (candidate in office)	Niskanen (1979)	1896–1972				$1.51^{**}\ln\left(\dfrac{Y_t + Y_{t-1} + Y_{t-2} + Y_{t-3}}{4}\right)$
Democratic candidates	Fair (1982)	1961–1980		$-0.68\lvert P_t - P_{t-2}\rvert/2P_{t-1}$		$0.98^{**}\Delta Y_t/Y_{t-1}$
Vote shares of candidate in office	Kirchgässner (1981)	1896–1976	0.49^{**}	$-0.12^{**}P_t^2$		

Dependent variable	Study	Period				
Incumbent party's share of vote	Peltzman (1990)	1952–1988		$-9.7^{**}\sum_{j=-48}^{-1}(P_{t+j}-\hat{P}_{t+j})^a$		$3.1^{**}\sum_{j=-48}^{-1}\Delta\ln Y_{t+j}$
Bush's vote-share by state	Abrams and Butkiewicz (1995)	1992	0.75**		$-0.61^{**}U_t$	$0.19^{**}(\Delta Y_t - \Delta Y_{t-1})^d$
Republican candidate's vote shares	Alesina and Rosenthal (1995)	1915–1988	0.74**			$1.14^{**}\Delta Y_t$
Incumbent party's candidate	Hibbs (2000)	1952–1996				$4.1^{**}\dfrac{\sum_{j=0}^{14}\lambda^j\Delta\ln Y_{t-j}^e}{\sum_{j=0}^{14}\lambda^j}$
Gubernatorial elections						
Incumbent's probability of reelection	Adams and Kenny (1989)	1946–1984				$0.007^*\sum_{j=-4}^{-1}(Y_{t+j}-\hat{Y}_{t+j})^a$
Incumbent party's share of vote	Peltzman (1990)	1952–1988		$-2.7^{**}\sum_{j=-48}^{-1}(P_{t+j}-\hat{P}_{t+j})^a$		$1.4^{**}\sum_{j=-48}^{-1}\Delta\ln Y_{t+j}$
Incumbent party's share of vote	Levernier (1992)	1970–1988	0.39*		$-0.15U_t$	$0.31^{**}\Delta Y_t$
Lower state legislatures						
Democrats percent of seats by state	Chubb (1988)	1940–1982	0.42**			$0.53^*Y_t^c$
Denmark						
Deviation from long-term trend of bigger party in power	Madsen (1980)	1920–1973		-0.43^*P_t	$-0.119(\Delta U_t -\Delta U_{t-1})$	
Norway						
Deviation of governing party from long-term average	Madsen (1980)	1920–1973		-0.36^*P_t	$-0.10U_t$	

(continued)

Table 19.1 (*continued*)

Country-dependent variable	Author(s)	Time period	Lagged dependent variable	Inflation rate (P)	Unemployment rate (U)	National income (Y)
Sweden						
Deviation of government party from long-term trend	Madsen (1980)	1920–1972		$-0.22P_t$	$-2.30^*(\Delta U_t - \Delta U_{t-1})$	$0.73^{**}Y_t$
France						
Left opposition parties	Rosa (1980)	1920–1973		$0.20^*\left(\dfrac{P_t + P_{t-1} + P_{t-2}}{3}\right)$	$+0.02^{**}\left(\dfrac{U_t + U_{t-1} + U_{t-2}}{3}\right)$	$-0.08^{**}\left(\dfrac{Y_t + Y_{t-1} + Y_{t-2}}{3}\right)$
Great Britain						
Incumbent party's share of vote	Hibbing (1987)	1945–1984		-0.49^*P_t	-0.50^*U_t	$-1.2^*\Delta Y_t$
England						
Labor Party/ Conservative Party share of vote	Fielding (2000)	1997[f]			1.02^*U_t	

Note: * Significant at 0.05 level, ** at 0.01 level, two-tailed tests. Variable definitions differ across studies. The reader must consult the original studies. X_t is current value of X, X_{t-i} is X lagged i period, $\Delta X_t = X_t - X_{t-1}$, $\bar{X}$ is a mean or trend value for X.

Note: [a] $\hat{P}_{t+j}$, $\hat{Y}_{t+j}$ is the predicted inflation rate or real income in period $t + j$.

[b] State economic conditions insignificant.

[c] National economic conditions when president is in same party.

[d] "Unexpected growth" in state real income per capita defined as growth from 1988–1992 (ΔY_t); less growth from 1984–1988 (ΔY_{t-1}).

[e] λ estimated to equal 0.95.

[f] Country-level, cross-sectional data. Conservative Party in office, predicted sign on U_t is positive.

Sources: Early studies are from Schneider and Frey (1988, Table 1). Reprinted with permission of Duke University Press.

432

in government receives. Although each variable is not significant in every study, and the coefficients bounce around a bit, the number of times that the coefficients on P, U, or Y are statistically significant and of the right sign compares favorably with other empirical studies of macrorelationships.

U.S. presidential elections occur once every four years, French presidential elections once in seven (now five). A British parliamentary election need not be held for up to five years. Thus, studies that try to predict the votes cast in national elections are constrained to small sample sizes, and often consequently small degrees of statistical significance. One way to avoid this problem is to do as Kramer did – estimate the relationships for lower offices of government where there are more contests. An alternative way to increase the reliability of one's estimates of the political consequences of macroeconomic performance is to use poll data rather than election data. Answers to questions like, "Do you think the president is doing a good job?" reflect at least in part a citizen's judgment about the state of the economy and the president's responsibility for it. And poll data are reliable, if not perfect, forecasts of election outcomes. Since polls are taken much more often than elections occur, they can be linked to quarterly and even monthly economic data. Table 19.2 lists several studies that have tested for a relationship between the government's or the president's popularity, as measured by pollsters and macroeconomic performance variables. The same pattern of results can be observed in Table 19.2 as exists in Table 19.1. Harold Wilson appears to have been right. A good macroeconomic performance increases the voters' approval of the government and increases its chances of reelection.

19.1.2 *Whom do voters hold responsible?*

Stigler (1973) attacked both the logic underlying Kramer's (1971) study of voting in House elections and its empirical findings. Reestimations of the basic equations for different time periods revealed the coefficients to be unstable.[1] An alternative explanation to the one given by Stigler for the weakness of the relationship between macroeconomic conditions and voting in House elections might be that voters do not hold their congressmen responsible for the state of the macroeconomy (Crain, Deaton, and Tollison, 1978). They might reasonably believe that their representative in the House is more directly responsible for the flow of redistribution dollars to and from them that arise due to pork-barrel programs, while the president is more directly responsible for macroeconomic policy.

This interpretation is supported by several cross-sectional analyses of panel survey data that fail to discern much of a relationship between voting in House elections and macroeconomic variables (Fiorina, 1978; Weatherford, 1978; Kinder and Kiewiet, 1979). Although Kramer (1983) is probably correct in arguing that errors in observation are particularly likely to obscure the relationship between the economic performance variables and voting in micro-cross-sectional analyses, these studies do nonetheless uncover the predicted relationships in Senate and presidential

[1] See also Arcelus and Meltzer (1975a,b), Bloom and Price (1975), and Goodman and Kramer (1975).

Table 19.2. *The effect of macroeconomic conditions on party (presidential) popularity*

Country-dependent variable[a]	Author(s)	Time period	Lagged dependent variable	Inflation rate (P)	Unemployment rate (U)	National income (Y)
United States						
Presidential, Q	Schneider (1978)	1961:1–1968:4		-2.61^*P_{t-2}	$-5.43^{**}U_{t-2}$	
Presidential, Q	Schneider (1978)	1969:1–1976:4		-2.15^*P_{t-2}	$-3.89^{**}U_{t-2}$	
ln[POP/(100-POP)], Q POP = presidential	Hibbs (1982c)	1961:1–1980:1	0.84^b	$-0.017^{**}\ln(P_t/P_{t-1})$	$-0.017^{**}\ln(U_t/U_{t-1})$	$0.015^{**}\ln(Y_t/Y_{t-1})$
ln[POP/(100-POP)], Q POP =	Hibbs (1987)	1961:1–1984:1				
Popularity among						
Democats			0.83^b	$-0.028^{**}\ln(P_t/P_{t-1})$	$-0.030^{**}\ln(U_t/U_{t-1})$	$0.011^{**}\ln(Y_t/Y_{t-1})$
Republicans			0.77^b	$-0.039^{**}\ln(P_t/P_{t-1})$	$-0.025^{**}\ln(U_t/U_{t-1})$	$0.018^{**}\ln(Y_t/Y_{t-1})$
Independents			0.84^b	$-0.031^{**}\ln(P_t/P_{t-1})$	$-0.015^{**}\ln(U_t/U_{t-1})$	$0.015^{**}\ln(Y_t/Y_{t-1})$
Presidential, Q	Smyth and Dua (1989)	1971–1978		$-1.47^{**}P_t$	$+7.0^*U_t - 0.60^{**}U_t^2$	
Presidential, M	Smyth, Dua, and Taylor (1994)	1981–1988	0.63^{**}	$-0.11^{**}P_t^2$	$-0.35^{**}U_t^2$	
France						
Presidential, M	Lewis-Beck (1980)	1960:1–1978:4		$-1.89^{**}P_{t-2}$	-0.56^*U_{t-2}	
ln[POP/(100-POP)], Q	Hibbs (1981)	1969:4–1978:4	0.8^b	$0.004^{**}P_t$	$-0.01^{**}U_t$	$0.017^{**}Y_t$
ln[POP/(100-POP)], M	Lafay (1984)	1974:10–1983:12		$-0.028^{**}P_t$	$-0.103^{**}U_{t-1}$	$0.029^{**}Y_{t-1}$
Australia						
Governing parties, Q	Schneider and Pommerehne (1980)	1960:2–1977:2	0.66^{**}	-0.47^*P_{t-1}	$-1.13^{**}U_{t-1}$	0.05^*Y_{t-1}
Denmark						
Governing parties, Q	Paldam and Schneider (1980)	1957:2–1968:1	0.67^{**}	$-0.41^*(P_t - P_{t-4})$	$-0.73^*(U_t - U_{t-4})$	$0.19^*(Y_t - Y_{t-4})$

Country / Dependent variable	Source	Period		P term	U term	Y term
Germany						
Governing party, M	Kirchgässner (1976)	1951:1–1966:10	0.67**	$-0.20^{**}P_t$	$-0.43^{**}U_t$	
Governing parties, M	Kirchgässner (1977)	1970:3–1976:10	0.61**	$-0.09^{*}P_t$	$-0.31^{**}U_t$	
Governing parties, Q ln[POP(100-POP)]	Hibbs (1982c)	1957:4–1978:4	0.88[b]	$-0.0044^{**}\ln(P_t/P_{t-1})$	$-0.006^{**}\ln(U_t/U_{t-1})$	$0.0051^{**}\ln(Y_t/Y_{t-1})$
Great Britain						
Government lead, Q (POP$_{GOV}$–POP$_{OPP}$)	Pissarides (1980)	1955:3–1977:4	0.52**	$-0.57^{**}(P_t - P_{t-1})$	$4.55^{*}(1/U_{t-2})$	$0.26^{*}Y_t$
Governing parties, Q ln[POP/(100-POP)]	Hibbs (1982c)	1959:4–1978:4	0.88[b]	$0.0038^{**}\ln(P_t/P_{t-1})$	$-0.21^{**}\ln(U_t/U_{t-1})$	$0.0081\Delta\ln(Y_t/Y_{t-1})$
Government lead, Q (POP$_{GOV}$–POP$_{OPP}$)	Minford and Peel (1982)	1959:1–1957:3		$1.95P_{t+1}^{c}$		$0.53Y_{t+1}^{c}$
Government, Q $\ln\left(\dfrac{POP}{1-POP}\right)$	Price and Sanders (1994)	1951–1989	0.87**	$-0.015^{**}P_t - 0.009^{*}P_{t-2}$	$-0.24^{*}\Delta\ln U_{t-1}$ $-0.28^{**}\Delta\ln U_{t-2}$	
Ireland						
Lead of main governing party over main opposition party, Q	Borooah and Borooah (1990)	1974–1987		$-1.86^{*}P_t$	$-0.008^{**}U_{t-1}$	$1.39^{*}Y_t$
Japan						
Governing parties (30 observations)	Inoguchi (1980)	1960–1976		$-0.68^{**}P_t$		$0.59^{*}Y_{t-2}$
Governing party, Q	Suzuki (1994)	1961–1987	0.81**	$0.008P_{t-1}$		$0.0003Y_{t-1}$
New Zealand						
Government lead, Q (POP$_{GOV}$–POP$_{OPP}$)	Ursprung (1983)	1970:1–1981:4	0.28	$-0.35^{*}(P_t - P_{t-1})$	$-2.12^{**}U_t$	$0.07Y_t/Y_{t-1}$
Government, Q	Smyth and Woodfield (1993)	1985–1990		$-0.039^{**}P_{t-4}^{2}$	$-0.79^{**}U_t^{2}$	

(continued)

435

Table 19.2 (*continued*)

Country-dependent variable	Author(s)	Time period	Lagged dependent variable	Inflation rate (P)	Unemployment rate (U)	National income (Y)
Sweden						
Social Democrats, M	Jonung and Wadensjoe (1979)	1967:3–1976:9	0.88**	-0.10^*P_{t-1}	$-0.73^{**}U_{t-1}$	
The Netherlands						
Popularity of 3 parties, M	Renaud and van Winden (1987a)	1970:1–1981:12				
Christian Democrats			0.83*	-2.23^*P_t	-1.09^*U_t	
Social Democrats			0.83*	-1.67^*P_t	-0.57^*U_t	
Liberal			0.83*	-0.78^*P_t	-0.36^*U_t	
Conservatives						

Notes: See Table 19.1.

[a] Q = quarterly; M = monthly.

[b] Estimated by iterative search for minimum sum of squared errors.

[c] Projected value assuming rational expectations.

Source: Schneider and Frey (1988, Tables 2 and 3) with additions and amendments. Reprinted with permission of Duke University Press.

voting. Peltzman's (1990) results presented in Table 19.1 are typical in this respect. Peltzman estimates the same model over the same time period using votes in presidential, Senate, and gubernatorial elections. Although the coefficients on unexpected inflation and income growth tend to be significant in all three sets of regressions, the coefficients in the presidential contests are much larger in absolute size. Alesina and Rosenthal (1995) obtain a significant relationship between income growth and votes in presidential races, but not in House contests.[2] Bennett and Wiseman (1991) find that economic conditions significantly affect a senator's chance for election only if he is from the same party as the president. Chressanthis and Shaffer (1993) can find no significant effects of any macroeconomic variables on votes in senatorial contests.

Weaker relationships between macroeconomic variables and party votes or popularity have also been observed in countries in which governments typically are formed by coalitions among several parties.[3] These findings again suggest that macroeconomic conditions only influence how citizens vote when the citizens can fairly readily hold a person or party responsible for these conditions. Thus, some discretion must be used when trying to interpret the importance of economic conditions for election outcomes, based on the results of vote- and popularity-function estimates.

19.2 Opportunistic politics

If voters weigh macroeconomic performance when deciding how to vote, then vote-seeking politicians will choose macroeconomic policies to win voters. One way to view this problem is to assume that inflation and unemployment are the only variables in the voter's utility function, and that a traditional long-run Phillips curve LL exists as in Figure 19.1. Since both inflation and unemployment are bad, voter indifference curves are concave to the origin with indifference curves closer to the origin representing higher utility levels.[4] LL is the effective opportunity set and, assuming two political parties, competition for votes between them leads to a single vote-maximizing point along LL. While each voter's indifference map might lead her to favor a different point along LL, with only U and P in the utility function, the inverse relationship between U and P inherent in the Phillips curve reduces the issue set to a single dimension, the choice, say, of U. Voters' preferences are single-peaked along LL, and the median voter theorem applies. If I_1 and I_2 are indifference curves of the median voter, then both parties will strive to adopt macro-stabilization policies that bring the economy to point M on the Phillips curve.

---

[2] Kramer (1971), on the other hand, observed a much better fit when results for congressional elections were used, than for presidential elections. See also Kuklinski and West's (1981) comparative results for House and Senate voting, and Fiorina's (1978, 1981) for House and presidential voting.

[3] See Alesina et al. (1997, ch. 6) and the discussion and references in Nannestad and Paldam (1994, pp. 233–4). Swank and Eisinga (1999) find evidence that parties in coalition governments in the Netherlands were punished for poor macroeconomic results, once they controlled for partisan effects.

[4] Smyth and Woodfield (1993) estimate indifference curves for New Zealand voters that resemble those in Figure 19.1. The indifference curves estimated by Smyth and Dua (1989) for the United States look like inverted Us.

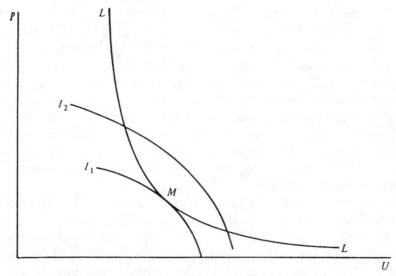

Figure 19.1. The trade-off between inflation (P) and unemployment (U).

19.2.1   *With myopic voters*

Thus, with choices constrained to a long-run Phillips curve like LL and fully informed, rational voters, two-party competition can be expected to result in a unique
unemployment/inflation combination regardless of which party is in office. The situation is somewhat different, however, if, say, quantities respond more rapidly to
changes in macroeconomic conditions than prices (Okun, 1981). The government
can then manipulate the macroeconomic levers so as to reduce unemployment in the
short run, with the full inflationary effect coming some time later. Governments face
a short-run Phillips curve like SS in Figure 19.2. If voters ignore or heavily discount

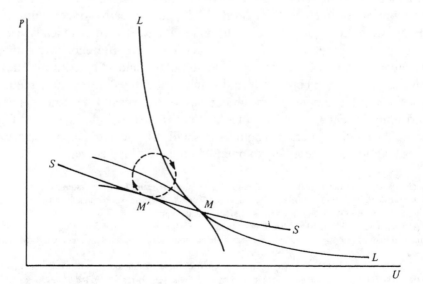

Figure 19.2. The political business cycle.

the future inflation that a movement along SS to the left of M must eventually bring, then the party in government can raise a substantial majority of voters' utilities in the short run by adopting policies that move the economy out along SS to, say, M'. The party in control of the government is in a position to increase its chances for reelection by reducing unemployment just before an election (Nordhaus, 1975; Lindbeck, 1976; MacRae, 1977; Fair, 1978; Tufte, 1978). In countries in which the government has some discretion in choosing when to call an election, the party in power has an even further advantage over the opposition in ensuring that elections occur under favorable economic conditions (Frey and Schneider, 1978b; Lächler, 1982).

Of course, after the election inflation rises and the economy returns to LL. But this higher inflation may be inherited by the opposition party, and even if the incumbent party wins, it can wring the inflation out of the economy after the election by sufficiently deflationary policies. Thus, the prediction emerges from our first opportunistic model of macroeconomic policy that incumbent parties deliberately create a political business cycle (PBC) with falling unemployment (rising national income) prior to an election, and rising unemployment (falling inflation) afterward, as depicted, say, by the dashed line in Figure 19.2.

19.2.2 *With rational voters*

The preceeding model of a political business cycle assumes that voters are myopic. They vote for the government at M' as if this combination of U and P were sustainable, even though the economy will soon change and bring them to lower levels of utility than at either M' or M. Moreover, they never learn from their mistakes. Each government tries to trick the voters into believing that it is able to deviate from the long-run Phillips curve, and voters regularly fall for the trick.

This kind of extreme voter myopia is difficult to reconcile with the assumption of rational actors upon which much of public choice is based, and the assumption of the rational expectations of all economic agents that has come to dominate the macroeconomic modeling in the years since the myopic voter/opportunistic PBC models first appeared. Following Rogoff and Sibert (1988) several variants of a rational voter/opportunistic PBC model have now appeared.[5] In these models parties or candidates differ in their abilities to macromanage the economy. Candidate A can achieve a greater rate of growth in income for a given level of inflation than can candidate B. If voters are fully informed, candidate A always wins the election. A PBC can be generated, however, if we assume that the voters are not fully informed. If A is the incumbent, she can signal her greater competence by inducing the economy to grow faster prior to the election. The voters can recognize that she is the more competent candidate, because it would be too costly for the less competent candidate to adopt this policy. Although this artificial acceleration in growth results in some unnecessary inflation or other costs after the election, the voters are still better off electing A since she is able to manage the economy better than her opponent.

---

[5] See also Lächler (1984), Persson and Tabellini (1990), Rogoff (1990), Alesina and Rosenthal (1995, ch. 9), and Sieg (1998).

This model thus predicts, as does the myopic voter model, that governments will increase certain categories of spending, run deficits, and perhaps create extra inflation just prior to an election.

19.3   Partisan politics

The two-party competition model just described assumes that voters have no loyalty to any party and parties have no loyalties toward specific groups of voters. Political competition is, like market competition, impartial. Voters vote for the party coming closest to their position on inflation and unemployment; parties court all voters with equal alacrity. Both parties would converge on the same combination of unemployment and inflation if constrained to points along the long-run Phillips curve; both parties try in the same way to manipulate the economy to their advantage just before elections.

A large body of evidence exists indicating that voters' choices of party are not as fluid as the preceding characterization suggests. Moreover, parties do not promise exactly the same policies. The attraction of voters for particular parties and ideological inertia of party goals can be explained by an extension of the voter-self-interest-party-competition model.

Blue-collar and unskilled workers are more likely to become unemployed and stay unemployed than are white-collar and professional groups. Thus, it is rational for lower-skilled groups to be more concerned about unemployment. That they are is illustrated in Figure 19.3 taken from Hibbs (1982b) (see also Tufte, 1978, pp. 83–4; and for the United States, Hibbs, 1979, p. 715, and 1987, p. 139). The vertical axis gives the percentage of individuals of a given occupational group who regarded unemployment as "a particularly important issue" or the "most important problem" at the time. Not surprisingly, unemployment is regarded as a more important issue in 1975 when the unemployment rate stood at 4.2 percent, than in 1969 or 1964 when the rates were 2.5 and 1.8 percent, respectively. But at any given point in time, the lower-status occupational groups show a greater concern about unemployment than the managerial and professional group.

Given their greater relative concern about unemployment, it is perhaps not surprising to find that the lower-status groups' support for the president or government in office is more sensitive to unemployment levels. Table 19.3 reports estimates of the effects of changes in unemployment, inflation, and real income on support for the president in the United States and governing party in the United Kingdom. In both countries, the response to changes in unemployment differs to a greater extent across occupational groups than it does for inflation. Indeed, there is little difference in the response of the different groups to changes in inflation within either country, while the responses to changes in unemployment differ by a factor of more than four in the United States and two in the United Kingdom. Note also that the coefficients on inflation are much higher relative to those on unemployment in the United States than in the United Kingdom. According to Hibbs's estimate, Americans on average are more concerned about inflation relative to unemployment than the British population. In even starker contrast to the United States, the New Zealanders appear to be

Table 19.3. *Changes in support for the U.S. president and U.K. governing party in response to macroeconomic performance*

Occupational group	Inflation rate	Unemployment rate	Real income growth rate
Gallop poll approval, U.S. presidents (1960–79)			
Blue-collar	−3.3	−2.2	+2.7
White-collar	−3.6	−1.6	+2.1
Nonlabor force	−3.2	−0.45	+1.2
Political support for U.K. governing party (1962–78)			
Semi- and unskilled workers, widows, and state pensioners	−1.9	−2.85	+1.0
Skilled workers	−1.8	−3.3	+1.3
Nonmanual employees	−1.7	−1.55	+0.55

Sources: Hibbs (1982a, Table 4; 1982b, Table 3). Figures are Hibbs's figures for a 2-percentage-point increase divided by 2. All figures are values for complete adjustment except U.K. real income change figure, which is after 8 quarters.

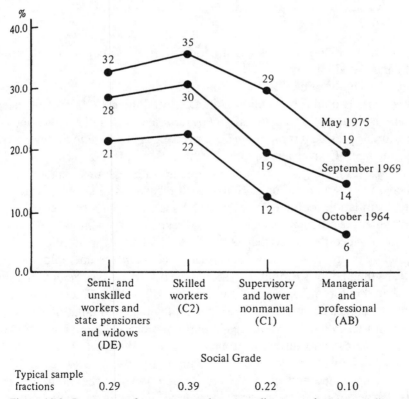

Figure 19.3. Percentage of survey respondents regarding unemployment as a "most serious problem." *Source:* Hibbs (1982b, p. 262).

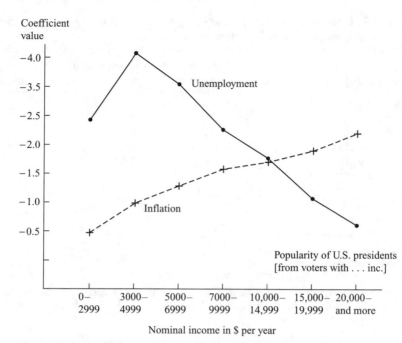

Figure 19.4. Coefficients for unemployment and inflation in U.S. presidential popularity equations (1969–76), seven income groups. *Source:* Schneider (1978); Schneider and Frey (1988).

willing to trade off large increases in inflation for small reductions in unemployment (Smyth and Woodfield, 1993).

Figure 19.4 plots the coefficients on unemployment and inflation by income group in a presidential popularity function estimated by Schneider (1978). Consistent with the relationship across occupational groups reported in Table 19.3, one finds that the support for the president is more sensitive to changes in unemployment the lower the group's income.[6] Conversely, support for the president is more sensitive to changes in inflation rates the higher a group's income is. Although there is more variability in the coefficients on inflation in Schneider's results than in Hibbs's, the line connecting the inflation coefficients in Figure 19.4 is flatter than the one connecting the unemployment coefficients. The differential response to unemployment changes is greater across income groups than is the differential response to inflation. Note that Schneider's results indicate a greater relative concern for unemployment among Americans than Hibbs's results. The absolute value of the coefficient on inflation is higher than that for unemployment for only two of the seven income groups.

These differences in attitudes toward unemployment and inflation across income classes will translate into differences in party platforms if, unlike in the Downsian model, parties cater to different groups of voters. Wittman (1973) was the first to modify the Downsian model by endowing party leaders with goals other than simply getting elected, and this behavioral assumption underlies all partisan politics models. Parties of the left are assumed to draw their political support from lower

---

[6] The anomalous coefficient for the lowest income group may come about because this group contains a disproportionate fraction of retirees who may be less concerned about unemployment.

occupational status and income groups. These groups are more concerned about unemployment and their support is more sensitive to changes in unemployment. Parties of the right draw their support from groups more concerned about and responsive to inflation. An analysis of left-of-center party membership should find them more responsive to unemployment, and right-of-center members to inflation – and it does. An increase in unemployment lowers the percentage of Democrats who approve of the president's performance by two to three times as much as it reduces the support of Republicans. On the other hand, an increase in the inflation rate reduces a president's approval among Republicans by somewhat more than it does among Democrats, although the differences are less dramatic (Hibbs, 1982a, Table 4; 1987, pp. 175–82).

19.3.1 *Partisan politics with retrospective voters*

The political scientist V.O. Key, Jr. is often cited as the originator of the retrospective voter hypothesis.

> The patterns of flow of the major streams of shifting voters graphically reflect the electorate in its great, and perhaps principal, role as an appraiser of past events, past performance, and past actions. It judges retrospectively; it commands prospectively only insofar as it expresses either approval or disapproval of that which has happened before.[7]

The first full development of a model of electoral politics with retrospective voters is due, however, to Fiorina (1977a, 1981). Hibbs (1981, 1982a,b,c, 1987, 1992, 1994, 2000) incorporates the same view of a rational, retrospective voter into his models of partisan politics. In deciding which party to vote for, the individual evaluates the performances of the competing parties on the issues of highest salience to her. For low-income and status groups this issue tends to be unemployment; for higher-income and status groups inflation. The former groups are drawn rationally to the left-of-center parties because these parties have better records at reducing unemployment, just as the higher-income and status groups are drawn to the right-of-center parties owing to their better performance at reducing inflation.

These behavioral assumptions may be captured with the following model. Each voter evaluates the performance of the incumbent party using the weights she places on unemployment and inflation. Letting E_{it} be the performance evaluation of the incumbent party by voter i at time t, we have

$$E_{it} = \alpha_i \left(\sum_{j=1}^{n} \lambda^j U_{t-j} \right) + \beta_i \left(\sum_{j=1}^{n} \lambda^j P_{t-j} \right), \tag{19.1}$$

where U_{t-j} and P_{t-j} are the unemployment and inflation levels at time $t - j$. If voter i comes from a lower socioeconomic class than voter k, then

$$\alpha_i > \alpha_k \quad \text{and} \quad \beta_i < \beta_k. \tag{19.2}$$

---

[7] Key (1966, p. 61). See discussion by Keech (1995, ch. 6).

Each voter evaluates the performance of the incumbent party at the time of the election, and votes for the incumbent party if its evaluated performance is higher than some benchmark level of performance that the voter expects that the opposition party might have obtained.

Given the differences in weights that the voters place on unemployment and inflation, if left-of-center parties do produce lower levels of unemployment and higher levels of inflation over time than do right-of-center parties, then they will win larger fractions of the votes of low-income voters. Note, however, that the model does incorporate a form of voters' reward for competence. If a right-of-center party manages to produce sufficiently low levels of inflation and unemployment, it will win votes from those voters on the left for whom the right-of-center party's performance evaluation exceeds the expected performance of the left-of-center party.

It should also be noted that, although voters are assumed to be backward looking, they are not assumed to be either irrational or necessarily myopic. Rather voters and parties are both assumed to recognize that they are essentially in a principal–agent relationship. Since the voters cannot write a contract that binds parties to good performance while in office, all of the incentives for good performance have to come at the time of "settling up," that is, when the party runs for reelection. Good performance is rewarded by reelection; bad performance is punished through the election of the opposition (Ferejohn, 1986).

How myopic these retrospective voters are depends on the sizes of n and λ in (19.1). This is, of course, an empirical question to which we shall return.

19.3.2 *Partisan politics with rational, forward-looking voters*

The first paper to introduce rational expectations into a form of partisan-politics model was by Minford and Peel (1982). The variant of this type of model that has received the most attention, however, is due to Alesina (1987). We shall outline here the formulation as it appears in Alesina and Rosenthal (1995).[8]

The first problem one faces when building rational expectations into a political economy model of macroeconomics is that with rational expectations both the Phillips curve and the political business cycle disappear (Detken and Gärtner, 1992). Voters anticipate and neutralize every possible partisan or opportunistic action by the government. To bring politics back into the picture, the strong form of the rational expectations assumption must be relaxed in some way. Alesina and Rosenthal do this in their model of U.S. politics by assuming that voters *and labor unions and employers* are uncertain about the outcome of a presidential election at the time that they vote. The wage contracts signed just prior to an election will, therefore, be based on an expected rate of inflation that is somewhere between the inflation rate that the Left Party favors and the rate favored by the Right Party. If the Left wins the election it can adopt a temporary policy of stimulating the economy and reducing unemployment at the cost of some additional inflation. A victory by the Right allows it to successfully reduce inflation by contracting the economy. When

---

[8] See also Alesina (1988a,b) and Alesina and Roubini with Cohen (1997).

Number of voters

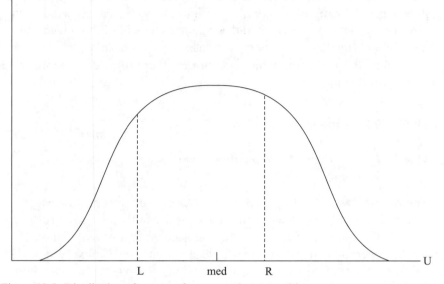

Figure 19.5. Distribution of voter preferences and party positions.

the mid-term election comes around, there is no longer any uncertainty about who is in the White House. The full force of rational expectations is at work. The economy is locked into its natural rate of unemployment.

The Alesina and Rosenthal model thus makes some very specific predictions about the patterns of unemployment and inflation over a four-year electoral cycle. If a Democratic administration takes office, unemployment should fall following the election and then return to its natural rate toward the end of the cycle. A victory by the Republicans has the exact opposite pattern over the first two years, but the economy winds up in exactly the same place at the next presidential election.

An important advantage of the Alesina and Rosenthal model comes in the way it allows them to analyze the interplay between Congress and the president. To see what is involved, consider Figure 19.5. Competition for votes takes place over a single-dimensional policy space. For our purposes we might think of this being the choice of the level of unemployment. The distribution of voters is assumed to be single peaked with the two parties having favored policy positions to the left and right of the policy preferred by the median voter. If the Left Party controls both the White House and the Congress, it implements its preferred policy, L. If the Right Party controls both branches, it implements R. With *divided government*, that is, one party in control of the White House and the other of Congress, Alesina and Rosenthal assume that a compromise on macroeconomic policy must be reached and some level of unemployment between L and R arises. This in turn means that some voters who prefer policy outcomes between L and R actually prefer to see different parties controlling each branch than one party in control of both.

This line of reasoning allows Alesina and Rosenthal to account for "split-ticket voting" and the "midterm cycle." A voter who prefers a policy between L and R

might rationally vote for one party for the office of president and the other for Congress to try and get a divided government. If one party, say the Left, wins the presidency, a swing of voters to the Right Party can be expected at the midterm election as some of the voters in the middle of the distribution try to strengthen the hand of the Right Party in Congress as a balance against the president. We turn now to see how these and the predictions of the other political economic models stand up against the data.

19.4   The evidence

19.4.1   *Do politicians try to manipulate the macroeconomic environment?*

The simplest way to operationalize the voter self-interest postulate is to assume that income is the only argument in the voter's utility function, and as Tufte (1978, p. 29) noted, "The quickest way to produce an acceleration of real disposable income is for the government to mail more people larger checks." Tufte (1978, ch. 2) provided ample evidence of the use of transfer payments to win votes in the United States, and Frey and Schneider (1978a,b, 1979) presented econometric evidence of increases in government expenditures before elections in both the United States and the United Kingdom. This early work was heavily criticized by Brown and Stein (1982) and Alt and Chrystal (1983), and several subsequent studies have failed to find evidence of cycles in expenditures, taxes, or transfers that are related to the electoral cycle (Paldam, 1979, 1981a,b; Golen and Poterba, 1980; Lowery, 1985; Sorensen, 1987).

As Blais and Nadeau (1992, pp. 391–2) point out, however, in these studies the coefficients on the key variables are often of the predicted sign and their lack of statistical significance may be simply due to the scant numbers of time series observations available. Blais and Nadeau avoid this problem by using data on the ten Canadian provinces from 1951 to 1984. They find significant increases in spending on roads and social services as well as in total spending. In election years budget deficits also increase. Their findings have been reconfirmed by Reid (1998) using provincial data from 1962 through 1992. Hibbs (1987, chs. 7 and 9) provides further evidence on the use of transfers to win votes in the United States. Bhattacharyya and Wassmer (1995) find that city government expenditures rise and taxes fall in election years. Yoo (1998) demonstrates that the Liberal Democratic Party systematically reduced taxes in election years in Japan from 1953 through 1992. Van Dalen and Swank (1996) observe significant increases in social security payments, defense expenditures, and outlays for public administration in election years. Finally, Schuknecht (2000), using data from 24, and Alesina and Roubini with Cohen (1997, ch. 7), using data from 18 OECD countries, find public spending and deficits rising just prior to elections.

The discretion governments have to manipulate fiscal policies is limited, of course, and thus the amounts by which expenditures rise or taxes fall at election times tend to be modest – typically of the order of 1 to 3 percent. With such small changes and heterogeneous behavior, it is quite possible that a statistically significant relationship will not be found in a given set of data, particularly when the data set is small. However, the most recent studies with longer time series and using pooled cross-section/time series data seem to confirm the early work of Tufte, Frey, and Schneider. It is difficult to avoid the conclusion that *some* politicians open the public spigots prior to at least some elections to win votes.[9]

Evidence that governments also speed up the printing press just prior to elections is more mixed, but still tilts in the direction of opportunistic increases of the money supply, usually measured as $M1$, prior to elections. Supportive evidence for the United States has been provided by Allen (1986), Richards (1986), Grier (1987, 1989a), Havrilesky (1987), Chappell and Keech (1988), Haynes and Stone (1989), Williams (1990), and Carlsen (1997); for Germany by Berger and Woitek (1997); and for 18 OECD countries by Alesina and Roubini with Cohen (1997, ch. 7). Counterevidence, all for the United States, comes from Golen and Poterba (1980), Beck (1984, 1987), and Hibbs (1987). Once again time series are often short, and even where evidence of opportunistic money supply increases is found, the statistical and/or economic significance is not overwhelming. But even in countries like the United States and Germany, where central bank independence is taken as a given, the central bankers do not appear to be totally oblivious to the electoral fortunes of their governments.

19.4.2 *Are there partisan biases?*

We reviewed the preceding evidence indicating that lower income groups tend to be more concerned about unemployment and upper income groups about inflation. Lower income groups have traditionally supported parties on the left and upper income groups parties on the right. Is this party allegiance rational? Do parties on the left promise to do more about unemployment than do parties on the right? Do they deliver? The answers to the latter two questions are unequivocally "yes".

A content analysis of the annual *Economic Report of the President and the Council of Economic Advisers* along with party platforms reveals far more emphasis on unemployment by the Democrats and far more emphasis on inflation by Republicans (Tufte, 1978, pp. 71–83). Evidence exists that the same differences are present in other countries (Kirschen, 1974).

These differences in rhetoric are matched by differences in policies. Using quarterly data over the period 1953 through 1990, Hibbs has estimated the apparent target growth rates under Democratic and Republican administrations. He found "that the inflation-neutral growth rate goals of the Democrats typically were about

---

[9] This action could also be interpreted as consistent with the Rogoff and Sibert (1988), and Rogoff (1990) rational-expectations PBC. One of the predictions from this model is, however, that "the incumbent leader has an incentive to bias pre-election fiscal policy toward easily observed consumption expenditures, and away from government investment" Rogoff (1990, p. 21). Several studies have found, however, that investment is one of the government outlays that does increase just before elections (Blais and Nadeau, 1992; van Dalen and Swank, 1996; Schuknecht, 2000), and is even favored over consumption (Reid, 1998).

6 to 7 percent above historical trend," while "aggregate demand changes under the Republicans generally were just big enough to perpetuate received real growth rates" (Hibbs, 1994, p. 10).

Monetary policy has been more expansionary in the United States when Democrats control the key banking committees in Congress and/or occupy the White House, although the differences in policies are not uniform across administrations (Hibbs, 1977, 1987; Beck, 1982c; Chappell and Keech, 1988; Grier, 1991, 1996; Havrilesky, 1993; Caporale and Grier, 1998). Alogoskougis, Lockwood, and Philippopoulos (1992) found that labor governments pursue more expansionary monetary polices in the United Kingdom and Alogoskougis and Philippopoulos (1992) found the same for Greece. Alesina and Roubini with Cohen (1997, ch. 7) found evidence of partisan bias in monetary policy in their study of 18 OECD countries. Berger and Woitek (1997) were not able to detect any partisan biases in Germany's monetary policy, however.

Alesina and Roubini with Cohen (1997, ch. 7) did not find that budget deficits were larger in their sample of 18 OECD countries when left-of-center parties were in power. On the other hand, Blais and Nadeau (1992) observed lower spending and smaller deficits in Canadian provinces controlled by right-wing governments. De Haan and Sturm (1994) found that EU countries controlled by left-wing governments spent more. Van Dalen and Swank (1996) found that left-wing governments in the Netherlands allocate more funds to social security and health care; right-wing governments spend more on infrastructure and defense. Allers, de Haan, and Sterks (2001) estimate high local property taxes in Dutch municipalities controlled by left-of-center parties. A governing party's ideology does appear to influence the policies it chooses.

What differences do these policies make? Since the thrust of the literature on politically driven macropolicies has been concerned with unemployment and inflation, it is natural to look at these indicators of macroeconomic performance. Table 19.4 reports unemployment U and inflation P rates in the fourth years of every presidential term since 1952. The middle portion of the table indicates that each of the seven Republican presidential terms resulted in an average increase of 1 percentage point in the unemployment rate, an increase of 20 percent over the figure in the year before the presidential term began. Inflation was reduced by an average of 1.4 percentage points, on the other hand. The five Democratic presidential terms brought unemployment down by an average of 1.2 percentage points per term, while raising inflation by 2.2 percentage points.

Perhaps the most revealing figures are at the bottom of the table for the four full Republican administrations and three Democratic ones. Since 1952 Republican presidential administrations have added 7.0 percentage points to the unemployment rate, while taking 8.9 percentage points off the rate of inflation. Democrats have added 11.1 percentage points to inflation while lowering unemployment by 6.0 percentage points.

A similar picture is obtained from Hibbs's time-series model for predicting unemployment and real output levels. Using quarterly data from 1953:1 through 1983:2,

Table 19.4. *Macroeconomic performance of U.S. economy under Republican and Democratic presidents (1952–2000)*

Year	U	P	Year	U	P
1952	3.0	0.9	1980	7.1	12.4
1956	4.1	2.9	1984	7.5	3.9
1960	5.5	1.5	1988	5.5	4.4
1964	5.2	1.2	1992	7.5	2.9
1968	3.6	4.7	1996	5.4	3.3
1972	5.6	4.4	2000	4.0	3.2
1976	7.7	4.8			

Changes in U and P by party of president for presidential terms

	Republican					Democratic			
	ΔU		ΔP			ΔU		ΔP	
Term	ABS.	%	ABS.	%	Term	ABS.	%	ABS.	%
52–56	+1.1	+31	+2.0	+105	60–64	−0.3	−6	−0.3	−22
56–60	+1.4	+29	−1.4	−64	64–68	−1.6	−36	+3.5	+119
68–72	+2.0	+43	−1.3	−32	76–80	−0.6	−8	+7.6	+88
72–76	+2.1	+32	+1.4	+34	92–96	−2.1	−33	+0.4	+13
80–84	+0.4	+5	−8.5	−104	96–00	−1.4	−26	−0.1	−3
84–88	−2.0	−31	+0.5	+12					
88–92	+2.0	+31	−1.5	−41					
Average	+1.0	+20	−1.4	−13		−1.2	−22	+2.2	+39

Changes in U and P by uninterrupted party control of presidency

	ΔU	ΔP
Republican administrations		
Eisenhower (1952–60)	+2.5	+0.6
Nixon-Ford (1968–76)	+4.1	+0.1
Reagan (1980–8)	−1.6	−8.0
Bush (1988–92)	+2.0	−1.5
Cumulative	+7.0	−8.8
Democratic administrations		
Kennedy-Johnson (1960–8)	−1.9	+3.2
Carter (1976)	−0.6	+7.6
Clinton (1992–2000)	−3.5	+0.3
Cumulative	−6.0	11.1

Source: Council of Economic Advisors, Economic Report of the President. Washington, D.C.: U.S. Government Printing Office, 1989, 2001. Figures for 2000 are preliminary.

Hibbs estimates that Democratic administrations have a long-run impact on the economy that tends to reduce unemployment by 2 percentage points and increase real output by around 6 percent.[10]

One can argue that Republicans concentrate on inflation when they take office because it is the most serious macroproblem the country faces at the time, and for

[10] Hibbs (1987, pp. 224–32). See also Hibbs (1994, Table 1, p. 4).

the same reason the Democrats concentrate on unemployment. But since Republicans take over from Democrats, and Democrats from Republicans, this observation hardly contradicts the partisan-bias hypothesis. Particularly revealing in this regard is the performance of the Reagan administration. One can argue that both unemployment (7.1 percent) and inflation (12.4 percent) were serious problems when Reagan took office. But it was inflation that received the highest priority. By the administration's second year the inflation rate had been cut by more than two thirds, while unemployment had risen to its highest level since World War II, 9.5 percent. It was six years before the unemployment rate fell below the level when Reagan took office.

A similar dichotomy is apparent in other countries. Hibbs (1977) presents data on unemployment and inflation rates for 12 Western democracies (Belgium, Canada, Denmark, Finland, France, Italy, the Netherlands, Norway, Sweden, the United Kingdom, the United States, and West Germany) and compares them with the percentage of time from 1945 to 1969 in which Socialist-Labor parties were in office. The correlation between left-of-center control and unemployment is −0.68. The correlation between left-of-center control and inflation is +0.74 (see also Beck, 1982b; Beetsma and van der Ploeg, 1996; Oatley, 1999).

These differences in performance in dealing with unemployment have not gone unnoticed by voters. In the United States, those who are more personally affected by unemployment, or who regard unemployment as a serious national issue, are more likely to vote Democratic, ceteris paribus (Kiewiet, 1981, 1983; Kuklinski and West, 1981). In Germany, high unemployment increases the percentage of the vote going to the left-of-center Social Democratic Party (Rattinger, 1981). In France, high unemployment increases the share of votes going to left-of-center parties, which are in opposition; high income lowers their share (Rosa, 1980).

Thus, competition for votes does not lead competing parties to converge on the same target with respect to unemployment and inflation rates. The prediction of a simple form of the median voter theorem applied to macroeconomic policy is not supported. What accounts for this observation?

One possible explanation is that the distribution of voter preferences is not unimodal. Hibbs has emphasized the importance of economic class in explaining voter support for political parties and the link between this support and macroeconomic policies. The existence of significant class distinctions might be interpreted as resulting in either a bi- or multimodal distribution of voter preferences with respect to unemployment and inflation. If voters abstain from supporting a party whose position is too far from their most favored position, competition for votes can pull party platforms away from one another, toward the modes in the distribution (see Downs, 1957, pp. 118–22; Davis, Hinich, and Ordeshook, 1970; and Chapter 11 of this volume). The threat of abstention is likely to be particularly effective in parliamentary systems with proportional representation, as the voter often has party options on both the left and the right of a given party, and new parties can more easily form than in the United States. Thus, one finds European parties to be more ideological than the two U.S. parties, and voters more closely tied to their parties (for example, Hibbs, 1982c).

A second explanation is that party platforms and the identities of candidates are determined by party activists, and these activists tend to be drawn more from the tails of the distribution of voters than from the center.[11]

19.4.3 *Which theories fit the data best?*

Since the opportunistic PBC models predict that both parties behave identically, the evidence reviewed in the previous subsection would appear to make them non-starters. Nevertheless, we shall consider their predictions and the evidence in support of them along with the two leading partisan PBC models.

Each model makes fairly specific predictions about the patterns of unemployment, inflation, and growth over the electoral cycle. Before discussing the econometric support for each, it is useful to compare their predictions with the experience for the United States. In Table 19.5 I have summarized the predictions of each hypothesis. Because the rational-voter, opportunistic PBC model only predicts policies around the time of the election, I have omitted it from consideration here. The Nordhaus/MacRae (NM) model predicts the same pattern, of course, regardless of which party is in office – rising unemployment until a peak is reached in the second year of the cycle and then a decline so that the party goes into the election with unemployment at its minimum.

Hibbs' partisan PBC predicts continually falling unemployment under the Democrats, and continually rising unemployment under the Republicans.[12]

The Alesina/Rosenthal model makes such strong predictions that it is difficult to make a fair comparison with the other two models. In terms of growth rates it predicts growth at the same, natural rate in the last two years of both types of administrations, with faster growth for the Democrats and slower for the Republicans in the first two years.[13] Since unemployment adjusts slowly, I have translated these predictions into an upward movement in unemployment under a Republican administration peaking in the second year, and then declining to the natural rate of unemployment and the exact opposite pattern for a Democratic administration. This pattern matches the pattern of changes in GDP estimated by Alesina and Roubini with Cohen (1997, Figure 4.1, p. 76) and would thus seem to be a reasonable depiction of this class of rational PBC models.[14] Note that when the Republicans hold the White House, the Nordhaus/MacRae PBC model and the Alesina/Rosenthal model make essentially the same predictions.

With the Alesina/Rosenthal model there is the additional complication of specifying the natural rate of unemployment. Up through the 1960s *full* employment was often thought to be around 4 percent. Once stagflation set in during the 1970s some economists raised their estimate of this figure to as high as 6 percent. The

---

[11] For further discussion of this and other explanations for why parties choose separate policy positions see Alesina and Rosenthal (1995, pp. 40–1).

[12] Of course, if several Democratic administrations followed one another, unemployment would eventually have to stop falling.

[13] See Alesina and Rosenthal (1995, pp. 171–8, and especially Figure 7.1 on p. 175).

[14] The pattern I depict for the Alesina/Rosenthal model is, however, *not* the one suggested by Paldam (1997, p. 355).

Table 19.5. *Scores for political business cycle models*

Year	Y1	Y2	Y3	Y4
Model	Democrats			
NM election cycle	Up	Max	Down	Min
Hibbs partisan cycle	Max	Down	Down	Min
AR partisan cycle	Down	Min	Up	Natural

Administration	Unemployment				NM	Hibbs	AR
Truman, 1949–52	5.9	5.3	3.3	3.0	3	4	0
Kennedy/Johnson, 1961–4	6.7	5.5	5.7	5.2	2	3	1
Johnson, 1965–8	4.5	3.8	3.8	3.6	2	4	2
Carter, 1977–80	7.1	6.1	5.8	7.1	1	3	1
Clinton, 1993–6	6.9	6.1	5.6	5.4	2	4	1
Clinton, 1997–2000	4.9	4.5	4.2	(4.0)[a]	2	4	2
Totals	average 4.7				12	22	7

Year	Y1	Y2	Y3	Y4
Model	Republicans			
NM election cycle	Up	Max	Down	Min
Hibbs partisan cycle	Min	Up	Up	Max
AR partisan cycle	Up	Max	Down	Natural

Administration	Unemployment				NM	Hibbs	AR
Eisenhower, 1953–6	2.9	5.5	4.4	4.1	2	2	3
Eisenhower, 1957–60	4.3	6.8	5.5	5.5	3	2	3
Nixon, 1969–72	3.5	4.9	5.9	5.6	0	3	0
Nixon/Ford, 1973–6	4.9	5.6	8.5	7.7	0	3	0
Reagan, 1981–4	7.6	9.7	9.6	7.5	4	1	3
Reagan, 1985–8	7.2	7.0	6.2	5.5	2	0	1
Bush, 1989–92	5.3	5.6	6.8	7.5	0	4	0
Totals	average 6.2				11	15	10
Totals both parties					23	37	17

[a] Preliminary.

Source: Council of Economic Advisors, Economic Report of the President. Washington, D.C.: U.S. Government Printing Office, 1989, 2000.

performance of the economy during the 1990s suggests that the 4 percent figure is in fact more appropriate. To define the natural rate of unemployment as any level between 4 and 6 percent would seem to rob the concept of all predictive value. Thus, for the purpose of comparison, I have defined the natural rate as anything between 4 and 5 percent.

The farthest right-hand-side columns in Table 19.5 give the scores on how many times the predictions of each model match the unemployment figures to the left.

Consistent with the picture painted by the figures in Table 19.4, the predictions of Hibbs' partisan model fit the data best. Unemployment tends to fall when the Democrats are in the White House, and rise when the Republicans occupy it.

The NM and AR models perform about the same under Republican administrations, of course, because they make the same predictions. Interestingly, although the original PBC models of Tufte and Nordhaus were probably inspired by the actions of the first Nixon administration – if "inspired" is the proper word – the performance of the economy during the two Nixon administrations does not match the predictions of the NM model in any year. The only perfect match to the NM model comes during the first Reagan administration.[15] In contrast, Hibbs's model perfectly characterizes the patterns of unemployment under four Democratic administrations and one Republican.

The AR model's relatively poor performance is in part due to the strong predictions it makes – in particular that under both types of administrations the economy grows at the same, natural rate over the last two years in the electoral cycle. I have interpreted this to imply that the unemployment rate reaches its natural level (4.0 to 5.0 percent) in the final year of an electoral cycle. A more generous range for the natural rate – 4.0 to 6.0 percent – would add five points to the AR model's score, raising it to rough equality with the NM model. But the difference in performance of the economy under the Democrats and Republicans observed in the last year of each electoral cycle is, I believe, a big strike against the AR model. It predicts identical performance under each party in the fourth year of an electoral cycle, where in fact the average unemployment rate under Republican administrations was 6.2 percent in this year, a full 1.5 percentage points above the mean under the Democrats.[16]

Table 19.5 presents the predictions of each hypothesis in their starkest form, and none of the authors of the different models would accept my characterization of their model. The pattern predicted by Alesina and Rosenthal, for example, depends in part on the degree of surprise over the outcome of the presidential election. Nordhaus' (1989) most recent formulation of a PBC model integrates partisan aspects into it. Hibbs's (1994) most recent formulation of a partisan model allows the goals of the parties in office to adjust to realized economic outcomes. Nevertheless, I think it is useful to observe the differences and similarities of the different models, and how well they match the gross patterns of economic change that have occurred, before considering the econometric evidence.

No government could manage the economy perfectly to produce just the levels of unemployment and inflation that it wanted at each stage in the electoral cycle. Unemployment and inflation rates in the United States since World War II have been affected by the Korean and Vietnam wars, the oil price increases of the 1970s, and still other shocks. A proper testing of each model requires an explicit formulation and rigorous econometric tests. Each set of authors has conducted such tests, and

---

[15] It is also interesting to note that when Nordhaus (1989) returns after more than a decade to examine how his PBC model stacks up against its new competitors, he concentrates on data from the Reagan years.

[16] The Alesina/Rosenthal model would fare somewhat better if we used growth in income as our performance measure – somewhat worse if we used price changes. See Drazen (2000, pp. 260–8).

Table 19.6. *Studies testing the PBC of Nordhaus and MacRae*

Support for	Against
Lächler (1978)	McCallum (1978)
Tufte (1978)	Golen and Poterba (1980)
Maloney and Smirlock (1981)	Dinkel (1982)
Richards (1986)	Beck (1982a,b,c)
Pack (1987)	Brown and Stein (1982)
Keil (1988)	Alt and Chrystal (1983)
Haynes and Stone (1989)	McGavin (1987)
	Lewis-Beck (1988)
	Berger and Woitek (1997)

each has found support for his/their version of the PBC model.[17] A full analysis of the empirical work of each author would require at least another chapter, if not another book. An alternative strategy is to examine how each type of model has fared in the hands of other scholars.

Unfortunately, only the opportunistic PBC of Nordhaus and MacRae has been subjected to extensive testing by other researchers. The results split right down the middle. Table 19.6 lists a sampling of studies on both sides of the divide.

Hibbs uses three kinds of evidence to support his partisan theory: (1) systematic differences in policy choices by left- and right-of-center parties, (2) systematic differences in policy outcomes under left- and right-of-center parties, and (3) voter response functions of the type presented in (19.1) in which voters exhibit fairly long memories (n) with relatively high weights (λ) placed on policy outcomes early in an electoral cycle. We have already amply illustrated the support for the theory that falls in the first two categories. We discuss the evidence pertaining to category (3) below.[18]

Since the rational voter models of Alesina (1987) assume the same sorts of partisan policy differences as Hibbs does, much of the evidence in support of the Hibbs model can also be interpreted as support for the rational/voter, partisan model. The key difference between the two comes in the *timing* of the policy changes. In the Alesina models all of the action comes in the first two years of the electoral cycle. Indirectly Paldam (1979, 1981b) was the first to provide support for this model – almost a decade before it was formulated – when he noted in trying to test the NM model that the biggest changes in the main variables came during the first two years following an election, and that these changes did not generally match the predictions of the NM model.

Alesina and Rosenthal (1995, pp. 178–87) and Alesina and Roubini with Cohen (1997, pp. 83–93) provide still more evidence. As an example consider the following regression results of Alesina and Roubini with Cohen (1997, p. 92):

$$U_t = .27^{**} + 1.66^{**}U_{t-1} - .89^{**}U_{t-2} + .19^{**}U_{t-3} + .13^{**}\text{DR6}$$
$$+ .01\text{DR6+},$$ (19.3)

$$R^2 = 0.96.$$

---

[17] See Nordhaus (1975, 1989); Hibbs (1977, 1986, 1987, 1992, 1994); Alesina and Sachs (1988); Alesina and Rosenthal (1995); and Alesina and Roubini with Cohen (1997).

[18] See also Beck (1982b) and Swank (1993) in support of the partisan model.

The equation is estimated with quarterly data over the period 1947:1 through 1993:4. The unemployment rate is significantly related to unemployment lagged over three quarters and to a dummy variable, DR6, that is a one for the second through seventh quarters of a Republican administration (** indicates significance at the 1 percent level). Equation (19.3) predicts unemployment to be significantly higher over roughly the first half of a Republican administration. The rational partisan model predicts no significant differences in unemployment between administrations over the last two years of the electoral cycle. DR6+ is a dummy variable, which is a one for quarters eight and above during a Republican administration. Alesina and Roubini with Cohen predict a zero coefficient for this variable, but argue that if Hibbs is correct, the coefficients on DR6 and DR6+ should be the same. They clearly are not the same, and this can be interpreted as evidence in favor of the Alesina/Rosenthal/Roubini/Cohen version of the partisan politics model.

On the other hand, inspection of Table 19.5 reveals that unemployment usually does continue to fall during the last two years of a Democratic administration, although perhaps at a dampened rate. Such dampening of the effects of partisan economic policies over the course of an electoral cycle is quite consistent with the early version of the Hibbs model, in which each party tries to reach a different location along a Phillips curve like the one depicted in Figure 19.1. If a Democratic administration takes office when unemployment is high and inflation is low, the initial impacts of its stimulation policies will produce large declines in unemployment at modest costs of inflation. As the economy moves up along the Phillips curve, however, each reduction in unemployment comes at a greater cost of higher inflation; the predicted declines in unemployment under a Democratic administration should become smaller, the farther into the electoral cycle it is. The reverse sort of dampening effect can be expected as a Republican administration moves down along the Phillips curve.[19]

19.4.4 *Additional evidence for the Alesina/Rosenthal model*

Alesina and Rosenthal's book is an ambitious effort to model the behavior of American voters and the interplay between Congress and the president on macroeconomic policy. In addition to making rather precise predictions about the patterns of economic growth and inflation over an electoral cycle, they make several predictions about how citizens will vote.

One interesting aspect of their theory is that it implies that for *some* voters divided government is an intended outcome and therefore that they will try and bring it about. A large group of voters with preferences between points *L* and *R* in Figure 19.5 will try to bring about a division in control over Congress and the White House in the hopes of obtaining a macroeconomic policy falling between these two extremes. One way to do this is to split their vote in a presidential election between a presidential candidate of one party and congressional candidate(s) of the other party. A plus

---

[19] See Hibbs (1992, pp. 369–70; 1994). For an early and unsupportive test of the rational partisan model, see Sheffrin (1989), and for a more recent one Heckelman (2001).

for the Alesina/Rosenthal theory is that it gives a rational voter account of this seemingly schizophrenic behavior.

A second plus comes in accounting for the midterm cycle. The share of the national vote going to the party of the president has declined in 19 of the 20 midterm elections since 1918 (see Figure 19.6).[20] Alesina and Rosenthal's (1995, ch. 4) account for this phenomenon is that voters are uncertain about the identity of the next president when they vote in a presidential election, but not when they vote in a midterm election. Thus, a middle-of-the-road voter *knows* at a midterm election that she must vote against the president's party in the congressional races to balance the strength of the White House, and this explains the midterm cycle. None of the other PBCs offers an explanation for this cycle, and thus this clearly supported prediction must be recorded as a big plus for the Alesina/Rosenthal theory.

Nevertheless, one must note that not all of the swings in voter support in midterm elections line up quite as nicely as Alesina and Rosenthal might like. Their model predicts *no* midterm cycle if the voters are certain of the outcome in the preceding presidential election. One expects, therefore, the biggest swings at midterm following the most uncertain presidential contests. No election outcome in the twentieth century was a bigger surprise than Harry Truman's victory in 1948, but the midterm swing in 1950 was roughly equal to the mean swing. Roosevelt's landslide win in 1936 must have been well anticipated, and yet it was followed by the second biggest swing over the period examined. All in all, however, the data on midterm cycles must be regarded as offering good support for the Alesina/Rosenthal theory.

Less successful is their attempt to explain voters' decisions in presidential elections as rational responses to judgments about the competence of the incumbent party. The data reject this formulation of the model and Alesina and Rosenthal (1995, p. 206) are forced to conclude that "the assumption of voter rationality is put into question by our results in the sense that *the American electorate seems to place 'too much' weight on the state of the economy in the election year when choosing a president*" (emphasis in the original).

19.4.5 *Discussion*

The seemingly irrational voter behavior described by Alesina and Rosenthal in the closing sentence of the previous subsection is, of course, precisely the kind of behavior that the Nordhaus/MacRae model presumes. Although this model has been subject to the most intense empirical scrutiny of all PBC models, and has the longest list of authors who reject it, one still gets the impression when reading through this literature that it is not totally at odds with the data. A more naive hypothesis about opportunistic political behavior than the one modeled by Nordhaus and MacRae would be that presidents try to improve the state of the economy going into election years. The literature on short-term changes in expenditures, transfers, taxes, and monetary policy reviewed earlier offers ample support for this hypothesis. A further

---

[20] Writing in the early 1990s Alesina and Rosenthal could claim that their prediction of a midterm loss for the president's party was *always* confirmed. But the 1998 election destroyed this perfect record.

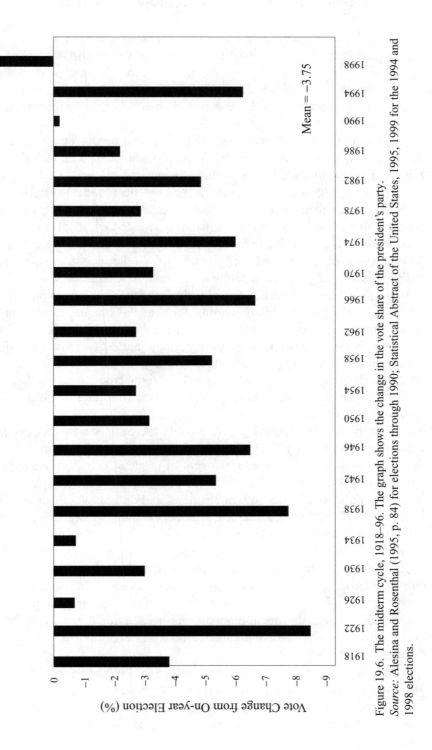

Figure 19.6. The midterm cycle, 1918–96. The graph shows the change in the vote share of the president's party.
Source: Alesina and Rosenthal (1995, p. 84) for elections through 1990; Statistical Abstract of the United States, 1995, 1999 for the 1994 and 1998 elections.

457

glance at Table 19.5 reveals that unemployment fell between the third and fourth years of ten of the thirteen presidential terms since 1948 and remained unchanged in one other. On the two occasions when it rose a president standing for reelection lost – Carter in 1980 and Bush in 1992. It is easy to reach the conclusion from these figures that presidents try to lower unemployment when going into an election, and are well-advised to do so.

The opportunistic PBC model predicts that both parties adopt the same set of macroeconomic policies. In his fierce bombardment of Kramer's (1971) article Stigler (1973) dismissed Kramer's findings in part because "there is no difference between the Republicans and Democrats with respect to the ardent pursuit of high levels of employment and high and steady rates of growth of real income." Empirically this must be one of the *least* well-founded of all of the great Stigler's observations. The evidence reviewed earlier indicates unequivocally that these two parties, and parties of the left and right in many other countries, generally pursue different goals and produce different macroeconomic outcomes.

What then are we to conclude from this evidence? Which model fits the data the best? One clear loser is the strong form of the rational expectations model, which predicts that governmental economic policies cannot affect real economic variables, because these policies are accurately anticipated and fully discounted. Democratically elected governments do not appear to believe that it is futile to try and alter unemployment and growth through macroeconomic policies. And the evidence suggests that each party in office does have some success in achieving its ideological goals.

With respect to the competing PBC models, there appears to be empirical support for both an opportunistic PBC and one which emphasizes partisan differences. Yet the premises upon which these two sets of models rest are quite different. The opportunistic PBC models follow Downs (1957, p. 28) in postulating that "parties formulate policies in order to win elections, rather than win elections in order to formulate policies." The partisan PBC models in contrast "assume that parties win elections in order to formulate policies" (Chappell and Keech, 1986, p. 881; see also Alesina and Rosenthal, 1995, pp. 16–19). A more fundamental difference in starting points would not seem possible. But perhaps both starting points are partly correct. Downs defended his assumption with the argument that a party could not pursue any goal if it did not win the election first. The fact that winning an election is a necessary condition for the pursuit of any additional goals may help explain why some politicians at some points in time undertake opportunistic actions to win elections.

Having won an election, a party may feel free to implement some of its ideological goals, and its sense of freedom may vary with the size of its electoral victory, its lead in the current polls, and the time to the next election. Each behavioral assumption may accurately characterize the motivation of different parties at different points in time.

One of the pioneering contributions to the PBC literature made exactly this sort of assumption. Frey and Lau (1968) posited that left-wing governments would spend more and right-wing governments less when their popularity was high, but that both would try to lower unemployment and expand national income as the election approached and/or their popularity fell below a critical value (assumed in empirical work to be 52 percent approval). Lower average unemployment rates and higher average inflation rates for left-of-center governments emerge from the Frey Lau model as a consequence of their ideological predilection to greater spending. Opportunistic behavior by incumbents would also be observed on at least some occasions. Empirical support for variants on this model, modified to capture country-specific economic and institutional factors, was presented for the United States (Frey and Schneider, 1978a), the United Kingdom (Frey and Schneider, 1978b, 1981a), West Germany (Frey and Schneider, 1979), and Australia (Schneider and Pommerehne, 1980; Pommerehne and Schneider, 1983). Some of the empirical findings were challenged, however (e.g., Chrystal and Alt, 1981), and the model seemed to have been discarded along with the other, early PBC models.

The model has, however, been recently rediscovered by a number of authors who have both improved upon the original formulations of it, and provided further empirical support (Blais and Nadeau, 1992; Davidson, Fratianni, and von Hagen, 1992; Carlsen 1997; Price, 1997). Davidson et al., for example, present a *satisficing* model with partisan differences, but in which a presidential administration adopts polices to lower unemployment in the fourth year of an electoral cycle if unemployment rose during the third year. They find support for their model using data for presidential elections back to 1916.

Any model that mixes ideological goals and opportunistic behavior, substitutes satisfying for maximizing behavior, myopic for rational expectations, and the like, is vulnerable to that most devastating of all criticisms – that it is *ad hoc*. My dictionary defines "ad hoc" as being "concerned with a particular end or purpose." The particular end or purpose to which this literature is concerned is explaining the impact of politics on macroeconomic variables, and the feedback of the macroeconomy back onto political outcomes. If a model that assumes steadfast maximizing and forward-looking, rational behavior does not explain all of the data, then perhaps one or more of these assumptions must be relaxed. My reading of the empirical results obtained so far suggests that some hybrid model of the polar alternatives fits the data best.

19.5   Voter behavior

19.5.1   *Myopic, retrospective, rational*

The different PBC models make quite different assumptions about the kind of information voters use when deciding how to vote, ranging all the way from a highly myopic voter who only considers the state of the economy just before she votes to a highly rational voter who at most uses recent economic performance to judge a party or administration's competence and to predict its likely future performance. In between these polar extremes is the rationally retrospective voter who ensures that her agents in government will perform their duties well into the future by rewarding good performance in the past.

The evidence in favor of some form of retrospective voter hypothesis consists of both survey studies, which ask voters questions about how their choices are formed, and the many vote- and popularity-function studies. As Tables 19.1 and 19.2 suggest, there is a great deal of support for the retrospective voter hypothesis from the latter sorts of studies. The main remaining issue in these studies would appear to be how much weight events in the distant past get relative to the recent past. Some studies like Fair (1978), Nordhaus (1989, pp. 28–39), and Borooah and Borooah (1990) suggest that only the current or more recent values of unemployment, inflation, and so on are important in explaining the vote for or popularity of a president.

Others like Hibbs (1982c, 1987, 2000) and Peltzman (1990) have estimated positive and economically meaningful weights on past performance over essentially the full electoral cycle. In considering his results for presidential elections, for example, Peltzman (1990, p. 42) drew the following conclusion: "These results are inconsistent with the notion that voters myopically weight only the most recent experience . . . the peak total weight never occurs before a two-year lag and usually occurs at a four year lag." I have included in Table 19.1 the estimates for the four-year lag.

Hibbs (2000) also reaches the conclusion that the data from the entire 48 months running up to an election are evaluated by voters when they cast their ballots. His estimate of 0.95 for λ in equation (19.1) implies, of course, very little decay in the weights given to past economic events. If one models voter decisions using (19.1) and one assumes that the parameters are stable over time – a rather big if, in this case, since parameter stability has not been one of the hallmarks of this literature – then the coefficient on a lagged dependent variable in a vote or popularity function with current values of the other variables included becomes an estimate λ. A glance back over the figures in Tables 19.1 and 19.2 reveals that several of the λs estimated in this way are also quite large – although, of course, several are also fairly small. Whereas all studies do not support the extreme positions of Peltzman and Hibbs, there is certainly additional evidence on their side in some of these other studies.

A few studies using cross-sectional panel data have found that expectations about financial conditions perform better in explaining voter decisions than current or past levels (Kuklinski and West, 1981; Hibbing, 1987). These findings offer support for the rational voter assumption. Unfortunately, however, these studies appear to be the exception rather than the rule. The safest generalization from this literature would seem to be that some form of the retrospective voter hypothesis receives the most support from the data, with some residual uncertainty over how far into the past voters look when making their choices.

19.5.2 *Sociotropic or egotropic*

The vote- and popularity-function studies use aggregate measures of inflation and so forth to explain how individuals vote or their opinions. Do people downgrade an administration that produces high inflation because they personally have been harmed by the inflation or because they regard high inflation as bad for society? After a careful analysis of survey responses Kinder and Kiewiet (1979) concluded that individuals rate presidents poorly because of high inflation or unemployment, and because of a concern about what is good for the country. That is, a person may vote against a presidential candidate because she thinks the country has been harmed by his policies, even though she herself is personally better off.

This behavior has come to be known as *sociotropic* voting in contrast to *egotropic* voting where the voter is only concerned about his own economic circumstances. Kinder and Kiewiet's study produced a sharp critique from Kramer (1983), but their findings have generally been substantiated with larger data sets for both the United States and other countries (Kinder and Kiewiet, 1981; Hibbing, 1987; Lewis-Beck, 1988; Markus, 1988). Some studies have, however, found *both* a voter's personal economic position and her perceptions of the nation's problems to be significant in explaining her party preferences (Fiorina, 1978, 1981; Kiewiet, 1981, 1983; Kirchgässner, 1985).

19.6 Politics and inflation

19.6.1 *Hypotheses*

In Section 19.2.1 we described a scenario in which party competition for votes leads to a stable PBC as hypothesized by MacRae (1977). This model assumes the existence of an L-shaped Phillips curve as depicted in Figures 19.1 and 19.2, however. The existence of such *long-run* trade-offs is now generally rejected in favor of a Phillips curve that is a vertical straight line, as in Figure 19.7. Even in the absence of any long-run trade-off, it still might be possible to "fool" economic agents temporarily. Suppose, for example, that the government can adopt short-run economic policies such that if it starts from point M it can reduce unemployment by moving out along S_1S_1 to point 1. A vote-maximizing government faced by myopic voters

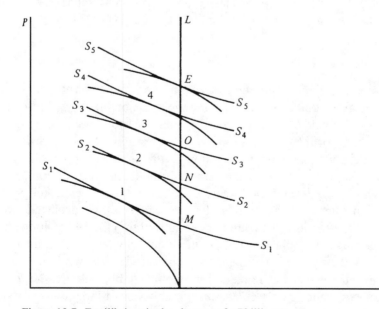

Figure 19.7. Equilibrium in the absence of a Phillips curve.

could then increase its chances of winning in the short run by going to point 1. Economic agents would then adjust their expectations of future inflation rates upward and one would return to LL at some higher point, N. If a new government could again surprise economic agents, the economy would move to point 2, and then, say, to O. As long as governments can find new ways to fool economic agents, the inflation rate would drift upward until some point like E was reached where inflation got so high that no short-run gains from reducing unemployment could be obtained, or until economic agents could no longer be fooled. This dynamic version of the PBC sees inflation steadily rising over time and eventually settling into a permanently high level (Nordhaus, 1975).

The preceding scenario relies upon a degree of voter myopia. Politics can introduce an inflationary bias into economic outcomes even without voter myopia, owing to the "time inconsistency problem" (Kydland and Prescott, 1977). To see what is involved, assume again the existence of a long-run vertical Phillips curve as in Figure 19.7. All citizens would prefer to be at point M along the curve than at higher points, and a vote-maximizing government that could commit itself to a set of macropolicies would promise this combination of unemployment and inflation. But because governments cannot truly commit to keep their promises, economic actors must always anticipate that a government will opportunistically attempt to stimulate the economy and produce temporarily lower levels of unemployment at the cost of higher future levels of inflation. Thus, when negotiating wage contracts workers will not demand wage increases based on the expectation that the inflation will be as represented at M, but will build into their demands the higher inflation rates that the opportunistic government would in the long run produce. Thus, the government does not go into an election at point M, but rather already at E, and its options to behave opportunistically are foreclosed. The economy experiences permanently higher inflation rates because of the government's inability to commit to more responsible macroeconomic policies.

19.6.2   *The facts*

Table 19.7 presents inflation and unemployment rates, and government deficits as a percentage of gross domestic product, for those major industrialized countries for which fairly complete data were available from 1951 to 1998. Two things stand out in the numbers for inflation: a great deal of variation across countries at any one point in time, and a dramatic acceleration in inflation rates across all countries beginning in the early 1970s. This acceleration was due in part, of course, to the OPEC oil price increases. But the direct impact of the increases in oil prices on country inflation rates was far smaller than the changes that occurred, and the higher levels of inflation in some countries lasted well into the 1980s, long after oil prices had collapsed. Why did Austria, Germany, and Switzerland's inflation rates return to roughly their pre-oil shock levels by the early 1980s, while in Denmark, Finland, Spain, and Sweden they remained at roughly double their pre-shock levels? Why did Israel experience such tremendously high levels of inflation over much of the post–World War II period?

Table 19.7. *Government deficits, inflation, and unemployment rates for 23 industrial countries, 1951–98*

Country	1951–5			1956–60			1961–5			1966–70			1971–5		
	D[a]	P	U	D	P	U	D	P	U	D	P	U	D	P	U
Australia	1.5	9.1	.	0.6	2.9	a	-1.7	1.8	.	-1.5	3.2	1.5	-0.4	10.3	2.5
Austria	-0.2	9.3	7.2	-1.8	2.0	4.8	-1.4	4.0	2.8	-2.0	3.2	2.7	-2.1	7.3	1.8
Belgium	.	2.2	10.5	-4.1[b]	1.8	7.6	-2.7	2.5	3.0	-2.4	3.4	3.5	-3.5	8.5	4.1
Canada	0.9	2.6	3.5	-0.9	1.9	5.6	-0.9	1.6	5.4	-0.5	3.9	4.6	-2.1[b]	7.4	6.1
Denmark	-0.7	4.5	9.8	0.9	2.4	6.5	1.0	5.0	3.4	1.3	5.0	3.4	1.4	9.3	2.6
Finland	0.2	3.2	.	0.0	6.8	2.3[b]	-1.4	8.4	1.4	-0.1	4.6	2.6	0.6	11.8	2.2
France	-4.7	5.8	.	-3.1	4.6	.	-1.1	3.7	.	-0.5	4.5	.	-1.2	8.9	.
Germany	0.6	2.0	7.4	-0.6	1.8	2.9	-0.4[b]	2.8	0.7	-0.5	2.7	1.2	-2.1	6.1	2.1
Greece															
Iceland	0.8[b]	7.4	.	0.1	6.0	.	0.8	10.9	.	.	12.3	3.8[b]	-4.2[b]	26.2	0.5
Ireland	-6.3	4.9	8.2	-4.0	2.7	8.0	-6.0	4.2	5.8	-5.7	5.3	6.6	-8.5	13.4	8.5
Israel	.	21.0	.	-5.2	4.0	.	-6.9	7.1	3.4	-17.1	4.1	6.4	-18.9	24.8	3.0
Italy	-4.1	4.2	9.6	-2.1	1.9	8.9	-2.6	4.9	4.7	-3.4	3.0	5.6	-11.3[b]	11.5	5.9
Japan	.	6.4	1.3	1.4	1.9	1.3	-0.8	6.2	1.3	-1.2	5.5	1.2	-2.5	11.7	1.4
Netherlands	1.8	3.6	2.3	0.3	2.7	1.5	-1.0	3.4	0.9	-2.4	5.0	1.5	1.1[b]	8.7	3.0
New Zealand	-2.4	7.1	.	-3.3	2.9	.	-3.6	2.7	.	-2.5	3.4	.	-4.4	10.3	.
Norway	-2.9[b]	6.3	1.3	-1.4	2.8	1.8	-1.0	4.1	1.4	-2.0	5.0	0.9	-2.9	8.4	1.0
Portugal															
Spain	.	2.9	.	.	8.3	.	-1.0	5.4	1.7[b]	-1.8	5.1	1.0	-1.2	12.1	2.5
Sweden	-1.3	2.6	2.4	-2.0	3.7	1.9	0.2	3.7	1.5[b]	-2.0	4.4	1.9	-3.8	8.0	2.3
Switzerland	0.1	1.7	0.8	0.8	1.2	.	0.3	3.2	.	0.0	3.5	.	-0.6	7.7	.
United Kingdom	-2.3	5.4	1.6	-0.3	2.7	1.8	-0.3	3.1	1.8	-0.3	4.6	2.2	-4.9	13.2	3.2
United States	0.0	2.2	3.7	-0.4	2.2	5.2	-0.8	1.3	5.5	-0.9	4.2	3.9	-1.8	6.6	6.1
Average (omitting Israel through 1990)	-1.1	4.7	5.0	-1.0	3.4	4.3	-1.2	4.5	3.0	-1.5	4.6	2.8	-2.8	10.8	3.3

(*continued*)

463

Table 19.7 (continued)

Country	1976–80 D[a]	1976–80 P	1976–80 U	1981–5 D	1981–5 P	1981–5 U	1986–90 D	1986–90 P	1986–90 U	1991–5 D	1991–5 P	1991–5 U	1996–8 D	1996–8 P	1996–8 U
Australia	−3.1	10.6	5.8	−2.3	8.3	7.9	0.6	9.3	7.3	−2.2	2.3	9.9	−0.3[b]	1.2	8.4
Austria	−5.0	5.3	2.0	−4.4	4.9	3.7	−4.5	2.3	5.3	−4.9	2.9	6.3	−4.1[b]	1.4	7.1
Belgium	−6.7	6.4	8.2	−11.9	7.0	11.0	−7.0	2.2	9.7	−5.2	2.9	12.5	.	1.6	13.2
Canada	−4.0	8.8	7.7	−5.4	7.2	8.5	−3.2	4.9	8.4	−4.0[b]	3.3	10.6	.	1.4	9.1
Denmark	−1.0	10.4	6.4	−6.6	7.9	9.8	2.0	4.2	8.8	−1.8	2.3	11.4	.	1.3	7.7
Finland	−1.6	10.8	5.7	−1.5	9.6	5.9	0.2	5.5	4.4	−11.0	2.0	14.8	−6.2[b]	1.1	14.1
France	−1.8	10.5	.	−3.1	8.4	8.7	−2.2	3.3	9.9	−4.7	2.7	8.9	−3.6[b]	3.3	12.2[b]
Germany	−3.5	4.0	4.2	−3.3	3.9	7.1	−1.1	1.4	8.5	−2.0	3.3	10.3[b]	−1.7[b]	1.4	12.2
Greece	.	.	.	−8.5	.	.	−11.3	24.5	7.4	−13.0	11.3	9.1	−9.8[b]	6.5	10.3[b]
Iceland	−2.7	42.2	0.4	−2.7	49.7	.	−2.8	30.0	1.0	−3.8	3.2	3.7	−0.6[b]	2.0	3.7
Ireland	−11.2	14.1	10.9	−13.2	12.4	14.8	−4.7	3.5	16.2	−1.1	2.3	16.2	0.4[b]	1.9	.
Israel	−13.8	65.2	3.8	−14.9	212.2	.	−4.4	58.2	7.6	−4.2	9.1	9.3	−4.0[b]	9.3	8.0
Italy	−11.5	16.4	7.3	−13.5	13.8	9.1	−11.1	6.4	11.7	−9.4	4.3	11.2	−3.7	2.7	12.2[b]
Japan	−6.8	6.6	2.1	−6.1	2.7	2.5	−3.0	1.4	2.5	0.1[b]	1.3	2.6	.	0.8	3.6
Netherlands	−3.6	6.1	5.3	−7.4	4.2	11.5	−4.4	0.7	9.1	−2.3	2.5	6.2	−1.2	2.1	6.0[b]
New Zealand	−5.9	14.8	.	−7.2	12.1	.	1.2[b]	12.8	5.7	1.4	1.9	8.9	4.7[b]	1.4	6.4[b]
Norway	−7.3	8.4	1.3	0.3	9.1	2.7	0.5	7.1	3.3	−2.9	2.2	5.5	5.1[b]	2.1	4.5[b]
Portugal	.	.	.	.	.	.	−6.7	14.2	5.5	−5.1	5.9	5.6	−2.3[b]	2.8	7.1[b]
Spain	−2.9	18.1	7.9	−6.3	12.4	17.8	−2.5	7.4	19.0	−4.7	4.5	20.9	−3.0	2.5	21.5[b]
Sweden	−4.9	10.5	1.9	−8.9	9.0	3.0	−0.3	6.0	1.8	−8.4	3.6	6.6	−1.5	0.3	7.5
Switzerland	−0.4	2.3	.	−0.3	4.3	.	4.3	2.6	0.7	−1.3	2.9	3.4	−0.8	0.4	4.6
United Kingdom	−5.6	14.4	6.2	−3.5	7.2	10.3	0.7	6.7	8.4	−4.6	3.1	9.2	.	3.1	6.0
United States	−2.9	8.9	6.7	−4.7	5.5	9.6	−3.6	4.1	5.9	−3.5	2.0	6.6	−0.2	2.3	5.0
Average (omitting Israel through 1990)	−4.6	11.5	5.3	−6.8	10.0	8.5	−2.7	7.3	7.6	−4.2	3.6	9.1	−1.8	2.3	8.7

Note: D = government deficit as percentage of Gross Domestic Product; P = percentage change of Consumer Price Index; U = unemployment rate. ". " signifies data missing.

[a] Deficit figures are for general government expenditures where available for most years, when not available for central government.

[b] Data for all five years were not available. Average is for the years that were.

Sources: Deficit, inflation, and recent unemployment data are from International Monetary Fund, *Financial Statistics*, October 1986, and Supplements on Economic Indicators, 1985, 1972, and *International Financial Yearbook*, 1999 (Washington, D.C.). Early unemployment data are from OECD, *Main Economic Indicators*, July 1983, 1986, January 1990, 1992 (Paris), and *Main Economic Indicators*, Historical Statistics, 1960–79, 1955–71 (Paris). United Nations, *Statistical Yearbook*, 1956, 1961, 1966, 1971, 1976, 1981 (New York).

Partial answers to these questions have already been given in our discussions of the PBC and partisan politics. Some governments do expand the money supply just prior to elections; left-wing governments generally pursue looser monetary policies and produce higher levels of inflation. We now consider some additional explanations that focus in particular on the question of why economically similar countries often reveal such significantly different rates of inflation.

19.6.3 *Central bank independence*

The explanation for inflation based on the time-inconsistency problem assumes that the government cannot credibly commit *not* to try to produce short spells of low unemployment by meddling with the macroeconomy. The result is lower popularity for the government and lower welfare for society. A Pareto improvement is possible *if* the government can tie its hands to prevent it from meddling with the economy. The creation of an independent central bank (CB) may be one way to accomplish this outcome (Rogoff, 1985). The government, which is the agent of the citizens, effectively creates yet another agent to carry out a task that it is unable to carry out properly – namely, a low-inflation monetary policy.

But if the government cannot commit itself not to meddle with macropolicy in general, how can it credibly commit itself not to meddle with the CB? How can an institution created by and dependent on the government remain independent?

The problem is not unlike the problem of creating an independent judiciary, and one approach to creating central bank independence (CBI) has been to make its directorship something like a judgeship with long terms of appointment and salaries set by formula.[21]

A second form of protection of CBI arises in democratic systems with effective checks and balances. When authority over the CB is shared, and the seats of authority differ in their monetary policy objectives, each may block the other leaving the CB free to pursue its preferred monetary policy (Moser, 2000, chs. 10 and 11).

The ultimate protection of CBI is to write it into the constitution, so that it is effectively guaranteed by the (hopefully also) independent judiciary. This is de facto the route that the European Monetary Union took when it created the European Central Bank, although the member countries may still be able to exert some influence through the appointment process for directors.

Empirically CBI appears to be positively correlated across countries with indexes of political freedom and political stability (Cukierman, 1992; Cukierman and Webb, 1995; de Haan and van 't Hag, 1995; de Haan and Siermann, 1996; Bagheri and Habibi, 1998). The less secure a nation's political freedoms are and the more unstable its politics, the more likely it is that some party or party leader finds it advantageous to sweep aside the institutions protecting the CB's independence and print money to win public support.

---

[21] For a discussion of the costs and benefits of this solution, see Waller and Walsh (1996). For a general discussion of creating independent and responsible governmental agents, see Mueller (1996a, ch. 19).

Numerous indexes of CBI have been constructed to determine whether CBI is related to price stability. The bulk of the studies find that it is, although whether a relationship is found and how strong it is depends on which measure of CBI one uses.[22] Moser (2000, pp. 146–50) finds that the lowest inflation rates are observed in countries like Germany and the United States, with both strong CBI and strong checks and balances on legislative action to reinforce CBI. These studies illustrate rather clearly the important role political institutions can play in insuring that political competition works to benefit citizens rather than to harm them.

19.7 Deficits

19.7.1 *The facts*

Table 19.7 presents budget deficit figures for most major industrial countries since World War II. As with the figures on inflation, considerable variation exists across countries. Nevertheless a general pattern is apparent. The first five-year period (1951–5) has more countries with government budgets in surplus than any other five-year period. The large deficits for France, Ireland, and Italy pull the average deficit up to slightly more than that for 1956–60. Starting with this five-year period, the average deficit rises steadily until by the early 1980s it is running at almost 7 percent of Gross Domestic Product (GDP). What is true of the average is also true of the individual countries. Over the first fifteen years of this period more than half of the countries either ran surpluses on average or had deficits of less than 1 percent of GDP. In the early 1980s only one country – Norway, with its huge oil revenues – ran a budget surplus. The average deficit has fallen since 1985, but it remains true that a substantial majority of the industrial countries continued to run deficits into the 1990s. Why did the pattern of government finances over the last fifty years shift to one in which governmental deficits have become the norm?[23] In the next subsection we present some hypotheses.

19.7.2 *Hypotheses*

19.7.2.1 *Fiscal illusion and Keynesian delusions.* Throughout the nineteenth and first half of the twentieth century voters held politicians responsible for keeping state finances in balance. Even FDR promised to balance the budget in his first campaign for the presidency. Then during the 1960s, Buchanan and Wagner (1977) argue the "Keynesian revolution" changed both economists' and the public's attitudes toward

---

[22] See Grilli, Dourato, and Tabellini (1991); Cukierman (1992); Alesina and Summers (1993); Havrilesky and Granato (1993); Al-Marhubi and Willett (1995); Cukierman and Webb (1995); and Iversen (1999). Banaian, Burdekin, and Willett (1998) have difficulty relating inflation rates to many of the measures of CBI proposed by Cukierman (1992). Of the eight different measures examined by Oatley (1999) a simple dichotomy between moderately strong and strong CBI, on the one hand, and weak CBI gave as good a fit as any other alternative.

[23] Webber and Wildavsky (1986, ch. 5 and p. 562 ff.) claim that states have confronted the problem of their revenues falling short of their expenditures throughout their entire history.

debt. Since Americans held most of the federal government's debt, they were both creditors and debtors and, so it was argued, this implied that the public debt did not really impose any fiscal burdens on the population. The logic of Keynesian economics implied further that running deficits could be good for the economy because they stimulated economic activity and reduced unemployment.

The rational individual lacks the incentive to make superrational calculations of the consequences of government policies. A check in the mail, an announced cut in taxes, or a fall in the unemployment rate are easily noticed and much publicized manifestations of government policies. The future inflation or future tax liabilities that these policies foreshadow are dimly perceived shadows for most voters. Thus when they were told that deficits were in fact good for the economy citizens stopped punishing politicians for running them, and the competition for votes led to an imbalance between taxes and expenditures, resulting in the government deficits and inflation depicted in Table 19.7.

19.7.2.2 *Political business cycles.* Although Buchanan and Wagner's explanation for the growth in budget deficits in the United States is an attempt to explain a one-time secular shift in governmental policies, its reliance on the concept of fiscal illusion introduces a form of voter myopia and thus makes their explanation somewhat related to the traditional PBC model. This model in both its myopic voter and rational voter forms predicts deficit spending prior to elections and thus could account for secular swings in deficits, if governments fail to reverse these policies fully after the elections.

19.7.2.3 *Partisan effects.* Left-of-center governments run deficits; right-of-center governments run surpluses (smaller deficits).

19.7.2.4 *Government paralysis.* Much of the PBC literature implicitly and even often explicitly assumes a two-party electoral system. If the voter is unhappy with the levels of unemployment and inflation, she can vote for the opposition party. If she has a high income, she is likely to favor the party of the Right and not the Left. In such two-party systems the incumbent party can always be held responsible for the current macroeconomic situation.

Most European countries, however, have multiparty systems that often lead to *the government* being formed by a coalition of two or more parties. In such coalition governments disagreements over policy choices, as say the proper response to an economic shock like the OPEC price increases, may arise. Each party has its own constituents and no party wants to appear to give in to a compromise that makes its constituents worse off than those of other members of the coalition. A form of "war of attrition" ensues, with each party holding out in the hopes that the other members of the coalition give in first (Alesina and Drazen, 1991). The result is that the needed policies to deal with the economic shock are delayed and the economy suffers the consequence.

This type of argument can explain why some countries were able to adjust rather quickly to the OPEC price increases and reduce inflation levels back to normal, while others adjusted more slowly. In the same way it could account for the growth in government deficits that began about the same time. Note that this hypothesis, unlike the previous two, also gives clear predictions about the causes for *different* sized deficits across countries.

19.7.2.5 *Budgetary rules.* The government paralysis described in the previous hypothesis arises because no party wants to take responsibility for the hard economic choices that sometimes must be made. In all parliamentary systems, however, there is a prime minister and a finance minister who at least nominally are responsible for the government's economic performance. They presumably have an incentive to see the government adopt responsible economic policies. Their ability to implement these polices will depend, however, on their authority over the individual ministers, the rules governing the amendment of budgets by the parliament, and so on (von Hagen, 1992).

19.7.3 *The evidence*

Buchanan and Wagner (1977) gave an explanation for the dramatic rise in the federal deficit that began in the United States during the 1960s. Although U.S. voters may have been fooled into voting for politicians who produced high deficits up through the 1980s, by the early 1990s the American voter seemed to have returned to the same sort of fiscal conservatism that Buchanan and Wagner saw disappearing during the 1960s.[24] An important clause in Newt Gingrich's "contract with America" that led to the Republicans' landslide victory in 1994 was the promise to eliminate the federal deficit. Bill Clinton also perceived there to be political gains from fiscal conservatism, and by the end of the 1990s the federal deficit was gone. American voters appear to have gotten over their illusions about the deficit.

Several of the studies cited in support of the PBC model have found government debt expanding prior to elections (Blais and Nadeau, 1992; Alesina and Roubini with Cohen, 1997, ch. 9; Franzese, 2000; Schuknecht, 2000). Partisan biases have been found in some studies (Blais and Nadeau, 1992), but not in others (de Haan and Sturm, 1994; Alesina and Roubini with Cohen, 1997, ch. 9), and at least one study has found some evidence of a reverse bias (Franzese, 2000).

Roubini and Sachs (1989) found that government deficits were larger in countries where government coalitions tended to be short and composed of many parties. Their findings have been supported in some additional studies (Grilli et al., 1991; Alesina and Perotti, 1995; Franzese, 2000),[25] but not in others (de Haan and Sturm, 1994; de Haan, Sturm, and Beekhuis, 1999).

Von Hagen's (1992) evidence on the importance of budgetary institutions in explaining deficits has been corroborated by several additional studies (e.g., de Haan and Sturm, 1994; Helland, 2000; Strauch, 2000).

---

[24] See also Peltzman (1992).

[25] Edin and Ohlsson (1991) claim that it is minority governments rather than coalition governments per se that produce large deficits.

Thus, as too often happens when competing hypotheses are tested, the evidence is somewhat equivocal as to what *the* determinants of governmental deficits are. Clearly no single hypothesis can account for all the differences.

19.8   Reflections

The basic models discussed in this chapter often make different assumptions about how voters behave, how parties behave, and how the economy behaves. Not surprisingly, these models often generate quite different predictions. Understandably, there are substantial differences of opinion among the proponents of the different models as to how well the data support their predictions.

As mentioned earlier, one possible explanation for the difficulties researchers have had in finding *one* model that is consistent with all the data may be that more than one model is needed. Some of the authors of the original opportunistic PBC models seem to have had the Nixon administration's macroeconomic policies in mind when they wrote down their models, and certainly Richard Nixon was every bit the opportunist. But perhaps other presidents behave differently than Nixon. Perhaps Nixon today would behave differently.

Juan Peron once offered the following advice to the president of Chile:

> My dear friend: Give to the people, especially the workers, all that is possible. When it seems to you that already you are giving too much, give them more. You will see the results. Everyone will try to scare you with the specter of an economic collapse. But all of this is a lie. There is nothing more elastic than the economy which everyone fears so much because no one understands it.
>
> (as quoted in Hirschman, 1979, p. 65)

Peron tested the elasticity of the Argentine economy on several occasions, and many other Latin American leaders have followed his advice. Although giveaway programs financed by increasing public debt or printing money might have been successful ways to maintain popularity and win elections at one time in Latin America, today they do not appear to be so. Latin American voters seem to have become more sophisticated in their understanding of the macroeconomy; Latin American politicians have consequently become more responsible in their choices of policy.

It would also appear from evidence presented by Suzuki (1994) that Japanese voters have become less myopic over the post-war period. Suzuki finds support for the opportunistic PBC in data from the early years of the Liberal Democratic Party's rule, but that by the 1980s this support had disappeared. It is also interesting in this regard to note how virtually every European government was able to meet the strict requirements regarding inflation rates and government deficits that were set down for entry into the European Monetary Union. Despite starting from such widely different levels of inflation and budget deficit as presented in Table 19.7, all 12 countries desiring entry save Greece were able to meet the criteria by 1998, and even Greece met them by 2001. If the stakes are high enough, politicians can control inflation and the budget deficit.

All of the models reviewed in this chapter have one thing in common – they assume that the only government policies that voters are concerned about are related to the macroeconomy, and that elections are fought on the basis of policies that affect the macroeconomy.[26] This feature makes these models quite different from much of the rest of the public choice literature and in some ways in conflict with it.

For example, Alesina and Rosenthal (1995) assume that a moderate Democrat, when deciding whether to vote for his incumbent Democratic congresswoman in a midterm election, might vote against her, even though she has an excellent record in bringing pork-barrel projects to her district, because the voter wants to balance the liberal macroeconomic policies of the incumbent Democratic president with a Republican Congress. This assumption is at odds with a large segment of the public choice/political science literature that sees voters interested in only the pork-barrel/ombudsman activities of their representatives in Congress, and the representatives catering to these interests (Ferejohn, 1974; Fiorina, 1977b).

The assumed voter calculus also seems to put into question the voter rationality assumption. Even if the voter would like to see the Democratic president balanced by a Republican Congress, he is likely to calculate that the party affiliation of his congresswoman – since she is only one of 435 – will have a much smaller impact on future macroeconomic policies than it does on the flow of pork-barrel projects to the district. Thus even if the voter considers macroeconomic issues to be far more important than local ones, if he is truly rational he will probably vote to return the incumbent congresswoman to office and enjoy the pork that she will provide, rather than trying to alter national macroeconomic policies by defeating her.

Also conspicuous by their absence from PBC models are interest groups. Their inclusion might help explain some of the puzzling findings in the literature. For example, several of the studies cited above have observed increases in certain outlays and cuts in taxes just prior to elections. These policies are consistent with the predictions of some of the PBC models. However, the changes in taxes and expenditures tend to be small, and thus it is much more difficult to observe the predicted PBC in the unemployment and inflation data than in the expenditures and tax data. Perhaps the purpose of the expenditure/tax changes is *not* to affect macroeconomic variables, but to benefit certain interest groups that have promised to support the government with votes and/or money. Integrating interest groups into the models might greatly improve their explanatory power,[27] but, of course, at the cost of increasing their complexity.

One of the most attractive features of most of the models reviewed in this chapter is how much they are able to explain with such relatively simple structures and a relatively small number of variables. An important point to be made is to remind the reader that the models are often extreme simplifications of reality, and that they

---

[26] Econometric studies that try to forecast election outcomes, like Fair (1982) and Hibbs (2000), do add in other variables to improve the accuracy of their predictions, but even here the work is notable for the sparsity of the additional variables included. Hibbs, for example, adds only one – troops killed in combat – beyond growth in income to predict the last half century's presidential elections.

[27] Frans van Winden (1983) has developed and simulated a model of private–public sector interaction allowing separate roles for labor, firms, the public bureaucracy, interest groups, and political parties.

often leave out much that is relevant. One important omission is certainly interest groups. In the next chapter we take up the activities of these groups. Here again we will find models that abstract from much that is relevant. Indeed, we will find models that assume that all government activity consists of selling legislation to interest groups and that all elections are determined by the wishes and actions of these organized interests. Macroeconomic policies that affect all citizens will vanish from view.

Bibliographical notes

This literature is huge and has led to the publication of at least one 800-page textbook. Drazen's *Political Economy in Macroeconomics* (2000) is an excellent introduction to and overview of the literature, although the book is somewhat mistitled, since it discusses virtually all topics from the public choice literature.

Several authors of the main PBC models have written their own partisan surveys of the literature (Schneider 1978, 1982; Schneider and Frey, 1988; Nordhaus, 1989; Hibbs, 1992; Alesina, 1988a; Alesina and Roubini with Cohen, 1997).

Additional surveys include Paldam (1981a, 1997), Alt and Chrystal (1983), Borooah and van der Ploeg (1984), Gärtner (1994, 2000), Keech (1993), and Nannestad and Paldam (1994).

CHAPTER 20

Interest groups, campaign contributions, and lobbying

The diversity in the faculties of men, from which the rights of property originate, is not less an insuperable obstacle to a uniformity of interests. The protection of these faculties is the first object of government. From the protection of different and unequal faculties of acquiring property, the possession of different degrees and kinds of property immediately results; and from the influence of these on the sentiments and views of the respective proprietors, ensues a division of the society into different interests and parties.

The latent causes of faction are thus sown in the nature of man; and we see them everywhere brought into different degrees of activity, according to the different circumstances of civil society. A zeal for different opinions concerning religion, concerning government, and many other points, as well of speculation as of practice; an attachment to different leaders ambitiously contending for pre-eminence and power; or to persons of other descriptions whose fortunes have been interesting to the human passions, have, in turn, divided mankind into parties, inflamed them with mutual animosity, and rendered them much more disposed to vex and oppress each other than to cooperate for their common good. So strong is this propensity of mankind to fall into mutual animosities, that where no substantial occasion presents itself, the most frivolous and fanciful distinctions have been sufficient to kindle their unfriendly passions and excite their most violent conflicts. But the most common and durable source of factions has been the various and unequal distribution of property. Those who hold and those who are without property have ever formed distinct interests in society. Those who are creditors, and those who are debtors, fall under a like discrimination. A landed interest, a manufacturing interest, a mercantile interest, a moneyed interest, with many lesser interests, grow up of necessity in civilized nations, and divide them into different classes, actuated by different sentiments and views. The regulation of these various and interfering interests forms the principal task of modern legislation, and involves the spirit of party and faction in the necessary and ordinary operations of the government.

James Madison

Karl Marx saw society as divided into two warring classes, and many observers of politics following Marx have seen class orientation in parties, class bias in voting, and so on. Several models of political business cycles assume that one party caters to the labor class and tries to keep unemployment low, while the other favors the capitalists and tries to keep interest rates low.

Over 200 years ago, James Madison also observed that "those who hold and those who are without property have . . . distinct interests in society." But he immediately went on to identify separate interests of creditors and debtors, "a landed interest, a manufacturing interest, a mercantile interest, a moneyed interest, [and] many lesser interests." Politics in the modern democratic state is not a confrontation between two polarized economic classes, but rather a struggle among a plethora of groups with divergent interests. In this chapter we focus on these groups. We begin by reviewing the hypotheses about interest groups put forward by Olson (1965) in one of the classics of the public choice literature.

20.1   The logic of collective action

Interest groups come in a wide variety of institutional forms and sizes. Some seek to further the objectives of their members as factors of production or producers. Labor unions, farmer associations, professional associations (doctors, dentists, accountants), retail trade associations (groceries, hardware, liquor), and industrial trade associations (petroleum, cement, coal) are examples of these. Others seek to influence public policy or public opinion with respect to particular public good–externality issues. Peace groups, environmental groups, and the National Rifle Association are examples of these. Often a group is organized to pursue one objective, and then once organized turns to other forms of activity of benefit to its members. Labor unions came into being to improve the bargaining power of workers vis-à-vis management. But once the large initial costs of organization had been overcome, unions engaged in additional activities of interest to their members, such as lobbying for legislation, which improves the position of workers. Still other groups seek to advance *all* the interests of particular groups of people who have a certain *social affinity* for one another due perhaps to their ethnic, religious, or geographic origins (Kristov, Lindert, and McClelland, 1992). Most recently, groups have appeared to promote the interests of members of a given sex, or those with particular sexual affinities. In every case the driving force behind the formation of an interest group is the belief that its members have *common* interests and goals, be they higher wages for truck drivers or for women, or cleaner rivers for those whose consumption activities are enhanced by this public policy (pp. 5–8).[1]

The commonality of the goals of an interest group's members makes the achievement of these goals a public good for the group, and thus gives rise to the same incentives to free-ride as exist in all public good–prisoners' dilemma situations. The individual steelworker and steel manufacturer benefit from a tariff on steel, whether they have contributed to the efforts to bring about the tariff or not (pp. 9–16).

Two important conclusions can be drawn from this observation: (1) it is easier to form an interest group when the number of potential members is small than when the number is large (pp. 9–16, 22–65). An effective interest group can be organized more readily for two dozen steel producers than for two hundred thousand steel workers; and (2) the appearance of organizations that effectively represent large numbers of individuals requires that "*separate and 'selective' incentive(s)*" be used to curb free-riding behavior (p. 51, italics in original). The archetypal example

---

[1] Page references in this section are to Olson (1965) unless otherwise noted.

of the use of selective incentives is the labor union. Unions have fought to have employers deduct dues from union members' wages, and for "closed shop" contracts forbidding employers from hiring nonunion labor (pp. 66–97). Where they have succeeded in forcing employers to abide by these rules, as in many states in the United States and countries in Europe, union membership has been relatively high and union workers have earned higher wages. In France, where these selective incentives encouraging union participation are absent, union membership has been much lower.[2] Perhaps the best evidence that such selective incentives are needed to avoid free-riding behavior is the importance union leaders place on getting legislation and/or contractual stipulations requiring closed-shop contracts, the collection of union dues, and the like. Worker solidarity does not suffice.

Where the benefits from collective action are not the same across all group members, *"there is a systematic tendency for 'exploitation' of the great by the small"* (p. 29). To see this, consider the following example. The automobile industry has four firms producing the following numbers of cars each year:

$$X_G = 4,000,000 \text{ cars}$$
$$X_F = 2,000,000 \text{ cars}$$
$$X_C = 1,000,000 \text{ cars}$$
$$X_A = 500,000 \text{ cars}.$$

Compliance with fuel economy standards issued by the Environmental Protection Agency (EPA) would raise the costs of producing cars by an average of $10 per car. Each firm independently considers opening up an office in Washington to lobby the EPA to delay enforcement of the fuel economy standard by one year. The cost of running a lobbying office is $1.5 million for the year. The probability that the industry will be successful in its lobbying effort increases with the number of lobbying offices opened, being 0.25 for one office, 0.4 for two, 0.5 for three, and 0.55 for four. Firm G realizes that if it does not profit from opening a lobbying office, no firm will. Its expected profit increase from opening a lobbying office is 0.25 times $40 million, which exceeds the $1.5 million cost of the office. Firm F realizes that it will not profit from opening an office unless G does and thus calculates its profits from opening the second lobbying office for the industry. The incremental probability that the lobbying will succeed is 0.15, which when multiplied by F's $20 million cost saving gives an expected profit increase of $3 million for F. This saving exceeds the $1.5 million cost of the lobbying office, so F also opens an office. Given that G and F have opened offices, neither C nor A find it profitable to do so, however. Both choose to free-ride on G and F's lobbying efforts, receiving, respectively, $4 million and $2 million increases in expected profits from G and F's lobbying. In this way the weak "exploit" the strong.

Note also that the amount of lobbying effort that arises from independent decisions is suboptimal from the point of view of the industry. A third and fourth lobbying office would bring the industry $7.5 and $3.75 million in expected profits,

---

[2] For a discussion of France in the context of Olson's work, see Asselain and Morrison (1983).

respectively. But these additional offices will be opened only if G and F can bribe C and A to do so. Moreover, since C and A know that G and F will open lobbying offices regardless of whether C and A do so, C and A can hold out for subsidies from G and F, which maintain their favorable ratio of benefits to costs.[3]

One of the counterintuitive predictions of Olson's theory is that small interest groups are much more effective at obtaining favors from government than large groups are. Dramatic support for this hypothesis is provided by the agricultural policies of nations around the world. In poor countries, where the agricultural sector is large and the group of middle-class urban dwellers is small, farmers receive small or even *negative* subsidies for their products – that is, the government often sees that the farmers receive less than world market prices. In the rich, developed countries where farmers make up a tiny fraction of the total workforce, they often receive giant subsidies. Van Bastelaer (1998) reports a range of effective subsidies for farmers over the period 1955–80 from −26.9 in Ghana to 85.9 percent in Switzerland. Van Bastelaer provides econometric support for the Olson hypothesis with data from 31 countries.[4] Additional evidence related to the Olson hypothesis is contained in the experimental literature on the free-rider problem reviewed in Chapter 2.

Although interest groups take center stage in much of Olson's work, he did not formally model how they operate in the political process and their effects on its outcomes. This void has been filled, however, by an army of scholars who have developed and tested models of interest group political behavior. We turn now to these models.

20.2 Models of interest group behavior in politics

An interest group enters the political process to advance the common interest of its members. It can accomplish this by providing candidates information as to what this common interest is, by delivering votes to a candidate who promises to support the group's interests after the election, and most importantly and conspicuously in recent years by supplying a candidate with money, which she can use to win an election.[5] By far the most controversial of these three activities of interest groups, from both a positive and a normative perspective, is their use of money to influence the outcomes of the political process. We take up the positive side of this question now, and return to the normative issues raised in a later section.[6]

What is uncontroversial is that candidates use the money that they receive to get (re)elected. Indeed, in the United States that is the only use to which these funds can be put. Thus, campaign contributions become campaign expenditures, and any

---

[3] For example, if C agrees to pay only 1/7 of the cost of its lobbying office with G and F paying 6/7, since that is the ratio of their benefits, and A agrees to pay only 1/15 of the cost of its lobbying office, with the other three sharing in proportion to their benefits, then C and A wind up enjoying 13.3 and 6.7 percent of the benefits from lobbying while paying but 6.9 and 1.7 percent of the costs, respectively.

[4] See also Krueger, Schiff, and Valdés (1991) from which some of van Bastelaer's data are drawn.

[5] Supplying a candidate with money that she can use for other purposes is, of course, not unknown in politics, although it is illegal in most democratic countries. We discuss bribes and corruption later in the chapter.

[6] Austen-Smith (1997, pp. 312–20) reviews the literature on interest group activity in supplying only information.

model which explains the one must explain the other. Under one interpretation of campaign contributions/expenditures, their only purpose is to determine the *outcome* of the election. Candidates preselect their positions, and interest groups contribute to the candidate whose position on the issues comes closest to their favored position. The election determines the winning candidate/position from the preselected set of options. This interpretation of campaign contributions has been called the "political man" theory (Welch, 1976), with contributors characterized as passive "consumers" of the positions selected by the candidates (Snyder, 1990). Alternatively, contributors have been characterized as "investors" who buy the positions of the candidates. In this "economic man" model of politics, a quid pro quo exists between the interest group, which contributes to a candidate's campaign for election, and the candidate who "supplies" the group with her position on the issues (Welch, 1976). The first question we wish to answer is which of these two models of the political process comes closest to its reality?

20.2.1 *Informative campaigning in a Downsian model*

Much of campaign spending today goes to buy time on television. The natural way for a political economist to think of this sort of "political advertising" is as an analogue to consumer advertising, and several writers have treated campaign expenditures as a form of advertising.[7] Within the advertising literature, the distinction is often made between *informative* and *persuasive* advertising. In a simple Downsian model, with a single-dimensional issue x, informative political advertising has a natural interpretation – a candidate informs voters of her position on x. If informed voters vote for the candidate who comes closest to their ideal point, and uninformed voters abstain, each candidate has an incentive to inform those voters with ideal points closest to her position of the location of this position. As more voters become informed, the candidate whose position is closest to the median voter's ideal point wins a larger fraction of the additional votes cast. The informative campaigning by both candidates increases the likelihood that the candidate nearest the ideal point of the median voter wins, and thus tends to drive both candidates to this median position.[8]

With both candidates selecting the ideal point of the median voter, all voters are indifferent as to which one wins. No person or group would contribute to a candidate to increase her chances of winning in this situation. Groups to the left of the median would have an incentive to contribute to candidate L *if* she would move to the left. But if L abandons the median position, and informs all voters she has done so, she *reduces* her chances of winning. Selective informing of just those on the left would be an attractive strategy, but unfortunately groups on the right then have an incentive to contribute to R so that he can inform his potential supporters. Thus, it is difficult in a simple Downsian world with only informative campaigning to derive the economic-man model of politics. No group has an incentive to contribute to

---

[7] See in particular Palda (1973, 1975) and Thomas (1989, 1990). The exposition given follows Mueller and Stratmann (1994).

[8] For formal models that produce this result, see Austen-Smith (1987) and Baron (1994).

either candidate if they both adopt the same position. No candidate has an incentive to leave the median position to raise campaign funds if the only thing she can do with these funds is to inform voters that she is not at the median position.

20.2.2 *Persuasive campaigning in a Downsian model*

With purely informative political advertising, a candidate increases the likelihood of some voters voting for her when she informs them of her position, but decreases the likelihood that some other voters vote for her. Obviously, she would prefer it if an advertising message would increase the likelihood that *every* voter would vote for her. Again using the analogy of consumer advertising, we can define this sort of campaign expenditure as *persuasive* campaigning. When a soft drink company informs potential customers that it sells a lemon/lime soda, it increases the probability that those who like lemon/lime flavors purchase its soda, but reduces the probability of those who prefer orange, cherry, or cola buying it. But when the same company advertises that its soft drink "tastes the best" or "better than the rest," it may increase the probability that all potential customers buy it.

The same may be true for certain kinds of political advertising. All citizens prefer honest politicians to crooks, competent politicians to buffoons, and so on. A politician who convincingly advertises that she is more honest than her rival may increase the probability of every voter's support *regardless* of her position along the x vector. In this section, we explore the implications of assuming that this sort of political advertising is possible.[9]

Let π_{iJ} be the probability that a member of group i votes for candidate J. Let IC_J and PC_J be J's informative and persuasive campaign expenditures. Then assuming that some members of each group are uncertain about the positions of the two candidates, the probability that a member of group i votes for candidate J is a function of the positions of both candidates, and their informative and persuasive campaign expenditures.

$$\pi_{iJ} = \pi_{iJ}(x_L, x_R, IC_L, IC_R, PC_L, PC_R) \qquad (20.1)$$

where $i = 1, 2, \ldots, m$ and $J = L, R$. The distinction between informative and persuasive campaigning lies in the signs of the partial derivatives of π_{iJ} with respect to the four campaign expenditures. An increase in L's persuasive campaign expenditures increases the probability that all members of group i vote for L, just as an increase in persuasive campaign expenditures by R decreases the probability of an i voting for L.

$$\partial \pi_{iL}/\partial PC_L > 0, \qquad \partial \pi_{iL}/\partial PC_R > 0, \qquad \text{for all } i. \qquad (20.2)$$

On the other hand, informative campaign expenditures increase the probabilities that some groups vote for a candidate, while reducing the probabilities that other

---

[9] Austen-Smith (1987) motivates a similar characteristic for campaign expenditures, while sticking with the assumption that they are informative in nature, by assuming that all risk-averse voters benefit from a reduction in uncertainty over a candidate's position.

groups vote for her. Letting f denote those groups favoring L when fully informed, and r those groups favoring R, we have

$$\partial \pi_{fL}/\partial IC_L > 0, \quad \partial \pi_{rL}/\partial IC_L < 0, \quad \partial \pi_{fR}/\partial IC_R < 0, \quad \partial \pi_{rR}/\partial IC_R > 0. \quad (20.3)$$

The attraction of persuasive campaign spending over informative spending is obvious. The latter, unless selectively targeted, must decrease the probability of some groups supporting the candidate, while it increases the probability of others' support. Persuasive campaign spending, on the other hand, holds out the promise of increasing the votes obtained from all groups.

Given this feature, we can represent J's probability of winning the election, π_J, as a function of her campaign expenditures, C_J, those of her opponent, and the positions of the two candidates,

$$\pi_L = \pi_L(x_L, x_R, C_L, C_R), \qquad \pi_R = \pi_R(x_R, x_L, C_R, C_L) \qquad (20.4)$$

with $\partial \pi_L/\partial C_L > 0, \partial \pi_L/\partial C_R < 0, \partial \pi_R/\partial C_R > 0, \partial \pi_R/\partial C_L < 0$.

Now consider the decision of a member of group i on whether to contribute to a given candidate. Let x_i be his ideal point for x, v_i his consumption of private goods,

$$U_i = U_i(x, v_i), \qquad \partial U_i/\partial v_i > 0, \qquad \partial^2 U_i/\partial v_i^2 < 0. \qquad (20.5)$$

Let us assume to begin with that the voter believes that the positions of the two candidates are fixed and that the only effect of his contribution is to change the probability of a candidate's victory. Voter i chooses the contribution C_i that maximizes his expected utility, $E(U_i)$, subject to the budget constraint ($y_i = v_i + C_i$), where y_i is i's income.[10]

$$E(U_i) = \pi_L U_i(x_L, v_i) + (1 - \pi_L)U_i(x_R, v_i). \qquad (20.6)$$

If i contributes only to L and $\partial U_i(x_L, v_i)/\partial v_i \approx \partial U_i(x_R, v_i)/\partial v_i$, then the first-order conditions from the maximization of (20.6) with respect to C_i and v_i imply[11]

$$\frac{\partial \pi_L}{\partial C_L}[U_i(x_L, v_i) - U_i(x_R, v_i)] = \frac{\partial U_i(x_L, v_i)}{\partial v_i}. \qquad (20.7)$$

The right-hand side of (20.7) is the marginal utility of private good consumption and is positive. The equation has a solution with $C_L > 0$, only if $U_i(x_L, v_i) > U_i(x_R, v_i)$.

---

[10] To simplify the discussion we ignore i's share of x's costs.

[11] $E(U_i) = \pi_L U_i(x_L, v_i) + (1 - \pi_L)U_i(x_R, v_i) + \lambda(y_i - v_i - C_i)$, where $\pi_L = \pi_L(x_L, x_R, C_L, C_R)$.
Maximizing with respect to C_i and v_i yields

$$\frac{\partial E(U_i)}{\partial C_i} = \frac{\partial \pi_L}{\partial C_L}U_i(x_L, v_i) - \frac{\partial \pi_L}{\partial C_L}U_i(x_R, v_i) - \lambda = 0$$

$$\frac{\partial E(U_i)}{\partial v_i} = \pi_L\frac{\partial U_i(x_L, v_i)}{\partial v_i} + (1 - \pi_L)\frac{\partial U_i(x_R, v_i)}{\partial v_i} - \lambda = 0.$$

Eliminating λ from each equation and assuming $\partial U_i(x_L, v_i)/\partial v_i = \partial U_i(x_R, v_i)/\partial v_i$ yields (20.7).

A campaign contribution increases a voter's expected utility only if the candidates' positions differ, and if their positions are fixed, the voter contributes only to that candidate whose position promises the higher utility. The voter contributes to L up to the point where the change in his expected utility from the increase in probability that his favored candidate wins just equals the reduction in utility from the reduction of his income.

Now consider the decision of a candidate. If she matches her opponent's position her campaign contributions are zero, and she has a 50/50 chance of winning. By moving away from her opponent's position, however, she attracts contributions possibly increasing the likelihood that she wins, although she must also recognize that by placing a distance between herself and her opponent she may induce contributions to her opponent. While competition for votes in a Downsian sense brings the candidates' platforms closer to the median, competition for money moves them away from it. Competition for votes leads to competition for money, and the latter pulls the two platforms apart.

Thus, in choosing a position, x_L, L must take into account its effect on both her own and her rival's campaign expenditures, that is, that $C_L = C_L(x_L, x_R)$ and $C_R = C_R(x_L, x_R)$. If x_R remains fixed, the x_L that maximizes L's chance of winning, π_L, satisfies

$$\frac{\partial \pi_L}{\partial C_L}\frac{\partial C_L}{\partial x_L} = -\frac{\partial \pi_L}{\partial x_L} - \frac{\partial \pi_L}{\partial C_R}\frac{\partial C_R}{\partial x_L}, \tag{20.8}$$

where π_L is defined as in (20.4). If campaign contributions for both candidates were zero, each would choose a position that maximized the probability of winning – the median position. If a candidate gains more votes by spending the campaign contributions she obtains and distancing herself from her opponent, she does so. Equation (20.8) states that L moves to the point where the marginal increase in the probability of winning from the additional contributions obtained by moving slightly farther from R just balances the combined reduction in probability of winning from the move itself, and the additional campaign contributions to R it induces. Thus, if campaign expenditures do generate votes, and campaign contributions are dependent on the positions of the candidates, candidates will take positions based on the expected contributions that they generate. Money will affect both the identity of the winning candidate and the positions both candidates take.

We can now see that when campaign spending generates additional votes, the distinction between the "political man" and the "economic man" models collapses. On the margin a dollar of campaign contributions changes both the expected votes *and* the positions of the candidates. Given that the positions of candidates are dependent on the expected contributions they induce, contributors take into account not only the effect of their contributions on the probability that a candidate wins, but the effect of their contributions on the positions of the two candidates. The probability that L wins can now be written $\pi_L[x_L(C_L, C_R), x_R(C_L, C_R), C_L, C_R]$ and U_i becomes $U_i[x_L(C_L, C_R), v_i]$ or $U_i[x_R(C_L, C_R), v_i]$ depending on whether

L or R wins the election. Substituting these functions into (20.6) and maximizing with respect to i's contribution to L and v_i yields

$$
\left(\frac{\partial \pi_L}{\partial x_L} \frac{\partial x_L}{\partial C_L} + \frac{\partial \pi_L}{\partial x_R} \frac{\partial x_R}{\partial C_L} + \frac{\partial x_R}{\partial C_L} \right) [U_i(x_L, v_i) - U_i(x_R, v_i)]
$$

$$
+ \pi_L \frac{\partial U_i(x_L, v_i)}{\partial x_L} \frac{\partial x_L}{\partial C_L} + (1 - \pi_L) \frac{\partial U_i(x_R, v_i)}{\partial x_R} \frac{\partial x_R}{\partial C_L} \qquad (20.9)
$$

$$
= \frac{\partial U_i(x_L, v_i)}{\partial v_i}.
$$

The first term in (20.9) represents i's expected change in utility from contributing to L as a result of this contribution's effect on L's probability of winning. If i favors R over L, that is, $U_i(x_L, v_i) - U_i(x_R, v_i) < 0$, the first term is negative and i would contribute nothing to L, assuming L's position were fixed.[12] But if the probability of L's winning (π_L) is large, and the increment in utility i experiences from a shift in x_L is large, the second term in (20.9) is large and positive and could offset a negative first term, inducing i to contribute to L even though he prefers R.[13] Thus, when candidate positions respond to campaign contributions, i might well contribute to *both* candidates, moving one toward his optimum position and reducing the distance that the other moves away. The outcome in which a voter contributes to both candidates can *only* arise when candidates' positions are influenced by the campaign contributions they receive. Thus, evidence that some PACs and interest groups contribute to both candidates in an election implies that candidate positions do shift to induce greater contributions.[14]

The results that we have just derived, in part if not in toto, have been derived by several authors under various assumptions. Grossman and Helpman (1996), for example, assume the existence of two groups of voters, instead of two types of campaign expenditures. One group is informed. Each voter is informed and votes as in the Downsian model for the candidate (party) with the closest platform to his ideal point. Uninformed voters, on the other hand, are "impressionable" and "can be swayed by the messages they receive in the course of the campaign" (p. 268). Thus, campaign expenditures in the Grossman-Helpman model have essentially the same property as persuasive campaigning in the model sketched above, and affect both the probabilities of each candidate's victory and the positions that the candidates take.[15]

Although we have illustrated the basic relationships with a one-dimensional spatial model, the important role played by uncertainty in the model makes the incorporation of interest groups and campaign contributions into the probabilistic voting

---

[12] The first factor in the first term is positive. If i's contribution to L increases x_L, it moves x_L toward x_R increasing π_L. If i's contribution to L reduces x_L, it also reduces π_L. Similar arguments hold for the second term in this factor, and $\partial \pi_L / \partial C_L > 0$.

[13] The third term's sign is ambiguous, since R could be right or left of i's ideal point, and thus his contribution to L could shift R away from or toward this point.

[14] See Jacobson and Kernell (1983, p. 36). Poole and Romer (1985, p. 95) provide modest support for this prediction.

[15] See also Ben-Zion and Eytan (1974); Bental and Ben-Zion (1975); Kau and Rubin (1982); Kau, Keenan, and Rubin (1982); Jacobson and Kernell (1983); Denzau and Munger (1986); Austen-Smith (1987); Congleton (1989); Hinich and Munger (1989, 1994, chs. 9 and 10); Morton and Cameron (1992); Grossman and Helpman (1994); and Ball (1999).

model of Chapter 12 fairly straightforward, and several of the papers just cited have established the existence of equilibria with multidimensional issue spaces using some variant of the probabilistic voting model.

These models of campaign contributions produce a rich set of predictions, and an immense literature has tried to test them. We examine some of its findings next.

20.3   Empirical studies of the causes and consequences of campaign contributions

The theoretical models of campaign contributions lead to three sets of predictions: (1) the positions candidates have taken on issues in the past, their ideologies, and perhaps their ability to help interest groups in the future should affect the amounts of money contributed to them; (2) campaign expenditures should increase the number of votes a candidate receives; and, to close the circle, (3) the actual voting behavior of representatives should be influenced by the magnitudes and sources of the campaign funds that they have received. The second prediction is pivotal. If political advertising does not *buy* votes, no candidate has a reason to undertake it and no interest group has a reason to contribute to a candidate. Given the vast amounts spent in campaigns, it would seem that proposition (2) must be true, and of the three relationships, this one is perhaps the most extensively researched. We begin, therefore, by examining the empirical work that tests the second prediction of the campaign expenditure model literature.

20.3.1   *Votes for a candidate are a function of campaign expenditures*

To test proposition (2), one might begin with (20.4). This equation implies that the number of votes a candidate receives is a function of her campaign expenditures, the expenditures of her opponent, and their positions on the issues. In addition to being sensitive to characteristics of her opponent, the relationship between expenditures and votes may depend on personal characteristics of the candidate herself, and perhaps of her district. For example, the effectiveness of a given amount of political advertising may vary with the education or income levels of citizens in a district. Catholic candidates may be more successful in districts with large fractions of Catholic voters. These considerations suggest that an empirical specification of (20.4) to be tested on cross-section data could take on a rather complex, nonlinear form (Coates, 1998, 1999).

In particular, we should expect the relationship between own expenditures and share of the votes won to be nonlinear. Here again the analogy between campaign expenditures and consumer advertising is relevant. An important goal of Coca-Cola's advertising is simply first to introduce and then to remind people of its brand name, so that it becomes the first brand name that pops into the consumer's mind when he orders a soft drink. The sales that this sort of advertising generates can be expected to follow an S-shaped curve. In particular, as the population becomes saturated with messages, the number of new customers reached and won from an additional message declines.

The same can be expected of political advertising. The most difficult challenge many new entrants into politics face is to get citizens to remember their names. Unless they are the son of a former president or an ex-wrestler, they start at the origin of the S-shaped vote function depicted in Figure 20.1.[16] At the beginning of a campaign, spending is highly productive as a candidate reaches those citizens who will vote for him once they learn something about him. As more and more citizens learn his name and his position on the issues, the number of new votes won per dollar of campaign spending declines, reaching perhaps zero at the level C_Z as depicted in the figure.

Two implications follow from this figure. First, assuming that the curve does not actually turn down, a candidate has the incentive to spend all of the money contributed to his campaign. Second, the goal of the candidate is to raise enough funds to reach a point like C_Z, where the marginal return to the candidate in votes is *zero*.

One more important prediction can be inferred from the analogy between political and consumer advertising. Advertising builds up a stock of goodwill.[17] An established brand like Coca-Cola needs to spend far less to maintain this stock, than a new brand must spend to build up a stock. This asymmetry creates an entry barrier in consumer markets and an important advantage for incumbents in politics. Where a challenger for a seat in Congress may start a campaign close to the origin in Figure 20.1, an incumbent may start at a point like C_I, and thus have a significant advantage over the challenger.

All of these predictions regarding campaign expenditures have found empirical support. Grier's (1989) study of U.S. Senate races from 1978 through 1984 captures several key features of the campaign expenditures model. His main findings are illustrated in the following regression explaining the incumbent's percentage share of the vote (V_t):

$$V_t = 48.3 + 4.37 \text{ D8284} + .19 V_{t-1} - 11.42 \text{ S} - .0760 \text{ CHAL}$$
$$\quad 10.95 \qquad 2.99 \qquad\quad 2.81 \qquad 3.12 \qquad\quad 7.65$$

$$+ .000059 \text{ CHAL}^2 + .0287 \text{ INC} - .000016 \text{ INC}^2, \qquad R^2 = 0.55$$
$$\qquad 5.07 \qquad\qquad 5.01 \qquad\qquad 4.26$$

where D8284 is a dummy variable for the two years 1982 and 1984, S is a dummy set equal to one for the one incumbent Senator caught in a scandal during this period, and CHAL and INC are the campaign expenditures of the challenger and the incumbent. The lagged vote share is included as in several other studies to account for district-specific factors. The two squared expenditure terms capture the anticipated

---

[16] The reader should think of this figure as drawn for a given level of spending for the other candidate.

[17] See Grier (1989) and Lott (1991). Here the distinction between informative and persuasive advertising is again important. Goodwill capital from informative advertising depreciates much more rapidly than goodwill capital from persuasive advertising. Today's ad that Coca-Cola is on sale for 99 cents a liter will have little impact on its sales six months from now. But an ad stating that "Coke tastes better" may have a long-lasting impact. A candidate's position on an increase in the sales tax in one campaign will have little impact on her votes four years later. Her image as an honest politician may carry over from one campaign to the next, however. Again see Mueller and Stratmann (1994).

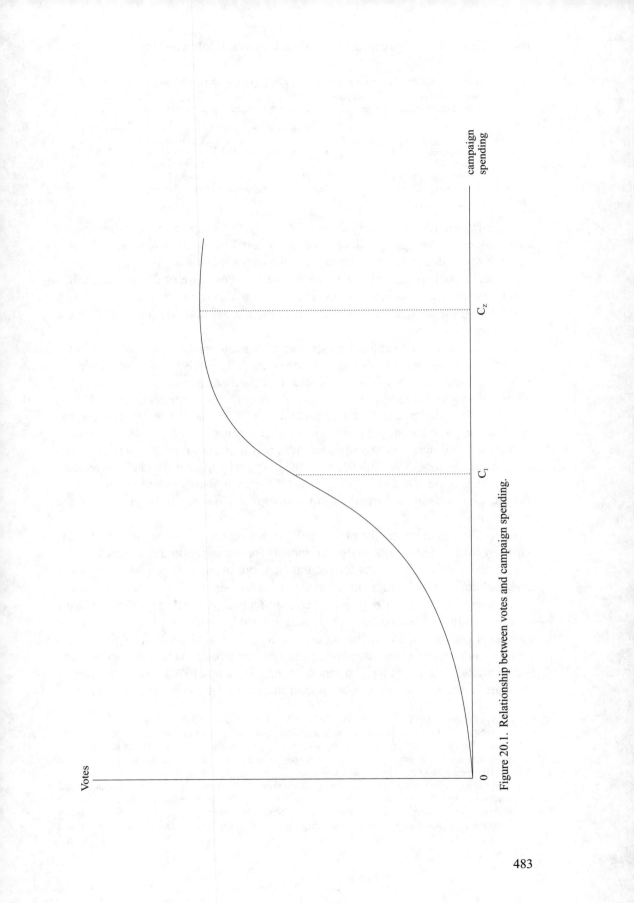

Figure 20.1. Relationship between votes and campaign spending.

483

Table 20.1. *Proportion of marginal effects on incumbents' votes shares, 1984 House of Representative elections*

	Significantly < 0	Insignificantly different from zero	Significantly > 0
Incumbents	0.14	0.86	0.000
Challengers	0.91	0.08	0.006

Source: Coates (1998).

diminishing returns to campaign expenditures. Both are significant. An increase in a challenger's campaign spending has a negative effect on an incumbent's share of the vote which decreases on the margin as the challenger's spending increases. The incumbent's own spending has a positive effect on her share of the vote, an effect which also decreases on the margin. The equation also indicates that at low levels of spending, the challenger's spending has much larger marginal impacts than the incumbent's spending.[18]

Although Grier's expenditure model captures some of the main anticipated relationships, it can be criticized for not correcting adequately for differences in the personal characteristics of the candidates and their states. As noted above, such corrections are likely to require quite complicated nonlinear models. Coates (1998) estimates one such model that contains numerous interaction terms between the expenditure variables and the candidate and district characteristics. Table 20.1 summarizes his findings with regard to the marginal impacts of the two sets of candidates' expenditures. Although 91 percent of the challengers would have benefitted from having more money to spend, *none* of the incumbents would have done so. Indeed, Coates estimates small negative marginal impacts for 14 percent of the incumbents.[19]

Tables 20.2 summarizes the major findings of a representative sample of studies. Virtually all find significant marginal impacts for the expenditures of challengers. A few find significant effects for incumbents, but even these tend to find larger marginal impacts for challengers than for the incumbents.

Another reason why it may have been difficult to estimate significant effects for the spending of both candidates is that the two expenditures tend to be highly correlated (Jacobson, 1978, 1985). This problem is magnified by bringing in the simultaneous relationship between expenditures and votes. Most incumbents win. For example, in the Glantz, Abramowitz, and Burkart (1976) study of contests for seats in the California legislature and the House of Representatives, only 16

---

[18] Abramowitz (1988) obtains similar results to Grier for Senate contests over the 1974–86 period. Welch (1976) and Jacobson (1985) have also reported results suggesting diminishing returns to campaign expenditures.

[19] Such negative marginal effects are of course possible if the curve in Figure 20.1 were to actually turn down beyond some level of spending. Coates argues that such turning points can exist, and that candidates may go beyond them because of ignorance of their location.

    Levitt (1994) adopted the ingenious strategy of eliminating all additive district- and candidate-specific characteristics by including in his sample only House contests in which both candidates compete against one another two or more times. Levitt finds zero marginal effects of incumbent spending and near-zero effects for challengers. His procedure can be faulted, however, for not allowing for interaction effects between expenditures and district or candidate characteristics (Coates, 1998, p. 64).

Table 20.2a. *Summary of main results linking votes for candidates to their campaign expenditures, U.S. House, Senate, and President*

Election	Effect of expenditures by		Study
	Challenger	Incumbent	
U.S. House			
1972	sig.	insig.	Glantz et al. (1976)
1972, 1974,	sig.	sig. (1974, OLS)	Jacobson (1978)
1978	sig.	sig., wrong sign	Kau, Keenan, and Rubin[b] (1982)
1972–82	sig.	insig. (usually)	Jacobson (1985)
1972–90	sig.	insig.	Levitt[c] (1994)
1984	sig.	insig.	Coates (1998)
1980	sig.	insig.	Kau and Rubin[b] (1993)
	Dem	*Rep*	
1972	sig.	sig.	Welch (1974, 1981)
1980–86	sig.	sig.[d]	Snyder (1990)
U.S. Senate			
1972, 1974	sig.	sig. (1972)	Jacobson (1978)
1972–82	sig.	insig. (usually)	Jacobson (1985)
1974–86	sig.	sig.	Abramowitz (1988)
	Dem	*Rep*	
1972	sig.	sig.	Welch (1974, 1981)
U.S. Presidential			
1972	sig.	sig.	Nagler and Leighly (1992)

Table 20.2b. *Summary of main results linking votes for candidates to their campaign expenditures, other contests*

Election	Effect of expenditures by			Study
	Challenger	Incumbent	Candidate	
Provincial Elections				
Quebec, 1966, 1970			sig.	Palda[a] (1973, 1975)
Manitoba, 1973			sig.	Palda[a] (1975)
California Assembly, 1972, 1974	sig.	sig. (1974)		Glantz et al. (1976)
Parliamentary seats, Scotland and Wales, 1974			mixed	Johnston (1978)
8 Provincial elections in Canada, 1973–7			sig.	Chapman and Palda (1984)
Canadian Federal Election (Ontario), 1979			sig.	Palda and Palda (1985)

[a] Palda (1973, 1975) uses votes for all candidates as the dependent variables. Incumbency treated as a dummy variable (significant).

[b] Kau, Keenan, and Rubin (1982), and Kau and Rubin (1993) regress winner's margin on winner's and loser's expenditures. Given high success rate of incumbents, I have interpreted their results for winners as pertaining to incumbents.

[c] Sample restricted to contests in which both candidates faced each other more than once. Coefficient on challenger spending much smaller than in other studies.

[d] Snyder regresses Democrat's share of vote on Democrat's share of expenditures. Significance of Republican spending inferred from significance of Democrat's spending share.

of 511 incumbents lost. Many are almost certain winners regardless of what they spend, and thus may receive and spend little. Those who face stiff challenges may receive more funds to help fight off the challenge. Thus incumbents facing tough challengers will spend more, but receive fewer votes than easy winners. A cross-sectional regression that includes the two types of incumbents may thus fail to capture the positive relationship between spending and votes in the close contests. This simultaneity problem may explain the surprising result observed by Palda and Palda (1998) in the 1993 French parliamentary election. Although they generally found that campaign spending increased votes for both incumbents and challengers, incumbents who spent large amounts of their own money did significantly less well. Palda and Palda interpret this result as implying that voters penalized incumbents who tried "to buy their reelection." An alternative interpretation is that incumbents did not spend their own money when they faced weak challenges, and thus that own spending proxies for a tight race, which explains its negative coefficient in a cross-section regression.[20]

One recent study that nicely accounts for the simultaneity between the closeness of the contest and the amount of campaign spending is by Nagler and Leighley (1992). They test Snyder's (1989) prediction that presidential candidates will allocate more funds to states that are pivotal in the electoral college, and are expected to have close votes. They estimate a two-equation model that explains money allocated to each state in the 1972 presidential election, and the responsiveness of votes won to money spent. Their model both predicts the allocation of funds by the two candidates across the states, and reveals large marginal effects of spending for both Nixon and McGovern.

Finally, we note that congressmen, when they vote on bills to curtail campaign spending, behave as if *they* at least believe that this spending has differential effects on their chances of being reelected (Bender, 1988, 1991).

20.3.2 *Determinants of campaign contributions*

Equation (20.9) has three implications with respect to the direction and levels of campaign contributions: (1) a contributor gives to the candidate whose position is closest to his own; (2) a contributor gives to a candidate who is willing to shift her position toward that favored by the contributor; (3) contributions to a candidate are higher, the higher her probability of winning. All three predictions have found support in an extensive literature.[21]

---

[20] Johnston (1978) emphasizes the difficulty of estimating the expenditure-vote relationship with cross-sectional data, and Welch (1981) and Jacobson (1985) review the simultaneity issue.

[21] Ben-Zion and Eytan (1974); Bental and Ben-Zion (1975); Crain and Tollison (1976); Jacobson (1978, 1985); Welch (1980, 1981); Kau and Rubin (1982, 1993); Kau, Keenan, and Rubin (1982); Palda and Palda (1985); Poole and Romer (1985); Poole, Romer, and Rosenthal (1987); Munger (1989); Grier, Munger, and Torrent (1990); Snyder (1990, 1992); Grier and Munger (1991); Stratmann (1991, 1992a, 1995, 1996b, 1998); Bennett and Loucks (1994); Kroszner and Stratmann (1998); and Hersch and McDougall (2000).

Also relevant are the studies that find that the total contributions of a firm or industry are positively related to their potential gains from public policies (Pittman, 1976, 1977; Mann and McCormick, 1980; Zardkoohi, 1985).

The prediction that contributions flow to candidates with high probabilities of winning is confirmed by the general finding that incumbents have extremely high probabilities of being reelected, and they receive most of the campaign contributions (Welch, 1980).

In a study that is noteworthy both for the sophistication of its methodology and the size of its sample, Poole and Romer (1985) found a strong relationship between the ideological positions of contributors and the ideological positions of the candidates to whom they offer contributions. Corporate and trade association PACs give to conservative candidates and labor unions to liberal candidates. Moreover, within these broad interest group categories campaign contributions break down even further into consistent ideologic patterns; some corporate PACs give exclusively to the most conservative candidates, others to moderate conservatives and liberals. Poole and Romer's general findings about the direction of flow of PAC contributions have been corroborated by Kau, Keenan, and Rubin (1982); Kau and Rubin (1982, 1993); Munger (1989); Grier, Munger, and Torrent (1990); Grier and Munger (1991); Stratmann (1991, 1992a, 1995, 1996b, 1998); Bennett and Loucks (1994); and Kroszner and Stratmann (1998).

The results from most of these studies seem to imply that contributors are not merely trying to increase the election probabilities of candidates whom they favor, but are trying to influence the votes that they will cast on specific issues, or to obtain specific political "favors" (Snyder, 1990). Stratmann (1992a) finds, for example, that agricultural PACs channel money to representatives who are likely to be undecided over how to vote on farm bills. Grier and Munger (1991) hypothesize that congressmen will feel more obligated to contributors who supply them with funds when they face a close race. Knowing this, contributors have a motivation to supply more funds to candidates involved in close races, or who come from districts with economic and ideological characteristics that lower the odds of getting reelected (Stratmann, 1996b). Poole and Romer (1985) also find that money flows to incumbents involved in tight races, and go on to state that "this result, together with a parallel one on challenger contributions, appears to be the most robust finding in the empirical literature on campaign contributions" (p. 101), citing Jacobson (1985) and Kau and Rubin (1982) in further support of their statement.

The economic-man, investor-contributor model of campaign contributions also finds empirical support in the many studies that observe systematic patterns between the economic interests of the contributors and the committee assignments of the recipients.[22] Building on Shepsle and Weingast's (1987) theory of standing committees, Kroszner and Stratmann (1998) posit the existence of long-run, exchange relationships between members of standing committees and the interest groups they

---

[22] See Munger (1989); Grier and Munger (1991); and Dow, Endersby, and Menifield (1998). Somewhat indirect support for the existence of long-run, exchange relationships between House committee members and interest groups is also provided by Grier, Munger, and Torrent's (1990) *failure* to detect systematic patterns of interest group contributions to senators. Their explanation for this is that the rules of the Senate are much different from those of the House, and that they reduce the value of committee membership. Poole and Romer (1985) found only a weak relationship between committee assignments and campaign contributions in the House, however.

regulate. They test their predictions using data on contributions from commercial and investment banks, security firms, and insurance companies to members of the House of Representatives from 1983 through 1992. The following results support their predictions:

1. The largest contributions from these PACs go to members of the House Banking Committee.
2. The contributions from PACs with opposing interests are negatively correlated for committee members, but positively correlated for all other congressmen.
3. The contributions from these PACs to a particular committee member fall dramatically when she leaves the banking committee.
4. Congressmen who are not successful in raising large amounts of contributions while on this committee tend to leave it.

If PACs from the financial sector and congressmen are involved in long-run, exchange relationships, commercial banks and insurance companies will know "who their friends are" on these committees and will concentrate their contributions accordingly (finding 2). Since no long-run exchange relationships exist between financial companies and members of Congress who are not on the banking committee, all of these PACs spread their campaign contributions around evenly and thinly to these other congressmen. Findings 3 and 4 offer clear support for the hypothesized exchange relationships.[23]

Snyder (1992) also finds evidence that PACs establish long-run, "investment" relationships with congressmen. A given PAC tends to give to the same subset of representatives every year, and this pattern of persistence is stronger for PACs with economic interests than for "ideological" PACs. Since older representatives are more likely to retire or die, they receive less from PACs, ceteris paribus, than young representatives.

Perhaps the strongest evidence of a quid pro quo relationship between interest group contributors and members of Congress comes in Stratmann's (1995, 1998) work on the timing of contributions. If contributors took the positions of congressmen on issues as fixed, and just gave to those congressmen who took positions that the interest groups favored, one might expect a steady flow of contributions to congressmen over the course of an electoral cycle, or a pattern correlated with the cycle. On the other hand, if interest groups attempt to influence the way representatives vote on specific issues, they might be expected to concentrate their giving around key votes on these issues either to "remind" a Congressman just before a vote is taken of the implicit exchange relationship between him and the interest-group contributor, or to reward him immediately after a vote has been taken. Stratmann (1998) finds that farm PAC contributions to members of the House were significantly clustered around the dates when key votes on farm legislation were taken.

---

[23] Bennett and Loucks (1994) also examine contributions to the House Banking Committee although in this case from financial institutions and savings & loan associations. They also find a concentration of contributions on members of this committee.

20.3.3 *Determinants of representative voting behavior – campaign contributions*

If campaign contributions are rational allocations of contributor income, then there should be payoffs in terms of the votes that winning candidates cast on issues of importance to the contributor. The evidence reviewed in the previous subsection certainly suggests that PACs *expect* the behavior of congressmen to be influenced by their contributions. Are these expectations vindicated? The cleanest test of this hypothesis comes on those issues that have a simple and obvious economic payoff to certain contributors, such as legislation on the minimum wage or cargo preference. Several studies have successfully conducted these sorts of tests.[24]

Evidence also exists indicating that some PACs, which do not represent narrow economic interests, nevertheless try to influence congressional voting through their contributions. Langbein (1993), for example, examined the patterns of contributions of both the National Rifle Association (NRA) and Handgun Control, a citizen PAC whose goal is stated in its name. One expects ideology to be important in the decisions of individuals to both join and contribute to these PACs, and thus that the political man or consumer contributor model might well apply here. Langbein (1993, p. 563) found, however, that "NRA contributions to pro-gunners and to gun controllers were both significant. The more NRA money a pro-gunner received, the fewer times he or she switched from the pure NRA position; this is consistent with expectation. By contrast, the more NRA money a gun-controller received, the more he or she switched from a pure gun-control position." Money matters even for an issue as ideological and emotionally charged as gun controls.

20.3.4 *Determinants of representative voting behavior – ideology or pure survival?*

"Buying" a congressman's vote through a campaign contribution is one way economic interests can make themselves felt. But even if campaign contributions were totally banned or, as several scholars claim, did not influence how congressmen vote, we would still expect economic interests to be important in determining how representatives vote. If voters vote their pocketbooks, then their representatives will take the economic interests of these voters into account when they vote. Representatives from districts with large fractions of dairy farmers will vote for price supports for milk; representatives from urban districts will vote against them. The studies that have tested whether campaign contributions affect how representatives vote have all included other variables to capture the economic interests and ideological preferences of the representatives' districts. Those studies that claim that campaign contributions do affect how representatives vote have found them to have

---

[24] See Silberman and Durden (1976); Chappell (1981); Kau, Keenan, and Rubin (1982); Kau and Rubin (1982, 1993); Peltzman (1984); Frendreis and Waterman (1985); Marks (1993); Stratmann (1991, 1995, 1996b); Kang and Greene (1999); and Baldwin and Magee (2000).

  Chappell (1982), Grenzke (1989), Wright (1990), and Dow and Endersby (1994), on the other hand, fail to detect significant relationships between PAC contributions and the votes cast by legislators.

a significant impact on representatives' voting *after* controlling for the characteristics of their districts. Studies that claim that campaign contributions do not affect how representatives vote have found that it is only the characteristics of the representatives' districts that have a significant impact on their voting.

Many studies have included only measures of the economic interests and ideological preferences of the representatives' districts. When voting is on legislation where the opposing economic interests are clearly defined, the economic interests of their districts have always been found to be important in determining how the congressmen vote.[25] Moreover, the *narrow* economic interests of representatives' constituents also appear to have a significant effect on how they vote on legislation with *broad* economic impacts. A ban on child labor would appear to have potentially broad economic consequences, and to entail a significant ideological component. Davidson, Davis, and Ekelund (1995) find, however, that Senate voting on the Child Labor Act of 1937 is related to the economic impacts of the legislation on each state. Senators from states adversely affected by the bill (states with many firms in interstate commerce, with many textile firms that were the primary employers of children, and with large numbers of children in domestic service) voted against the bill. Senators from states where beneficial effects from the bill were identified voted for it. Libecap (1992) has made similar claims with respect to the Sherman Antitrust Act of 1890, as have Ramírez and Eigen-Zucchi (2001) with respect to the Clayton Act in 1914.[26]

In an extremely ambitious paper, Peltzman (1985) sets out to explain "the history of Congressional voting in the twentieth century." He finds that the "profound political changes" over this century can to a "remarkably close degree . . . be attributed to changes in economic interest" (p. 669), that is, changes in the economic interests of states and congressional districts explain changes in voting patterns in the House and Senate. Peltzman also identifies a "'persistent historical' element" in the voting behavior of representatives from different states and regions that one might associate with underlying ideological differences. Moreover, Peltzman confines his analysis to congressional voting on tax and expenditure bills, issues upon which one might expect economic interests to dominate. Conceivably voting on more ideological issues like prohibition, civil rights, gun controls, and so on might reveal even more persistent regional/ideological differences.

Thus, it seems likely that both the economic interests and the ideological preferences of a representative's constituents are likely to influence how she votes in the legislature. We might then reasonably model the vote of representative r on issue i as

$$V_{ri} = \alpha I_C + \beta E I_C + \mu_i, \qquad (20.10)$$

where I_C is a vector measuring the ideological preferences of different legislative districts, and $E I_C$ is a vector that measures their economic interests. Quite

[25] In addition to the studies already cited, see Richardson and Munger (1990) explaining voting social security legislation; Harper and Aldrich (1991) votes on sugar bills; Marks (1993) voting on trade bills; Kahane (1996) voting on fast-track authority for NAFTA; Basuchoudhary, Pecorino, and Shughart II (1999) voting on funding for a superconducting supercollider; Fishback and Kantor (1998) on the adoption of workers' compensation; Irwin and Kroszner (1999) on Republican voting on free trade; and Jenkins and Weidenmier (1999) voting for the Bank of the United States from 1811 to 1816.

[26] See also Delorme, Frame, and Kamerschen (1997).

obviously, from the preceding discussion, there is no reason to assume that a single set of ideological and economic interest variables explains voting on all issues. The fraction of dairy farmers in a district may be important in explaining votes on milk price supports, but not on restrictions on abortions. The fraction of Baptists in a district may be related to votes on abortion issues, but not to milk price supports. Different variables and different coefficients can be expected for different sorts of issues.

A strong form of the Downsian model would predict that it is *only* the economic interests and ideological preferences of a representative's constituents that explain her voting. Each representative is only concerned about getting reelected and fears that any deviation from her constituents' preferences will be punished with defeat in the next election. Peltzman's (1984, 1985) work is consistent with this Darwinian interpretation of political competition.

The alternative position sees political competition as less Darwinian. The high probabilities of reelection that incumbents enjoy create "slack" in the political process, which allows representatives on occasion to "shirk" on their obligations as representatives and vote as their own preferences dictate, even when this runs counter to the preferences of their constituents.[27] One way to test this hypothesis would be to construct a vector of variables to measure a representative's personal economic interests and ideology (I_r) – whether she is a Baptist or a dairy farmer – and add it to (20.10).

Most studies that have tried to account for the personal ideology of a representative have not followed this approach, however, but rather have used the scores given to representatives by various ideological interest groups based on their past votes on key, ideologically important issues. One difficulty with this approach, however, is that a representative's ideological score may simply reflect the economic interests and ideological preferences of her constituents. If this is the case, there may be significant collinearity between I_r and the other variables in (20.10).

Kalt and Zupan (1990) have treated I_r as part of the residual from (20.10), and tested to see whether it behaves systematically, as it should, if a representative's ideology matters. They first specified a vector of variables to include in (20.10) and used it to predict how members of the Senate would vote during the 1977–8 legislative period. They then summed the residuals from this regression and tested to see whether they were systematically related to the American for Democratic Action's ideological categorization of issues during this period. The pattern of residuals was not random. Some senators consistently voted more liberally than the characteristics of her state predicted she would, and others more conservatively. George McGovern, the Democratic nominee for president in 1972 who lost in a landslide to Richard Nixon, consistently voted more liberally than his South Dakota constituency's characteristics predicted he would. Barry Goldwater, the Republican nominee for president in 1964 who lost in a landslide to Lyndon Johnson, consistently voted more conservatively than his Arizona constituency's characteristics predicted.[28]

As Higgs (1989) has pointed out, the strong form of the Darwinian model seems to be resoundingly rejected by the fact that the two Senators from a state often vote

[27] See Kau and Rubin (1979); Kau, Keenan, and Rubin (1982); and Kalt and Zupan (1984, 1990).
[28] See also Carson and Oppenheimer (1984), Kalt and Zupan (1984), and Garrett (1999).

differently on an issue – *37 percent* of the time on 465 defense-related votes in 1987. Since the constituency characteristics for a single state that go into (20.10) are identical, this equation must predict the same vote on any given issue. Such a large number of splits casts considerable doubt on the explanatory power of *all* possible sets of state characteristics that one might choose.

Some of those who discount the representative-ideology/shirking hypothesis have responded by arguing that the senators from a given state actually represent *different* constituencies (Peltzman, 1984; Dougan and Munger, 1989; Lott and Davis, 1992). If one thinks of constituents as potential voters, then this argument is either patently false or it undermines all of the empirical work that has tried to explain voting in the House and Senate using characteristics of the populations in each district or state as explanatory variables.[29] Indeed, one attempt to identify different reelection constituencies relies on the same sort of examination of residuals that has been used to measure representative ideology (Stratmann, 1996b).

One way to explain why two Senators from the same state vote differently is to posit the existence of a *geographic* constituency of potential voters and an *economic and ideological* constituency of interest groups that lobby her and contribute money to her campaign.[30] These might include interest groups based within a senator's state, but could also include interests from outside the state. An additional vector, *PAC*, measuring campaign contributions and possibly lobbying efforts of interest groups must then be added to (20.10) to give us

$$V_i = \alpha I_C + \beta E I_C + \delta I_r + \gamma PAC + \mu_i. \tag{20.11}$$

Equation (20.11) would carry the prediction that *all* of the split voting by senators from the same state can be explained either by differences in their personal ideologies or in their relationships with interest groups.

Several studies have attempted to test for the importance of a representative's personal ideology by testing whether a representative who announces her retirement votes differently in her final term. Once she decides to retire, a representative is freed from *both* the implicit contracts to deliver votes to contributors of campaign funds *and* the need to satisfy the preferences of her constituents. I_C, $E I_C$, and *PAC* all drop out of (20.11) leaving the representative's personal ideology, I_r, as the sole variable to explain how she votes. Several studies that have performed such tests claim that representatives *do not* vote significantly differently in their final terms than they did before,[31] while a second group of studies claims that they do.[32] In one

---

[29] Following Peltzman (1984), one might want to adjust the state data to take into account the different propensities for groups to vote, but this alone does not lead to different predictions for how the two senators from a state vote.

[30] See, for example, Fort, Hallagan, Morong, and Stegner (1993).

[31] See Lott (1987, 1990), van Beek (1991), Lott and Davis (1992), Lott and Bronars (1993), and Poole and Romer (1993).

[32] One problem with focusing on last period voting is that representatives tend to vote much less frequently after they have announced their retirement (Lott, 1987, 1990). If the characteristics of a representative's district imply that she should vote against the defense appropriation bill, but her implicit contract with defense PACs over the years implies that she should vote in favor of it, if the representative votes she must disappoint either her geographic constituents or her financial ones. By not voting at all, she avoids overtly offending both

of the most recent contributions falling into the latter category, Tien (2001) used an improved index of ideology and found evidence of shirking by members of the House who voluntarily retired between 1983 and 1990. Besley and Case (1995) also found evidence of significant differences in the behavior of those who involuntarily retired because of constitutional prohibitions against running for reelection.[33]

A somewhat different way to test for shirking is to see whether congressmen who have secure seats deviate in their voting away from their constitutent preferences more than do congressmen who face tough races. Coates (1995), examining votes on radioactive disposal, and Coates and Munger (1995), examining votes on anti-strip mining legislation, both found significant differences in the voting behavior of legislators with safe seats. Both studies found that economic interest variables were also significant. And, finally, Figlio (2000) found more evidence of senators shirking in the early portion of the electoral cycle than shortly before they would stand for reelection. This behavior appears rational, since he also found that shirking early in a senator's six-year term was less severely punished by voters. All in all, one must conclude that the evidence suggests that elected politicians do indulge their own personal ideological preferences to a greater degree when the likely costs of such indulgence at the next election are reduced or eliminated.

20.3.5 *Evaluation*

The interest group model of political competition rests on three legs: (1) an equation to explain how interest groups allocate their campaign contributions, (2) an equation to explain the effect of campaign contributions on the way representatives vote, and (3) an equation to explain the effect of campaign contributions on the outcomes of electoral contests. All three legs of the model have found empirical support. All three, however, have also been challenged on the basis of empirical evidence of one sort or another. Of the three, the least controversial would appear to be the prediction that PACs and other contributors distribute their funds selectively. Although some disagreement exists over *which* characteristics of a representative affect the size and source of his contributions, no one who has examined the data on contributions has concluded that they are allocated randomly.

If contributors are rational and they have rational expectations, then the evidence that they selectively channel their contributions to certain legislators implies support for at least one if not both of the other legs of the interest group model. Contributors must expect to influence either the outcome of an election or the way a legislator votes by contributing to his campaign.[34]

The evidence that campaign spending is effective in increasing a candidate's chances of winning an election also seems quite strong, at least for challengers of incumbents and in open seat elections. The much weaker findings with respect to

constituencies. Representative shirking in the final term may manifest itself as a *nonrandom* choice of issues on which to abstain. Support for this interpretation is provided by Calcagno and Jackson's (1998) evidence that PAC contributions increase senators' participation rates in roll call votes.

[33] See also Kalt and Zupan (1990), and Zupan (1990).

[34] A caveat here is Snyder's (1990) hypothesis that the contributor is buying nonlegislative favors.

the effects of spending by incumbents can also be interpreted as support for the interest group model, since incumbents receive such large amounts of campaign funds that they probably are operating at the top of the vote/expenditures mountain, where the marginal impact of another dollar of political advertising is zero.

The biggest disagreement in the literature is over the determinants of a representative's voting in the legislature and the relative importance of constituent interests, money, and ideology as determinants. At one extreme would be the studies that include only measures of the economic interests in each state or district, and thus implicitly assume that neither the representative's own ideology nor that of his district matters. If the ideologies of voters affect how they vote, however, even a strong form of the Downsian model would predict that representative voting would have an ideological component. The Downsian version of (20.11) would have both I_C and EI_C as right-hand-side variables. Most observers would now seem to agree that voter ideologies play an important role in politics, and thus that I_C belongs in a model to explain representatives' voting.[35]

The interest group model predicts that candidates will shift their positions on issues to obtain additional campaign funds *if* by spending these funds they can increase their chances of getting reelected. The studies that find a positive impact of incumbent spending on their chances of winning support the hypothesis that PAC contributions affect representatives' voting. Several studies find direct support for this hypothesis, but several others fail to support it. The evidence that contributions are timed to coincide with important votes in Congress strongly suggests, however, that contributors *expect* their contributions to affect how legislators vote.

By far the most controversial of the components of (20.11) is I_r, a representative's personal ideology. The studies that claim that representatives vote the same way after they announce their retirements as before seem to imply that I_r is *all* that matters in explaining how representatives vote, since all other variables drop out of the equation for a retiring representative. If the ADA index of voting is a good measure of how a representative will vote, and it also measures I_r, then all one should need to explain a representative's ADA index in period t is her index in $t - 1$. Krehbiel (1993) comes close to suggesting that this is the case, and it is a direct implication of Poole and Rosenthal's (1997) research establishing the importance of a *single* ideological dimension in congressional voting patterns. Tien (2001), on the other hand, records a significant decline in the coefficient on a representative's lagged ADA rating once she announces that she will retire.

Even if a representative's voting is heavily autoregressive, it might be consistent with a Darwinian version of political competition. Assume, for example, that the only two factors that affect whether a citizen votes for incumbent i when he runs for reelection are his voting record in the legislature, V_i, and his campaign expenditures. If in turn his flow of campaign funds depends solely on his voting record, the probability that an incumbent is reelected will depend only on his voting record,

$$\pi_i = f(V_i) + \mu_i. \tag{20.12}$$

---

[35] Hinich and Munger (1994) place ideology at the center of their theory of politics.

With sufficiently intense political competition only those incumbents with voting records that maximize (20.12) will survive. Whether candidates are devoid of personal ideologies and consciously *choose* a pattern of voting that maximizes (20.12), or are slaves to their personal ideologies and only survive in office if their ideologies happen to lead to a mix of votes in the legislature that maximizes (20.12), is irrelevant for explaining how representatives vote in the long run. V_i in (20.11) will be dependent on only I_C, EI_C, and PAC. The ideological score this voting record produces, as measured by the ADA, will also be solely explained by I_C, EI_C, and PAC. Thus, I_r, as measured by a legislator's ADA score, should also be determined subject to a random error by I_C, EI_C, and PAC. One should be able to explain a legislator's voting record with an equation that includes *either* I_C, EI_C, and PAC, or I_r, *if* the level of political competition is strong enough.

Several studies have tested the strength of the Darwinian process by using the residuals from equations like (20.11) that omit I_r to explain the probability that an incumbent is reelected. These studies uniformly find that legislators are "strongly punished" for their shirking. Lott and Davis (1992, p. 470) found "that those who are eventually sorted out of office deviated from the interests of their constituents by only 1.27 percentage points."[36]

The fact that shirking does get punished implies, of course, that *some* shirking does take place. Equation (20.11), if estimated without a measure of I_r, will produce residuals that are correlated with the representatives' personal ideologies (Carson and Oppenheimer, 1984; Kalt and Zupan, 1984, 1990). Although the results of Lott and Davis and others imply that shirking is fairly unimportant when measured across a large set of votes, it is possible that when shirking occurs, it is on issues of considerable ideological salience and importance. A representative's personal ideology has been found to be important, for example, in explaining voting on a constitutional amendment to ban flag burning (Lascher, Kelman, and Kane, 1993); on superfund legislation to clean up toxic waste sites (Gibson, 1993); on funding for a superconducting supercollider (Basuchoudhary, Pecorino, and Shughart II, 1999); on protectionist legislation (Nollen and Iglarsch, 1990); and on abortion (Brady and Schwartz, 1995).[37]

Thus, it seems fair to conclude that a representative's personal ideology does affect how she votes on at least some issues. At doubt is the number and significance of these issues. Because ideology must inevitably be measured as a residual to an equation like (20.10), like all residuals it is to some extent a measure of our ignorance and subject to question (Jackson and Kingdon, 1992). What we measure as the persistent ideological preference of a representative may simply be a persistently unaccounted for economic interest of his constituents or pressure from a lobbyist. Pending the assembly of a set of variables that can explain legislative voting without leaving a systematic component that can be related to an index of ideology, however,

---

[36] Corroboration is provided by Kau and Rubin (1993), Lott and Bronars (1993), and Wright (1993). Figlio (2000) observes, however, that it is only shirking in the last two years of senators' six-year terms that gets punished.

[37] Brady and Schwartz show that voting on abortion bills is much closer to constituent preferences when these are adjusted to allow for the primary system. Brady and Schwartz's adjustments reduce the explanatory power of a representative's personal ideology in explaining how she votes, but do not eliminate it entirely.

we must allow for the possibility that a representative's ideology also plays a role in determining how he votes.

20.4   Lobbying

Wright (1990) found in his detailed study on voting in the House Agricultural and Ways and Means Committees that interest group lobbying was more important in explaining how committee members vote than campaign contributions. Interest groups also appear to devote far more money to lobbying than they contribute to congressional campaigns. Thus, interest group lobbying is yet another factor that can affect how representatives vote.

Lobbying is essentially a one-way transmission of information from an interest group to members of the government. This information may pertain to the preferences of the interest group or to "states of the world." Although interest groups have no incentive to falsify information about their preferences – other than perhaps to exaggerate their intensity – they may under certain circumstances have an incentive to distort information in their possession regarding states of the world. Suppose, for example, that the speed limit in a state is 55 mph. This imposes a cost on the trucking industry of $200 million per year because of the extra time spent transporting goods. By lobbying the state's legislature to raise the speed limit, the trucking industry informs the legislature that the industry stands to gain from the speed limit change, and this may translate into votes and campaign funds. But the industry may go even further and provide the legislature with estimates of the cost savings for the industry and private motorists from a higher speed limit, and the likely increase in accidents and highway fatalities from a higher speed limit. Here, of course, the industry may have an incentive to distort the "facts" that it provides the legislature to make the increase in the speed limit more attractive to the legislators.

If, however, the industry *always* distorts the facts, the legislators have no incentive to give weight to the "information" provided by the industry. Since lobbying costs money, the industry has no incentive to lobby the legislature if it is going to be ignored. Thus, the industry has an incentive to provide the legislature with accurate information at least some of the time, so that the legislature will consider the information provided by the industry. Thus, when facts about the true state of the world are likely to change a legislature's policies in favor of a particular interest group, it sometimes has an incentive to provide truthful information through lobbying.[38]

If the industry expects that the legislature will raise the speed limit even without its lobbying, it will of course not lobby for a change, since lobbying costs money. And it will not lobby for a change if it prefers – say, for safety reasons – the lower speed limit. Thus, both the lobbying efforts of an industry and the absence of such efforts can provide accurate information to the legislature. When an industry does not lobby for a change in policy, the legislature can assume that it either will not benefit from a change, or that the information it has is such that it does not expect to effect a change in policy by lobbying.

---

[38] But only sometimes, because the costs of gathering and supplying the information may be too large relative to their effect on the probability of a change in policy.

Potters and van Winden (1992) and Potters (1992) have modeled the decision of a single interest group to lobby, and Austen-Smith and Wright (1992) have modeled lobbying by two interest groups with opposing interests. Counter perhaps to one's priors, interest groups often have the incentive to provide true information through their lobbying efforts and lobbying by groups with conflicting interests tends to improve the quality of information provided to the legislature. Austen-Smith and Wright (1994) have found support for their model in data on lobbying and the Senate's voting on Robert Bork's nomination to the U.S. Supreme Court.

20.5 The welfare effects of interest group activities

Total spending on congressional campaigns over the 1999/2000 electoral cycle amounted to over $1 billion, up from the $740 million spent over the 1997/8 cycle. Add to these funds the more than $500 million spent in the presidential primaries leading up to the 2000 election and by the three final candidates, and one has more than $1.5 billion being spent in the two years prior to a presidential election by candidates for this office and seats in Congress.[39] If Wright's (1990, p. 420) speculation that lobbying expenditures add up to 10 times the amount spent by congressional candidates is anywhere near correct, then some $5 billion is being spent each year to affect the probabilities that congressmen are reelected, and the way they vote in office, with another half billion being spent by presidential candidates in election years. To this one could add the money spent in gubernatorial and state legislature elections, in elections for city mayors and councils, county councils, sheriffs, school boards, and so on. Lobbying takes place here, too, so that the annual outlays in the United States to decide who will occupy public office and how they behave could easily amount to as much as $10 billion. Does this money buy better democratic government or worse? Do the campaign contributions and lobbying efforts of business, trade, and professional associations, of labor unions, and of all of the other groups with special economic or ideological interests lead to better political outcomes, and if so, in what sense are they better?

One way to define better and best is in terms of a social welfare function (SWF). Our question now becomes whether the activities of interest groups move us closer to the maximum value for this function. To begin to answer this question, let us return to the simple case in which each individual i has a concave utility function, $U_i(x)$, defined over a single-dimensional issue x. Let x_i be the value of x at which $U_i(x)$ obtains its maximum – i's ideal point. If then our SWF is a weighted Benthamite function

$$W = \alpha_1 U_1 + \alpha_2 U_2 + \cdots + \alpha_i U_i + \cdots + \alpha_n U_n, \tag{20.13}$$

the optimal $x - x_{SWO}$ – will satisfy the following first-order condition:

$$\alpha_1 U_1' + \alpha_2 U_2' + \cdots + \alpha_n U_n' = 0 \tag{20.14}$$

where α_i is the positive weight placed on the utility of voter i in the SWF.

---

[39] Figures are taken from the Federal Elections Committee's Web site.

Now the first thing to note is that there is no reason to expect x_{SWO} to coincide with x_m, the ideal point of the median voter, and the outcome that we would expect if two candidates compete for votes without campaign contributions. Equation (20.14) implies that the socially optimal x will be pulled away from x_m in the direction of voters with either high α_is or high marginal utilities from changes in the quantity of x. If we assume that those groups who will experience the most utility gain from a change in x away from x_m contribute the most to candidate campaigns and devote the most resources to lobbying, then campaign spending and lobbying can be justified on normative grounds, since it moves the social choice toward the social welfare optimum.

Once we take into account Olsonian differences in the abilities of groups to organize, and differences in their commands over resources, the consequences from campaign spending and lobbying become less sanguine. The social choice of x is shifted toward the most preferred quantity of x of the best organized and financed interest groups. Campaign spending and lobbying have the same effect on the outcome of the political process as would arise if the utilities of the well-organized and well-healed groups are given heigher weights in the Benthamite SWF that is implicitly maximized.

If our definition of the best social outcome merely requires it to satisfy the Pareto-optimality condition, then interest group activities will have *no* normative significance, since both the median voter's optimal x and any other choice that might arise as a result of interest group activities satisfy the Pareto condition in our simple, single-dimensional world. Indeed, *all* choices of x within the range of voter ideal points are Pareto optimal. Analogous conclusions can be drawn for a multidimensional issue space if we assume that political competition leads to the sorts of equilibria expected from the probabilistic voting models.[40]

Campaign spending and lobbying do more than just affect the choice of x; they use up resources in the process. Indeed, in this respect these activities are just another form of rent seeking. In the pure rent-seeking model, competition among interest groups is over a rent rectangle generated by some monopoly power (see Chapter 15). This rent represents the foregone utility of one group – the consumers – which is transferred to another group – the owners of the monopoly. When interest group campaign contributions and lobbying alter political outcomes, that is, they change x, they also effectively transfer utility from one group to another and the resources used to bring about the transfer are potentially wasted.

To see what is involved, consider Matrix 20.1. To simplify the discussion, assume that each candidate has only two options – to raise campaign funds and spend them all or to raise and spend nothing. If both spend nothing, the incumbent's share of the vote is 65 percent. If the incumbent were to continue to spend nothing while the challenger raised and spent funds, the challenger could raise his chances of winning to 50/50. If both spend, however, the challenger's odds fall back to 35/65. The matrix

---

[40] A more attractive role for lobbying groups can be defined, if we assume that candidates are ignorant of some possible dimensions of the issue space. Pareto-preferred outcomes might then arise from interest group lobbying if this lobbying informs those in government about new public goods that when provided make all citizens better off.

Matrix 20.1. *Outcomes from an election with and without campaign spending*

		Challenger			
		Spends all funds		Spends nothing	
Incumbent	Spends all funds	65	35	75	25
	Spends nothing	50	50	65	35

has the configuration of a prisoners' dilemma with the familiar implication that the two candidates select the dominant strategy and raise and spend campaign funds even though they have no net effect on the election outcome. The spend/spend equilibrium is dominated by the outcome when both spend nothing because of the assumption, in this example, that the spending does not alter the probabilities of the two candidates' victories, and thus all of the money spent has gone for naught.

Of course, it is likely that the spending of both candidates will change the probabilities of victory – *slightly*. The conclusion that society would be better off if both candidates spent nothing is, however, not likely to be overturned if the two entries in the spend/spend box are, say, 62 and 38. With reelection rates running as high as 97 percent or more in the House of Representatives, and over 90 percent in the Senate, there is not much scope for a dramatic *decline* in the success rate of challengers from lower expenditures.[41]

Much the same conclusion follows if we think of the effects of campaign spending being to change policy outcomes rather than to change the identities of representatives. If interest groups are located on both sides of the median voter's ideal point, then their efforts to change x must partly offset one another. Much money may go to candidates and be spent at election time with a very small net movement in x as a consequence, just as much of Coca-Cola's and Pepsi-Cola's advertising cancels itself out leaving the market shares of the two firms largely unchanged. But the tendency for wasteful overspending in the political marketplace is even greater than in private goods' markets. When Coca-Cola and Pepsi-Cola advertise they spend money that could have been paid out to their shareholders in higher dividends or to the managers in higher salaries. There is an opportunity cost to these funds. But when candidates spend money that interest groups have given them, they spend money that has no other use. They spend other people's money and the incentive is certainly to spend it all until the point of *negative* marginal returns is reached.[42]

Beyond their effects on the identities of winning candidates and policy outcomes, lobbying and campaign spending may have additional social value by "educating" voters. The issue of campaign spending is more complicated than is suggested by Matrix 20.1. On the other hand, the activities of interest groups do have a rent-seeking character, and political advertising, like the advertising of private goods,

---

[41] See Levitt's (1994) discussion of the potential social gains from limits on campaign spending.
[42] I abstract here, of course, from the costs candidates incur in raising campaign funds.

has much the same characteristics as a prisoners' dilemma game. Twice as much was spent on congressional campaigns over the 1997/8 electoral cycle than was spent over the 1981/2 cycle. Six times as much was spent in 1988 as in 1976. Although data from before the 1970s are not available, it seems reasonable to expect that at least 10 times as much money was spent on the presidential and congressional races in the year 2000 as was spent in the year that John F. Kennedy was elected. As one contemplates this growth in spending on political campaigns over the last 40 years, one cannot help but wonder whether the quality of the democratic process in the United States, and the outcomes that it produces, have improved proportionally.

Bibliographical notes

Hinich and Munger (1994) both justify the importance of ideology and integrate it into a formal spatial model of political competition.

The literature on interest groups and campaign contributions has been surveyed by Morton and Cameron (1992), Potters and Sloof (1996), Austin-Smith (1997), and van Winden (1999). Bender and Lott (1996) provide a critical review of the literature on ideological shirking. Grossman and Helpman (2001) present a comprehensive theoretical treatment on interest group activities.

Although most of the literature on interest groups focuses upon their behavior as contributors to political parties and recipients of messages and legislation from them, Lohmann (1993) explores how protest groups can affect political outcomes by *signaling* the nature and intensity of their positions on issues.

CHAPTER 21

The size of government

Politicians are the same all over. They promise to build a bridge even where there is no river.

Nikita Khruschev

Much attention in both lay and academic discourse has been given to the question of the proper size of government and the reasons for its growth. Public choice, the economic analysis of political institutions, would seem to be the natural tool for answering these questions, and it has frequently been employed in this task. A review of these efforts follows.

21.1 The facts

That government has grown, and grown dramatically in recent years, cannot be questioned. Total government expenditure in the United States in 1999 as a percentage of GNP was 28.3 percent, up from 23 percent in 1949 and 10 percent in 1929 (see Table 21.1). Moreover, this growth is confined neither to this century nor to the United States. Federal government expenditures as a percentage of national income in the United States were only 1.4 percent of national income in 1799. They rose to double that figure by the end of the nineteenth century, but were still only 3 percent of the GNP in 1929. Starting in the 1930s, however, federal expenditures took off, rising sevenfold as a percentage of the GNP over the next 70 years.

The government sector has also grown outside of the United States with this growth beginning at least as far back as the nineteenth century. Table 21.2 presents figures from Tanzi and Schuknecht (2000) for 16 countries in addition to the United States. As can be readily seen, the size of the public sector increased substantially in several countries like Austria, France, and Germany, between roughly 1870 and the start of World War I. Between the beginning and the end of this war there was a further overall expansion of the public sector, largely reflecting military outlays. But government sectors *did not* fall back to their pre-war levels. In 1937, the size of the government sector was larger than in 1913 for 13 of the countries for which a comparison is possible.[1]

---

[1] In one of the seminal contributions to the growth-of-government literature, Peacock and Wiseman (1961) hypothesized the existence of a ratchet effect of wars. Once the government sector expands due to a war, it does not fall back to its original level. Despite the support for this hypothesis apparent in Table 21.2, it has not stood up to more rigorous econometric testing (Henrekson, 1990).

Table 21.1. *Government expenditure in relation to national income and GDP in the United States, 1799–1999*

Year	(1) Total federal expenditures in millions of dollars	(2) Total federal expenditures as percentage of national income	(3) Total federal expenditures as percentage of GDP	(4) Federal, state, and local expenditures	(5) Federal, state, and local expenditures as percentage of GDP	(6) Federal, state, and local consumption expenditures in billions of dollars	(7) Government transfer payments in billion dollars	(8) Total government consumption plus transfers in billions of dollars (6) + (7)	(9) Total government consumption plus transfers as percentage of GDP
1799	10	1.4							
1809	10	1.1							
1819	21	2.4							
1829	15	1.6							
1839	27	1.6							
1849	42	1.7							
1859	66	1.5							
1869	316	4.6	5.0						
1879	267	3.7	3.2						
1889	309	2.9	2.6						
1899	563		3.4						
1909	694		2.3						
1919	12.402		16.7						
1929	3.100		3.0	10.3	10.0				
1939	8.800		11.7	17.6	19.4				
1949	38.800		16.2	59.3	23.0				
1959	92.100			131.0	26.8	112.5	24.7	137.2	27.0
1969	183.600			286.8	30.4	224.6	60.6	285.2	28.9
1979	503.500			750.8	31.1	503.5	230.2	733.7	28.6
1989						1100.2	529.6	1629.8	29.7
1999						1634.4	998.1	2632.5	28.3

Sources: Figures for columns 2 and 3 are from Kendrick (1955, pp. 10–12). Figures for columns 4–9 are from United States, *Economic Report of the President*, 1985, 1989, Tables B-1, B-72, and B-79, and 2001 Tables B1 and B83.

Table 21.2. *Growth of general government expenditure, 1870–1996 (percent of GDP)*

| | About 1870 | Pre– World War I | | Pre– Post– World War II | | | | |
		1913	1920	1937	1960	1980	1990	1996
General government for all years								
Australia	18.3	16.5	19.3	14.8	21.2	34.1	34.9	35.9
Austria	10.5	17.0	14.7	20.6	35.7	48.1	38.6	51.6
Canada	–	–	16.7	25.0	28.6	38.8	46.0	44.7
France	12.6	17.0	27.6	29.0	34.6	46.1	49.8	55.0
Germany	10.0	14.8	25.0	34.1	32.4	47.9	45.1	49.1
Italy	13.7	17.1	30.1	31.1	30.1	42.1	53.4	52.7
Ireland	–	–	18.8	25.5	28.0	48.9	41.2	42.0
Japan	8.8	8.3	14.8	25.4	17.5	32.0	31.3	35.9
New Zealand	–	–	24.6	25.3	26.9	38.1	41.3	34.7
Norway	5.9	9.3	16.0	11.8	29.9	43.8	54.9	49.2
Sweden	5.7	10.4	10.9	16.5	31.0	60.1	59.1	64.2
Switzerland	16.5	14.0	17.0	24.1	17.2	32.8	33.5	39.4
United Kingdom	9.4	12.7	26.2	30.0	32.2	43.0	39.9	43.0
United States	7.3	7.5	12.1	19.7	27.0	31.4	32.8	32.4
Average	10.8	13.1	19.6	23.8	28.0	41.9	43.0	45.0
Central government for 1870–1937, general government thereafter								
Belgium	–	13.8	22.1	21.8	30.3	57.8	54.3	52.9
Netherlands	9.1	9.0	13.5	19.0	33.7	55.8	54.1	49.3
Spain	–	11.0	8.3	13.2	18.8	32.2	42.0	43.7
Average	9.1	11.3	14.6	18.0	27.6	48.6	50.1	48.6
Total average	**10.7**	**12.7**	**18.7**	**22.8**	**27.9**	**43.1**	**44.8**	**45.6**

Source: Tanzi and Schuknecht (2000, Table 1.1).

The big acceleration in the growth of the public sector began, however, around 1960. Where its average size grew by 22 percent over the roughly 20 years between 1937 and 1960, this average grew by 54 percent over the next 20 years. *None* of the 17 countries in Table 21.2 had a smaller government sector in 1980 than in 1960. Moreover, in several cases the growth was quite spectacular. In Belgium, Japan, Sweden, and Switzerland, the government sector was nearly twice as large in 1980 as in 1960.

After 1980 this spectacular growth came to a halt. The average size of the public sector in the 17 countries was only 6 percent larger in 1996 as in 1980, and in two of them it was actually smaller in 1996 than in 1980 (Belgium and the Netherlands).

It is also worth noting that the figures in Table 21.2 tend to *understate* the fiscal impact of government in each country by failing to report their *tax expenditures*. By tax expenditures we mean transfers to different groups that take the form tax deductions or credits rather than budgetary transfers. To see what is involved, consider the following simple example. Let countries *A* and *B* each have a gross national income of 100. Each imposes a tax on income of 50 percent. This tax raises 50 in tax revenue in A, which the government allocates as follows:

Country A	Official	Full
Government consumption	20	20
Transfers to pensioners	20	20
Transfers to children	10	10
Spending	50	50
Tax revenue	50	50

The government's consumption expenditures include defense, education, and the like, and make up 40 percent of both the tax revenue and the spending of the government. Another 40 percent takes the form of cash transfers to people on pensions, and the remaining 20 percent is cash transfers to people with children below a certain age. Total tax revenue equals 50 and this equals total government spending defined to include both government consumption and cash transfers.

Now consider country B. It also levies a 50 percent tax on all incomes, but it allows those with children to make deductions before paying their taxes that amount to 10. Its governmental consumption and transfers to pensioners are exactly the same as in country A. B's allocations are as follows:

Country B	Official	Full
Government consumption	20	20
Transfers to pensioners	20	20
Transfers to children		10
Spending	40	50
Tax revenue	40	50

Because B chooses to subsidize those with children by granting their families tax breaks rather than by first collecting the funds in taxes and transferring the money back to these families, as it does with the pensioners, the amount of tax revenue officially raised and spent in B appears to be less than in A. But clearly, the fiscal impact of the state is identical in both countries. In both A and B, the state has command over 50 percent of national income, and in both it allocates these funds identically among government consumption, and transfers to children and pensioners. The fact that in the one case the allocation is in the form of transfers of collected tax revenues, while in the other it is in the form of uncollected taxes, is immaterial as far as the determination of who gets what. The size of the public sector in both countries should be judged to be the same, and the most appropriate figure is obvioulsy 50 percent.

To calculate the full scale of the government sector, one must add to the expenditures and transfers that governments actually make, the implicit expenditures

Table 21.3. *Official and full tax, transfer, and expenditures as a percentage of GNP for 22 OECD countries, 1992*

Country	T^0	T	T_{MAX}	Year[a]	R^0	R	R_{MAX}	Year[a]	S^0	S	S_{MAX}	Year[a]
Australia	24	46	51	(1985)	30	52	58	(1985)	36	58	64	(1985)
Austria	41	59	61	(1983)	44	61	63	(1984)	50	68	71	(1986)
Belgium	34	63	73	(1984)	46	74	78	(1985)	54	82	92	(1984)
Canada	32	53	54	(1982)	38	60	61	(1991)	45	67	71	(1991)
Denmark	44	63	71	(1982)	51	71	77	(1986)	55	74	82	(1982)
Finland	60	70	70	(1992)	49	59	66	(1988)	66	76	76	(1992)
France	39	56	58	(1986)	44	61	63	(1986)	49	66	68	(1986)
Germany	40	54	56	(1982)	43	57	60	(1985)	48	62	64	(1982)
Ireland	33	52	71	(1983)	41	61	67	(1985)	45	65	86	(1985)
Italy	36	54	58	(1987)	43	62	62	(1992)	55	73	73	(1992)
Japan	26	40	43	(1986)	29	43	45	(1986)	31	45	50	(1986)
Luxembourg	45	69	69	(1992)	36	59	59	(1984)	47	71	71	(1992)
Netherlands	42	51	67	(1983)	47	56	65	(1983)	53	62	79	(1983)
New Zealand	36	41	60	(1975)	37	43	55	(1976)	44	49	67	(1975)
Norway	43	53	68	(1988)	48	58	72	(1986)	48	58	75	(1979)
Portugal	27	35	47	(1985)	38	47	51	(1988)	41	50	64	(1985)
Spain	32	47	50	(1990)	36	51	53	(1989)	42	56	58	(1990)
Sweden	42	49	75	(1980)	52	59	74	(1976)	56	63	84	(1982)
Switzerland	28	42	44	(1984)	31	45	48	(1986)	32	46	48	(1984)
Turkey	23	46	50	(1985)	23	46	47	(1985)	30	53	55	(1985)
United Kingdom	28	40	55	(1975)	35	47	56	(1975)	40	52	67	(1975)
United States	19	28	37	(1978)	29	38	47	(1978)	34	42	49	(1978)

Notes: T^0, R^0, S^0 = Official Transfers, Tax Revenue, and Spending; T, R, S = Full Transfers, Tax Revenue, and Spending; T_{MAX}, R_{MAX}, S_{MAX} = Maximum Full Transfers, Tax Revenue, and Spending.
[a] Year in which maximum occurred.
Source: Hansson and Stuart (forthcoming, Tables 1 and 3).

that they make via tax reductions. Table 21.3 presents a set of estimates of this type made by Hansson and Stuart (forthcoming) for 1992. Table 21.3 presents both the official transfers (T^0), tax revenue (R^0), and spending (S^0) for each country, and the comparable *full* levels of transfers, T, revenue, R, and spending, S. The table also lists the peak value for each full figure and the year in which it occurred. As can easily be seen, the official budgetary figures understate the fiscal impact of governments to a considerable degree. Although transfers appear to constitute only 19 percent of the GNP in the United States in 1992 when one looks at the money passed through the government, transfers accounted for 28 percent of the GNP when one adds in the money allocated by the government to different groups through tax breaks, and total spending rises to some 42 percent of the GNP. More or less, the rankings remain the same, with Japan, Switzerland, and the United States having the three smallest government sectors. Only they and New Zealand had full government spending figures in 1992 that accounted for less than 50 percent of the GNP. Australia and Turkey, which seem to have relatively small government sectors when one looks at the official figures, wind up with government spending of more than 50 percent of the GNP once their tax expenditures are added.

The upper echelons of government activity remain about the same except that Belgium and Luxembourg now join the high-spending elite. Sweden, on the other hand, drops into tenth place with full government spending amounting to *only* 63 percent of the GNP in 1992, barely three-fourths of the 82 percent of GNP that Belgium's full government spending accounted for in that year. Belgium also takes the prize for the largest amount of full government spending between 1972 and 1992 – 92 percent in 1984.

The full-impact figures in Table 21.3 reveal a decline in outlays and transfers from an earlier peak for several countries other than Belgium. These figures, along with those in Tables 21.1 and 21.2, suggest the following four questions: What caused the increase in the relative size of government over the past two centuries? What caused the growth of government to accelerate after World War II? What has caused the size of government, as measured by its full fiscal impact, to stop growing and in some cases to decline in the last few years? What explains the large disparities in the sizes of the government sectors across the developing countries? This chapter examines some of the answers that have been given to these questions.

21.2   Explanations for the size and growth of government

The same explanations that have been given for why government exists should, logically, explain why it attains a given size in one country and not in another, or why it starts to grow at a more rapid rate at a particular time. Thus, in reviewing the hypothesized causes for the size and growth of government, one is essentially reviewing the explanations for the existence of government. If each explanation is represented as a variable or a variable set, then differences in size and rates of growth must be explained by differences in these variables.

21.2.1   *The government as provider of public goods and eliminator of externalities*

The traditional explanation for why governments exist is to provide public goods and eliminate or alleviate externalities. Let us assume that this is the only function governments perform. Each citizen can then be posited to have a demand for the public goods, which is a function of the individual's income, the relative price of public to private goods, and perhaps other taste variables. If it is assumed that voting takes place using majority rule, that citizens vote directly on the government expenditure issue, and that the only issue to be decided is the level of government expenditures, then one can apply the median voter theorem and write government expenditures as a function of the characteristics of the median voter.[2] Letting X be a composite of private goods and G the composite of public goods (with P_x

---

[2] See Barr and Davis (1966), Davis and Haines (1966), Borcherding and Deacon (1972), Bergstrom and Goodman (1973), and Deacon (1977a,b).

and P_g being their respective prices), Y_m the income of the median voter, and Z a vector of taste parameters, then one can write a government expenditure equation in logarithms for the median voter:

$$\ln G = a + \alpha \ln P_g + \beta \ln Y_m + \gamma \ln Z + \mu. \tag{21.1}$$

An explanation for the relative growth of government can be obtained from (21.1) if any of the following conditions are met:

- The demand for public goods is inelastic ($-1 < \alpha < 0$), and P_g has risen relative to P_x.
- The demand for public goods is elastic ($-1 > \alpha$), and P_g has fallen relative to P_x.
- Because Y_m has been increasing over time, if changes in Y_m are to explain growing G relative to X, β must be greater than unity.
- Some taste variable could change in the appropriate way, given the sign of γ.[3]

21.2.1.1 *"Taste variables"*. Let us start with the last possibility. In Chapter 3 we described how government redistribution policies can be a form of insurance that benefits all citizens and thus has the property of a public good ex ante, even though ex post these insurance programs constitute a form of redistribution. Rodrik (1998) has recently presented empirical support for this explanation for the growth of government. Rodrik focuses upon the risks to individual incomes that arise in open economies, whose export and import prices can vary dramatically producing large shifts in incomes and employment. Column 1 of Table 21.4 presents one of his regression results for a sample of 97 developed and developing countries. OPEN is a measure of the openness of the economy (exports + imports divided by GDP). TTRISK measures the terms of trade risk (the variance in export prices/import prices). The dependent variable is government consumption (administrative expenditures, police, national defense, health, education, and so forth). Open economies with high terms of trade risk had significantly larger government consumption. Although OPEN and TTRISK had positive effects on government consumption when entered separately, both of their coefficients turn negative when the interaction term between them is added to the equation. It is the joint presence of a highly open economy and high terms of trade risk that leads to higher government consumption expenditures.

One might expect government programs to offset the risks of operating in an open economy to take the form of unemployment compensation and other "social insurance" programs. Rodrik (p. 1019) argues that many developing countries lack the administrative capacity to manage such programs, and thus simply expand employment in the more stable public sector to reduce employment risk. Columns 2 through 5 in Table 21.4 present evidence consistent with this interpretation. The interaction term, OPEN·TTRISK, is positively and significantly related to social security and welfare

---

[3] For discussion of these possibilities relative to the growth of government issue, see Borcherding (1977a, 1985), Buchanan (1977), and Bennett and Johnson (1980b, pp. 59–67).

Table 21.4. *Trade risk and government size*

Dependent variable as a percentage of GDP	Developed + developing countries Government consumption 1990–2	Sample OECD countries		Developed + developing countries	
		Social security + welfare 1985	Government consumption 1985	Social security + welfare 1985	Government consumption 1985
Independent variable	(1)	(2)	(3)	(4)	(5)
OPEN	−0.003	−0.170*	−0.005	−0.018	−0.002
	(0.002)	(0.043)	(0.010)	(0.013)	(0.003)
TTRISK	−3.053*	−134.09*	−9.371***	−16.484*	−2.953**
	(1.087)	(22.15)	(5.198)	(5.665)	(1.391)
OPEN·TTRIKS	0.053*	1.869*	0.069	0.183***	0.48**
	(0.017)	(0.431)	(0.101)	(0.096)	(0.023)
Observations	97	19	19	68	68
$\bar{R}^2$	0.438	0.75	0.35	0.48	0.50

Notes: Equations in columns 1, 4, and 5 omit other control variables. Independent variables for column 1 are averages over 1980–9, for columns 2–5 over 1975–84.
Standard errors in parentheses.
* Significant at the 99 percent level
** Significant at the 95 percent level
*** Significant at the 90 percent level.
Source: Rodrik (1998, Tables 4 and 6).

payments in a subsample of rich OECD countries; government consumption is *not* significantly related to this variable for these countries. In the somewhat reduced full sample, both social security/welfare expenditures and government consumption are positively and significantly related to the openness/terms-of-trade-risk interaction term.

Rodrik's empirical results are impressive.[4] I doubt, however, if many European economic historians would accept Rodrik's hypothesis as *the major* explanation for the growth of government in Europe. The redistributive/insurance programs that one associates with the welfare state have their origins in the "class struggles" of nineteenth century Europe, and seem better explained as an effort to "insure" workers against the risks of unemployment and poverty in an industrial society. Similarly, the major welfare programs in the United States were introduced during the Great Depression in response to the collapse of the domestic economy (which albeit was worsened by the simultaneous collapse in world trade). An interpretation of Rodrik's findings that would be consistent with these events would be that *once*

---

[4] For related empirical work that is consistent with that of Rodrik, see Cameron (1978), Saunders and Klau (1985), and Rice (1986). Katsimi (1998) develops a model that assumes greater employment volatility in the private sector than in the public sector to explain voter preferences for a larger public sector, and offers time series evidence for Greece that fits this model.

the basic institutions of the welfare state were in place, greater exposure to the risks of foreign trade would lead to greater expansion of this sector.[5]

A second plausible candidate for a "taste" variable in the public goods demand equation is population density. The very definitions of public goods and externalities connote geographic proximity. The smoke from a factory harms more individuals in a densely populated community than in a population thinly dispersed around the factory. A park is easier to reach and probably of more utility in a densely populated community than in a rural area. Increasing urbanization has occurred throughout the last century in every developed country and has been taking place for well over a century in most. Urbanization or population density is an obvious choice for a Z variable with a predicted positive sign on its γ. It is surprising, therefore, to find so little empirical support for this hypothesis.[6] No other "taste" variable has garnered both compelling a priori and empirical support.

21.2.1.2 *Income.* For increases in income to explain increases in the relative size of government, the income elasticity of demand for government services must be greater than one. Although some estimates of β meet this criterion,[7] a greater number do not, and very few estimates of β are significantly greater than one.[8]

Existing studies all estimate β using data from state and local government jurisdictions.[9] Most redistribution takes place at the national level, however, and

---

[5] One might question why the employment risks of international trade (Rodrik), or the private sector more generally (Katsimi), lead workers to seek protection in the "political marketplace," with its high costs of collective action, rather than in the labor market, where each worker can act alone. If the employment risks of the private sector are large relative to the public sector, why do more workers not simply seek employment in the public sector? As the supply of workers to the public sector increases, public sector wages should fall relative to the private sector. Given that the demand for the services of the public sector appears to be price inelastic (see following discussion), this change in relative wages should, ceteris paribus, *reduce* the relative size of the public sector.

[6] See Borcherding (1977a, 1985), Deacon (1977b), and Holsey and Borcherding (1997), and for a critique of this literature, Oates (1988a). Most work in estimating equation (21.1) has been at the local governmental unit level, and many problems in public goods and externalities may be resolved at higher levels of governmental aggregation. But Mueller and Murrell (1985) did not find a positive relationship between government expenditures and urbanization across countries, and Rodrik (1998, Table 1, p. 1003) found a *negative* one.

[7] Deacon (1977b) has noted that in most studies park and recreation expenditures appear to be income-elastic.

[8] There is good reason to believe that existing estimates of the income elasticity of demand for G, based on state and local cross-sectional data, are biased downward. Most studies assume that the cost of providing government services is the same across communities. But a given level of safety may be provided more cheaply in a wealthy community than in a poor one. Thus the price of safety is lower in wealthy communities and, given that the price elasticity of this service is less than unity, wealthy communities will consume less, other things being equal. With the price of government services held constant across all communities, this wealth-price effect is shifted to the income elasticity, biasing it downward (Hamilton, 1983). Schwab and Zampelli (1987) observed a jump in β from near zero to unity when this income-price relationship was properly estimated. But in terms of accounting for the long-run growth of government, this adjustment merely shifts some of the explanation of government growth, using equation (21.1), from the price term to the income term. The Hamilton-Schwab-Zampelli critique implies that the growth of income should, other things being equal, bring down the cost of providing government services, thus partly offsetting the Baumol effect on price discussed in the next subsection. The total effect of changes in income on expenditures measured by Schwab and Zampelli was roughly zero.

[9] Mueller and Murrell (1986) estimated government size relative to GDP at the national level. Although always positive and often significant, the coefficients on income in their equations were too small to provide much of an explanation of the growth of government. Rodrik (1998) found a consistently negative and sometimes significant relationship between GDP per capita and government consumption as a percent of GDP.

redistribution has been one of the most rapidly growing components of federal expenditures. Estimates of β based on state and local government data may not be reasonable approximations of the income elasticity of redistribution expenditures at the national level. However, estimates of the income elasticity of charity contributions also tend to lie below unity, suggesting that this adjustment would not account for the growth of government (Clotfelter, 1985, ch. 2).

21.2.1.3 *The Baumol effect.* The remaining candidate for explaining government growth is the price elasticity of demand. Most estimates of α suggest that it is significantly greater than -1 and thus imply a relative growth in government if there has been a relative increase in its price. Baumol (1967a) has argued that we might expect a relative increase in the price of government-provided "goods," given that many of them (education, police protection) are services. Because productivity increases come largely from technological change, and this in turn is typically embodied in capital equipment, there is less potential for productivity advances in service sectors such as the government.

Although the argument has intuitive plausibility, it is not clear how far it can be pushed. The military services are quite capital-intensive today and spend vast sums on productivity-enhancing research and development. Similarly, computers, xerography, and other innovations have brought productivity increases in many white-collar jobs. Thus it is not apparent a priori that productivity increases in government could not keep pace with those in the private sector, at least with those in the private service sector. But it appears that they have not. A fair consensus exists among studies of government productivity that suggests that government productivity lags private sector productivity and may in fact be zero or negative.[10] As Buchanan (1977, pp. 8–9) has noted, lagging productivity in the government sector may be more symptomatic of why government growth is a "problem" than the cause of it.

Whatever the cause of the relative rise in the price of government-provided goods, this rise does appear to account for some of the growth of government. Estimates of significant "Baumol effects" have been obtained for the United States (Tussing and Henning, 1974; Berry and Lowery, 1984; and Ferris and West, 1996), Switzerland (Pommerehne and Schneider, 1982), Sweden (Henrekson, 1988), and Austria (Neck and Schneider, 1988). Lybeck (1986, ch. 5) finds support for the Baumol effect in his pooled, cross-sectional time-series analysis of 12 OECD countries, as well as in 9 of the 12 individual countries examined: Australia, Austria, Belgium, Canada, Federal Republic of Germany (weak), Italy, the Netherlands, Norway, and the United Kingdom. The effect was not found in France, Sweden, or the United States (my judgment, according to results for supply equations explaining government expenditures *excluding* transfers).

Although Ferris and West (1996) found evidence of the Baumol effect, it did not account for all of the increase in the costs of government services relative to private goods between 1959 and 1984 in the United States – only two-thirds. One-third of

---

[10] See in particular Fuchs (1968), Gollop and Jorgenson (1980), Ross and Burkhead (1974, ch. 6), and the discussion in Pommerehne and Schneider (1982, pp. 312–13).

the increase in the relative costs of government services was due to increases in wages in the public sector relative to the private sector. Here we have an example of the "dead hand of monopoly" working in the public sector. The monopoly or near-monopoly government has in the provision of some public services, like education and health care, to pass on cost increases to citizen/consumers and encourages monopoly/public sector unions to demand higher wages. Ferris and West (1996) cite evidence of larger increases in teacher salaries in unionized school districts than in nonunionized districts. Their work underscores the point made earlier: all of the relative increase in the cost of the public services cannot be assumed to be exogenously determined.

Assuming now that significant Baumol effects exist, the next question is how much of the growth of government can they explain? Some parts of the government budget (for example, pure transfers and interest payments) are difficult to think of as "goods" whose prices rise relative to private goods. The budget component for which Baumol's effect seems most appropriate is perhaps what the OECD characterizes as "final consumption" – that is, the goods and services actually absorbed by government. Final consumption expenditures for the OECD countries from 1960 through 1995 are presented in Table 21.5. All but one country – the United States – saw their government consumption expenditures rise as a percent of GDP over this period. Estimates of the relative increase in the cost of government services due to the Baumol effect cluster around 1.5 percent per year.[11] Over the 1960 to 1995 period, a 1.5 percent annual increase compounds to a 68.4 percent increase in the cost of government services relative to private goods. Assuming a price elasticity of demand for government services of -0.5,[12] the Baumol effect should have resulted in a 29.8 percent relative increase in final consumption expenditures. Twenty of the 25 countries in Table 21.5 experienced higher percentage increases in government consumption than this figure (see last column). Eight had an increase that was more than double this figure. Thus, the Baumol effect seems capable of explaining the full increase in final government consumption expenditures for only a handful of OECD countries, although it probably explains a part of the increase for all.[13]

21.2.2 *The government as redistributor of income and wealth*

The government giveth and it taketh away.

Several writers have criticized the view that government exists to provide public goods and alleviate externalities, arguing that this is essentially a normative description of government – a theory of what government ought to do – not a description of what it actually does. These writers argue that a positive theory of government must analyze the redistributive nature of its activity. Aranson and Ordeshook (1981)

---

[11] See Holsey and Borcherding (1997, p. 568) for discussion and references.

[12] This figure seems reasonable from the studies surveyed by Borcherding (1977a, p. 49; 1985, pp. 364–5).

[13] A large component of the fall in government consumption in the United States between 1960 and 1995 came in defense expenditures. In the context of equation (21.1) this fall must be interpreted as a shift in the government's demand schedule for defense due to a change of "tastes" brought about by the end of the cold war, rather than as a repudiation of the Baumol effect. In other components of U.S. government consumption – like education (Ferris and West, 1996) – the Baumol effect seems alive and well.

Table 21.5. *Government final consumption expenditure as a percentage of GDP, 1960–95*

Country	1960	1968	1974	1985	1990	1995	Percentage increase
United States	16.6	18.5	17.6	17.8	17.6	15.8	−4.8
Japan	8.0	7.4	9.1	9.6	9.0	9.8	22.5
Germany	13.7	15.9	19.8	20.5	19.4	19.5	42.3
France	14.2	14.8	15.4	19.4	18.0	19.3	35.9
Italy	12.3	13.9	14.0	16.7	17.6	16.3	32.5
United Kingdom	16.4	18.0	20.5	21.1	20.6	21.3	29.9
Canada	13.4	16.9	18.1	20.1	20.3	19.6	46.3
Average of above countries	14.9	16.2	16.4	17.1	16.6	16.0	
Australia	11.1	14.1	15.6	18.5	17.2	17.3	55.9
Austria	13.1	14.9	15.9	19.3	18.6	20.2	54.2
Belgium	12.4	13.6	14.7	17.0	14.1	14.8	19.4
Denmark	13.3	18.6	23.4	25.3	25.3	25.2	89.5
Finland	11.9	15.3	15.2	20.2	21.1	21.9	84.0
Greece	8.3	9.1	9.8	14.4	15.3	14.1	69.9
Iceland	10.4	12.9	15.9	17.5	19.2	20.8	100.0
Ireland	11.9	12.8	16.5	17.8	14.8	14.7	23.5
Luxembourg	8.3	10.2	9.7	13.3	13.4	13.1	57.8
Mexico	5.7	6.9	8.3	9.0	8.4	10.4	82.5
Netherlands	12.2	14.4	15.7	15.8	14.5	14.3	17.2
New Zealand	10.5	13.0	14.7	16.2	17.0	14.3	36.2
Norway	12.4	16.0	17.7	18.2	20.8	21.1	70.2
Portugal	9.7	12.1	13.0	14.3	15.7	18.1	86.6
Spain	8.4	9.1	9.9	14.7	15.6	16.6	97.6
Sweden	16.1	20.8	23.5	27.9	27.4	25.8	60.2
Switzerland	9.6	11.3	12.7	14.5	14.6	15.0	56.2
Turkey	7.6	9.0	10.2	8.9	11.0	10.8	42.1
Average of above countries	10.4	12.2	13.4	15.4	15.2	15.6	
Total EU 15	13.7	15.2	16.8	19.0	18.5	18.7	
Total OECD	14.2	15.5	15.8	16.8	16.3	15.9	

Source: OECD Economic Outlook: Historical Statistics, 1960–1995, p. 70.

pressed the point most forcefully, emphasizing that all government expenditures have a redistributive component. Roads must be built in this location or that. Construction contracts are given to one set of firms, to the loss of all others. As Aranson and Ordeshook view it, to understand what government is and why it grows, one must analyze its redistributive activities.

21.2.2.1 *The Meltzer and Richard model.* Meltzer and Richard (1978, 1981, 1983) have presented perhaps the simplest and yet most elegant public choice analysis of the growth of government. Their model presumes that all government activity consists of redistribution. This redistribution occurs by means of per capita lump-sum grants of r, financed from a proportional tax of t levied on all earned income. If $\bar{y}$ is mean per capita income, a balanced government budget implies

$$r = t\bar{y}. \tag{21.2}$$

An individual's utility depends on his consumption, c, and leisure, l. Letting n be the fraction of total time worked, we have the identities

$$l = 1 - n \tag{21.3}$$
$$c = (1 - t)y + r. \tag{21.4}$$

Meltzer and Richard assumed that income depends on an ability or productivity factor x, which is randomly distributed across the population. Given the hours one works, n, one's income is higher, the higher one's x factor:

$$y = nx. \tag{21.5}$$

Given t and r, an individual's only choice is how much to work, n. Maximizing $U(c, l)$ with respect to n, given (21.3)–(21.5), one gets, as a first-order condition,

$$U_c(1 - t)x = U_l \tag{21.6}$$

or

$$\frac{U_l}{U_c} = (1 - t)x. \tag{21.7}$$

The marginal rate of substitution between leisure and consumption is equated to the net-of-tax marginal product of an individual's time. From (21.7) one can obtain the number of hours an individual works. For the specific case of a Stone-Geary utility function, $U = \ln(c + \gamma) + a \ln(l + \lambda)$, one obtains for optimal n

$$n = \frac{(1 - t)(1 + \lambda)x - a(r + \gamma)}{(1 - t)(1 + a)x}. \tag{21.8}$$

The denominator of (21.8) must be postive, but with small enough x the numerator can be negative. Obviously n cannot be negative; thus there is a critical level of ability, x_o, at which optimal $n = 0$; we can derive from (21.8) that

$$x_o = \frac{a(r + \gamma)}{(1 - t)(1 + \lambda)}. \tag{21.9}$$

Although r and t are exogenous from the point of view of the individual, they are endogenous to the political system. Substituting (21.8) back into the individual's utility function demonstrates that the individual's utility ultimately depends on r and t. When choosing r and t, the rational voter considers this and takes into account the relationship between r and t given by (21.2). Now $\partial \bar{y}/\partial t < 0$. Mean income falls as the tax rate rises because of the negative incentive effects of higher taxes on effort.[14] Thus r is a function of t, rising at a diminishing rate until $-d\bar{y}/dt = \bar{y}/t$ and then falling (see Figure 21.1). Voters who work have positively sloped indifference curves such as U^1 and U^2 ($U^2 > U^1$), since higher taxes lower utility and

---

[14] Note that as t rises more individuals choose not to work:

$$\partial x_o/\partial t = a(r + \gamma)/(1 + \lambda)(1 - t)^2 > 0.$$

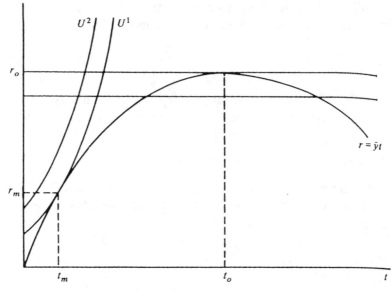

Figure 21.1. The optimal choice of t.

increased subsidies raise it. Voters who do not work do not have their utilities affected by changes in t. Their indifference curves are horizontal straight lines such as U^3 and U^4, with $U^4 > U^3$. Each rational voter recognizes that $r = \bar{y}t$ constitutes the opportunity set in choosing t (or r). Each voter chooses the $t - r$ combination along the $r = \bar{y}t$ curve that maximizes her utility. Voters who do not work all choose the t_0 that maximizes the lump-sum transfer. The voter with $x > x_0$ favors a lower t than t_0. If all voters have the same utility function and differ only in their ability factors, x, voters with higher x have steeper utility functions and favor a lower t. The voters are in essence confronted with a one-dimensional choice, with t uniquely defining r. A variant on the median voter theorem, first proved by Roberts (1977), can be used to establish the existence of an equilibrium under majority rule. If U^1 and U^2 are indifference curves for the median voter, then $t_m - r_m$ is the optimal tax-subsidy combination.

21.2.2.2 *Additional redistribution–growth-of-government hypotheses.* Three additional hypotheses linking government size to redistribution must be mentioned. Most closely related to Meltzer and Richard's hypothesis is that of Cusack (1997). Left-of-center governments are assumed to favor more redistribution and larger budgets than right-of-center governments. Pooled cross-section/time-series regressions for 15 (16) OECD countries for the period 1955–89 (1961–89) confirm this prediction. Of course this hypothesis cannot explain the secular *growth* in government without an auxillary hypothesis that parties' (voters') ideological positions have shifted leftward over time.

Instead of viewing redistribution as simply involuntary taking from the rich by the poor, Kristov, Lindert, and McClelland (1992) see redistribution as a function of the *social affinity* between different groups in the income distribution. Their hypothesis comes closer to the Pareto-optimal and insurance motives for redistribution. They also rely on the median voter model, and hypothesize that the middle class has a closer affinity to the upper class, the smaller is the gap between the upper and middle classes' incomes, and thus that the scale of government redistribution is positively related to this gap. Similarly, the middle class has a closer affinity to the poor, the smaller the gap is between the lowest and middle classes' incomes, and thus that the scale of government redistribution is negatively related to the size of this gap. They also argue that there will be less social affinity with the poor, and thus less income redistribution, the faster income is growing. Kristov, Lindert, and McClelland (1992) predict a relationship between the shape of the income distribution and the amount of redistribtion, but it is not the same relationship predicted by Meltzer and Richard.

Peltzman (1980) has presented yet another explanation for the growth of government that depends on the shape of the distribution of income. Peltzman's explanation, however, does not make use of the median voter theorem. A form of representative government is envisaged in which candidates compete for votes by promising to redistribute income toward groups of voters that agree to join the candidate's coalition of supporters. Peltzman reasoned that the more equal the distribution of income among the potential supporters of a candidate, the more bargaining strength they would have. Thus the candidate must promise a greater amount of redistribution, the more equal is the initial distribution of income among voters. Peltzman pointed to the spread of education as an important factor, increasing the equality of pretransfer incomes and thus leading to a growth in the size of government. Peltzman's hypothesis depends on increasing equality of income among potential coalition members to drive the growth of government, whereas Meltzer and Richard's rests on increasing inequality of the income distribution across enfranchised voters.

21.2.2.3 *Some logical/empirical difficulties with the redistribution–growth-of-government hypothesis.* Both the Meltzer-Richard and Peltzman papers discussed the role of government as if government were exclusively engaged in redistribution. Aranson and Ordeshook (1981), Brunner (1978), and Lindbeck (1985) also placed primary emphasis on government's redistributive activities. But if redistribution is the primary activity of government, then some additional logical arguments are missing to explain the growth in government to the sizes now observed in different countries. Alternatively, government activity is not exclusively redistributive.

Government has grown to far greater size than is necessary just to achieve redistribution. If one group or a coalition of groups can make use of the democratic machinery of government to achieve a greater share of the pie, then one would think that the group or coalition ought to be able to do so in such a way as not to use up such a large fraction of the pie in bringing about the redistribution. The number of programs and people making up government seems much larger than necessary just to achieve redistribution.

Meltzer and Richard, Peltzman, and to some extent Kristov, Lindert, and McClelland (1992) assume that all redistribution is from rich to poor.[15] But this

---

[15] Peltzman (1980) backs away from this assumption at the end of his paper, however (pp. 285–7).

characterization of government redistribution does not fit the facts. As we saw in Chapter 3, recipients of governmental transfers are located across the distribution of income, with the upper quintile in some countries receiving more transfers than the lowest quintile.[16] Indeed, if all government activity can be characterized as some form of redistribution, its most salient feature is probably the lack of a uni-directional flow (Aranson and Ordeshook, 1981; Brunner, 1978).

The multidimensional character of government redistribution makes it difficult to rationalize *all* government activity as *purely* redistributionally motivated. If all government programs simply take from one group and give to another, and if all citizens participate at both ends of the redistributional process, who gains from the process? Why do not citizens simply abolish the government and save the tremendous deadweight losses from zero-sum redistribution? Either there must be some clear gainers from the redistributional process, who are in a position to sustain and enlarge their gains, or all government activity is not purely redistributional in character. If the former possibility explains the growth of government, who are those gaining from government and how do they achieve their goals within the rules of a democratic process? If some significant proportion of government activity is not purely redistributional, but, say, is directed at providing public goods, then one again has a logical problem in explaining government growth as a result of redistributional struggles. Once it is admitted that a large component of government expenditure is to provide public goods, then all redistributional objectives can be achieved simply by changing the tax shares of individuals or groups of individuals.[17] One typically does not have to spend money on, or give money to, a group to give that group greater command over private goods.

An assumption of both the Meltzer-Richard and Peltzman models is that the beneficiaries of government growth support government growth. In the Meltzer-Richard model, all voters with incomes below the median favor increased government transfers. Yet, survey evidence indicates that obvious beneficiaries of government growth, such as public employees and welfare recipients, do not have significantly different preferences for tax limitation proposals from other voters (Courant, Gramlich, and Rubinfeld, 1981; Gramlich and Rubinfeld, 1982b).

21.2.2.4 *Direct empirical tests of the redistribution–government-size hypothesis.* One piece of evidence that Meltzer and Richard cite in support of their thesis is the increasing expansion of the voting franchise over the past two centuries. Justman and Gradstein (1999) have developed a model of voter participation and government redistribution policies that fits the Meltzer and Richard hypothesis

---

[16] Fratianni and Spinelli (1982) emphasize the increasing importance of special programs to help business in their discussion of the growth of government in Italy.

[17] See Mueller and Murrell (1985). Of course those groups that pay no taxes to finance the public goods portion of the budget can be subsidized further only by an expenditure or transfer program, but not enough groups such as this exist to account for current government activity in most countries. One might object that tax cuts cannot always be designed to benefit specific groups, but the number of tax loopholes and the complexity of tax-loophole legislation belie this point.

Hettich and Winer (1988, 1999) analyze the effect of political pressure to achieve redistribution on tax structure.

and also can account for Kuznets' (1955) famous inverted-U relationship between income inequality and the per capita income of a country. This inverted-U pattern fits the historical record of Great Britain quite well.[18] Justman and Gradstein argue that the income of the median voter was *above* the mean in Great Britain at the beginning of the nineteenth century, as only a sixth or so of the population was eligible to vote. Redistribution policy at that time was *regressive* and led to an increase in income inequality. The increase in average income that occurred throughout the nineteenth century resulted in a continual extension of the franchise to a larger fraction of the population until the median voter's income was *below* the mean, and governmental redistribution policies became progressive.

Husted and Kenny (1997), Abrams and Settle (1999), and Lott and Kenny (1998) also offer explanations for the growth of government that rely on changes in the franchise and voter participation that bring poorer-than-average citizens to the polls and thus increase the demand for government services. Husted and Kenny emphasize the impact of the elimination of the poll tax and literacy tests in the South, while Abrams and Settle and Lott and Kenny focus upon the extension of suffrage to women in Switzerland and the United States.

A logical difficulty with the Meltzer-Richard-Justman-Gradstein-Abrams-Settle-Lott-Kenny hypotheses is that by extending the franchise to larger and larger fractions of the population over the nineteenth and twentieth centuries, the median voter made himself worse and worse off.[19] Why, for example, did he (there were no she voters in Great Britain in the nineteenth century), as represented in Parliament, vote for the "watershed ... Second Reform Act of 1867 which enfranchised higher-skilled labor, in consequence of which the new median voting family earned less than the average family income, and had a vested interest in redistribution, [which] signalled the beginning of a dramatic shift in the redistributive bias of economic policy that culminated in the foundation of the modern welfare state after the turn of the century"? One possible answer is that the median voter of 1867 feared that the alternative to the slow erosion of his position within the democratic process was a dramatic reversal of his fortunes through more revolutionary channels. Similarly, the median *male* voter in each of the developed democratic countries over the course of the nineteenth and early twentieth centuries may have grown weary of seeing his wife and other female relatives protesting on the streets and complaining at home, and eventually opted for short-run peace of mind over long-run economic advantage and voted to give women the right to vote. Not all democratic history can be captured by a model that assumes that the preferences of a narrowly selfish median voter dictate political outcomes.

A more direct and rigorous test of the Meltzer-Richard hypothesis is to test its prediction of a positive relationship between the ratio of mean to median income

---

[18] It also fits that of a few other countries (see e.g., Lindert and Williamson, 1985), but in general subsequent research has not been kind to the "Kuznets' hypothesis" (see Anand and Kanbur, 1993; Deininger and Squire, 1996).

[19] This logical difficulty does not arise with the Husted-Kenney argument insofar as it hinges on the abolition of the poll tax and literacy tests in the southern United States, and these changes were forced upon the southern states by the federal courts.

Table 21.6. *A. Estimates of the Meltzer–Richard model using U.S. time series data, 1937–40, 1946–76*

	Independent variables		
Dependent variable	$\ln(\bar{y}/y_{m-1})$	$1/y_m$	R^2
$\ln t(1-F)$	0.57	−1,081	0.80
	9.1	5.0	
$\ln t_2(1-F)$	0.48	28.3	0.73
	9.2	0.16	
$\ln t_3(1-F)$	0.67	−3,461	0.79
	5.5	8.1	

B. Estimates of the Meltzer–Richard model using pooled state data, 1979–91

	Independent variables		
Dependent variable	$\ln(\bar{y}/y_{m-1})$	$1/y_m$	R^2
$\ln t(1-F)$	−0.05	9,879	0.93
	5.77	11.96	
$\ln t_2(1-F)$	−0.007	4,290	0.91
	0.52	3.43	
$\ln t_3(1-F)$	−0.076	12,175	0.92
	6.91	12.32	

Notes: $\bar{y}$-mean income; y_m-median income; F = dependency rate; t_2 = public provision of private goods; t_3 = income transfers; $t = t_2 + t_3$; t-statistics under coefficients.

Sources: Part A: Meltzer and Richard (1983, Table 1).
Part B: Gouveia and Masia (1998, Table 4).

$\bar{y}/y_m$ and government size. Meltzer and Richard (1983) test this hypothesis using time-series data for the United States from 1938 to 1976. The empirical realization of their model involves regressing various measures of government transfers as a percentage of GDP adjusted for the dependency ratio, F, the fraction of the population that does not pay taxes, onto $\bar{y}/y_m$ and $1/y_m$. This equation is a linear approximation to the complicated expression for transfers that one derives from their model. The three transfer measures are

t_2 = public provision of private goods

t_3 = pure transfers

$t = t_2 + t_3$.

The term containing $\bar{y}/y_m$ should have a coefficient of 1.0. Its coefficient is <1, but positive and significant for all three definitions of transfers, offering some support for the Meltzer-Richard hypothesis (see Table 21.6, Part A).

The ratio $\bar{y}/y_m$ is essentially a measure of the skewness of the income distribution. As Tullock (1983) pointed out, this ratio has been virtually constant since World War II, yet it "explains" a significant fraction of the growth of government. Meltzer and Richard's test essentially amounts to regressing one long-run trend variable on

and regulations that reduce competition has been established. *None* of these government interventions directly affects the size of government as we have been discussing it in this chapter – expenditures or taxes over GDP – however.[21] An ideal measure of government size would include its regulatory impact on the economy, but so far no one has constructed such a measure.

If we confine our attention to the size of government as measured by expenditures and taxes, we obtain contradictory predictions. Some interest groups favor higher government expenditures (automobile and truck drivers want larger highway expenditures), but others favor lower expenditures (environmental groups oppose highway construction). *Everyone* prefers to receive higher subsidies, but to pay lower taxes. Some interest groups are effective in obtaining each. Such efforts might simply shift tax burdens and subsidy benefits around without changing their overall magnitudes. The *net effect* of interest groups on the size of government cannot be determined a priori. It is an empirical question.

Casual observation suggests that pressure groups are successful in reducing their tax burdens. Until recently, oil production in Western Europe has been trivial relative to in the United States, and taxes on petroleum products in Western Europe have been dramatically higher. Tobacco-producing states have lower cigarette taxes than nonproducing states. Hunter and Nelson (1989) present evidence for Louisiana indicating that farmers and wealthy homeowners are able to lower their tax burdens.

Rice (1986) presented evidence suggesting that labor unions and other interest groups were able to induce governments to introduce programs to offset economic hardships, and that these programs helped to explain the growth of the government sectors in European countries between 1950 and 1980. Naert (1990) also found that from 1961 to 1984 Belgian labor unions were able to secure significant increases in certain budgetary items that benefitted their members, like social services and public health. Congleton and Bennet (1995), on the other hand, found that interest group influence on state highway expenditures was pretty much a wash. Truck drivers were able to exert a positive influence on these expenditures, but railroad workers were even more effective in bringing about reductions, as were members of the Sierra Club. Together interest group variables added little explanatory power to a standard, median voter model of highway expenditures.

Several studies have attempted to relate overall interest group strength to government size. North and Wallis (1982), for example, drew a parallel between the growth of government and the growth of white-collar and managerial employment in the private sector. Both were seen as a response to the greater transaction costs from organizing a market economy with increasing specialization (see also North, 1985): "Growing specialization also created a host of new interest groups" (North and Wallis, 1982, p. 340). The demands that these groups press on government are not simply for a redistributive handout, but are to alleviate the transaction costs these groups bear within an increasingly specialized society. Thus, the influence of interest groups on government activity is seen as having both an efficiency-enhancing dimension as well as a redistributive dimension. North and Wallis substantiated their

---

[21] Of course, an agricultural price support program may lead to a larger Department of Agriculture, but these indirect effects on government size are not likely to be substantive.

argument with data showing that nondefense, nontransfer expenditures of government have grown faster than total government has grown since World War II, and almost as fast as transfers.

The transaction costs explanation for the growth of government is the most general. Our analysis in Chapter 2 revealed that the existence of externalities and public goods was not sufficient to warrant the creation of the state. Rather, the state emerged as the lowest transaction costs institution for providing public goods and eliminating externalities. Logically, therefore, increasing governmental efforts to reduce transaction costs are the best explanation for the growth in the state. But the very generality of the transaction costs notion makes it difficult to pinpoint more accurately the particular transaction costs that have to be reduced, and the budget items that will grow to accomplish this task. For example, all industrialized countries can make use of income taxation, yet this efficient source of revenue collection leads to vastly different government sizes in Japan and Switzerland compared with Sweden and Holland. Do the transaction costs of organizing interest groups differ greatly across countries?

Mueller and Murrell (1985, 1986) presented empirical evidence that interest groups affect the size of government. They described a political process in which parties supply interest groups with favors in exchange for the interest groups' support. When these favors take the form of goods targeted to specific interest groups, but with some spillovers for other groups, government grows larger. The number of organized interest groups in a country was shown to have a positive and significant effect on the relative size of the government sector in a cross-sectional sample of OECD countries for the year 1970.

Lybeck (1986, pp. 88–96) found that the relative size of government in Sweden varied over time with the relative fraction of employees who were members of interest groups. McCormick and Tollison (1981, pp. 45–9) found that the extent of economic regulation within a state varied directly with the number of trade associations registered in the state.

To explain the *growth* of government over time using one of these hypotheses, one must of course argue that interest groups' bargaining strength has grown over time, governments have become less cohesive over time, or some combination of the two.

The aforementioned studies do not provide evidence of these secular changes. Olson (1982) did discuss the conditions favoring the growth of interest groups, however, and Murrell (1984) presented evidence consistent with Olson's hypotheses concerning the causes of interest group formation. The stable economic and political environment in Western developed countries since World War II facilitated the growth in interest groups, according to Olson's thesis, and this growth in turn may help to explain the relatively poor macroeconomic performance of many European countries in the last quarter of the twentieth century. If the number of effective interest groups in developed countries has grown since World War II, then their growth could also help to explain the relative growth of government.[22] Government

---

[22] Mueller and Murrell (1985, 1986) made allowance for interest groups and government size, both being endogenous variables.

growth and macroeconomic inefficiency would, in turn, be tied together. This interconnection is taken up in the next chapter.

21.2.4 *Bureaucracy and the growth of government*

Government programs do not come into existence merely because some interest group wants them and the legislature authorizes them. They must be "manufactured." More often than not, the supplier of a program is part of the government itself – a government bureau. Government may grow not only because increasing expenditures are demanded by citizens, interest groups, or legislators, but also because they are demanded by the bureaucracy supplying government programs. The government bureaucracies are an independent force, which possibly may lead to increasing government size.

In Chapter 16 we examined several hypotheses as to why bureaucrats might seek a larger budget and considered some evidence in a specific situation when the bureaucrats have the power to set the agenda where they do. Thus, the bureaucracy appears to be a plausible candidate as an independent source for the growth of government.

Nevertheless, some logical difficulties exist when applying the bureaucracy models to explain the size of government and its growth. The Niskanen (1971) model predicts a government budget as much as twice as large as that demanded by the bureau's sponsor. It is easy to see why a bureau would wish to charge a higher price for a given output. The extra revenue could be used to offer higher salaries, more leisure (because of a large staff), more perquisites (paid travel to conventions), and a whole host of amenities that might make a bureaucrat's life on and off the job more pleasant. But the power of the bureaucracy to obtain these benefits should not be exaggerated. Salary increases are very visible exercises of bureaucratic power; travel and other perquisites can often be easily monitored. A wise legislature should be capable of exercising some control over such budget items.

One way sometimes used to justify a larger salary is to expand the bureau's output, and then to demand higher salaries that allow for the expanded demands placed on the bureaucracy. Niskanen (1971, p. 38) postulated that a bureaucrat's "salary, perquisites of the office, public reputation, power [and] patronage" are all positively related to the size of the bureau. Niskanen uses this postulate to analyze the consequences of assuming that bureaucrats maximize the size of their budgets. Not surprisingly, the model implies larger budgets than are desired by the legislative demanders. Niskanen's analysis has become the theoretical underpinning for an important part of the literature on the growth of government.

The model of the budget-maximizing bureaucrat has a certain resonance with models of the corporation that assume that managers maximize the corporation's

Wallis and Oates (1988) indirectly test the hypothesis linking the size of government to the growth of interest groups. Following Olson (1982), they assume stronger interest groups in old states. Following Mueller and Murrell, they assume bigger government sectors in states with stronger interest groups. Yet they find the government sectors to be larger in *younger* states, thus contradicting one of the links in the causal chain. Gray and Lowery's (1986) results suggest that it is the relationship between age of state and number of interest groups that breaks down.

size, its growth in size, or other size-related variables such as white-collar staff (Baumol, 1959; Marris, 1964; Williamson, 1964). The behavioral underpinning and empirical support for these models can to some extent be cited in support of the postulate of the budget-maximizing bureaucrat. But one must not be too quick to generalize.

The manager of a company with $10 billion in sales may be able to justify to the board of directors and stockholders a larger salary than she could if the company had sales of $1 billion and company size and managerial compensation are positively correlated. But the head of a bureau with a budget of $10 billion does not necessarily get paid more than the head of a bureau with a budget of $1 billion. Salaries across government bureaucracies tend to be much more uniform than are salaries across companies. Moreover, the top officers in bureaus are typically political appointees who stay at the bureau for four years at most. Thus expanding the size of the bureau, even if size and salary were positively related, would not be likely to benefit directly the bureaucrat who brought about the increase. If the growth of bureaus benefits the top members of the bureaucracy, it must in general be from the nonpecuniary dimensions of a bureaucrat's rewards that accompany a bureau's growth.

Even at middle levels, salaries do not differ much across bureaus. Undersecretaries earn the same regardless of which department they are in. But the chances for promotion in a rapidly growing bureau are certainly greater than in a shrinking one. Thus, middle-level bureaucrats do have a financial incentive to encourage the rapid expansion of their bureaus because it increases the likelihood of their promotion to a higher rank. Career bureaucrats are also likely to be with the bureau long enough to benefit directly from the expansion, unlike their short-term superiors.

Although this analysis provides a rationale for the promotion of growth in size by middle-level career bureaucrats, it greatly complicates the story of why these individuals are allowed to fulfill their goals to the loss of society. If the bureaucrats at the top of the bureau do not benefit from the growth in bureau size, why do they not curtail its growth? Are middle-level bureaucrats able to deceive both the legislative overseers of the bureau and their superiors within the bureau about the true quantities of the bureau's output and its unit costs?[23]

Bureaucrats and interest groups stand equally high on all lists of the causes of the growth of government, and much case study evidence is consistent with these hypotheses. For example, Miller's (1981, ch. 3) study of city incorporations in Los Angeles County reveals both city and county bureaucrats to be driven by the goal of expanding the size and scope of their jurisdictions, and resisting attempts to contract them.

In much the same spirit Johnson and Libecap (1991) argue government workers have more to gain from voting, and that this explains why participation rates are higher for government employees than for citizens who are dependent on the private sector for their employment. They interpret higher turnouts by state and local employees relative to federal employee participation rates as further evidence

---

[23] For further critical discussion of the hypothesis linking the size of government to the bureaucracy, see Musgrave (1981, pp. 91–5).

consistent with this hypothesis, because the probability of government workers being decisive is greater in state and local elections than it is in federal elections, owing to the smaller sizes of the electorates at state and local levels. Johnson and Libecap were not able to show, however, that state and local government employees were able to convert their voting power to their personal advantage. Federal employees earn *higher* salaries than their compatriots at lower levels of government despite the latter's higher participation rates.

Several studies have tested the hypothesis that the *voting* power of bureaucrats in and of itself leads to larger government budgets. The bigger the government is, the larger the fraction of voters who work for it and, if they perceive their interests advanced by increasing government size, the more votes there are for this outcome. Borcherding, Bush, and Spann (1977) were perhaps the first to test this hypothesis, and presented supporting evidence for the United States; Lowery and Berry (1983) and Berry and Lowery (1984) use U.S. data to contradict the hypothesis, however. Ferris and West (1996) use U.S. time-series data from 1959–89 to support the hypothesis, but when they expand the data series to 1949–89, they are unable to uncover a significant relationship between number of public employees and government size (Ferris and West, 1999).

Evidence from other countries is equally contradictory. Henrekson (1988) finds that public employment is positively related to local levels of government consumption expenditures in Sweden, but not to transfers. This result seems plausible, since bureaucrats are presumably more interested in increasing the money spent within government than the money passing through it. But Renaud and van Winden (1987b) come up with entirely opposite results for Holland. Neck and Schneider (1988) are not able to sustain the hypothesis on Austrian data, nor are Frey and Pommerehne (1987) able to find any measurable effect of bureaucrats' voting power in Swiss municipalities.

Santerre (1993) was able to discern an influence of bureaucrats on political outcomes in his investigation of Connecticut municipalities. But here the impact of government employees on the democratic process did not appear to be simply through their raw numbers, but through their active participation in town meetings. The number of public school employees was significantly related to the size of school budgets where town-meeting direct democracy prevailed, but not where representative government existed. Through active participation in town meetings bureaucrats appeared able to influence how other citizens voted, and thereby the outcomes of the process.

The bureaucracy models of Niskanen (1971), Romer and Rosenthal (1978, 1979b, 1982), and others are static. They explain why government might be larger than the legislature would prefer if it knew the unit costs of the outputs it thought it was buying, and why the level of outputs might be larger than the median voter's most preferred quantity. They do not directly explain why government grows.

Indirectly, however, they perhaps do offer an explanation. The bureaucracy's ability to expand the budget beyond the amount the legislature or citizens demand depends in part on its ability to misrepresent the true prices and quantities of publicly provided goods. The ability to misrepresent is likely to depend in turn on the size and complexity of the budget itself. The bigger the bureaucracy, the more difficult it is for outsiders to monitor its activity, and the more insiders there are who are working to increase the size of the bureaucracy. Thus the growth of the bureaucracy is likely to depend on its absolute size.

To see this relationship, let us define G_t as the amount of publicly provided goods that the citizens or legislature truly demand. Let B_t be the total size of the budget. B_t is greater than G_t to the extent to which the bureaucracy is capable of forcing a greater flow of resources toward the bureaucracy than is demanded; that is,

$$B_t = \alpha_t G_t, \qquad \alpha_t \geq 1. \tag{21.10}$$

Now let

$$\alpha_t = e^{aB_t} \tag{21.11}$$

and let the amount of publicly provided goods demanded grow at a constant rate n equal to, say, the growth in national income:

$$G_t = ce^{nt}. \tag{21.12}$$

Then

$$B_t = ce^{aB_t} e^{nt}. \tag{21.13}$$

The growth in the budget, g, is then

$$g = \ln B_t - \ln B_{t-1} = a(B_t - B_{t-1}) + n. \tag{21.14}$$

The growth rate of the budget both exceeds the growth in national income, n, and increases with the absolute difference between this period's and last period's budget. Other functional forms for α_t will yield other relationships between g and B_t; as long as α_t increases with budget size, however, the growth in the size of the budget can be expected to increase with its absolute size.

The Niskanen-type models lead one naturally to think of bureaucrats exercising their power by expanding the *outputs* of their bureaus. Ferris and West (1996) show, however, that real government output in the United States has actually *fallen* since 1959. It is only the nominal size of the government that has expanded. Government bureaucrats have succeeded in increasing their salaries and budgets, while at the same time *reducing* their outputs. Direct evidence of this is found in the many studies that show that government bureaucracies have higher unit costs than private firms when they both supply comparable and measurable outputs, such as tons of garbage collected. Borcherding (1977, p. 62) describes this as "the Bureaucratic Rule of Two" – "removal of an activity from the private sector will double its unit costs of production."[24] If unit costs rise by this much when direct comparisons with private sector alternatives are possible, how much more are they inflated when the bureaucracy knows it cannot be subjected to a comparison with private market alternatives?

---

[24] For summaries of the evidence, see Orzechowski (1977); Borcherding, Pommerehne, and Schneider (1982); and Chapter 16.

Additional evidence of the bureaucracy's ability to use its power over its monitors to increase its salaries is provided by Ferris and West (1999). Using time-series data for the United States from 1949 to 1989 they first confirm the Kau and Rubin (1981, 1999) hypothesis that falling costs of collecting taxes over this time leads to increases in government size. They then relate increases in government employee salaries to these cost decreases. Members of the government bureacracy were able to convert possible reductions in taxes or expansions in government outputs into increases in their own incomes.

21.2.5 *Fiscal illusion*

The hypothesis that bureaucratic power increases the size of government presumes that the bureaucracy can deceive the legislature about the true costs of supplying different levels of output. The fiscal illusion hypothesis presumes that the legislature can deceive the citizens about the true size of government.

The fiscal illusion explanation for government size assumes that citizens measure the size of government by the size of their tax bill. To bring about an increase in government size, for which the citizens are not willing to pay voluntarily, the legislative-executive entities must increase the citizens' tax burden in such a way that the citizens are unaware that they are paying more in taxes, or be willing to pay the price of citizen displeasure at the next election. If tax burdens can be disguised in this way, citizens have the illusion that the burden of government is smaller than it actually is, and government can grow beyond the levels citizens prefer.

The fiscal illusion hypothesis follows logically from the assumption that voters are rationally ignorant (Congleton, 2001). A renter pays no property tax directly. If she is a rationally ignorant voter, she may not gather enough information about the government's finances even to know that property taxes exist. Even if she knows that property taxes exist, she may not devote sufficient time and effort to determine the extent to which a tax on the owner of the property that she rents gets passed on to her. She might then vote for increased school budgets – to be financed out of increased property taxes – not realizing that she will be paying more in taxes.

Although this argument is reasonable enough, to develop it into a model for explaining the size of government one must make some specific assumptions about the kinds of tax burdens that can be disguised. Mill (1861) felt that direct taxes were more visible and, by implication, that excessive government growth would have to rely on indirect taxes. But the citizens of Boston had no illusions about the burden of the British tax on tea two centuries ago, and one can argue that employer withholding of income taxes, like bank collection of property taxes with mortgage payments, makes these forms of direct taxation less visible than some types of indirect taxation, such as liquor and cigarette taxes. The issue of what sources of revenue are less visible to citizens, as well as the magnitude of any fiscal illusion caused, must be regarded as largely empirical.

In his comprehensive survey of the empirical literature on fiscal illusion Oates (1988b) identifies five categories of fiscal illusion: (1) a tax burden is more difficult to judge the more complex the tax structure; (2) renters are less able to judge their share of property taxes in the community than are homeowners; (3) built-in tax increases because of the progressivity of the tax structure are less clearly perceived than are legislated changes, making elastic tax structures more conducive to government growth than are inelastic structures; (4) the implicit future tax burdens inherent in the issuance of debt are more difficult to evaluate than are equivalent current taxes; (5) citizens do not treat lump-sum cash subsidies to their government as being as much theirs as they would a cash subsidy to themselves (the "flypaper" effect). Each of these hypotheses implies a relationship between the size or growth of government and the relevant fiscal illusion variable. Oates carefully examined the evidence in support of each and concluded "that although all five cases entail plausible illusion hypotheses, none of them have very compelling empirical support" (Oates, 1988b). I tend to agree with this conclusion for all of the five categories of fiscal illusion, save the last. The logic against a flypaper effect is compelling, but the empirical evidence refuses to give in to this logic. Grants from the central government do seem to be treated by lower levels of government as "gifts from heaven" and, so as not to offend the giver, tend "to stick where they land."[25]

Direct evidence of fiscal illusion has been obtained recently in experiments by Tyran and Sausgruber (2000). They designed a market experiment involving tax/transfer proposals. A tax could be leveled on either the buyers or the sellers with part of the tax revenue transferred to the buyers and the other part going to the sellers. The demand schedule was perfectly inelastic and so in both cases all of the tax fell on the buyers, and thus in both cases the buyers were better off rejecting the tax/transfer proposal. Most buyers correctly perceived that they would be made worse off by the proposal when the tax was levied on them and voted against it. A significant fraction voted for the tax/transfer proposal, however, when the tax was levied on the sellers. The way in which the tax part of the proposal was framed had a significant impact on how the participants in the experiments voted. Tyran and Sausgruber's findings have obvious implications for the likelihood of fiscal illusion existing for property taxes on rental property, employment taxes paid by employers, and so forth.

Mention should also be made of Peter Swann's finding of a strong relationship between the elasticity of the Australian tax system and the growth in the size of its government. Swann argues that essentially *all* of the relative growth of government in Australia since World War II can be explained by the disguised tax increases that occurred as a result of inflation, which shifted individuals into ever higher tax brackets and thus expanded the tax take of the state. Unfortunately for this version of the fiscal illusion hypothesis, Swann's impressive time series results for Australia – like Meltzer and Richard's (1983) time series results – have not been confirmed using pooled cross-sectional data in Flanders (Heyndels and Smolders, 1994) and the United States (Hunter and Scott, 1987; Greene and Hawley, 1991).

The lack of strong empirical support for the fiscal illusion hypothesis, despite its intuitive appeal, may be due to the rather vague way in which it has been defined and modeled in the literature. For example, it is not clear whether fiscal illusion is a

---

[25] The empirical evidence regarding the flypaper effect is reviewed in Chapter 10.

kind of short-run myopia on the part of voters that allows for temporary increases in expenditures, or a permanent astigmatism indefinitely obscuring the true size of government. The latter is obviously a much stronger hypothesis. The tax revolts in both Europe and the United States in the 1970s, and Newt Gingrich's successful "contract with America" to reduce taxes and the deficit in the United States in the early 1990s, suggest that fiscal illusion may not permanently impair voters' vision. By the end of the twentieth century, the U.S. federal deficit had disappeared, and government's share of the GDP had stopped growing. Eventually, citizens may be able to recognize the true scale of Leviathan and rise up to chain it. (For further discussion of the fiscal illusion hypothesis, see Musgrave, 1981, pp. 98–104, and Oates, 1988b.)

21.2.6 *Tax elasticity*

Our last hypothesis about the growth of government is not so much about the motivation of those who bring about this growth, but about the means of their doing so. Kau and Rubin (1981, 1999), whose work has already been mentioned, assume that the supply of government services and transfers is provided by those who seek to maximize government size as in the Brennan and Buchanan (1980) Leviathan model or Niskanen's (1971) bureaucracy model. The chief constraint these budget maximizers face is a technical one – how can they extract the maximum amount of revenue from the population? Luckily for the budget maximizers, several economic and social developments over the last century have made their task much easier. The movement of workers from farms into factories makes it easier for the government to measure and tax their incomes; the movement of women from employment at home into employment in the marketplace allows government to measure and tax their incomes; the development of computers and other technological changes makes it easier for the government to monitor – and thus to tax – economic activity. In their most recent test of these propositions, Kau and Rubin (1999) found that variables measuring these developments accounted for two-thirds of the changes in government size in the United States over the period 1947–93. A measure of the ideology of members of Congress, included to account for changes in the *demand* for government, was insignificant. *All* of the changes in government that Kau and Rubin were able to explain were accounted for by their proxies for the government's ability to raise tax revenue.[26]

The importance of the elasticity of the tax system is also emphasized by Hansson and Stuart (forthcoming) in their explanation for why the size of the government sector has *declined* in several OECD countries from peaks attained during the 1980s. Hansson and Stuart argue that in these countries those in government overestimated the elasticity of tax revenue and raised taxes beyond the level at which they could be sustained indefinitely. Hence, they were forced to retreat. We discuss some factors that determine these limits to taxation in the next chapter.

---

[26] Kau and Rubin first presented evidence that these measures of tax elasticity could explain the intertemporal movements in government size in the United States in 1981 using a data set from 1929 through 1970. Additional support for the tax-elasticity side of their hypothesis is provided by Ferris and West (1996).

21.3   Conclusions

The six explanations of government size reviewed in this chapter stem from two quite different conceptualizations of the state. The first three hypotheses (the government as a provider of public goods and eliminator of externalities, the government as a redistributor of income and wealth, and interest groups as inducers of government growth) are essentially drawn from a classical theory of the democratic state (Pateman, 1970). Ultimate authority lies with the citizens. The state exists to carry out "the will of the people." State policies are reflections of the preferences of individual voters. In the public choice literature, the state often appears as simply a voting rule that transforms individual preferences into political outcomes. Most of the classic works on public choice – beginning with Arrow (1951), Downs (1957), Black (1958), and Buchanan and Tullock (1962) – are based on this citizen-over-state view of the polity, and it continues dominant in the most recent literature in the many works that employ the median voter model, probabilistic voting models, and the like.

The last three hypotheses reviewed here place the state above the citizens. It is the preferences of the state, or of the individuals in the government, that are decisive. Citizens' preferences and political institutions constitute at most (loose) constraints against which political leaders and bureaucrats pursue their own personal interests. Indeed, in the extreme version of this view of the state, the only binding constraint on it is its ability to extract tax revenue from the citizens. This state-rules-citizen view of politics underlies Puviani's (1903) work and characterizes that of Niskanen (1971) and Brennan and Buchanan (1980).

If either of these two conceptions of the state is fully accurate,[27] then the other must be rejected – and so, too, the set of hypotheses associated with it in this chapter. But both views might be correct to some degree. Government officials and bureaucrats may have some discretionary power to advance their own interests at the citizens' expense, but citizens' preferences, as registered through existing political institutions, may also constitute a consequential constraint. If so, then all six hypotheses may help to explain the size and growth of government. Certainly, the huge growth in the redistribution component of the state budgets seems likely to be explained by some combination of the hypotheses reviewed here: (1) insurance against the risks to incomes from living in highly developed and interdependent economies, (2) insurance against the risks to incomes from living in economies that are highly dependent on international trade, (3) involuntary redistribution from those above the median income to those below, and (4) involuntary redistribution from groups with weak political power to more powerful groups.

Several studies have tested for the relative strengths of demand and supply factors in explaining government growth. Henrekson (1988) found evidence of both the Baumol effect and the voting power of government bureaucrats in his time-series

---

[27] Tanzi (1980) has discussed both of these conceptions of the state – as well as a third, the paternalistic state – in the context of the fiscal illusion issue.

analysis of Sweden. Although the fiscal illusion variables did not prove to be very robust, the supply side variables did have somewhat more explanatory power than the demand variables.

Ferris and West (1996) estimated demand and supply equations using time-series data for the United States. They also included a third equation to explain the level of government employment. Neither price nor income was significant in the demand equation with the latter result contradicting Wagner's law. The numbers of government employees and farm population were significant interest group "taste factors" in the demand equation. The Baumol cost effect was significant in the supply equation.

Lybeck (1986) estimated an integrated demand and supply of government model for 12 OECD countries. Demand factors appeared to dominate in Sweden and the United Kingdom; supply factors in Canada, France, and the United States; and both were of about equal importance in the remaining countries (Australia, Austria, Belgium, the Federal Republic of Germany, Italy, the Netherlands, and Norway). Impressive support for the Baumol effect was again found. Interest group strength, as measured by the number of interest groups in a time-series analysis of Sweden (Lybeck, 1986, pp. 58–82), and by the degree of unionization in a pooled cross-sectional time-series analysis of all 12 countries (pp. 96–106), was highly significant. The number of public employees, another interest group measure, proved significant in several countries. In the pooled regressions, population size (negatively related) and unemployment (positively related) were the remaining significant variables. The former appears in the demand side of the model and implies that government size declines relatively as population grows, as one would expect if government output resembles a pure public good. The unemployment rate appears in the supply side of the model, as hypothesized in political-business-cycle models. Other hypotheses (Wagner's law, redistribution, fiscal illusion) received very mixed support.

Pommerehne and Schneider (1982) incorporated both of the views of the state in their model. The demand for government for 48 Swiss municipalities that operate under direct (as opposed to representative) democracy was first estimated. The estimated coefficients from this equation were then used to simulate what the levels of government expenditure would be in the 62 Swiss municipalities that have representative democracy. They found that *all* of the individual spending categories are underestimated from the parameter estimates based on the direct democracies. The representative democracies spent 28 percent more than predicted by the expenditure equation estimated over the direct democracies. The use of a representative form of government changes the nature of the political outcomes substantially, making government considerably larger than it would be if citizens directly determined outcomes. Moreover, in those Swiss municipalities in which representative democracy exists, the size of government is smaller if the citizens have the right to call a referendum and thereby reverse a government decision. These results of Pommerehne and Schneider suggest rather strongly that the existence of a layer of representative government between the citizens and political outcomes expands the size of the public sector considerably. They would appear to support the state-over-citizen view of government, and Pommerehne and Schneider (1982, pp. 319–22) interpret their results as indicating the importance of "the supply side of local services."

Santerre's (1989) study of Connecticut suburbs provides further support for the Pommerehne/Schneider results. Suburbs with representative democracy had *larger* budgets than those governed by direct town-meeting democracy, but actually spent *less* per pupil for schooling – the major component of the local budget. Farnham (1990), on the other hand, did not observe a better fit to the median voter model in small U.S. communities that used other instruments of direct democracy – the initiative, referenda, and recall.

It is also possible that the existence of representative democracy facilitates the attainment of private gains by interest groups. Both Peltzman (1980) and Mueller and Murrell (1985, 1986) have seen the growth of government as a by-product of the competition for votes between candidates and parties. Thus government growth (or size) in these models is dependent on the representative nature of the democratic process, although the models assume that citizens' preferences, as channeled by interest group representation, are the driving force behind government programs.

Work by Roubini and Sachs (1989), Cusack (1997), and Persson and Tabellini (1999, 2000b) suggests that it is not only the existence of representative democracy per se that affects the size of the government sector, but that the *structure* of the institutions of representative government is important. Roubini, Sachs, and Cusack argue that lack of government cohesion in multiparty or presidential systems leads to more logrolling and larger budgets. Persson and Tabellini make almost exactly the opposite predictions. They argue that the checks and balances that exist in a presidential system lead to more competition among the different branches of government and that this competition helps constrain the rent-seeking activities of those in government. They also predict smaller budgets in "majoritarian" (two-party) systems than in multiparty systems because the competition for votes in majoritarian systems focuses on the marginal districts rather than the entire nation, and thus politicians tend to make more targeted and in the aggregate smaller commitments in majoritarian systems. All three studies claim support for their hypotheses.

Although as almost always the theoretical underpinning for these models is more impressive than their empirical support, this recent work on the importance of electoral systems alongside Pommerehne and Schneider's earlier results demonstrates what may be regarded as the single most important message that public choice has to teach – the rules of the game *do* affect the outcomes of the game. Institutions matter. In Switzerland, the more direct the citizen's influence on political outcomes is, the smaller is the scale of government. Among the developed countries, citizens of Switzerland are able to exercise control over government more effectively than anywhere else. Only Switzerland makes much use of direct democracy and the referendum, and it has the strongest federalist system in the world. It also has the smallest public sector in Western Europe (see Table 21.2). The results of Pommerehne and Schneider as well as those of Santerre (1986, 1989) suggest that these facts are related.

Corroborative evidence that more direct citizen control effectively constrains government may be inferred from the many studies that have found that more federalized or decentralized government structures are associated with smaller or slower growing government sectors.[28] At the national level, the effects of federalism on government size are almost impossible to measure, since there are so few countries that fulfill the essential criteria for federalism – citizens are represented at each level of government and their representatives can decide both the expenditures and taxes at each respective level. In the so-called federalist states of Europe – like Austria and Germany – lower levels of government have limited authority to set their own tax rates, and thus citizens cannot put pressure on them to lower taxes. Only one country in Western Europe has a federalist structure in which citizens at each level can determine both expenditures and taxes – Switzerland – and it "happens" to have the smallest government sector in Western Europe. Worldwide, of the four developed countries with the smallest government sectors, three fulfill this criterion of federalism – Switzerland, the United States, and Australia (Table 21.2). Canada would appear to provide an important counterexample, as it too meets the criterion, but the disciplinary potential of federalism in Canada has been dramatically curtailed since World War II by a federally led program of introducing "tax uniformity" across the provinces. Grossman and West (1994) claim that this program was the product of collusion among the provincial governments, and provide evidence that it led to an increase in the size of the government sector in Canada since World War II.

Blankart (2000) recounts a similar story for Germany. The German regional governments have happily allowed the federal government to usurp their taxing authority over the last 50 years as this centralization of taxation has removed tax competition among them and thus increased the size of their budgets. Blankart argues that this centralization of tax authority accounts for the faster growth in the size of Germany's public sector relative to Switzerland's.[29] Consistent with the Canadian and German experiences, we find that the response of governments in the European Union to the "threat" of tax competition posed by the greater integration of their economies has been to press for the elimination of this competition through "tax harmonization" within the Union.

Thus we see that all of the institutions of democracy – electoral rules, institutions of direct democracy, and federalist institutions – seem to be important in determining the size of government. These institutions differ across countries, and their efficacy changes over time as the economic and political environment of a country change. The citizen's role in a representative democracy is more passive than in a direct democracy, and even this difference seems to lead to a significant fillip to government size. Today's citizen, confronted by expanded and more complex government structures at the local, state, and federal levels, must feel that he is more of a

---

[28] See Cameron (1978), Saunders (1986), Schneider (1986), Nelson (1987), Zax (1989), Marlow (1988), Joulfaian and Marlow (1990), and Vaubel (1996). Here, as so often is the case, one can cite contradictory evidence (see again the discussion in Oates, 1988b).

[29] Joulfian and Marlow (1990) provide additional evidence of the effects of collusion using U.S. data.

passive spectator of the democractic process, as he watches a campaign commercial on television, than did the citizen of 150 years ago. How much of the growth of government in the intervening years can be explained by a slackening of the reins of government in citizens' hands, how much is a reflection of the preferences of citizens transmitted through the political process, and how much reflects merely the preferences of those within the government remains a somewhat open question.

Bibliographical notes

Holsey and Borcherding (1997) survey the public choice literature on the growth of government. Tanzi and Schuknecht (2000) provide a wealth of data on the size and composition of government expenditures and taxes in different countries from the end of the nineteenth century up to the present, and analyze the causes and consequences of these fiscal developments.

CHAPTER 22

Government size and economic performance

I sit on a man's back, choking him and making him carry me, and yet assure myself
and others that I am very sorry for him and wish to lighten his load by all possible
means – except by getting off his back.

Leo Tolstoi

In the previous chapter we documented how governments have grown around the
world – until in Europe; they now generally absorb half the national income or more.
What have been the consequences of this growth for the welfare of the citizens of
these countries? What have been the consequences for the economic performance
of the countries? The first question is, of course, the most relevant one. Since the
end of World War II, the United States has spent over $8 trillion on defense. If these
expenditures prevented a third world war, led to the collapse of Communism in
East Europe and the Soviet Union, and thereby preserved democracy and freedom
in the West, most Americans would probably say that the money was well spent.
But if the same events would have transpired if the United States had spent only a
tenth as much on defense, then more than $7 trillion would have been wasted, and
Americans are that much worse off as a result.

The very "nonmarket" nature of many of the goods and services government
supplies makes it difficult to measure their effects on welfare. One can measure the
amounts of money given out as unemployment compensation and social security
payments, but how does one measure the peace of mind to all of those who were not
unemployed and yet did not have to fear unemployment because of the existence of
unemployment benefits? How does one measure the peace of mind of knowing that
one will not live in poverty in one's old age?

Economists and public choice scholars have not tried to answer these questions.
Just as in the political business cycle literature they have focused on the *economic*
causes of government popularity; they have focused on the economic consequences
of government growth or size. Although these include only a small portion of the
welfare effects of government, they constitute important components of performance and ones which we can measure with some accuracy. In this chapter we
examine some of these consequences. We begin at the microlevel and work our way
up to the macrolevel.

22.1   The welfare losses from taxation

All taxes, with the exception of the much discussed but seldom used lump-sum tax, distort individual behavior and reduce welfare as a result of these distortions. Consider first the case of a commodity tax. In Figure 22.1a the compensated demand schedule for commodity x is depicted. It is produced with constant marginal costs, c, and under perfect competition. In equilibrium, x_c units are sold at a price of P_c. Now let the government introduce a commodity tax of t_1 per unit. Price rises by this amount, the government takes in the long rectangle between t_1 and P_c in tax revenue, and consumers suffer the additional loss in consumers' surplus on the units of x not purchased as measured by triangle L_1. The welfare loss triangle is small relative to the tax revenue raised.

The maximum tax revenue that the government can raise from this commodity tax occurs at the tax t_m, where the price of the commodity including the tax has risen to the profit-maximizing price of a monopolist. The government takes in the rectangle R_m falling between the t_m and P_c lines. The welfare loss from the distortionary effect of this tax has now risen to L_m, however, and equals half of the revenue from the tax. The welfare loss from taxation rises relative to the revenue from the tax as the tax increases.

To see this relationship more clearly, let us examine the algebra involved. The compensated demand schedule for x can be written as

$$P = a - bx. \tag{22.1}$$

With perfect competition price equals marginal costs,

$$P_c = c = a - bx, \tag{22.2}$$

yielding a competitive output x_c:

$$x_c = \frac{a - c}{b}. \tag{22.3}$$

Adding the tax t we obtain the output x_t:

$$x_t = \frac{a - (c + t)}{b}. \tag{22.4}$$

The tax revenue raised by the state equals this output times the tax:

$$R = \frac{a - (c + t)}{b}t = \frac{(a - c)t - t^2}{b}. \tag{22.5}$$

Maximizing (22.5) with respect to t, we obtain the tax t^* that maximizes tax revenue

$$t^* = \frac{a - c}{2}, \tag{22.6}$$

which yields the maximum tax revenue of

$$R^* = \frac{(a - c)^2}{4b}. \tag{22.7}$$

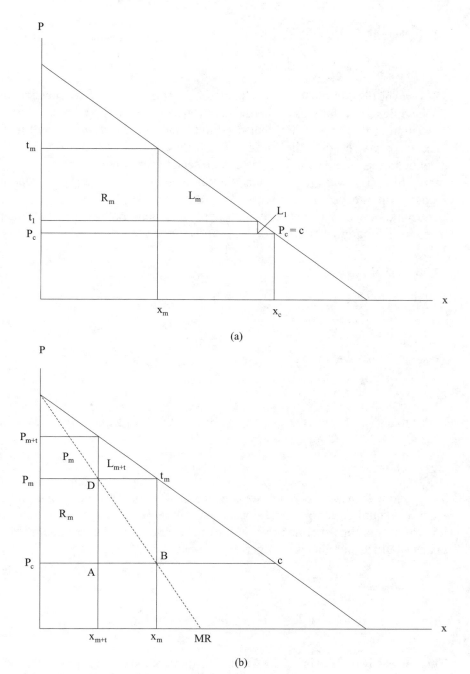

Figure 22.1. The distortionary effects of taxation.

The welfare loss from taxation is one-half the change in output caused by the tax times the tax. The change in output caused by the tax is

$$\triangle x_t = \frac{a-c}{b} - \frac{a-(c+t)}{b} = \frac{t}{b} \tag{22.8}$$

with the welfare loss thus being

$$L = \frac{1}{2}\frac{t}{b}t = \frac{t^2}{2b}. \tag{22.9}$$

The revenue raised from the tax is a quadratic function of t which reaches a maximum at t^*, while the welfare loss from the tax grows exponentially with it.

Assuming that the government does not charge a tax *greater* than that which maximizes tax revenue, the welfare loss from taxation is at most half of the tax revenue raised with a straight line demand schedule *and* perfect competition in the supply of x. The welfare loss from taxation increases, however, if the suppliers of x possess market power.

Assume now that x is sold by a monopoly. Absent any tax it equates marginal revenue and marginal cost and sells x_m at the price P_m, where

$$x_m = \frac{a - c}{2b}. \tag{22.10}$$

The monopolist's profit-maximizing output is

$$x_{m+t} = \frac{a - (c + t)}{2b}. \tag{22.11}$$

The state's tax revenue is now

$$R = \frac{a - (c + t)}{2b}t = \frac{(a - c)t - t^2}{2b}. \tag{22.12}$$

Maximizing (22.12) with respect to t, we obtain the exact same t^* that we did before,

$$t^* = \frac{a - c}{2}. \tag{22.6}$$

This yields a tax revenue for the state, however, which is only one-half of that raised when x is supplied competitively, because the monopolist still chooses to maximize its profits, and thus supplies only half of the output with the revenue-maximizing tax as would be supplied under perfect competition.

$$R^*_{m+t} = \frac{(a - c)^2}{8b} \tag{22.13}$$

$$x_{m+t} = \frac{a - \left(c + \frac{a-c}{2}\right)}{2b} = \frac{a - c}{4b}. \tag{22.14}$$

This can easily be seen in Figure 21.1b. The monopolist charges price P_{m+t} with the tax and sells x_{m+t}. The government's tax revenue is the rectangle R_m. The welfare loss from the tax now *exceeds* the revenue it raises, however. This welfare loss equals the rectangle ABt_mD, which represents the profits that the monopolist would have earned on units of x that now go unsold as a result of the tax, plus the consumers' surplus triangle, L_{m+t}, on these unsold units. As R_m equals ABt_mD, the welfare loss exceeds the tax revenue by the triangle L_{m+t}.

Of course, these results for monopoly constitute an upper bound on the losses from a commodity tax, just as the results for perfect competition constitute a lower bound. Most industries fall in between these two extremes. The results indicate, however, that the welfare losses from taxation can become relatively large when the government attempts to maximize its revenue from the tax, and are larger, the larger the market power enjoyed by firms subject to the tax.

A commodity tax creates a welfare loss by distorting a consumer's pattern of consumption. General commodity taxes distort choices between consumption and leisure; income taxes distort choices between work and leisure; and so on. All taxes in common use lead to some distortions in choices and losses in welfare.

Of particular interest in this regard are the distortionary effects of income taxes. Browning (1987), using an analysis similar to the one employed here but with respect to the supply of labor, has calculated a range of possible *marginal* welfare losses from income taxes in the United States of from roughly 10 to over 300 percent, depending on the assumptions made about the elasticity of the labor supply curve, the effective tax rate, and so on. Browning's "preferred estimates" based on the plausibility of the assumed parameters range from 31.8 to 46.9 percent.[1]

These estimates imply a rather substantial welfare loss on the margin from the taxation of income in the United States. Given that labor and income from labor is much more heavily taxed in Europe than it is in the United States, and that welfare losses increase exponentially with the tax rate, the marginal welfare losses from taxes on labor in Europe must be substantially higher. Alesina and Perotti (1997) have not measured welfare losses in the same way that Browning does, but they nevertheless find a very significant distortionary effect from taxes on labor. Taxes on labor significantly increase labor costs causing higher unemployment and an overall loss in competitiveness for a country.

22.2 Government size and black market activity

The previous section demonstrated how taxes reduce economic efficiency and social welfare by distorting choices among consumption goods, between work and leisure, and so forth. Taxes and other forms of government intervention and regulation can, however, have other distortionary effects. Rather than working less to avoid paying income taxes, for example, people may simply *report* less income. In the United States roughly 17 percent of the potential revenue from the federal income tax is lost because of this form of tax evasion (Andreoni, Erard, and Feinstein, 1998, p. 819).

More generally, taxes and regulations can affect the choice between conducting an activity in the "legitimate economy" and conducting it in the "underground economy." The underground economy includes both legitimate activities, like hiring someone to paint an apartment, that go unreported, and illegal activities, like the purchase of cocaine. The underground economy has been called the shadow economy, the informal sector, the irregular sector, the unreported sector, the black or gray economy (market), and, for some activities, the illegal or criminal sector.[2] The economic activity described by these terms is underground in the sense that the

---

[1] Additional estimates of similar magnitude have been made by Stuart (1984) and Ballard, Shoven, and Whalley (1985). Ng (2000) argues, however, that these sorts of estimates are too high.

[2] See discussion in Feige (1989b) and Thomas (1992).

persons engaged in it, both buyers and sellers, try and conceal the activity from the government. They do this to avoid having to obtain any licenses that are needed to engage in the activity, to avoid regulation, and to avoid paying taxes.

When economic activity is driven into the underground economy, there can be several adverse effects on economic efficiency:

1. Going underground brings with it its own distortions. For example, buyers of merchandise in the black market may have to travel greater distances to make their purchases, devote more time to the transactions, and may not receive goods of the same quality and be accorded the same warranty protection that accompanies goods purchased from legitimate businesses. When safety and environmental regulations are circumvented by going underground, social welfare is reduced through the greater risks consumers or employees bear, or by the environmental damage done.

2. The state loses the tax and license revenue that it could have collected. This loss may force the state to set higher tax rates or to introduce additional taxes to cover its expenditures leading to more distortions and driving more activity underground.

3. Because the scale of the underground economy is difficult to measure, those in government may make erroneous judgments about economic policies based on the figures for the legitimate economy. Suppose, for example, that heavy income and social insurance taxes lead some people who are unemployed to work in the underground economy. They continue to pretend to look for work so as to be able to claim unemployment benefits, but refuse to take jobs offered to them, so long as the net of tax income from a job in the legitimate sector is less than the unemployment benefits plus the tax-free income in the underground economy. These people can truthfully be said to be "voluntarily unemployed." Official unemployment figures overestimate the number of people actively seeking employment, and government policies to reduce official unemployment are likely to be less effective than the designers of these policies anticipate.

4. Each person who participates in the underground economy is breaking a governmental law or regulation, and perhaps certain mores of the community. Once a person breaks one law and "gets away with it," she may be tempted to break others. Thus, one set of illegitimate activies in the underground economy may encourage others, and the legal and moral fabric of a community will be harmed.

How big is the underground economy? This obvious and basic question is, unfortunately, very difficult to answer. The fact that it is underground or in the shadows makes it difficult to observe and to measure its size. Several approaches have been tried. The simplest is to ask people directly. Many surveys have been conducted that, for example, ask people to report the amount of income that they earn that must be or is reported to the government and how much is not reported. One expects that some people may be reluctant to admit that they conceal income from the government – even in a survey where anonymity is promised – and thus that there is a downward bias in the estimates of the size of the underground sector using survey data. This downward bias is likely to be particularly large for activities for which there is strong social approbation or large legal penalties, for example, questions about the purchase or sale of illegal drugs. Not surprisingly, therefore, estimates of the size of the underground economy based on surveys tend to be the smallest of all of the procedures used.

The most frequently used method for estimating the size of the underground economy tries to identify an easily observed and measured activity or commodity that is complementary to economic activity in both the above- and underground economies. Money might be such a commodity, for example. Let us assume that the quantity theory of money holds, and thus that the demand for money balances can be written as $M = kY$, where M stands for money balances, Y for gross domestic product, and k is a constant representing the amount of money balances people wish to hold relative to the level of economic activity that they carry out. Let us assume now that at some past point in time, $t - n$, we believe that the size of underground economy was zero, but at time t it is positive. We further believe that the k for transactions in the aboveground economy is the same as for the underground economy, and that k is the same in t as it was in $t - n$. Data for the gross domestic product (PT) and money balances in period $t - n$ can then be used to estimate k. Given this estimate of k and the level of observed money balances in t, we can predict what gross domestic product is in t. This will be an estimate of the size of the official and underground economies combined. The difference between this figure and the offical government estimate of GDP is a measure of the size of the underground economy.

There are several possible ways in which this estimate may be in error.[3] The underground economy may not have been zero in $t - n$,[4] k may differ between the two sectors, k may change over time, and so on. Thus, other proxies have been tried.

One popular choice is the consumption of electricity. Electricity is a basic input to many production and consumption activities, and its consumption is easy to measure. If E_t is the amount of electricity consumed at time t, and Y_t is gross domestic product at t, then electricity consumption can be reasonably accurately predicted by the equation, $E_t = kY_t$. The electricity-consumption approach then proceeds like the demand-for-money-balances approach. The parameter k is estimated at a point in time, $t - n$, when the underground economy is thought to be of size X, where X might equal zero. The consumption of electricity at time t is then used to predict Y_t, assuming that k has not changed. The difference between the gross domestic product predicted from the use of electricity and the official GDP is the measured size of the underground economy.

The electricity-consumption approach has also been critized. Schneider and Enste (2000) discuss the merits and faults of nine approaches that have been tried. We shall not review each approach. Suffice it to say that they yield a broad range of estimates, with household surveys producing the smallest estimates, and variants on

[3] See Porter and Bayer (1989) and Schneider and Enste (2000).
[4] One might employ the procedure and assume some nonzero value for the underground economy in $t - n$, but the estimate for t would still be sensitive to this assumption.

Table 22.1. *Average size of the underground economy in developing, transition, and OECD countries*

Countries	Ranges of the size of the underground economy, 1990–3
Developing countries	
Africa	39–76% of GDP
Central and South America	25–60% of GDP
Asia	13–70% of GDP
Transition countries	
Former Soviet Union	20–43% of GDP
Central Europe	9–28% of GDP
OECD countries	8–30% of GDP

Note: Estimates based on electricity or currency demand approaches.
Source: Schneider and Enste (2000, Table 2).

the demand-for-money approach producing the largest estimates. Estimates of the size of the underground economy as a percent of GDP for Canada in the late 1980s range, for example, from 1.4 percent based on a household survey to 21.2 percent using the transactions approach.[5] Similarly, wide ranges of estimates are reported for Germany, Great Britain, Italy, and the United States (Schneider and Enste, 2000, Table 8).

Despite these large differences across the various approaches, two conclusions can safely be drawn from the existing literature. The first is that the relative size of the underground economy is much larger in developing and transition economies than in the developed countries. Table 22.1 presents ranges for the three groups of countries. The underground economies in the developing countries of Africa, Asia, and Latin America average to roughly 40 percent of total GDP, while in the OECD they average only around 15 percent of GDP. Estimates for the transition countries fall midway between these two figures.

The second conclusion that can safely be drawn is that the underground sectors have been growing. Table 22.2 presents estimates of the size of the underground economy in several OECD countries at different points in time.[6] In each of the 15 countries, the underground economy has grown. In Norway and Sweden it has grown from an insignificant 1 to 2 percent of GDP in 1960 to around 18 percent of GDP in 1994. In only 3 of the 15 countries – Austria, Switzerland, and the United States – was the underground economy estimated to be less than 10 percent of GDP in 1994. The highest estimate was over 25 percent for Italy.

These figures suggest the same two questions that we tried to answer about the size of the government sector in the previous chapter. What accounts for the relative growth in size of the shadow economy, and what accounts for the wide dispersion of estimated sizes across countries?

[5] This approach uses the variant on the quantity theory of money, $MV = PT$, where M stands for money balances, V for the velocity of money, P for prices, and T for transactions. The size of the shadow economy is estimated by comparing actual and predicted levels of T.

[6] Table 22.2 is taken from the working paper version of Schneider and Enste (2000) because it contains more countries and data points.

Table 22.2. *Estimates of the size of the underground economy in selected OECD countries, 1960–94*

Countries	Currency demand approach Size of the underground economy (as % of official GDP) in the years						
	1960	1970	1975	1978	1980	1990	1994
Austria	0.4	1.8	1.9	2.6	3.0	5.1	6.8
Belgium	–	10.4	15.2	–	16.4	19.6	21.4
Canada	–	–	5.8–7.2	–	10.1–11.2	13.6	14.6
Denmark	3.8–4.8	5.3–7.4	6.4–7.8	6.7–8.0	6.9–10.2	9.0–13.4	17.6
Germany	2.0–2.1	2.7–3.0	5.5–6.0	8.1–9.2	10.3–11.2	11.4–12.0	13.1
France	–	3.9	–	6.7	6.9	9.4	14.3
Ireland	–	4.3	6.9	–	8.0	11.7	15.3
Italy	–	10.7	–	–	16.7	23.4	25.8
Netherlands	–	4.8	–	–	9.1	12.9	13.6
Norway	1.3–1.7	6.2–6.9	7.8–8.2	9.6–10.0	10.2–10.9	14.5–16.0	17.9
Spain	–	–	–	18.0	–	21.0	22.3
Sweden	1.5–1.8	6.8–7.8	10.2–11.2	12.5–13.6	11.9–12.4	15.8–16.7	18.3
Switzerland	1.2	4.1	6.1	6.2	6.5	6.6	6.9
United Kingdom	–	2.0	6.5	7.8	8.4	10.2	12.4
United States	2.6–4.1	2.6–4.6	3.5–5.2	3.7–5.3	3.9–6.1	5.1–8.6	9.4

Source: Schneider and Enste (1998, Table 3.3.2).

When deciding whether "to go underground" the rational actor must trade off the benefit from operating in the underground economy versus the potential cost, if she is caught and must pay the appropriate penalty. The relatively large size of the underground economy in developing countries should, therefore, be explained by the heavy costs of regulation and taxation born by individuals and businesses in these countries, which lead to large benefits from going underground, and/or the low penalties from being caught.

These predictions are supported by Johnson, Kaufmann, and Zoido-Lobatón (1998). They relate different measures of the size of the underground economy relative to GDP to indexes of the burdens of regulation, taxation, and corruption in a sample of up to 49 countries in Latin America, the former Soviet Union, and the OECD. They find that the underground sector's size is larger (1) the larger the degree of regulation in a country, (2) the greater the burden of taxation, (3) the weaker "the rule of law" is (property rights are clearly defined, laws impartially enforced), and (4) the more corruption there is in the government bureaucracy. The first two sets of variables tend to measure the benefits of going into the underground sector to avoid government interference and taxation; the second two are related to the likelihood of getting caught and punished. The weaker the rule of law is and the more corrupt government officials are, the more likely it is that the law can be bent or an official bribed to avoid a penalty. Johnson, Kaufmann, and Zoido-Lobatón's findings are corroborated by Johnson, Kaufmann, and Shleifer's (1997) more intensive analysis of 15 former Soviet Union/bloc countries.

Johnson, Kaufmann, and Shleifer (1997, pp. 209–10) identify "three types of transition economies in Eastern Europe and the former Soviet Union. First, there are politically repressed economies with highly distortionary taxes, low provision of public goods, but still, a small unofficial sector. Second, there are economies with relatively fair taxes, relatively light regulation, high tax revenues, and relatively good provision of public goods in the official sector; these are concentrated in Eastern Europe. Third, there are economies with relatively unfair taxes, relatively onerous regulation, low tax collection, and relatively poor public goods; these are concentrated in the former Soviet Union. Comparing the second and third groups, the former has a lower share of unofficial activity and faster economic growth than the latter."

The last observation draws a link between the size of the underground economy and the economic performance of a country. One reason given for why some poor countries fail to develop is that their public sectors are so corrupt and their tax and regulation systems so oppressive that their private sectors are not only driven underground, but out of existence. Evidence of a negative effect of corruption on the level of investment in a country is consistent with this interpretation.[7]

It is tempting when thinking of the second of the two questions posed above – Why has the underground sector grown so rapidly across all countries? – to seek an answer in the tremendous growth in government that has occurred since 1960. The growth of government regulations and taxation has driven the private sector out of sight. Some support for this answer seems to be present in Table 22.2. The government sector is much smaller in Switzerland and the United States than in the other countries in the table, and these two countries are among the three whose underground economies make up less than 10 percent of the GNP. But the third country with an underground sector that is less than 10 percent of the GNP is Austria, and its government sector is about in the middle of those in the sample. The growth in relative size of the government sector has been about the same in Sweden and the Netherlands, yet the growth in the underground economy seems much larger in Sweden. Linking up the size and growth of the government sector to the size and growth of the underground economies of the developed countries remains a challenging research task.

22.3   Government size and corruption

Transactions in the underground economy represent illegal activity by the citizens. Corruption constitutes illegal activity by those in government. As we have seen in the previous section, corruption raises the costs of doing business and tends to drive legitimate economic activity underground. Thus, corruption is generally regarded as a conspicuous example of government failure, and a justification for *not* resorting to government intervention.

Acemoglu and Verdier (2000) have pointed out, however, that corruption can be regarded as a form of *transaction cost* from using government to rectify market failures, and one which will be well worth paying if the market failure is significant.

---

[7] See Mauro (1995), and more generally regarding the quality of government and investment Clague, Keefer, Knack and Olson (1996) and Keefer and Knack (1995).

To see their point, consider the provision of a typical public good like a bridge. The local legislature votes to construct a bridge to be paid for at first by a bond issue with the bonds amortized through the subsequent collection of tolls for the use of the bridge. Even if a private firm is engaged to construct the bridge, the government must decide which private firm to engage. A bureaucracy, or at minimum a bureaucrat, paid for by the state, must choose a private firm to construct the bridge. The members of the legislature and the citizens whom they represent are thrust into a principal/agent relationship with respect to the bureaucrats making this choice. Lacking information about all the characteristics of the firms bidding for the construction contract, the legislature will in general not be in a position to determine whether the bureaucrats have chosen the bidder offering the best combination of quality and price. The legislature also will not be in a position to determine whether the bureaucrats' choice of a bidder was solely determined by the characteristics of the bid, or by the size of the bribe that accompanied it. Thus, corruption is almost an inevitable consequence of the existence of government and the principal/agent problems that come with it. Few, if any, activities of government give rise to more cases of corruption than the awarding of construction contracts.

To reduce the likelihood that bureaucrats sacrifice the public's interest for their own, they must be offered a wage *above* their opportunity costs in the private sector. By offering bureaucrats rents, and threatening them with dismissal should they be discovered to be corrupt, the principals in the legislature can reduce the incidence of corruption. As always, however, there are trade-offs – this time between the costs of paying all bureaucrats higher wages and the costs of having some corrupt bureaucrats – and thus the optimal wage for bureaucrats will not be so high as to eliminate all corruption.[8]

The illegal nature of corruption, like that of activity in the underground economy, makes it difficult to measure. Most studies use surveys of the victims of corruption – heads of businesses. Using such measures Persson and Tabellini (2000c) find corruption to be more prevalent in countries that use proportional representation electoral systems. They reason that PR systems are more prone to corruption due to the weaker accountability of individual politicians in the typical PR-list system in which voters can only choose among parties.

Goel and Nelson (1998) use convictions for public abuse of office as an index of corruption, and find that corruption at the state level in the United States increases with the size of state governments. Consistent with Acemoglu and Verdier's theory, Goel and Nelson find corruption to be inversely related to the wages paid to state employees.

22.4 Government size and economic productivity

Government should provide goods and services that lift citizens out of anarchy to higher levels of economic and social welfare. Many public goods can have direct positive effects on the efficiency of the private economic sector. Roads, canals, and

---

[8] See Acemoglu and Verdier (2000) for further discussion and results.

airports facilitate the transport of goods, a legal system can facilitate the exchange of goods and enforcement of contracts, education can improve the productivity of the workforce, and so on.

In addition to these direct effects on economic productivity, government activity can lead to productivity increases by (1) increasing the rate of utilization of the existing capital stock in a country prone to stagnation and unemployment, (2) reducing social conflict by reducing economic inequality and poverty, and (3) inducing higher work efforts due to the negative income effects of high taxation.[9]

Of course, government activity can also have negative effects on economic productivity by (1) inducing lower work efforts and savings due to the substitution effects of high taxation, (2) diverting profit-creating activities into rent-seeking activities, and (3) crowding out private sector investment and production (Hansson and Henrekson, 1994, p. 384).

These considerations suggest an inverted-U relationship between government activity and economic productivity as depicted in Figure 22.2. When the government sector is very small, roads and other infrastructure are low leading to low productivity. As the government sector expands infrastructure improves and productivity rises. Once the government sector expands beyond the optimal ratio g^*, productivity begins to decline as the disincentive effects of high taxation and government crowding out begin to dominate. When all of the gross domestic product is devoted to building roads and the like, economic productivity is again at a very low level.

Peden (1991) has estimated the relationship between labor productivity and the size of the government sector using aggregate data for the United States from 1929 to 1986. The data reveal an inverted-U relationship as in Figure 22.2, with the productivity peak coming at a ratio of government activity to GDP of 17 percent. During the first portion of the time period analyzed, the government sector fell short of its optimal size and productivity expanded with government growth. The optimal ratio was passed during the New Deal in the early 1930s, and since then the government sector has been a drag on productivity. Peden attributes the celebrated productivity slowdown that began at the end of the 1960s to the rapid expansion of the goverment sector in the United States that preceded it.[10]

Hansson and Henrekson (1994) have estimated the relationship between government activity and productivity at the industry level. By looking at productivity in the private sector, they avoid the problem of regressing government outputs onto government outputs, which occurs when aggregate output or productivity is regressed on government outlays. Their sample includes data on 14 industries and 14 OECD countries for the periods 1965–82 and 1970–87. Hansson and Henrekson do not estimate a nonlinear relationship between productivity and government expenditures but, given the nature of their sample, it is safe to assume that the government sectors in *none* of the 14 OECD countries was *smaller* than optimal size. Thus, assuming the nonlinear relationship between government size and productivity of

[9] For further discussion and references to the literature, see Hansson and Henrekson (1994), pp. 382–3.

[10] Some caution must be exercised in accepting Peden's estimate of optimal government size, given the very few observations he had when the government sector was smaller than 17 percent of national income. For related evidence, see Peden and Bradley (1989).

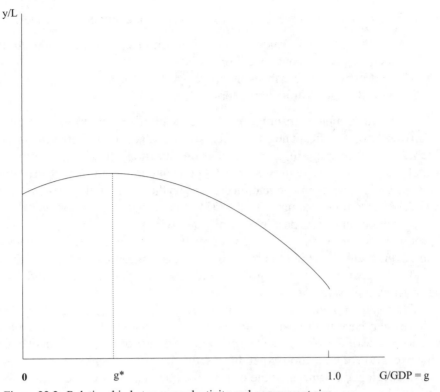

Figure 22.2. Relationship between productivity and government size.

Figure 22.2 is valid, the Hansson and Henrekson estimates should fall along the declining portion of the curve.

Equation (22.15) contains a representative example of Hansson and Henrekson's (1994, Table 5) results for the 1965–82 period (t-statistics are given below coefficients):

$$\text{TFPG} = 0.042 + 0.023\,\dot{k} + 6905\,\dot{l} - 0.001\,\text{CATCH}$$
$$ 4.52 2.26 9.34 2.69$$
$$- 0.168(\text{GC-GE}) + 0.278\,\text{GE} - 0.050\,\text{GI} - 0.083\,\text{GTR} \quad (22.15)$$
$$ 4.24 2.01 0.45 2.76$$
$$\bar{R}^2 = 0.543, \qquad n = 153.$$

The dependent variable is total factor productivity growth (TFPG). The $\dot{k}$ and $\dot{l}$ variables are the share-weighted percentage changes in capital and labor, which have the predicted positive signs. CATCH is the log of the ratio of TFP in an industry and country divided by the highest TFP for that industry in the sample. CATCH is intended to capture the "catch-up" hypothesis. The lower the TFP in an industry in a particular country relative to the highest productivity for this industry, the greater the increase in productivity that can come about by the industry merely copying the available technologies in other countries and thereby catching up. CATCH has the predicted negative sign.

Our main interest, however, is in the government expenditure variables:

$GC - GE$ = government consumption minus government education outlays
GE = government education outlays
GI = government investment
GTR = government transfers.

Both government consumption less education expenditures and government transfers have significant negative effects on industry productivity growth. A ten percentage point increase in government's noneducation consumption outlays reduces total factor productivity growth by 1.68 percent per annum. A ten percentage point increase in government's education outlays, on the other hand, *increases* TFP growth by 2.78 percent per annum. The 14 OECD countries in Hansson and Henrekson's sample would appear to be aligned along the *rising* portion of the government sector-productivity curve of Figure 22.2 with respect to education outlays. The coefficient on government investment is insignificant suggesting that the 14 OECD countries tend to be near the top of the government sector-productivity curve with respect to government investment.[11]

The results of Peden and Hansson and Henrekson reveal that government expenditures can have both positive and negative effects on productivity depending on both the size of the government sector and the nature of the government outlay. With the exception of education expenditures, the scale of government activity within the most developed countries of the world appears to have grown beyond the point that maximizes factor productivity.

Most developing countries have small government sectors, and should therefore be on the rising portion of the inverted-U in Figure 22.2. All governments are not alike, however, with respect to corruption and other attributes of government quality. Olson, Sarna, and Swamy (2000) show for a sample of developing countries that productivity growth is positively related to the quality of government institutions.[12] Both the size of government and the quality of its institutions appear to matter.

22.5   Government size and economic growth

22.5.1 *Methodological issues*

Several studies have tested for a relationship between government activity and a country's growth in income. Behind such tests is an assumption, as in the literature relating government size to productivity, of an inverted-U relationship between the scale of government and economic growth. This assumption is reasonable if we assume that the size of the government sector in each country is exogenously determined, or at least is chosen for reasons other than to maximize a country's rate of

[11] The 14 countries in Hansson and Henrekson's sample were Australia, Belgium, Canada, Denmark, Finland, France, Italy, Japan, the Netherlands, Norway, Sweden, the United Kingdom, the United States, and West Germany.

[12] They use an index of International Country Risk, which combines various factors of government policy that are of concern to international investors, to measure the quality of government institutions.

economic growth. Countries with small government sectors lack the infrastructure to achieve the maximum possible rate of growth (see Figure 22.3a – each point represents an observation for a country). These might be developing countries, which lack even the infrastructure to bring in sufficient tax revenue to supply needed government services (Kau and Rubin, 1981). Countries arrayed along the falling portion of the inverted-U have government sectors that are larger than optimal as far as economic growth is concerned, perhaps because their citizens have chosen to trade off growth for security in the form of a large redistributive government sector, perhaps because their government bureaucracies have succeeded in expanding the government sector beyond the point which the citizens would wish, or perhaps the government sector has grown *too large* for one of the other reasons discussed in the preceding chapter. Under the assumption that a single, inverted-U relationship exists between government size and growth, it does not really matter *why* government sectors are too large or too small; what matters is that both possibilities exist, that is, that countries are located all along the curve.

Alternatively, government leaders or citizens might choose the size of the government sector to maximize the rate of economic growth. If a single, inverted-U relationship between government size and growth exists for all countries, then all wish to have government sectors of the same size. Differences among countries reflect random shocks. The data consist of a cluster of points around the peak of the curve, and no statistical relationship can be observed between the two variables.[13] Given that government sectors range from under 20 percent of the GDP to more than 70 percent, this possibility does not seem likely – at least with respect to total government activity.

A third possibility is that there are several different relationships between government size and economic growth depending on other factors, like the level of economic development in a country. This possibility is illustrated in Figure 22.3b. Curve *L* depicts the relationship between government size and growth in countries with low levels of economic development, *M* in countries with middle levels of economic development, and *H* in highly developed countries. Countries with low levels of economic development typically have low literacy rates, large agricultural sectors, and other attributes that limit their potential rates of growth. Providing the levels of government infrastructure that lead to high growth in a middle-level development country will not do so in a low-level development country. Middle-level countries have the greatest potential for growth, as they can play the "catch-up" game of adopting the technologies of the highly developed countries. The latter cannot, of course, play the catch-up game, and thus their growth potential is more limited.

If within each level of development, countries were arrayed along the full range of the curve as in Figure 22.3a, each curve's parameters could be estimated by separating the data into subsamples of countries of similar levels of economic development. Any relationship estimated for the pooled sample would be spurious.

The same is true, if the size of the government sector is chosen in each country to maximize the rate of economic growth. Under this assumption observations for

---

[13] See Barro (1990, pp. S120–1), and for a more general methodological discussion, Slemrod (1995, pp. 381–9).

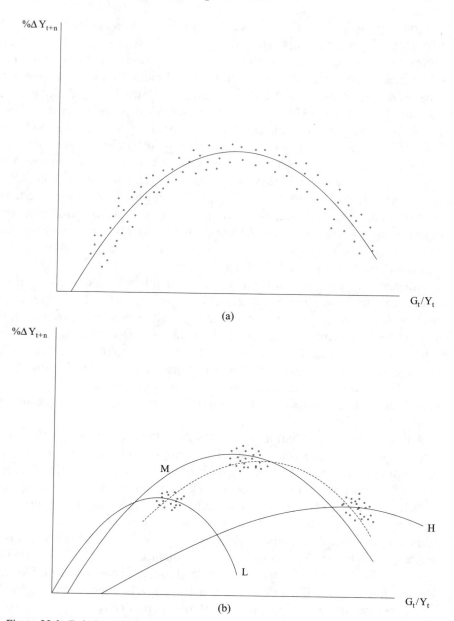

Figure 22.3. Relationships between government size and growth.

countries at each level of development would cluster at the peaks of their respective curves, as illustrated in Figure 22.3b. *If* the positions of the three curves were as shown in this figure, the dashed-inverted-U relationship between government size and growth would be estimated. The implications of this estimated relationship – that low-level development countries would grow faster with larger government sectors, and highly developed countries would grow faster with smaller government sectors – would both be false, however. Each country would have the optimal-sized government sector, given its level of economic development.

These considerations suggest that any systematic relationship that exists between the size of the government sector and economic growth may be difficult to uncover in cross-national data sets. To do so, one must specify carefully the various other control factors – like level of economic development – that may affect the relationship. The next subsection reviews the main findings in this literature.

22.5.2 *The evidence*

Problems of intercountry heterogeneity do not arise, of course, if one estimates the relationship between government size and growth using time-series data for a single country. Grossman (1987, 1988a, 1988b) has done this for the United States and Australia, and his results are consistent with the inverted-U prediction. His estimates for the United States reveal an inverted-U relationship between government size and growth and, like those of Peden (1991) using productivity data, imply that the government sector in the U.S. was *smaller* than the optimal size, in 1929. Grossman's figures suggest that the government sector grew too large, as far as maximizing the growth of income is concerned, during the 1940s.

Barro (1991) tested for the effects of both government size and political stability on the growth of real GDP per capita in 98 countries over the period 1960–85. A representative result from his study is presented in Table 22.3. As control variables Barro used initial income, secondary and primary education enrollment rates, and whether a country was located in Africa or Latin America. Initial income tests the catch-up hypothesis. The lower a country's initial income, the faster it grew. Several studies have failed to find evidence of a catch-up effect. In Barro's it appears only when initial levels of primary and secondary education are controlled for. Here we see evidence of the possible *positive* effects of government on growth, when governments provide primary and secondary education. Holding these and the four political variables constant, there appear to be elements in the African and Latin American cultural/political environments that lead to slower economic growth.

Turning to the political variables we see that the scale of government consumption in a country is *negatively* related to its growth in income. Barro defines government consumption *net* of education and defense expenditures, and thus includes only those activities that are least likely to affect growth positively. Barro argues that it is the distortionary effects of taxes to finance this consumption that leads to slower growth. Distortionary governmental regulation, as proxied by an index of price distortions, also has a negative impact on growth. Political instability, as measured by numbers of revolutions and assassinations, also affects growth adversely.

Barro also tested for a cross-sectional relationship between government investment and economic growth, and found none. Since government investment should have the most direct relationship to economic growth of all components of the public budget, this finding of Barro is consistent with the hypothesis that all governments select the optimal levels of investment for growth, and thus that no cross-section pattern can be observed.

Additional cross-national evidence of a negative relationship between government size, somehow measured, and economic growth has been provided by

Table 22.3. *Growth in income per capita and government size (dependent variable is growth rate of real GDP per capita, 1960–85)*

Coefficient (standard errors)	Explanatory variables
0.0345 (0.0067)	Constant
	Economic and cultural control variables
−0.0068 (0.0009)	GDP per capita (real) in 1960
0.0133 (0.0070)	Secondary school enrollment rate, 1960
0.0263 (0.0060)	Primary school enrollment rate, 1960
−0.0114 (0.0039)	African nation dummy
−0.0129 (0.0030)	Latin American nation dummy
	Political variables
−0.094 (0.026)	Government consumption/GDP
−0.0167 (0.0062)	Revolutions per year
−0.0201 (0.0131)	Political assassinations per million of population and year
−0.0140 (0.0046)	Price distortions index
$R^2 = 0.62$, n = 98	

Source: Barro (1991, Table 1, eq. 14).

Landau (1983), Weede (1984), Grier and Tullock (1989), Scully (1989), Grossman (1990), Fölster and Henrekson (1999, 2001), and Mueller and Stratmann (2000). Of particular interest is the study by Grossman. He, like Barro, attempts to separate the positive and negative impacts of government on growth. Like Barro, he also argues that the negative impacts are due to distortionary taxes. He thus introduces the relative levels of taxation across countries as a separate variable, and finds that it does indeed have a negative and significant effect on growth. Holding this tax effect constant, government consumption expenditures (including education and defense) have a *positive* effect.

Positive effects of government size on growth have also been measured by Ram (1986) and Aschauer (1989), while Kormendi and Meguire (1985), Easterly and Rebelo (1993), and Agell, Lindh, and Ohlsson (1997) essentially find no relationship. Agell, Lindh, and Ohlsson are highly critical of the econometric techniques used in the earlier studies, but more careful econometric tests reveal that, at least for the OECD countries, higher taxes and larger government sectors have a significant negative effect on economic growth (Fölster and Henrekson, 1999, 2001).

Further, although somewhat indirect, corroboration for this statement is provided by the studies of Alesina and Rodrik (1994) and Persson and Tabellini (1994). They argue that government taxation and other sorts of interventions to bring about income inequality are likely to be greater, the greater the initial level of income inequality is. Since these redistribution policies introduce distortions that harm growth, a negative relationship between income inequality and economic growth is predicted and observed.

Persson and Tabellini find that the negative relationship between income inequality and economic growth holds only for democracies.[14] This result is plausible, since the ability of the poor to pressure the government for redistribution is likely to be greater in a democracy. This observation in turn raises the question of the possible effects of democratic institutions on economic growth independent of the size of the government sector. This question was addressed in Chapter 18 and is, therefore, only briefly discussed here.

Some studies have distinguished between democratic and nondemocratic forms of government; others have constructed indexes of economic and political liberties. As with the government size/growth literature, studies can be cited that find a positive relationship between growth and democracy/liberty, a negative relationship, or no relationship whatsoever.[15]

As Levine and Renelt (1992), de Haan and Siermann (1995, 1998), and Heckelman and Stroup (2000) show, the relationship one estimates seems to be very sensitive to the measures of economic liberty and democracy that one uses and the additional explanatory variables included in the equation. Nevertheless, at least with respect to the effect of *economic* liberties on growth, the most recent studies paint a fairly consistent picture. Both Abrams and Lewis (1995) and Knack (1996), for example, find that low-income countries do indeed grow faster than the high-income countries, as the catch-up hypothesis predicts, *if* they have high levels of economic liberties, or in the Abrams/Lewis study are not classified as planned economies.

To measure the strength of market institutions, Knack used the index of International Country Risk (ICR) described earlier. When he omitted this index, he obtained the following results for a sample of the 24 richest, non-OECD countries in 1960.

$$GR6089 = 1.98 - 0.179 \log GDP60, \qquad \bar{R}^2 = -0.04$$
$$(0.20)$$
(22.16)

where GR6089 is the growth in income per capital between 1960 and 1989, and GDP60 is income per capita in 1960. The number in parentheses below the coefficient on logGDP60 is the t-ratio. Without the ICR index, there is no evidence of

[14] Alesina and Rodrik, on the other hand, find that the relationship holds regardless of a country's form of government.

[15] Positive effects of democracy and/or liberty on growth have been reported by Pourgerami (1988, 1992), Scully (1988, 1989, 1992), Grier and Tullock (1989), Dasgupta (1990), De Vanssay and Spindler (1994), Abrams and Lewis (1995), Keefer and Knack (1995), Knack (1996), and Heckelman and Stroup (2000); negative effects have been reported by Landau (1983, 1986), Sloan and Tedin (1987), and Barro (1997); no systematic effects of democracy and/or liberty on growth have been reported by Kormendi and Meguire (1985), Marsh (1988), Levine and Renelt (1992), and de Haan and Siermann (1995).

catch-up. When the index is added, however, a significant catch-up effect appears, and the index itself has a positive effect on growth.

$$GR6089 = 1.43 - 1.93 \log GDP60 + 0.09 ICR.$$
$$\qquad\qquad (2.49) \qquad\qquad (4.89)$$

(22.17)

The signifcant effect of this index of the strength of market institutions holds up with the addition of the measures of school enrollment used by Barro. The works of Barro, Abrams and Lewis, and Knack highlight the positive things governments of developing countries can do to increase the likelihood that they catch up to the richest countries – provide primary and secondary education, free up and protect market institutions.

In closing this review, mention must be made of the recent tests for the robustness of the relationship between economic liberty and growth by de Haan and Siermann (1998). They found that all *nine* of the different measures of economic liberty that they tried had a positive effect on growth, and at least three of them were robust to the inclusion of other variables in the equation. Although uncertainty may remain concerning the *magnitude* of the impact of economic liberties and market institutions on growth, there seems now to be little reason to doubt that their impact is positive.[16]

22.6   Government activity and the economic decline of nations

22.6.1   *The logic*

Where much of the literature relating democracy and economic liberties to growth is concerned with why developing countries do or do not succeed in catching up to the rich countries, Olson (1982) put forward an explanation for why some rich countries "catch up" to poorer ones – why some rich countries enter into economic decline. Although the title of the book in which Olson developed this hypothesis is *The Rise and Decline of Nations*, the novelty of the work lies mostly in Olson's account of the causes of economic decline. Olson's hypothesis builds on his analysis of interest group formation, which we discussed in Chapter 20. Most interest groups pursue redistributive objectives. Business, trade, and professional associations are primary examples of such groups, as are unions. In each case, much of the activity of these groups, insofar as it impinges on others in society, is devoted to creating or preserving monopoly positions. Medical associations seek to restrict entry into medical schools and the licensing of foreign-trained physicians. Unions seek to force employers to hire only union members and to determine wages and other employee benefits by bargaining with the union. Business associations and unions both seek to protect their members from foreign competition by obtaining tariffs and quotas on imports; and by obtaining regulations requiring that the government favor domestic producers in its purchases, government workers favor the nation's flagship airline in their travel, and the like. Thus, much of the activity of the economically oriented interest groups falls under the heading of rent seeking (p. 44).[17]

---

[16] See also Wu and Davis (1999) and Leschke (2000).
[17] All remaining page references in this section are to Olson (1982) unless otherwise noted.

Many interest groups that are not organized along business, trade, or occupational lines, nevertheless, have goals that are, at least in part, distributional. The objectives of associations of the handicapped, the aged, and welfare recipients are largely distributional. Women's and ethnic groups have sought legislation imposing de facto if not de jure hiring quotas on employers.

The heavy emphasis that interest groups place on distributional goals has the consequence that their activities lead largely to jockeying for positions along the utility possibility frontier, not to shifts outward in the frontier. Moreover, each restriction on entry, each quota, and each regulation creates an efficiency loss that shifts inward the utility possibility frontier (pp. 41–7). As more and more energy is devoted to carving up the pie, the pie gets smaller.

Olson uses this redistribution-efficiency loss argument to explain differences in growth rates across nations. Not only does the activity of interest groups (Olson names them "distributional coalitions") shift the production possibility frontier inward, it retards the speed at which it moves outward as a result of the normal growth process. Interest groups tend to be democratic in varying degrees and thus are slow to reach decisions. They are therefore slow to respond to change, and impede the speed with which the organizations that they affect can react to or implement changes. The consequence is that "*distributional coalitions slow down a society's capacity to adopt new technologies and to reallocate resources in response to changing conditions and thereby reduce the rate of economic growth.*"[18]

From this important proposition it follows that a country's growth rate varies inversely with the level of interest group activity ceteris paribus. It takes time to overcome free-rider inertia and to discover the combinations of collective benefits and selective incentives that can induce active involvement in interest group activities. Long periods over which the social and political environment of a country remains stable are conducive to the appearance of new interest groups and the strengthening of existing ones. Periods of social and political stability give rise to growing numbers of interest groups, growing distributional conflicts, and a slowing of economic growth. Conversely, a country whose interest groups were somehow destroyed or institutionally constrained from pursuing their institutional objective would grow faster than one heavily burdened by interest group activity, with again the important ceteris paribus proviso. Olson uses this argument to explain differences in growth rates over the first 25 years after World War II across developed democracies. Germany, Italy, and Japan suffered the greatest devastation to their economic and political institutions, and their growth performance was among the best of the developed countries up through 1970. The occupied, continental European countries also had their interest group structures disrupted to a degree by the war, and then the strength of their interest groups was further eroded by the formation of the Common Market. They, too, had impressive growth rates in the fifties and sixties. Ironically, or so it would seem, it was the countries whose economies and social-institutional structures were least damaged by the war (Australia, New Zealand, the United Kingdom, and the United States) that performed most poorly in terms

---

[18] Bowles and Eatwell (1983) question the leap from arguments related largely to static efficiency to conclusions regarding dynamic performance. Olson defends himself on pages 61–5, and also cites Hicks (1983) in support.

of economic growth up through the early seventies.[19] The power in Olson's thesis comes in explaining why this fact should *not* be viewed with surprise. Indeed, it is precisely because the fabric of interest group structures existing prior to the war was left untorn that these Anglo-Saxon countries performed so poorly relative to both the countries suffering defeat in the war and those that suffered occupation (ch. 4).

Olson employs the logic of his thesis to explain both the exhilarating effect on economic performance of forming a larger economic federation or customs union (ch. 5), and the debilitating effects of discriminatory practices (ch. 6). An intriguing and somewhat controversial example of the latter is Olson's explanation for India's poor economic development performance alongside that of some of its Asian neighbors. Olson attributes India's relatively poor economic performance to an important degree to the rigidities growing out of the caste system. Olson argues that the castes emerged from guilds and other occupational groupings and have functioned like other distributional coalitions trying to protect whatever monopoly or monopsony power its members have. Restricting marriages to members of one's own caste was a form of entry barrier to control the size of the caste and protect its monopoly position. The heavy concern with distributional issues as reflected in the caste system has had the same debilitating effect on India's growth that the distributional struggles among organized interests have had on India's former ruler, Great Britain (pp. 152–61).

22.6.2 *Empirical evidence*

Several attempts have been made to test Olson's theory empirically. The chief challenge comes in trying to measure the strength of interest group activity (Abramovitz, 1983; Pryor, 1983). In initially setting forth the theory, Olson argued that Italy, Germany, and Japan's strong postwar economic performance could be explained by the destruction of their interest group structures wrought by the war and immediate postwar occupation. These examples suggest the hypothesis that interest group strength can be measured by the length of time that has elapsed since a nation's inception, or since its rebirth following a war or revolution. Most tests of the thesis have thus used some time-dependent proxy for interest group strength. Choi (1983) constructed an index of "institutional sclerosis" for 18 OECD countries based on (1) the point in time when common-interest groups begin to accumulate, (2) what and when major disruptions occurred, and how long they lasted, and (3) how strong each disruption was. An example of the results Choi obtained is presented as (22.18) (Choi, 1983, p. 73, equation 14):

$$Y = 7.75 - 0.074\,\mathrm{IS} \qquad R^2 = 0.59, \qquad n = 18. \tag{22.18}$$
$$ (8.81)\ \ (4.78)$$

The dependent variable is the growth in income per capita from 1950 to 1973 and IS is one of Choi's measures of institutional sclerosis, defined to fit a logistic curve so

---

[19] See, for example, Pryor (1983, Tables 5.3 and 5.4, p. 99). Logically, Canada might also be expected to be in this group, since its borders were not crossed during the war. But its growth performance, although not above the average, was also not below.

that it already incorporates a diminishing impact of time on interest group strength after some point. The negative and significant impact of institutional sclerosis proved resilient to (1) how this variable was measured, (2) the choice of dependent variable, and (3) the composition of the sample.

The best example of a nation suffering from acute institutional sclerosis after World War II was the United Kingdom. The best examples of nations rejuvenated by the destruction of their interest group structures were the three axis nations. Murrell (1983) presented yet another test of the hypothesis by more closely examining the U.K. and West German economies.

Murrell reasoned that interest group strength in the United Kingdom would be weakest in the newest industries to have formed, since in these industries interest groups have had the shortest time to develop. Thus, the performances of U.K. industries should be the most comparable to that of West Germany in "young" industries, the furthest behind in "old" industries.

To test the hypothesis, Murrell compared the growth rates of young (j) and old (k) industries in the United Kingdom (UK) and West Germany (WG), standardizing for differences in the average (A) growth rate in each country. The hypothesis was that the growth rates of young industries in the United Kingdom would be relatively higher; that is, the inequality in (22.19) would hold, where G stands for an industry or commodity growth rate from 1969 through 1973:

$$\frac{G_j^{UK} - G_k^{UK}}{G_A^{UK}} > \frac{G_j^{WG} - G_k^{WG}}{G_A^{WG}}. \tag{22.19}$$

The proportions of cases in which (22.19) is satisfied are all significantly above the 0.5 predicted by the null hypothesis, and thus support the hypothesis that institutional sclerosis in the United Kingdom is most advanced in the older industries.

Olson reported results analogous to those obtained by Choi for the 48 contiguous states. A representative example is presented as (22.20):[20]

$$Y = 10.01 - 2.69\,\text{STACIV1} \qquad R^2 = 0.52, \qquad n = 48.$$
$$(7.02) \tag{22.20}$$

The dependent variable is the growth rate of per capita private nonfarm income during 1965–78. STACIV1 is the number of years since statehood divided by 178, with all Confederate states having been assumed to be reborn in 1865. As with Choi's results for the OECD, the significant negative effect of a state's age remains reasonably robust to changes in the definition of the dependent and independent variables (Olson, 1982, pp. 98–108).

As Pryor (1987, pp. 223–4) noted, one might have expected from Olson's theory that the "rise of the South" following its defeat in the Civil War would have begun before the end of World War II, yet the South underperformed the North up through the 1930s.[21] In general, tests of Olson's theory using state data from the United States have tended to reject its implications. Gray and Lowery (1986) found a complete collapse of the Olson model using state data, when it was tested over

---

[20] Equation (24), Table 4.1, p. 104. Olson credits Kwang Choi with having done the regression work.
[21] Quiggin (1992, p. 271) makes a similar point.

a later time period and other variables were added to the equation, as did Wallis and Oates (1988) when population growth by state was treated as an exogenous variable. Nardinelli, Wallace, and Warner (1987) found little support for Olson's hypothesis once differences in income across states were included. On the other hand, corroborative evidence using state data was presented by Vedder and Gallaway (1986), and by Dye (1980).

By and large, tests of Olson's theory using cross-national data have tended to confirm it. Lane and Ersson (1986) found that Choi's measure of institutional sclerosis maintains its significance as other variables are placed alongside of it and the dependent variable is measured over different time periods. Additional studies reporting evidence for the Olson hypothesis based on cross-national comparisons include Whiteley (1983), Paloheimo (1984a,b), Weede (1984, 1986, 1987), Datta and Nugent (1985), Lange and Garrett (1985), Lehner (1985), Goldsmith (1986), McCallum and Blais (1987), Jankowski (1993), and Heckelman (2000b). Quiggen (1992) argues that the hypothesis should be tested using income *levels* rather than growth rates, and rejects the "strong form" of the hypothesis using income levels as the dependent variable, and cross-national data.[22]

An important component of the Olson hypothesis is that interest group strength increases with the number of years over which a country experiences political stability. Kennelly and Murrell (1987) supported this part of the theory by showing that interest group numbers are larger in those industries in which the redistributive gains from interest group action are potentially larger. Murrell (1984) has also established that the number of organized interest groups in a country is positively related to the number of years that a country has had a modern political system receptive to pressure from interest groups. On the other hand, Gray and Lowery (1986) did *not* find a relationship between the age of a state and the number of interest groups in it. Their finding may explain the breakdown of the hypothesis when state data are used.

Many objections to Olson's theory stem from observations of a given country, whose growth record and interest group structures do not accord with what Olson's theory seems to predict, or that argue for a more complicated formulation of the theory (Asselain and Morrison, 1983; Lehner, 1983; Rogowski, 1983; Schuck, 1984; Gustafsson, 1986; Rasch and Sorensen, 1986; Pryor, 1987; Quiggin, 1992). Of particular interest in this regard is the case of Switzerland. Switzerland had the fourth highest index of institutional sclerosis in Choi's list of 18 OECD countries (1983, p. 70), and "has a very differentiated, pluralist structure of interest organization" (Lehner, 1983, p. 204). Yet, its degree of tariff protection was lowest among the 18 OECD countries (Olson, 1982, p. 134), and its growth rate above average over the fifties and sixties (Lehner, 1983, p. 70). The explanation for this apparent inconsistency with Olson's theory is found in the strong federalist nature of its political structure, and the importance of direct democracy at the local level or in the form of the referendum. Since legislative decisions either must be subjected to a referendum vote or can be petitioned to a referendum vote, interest groups cannot

---

[22] Pryor (1983) should also be cited here, but he did not test for the impact of some time-of-stability variable on growth, but rather tested for the impact of several additional variables that he claimed should be correlated with growth if Olson's theory is correct: population size, communist rule, ethnic heterogeneity, and religious heterogeneity. None of these had a significant impact on country growth rates.

strike a bargain with the parties in Parliament or with members of key legislative committees, and obtain redistributional favors, unless a majority of the citizens are willing to ratify the bargain. With the outcomes of referenda being hard to predict, forming a minimum winning coalition is a precarious strategy and the legislature strives for consensual policies (Lehner, 1983). The result is that redistributional struggles do not figure prominently in Swiss political life, despite the strength of their interest group structure.

Thus, one can conclude that Switzerland does not run counter to the main tenets of Olson's theory. The political institutions of Switzerland protect it from the undesirable consequences of the distributional struggles that would otherwise ensue given its fractionalized interest group structure. But the example of Switzerland does point to an important lacuna in Olson's argument. Olson focuses almost exlusively on interest groups and leaves out an analysis of how interest group pressure is channeled by the political and economic institutions of a country to produce the outcomes his theory predicts (Paloheimo, 1984a,b; Lehner, 1985).

This latter point has been pressed by Tang and Hedley (1998) in one of the most recent tests of Olson's theory. Tang and Hedley criticize Olson for neglecting the positive stimulus to growth that government policies can have *when interest groups are weak*. They hypothesize that Olson-type measures of sclerosis will have the predicted impact on growth only in countries where the state has the strength to play an active role in promoting growth. They find support for this hypothesis in a sample of Asian and Latin American countries. The higher growth rates in the Asian countries over the last few decades are attributed to the positive roles government has played in stimulating growth *and* the weak interest group strength in these countries.

In Olson's 1982 book, Germany's economic success was attributed to the destruction of its interest groups during World War II, and Sweden's success was attributed to the cooperation among its large, "encompassing" interest groups. Over the last quarter of the twentieth century, the growth rates of Germany and Sweden have not exceeded those of Great Britain and the United States, and over the last decade of the century even Japan showed signs of sclerosis. If Olson's theory is valid, then we must conclude that interest groups have had sufficient time to entrench themselves in Germany and Japan and thereby have brought on sclerosis, and that interest groups have become less encompassing and cooperative in Sweden.[23] One might buttress the argument further in favor of the Olson hypothesis, by arguing that the Reagan and Thatcher "revolutions" in the United States and the United Kingdom had the kind of interest-group-destroying impact on labor unions that Olson's theory requires for growth. Despite the many tests of Olson's theory that have been made, it still invites more testing.

22.7 Conclusions

In this chapter we have examined several possible effects of government policies on economic activity. The emphasis has been on the negative effects of government

---

[23] For a discussion of Germany's "decline" that is consistent with this interpretation, see Giersch, Paque, and Schmieding (1994). For a discussion of the weakening of cooperation among Sweden's major economic interest groups and the country's relative decline, see Lindbeck (1997).

intervention into the economy. As with almost all questions, the empirical literature that tries to measure these effects does not speak with a clear and unequivocal voice. Nevertheless, the weight of the evidence to date allows us to draw some general conclusions. (1) Taxes distort choices wherever they are levied, and thereby reduce welfare. The magnitude of these welfare losses is in doubt, but it seems likely that it is substantial. (2) The underground economy has, like the government sector, been growing in both developed and developing countries since at least 1960. In some of the developing countries it accounts for as much economic activity as the official sector. High levels of regulation, taxation, heavy-handed and arbitrary administration of regulations, and corruption all encourage the growth of the underground economy. (3) The relationship between the relative size of the public sector and economic performance, as measured by either productivity in the private sector or growth in GDP per capita, is an inverted-U. Too small of a government sector can harm economic performance by denying the economy infrastructure and the educated labor force that it needs to perform optimally. Beyond some point, however, the adverse incentive effects of government activity begin to outweigh its positive effects on economic performance. All of the highly developed countries in the world appear to be in the downward sloping part of the curve.

More tentative are the conclusions one can draw about the effects of democracy on economic performance. Here there is evidence that some forms of bureaucratic, authoritarian governments can bring about faster economic growth than can democratic governments, but the conclusions one can draw depend on both how the different forms of government are categorized, and the composition of one's sample. Equally tentative are the conclusions one can draw from the empirical literature regarding the long-run effects of democratic stability on economic growth. Although democratic stability does appear to have produced "economic sclerosis" in the developed countries of the world in the post–World War II period, the extent to which the "Olson hypothesis" applies to other countries and other time periods is still not clear.

Less controversial is the proposition that *economic liberty* fosters economic growth. Independent of whether their governments are democratically chosen or not, countries with institutions in place that underpin market exchange by ensuring property rights, enforcing contracts, and the like have higher growth rates in GDP per capita.

Virtually all of the works discussed in this chapter have appeared since 1980, and a good number since 1990. This research can be expected to continue to grow at a brisk rate in the years ahead.

Bibliographical notes

Rose-Ackerman (1999) provides a nice overview of the problem of corruption in government. Bardhan (1997) surveys the literature on corruption in developing countries.

Barro (1997) updates his earlier work discussed in the text.

Aghion, Caroli, and Garcia-Peñalosa (1999) survey the literature on economic inequality and growth.

PART V

Normative public choice

CHAPTER 23

Social welfare functions

The interest of the community then is – what? The sum of the interests of the several members who compose it.

Jeremy Bentham

Whereas one can speak of *the* positive theory of public choice, based upon economic man assumptions, one must think of normative *theories* of public choice, for there are many views of what the goals of the state should be and how to achieve them. This potential multiplicity has been the focus of much criticism by positivists, who have argued for a "value-free" discipline. For the bulk of economics, it might be legitimate to focus on explanation and prediction, and leave to politics the explication of the goals of society. For the study of politics itself, in toto, to take this position is less legitimate; thus the interest in how the basic values of society are or can be expressed through the political process. The challenge that normative theory faces is to develop theorems about the expression and realization of values, based on generally accepted postulates, in the same way that positive theory has developed explanatory and predictive theorems from the postulates of rational egoistic behavior. Part V reviews some efforts to take up this challenge.

23.1 The Bergson-Samuelson social welfare function

The traditional means for representing the values of the community in economics is to use a social welfare function (SWF). The seminal paper on SWFs is by Bergson (1938), with the most significant further explication by Samuelson (1947, ch. 8). The SWF can be written as follows:

$$W = W(z_1, z_2, \ldots, z_n),$$

where W is a real valued function of all variables, and the z_is and W are chosen to represent the ethical values of the society or of the individuals in it (Samuelson, 1947, p. 221). The objective is to define a W and set of z_is, and the constraints thereon, to yield meaningful first- and second-order conditions for a maximum W. Although in principle any variables that are related to a society's well-being (e.g., crime statistics, weather data, years of schooling) might be included in the SWF, economists have focused on economic variables. Thus, the SWF literature has adopted the same assumptions about consumers, production functions, and so on, that underlie the bulk of economics and public choice and has made these the focal point of its analysis.

The only value postulate upon which general agreement has been possible has been the Pareto postulate. This postulate suffices to bring about a set of *necessary* conditions for the maximization of W, which limit social choices to points along the generalized Pareto frontier. The proof is analogous to the demonstration that movement from off the contract curve to points on it can be Pareto improvements, and the necessary conditions are also analogous. With respect to production, these conditions are

$$\frac{\partial X_i / \partial V_{1i}}{\partial X_k / \partial V_{1k}} = \cdots = \frac{\partial X_i / \partial V_{mi}}{\partial X_k / \partial V_{mk}} = \frac{T_{xk}}{T_{xi}}, \tag{23.1}$$

where $\partial X_i / \partial V_{mi}$ is the marginal product of factor V_m in the production of output X_i, and T is the transformation function defined over all products and inputs (Samuelson, 1947, pp. 230–3).

> In words this takes the form: *productive factors are correctly allocated if the marginal productivity of a given factor in one line is to the marginal productivity of the same factor in a second line as the marginal productivity of any other factor in the first line is to its marginal productivity in the second line. The value of the common factor of proportionality can be shown to be equal to the marginal cost of the first good in terms of the (displaced amount of the) second good.* (Samuelson, 1947, p. 233; italics in original)

These conditions ensure that the economy is operating on the production possibility frontier. If these conditions were not met, it would be possible to transfer factors of production from one process to another and obtain more of one product without giving up any amounts of another. Such possibilities are ruled out by the Pareto principle.

The necessary conditions for consumption require that the marginal rate of substitution between any two private goods, i and j, be the same for all individuals consuming both goods:

$$\frac{\partial U_1 / \partial X_i}{\partial U_1 / \partial X_j} = \frac{\partial U_2 / \partial X_i}{\partial U_2 / \partial X_j} = \cdots = \frac{\partial U_s / \partial X_i}{\partial U_s / \partial X_j}, \tag{23.2}$$

where $(\partial U_k / \partial X_i)/(\partial U_k / \partial X_j)$ is voter k's marginal rate of substitution between i and j (Samuelson, 1947, pp. 236–8). If (23.2) were not fulfilled, gains from trade would exist, again violating the Pareto postulate. Thus, choice is limited to points along the production possibility frontier – distributions of final products that bring about equality between the marginal rate of transformation of one product into another, and individual marginal rates of substitution (Samuelson, 1947, pp. 238–40).

Through the appropriate set of lump-sum taxes and transfers it is possible to sustain any point along the Pareto-possibility frontier as a competitive equilibrium. Thus, the normative issue to be resolved with the help of the SWF is which point along the generalized Pareto-possibility frontier should be chosen; what set of lump-sum taxes and subsidies is optimal. Both Bergson and Samuelson speak of solving this question with the help of a variant of the SWF in which the utility indexes of each individual are direct arguments in the welfare function

$$W = W(U_1, U_2, \ldots, U_s). \tag{23.3}$$

The issue then arises as to what form W takes, and what the characteristics of the individual utility functions are. In particular, one wants to know whether ordinal utility functions are sufficient, or whether cardinal utility indexes are required, and if the latter, whether interpersonal comparability is required as well. Since the evolution of utility theory over the last century has led to an almost unanimous rejection of cardinal, interpersonally comparable utility functions throughout much of economics, the hope is, of course, that they will not be needed here. But, alas, that hope is in vain.

To see why this is so consider the following simple example: six apples are to be divided between two individuals. On the basis of knowledge of the positions of the two individuals, their tastes for apples, and the ethical values and norms of the community, we believe that social welfare will be maximized with an even division of the apples. The question then is whether an ordinal representation of individuals 1 and 2's preferences can be constructed that always yields this result. Consider first the additive welfare function

$$W = U_1 + U_2. \tag{23.4}$$

We wish to select U_1 and U_2 such that

$$U_1(3) + U_2(3) > U_1(4) + U_2(2). \tag{23.5}$$

Inequality (23.5) implies

$$U_2(3) - U_2(2) > U_1(4) - U_1(3). \tag{23.6}$$

If U_1 is an ordinal utility function, it can be transformed into an equivalent ordinal function by multiplying it by k. This transformation multiplies the right-hand side of (23.6) by k, however, and given any choice of U_2 that is bounded, a k can always be found that will reverse the inequality in (23.6), assuming $U_1(4) - U_1(3) > 0$.

The same holds if W is multiplicative. We then seek a U_1 and U_2 such that

$$U_1(3) \cdot U_2(3) > U_1(4) \cdot U_2(2), \tag{23.7}$$

which is equivalent to

$$\frac{U_2(3)}{U_2(2)} > \frac{U_1(4)}{U_1(3)}. \tag{23.8}$$

However, the ordinality of U_2 is not affected by adding a constant to it, so that (23.8) should also hold for

$$\frac{U_2(3) + k}{U_2(2) + k} > \frac{U_1(4)}{U_1(3)}. \tag{23.9}$$

But the left-hand side of (23.9) tends toward one as k becomes larger, and the inequality will thus reverse for some sufficiently large k if individual 1 experiences some positive utility from consuming the fourth apple.

Other algebraic forms of W are possible, but it should be obvious that the pliability of an ordinal utility function is such that these, too, will be incapable of yielding a maximum at (3,3) under every possible transformation that preserves the ordinality of the Us. The same arguments could be repeated with respect to a comparison of the distribution (4,2) with (5,1), and the distribution (5,1) and (6,0). The only way we will get a determinant outcome from an SWF whose arguments are ordinal utility indicators is to define it lexicographically, that is, to state that society prefers any increase in 1's utility, however small, to any increase in 2's utility, however large, and have this hold independently of the initial utility levels (distribution of income and goods); which is to say, an SWF defined over ordinal utility indexes must be dictatorial if it is to select a single outcome consistently. This result was first established by Kemp and Ng (1976) and Parks (1976) with proofs that follow the Arrow impossibility proofs discussed in Chapter 24 (see also Hammond, 1976; Roberts, 1980c).

The very generality of the ordinal utility function, which makes it attractive for the analysis of *individual* decisions, makes it unsuitable for the analysis of *social* decisions, where trade-offs *across individuals* are envisaged. To make these trade-offs, *either* the relative positions of individuals must be compared directly in terms of the bundles of commodities or command over these commodities they enjoy using the ethical norms of the community, or, if utility indexes are employed, these must be defined in such a way as to make cardinal, interpersonal comparisons possible.

All of this would appear to have been known for some time. Although Bergson's initial exposition of the SWF seems to have led to some confusion over the need for cardinal utilities and interpersonal comparisons,[1] this need was emphasized by Lerner (1944, ch. 3) and clearly addressed by Samuelson (1947, p. 244) in his initial

---

[1] At several places Bergson emphasizes that only ordinal utility indexes are required when deriving the optimality conditions for the SWF and he states directly, "In my opinion the utility calculus introduced by the Cambridge economists [i.e., cardinality] is not a useful tool for welfare economics" (1938, p. 20). From these statements undoubtedly arises the view that Bergson claimed that welfare judgments could be based on ordinal utility indicators. Thus, for example, we have Arrow (1963, p. 110) stating, "It is the great merit of Bergson's 1938 paper to have carried the same principle [Leibnitz's principle of the identity of indiscernibles] into the analysis of social welfare. The social welfare function was to depend only on indifference maps; in other words, welfare judgments were to be based only on interpersonally observable behavior." But the clauses preceding and following "in other words" are not equivalent. And, in fact, Bergson goes on following his attack on the Cambridge economists' use of cardinal utility to argue not for the use of ordinal utility indexes or "interpersonally observable *behavior*," but for interpersonal comparisons of "relative economic positions" and "different commodities." Thus, in rejecting cardinal utility, Bergson opts not for a W defined over ordinal Us but for W defined over the actual physical units, that is, $W(z_1, z_2, \ldots, z_n)$. This leaves the status of W defined over individual, ordinal utility indexes indeterminate, at best.

In his discussion of Arrow's theorem in 1954, Bergson states quite clearly, to my mind, that interpersonal cardinal utility comparisons are required (see, in particular, his discussion of the distribution of wine and bread on pp. 244–5, and n. 8), but Arrow (1963, pp. 111–12) would not agree.

exploration of the SWF:

> An infinity of such positions [points along the generalized contract locus] exists ranging from a situation in which all of the advantage is enjoyed by one individual, through some sort of compromise position, to one in which another individual has all the advantage. Without a well-defined W function, i.e., without assumptions concerning interpersonal comparisons of utility, it is impossible to decide which of these points is best. In terms of a given set of ethical notions which define a *Welfare function* the best point on the generalized contract locus can be determined, and only then. (Italics in original)

And we have Samuelson's (1967) subsequent proof that cardinality alone will not suffice; that is, cardinality *and* interpersonal comparability are required. The issue of whether the arguments of the SWF can be ordinal utility indexes would seem to be finally closed with the appearance of the papers by Kemp and Ng and Parks, were it not that these articles sparked a controversy over precisely the cardinality-ordinality issue involving, perhaps surprisingly, Samuelson (and indirectly Bergson, also). Given the personages involved and the issues at debate, it is perhaps useful to pause and examine their arguments.

The main purpose of Samuelson's (1977) attack on the Kemp-Ng and Parks theorems is, as the title of his note states, to reaffirm the existence of "reasonable" Bergson-Samuelson SWFs. And the note is clearly provoked by the claims by Kemp and Ng and Parks of having established nonexistence or impossibility theorems. In criticizing their theorems, Samuelson focuses on the particular form of axiom Kemp and Ng use to capture ordinality in a Bergson-Samuelson SWF, an axiom that implies that the SWF must be lexicographic. Samuelson is obviously correct in deriding an axiom that makes one individual an "ethical dictator," but his criticism of the theorems of Kemp-Ng, and Parks is misplaced. As Parks's proof most clearly shows, all Bergson-Samuelson SWFs based on ordinal preferences make one individual an ethical dictator.

A careful reading of the Kemp and Ng and Parks papers indicates that they do not claim the nonexistence of *all* reasonable Bergson-Samuelson SWFs, but only of those whose arguments are ordinal, individual utility indicators. Interestingly enough, Kemp and Ng (1976, p. 65) cite Samuelson himself as one of those holding "the apparently widely held belief that Bergson-Samuelson SWFs can be derived from individual ordinal utilities." They cite page 228 of the *Foundations*, the same page, incidentally, that Arrow (1963, pp. 10, 110, n. 49) cites, to indicate that the SWF *is* based on ordinal utilities. On this page appears the following:

> Of course, if utilities are to be added, one would have to catch hold of them first, but there is no need to add utilities. The cardinal utilities enter into the W function as independent variables if assumption (5) [individuals' preferences are to "count"] is made. But the W function is itself only ordinally determinable so that there are an infinity of equally good indicators of it which can be used. Thus, if one of these is written as
>
> $$W = F(U_1, U_2, \ldots),$$

and if we were to change from one set of cardinal indexes of individual utility to another set $(V_1, V_2, \ldots)$, we should simply change the form of the function F so as to leave all social decisions invariant.

This passage clearly states that W is ordinal and seems to imply that the individual utility arguments need not be interpersonally comparable. But the passage appears in the section in which the necessary conditions defining points *along the generalized Pareto-possibility frontier* are derived, and is obviously superseded, or amplified by the passage appearing later in the book on p. 244 and quoted above, where Samuelson makes clear that one *must* "catch hold" of the individual utilities and compare them if a single point out of the Pareto set is to be chosen. However, subsequent statements by Samuelson and his vigorous attack on the Kemp-Ng-Parks theorems would seem to imply that he believes that Bergson-Samuelson SWFs are well defined even when they have the ordinal utility functions of individuals as arguments.[2] The theorems of Kemp and Ng (1976), Parks (1976), Hammond (1976), Roberts (1980c), and still others deny this interpretation. Rather, one must conclude (1) that ordinal utility functions are sufficient as arguments of W when deriving the necessary conditions for a Pareto optimum, but (2) that cardinal, interpersonally comparable arguments are required to select a single, best point from among the infinity of Pareto optima.

23.2   Axiomatic social welfare functions

Kemp and Ng (1976) and Parks (1976) prove their impossibility theorems by demonstrating that it is impossible to have an SWF that satisfies a particular set of axioms, which among other things imply that the arguments of the function are ordinal utility functions. Their theorems naturally raise the question of the sorts of axioms we need to impose to obtain a *reasonable* SWF. In this section we review some of the answers that have been given to this question.

23.2.1   *Fleming's social welfare function*

The pioneering axiomatic treatment of SWFs was by Fleming (1952). Fleming proved that any SWF satisfying the Pareto principle and the elimination of indifferent individuals axiom (EII) must be of the following form:

$$W = f_1(U_1) + f_2(U_2) + \cdots + f_s(U_s). \tag{23.10}$$

Elimination of indifferent individuals axiom: *Given at least three individuals, suppose that i and j are indifferent between x and x', and between y and y', but i prefers x to y, and j prefers y to x. Suppose that all other individuals*

---

[2] See Samuelson (1967, 1977, 1981). Samuelson also attributes this position to Bergson (Samuelson, 1967, pp. 44–5, 48–9), but see my discussion in n. 1.

are indifferent between x and y, and x' and y' (but not necessarily between x and x', and y and y'). Then social preferences must always go in the same way between x and y as they do between x' and y'. (Name and statement follow Ng's (1981b) simpler presentation.)

EII has two important properties. First, as its name implies, it does eliminate individuals who are indifferent between x and y. Second, it requires that whatever convention is used to decide whether i's preferences regarding x and y override j's, it must also decide the pair (x', y') given i and j's indifference between x and x', and y and y'. One sort of convention for deciding whose preferences are overriding would, of course, be to make one person a dictator. An alternative convention would be to posit interpersonally comparable cardinal utility functions for i and j.

The value of W in (23.10) is obviously independent of the ordering of individuals in the $1, s$ sequence, and so the theorem satisfies the anonymity axiom. But the theorem does not tell us much about the functional form of W. In particular, if

$$f_i(U_i) = a_i U_i, \tag{23.11}$$

then (23.10) becomes an additive W. If

$$f_i(U_i) = log(U_i), \tag{23.12}$$

we have essentially a multiplicative W.[3] To specify the SWF more precisely we need additional axioms.

23.2.2 *Harsanyi's social welfare function*

Harsanyi (1953, 1955, 1977) derives an SWF from the following three assumptions:

1. Individual personal preferences satisfy the von Neumann–Morgenstern–Marschak axioms of choice involving risk.
2. Individual ethical preferences satisfy the same axioms.
3. If two prospects P and Q are indifferent from the standpoint of every individual, they are indifferent from a social standpoint.

An individual's personal preferences are those he uses when making his day-to-day decisions. His ethical preferences are used on those more seldom occasions when he makes moral or ethical choices. In making the latter decisions, the individual must weigh the consequences of a given decision on other individuals, and thus must engage in interpersonal utility comparisons.

---

[3] The summation of the logs of the U_is equals the log of their product. Thus the transformation given in (23.12) makes W equal to the log of the product of the individuals' utilities. Since $log(x)$ obtains a maximum when x does, both a W defined as the product of s individuals' utility functions and a W defined as the log of this product will carry the same implications for the optimal values of the arguments of the individual utility functions.

From these three postulates Harsanyi proves the following theorem concerning the form of the SWF, W:

Theorem: *W is a weighted sum of the individual utilities of the form*

$$W = a_1 U_1 + a_2 U_2 + \cdots + a_s U_s, \tag{23.13}$$

where a_i stands for the value that W takes when $U_j = 0$, for all $j \neq i$ (Harsanyi, 1955, p.52).

This is clearly a rather powerful result given the three postulates. As always, when powerful results follow from seemingly weak premises one must reexamine these premises to see whether they perhaps contain a wolf in disguise.

The first assumption simply guarantees a form of individual rationality in the face of risk and seems innocuous as such. When deciding whether to go to the beach or stay home, the rational individual first computes his expected utility from being at the beach. If π_r is the probability that it will rain and π_s is the probability that the sun shines, and U_r and U_s are her utilities in these two states of the world, then her expected utility from being at the beach is $U_B = \pi_r U_r + \pi_s U_s$. The rational individual goes to the beach if this expected utility exceeds the (let us assume) certain utility from staying at home.

The second assumption extends the concept of rationality in the face of risk from the individual's personal preferences to her ethical ones. When making a decision about whether to give \$100 to a poor person, the rational, ethical individual envisages the utility that she would experience if she were a poor person and received \$100, and the utility she would experience if she had \$100 less, and places the appropriate probabilities on each state of the world. The assumption that an individual's preferences satisfy the von Neumann-Morgenstern-Marschak axioms of choice induces the ethical person to add individual utilities when making ethical choices.

Harsanyi's second assumption can be criticized as an illegitimate extension of the notion of individual rationality to social choices. Pattanaik (1968) made this criticism of Harsanyi's SWF and Buchanan (1954a) made a similar criticism of Arrow's SWF, which we shall take up in the next chapter. But this objection seems to carry less weight against Harsanyi than against Arrow. Harsanyi is assuming *individual* evaluations of different social states in both cases; no aggregate will or organic being is even implicitly involved as arguably is the case with Arrow's SWF. The W in Harsanyi's theory is a subjective W in the mind of the individual. If individuals differ in their subjective evaluations, there will be different Ws for different individuals. A collective W need not exist.

Under the assumption that individuals make decisions involving risk by maximizing the expected value of their subjective utilities, Ng (1984a) has established an equivalence between von Neumann-Morgenstern utility indexes and subjective utility indexes. Thus, Harsanyi's first two assumptions effectively introduce interpersonally comparable, cardinal utilities into the SWF.[4]

---

[4] See also Binmore (1994, ch. 4).

The third postulate introduces the individualistic values that underlie Harsanyi's SWF. What is remarkable about Harsanyi's theorem is that he has been able to derive the intuitively plausible additive SWF from these three rather modest looking sets of assumptions.

Knowing that the SWF is additive is only the first, even though large, step in determining the optimal social outcome, however. The weights to be placed on each individual's utility index must be decided, and the utility indexes themselves must be evaluated. It is here that Harsanyi derives the ethical foundation for his SWF. He suggests that each individual evaluate the SWF at each possible state of the world by placing himself in the position of every other individual and mentally adopting their preferences. To make a selection of a state of the world impartial, each individual is to assume that he has an equal probability of being any other person in society (Harsanyi, 1955, p. 54).

The selection of a state of the world is to be a lottery with each individual's utility – evaluated using her own preferences – having an equal probability. "This implies, however, without any additional ethical postulates that an individual's impersonal preferences, if they are rational, must satisfy Marschak's axioms and consequently must define a cardinal social welfare function equal to the arithmetic mean of the utilities of all individuals in society" (Harsanyi, 1955, p. 55). Thus, the *Gedankenexperiment* of assuming that one has an equal probability of possessing both the tastes and position of every other person solves both of our problems. The utility functions are evaluated using each individual's own subjective preferences, and the weights assigned to each, the a_i, are all equal. The SWF can be written simply as the sum of all individual utilities:

$$W = U_1 + U_2 + \cdots + U_s. \tag{23.14}$$

Of course, there are serious practical problems of getting people to engage in this form of mental experiment of evaluating states of the world using other individuals' subjective preferences, and Harsanyi (1955, pp. 55–9; 1977, pp. 57–60) is aware of them. Nevertheless, he holds the view that with enough knowledge of other individuals, people could mentally adopt the preferences of others, and the U_i terms in each individual's evaluation of social welfare would converge. The mental experiment of adopting other individuals' preferences combined with the equiprobability assumption would lead all individuals to arrive at the same, impartial SWF (Harsanyi, 1955, p. 59). Later both Rawls (1971) and Buchanan and Tullock (1962) would introduce uncertainty over future position to bring about unanimous agreement over a social contract and a constitution, respectively. Their work is discussed in Chapters 25 and 26.

23.2.3 *Two criticisms of Harsanyi's social welfare function*

23.2.3.1 *Should individual attitudes toward risk count?* Writing before Harsanyi derived his SWF, but in clear anticipation that the then newly invented von Neumann-

Morgenstern utility indexes would be used to create an SWF, Arrow (1951, 2nd ed. 1963, pp. 8–11) raised the following objection against this use of them:

> This [the von Neumann-Morgenstern theorem] is a very useful matter from the point of view of developing descriptive economic theory of behavior in the presence of random events, but it has nothing to do with welfare considerations, particularly if we are interested primarily in making a social choice among alternative policies in which no random elements enter. To say otherwise would be to assert that the distribution of social income is to be governed by the tastes of individuals for gambling. (Arrow, 1963, p. 10)

More generally, as Sen (1970a, p. 97) notes, the use of the von Neumann-Morgenstern axioms introduces a degree of arbitrariness that is inherent in all cardinalization of utilities.

Whether social choices *should* depend on individual attitudes toward risk is a knotty question. If Jane's attitude toward risk affects her decision about whether to go to the beach or not, then presumably her attitude toward risk may also affect her willingness to give to the poor, assuming that she makes this choice after engaging in the kind of mental experiment that Harsanyi described. Conceivably her attitude toward risk might also affect how she votes on redistribution legislation. To say "that the distribution of the social income" *should not* be governed by such tastes would assume that the preferences of individuals formed in this way should not count. The specter of a "social planer" deciding what the distribution of the social income should be using the "proper" preferences as given in *his or her* SWF arises.

More generally, once we decide that an individual's attitudes toward risk should not count, we must inquire what other preferences of hers should not count – for pornography, for education? Here the conflict between the elitist view of social choice as represented by the social planer choosing social outcomes using an SWF, and the individualistic view of social choice as the outcome of a voting process in which each individual's preferences are counted becomes apparent.

The knowledge that Jane would pay X for a p probability of winning Y tells us something about her preferences for X and Y, just as the knowledge that she prefers Y to X does. The former knowledge actually contains more information than the latter, and this information does not seem a priori inherently inferior to knowledge of simple preference orderings. At least the inferiority of the former sort of information would seem to require further justification.[5]

23.2.3.2 *Can individuals agree on a value for W?* The dependence of the individually determined Ws on individual risk preferences has led both Pattanaik (1968) and Sen (1970a, pp. 141–6) to question whether individuals who engaged in Harsanyi's equiprobability experiment would unanimously agree on which state of the world maximizes W.

---

[5] For additional criticism and discussion of the role of risk preferences in the Harsanyi SWF, see Diamond (1967), Pattanaik (1968), and Sen (1970a, pp. 143–5). For a defense of the use of von Neumann-Morgenstern utilities in social choice analysis, see Binmore (1994, pp. 51–4, 259–99).

Table 23.1. *Outcomes in dollars*

State of the world	T	W
Person		
R	60	100
P	40	10

To see the problem, consider the following example. Let there be two individuals in the community, rich (R) and poor (P), and two possible states of the world, with a progressive tax (T) and without one (W). Table 23.1 gives the possible outcomes in dollar incomes.

In Table 23.2 the von Neumann-Morgenstern utilities for each outcome are presented, scaled in such a way as to make them interpersonally comparable. R is assumed to have constant marginal utility of income; P diminishing marginal utility. If each individual now assumes that he has an equal probability of being R or P in either state of the world, then the von Neumann-Morgenstern postulates of rationality dictate the following evaluation of the two possible states:

$$W_T = 0.5(0.6) + 0.5(0.4) = 0.5$$

$$W_W = 0.5(1.0) + 0.5(0.2) = 0.6.$$

The state of the world without the progressive tax provides the highest expected utility and would, according to Harsanyi, be selected by all impartial individuals. But, reply Pattanaik and Sen, P might easily object. He is clearly much worse off under W than T and experiences a doubling of utility in shifting to T, while R loses less than 1/2. The utility indexes in Table 23.2 reveal P to be risk averse. Given a choice, he might refuse to engage in a fair gamble of having R or P's utility levels under T and W, just as a risk-averse person refuses actuarially fair gambles with monetary prizes. Although the Harsanyi SWF incorporates each individual's risk aversion into the evaluations of the U_i, it does not allow for differences in risk aversion among the impartial observers who determine the SWF values. If they differ in their preferences toward risk, so too will their evaluations of social welfare under the possible states of the world, and unanimous agreement on the SWF will not be possible (Pattanaik, 1968).

The Pattanaik-Sen critique basically challenges Harsanyi's assumption that the von Neumann-Morgenstern-Marschak axioms can reasonably be assumed to hold for the ethical choices individuals make when uncertain of their future positions. In defense of postulating that these axioms hold at this stage of the analysis, one

Table 23.2. *Outcomes in utility units*

State of the world	T	W
Person		
R	0.6	1.0
P	0.4	0.2

Table 23.3. *Outcomes in utility units*
(second round of averaging)

State of the world	T	W
Person		
N	0.5	0.6
A	0.44	0.42

can reiterate that the utilities that make up the arguments of W *already* reflect individual attitudes toward risk. To argue that special allowance for risk aversion must be made in determining W from the individual U_is is to insist that social outcomes be discounted twice for risk, a position that requires its own defense (Harsanyi, 1975b; Ng, 1984a).

An alternative response to the Pattanaik-Sen critique is to extend the logic of Harsanyi's mental experiment and assume that each individual uses not his own risk preferences, but that he assumes that he has an equal probability of having the risk preferences of every other individual. Suppose that in our example one individual was risk neutral (N) and the other risk averse (A). Their evaluations of the alternative states of the world might then look something like the figures in Table 23.3.

The elements of row N represent the simple expected values of states T and W occurring, assuming that an individual has the same probability of being R or P and is risk neutral. Row A presents the lower evaluations that a risk-averse person might place on the possible outcomes. The social welfare levels under these two states of the world, assuming that each individual has an equal probability of being rich and poor *and of being risk averse or risk neutral*, would then be

$$W_T = 0.5(0.5) + 0.5(0.44) = 0.47$$

$$W_W = 0.5(0.6) + 0.5(0.42) = 0.51.$$

The state of the world without the tax is again preferred, although by a narrower margin.

The same objection to this outcome can be raised, however, as was raised to the first. A risk-averse person will recognize that the tax alternative favoring the rich has a greater likelihood of being selected under risk-neutral preferences than under risk-averse preferences. He might then object to being forced to accept a gamble that gave him an equal chance of having risk-neutral or risk-averse preferences, in the same way that he would reject a fair gamble of experiencing the utility levels of the rich and poor. This objection can be met in the same way as the previous objection, however. Reevaluate the two states of the world assuming each individual has an equal probability of being risk neutral or risk averse using the utility levels from the previous round of averaging as this round's arguments for the utility functions. If the utility functions are smooth and convex, convergence on a single set of values for W_T and W_W can be expected.[6]

---

[6] Vickrey (1960, pp. 531–2) was the first to suggest repeated averaging of welfare functions to bring about consensus. Mueller (1973) and Mueller, Tollison, and Willett (1974a) have proposed using this technique as an

Here the reader may begin to feel his credulity stretching. Not only is an ethically minded citizen supposed to take on the subjective preferences of all other citizens, these preferences must be defined over both physical units (like apples and money) and the interpersonally comparable cardinal utility units of each individual, and he must be prepared to engage in a potentially infinite series of mental experiments to arrive at *the* social welfare evaluation to which all impartial citizens agree. The price of unanimity is high.

Although this type of criticism cannot be readily dismissed, it must be kept in mind that what we seek here is not a formula for evaluating social outcomes that each individual can apply to come up with a unique number. What we seek is a way of conceptualizing the problem of social choice to which we all might agree, *and* which might help us arrive at an agreement over actual social choices were we to apply the principles emerging from this form of mental experiment. The difference between the straight application of the Harsanyi SWF to a social choice problem, and a version of it modified to take into account the criticisms of Pattanaik and Sen involves simply the question of how much weight should be placed on the preferences of risk-averse individuals. For example, if one individual in the community is maximin risk averse, repeated averaging will result in the selection of the state of the world that maximizes the welfare of the worst-off individual (Mueller, Tollison, and Willett, 1974a). This is essentially the *just* social outcome, which Rawls (1971) obtains from a similar starting position as that assumed by Harsanyi, but without the use of any utility calculations.

Thus, in evaluating the "realism" of the Harsanyi approach, the issues are these:

1. Can one envisage individuals obtaining sufficient information about the positions and psychology of other individuals to allow them to engage in the interpersonal comparisons inherent in the approach?
2. Can individuals assume an impartial attitude toward all individuals in the community, and from this impartial stance agree on a set of weights (a common attitude toward risk) to be attached to the positions of each individual when making the social choice?

If for some social choices it is reasonable to assume that the answers to these two questions are both "yes," then for these choices the Harsanyi SWF can be a useful analytic construct.

23.2.4 *Ng's social welfare function*

Ng (1975) has derived an additive SWF in which the utilities of each individual are measured in "finite sensibility" units. The concept of a finite sensibility unit is built on "the recognition of the fact that human beings are not finitely discriminative"

answer to Pattanaik and Sen's objections to the Harsanyi SWF. Vickrey set up the problem of maximizing social welfare as the choice of a set of rules for a community that one is about to enter not knowing one's position in it. The setting is obviously similar to that envisaged by Harsanyi, and not surprisingly we find Vickrey arguing for a weighted summation of von Neumann-Morgenstern (or "Bernoullian") utility functions. Vickrey resorts to repeated averaging in the event that there is disagreement over the values of the weighted sums.

(p. 545). Thus, for a small enough change in x to x' an individual is indifferent between x and x' even though $x \neq x'$. Individuals are capable of perceiving changes in x only for discrete intervals in x. These discrete steps in an individual's perceptions of changes in x become the building blocks for a cardinal utility index measured in finite sensibility units. To the finite sensibility postulate Ng adds the weak majority preference criterion.

Weak majority preference criterion: *If a majority prefers x to y, and all members of the minority are indifferent between x and y, then society prefers x to y.*

The weak majority preference criterion incorporates the ethical values built into the SWF. It is obviously a combination of both the Pareto principle and the majority rule principle that is at once significantly weaker than both. In contrast to the Pareto criterion, it requires a majority to be better off, not just one person, to justify a move. And, in contrast to majority rule, it allows the majority to be decisive only against an indifferent minority. In spite of this apparent weakness, the postulate nevertheless proves strong enough to support a Benthamite SWF whose arguments are unweighted individual utilities measured in finite sensibility units, that is, equation (23.14). For those who dismiss Harsanyi's theorem justifying (23.14), because it introduces attitudes toward risk through the use of von Neumann-Morgenstern utility indexes, Ng's theorem offers a powerful alternative justification for the Benthamite SWF, which does not introduce risk in any way.

From the perspective of public choice, the theorems of Harsanyi and Ng are the most important justifications for the additive SWF, since their basic axioms are easily interpretable as conditions one might wish to incorporate into a set of constitutional rules, and in Harsanyi's case, the whole context in which the SWF is derived resembles the settings from which Rawls and Buchanan and Tullock derive their social contract and constitution, respectively. In Chapter 26 we shall analyze the differences and similarities in the three approaches.

23.2.5 *Nash's and other multiplicative social welfare functions*

Where the additive SWF is most often associated with the name Jeremy Bentham, the multiplicative SWF is most often associated with the name John Nash. Nash's (1950) objective, however, was not to derive an SWF, but rather to come up with a solution to a two-person "bargaining problem." When generalized to s persons, however, Nash's solution to bargaining problems can be regarded as a multiplicative SWF (Luce and Raiffa, 1957, pp. 349–50).

$$W = (U_1 - U_1^*)(U_2 - U_2^*) \cdots (U_s - U_s^*). \tag{23.15}$$

The utilities that go into the welfare function are defined relative to a status quo point at which $U_i = U_i^*$ for all i. This formulation is natural for the bargaining problem that Nash first addressed. Should a bargain not be reached, the status quo is the outcome of the game. All gains from the bargain are measured relative to this status quo starting point.

The axioms needed to derive the Nash SWF are few and rather innocuous. The utility functions must, of course, be cardinal, and the Pareto principle, an α-contraction property and a symmetry condition, must also be satisfied.

Property α: *If x is a member of the choice set defined over the full set of alternatives S, then x is a member of the choice set of any proper subset of S of which it is a member* (Sen, 1969).

Symmetry: *If an abstract version of a bargaining game places the players in completely symmetric roles, the arbitrated value shall yield them equal utility payoffs, where utility is measured in units which make the game symmetric* (Luce and Raiffa, 1957, p. 127).

Nash's solution to the bargaining problem was put forward more as a description of the outcome of a game than as a prescription as to what the outcome ought to be. On the other hand, Nash does argue that the outcome is fair, and it is because of the inherent fairness of the outcome, which should be apparent to both sides, that one expects the solution satisfying (23.15) to emerge (Luce and Raiffa, 1957, pp. 128–32).

However, the delimitation of the gains to be shared is sensitive to the choice of the status quo point. The important role played by the status quo in the Nash SWF has led to its criticism as a normative construct by Sen (1970a, pp. 118–21). If bargaining on social choices takes place, given market-determined income and wealth and presently defined property rights, then the scope for alleviating current inequities through collective action will be greatly restricted.

On the other hand, conceptualizing the problem of selecting a set of rules to govern the political game as a "bargaining problem" does seem to be a reasonable way to view the writing of a constitution or a social contract by individuals *who are not uncertain about their future preferences and/or positions*. Were one to think of the social contract as being the set of rules selected from a hypothetical or real state of anarchy, then the status quo point would be the "natural distribution" of property that would exist under anarchy (Bush, 1972; Buchanan, 1975a). The gains from cooperation would then be enormous and a rather egalitarian sharing of these gains as implied by the Nash SWF might indeed be deemed fair, as Nash thought it would be.

Viewing the status quo as the starting position from a state of anarchy resembles the setup in the Kaneko and Nakamura (1979) theorem. They derive conditions for an SWF of the Nash form as in (23.15), but $(U_1^*, U_2^*, \ldots, U_s^*)$ is defined not as the status quo, but as the worst possible state for each individual that we can imagine. It is doubtful if modern man were thrust into true anarchy that his utility would be much higher than that envisaged by Kaneko and Nakamura. As with all of the SWFs that we have been considering, the Kaneko/Nakamura SWF satisfies anonymity and the Pareto postulate. They also assume a form of the independence of irrelevant alternatives axiom, which we shall examine at length in the next chapter, and make the "fundamental assumption that we evaluate the social welfare by considering relative increases of individuals' welfare from the origin" (p. 426). This assumption, combined with their use of von Neumann-Morgenstern utility indexes, forces one to compare ratios of utilities across individuals rather than absolute differences and obviously goes most of the way toward requiring an SWF in multiplicative form.

The most general characterization of a multiplicative SWF is by DeMeyer and Plott (1971). They measure intensity differences as ratios of utilities (relative utilities) and go on to derive an SWF of the form

$$W = U_1^K \cdot U_2^K \cdots U_s^K, \tag{23.16}$$

where K is a real number.

23.3   What form of social welfare function is best?

We have now seen that it is possible to derive either an additive or a multiplicative SWF from a few basic axioms. In both cases we need to assume that their arguments are some form of cardinal, interpersonally comparable utility indexes if we are going to use them to select optimal states of the world, or optimal political institutions. Both types of SWF satisfy the Pareto postulate; both also satisfy an anonymity axiom. Each differs from the other, however, in some important ways with respect to their other axiomatic properties. Rather than analyze each axiom in detail, we shall close this chapter by considering some simple examples that illustrate the properties of these two different types of SWFs. We shall confine our attention to the simplest form of each.

$$W = U_1 + U_2 + \cdots + U_s \tag{23.17}$$
$$W = U_1 \cdot U_2 \cdots U_s. \tag{23.18}$$

Consider now Table 23.4. Each entry represents the cardinal, interpersonally comparable utility level of either individual i or j in the two possible states of the world G and M. These utility levels allow for any diminishing marginal utility of income, and thus i's income in state G might be 3, 4, or 10 times her income in M, even though her utility level in G is only double her utility in M. If a social choice had to be made between G and M, which state should be chosen? An additive W selects M – a multiplicative G.

Regardless of which choice the reader makes, it should be obvious that it is possible that other readers will make the opposite choice. To see this point more clearly, assume that i and j are really the same person at two different times in her life, and G and M are two alternative career paths. Path G is a job in government with somewhat lower income and utility at the start than later. Path M is a career in medicine with lower utility at the start than the government job, but much higher utility later. Given full knowledge of the utility payoffs to each career choice, it is conceivable that some rational, self-interested individuals favor the career in government,

Table 23.4.

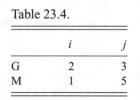

	i	j
G	2	3
M	1	5

Table 23.5.

		Individuals				
		1	2	3	4	5
	A	1	1	1	1	1
States	B	0.0001	10,000	1	1	1
	C	0.0001	10	10	10	10

others medicine; if this is true, then some will probably prefer a multiplicative welfare function, others an additive.

As this example suggests, the choice of the multiplicative welfare function is likely to hinge on one's values with regard to how egalitarian the distribution of *utilities* ought to be. Recall that the entries in Table 23.4 are in utilities, not incomes. If the marginal utility of income declines, the differences in the utility levels i and j experience are smaller than the differences in their incomes. A choice of G over M as a state of the world (career) indicates a strong preference for egalitarian outcomes.

With a multiplicative SWF, a doubling of i's utility is offset by a halving of j's. An increase in i's utility from 100 to 200 is fully offset by a decline in j's from 100 to 50. Requiring that such trade-offs be made in the SWF has been criticized by Ng (1981b) on the grounds that it can lead some individuals to make very large sacrifices to avoid very small *absolute* declines in utility for others. Suppose, for example, that a society of five faces the choice among the three states of the world A, B, and C as in Table 23.5. In state A, all five experience a relatively modest level of welfare. In B, one is utterly miserable (almost to the point of suicide), two are ecstatic, and the other three individuals are as in state A. In C, one is again miserable, but all four of the other individuals are 10 times better off than in A. An additive welfare function ranks B above C, and places both above A. The multiplicative regards A, B, and C as socially indifferent.

Those who object to the choice of B over A argue that the use of the additive welfare function in this situation allows individual 1 to be used as a *means* to 2's gain in violation of Kant's fundamental dictum.[7] Indeed, with an additive W, a maximum could arise at which some individuals have zero or negative utilities. Killing a wealthy invalid and redistributing her property to the healthy poor could easily raise an additive W. If j were a sadist, then j's torture of i so that i has negative utility (wishes he were dead) could raise W. With a multiplicative W, no state with any $U_i \leq 0$ could ever be chosen as long as some states are feasible for which all $U_i > 0$.

As a counterargument to these examples, note that although increases in W can easily be envisaged as involving murder and torture, that maximum W would occur at these points is less plausible. If i is not a masochist, then a less costly (in terms of the interpersonally comparable U's) way of increasing U_j is probably available, than by letting j torture i.

---

[7] See, in particular, Rawls (1971). Sen's (1979) critique of welfarism is also relevant here. Rawls does not argue for a multiplicative welfare function, but rather a lexicographic one (setting aside his objections to utilitarianism). Rawls's theory is discussed in Chapter 25.

The same logic and arithmetic that make A and B equal with multiplicative W, make C not better than A, although here the exchange of making four people considerably better off for making one modestly worse off in absolute terms may strike some as reasonable. Note again that one could well imagine individuals making such a trade-off for themselves. If at the age of 21 the reader were given a choice between living the next 50 years at, say, the poverty line, versus living 10 of those years at the margin of existence and 40 in the affluence of the upper middle class, it is more than conceivable that the reader would make the Faustian choice for the second alternative. If these options are represented reasonably by the utility numbers in rows A and C in Table 23.5, then the reader has made the choice using a criterion that is closer to the additive than to the multiplicative SWF. If the reader would make choices such as these by implicitly adding the different utility levels, why would it be wrong for society to use the same criterion?

One possible reply to this question is to argue that, although it is perfectly acceptable for an individual to make choices by adding her utility levels at different points in time, since she is making choices for herself and may compare her utilities at different points in time any way she wants, when the welfare levels of *different* persons are to be compared, the trade-offs inherent in the additive W are unacceptable for the means-ends reason given above. A different criterion, one more protective of individual rights as in the multiplicative W, is required when one makes interpersonal welfare choices, from that which may be reasonable or acceptable for making intrapersonal choices.

This reply raises indirectly the issue of the context in which the SWF is used. Many observers seem to think of an SWF as an analytic tool to be used by a policymaker, who plugs in the U_is and then maximizes; that is, some unknown third party is making social choices *for* society. In this setting, the issues of how the U_is are measured and what trade-offs in utility are allowed across individuals are salient. Constraints on the choices that protect individuals from having their welfare lowered for the benefit of others in the community, as introduced through a multiplicative W, have much appeal.

An alternative way to view W, however, is to see it as a guide to writing the constitution, the set of rules by which the society makes collective decisions. If one views these rules as being chosen by self-interested individuals who are uncertain of the future positions they will hold when the rules are in effect, then in choosing an SWF (that is, a set of rules to implement an SWF), one is not making an interpersonal choice but rather an *intra*personal one. One is choosing a set of rules to maximize one's own welfare, given that one is uncertain about what position and utility function one will possess. In this context, an additive W would seem appropriate as a social welfare function if individual choices tend to be made by comparing differences in utility levels at different points in time.

The context in which the SWF is to be used is also relevant to the issue of whether and how cardinal utilities are to be measured. The abhorrence of economists for the concept of cardinal utility would seem to stem from a fear that some bureaucrat would go about metering and somehow combining individual utilities to reach decisions on social policies. Evidence from the psychological literature and sensitivity studies that indexes of cardinal utility can be constructed might from this perspective be viewed more with alarm than enthusiasm.

But if one views the SWF as a construct to guide an individual's choice in selecting a constitution, a choice made from behind a veil of ignorance concerning one's future position and utility function, then the issue is whether people can conceptualize being a slave and a slave owner, and compare their utilities in both roles. If they can, then choosing a set of rules to implement a W of whatever functional form is at least a hypothetical possibility. This is the setting in which Rawls (1971) and Buchanan and Tullock (1962) envisage a social contract and set of constitutional rules being chosen, and Harsanyi an SWF. It is the context in which the concept of an SWF seems most useful to the study of collective decision making. We return to these issues in Chapters 25 and 26.

Bibliographical notes

Following the pioneering papers by Parks (1976) and Kemp and Ng (1976), several papers appeared reestablishing the impossibility of a Bergson-Samuelson SWF with ordinal utility arguments, or the necessity of using cardinal, interpersonally comparable utility indexes (D'Aspremont and Gevers, 1977; Pollack, 1979; Roberts, 1980a,b,c); for a survey see Sen (1977b).

I have been of the opinion, ever since I read Bergson (1938) and Samuelson (1947, ch. 8) on SWFs, that cardinal, interpersonal utility comparisons were necessary to select a single allocation as best among those in the Pareto set. Moreover, I believe this opinion was commonly shared among welfare-public choice theorists. The papers of Kemp and Ng (1976) and Parks (1976) appeared to me to be important not so much because they brought startling new results to light, but because they proved formally what had been known or suspected for some time. I thus confess to some befuddlement at the nature and tone of the Samuelson (1977, 1981) and Kemp and Ng (1977, 1987) debate.

The seminal contributions of Harsanyi appeared in 1953 and 1955. The argument has been reviewed and alternative proofs of the theorem presented in Harsanyi (1977, ch. 4).

Sugden and Weale (1979) link their SWF theorem directly to the constitutional-contracting setting. Their theorem resembles Fleming's (1952).

Ng's (1975) original theorem reviewed here, and his subsequent elaborations thereon (1981b, 1982, 1983, 1984b, 1985a, 2000), constitute a most forceful defense of the additive SWF.

The literature on experimentally measuring utilities is reviewed in Vickrey (1960) and Ng (1975).

For axiomatic derivations of the Nash SWF, besides Nash's (1950) own, see Luce and Raiffa (1957, pp. 124–32, 349–50) and Sen (1970a, pp. 118–21, 126–8).

Section 23.3 draws heavily on Ng (1981b). See also Bergson (1938), Samuelson (1947), Little (1957), Sen (1979), and Ng (1981a).

Binmore's (1994, 1998) two-volume treatise contains a broad-ranging discussion of utility indexes, cardinal and ordinal, and their use in normative analysis.

CHAPTER 24

The impossibility of a social ordering

The only orthodox object of the institution of government is to secure the greatest degree of happiness possible to the general mass of those associated under it.

Thomas Jefferson

A really scientific method for arriving at the result which is, on the whole, most satisfactory to a body of electors, seems to be still a *desideratum*.

Charles Dodgson
(Lewis Carroll)

The Bergson-Samuelson SWF has been constructed analogously to the individual's utility function. Just as the individual chooses bundles of commodities to maximize his utility, society must choose an allocation of commodities across individuals to maximize its welfare. That consumers make choices to maximize their utility follows almost tautologically from the definition of rationality. In extending the idea of maximizing an objective function to the level of society, however, more is involved than just rationality. Embedded in the characteristics of the welfare function and the nature of the data fed into it are the value judgments that give the SWF its normative content, as the discussions of Bergson (1938) and Samuelson (1947, ch. 8) make clear.

An alternative way of analyzing individual behavior from assuming that individuals maximize their utility is to assume various postulates about individual rationality that suffice to define a preference ordering, and allow one to predict which bundle an individual will choose from any environment. Again by analogy, one can make various postulates about social decision making and analyze society's decisions in terms of social preference orderings. What choice should a society make from a given environment? Again, however, in shifting from the individual to the societal level, the postulates change from simply defining rationality to expressing the ethical norms of the community. This is important to keep in mind because some of the axioms *sound as if* they simply require collective rationality, and some writers have so interpreted them. This is not the course followed here. In discussing each axiom, we emphasize its normative content.

The first and most important attempt to define an SWF as a social ordering satisfying a few, basic ethical axioms was made by Arrow in 1951 (rev. ed. 1963). Although some of Arrow's discussion of the individual axioms seems to mix ethical and rational considerations, the overriding objective of the inquiry is normative, and our emphasis on the normative characteristics of the axioms does not seem out of place. Arrow, himself, has accepted the interpretation of these axioms as indicating the basic value judgments to be incorporated in the community's social contract or constitution,[1] and this is perhaps the best way to look at them. The question then is this: What ethical norms are we to impose on the social choice process, and what collective choice processes satisfy these axioms? The answer is disappointing. Given but a few fairly weak and ethically uninspiring axioms, no process (voting, the market, or otherwise) exists that satisfies them.

We begin by briefly stating the axioms and sketching the impossibility proof, after which we turn to a more detailed examination of the axioms.

24.1 Logic of the proof

I follow Vickrey's (1960) restatement of the postulates and proof, since they are simpler and shorter.

1. *Unanimity* (the Pareto postulate): If an individual's preference is unopposed by any contrary preference of any other individual, this preference is preserved in the social ordering.
2. *Nondictatorship*: No individual enjoys a position such that whenever he expresses a preference between any two alternatives and all other individuals express the opposite preference, his preference is always preserved in the social ordering.
3. *Transitivity*: The social welfare function gives a consistent ordering of all feasible alternatives. That is, $(aPbPc) \rightarrow (aPc)$, and $(aIbIc) \rightarrow (aIc)$.
4. *Range* (unrestricted domain): There is some "universal" alternative u such that for every pair of other alternatives x and y and for every individual, each of the six possible strict orderings of u, x, and y is contained in some admissible ranking of all alternatives for the individual.[2]
5. *Independence of irrelevant alternatives*: The social choice between any two alternatives must depend only on the orderings of individuals over these two alternatives, and not on their orderings over other alternatives.[3]

---

[1] This interpretation was first put forward by Kemp and Asimakopulos (1952) and was subsequently endorsed by Arrow (1963, pp. 104–5).

[2] Arrow's statement of the axiom is as follows:

> Among all the alternatives there is a set S of three alternatives such that, for any set of individual orderings $T_1, \ldots, T_n$ of the alternatives in S, there is an admissible set of individual orderings $R_1, \ldots, R_n$ of all alternatives such that, for each individual i, $x R_i y$ if and only if $x T_i y$ for x and y in S (Arrow, 1963, p. 24).

[3] Vickrey states this postulate somewhat differently, but his proof relies on it in this form. This statement of the axiom also differs from Arrow's original statement of it, and others existing in the literature. Arrow's statement is as follows:

> Let $R_1, \ldots, R_n$ and $R'_1, \ldots, R'_n$ be two sets of individual orderings and let $C(S)$ and $C'(S)$ be the corresponding social choice functions. If, for all individuals i and all x and y in a given environment S, $x R_i y$ if and only if $x R'_i y$, then $C(S)$ and $C'(S)$ are the same (Arrow, 1963, p. 27).

For a statement of the axiom in the present way, and impossibility proofs based on it, see Sen (1970a).

Condition 4 perhaps requires an additional word of explanation. The notion of a universal alternative is not crucial here. What is implied by the range axiom is that the social choice process allows any possible ordering of the three alternatives x, y, and u. The process is not established in such a way as to rule out possible orderings.

The theorem states that no SWF satisfies these five postulates. To understand the significance of the theorem, it is useful to run through the proof, again following Vickrey. We first define a decisive set D.

Definition of decisive set: *A set of individuals D is decisive, for alternatives x and y in a given social welfare function, if the function yields a social preference for x over y, whenever all individuals in D prefer x to y, and all others prefer y to x.*

Proof:

Step	Justification
1. Let D be a set of individuals decisive for x and y	Assumption
2. Assume for all members of D $xPyPu$, and for all others (those in C) $yPuPx$	Range
3. For society xPy	Definition of D
4. For society yPu	Unanimity
5. For society xPu	Transitivity
6. But for only members of D is xPu	Assumption
7. Society must prefer x to u regardless of changes in rankings of y or any other alternatives	Independence
8. D is decisive for x and u	Definition
9. D is decisive for all pairs of alternatives	Repetition of steps 2–8
10. D must contain two or more persons	Nondictatorship
11. Divide D into two nonempty subsets A and B	Assumption
12. Assume for A $x'Py'Pu'$ for B $y'Pu'Px'$ for C $u'Px'Py'$	Range
13. Since for members of A and B, $y'Pu'$, for society $y'Pu'$	Definition of D
14. If for society $y'Px'$, B is decisive for y' and x'	Definition of D
15. If for society $x'Py'$, then for society $x'Pu'$	Transitivity
16. But then A is decisive for x' and u'	Definition of D

In either case, one of the proper subsets of D is decisive for a pair of issues, and therefore by step 9 for all issues. Steps 10–16 can be repeated for this new decisive set and then continued until the decisive set contains but one member, thus contradicting the nondictatorship postulate.[4]   □

---

[4] This literature is replete with this form of "Chinese boxes" proof to uncover the dictator. For an important variant thereon with infinite numbers of voters, see Kirman and Sondermann (1972).

The intuition underlying the proof runs as follows: the unrestricted domain assumption allows any possible constellation of ordinal preferences. When a unanimously preferred alternative does not emerge, some method for choosing among the Pareto-preferred alternatives must be found. The independence assumption restricts attention to the ordinal preferences of individuals for any two issues when deciding those issues. But as we have seen in our discussions of majority rule, it is all too easy to construct rules that yield choices between two alternatives but produce a cycle when three successive pairwise choices are made. The transitivity postulate forces a choice among the three, however. The social choice process is not to be left indecisive (Arrow, 1963, p. 120). However, with the information at hand – that is, individual ordinal rankings of issue pairs – there is no method for making such a choice that is not imposed or dictatorial.

24.2   Relaxing the postulates

To avoid the impossibility result, the postulates must be relaxed. Before doing so, however, let us consider the significance of the theorem as it stands, for its significance stems precisely from the weakness of the postulates as now stated. Although, as we shall see, these axioms are somewhat stronger than they might first appear, they are far weaker than one would wish to impose at the constitutional stage to satisfy reasonable notions of distributional equity. For example, there is nothing in the axioms to preclude one group of individuals, as long as it has more than one member, from tyrannizing over the others, if it stays on the Pareto frontier.[5] Even allowing this and still other violations of our ideas of equity, we cannot find a process to choose from among the Pareto-optimal set that satisfies these axioms.

Space precludes a complete review of all modifications of the postulates that have been made to produce either possibility theorems or new impossibility results. Instead, we focus on modifications of particular relevance to public choice.

Relaxing unanimity and nondictatorship hardly seems worth discussing if the ideals of individualism and citizen sovereignty are to be maintained.[6] These two axioms clearly illustrate that what we are engaged in here is a normative exercise. There is nothing particularly irrational about selecting one individual and allowing him to make all decisions for the community; indeed, arguments for an omniscient dictator have been around at least since Plato's eloquent defense of this alternative in *The Republic*.[7] But such arguments are inconsistent with our most basic democratic ideals. Special mention should also be made of Hobbes's defense of monarchy (1651). To Hobbes, there was one issue on which all preferences were identical: life in anarchy was terrible and inferior to life under a unanimously accepted dictator. If one made the other postulates part of the Hobbesian contract, one might construct a new defense of autocracy; and, of course, in practice the dictatorial solution to the

---

[5] See Sen's amusing example (1977a, p. 57).

[6] However, see Little (1952).

[7] Bell (1973) presents the modern version of this position. After citing Arrow's proof at a number of places to indicate the difficulty that purely democratic processes have reaching decisions, he opts for choice by technocratic experts who form the ruling elite in the postindustrial society.

uncertainties and deadlocks of social choice is very popular. Empirically, it might be interesting to investigate the frequency with which dictatorial governments replace democratic ones following apparent deadlocks of the latter stemming from voting paradoxes. The other three axioms require more detailed discussion.

24.2.1 *Transitivity*

Arrow's reasons for requiring that the social choice process produce a consistent social ordering appear to be (1) "that some social choice be made from any environment" (1963, p. 118), and (2) that this choice be independent of the path to it (p. 120). These are in fact different requirements, and neither of them requires the full force of transitivity.

The requirement that the social choice process should be able to make some choice from any environment seems the easiest to defend, deadlocks of democracy being an open invitation to dictatorship. But to achieve the goal one does not have to assume the existence of a social preference ordering defined on the basis of all individual preference orderings. To make choices one needs only a *choice function* that allows one to select a best alternative from any set of feasible alternatives (Sen, 1970a, pp. 47–55; Plott, 1971, 1976). Transitivity is not required. Either quasi-transitivity or acyclicity will suffice (Sen, 1970a, pp. 47–55). Both of these conditions are milder than transitivity. Quasi-transitivity requires transitivity of the preference relation, but not of indifference; acyclicity allows x_1 to be only "at least as good as" x_n even though $x_1 P x_2 P x_3, \ldots, x_{n-1} P x_n$. Possibility theorems have been proven by replacing transitivity by either of these and retaining the other Arrow axioms. Gibbard (1969) has shown, however, that requiring a quasi-transitive ordering of the social choice function produces an oligarchy that can impose its unanimous preference on the rest of the community; and Brown (1975) has shown that acyclicity gives veto power to *every* member of a subset of the committee that Brown calls a "collegium."[8] Thus, as one relaxes the consistency requirement from transitivity to quasi-transitivity, and then to acyclicity, dictatorial power becomes spread and transformed, but does not disappear entirely. Requiring the social decision process to be decisive in some sense vests one individual or a subset of individuals with the power to decide, or at least block, any outcome.[9]

Although relaxing the transitivity axiom has some advantage in spreading dictatorial power across a wider group, it incurs the additional cost of introducing a degree of arbitrariness into the process (Sen, 1970a, pp. 47–55). Under quasi-transitivity, for example, *aIb* and *bIc* can exist along with *aPc*. Then, in a choice between *a* and *b*, society can pick either, but if *c* is added to the set, society must pick only *a*. If *a*, *b*, and *c* are points on the Pareto frontier, there will be distributional consequences to the choice of any one. Those favored under *b* may question the ethical underpinnings of a process that makes their fate dependent in such a seemingly capricious way on the set of alternatives under consideration.

---

[8] See also Blau and Deb (1977).

[9] For further discussion of this point, see Brown (1973), Plott (1976, pp. 543–6), and Sen (1977a, pp. 58–63).

The gain from relaxing the transitivity axiom is further reduced when one considers the restrictions that must be placed on the patterns of individual preference orderings to ensure that either quasi-transitivity or acyclicity holds. For majority rule, at least, the conditions that are necessary and sufficient for acyclicity are the same as those required for quasi-transitivity, and these in turn will also ensure transitivity when the number of individuals is odd.[10] Thus, if the property of having a choice made from every environment is to be maintained, there appears to be little lost by sticking to the full transitivity requirement.

The intuition behind requiring the final outcome to be independent of the path to it is somewhat different. Here, to begin with, a *path to* the final outcome is obviously assumed. That is, a choice is not made from the full set of all possible candidates, but instead winners are selected from subsets of the full issue set. These in turn are pitted against one another in some manner, and a given path is followed until a final choice set is found. The requirement that the social choice process should be path independent amounts to the requirement that the final choice set should be independent of how the initial subsets are formed out of the full issue set (Plott, 1973).

Path independence is related to and in fact implies another condition that has received much attention in the literature, Sen's (1969) property α, already introduced in Chapter 23. Property α states that if x is a member of the choice set defined over the full set of alternatives S, then x is a member of the choice set of any proper subset of S of which it is a member. Property α is one of a group of *contraction-consistent* properties that have been investigated.[11] As the set of alternatives is contracted, x must continue to be chosen as long as it is one of the alternatives. The intuitive notion here is perhaps obvious: if x is the best chess player in the world, then he is also the best chess player in London. Path independence in this context requires that x's emergence as champion be independent of how the original runoff matches were ordered. This latter requirement is obviously stronger than the former, which explains why path independence implies the α-property, but not the reverse.

Complementary to α and the other contraction-consistent properties are a set of *expansion-consistent* properties such as the β property (Sen, 1969, 1970a, 1977a). The β property states that if x and y are both members of the choice set for some subset S_1 of the full set S, then x can be a member of the choice set of S if and only if y is. Returning to our chess champion examples, if x and y tie for the chess championship of England, then the β property requires that they both be among those who tie for the chess championship of the world, if either one of them ties for the world championship. As Sen pointed out, it is quite plausible in examples such as these for two individuals to tie in a local contest, but one goes on to beat all others and emerge the world champion. Thus, although β may be a reasonable constraint to place on some choice processes, as when contestants are measured in a single dimension like weight, it does not seem as reasonable when the candidates are measured (or compete) in several dimensions. Since issues arising in a social choice context are likely to take the latter form, it is quite possible that a social

[10] See Sen and Pattanaik (1969), Inada (1970), and Sen (1977a).
[11] See Sen (1977a, pp. 63–71).

decision process would violate property β and still not seem inherently irrational or unfair.

Thus, of the two types of properties, the intuitive support for contraction-consistent or path-independent properties seems much stronger than for expansion-consistent properties of the β type. What we seek is the social choice, or set of choices, that defeats all others. Having found such a choice, it would be comforting to know that its selection was independent of the chance way in which earlier contests were established (path independence), and that it could compete again against any subset of losers and still emerge a winner (α property). Unfortunately, it is path independence and the α properties, even in their weakest forms, that lead to dictatorial or oligarchical social preference orderings; the only possibility theorems that have been proven impose only expansion-consistent properties of the β type.[12]

Let us consider somewhat further what is at stake if we abandon all vestiges of the transitivity axiom. Requiring that the social choice process satisfy this axiom is motivated in part by the desire to avoid the embarrassment of inconsistency and arbitrariness. But this view in turn seems to stem from the belief that, just as it is *irrational* for an individual to exhibit inconsistent preference orderings, it is *wrong* for society to do so. Buchanan (1954a) made an early attack on Arrow's generalization of the concept of individual rationality to collective choice processes focusing precisely on this axiom, and Plott (1972) has extended and generalized this line of criticism. If the transitivity axiom is to earn a place in our constitutional set of constraints on the social choice process, then it must do so by demonstrating that the arbitrary outcomes arising from cyclic preference orderings violate some basic ethical norm. This need not be true. Small committees often resort to random processes such as the flip of a coin, or the drawing of straws to resolve issues of direct conflict. Although obviously arbitrary, the general popularity of random decision procedures to resolve conflictual issues suggests that "fairness" may be an ethical norm that is more basic than the norm captured by the transitivity axiom for decisions of this sort. One might then think of replacing Arrow's notion of collective rationality with the requirement that the social decision process be fair. Transitivity could then be relaxed by simply declaring society indifferent to all choices along the Pareto frontier. Any choice among them will be somewhat arbitrary, but it just might meet with general acceptance. The winners of chess, tennis, and similar elimination tournaments may on occasion be dependent on the particular set of drawings (paths) occurring. This does not seem to detract from the widespread acceptability of this form of tournament for determining the "best" player, however, since the method of determining a sequence of plays is regarded as fair, and the nature of the process precludes the determination of which of the contests were, in fact, path dependent. Thus, it is possible that a social decision process which was intransitive or path dependent, but had additional desirable properties such as fairness, could be widely acceptable. If there is more general agreement concerning these rules than for transitivity or the other consistency properties, the Arrow problem is solved (Kemp, 1954).

---

[12] Plott (1976, pp. 569–75); Sen (1977a, pp. 71–5).

24.2.2 *Unrestricted domain*

The justification for requiring this axiom is something akin to requiring freedom of choice or expression. Each individual should be free to have any preference ordering he might select and the collective choice process should be capable of reflecting these preferences in accordance with the other axioms. Although freedom of choice strikes a responsive chord, we have seen how quickly conflict can arise when individuals have different preference orderings even over how a given piece of public land is to be used. A set of cyclic preferences is quite possible, and if we also require transitivity, we are well on the way to an impossibility result. It should be obvious that some preference orderings are diametrically opposed to one another. This must follow almost of necessity from Axiom 1, which limits consideration to points along the Pareto frontier, that is, to pure distributional issues. Establishing a committee procedure to resolve these issues, without placing any constraints on the preferences that the individuals can express, seems doomed to failure from the start. Indeed, Saari (1994, p. 327) has observed that the combination of unrestricted domain plus the independence of the irrelevant alternatives axiom allows individual preference orderings to be intransitive. Is it any wonder that the social ordering may violate transitivity?

There are two ways around this problem. One is to replace unrestricted domain with other axioms limiting the types of preference orderings that the collective choice process is capable of reflecting. In the context of public choice, this implies placing constitutional constraints on the types of issues that can come up before the collective. The protection of certain property rights is one example of this type of constraint. Everyone can be a member of the community, but not every preference can be satisfied or necessarily even recorded as part of the collective choice process. The alternative solution is to restrict entry into the community to those having preference orderings that do make collective choices possible.

The first thing to note in this context is that requiring that individual preferences be transitive will *not* solve our problem. Something more, like extremal restriction, is required.[13] Single-peakedness ensures that majority rule produces an outcome, namely, the median, and single-peakedness along with the other four axioms produces a nondictatorial SWF. But this way out of the dilemma requires strict restrictions on both the selection of issues to be decided and the voters to decide them (Slutsky, 1977b). Issues must all be of the one-dimensional variety: the number of guns, the number of schoolbooks. The voters cannot simultaneously consider both the number and kinds of books; and their preferences must be single-peaked in this one dimension. If fate provides voters of this type, these kinds of issues can be resolved by majority rule without violating the other axioms, although we are still left with a plethora of multidimensional issues to resolve in some other way. If some individuals' preferences have multiple peaks, these individuals must somehow be isolated and excluded from the community, or an impossibility result can again emerge.

---

[13] See Chapter 5.

The single-peakedness and extremal-restriction conditions implicitly introduce a degree of homogeneity of tastes assumption, for there must be a consensus over how the social choices are ordered along some left–right dimension.[14] More generally, the experimental work on majority rule cycles reviewed in Chapter 5 indicates that the probability of a cycle occurring decreases as voter preferences become more "homogeneous," and increases with increasing voter "antagonism" (Plott, 1976, p. 532). These results suggest searching for ways of restricting membership in the polity to those with sufficiently homogeneous or complementary preferences to avoid the impossibility result. The theories of clubs and voting-with-the-feet describe processes by which groups with homogeneous tastes might form. In the absence of externalities across clubs (local communities), and with perfect mobility, free entry, and so on, such a process might avoid the Arrow problem. But, as we have seen, when spillovers exist, some decisions may have to be made by the aggregate population, and the impossibility problem will apply here, even when "solved" in the smaller ones. In such likely circumstances, homogeneity of preferences can be brought about only if individuals adopt or already have a common set of values (Bergson, 1954). Appeals to reason, à la Kant, or uncertainty, à la Rawls (1971) and Harsanyi (1955), are along these lines.

24.2.3 *Independence of irrelevant alternatives*

Of all the axioms, the independence of irrelevant alternatives has been the subject of the most discussion and criticism.[15] In justifying this axiom Arrow (1963, p. 110) made the following argument:

> The Condition of Independence of Irrelevant Alternatives extend the requirements of observability one step farther. Given the set of alternatives available for society to choose among, it could be expected that ideally, one could observe all preferences among the available alternatives, but there would be no way to observe preferences among alternatives not feasible for society . . . clearly, social decision processes which are independent of irrelevant alternatives have a strong practical advantage. After all, every known electoral system satisfies this condition.

Here Arrow defends the axiom in terms of limiting attention to feasible alternatives only, and this objective of the axiom has led Plott (1971, 1976) to restate and rename the axiom specifically in terms of infeasible alternatives. But in his original discussion of the axiom, Arrow presents an example using the rank-order or Borda method discussed in Chapter 7, in which candidates are ranked according to their position in each voter's preferences. In the example Arrow (1963, p. 27) gives, x wins from a slate of x, y, z and w, but draws with z when y is dropped from the list. Thus, under the Borda method the outcome depends on the nature of the full list of candidates. One of Arrow's objectives for invoking the independence axiom would appear to be to eliminate procedures like the Borda method so that "Knowing the

---

[14] Arrow (1963, p. 80) and Sen (1970a, pp. 166–71).
[15] As noted in n. 3, Arrow's statement of the axiom differs from the one presented here.

social choices made in pairwise comparisons in turn determines the entire social ordering and therefore the social choice function $C(S)$ for all possible environments" (p. 28). Now this is precisely what the independence axiom stated earlier (condition 5) achieves, and it does eliminate procedures like the Borda method from consideration. Thus, our use of this form of the independence axiom would appear to be fully consistent with Arrow's objectives in introducing it.[16] The question then is, what is the normative value to limiting the informational content of collective choice processes in this way?

The outcomes under the Borda procedure and similar schemes depend on the specific (and full) set of issues to be decided. Thus, abandonment of the independence axiom raises the importance of the process that selects the issues to be decided in a way that its acceptance does not. When the choice between x and y can be made by considering voter preferences on only x and y, the rest of the agenda need not be known. This property of the independence axiom has an appealing economy to it, but it is this property that opens the door to endless cycling over these *other* items in the agenda.

By restricting the choice between two alternatives to information on individual rankings of these two alternatives, the independence axiom excludes all information with which one might cardinalize and interpersonally compare utilities (Sen, 1970a, pp. 89–91). It was the desire to establish a welfare function that was not based on interpersonal utility comparisons that first motivated Arrow (1963, pp. 8–11, 109–11). There would appear to be two distinct justifications for wishing to exclude cardinal utility information from a collective choice process. The first is that the measurement of cardinal utilities is difficult and arbitrary, and any process that was based on combining interpersonally comparable, cardinal utilities would be vulnerable to abuse by those making the cardinal utility measurements. This would appear to be Arrow's chief fear (pp. 8–11). It rests on Arrow's view of the collective choice process as one in which information is gathered by public officials who make the actual choices for the collective (pp. 106–8). Allowing these officials to engage in cardinal, interpersonal utility comparisons would vest them with a great deal of discretionary power and might be something to be avoided.

The danger of an abuse of discretionary power does not arise, however, if the cardinal utility information is provided by the voters themselves, as when they take part in the process using, say, the point voting procedure discussed in Chapter 8. Now a different problem arises, however. Such procedures are vulnerable to the strategic misrepresentation of preferences. The independence axiom eliminates not only these strategy-prone procedures, but all voting procedures that are vulnerable to strategizing. This property is sufficiently important to warrant separate treatment.

---

[16] As Plott (1971, 1976) and Ray (1973) have shown, however, Arrow's original statement of the axiom as given in n. 3 does not exclude the Borda procedure limited to outcomes in the feasible set. It does eliminate the Borda procedure when the ranks are assigned over the set of all possible alternatives, feasible and infeasible, and thus does limit some of this procedure's scope for strategic behavior (Plott, 1976). For additional comment on this axiom, see Bergson (1954), Blau (1972), Hansson (1973), Kemp and Ng (1987), and Saari (1994).

24.3   Strategy-proof social welfare functions

The preceding discussion indicates that an important objective of Arrow in imposing the independence of irrelevant alternatives axiom was to eliminate the possibility of individuals being made better off under a collective decision procedure if they did not state their true preferences as inputs into the collective decision process. Vickrey (1960, pp. 517–19) speculated that immunity to strategic manipulation and satisfying the independence axiom were logically equivalent, and subsequently this insight was rigorously established by Gibbard (1973) and Satterthwaite (1975).

The relationship between independence of irrelevant alternatives (IIA) and strategy proofness (SP) is brought out most clearly by Blin and Satterthwaite (1978).

Strategy proofness (SP): *Let M_i be the message i supplies the voting procedure when she states her true preferences. Let M_i' be any misstatement of i's preferences. Let x be the social outcome from the voting procedure when i states M_i and all other voters j state their true preferences M_j. Let y be the social outcome when i states M_i' and all other voters state their true preferences M_j. Then a voting procedure is strategy proof, if and only if for all possible M_i' there exists no y such that $y P_i x$.*

Another way to think of strategy proofness is that every profile of true preferences must be a Nash equilibrium under the voting procedure (Blin and Satterthwaite, 1978, p. 257, n. 10).

Blin and Satterthwaite first prove an Arrow-type impossibility theory for the three axioms, nondictatorship (ND), Pareto optimality (PO), and IIA, and two not yet defined axioms, rationality (R) and positive association (PA). R states simply that the voting procedure must define a social preference ordering and subsumes transitivity. PA requires that if x is chosen under one profile of individual preferences, then it must also be chosen under a second profile of preferences that differs from the first only in that x has gone up in one or more individuals' preference orderings.[17]

They then show that the three axioms R, IIA, and PA are equivalent to R and SP. Thus, SP and IIA are not equivalent, but when one demands that the voting process be rational, that is, that it define a consistent social ordering, they come close to being so.

Because R, IIA, and RP are equivalent to R and SP, and it is impossible to have a voting procedure that satisfies R, IIA, RP, ND, and PO, it is impossible to have a voting procedure that satisfies R, SP, ND, and PO. To see the logic of this result, consider a simple example, where we have but two voters (1 and 2) and three alternatives (x, y, z).[18] Each voter can order the three alternatives in six possible ways. Thus, there are 36 possible combinations of the two voters' preference

---

[17] Note that this axiom is not the same as the positive responsiveness axiom used in May's (1952) theorem on majority rule (discussed earlier in ch. 6). Rather, it resembles nonnegative responsiveness as defined by Sen (1970a, pp. 68–9, 74–7).

[18] With this example we follow the exposition of Feldman (1979, pp. 465–72). Kalai and Muller (1977) show that a strategy-proof SWF exists for a group of $n > 2$, if and only if it exists for a group of two. Thus, a complete proof for a committee of two would suffice for the general case.

Table 24.1. *Possible orderings (6 of 36) of two voters'*
preferences over three issues

1	2	1	2	1	2	1	2	1	2	1	2
x	x	x	x	x	y	x	y	x	z	x	z
y	y	y	z	y	x	y	z	y	x	y	y
z	z	z	y	z	z	z	x	z	y	z	x

orderings, of which six are presented in Table 24.1. Voter 1's preferences are the
same in all six cases, $x P_1 y P_1 z$, and 2's preferences run through the full set of six
possible orderings. In the first two combinations or orderings, both voters rank x
highest. Thus, by the Pareto principle, x must be the social choice if both voters state
either of these sets of preferences. By further application of the Pareto principle, we
establish the following restrictions on the social choice for the six combinations of
preferences.

$$x \quad x \quad x \text{ or } y \quad x \text{ or } y \quad x \text{ or } z \quad x \text{ or } y \text{ or } z.$$

Voter 1's preferences are the same in all six cases. If 1 honestly states this preference ordering, then any differences in the outcomes that come about must be due
to differences in 2's stated preferences. Now consider the third case, where 2's preferences are $y P_2 x P_2 z$. This preference ordering in conjunction with 1's must yield
either x or y as the social choice to be consistent with the Pareto principle. Suppose
from this third case the social outcome were x. Voter 2 prefers y to x under the
preferences given in this third case. If they are his true preferences, and the voting
rule were such that y would be the outcome if 2 stated any of the preferences 4, 5, or
6, then the procedure would not be strategy-proof; 2 would then state the preference
ordering that produced y, given 1's honestly stated ordering. Thus, given that x is
the social outcome in case 3, y cannot be the outcome in cases 4, 5, and 6, and
we now have the following constraints on the social outcome imposed by strategy
proofness.

$$x \quad x \quad x \quad x \quad x \text{ or } z \quad x \text{ or } z.$$

Under the preferences of case 4 ($y P_2 z P_2 x$), 2 prefers z to x. Were these 2's true
preferences, and z were the social choice for either case 5 or 6, 2 would again have
an incentive to misstate his preferences so they appear as in either 5 or 6 when they
are really as in 4. Thus, strategy proofness requires x to be the social choice for the
pairs of preference orderings in cases 5 and 6. But that implies that x is the social
choice when 1's preferences are $x P_1 y P_1 z$ regardless of what 2's preferences are,
which is to say that 1 is a dictator.

Had we assumed that y was the outcome from case 3, we could have shown that
nonmanipulation required 2 to be a dictator. The remaining 30 cases can be handled
in a similar manner.

The close relationship between strategy proofness and independence of irrelevant
alternatives is apparent from this example. In the third combination of individual

preferences depicted in Table 24.1, the two individuals disagree only with respect to whether x is better than y, or the reverse. The independence axiom confines the social choice to using only information from the two individuals' rankings of this pair when choosing the socially preferred outcome. If the social choice process picks x in this situation, it effectively makes 1's preferences dominant over 2's, and 1 becomes the dictator. If y is the social choice, 2 is effectively a dictator.

If the voting procedure's selection of an alternative is sensitive to the voter's full statement of preferences over the 3 or more issues in the issue set, the scope for strategic manipulation of the procedure exists *unless* one voter is treated as a dictator. The dictator has an incentive to be honest, and the preferences of the other voters do not matter. When the voting procedure processes information on only individual, ordinal preferences on issue pairs, as required by the independence axiom, and the procedure is positively responsive, voters will honestly state their true preferences. But information on ordinal preferences on issue pairs does not in general suffice to determine a consistent social preference ordering over the full set of issues. One must make one voter a dictator to ensure transitive social preferences.

The public choice literature builds on the behavioral postulate that individuals rationally and slavishly pursue their self-interests. Whenever the outcome of a voting procedure can be manipulated by cheating, this postulate requires that we assume that voters will cheat – thus, the concern in the public choice literature with finding cheat-proof voting procedures, and the importance of the theorems establishing the impossibility of finding such procedures.

But the negative side to these theorems should not be overdrawn. We saw in Chapter 14 that the rational, self-interest assumption does not give us a very satisfactory predictive theory of voter behavior. Individuals appear to be conditioned to behave in ways that do not fit a narrow definition of self-interested behavior. To what extent individuals who vote out of a sense of "civic duty" would vote strategically is not clear, even if they could figure out what their strategic vote should be.[19]

The more sophisticated voting procedures discussed in Chapter 8 require manipulative strategies that are likely to go beyond the capacities of most voters. The obvious strategy of overloading one's vote points on one's most preferred candidates is curbed in Hylland and Zeckhauser's (1979) version of point voting by the use of a square-root aggregation procedure. The demand revelation process is strategy-proof, although perhaps not Pareto optimal.[20] Voting by veto is strategy-proof, but does not define a social preference ordering.[21] The significance of the impossibility results regarding strategy proofness must be examined in each case. Vernon Smith's (1977) experimental results indicating that students using the auction method of

---

[19] Cox (1997) presents considerable evidence implying that a small, but nontrivial fraction of citizens do vote strategically in some elections.

[20] The demand revelation process also violates the unrestricted domain assumption by placing certain constraints on individual preferences; for example, they prefer paying less taxes than more. See Sugden (1981, pp. 164–5).

[21] Voting by veto attaches probabilities to the outcomes in the feasible set rather than defining a social ordering over them (Mueller, 1984). In general, probabilistic voting rules that satisfy a positive association condition, as does voting by veto, fare much better with regard to strategy proofness than do deterministic rules. See Gibbard (1977) and Barbera (1977). Note also the similarity between this finding and the results for the political competition models (Chapters 11 and 12).

voting did not behave strategically must again be cited as evidence showing that what one can prove to be a certain hypothetical possibility does not always happen.

24.4   Implications for public choice

The Arrow theorem rests on five axioms that appear to be fairly moderate and reasonable restrictions to place on the collective choice process. The theorem states that no process can exist that satisfies all five axioms simultaneously. In designing a collective choice process, writing our political constitution, we must violate one or more of the axioms – although in so doing we may be able to satisfy the others – and still more to be added to the list.

From a public choice perspective, two promising avenues might be followed out of the Arrow paradox. One is to drop the transitivity axiom and abandon the search for a *best* alternative, *the* social preference. In its place could then be substituted the requirement that the social choice process be fair or accord with some other generally held democratic value. For example, one of the probabilistic voting procedures with desirable normative properties like voting by veto could be substituted for the deterministic ones (see n. 21). Alternatively, if a social ordering must be made, then either the independence axiom or unrestricted domain must be relaxed.

If we continue to interpret these axioms as restrictions on the collective choice process written into the constitution, then these conclusions have the following implications. Axiom 1 limits consideration to points along the Pareto frontier. But a choice from among these involves distributional issues directly, and cycles will occur under any voting process requiring less than full unanimity. Thus, if the majority rule or any other less-than-unanimity rule is chosen, some fair or otherwise generally accepted way for breaking cycles must be included in the constitution.

Relaxing the unrestricted domain assumption to allow only single-peaked preferences does not seem to be a very promising way out of the paradox, since so few issues can realistically be thought of as unidimensional. When collective decisions are restricted to the provision of public goods, the restrictions on preferences that underlie Caplin and Nalebuff's (1988) theorem seem likely to be satisfied, and cycles could be avoided by requiring majorities in excess of 64 percent to pass issues. Some other voting rule would still be needed to deal with redistribution issues.

Alternatively, one can think of designing the constitution in such a way as to allow for the revelation of preferences for public goods via voluntary association in private and local clubs. This solution solves the problem by imposing a form of unanimity condition, but again leaves aside all distributional considerations, and the problems of resolving differences of opinion on global public goods.

Where strategic behavior is not a problem, one of the procedures that gathers information on the voters' preferences over the full set of alternatives, like the Borda procedure or point voting, can be used. As we noted in Chapter 8, however, the normative properties of these procedures depend heavily on what issues are allowed into the decision set. Thus, relaxing either the unrestricted domain assumption or independence of irrelevant alternatives raises questions as to what issues are to be decided, who is to decide, and of those who decide, which preferences shall be weighed and with what weights. Such choices directly or indirectly involve interpersonal utility comparisons and must rest on some additional value postulates which, if explicitly introduced, would imply specific interpersonal utility comparisons. The latter cannot be avoided if a preferred social choice is to be proclaimed.[22]

We close our discussion of the Arrow axiomatic SWF at the same point we were at with the Bergson-Samuelson real-valued SWF.

Bibliographical notes

The difference between Arrow's SWF and the Bergson-Samuelson SWF has been the subject of much discussion (Arrow, 1963, pp. 23–4; Samuelson, 1967; Sen, 1970a, pp. 33–6).

Numerous books and articles survey and extend the impossibility result first established by Arrow. See, in particular, Riker (1961, 1982b), Rothenberg (1961), Arrow (1963, ch. 8), Sen (1970a, 1977a,b, 1999), Pattanaik (1971, 1997), Taylor (1971), Fishburn (1973), Plott (1976), Kelly (1978), MacKay (1980), Suzumura (1983), and Saari (1994).

---

[22] Kemp and Asimakopulos (1952), Hildreth (1953), Bergson (1954), Sen (1970a, pp. 123–5, 1974, 1977b).

CHAPTER 25

A just social contract

A republican constitution is a constitution which is founded upon three principles. First, the principle of the *freedom* of all members of a society as men. Second, the principle of the *dependence* of all upon a single common legislation as subjects, and third, the principle of the *equality* of all as *citizens*. This is the only constitution which is derived from the idea of an ongoing contract upon which all rightful legislation of a nation must be based. (Italics in original)

Immanuel Kant

One of the most influential studies of the first stages of the social choice process has been Rawls's *A Theory of Justice* (1971). This book is at once a contribution to moral and to political philosophy. Rawls relies on work and results appearing in various branches of the social sciences, however, and applies his theory to several of the major issues of the day. For this reason, Rawls's work has been widely read and discussed and has had a substantial impact on the economics literature in general, and on collective choice in particular.

Rawls's theory differs from those that we have discussed up to now in its focus on the *process* or *context* in which decisions are made as much as, if not more than, on the outcomes of this process. The goal is to establish a set of just institutions in which collective decision making can take place. No presumption is made that these institutions or the decisions emerging from them will in any sense maximize the social good (pp. 30–1, 586–7).[1] Here we see a clear break with the social welfare function approach. More generally, Rawls challenges the utilitarian philosophy that underlies the SWF methodology and that has reigned in discussions of these topics over the past two centuries.[2]

Rawls sets out to develop a set of principles to apply to the development of "the basic structure of society. They are to govern the assignment of rights and duties and regulate the distribution of social and economic advantages" (p. 61). These principles form the foundation of the social contract, and Rawls's theory is clearly

---

[1] This and all subsequent page references in this chapter are to Rawls (1971) unless otherwise indicated.

[2] Bruce Ackerman (1980) is critical of both utilitarianism and contractarianism as approaches to deriving principles of justice. Instead, he emphasizes dialogue as the *process* by which these principles are established.

His criticism of contract theory seems overdrawn, however. Unless dialogue eventually leads to a consensus on the principles that underlie the liberal state, the liberal state can never come into being. If agreement on principles is ultimately achieved, that agreement becomes a form of social contract that binds the citizens of the liberal state together. Dialogue is an important part of the process by which agreement is obtained, but not a substitute for the agreement.

one of the major, modern reconstructions of the contractarian argument. The theory is developed in two parts: first, the arguments in favor of the contractarian approach are established. Here the focus is upon the characteristics of the original position from which the contract is drawn. The moral underpinning of the social contract rests on the nature of the decision process taking place within the *original position*, which in turn depends upon the setting in which the original position is cast. The second part of the theoretical argument develops the actual principles embedded in the social contract. Rawls emphasizes the independence of these two arguments. One can accept either part without necessarily committing oneself to the other (pp. 15 ff.). This point is important to keep in mind since the different parts have been attacked in different ways and one might feel more comfortable about one set of arguments than another. This two-part breakdown forms a natural format by which to review Rawls' theory. Following this review, we examine some of the criticisms of the theory that have been made.

25.1   The social contract

Perhaps the easiest way to envisage how the social contract comes about in Rawls's theory is to think of a group of individuals sitting down to draw up a set of rules for a game of chance, say, a game of cards, in which they will subsequently participate.[3] Prior to the start of the game, each individual is ignorant of the cards to be dealt to him and uncertain of his skills relative to those of other players. Thus, each is likely to favor rules that are neutral or fair with respect to the chances of each player, and all might be expected to agree to a single set of fair rules for the game. Here the incentive "to get on with the game" can be expected to encourage this unanimous agreement.

In Rawls's theory, life is a game of chance in which Nature deals out attributes and social positions in a random or accidental way (pp. 15, 72, 102 ff.). Now this natural distribution of attributes and chance determination of social position is neither just nor unjust (p. 102). But it is unjust for society simply to accept these random outcomes, or to adopt institutions that perpetuate and exaggerate them (pp. 102–3). Thus, a set of just institutions is one that mitigates the effects of chance on the positions of individuals in the social structure.

To establish such a set of institutions, individuals must divorce themselves from knowledge of their own personal attributes and social positions by stepping through a *veil of ignorance* that screens out any facts that might allow an individual to predict his position and benefits under a given set of principles (pp. 136 ff.). Having passed through the veil of ignorance, all individuals are in an *original position* of total equality in that each possesses the same information about the likely effects of different institutions on his own future position. The original position establishes a status quo of universal equality from which the social contract is written (pp. 3–10).

Individuals in the original position about to choose a set of principles to form a social contract resemble individuals about to draw up rules for a game of

---

[3] The analogy between a social contract or constitution and drawing up rules for a parlor game is often used by Buchanan. See, for example, Buchanan (1966) and Buchanan and Tullock (1962, pp. 79–80).

chance – with one important difference. Individuals choosing rules for a game of chance are ignorant of their future positions by necessity, and thus can be expected to adopt fair rules out of self-interest. Individuals in the original position are ignorant of their present and likely future positions, because they consciously suppress this information by voluntarily passing through the veil of ignorance. Although they may choose institutions out of self-interest once they are in the original position, the act of entering *the original position* is a moral one, whose ethical content rests on the argument that information about the distribution of certain "factors [is] arbitrary from a moral point of view" (p. 72). Justice is introduced into the social contract via the impartiality incorporated into the collective decision process through the nature of the information made available to individuals in the original position. Thus emerges the fundamental notion of *justice as fairness*.

What, then, is the nature of the information screened out by the veil of ignorance? Rawls's views here are rather strict. Not only is knowledge of their natural talents, tastes, social position, income, and wealth denied them, but also information about the generation to which they belong, the state of economic and political development of their society, and other fairly general information that Rawls argues might nevertheless bias an individual's choice in the direction of one set of principles over another. For example, knowledge of the generation in which an individual lives might lead him to favor a particular type of public investment policy, or social discount rate, thereby benefitting his generation at the expense of others. Given the very general nature of the information that individuals have in the original position, it is plausible to assume that the principles on which they agree are impartial with respect to the advantages they provide, not only for specific individuals, or individuals in well-defined positions, but even for individuals in different generations and living under different economic and political systems. Since all individuals have access to the same information once they have passed through the veil of ignorance, all will reach the same conclusions as to the set of just principles that ought to be embedded in the social contract. Equality in the original position leads to unanimity over the social contract.

25.2   The two principles of justice

Given the information available in the original position, Rawls argues that the following two principles will be chosen as the pillars of the just social contract:

> *First:* each person is to have an equal right to the most extensive basic liberty compatible with a similar liberty for others.
> *Second:* social and economic inequalities are to be arranged so that they are both (a) reasonably expected to be to everyone's advantage, and (b) attached to positions and office open to all. (p. 60) [These] two principles (and this holds for all formulations) are a special case of a more general conception of justice that can be expressed as follows. All social values – liberty and opportunity, income and wealth, and the bases of self-respect – are to be distributed equally unless an unequal distribution of any, or all, of these values is to everyone's advantage. (p. 62)

It is perhaps intuitively obvious that something like the "more general conception of justice" appearing on page 62 would emerge from a collective decision process in which the individuals were ignorant of their future positions and thus were induced to act impartially. Indeed, in some ways the setting of the original position resembles the familiar cake-cutting problem in which one individual divides the cake and the other chooses the first piece. By analogy with this example, one would expect the principles emerging from the original position to have an egalitarian tone, as is present in the more general conception. Rawls adds flesh to his theory, however, by deriving the two, more specific principles quoted above as part of the *special* conception of justice that is thought to hold once a society has reached a point of moderate scarcity, and by further arguing that these two principles will be chosen in lexicographical order. The first principle always has precedence over the second (pp. 61 ff., 151 ff., 247–8).

Rawls defends the lexicographical ordering of these two principles as follows:

> Now the basis for the priority of liberty is roughly as follows: as the conditions of civilization improve, the marginal significance for our good of further economic and social advantages diminishes relative to the interests of liberty, which become stronger as the conditions for the exercise of the equal freedoms are more fully realized. Beyond some point it becomes and then remains irrational from the standpoint of the original position to acknowledge a lesser liberty for the sake of greater material means and amenities of office. Let us note why this should be so. First of all, as the general level of well-being rises (as indicated by the index of primary goods the less favored can expect) only the less urgent wants remain to be satisfied by further advances, at least insofar as men's wants are not largely created by institutions and social forms. At the same time the obstacles to the exercise of the equal liberties decline and a growing insistence upon the right to pursue our spiritual and cultural interests asserts itself. (pp. 542–3)

Thus, Rawls sees society as better able to "afford" the extension of equal liberties to all citizens as it develops; that is, he sees liberty as essentially a luxury good in each individual's preference function. With increasing levels of income, the priority of liberty over other psychological and material needs rises, until at some level of development it takes complete precedence over all other needs.

The second principle of justice, which Rawls names the difference principle, also contains a lexicographic ordering. The welfare of the worst-off individual is to be maximized before all others, and the only way inequalities can be justified is if they improve the welfare of this worst-off individual or group. By simple extension, given that the worst-off is in his best position, the welfare of the second worst-off will be maximized, and so on. The difference principle produces a lexicographical ordering of the welfare levels of individuals from lowest to highest. It is important to note that Rawls defines welfare levels not in terms of utility indexes or some similarly subjective concept, but in terms of *primary goods*. These are defined as the basic "rights and liberties, powers and opportunities, income and wealth" that a society has to distribute (p. 62; see also pp. 90–5). Here we have another

Table 25.1. *Payoff possibilities*

	W	B
S_1	0	n
S_2	$1/n$	1

example of the break that Rawls is trying to establish between his theory and classical utilitarianism. The principles embedded in the social contract must be general. They must apply to all and be understandable by all (p. 132). This requirement places a bound on the complexity that can be allowed to characterize the basic principles of the social contract. The lexicographical nature of the difference principle and its definition in terms of objectively discernible primary goods make it easy to apply.

The difference principle is closely related to the maximin strategy of decision theory. This strategy dictates that an individual should always choose the option with the highest minimum payoff regardless of what the other payoffs are or the probabilities of obtaining them. The force of the strategy can easily be seen in an example Rawls himself uses when discussing the principle (pp. 157–8). Let W and B be two possible states of the world, say, the drawing of a white or black ball from a sack. Let S_1 and S_2 be the strategy options with prizes as given in Table 25.1. The maximin strategy requires that one always pick strategy S_2, regardless of the value of n and regardless of the probability, p, of a white ball being drawn, as long as $n < \infty$, and $p > 0$. One will never pay an amount, however small, to win a prize, however large, no matter what the probability of winning is, as long as it is not a sure thing.

Given the conservatism inherent in the maximin decision rule, Rawls goes to great pains to rationalize incorporating this rule into his basic principle of distributive justice. His reasons are three:

> First, since the rule takes no account of the likelihoods of the possible circumstances, there must be some reason for sharply discounting estimates of these probabilities. (p. 154)
>
> Now, as I have suggested, the original position has been defined so that it is a situation in which the maximin applies [and] the veil of ignorance excludes all but the vaguest knowledge of likelihoods. The parties have no basis for determining the probable nature of their society, or their place in it. Thus they have strong reasons for being wary of probability calculations if any other course is open to them. They must also take account of the fact that their choice of principles should seem reasonable to others, in particular their descendants, whose rights will be deeply affected by it. (p. 155)
>
> The second feature that suggests the maximin rule is the following: the person choosing has a conception of the good such that he cares very little, if anything, for what he might gain above the minimum stipend that he can, in fact, be sure of by following the maximin rule. It is not worthwhile for him to take a chance for

the sake of a further advantage, especially when it may turn out that he loses much that is important to him. This last provision brings in the third feature, namely, that the rejected alternatives have outcomes that one can hardly accept. The situation involves grave risks. (p. 154)

Thus Rawls's arguments for the difference principle rest heavily upon his assumptions about the information available in the original position, and the economic conditions facing society. Society is in a state of "moderate scarcity"; the poor can be made better off without great sacrifice to the rich (pp. 127–8). The assumption of moderate scarcity also plays an important role in justifying the lexicographic priority of the liberty principle over the difference principle, as already noted (pp. 247–8). Obviously, situations could be envisaged in which an individual would be willing to give up a certain degree of liberty for an increase in material goods, or risk being slightly poorer for a chance to be substantially richer. Rawls assumes, however, that the marginal utility of material gains declines rapidly enough as prosperity increases, and that society is already wealthy enough, so that these trade-offs and gambles at unknown odds are no longer appealing.

25.3   Extensions of the theory to other political stages

Rawls extends his theory to consider the characteristics of subsequent stages in the political process: the constitutional stage, the parliamentary stage, and administrative and judicial stages. In each subsequent stage, the veil of ignorance is lifted to some extent and individuals are given more information with which to make collective decisions. For example, in the constitutional stage, individuals are allowed to know the type of economic system with which they are dealing, the state of economic development, and so on. At each subsequent stage, however, knowledge of specific individual positions and preferences are denied to individuals making collective decisions. Impartiality is thus preserved, and the two principles of justice continue on into subsequent stages of the political process in precisely the same form in which they appear in the social contract. Thus, the social contract forms the ethical foundation for all subsequent political stages. As with the social contract stage itself, Rawls does not envisage actual political processes at work, but rather a form of *Gedankenexperiment* in which individuals reflect upon the principles that *ought* to underlie the social contract, constitution, or subsequent stages. In the original position, as defined for the constitutional stage, a hypothetical, just constitution is drafted in the same way that a hypothetical, just social contract is drafted by individuals at this earlier stage. This just constitution, once drafted or conceptualized, can then be compared with actual constitutions to determine in what respect they are in accord with the ethical principles contained in this hypothetical constitution. Of course, once one has specified the principles underlying a just constitution, and assuming that all can agree on them, one would be free to redraft actual constitutions to conform to these principles. But the leap from hypothetical constitutions formulated introspectively to actual constitutions written by individuals with real conflicts of interest may be a great one.

25.4   Critique of the Rawlsian social contract

A *Theory of Justice* has precipitated so much discussion and critical evaluation that we cannot hope to survey all of this material here. Instead, we focus on those issues that are most relevant to the public choice literature. Again the material can be most easily organized around Rawls's arguments in favor of the contractarian approach and the two principles underlying the contract formed.

25.4.1   *The social contract*

Until the appearance of Rawls's book, social contract theory had fallen into disrepute. The historical version of the theory had been fully discredited for over a century, and as a purely theoretical account for the existence of the state it was thought by many to be redundant.[4] This latter criticism is certainly valid from a public choice perspective. The theory of public goods, the prisoners' dilemma, externalities, the existence of insurable risks, and a variety of similar concepts suffice to explain why individuals might out of self-interest reach unanimous collective agreements. Now a contract is nothing more than a unanimous collective agreement to the provisions specified in it. Thus, any decision that can be explained via the creation of a contract can probably be explained just as well as a unanimous collective decision (vote). Not all public good and prisoners' dilemma situations require the existence of a state, of course. But one does not have to think very long to come up with *some* public goods with sufficiently strong joint supply and nonexclusion properties to require the participation of *all* members of a given geographic area. If such collective goods exist, then we have an explanation for a unanimous agreement to provide them.[5]

We have seen, however, how the provision of public goods is plagued by the free-rider problem; the cooperative solution to the prisoners' dilemma game is dominated. The notion of a social contract, with the connotation of mutual obligations and rewards and penalties for abiding by the contract, may serve a useful purpose in winning adherence to the provisions of the collective agreement.

Rawls is concerned throughout much of the latter part of his book with the problem of obtaining a stable, well-ordered, just society (pp. 453–504). To do so, individuals must adhere to the principles of justice incorporated in the social contract not only in the original position, but also, by and large, in daily life when they are cognizant of their actual positions. One of the important advantages claimed for the principles derived from the original position is that they stand a greater chance of compliance in the real world than any of their competitors (pp. 175–80). For this to be true, however, it is necessary that the principles be formulated so that all individuals can determine fairly readily what conduct compliance requires, and of course, all must be compelled by the nature of the arguments for compliance based on a consensus reached in the original position.

---

[4] For a review of this literature, see Gough (1957).
[5] For a reluctant demonstration that this is so for at least one category of public goods, see Nozick (1974).

To see that the first condition may be a problem in the Rawlsian system, consider the following example presented by Hart (1973). The application of Rawls's (pp. 201–5) first principle requires that one liberty be constrained only for the advancement of another. This requires that individuals in the original position trade off the benefits from advancing one liberty against the costs of constraining another. Private property, including the right to own land, is one of the possible freedoms that Rawls allows in his system. But the right to own land might be defined to include the right to exclude trespassers, and this in turn would conflict with the right of free movement. Thus, rights to exclude trespassers and rights to free movement are among those that would have to be sorted out at the original position. Now suppose that a farmer and a hiker get into conflict over the hiker's right to cross the farmer's field. The priority of liberty principle will do nothing to promote compliance with the social contract if the farmer and hiker, or any two people selected at random, are not likely to agree on whose right is to be preserved upon adopting the reflective frame of mind called for in the original position. But, as defined, the original position does not seem to contain enough information to allow one to sort out the priority of different liberties, and thus compliance with these important stipulations of the social contract cannot be presumed.[6]

It might be possible to resolve this kind of conflict from the original position if more information were available to individuals in this position. If they knew the amount of land available, population densities, the impact of trespassing on agricultural productivity, the alternatives to trespassing and their costs, and the like, they might be able to specify whether the right to own property took precedence or not, or even work out mixed cases in which trespassing was prohibited on land smaller than some size, but public pathways were required on larger plots. However, allowing this kind of information would in effect allow individuals to make probability calculations, and this is precluded from the original position by the characteristics of the veil of ignorance. Thus, at the level of generality at which they are derived, the principles inherent in Rawls's social contract may be an imperfect guide for compliance.

The problem of compliance can be likened to the existence of a core in a game in which individuals behind the veil of ignorance choose principles to govern the distribution of resources once the veil is lifted. If a core exists, no individual or coalition of individuals will choose to return behind the veil of ignorance and draft new principles. Howe and Roemer (1981) show that the difference principle, defined as maximizing the *incomes* of the lowest income group, yields a core to the game if all individuals are extremely risk-averse in the sense that they will join a new coalition only when they can *guarantee* themselves a higher income. Less extreme risk aversion leads to less extreme (egalitarian) principles of justice.

Rawls explicitly rejects a defense of the difference principle based on individual attitudes toward risk and similar utilitarian concepts (p. 172). Rather, he argues for greater compliance with his social contract than with a set of principles based on utilitarianism on the grounds that one could not expect compliance from the

---

[6] Ackerman raises similar criticisms of the problem of conceptualizing what principles the impartial or ethical observer arrives at, even assuming that one is able to assume an impartial frame of mind (1980, pp. 327–42).

poor under any set of principles requiring them to make sacrifices for the rich, as might occur under a set of utilitarian principles (pp. 175–80). But, under the difference principle, the rich are to be asked to make sacrifices (possibly quite large) for the benefit (possibly quite small) of the poor. This could lead to a problem of noncompliance by the rich.[7] Rawls (1974, p. 144) has responded to this form of criticism by noting that the "better situated . . . are, after all, more fortunate and enjoy the benefits of that fact; and insofar as they value their situation relatively in comparison with others, they give up much less." However plausible this argument is in its own right, it does not seem adequate as a part of a defense of the difference principle within the context of Rawls's theoretical framework. The latter would seem to dictate that the appeal for compliance rests on the inherent justness (fairness) of the principle's application and the proposition that the rich would agree to this principle from behind the veil of ignorance. But here we have a difficulty. The gains to the rich are excluded from consideration under alternative distributions because probability information is barred from the original position.

The exclusion of probability information cannot be defended entirely on the grounds that it would lead to principles favoring one *individual against another*. Knowing the numbers of rich and poor in the country and yet not knowing one's own income could still lead one to select a set of rules that were impartial with respect to one's own future position. But these rules would undoubtedly not include the difference principle.[8] As Rawls's three arguments in defense of the difference principle indicate, in the presence of general knowledge about probabilities something more akin to a utilitarian principle of distribution giving some weight to the interests of rich as well as poor would be selected. Rawls's chief reason for ruling out information about probabilities from the original position would thus appear to be to remove rational calculations of an average utility sort. But, as Nagel pointed out (1973, pp. 11–12), the elimination of competing principles is supposed to be a *consequence* of the working out of the justice-as-fairness concept, not a presupposition of the analysis.[9] Note also that Rawls does allow individuals in the original position certain pieces of information that are particularly favorable to the selection of his twin principles, for example, a period of moderate scarcity reigns, and individuals care little for what they receive above the base minimum. A utilitarian might ask that this information be excluded from the original position along with the general probability information that serves to handicap the selection of utilitarian rules. In any event, the construction of the arguments in favor of the difference principle is such that an individual more favorably situated than the worst-off individual in the society might question whether his interests have been fairly treated in the original position. If he does, we have a compliance problem. Rawls's social contract and his arguments in support seem to be constructed entirely for the purpose of achieving the compliance of only one group, the worst-off individuals (pp. 175–80).

---

[7] Nagel (1973, p. 13); Scanlon (1973, pp. 198 ff.); Klevorick (1974); Mueller, Tollison, and Willett (1974a); Nozick (1974, pp. 189–97).

[8] Nagel (1973); Mueller, Tollison, and Willett (1974a); Harsanyi (1975a).

[9] See, also, Hare (1973, pp. 90–1) and Lyons (1974, pp. 161 ff.).

Problems of compliance could also arise among the various candidates for the worst-off position (Klevorick, 1974). As Arrow (1973) and Harsanyi (1975a) have noted, these are likely to include the mentally and physically ill and handicapped as well as the very poor. But with the set of primary goods defined over several dimensions, individuals in the original position will be forced into interpersonal utility comparisons of the type Rawls seeks to avoid (Arrow, 1973; Borglin, 1982). Should individuals disagree in their rankings, then the problem of noncompliance could again arise, since those who fail to qualify as the worst off under Rawls's difference principle receive no weight whatsoever in the social outcome. If someone truly believed that the affliction he bore was the worst that anyone could possibly bear, it is difficult to see how one could make a convincing argument to him that his position was ignored in the meting out of social justice, on the grounds that from an original position, in which he did not know he had this affliction, he would weigh it below some other. He in fact has it, and the knowledge this imparts to him convinces him that he is the worst off.

Inevitably, in trying to justify an actual implementation of the difference principle and win compliance, one is led to appeal for compliance by an individual by pointing to another who is unquestionably worse off. This resembles Varian's (1974, 1976) suggestion that the difference principle should be defined in terms of envy; the worst-off individual is the one that no one envies. Here, of course, we can still have conflicts. The blind may envy those who are paralyzed but can see, and the latter may envy those who can walk but are blind. Even if the envy relationship is, from behind the veil of ignorance, transitive, the risk here is that the individual selected as the worst off will be someone who is very bad off indeed – someone perhaps like the pathetic creature in Trumbo's *When Jonny Comes Marching Home*. Literal application of the procedure to someone in this position could lead to the expenditure of immense resources to achieve a very modest improvement in individual welfare. Arrow (1973) is undoubtedly right in arguing that this is the type of special case to which Rawls's principles are not meant to apply. But the number of special cases is likely to be large, and it is particularly awkward to set aside these often pitiable and ethically difficult cases from the application of the principles of justice, because it is precisely these kinds of cases that one would like an ethical theory to handle.

These problems are all variants on the general problem of compliance raised in the example of the rich and poor. Much of Rawls's discussion of the difference principle seems to be couched in a comparison of *the* rich and *the* poor, as if there were but two groups to compare and one criterion by which to compare them. But in reality there are many possible groupings of individuals and many possible dimensions over which their welfares can be defined. Thus, a line must be drawn on the basis of some sort of interpersonal utility comparisons, around those who are to be categorized as *the* worst off. Unless a fair consensus exists on where this line is to be drawn, compliance with the principles of justice may not be forthcoming (Klevorick, 1974), for the difference principle treats all of those outside of the line, the rich and the not so rich, as being equally rich. This may lead to compliance problems among the very rich, who have to make great sacrifices for the worst off, and among the fairly poor, who receive no special treatment at all. In this way, a utilitarian principle, which weighed each individual's welfare to some degree, might achieve greater compliance than the difference principle, which ignores the welfare of all but a single group (Harsanyi, 1975a).

25.4.2 *The two principles of justice*

Even if we accept the preceding criticisms of the social contract aspect of Rawls's theory, it is still possible to consider the two principles of justice based on the justice-as-fairness argument as candidates for a set of political institutions. The question then is, can the arguments behind these two principles be sustained?

The ethical support for these two principles is derived from the impartiality characterizing the original position and the unanimity that stems from it. Is, then, the original position truly impartial with respect to all competing principles of justice? In setting up the problem as one in which "free and equal persons" voluntarily assent to principles to govern their lives, liberty seems to receive a prominent position from the start.[10] It is perhaps no surprise, therefore, that liberty is "chosen" as the top-priority principle from the original position.

A similar argument has been made by Nozick (1974, pp. 198–9) against the difference principle: "A procedure that founds principles of distributive justice on what rational persons who know nothing about themselves or their histories would agree to *guarantees that end-state principles of justice will be taken as fundamental*" (italics in original). Given that people know nothing about the economic structure of society, about how primary goods and the other outcomes of economic and social interaction are produced, they have no choice but to ignore these intermediate steps, and any principles of justice that might govern them, and focus on final outcomes, the end distribution of primary goods. Nozick argues that this conceptualization of the setting for choosing principles of justice excludes consideration of principles that would govern the *process* of economic and social interaction. In particular, it excludes consideration of an *entitlement* principle of distributive justice, in which individuals are entitled to their holdings as long as they came to them via voluntary transfers, exchanges, and cooperative productive activity, that is, by legitimate means (Nozick, 1974, pp. 150–231). To choose such a principle, one would have to know something about how the society functions, information unavailable in the original position.

The flavor of Nagel's and Nozick's criticisms can possibly be captured by returning to our example of the rule-making card game. In this particular example, it is highly unlikely that the players choose rules to bring about particular end-state distributions. If they did, they would probably agree to have all players wind up with an equal number of chips, or points. But this would destroy much of the purpose of the game, which is presumably to match each player or couple's skill against that of the other players, given the chance distribution of the cards. The fun of the game is in the playing, and *all* of the rules would govern the *process* by which winners are selected and not the *final positions* of the winners.

My point here is not to argue that life is like a game of cards and thereby defend Nozick's entitlement theory. But it is valid to argue that individuals may want to

---

[10] Nagel (1973, pp. 5–11). The quoted words are from Rawls (p. 13).

consider the *context* and *process* by which outcomes are determined, perhaps along with these outcomes, in choosing principles of justice.[11] It is ironic that Rawls's theory, which derives its conception of justice from the process by which principles are chosen, rules out all consideration of principles that deal with the subsequent process of social interaction (except for those contained in the equal liberty principle) (Nozick, 1974, p. 207). Indeed, the theory based on the notion of justice as fairness seems to exclude the selection of a principle of justice that would give to each individual anything that he had acquired by fair means, a principle that does resemble Nozick's entitlement principle.

Even if we accept Rawls's constraints on the information available in the original position and view the problem as one of selecting an end-state distribution principle, it is not clear that the difference principle is the one that would necessarily be chosen. As Harsanyi (1975a) and Binmore (1994, pp. 327–33) have argued, in the absence of objective probability information, we implicitly and almost instinctively apply subjective probability estimates, or act as if we do, when making decisions. Suppose that the prize for correctly identifying the color of the ball drawn from a bag in our previous example is $5, and nothing is paid, or charged, if the color is incorrectly guessed. Since the game is free, even a person who is maximin risk-averse will play. If she chooses white, she is implicitly assuming that the probability of a white ball being chosen is equal to or greater than 0.5. If she chooses black, the reverse. If she is indifferent between the choice of color and perhaps uses a fair coin to decide, she is implicitly applying the principle of insufficient reason. It is difficult to believe that individuals in the original position will not form probability estimates of this sort, perhaps to eliminate the awkward special cases of physical and mental illness discussed above, and if they do they are unlikely to choose the maximin rule.[12]

It is also possible, under the assumptions that Rawls makes about the original position, that utilitarianism would give outcomes rather similar to those of Rawls's system.[13] To assume that "the person choosing has a conception of the good such that he cares very little, if anything, for what he might gain above the maximum stipend that he can, in fact, be sure of by following the maximin rule" is equivalent to assuming rapidly diminishing marginal utility of income (primary goods). Incorporated into von Neumann-Morgenstern utility indexes, this assumption implies extreme risk aversion and would undoubtedly lead to fairly egalitarian redistribution rules, although probably not the difference principle as long as individuals care something for what lies above the minimum. More generally, under the rather favorable economic conditions that exist when the special conception of justice, including the difference principle and the lexicographic ordering of the two principles,

---

[11] "The suppression of knowledge required to achieve unanimity is not equally fair to all the parties.... [It is] less useful in implementing views that hold a good life to be readily achievable only in certain well-defined types of social structure, or only in a society that works concertedly for the realization of certain higher human capacities and the suppression of baser ones, or only certain types of economic relations among men" (Nagel, 1973, p. 9).

[12] For additional discussion of the implausibility of the maximin criterion even under the assumptions Rawls makes, see Sen (1970a, pp. 135–41); Arrow (1973); Hare (1973); Nagel (1973); Mueller, Tollison, and Willett (1974a); Harsanyi (1975a); and Binmore (1994, pp. 315–33).

[13] Arrow (1973), Lyons (1974), and Harsanyi (1975a).

is chosen, it is likely that utilitarianism would also greatly favor liberty and substantial redistribution. Arrow (1973) points out that an additive social welfare function will order liberty lexicographically over all other wants, if all individuals do, as they might given enough wealth. Rawls's arguments that utilitarianism would produce significantly different outcomes, for example, slavery, often seem to rest on the assumption that utilitarianism is operating in the harsher economic environment under which only Rawls's *general* conception of justice applies. But this general conception of justice also allows trade-offs between liberty and economic gain and thus resembles utilitarianism to this extent (Lyons, 1974).

25.4.3 *Experimental evidence*

The critiques of the maximin principle discussed in the previous subsection revolve around the plausibility of the assumption that individuals choose this principle from behind the veil of ignorance. An alternative to merely speculating about what principle individuals *would* choose is to run experiments to see what they *do* choose.

Frohlich, Oppenheimer, and Eavey (1987) presented students with four possible redistribution rules (Rawls's rule of maximizing the floor, maximizing the average, maximizing the average subject to a floor constraint, and maximizing the average subject to a range constraint). The students were made familiar with the distributional impacts of the four rules and were given time to discuss the merits and demerits of each. In 44 experiments in which students were uncertain of their future positions in the income distribution, the five students in each experiment reached unanimous agreement on a redistributive rule to determine their final incomes. Not once did they choose Rawls's rule of maximizing the floor. The most popular rule, chosen 35 out of 44 times, was to maximize the average subject to a floor constraint. Similar experiments conducted in Canada, Poland, and the United States have all found (1) that individuals can unanimously agree on a redistributive rule, and (2) that it is almost never Rawls's maximin rule, but rather some more utilitarian rule like maximizing the mean subject to a floor (Frohlich and Oppenheimer, 1992).

Hoffman and Spitzer (1985) also found that students in an experimental setting employ a principle of distributive justice that is neither straight Rawlsian egalitarianism nor simple utilitarianism. Rather, in the context of their experiment, students employed what appeared to be a "just desserts" principle, a principle consistent with Nozick's entitlements principle. Some of the results in Frohlich and Oppenheimer's (1992, ch. 9) experiments can also be interpreted as supporting the selection of a just-desserts principle from behind a veil of ignorance.

25.5   Two utilitarian defenses of the maximin principle

25.5.1 *Maximin as a means to obtain compliance*

As we have already discussed at length, Rawls places great emphasis on the importance of including provisions in the social contract that induce subsequent compliance with it. His total rejection of utilitarian calculations is largely motivated by this goal of compliance.

Binmore (1994) recently developed a social contract theory that – like that of Rawls – places great emphasis on compliance, but follows Harsanyi in assuming that individuals are capable of making cardinal, interpersonal utility comparisons and of calculating the probabilities that they will occupy different positions once they remove the veil of ignorance. On the other hand, he also seeks to distinguish his social contract theory from their theories.

> In particular, the term *social contract* shall not be understood in the quasi-legal sense adopted, for example, by Harsanyi and Rawls. I shall emphatically *not* argue that members of society have an *a priori* obligation or duty to honor the social contract. On the contrary, it will be argued that the only viable candidates for a social contract are those agreements, explicit or implicit, that police *themselves*. Nothing enforces such a self-policing social contract beyond the enlightened self-interest of those who regard themselves as a party to it. (Binmore, 1994, p. 30, emphasis in the original)

Binmore assumes a thin veil of ignorance, which only conceals the future identities of those bargaining in the original position. Each person knows her current utility level, the utility levels of all future persons in every possible state of the world, and each person can calculate the probability that she will be any one of these future persons. Thus, all of the information needed to maximize a Harsanyi SWF is present in the original position, and rational individuals would write a social contract that achieved this end *if* the provisions of this contract could be enforced. But there is no way to enforce these provisions, and so the social contract must be written in such a way as to make it self-enforcing when people follow their enlightened self-interest (Binmore, 1994, pp. 52–3).

To illustrate the nature of Binmore's arguments, consider the following example involving a community of two. In the absence of a social contract Adam and Eve would experience utility levels of 1 and 2, respectively. By agreeing to cooperate in certain prisoners' dilemma situations three possible alternative states of the world are possible – $x(6, 8)$, $y(5, 10)$, and $z(4, 12)$ – where the first number in parentheses is the utility level experienced by Adam, the second the level experienced by Eve.[14] Because Adam and Eve are in a bargaining situation, they consider only the utility *gains* that they would experience under each possible social contract. Thus, in the absence of any form of uncertainty, they might be expected to reach the outcome predicted by Nash's (1950) solution to the bargaining problem – the outcome maximizing the Nash SWF (see ch. 23). The values for the three possible social outcomes are

$$W_N(x) = (6 - 1)(8 - 2) = 30,$$
$$W_N(y) = (5 - 1)(10 - 2) = 32, \qquad\qquad (25.1)$$
$$W_N(z) = (4 - 1)(12 - 2) = 30.$$

---

[14] We are, of course, dealing with cardinal interpersonally comparable utilities here. Binmore (1994, 1998) devotes a lot of space to discussing the advantages and difficulties with these measures.

Adam and Eve would select y if they were certain of their future identities and could commit not to cheat on the terms of the contract in the future.

If Adam and Eve could commit not to cheat on the terms of the contract in the future, but assumed that they had an equal probability of being one another, they would ignore the status quo distribution and select z as it maximizes the Harsanyi SWF

$$W_H(x) = 6 + 8 = 14, \qquad W_H(y) = 5 + 10 = 15, \qquad W_H(z) = 4 + 12 = 16.$$
(25.2)

However, since Adam and Eve cannot commit not to cheat on the terms of the contract in the future, they select the social contract that produces x – the maximin outcome in terms of increments in utility – as the provisions of this choice, according to Binmore, are self-enforcing.

Binmore, like Rawls, assumes that the only threat to the stability of the social contract comes from the worst-off individual. Adam will not violate the contract that produces x because his gain is smaller under both alternative social contracts. But might x not be overturned by Eve, once she knows her identity, because her gain would be greater under either alternative social contract? Note that x is the maximin choice even if Eve's payoff under y is 100 or 100 million. Conceivably there might exist some utility payoff to Eve under a different state from x that would induce her to take the plunge of throwing the community back into the state of anarchy, in the hopes that a different social contract would be chosen. If this is so, then the defense of the maximin criterion as a guarantee for compliance fails. We present some other criticisms of Binmore's approach below.

25.5.2 *Maximin as a redistribution principle*

Consider now the theory of Pareto-optimal redistribution first proposed by Hochman and Rodgers (1969). Rich Mutt gives to poor Jeff because Jeff's utility is an argument in Mutt's utility function. Assuming that Jeff's utility is positively related to his income, we can write Mutt's utility as a function of both Mutt's and Jeff's incomes:

$$U_M = U(Y_M, Y_J).$$
(25.3)

Given such a utility function, we can expect rich Mutt to make voluntary transfers to poor Jeff if the latter figures heavily enough in Mutt's utility function. In a world of more than one Jeff, Mutt will receive the highest marginal utility from giving a dollar to the poorest Jeff. Thus, although the Pareto-optimal approach to redistribution does not fully justify the maximin principle, it does justify a redistribution policy that focuses sole attention on the worst-off individual or group (von Furstenberg and Mueller, 1971). An altruistic utilitarian and a Rawlsian will both consider the welfare of only the worst-off individual(s) in society.[15]

---

[15] For two additional utilitarian defenses of the difference principle, see Buchanan (1976) and Chu and Liu (1998).

25.6   The social contract as a constitution

From a public choice perspective what is of most interest from the literature on social contracts is the potential insights it may yield for the design of political institutions. If we agree with Rawls that the basic institutions of society, including its political institutions, *ought* to be selected from behind a veil of ignorance, what should those institutions look like? What do Rawls's two principles of justice imply regarding the optimal design of a constitution?

The implications of the first principle seem fairly clear. The social contract, and by logical extension the constitution, should protect liberty. Rights to free speech, privacy, and the like come readily to mind as political embodiments of Rawls's equal liberty principle.

What about the second principle? What set of political institutions would embody the intent of the difference principle? This principle has quite obvious implications for the distribution of income and wealth or, as Rawls prefers, of primary goods, and much of the discussion of it by both Rawls and Binmore can be most easily understood in this context. Distributional questions are not the only issues a society must resolve, however. What are the implications of the difference principle or the maximin criterion for the provision of public goods, or for the resolution of conflict issues that do not involve the distribution of income or primary goods? What electoral and voting rules does the difference principle imply?

The most straightforward application of the difference principle to choosing a voting rule to decide public goods issues suggests that the unanimity rule should be chosen. Who is the worst-off person when a public good is provided using a qualified majority rule – one of the persons who votes against its provision. Because it is always possible to determine a set of tax shares and public good quantity so that every person is made better off, maximizing the welfare of the worst-off individual would seem to require a continual reformulation of the issue until a set of tax shares and a public good quantity is found to which all agree. But against this interpretation of the difference principle all of the objections that have been made against the unanimity rule can be levied.

Consider next a simple, conflictual issue – the maximum speed to be allowed on the public highways. Who is harmed by high speed limits? – those injured in accidents with the worst-off person clearly being someone killed in a road accident. What speed limit would maximize the welfare of the worst off individual? – a limit so low that it precluded any serious accidents. The extreme aversion to risk that characterizes the maximin criterion as a principle for making choices in the face of uncertainty is readily apparent here, as is the impracticality of applying it either to specific issues of conflict or as a guide for choosing a voting rule to resolve such issues.

The same can be said of Binmore's application of the maximin criterion. Recall that Binmore's derivation of the optimality of this criterion does not hinge on individual attitudes toward risk, but rather stems from his concern for avoiding defections from the social contract's provisions, once the veil of ignorance is lifted. This goal would also seem to imply the application of the unanimity rule in the postagreement stage. Who are the most likely people to defect from a decision made under some alternative, qualified majority rule? – the losers under this rule, those "tyrannized" by the application of a less-than-unanimity rule, when unanimity is possible. Who are the most likely to defect from a decision to allow cars to travel at speeds that produce some fatal accidents? – those who do not own cars and experience only the costs from such a decision. To avoid the possibility of future defections from collective decisions, one must avoid creating losers from these decisions, and this implies using the unanimity rule whenever consensus is possible.

These observations are not made as criticisms of the social contract theories of Rawls and Binmore, for these theories were not intended to produce principles that allow society to set speed limits or even to choose a voting rule to determine speed limits. But these examples make clear that these social contract theories are not going to be of much help in making these more mundane collective choices. Indeed, when Rawls comes to discuss why the simple majority rule would be included in a constitution written in accordance with his principles of justice, he *does not* demonstrate how this rule follows logically from these principles. Instead, Rawls assumes that all citizens and legislators have already joined the just social contract, so that "legislative discussion must be conceived not as a contest between interests, but as an attempt to find the best policy as defined by the principles of justice. I suppose, then, as part of the theory of justice, that an impartial legislator's only desire is to make the correct decision in this regard" (p. 357). If all legislators were fully informed, they would all know what the correct decision is, and the unanimity rule could be used. The only reason not to use it is that legislators are not fully informed. Therefore Rawls opts for the simple majority rule using Condorcet's original defense of this rule. It is used as a sampling procedure to aggregate the views of the impartial legislators and thereby to obtain "a best judgment" as to what the correct decision is (pp. 357–8).[16]

I assume that very few readers who have come this far with me will share Rawls's belief that legislators are impartial seekers of the correct decisions for the community, and that the only task of politics is to sort out what these correct decisions are.[17] We need to consider the political institutions to be chosen from behind the veil of ignorance under the assumption that politics *is* a "contest between interests," and entertain the possibility that these interests are narrowly defined. This was, in fact, the exercise that Buchanan and Tullock (1962) set for themselves when writing *The Calculus of Consent*. We take it up in Chapter 26.

Bibliographical notes

Daniels (1974) contains an excellent set of papers analyzing and criticizing Rawls. (Page references in this chapter are to the reprinted versions in Daniels.) The books by Nozick (1974), Wriglesworth (1985), Gauthier (1986), and Barry (1989) can be

---

[16] Condorcet's arguments are reviewed in ch. 6.

[17] Not surprisingly, Rawls does not regard public choice as an appropriate methodology for determining the optimal design of just political institutions, as the following statement reveals: "the application of economic theory to the actual constitutional process has grave limitations insofar as political theory is affected by men's sense of justice" (p. 360).

said to have been inspired by Rawls's theory. Binmore's (1994, 1998) two-volume treatise links modern game theory to the classical social contract theory from Hobbes on up to Rawls. It also shows the relationship between this work and the SWF of Harsanyi. It contains an exhaustive discussion of von Neumann-Morgenstern utility indexes and of cardinal, interpersonal utility comparisons. John Rawls's recent thoughts on social justice are presented in his 1999 book.

CHAPTER 26

The constitution as a utilitarian contract[1]

The individuals themselves, each in his own personal and sovereign right, entered into a compact with each other to produce a government; and this is the only mode in which governments have a right to arise and the only principle on which they have a right to exist.

Thomas Paine

The ideally perfect constitution of a public office is that in which the interest of the functionary is entirely coincident with his duty. No mere system will make it so, but still less can it be made so without a system, aptly devised for the purpose.

John Stuart Mill

We have already discussed several works that have assumed uncertainty over future position to derive a normative theory of social choice. Rawls's (1971) theory discussed in Chapter 25 uses uncertainty over future position to derive principles of justice to be included in a social contract; Harsanyi (1953, 1955, 1977) uses it to derive an additive SWF (see Chapter 23).

Buchanan and Tullock (1962) develop a theory of constitutional government in which the constitution is written in a setting resembling that depicted by Harsanyi and Rawls. Individuals are uncertain about their future positions and thus are led out of self-interest to select rules that weigh the positions of all other individuals (Buchanan and Tullock, 1962, pp. 77–80).[2] Buchanan and Tullock's theory is at once positive and normative. Its authors state: "The uncertainty that is required in order for the individual to be led by his own interest to support constitutional provisions that are generally advantageous to all individuals and to all groups seems likely to be present at any constitutional stage of discussion" (Buchanan and Tullock, 1962, p. 78). And the tone of their entire manuscript is strongly positivist in contrast to, say, the works of Rawls and Harsanyi. But they also recognize the normative antecedents to their approach in the work of Kant and the contractarians (see, especially, Buchanan and Tullock, 1962, Appendix 1). Indeed, they state that the normative content of their theory lies precisely in the unanimity achieved at the constitutional stage (p. 14).

---

[1] This chapter draws heavily from Mueller (2001).

[2] Leibenstein (1965) achieves the same effect by envisaging collective decisions being made by a group of aging individuals for their descendants. Vickrey (1960) assumes people are moving to an island and are uncertain of their positions on the island.

One of the important contributions of Buchanan and Tullock's book is that it demonstrates the conceptual usefulness of the distinction between the constitutional and parliamentary stages of democratic decision making. If unanimous agreement can be achieved behind the veil of uncertainty that shrouds the constitutional stage, then a set of rules can be written at this stage that will allow individuals to pursue their own self-interests at the parliamentary stage in full possession of knowledge of their own tastes and positions. This obviously requires that any redistribution which is to take place be undertaken at the constitutional stage, where uncertainty over future positions holds (Buchanan and Tullock, 1962, ch. 13). Here the similarity to Rawls is striking. Unlike Rawls, however, Buchanan and Tullock allow individuals not just *more* information about themselves at the parliamentary stage, but full information.

The differences in the degrees of uncertainty assumed by Harsanyi, Rawls, and Buchanan and Tullock lead them in quite different directions in describing the principles and institutions that are optimal for making social choices. In this chapter we spell out these differences and draw out their implications. In so doing we outline a general theory of constitutional choice that builds on the Buchanan and Tullock mode of analysis.

26.1   The constitutional context

Each individual R can undertake one of n possible actions, a_{rj}, $j = 1, n$. These can range from very private actions like scratching one's ear, to very public ones like bombing the local pub. Among the set of actions might be paying a tax to provide a pure public good. Thus, all *collective* action questions can be viewed as decisions about *individual* actions. A law against driving above 65 mph restricts one's freedom to drive fast. A tax on gasoline to finance highway construction both restricts one's ability to purchase gasoline, and expands one's driving opportunities. All *collective choices* are decisions about individual actions.

All actions fall into one of three categories: *neutral* actions that affect only the welfare of the actor; *negative externalities*, actions that make other parties worse off; and *positive externalities*, actions that make other parties better off. Since we deal with situations involving risk and uncertainty, we assume that individual utility functions satisfy the von Neumann-Morgenstern utility axioms, and thus that the utilities of each individual can be regarded as *cardinal* indices (Ng, 1984a; Binmore, 1994, ch. 4).

The community can make three mutually exclusive decisions with respect to any individual R and her action a_{rj}: (1) it can *allow* R the freedom to make the action or not, (2) it can *ban* R from undertaking the action, or (3) it can *obligate* R to undertake it. A ban of an action can be regarded as setting an infinite price on the action.

Any action that creates an externality can lead to conflict in the post-constitutional stage over whether to ban or compel this action, and at the constitutional stage over the political institutions to be used to resolve this postconstitutional conflict. This sort of conflict at the constitutional stage can prevent unanimity over the constitutional contract. Following Harsanyi (1955), Rawls (1971), and Buchanan and Tullock (1962) unanimity can be obtained by assuming uncertainty over future positions at the constitutional stage. Each of these authors defended this assumption in different ways and, at least insofar as Harsanyi and Rawls are concerned, assumed different thicknesses in the *veil of ignorance*, which screens out information about the future. The assumptions one makes about the "thickness" of the veil of ignorance, that is, the information citizens have at the constitutional stage, have important consequences for the types of institutions that are placed in the constitution.

At the constitutional stage individuals choose bans, obligations, and voting rules to maximize their *expected* utilities. The agreement on the constitution must be unanimous, the existence of uncertainty ensures that this unanimity is obtained. At the post constitutional stage individuals know who they are, what their preferences are, and so forth. All private actions have the goal of maximizing utility, as do all collective actions under the voting rules established in the constitution. It is of course possible that an individual will vote to ban an action at the constitutional stage, when she is uncertain about her future preferences, and then in the postconstitutional stage, when she knows her preferences, try to violate the ban. Thus, the community obviously must include in the constitution institutions to ensure *compliance* with it. The compliance issue is taken up in Section 26.8.

26.2 The two-action case

Assume that there are only two groups of individuals, Rows (R) and Columns (C). Each can undertake any one of n possible actions, a_{rj}, $j = 1, n$, and a_{cj}, $j = 1, n$. Each individual in a group has the identical utility function defined over his own action and the action of the players in the other group, $U_i(a_{rj}, a_{cj})$, $i = R, C$. Since all Rs have identical utility functions, if one R experiences a higher utility from undertaking action a_{rj}, then all Rs do, and so we can think of $U_i(a_{rj}, a_{ck})$ as the utility an i experiences when all Rs undertake a_{rj}, and all Cs undertake a_{ck}. Each individual undertakes only one action at a time. Actions a_{rn} and a_{cn} are defined as no action and are assumed to produce no externalities.

Now consider the possible consequences of Rs and Cs undertaking the actions a_{rj} and a_{cj} versus the nonactions a_{rn} and a_{cn}. Action a_{rj} has three possible consequences for an R: (1) it raises his utility relative to when he undertakes a_{rn} – we represent this situation as $u_{rj} > 0$; (2) action a_{rj} does not alter R's utility, $u_{rj} = 0$; or (3) action a_{rj} reduces R's utility, $u_{rj} < 0$. These utility changes can be thought of as the combined effect on R of his own gain or loss from action a_{rj}, and any gain or loss he experiences from contemplating the effect of this action on the Cs. For example, suppose a_{rj} is R's smoking a cigar, although he knows this makes all Cs worse off. If R suffers sufficient disutility from the knowledge that Cs suffer from his smoking cigars, then $u_{rj} < 0$ for this action even though in the absence of any Cs, an R would get positive utility from smoking. The same three possible utility payoffs exist for the action a_{cj} by the Cs.

Each action by an R or a C can have no effect on the other group, or a positive or negative externality. Let us call e_{rj} the utility change a C experiences from the action a_{rj} by the Rs. A positive externality thus implies $e_{rj} > 0$, with $e_{rj} = 0$,

Matrix 26.1. *Collective action options when external effects are separable*

			Column					
			1	*2*	*3*	*4*	*5*	*6*
			$u_{cj} > 0$	$u_{cj} > 0$	$u_{cj} \leq 0$	$u_{cj} \leq 0$	$u_{cj} > 0$	$u_{cj} \leq 0$
			$e_{cj} > 0$	$e_{cj} = 0$	$e_{cj} < 0$	$e_{cj} = 0$	$e_{cj} < 0$	$e_{cj} > 0$
	1	$u_{rj} > 0$ $e_{rj} > 0$	NN	NN	NN	NN	NB	NO
	2	$u_{rj} > 0$ $e_{rj} = 0$	NN	NN	NN	NN	NB	NO
R	3	$u_{rj} \leq 0$ $e_{rj} < 0$	NN	NN	NN	NN	NB	NO
o	4	$u_{rj} \leq 0$ $e_{rj} = 0$	NN	NN	NN	NN	NB	NO
w	5	$u_{rj} > 0$ $e_{rj} < 0$	BN	BN	BN	BN	BB	BO
	6	$u_{rj} \leq 0$ $e_{rj} > 0$	ON	ON	ON	ON	OB	OO

Notes: N = No action required; B = ban of the action; O = obligation to act.
First letter applies to Rows, second to Columns

and $e_{rj} < 0$ representing neutral actions and negative externalities. To begin we make the simplifying assumption that the utility functions are separable. Under this assumption the effects of R's action, a_j, and the external effects of C's action, a_j, are both constants, and their combined effect on R's utility is simply the sum of the two effects, $u_{rj} + e_{cj}$.

Action a_{rj} has three possible utility consequences for each R, and three possible external effects producing nine combinations of own effect and externality. The same holds for the Cs, giving 81 combinations of utility payoffs taking into account the possible actions and interactions of the two groups. The number of combinations can be reduced to 36, however, if we assume that an R does not voluntarily undertake a_{rj} when $u_{rj} = 0$, and likewise for C when $u_{cj} = 0$. The remaining 36 combinations are depicted in Matrix 26.1.

Of the 36 possible situations, 16 require no collective action. The matrix has been constructed so that these cases appear in the upper left-hand portion of the matrix, and are indicated by an NN. The first N indicates that *no* collective decision need be taken with respect to a Row's action a_{rj}; the second N has the same implication with respect to a Column's action. In the row 3, column 1 entry, for example, R's undertaking a_{rj} would create a negative externality for the Cs, while a C's undertaking a_{cj} creates a positive externality for the Rs. Since $u_{rj} \leq 0$, however, and $u_{cj} > 0$, the Rs find it in their own interest not to undertake the action, while the Cs find it in their interest to do so, and the optimal outcome occurs without the need for any collective decision.[3]

---

[3] Recall, however, that the reason why $u_{rj} \leq 0$ may be that the Rs suffer disutility if they create a negative externality, that is, because $e_{rj} < 0$.

For all entries containing a B, a ban on a group's undertaking the action *may be optimal*. In row 5, column 1, for example, Rs obtain positive utility from undertaking the action, $u_{rj} > 0$, but the action also produces a negative externality, $e_{rj} < 0$. If e_{rj} is large enough relative to u_{rj}, a ban on the R's undertaking the action may be socially optimal. Note that when the Cs commit the same action it produces a positive externality, so that *if* a ban in this situation were optimal, it would be an *asymmetric* ban against only the Rs. Entries containing an O designate situations in which an obligation *might be optimal* because of the existence of positive externalities, with the two squares labeled OB and BO representing the unusual cases of a simultaneous asymmetric ban and obligation being optimal. We return to these and the other asymmetric cases below.

The 16 entries with an NN designate situations in which collective action is *never required*, because each group acting independently of the other produces the optimal outcome. The 20 additional entries designate situations in which bans or obligations *may be optimal*. It is, of course, conceivable that no collective action of any kind is necessary. A single R, Robinson, and C, Crusoe, inhabit an island that is so bountiful that no collective action produces benefits that exceed its costs, and the island is big enough so that all negative externalities are small in comparison with the gains to the perpetrator of the externality. Blissful anarchy is a logical possibility.

In more populous communities and harsher environments, one expects potential gains from collective action. We now explore how optimal collective agreements might emerge out of a two-stage constitutional process in which individuals in the first stage are uncertain over future positions.

26.3 The constitutional contract

In the context of a two-stage democratic process, uncertainty can take several forms. The minimum uncertainty needed to produce unanimous agreement on a constitution covering the full spectrum of possible actions is over future identities. Assume that each individual at the constitutional stage can forecast all possible future collective actions and their consequences, that is to say, the entries in Matrix 26.1 and all similar matrices for all other pairs of future actions, including the utility payoffs to the different players. Since each possible "state of the world" is a pair of actions by Rows and Columns, this assumption is equivalent to assuming that each individual at the constitutional stage can envisage all possible future states of the world. Each individual at the constitutional stage knows the u_{rj}, u_{cj}, e_{rj}, and e_{cj} in Matrix 26.1 for every possible pair of actions, and the numbers of Row and Column players, n_r and n_c. Each individual at the constitutional stage knows *everything* about the future *except* whether she will be an R or a C player. We refer to this situation as one of *identity uncertainty*. One way to think of identity uncertainty arising is to think of individuals choosing a constitution for their future children. Let R stand for female and C for male. It may be possible to envisage the utilities men and women will experience from a given pair of actions, and the numbers of men and women in the future. But it may not be possible at the constitutional stage to predict the sex of one's unborn children. If so, then identity uncertainty exists.

If individuals at the constitutional stage know the numbers of Row and Column players, the n_r and n_c, then they can calculate the probabilities that they are an R or a C. A further degree of uncertainty is added by assuming that these numbers are unknown. R and C now represent ethnic groups and the future population growth of each group is unknown. We refer to this as *numbers uncertainty*.

The degree of uncertainty is increased still further by assuming that individuals at the constitutional stage are uncertain about the future utility payoffs – the u_{rj}, u_{cj}, e_{rj}, and e_{cj} – in different situations. We refer to this situation as one of *payoff uncertainty*. A person at the constitutional stage can make no judgment about the likely suffering of a future slave or the benefits to her master.

Each of these types of uncertainty leads to a different institutional solution to the collective action problem.

26.3.1 *Optimal collective action with only identity uncertainty*

Every individual at the constitutional stage can envisage the kinds of issues that will come up in the future, the numbers of individuals in each group, and their utility payoffs. They are uncertain over only whether they will be an R or C. Thus, each individual at the constitutional stage can predict for every possible pair of future actions (a_{rj}, a_{cj}) the box in Matrix 26.1 in which the community will be located. If the box is one of those containing an NN, no collective decision is necessary. Many actions are likely to fall into these 16 boxes, so many that the constitution framers are likely to include a clause that allows everyone to do anything he chooses *unless the constitution or a law passed in accordance with the constitution specifically forbids or requires a certain action*, thereby handling all of the possible actions an individual can undertake that affect no one's welfare other than the actor, or have positive external effects on others.

Now consider an action in one of the remaining 20 boxes, say row 5, column 1. Column's action creates a positive externality and gives Column positive utility. Thus, C need not be compelled to undertake the action and should not be prevented from doing so. Row's action, on the other hand, creates a negative externality while giving Row positive utility. The rational individual at the constitutional stage, uncertain over whether she will be a future R or C player, chooses to ban future Rs from undertaking the action if the expected utility from such a ban is positive. The probability that an individual is an R is $\pi_r = n_r/(n_r + n_c)$, while the probability that she is a C is $\pi_c = n_c/(n_r + n_c)$. Her expected utility from the action is then

$$\mathcal{E}(U) = \pi_r u_{rj} + \pi_c e_{rj}. \tag{26.1}$$

If (26.1) is negative for an action leading to a box in row 5, the constitution should ban R's undertaking this action. If (26.1) is negative, then so too is (26.2), which is just (26.1) multiplied by $(n_r + n_c)$.

$$n_r u_{rj} + n_c e_{rj} < 0. \tag{26.2}$$

Condition (26.2) reveals the close link between the expected utility maximizing choices of an individual at the constitutional stage and the Benthamite SWF; the optimal collective decision regarding action a_{rj} maximizes the sum of the utility changes caused by this action.

If (26.3) holds for an action leading to any box in row 6, the constitution framers should agree to obligate R to undertake the action.

$$n_r u_{rj} + n_c e_{rj} > 0. \tag{26.3}$$

Analogous inequalities with respect to entries in columns 5 and 6 define the conditions under which actions by C should be banned or compelled. Notice that only the boxes in (row 5, column 5) and (row 6, column 6) can *possibly* lead to *symmetric* bans or obligations on all citizens. We discuss symmetric and asymmetric bans and obligations in the next section.

If the only information individuals at the constitutional stage lacked was knowledge of which future citizen they would be, then the constitution could contain all of the bans and obligations that would ever be needed. Strictly speaking, such a situation involves only Knightian risk, rather than true uncertainty, and individuals at the constitutional stage have all of the information they need to calculate their expected utilities for every pair of actions by Rows and Columns (Knight, 1921). If in 20 or 100 years time, the threat of a flood would require the construction of a dike, the constitution framers could forecast this event, the future preferences of citizens, and determine their tax and effort obligations. These could then be written into the constitution. No second stage in the democratic process would be needed. From the point of view of individuals at the constitutional stage, the constitution could optimally resolve all issues for all time.

Proposition 1: *Identity uncertainty combined with full knowledge of preferences and numbers of all future citizens allows individuals at the constitutional stage to specify all future bans and obligations so as to maximize their expected utility in the postconstitutional stage. No second stage of collective decision making is required.*

The assumptions in Proposition 1 are essentially those that Harsanyi (1955, 1977) made in determining principles for moral choices. Each individual can envisage the utility of every individual in every possible future state of the world, and the probabilities that she will be any of those individuals. She chooses that social state, that is, a combination of actions for Rows and Columns, that maximizes her expected utility. This choice maximizes the sum of the future utilities of the community, and thus can be viewed as maximizing a Benthamite SWF.[4] If only identity uncertainty is present at the constitutional stage, then the constitution specifies all actions for all future citizens so as to maximize the Benthamite sum of individual utilities. The social contract/constitution specifies all of the necessary actions of those who are a party to it. No second stage of the political process is needed.

---

[4] With a few additional axioms Harsanyi (1955) proves that the ethical choices of individuals, which consist of maximizing their expected utilities under the assumption that they have an equal probability of being any future citizen, are equivalent to maximizing a Benthamite SWF. See ch. 23.

26.3.2 *Optimal collective action with identity and numbers uncertainty*

We continue to assume that individuals at the constitutional stage know and can compare the u_{rj}, u_{cj}, e_{rj}, and e_{cj} associated with all future actions by members of the two groups. Thus, the optimal collective decision with respect to an R's action that leads to a box in rows 5 or 6 in Matrix 26.1 must still satisfy equations (26.2) or (26.3). Equation (26.2) requires that the following condition be satisfied:

$$n_r/n_c < -e_{rj}/u_{rj} \tag{26.4}$$

and with respect to a ban of a_{cj},

$$n_c/n_r < -e_{cj}/u_{cj}. \tag{26.5}$$

Since the right-hand sides of (26.4) and (26.5) are assumed to be known, the optimal collective choices can be made once the numbers of individuals in the two groups are established. This information can be obtained simply by citizens voting in the second stage of the political process on the bans. It is in an R's interest to vote against a ban of a_{rj}, and in a C's interest to vote for it. The constitution framers can ensure that the optimal collective choice is made with respect to the ban on R's action by requiring a referendum with a majority of votes in favor of a ban satisfying (26.4). For example, if the utility gain to an R from a_{rj} is known to be three times the loss imposed on a C from the action ($u_{rj} = -3e_{rj}$), then the expected utility of the constitution framers is maximized by requiring that a future ban against Rows undertaking this action obtain a three-fourths majority or more.

Proposition 2: *With $u_{rj} > 0$, $u_{cj} > 0$, $e_{rj} < 0$, and $e_{cj} < 0$, identity and numbers uncertainty combined with full knowledge of the preferences of all future citizens allows individuals at the constitutional stage to maximize their expected utility by specifying a voting rule for the second stage of collective decision making to decide all future bans against $a_{rj}(a_{cj})$ such that condition (26.4) [(26.5)] is satisfied.*

From (26.3) we can analogously derive the conditions for obligating a_{rj} and a_{cj}:

$$n_r/n_c > -e_{rj}/u_{rj} \tag{26.6}$$

$$n_c/n_r > -e_{cj}/u_{cj}, \tag{26.7}$$

from which we obtain

Proposition 3: *With $u_{rj} < 0$, $u_{cj} < 0$, $e_{rj} > 0$, and $e_{cj} > 0$, identity and numbers uncertainty combined with full knowledge of the preferences of all future citizens allows individuals at the constitutional stage to maximize their expected utility by specifying a voting rule for the second stage of collective decision making to decide all future obligations of $a_{rj}(a_{cj})$ such that condition (26.6) [(26.7)] is satisfied.*

In the special case that $u_{rj} = -e_{rj} > 0$ the expected utility of an individual at the constitutional stage is maximized if the ban against a_{rj} is decided using the simple majority rule. This is essentially the Rae-Taylor theorem in favor of the simple majority rule, which we discussed in Chapter 6, and rests clearly on the assumption of equal intensities on both sides of the issue.[5]

When the equal intensity condition holds with respect to symmetric negative externalities, that is, $u_{rj} = -e_{rj} > 0$ and $u_{cj} = -e_{cj} > 0$, then the simple majority rule is the optimal voting rule to decide whether to ban action a_{rj} by Row players, and a_{cj} by Column players. If Rows are in the majority they will vote to ban a_{cj} and to allow themselves to undertake a_{rj}. The relentless logic of expected utility maximization coupled with the equal intensity assumption leads to "a tyranny of the majority" as the optimal outcome of the process of choosing a voting rule that maximizes the expected utility of a citizen at the constitutional stage. The majority votes to allow themselves to do that which it forbids the minority from doing.

Proposition 4: *With symmetric negative (positive) externalities and equal intensities on the two sides of the issue (that is, $u_{rj} = -e_{rj}$, and $u_{cj} = -e_{cj}$), identity and numbers uncertainty combined with full knowledge of the preferences of all future citizens implies that the simple majority rule is the optimal voting rule to decide whether to ban (obligate) actions a_{rj} and a_{cj} by future Row and Column players. The application of this voting rule in the second stage of collective decision making under these assumptions* must *lead to an* asymmetric *ban (obligation) of the actions a_{rj} and a_{cj}. (Note that the equal intensities assumptions imply that the right-hand sides of both (26.4) and (26.5) equal 1. For a symmetric ban to be optimal, $n_r/n_c < 1$ and $n_c/n_r < 1$ would both need to hold, which is impossible.)*

Conversely, we can see that a symmetric ban can be optimal with identity and numbers uncertainty, only when the payoffs are *known* and are such as to make *different* voting rules optimal for the respective bans. For example, if $u_{rj} > 0$, $u_{cj} > 0$, $-e_{rj}/u_{rj} = 1$, and $-e_{cj}/u_{cj} = 2$, then the simple majority rule would be optimal for banning a_{rj}, while a_{cj} should be banned if even a third of the community chooses to do so. If $1 < n_c/n_r < 2$, Columns are able to ban a_{rj} but are not able to block Rows from banning a_{cj}.

Conditions (26.4) and (26.5) require that the majority required to ban an action be higher, the smaller the gain in utility to an individual in favor of a ban relative to the gain in utility for the person who is allowed to act. In the limit, as the right-hand sides of (26.4) and (26.5) approach infinity, the constitution framers would allow a future ban only if the community unanimously voted in favor of it.

Conversely, as $-e_{rj}$ grows large relative to u_{rj} the constitutional convention will wish to establish a presumption against action a_{rj}. This could be accomplished through a constitutional ban on a_{rj} with a provision that it could be lifted with a majority of $m_j \geq -e_{rj}/(-e_{rj} + u_{rj})$. In the limit, as the utility loss to a Column becomes very large relative to the gain to a Row from the action, its constitutional ban could be lifted only by a unanimous vote of the community.

Analogous considerations once again apply with respect to obligations.

---

[5] See Rae (1969), Taylor (1969), and Rae and Schickler (1997). Buchanan and Tullock (1962, pp. 128–30) also stress the importance of assuming equal intensities in choosing the simple majority rule.

26.3.3   *Optimal collective action with identity, numbers, and payoff uncertainty*

For many sorts of actions the most realistic assumption to make is that an individual at the constitutional stage is uncertain over identities, numbers, and future utility payoffs from these actions. For example, it might be reasonable to assume that in 1787 an individual could compare the utility he perceived a smoker obtained from smoking, and the negative externality this action caused at that time, but he would not have been able to envisage very accurately future citizens' utilities and disutilities from smoking, or the numbers of smokers and nonsmokers. More generally, he could not anticipate whether other stimulants similar to tobacco would be discovered, their positive and negative effects, and so on. Both the e_js and the u_js in (26.2) and (26.3) are in these situations unknown.

If the constitution framers can envisage the distribution of utility changes associated with a particular action, then we can simply substitute the expected values of the e_js and u_js into our optimality conditions, and proceed as above. If we think of the constitution as governing the collective decisions of the community over a very long period, however, even this assumption may be questionable. On the other hand, if all elements in the equations defining the optimality conditions are unknowns, no voting rule specifying a qualified majority for making future collective choices can be written into the constitution that maximizes the expected utility of someone at the constitutional stage.

Thus, when reasonable predictions of the utility gains and losses from particular actions cannot be made, the constitution might simply be silent on how future generations should decide them. Although this approach would be intellectually honest, it would impose on future generations the difficult task of both choosing and applying voting rules to deal with many potentially divisive issues, once their preferences were fully known.

Rather than saddle future generations with such choices, the constitution framers might make "an educated guess" as to the magnitudes of the $-e_j$ and u_j and define a voting rule accordingly. But what is a reasonable guess? $-e_{rj}$ is half of u_{rj}, three times as great? Assuming they are of equal magnitude constitutes a form Schelling point, or alternatively might be interpreted as an application of the principle of insufficient reason to this problem. With $-e_{rj}$ and u_{rj} equal, condition (26.4) requires that any ban of an action that fits entries in row 5 be resolved using the simple majority rule. Condition (26.6) demands the simple majority rule for obligations in situations that fit entries in row 6. We have then a normative justification for the ubiquitous use of this voting rule. Unable to estimate the future gains and losses from many collective decisions, the constitution writers assume that they are equal and opt for the voting rule that maximizes their expected utility under this assumption.

26.4   Symmetric and asymmetric bans and obligations

Although asymmetric bans or obligations are likely to be optimal from the point of view of an individual at the constitutional stage who is uncertain of her future identity, they may often be infeasible. Suppose that both Rows and Columns get utility out of being free to drive faster than 65 mph when they so choose ($u_{rj} > 0$ and $u_{cj} > 0$). Rows are skillful and prudent drivers and only drive at these speeds when there is no danger of their harming anyone ($e_{rj} = 0$). Columns, on the other hand, are poor and somewhat reckless drivers ($e_{cj} < 0$). From behind the veil of ignorance, the community could unanimously agree to ban Columns from driving at more than 65 mph, while allowing Rows to drive at whatever speed they choose. But unless Rows and Columns can be identified prior to their stepping behind the wheel, such a ban will be unenforceable. Since both Rows and Columns prefer having the freedom to drive above 65, Columns will simply pretend to be Rows. Given the infeasibility of enforcing an asymmetric ban, a symmetric ban may be optimal. This will be the case when the expected utility of someone at the constitutional stage from a total ban is positive, that is, when (26.8) is satisfied:

$$n_r u_{rj} + n_c e_{rj} + n_c u_{cj} + n_r e_{cj} < 0. \tag{26.8}$$

When (26.8) does not hold the optimal rule will be a symmetric freedom to drive above 65. An analogous condition with the inequality reversed applies to symmetric obligations in the presence of positive externalities. Thus, owing to the transaction costs of enforcing asymmetric bans and obligations, more rules must be applied symmetrically than is suggested by Matrix 26.1.

Identifying those who have different preferences and/or who generate different externalities is, on the other hand, often feasible, thus so too are asymmetric bans, for example, a ban against those who are under 21 consuming alcohol. Thus, an expected utility-maximizing constitution would impose asymmetric bans whenever differences in utility payoffs and external effects from actions can be readily identified.

Row 6, column 5, and row 5, column 6 in Matrix 26.1 contain entries that may seem highly unlikely – a simultaneous ban and obligation for the two groups with respect to the same action. Nevertheless, such asymmetric treatments of different groups are both logically possible and observable in practice. A somewhat archaic and sexist example of this sort of asymmetry would be a constitutionally defined obligation for men to serve in the army, and a ban against women serving. Such asymmetric treatment of these two groups could arise if men got negative utility from being in the army but their service generated positive externalities, while women fancied being in the army but their service generated negative externalities. Under these conditions, citizens who were uncertain of their future sex could unanimously agree on an asymmetric ban and obligation regarding military service.

26.5 Continuous actions with interdependent utilities

The assumptions of binary actions and separable external effects have allowed us to illustrate rather simply several important features of the optimal political institutions in a utility-maximizing constitution. Moreover, these assumptions are realistic with respect to many collective choices. Slavery, abortion, and legalized drugs are just three examples of issues that many people view as binary choices. The loss Column experiences when a Row steals from him may reasonably be assumed to be independent of whether Column is also a thief.

In other situations more complex relationships must be assumed to exist, however. The risk of harm that Rs experience from Cs' driving depends on whether the Rs are also driving. Cars can be driven at any one of a continuous range of speeds. Money to provide a pure public good can be contributed in various amounts. To handle such cases, we need to think of a_j as a continuous variable. To see what is involved, let us assume that Rows and Columns have twice differentiable utility functions defined over the two scalars a_{rj} and a_{cj} of the following forms:

$$U_R = U_R(a_{rj}, a_{cj}) \text{ and } U_C = U_C(a_{cj}, a_{rj}). \tag{26.9}$$

An individual at the constitutional convention wishes to maximize his expected utility, which again amounts to maximizing the Benthamite function

$$W = n_r U_R(a_{rj}, a_{cj}) + n_c U_C(a_{cj}, a_{rj}), \tag{26.10}$$

which yields the first-order conditions

$$\frac{\partial W}{\partial a_{rj}} = n_r \frac{\partial U_R}{\partial a_{rj}} + n_c \frac{\partial U_C}{\partial a_{rj}} = 0$$

$$\frac{\partial W}{\partial a_{cj}} = n_r \frac{\partial U_R}{\partial a_{cj}} + n_c \frac{\partial U_C}{\partial a_{cj}} = 0. \tag{26.11}$$

If both the utility functions and the numbers of Row and Column players are known, we again have essentially the situation first analyzed by Harsanyi (1955), and the constitution framers stipulate the levels of each action (a_{rj}, a_{cj}) so as to maximize the SWF in (26.10).

When the utility functions U_R and U_C are known, but the n_r and n_c are not, one might wish to define a voting rule to reveal the n_r and n_c. When U_R and U_C are continuous functions of a_{rj} and a_{cj}, however, such an option no longer exists. From (26.11) we can solve for the optimal relationships between the numbers of individuals in each group and the marginal utilities from each action.

$$\frac{n_r}{n_c} = -\frac{\partial U_C / \partial a_{rj}}{\partial U_R / \partial a_{rj}}$$

$$\frac{n_r}{n_c} = -\frac{\partial U_C / \partial a_{cj}}{\partial U_R / \partial a_{cj}}. \tag{26.12}$$

If both marginal utilities from a_j are positive ($\partial U_R / \partial a_{rj} > 0$ and $\partial U_C / \partial a_{cj} > 0$) and the actions cause negative externalities, then (26.12) defines conditions that determine the optimal levels of both actions. But no voting rule leads to this outcome. If the simple majority rule is used to decide the levels of a_{rj} and a_{cj}, and the Rows are in the majority, they will not choose to require levels of a_{rj} and a_{cj} that satisfy (26.12). Instead they will allow themselves full freedom to act, so that $\partial U_R / \partial a_{rj} = 0$, and the right-hand side of the first equation in (26.12) goes to infinity, while totally banning a_{cj}. When multiple degrees of an action are possible and utility varies with the level of the action, no qualified majority rule *alone* can be relied upon to determine the optimal level of the action.

The potential scope for a tyranny of the majority is obviously great when the levels of action vary over a wide range. Moreover, unlike the situation when only two choices exist – action or no action – with multiple actions the simple majority rule is likely to produce an outcome that deviates greatly from that which would maximize the expected utility of an individual at the constitutional stage. A closer approximation to the levels of actions that are optimal might be achieved in this situation if the constitution coupled the choice of a qualified majority to decide the level of an action with a symmetry constraint. Whatever level of the action that is allowed (required) of one group must pertain to the other. With this symmetry condition, the simple majority rule in use, and Rows, say, in the majority, they would choose a level of a_j such that $\partial U_R/\partial a_{rj} = -\partial U_R/\partial a_{cj}$, that is, a level that equates the denominators of the right-hand sides of the two equations in (26.12). If the utility functions of the Rows and Columns were similar, then this level of activity would also equate the numerators, and the right-hand sides of (26.12) would both equal 1. Although the levels of a_{rj} and a_{cj} would not maximize (26.10), given n_r and n_c, they would most likely come much closer to achieving this outcome than allowing one group to set different levels of a_j for each group so as to maximize its utility.[6]

We conclude that a constitutional convention that expected future members of the community to have similar utility functions defined over continuous levels of different activities could achieve a higher level of expected utility at the constitutional stage, if it coupled the use of the simple majority rule to the requirement that decisions made with this rule apply uniformly to all members of the community.

26.6   Decision-making costs

Consider again the entries in row 5 of Matrix 26.1. Rows obtain positive utility from an action that causes a negative externality. It is tempting to argue that no collective action is necessary in these cases, and to rely on the Coase theorem to ensure that a Pareto-optimal outcome is obtained.[7] Columns can simply bribe Rows not to act.

In thinking about the resolution of these conflicts at the constitutional stage, however, such a way around these sorts of difficulties seems illegitimate, at least with respect to the first four entries in row 5. To prevent Rows from acting Columns must offer them a sufficiently large bribe. But with what can Columns bribe Rows if, at the constitutional stage, property rights are not yet secure? Thus, with respect to the kinds of *conflict* issues that are represented in the first four boxes of rows 5 and 6, it seems reasonable to assume that Coasian solutions are not feasible, and provision in the constitution must be made for their optimal resolution.

---

[6] With diminishing marginal utility from undertaking a_{rj}, the gain to a Row from going from the constrained level of a_{rj}, where $\partial U_R/\partial a_{rj} = -\partial U_R/\partial a_{cj}$, to the level of a_{rj}, where Rs are unconstrained ($\partial U_R/\partial a_{rj} = 0$), will tend to be less than the loss in utility if Columns are constrained and $a_{cj} = 0$.

    Buchanan and Congleton (1998) present examples of situations in which the imposition of a symmetry constraint can improve the realized aggregate utilities of a community.

[7] See Coase (1960), Bernholz (1997a), and the discussion in Chapter 2.

This argument does not hold for the four entries in the bottom right-hand corner of Matrix 26.1, where rows 5 and 6, and columns 5 and 6 intersect. Now each person does have something to trade – her freedom to undertake action a_j. These four cases can give rise to different forms of prisoners' dilemmas, and the optimal outcome could conceivably be reached by requiring that bans and obligations of these actions be made jointly using the unanimity rule. In discussing the possible problems raised by decision-making costs, therefore, we distinguish between the four boxes in Matrix 26.1 which potentially give rise to prisoners' dilemmas (the intersections of rows 5 and 6 with columns 5 and 6), and the other 16 entries in these two rows and columns, which we refer to as *conflict* issues.

26.6.1   *Prisoners' dilemmas*

In a prisoners' dilemma, a unanimous agreement to adopt the cooperative strategies is possible *without* any uncertainty over who the players are or their utility payoffs (Müller, 1998). Thus, *even* when none of the three forms of uncertainty is present at the constitutional stage, for actions giving rise to prisoners' dilemmas, the players have the incentive to agree to the jointly cooperative actions, and this agreement can, in principle, be written directly into the constitution.

Unfortunately, of course, in prisoners' dilemma situations each individual has an incentive to break the agreement in the postconstitutional stage. To achieve the gains from cooperation in prisoners' dilemmas, agreements must also include incentives to cooperate as, for example, penalties for noncooperation. An effective ban of stealing must stipulate the penalty to be imposed if the ban is violated. The optimal penalties to deter stealing a loaf of bread may differ from those to deter robbing a bank. Thus, collective decisions in many prisoners' dilemma situations do not simply involve the specification of the desired actions by each party – do not steal – they also involve multiple, possible retaliatory actions by the community.

Contributions to the provision of a pure public good also have the characteristics of a prisoners' dilemma, but in this case the *action* involved – how much each person contributes – is essentially a continuous variable. The optimal contribution of each citizen depends on her preferences and income, and the number of groups with different preferences for the public good is likely to exceed two. In communities with large numbers of individuals with different preferences and incomes, the *decision-making costs* of determining each individual's contribution, the penalty for failing to contribute, and so on will be large. When these costs are taken into account, some less-than-unanimity rule may prove optimal.

Once collective decisions are made with a qualified majority rule, however, an individual loses the protection afforded by the unanimity rule against decisions that make her worse off. She becomes exposed to the *external costs of collective decision making*.[8] Thus, the decision-making costs associated with the unanimity rule convert a potentially cooperative game to find a Pareto-preferred set of actions into a conflict between those in the winning coalition who obtain net benefits from the collective action, and those in the losing coalition who do not. Uncertainty

---

[8] See Buchanan and Tullock (1962, pp. 63–91) and discussion in Chapter 4.

reappears at the constitutional stage over whether a given individual will be in a future winning or losing coalition.

The impact of decision-making costs on the choice of collective decision rule can be studied under the assumption that there are again only two groups in the community, the winners and the losers under a given collective decision. Let w be the gain in utility an individual at the constitutional stage expects from a particular collective action should he be on the winning side on this issue, and s the loss if he is on the losing side. The probability that the individual is on the winning side of issue j, $p(m_j)$ is a function of the majority required to pass it, m_j, where $p'(m_j) > 0$, and $p''(m_j) < 0$ up to $m_j = 1$. In choosing a voting rule to decide this issue, an individual at the constitutional stage must weigh the gain in utility he expects from increasing the majority required to pass an issue, and thus his chances of being on the winning side, against the decision-making costs of finding a set of actions that can win a higher majority. Let us call these $d(m_j)$, where it is reasonable to assume $d'(m_j) > 0$, and $d''(m_j) > 0$ up to $m_j = 1$. A member of the constitutional convention must thus choose m_j to maximize

$$\mathcal{E}(U) = p(m_j)w - [1 - p(m_j)]s - d(m_j), \tag{26.13}$$

which yields the m_j satisfying

$$p'(m_j)(w + s) = d'(m_j). \tag{26.14}$$

The left-hand side of (26.14) is the marginal gain in utility expected from increasing the required majority; the right-hand side is the marginal increase in decision-making costs. The voting rule that maximizes the expected utility of someone at the constitutional stage balances these marginal gains and costs of alternative required majorities.

If we think of the voting process as a search for information about individual preferences, for example, the willingness of each individual to contribute to the provision of a public good, it seems reasonable to think of marginal decision-making costs rising continuously with the majority required to pass an issue, as it becomes more and more difficult to discover a contribution that makes an individual with outlier preferences better off, and the incentive to engage in strategic holdouts increases. An alternative way to envisage the process, however, is as a search for winning coalitions. Each new proposal may be quite different from its predecessor and win support from a quite different set of voters. When the voting process is of this form, the possibility of cycling must be entertained. Decision-making costs might then actually *fall* as the required majority is increased over some range of m_j, because increasing m_j lowers the probability of a cycle. This is particularly likely if the issues to be decided resemble the determination of the quantities of pure public goods, and thus it is reasonable to assume that the conditions needed to invoke Caplin and Nalebuff's (1988) theorem are satisfied. In this case the probability of cycles can be expected to fall as the required majority increases, reaching zero at an m_j of 0.64. This implies that marginal decision-making costs are U-shaped with the bottom of the U perhaps somewhere around 0.64 (see Figure 26.1). The marginal benefits from increasing m_j, $p'(m_j)(w + s)$, are then likely to cut $d'(m_j)$

630

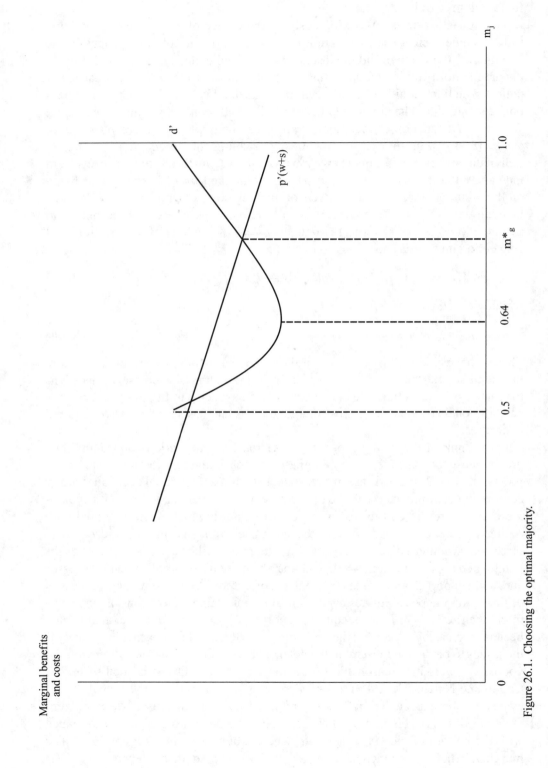

Figure 26.1. Choosing the optimal majority.

twice with the optimal m_j^* being somewhere around or above 0.64. Taking into account the possibility of cycling and the decision-making costs it causes would lead a constitutional convention to reject the simple majority rule for public good–prisoners' dilemma issues in favor of a higher qualified majority rule.[9]

26.6.2 *Direct conflicts*

The other 16 entries in rows and columns 5 or 6 of Matrix 26.1 involve one-way externalities. Entries in row or column 5 involve negative externality issues like smoking in public places and driving at high speeds; entries in row or column 6 positive externalities. These issues can be thought of as single-dimensional, ranging from out right prohibitions and obligations to blanket freedoms. The collective action involves the resolution of a conflict among the citizens over the optimal severity of a ban or obligation. It is reasonable to assume that individuals have single-peaked preferences with respect to these sorts of issues; that is, each person favors a ban or obligation of a particular degree of severity with utility falling off as the severity chosen deviates from this ideal level. The unanimity rule is not an option for resolving such conflicts unless side payments are also allowed as a way of securing a Coasian exchange.

With a single-dimensional issue an individual has an incentive to vote sincerely. Proposals to restrict an action can be made in increasing degrees of severity. The winning proposal under an m_j-qualified majority rule will impose a restriction corresponding to the ideal point of the voter at the m_jth percentile of the distribution of voter ideal points. The choice of m_j amounts to the choice of the percentile of the distribution of ideal points where the restriction will lie. The time required to select one percentile should not differ much from the time to select another; $d'(m_j)$ might reasonably be assumed to be zero. The constitutional convention can treat decision-making costs as a constant deadweight loss. When choosing the optimal majority to resolve single-dimensional conflict issues, only the effects of this choice on the expected utility payoffs need be weighed. Future decision-making costs should not be a factor.

26.7 Rights and obligations

Consider equation (26.4) once again. As the right-hand side approaches zero, the majority required to prohibit a_{rj} approaches unanimity. Now there are two ways in which the right-hand side of (26.4) might approach zero. First, of course, it equals zero if $e_{rj} = 0$. If C's utility is unaffected by a_{rj}, then R should be free to act, and (26.4) calls for a unanimous vote of the community in the second stage of the political process to prohibit her from doing so. But there are a myriad of actions, a_{rj}, that benefit R and have no impact on others. It would be impossible for the constitution to list all of these and specify that they could be abridged only through a unanimous vote of the community. As noted above, such actions seem

---

[9] See discussion in Chapter 5.

most efficiently handled through a blanket provision that allows all actions that have not been specifically prohibited.

The ratio $-e_{rj}/u_{rj}$ also approaches zero even when $-e_{rj} > 0$, as u_{rj} becomes very large. In this case individuals at the constitutional stage who thought that they might be a future R could not simply count on a broadly defined freedom to do what one chooses to protect their freedom to do a_{rj}. Because Cs experience a utility decline from a_{rj}, future Cs may try to prohibit Rs from doing a_j. Such restrictions might be imposed by a simple majority vote and result in a loss in net utility if an R's freedom to do a_j were not explicitly protected. Individuals who are uncertain of whether they would be a future R or C would maximize their expected utility at the constitutional stage by explicitly requiring that a proposal to restrict the freedom to do a_j must pass by a supramajority, which could range up to unanimity (see Figure 26.2).

If Rs experience a great loss from not doing a_j, they would only vote for a proposal to restrict their freedom to do a_j if they were compensated for this loss or cajoled into accepting it. Although one can imagine groups being somehow convinced to give up their veto powers in such situations, one expects this to be rare if the constitutional convention correctly anticipated the relative payoffs from the action when it chose to protect it by invoking the unanimity rule. Rs would nearly always vote down proposed restrictions. Time spent debating and voting on such restrictions would be wasted. Anticipating that most future proposals to restrict this action would lose under the unanimity rule, future decision-making costs could be economized by defining a constitutional *right* guaranteeing Rs the freedom to do a_j. This guarantee would prohibit any future political or private attempts to infringe on an R's freedom to commit the defined action, or if the analogous condition holds for Cs, on anyone's freedom. Since a right always carries with it the freedom *not* to undertake the action, the community could still try and bribe or persuade a group to refrain from a particular action, and so both outcomes possible under the unanimity rule are still open to the community after it defines a right.

Several features of constitutional rights under this theory are to be noted. First, explicit rights are defined only for actions capable of generating sufficiently strong negative externalities to elicit efforts by some members of the community to restrict the actions. In the absence of possible negative externalities, even actions that provide considerable benefits for the actor will not be challenged and need not be protected. Second, there is an inherent tension between constitutional rights and the principle of majoritarian democracy. When the institutions of explicitly defined rights and the simple majority rule are both found in the constitution to deal with situations where individual interests conflict, these situations will differ dramatically in the perceived losses imposed on the different sides from curtailing the action. The simple majority rule is optimal for resolving a negative externality when an individual at the constitutional stage expects the utility gain from undertaking the action to equal the loss it causes. Rights are defined precisely where the simple majority rule is not optimal, because the expected gains and losses from a ban are dramatically different and the constitution framers wish to preclude its use. Because rights will be defined only when significant losses are expected for those prevented from acting relative to the losses imposed on others, disputes over rights are likely to

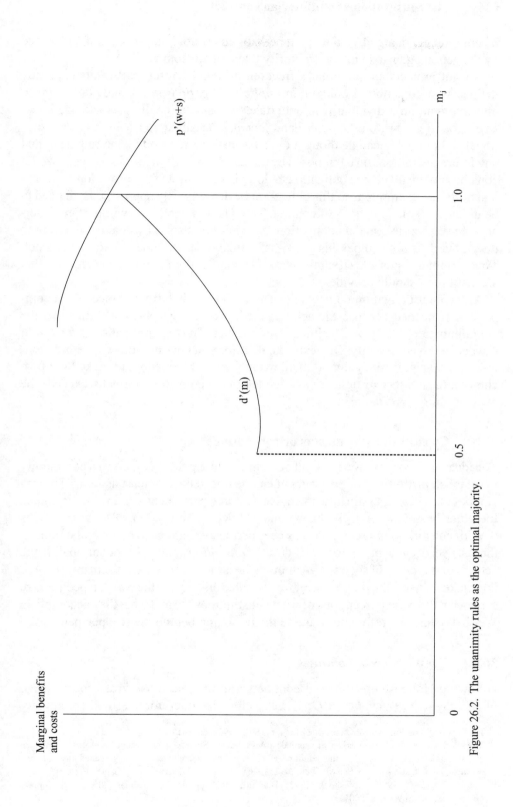

Figure 26.2. The unanimity rules as the optimal majority.

be emotionally charged, as they pit a perhaps substantial majority that feel harmed by the action against an intense minority that benefit from it.[10]

A right protects an individual's freedom *to act*. Therefore, all rights explicitly defined in a constitution contain an *implicit obligation* on all individuals *not* to interfere with an individual who undertakes a constitutionally protected action.[11] *Explicit obligations*, on the other hand, *compel* certain actions. Just as a constitutional right to do a_j can be thought of as a substitute for a provision requiring that any future restrictions on a_j imposed by the community be unanimously approved, a constitutionally mandated obligation to do a_j is a substitute for a provision requiring that all future exemptions to this obligation be unanimously approved. Both need to be defined only in situations of conflict. There is, however, a very important difference between a right and an obligation. A right *allows* an individual the freedom to do a_j, but does not compel this *choice*. The individual remains free to do a_j or not. Thus a right extends and strengthens the blanket freedom to do as one chooses that a constitution should provide.

An explicit obligation compels a_j. The individual is left no choice. Such compulsion is needed because the actor is made worse off to benefit the rest of the community, that is, only in a situation of conflict. Thus, an obligation is a form of slavery to the community. One expects, therefore, in communities where individuals perceive significant gains from allowing people the freedom to make their own choices, the number of rights *to act* defined in the constitution greatly exceeds the explicit obligations *to act*.

26.8   Constitutions: contracts or conventions?

The idea that a constitution is a kind of contract among the members of a community to establish institutions of government can be traced back at least as far as Thomas Hobbes (1651) and, as already noted, has featured prominently in the public choice literature beginning with Buchanan and Tullock's *The Calculus of Consent*. This view of constitutions as contracts has been seriously challenged by several writers in the last decade, who prefer to think of it as a *convention* or *device* for coordinating the actions of members of society.[12] Although the issue is partly one of semantics, more is at stake than just the proper use of words, since underlying the two perspectives are somewhat different perceptions of what constitutions are and what they accomplish. We shall pause, therefore, to examine the reasoning behind the two perspectives.

26.8.1   *Constitutions as contracts*

Following Hobbes constitutional contracts are often seen as agreed to in a state of anarchy (e.g., Buchanan, 1975a). Let us imagine, therefore, a small community

---

[10] For further discussion of these issues, see Mueller (1991, 1996a, ch. 14).

[11] The word "rights" is often used today in reference to entitlements. Such "economic rights" can also be defended as constitutional provisions. Here the definition of an action must encompass obtaining needed medical care, an adequate diet, and so forth. See Mueller (1991, 1996a, ch. 16), and discussion in Chapter 3 of this book.

[12] See Hardin (1989, 1990); Ordeshook (1992); Binmore (1994, pp. 28–31); Kolmar (2000); and Filippov, Ordeshook, and Shvestova (2001).

living in anarchy that considers creating political institutions to facilitate making future collective decisions. The community is small enough so that all members can meet in assembly, and it meets to draft a constitution. It is soon decided that future collective decisions will also be made in an assembly composed of all members of the community. The question of the voting rule to be used in the future takes more time to resolve. Some favor the simple majority rule, others a three-fourths majority, a few full unanimity. After much debate the assembly agrees – unanimously – to require a two-thirds majority for all future collective decisions.

Why might the community *require* that the choice over the future voting rule be unanimous at this first meeting? There are at least two reasons. The first is to solve the infinite regress problem. What voting rule should be used to choose a voting rule? *If* the community can unanimously agree on a voting rule for making future collective decisions the infinite regress is broken.[13] The second reason for requiring unanimous agreement at the constitutional stage is to increase the likelihood of future compliance with the constitution's provisions. If the two-thirds majority rule is chosen, then there will be some people who are harmed by future collective decisions. How can one be sure that they will go along with the community's decision? The answer, of course, is that one can never be sure, but the likelihood is higher if the losers on a future decision agreed to this choice of voting rule, because in agreeing they endorsed a procedure that they knew would allow some people to be harmed by collective decisions and at least implicitly agreed to be among those harmed.[14]

To further enhance the likelihood of compliance, one could well imagine all members of the community *signing* the constitution after it was voted upon, just as they would sign a private contract. In engaging in this symbolic act each citizen would further commit herself to abide by the constitution.

This point might be buttressed by drawing an analogy between constitutions and marriages.[15] Today a man and woman often live together for several years without being married, and then decide to marry even though this act will not alter their day-to-day life-style. Why do they go through the bother and expense of a formal marriage? One explanation is that they have decided to make a deeper commitment to the relationship, and to symbolize this deeper commitment by formally wedding. By so doing they both signal to one another a willingness to live together for a long period of time, "for better or worse," and so on. Signing the marriage contract may strengthen each party's commitment to the relationship, just as signing a constitution – or voting to ratify one – might strengthen each citizen's commitment to it. For some people such symbolic acts have meaning.

In communities that are too large to function solely as direct democracies, a second form of compliance problem arises. How can one ensure that the future representatives of the citizens will make decisions that advance the citizens' interests

---

[13] See Buchanan and Tullock (1962, pp. 6–8).

[14] Rawls (1971) is much concerned about the question of ensuring compliance in his theory of the *social contract*, as is Buchanan (1975a) in his Hobbesian theory of constitutions.

[15] Although highly critical of the contractarian approach to constitutions, Filippov, Ordeshook, and Shvestova (2001) draw the same analogy.

and not simply their own? Here again we can think of a constitution as a contract, but now as a *principal–agent contract*. As in all principal–agent contracts the question of creating the proper incentives for the agents is salient. Competitive elections are one obvious device – constitutional checks and balances another.

Thus, the constitution-as-contract approach to constitutional analysis can be seen to have three possible conceptual advantages: (1) it solves the infinite regress problem of the choice of voting rule, (2) it gives a motive for why citizens might comply with the constitution, and (3) it highlights the principal–agent nature of representative government and the need, therefore, to design institutions that align representatives' interests with those of the citizens.

26.8.2   *Constitutions as conventions*

Ordeshook is concerned with a different sort of infinite regress problem from the one described above.

> But if contracts ensure that people do things that they would not otherwise do, it is difficult to isolate the ultimate source of a constitution's durability. Are its provisions enforced by yet a second contract, that is enforced by a third, and so on? Are they enforced from within, by the police, the courts and the military? Or must they be enforced by force to be administered by an oligarchy that stands removed from constitutional limits? The answer to the first question is obviously "No," the second question merely pushes the problem back a step so that we must ask, "How are the provisions enforcing those enforcement mechanisms enforced?"
>
> Ordeshook (1992, p. 144)

According to Ordeshook the only solution to this infinite regress problem is for the constitution to be *self-enforcing*. The constitution must consist of a set of *devices* or *conventions*, which provide the proper incentives for their self-enforcement.[16]

All of those who reject the constitution-as-contract perspectives emphasize the game-theoretic nature of the problem of constitutional design. Society confronts a plethora of recurring social dilemmas, and it must somehow settle in on one of the many possible equilibria to these supergames. A constitution is a mechanism, a set of conventions, that selects the equilibria.[17]

A frequently used example of a convention is whether a community drives on the right or left side of the road. Young (1993) has employed evolutionary game theory to demonstrate how a community would converge on one of the two possible equilibria in a supergame, even without any communication among the citizens. Such convergence is likely to be much quicker, however, if the citizens do communicate. Imagine, therefore, that the automobile is about to be introduced into our small community. It has observed what has happened in other communities when

---

[16] See also Filippov, Ordeshook, and Shvestova (2001, especially ch. 5).

[17] Given his emphasis on game theory as a tool for analyzing constitutions, one might expect Cooter (2000) to commit himself to the constitutions-are-conventions position. But he also recognizes the advantage of the constitutions-are-contracts idea in fostering compliance (pp. 273–6).

the automobile was introduced, and wishes to avoid the many accidents that occur through its anarchic use. A meeting is called to decide which side of the road cars should drive on.

As each person enters the meeting she has a preference for either the right side or the left. Each also knows, however, that if her favored side is not chosen her loss will not be great. The first decision that the meeting must make is to choose a voting rule for making the choice of road side. The community unanimously agrees to use the simple majority rule for this choice, because no one wants to spend a lot of time deciding this issue. A motion is then made, a vote taken, and a side of the road is chosen. The meeting is over quickly.

This simple example illustrates the main characteristics of the constitutions-are-conventions perspective. There are multiple (two) equilibria from which to choose. Once a selection is made, the rule becomes self-enforcing. No one has an incentive to break the convention. Note also that there would be little gained in thinking of this decision as being some sort of contract. It would be far less likely than in the first example that anyone would suggest that everyone should *sign* a proclamation that all citizens should drive on the left side of the road. No symbolic acts of commitment are needed because of the self-enforcing nature of the convention.

26.8.3 *Discussion*

Constitutions are contracts. Constitutions are conventions. Both statements are metaphors, and like all metaphors neither one is literally true. On the other hand, each does connote a set of ideas that helps reveal important underlying characteristics of constitutions. Constitutions resemble *both* contracts and conventions.

A provision in a constitution that the head of state should be elected every four years fits the metaphor that constitutions are conventions nicely. There are a variety of terms of office that might be chosen – three years, four years, life. Each can be thought of as resulting in a different long-run equilibrium. By establishing four years as the convention, the constitution effectively selects one of these equilibria. Once it becomes established, it is likely to be self-enforcing. There are many elements in most constitutions that resemble this one.

Now consider, however, a constitutional ban of divorces. Such a provision does not seem to be reasonably characterized as a convention. Certainly it is not likely to be self-enforcing. At some time, some people are likely to want to get divorced, and if this provision of the constitution is to be enforced it will have to be by the police, the courts, and/or the military. If the constitution includes provisions like this one it will also have to create agencies to enforce them, and the infinite regress problem described by Ordeshook raises its ugly head. Once the police, courts, and military can prevent divorces, what stops them from preventing the use of birth control devices, sexual relationships out of marriage, and many other actions that are *not* banned in the constitution?

All constitutions contain provisions that require enforcement agencies for them to be effective. Their inclusion in the constitution immediately thrusts the citizenry into a principal–agent relationship with the state, and the metaphor of constitutions as contracts begins to have value. Why would a community ever ban divorces? Why would a community ever ban slavery? The two-stage theory of constitutions presented in this chapter gives some insight into possible answers to these questions. A community might ban divorces or slavery if it believed that the future gains to anyone seeking a divorce or wishing to own slaves would be very small relative to the losses imposed on others by these actions. When placing such provisions into the constitution, the citizens must also create agencies to enforce these bans, and thus also include provisions that give the agents incentives to abide by the constitutional contract. The principal–agent nature of the constitutional contract must be faced head on.[18]

One danger in thinking of constitutions as self-enforcing conventions is that one obtains the impression that these "mechanisms" or "devices" for coordinating actions will – if properly designed – run forever. The value of thinking of them as contracts is that one recognizes that contracts often need to be rewritten to reflect changing situations, *and* one immediately identifies who it is that should do the rewriting. If the community thought when it first wrote the constitution 200 years ago that a ban of divorces should be included, and today it feels differently, then it should meet again and change the constitution. This in turn implies that when the constitution is first written, provisions should be made that allow the community to rewrite the constitution as conditions change.[19] In contrast, the metaphor of constitutions as conventions connotes an evolutionary process of selecting conventions and equilibria, which is somehow out of the hands of the citizens.

Although all constitutions have the attributes of both contracts and conventions, they differ in the extent to which they exhibit these attributes. The British Constitution comes closest to resembling a set of conventions that serves to coordinate the political activity of the nation. Except for the signing of the Magna Carta at Runnymede in 1215, there are no "constitutional moments" in British history which might be identified as instances of contractual agreement among the citizens.[20] The unwritten nature of the British Constitution gives it a great deal of flexibility in responding to changes in the environment. Over time the convention has evolved that a national election must be held at least once every five years, but in times of war or national crisis national elections have occasionally been suspended. The British Constitution is a flexible and evolving set of conventions.

In contrast U.S. history does contain that great "constitutional moment" at the end of the eighteenth century, when the U.S. Constitution was written and ratified. The quotation from Thomas Paine at the opening of this chapter reveals that he thought of the Constitution as a "compact," and this was probably true for many of those involved in its writing and ratification. Many Americans today probably also

---

[18] The problem of constraining the agents in government is central in the contractarian approach to constitutions of Brennan and Buchanan (1980, 1985). Merville and Osborne (1990) also stress the principal-agent nature of the constitutional contract, and emphasize that the contract must be self-enforcing. Thus, the need for constitutions to be self-enforcing is *not* what divides the contractarians and the conventiontarians.

[19] See my proposals in Mueller (1996a, ch. 21). One of the great weaknesses of the U.S. Constitution has proved to be the difficulty of changing it. See Ackerman (1998).

[20] Even the signing at Runnymede involved only the king and some barons.

feel that they are willing parties to this compact owing to the illustrious status of the "Founding Fathers." And this sense of belonging may help explain the reverence with which so many Americans hold their Constitution and thus its durability.

26.9 Conclusions regarding two-stage theories of social choice

In this chapter we have described the basic elements of a two-stage theory of social choice, where decisions in the first stage are made behind a veil of ignorance, while decisions in the second stage are made with each individual in full knowledge of her personal preferences. We have seen that the implications of this theory depend crucially on the nature of the uncertainty assumed in the first stage. If participants at the constitutional convention can envisage the utilities of every future individual for every possible future action, and are uncertain only with regard to which of these future individuals they will be, they can write all rules governing future actions into the constitution. Postconstitutional politics disappears, and the constitution maximizes a Harsanyian social welfare function. Government will not disappear entirely, because individuals in the postconstitutional stage may have incentives to disobey the stipulations of the constitution, and such cheating must be punished. However, no additional collective choices and thus political institutions need be defined.

On the other extreme, if the constitution framers lack all information for calculating future probabilities and utility payoffs, they are incapable of writing rules into the constitution that will maximize their expected utilities. They are then thrust into Rawls's world, and some additional normative principles – like Rawls's two principles of justice – must be invoked to select political institutions for making future collective choices and resolving future conflicts.

If the middle degree of uncertainty is assumed – individuals can judge the likely utilities associated with different future actions, but cannot determine the numbers of individuals who will benefit or be harmed by each action – it may be possible to select voting rules to reveal this information in the postconstitutional stage. It is in this middle area of uncertainty that the principles of public choice come into play. Implicitly it was this middle degree of uncertainty that Buchanan and Tullock (1962) assumed in their analysis of the choice of voting rules and other political institutions at the constitutional stage.

Although we have been able to derive some very precise conditions for the selection of a particular voting rule or the specification of a right to act, we have done so under rather restrictive assumptions – there are only two groups of individuals, they are able to make interpersonal cardinal utility comparisons, and so on. If we were to expand the number of groups with different preferences our ability to define voting rules that would maximize the expected utility of someone at the constitutional stage would decline rapidly (Mueller, 2001). Thus, the real lesson to be learned from this exercise is not that it is possible in a utilitarian theory of constitutions to derive conditions under which a voting rule like the simple majority rule is optimal, but rather how restrictive the assumptions are that one must make to accomplish this task.

On the other hand, we have also limited consideration to the family of qualified majority rules running from dictatorship up to unanimity. The potential for specifying voting rules that maximize the expected utility of someone at the constitutional stage is greatly enhanced once one allows the constitution framers to consider some of the procedures for revealing individual preferences that have been invented. For example, the point voting procedure discussed in Chapter 8 can be designed to maximize a Benthamite SWF and thus would be an attractive option for individuals at a constitutional convention who wished to select a voting rule that would reveal their preferences for public goods issues in the postconstitutional stage. Under the assumptions that support the probabilistic voting model discussed in Chapter 12, a set of electoral rules that would produce a two-party system would also maximize an SWF. In the forty years since Buchanan and Tullock wrote *The Calculus of Consent* public choice has produced a wide range of candidates for institutions that could be chosen by a group of individuals who sought to write a constitution to maximize their expected utilities when they were uncertain of their future positions under the constitution.[21]

26.10   From the normative, two-stage theory of constitutions to hypothesis testing

As noted at the beginning of this chapter, Buchanan and Tullock's *The Calculus of Consent* can be regarded as both a normative and a positive theory of constitutions. Most of the analysis of two-stage theories of constitutions has tended to be normative, and that has been the approach taken in this chapter. Before leaving these two-stage theories we shall briefly discuss the extent to which they can or have been tested empirically.

There are two ways of thinking about testing the implications of constitutional theories. The first is to think of them as theories about how political rules or institutions translate into outcomes.

$$\text{Rules} \longrightarrow \text{Outcomes.}$$

Much public choice can be regarded as developing and testing theories about this aspect of constitutional political economy. For example, the theories of how different electoral rules determine the number of parties represented in the legislature discussed in Chapter 13 fall into this category. Whether or not a country has a two-party or a multiparty system, or a presidential or a parliamentary system in turn will affect the size and composition of its governmental outlays.[22]

The second way to think about constitutional theories is as theories about how individual preferences translate into political rules, where the relevant preferences in this case pertain to the individuals who write the constitution.

$$\text{Preferences} \longrightarrow \text{Rules.}$$

It is this way of viewing the theory of constitutions that is most closely related to the two-stage theory outlined above. For example, the two-stage theory of constitutions predicts that individuals place rights to undertake specific actions into the

---

[21] See Mueller (1996a).
[22] See Persson and Tabellini (2000a) and the discussion in ch. 21.

constitution if they envisage significant losses to those prevented from undertaking the action relative to any externality it might cause, and *if* they are uncertain over whether it will be they or someone else whom the community might try to prevent from undertaking the action. The United States was settled in part by people who had escaped from religious persecution in Europe, and at the time its constitution was written, many might still have feared that some future majority might try and prevent them from practicing their religion and thus that the freedom to do so required protection in the constitution. Similarly, many had been subject to arbitrary arrest under British rule and thus might also have felt uncertain about this sort of danger. The existence of several of the rights to act protected in the Bill of Rights of the U.S. Constitution is easily accounted for by the two-stage theory of constitutions.

Slavery also has the characteristics that would from the theory lead us to anticipate a constitutional ban against it – large expected utility losses for those prevented from acting, and relatively small gains from those benefiting from slavery. Why then did the U.S. Constitution originally fail to ban slavery? The obvious answer is that there was no uncertainty among those who wrote and ratified the Constitution about their ever becoming slaves in the future. Uncertainty about future position – real or self-imposed – is an essential element in the two-stage theory of constitutions.

McGuire and Ohsfeldt (1986, 1989) and McGuire (1988) have had some success in explaining voting at the Philadelphia Convention and at the ratifying conventions in terms of the self-interest of the participants. Although some of their interpretations of the data can be questioned (Mueller, 1996a, pp. 62–3), they provide convincing evidence that the Founding Fathers of the United States did not suppress all aspects of narrow self-interest when writing and ratifying the Constitution. Unfortunately, constitutional conventions are such rare events that empirical testing of hypotheses about voting on constitutional provisions is likely to remain an "infant industry" in the public choice field.[23]

Bibliographical notes

The number of papers that have implicitly adopted the constitutional stage decision as a point of reference is large. See, in particular, Rae (1969); Mueller (1971, 1973, 1996a); Mueller, Tollison, and Willett (1974a,b, 1976); and Abrams and Settle (1976). The field of constitutional political economy now has its own journal, *Constitutional Political Economy*, and the entire 90th volume of the journal *Public Choice* (March 1997) was devoted to the topic.

James Buchanan has expounded upon and defended the two-stage constitutional approach to public choice in numerous essays down through the years. A good sampling of these is contained in the two volumes published in 1986 and 1991. The Liberty Fund is in the process of republishing all of his writings. Riley (2001) presents an excellent analysis of the two-stage approach to constitutions.

Coleman (1988) critically discusses constitutional political economy from a legal perspective. Cooter (2000) applies concepts from game theory to the analysis

---

[23] For an innovative attempt to test propositions about constitutional design using data on the democratic rules used in condominiums, see Sass (1992).

of constitutional institutions. Ferejohn, Rakove, and Riley (2001) contains several interesting essays on constitutional issues.

Beard's (1913) *An Economic Interpretation of the Constitution* of the United States might well be regarded as a, if not *the*, pioneering contribution to both public choice and constitutional political economy. Certainly, this book can be characterized as "constitutional political economy without romance" to paraphrase a characterization of public choice that James Buchanan has often made. Beard clearly anticipated some of the hypotheses and results of McGuire and Ohsfeldt (1986, 1989) and McGuire (1988), and his book shares with all "economic theories of politics" a certain cynicism about individual motivations and their effects on political outcomes. But Beard's work has been essentially ignored by students of both public choice and constitutional political economy.

Voigt (1997, 1999) has been one of the leading proponents of the development of the positive dimension to constitutional political economy.

CHAPTER 27

Liberal rights and social choices

... there is a sphere of action in which society, as distinguished from the individual, has, if any, only an indirect interest; comprehending all that portion of a person's life and conduct which affects only himself, or if it also affects others, only with their free, voluntary, and undeceived consent and participation.

... there is ... in the world at large an increasing inclination to stretch unduly the powers of society over the individual, both by the force of opinion and even by that of legislation; and as the tendency of all the changes taking place in the world is to strengthen society, and diminish the power of the individual, this encroachment is not one of the evils which tend spontaneously to disappear, but, on the contrary, to grow more and more formidable.

John Stuart Mill

In Chapter 26 we illustrated why individuals might choose to define certain rights to act in the constitution. The existence of these sorts of constitutionally protected rights is often regarded as an essential prerequisite for a free society. Such rights protect the liberty of all citizens and are associated with classic definitions of *liberalism* as put forward by John Stuart Mill (1859). In a short note published in 1970, Nobel prize-winner Amartya Sen (1970b) explored the notion of liberalism from a public/social choice perspective. This note proved yet another impossibility theorem of the Arrow variety, and precipitated a lengthy and often vigorous debate over both the implications of the theorem and the concept of liberalism itself. In this chapter we explore some of the issues raised in this debate. We begin with the theorem itself.

27.1   The theorem

Arrow's theorem states that it is impossible to satisfy four reasonable constraints on the social choice process without making one person a dictator over all social choices (see Chapter 24). Sen (1970a,b) sought to allow each person to be dictator over a single "social" choice, for example, the color of paint in one's own bathroom, and arrived at yet another impossibility theorem.

More specifically, Sen (1976, p. 217) set out to find a social decision function that would satisfy the following property:

Acceptance of personal liberty: there are certain personal matters in which each person should be free to decide what should happen, and in choices over these things whatever he or she thinks is better must be taken to be better for the society as a whole, no matter what others think.

He formalizes this condition by allowing each individual to be decisive for the social choice over one pair of alternatives, and shows that this condition, unrestricted domain, and the Pareto principle are sufficient to produce a cyclic social decision function (1970a,b). The theorem is remarkable, as in the Arrow case, in that it achieves so much from so few constraints. Neither transitivity (only acyclicity) nor the independence of irrelevant alternatives is involved (but see below).

Sen illustrates his theorem with the following example: a copy of *Lady Chatterley's Lover* is available to be read and the following three social states are possible:

    a.   *A* reads *Lady Chatterley's Lover* and *B* does not.
    b.   *B* reads *Lady Chatterley's Lover* and *A* does not.
    c.   Neither reads it.

A, the prude, prefers that no one reads it, but would rather read it himself than have *B* read it. Lascivious *B* prefers most that prudish *A* read the book, but would rather read it himself than see it left unread, that is,

        for *A*: *c* P *a* P *b*, and
        for *B*: *a* P *b* P *c*.

Invoking the liberal rule to allow *B* to choose whether he reads the book or not results in

        b P *c*.

Doing the same for *A* results in

        c P *a*.

But both *A* and *B* prefer *a* to *b*; thus, by the Pareto principle,

        a P *b*

and we have a cycle.

27.2   Resolving the paradox

27.2.1 *Rights over Pareto*

There are several ways out of or around the paradox, of which we discuss three.

Sen's own preferred solution is to require that the Pareto principle defer to liberal rights in certain situations.

> Let me be "prude" (Mr. *A*) . . ., while you are "lascivious" (Mr. *B*). I would rather not read the stuff by myself (i.e. I prefer c to a), and I would rather you would not (i.e. I prefer c to b), but I decide to "respect" your tastes on what I agree is

your benighted business (while wondering whether "respect" is quite the word), conceding that my preference for c over b be ignored. My dislike of your floating over "muck" was so strong that I would have preferred to read the work myself to stop you from falling into this (i.e., I preferred a to b), but being a consistent kind of man, I notice that, if I insist that my preference for c over a should count as well as my preference, for a over b, then there is not much point in my "renouncing" my preference for c over b. So I may decide not to want my preference for a over b to count, even though the choice over the pair (a,b) is not exclusively your business.

On a similar ground, you might not want your preference for a over b to count, since you do wish your preference for b over c to count and decide not to want that your preference for a over c should count (since it is my business). But the Pareto preference for a over b is built on counting my preference and yours over a and b (Sen, 1976, 1982, pp. 313–4; case designation altered to conform to our example).

Thus, Sen solves the paradox by assuming that the individuals, although meddlesome in nature, have liberal values that they impose upon themselves so that parts of their preferences "do not count" or receive "different weight." Liberal B might state, for example, that the only choice relevant for him is b or c, and state

> liberal B b P c

while liberal A states

> liberal A c P a.

The social ordering is now transitive with the liberally constrained outcome being the plausible one that B reads LCL and A does not.

Sen chooses to treat the meddlesome preferences of A and B as in some sense their "true" preferences for the purposes of defining Pareto optimality, with liberalism a constraint or weight placed on true preferences. Alternatively, one could regard meddlesomeness and liberalism as both attributes of a single set of preferences with one dominating the other (Mueller, 1996b).

Liberal A might simply state that if B prefers reading LCL to not reading it, A as a liberal is willing to respect that choice so that his ordering of b and c becomes

> liberal A b P$'$$c$

and likewise for liberal B

> liberal B c P$'$$a$.

Prudish A would rather not read the book

> for A: c P$'$$a$

while lacivious B rather would

> for B: b P$'$$c$.

Combining their liberal preferences over what the other person does and their personal preferences with respect to their own actions, we obtain for both prudish A

and lascivious B:

$$b \; \mathrm{P}'c \; \mathrm{P}'a.$$

If A and B are liberals, they unanimously agree that the best social outcome is for lascivious B to read LCL, and for A not to read it.[1]

Thus, the same outcome emerges if we assume liberalism is a part of a person's preferences or a constraint upon them. Which way one views the problem is an issue of methodological preference (Mueller, 1996b). I enjoy a cigarette after dinner, and always smoke one when I dine alone. But tonight I am dining with you, and you are offended by the smoking of others. I choose not to smoke. Is this choice best described as the unconstrained maximum of my utility function, which includes as arguments both my pleasure from smoking and my displeasure from watching your reaction to my smoking, or as the maximum to my utility function that includes only my pleasure from smoking, but with the solution being derived under the constraint that I not cause you discomfort?

Our first solution to the liberal paradox solves the paradox by assuming that the individuals themselves are willing to behave in such a way as to avoid what would otherwise be a paradox. Were individuals resolutely selfish and meddlesome, a conflict between liberal principles and Pareto optimality would remain. But if both individuals' behaviors (preferences) are controlled by liberal principles, no inconsistency with an (un)constrained Pareto principle arises. The next solution to the paradox relies entirely on the selfish interests of the individuals.

27.2.2 *Pareto trades of actions*

As the original example was posed, it appears as if there is but one copy of the book to read, and the collective choice to be made is over who should read this book. This makes somewhat artificial the presentation of this choice to both individuals, since both cannot decide to read the book at the same time. If there is but one book to read, the decision of who reads it is obviously a collective decision from the start, and cannot be a purely personal matter for both individuals at the same time (see Buchanan, 1996; de Jasay and Kliemt, 1996).

This difficulty can be gotten around by assuming that the book is available to both, and redefining the liberalism axiom to require that each individual is decisive over an element pair (whether he reads *Lady Chatterley* or not) in all possible social states, that is, independent of the other's choice.[2] The decision options can now be illustrated by Matrix 27.1 in which the possibility

d. Both A and B read *Lady Chatterley's Lover*

has been added. Whereas Sen's condition grants A the choice of either row *given that B is constrained to the first column*, the modified liberalism condition gives A

---

[1] Resolution of the paradox does not require that both individuals be liberals, but the social outcome can depend on which individual is the liberal, when only one is (Suzumura, 1978; Austen-Smith, 1982).

[2] See Bernholz (1974c); Seidl (1975); Breyer (1977); Craven (1982); Sugden (1985, 1993); Gaertner, Pattanaik, and Suzumura (1992); Buchanan (1996); Fleurbaey and Gaertner (1996); Pattanaik (1996); and Suzumura (1996).

Matrix 27.1.

		B, the lascivious	
		Does not read LCL	Reads LCL
A, the prude	Reads *LCL*	a	d
	Does not read *LCL*	c	b

the choice of row regardless of what column B chooses, and assigns the analogous right to B with respect to the choice of column.

Since this new liberalism condition is stronger than Sen's, it obviously does not overturn his theorem. Applying the condition to A, we have

$$(c, b) \, P \, (a, d)$$

and from B's preference ordering

$$(d, b) \, P \, (a, c).$$

The intersection of these two choice sets is b, which is Pareto inferior to a. Notice that Pareto-optimal a is the only social state ruled out entirely by the application of this modified liberalism principle.

Although this new liberalism principle does not solve the liberal's paradox, it does suggest a way out of it. Matrix 27.1 is a prisoners' dilemma matrix, and the Pareto-inferior outcome at b comes about from each individual's *independent* decision to exercise his own liberal rights without regard for the externalities that this decision inflicts on the other (Fine, 1975; Buchanan, 1996). A way out of the dilemma, as in the case of other externalities, is to invoke another liberal axiom – all individuals are free to engage in mutually beneficial trades – and allow A and B to form a contract in which B agrees not to read the book in exchange for A's reading it (Coase, 1960). The power to form such contracts requires that the liberalism axiom be redefined to allow an individual either to exercise his assigned right or trade it away, that is, agree not to exercise it.[3]

Sen (1986, pp. 225–8) raises two objections to allowing individuals to trade away their liberal rights to achieve Pareto optimality. First, if A and B have liberal values, they might refuse to form such a contract despite its seeming attractiveness. The inherent intrusiveness of the contract may be such an affront to A's and B's liberal beliefs that they refuse to join the contract, even though they would experience higher utilities if the provisions of the contract were to arise without their having to join it.[4] In this case, the only possible resolution of the paradox is Sen's preferred solution, namely, if liberal values dominate pure selfish preferences. Whether one regards this

---

[3] See Gibbard (1974), Kelly (1976), Buchanan (1996), Nath (1976), Breyer (1977), Barry (1986), Harel and Nitzan (1987), Hardin (1988), de Jasay and Kliemt (1996), and Bernholz (1997a).

[4] See also Suzumura (1991, 1996) and Sen (1992, 1996).

solution as a violation of the Pareto principle or a consistent application of it still depends, however, on the methodological choice of incorporating an individual's liberal values into her preferences, or treating them as a constraint upon them.

Sen's second objection to the efficient-Pareto-trades resolution of the paradox is that the needed contract is difficult if not impossible to enforce. Prudish *A* may feign reading the book but avert his eyes at the juiciest passages. Lascivious *B* may surreptitiously devour a purloined copy of the book. Moreover, the enforcement of such a contract by even an impartial third party would in itself violate liberal values in a most fundamental way. Consider just how carefully and continuously *B* would have to be monitored to ensure that he never read the book.

This second objection to the trading solution to the paradox is certainly valid, but in accepting it the paradox in not achieving Pareto optimality becomes less paradoxical. We have seen in our discussion of externalities and public goods in Chapter 2 that Pareto-optimal allocations of resources are always in principle attainable through unanimous agreements among all concerned parties. "All" that stands in the way of reaching these agreements are transaction costs. The failure to achieve potentially Pareto-optimal allocations due to transaction costs does not constitute a paradox. It is a fact of our collective lives. Indeed, one might better describe the resulting allocations as Pareto optimal *given the existence of transaction costs* (Dahlman, 1979).

The costs of making and enforcing a contract to produce the Pareto-preferred outcome *a* could prevent its realization *even in the absence of liberal rights*. If every decision as to who reads what had to be made as a collective agreement between *A* and *B* and neither had the right to do anything on his own, the prisoners' dilemma nature of their preference structure would still provide incentives for both to cheat on the agreement to obtain *a*. The problem of enforcing such a contract exists with or without the assignment of liberal rights.

27.2.3 *Pareto trades of rights*

The resolution of the liberal paradox discussed in the previous subsection envisages individuals being assigned rights, and contracting away their freedom to exercise their rights or not – individuals *trade away* their freedom to act. Harel and Nitzan (1987) have proposed a resolution of the paradox that allows individuals to trade their *rights* away.

To see what is involved, assume again that there are two individuals, *A* and *B*, and four possible states of the world:

> *x*. *A* eats an apple, and *B* does not eat an apple
> *y*. *A* eats an orange, and *B* does not eat an orange
> *z*. *B* eats an apple, and *A* does not eat an apple
> *w*. *B* eats an orange, and *A* does not eat an orange

A prefers eating an apple to eating an orange, and prefers seeing *B* eat an orange to *B*'s eating an apple. That is, *A*'s preferences are

> for *A*: x P y P w P z

B's preferences, on the other hand, are

for *B*: w P z P x P y.

As with Sen's theorem, a person i has a liberal right to decide between the two states of the world (u, v), if $\{u \text{ P}_i v\} \rightarrow \{u \text{ P } v\}$, and $\{v \text{ P}_i u\} \rightarrow \{v \text{ P } u\}$. Each person assumes that all states of the world, which she is unable to control by exercising her preassigned rights, are equally likely. Under this assumption, a right over the pair (x, z) is more valuable for *A* than a right over the pair (x, w), since *A* prefers w to z. If *A* has the right to decide between the $(x - z)$ pair, she can make sure that her least preferred state of the world does not occur. Thus, each person can be viewed as having preferences defined over the assignment of rights. If then, we allow individuals to exchange these rights, they may be able to achieve superior outcomes – they may be able to avoid the liberal paradox.

To illustrate, assume that *A* is initially given the right to decide the (y, w) pair and *B* the (x, z) pair. *A* can decide whether she eats an apple or *B* does. *B* gets to decide who eats the orange. *A* prefers w to z, and thus prefers the right to decide (y, z) over (y, w). *B* prefers the right over (x, w) to (x, z). *A* and *B* swap w for z. This results in the new pairs of rights (y, z) for *A* and (x, w) for *B*. This assignment is still not optimal, however, and *A* and *B* now trade y for x giving both the right to choose between their most and least preferred outcomes, that is, for *A* (x, z) and for *B* (w, y). *A* gets to eat an orange, *B* an apple. Harel and Nitzan extend the definition of liberalism to allow for the possibility of trades such as these, and establish conditions under which this modified definition of liberalism is compatible with the Pareto principle, unrestricted domain, and the absence of cycles.[5]

It should be noted, however, that such trading of rights *cannot* get around the problem inherent in Sen's *Lady Chatterley* example. Assume again that *A*'s and *B*'s preferences are as follows:

for *A*: c P a P b P d
for *B*: d P a P b P c.

Assign *A* the right over the (b, d) pair and *B* over (a, c), that is conditional on *B*'s reading the book, *A*, the prude, can choose to read it or not; conditional on *A*'s not reading it, *B* has the right to read it or not. *A* would like to trade his right over b for either a or c, but *B* prefers the right over (a, c) over either (a, b) or (b, c). No trade is possible.

Note also that *A* and *B* cannot *both* exercise their rights over their assigned pairs of states of the world, since only one of the four states is possible.[6] *A* cannot choose not to read the book, while *B* selects that they both read it. *One* person's right must take precedence over the other's. Thus, one of the actors must be selected as the

---

[5] See, however, the critiques of Breyer (1990) and Seidl (1990).

[6] This difficulty does not arise in Harel and Nitzan's formulation of liberal rights, as our apple and orange example illustrates. More than one state of the world is possible, and thus meaningful assignments of rights can be made.

social dictator even without invoking the Pareto principle.[7] This feature of Sen's *Lady Chatterley* example arises because of his assumption that individuals have rights over the choice of *states of the world*. We next consider this assumption in greater detail.

27.3   Rights over social states versus rights over actions

Sen set up the paradox by formulating the question as a problem of *social* choice. As with Arrow's impossibility result, the question is one of choosing a *state of the world*, whereby state of the world we mean a complete description of the position of everyone in society: A is wearing a blue shirt and reading *LCL*, and B is wearing a white shirt and is also reading *LCL*. It is natural in this context to define rights in terms of individual choices over states of the world.

Returning to Sen's original formulation of the *LCL* example let us define a, b, and c as social states, such that in

a. A reads *Lady Chatterley's Lover* and B does not.
b. B reads *Lady Chatterley's Lover* and A does not.
c. Neither reads it.

A is decisive over (a, c) and B is decisive over (b, c). That is to say, *given that B is not reading LCL*, A can choose whether or not to read it, and *given that A is not reading LCL*, B can choose whether or not to read it.

When rights are defined over social states, they are always *conditional*. Since social state b is a complete description of *all* of the attributes of the environment and actions of individuals in situation b, giving someone a right to select b or c must be conditional on everyone in society doing what they are described as doing in the definitions of b and c. If B somehow manages to get a hold of *LCL* and read it, A's right to choose whether to read the book or not becomes of no consequence, since it is contingent on B's not reading it. The conditional nature of rights, and the presence of option c in both A's and B's assigned rights is what bothers Buchanan (1996) and de Jasay and Kliemt (1996). If A's right is contingent on B's not reading the book, how can we say that B is free – has the right – to read the book or not?

Gaertner, Pattanaik, and Suzumura (1992) point out that this way of formulating liberalism or liberal rights runs counter to most intuitive notions of rights, namely, that A is free to read *LCL* or not *independently* of what B does. Rights are *unconditional* freedoms to act. This more intuitive notion of rights can be best captured by adopting a game theoretic approach, and defining rights as choices over *admissable actions*. In the two-person case, think of A as the row player and B as the column player. In the normal form of the game, A confronts a matrix containing n possible actions on his part, a_{Ai}, and B confronts the same matrix containing, say, m possible

---

[7] Breyer (1996) criticizes Buchanan (1996) and de Jasay and Kliemt (1996) for thinking of liberal rights, as defined by Sen, as entitling individuals to make choices *for society*. Instead, Breyer claims that they are to be interpreted as a guide for the social planner, who is charged with choosing the optimal social state. This alternative interpretation does not remove the difficulty, however, since the assignment of rights to both A and B forces the social planner to favor one of the two persons over the other.

actions on her part, a_{Bi}. If A and B are the only two persons in the society, then the natural way to think of rights is to assume that A has a right to undertake some a_{Ai} or not to do so, with B having a similar right to some action a_{Bj}. If both of them choose to exercise their rights by undertaking the actions a_{Ai} and a_{Bj}, then the social state defined by the joint pair of actions (a_{Ai}, a_{Bj}) results. Neither A nor B has chosen this social state, however, nor does either have a right to choose it. Each is empowered only to choose one attribute of the resulting social state, namely, his action in it. As we illustrated with the prisoners' dilemma matrix in the previous section, when liberalism is defined in these game-theoretic terms, it remains possible to construct examples in which the social outcome – the intersection of each player's strategy choice – is not Pareto optimal.[8]

Which way of conceptualizing rights is better? The answer to this question depends in part on the nature of the conditions included in the social-state description of rights, and in part on our intuitions as to what the word "rights" connotes. In many contexts our intuitions will normally imply an unconditional freedom to act, as say in choosing what book to read or what color shirt to wear. In others, a conditional right may seem more appropriate. X has the right to kiss Y, conditional on Y's being willing to be kissed by X.[9]

Sen (1996) accepts that treating liberalism as conferring rights to choose actions rather than social states often comes closer to capturing commonly held notions about rights, but goes on to maintain that our reasons for defining or defending rights also sometimes arise out of a concern for the *consequences* of the actions, which in turn depend on the characteristics of the social state that arises when each person chooses a particular action. He gives the following example:

> When John Stuart Mill (1859) discusses the liberty of people of different faith to eat pork, while guaranteeing the liberty of non-Muslims to eat pork (Mill 1859, pp. 152–5), problems can arise because of a person's not knowing what each particular cooked dish consists of. In making sure that the rights of Muslims and non-Muslims are being respectively realized, we have to go beyond simply giving each person the freedom of action. The emergence of the right outcome will be important for the fulfillment of liberty in this case . . .
>
> (Sen, 1996, p. 158)

Thus, in this example Sen is emphasizing that the Muslim's ability to exercise his right not to eat pork is contingent in an important way on his knowing the content of the foods placed before him.

27.4 Liberal rights and obligations

All protections of rights to act imply obligations for the rest of society passively to allow these actions. My right to read a particular book depends on everyone else not trying to take this book from me, not gouging my eyes out, and most importantly in

---

[8] See also discussion by Nozick (1974, pp. 165–6).

[9] See Sen's (1992) discussion of examples of rights to sing with a group or have uncovered hair in public.

the context of constitutionally protected rights, not passing laws that ban the book's publication or my reading of it.

In some of his examples, Sen seems to want to go beyond such *passive* notions of obligations not to interfere with an action, when it is protected by a right, to a more *active* notion of social obligations. In the Muslim example Sen seems to be implying that society has an obligation to provide the Muslim with information about food content to ensure that his act of eating has the desired consequence. This more active interpretation of rights leads directly to what many have called "economic rights" – providing people with not only the freedom to undertake certain actions, but also the resources to act. Returning to the reading example, one might argue that the freedom to read what one wishes is meaningless unless one can afford to buy books, and thus that society is obligated to couple rights of free speech with, say, public libraries so that the poor have access to books. The freedom to read what one wishes is meaningless if one is blind and of modest means, and thus society is obligated to couple rights of free speech with subsidies for the publication of books in braille, or perhaps society must hire people to read aloud to the blind. In the religious context, this might imply society's building a mosque for the Muslim to worship in, if none exists. In situations like these, the objective sought in defining a right is contingent in a nontrivial way on specific elements in the *social state*, and these attributes of the desired social state may imply certain active obligations for society.

Although most people will agree that a right to eat what one chooses is of little value to a person who cannot afford food, many will at the same time balk at the notion that all rights to choose actions imply specific, active obligations for society. Each of us might feel that X is at liberty to travel to the moon, if she so chooses, but we will object to having to pay for a rocket to improve her chances of completing the journey safely. How does a society determine which rights to act require active involvement by society, and which only warrant passive nonintervention? One way to proceed is obviously to try and determine the benefits for the actor and costs imposed on the rest of society. This takes us into the kind of *welfarist* analysis of constitutional rights in which we engaged in Chapter 26. We close this chapter by applying that analysis to the question of liberal rights.

27.5   Constitutional rights and liberal rights

The literature on the liberal paradox treats both the assignment of rights and the preferences of individuals as exogenous. The desirability of enforcing the assigned rights is taken for granted, and given the assumed preferences a paradox ensues. From whence come these rights, however? If they are embedded in the constitution, how was it possible that these individuals ever agreed on the definition of rights?

To see the problem consider again the apple and orange example, but assume that both individuals have identical preferences, and both prefer eating an orange to an apple. Then no trade of rights occurs. The person assigned the right to decide who eats the orange will select herself. Moreover, *no unanimous agreement on the assignment of rights* at the constitutional stage will be possible, without invoking some form of veil of ignorance that conceals the future identities of the individuals.[10]

Once we think of rights as being themselves the subject of social choice, as in a constitution, then the questions arise in the context of the *LCL* example, of whether individuals with meddlesome preferences, like the prudish *A* and lascivious *B*, would ever define a right to read a book of one's choosing, knowing that books like *LCL* sometimes appear, or conversely, if a society is sufficiently liberal to protect in its constitution the right to read what one chooses, is it likely to contain persons with the meddlesome preferences, which give rise to the paradox? More fundamentally, we might ask if rational, self-interested individuals were to write a constitution would they define rights to act that would lead to Pareto inefficiencies?

The theory of constitutional rights presented in Chapter 26 provided an explanation for why rights to act might be singled out for explicit protection by rational individuals seeking to maximize their expected utilities at the constitutional stage. Explicit protection is called for when the action is expected to provide a great increase in utility for the actor, but at the same time may generate a negative externality of sufficient strength to induce some individuals to attempt to prohibit the action through collective action. Explicit rights protection bars future majorities from attempting to ban the action. Publishing and even reading certain books have led to efforts to ban these activities in many countries, and one can anticipate that they would arise again with respect to certain books. If from behind the veil of ignorance one believed that the utility gains from reading and publishing books were generally much greater than any utility losses that these activities imposed on third parties, one would support a free-speech clause in the constitution to protect these actions.

Although some of the examples in the literature on the liberal paradox, like the original one involving *Lady Chatterley's Lover*, relate to actions that are typically explicitly protected in constitutions, others, like the choice of tiles in the bathroom, the color of one's shirt, whether one sleeps on one's back or not, relate to actions that are never *explicitly* protected in constitutions. The theory of constitutional rights would explain why these actions are not explicitly protected by their being highly unlikely to generate sufficiently strong negative externalities to induce future efforts to ban them. Not anticipating that a future majority would ever try to ban people from wearing blue shirts, the writers of the constitution choose not to protect this action explicitly.

If we assume that individuals act in their enlightened self-interest when they write a constitution, and that liberal rights are collectively agreed upon at the constitutional stage by the individuals who will later exercise them, then there cannot be a conflict between liberal rights and an *ex ante* application of the Pareto principle. A constitutional contract unanimously joined by all citizens must be Pareto optimal. The unrestricted preference domain assumption implies that we cannot assume that situations like that described in the example involving *Lady Chatterley's Lover* will never arise, however. When they do, a possible conflict between each person's exercising her right to read what she wants to read and the Pareto principle cannot

---

[10] Breyer (1990) emphasizes the problem of agreeing to the initial assignment of rights.

be ruled out. If, for whatever reasons, those involved are unable to circumvent the Pareto inefficiency through Coasian contracts, a Pareto inefficiency may survive. Those who propose that liberal values *ought* to prevail over welfarist calculations can applaud this outcome. Those who steadfastly defend welfarism can, on the other hand, still take some solace from the knowledge that such Pareto-inefficient situations are likely to be rare, if those who wrote the constitution correctly identified the categories of actions that should be protected by the explicit definition of rights.

Thus, there does not appear to be a fundamental inconsistency between the existence of rights to undertake certain actions and the assumption that individuals make collective decisions with the goal of maximizing their utility. Conflicts between the exercise of liberal rights and the Pareto principle will occur under this interpretation in only exceptional cases. An advantage to this way of viewing rights is that it allows us to incorporate them into our rational actor models of collective decisions without having to modify the basic premises upon which these models rest. Moreover, we have both a normative theory of rights, based on their contractarian nature, and a positive theory to the extent that self-interested individuals participate in the process of defining rights.

Amartya Sen and some of the other participants in the debates over liberal rights appear to prefer treating rights as principles that cannot be derived from a utility-maximizing calculus. Rights and the Pareto principle can under this interpretation come into conflict, and when they do, Sen at least would favor having the exercise of a right override the Pareto principle. Although this approach has some advantages insofar as it provides clear prescriptions with respect to the correct social choices to be made whenever rights are clearly defined, it gives us no indication as to where rights come from in the first place. Is the choice of one's shirt color a protected right? Is it on an equal footing with reading a book of one's choice, or praying as one wishes? From whence do such rights arise? The existing literature on liberal rights does not give us any answers. The constitutional political economy approach developed in Chapter 26 provides one explanation for and characterization of rights. This theory does not place rights above the Pareto principle, however, but rather makes them a consequence of its application at an earlier stage in the collective decision process.

Bibliographical notes

Sen's original six-page note posing the liberal paradox has spawned an immense literature. Sen (1976) surveys the results up through 1976. Wriglesworth (1985) also surveys the terrain. Pattanaik (1997) reviews the literature along with that concerning the Arrow theorem. The September 1996 issue of *Analyse & Kritik* is entirely devoted to the topic.

For an optimistic statement concerning the potential for embedding liberal values in a set of democratic institutions, see Riley (1985).

PART VI

What have we learned?

CHAPTER 28

Has public choice contributed anything to the study of politics?

> The human understanding when it has once adopted an opinion draws all things else to support and agree with it. And though there be a greater number and weight of instances to be found on the other side, yet these it either neglects or despises, or else by some distinction sets aside and rejects, in order that by this great and pernicious predetermination the authority of its former conclusion may remain inviolate.
>
> Sir Francis Bacon

In the fifty some years since the field of public choice was launched with the works of Black (1948a,b), Buchanan (1949), and Arrow (1951), it has grown tremendously in both breadth and depth. A comparison of the lengths of *Public Choice* published in 1979, *Public Choice II* published in 1989, and *Public Choice III* actually *understates* the growth of the field, since the current text leaves uncovered or only lightly covered a far greater fraction of the literature than did the one published in 1979.

The growth of the literature also reflects a growth in the number of people working in the field. This growth has been particularly conspicuous in political science. Three of the major figures in the field – Kenneth Arrow, James Buchanan, and Amartya Sen – have been awarded Nobel prizes. It would seem reasonable to conclude from these developments that the experiment of introducing rational actor models into the study of politics has been a success.

Not all observers would agree, however. From early on, the public choice or economic approach to politics has had its critics [for example, Stokes (1963) and Barry (1965, 1970)], and if anything criticism of the public choice approach has become more strident in recent years. It seems warranted, therefore, before closing this review of public choice to address some of the criticisms that have been launched against it. The weary reader will be happy to know that I shall not try to take up *all* of the criticisms that have been made against the public choice approach – that would require a book at least as long as the present one. Instead, I shall focus upon the attack of Green and Shapiro (1994), two political scientists, since theirs is a frontal assault on the public choice approach, and it subsumes many of the criticisms leveled by others.[1] Any reader who has been persuaded that public choice does have something to offer to the study of politics and is not interested in methodological disputes should skip to the final chapter.

---

[1] From here on I shall refer to the authors as simply G&S with apologies to fans of Gilbert and Sullivan. All unidentified page references in this chapter are to their book.

28.1   The failures of rational actor models of politics

G&S

> ... contend that much of the fanfare with which the rational choice approach has been heralded in political science must be seen as premature once the question is asked: What has this literature contributed to our understanding of politics? ... To date, a large proportion of the theoretical conjectures of rational choice theorists have not been tested empirically. Those tests that have been undertaken have either failed on their own terms or garnered theoretical support for propositions that, on reflection, can only be characterized as banal: they do little more than restate existing knowledge in rational choice terminology. (p. 6)

To support these claims, G&S focus on three of the classics in the public choice field: Arrow's *Social Choice and Individual Values*, Downs's *An Economic Theory of Democracy*, and Olson's *The Logic of Collective Action*. Clearly, if these three works have not contributed to our understanding of political processes, it is unlikely that lesser works have done so, and thus it pays to consider whether G&S have indeed made their case. Have we learned little or nothing over and above what was already known in political science from these works and the literatures that they spawned?

G&S examine the empirical support for four predictions, which they claim emerge from the above three books: (1) that cycling will be widespread in legislatures (Arrow), (2) that rational citizens will vote only when the expected, instrumental gains from the outcome of the election exceed the cost of voting (Downs), (3) that candidates compete in issue spaces and converge upon identical platforms in two-party systems (Downs), and (4) that rational individuals will not join groups that provide public goods without selective incentives, that is, that they free-ride (Olson).

G&S argue that the public choice literature has failed to produce much in the way of empirical support for any of these predictions and, more generally, "has yet to get off the ground as a rigorous empirical enterprise." The reason for this is, according to G&S, that empirical testing of the implications of rational choice models has suffered from several, fundamental "methodological pathologies" (p. 33). These include: (1) post hoc theorizing (pp. 34–8). When confronted with evidence, which is inconsistent with the predictions of a model, the rational choice scholar introduces some auxiliary assumption which "rescues" the theory from being rejected by the data. G&S use the introduction of a "taste for civic duty" into the Downsian rational voter model to avoid the awkward prediction that no one will vote as one example (p. 50 ff.); (2) formulating untestable theories. "Those who seek to derive testable propositions from rational choice models frequently find ... that these theories are constructed in ways that insulate them against untoward encounters with evidence" (p. 38); (3) selecting and interpreting the evidence. Rational choice scholars are accused of searching for evidence that will confirm their theories (pp. 42–3), of projecting evidence from their theories (pp. 43–4), and of placing arbitrary restrictions on the domain over which their theories are applicable (pp. 44–6). An example of the latter would be an argument that the prediction of free-riding in the voluntary provision of public goods is not refuted by individuals participating in mass demonstrations, since this behavior is "irrational" and thus falls outside of the theory (p. 88).

Before discussing these criticisms of G&S, it is perhaps worth pausing to consider what the methodology of the rational choice approach is exactly, and its potential and limitations.

28.2 The rational choice approach to modeling

The fundamental assumption of the rational choice approach to modeling is, of course, that people are rational. In most applications of the approach this translates into assuming that they are *maximizers*. To be a maximizer you have to have something to maximize. Thus, before the rational choice analyst begins to model human behavior, she must decide what it is that the people whose behavior she wishes to explain are maximizing. She must postulate an objective function.

Now the first thing to note about the necessity to posit an objective function is that this must come from *outside* the theory to be tested. Most often the rational choice analyst chooses the arguments to go into the objective function by introspection or by simply using the objective function, which has become standard in the literature (firms maximize profits, workers maximize utility, which is a function of income and leisure). But she might also consult sociology or psychology to see what is a reasonable assumption to make about the particular group she is studying. While *some* economists might study the Catholic church by positing that it maximizes profits, and the behavior of priests assuming that they are only concerned about income and leisure, other more daring and ambitious scholars might try to determine from other sources what are reasonable assumptions about the goals of these actors. The rational choice approach does not require that the rational choice scholar refrain from using knowledge from other disciplines that might help her specify the goals of indiviuals.

The second step in constructing a rational actor model is to specify what, if any, constraints exist within which the actor must operate. Once again there are standard assumptions regarding the choice of constraints in economic modeling (consumers have limited budgets), but in applying the approach in new areas the analyst will need to find out what are reasonable assumptions. Here again, appeal to other branches of the social sciences may be in order.

Once the rational choice analyst has specified the arguments of the objective function and the relevant constraints, she can maximize this function. This gives her one equation – the first-order condition from the maximization problem – with which to make predictions. In some cases, the second-order condition may give her some additional, predictive power. Still more analytic power can be brought to bear on the problem if the analyst can assume that the aggregated behavior of all individuals in the system leads to an equilibrium outcome. This gives the analyst two equations instead of one, and increases the possibility of deriving refutable propositions. The great interest of the rational choice analyst in determining whether political competition is likely to produce an equilibrium or not arises from the greater predictive content of models with equilibria.

Armed with these two equations, the rational choice analyst can, ideally, derive predictions from her model and test them with the relevant data. Very often, however, the fairly simple objective function specified for the actors and the other elements of the model lead to rather general predictions. For example, the usual assumptions that economists make about consumer utility functions lead to the prediction that consumer demand schedules have negative slopes. Consumers buy more of a good at a lower price. This is certainly one of the "banal" predictions from rational choice models that "do little more than restate existing knowledge." Moreover, any estimate of the elasticity of demand for a good between −0.001 and −1000 could be interpreted as "consistent with the theory's predictions," and thus support for rational choice models in general. Such flexibility in empirical testing is part of what disturbs G&S. To derive more precise predictions, however, one must build more into the model. How one chooses to modify the model to obtain more accurate predictions will depend on the questions one wishes to answer with it.

Consider the following example: suppose that an economist at the University of Iowa decides to estimate the demand schedule for pork in Iowa, and the fraction of consumers' food budgets that goes to the purchase of pork. He gathers data on consumer incomes, prices and quantities of pork sold, prices of substitute products like beef, and so forth and estimates the parameters of his model. The fit to the data is so good that he has great confidence in the accuracy of his estimates. He sets up a consulting firm and begins to use the model to predict pork sales in other states and countries. He has great success in some states and countries, but the model does very poorly in explaining purchases of pork in Israel and Egypt. A sociologist friend of the economist suggests that this may be because the Jewish and Moslem religions forbid eating pork.

What to do? One possibility would be to refuse to use the model in countries with large Jewish or Moslem populations on the grounds that it is "irrational" to allow one's religious beliefs to affect one's food consumption and the economist's model of demand assumes rational individual behavior. This would be an example of the kind of domain restriction of which G&S are highly critical. A more pragmatic response would be to introduce some variables, like the percentages of the population that are Jewish or Moslem, to account for the differences in "tastes for pork" by these consumers. G&S would also be unhappy with this amendment to the rational actor model to improve its explanatory power, and would dismiss it as just another example of the kind of post hoc theorizing that rational choice scholars resort to when their models fail to perform well empirically. Their position seems to be that once the rational choice theorist has constructed a simplified model to explain one phenomenon – demand schedules have negative slopes – she cannot modify this model to improve its performance in specific applications. If the only relevant variables in the simplified model were income and prices, then income and prices must explain equally well the demand for all groups for all sorts of goods.[2]

Many economists would agree with them. Extreme in this regard is the position of Stigler and Becker (1977), whom G&S cite, who regard any appeal to

---

[2] See the discussion of Chong (1996) and Diermeier (1996).

changes in preferences to explain anomalous empirical findings as unscientific. Many economists also regard any assumption about the motives of managers, other than that they maximize profits, as ad hoc. But some managerial decisions, like paying high premia to acquire firms in unrelated industries, seem difficult to explain as attempts by managers to maximize profits. The investment and merger activity of large corporations is easier to explain by assuming that managers maximize an objective function that includes the growth of the firm in it, and thus some economists, like myself, have chosen to posit this sort of objective function when modeling corporate investment and merger activity. Such models are no less a part of the rational actor literature than are models that assume profits maximization. There is nothing in the rational actor methodology that demands that we assume that there is only one argument in an actor's objective function, and that the analyst is constrained in her choice of what this one argument should be by the choices made by previous analysts.

This point is particularly important to keep in mind when considering the application of rational actor modeling to politics. What, for example, should the rational choice analyst assume goes into the objective function of a rational bureaucrat? To answer this question she can contemplate what goals she would pursue if she were a bureaucrat, she can consult sociology and psychology books dealing with bureaucracies, read Franz Kafka or other novelists who have written about bureaucracy, and so on. Niskanen (1971), having worked in the Defense Department, came to the conclusion that bureaucrats maximize the size of their budgets and developed a theory of bureaucracy based on this assumption. This behavioral assumption is obviously similar to that mentioned above used to explain the investment and merger activity of large firms. But it may not explain the behavior of all bureaucrats in all settings. Perhaps if Niskanen had worked in a different bureaucracy with different constraints and opportunities, he would have concluded that bureaucrats maximize leisure, or the probability of not being fired.

Niskanen was the first person in the public choice field to develop a model of bureaucracy, and many who have followed him have also assumed that bureaucrats are budget maximizers. A number have also claimed to find empirical support for this hypothesis. We shall reexamine one set of studies that provides this support below. It would be wrong to argue, however, because Niskanen was the first to model bureaucratic behavior and he assumed that bureaucrats are budget maximizers, and because several other studies have made the same assumption, that the application of the methodology of rational choice *requires* that one assume that all bureaucrats maximize their budgets, and only their budgets. It would be equally wrong to interpret any evidence that is inconsistent with the predictions of a model of budget-maximizing bureaucrats as rejecting *both* the assumptions of this model and the rational choice approach to the study of bureaucracy.

A good positive theory derives strong and refutable predictions from a relatively small set of assumptions. Arrow's essay is not intended to be a contribution to positive theory, and it is a bit misleading to argue against it on the basis of empirical studies as I shall explain in the following test. Downs's and Olson's contributions are positive theories and they meet the criterion for good positive theory – they make strong predictions from a few assumptions – no one votes, two candidates adopt identical platforms, no one contributes anything voluntarily to the provision of a public good.[3] G&S appear to want to reject both these theories and the rational choice approach to politics, because the theories' strong predictions are not born out by the data. But such a step is premature. Neoclassical economics also makes strong predictions. Under the assumptions that firms maximize profits and markets are competitive, for example, all firms should earn zero profits. Should one reject all neoclassical economics and the rational choice approach to human behavior if one observes some firms earning positive or negative profits?

Before doing so one must answer three questions: (1) Are the predictions of the theory so wide from the mark that it is impossible to believe that the theory accounts for the data? (2) Are there additional, plausible assumptions that one can make which are consistent with the rational choice methodology and that will account for the discrepancies between the model's predictions and the empirical evidence? (Some markets are not perfectly competitive, some managers maximize objective functions that include additional or other arguments than profits.) (3) Is there an alternative theory that explains the data better? Only if the answers to these three questions are yes, no, and yes is one justified in abandoning the rational choice approach. G&S claim that this is the case for the theories of Arrow, Downs, and Olson. Let us examine their arguments further.

28.3   The prediction of cycling

G&S cite Arrow (1951) as the source of the prediction that democracy is unstable, and in particular that legislatures will be plagued by cycles. As noted earlier, Arrow's book is a contribution to normative theory. It makes *no* predictions about what one might observe in practice. The impossibility theorem states that it is not possible to devise a process for aggregating individual preferences that both defines a social ordering and satisfies the famous five axioms (see Chapter 24). The only empirical prediction from this theorem that is possible is that any actual system for aggregating individual preferences must violate at least one of the axioms, *assuming, that is, that the system defines a social ordering.* Since it is unlikely that any political system truly defines a social ordering, that is, a ranking of all feasible social states, no "prediction" from the theory is truly testable. If, on the other hand, we assume that all political systems are capable of defining a social ordering, then the theory still only predicts that at least one of the axioms is violated. It is just as legitimate to claim that Arrow's theorem predicts that all political systems will be dictatorships as it is to claim that it predicts that all legislatures will get caught in voting cycles. Since until very recently most of the world's political systems have been dictatorships of one form or another, it might be argued that this "prediction of the Arrow theorem" is well supported.

---

[3] Strictly speaking neither Downs's model of the rational voter nor Olson's model predict zero participation. The voluntary-contribution-to-a-public-good model presented in Chapter 2, for example, predicts *positive* contributions when the group's size is finite. See Lohmann (1996).

When the underlying preferences of the members of a committee are such as to produce a cycle over all of the feasible outcomes, it would be possible for the committee to cycle endlessly over these outcomes. Since rational people will not want to spend endless amounts of time voting on a given set of issues, one expects a committee made up of rational people to establish procedures that reduce, if not eliminate, the probability of a cycle. The questions Arrow's theorem raises about these procedures are, do they in fact eliminate cycles, and if so how? Do they eliminate cycles, for example, by producing arbitrary outcomes – the outcome chosen depends on the chance order in which issues come to a vote in a constrained agenda; dictatorial outcomes as the result of agenda manipulation; or Pareto-dominated outcomes because the agenda has been so restricted to avoid a cycle that a Pareto-optimal outcome cannot come to a vote? G&S are highly critical of the efforts by rational choice scholars to answer these questions. Some of their criticisms are well taken, but they do not undermine the importance of determining the answers to these questions. Had Arrow (and Black) not alerted us to the potential for cycling and its dangers, we would not even be in a position to pose the right questions about the impact of legislative procedures, let alone answer them.

It should also be noted that cycling *can* be observed in situations in which political institutions have *not* been designed to prevent them. The formation of a cabinet in a multiparty system has the characteristics of a zero-sum game. There are a fixed number of cabinet positions, and a majority coalition must form to determine how the positions are allocated. When an election results in the possibility of three or more assignments of cabinet seats, the stage is set for a cycle. The frequent turnover of governments in countries like Italy and Fourth Republic France looks a lot like what coalition theory leads us to expect in the absence of a core.

Simulation studies indicate that the probability of a cycle rises with the degree of heterogeneity of the preferences of the committee members, and with the size of the issue set (see Chapter 4). Thus, the findings that cabinet stability declines as the degrees of fractionalization and polarization in multiparty parliaments increase is consistent with what one expects from rational choice theory.[4] Cycling can and does occur in more unstructured settings, and thus it is important to find out if it occurs in legislatures like the U.S. Congress, and if not why not.

28.4 The predictions of spatial models

The Downsian model of two-party competition with a single-dimensional issue space predicts that both parties adopt the position favored by the median voter (see Chapter 11). Most probabilistic voting models of two-party competition also predict that both parties adopt the same position, although now it is some sort of *mean* of the voters' ideal points (see Chapter 12). Almost everyone probably agrees that U.S. presidential candidates and the leading two parties in Britain do not adopt identical platforms. Once again the rational actor model is hoisted with the petard it has created by making too precise of a prediction. But before tossing aside these

---

[4] See Grofman and van Roozendaal (1997) and Chapter 13, this book.

models and the rational actor methodology that they employ, let us try to answer the three questions just posed: (1) Are the predictions so wide from the mark that it is impossible to accept the theory? (2) Are there additional, plausible assumptions that one can make that are consistent with the rational choice methodology and will account for the discrepancies between the model's predictions and the empirical evidence? (3) Is there an alternative theory that explains the data better?

Let us start with the first question. How close must the platforms of two candidates be for us to say that they are close enough to accept the theory? Now the first problem in answering this question is, of course, that differences between candidate platforms cannot be measured as easily as, say, distances between vendors on a beach. Closeness is to some extent in the eye of the beholder, and G&S emphasize that rational choice scholars are not of one opinion on this matter (pp. 153–4).

Let us leave this measurement problem aside, however, and assume that we can measure distances between candidates objectively. One way to try and answer the question of whether the two candidates' platforms are close enough to one another to accept rational choice theory is to compare its prediction to that of a competing theory that does not assume that voters and candidates are rational actors. What is a reasonable alternative model of two-candidate competition? What is a reasonable null hypothesis?

Perhaps a good way to begin to answer these questions is to consider the problem first addressed by Hotelling (1929) in his classic article on spatial competition. Although Hotelling's article is often cited as the first spatial model of voting, he did not set out to examine this problem, but rather a seemingly simpler and yet more intriguing question – the choice of location of sellers in a spatial market. Imagine bathers evenly distributed along a straight stretch of beach of length d. Two ice cream vendors set up stands along the beach. Where does one expect them to set up their stands?

The simplest hypothesis would be to assume that they choose locations at random. This would lead us to expect that we would find each vendor at a different location on the beach each day. The distance between them, b, would be a random variable, but over time we would predict that the mean of b would equal one half of d.

An alternative hypothesis would be that the vendors seek to minimize the distance bathers must walk to purchase an ice cream. This might be called "the public interest theory" of vending.[5] This hypothesis leads to the prediction that the vendors locate their stands one-fourth of the distance from the two ends of the beach. Now we would predict that the vendors choose the same locations every day, and that $b = d/2$ every day.

What other predictions are reasonable? If one described this problem to a random sample of people passing through Times Square, I doubt that many of them would predict that the two vendors would locate adjacent to one another at the center of the beach. Yet this is the prediction of the Hotelling model. Suppose now we went to a beach that was 100 meters long, and observed two vendors located adjacent

---

[5] Hotelling (1929, pp. 52–3) discusses this possibility as the outcome one would expect under socialism and characterizes it as "an argument to the socialist side."

to the center of the beach five meters apart. Would we reject Hotelling's model because they were not located literally next to one another, or would we say that the observed b is so much smaller than 50 $(d/2)$ that we accept the model over its rivals, leaving open of course the possibility that some other model may come along that outperforms Hotelling's in predicting the locations of the two vendors?

Returning to the problem of two-party competition, I suspect that estimates of b and d for two-party systems would reveal that b tends to be significantly less than $d/2$. Is this sufficient for us to accept the simplified version of the Hotelling/Downs model of two-party competition? For some it will be, for others not. Some will wish to predict b more accurately and thus will choose to modify the simple version of the model.

The Hotelling/Downs model assumes that there is but one election, and that the candidates are free to choose any position in the issue space. In the United States a person must win two contests to become president – the one to become the candidate of her party and then the one to become president. A direct extension of the Downsian model to take into account the nomination process leads to the prediction that candidates would adopt the position favored by the median voter *in their party* to win its nomination, and then move to the median voter's position in the full electorate. If one adds the reasonable auxiliary assumption that it is not possible for a candidate to move all of the distance between the median for her party and the median for the country during the short span of time between party conventions and presidential elections, then one reaches the following predictions: (1) prior to being nominated candidates adopt positions far removed from one another, (2) after their nominations they move toward the center, and (3) at the election they are located nearer to one another than when they were nominated, but they still do not adopt identical positions.[6] These predictions would seem to fit the facts of American presidential elections fairly well. G&S do not discuss these extensions of the Downsian model by rational choice scholars, but I expect that G&S would also dismiss this work as "post hoc theorizing."

In Chapter 19 we discussed one attempt by rational choice scholars to develop a model of two-party competition that explicitly took into account the ideological differences between parties, which led them to adopt different policies – namely, the work of Alesina (1988b) and Alesina and Rosenthal (1995). The Alesina and Rosenthal model makes some very precise predictions about the patterns of income growth over the electoral cycle under Republican and Democratic administrations, and not all their predictions are supported by the data. Yet the model accounts for a number of phenomena, like the midterm cycle, that other observers of politics have had trouble explaining.

G&S concentrate on the attempts by rational choice scholars to explain outcomes in two-party systems. The Downsian spatial model has been adapted to study competition in multiparty systems, however, with considerable success (see discussion in Chapter 13). van Roozendaal's (1990, 1992, 1993) prediction that "central parties" will always be part of a coalition government is a fairly straightforward extension of

---

[6] See discussion and references in Chapter 11, Section 11.1.

the logic of the median voter theorem to cabinet formation, and one that has proven to be accurate roughly 85 percent of the time (Laver and Schofield, 1990, p. 113). Is 85 percent a sufficiently high success rate to vindicate the use of spatial models and coalition theories to predict cabinet compositions in multiparty systems? Is there a nonspatial model that does better?

Laver and Shepsle's (1996) model of cabinet formation extends the median voter model to a multidimensional issue space, and Schofield's (1993a,b, 1995) concept of the "heart" is yet another development using spatial theory and rational choice models to predict which parties will form the governments in multiparty systems. The predictive power of these models seems sufficiently strong to warrant retaining the rational choice approach and spatial theory in the study of multiparty systems – pending the appearance of models with greater explanatory power that do not employ this methodology.[7]

28.5   Predicting voting and free-riding

In Chapter 14 we reviewed the public choice literature explaining voter turnouts. As the reader will recall, the simple Downsian rational-voter model, in which the voter weighs the expected benefits from bringing about the victory of his favored candidate against the cost of voting, does not offer an adequate explanation of why people vote. Moreover, some of the attempts to modify the theory by proponents of the rational choice approach raise more questions than they answer. G&S make much of these failures of the rational choice approach and many of their points are well taken (pp. 50–68).

G&S also question the empirical support for the prediction, often associated with Olson (1965), that people will not voluntarily contribute to the provision of a pure public good, as their receipt of the benefits from its provision are independent of their contribution. Among the evidence that they cite against the free-rider hypothesis are the many public good-provision experiments that find participants making far greater contributions than the rational choice hypothesis predicts.[8]

There is no question that these sorts of results constitute a great challenge to the rational choice approach to politics. Many practitioners of this approach have been disturbed by these findings and have gone to great (excessive) lengths to explain them away. But the proper response to such contradictory evidence is neither to dismiss it as irrelevant nor, as G&S would seem to have us do, to discard the rational choice approach in its entirety. The proper reaction is to reconsider this approach's premises and try to determine which of them is sufficiently far from reality to account for the predictive failures. Once again, it is also necessary to compare the predictive power of the rational actor model with that of alternative approaches.

What prediction, for example, would a student of politics who is not a follower of the rational choice approach make as to the likely contribution of someone in a public goods experiment? One possibility, of course, would be to assume that people *do not*

---

[7] See also Schofield (1996b).
[8] See G&S (pp. 88–93) and our discussion in Chapter 2.

free-ride. They pursue the public interest rather than their own, narrowly defined self-interest. If the contribution that maximizes the payoffs to the group is 100, and the contribution that maximizes the payoff to an individual contributor is 1, this public interest model would predict an individual contribution of 100. Since the typical outcome from a public goods experiment is an average contribution of around 50, the prediction of the public interest model is as far off the mark as is the selfish-individual, rational choice model. Both need to be significantly modified to account for the findings in public goods experiments.

Note that both the public interest and the rational choice models assume that people are maximizing some sort of objective function and thus yield very precise predictions. Because of their preciseness they are very easy to reject. But before discarding either model, we must again ask what the predictions of the alternative models are. If one claims that the nonrational choice approach would predict some contribution between 1 and 100, one stacks the cards in favor of this approach. And even this vacuous interpretation of the alternative to rational choice models would not help us to predict *which* people would contribute more than 50, which less.[9]

In Chapter 14 I proposed modeling individual behavior under the assumption that people acted *as if* they were maximizing an objective function of the following form:

$$O_i = U_i + \theta_i \sum_{j \neq i} U_j. \tag{28.1}$$

Many sorts of behavior, like individual choices in market experiments, can be adequately explained assuming θ equals zero. A contribution of 30 by one person and 60 by another in a public goods experiment would, on the other hand, imply both positive and different θs for each person.

Of course, such a model would merely allow us to offer a post hoc rationalization for deviations from the predictions of the selfish, rational actor model, unless we are able to explain why one person has a θ of 0.3 and someone else 0.6. Moreover, to construct a general theory that can predict human actions, we would need to be able to explain why a given individual might behave in one situation as if θ were zero, and in another as if it were one. Such explanations are more likely to be found in the field of psychology than in the rational choice literature. The key difference between such a behavioral approach and the usual application of rational actor models is that it forces the investigator to examine the *past* histories of the people whose behavior he wishes to explain, and not just focus upon the entries in the different cells of the game's payoff matrix. Human behavior is viewed as being adaptive and only approximates the purely forward-looking behavior depicted in rational actor models.

This adaptive approach would remove some of the surprise from experiments such as those of Marwell and Ames (1981), who found that graduate students in

---

[9] Strong proponents of the rational choice approach can take solace from the fact that mixed-strategy equilibria to this sort of game exist in which some participants make contributions greater than one (Lohmann, 1996). G&S (pp. 125–8) will only lament that this is just another example of the failure of game-theoretic approaches to generate refutable hypotheses.

economics contributed significantly less than other students in public goods experiments, or of Blais and Young (1999), who found that Canadian students were significantly less likely to vote after having listened to a lecture explaining the Downsian voter model.

Many proponents of rational choice modeling, like Stigler and Becker (1977), would reject any attempt to improve the predictive power of a rational choice model by allowing preferences to be malleable, and Riker (1990), whom G&S cite (pp. 185–6), explicitly rejects behaviorism as an alternative to rational choice modeling. Thus, anyone who would follow the route that I have suggested would take a long step away from the pure forms of rational choice analysis, and indeed a step in the direction of the approach advocated by G&S, which tries to identify "cognitive or social-psychological factors that affect the degree to which actors follow impulse, habit, or the lead of others . . . ." But this approach would not force one to abandon the search for a universal theory of human behavior, which G&S would have us do, nor would one have to sacrifice the potential for analytical rigor that comes by modeling individuals as maximizing explicitly defined objective functions.

28.6   Can public choice contribute to the positive study of political institutions?

G&S's book is filled with examples of empirical studies by public choice scholars who, G&S claim, made fundamental methodological errors that robbed their work of scientific value. In closing their book, they offer these scholars the following advice:

> More fruitful than asking "How might a rational choice theory explain X?" Would be the problem-driven question: "What explains X?" (p. 203)

In this section we describe a few studies that have employed the rational choice approach to explain X and, I believe, have done a relatively good job of it.

In the state of Oregon local school boards are free to spend any amount of money up to an amount defined by a specific formula. This formula-set limit is called the reversion budget, R. If a school board wishes to spend more than its R, it must seek the approval of the voters in its district. Some school boards propose amounts above their R, some do not. Some proposals are greatly above R, some are not. How might one predict when a school board would call a referendum to approve a higher budget, and by how much it would deviate from the reversion level?

Romer and Rosenthal (1978, 1979b, 1982) addressed these questions using the public choice approach.[10] They first had to posit an objective function for the school board. Following Niskanen (1971) they assumed that school board members were bureaucrats who maximized their budgets. Romer and Rosenthal then utilized the median voter model to predict the maximum possible budget a school board could get approved in a referendum. With these two elements of the model in place, they

---

[10] Their work is discussed in more detail in Chapter 16.

were able to generate several quite specific predictions as, for example, that the amount by which a proposed budget exceeds that favored by the median voter will be higher, the lower R is relative to the median voter's preferred expenditure; and that referenda will not be called when R exceeds the expenditure favored by the median voter. Their predictions were supported by the data.

Note that Romer and Rosenthal committed all of the sins outlined by G&S. They assumed that bureaucrats were budget maximizers and voters were utility maximizers. They assumed that the collective choice problem could be analyzed using a spatial model with a single-dimensional issue space. They invoked the median voter theorem.

How should one proceed if one does not want to commit these sins? Does one posit an objective for a school board, and if so, what is it? Lane (1996, p. 123) criticizes the rational choice approach for assuming "that managers of public enterprises are motivated by personal self-interest." Instead, he claims that they internalize the goals of their organization, citing Wolf (1988) in support. Applying this assumption to school boards one might assume that each seeks to provide the students in its district with a "good education." If so what model does one use to predict the amount needed in each district? Does one proceed inductively, and set up a probit model to predict when a school board calls a referendum and collect data on all possible relevant variables (number of school-age children in a district, income of the district, and so on). With considerable diligence and luck one might come up with enough variables to provide a reasonable fit to the data. But one would not really understand why the school boards behaved as they did. One would also not be able to pass judgment over whether the school budgets were larger or smaller than they should be. Indeed, through one's choice of motivation for the school board, one would have essentially already assumed that each school budget was at its optimal level.

One of the advantages of a rational choice approach over a purely inductive approach to modeling is that the rational choice approach often can identify whether policy outcomes are inefficient or suboptimal in some other way. If one adheres to the view that the government ought to do that which the median voter desires, then one must conclude from Romer and Rosenthal's work that school budgets in Oregon are systematically larger than they should be.

In *The Theory of Political Coalitions* (1962) Riker followed exactly the procedure G&S recommend – he chose as the subject to be analyzed a puzzle from the real world. Why are grand coalitions so short lived? He deviated from their recommendations by applying rational choice analysis to this problem. Using this approach he developed his "theory of minimum winning coalitions." I know of no better analysis of this question. G&S are critical of Riker's applications of rational choice analysis to the study of politics at several places in their book, but curiously they omit any reference to this application, Riker's most famous contribution to the literature.

Observers of U.S. politics have long believed that congressmen trade votes on bills. How can one test whether this in fact is true? Does logrolling occur on all bills, or only on some? If only on some, how does one determine which issues are the result of vote trades and which are not?

The public choice analysis of logrolling provides a rigorous means to test whether it occurs. From the definition of a logrolling situation we predict that issues X and Y would lose, if individuals would sincerely state their preferences, and pass as a result of vote trades.[11] This precise definition of logrolling leads to the prediction that trading should only occur on issues where the vote is close *and* the votes of the traders are crucial to the victory of the winning issues. Thus to test for the presence of logrolling one first needs to construct a model to predict how representatives will vote in the absence of a trade. This, in turn, requires us to model the voting behavior of representatives, and thus to make some assumption about their motivation. The work of Stratmann (1992b, 1995) indicates that logrolling occurs on some issues, but not on others. It allows us to provide precise answers to the above questions. How one would answer these questions without employing the analytical tools provided by public choice is difficult to imagine.

One could cite other examples from the literature on voting-with-the-feet (Chapter 9), rent seeking (Chapter 15), campaign contributions (Chapter 20), government size (Chapter 21), and still more.[12] However, I hope that these examples will suffice to convince the reader that the methodology of public choice is capable of providing rigorous empirical tests of hypotheses about politics, and that at least *some* practitioners in the field have conducted such tests.

28.7   Has public choice contributed anything to the normative study of political institutions?

Just as challenging for the student of politics as the question of why government sizes differ so much across countries, is the question of why the choice of voting rules differs *so little*. Why does virtually every legislature and other sort of committee employ the simple majority rule for most, if not all, of its collective decisions? This question obviously *cannot* be approached empirically, because there is little or no variation in the variable that one wishes to explain. The answer must be sought in a normative analysis of the simple majority rule. The simple majority rule must be presumed to be the best voting rule because it is the rule preferred by all forms of committees. But in what sense is it best?

Public choice has offered several answers to this question (see Chapters 4 and 6). The most elegant of these is May's (1952) proof of the equivalence between the simple majority rule and four axioms. If one believes that a voting rule should satisfy these four axioms, then one should advocate the use of the simple majority rule for making collective decisions.

May's theorem is valid only for binary choices. Should a committee need to decide among three or more alternatives, it must consider the possibility of cycles under the simple majority rule. The normative case for the simple majority rule is weakened, and we enter the realm of Arrow's (1951) impossibility theorem. Even if we assume with G&S that cycling is not often observed in some legislatures, like the U.S. Congress, this observation in no way detracts from the significance of the

---

[11] For a full statement of the definition and discussion, see Chapter 5.

[12] See also the examples cited by Fiorina (1996, p. 90), Ordeshook (1996, p. 176), Shepsle (1996, p. 218), Cox (1999), and discussion in Mueller (1997b).

Arrow theorem. This "fact" merely alerts us to another fact – that one or more of the five axioms of the theorem must generally be violated.

New democracies appear from time to time and must decide which voting rule(s) to inscribe in their constitutions. Old democracies sometimes amend their constitutions. Should the student of politics recommend the simple majority rule, some venerable rule like the Borda count, or some newly invented rule like approval voting, the demand revelation process, or voting by veto? I do not see how one can offer an adequate answer to this question unless one understands the formal properties of each voting rule.[13]

28.8   Conclusions

Suppose that you were asked to explain why the OPEC countries sometimes agree to cut petroleum output significantly and oil prices rise to great heights, and at other times they expand their outputs driving petroleum prices into great troughs. These are decisions by governments and thus by definition political decisions. A good student of politics ought to be able to explain them. How should a good student proceed?

The good student might first inquire as to the likely motivation behind the decisions for each government. Oil revenues are higher when oil prices are higher, and so one might posit that the OPEC countries are trying to increase their revenues when they cut outputs to raise prices. A reasonable beginning would be to assume that each OPEC country is a revenue maximizer, and that the periodic meetings of representatives from each country in Vienna are attempts to set outputs so as to maximize the joint revenues of the OPEC members.

The astute student might next observe that cartels have the characteristics of a prisoners' dilemma, and thus are vulnerable to free-riding if each country is maximizing its revenues. A first start to the problem would be to develop, or locate within the literature, a model of cartel behavior that predicts that cartels will sometimes succeed in restricting output and raising revenues, but then breakdown as individual members engage in free-riding behavior.

Should one not also allow for the fact that Saudi Arabia is an Arab, Moslem country and Venezuela is Catholic; that Kuwait is rich and Nigeria poor; that some country leaders are empire-builders, while other leaders appear content to preserve their monarchies? Perhaps, but before doing so most rational choice scholars would first want to see how well the simpler model explains the data, the model that assumes only that each country seeks to maximize its revenue, and together they are caught in a recurring prisoners' dilemma. Only if this model fails to account for the observed pattern of prices and quantities adequately would it be necessary to bring in other factors.

Great theorists provide clear answers to important questions that often arise not as a result of their reading of the latest issue of a technical journal, but from reading the latest newspaper and observing the world around them. Riker (1962) was puzzled by the short lives of grand coalitions, and developed a theory to explain why they so quicky come apart. Olson (1982) was puzzled by the relative economic success

---

[13] See also Schofield (1996b, pp. 190–1).

of the countries which lost World War II compared to the winners, and developed a theory to explain the losers' superior performance. In both cases they found answers to the questions they tackled through the application of rational choice analysis.

John Maynard Keynes (1936) was puzzled as to how widespread unemployment could arise and persist. He did not find an answer in the prevailing economic models with their predictions of market equilibria. He compared the premises of these models with the facts of the world around him and found some of the premises wanting. Wages were not as flexible as the competitive model assumed; interest rates sometimes got stuck in a "liquidity trap." Investors were not the rational, cool, calculating individuals who appeared in economic models, but rather mortals whose "animal spirits" sometimes got the best of them. By abandoning some of the assumptions contained in the reigning paradigm, Keynes created a model of the economy which could account for the existence of widespread and persistent unemployment. His modification of the reigning paradigm was attacked by its adherents from the start, and debate continues to the present day over how best to model the macroeconomy. Regardless of one's views on this question, one should recognize that Keynes's methodological approach is the one to follow. Stick to the prevailing model so long as it is able to explain the phenomena which one wishes to explain. Reexamine its premises when it cannot explain these phenomena, and substitute other premises that fit reality more closely. Continue to modify the existing model until it can adequately account for the data. Abandon the old model (paradigm) in favor of a new one if one comes along which offers a better solution to the puzzle.

The social scientist who wishes to explain the behavior of individuals as consumers, workers, voters, bureaucrats, priests, politicians, stockbrokers, soldiers, and drug addicts has a series of options. At one extreme is the universal, rational actor model – all individuals maximize an objective function (O). The starkest form of such a model would have a single variable in the objective function: all individuals maximize their own personal wealth (W),

$$O = W. \tag{28.2}$$

A slightly more general version of this model would be that all individuals maximize a utility function that includes wealth and one or two additional variables depending on the type of decisions being analyzed,

$$O = U(W, X_1, X_2, \ldots). \tag{28.3}$$

Moving farther away from the strongest version of a universal theory we would have

$$O = U(X_1, X_2, \ldots). \tag{28.4}$$

All arguments of the utility function are at the analyst's discretion. And moving still farther we have the approach suggested above to account for altruistic and similar sorts of behavior in situations where this behavior is anticipated,

$$O_i = U_i + \theta_i \sum_{j \neq i} U_j. \tag{28.5}$$

When one takes into account that the analyst is also free to choose the shape of the utility function and a set of constraints and auxiliary conditions under which the maximization process takes place, one sees that an approach to modeling human behavior that is universal insofar as it posits that individuals maximize an objective function can be quite flexible.

At the other extreme of the methodological spectrum is a pure inductive approach. The analyst who wishes to explain the behavior of individuals in the ten contexts just listed constructs ten different models, each one containing the set of variables that best explains the behavior of the group in question. The choice of variables in each case is determined from an examination of the relevant literatures in sociology and psychology, what has "worked" in previous studies, or simple trial and error. As one adds more arguments to the objective function, and more auxiliary assumptions, the power of the maximizing assumption is diluted and the model estimated under this approach begins to resemble that obtained by proceeding inductively. Where each scholar chooses to place herself along the spectrum running from (28.2) to the pure inductive model is largely a matter of scientific taste – one's willingness to live with weak explanatory power in some situations for the cleanness and beauty of a simple, elegant model of human behavior versus one's desire for high explanatory power in all situations at the cost of analytic consistency and clarity.

Earlier in this chapter we discussed several examples of behavior like voting and free-riding, which cannot be well explained with a simple version of the selfish, rational actor model. My proposal was to replace this model in these situations with a model in which individuals acted *as if* they were maximizing an objective function that included their own utility and a weighted sum of everyone else's utility. This could be used to explain human behavior in all situations, even those where the traditional rational, self-interest model does well, since it allows for the possibility that the weight on other people's utility is zero.

My proposal would constitute a step away from the pure rational actor model, but would retain some of the advantages of this approach in terms of making clear predictions that are subject to falsification. A more radical step is to abandon the assumption of maximizing behavior entirely. Simon (1947) won a Nobel prize for his studies of organizational behavior that built on the assumption that individuals are "satisficers" instead of maximizers. G&S seem sympathetic to Simon's approach (pp. 22, 29, 186), and Lane (1996, p. 126) cites with favor an early application of it by Cyert and March (1963) who analyzed a single firm under the assumption that five different goals had to be satisfied. The model did extremely well at explaining the behavior of *this* firm, but it appeared that a different model might be needed for each firm in the economy, and the Cyert and March approach was not pursued by the economics profession. Applying the satisfying approach to, say, the study of public bureaucracies would seem likely to suffer a similar fate. Although with enough interviews and data, a team of economists, psychologists, and other social scientists might be able to construct a simulation model that would track decisions at the Defense Department accurately, one would not know whether it would do as well at other departments. A collection of ten simulation models, each tailored to a different government bureaucracy, *might* provide some insights to a general theory of bureaucracy, but the likelihood seems small relative to the costs of putting such a collection together. The rational social scientist with scarce research time and resources seems well advised to avoid this research strategy.

Most parents exaggerate their children's accomplishments and overlook their failings. The same holds true for scientists with respect to their intellectual offspring. The same also holds true with respect to the scientific methodologies that they employ. It is perhaps some small comfort that these deficiencies appear to be as old as science itself, as the opening quotation of this chapter from Sir Francis Bacon reveals.

Several proponents of the rational choice approach to the study of both economics and politics can be accused of overstating the explanatory power of this approach, and of being blind to its shortcomings. G&S are justified in accusing them of hubris in the extreme. But in pressing their attack on the rational choice approach, G&S appear to ignore the weaknesses of the alternative approaches which they, implicitly, seem to advocate. They criticize rational choice scholars for seeking to develop and apply a *universal* model to explain the behavior of political actors. Although G&S make many valid criticisms of the way in which some researchers have tested such models, they offer no concrete, alternative research strategy. Thus, I expect that those working in the public choice field will continue to employ rational actor models to the study of politics modifying them as need be to explain individual actions in different situations. And I expect that many fine young scholars entering into the study of politics will continue to gravitate toward the rational choice approach precisely because it offers a more unified and compelling explanation of political behavior than do rival approaches.[14]

Bibliographical notes

Friedman (1996) has assembled 14 essays both supporting and taking issue with G&S, plus a concluding reply from them. Hogarth and Reder (1987) contains the proceedings of a conference in which several distinguished proponents and opponents of rational actor models made contributions. Mansbridge's (1990) anthology also includes a distinguished list of contributors who are mostly drawn from the critical side.

Both Frank (1988) and Thaler (1991) have sought to weaken or adapt the notion of rational behavior to make rational or "quasi-rational" actor models more consistent with the evidence on how humans behave arising from the psychology and experimental literatures.

Sen (1995) discusses both individual and collective rationality, and the importance of the distinction between social *preferences* and social *judgments* in the context of the Arrow Impossibility Theorem.

---

[14] Both Ferejohn and Satz (1996) and Schofield (1996b) defend the scientific importance of universal theories.

CHAPTER 29

Allocation, redistribution, and public choice

Some men look at constitutions with sanctimonious reverence, and deem them like the ark of the covenant, too sacred to be touched. They ascribe to the men of the preceding age a wisdom more than human, and suppose what they did to be beyond amendment. I knew that age well; I belonged to it; and labored with it. It deserved well of its country. It was very like the present, but without the experience of the present; and forty years of experience in government is worth a century of book-reading; and this they would say themselves, were they to rise from the dead. I am certainly not an advocate for frequent and untried changes in laws and constitutions. I think moderate imperfections had better be borne with; because, when once known, we accommodate ourselves to them, and find practical means of correcting their ill effects. But I know also, that laws and institutions must go hand in hand with the progress of the human mind. As that becomes more developed, more enlightened, as new discoveries are made, new truths disclosed, and manners and opinions change with the change of circumstances, institutions must advance also, and keep pace with the times. We might as well require a man to wear still the coat which fitted him when a boy, as civilized society to remain ever under the regimen of their barbarous ancestors.

Thomas Jefferson

Rules for collective decision are needed, quite simply, because people live together. Their mere grouping into circumscribed geographic areas creates the potential and necessity for collective action. Some collective decisions can benefit all individuals involved; other decisions benefit only some. Even when everyone benefits, some do so more than others, raising an issue of how the "gains from trade" are shared. Thus, collective choices can be grouped into two categories: those benefiting all members of the community and those benefiting some and hurting others. These two categories correspond to the familiar distinction between moves from off the Pareto frontier to points on it and moves along the frontier – that is, to allocation and redistribution.

The potential to make collective decisions benefiting all members of a community has undoubtedly existed for as long as it has been legitimate to call a group of humans living in proximity to one another a community. So, too, has the potential for redistribution. Did the state come into existence to enable its members to better achieve the allocative efficiency gains that social organization and technology made possible? Did the state come into existence so that some members of the community could exploit their neighbors? Does the modern state grow by providing an ever-increasing amount of collective benefits to the community, or does its growth reflect an escalating series of programs for transferring wealth from one segment of the community to another? Do the rent-seeking and wealth-transferring efforts of different groups in society stifle the potential for making moves that benefit all society? These questions have puzzled anthropologists, economists, and political scientists. They lie at the heart of the public choice literature.

It was one of Wicksell's (1896) great insights to recognize the importance of the distinction between allocation and redistribution decisions, *and* to recognize the need to make these decisions by separate voting procedures. More fundamentally, his contribution to the literature can be seen as the recognition that the characteristics of the outcomes of government action, the allocation or redistribution decisions, cannot be discussed without taking into account the inputs from the citizens via the voting process bringing these outcomes about. This latter contribution was virtually ignored by the profession for half a century until the public choice literature began to appear. It may be regarded as one of the cornerstone postulates of this literature.

Although Wicksell made use of the distinction between allocation and redistribution decisions, his analysis focused on the former. The redistribution decisions were assumed to have been justly decided at some prior point in time. This left only the allocative efficiency improvements to resolve, decisions of potential benefit to all. Here Wicksell's work takes on a distinctly contractarian and individualistic tone. Each citizen takes part in the collective decision process to advance his own ends, and via the quid pro quo of collective decision-making outcomes are reached to the mutual benefit of all. Voting achieves in the market for public goods the same outcome as exchange achieves in markets for private goods. This contractarian, quid pro quo approach to government has underlain much of public choice and the public expenditure theory of public finance, most visibly in the work of Buchanan and Musgrave.

Often this literature takes on a very optimistic tone concerning the potential of collective decision making. In *The Calculus of Consent* Buchanan and Tullock describe government institutions that bear more than a passing resemblance to those of the United States and that seem capable of satisfying a society's collective wants. Redistribution decisions are separated from allocative efficiency decisions, however, and unanimously resolved at the constitutional stage. Thus, the day-to-day work of parliament is limited to deciding those issues in which unanimity is potentially possible. In the past 30 years several new and "superior" voting procedures have been put forward. All have attractive properties that seem to circumvent most if not all of the paradoxes of collective choice. All are capable of achieving this magic only when limited to deciding allocative efficiency improvements.

The literature that focuses upon redistribution, or ignores the distinction between redistribution and allocation, thereby implicitly combining the two, has a discernibly more pessimistic tone. Equilibria do not exist. Their absence enables agenda setters to dictate outcomes. Outcomes of all voting procedures can be manipulated by strategic misrepresentation of preferences unless someone is allowed to be dictator. Outcomes may be Pareto inefficient. The mood of this new "dismal" science is accurately captured by Riker (1982b). It is interesting to note that while Green and

Shapiro (1994) cite Arrow's work in their attack on the rational choice approach to politics, Riker, one of this approach's strongest proponents, makes heavy reference to the Arrow impossibility theorem and subsequent developments in the social choice literature to question, if not attack, "populist democracy." Majoritarian democracy cannot produce outcomes that maximize any sort of SWF that satisfy "the will of the people"; the most that society can hope for is to develop and maintain political institutions capable of deposing bad leadership – some of the time.

It is difficult to reject Riker's pessimistic interpretation of the implications of the social-public choice literature. Moreover, his examples and countless others that one could present illustrate too vividly that the instabilities, inefficiencies, manipulated agendas, and other diseases of democratic decision making, which public choice predicts, do sometimes occur. But I am reluctant to write off the achievements of the first 50 years of public choice as a catalogue of the deficiencies of democratic decision making. There are strands in this literature that suggest a more optimistic picture, a picture perhaps more of what might be than of what is. We close by sketching this picture.

To begin with, one must distinguish between decisions to improve allocative efficiency and to redistribute income and wealth. Certainly one of the major achievements of the public choice literature has been to underline the importance of this distinction first recognized by Wicksell. Not to make use of it when designing political institutions is to handicap the exercise from the start. Second, one must distinguish clearly between designing institutions for direct democracy and designing institutions for electoral politics.

Nowhere is the importance of the distinction between allocative efficiency and redistribution made more vivid than in the literature on clubs and voting-with-the-feet. Allocative efficiency can be improved when individuals with homogeneous tastes for bundles of public goods form clubs and local polities. When local polities attempt to provide redistribution programs and other programs unwanted by some taxpayers, individuals vote with their feet and move to communities where such programs do not exist. In a mobile society significant amounts of redistribution at the local level cannot occur if those who must pay for the redistribution are unwilling to do so. Just as redistribution proposals would be screened out under a unanimity rule leaving only proposals to improve allocative efficiency, the unanimity achieved silently through voting-with-the-feet eliminates redistribution programs from local budgets. If significant redistribution is to occur, it must take place at higher levels of government.

Much of the pessimism regarding the potential of democratic institutions stems from Arrow's theorem and the flood of theorems in its aftermath. The objective of Arrow's search was to find an SWF that based its rankings of alternatives on the aggregation of individual ordinal rankings. That none was found indicates that interpersonal utility comparisons must be made either directly via the decision rule, or indirectly through restrictions placed on the preference domain or the types of issues that can be decided.

The same conclusion emerges from the literature on real-valued welfare functions. Ordinal utility functions plus the Pareto postulate do not allow one to choose from among the set of points along the Pareto frontier. To make such a choice, additional postulates must be introduced incorporating stronger value judgments than contained in the Pareto postulate. Most writers have shied away from making these additional value judgments and have stopped short of defining an SWF that will select from among the Pareto-preferred set. Those who have introduced additional value postulates, for example, Harsanyi (1955) and Ng (1975), have invariably come up with additive SWFs whose arguments are the cardinal, interpersonally comparable utilities of the citizens.

Several of the new voting procedures aggregate cardinal utility information supplied by the voters (the demand revelation process, Smith's auction process, Hylland and Zeckhauser's point voting). If their use is restricted to decisions that could improve allocative efficiency, then they contain the potential for achieving Pareto-optimal allocations of resources. Experimental work and some limited applications indicate that they can work as theory predicts. Although each is potentially vulnerable to strategic and coalitional manipulation, such strategic behavior is both complicated and risky. The extent to which these procedures would be manipulated needs to be demonstrated experimentally rather than assumed on the basis of hypothetical examples and impossibility proofs. Voting by veto is strategy-proof and relies only on ordinal utility information. It thus provides another option for achieving a Pareto-optimal allocation of resources in deciding public good-externality issues, an option that would allow one to avoid the implicit weighting of cardinal utilities in proportion to initial incomes inherent in the demand revelation and auction procedures. Even a two-thirds (64 percent) majority rule can avoid cycles and achieve Pareto-optimal allocations *if* its use is restricted to certain classes of allocative efficiency issues like choosing public goods quantities when tax rates are fixed.

These voting procedures all assume that voting is by those whose welfare is affected by the outcomes of the voting process, as in a direct democracy. Were these procedures to be employed by a committee of representatives, then these representatives should be chosen in such a way that each group of citizens is represented in proportion to their number in the polity. A form of proportional representation is required. To ensure that the representatives do vote in accordance with the preferences of those they represent, their (re)election should depend on their record of voting on the public good-externality issues to be decided. The function of choosing a government (executive) should be separated from that of deciding allocative efficiency issues. Under such a reform the ideal proportional representation system would differ from those now extant. So be it. The proportional representation systems functioning today reflect the best ideas of political theorists of a century and a half ago. We know more today than we did then. We know that deciding levels of national defense, police protection, and other public goods are positive-sum games in which all can possibly gain. Forming a cabinet by majority rule is a zero-sum game in which nearly half of the parties represented must lose. The same institution and voting rule are not optimal for both tasks.[1]

---

[1] For further discussion see Mueller (1996a, chs. 8–10).

If one assumes that political institutions can be designed to reveal preferences on allocative efficiency changes adequately, the question remains how to resolve redistributional questions. In answering this question it is again critical to recognize that the procedures required are different from those employed for allocative efficiency gains. Beyond this important insight, the public choice literature points in two distinct directions. First, the uncertainty inherent in the long-run nature of constitutional decisions can induce individuals, out of self-interest, to incorporate certain redistributional measures and the protection of civil liberties into the constitution. The potential for this kind of redistribution could be enhanced by organizing a constitutional convention in such a way as to maximize uncertainty over future positions or impartiality (e.g., have the constitution not go into effect until several years after ratification). Parliaments could be freed to concentrate on allocative efficiency improvements by confining redistributional measures to constitutional guarantees.

The literature on majority rule suggests a second way of handling redistributional property rights issues. When these issues are of a binary nature and equal intensities can be assumed by individuals on both sides, then majority rule can be an attractive rule for settling distributional questions. The requirement that issues be binary immediately suggests a court of law, and the Supreme Court in the United States has used majority rule to resolve distributional questions (e.g., abortion and desegregation of schools). Other institutional arrangements can be envisaged once one recognizes the need to resolve redistributional questions using a procedure different from that used for allocative efficiency improvements.

An alternative to institutionally separating allocative efficiency and redistribution issues and allowing the citizens to decide them directly is to limit the citizen's role to that of selecting an agent or set of agents, and to have the agent(s) decide the issues. The models of Chapters 11 and 12 are relevant here, and this literature contains a more optimistic view of the results of voting than does the literature on committee voting in the Arrow tradition. When voting is limited to a pair of candidates or parties that compete for the privilege of running (forming) the government, an equilibrium pair of platforms exists (Chapter 12). The properties of this equilibrium (Pareto optimality, the maximization of a particular SWF) are not obviously inferior to those achieved by (claimed for) the market, or to those one might reasonably demand of a collective choice process. These results place the outcomes from collective decision procedures in a radically different light.

There is much evidence consistent with this model of electoral competition. Although the cycling literature implies that a candidate forced to run on her record is always doomed to defeat, incumbents generally face much better odds. The evidence reviewed in Chapters 12, 15, 19, and 20 indicates that intense efforts are made by candidates to win votes, and by interest groups to influence candidates. Political competition is real and results in predictable and stable outcomes with reasonable normative properties. Wittman (1995) goes so far as to argue that political competition produces the same sorts of efficient outcomes as market competition does. Breton (1996) makes similar claims placing heavy emphasis upon the competition among governments that exists in federalist systems.

Competition between candidates increasingly takes the form of spending money to "buy" votes. This money comes from interest groups that seek to "buy" legislation. The weights given to individual utilities in the SWF that political competition maximizes depend on the resources and organizational skills of the interest groups to which individuals belong. Although the process of competition for votes may achieve a welfare maximum of sorts, it is not necessarily one in which all will be happy with the weights their interests receive in the resulting equilibrium.

Moreover, the money candidates spend does not really buy votes. It buys television commercials, posters, placards and buttons, pollsters, canvassers, and consultants. It buys all of the instruments that modern marketing can devise to influence how an individual votes on election day. But in the end it is the decision the voter makes that determines the outcome of the election. The quality of these outcomes rests on the quality of this choice.

An important implication of the rational choice approach to politics is that it is irrational for an individual to vote if the act of voting is predicated on the assumption that the individual's vote will affect the outcome of the election. Given this observation, voting must be explained as satisfying some motivation of individuals other than one directly tied to the outcomes of the election. Several hypotheses have been put forward that do not rely on the assumption that the voter believes that her vote will "make a difference." None of these hypotheses guarantees, however, that voters gather sufficient information to make a discriminating choice. Nor is the "information" supplied to them by the candidates likely to aid in this task. Candidate competition may lead to an equilibrium set of platforms defined over an "issue" space, but the nature of the issues over which this competition takes place is undefined; thus, also, is the significance of the welfare maximum achieved through this competition.

The candidate competition models help to dispel concern over the existence of an equilibrium in policy space. They raise questions, however, about the nature of the policy space over which competition takes place, and about the weights given to individual preferences in the welfare function that this competition implicitly maximizes. More generally, they suggest that the emphasis in public choice research needs to shift from the outputs of the political process to its inputs, to shift from an emphasis upon the quality of the aggregation process to what it is that is being aggregated.[2] Much of the public choice literature has analyzed outcomes of procedures in which each individual's vote(s) receives equal weight and all voters are well informed about the issues. But in representative democracies, rules of representation and the nature of competition give radically different weights to voter interests, and these are often poorly defined and expressed.

Thus, a number of important issues in public choice require further research. In its first 50 years, a rich harvest of results has been brought forth. Most do seem to be rather disheartening descriptions of how political institutions function and malfunction. But I have tried to suggest that there is also a brighter side to the public choice literature. Some parts offer insights into when and why political institutions work well.

---

[2] See Sen (1995) and Schofield (1996b).

Other parts make proposals to improve the performance of political institutions. To some, this latter literature will appear utopian. And so it is. But the constitutional governments of Switzerland and the United States today would have seemed utopian to a vassal living in Europe during the Middle Ages, and even today must seem utopian to some citizens living under autocracy and other nondemocratic forms of government.

Indeed, what is most utopian of all is the idea that knowledge is cumulative, and that from a knowledge of past mistakes we can design institutions that will avoid similar mistakes in the future. Public choice does provide us with this knowledge. Because of this, I remain optimistic not only about the ability of the field to continue to attract fine scholars, and about the ability of these scholars using the methodology of public choice to make contributions of high quality to the scientific study of politics, but I even am optimistic that this research may someday help to improve the democratic institutions by which we govern ourselves.

References

Aaron, Henry and George M. von Furstenberg, "The Inefficiency of Transfers in Kind," *Western Economic Journal* 9, June 1971, 184–91.

Abramovitz, Moses, "Notes on International Differences in Productivity Growth Rates," in D. C. Mueller, ed., 1983, 79–89.

Abramowitz, Alan I., "Explaining Senate Election Outcomes," *American Political Science Review* 82, June 1988, 385–403.

Abrams, Burton A. and James L. Butkiewicz, "The Influence of State-Level Economic Conditions on the 1992 U.S. Presidential Election," *Public Choice* 85, October 1995, 1–10.

Abrams, Burton A. and Kenneth A. Lewis, "Cultural and Institutional Determinants of Economic Growth: A Cross-Sectional Analysis," *Public Choice* 83, June 1995, 273–89.

Abrams, Burton A. and Russell F. Settle, "A Modest Proposal for Election Reform," *Public Choice* 28, Winter 1976, 37–53.

Abrams, Burton A. and Russell F. Settle, "Women's Suffrage and the Growth of the Welfare State," *Public Choice* 100, September 1999, 289–300.

Abrams, Robert, "The Voter's Paradox and the Homogeneity of Individual Preference Orders," *Public Choice* 26, Summer 1976, 19–27.

Abramson, Paul R. and John H. Aldrich, "The Decline of Electoral Participation in America," *American Political Science Review* 76, September 1982, 502–21.

Acemoglu, Daron and Thierry Verdier, "The Choice between Market Failures and Corruption," *American Economic Review* 90, March 2000, 194–211.

Acheson, K. and J. Chant, "Bureaucratic Theory and the Choice of Central Bank Goals," *Journal of Money, Credit and Banking* 5, 1973, 637–55.

Ackerman, Bruce A., *Social Justice in the Liberal State*, New Haven: Yale University Press, 1980.

Ackerman, Bruce A., *We the People: Transformations*, Cambridge, MA: Harvard University Press, 1998.

Adams, James, "An Assessment of Voting Systems under the Proximity and Directional Models of the Vote," *Public Choice* 98, January 1999, 131–51.

Adams, James, "Multicandidate Equilibrium in American Elections," *Public Choice* 103, June 2000, 297–325.

Adams, James D. and Lawrence W. Kenny, "The Retention of State Governors," *Public Choice* 62, July 1989, 1–13.

Adelman, Irma and Cynthia Morris, *Society, Politics, and Economic Development*, Baltimore: Johns Hopkins University Press, 1973.

Agell, Jonas, Thomas Lindh, and Henry Ohlsson, "Growth and the Public Sector: A Critical Review Essay," *European Journal of Political Economy* 13, February 1997, 33–52.

Aghion, Philippe, Eve Caroli, and Cecilia Garcia-Peñalosa, "Inequality and Economic Growth: The Perspective of the New Growth Theories," *Journal of Economic Literature* 37, December 1999, 1615–60.

Ahlbrandt, Roger S., Jr., "Efficiency in the Provision of Fire Services," *Public Choice* 16, Fall 1973, 1–15.

Ahmed, Sultan and Kenneth V. Greene, "Is the Median Voter a Clear-Cut Winner?: Comparing the Median Voter Theory and Competing Theories in Explaining Local Government Spending," *Public Choice* 105, December 2000, 207–30.

Ahn, T. K., Elinor Ostrom, David Schmidt, Robert Shupp, and James Walker, "Cooperation in PD Games: Fear, Greed, and History of Play," *Public Choice* 106, January 2001, 137–55.

Aivazian, Varouj A. and Jeffrey L. Callen, "The Coase Theorem and the Empty Core," *Journal of Law and Economics* 24, April 1981, 175–81.

Aivazian, Varouj A. and Jeffrey L. Callen, "The Coase Theorem and Transaction Costs: The Core Revisited," mimeo, University of Toronto, 2000.

Akerlof, George A., "The Market for 'Lemons': Qualitative Uncertainty and the Market Mechanism," *Quarterly Journal of Economics* 84, August 1970, 488–500.

Alchian, Armen, "Uncertainty, Evolution and Economic Theory," *Journal of Political Economy* 58, June 1950, 211–21.

Aldrich, John H., "Rational Choice and Turnout," *American Journal of Political Science* 37, 1993, 246–78.

Aldrich, John H., *Why Parties? The Origin and Transformation of Party Politics in America*, Chicago: University of Chicago Press, 1995.

Aldrich, John H., "When is it Rational to Vote?" 1997, in D. C. Mueller, ed., 1997a, 373–90.

Alesina, Alberto, "Macroeconomic Policy in a Two-Party System as a Repeated Game," *Quarterly Journal of Economics* 102, June 1987, 651–78.

Alesina, Alberto, "Macroeconomics and Politics," in S. Fischer, ed., *NBER Macroeconomic Annual 1988*, Cambridge, MA: MIT Press, 1988a, 13–61.

Alesina, Alberto, "Credibility and Policy Convergence in a Two-Party System with Rational Voters," *American Economic Review* 78(4), September 1988b, 796–805.

Alesina, Alberto and Allan Drazen, "Why are Stabilizations Delayed?" *American Economic Review* 81, December 1991, 1170–88.

Alesina, Alberto and Roberto Perotti, "Fiscal Expansions and Adjustments in OECD Countries," *Economic Policy* 21, 1995, 207–48.

Alesina, Alberto and Roberto Perotti, "The Welfare State and Competitiveness," *American Economic Review* 87, December 1997, 921–39.

Alesina, Alberto and Dani Rodrik, "Distributive Politics and Economic Growth," *Quarterly Journal of Economics* 109, May 1994, 465–90.

Alesina, Alberto and Howard Rosenthal, *Partisan Politics, Divided Government and the Economy*, Cambridge: Cambridge University Press, 1995.

Alesina, Alberto, Uriel Roubini with Gerald D. Cohen, *Political Cycles and the Macroeconomy*, Cambridge, MA: MIT Press, 1997.

Alesina, Alberto and Jeffrey Sachs, "Political Parties and the Business Cycle in the US, 1948–1984," *Journal of Money, Credit and Banking* 20, 1988, 63–82.

Alesina, Alberto and Lawrence H. Summers, "Central Bank Independence and Macroeconomic Performance," *Journal of Money, Credit and Banking* 25, 1993, 151–62.

Alexander, Barbara J., "Mechanisms for Rent Transfers: Subcontracting among Military Aircraft Manufacturers," *Public Choice* 91, June 1997, 251–69.

Alger, Dan, "Laboratory Tests of Equilibrium Predictions with Disequilibrium Data," *Review of Economic Studies* 54, 1987, 105–45.

Allen, Stuart D., "The Federal Reserve and the Electoral Cycle," *Journal of Money, Credit and Banking* 18, 1986, 88–94.

Allers, Maarten, Jakob de Haan, and Cees Sterks, "Partisan Influence on the Local Tax Burden in the Netherlands," *Public Choice* 106, March 2001, 351–63.

Al-Marhubi, Fahim and Thomas D. Willett, "The Anti Inflationary Influence of Corporatist Structures and Central Bank Independence: The Importance of the Hump Shaped Hypothesis," *Public Choice* 84, July 1995, 152–62.

Alogoskougis, George S., Ben Lockwood, and Aposlolis Philippopoulos, "Wage Inflation, Electoral Uncertainty and the Exchange Rate Regime: Theory and U.K. Evidence," *Economic Journal* 102, November 1992, 1370–94.

Alogoskougis, George S. and Aposlolis Philippopoulos, "Inflationary Expectations, Political Parties and the Exchange Rate Regime: Greece 1958–89," *European Journal of Political Economy* 8, October 1992, 375–99.

Alt, James E., "The Impact of the Voting Rights Act on Black and White Voter Registration in the South," in C. Davidson and B. Grofman, eds., 1994, 351–77.

Alt, James E. and K. Alec Chrystal, *Political Economics*, Brighton: Wheatsheaf Books, 1983.

Alvarez, R. Michael and Jason L. Saving, "Congressional Committees and the Political Economy of Federal Outlays," *Public Choice* 92, July 1997, 55–73.

Amihud, Yakov and Baruch Lev, "Risk Reduction as a Managerial Motive for Conglomerate Mergers," *Bell Journal of Economics* 12, Autumn 1981, 605–17.

Amy, Douglas J., *Real Choices/New Choices*, New York: Columbia University Press, 1993.

Anand, Sudhir and S. M. R. Kanbur, "The Kuznets Process and the Inequality-Development Relationship," *Journal of Development Economics* 40, 1993, 25–52.

Anderson, Kym, "The Political Market for Government Assistance to Australian Manufacturing Industries," *Economic Record* 56, 1980, 132–44.

Andreoni, James, Brian Erard, and Jonathan Feinstein, "Tax Compliance," *Journal of Economic Literature* 36, June 1998, 818–60.

Ansolabehere, Stephen and James M. Snyder, Jr., "Valence Politics and Equilibrium in Spatial Election Models," *Public Choice* 103, June 2000, 327–36.

Aranson, Peter H., "Federalism at Founding," mimeo, Emory University, Atlanta, 1992a.

Aranson, Peter H., "Federalism: Doctrine against Balance," mimeo, Emory University, Atlanta, 1992b.

Aranson, Peter H. and Peter C. Ordeshook, "Spatial Strategies for Sequential Elections," *Decision-Making*, Columbus: Merrill, 1972.

Aranson, Peter H. and Peter C. Ordeshook, "Regulation, Redistribution, and Public Choice," *Public Choice* 37(1), 1981, 69–100.

Arcelus, Frank and Allan H. Meltzer, "The Effect of Aggregate Economic Variables on Congressional Elections," *American Political Science Review* 69, December 1975a, 1232–65.

Arcelus, Frank and Allan H. Meltzer, "Aggregate Economic Variables and Votes for Congress – Reply," *American Political Science Review* 69, December 1975b, 1266–9.

Arnold, R. Douglas, *Congress and the Bureaucracy: A Theory of Influence*, New Haven: Yale University Press, 1979.

Arrow, Kenneth J., *Social Choice and Individual Values*, 1951, New York: John Wiley & Sons, rev. ed. 1963.

Arrow, Kenneth J., "Uncertainty and the Welfare Economics of Medical Care," *American Economic Review* 53, December 1963, 941–73.

Arrow, Kenneth J., "Some Ordinalist-Utilitarian Notes on Rawls' *Theory of Justice*," *Journal of Philosophy* 70, May 1973, 245–63.

Arrow, Kenneth J. and Robert C. Lind, "Uncertainty and the Evaluation of Public Investment Decisions," *American Economic Review* 60, June 1970, 364–78.

Arrow, Kenneth J. and Tibor Scitovsky, eds., *Readings in Welfare Economics*, Homewood, IL: Richard D. Irwin, 1969.

Asch, Peter, Gary A. Gigliotti, and James A. Polito, "Free Riding with Discrete and Continuous Public Goods: Some Experimental Evidence," *Public Choice* 77, October 1993, 293–305.

Aschauer, David A., "Is Public Expenditure Productive?" *Journal of Monetary Economics* 23, 1989, 177–200.

Ashenfelter, Orley and Stanley Kelley, Jr., "Determinants of Participation in Presidential Elections," *Journal of Law and Economics* 18, December 1975, 695–733.

Asselain, J.-C. and C. Morrison, "The Political Economy of Comparative Growth Rates: The Case of France," in D. C. Mueller, ed., 1983, 157–75.

Atkinson, Anthony B., Lee Rainwater, and Timothy M. Smeeding, *Income Distribution in OECD Countries*, Paris: OECD, 1995.

Atkinson, Scott E. and Robert Halvorsen, "The Relative Efficiency of Public and Private Firms in a Regulated Environment: The Case of U.S. Electric Utilities," *Journal of Public Economics* 29, April 1986, 281–94.

Austen-Smith, David, "Voluntary Pressure Groups," *Economica* 48, May 1981a, 143–53.

Austen-Smith, David, "Party Policy and Campaign Costs in a Multi-Constituency Model of Electoral Competition," *Public Choice* 37(3), 1981b, 389–402.

Austen-Smith, David, "Restricted Pareto Rights," *Journal of Economic Theory* 26, February 1982, 89–99.

Austen-Smith, David, "Interest Groups, Campaign Contributions, and Probabilistic Voting," *Public Choice* 52(2), 1987, 123–39.

Austen-Smith, David, "Refinements of the Heart," in N. Schofield, ed., 1996a, 221–36.

Austen-Smith, David, "Interest Groups: Money, Information, and Influence," 1997, in D. C. Mueller, ed., 1997a, 296–321.

Austen-Smith, David and Jeffrey S. Banks, "Information Aggregation, Rationality, and the Condorcet Jury Theorem," *American Political Science Review* 90, March 1996, 34–45.

Austen-Smith, David and John R. Wright, "Competitive Lobbying for a Legislator's Vote," *Social Choice and Welfare* 9, 1992, 229–57.

Austen-Smith, David and John R. Wright, "Counteractive Lobbying," *American Journal of Political Science* 38, 1994, 25–44.

Auster, R. D. and M. Silver, *The State as a Firm*, Boston: Kluwer, 1979.

Averch, Harvey and L. L. Johnson, "Behavior of the Firm under Regulatory Constraint," *American Economic Review* 52, December 1962, 1052–69.

Axelrod, Robert, *Conflict of Interest*, Chicago: Markham, 1970.

Axelrod, Robert, *The Evolution of Cooperation*, New York: Basic Books, 1984.

Baack, B. D. and Edward J. Ray, "The Political Economy of Tariff Policy: A Case Study of the United States," *Explorations in Economic History* 20, 1983, 73–93.

Bagheri, Fatholla M. and Nader Habibi, "Political Institutions and Central Bank Independence: A Cross-Country Analysis," *Public Choice* 96, July 1998, 187–204.

Bagnoli, Mark and Michael McKee, "Voluntary Contribution Games: Efficient Private Provision of Public Goods," *Economic Inquiry* 29, 1991, 351–66.

Baharad, Eyal and Shmuel Nitzan, "Alleviating Majority Tyranny through Expression of Preference Intensity," mimeo, Bar Ilan University, 2001.

Baik, Kyung Hwan and Jason F. Shogren, "Strategic Behavior in Contests: Comment," *American Economic Review* 82, March 1992, 359–62.

Baik, Kyung Hwan and Jason F. Shogren, "Competitive-Share Group Formation in Rent-Seeking Contests," *Public Choice* 83, April 1995, 113–26.

Bailey, Martin J., "The Demand-Revealing Process: To Distribute the Surplus," *Public Choice* 91, April 1997, 107–26.

Bailey, Stephen J. and Stephen Connolly, "The Flypaper Effect: Identifying Areas for Further Research," *Public Choice* 95, April 1998, 335–61.

Bails, Dale, "Provision of Transportation Services," *Public Choice* 34(1), 1979, 65–8.

Baldwin, Robert E., *The Political Economy of U.S. Import Policy*, Cambridge, MA: MIT Press, 1985.

Baldwin, Robert E. and Christopher S. Magee, "Is Trade Policy for Sale? Congressional Voting on Recent Trade Bills," *Public Choice* 105, October 2000, 79–101.

Balinsky, M. L. and H. Peyton Young, "Stability, Coalitions and Schisms in Proportional Representation Systems," *American Political Science Review* 72, September 1978, 848–58.

Balinsky, M. L. and H. Peyton Young, *Fair Representation*, New Haven: Yale University Press, 1982.

Balisacan, Arsenio M. and James A. Roumasset, "Public Choice of Economic Policy: The Growth of Agricultural Protection," *Weltwirtschaftliches Archiv, Review of World Economics* 123, 1987, 232–48.

Ball, Richard, "Opposition Backlash and Platform Convergence in a Spatial Voting Model with Campaign Contributions," *Public Choice* 98, March 1999, 269–86.

Ballard, Charles L., John B. Shoven, and John Whalley, "General Equilibrium Computations of the Marginal Welfare Costs of Taxes in the United States," *American Economic Review* 75, March 1985, 128–38.

Banaian, King, Richard C. K. Burdekin, and Thomas D. Willett, "Reconsidering the Principal Components of Central Bank Independence: The More the Merrier?" *Public Choice* 97, October 1998, 1–12.

Barbera, Salvador, "The Manipulation of Social Choice Mechanisms that Do Not Leave 'Too Much' to Chance," *Econometrica* 45, October 1977, 1573–88.

Bardhan, Pranab, "Corruption and Development: A Review of the Issues," *Journal of Economic Literature* 35, September 1997, 1320–46.

Baron, David P., "Government Formation and Endogenous Parties," *American Political Science Review* 87, 1993, 34–48.

Baron, David P., "Electoral Competition with Informed and Uninformed Voters," *American Political Science Review* 88, 1994, 33–47.

Baron, David P. and John Ferejohn, "Bargaining and Agenda Formation in Legislatures," *American Economic Review* 77, May 1987, 303–9.

Barr, James L. and Otto A. Davis, "An Elementary Political and Economic Theory of the Expenditures of Local Governments," *Southern Economic Journal* 33, October 1966, 149–65.

Barro, Robert J., "Government Spending in a Simple Model of Endogenous Growth," *Journal of Political Economy* Supplement 98, 1990, 103–25.

Barro, Robert J., "Economic Growth in a Cross Section of Countries," *Quarterly Journal of Economics* 106, May 1991, 407–43.

Barro, Robert J., "Democracy and Growth," *Journal of Economic Growth* 1, March 1996, 1–27.

Barro, Robert J., *Determinants of Economic Growth: A Cross-Country Empirical Study*, Cambridge, MA: MIT Press, 1997.

Barry, Brian, *Political Argument*, London: Routledge and Kegan Paul, 1965.

Barry, Brian, *Sociologists, Economists, and Democracy*, London: Collier-Macmillan, 1970.

Barry, Brian, "Lady Chatterley's Lover and Doctor Fischer's Bomb Party: Liberalism, Pareto Optimality, and the Problem of Objectionable Preferences," in J. Elster and A. Hylland, eds., 1986, 11–43.

Barry, Brian, *Theories of Justice*, Berkeley: University of California Press, 1989.

Barzel, Yoram, "Private Schools and Public School Finance," *Journal of Political Economy* 81, January 1973, 174–86.

Barzel, Yoram and Robert T. Deacon, "Voting Behavior, Efficiency, and Equity," *Public Choice* 21, Spring 1975, 1–14.

Barzel, Yoram and E. Silberberg, "Is the Act of Voting Rational?" *Public Choice* 16, Fall 1973, 51–8.

Basuchoudhary, Atin, Paul Pecorino, and William F. Shughart, II, "Reversal of Fortune; The Politics and Economics of the Superconducting Supercollider," *Public Choice* 100, September 1999, 185–201.

Baumol, William J., *Business Behavior, Value and Growth*, New York: Macmillan, 1959; rev. ed. 1967a.

Baumol, William J., *Welfare Economics and the Theory of the State*, 2nd ed., Cambridge, MA: Harvard University Press, 1967b.

Baumol, William J., "On Taxation and the Control of Externalities," *American Economic Review* 62, June 1972, 307–22.

Baye, Michael R., Dan Kovenock, and Casper G. de Vries, "Rigging the Lobbying Process: An Application of the All-Pay Auction," *American Economic Review* 83, March 1993, 289–94.

Baye, Michael R., Dan Kovenock, and Casper G. de Vries, "The Solution to the Tullock Rent-Seeking Game when R > 2: Mixed-Strategy Equilibria and Mean Dissipation Rates," *Public Choice* 81, December 1994, 363–80.

Baye, Michael R., Dan Kovenock, and Casper G. de Vries, "The Incidence of Overdissipation in Rent-Seeking Contests," *Public Choice* 99, June 1999, 439–54.

Beard, Charles A., *An Economic Interpretation of the Constitution of the United States*, New York: Macmillan, 1913; reprinted 1941.

Beck, Nathaniel, "The Paradox of Minimax Regret," *American Political Science Review* 69, September 1975, 918.

Beck, Nathaniel, "Does There Exist a Business Cycle: A Box-Tiao Analysis," *Public Choice* 38(2), 1982a, 205–9.

Beck, Nathaniel, "Parties, Administrations, and American Macroeconomic Outcomes," *American Political Science Review* 76, March 1982b, 83–93.

Beck, Nathaniel, "Presidential Influence on the Federal Reserve in the 1970s," *American Journal of Political Science* 26, 1982c, 415–45.

Beck, Nathaniel, "Domestic Sources of American Monetary Policy: 1955–82," *Journal of Politics* 46, 1984, 786–871.

Beck, Nathaniel, "Elections and the FED: Is There a Political Monetary Cycle?" *American Journal of Political Science* 31, 1987, 194–216.

Beck, R. L. and T. M. Connolly, "Some Empirical Evidence on Rent Seeking," *Public Choice* 87, April 1996, 19–33.

Becker, E., "The Illusion of Fiscal Illusion: Unsticking the Flypaper Effect," *Public Choice* 86, 1996, 85–102.

Becker, Edmund R. and Frank A. Sloan, "Hospital Ownership and Performance," *Economic Inquiry* 23, January 1985, 21–36.

Becker, Gary S., "Comment" (on Peltzman, 1976), *Journal of Law and Economics* 19, August 1976, 245–8.

Becker, Gary S., "A Theory of Competition among Pressure Groups for Political Influence," *Quarterly Journal of Economics* 98, August 1983, 371–400.

Becker, Gilbert, "The Public Interest Hypothesis Revisited: A New Test of Peltzman's Theory of Regulation," *Public Choice* 49(3), 1986, 223–34.

Beetsma, Roel M. W. J. and Frederick van der Ploeg, "Does Inequality Cause Inflation?: The Political Economy of Inflation, Taxation and Government Debt," *Public Choice* 87, April 1996, 143–62.

Bell, Daniel, *Coming of Post-Industrial Society*, New York: Basic Books, 1973.

Bell, R., D. V. Edwards, and R. H. Wagner, eds., *Political Power*, New York: Free Press, 1969.

Bender, Bruce, "An Analysis of Congressional Voting on Legislation Limiting Congressional Campaign Expenditures," *Journal of Political Economy* 96, October 1988, 1005–21.

Bender, Bruce, "The Influence of Ideology on Congressional Voting," *Economic Inquiry* 29, July 1991, 416–28.

Bender, Bruce and John R. Lott, Jr., "Legislator Voting and Shirking: A Critical Review of the Literature," *Public Choice* 87, April 1996, 67–100.

Bendor, Jonathan, Serge Taylor, and Roland van Gaalen, "Bureaucratic Expertise versus Legislative Authority: A Model of Deception and Monitoring in Budgeting," *American Political Science Review* 79, December 1985, 1041–60.

Bennett, Elaine and David Conn, "The Group Incentive Properties of Mechanisms for the Provision of Public Goods," *Public Choice* 29-2 (special supplement), Spring 1977, 95–102.

Bennett, James T. and Manuel H. Johnson, "Public versus Private Provision of Collective Goods and Services: Garbage Collection Revisited," *Public Choice* 34(1), 1979, 55–64.

Bennett, James T. and Manuel H. Johnson, "Tax Reduction without Sacrifice: Private-Sector Production of Public Services," *Public Finance Quarterly* 8, October 1980a, 363–96.

Bennett, James T. and Manuel H. Johnson, *The Political Economy of Federal Government Growth, 1959–1978*, College Station: Texas A&M University Press, 1980b.

Bennett, Randall W. and Christine Loucks, "Savings and Loan and Finance Industry PAC Contributions to Incumbent Members of the House Banking Committee," *Public Choice* 79, April 1994, 83–104.

Bennett, Randall W. and Clark Wiseman, "Economic Performance and U.S. Senate Elections, 1958–86," *Public Choice* 69, February 1991, 93–100.

Benson, Bruce L. and M. D. Faminow, "The Impact of Experience on Prices and Profits in Experimental Duopoly Markets," *Journal of Economic Behavior and Organization* 9, 1988, 345–65.

Bental, Benjamin and Uri Ben-Zion, "Political Contributions and Policy: Some Extensions," *Public Choice* 19, Winter 1975, 1–12.

Bentley, A. F., *The Process of Government*, Chicago: University of Chicago Press, 1907.

Ben-Yashar, Ruth and Shmuel I. Nitzan, "The Optimal Decision Rule for Fixed Size Committees in Dichotomous Choice Situations – The General Result," *International Economic Review* 38, February 1997, 175–87.

Ben-Zion, Uri and Zeev Eyton, "On Money, Votes, and Policy in a Democratic Society," *Public Choice* 17, Spring 1974, 1–10.

Berg, Sven, "Condorcet's Jury Theorem, Dependency among Jurors," *Social Choice and Welfare* 10, 1993, 87–95.

Berger, Helge and Ulrich Woitek, "Searching for Political Business Cycles in Germany," *Public Choice* 91, April 1997, 179–97.

Berggren, Niclas, "Economic Freedom and Equality: Friends or Foes?" *Public Choice* 100, September 1999, 203–23.

Berglas, Eitan, "On the Theory of Clubs," *American Economic Review* 66(2), May 1976, 116–21.

Bergman, Torbjörn, Wolfgang Müller, and Kaare Strøm, eds., "Parliamentary Democracy and the Chain of Delegation," *European Journal of Political Research* 37, May 2000, 255–429.

Bergson, Abram, "A Reformulation of Certain Aspects of Welfare Economics," *Quarterly Journal of Economics* 52(7), February 1938, 314–44.

Bergson, Abram, "On the Concept of Social Welfare," *Quarterly Journal of Economics* 68, May 1954, 233–53.

Bergstrom, Theodore C., "When Does Majority Rule Supply Public Goods Efficiently," *Scandinavian Journal of Economics* 81, October 1979, 217–26.

Bergstrom, Theodore C. and Robert P. Goodman, "Private Demands for Public Goods," *American Economic Review* 63, June 1973, 280–96.

Bernholz, Peter, "Logrolling, Arrow Paradox and Cyclical Majorities," *Public Choice* 15, Summer 1973, 87–95.

Bernholz, Peter, "Logrolling, Arrow Paradox and Decision Rule – A Generalization," *Kyklos* 27, 1974a, 49–61.

Bernholz, Peter, *Grundlagen der Politischen Ökonomie*, vol. 2, Tübingen: Mohr Siebeck, 1974b.

Bernholz, Peter, "Is a Paretian Liberal Really Impossible?" *Public Choice* 20, Winter 1974c, 99–107.

Bernholz, Peter, "Logrolling and the Paradox of Voting: Are They Logically Equivalent?" *American Political Science Review* 69, September 1975, 961–2.

Bernholz, Peter, "Prisoner's Dilemma, Logrolling and Cyclical Group Preferences," *Public Choice* 29, Spring 1977, 73–84.

Bernholz, Peter, "On the Stability of Logrolling Outcomes in Stochastic Games," *Public Choice* 33(3), 1978, 65–82.

Bernholz, Peter, "The Constitution of Totalitarianism," *Journal of Institutional and Theoretical Economics* 147, September 1991, 425–40.

Bernholz, Peter, "Property Rights, Contracts, Cyclical Social Preferences, and the Coase Theorem: A Synthesis," *European Journal of Political Economy* 13, 1997a, 419–42.

Bernholz, Peter, "Ideology, Sects, State and Totalitarianism: A General Theory," in H. Maier and M. Schäfer, eds., *Totalitarismus und Politische Religionen*, Paderborn: Ferdinand Schöningh, 1997b, 271–98.

Bernholz, Peter, "The Generalized Coase Theorem and Separable Individual Preferences: A Comment," mimeo, University of Basel, 1998.

Berry, W.O. and D. Lowery, "The Growing Cost of Government: A Test of Two Explanations," *Social Science Quarterly* 65, September 1984, 735–49.

Besley, Timothy and Anne Case, "Does Electoral Accountability Affect Economic Policy Choices? Evidence from Gubernatorial Term Limits," *Quarterly Journal of Economics* 110, August 1995, 769–98.

Besley, Timothy and Stephen Coate, "Public Provision of Private Goods and the Redistribution of Income," *American Economic Review* 81, September 1991, 979–84.

Besley, Timothy and Stephen Coate, "An Economic Model of Representative Democracy," *Quarterly Journal of Economics* 112, February 1997, 85–114.

Bhagwati, Jagdish N., "Directly Unproductive, Profit-seeking (DUP) Activities," *Journal of Political Economy* 90, October 1982, 988–1002.

Bhagwati, Jagdish and Peter Rosendorff, eds., *Readings in the Political Economy of Trade Policy*, Cambridge, MA: MIT Press, 2001.

Bhagwati, Jagdish N. and T. N. Srinivasan, "Revenue Seeking: A Generalization of the Theory of Tariffs," *Journal of Political Economy* 88, December 1980, 1069–87.

Bhattacharyya, D. K. and Robert W. Wassmer, "Fiscal Dynamics and Local Elected Officials," *Public Choice* 83, June 1995, 221–49.

Binmore, Ken, *Game Theory and the Social Contract, I: Playing Fair*, Cambridge, MA: MIT Press, 1994.

Binmore, Ken, *Game Theory and the Social Contract, II: Just Playing*, Cambridge, MA: MIT Press, 1998.

Black, Duncan, "On the Rationale of Group Decision Making," *Journal of Political Economy* 56, February 1948a, 23–34; reprinted in K. J. Arrow and T. Scitovsky, 1969, 133–46.

Black, Duncan, "The Decisions of a Committee Using a Special Majority," *Econometrica* 16, 1948b, 245–61.

Black, Duncan, *The Theory of Committees and Elections*, Cambridge: Cambridge University Press, 1958.

Blais, André, "The Debate Over Electoral Systems," *International Political Science Review* 12, 1991, 239–60.

Blais, André and R. K. Carty, "The Effectiveness of the Plurality Rule," *British Journal of Political Science* 18, 1988, 550–3.

Blais, André and R. K. Carty, "Does Proportional Representation Foster Voter Turnout?" *European Journal of Political Research* 18, 1990, 167–81.

Blais, André and Richard Nadeau, "The Electoral Budget Cycle," *Public Choice* 74(4), December 1992, 389–403.

Blais, André and Robert Young, "Why Do People Vote? An Experiment in Rationality," *Public Choice* 99, April 1999, 39–55.

Blais, André, Robert Young, Christopher Fleury, and Miriam Lapp, "Do People Vote on the Basis of Minimax Regret?" *Political Research Quarterly* 48, December 1995, 827–36.

Blank, Rebecca M., "The Impact of State Economic Differentials on Household Welfare and Labor Force Behavior," *Journal of Urban Economics* 24, 1988, 186–211.

Blankart, Charles B., "The Process of Government Centralization: A Constitutional View," *Constitutional Political Economy* 11(1), March 2000, 27–39.

Blau, J. H., "A Direct Proof of Arrow's Theorem," *Econometrica* 40, January 1972, 61–7.

Blau, J. H. and R. Deb, "Social Decision Functions and the Veto," *Econometrica* 45, May 1977, 871–9.

Blin, Jean-Marie and M. A. Satterthwaite, "Individual Decisions and Group Decisions," *Journal of Public Economics* 10, October 1978, 247–67.

Bloom, Howard S., "Public Choice and Private Interest: Explaining the Vote for Property Tax Classification in Massachusetts," *National Tax Journal* 32, December 1979, 527–34.

Bloom, Howard S. and H. Douglas Price, "Voter Response to Short-Run Economic Conditions: The Asymmetric Effect of Prosperity and Recession," *American Political Science Review* 69, December 1975, 1266–76.

Boardman, Anthony E. and Aidan R. Vining, "Ownership and Performance in Competitive Environments: A Comparison of the Performance of Private, Mixed and State-owned Enterprises," *Journal of Law and Economics* 32(1), April 1989, 1–33.

Bohara, Alok K. and William H. Kaempfer, "A Test of Tariff Endogeneity in the United States," *American Economic Review* 81, September 1991, 952–60.

Bohm, Peter, "Estimating Demand for Public Goods: An Experiment," *European Economic Review* 3, March 1972, 111–30.

Borcherding, Thomas E., ed., *Budgets and Bureaucrats: The Sources of Government Growth*, Durham: Duke University Press, 1977.

Borcherding, Thomas E., "The Causes of Government Expenditure Growth: A Survey of the U.S. Evidence," *Journal of Public Economics* 28, December 1985, 359–82.

Borcherding, Thomas E., and Robert T. Deacon, "The Demand for the Services of Non-Federal Governments," *American Economic Review* 62, December 1972, 891–901.

Borcherding, Thomas E., W. C. Bush, and R. M. Spann, "The Effects of Public Spending on the Divisibility of Public Outputs in Consumption, Bureaucratic Power, and the Size of the Tax-Sharing Group," 1977b, in T. E. Borcherding, 1977a, 211–28.

Borcherding, Thomas E., Werner W. Pommerehne, and Friedrich Schneider, "Comparing the Efficiency of Private and Public Production: The Evidence from Five Countries," *Zeitschrift für Nationalökomie* 89, 1982, 127–56.

Bordley, Robert F., "A Pragmatic Method for Evaluating Election Schemes through Simulation," *American Political Science Review* 77, March 1983, 123–41.

Borglin, Anders, "States and Persons – On the Interpretation of Some Fundamental Concepts in the Theory of Justice as Fairness," *Journal of Public Economics* 18, June 1982, 85–104.

Borooah, Vani K. and Vidya Borooah, "Economic Performance and Political Popularity in the Republic of Ireland," *Public Choice* 67, October 1990, 65–79.

Borooah, Vani K. and F. van der Ploeg, *Political Aspects of the Economy*, Cambridge: Cambridge University Press, 1983.

Bös, Dieter and Martin Kolmar, "Anarchy, Efficiency, and Redistribution," *Journal of Public Economics*, forthcoming.

Bowen, H. R., "The Interpretation of Voting in the Allocation of Economics Resources," *Quarterly Journal of Economics* 58, February 1943, 27–48; reprinted in K. J. Arrow and T. Scitovsky, 1969, 115–32.

Bowler, Shaun and Bernard Grofman, eds., *Elections in Australia, Ireland, and Malta under the Single Transferable Vote*, Ann Arbor: University of Michigan Press, 2000a.

Bowler, Shaun and Bernard Grofman, "Introduction: STV as an Imbedded Institution," 2000b, in S. Bowler and B. Grofman, eds., 2000a, 1–14.

Bowles, Samuel and John Eatwell, "Between Two Worlds: Interest Groups, Class Structure, and Capitalist Growth," in D. C. Mueller, ed., 1983, 217–30.

Brady, David and Edward P. Schwartz, "Ideology and Interests in Congressional Voting: The Politics of Abortion in the U.S. Senate," *Public Choice* 84, July 1995, 25–48.

Brainard, S. Lael and Thierry Verdier, "The Political Economy of Declining Industries: Senescent Industry Collapse Revisited," *Journal of International Economics* 42, February 1997, 221–37.

Braithwaite, R. B., *Theory of Games as a Tool for the Moral Philosopher*, Cambridge: Cambridge University Press, 1955.

Brams, Steven J., *Game Theory and Politics*, New York: Free Press, 1975.

Brams, Steven J. and Peter C. Fishburn, "Approval Voting," *American Political Science Review* 72, September 1978, 831–47.

Brams, Steven J. and Peter Fishburn, *Approval Voting*, Boston: Birkhäuser, 1983.

Brams, Steven J., Peter C. Fishburn, and Samuel Merrill, III, "The Responsiveness of Approval Voting: Comments on Saari and van Newenhizen," *Public Choice* 59, November 1988, 121–31.

Brennan, Geoffrey and James M. Buchanan, *The Power to Tax: Analytical Foundations of a Fiscal Constitution*, Cambridge: Cambridge University Press, 1980.

Brennan, Geoffrey and James M. Buchanan, "Voter Choice: Evaluating Political Alternatives," *American Behavioral Scientist* 28, November/December 1984, 185–201.

Brennan, Geoffrey and James M. Buchanan, *The Reason of Rules*, Cambridge: Cambridge University Press, 1985.

Brennan, Geoffrey and Alan Hamlin, *Democratic Devices and Desires*, Cambridge: Cambridge University Press, 2000.

Brennan, Geoffrey and Loren Lomasky, *Democracy and Decision*, Cambridge: Cambridge University Press, 1993.

Brennan, Geoffrey and Cliff Walsh, "A Monopoly Model of Public Goods Provision: The Uniform Pricing Case," *American Economic Review* 71, March 1981, 196–206.

Breton, Albert, *The Economic Theory of Representative Government*, Chicago: Aldine, 1974.

Breton, Albert, *Competitive Governments*, Cambridge: Cambridge University Press, 1996.

Breton, Albert and Gianluigi Galeotti, "Is Proportional Representation Always the Best Electoral Rule?" *Public Finance* 40(1), 1985, 1–16.

Breton, Albert and Anthony Scott, *The Economic Constitution of Federal States*, Toronto: University of Toronto Press, 1978.

Breton, Albert and Ronald Wintrobe, "The Equilibrium Size of a Budget Maximizing Bureau," *Journal of Political Economy* 83, February 1975, 195–207.

Breton, Albert and Ronald Wintrobe, *The Logic of Bureaucratic Control*, Cambridge: Cambridge University Press, 1982.

Breyer, Friedrich, "Sen's Paradox with Decisiveness over Issues in Case of Liberal Preferences," *Zeitschrift für Nationalökonomie* 37(1–2), 1977, 45–60.

Breyer, Friedrich, "On the Existence of Equilibria in a Three-party System with Plurality Voting," in M. J. Holler, ed., *The Logic of Multiparty Systems*, Dordrecht: Kluwer, 1987, 113–28.

Breyer, Friedrich, "Can Reallocation of Rights Help Avoid the Paretian-Liberal Paradox?" *Public Choice* 65, June 1990, 267–71.

Breyer, Friedrich, "Comment on the Papers by Buchanan and by de Jasay and Kliemt," *Analyse & Kritik* 18, September 1996, 148–52.

Brittan, Samuel, "The Economic Contradictions of Democracy," *British Journal of Political Science* 5, April 1975, 129–59.

Brody, R. A. and B. I. Page, "Indifference, Alienation and Rational Decisions," *Public Choice* 15, Summer 1973, 1–17.

Brooks, Michael A. and Ben J. Heijdra, "In Search of Rent-Seeking," mimeo, University of Tasmania, 1986.

Brown, D. J., *Acyclic Choice*, New Haven: Cowles Foundation, 1973.

Brown, D. J., "Aggregation of Preferences," *Quarterly Journal of Economics* 89, August 1975, 456–69.

Brown, T. A. and A. A. Stein, "The Political Economy of National Elections," *Comparative Politics* 14, 1982, 479–99.

Browne, Eric C., John P. Frendreis, and Dennis W. Gleiber, "The Process of Cabinet Dissolution: An Exponential Model of Duration and Stability in Western Democracies," *American Journal of Political Science* 30, 1986, 628–50.

Browning, Edgar K., "On the Marginal Welfare Cost of Taxation," *American Economic Review* 77, March 1987, 11–23.

Browning, Edgar K., "Inequality and Poverty," *Southern Economic Journal* 55, April 1989, 819–30.

Brubaker, Earl R., "On the Margolis 'Thought Experiment', and the Applicability of Demand-Revealing Mechanisms to Large-Group Decisions," *Public Choice* 41(2), 1983, 315–9.

Brubaker, Earl R., "Efficient Allocation and Unanimous Consent with Incomplete Demand Disclosures," *Public Choice* 48(3), 1986, 217–27.

Brueckner, Jan K., "A Test for Allocative Efficiency in the Local Public Sector," *Journal of Public Economics* 19, December 1982, 311–31.

Brueckner, Jan K., "Welfare Reform and the Race to the Bottom: Theory and Evidence," *Southern Economic Journal* 66, January 2000, 505–25.

Brunner, Karl, "Reflections on the Political Economy of Government: The Persistent Growth of Government," *Schweizerische Zeitschrift für Volkswirtschaft und Statistik* 114, September 1978, 649–80.

Buchanan, James M., "The Pure Theory of Government Finance: A Suggested Approach," *Journal of Political Economy* 57, December 1949, 496–506.

Buchanan, James M., "Federalism and Fiscal Equity," *American Economic Review* 40, September 1950, 538–600.

Buchanan, James M., "Federal Grants and Resource Allocation," *Journal of Political Economy* 60, June 1952, 201–17.

Buchanan, James M., "Social Choice, Democracy, and Free Markets," *Journal of Political Economy* 62, April 1954a, 114–23.

Buchanan, James M., "Individual Choice in Voting and the Market," *Journal of Political Economy* 62, August 1954b, 334–43.

Buchanan, James M., "An Economic Theory of Clubs," *Economica* 32, February 1965a, 1–14.

Buchanan, James M., "Ethical Rules, Expected Values, and Large Numbers," *Ethics* 76, October 1965b, 1–13.

Buchanan, James M., "An Individualistic Theory of Political Process," in D. Easton, ed., *Varieties of Political Theory*, Englewood Cliffs, NJ: Prentice-Hall, 1966, 25–37.

Buchanan, James M., *Public Finance in a Democratic Process: Fiscal Institutions and the Individual Choice*, Chapel Hill: University of North Carolina Press, 1967.

Buchanan, James M., "Notes for an Economic Theory of Socialism," *Public Choice* 8, Spring 1970, 29–43.

Buchanan, James M., "Principles of Urban-Fiscal Strategy," *Public Choice* 11, Fall 1971, 1–6.

Buchanan, James M., *The Limits of Liberty: Between Anarchy and Leviathan*, Chicago: University of Chicago Press, 1975a.

Buchanan, James M., "Public Finance and Public Choice," *National Tax Journal* 28, December 1975b, 383–94.

Buchanan, James M., "A Hobbesian Interpretation of the Rawlsian Difference Principle," *Kyklos* 29, 1976, 5–25.

Buchanan, James M., "Why Does Government Grow?" in Borcherding, 1977a, 3–18.

Buchanan, James M., "Rent Seeking and Profit Seeking," in J. M. Buchanan, R. D. Tollison, and G. Tullock, 1980, 3–15.

Buchanan, James M., *Liberty, Market and State*, New York: New York University Press, 1986.

Buchanan, James M., *The Economics and the Ethics of Constitutional Order*, Ann Arbor: University of Michigan Press, 1991.

Buchanan, James M., "An Ambiguity in Sen's Alleged Proof of the Impossibility of a Pareto Libertarian," *Analyse & Kritik* 18, September 1996, 118–25.

Buchanan, James M. and Roger D. Congleton, *Politics by Principle, Not Reason*, Cambridge: Cambridge University Press, 1998.

Buchanan, James M. and C. J. Goetz, "Efficiency Limits of Fiscal Mobility: An Assessment of the Tiebout Model," *Journal of Public Economics* 1, April 1972, 25–43.

Buchanan, James M. and W. C. Stubblebine, "Externality," *Economica* 29, November 1962, 371–84; reprinted in K. J. Arrow and T. Scitovsky, 1969, 199–212.

Buchanan, James M., Robert D. Tollison, and Gordon Tullock, eds., *Toward a Theory of the Rent-Seeking Society*, College Station: Texas A&M Press, 1980.

Buchanan, James M. and Gordon Tullock, *The Calculus of Consent*, Ann Arbor: University of Michigan Press, 1962.

Buchanan, James M. and Richard E. Wagner, "An Efficiency Basis for Federal Fiscal Equalization," in J. Margolis, ed., *The Analysis of Public Output*, New York: National Bureau of Economic Research, 1970.

Buchanan, James M. and Richard E. Wagner, *Democracy in Deficit*, New York: Academic Press, 1977.

Buckwell, A., David R. Harvey, Kenneth J. Thomson, and Kenn A. Parton, *The Costs of the Common Agricultural Policy*, London: Croom House, 1982.

Budge, Ian, *Parties, Policies and Democracies*, Boulder, CO: Westview Press, 1994.

Budge, Ian, David Robertson, and Derek Hearl, eds., *Democracy, Strategy and Party Change*, Cambridge: Cambridge University Press, 1987.

Budge, Ian, David Robertson, and Derek Hearl, *Ideology, Strategy and Party Change*, Cambridge: Cambridge University Press, 1997.

Bundesrechnungshof, Bemerkungen des Bundesrechnungshofs zur Bundeshaushaltsrechnung (einschließlich Bundesvermögensrechnung) für das Haushaltsjahr 1972, Bundestagsdrucksache 7/2709, 110–111.

Bundesregierung Deutschland, Agrarbericht 1976, Bundestagsdrucksache 7/4680, pp. 63–65; Bundestagsdrucksache 7/4681, p. 146.

Burns, Michael E. and Cliff Walsh, "Market Provision of Price-excludable Public Goods: A General Analysis," *Journal of Political Economy* 89, February 1981, 166–91.

Bush, Winston C., Individual Welfare in Anarchy, in G. Tullock, ed., *Explorations in the Theory of Anarchy*, Blacksburg: Center for the Study of Public Choice, 1972, 5–18.

Bush, Winston C. and L. S. Mayer, "Some Implications of Anarchy for the Distribution of Property," *Journal of Economic Theory* 8, August 1974, 401–12.

Calcagno, Peter T. and John D. Jackson, "Political Action Committee Spending and Senate Roll Call Voting," *Public Choice* 97, December 1998, 569–85.

Calvert, R., "Robustness of the Multidimensional Voting Model: Candidates' Motivations, Uncertainty, and Convergence," *American Journal of Political Science* 29, 1985, 69–95.

Calvert, R., *Models of Imperfect Information in Politics*, Chur: Harwood Academic Publishers, 1986.

Cameron, Charles M., *Veto Bargaining*, Cambridge: Cambridge University Press, 2000.

Cameron, David R., "The Expansion of the Public Economy: A Comparative Analysis," *American Political Science Review* 72, December 1978, 1243–61.

Campbell, A., P. E. Converse, W. E. Miller, and D. E. Stokes, *The American Voter*, New York: Wiley, 1964.

Campbell, Colin D., "New Hampshire's Tax-Base Limits: An Example of the Leviathan Model," *Public Choice* 78, February 1994, 129–44.

Campbell, D. E., "On the Derivation of Majority Rule," *Theory and Decision* 14, June 1982, 133–40.

Caplin, Andrew and Barry Nalebuff, "On 64%-Majority Rule," *Econometrica* 56, July 1988, 787–814.

Caplin, Andrew and Barry Nalebuff, "Aggregation and Voter Choice: A Mean Voter Theorem," *Econometrica* 59, January 1991, 1–23.

Caporale, Tony and Kevin B. Grier, "A Political Model of Monetary Policy with Applications to the Real Fed Funds Rate," *Journal of Law and Economics* 41, October 1998, 409–28.

Capron, Henri and Jean-Louis Kruseman, "Is Political Rivalry an Incentive to Vote?" *Public Choice* 56, January 1988, 31–43.

Carlsen, Fredrik, "Opinion Polls and Political Business Cycles: Theory and Evidence for the United States," *Public Choice* 92, September 1997, 389–406.

Carroll, Kathleen A., "Industrial Structure and Monopoly Power in the Federal Bureaucracy: An Empirical Analysis," *Economic Inquiry* 27, October 1989, 683–703.

Carroll, Kathleen A., "Bureau Competition and Efficiency," *Journal of Economic Behavior and Organization* 13, January 1990, 21–40.

Carson, R. T. and Joe A. Oppenheimer, "A Method of Measuring the Personal Ideology of Political Representatives," *American Political Science Review* 78, March 1984, 163–78.

Carstairs, Andrew McLaren, *A Short History of Electoral Systems in Western Europe*, London: Allen & Unwin, 1980.

Carter, John R. and Stephen D. Guerette, "An Experimental Study of Expressive Voting," *Public Choice* 73, April 1992, 251–60.

Caves, Douglas W. and Laurits R. Christensen, "The Relative Efficiency of Public and Private Firms in a Competitive Environment: The Case of Canadian Railroads," *Journal of Political Economy* 88, October 1980, 958–76.

Caves, Richard E., "Economic Models of Political Choice: Canada's Tariff Structure," *Canadian Journal of Economics* 9, May 1976, 278–300.

Cebula, Richard J., *The Determinants of Human Migration*, Lexington: Lexington Books, 1979.

Cebula, Richard J., "A Brief Empirical Note on the Tiebout Hypothesis and State Income Tax Policies," *Public Choice* 67, October 1990, 87–9.

Cebula, Richard J., "A Brief Note on Welfare Benefits and Human Migration," *Public Choice* 69, March 1991, 345–9.

Cebula, Richard J. and Milton Z. Kafoglis, "A Note on the Tiebout-Tullock Hypothesis: The Period 1975–1980," *Public Choice* 48(1), 1986, 65–9.

Cebula, Richard J. and James V. Koch, "Welfare Policies and Migration of the Poor in the United States: An Empirical Note," *Public Choice* 61, May 1989, 171–6.

Cebula, Richard J. and D. R. Murphy, "The Electoral College and Voter Participation Rates: An Exploratory Note," *Public Choice* 35(2), 1980, 185–90.

Chamberlin, John R. and Paul N. Courant, "Representative Deliberations and Representative Decisions: Proportional Representation and the Borda Rule," *American Political Science Review* 77, September 1983, 718–33.

Chant, John F. and Keith Acheson, "The Choice of Monetary Instruments and the Theory of Bureaucracy," *Public Choice* 12, 1972, 13–33.

Chant, John F. and Keith Acheson, "Mythology and Central Banking," *Kyklos* 26, 1973, 362–79.

Chapman, Randall G. and Kristian S. Palda, "Electoral Turnout in Rational Voting and Consumption Perspectives," *Journal of Consumer Research* 9, March 1983, 337–46.

Chapman, Randall G. and Kristian S. Palda, "Assessing the Influence of Campaign Expenditures on Voting Behavior within a Comprehensive Electoral Market Model," *Marketing Science* 3, 1984, 207–26.

Chappell, Henry W., Jr., "Campaign Contributions and Voting on the Cargo Preference Bill: A Comparison of Simultaneous Models," *Public Choice* 36(2), 1981, 301–12.

Chappell, Henry W., Jr., "Campaign Contributions and Congressional Voting. A Simultaneous Probit-Tobit Model," *Review of Economics and Statistics* 64, February 1982, 77–83.

Chappell, Henry W., Jr. and William R. Keech, "Party Differences in Macroeconomic Policies and Outcomes," *American Economic Review* 76, May 1986, 71–4.

Chappell, Henry W., Jr. and William R. Keech, "The Unemployment Rate Consequences of Partisan Monetary Policies," *Southern Economic Review* 55, 1988, 107–22.

Chernick, Howard A., "An Economic Model of the Distribution of Public Grants," in P. Mieszkowski and W. H. Oakland, eds., *Fiscal Federalism and Grants-in-Aid*, Washington, D.C.: Urban Institute, 1979, 81–103.

Choi, Kwang, "A Statistical Test of Olson's Model," in D. C. Mueller, ed., 1983, 57–78.

Chong, Dennis, "Rational Choice Theory's Mysterious Rivals," in J. Fiedman, ed., 1996, 37–57.

Chressanthis, George A. and Stephen D. Shaffer, "Economic Performance and U.S. Senate Elections: A Comment," *Public Choice* 75, March 1993, 263–77.

Chrystal, Alec K. and James E. Alt, "Some Problems in Formulating and Testing a Politico-Economic Model of the U.K.," *Economic Journal* 91, September 1981, 730–6.

Chu, C. Y. Cyrus and Wen-Fang Liu, "A Dynamic Characterization of Rawls' Maximin Principle: Theory and Applications," *Constitutional Political Economy* 12, September, 2001, 255–72.

Chubb, John E., "Institutions, the Economy, and the Dynamics of State Elections," *American Political Science Review* 82, March 1988, 133–54.

Chubb, John E. and Terry M. Moe, *Politics, Markets, and America's Schools*, Washington, D.C.: Brookings Institution, 1990.

Clague, Christopher, Philip Keefer, Stephen Knack, and Mancur Olson, Jr., "Property and Contract Rights in Autocracies and Democracies," *Journal of Economic Growth* 1, 1996, 243–76.

Clark, Kenneth and Martin Sefton, "The Sequential Prisoner's Dilemma: Evidence on Reciprocation," *Economic Journal* 111, January 2001, 51–68.

Clarke, Edward H., "Multipart Pricing of Public Goods," *Public Choice* 11, Fall 1971, 17–33.

Clarke, Edward H., "Multipart Pricing of Public Goods: An Example," in S. Mushkin, ed., *Public Prices for Public Products*, Washington, D.C.: The Urban Institute, 1972, 125–30.

Clarke, Edward H., "Some Aspects of the Demand-Revealing Process," *Public Choice* 29-2 (special supplement), Spring 1977, 37–49.

Clarkson, Kenneth W., "Some Implications of Property Rights in Hospital Management," *Journal of Law and Economics* 15, October 1972, 363–84.

Clarr, Victor V., "An Incentive-Compatibility Approach to the Problem of Monitoring a Bureaucrat," *Public Finance Review* 26, November 1998, 599–610.

Clotfelter, C. J., *Public Spending for Higher Education*, College Park: University of Maryland Press, 1976.

Clotfelter, Charles T., *Federal Tax Policy and Charitable Giving*, Chicago: University of Chicago Press, 1985.

Coase, Ronald H., "The Nature of the Firm," *Economica* 4, November 1937, 386–405; reprinted in K. E. Boulding and G. J. Stigler, *Readings in Price Theory*, Homewood, IL: Irwin, 1952, 331–51.

Coase, Ronald H., "The Problem of Social Cost," *Journal of Law and Economics* 3, October 1960, 1–44.

Coate, Malcolm B., Richard S. Higgins, and Fred S. McChesney, "Bureaucracy and Politics in FTC Merger Challenges," *Journal of Law and Economics* 33, October 1990, 463–82.

Coates, Dennis, "Electoral Support and the Capture of Legislators: Evidence from North Carolina's Vote on Radioactive Waste Disposal," *RAND Journal of Economics* 26, Autumn 1995, 502–18.

Coates, Dennis, "Additional Incumbent Spending Really Can Harm (at Least Some) Incumbents: An Analysis of Vote Share Maximization," *Public Choice* 95, April 1998, 63–87.

Coates, Dennis, "The Effects of Campaign Spending on Electoral Outcomes: A Data Envelopment Analysis," *Public Choice* 99, April 1999, 15–37.

Coates, Dennis and Michael Munger, "Legislative Voting and the Economic Theory of Politics," *Southern Economic Journal* 61, January 1995, 861–72.

Coggins, Jay S. and C. Federico Perali, "64% Majority Rule in Ducal Venice: Voting for the Doge," *Public Choice* 97, December 1998, 709–23.

Cohen, Linda R., "Cyclic Sets in Multidimensional Voting Models," *Journal of Economic Theory* 20, February 1979, 1–2.

Cohen, Linda R. and Roger G. Noll, *The Technology Pork Barrel*, Washington, D.C.: Brookings Institution, 1991.

Coleman, James S., "Foundations for a Theory of Collective Decisions," *American Journal of Sociology* 71(1), May 1966a, 615–27.

Coleman, James S., "The Possibility of a Social Welfare Function," *American Economic Review* 56, December 1966b, 1105–22.

Coleman, James S., "Political Money," *American Political Science Review* 64, December 1970, 1074–87.

Coleman, James S., "Internal Processes Governing Party Positions in Elections," *Public Choice* 11, Fall 1971, 35–60.

Coleman, James S., "The Positions of Political Parties in Elections," in R. G. Niemi and H. F. Weisberg, eds., *Probability Models of Collective Decision-Making*, Columbus: Merrill, 1972.

Coleman, James S., "Recontracting, Trustworthiness, and the Stability of Vote Exchange," *Public Choice* 40(1), 1983, 89–94.

Coleman, Jules L., *Markets, Morals and the Law*, Cambridge: Cambridge University Press, 1988.

Collins, John N. and Bryan T. Downes, "The Effect of Size on the Provision of Public Services: The Case of Solid Waste Collection in Smaller Cities," *Urban Affairs Quarterly* 12, March 1977, 333–47.

Comanor, William S., "The Median Voter Rule and the Theory of Political Choice," *Journal of Public Economics* 5, January/February 1976, 169–77.

Comanor, William S. and Harvey Leibenstein, "Allocative Efficiency, X-Efficiency and the Measurement of Welfare Losses," *Economica* 36, August 1969, 304–9.

Congleton, Roger D., "Evaluating Rent-Seeking Losses: Do the Welfare Gains of Lobbyists Count?" *Public Choice* 56(2), February 1988, 181–4.

Congleton, Roger D., "Campaign Finances and Political Platforms: The Economics of Political Controversy," *Public Choice* 62, August 1989, 101–18.

Congleton, Roger D., "Rational Ignorance, Rational Voter Expectations, and Public Policy: A Discrete Informational Foundation for Fiscal Federalism," *Public Choice* 107, April 2001, 35–64.

Congleton, Roger D. and Randall W. Bennett, "On the Political Economy of State Highway Expenditures: Some Evidence of the Relative Performance of Alternative Public Choice Models," *Public Choice* 84, July 1995, 1–24.

Congleton, Roger D. and Bernard Steunenberg, "Voter Discernment and Entry in Pluralitarian Election," *Public Choice* 95, June 1998, 287–305.

Congressional Quarterly, *Gubernatorial Elections 1787–1997*, Washington, D.C., 1998.

Conn, David, "The Scope of Satisfactory Mechanisms for the Provision of Public Goods," *Journal of Public Economics* 20, March 1983, 249–63.

Conway, Karen Smith and Andrew J. Houtenville, "Do the Elderly 'Vote with Their Feet'?" *Public Choice* 97, December 1998, 663–85.

Cooter, Robert D., *The Strategic Constitution*, Princeton: Princeton University Press, 2000.

Cornes, Richard and Todd Sandler, *The Theory of Externalities, Public Goods and Club Goods*, Cambridge: Cambridge University Press, 1986.

Coughlin, Cletus C., "Domestic Content Legislation: House Voting and the Economics of Regulation," *Economic Inquiry* 23, July 1985, 437–48.

Coughlin, Peter, "Pareto Optimality of Policy Proposals with Probabilistic Voting," *Public Choice* 39(3), 1982, 427–33.

Coughlin, Peter, "Expectations about Voter Choices," *Public Choice* 44(1), 1984, 49–59.

Coughlin, Peter, "Elections and Income Redistribution," *Public Choice* 50(1–3), 1986, 27–99.

Coughlin, Peter, *Probabilistic Voting Theory*, Cambridge: Cambridge University Press, 1992.

Coughlin, Peter, Dennis C. Mueller, and Peter Murrell, "A Model of Electoral Competition with Interest Groups," *Economic Letters* 32, 1990, 307–11.

Coughlin, Peter and Shmuel Nitzan, "Electoral Outcomes with Probabilistic Voting and Nash Social Welfare Maxima," *Journal of Public Economics* 15, 1981a, 113–22.

Coughlin, Peter and Shmuel Nitzan, "Directional and Local Electoral Equilibria with Probabilistic Voting," *Journal of Economic Theory* 24, April 1981b, 226–39.

Courant, Paul N., Edward M. Gramlich, and Daniel L. Rubinfeld, "The Stimulative Effects of Intergovern-mental Grants: Or Why Money Sticks Where It Hits," in P. Mieszkowski and W. H. Oakland, eds., *Fiscal Federalism and Grants-in-Aid*, Washington, D.C.: Urban Institute, 1979, 5–21.

Courant, Paul N., Edward M. Gramlich, and Daniel L. Rubinfeld, "Why Voters Support Tax Limitations Amendments: The Michigan Case," *National Tax Journal* 33, 1980, 1–20.

Courbois, Jean-Pierre, "The Effect of Predatory Rent Seeking on Household Saving and Portfolio Choices: A Cross Section Analysis," *Public Choice* 70, June 1991, 251–65.

Coursey, D. L., Elizabeth Hoffman, and Matthew L. Spitzer, "Fear and Loathing in the Coase Theorem: Experimental Tests Involving Physical Discomfort," *Journal of Legal Studies* 16, January 1987, 217–48.

Cowling, Keith and Dennis C. Mueller, "The Social Costs of Monopoly Power," *Economic Journal* 88, December 1978, 727–48.

Cox, Gary W., "Electoral Equilibrium under Approval Voting," *American Journal of Political Science* 29, 1985, 112–18.

Cox, Gary W., "Electoral Equilibrium under Alternative Voting Systems," *American Journal of Political Science* 31, 1987, 82–108.

Cox, Gary W., *Making Votes Count*, Cambridge: Cambridge University Press, 1997.

Cox, Gary W., "The Empirical Content of Rational Choice Theory," *Journal of Theoretical Politics* 11, 1999, 147–69.

Cox, Gary W. and Richard McKelvey, "A Ham Sandwich Theorem for General Measures," *Social Choice and Welfare* 1, 1984, 75–83.

Cox, Gary W. and Michael C. Munger, "Closeness, Expenditures, and Turnout in the 1988 U.S. House Elections," *American Political Science Review* 83, 1989, 217–31.

Crain, W. Mark and Thomas H. Deaton, "A Note on Political Participation as Consumption Behavior," *Public Choice* 32, Winter 1977, 131–5.

Crain, W. Mark, Thomas H. Deaton, and Robert D. Tollison, "Macroeconomic Determinants of the Vote in Presidential Elections," *Public Finance Quarterly* 6, October 1978, 427–38.

Crain, W. Mark, D. R. Leavens, and L. Abbot, "Voting and Not Voting at the Same Time," *Public Choice* 53, 1987, 221–9.

Crain, W. Mark and Robert D. Tollison, "Campaign Expenditures and Political Competition," *Journal of Law and Economics* 19, April 1976, 177–88.

Crain, W. Mark and Asghar Zardkoohi, "A Test of the Property-Rights Theory of the Firm: Water Utilities in the United States," *Journal of Law and Economics* 21, October 1978, 395–408.

Craven, John, "Liberalism and Individual Preferences," *Theory and Decision* 14, December 1982, 351–60.

Crombez, Christopher, "Legal Procedures in the European Community," *British Journal of Political Science* 26, 1996, 199–228.

Crombez, Christopher, "Policy Making and Commission Appointment in the EU," *Aussenwirtschaft* 52, June 1997, 63–82.

Crozier, Michel, *The Bureaucratic Phenomenon*, Chicago: University of Chicago Press, 1964.

Cukierman, Alex, *Central Bank Strategy, Credibility, and Independence: Theory and Evidence*, Cambridge, MA: MIT Press, 1992.

Cukierman, Alex and Steven B. Webb, "Political Influence on the Central Bank: International Evidence," *World Bank Economic Review* 9, 1995, 397–423.

Cusack, Thomas R., "Partisan Politics and Public Finance: Changes in Public Spending in the Industrialized Countries, 1955–1989," *Public Choice* 91, June 1997, 375–95.

Cyert, Richard M. and James G. March, *A Behavioral Theory of the Firm*, Englewood Cliffs, NJ: Prentice-Hall, 1963.

Dahl, Robert A., *Who Governs? Democracy and Power in an American City*, New Haven: Yale University Press, 1961.

Dahl, Robert A., "The Concept of Power," *Behavioral Science* 2, 1957, 201–15; reprinted in R. Bell, D. V. Edwards, and R. H. Wagner, 1969, 79–93.

Dahlman, Carl J., "The Problem of Externality," *Journal of Law and Economics* 22, April 1979, 141–62.

Daniels, Norman, ed., *Reading Rawls*, New York: Basic Books, 1974.

Darvish, Tikva and Jacob Rosenberg, "The Economic Model of Voter Participation: A Further Test," *Public Choice* 56, February 1988, 185–92.

Das, Sanghamitra and Satye P. Das, "Quantitative Assessment of Tariff Endogeneity," *Economic Letters* 44, 1994, 139–46.

Dasgupta, P., "Well-Being and the Extent of Its Realization in Poor Countries," *Economic Journal* 100, 1990, 1–32.

D'Aspremont, Claude and Louis Gevers, "Equity and the Informational Basis of Collective Choice," *Review of Economic Studies* 44, 1977, 199–209.

Datta, Samar K. and Jeffrey B. Nugent, "Adversary Activities and Per Capita Income Growth," mimeo, University of Southern California, 1985.

Davidson, Audrey B., Elynor D. Davis, and Robert B. Ekelund, Jr., "Public Choice and the Child Labor Statute of 1938: Public Interest or Interest Group Legislation?" *Public Choice* 82, January 1995, 85–106.

Davidson, Chandler and Bernard Grofman, eds., *Quiet Revolution in the South*, Princeton: Princeton University Press, 1994.

Davidson, Lawrence S., Michele Fratianni, and Jürgen von Hagen, "Testing the Satisficing Version of the Political Business Cycle 1905–1984," *Public Choice* 73, January 1992, 21–35.

Davies, David G., "The Efficiency of Public Versus Private Firms: The Case of Australia's Two Airlines," *Journal of Law and Economics* 14, April 1971, 149–65.

Davies, David G., "Property Rights and Economic Efficiency: The Australian Airlines Revisited," *Journal of Law and Economics* 20, April 1977, 223–6.

Davies, David G., "Property Rights and Economic Behavior in Private and Government Enterprises: The Case of Australia's Banking System," *Research in Law and Economics* 3, 1981, 111–42.

Davies, David G. and P. F. Brucato, Jr., "Property Rights and Transaction Costs: Theory and Evidence on Privately-Owned and Government-Owned Enterprises, *Journal of Institutional and Theoretical Economics* 143, March 1987, 7–22.

Dávila, Alberto, José A. Pagán, and Montserrat Viladrich Grau, "Immigration Reform, the INS, and the Distribution of Interior and Border Enforcement Resources," *Public Choice* 99, June 1999, 327–45.

Davis, Douglas D. and Charles A. Holt, *Experimental Economics*, Princeton: Princeton University Press, 1993.

Davis, J. R., "On the Incidence of Income Redistribution," *Public Choice* 8(1), Spring 1970, 63–74.

Davis, Otto A., M. H. DeGroot, and Melvin J. Hinich, "Social Preference Orderings and Majority Rule," *Econometrica* 40, January 1972, 147–57.

Davis, Otto A. and G. H. Haines, Jr., "A Political Approach to a Theory of Public Expenditures: The Case of Municipalities," *National Tax Journal* 19, September 1966, 259–75.

Davis, Otto A., Melvin J. Hinich, and Peter C. Ordeshook, "An Expository Development of a Mathematical Model of the Electoral Process," *American Political Science Review* 64, June 1970, 426–48.

Deacon, Robert T., "Private Choice and Collective Outcomes: Evidence from Public Sector Demand Analysis," *National Tax Journal* 30, December 1977a, 371–86.

Deacon, Robert T., "Review of the Literature on the Demand for Public Services," in National Conference on Nonmetropolitan Community Services Research, paper prepared for U.S. Senate, Committee on

Agriculture, Nutrition and Forestry, 95th Congress, July 12, 1977b, Washington, D.C.: U.S. Government Printing Office, 207–30.

Deacon, Robert T., "A Demand Model for the Local Public Sector," *Review of Economics and Statistics* 60, May 1978, 184–92.

Deacon, Robert T., "The Expenditure Effect of Alternative Public Supply Institutions," *Public Choice* 34(3–4), 1979, 381–98.

de Borda, J. C., *Memorie sur les Elections au Scrutin*, Paris: Historie de l'Academie Royale des Sciences, 1781.

de Condorcet, Marquis, *Essai sur l'Application de L'Analyse à la Probabilité des Décisions Rendues à la Pluraliste des Voix*, Paris, 1785.

de Haan, Jakob and Clemens L. J. Siermann, "A Sensitivity Analysis of the Impact of Democracy on Economic Growth," *Empirical Economics* 20, 1995, 197–215.

de Haan, Jakob and Clemens L. J. Siermann, "Central Bank Inflation and Political Stability in Developing Countries," *Journal of Policy Reform* 1, 1996, 135–47.

de Haan, Jakob and Clemens L. J. Siermann, "Further Evidence on the Relationship between Economic Freedom and Economic Growth," *Public Choice* 95, June 1998, 363–80.

de Haan, Jakob and Jan-Egbert Sturm, "Political and Institutional Determinants of Fiscal Policy in the European Community," *Public Choice* 80, July 1994, 157–72.

de Haan, Jakob and Jan-Egbert Sturm, "On the Relationship between Economic Freedom and Economic Growth," *European Journal of Political Economy* 10, 2000, 215–41.

de Haan, Jakob, Jan-Egbert Sturm, and Geert Beekhuis, "The Weak Government Thesis: Some New Evidence," *Public Choice* 101, December 1999, 163–76.

de Haan, Jakob and Gert Jan van 't Hag, "Variation in Central Bank Independence across Countries: Some Provisional Empirical Evidence," *Public Choice* 85, December 1995, 335–51.

Deininger, K. and L. Squire, "A New Data Set Measuring Income Inequality," *World Bank Economic Review* 10, 1996, 565–91.

de Jasay, Anthony and Hartmut Kliemt, "The Paretian Liberal, His Liberties and His Contracts," *Analyse & Kritik* 18, September 1996, 126–47.

de Jouvenal, B., "The Chairman's Problem," *American Political Science Review* 55, June 1961, 368–72.

Delorme, Charles D., Jr., W. Scott Frame, and David R. Kamerschen, "Empirical Evidence on a Special-Interest-Group Perspective to Antitrust," *Public Choice* 92, 1997, 317–35.

DeMeyer, F. and Charles Plott, "The Probability of a Cyclical Majority," *Econometrica* 38, March 1970, 345–54.

DeMeyer, F. and Charles Plott, "A Welfare Function Using Relative Intensity of Preference," *Quarterly Journal of Economics* 85, February 1971, 179–86.

DeNardo, James, *Power in Numbers: The Political Strategy of Protest and Rebellion*, Princeton: Princeton University Press, 1985.

Dennis, J., "Support for the Institution of Elections by the Mass Public," *American Political Science Review* 64, September 1970, 269–80.

Deno, Kevin T. and Stephen Mehay, "Municipal Management Structure and Fiscal Performance: Do City Managers Make a Difference?" *Southern Economic Journal* 53, January 1987, 627–42.

Denzau, Arthur and Kevin Grier, "Determinants of Local School Spending: Some Consistent Estimates," *Public Choice* 44(2), 1984, 375–83.

Denzau, Arthur and Amoz Kats, "Expected Plurality Voting Equilibrium and Social Choice Functions," *Review of Economic Studies* 44, June 1977, 227–33.

Denzau, Arthur T. and Robert J. Mackay, "Gatekeeping and Monopoly Power of Committees: An Analysis of Sincere and Sophisticated Behavior," *American Journal of Political Science* 27, 1983, 740–61.

Denzau, Arthur and Michael Munger, "Legislators and Interest Groups: How Unorganized Interests Get Represented," *American Political Science Review* 80, 1986, 89–106.

de Palma, A., Gap-Seon Hong, and J.-F. Thisse, "Equilibria in Multi-Party Competition under Uncertainty," *Social Choice and Welfare* 7, 1990, 247–59.

de Swaan, Abram, *Coalition Theories and Cabinet Formations*, Amsterdam: Elsevier, 1973.

de Swaan, Abram, "A Classification of Parties and Party Systems According to Coalitional Options," *European Journal of Political Research* 3, 1975, 361–75.

de Swaan, Abram and Robert J. Mokken, "Testing Coalition Theories: The Combined Evidence," in L. Lewin and E. Vedung, eds., *Politics as Rational Action*, Dordrecht: Reidel, 1980, 199–215.

Detken, Carsten and Manfred Gärtner, "Governments, Trade Unions and the Macroeconomy: An Expository Analysis of the Political Business Cycle," *Public Choice* 73, January 1992, 37–53.

De Vanssay, Xavier and Z. A. Spindler, "Freedom and Growth: Do Constitutions Matter?" *Public Choice* 78, March 1994, 359–72.

Diamond, Peter, "Cardinal Welfare, Individualistic Ethics, and Interpersonal Comparisons of Utility: A Comment," *Journal of Political Economy* 75, October 1967, 765–6.

Diermeier, Daniel, "Rational Choice and the Role of Theory in Political Science," in J. Friedman, ed., 1996, 59–70.

Di Lorenzo, Thomas J. and Ralph Robinson, "Managerial Objectives Subject to Political Market Constraints: Electric Utilities in the U.S.," *Quarterly Review of Economics and Business* 22, Summer 1982, 113–25.

Dinkel, H., *Ein Politisches-Ökonomisches Modell der Bundesrepublik*, Tübingen: J.C.B. Mohr, 1982.

Dixit, Avinash, "Strategic Behavior in Contests," *American Economic Review* 77, December 1987, 891–8.

Dixit, Avinash and Mancur Olson, "Does Voluntary Participation Undermine the Coase Theorem?" *Journal of Public Economics* 76, June 2000, 309–35.

Dodge, David R., "Impact of Tax, Transfer and Expenditure Policies of Government on the Distribution of Personal Income in Canada," *Review of Income and Wealth* 21, March 1975, 1–52.

Dodgson, C. L., *A Method of Taking Votes on More than Two Issues*, 1876; reprinted in Black, 1958, 224–34.

Dougan, William R., "Tariffs and the Economic Theory of Regulation," *Research in Law and Economics* 6, 1984, 187–210.

Dougan, William R. and Michael C. Munger, "The Rationality of Ideology," *Journal of Law and Economics* 32, 1989, 119–42.

Dougan, William R. and James M. Snyder, "Are Rents Fully Dissipated?" *Public Choice* 77, December 1993, 793–813.

Douglas, George W. and James C. Miller, III, *Domestic Airline Regulation: Theory and Policy*, Washington, D.C.: Brookings Institution, 1974.

Dow, Jay K. and James W. Endersby, "Campaign Contributions and Legislative Voting in the California Assembly," *American Politics Quarterly* 22, 1994, 334–53.

Dow, Jay K., James W. Endersby, and Charles E. Menifield, "The Industrial Structure of the California Assembly: Committee Assignments, Economic Interests, and Campaign Contributions," *Public Choice* 94, January 1998, 67–83.

Dowding, Keith and Peter John, "Exiting Behavior under Tiebout Conditions: Towards a Predictive Model," *Public Choice* 88, September 1996, 393–406.

Dowding, Keith, Peter John, and S. Biggs, "Tiebout: A Survey of the Empirical Literature," *Urban Studies* 31, 1994, 767–97.

Downs, Anthony, *An Economic Theory of Democracy*, New York: Harper & Row, 1957.

Downs, Anthony, "In Defense of Majority Voting," *Journal of Political Economy* 69, April 1961, 192–9.

Downs, Anthony, *Inside Bureaucracy*, Boston: Little, Brown, 1967.

Drazen, Allan, *Political Economy in Macroeconomics*, Princeton: Princeton University Press, 2000.

Drèze, Jacques and D. de la Vallée Poussin, "A Tâtonnement Process for Public Goods," *Review of Economic Studies* 38, April 1971, 133–50.

Dryzek, John and Robert E. Goodin, "Risk-Sharing and Social Justice: The Motivational Foundations of the Post-War Welfare State," *British Journal of Political Science* 16, January 1986, 1–34.

Duncombe, William, Jerry Miner, and John Ruggiero, "Empirical Evaluation of Bureaucratic Models of Inefficiency," *Public Choice* 93, October 1997, 1–18.

Durden, Garey C. and Patricia Gaynor, "The Rational Behavior Theory of Voting Participation: Evidence for the 1970 and 1982 Elections," *Public Choice* 53, 1987, 231–42.

Duverger, Maurice, *Political Parties: Their Organization and Activity in the Modern State*, New York: Wiley, 1954.

Dye, Thomas R., "Taxing, Spending and Economic Growth in American States," *Journal of Politics* 42, November 1980, 1085–1107.

Easterly, William and Sergio Rebelo, "Fiscal Policy and Economic Growth: An Empirical Investigation," *Journal of Monetary Economics* 32, December 1993, 417–58.

Eavey, Cheryl L. and Gary J. Miller, "Bureaucratic Agenda Control: Imposition or Bargaining?" *American Political Science Review* 78, September 1984, 719–33.

Eberts, R. W. and T. J. Gronberg, "Jurisdictional Homogeneity and the Tiebout Hypothesis," *Journal of Urban Economics* 10, September 1981, 227–39.

Edel, Matthew and Elliott Sclar, "Taxes, Spending, and Property Values: Supply Adjustment in a Tiebout-Oates Model," *Journal of Political Economy* 82, September/October 1974, 941–54.

Edin, Per-Anders and Henry Ohlsson, "Political Determinants of Budget Deficits: Coalition Effects versus Minority Effects," *European Economic Review* 35, December 1991, 1597–1603.

Edwards, Franklin R. and Barbara J. Stevens, "The Provision of Municipal Sanitation by Private Firms: An Empirical Analysis of the Efficiency of Alternative Market Structures and Regulatory Arrangements," *Journal of Industrial Economics* 27, December 1978, 133–47.

Eichenberger, Reiner and Felix Oberholzer-Gee, "Rational Moralists: The Role of Fairness in Democratic Economic Politics," *Public Choice* 94, January 1997, 191–210.

Eisner, M. A. and K. J. Meier, "Presidential Control Versus Bureaucratic Power," *American Journal of Political Science* 34, 1990, 269–87.

Ekelund, Robert B., Jr., Robert F. Hébert, Robert D. Tollison, Gary M. Anderson, and Audrey B. Davidson, *Sacred Trust: The Medieval Church as an Economic Firm*, Oxford: Oxford University Press, 1996.

Elazar, Daniel J., *American Federalism: A View from the States*, New York: Crowell, 1966.

Election Research Center, *America Votes, 1984*, Washington, D.C., 1985.

Ellickson, Brian, "A Generalization of the Pure Theory of Public Goods," *American Economic Review* 63, June 1973, 417–32.

Elster, Jon, *Political Psychology*, Cambridge: Cambridge University Press, 1993.

Elster, J. and A. Hylland, eds., *Foundations of Social Choice Theory*, Cambridge: Cambridge University Press, 1986.

Elvik, Rune, "Explaining the Distribution of State Funds for National Road Investments between Counties in Norway: Engineering Standards or Vote Trading," *Public Choice* 85, December 1995, 371–88.

Enelow, James M., "An Expanded Approach to Analyzing Policy-Minded Candidates," *Public Choice* 74(4), December 1992, 425–45.

Enelow, James M., "Cycling and Majority Rule," 1997, in D. C. Mueller, ed., 1997a, 149–62.

Enelow, James M. and Melvin J. Hinich, *The Spatial Theory of Voting*, Cambridge: Cambridge University Press, 1984.

Enelow, James M. and Melvin J. Hinich, "A General Probabilistic Spatial Theory of Elections," *Public Choice* 61, May 1989, 101–13.

Enelow, James M. and Melvin J. Hinich, "A Test of the Predictive Dimensions Model in Spatial Voting Theory," *Public Choice* 78, February 1994, 155–69.

Enelow, James M. and David H. Koehler, "Vote Trading in a Legislative Context: An Analysis of Cooperative and Noncooperative Strategic Voting," *Public Choice* 34(2), 1979, 157–75.

Epple, Dennis and Thomas Romer, "Mobility and Redistribution," *Journal of Political Economy* 99, August 1991, 828–58.

Epple, Dennis, Allan Zelenitz, and Michael Visscher, "A Search for Testable Implications of the Tiebout Hypothesis," *Journal of Political Economy* 86, June 1978, 405–25.

Epstein, David and Sharyn O'Halloran, *Delegating Powers*, Cambridge: Cambridge University Press, 1999.

Escarraz, D.R., "Wicksell and Lindahl: Theories of Public Expenditure and Tax Justice Reconsidered," *National Tax Journal* 20, June 1967, 137–48.

Etzioni, Amitai, "The Case for a Multiple Utility Conception," mimeo, George Washington University, 1986.

Fair, Ray C., "The Effect of Economic Events on Votes for President," *Review of Economics and Statistics* 60, May 1978, 159–73.

Fair, Ray C., "The Effect of Economic Events on Votes for President: 1980 Results," *Review of Economics and Statistics* 64, May 1982, 322–5.

Faith, Roger L., D. L. Leavens, and Robert D. Tollison, "Antitrust Pork Barrel," *Journal of Law and Economics* 25, October 1982, 329–42.

Farnham, Paul G., "The Impact of Citizen Influence on Local Government Expenditures," *Public Choice* 64, March 1990, 201–12.

Farquharson, R., *Theory of Voting*, New Haven: Yale University Press, 1969.

Feddersen, Timothy J., Itai Sened, and Stephen G. Wright, "Rational Voting and Candidate Entry under Plurality Rule," *American Journal of Political Science* 34, 1990, 1005–16.

Feenstra, Robert C. and Tracy R. Lewis, "Distributing the Gains from Trade with Incomplete Information," *Economics and Politics* 3, March 1991, 21–39.

Feige, Edgar L., ed., *The Underground Economies*, Cambridge: Cambridge University Press, 1989a.

Feige, Edgar L., "The Meaning and Measurement of the Underground Economy," 1989b, in E. L. Feige, ed., 1989a, 13–56.

Feigenbaum, Susan and Ronald Teeples, "Public versus Private Water Delivery: A Hedonic Cost Approach," *Review of Economics and Statistics* 65, November 1983, 672–8.

Feld, Scott L. and Bernard Grofman, "The Borda Count in n-Dimensional Issue Space," *Public Choice* 59, November 1988, 167–76.

Feld, Scott L., Bernard Grofman, Richard Hartly, Marc Kilgour, Nicholas Miller, and Nicholas Noviello, "The Uncovered Set in Spatial Voting," *Theory and Decision* 23, 1987, 129–55.

Feldman, Alan, "Manipulating Voting Procedures," *Economic Inquiry* 17, July 1979, 452–74.

Ferejohn, John, *Pork Barrel Politics: Rivers and Harbors Legislation, 1947–1968*, Stanford: Stanford University Press, 1974.

Ferejohn, John A., "Incumbent Performance and Electoral Control," *Public Choice* 50(1–3), 1986, 5–25.

Ferejohn, John A. and Morris P. Fiorina, "The Paradox of Not Voting: A Decision Theoretic Analysis," *American Political Science Review* 68, June 1974, 525–36.

Ferejohn, John A. and Morris P. Fiorina, "Closeness Counts Only in Horseshoes and Dancing," *American Political Science Review* 69, September 1975, 920–5.

Ferejohn, John, R. Forsythe, and Roger Noll, "Practical Aspects of the Construction of Decentralized Decision-Making Systems for Public Goods," in C. S. Russell, ed., *Collective Decision Making*, Baltimore: Johns Hopkins University Press, 1979.

Ferejohn, John, Jack N. Rakove, and Jonathan Riley, eds., *Constitutional Culture and Democratic Rule*, Cambridge: Cambridge University Press, 2001.

Ferejohn, John A. and Debra Satz, "Unification, Universalism, and Rational Choice Theory," in J. Friedman, ed., 1996, 71–84.

Ferejohn, John A. and Barry R. Weingast, "Limitation of Statutes: Strategic Statutory Interpretation," *The Georgetown Law Journal* 80, 1992a, 565–82.

Ferejohn, John A. and Barry R. Weingast, "A Positive Theory of Statutory Interpretation," *International Review of Law and Economics* 12, June 1992b, 263–79.

Ferris, J. Stephen and Edwin G. West, "Testing Theories of Real Government Size: U.S. Experience, 1959–89," *Southern Economic Journal* 62, January 1996, 537–53.

Ferris, J. Stephen and Edwin G. West, "The Cost Disease and Government Growth: Qualifications to Baumol," *Public Choice* 89, October 1996, 35–52.

Ferris, J. Stephen and Edwin G. West, "Cost Disease versus Leviathan Explanations of Rising Government Cost: An Empirical Investigation," *Public Choice* 98, March 1999, 307–16.

Fielding, David, "Social and Economic Determinants of English Voter Choice in the 1997 General Election," *Public Choice* 102, March 2000, 271–95.

Figlio, David N., "Political Shirking, Opponent Quality and Electoral Support," *Public Choice* 103, June 2000, 272–84.

Filer, John E., Lawrence W. Kenny, and Rebecca B. Morton, "Voting Laws, Educational Policies, and Minority Turnout," *Journal of Law and Economics* 34, October 1991, 371–93.

Filer, John E., Lawrence W. Kenny, and Rebecca B. Morton, "Redistribution, Income and Voting," *American Journal of Political Science* 37, February 1993, 63–87.

Filimon, Radu, "Asymmetric Information and Agenda Control," *Journal of Public Economics* 17, February 1982, 51–70.

Filippov, Mikhial, Peter C. Ordeshook, and Olga Shvestova, *Designing Federalism: A Theory of Self-Sustainable Federal Institutions*, mimeo, St. Louis: Washington University, 2001.

Findlay, Ronald J. and Stanislaw Wellisz, "Endogenous Tariffs, the Political Economy of Trade Restrictions and Welfare," in J. N. Bhagwati, ed., *Import Competition and Response*, Chicago: University of Chicago Press, 1982.

Findlay, Ronald J. and Stanislaw Wellisz, "Tariffs, Quotas and Domestic Content Protection: Some Political Economy Considerations," *Public Choice* 50(1–3), 1986, 221–42.

Fine, Benjamin J., "Individual Liberalism in a Paretian Society," *Journal of Political Economy* 83, December 1975, 1277–82.

Finger, J. Michael, H. Keith Hall, and Douglas R. Nelson, "The Political Economy of Administered Protection," *American Economic Review* 72, June 1982, 452–66.

Finney, Louis D., "A Rational Choice Theory of Revolution and Political Violence," Ph.D. dissertation, University of Maryland, 1987.

Finsinger, Jörg, "Competition, Ownership and Control in Markets with Imperfect Information: The Case of the German Liability and Life Insurance Markets," mimeo, International Institute of Management, Berlin, 1981.

Finsinger, Jörg, Elizabeth Hammond, and Julian Tapp, *Insurance: Competition or Regulation*, London: Institute for Fiscal Studies, 1985.

Fiorina, Morris P., "The Voting Decision: Instrumental and Expressive Aspects," *Journal of Politics* 38, 1976, 390–415.

Fiorina, Morris P., "An Outline for a Model of Party Choice," *American Journal of Political Science* 21, August 1977a, 601–25.

Fiorina, Morris P., *Congress: Keystone of the Washington Establishment*, New Haven: Yale University Press, 1977b.

Fiorina, Morris P., "Economic Retrospective Voting in American National Elections: A Micro-Analysis," *American Journal of Political Science* 22, May 1978, 426–43.

Fiorina, Morris P., *Retrospective Voting in American National Elections*, New Haven: Yale University Press, 1981.

Fiorina, Morris P., "Legislative Choice of Regulatory Forms: Legal Process or Administrative Process?" *Public Choice* 39, 1982a, 33–66.

Fiorina, Morris P., "Rational Choice, Empirical Contributions, and the Scientific Enterprise," in J. Friedman, ed., 1996, 85–94.

Fiorina, Morris P., "Voting Behaviour," 1997, in D. C. Mueller, ed., 1997a, 391–414.

Fiorina, Morris P. and Charles R. Plott, "Committee Decisions under Majority Rule: An Experimental Study," *American Political Science Review* 72, June 1978, 575–98.

Fisch, Oscar, "Optimal City Size, the Economic Theory of Clubs and Exclusionary Zoning," *Public Choice* 24, Winter 1975, 59–70.

Fischer, A. J., "A Further Experimental Study of Expressive Voting," *Public Choice* 88, July 1996, 171–84.

Fischer, A. J., "The Probability of Being Decisive," *Public Choice* 101, December 1999, 267–83.

Fischer-Menshausen, H., "Entlastung des Staates durch Privatisierung von Aufgaben," *Wirtschaftsdienst* 55, 1975, 545–52.

Fishback, Price V. and Shawn Everett Kantor, "The Adoption of Workers' Compensation in the United States, 1900–1930," *Journal of Law and Economics* 41, October 1998, 305–41.

Fishburn, Peter C., *The Theory of Social Choice*, Princeton: Princeton University Press, 1973.

Fishburn, Peter C. and Steven J. Brams, "Approval Voting, Condorcet's Principle, and Runoff Elections," *Public Choice* 36(1), 1981a, 89–114.

Fishburn, Peter C. and Steven J. Brams, "Efficiency, Power, and Equity under Approval Voting," *Public Choice* 37(3), 1981b, 425–34.

Fishburn, Peter C. and W. V. Gehrlein, "Social Homogeneity and Condorcet's Paradox," *Public Choice* 35(4), 1980, 403–19.

Fisher, I. W. and G. R. Hall, "Risk and Corporate Rates of Return," *Quarterly Journal of Economics* 83, February 1969, 79–92.

Fisher, Joseph, R. Mark Isaac, Jeffrey W. Schatzenberg, and James M. Walker, "Heterogeneous Demand for Public Goods: Behavior in the Voluntary Contributions Mechanism," *Public Choice* 85, December 1995, 249–66.

Fisher, Ronald C., "Income and Grant Effects on Local Expenditure: The Flypaper Effect and Other Difficulties," *Journal of Urban Economics* 12, November 1982, 324–45.

Flatters, Frank, B. Henderson, and Peter Mieszkowski, "Public Goods, Efficiency, and Regional Fiscal Equalization," *Journal of Public Economics* 3, May 1974, 99–112.

Fleming, M., "A Cardinal Concept of Welfare," *Quarterly Journal of Economics* 66, August 1952, 366–84.

Fleurbaey, Marc and Wulf Gaertner, "Admissibility and Feasibility in Game Forms," *Analyse & Kritik* 18, September 1996, 54–66.

Flowers, Marilyn R., "Shared Tax Sources in a Leviathan Model of Federalism," *Public Finance Quarterly* 16, 1988, 67–77.

Fölster, Stefan and Magnus Henrekson, "Growth and the Public Sector: A Critique of the Critics," *European Journal of Political Economy* 15, June 1999, 337–58.

Fölster, Stefan and Magnus Henrekson, "Growth Effects of Government Expenditure and Taxation in Rich Countries," *European Economic Review* 45, August 2001, 1501–20.

Forsyth, P. J. and R. D. Hocking, "Property Rights and Efficiency in a Regulated Environment: The Case of Australian Airlines," *The Economic Record* 56, June 1980, 182–5.

Fort, Rodney D., "The Median Voter, Setters, and Non-Repeated Construction Bond Issues," *Public Choice* 56(3), March 1988, 213–31.

Fort, Rodney, "A Recursive Treatment of the Hurdles to Voting," *Public Choice* 85, October 1995, 45–69.

Fort, Rodney, William Hallagan, Cyril Morong, and Tesa Stegner, "The Ideological Component of Senate Voting: Different Principles of Different Principals," *Public Choice* 76, June 1993, 39–57.

Foster, Carroll B., "The Performance of Rational Voter Models in Recent Presidential Elections," *American Political Science Review* 78, September 1984, 678–90.

Frank, Robert H., *Passions with Reason: The Strategic Role of the Emotions*, New York: Norton, 1988.

Franzese, Robert J., Jr., "Electoral and Partisan Manipulation of Public Debt in Developed Democracies, 1956–90," in R. A. Strauch and J. von Hagen, eds., 2000, 61–83.

Fraser, J., "Political Participation and Income Level: An Exchange," *Public Choice* 13, Fall 1972, 115–18.

Fratianni, M. and F. Spinelli, "The Growth of Government in Italy: Evidence from 1861 to 1979," *Public Choice* 39 1982, 221–43.

Frech, Harry E., III, "The Property Rights Theory of the Firm: Empirical Results from a Natural Experiment," *Journal of Political Economy* 84, February 1976, 143–52.

Frech, Harry E., III, "The Property Rights Theory of the Firm: Some Evidence from the U.S. Nursing Home Industry," *Journal of Institutional and Theoretical Economics* 141, March 1985, 146–66.

Freedom House, "Freedom in the World," *Freedom Review*, New York: Freedom House, 1997.

Frendreis, John P. and Richard W. Waterman, "PAC Contributions and Legislative Behavior: Senate Voting on Trucking Deregulation," *Social Science Quarterly* 66, 1985, 401–12.

Frey, Bruno S., "Why do High Income People Participate More in Politics?" *Public Choice* 11, Fall 1971, 101–5.

Frey, Bruno S., "Political Participation and Income Level: An Exchange, Reply," *Public Choice* 13, Fall 1972, 119–22.

Frey, Bruno S., *International Political Economics*, Oxford: Basil Blackwell, 1984.

Frey, Bruno S., *Internationale Politische Ökonomie*, Munich: Vahlen, 1985.

Frey, Bruno S., *Economics as a Science of Human Behavior*, Dordrecht: Kluwer, 1992.

Frey, Bruno S., "Direct Democracy: Politico-Economic Lessons from Swiss Experience," *American Economic Review* 84, May 1994, 338–42.

Frey, Bruno S., *Not Just for the Money*, Cheltenham: Edgar Elgar, 1997a.

Frey, Bruno S., "A Constitution for Knaves Crowds Out Civic Virtues," *Economic Journal* 107, July 1997b, 1043–53.

Frey, Bruno S. and Reiner Eichenberger, "Competition among Jurisdictions: The Idea of FOCJ," in L. Gerken, ed., *Competition among Institutions*, London: Macmillan, 1995, 209–29.

Frey, Bruno S. and Reiner Eichenberger, *The New Democratic Federalism for Europe*, Cheltenham: Edward Elgar, 1999.

Frey, Bruno S. and L. J. Lau, "Towards a Mathematical Model of Government Behavior," *Zeitschrift für Nationalökonomie* 28, 1968, 355–80.

Frey, Bruno S. and Friedrich Schneider, "An Empirical Study of Politico-Economic Interaction in the U.S.," *Review of Economics and Statistics* 60, May 1978a, 174–83.

Frey, Bruno S. and Friedrich Schneider, "A Politico-Economic Model of the United Kingdom," *Economic Journal* 88, June 1978b, 243–53.

Frey, Bruno S. and Friedrich Schneider, "An Econometric Model with an Endogenous Government Sector," *Public Choice* 34(1), 1979, 29–43.

Frey, Bruno S. and Friedrich Schneider, "A Politico-Economic Model of the U.K.: New Estimates and Predictions," *Economic Journal* 91, September 1981, 737–40.

Frey, Bruno S. and Werner W. Pommerehne, "How Powerful are Public Bureaucrats as Voters?" *Public Choice* 38 1982, 253–62.

Fridstøm, Lasse and Rune Elvik, "The Barely Revealed Preference behind Road Investment Priorities," *Public Choice* 92, July 1997, 145–68.

Friedman, Jeffrey, ed., *The Rational Choice Controversy*, New Haven: Yale University Press, 1996.

Friedrich, Carl J., *Trends of Federation in Theory and Practice*, New York: Prager, 1968.

Frohlich, Norman and Joe A. Oppenheimer, "I Get by with a Little Help from My Friends," *World Politics* 23, October 1970, 104–20.

Frohlich, Norman and Joe A. Oppenheimer, *Choosing Justice: An Experimental Approach to Ethical Theory*, Berkeley: University of California Press, 1992.

Frohlich, Norman, Joe A. Oppenheimer, and Cheryl L. Eavey, "Laboratory Results on Rawls's Distributive Justice," *British Journal of Political Science* 17, January 1987, 1–21.

Frohlich, Norman, Joe A. Oppenheimer, J. Smith, and O. R. Young, "A Test of Downsian Voter Rationality: 1964 Presidential Voting," *American Political Science Review* 72, March 1978, 178–97.

Fuchs, V. R., *The Service Economy,* New York: Columbia University Press, 1968.

Funkhouser, Richard and Paul W. MacAvoy, "A Sample of Observations on Comparative Prices in Public and Private Enterprises, *Journal of Public Economics* 11, June 1979, 353–68.

Furstenberg, George M. von and Dennis C. Mueller, "The Pareto Optimal Approach to Income Redistribution: A Fiscal Application," *American Economic Review* 61, September 1971, 628–37.

Gächter, Simon and Ernst Fehr, "Collective Action as a Partial Social Exchange," mimeo, University of Zürich, 1997.

Gärtner, Manfred, "Democracy, Elections and Macroeconomic Policy: Two Decades of Progress," *European Journal of Political Economy* 10, May 1994, 85–109.

Gärtner, Manfred, "Political Macroeconomics: A Survey of Recent Developments," *Journal of Economic Surveys* 14, December 2000, 527–61.

Gaertner, Wulf, Prasanta K. Pattanaik, and Kotaro Suzumura, "Individual Rights Revisited," *Economica* 59, May 1992, 161–77.

Gardner, Bruce L., "The United States," in F. H. Sanderson, ed., 1990, 19–63.

Gardner, Grant W. and Kent P. Kimbrough, "The Behavior of U.S. Tariff Rates," *American Economic Review* 79, March 1989, 11–18.

Garman, M. B. and Morton I. Kamien, "The Paradox of Voting: Probability Calculations," *Behavioral Science* 13, July 1968, 306–17.

Garrett, Thomas A., "A Test of Shirking under Legislative and Citizen Vote: The Case of State Lottery Adoption," *Journal of Law and Economics* 42, April 1999, 189–208.

Gauthier, David, *Morals by Agreement*, Oxford: Oxford University Press, 1986.

Gehrlein, W. V. and Peter C. Fishburn, "Condorcet's Paradox and Anonymous Preference Profiles," *Public Choice* 26, Summer 1976a, 1–18.

Gehrlein, W. V. and Peter C. Fishburn, "The Probability of the Paradox of Voting: A Computable Solution," *Journal of Economic Theory* 13, August 1976b, 14–25.

Gibbard, Allan, "Intransitive Social Indifference and the Arrow Dilemma," mimeo, 1969.

Gibbard, Allan, "Manipulation of Voting Schemes: A General Result," *Econometrica* 41, July 1973, 587–602.

Gibbard, Allan, "A Pareto-Consistent Libertarian Claim," *Journal of Economic Theory* 7, April 1974, 388–410.

Gibbard, Allan, "Manipulation of Schemes that Combine Voting with Chance," *Econometrica* 45, April 1977, 665–8.

Gibson, John, "Equity Concerns and the Political Economy of Protection in New Zealand," *Public Choice* 77, October 1993, 323–32.

Giersch, Herbert, Karl-Heinz Paque, and Holger Schmieding, *The Fading Miracle*, Cambridge: Cambridge University Press, 1994.

Giertz, J. Fred, "A Limited Defense of Pareto Optimal Redistribution," *Public Choice* 39(2), 1982, 277–82.

Gillespie, W. I., "Effect of Public Expenditures on the Distribution of Income," in Richard A. Musgrave, ed., *Essays in Fiscal Federalism*, Washington, D.C.: Brookings Institution, 1965, 122–86.

Gillespie, W. I., "On the Redistribution of Income in Canada," *Canadian Tax Journal* 24, July/August 1976, 419–50.

Gillette, Clayton P., "The Exercise of Trumps by Decentralized Governments," *Virginia Law Review* 83, October 1997, 1347–417.

Gist, John R. and R. Carter Hill, "The Economics of Choice in the Allocation of Federal Grants: An Empirical Test," *Public Choice* 36(1), 1981, 63–73.

Glaeser, Edward L., David I. Laibson, José A. Scheinkman, and Christine L. Soutter, "Measuring Trust," *Quarterly Journal of Economics* 115, August 2000, 811–46.

Glantz, Stanton A., Alan I. Abramowitz, and Michael P. Burkart, "Election Outcomes: Whose Money Matters?" *Journal of Politics* 38, November 1976, 1033–8.

Glashan, R., *American Governors and Gubernatorial Elections, 1775–1978*, Westport: Meckler Books, 1979.

Glazer, Amihai and Bernard Grofman, "Why Representatives Are Ideologists Though Voters Are Not," *Public Choice* 61, April 1989, 29–39.

Glazer, Amihai and Susanne Lohman, "Setting the Agenda: Electoral Competition, Commitment of Policy, and Issue Salience," *Public Choice* 99, June 1999, 377–94.

Godek, Paul E., "Industry Structure and Redistribution through Trade Restrictions," *Journal of Law and Economics* 28, 1985, 687–703.

Goel, Rajeev K. and Michael A. Nelson, "Corruption and Government Size: A Disaggregated Analysis," *Public Choice* 97, October 1998, 107–20.

Goff, Brian L. and Kevin B. Grier, "On the (Mis)measurement of Legislator Ideology and Shirking," *Public Choice* 76, June 1993, 5–20.

Goldberg, Pinelopi Koujianou and Giovanni Maggi, "Protection for Sale: An Empirical Investigation," *American Economic Review* 89(5), December 1999, 1135–55.

Goldsmith, Arthur A., "Democracy, Political Stability, and Economic Growth in Developing Countries," *Comparative Political Studies* 18, January 1986, 517–31.

Golen, D. G. and James M. Poterba, "The Price of Popularity: The Political Business Cycle Reexamined," *American Journal of Political Science* 24, 1980, 696–714.

Gollop, F. M. and D. W. Jorgenson, "U. S. Productivity Growth in Industries, 1947–73," in J. W. Kendrick and B. B. Vaccara, eds., *New Developments in Productivity Measurement and Analysis,* Chicago: University of Chicago Press, 1980, 17–124.

Good, I. J. and L. S. Mayer, "Estimating the Efficacy of a Vote," *Behavioral Science* 20, 1975, 25–33.

Goodin, Robert E., *Reasons for Welfare*, Princeton: Princeton University Press, 1988.

Goodin, Robert E. and K. W. S. Roberts, "The Ethical Voter," *American Political Science Review* 69, September 1975, 926–8.

Goodman, S. F., *The European Union*, 3rd ed., London: Macmillan, 1996.

Goodman, Samuel and Gerald H. Kramer, "Comment on Arcelus and Meltzer," *American Political Science Review* 69, December 1975, 1277–85.

Goss, C. F., "Military Committee Membership and Defense-Related Benefits in the House of Representatives," *Western Political Quarterly* 25, 1972, 215–61.

Gough, J. W., *The Social Contract*, 2nd ed., Oxford: Clarendon Press, 1957.

Gouveia, Miguel, "Majority Rule and the Public Provision of a Private Good," *Public Choice* 93, December 1997, 221–44.

Gouveia, Miguel and Neal A. Masia, "Does the Median Voter Model Explain the Size of Government?: Evidence from the States," *Public Choice* 97, October 1998, 159–77.

Gradstein, Mark, "Optimal Contest Design: Volume and Timing of Rent Seeking Contests," *European Journal of Political Economy* 14, November 1998, 575–85.

Gramlich, Edward M., "The Effects of Grants on State-Local Expenditures: A Review of the Econometric Literature," National Tax Association, *Proceedings of the Sixty-Second Annual Conference on Taxation*, 1969 (1970), 569–93.

Gramlich, Edward M., "Intergovernmental Grants: A Review of the Empirical Literature," in W. Oates, ed., *The Political Economy of Fiscal Federalism*, Lexington, MA: Lexington Books, 1977, 219–39.

Gramlich, Edward M. and Harvey Galper, "State and Local Fiscal Behavior and Federal Grant Policy," *Brookings Papers on Economic Activity* 1, 1973, 15–58.

Gramlich, Edward M. and D. Laren, "Migration and Income Redistribution Responsibilities," *Journal of Human Resources* 19, 1984, 489–511.

Gramlich, Edward M. and Daniel L. Rubinfeld, "Micro Estimates of Public Spending Demand Functions and Tests of the Tiebout and Median-Voter Hypothesis," *Journal of Political Economy* 90, June 1982a, 536–60.

Gramlich, Edward M. and Daniel L. Rubinfeld, "Voting on Spending," *Journal of Policy Analysis and Management* 1, Summer 1982b, 516–33.

Gray, Virginia and David Lowery, "Interest Group Politics and Economic Growth in the American States: Testing the Olson Construct," mimeo, University of North Carolina, Chapel Hill, 1986.

Green, Donald P. and Ian Shapiro, *Pathologies of Rational Choice Theory*, New Haven: Yale University Press, 1994.

Green, Jerry and Jean-Jaques Laffont, "Characterization of Satisfactory Mechanisms for the Revelation of Preferences for Public Goods," *Econometrica* 45, March 1977a, 427–38.

Green, Jerry and Jean-Jacques Laffont, "Imperfect Personal Information and the Demand Revealing Process: A Sampling Approach," *Public Choice* 29-2 (special supplement), Spring 1977b, 79–94.

Green, Jerry and Jean-Jacques Laffont, *Incentives in Public Decision-Making*, Amsterdam: North-Holland, 1979.

Greenberg, Joseph, "Consistent Majority Rule over Compact Sets of Alternatives," *Econometrica* 47, 1979, 627–36.

Greenberg, Joseph, Robert Mackay, and T. Nicolaus Tideman, "Some Limitations of the Groves-Ledyard Optimal Mechanism," *Public Choice* 29-2 (special supplement), Spring 1977, 129–37.

Greenberg, Joseph and Shlomo Weber, "Multiparty Equilibria under Proportional Representation," *American Political Science Review* 81, 1985, 525–38.

Greene, Kenneth V. and Brian K. Hawley, "Personal Income Taxes, Elasticities and Fiscal Illusion," *Public Choice* 72, December 1991, 101–11.

Greene, Kenneth V. and Oleg Nikolaev, "Voter Participation and the Redistributive State," *Public Choice* 98, January 1999, 213–26.

Grenzke, Janet M., "PACs and the Congressional Supermarket: The Currency is Complex," *American Journal of Political Science* 34, 1989, 1–24.

Grier, Kevin B., "Presidential Elections and Federal Reserve Policy: An Empirical Test," *Southern Economic Journal* 54, 1987, 475–86.

Grier, Kevin B., "On the Existence of a Political Monetary Cycle," *American Journal of Political Science* 33, 1989a, 376–489.

Grier, Kevin B., "Campaign Spending and Senate Elections, 1978–84," *Public Choice* 63, December 1989b, 201–19.

Grier, Kevin B., "Congressional Influence on U.S. Monetary Policy," *Journal of Monetary Economics* 28, 1991, 201–20.

Grier, Kevin B., "Congressional Oversight Committee Influence on U.S. Monetary Policy Revisited," *Journal of Monetary Economics* 38, 1996, 571–9.

Grier, Kevin B. and Joseph P. McGarrity, "The Effect of Macroeconomic Fluctuations on the Electoral Fortunes of House Incumbents," *Journal of Law and Economics* 41, April 1998, 143–63.

Grier, Kevin B. and Michael C. Munger, "Committee Assignments, Constituent Preferences, and Campaign Contributions," *Economic Inquiry* 29, January 1991, 24–43.

Grier, Kevin B., Michael C. Munger, and Gary M. Torrent, "Allocation Patterns of PAC Monies: The U.S. Senate," *Public Choice* 67, November 1990, 111–28.

Grier, Kevin B. and Gordon Tullock, "An Empirical Analysis of Cross-National Economic Growth, 1951–80," *Journal of Monetary Economics* 24, 1989, 259–76.

Grilli, Vittorio, Masciandaro Dourato, and Guido Tabellini, "Political and Monetary Institutions and Public Financial Policies in the Industrial Countries," *Economic Policy* 6(2), October 1991, 343–92.

Grofman, Bernard, ed., *Information, Participation, and Choice*, Ann Arbor: University of Michigan Press, 1993a.

Grofman, Bernard, "Is Turnout the Paradox That Ate Rational Choice Theory?" 1993b, in B. Grofman, ed., 1993a, 93–103.

Grofman, Bernard, Christian Collet, and Robert Griffin, "Analyzing the Turnout-Competition Link with Aggregate Cross-Sectional Data," *Public Choice* 95, June 1998, 233–46.

Grofman, Bernard, Sung-Chull Lee, Edwin A. Winckler, and Brian Woodall, eds., *Elections in Japan, Korea, and Taiwan under the Single Non-Transferable Vote*, Ann Arbor: University of Michigan Press, 1999.

Grofman, Bernard and Arend Lijphart, eds., *Electoral Laws and Their Political Consequences*, New York: Agathon Press, 1986.

Grofman, Bernard, Guillermo Owen, and Scott L. Feld, "Thirteen Theorems in Search of the Truth," *Theory and Decision* 15, 1983, 261–78.

Grofman, Bernard and Andrew Reynolds, "Electoral Systems and the Art of Constitutional Engineering: An Inventory of Main Findings," in R. Mudambi, P. Navarra, and G. Sobbrio, eds., *Rules and Reasons: Perspectives on Constitutional Political Economy*, Cambridge: Cambridge University Press, 2001.

Grofman, Bernard and Peter van Roozendaal, "Review Article: Modeling Cabinet Durability and Termination," *British Journal of Political Science* 27, July 1997, 419–51.

Grossman, Gene M. and Elhanan Helpman, "Protection for Sale," *American Economic Review* 84(4), September 1994, 833–50.

Grossman, Gene M. and Elhanan Helpman, "Electoral Competition and Special Interest Politics," *Review of Economic Studies* 63, April, 1996, 265–86.

Grossman, Gene M. and Elhanan Helpman, *Special Interest Politics,* Cambridge MA: MIT Press, 2001.

Grossman, Philip J., "The Optimal Size of Government," *Public Choice* 53, 1987, 131–47.

Grossman, Philip J., "Government and Economic Growth: A Nonlinear Relationship," *Public Choice* 56, February 1988a, 193–200.

Grossman, Philip J., "Growth in Government and Economic Growth: The Australian Experience," *Australian Economic Papers* 27, June 1988b, 33–43.

Grossman, Philip J., "Federalism and the Size of Government," *Southern Economic Journal* 55, January 1989a, 580–93.

Grossman, Philip J., "Fiscal Decentralization and Government Size: An Extension," *Public Choice* 62, 1989b, 63–70.

Grossman, Philip J., "Government and Growth: Cross-Sectional Evidence," *Public Choice* 65, June 1990, 217–27.

Grossman, Philip J. and Edwin G. West, "Federalism and the Growth of Government Revisited," *Public Choice* 79, April 1994, 19–32.

Groves, Theodore, "Incentives in Teams," *Econometrica* 41, July 1973, 617–31.

Groves, Theodore, "Efficient Collective Choice When Compensation is Possible," *Review of Economic Studies* 46, April 1979, 227–41.

Groves, Theodore and John O. Ledyard, "Optimal Allocation of Public Goods: A Solution to the 'Free Rider' Problem," *Econometrica* 45, May 1977a, 783–809.

Groves, Theodore and John O. Ledyard, "Some Limitations of Demand Revealing Processes," *Public Choice* 29, Spring 1977b, 107–24.

Groves, Theodore and John O. Ledyard, "Reply," ibid., 1977c, 139–43.

Groves, Theodore and Martin Loeb, "Incentives and Public Inputs," *Journal of Public Economics* 4, August 1975, 211–26.

Grubb, W. N., "The Dynamic Implications of the Tiebout Model – the Changing Composition of Boston Communities, 1960–1970," *Public Finance Quarterly* 10, 1982, 17–38.

Güth, Werner, Rolf Schmittberger, and Bernd Schwarze, "An Experimental Analysis of Ultimatum Bargaining," *Journal of Economic Behavior and Decision* 3, 1982, 367–88.

Güth, Werner and Reinhard Tietz, "Ultimatum Bargaining for a Shrinking Cake: An Experimental Analysis," in R. Tietz, W. Albers, and R. Selten, eds., *Bounded Rational Behavior in Experimental Games and Markets*, Berlin: Springer, 1988.

Güth, Werner and Reinhard Tietz, "Ultimatum Bargaining Behaviour: A Survey and Comparison of Experimental Results," *Journal of Economic Psychology* 11, 1990, 417–49.

Gugler, Klaus, "Corporate Ownership Structure in Austria," *Empirica* 25(3), 1998, 285–307.

Guha, A. S., "Neutrality, Monotonicity and the Right of Veto," *Econometrica* 40, September 1972, 821–6.

Gunning, J. Patrick, "An Economic Approach to Riot Analysis," *Public Choice* 13, Fall 1972, 31–46.

Gustafsson, Agne, "Rise and Decline of Nations: Sweden," *Scandinavian Political Studies* 9, March 1986, 35–50.

Haas, J., *The Evolution of the Prehistoric State*, New York: Columbia University Press, 1982.

Haefele, Edwin T., "A Utility Theory of Representative Government," *American Economic Review* 61, June 1971, 350–67.

Hagen, Jürgen von, *Budgeting Procedures and Fiscal Performance in the European Communities*, Brussels: EEC, 1992.

Hall, J. and Bernard Grofman, "The Committee Assignment Process and the Conditional Nature of Committee Bias," *American Political Science Review* 84, 1990, 1149–66.

Hallett, George H., Jr., "Proportional Representation with the Single Transferable Vote: A Basic Requirement for Legislative Elections," in A. Lijphart and B. Grofman, eds., 1984, 113–25.

Hamburger Senat, *Abschlußbericht des Beauftragten zur Gebäudereinigung*, Hamburg, 1974.

Hamilton, Bruce W., "The Effects of Property Taxes and Local Public Spending on Property Values: A Theoretical Comment," *Journal of Political Economy* 84, June 1976, 647–50.

Hamilton, Bruce W., "The Flypaper Effect of Property Taxes and Local Public Spending on Property Values: A Theoretical Comment," *Journal of Public Economics* 22, December 1983, 347–61.

Hamilton, Bruce W., Edwin S. Mills, and David Puryear, "The Tiebout Hypothesis and Residential Income Segregation," in E. S. Mills and W. E. Oates, eds., *Fiscal Zoning and Land Use Controls*, Lexington: Lexington Books, 1975, 101–18.

Hamlin, Alan, *Ethics, Economics and the State*, New York: St. Martin's Press, 1986.

Hamlin, Alan and Michael Hjortlund, "Proportional Representation with Citizen Candidates," *Public Choice* 103, June 2000, 205–30.

Hammond, Peter J., "Why Ethical Measures of Inequality Need Interpersonal Comparisons," *Theory and Decision* 7, October 1976, 263–74.

Hammond, Thomas H. and Gary J. Miller, "The Core of the Constitution," *American Political Science Review* 81, 1987, 1155–74.

Hansen, J. M., "Taxation and the Political Economy of the Tariff," *International Organization* 44, 1990, 527–52.

Hansen, Stephen, Thomas R. Palfrey, and Howard Rosenthal, "The Downsian Model of Electoral Participation: Formal Theory and Empirical Analysis of the Constituency Effect," *Public Choice* 52, 1987, 15–33.

Hansson, Åsa and Charles Stuart, "Peaking of Fiscal Sizes of Government," *European Journal of Political Economy*, forthcoming.

Hansson, B., "The Independence Condition in the Theory of Choice," *Theory and Decision* 4, September 1973, 25–49.

Hansson, Ingemar and Charles Stuart, "Voting Competitions with Interested Politicians: Platforms Do Not Converge to the Preferences of the Median Voter," *Public Choice* 44(3), 1984, 431–41.

Hansson, Pär and Magnus Henrekson, "A New Framework for Testing the Effect of Government Spending on Growth and Productivity," *Public Choice* 81, December 1994, 381–401.

Hardin, Russell, "Collective Action as an Agreeable n-Prisoners' Dilemma," *Behavioral Science* 16, September 1971, 472–81.

Hardin, Russell, *Collective Action*, Baltimore: Johns Hopkins University Press, 1982.

Hardin, Russell, *Morality within the Limits of Reason*, Chicago: University of Chicago Press, 1988.

Hardin, Russell, "Why a Constitution?" in B. Grofman and D. Wittman, eds., *The Federalist Papers and the New Institutionalism*, New York: Agathon Press, 1989, 100–20.

Hardin, Russell, "Contractarianism: Wistful Thinking," *Constitutional Political Economy* 1(2), Spring/Summer 1990, 35–52.

Hardin, Russell, "Economic Theories of the State," 1997, in D. C. Mueller, ed., 1997a, 21–34.

Hare, R. M., "Rawls' Theory of Justice," *Philosophical Quarterly* 23, April 1973, 144–55; reprinted in N. Daniels, ed., 1974, 81–107.

Harel, A. and Shmuel Nitzan, "The Libertarian Resolution of the Paretian Paradox," *Zeitschrift für Nationalökonomie* 47, 1987, 337–52.

Harper, Richard K. and John Aldrich, "The Political Economy of Sugar Legislation," *Public Choice* 70, June 1991, 299–314.

Harrington, Joseph E., Jr., "The Power of the Proposal Maker in a Model of Endogenous Agenda Formation," *Public Choice* 64, January 1990, 1–20.

Harrison, Glenn W. and Jack Hirshleifer, "Experiments Testing Weakest-Link/Best-Shot Models for Provision of Public Goods," UCLA Working Paper 372A, February 1986.

Harrison, Glenn W. and Michael McKee, "Experimental Evaluation of the Coase Theorem," *Journal of Law and Economics* 28, October 1985, 653–70.

Harsanyi, John C., "Cardinal Utility in Welfare Economics and in the Theory of Risk-Taking," *Journal of Political Economics* 61, October 1953, 434–5.

Harsanyi, John C., "Cardinal Welfare, Individualistic Ethics, and Interpersonal Comparisons of Utility," *Journal of Political Economics* 63, August 1955, 309–21; reprinted in K. J. Arrow and T. Scitovsky, 1969, 46–60.

Harsanyi, John C., "Can the Maximin Principle Serve as a Basis for Morality? A Critique of John Rawls' Theory," *American Political Science Review* 69, June 1975a, 594–606.

Harsanyi, John C., "Nonlinear Social Welfare Functions," *Theory and Decision* 6, August 1975b, 311–32.

Harsanyi, John C., *Rational Behavior and Bargaining Equilibrium in Games and Social Situations*, Cambridge: Cambridge University Press, 1977.

Harstad, R. M. and M. Marrese, "Behavioral Explanations of Efficient Public Good Allocations," *Journal of Public Economics* 19, December 1982, 367–83.

Hart, H. L. A., "Rawls on Liberty and Its Priority," *University of Chicago Law Review* 40, Spring 1973, 534–55; reprinted in N. Daniels, ed., 1974, 230–52.

Havrilesky, Thomas M., "A Partisanship Theory of Fiscal and Monetary Regimes," *Journal of Money, Credit and Banking* 19, 1987, 308–25.

Havrilesky, Thomas M., *The Pressures of American Monetary Policy*, Boston, MA: Kluwer, 1993.

Havrilesky, Thomas M. and James Granato, "Determinants of Inflationary Performance: Corporatist Structures vs. Central Bank Autonomy," *Public Choice* 76, July 1993, 249–61.

Hayami, Yujiro, "Japan," in F. H. Sanderson, ed., 1990, 181–218.

Hayes, Kathy J., Laura Razzolini, and Leola B. Ross, "Bureaucratic Choice and Nonoptimal Provision of Public Goods: Theory and Evidence," *Public Choice* 94, January 1998, 1–20.

Hayes, Kathy J. and L. L. Wood, "Utility Maximizing Bureaucrats: The Bureau's Point of View," *Public Choice* 82, January 1995, 69–83.

Haynes, S. A. and J. A. Stone, "An Integrated Test for Electoral Cycles in the US Economy," *Review of Economics and Statistics* 71, 1989, 426–34.

Head, J. G., "Public Goods and Public Policy," *Public Finance* 17, 1962, 197–221.

Head, J. G., "Lindahl's Theory of the Budget," *Finanzarchiv* 23, October 1964, 421–54.

Heckelman, Jac C., "The Effect of the Secret Ballot on Voter Turnout Rates," *Public Choice* 82(1–2), January 1995, 107–24.

Heckelman, Jac C., "Revisiting the Relationship between Secret Ballots and Turnout," *American Politics Quarterly* 28, April 2000a, 194–215.

Heckelman, Jac C., "Consistent Estimates of the Impact of Special Interest Groups on Economic Growth," *Public Choice* 104, September 2000b, 319–27.

Heckelman, Jac C., "The Econometrics of Rational Partisan Theory," *Applied Economics* 33, 2001, 417–26.

Heckelman, Jac C. and Michael D. Stroup, "Which Economic Freedoms Contribute to Growth?" *Kyklos* 53, 2000, 527–44.

Helland, Leif, "Fiscal Constitutions, Fiscal Preferences, Information and Deficits: An Evaluation of 13 West-European Countries 1978–95," in R. A. Strauch and J. von Hagen, eds., 2000, 107–38.

Henderson, J. V., "Theories of Group, Jurisdiction, and City Size," in P. Mieszkowski and M. Straszheim, eds., *Current Issues in Urban Economics*, Baltimore: Johns Hopkins University Press 1979, 235–69.

Henrekson, M. "Swedish Government Growth: A Disequilibrium Analysis," in J. A. Lybeck and M. Henrekson, eds., *Explaining the Growth of Government*, Amsterdam: North-Holland, 1988, 93–132.

Henrekson, Magnus, "The Peacock and Wiseman Displacement Effect," *European Journal of Political Economy* 6, 1990, 245–60.

Hermens, Ferdinand A., *Demokratie und Wahlrecht*, Paderborn, Germany: Schöning, 1933.

Hermens, Ferdinand A., *Democracy or Anarchy?* Notre Dame, IN: University of Notre Dame Press, 1941.

Hermens, Ferdinand A., *Europe between Democracy and Anarchy*, Notre Dame, In: University of Notre Dame Press, 1951.

Hermsen, Hanneke and Albert Verbeek, "Equilibria in Multi-party Systems," *Public Choice* 73, March 1992, 147–65.

Hersch, Philip L. and Gerald S. McDougall, "Determinants of Automobile PAC Contributions to House Incumbents: Own *Versus* Rival Effects," *Public Choice* 104, September 2000, 329–43.

Hettich, Walter and Stanley L. Winer, "A Positive Model of Tax Structure," *Journal of Public Economics* 24, 1984, 67–87.

Hettich, Walter and Stanley L. Winer, "Economic and Political Foundations of Tax Structure," *American Economic Review* 78, September 1988, 701–12.

Hettich, Walter and Stanley L. Winer, "The Political Economy of Taxation," 1997, in D. C. Mueller, ed., 1997a, 481–505.

Hettich, Walter and Stanley L. Winer, *Democratic Choice and Taxation*, Cambridge: Cambridge University Press, 1999.

Heyndels, Bruno and Carine Smolders, "Fiscal Illusion at the Local Level: Empirical Evidence for the Flemish Municipalities," *Public Choice* 80, September 1994, 325–38.

Heyndels, Bruno and Carine Smolders, "Tax Complexity and Fiscal Illusion," *Public Choice* 85, October 1995, 127–41.

Hibbing, John R., "On the Issues Surrounding Economic Voting: Looking to the British Case for Answers," *Comparative Political Studies* 20, April 1987, 3–33.

Hibbs, Douglas A., Jr., "Political Parties and Macroeconomic Policy," *American Political Science Review* 71, December 1977, 1467–87.

Hibbs, Douglas A., Jr., "The Mass Public and Macroeconomic Performance: The Dynamics of Public Opinion toward Unemployment and Inflation," *American Journal of Political Science* 23, November 1979, 705–31.

Hibbs, Douglas A., Jr., "Economics and Politics in France: Economic Performance and Mass Political Support for Presidents Pompidou and Giscard d'Estaing," *European Journal of Political Research* 9, 1981, 133–45.

Hibbs, Douglas A., Jr., "The Dynamics of Political Support for American Presidents among Occupational and Partisan Groups," *American Journal of Political Science* 26, May 1982a, 312–32.

Hibbs, Douglas A., Jr., "Economic Outcomes and Political Support for British Governments among Occupational Classes: A Dynamic Analysis," *American Political Science Review* 76, June 1982b, 259–79.

Hibbs, Douglas A., Jr., "On the Demand for Economic Outcomes: Macroeconomic Performance and Mass Political Support in the United States, Great Britain, and Germany," *Journal of Politics* 44, May 1982c, 426–62.

Hibbs, Douglas A., Jr., "Political Parties and Macroeconomic Policies and Outcomes in the United States," *American Economic Review* 76, May 1986, 66–70.

Hibbs, Douglas A., Jr., *The Political Economy of Industrial Democracies*, Cambridge, MA: Harvard University Press, 1987.

Hibbs, Douglas A., Jr., "Partisan Theory after Fifteen Years," *European Journal of Political Economy* 8, October 1992, 361–73.

Hibbs, Douglas A., Jr., "The Partisan Model of Macroeconomic Cycles: More Theory and Evidence for the United States," *Economics and Politics* 6, March 1994, 1–23.

Hibbs, Douglas A., Jr., "Bread and Peace Voting in U.S. Presidential Elections," *Public Choice* 104, July 2000, 149–80.

Hibbs, Douglas A., Jr. and Heino Fassbender, eds., *Contemporary Political Economy*, Amsterdam: North-Holland, 1981.

Hicks, John, "Structural Unemployment and Economic Growth: A 'Labor Theory of Value'," in D. C. Mueller, ed., 1983, 53–6.

Higgs, Robert, "Do Legislators' Votes Reflect Constituency Preference? A Simple Way to Evaluate the Senate," *Public Choice* 63, November 1989, 175–81.

Hildreth, C., "Alternative Conditions for Social Orderings," *Econometrica* 21, January 1953, 81–94.

Hillman, Arye L., "Declining Industries and Political-Support Protectionist Motives," *American Economic Review* 72, 1982, 1180–7.

Hillman, Arye L., *The Political Economy of Protection*, Chur/New York: Harwood Academic Publishers, 1989.

Hillman, Arye L. and Eliakim Katz, "Risk-Averse Rent Seekers and the Social Cost of Monopoly Power," *Economic Journal* 94, March 1984, 104–10.

Hillman, Arye L. and John G. Riley, "Politically Contestable Rents and Transfers," *Economics and Politics* 1, Spring 1989, 17–39.

Hillman, Arye L. and Dov Samet, "Dissipation of Contestable Rents by a Small Number of Contenders," *Public Choice* 54(1), 1987, 63–82.

Hillman, Arye L. and Heinrich W. Ursprung, "Domestic Politics, Foreign Interests and International Trade Policy," *American Economic Review* 78(4), September 1988, 729–45.

Hillman, Arye L. and Heinrich W. Ursprung, "Political Culture and Economic Decline," *European Journal of Political Economy* 16, June 2000, 189–213.

Hines, James R., Jr. and Richard H. Thaler, "Anomolies: The Flypaper Effect," *Journal of Economic Perspectives* 9, Fall 1995, 217–26.

Hinich, Melvin J., "Equilibrium in Spatial Voting: The Median Voter Result Is an Artifact," *Journal of Economic Theory* 16, December 1977, 208–19.

Hinich, Melvin J., John O. Ledyard, and Peter C. Ordeshook, "Nonvoting and the Existence of Equilibrium under Majority Rule," *Journal of Economic Theory* 4, April 1972, 144–53.

Hinich, Melvin J., John O. Ledyard, and Peter C. Ordeshook, "A Theory of Electoral Equilibrium: A Spatial Analysis Based on the Theory of Games," *Journal of Politics* 35, February 1973, 154–93.

Hinich, Melvin J. and Michael C. Munger, "Political Investment, Voter Perceptions, and Candidate Strategy: An Equilibrium Spatial Analysis," in P. C. Ordeshook, ed., *Models of Strategic Choice in Politics*, Ann Arbor: University of Michigan Press, 1989.

Hinich, Melvin J. and Michael C. Munger, *Ideology and the Theory of Political Choice*, Ann Arbor: University of Michigan Press, 1994.

Hinich, Melvin J. and Peter C. Ordeshook, "Plurality Maximization vs. Vote Maximization: A Spatial Analysis with Variable Participation," *American Political Science Review* 64, September 1970, 772–91.

Hinich, Melvin J. and Walker Pollard, "A New Approach to the Spatial Theory of Electoral Competition," *American Journal of Political Science* 25, 1981, 323–41.

Hirsch, Werner Z., "Cost Functions of Urban Government Services: Refuse Collection," *Review of Economics and Statistics* 47, February 1965, 87–92.

Hirschman, Albert O., *Exit, Voice, and Loyalty*, Cambridge, MA: Harvard University Press, 1970.

Hirschman, Albert O., "The Turn to Authoritarianism in Latin America and the Search for Its Economic Determinants," in D. Collier, ed., *The New Authoritarianism in Latin America*, Princeton, NJ: Princeton University Press, 1979, 61–98.

Hirshleifer, Jack, "The Private and Social Value of Information and the Reward to Inventive Activity," *American Economic Review* 61, September 1971, 561–574.

Hirshleifer, Jack, "From Weakest-Link to Best-Shot: The Voluntary Provision of Public Goods," *Public Choice* 41(3), 1983, 371–86.

Hirshleifer, Jack, "The Voluntary Provision of Public Goods – Descending-Weight Social Composition Functions," UCLA Working Paper 326, May 1984.

Hirshleifer, Jack, "Conflict and Rent-Seeking Success Functions: Ratio vs. Difference Models of Relative Success," *Public Choice* 63, November 1989, 101–12.

Hobbes, Thomas, *Leviathan*, London, 1651; reprinted in *The English Philosophers*, New York: Modern Library, 129–234.

Hochman, Harold M. and James D. Rodgers, "Pareto Optimal Redistribution," *American Economic Review* 59, September 1969, 542–57.

Hochman, Harold M. and James D. Rodgers, "Pareto Optimal Redistribution: Reply," *American Economic Review* 60, December 1970, 977–1002.

Hoffman, Elizabeth, "Public Choice Experiments," 1997, in D. C. Mueller, ed., 1997a, 415–26.

Hoffman, Elizabeth and Matthew L. Spitzer, "The Coase Theorem: Some Experimental Tests," *Journal of Law and Economics* 25, April 1982, 73–98.

Hoffman, Elizabeth and Matthew L. Spitzer, "Entitlements, Rights, and Fairness: An Experimental Examination of Subjects' Concepts of Distributive Justice," *Journal of Legal Studies* 14, June 1985, 259–97.

Hoffman, Elizabeth and Matthew L. Spitzer, "Experimental Tests of the Coase Theorem with Large Bargaining Groups," *Journal of Legal Studies* 15, January 1986, 149–71.

Hogarth, Robin M. and Melvin W. Reder, eds., *Rational Choice*, Chicago: University of Chicago Press, 1987.

Holcombe, Randall G., "An Empirical Test of the Median Voter Model," *Economic Inquiry* 18, April 1980, 260–74.

Holcombe, Randall G. and Asqhar Zardkoohi, "The Determinants of Federal Grants," *Southern Economic Journal* 48, October 1981, 393–9.

Holsey, Cheryl M. and Thomas E. Borcherding, "Why Does Government's Share of National Income Grow? An Assessment of the Recent Literature on the U.S. Experience," 1997, in D. C. Mueller, ed., 1997a, 562–89.

Holt, Charles A., "Industrial Organization: A Survey of Laboratory Research," in J. H. Kagel and A. E. Roth, eds., 1995, 349–443.

Horn, Murray J., *The Political Economy of Public Administration*, Cambridge: Cambridge University Press, 1995.

Hotelling, Harold, "Stability in Competition," *Economic Journal* 39, March 1929, 41–57.

Howe, R. E. and J. E. Roemer, "Rawlsian Justice as the Core of a Game," *American Economic Review* 71, December 1981, 880–95.

Hoyer, R. W. and L. Mayer, "Comparing Strategies in a Spatial Model of Electoral Competition," *American Journal of Political Science* 18, August 1974, 501–23.

Hudson, John, "Preferences, Loyalty, and Party Choice," *Public Choice* 82, March 1995, 325–40.

Hudson, John and Philip R. Jones, "The Importance of the 'Ethical Voter': An Estimate of 'Altruism'," *European Journal of Political Economy* 10, 1994, 499–509.

Hume, David (1751), *An Inquiry Concerning the Principles of Morals*, Indianapolis: Bobbs-Merrill, 1957.

Humes, Brain D., "Multi-party Competition with Exit: A Comment on Duverger's Law," *Public Choice* 64, March 1990, 229–38.

Hunter, William J. and Michael A. Nelson, "Interest Group Demand for Taxation," *Public Choice* 62, 1989, 41–61.

Hunter, William J. and Charles E. Scott, "Statutory Changes in State Income Taxes: An Indirect Test of Fiscal Illusion," *Public Choice* 53, 1987, 41–51.

Hurwicz, Leonid, "On Allocations Attainable through Nash Equilibria," *Journal of Economic Theory* 21, August 1979, 140–65.

Husted, Thomas A. and Lawrence W. Kenny, "The Effect of the Expansion of the Voting Franchise on the Size of Government," *Journal of Political Economy* 105, February 1997, 54–82.

Hylland, Aanund and Richard Zeckhauser, "A Mechanism for Selecting Public Goods When Preferences Must Be Elicited," KSG Discussion Paper 70D, Harvard University, August 1979.

Inada, K.-I., "The Simple Majority Decision Rule," *Econometrica* 37, July 1969, 490–506.

Inada, K.-I., "Majority Rule and Rationality," *Journal of Economic Theory* 2, March 1970, 27–40.

Ingberman, Daniel E. and Dennis A. Yao, "Circumventing Formal Structure through Commitment: Presidential Influence and Agenda Control," *Public Choice* 70, May 1991, 151–79.

Inman, Robert P., "Testing Political Economy's 'As If' Proposition: Is the Median Income Voter Really Decisive?" *Public Choice* 33(4), 1978, 45–65.

Inman, Robert P., "The Fiscal Performance of Local Governments: An Interpretative Review," in P. Mieszkowski and M. Straszheim, eds., *Current Issues in Urban Economics*, Baltimore: Johns Hopkins University Press, 1979, 270–321.

Inman, Robert P., "Markets, Governments, and the 'New' Political Economy," in A. J. Auerbach and M. Feldstein, eds., *Handbook of Public Economics*, Amsterdam: North-Holland, 1987, 647–777.

Inman, Robert P. and Daniel L. Rubinfeld, "The Political Economy of Federalism," 1997, in D. C. Mueller, ed., 1997, 1997a, 73–105.

Inoguchi, Tanaka, "Economic Conditions and Mass Support in Japan," in P. Whitely, ed., *Models of Political Economy*, London: Sage, 1980, 121–54.

Intriligator, M.D., "A Probabilistic Model of Social Choice," *Review of Economic Studies* 40, October 1973, 553–60.

Ippolito, Richard A. and Robert T. Masson, "The Social Cost of Government Regulation of Milk," *Journal of Law and Economics* 21, April 1978, 33–65.

References

713

Irwin, Douglas A. and Randall S. Kroszner, "Interests, Institutions, and Ideology in Securing Policy Change: The Republican Conversion to Trade Liberalization after Smoot-Hawley," *Journal of Law and Economics* 42, October 1999, 643–73.

Isaac, R. Mark, David Schmidtz, and James M. Walker, "The Assurance Problem in a Laboratory Market," *Public Choice* 62, 1989, 217–36.

Isaac, R. Mark, James M. Walker, and Arlington W. Williams, "Group Size and the Voluntary Provision of Public Goods: Experimental Evidence Utilizing Large Groups," *Journal of Public Economics* 54, 1994, 1–36.

Iversen, Torben, "The Political Economy of Inflation: Bargaining Structure or Central Bank Independence?" *Public Choice* 99, 1999, 237–58; corrected version published in vol. 101, December.

Jackman, Robert W., "Political Institutions and Voter Turnout in the Industrial Democracies," *American Political Science Review* 81, June 1987, 405–23.

Jackson, John E. and J. W. Kingdon, "Ideology, Interest Group Scores, and Legislative Voters," *American Journal of Political Science* 36, August 1992, 805–23.

Jacobson, Gary C., "The Effect of Campaign Spending in Congressional Elections," *American Political Science Review* 72, June 1978, 469–91.

Jacobson, Gary C., "Money and Votes Reconsidered: Congressional Elections, 1972–1982," *Public Choice* 47(1), 1985, 7–62.

Jacobson, Gary C. and S. Kernell, *Strategy and Choice in Congressional Elections*, New Haven: Yale University Press, 1983.

Jankowski, Richard, "Resposible, Irresposible and Westminster Parties: A Theoretical and Empirical Evaluation," *British Journal of Political Science* 23, January 1993, 107–29.

Jenkins, Jeffrey A. and Mark Weidenmier, "Ideology, Economic Interests, and Congressional Roll-Call Voting: Partisan Instability and Bank of the United States Legislation, 1811–1816," *Public Choice* 100, September 1999, 225–43.

Jensen, Michael and William H. Meckling, "The Theory of the Firm: Managerial Behavior, Agency Costs and Ownership Structure," *Journal of Financial Economics* 3, October 1976, 305–60.

Johansen, L., "Some Notes on the Lindahl Theory of Determination of Public Expenditures," *International Economic Review* 4(7), September 1963, 346–58.

John, Peter, Keith Dowding, and S. Biggs, "Residential Mobility in London: A Micro-Level Test of the Behavioural Assumptions of the Tiebout Model," *British Journal of Political Science* 25, 1995, 379–97.

Johnson, Ronald N. and Gary D. Libecap, "Agency Growth, Salaries, and the Protected Bureaucrat," *Economic Inquiry* 27, 1989, 431–51.

Johnson, Ronald N. and Gary D. Libecap, "Public Sector Employee Voter Participation and Salaries," *Public Choice* 68, January 1991, 137–50.

Johnson, Simon, Daniel Kaufmann, and Andrei Shleifer, "The Unofficial Economy in Transition," *Brookings Papers on Economic Activity* 2, 1997, 159–212.

Johnson, Simon, Daniel Kaufmann, and Pablo Zoido-Lobatón, "Regulatory Discretion and the Unofficial Economy," *American Economic Review* 88, May 1998, 387–92.

Johnston, R. J., "Campaign Spending and Votes: A Reconsideration," *Public Choice* 33(3), 1978, 83–92.

Johnston, R. J., "Seats, Votes, Redistricting, and the Allocation of Power in Electoral Systems," in A. Lijphart and B. Grofman, eds., 1984, 59–69.

Jonung, Laro and Eskil Wadensjö, "The Effect of Unemployment, Inflation and Real Income Growth on Government Popularity in Sweden," *Scandinavian Journal of Economics* 81(2), 1979, 343–53.

Joslyn, Richard A., "The Impact of Decision Rules in Multi-Candidate Campaigns: The Case of the 1972 Democratic Presidential Nomination," *Public Choice* 25, Spring 1976, 1–17.

Joulfaian, David and Michael L. Marlow, "Government Size and Decentralization: Evidence from Disaggregated Data," *Southern Economic Journal* 56, April 1990, 1094–102.

Justman, Moshe and Mark Gradstein, "The Industrialization Revolution, Political Transition and the Subsequent Decline in Inequality in 19th Century Britain," *Explorations in Economic History* 36, April 1999, 109–27.

Kadane, Joseph B., "On Division of the Question," *Public Choice* 13, Fall 1972, 47–54.

Kagel, John H. and Alvin E. Roth, eds., *The Handbook of Experimental Economics*, Princeton: Princeton University Press, 1995.

Kahane, Leo H., "Senate Voting Patterns on the 1991 Extension of the Fast-Track Trade Procedures: Prelude to NAFTA," *Public Choice* 87, April 1996, 35–53.

Kahn, Alfred E., *The Economics of Regulation*, Vol. 1, New York: Wiley, 1970.

Kahneman, Daniel, Jack L. Knetsch, and Richard Thaler, "Fairness and the Assumptions of Economics," *Journal of Business* 59, 1986, 285–300.

Kahneman, Daniel and Amos Tversky, "Prospect Theory: An Analysis of Decision under Risk," *Econometrica* 47, 1979, 263–91.

Kahneman, Daniel and Amos Tversky, "Choices, Values, and Frames," *American Psychologist* 4, 1984, 341–50.

Kalai, Ehud and Eitan Muller, "Characterizations of Domains Admitting Nondictatorial Social Welfare Functions and Nonmanipulable Voting Procedures," *Journal of Economic Theory* 16, December 1977, 457–69.

Kalt, Joseph P. and Mark A. Zupan, "Capture and Ideology in the Economic Theory of Politics," *American Economic Review* 74, June 1984, 279–300.

Kalt, Joseph P. and Mark A. Zupan, "The Apparent Ideological Behavior of Legislators: Testing for Principal-Agent Slack in Political Institutions," *Journal of Law and Economics* 33, April 1990, 103–31.

Kamath, Shyam J., "Concealed Takings: Capture and Rent Seeking in the Indian Sugar Industry," *Public Choice* 62, August 1989, 119–38.

Kandori, Michihiro, George Mailath, and Rafael Rob, "Learning, Mutation, and Long Run Equilibria in Games," *Econometrica* 61, January 1993, 29–56.

Kaneko, Mamoru and Kenjiro Nakamura, "The Nash Social Welfare Function," *Econometrica* 47, March 1979, 423–35.

Kang, In-Bong and Kenneth Greene, "A Political Economic Analysis of Congressional Voting Patterns on NAFTA," *Public Choice* 98, March 1999, 385–97.

Kats, Amos and Shmuel Nitzan, "Global and Local Equilibrium in Majority Voting," *Public Choice* 26, Summer 1976, 105–6.

Katsimi, Margarita, "Explaining the Size of the Public Sector," *Public Choice* 96, July 1998, 117–44.

Katz, Richard S., "The Single Transferable Vote and Proportional Representation," in A. Lijphart and B. Grofman, eds., 1984, 135–45.

Kau, James B., D. Keenan, and Paul H. Rubin, "A General Equilibrium Model of Congressional Voting," *Quarterly Journal of Economics* 97, May 1982, 271–93.

Kau, James B. and Paul H. Rubin, "The Electoral College and the Rational Vote," *Public Choice* 27, Fall 1976, 101–07.

Kau, James B. and Paul H. Rubin, "Self-Interest, Ideology, and Logrolling in Congressional Voting," *Journal of Law and Economics* 22, October 1979, 365–84.

Kau, James B. and Paul H. Rubin, "The Size of Government," *Public Choice* 37(2), 1981, 261–74.

Kau, James B. and Paul H. Rubin, *Congressmen, Constituents, and Contributors*, Boston: Martinus Nijhoff, 1982.

Kau, James B. and Paul H. Rubin, "Ideology, Voting, and Shirking," *Public Choice* 76, June 1993, 151–72.

Kau, James B. and Paul H. Rubin, "The Growth of Government: Sources and Limits," mimeo, Emory University, 1999.

Keech, William, *Economic Politics: The Costs of Democracy*, Cambridge: Cambridge University Press, 1995.

Keefer, Philip and Stephen Knack, "Institutions and Economic Performance: Cross-Country Tests Using Alternative Institutional Measures," *Economics and Politics* 7(3), 1995, 207–27.

Keeler, Theodore E., "Theories of Regulation and the Deregulation Movement," *Public Choice* 44(1), 1984, 103–45.

Keil, Manfred W., "Is the Political Business Cycle Really Dead?" *Southern Economic Journal* 55, 1988, 86–99.

Kellett, J. and K. Mott, "Presidential Primaries: Measuring Popular Choice," *Polity* 9, Summer 1977, 528–37.

Kelley, S., Jr., R. E. Ayres, and W. G. Bowen, "Registration and Voting: Putting First Things First," *American Political Science Review* 61, June 1967, 359–79.

Kelly, Jerry S., "Rights Exercising and a Pareto-Consistent Libertarian Claim," *Journal of Economic Theory* 13, August 1976, 138–53.

Kelly, Jerry S., *Arrow Impossibility Theorems*, New York: Academic Press, 1978.

Kemp, Murray C., "Arrow's General Possibility Theorem," *Review of Economic Studies* 21(3), 1954, 240–3.

Kemp, Murray C. and A. Asimakopulos, "A Note on 'Social Welfare Functions' and Cardinal Utility," *Canadian Journal of Economic and Political Science* 18, May 1952, 195–200.

Kemp, Murray C. and Yew-Kwang Ng, "On the Existence of Social Welfare Functions: Social Orderings and Social Decision Functions," *Economica* 43, February 1976, 59–66.

Kemp, Murray C. and Yew-Kwang Ng, "More on Social Welfare Functions: The Incompatibility of Individualism and Ordinalism," *Economica* 44, February 1977, 89–90.

Kemp, Murray C. and Yew-Kwang Ng, "Arrow's Independence Condition and the Bergson-Samuelson Tradition," in G. Feiwel, ed., *Arrow and the Foundations of the Theory of Economic Policy*, London: Macmillan, 1987, 223–41.

Kemper, Peter and John M. Quigley, *The Economics of Refuse Collection*, Cambridge, MA: Ballinger Publishing Co., 1976.

Kendall, Wilmore, *John Locke and the Doctrine of Majority Rule*, Urbana: University of Illinois Press, 1941.

Kendrick, M. Slade, *A Century and a Half of Federal Expenditures*, New York: National Bureau of Economic Research, 1955.

Kennedy, Kenneth F. and Robert I. Mehr, "A Case Study in Private v. Public Enterprise: The Manitoba Experience with Automobile Insurance," *Journal of Risk and Insurance* 4, December 1977, 595–621.

Kennelly, B. and Peter Murrell, "The Sources of Collective Action: An Empirical Investigation of the Relationship between Industry Characteristics and Interest Group Formation," mimeo, University of Maryland, 1987.

Kenny, Lawrence W. and Mark Toma, "The Role of Tax Bases and Collection Costs in the Determination of Income Tax Rates, Seigniorage, and Inflation," *Public Choice* 92, July 1997, 75–90.

Kenny, P. J. and T. W. Rice, "An Empirical Examination of the Minimax Hypothesis," *American Politics Quarterly* 17, 1989, 153–62.

Key, V. O., Jr., *The Responsible Electorate*, New York: Vintage Books, 1966.

Keynes, John Maynard, *The General Theory of Employment, Interest and Money*, New York: Harcourt, Brace & World, 1936.

Kiewiet, D. Roderick, "Policy-Oriented Voting in Response to Economic Issues," *American Political Science Review* 75, June 1981, 448–59.

Kiewiet, D. Roderick, *Macroeconomics and Micropolitics*, Chicago: University of Chicago Press, 1983.

Kiewiet, D. Roderick and Mathew D. McCubbins, "Presidential Influence on Congressional Appropriations Decisions," *American Journal of Political Science* 32, 1988, 713–36.

Kinder, Donald R. and Donald R. Kiewiet, "Economic Discontent and Political Behavior: The Role of Personal Grievances and Collective Economic Judgments in Congressional Voting," *American Journal of Political Science* 23, August 1979, 495–517.

Kinder, Donald R. and Donald R. Kiewiet, "Sociotropic Politics: The American Case," *British Journal of Political Science* 11, 1981, 129–61.

King, G., J. Alt, N. Burns, and Michael Laver, "A Unified Model of Cabinet Dissolution in Parliamentary Democracies," *American Political Science Review* 34, 1990, 846–71.

Kirchgässner, Gebhard, Rationales Wählerverhalten und optimales Regierungsverhalten, Ph.D. dissertation, University of Constance, 1976.

Kirchgässner, Gebhard, "Wirtschaftslage und Wählerverhalten," *Politische Vierteljahresschrift* 18, 1977, 510–36.

Kirchgässner, Gebhard, "The Effect of Economic Events on Votes for President – Some Alternative Estimates," mimeo, Swiss Federal Institute of Technology, Zürich, 1981.

Kirchgässner, Gebhard, "Causality Testing of the Popularity Function: An Empirical Investigation for the Federal Republic of Germany, 1971–1982," *Public Choice* 45(2), 1985, 155–73.

Kirchgässner, Gebhard, "Probabilistic Voting and Equilibrium: An Impossibility Result," *Public Choice* 103(1–2), April 2000, 35–48.

Kirchgässner, Gerhard and Jörg Schimmelpfennig, "Closeness Counts if it Matters for Electoral Victory: Some Empirical Results for the United Kingdom and the Federal Republic of Germany," *Public Choice* 73(2), April 1992, 283–99.

Kirchsteiger, Georg, "The Role of Envy in Ultimatum Games," *Journal of Economic Behavior and Organization* 25, 1994, 373–89.

Kirman, Alan P. and Dieter Sondermann, "Arrow's Theorem, Many Agents, and Invisible Dictators," *Journal of Economic Theory* 5, October 1972, 267–77.

Kirschen, E.S., ed., *Economic Policies Compared: West and East*, vol. 1, *General Theory*, Amsterdam: North-Holland, 1974.

Kitchen, Harry M., "A Statistical Estimation of an Operating Cost Function for Municipal Refuse Collection," *Public Finance Quarterly* 4, January 1976, 56–76.

Klevorick, Alvin K., "Discussion," *American Economic Review* 64, May 1974, 158–61.

Knack, Steve, "Civic Norms, Social Sanctions, and Voter Turnout," *Rationality and Society* 4, 1992, 133–56.

Knack, Stephen, "The Voter Participation Effects of Selecting Jurors from Registration Lists," *Journal of Law and Economics* 36, April 1993, 99–114.

Knack, Steve, "Does the Rain Help the Republicans? Theory and Evidence on Turnout and the Vote," *Public Choice* 79, April 1994, 187–209.

Knack, Steve, "Institutions and the Convergence Hypothesis: The Cross-National Evidence," *Public Choice* 87, June 1996, 207–28.

Knack, Stephen, "Deterring Voter Registration through Juror Selection Practices: Evidence from Survey Data," *Public Choice* 103, April 2000, 49–62.

Knack, Stephen and Philip Keefer, "Institutions and Economic Performance: Cross-Country Tests Using Alternative Institutional Measures," *Economics and Politics* 7, 1995, 207–28.

Knight, Frank H., *Risk, Uncertainty and Profit*, New York: Harper & Row, 1965; first edition, 1921.

Knight, Frank H., "Profit," in *Encyclopedia of Social Sciences*, 1934; reprinted in W. Fellner and B. F. Haley, *Readings in the Theory of Income Distribution*, Homewood, IL: Richard D. Irwin, 1951, 533–46.

Koehler, D. H., "Vote Trading and the Voting Paradox: A Proof of Logical Equivalence," *American Political Science Review* 69, September 1975, 954–60.

Koester, Ulrich and Stefan Tangermann, "The European Community," in F. H. Sanderson, ed., 1990, 64–111.

Koford, Kenneth J., "Centralized Vote-Trading," *Public Choice* 39(2), 1982, 245–68.

Koford, Kenneth J., "Dimensions in Congressional Voting," *American Political Science Review* 83, September 1989, 949–62.

Koford, Kenneth J., "Dimensions, Transaction Costs and Coalitions in Legislative Voting," *Economics and Politics* 2, 1990, 59–82.

Kollman, Ken, John H. Miller, and Scott E. Page, "Adaptive Parties in Spatial Elections," *American Political Science Review* 86, 1992, 929–37.

Kolmar, Martin, "Constitution as Commitment or Coordination Device? Comment on C. Azariadis and V. Galasso: Constitutional 'Rules' and Intergenerational Fiscal Policy," *Constitutional Political Economy* 11, December 2000, 371–4.

Konrad, Kai A. and Harris Schlesinger, "Risk Aversion in Rent-Seeking and Rent-Augmenting Games," *Economic Journal* 107, November 1997, 1671–83.

Kormendi, Roger C., "A New Remedy for the Free Rider Problem? – Flies in the Ointment," *Research in Law and Economics* 1, 1979, 115–30.

Kormendi, Roger C., "Further Thoughts on the Free Rider Problem and Demand Revealing Processes," *Research in Law and Economics* 2, 1980, 219–25.

Kormendi, Roger C. and Philip G. Meguire, "Macroeconomic Determinants of Growth: Cross-Country Evidence," *Journal of Monetary Economics* 16(2), September 1985, 141–63.

Kramer, Gerald H., "Short Run Fluctuations in U.S. Voting Behavior, 1896–1964," *American Political Science Review* 65, March 1971, 131–43.

Kramer, Gerald H., "Sophisticated Voting over Multidimensional Choice Spaces," *Journal of Mathematical Sociology* 2, July 1972, 165–80.

Kramer, Gerald H., "On a Class of Equilibrium Conditions for Majority Rule," *Econometrica* 41, March 1973, 285–97.

Kramer, Gerald H., "A Dynamic Model of Political Equilibrium," *Journal of Economic Theory* 16, December 1977, 310–34.

Kramer, Gerald H., "The Ecological Fallacy Revisited: Aggregate- versus Individual-level Findings on Economics and Elections, and Sociotropic Voting," *American Political Science Review* 77, March 1983, 92–111.

Kramer, Gerald H. and A. H. Klevorick, "Existence of a Local Cooperative Equilibrium in a Class of Voting Games," *Review of Economic Studies* 41, October 1974, 539–47.

Krehbiel, Keith, *Information and Legislative Organization*, Ann Arbor: University of Michigan Press, 1991.

Krehbiel, Keith, "Constituency Characteristics and Legislative Preferences," *Public Choice* 76, June 1993, 21–37.

Krehbiel, Keith, *Pivotal Politics*, Chicago: University of Chicago Press, 1998.

Kress, Shirley E., "Niskanen Effects in the California Community Colleges," *Public Choice* 61, May 1989, 127–40.

Kristov, Lorenzo, Peter Lindert, and Robert McClelland, "Pressure Groups and Redistribution," *Journal of Public Economics* 48, July 1992, 135–63.

Kroszner, Randall S. and Thomas Stratmann, "Interest-Group Competition and the Organization of Congress: Theory and Evidence from Financial Services' Political Action Committees," *American Economic Review* 88, December 1998, 1163–87.

Krueger, Anne O., "The Political Economy of the Rent-Seeking Society," *American Economic Review* 64, June 1974, 291–303; reprinted in J. M. Buchanan, R. D. Tollison, and G. Tullock, eds., 1980, 51–70.

Krueger, Anne, Maurice Schiff, and Alberto Valdés, *The Political Economy of Agricultural Pricing Policy*, Baltimore: Johns Hopkins University Press, 1991.

Kuga, K. and H. Nagatani, "Voter Antagonism and the Paradox of Voting," *Econometrica* 42, November 1974, 1045–67.

Kuklinski, James H. and Darrell M. West, "Economic Expectations and Voting Behavior in United States House and Senate Elections," *American Political Science Review* 75, June 1981, 436–47.

Kunreuther, H. et al., *Disaster Insurance Protection*, New York: Wiley, 1978.

Kurnow, E., "Determinants of State and Local Expenditures Reexamined," *National Tax Journal* 16, 1963, 252–5.

Kurrild-Klitgaard, Peter, "The Constitutional Economics Autocratic Succession," *Public Choice* 103, April 2000, 63–84.

Kurrild-Klitgaard, Peter, "An Empirical Example of the Condorcet Paradox of Voting in a Large Electorate," *Public Choice* 107, April 2001, 135–45.

Kurth, James R., "The Political Consequences of the Product Cycle: Industrial History and Political Outcomes," *International Organizations* 33, 1979, 1–34.

Kydland, E. Finn and Edward C. Prescott, "Rules Rather than Discretion: The Inconsistency of Optimal Plans," *Journal of Political Economy* 85, 1977, 473–91.

Laakso, Markuu and Rein Taagepera, "Effective Number of Political Parties: A Measure with Applications to Western Europe," *Comparative Political Studies* 12, 1979, 3–27.

Laband, David N. and John P. Sophocleus, "The Social Cost of Rent Seeking: First Estimates," *Public Choice* 58, 1988, 269–75.

Lächler, Ulrich, "The Political Business Cycle: A Complementary Study," *Review of Economic Studies* 45, 1978, 369–75.

Lächler, Ulrich, "On Political Business Cycles with Endogenous Election Dates," *Journal of Public Economics* 17, 1982, 111–17.

Lächler, Ulrich, "The Political Business Cycle under Rational Voting Behavior," *Public Choice* 44, 1984, 411–30.

Ladha, Krishna K., "The Condorcet Jury Theorem, Free Speech, and Correlated Votes," *American Journal of Political Science* 36, August 1992, 617–34.

Ladha, Krishna K., "Condorcet's Jury Theorem in Light of de Finetti's Theorem: Majority-Rule Voting with Correlated Votes," *Social Choice and Welfare* 10, 1993, 69–85.

Ladha, Krishna K., "Coalitions in Congressional Voting," *Public Choice* 78, January 1994, 43–63.

Ladha, Krishna K., "Information Pooling through Majority-Rule Voting: Condorcet's Jury Theorem with Correlated Votes," *Journal of Economic Behavior and Organization* 26, 1995, 353–72.

Ladha, Krishna K., Gary Miller, and Joe Oppenheimer, "Democracy: Turbo-Charged or Shackled? Information Aggregation by Majority Rule," mimeo, University of Maryland, 1995.

Lafay, Jean-Dominique, "Important Political Change and the Stability of the Popularity Function: Before and after the French General Election of 1981," mimeo, University of Poitiers, 1984.

Laffont, Jean-Jacques and Eric Maskin, "A Differential Approach to Dominant Strategy Mechanisms," *Econometrica* 48, September 1980, 1507–30.

Lakeman, Enid, *How Democracies Vote – A Study of Electoral Systems*, 4th ed., London: Faber and Faber, 1974.

Lampert, S. I., Shmuel Nitzan, and J. Paroush, "The Sensitivity of Political Outcomes to Electoral Decision Rules," *Political Methodology* 10(3), 1984, 337–56.

Landau, Daniel L., "Government Expenditure and Economic Growth: A Cross-Country Study," *Southern Economic Journal* 49, January 1983, 783–92.

Landau, Daniel L., "Government and Economic Growth in the Less Developed Countries: An Empirical Study for 1960–1980," *Economic Development and Cultural Change* 35, October 1986, 35–75.

Landes, William M. and Richard A. Posner, "The Independent Judiciary in an Interest-Group Perspective," *Journal of Law and Economics* 18, December 1975, 875–901.

Lane, Jan-Erik and Svante Ersson, "Political Institutions, Public Policy and Economic Growth," *Scandinavian Political Studies* 9, March 1986, 19–34.

Lane, Robert E., "Political Involvement through Voting," in B. Seasholes, ed., *Voting, Interest Groups, and Parties*, Glenview, IL: Scott, Foresman, 1966.

Lane, Robert E., "What Rational Choice Explains," in J. Friedman, ed., 1996, 107–26.

Langbein, Laura I., "PACs, Lobbies and Political Conflict: The Case of Gun Control," *Public Choice* 77, November 1993, 551–72.

Lange, Peter and Geoffrey Garrett, "The Politics of Growth: Strategic Interaction and Economic Performance in the Advanced Industrial Democracies, 1974–80," *Journal of Politics* 47, August 1985, 792–827.

Lascher, Edward L., Jr., Steven Kelman, and Thomas J. Kane, "Political Views, Constituency Pressure, and Congressional Action on Flag Burning," *Public Choice* 76, June 1993, 79–102.

Laver, Michael and Norman Schofield, *Multiparty Government*, Oxford: Oxford University Press, 1990.

Laver, Michael and Kenneth A. Shepsle, *Making and Breaking Governments*, Cambridge: Cambridge University Press, 1996.

Ledyard, John O., "The Paradox of Voting and Candidate Competition: A General Equilibrium Analysis," in G. Hornwich and J. Quirk, eds., *Essays in Contemporary Fields of Economics*, West Lafayette: Purdue University Press, 1981.

Ledyard, John O., "The Pure Theory of Large Two-Candidate Elections," *Public Choice* 44(1), 1984, 7–41.

Ledyard, John O., "Public Goods: A Survey of Experimental Research," in J. H. Kagel and A. E. Roth, eds., 1995, 111–251.

Lee, Sanghack, "Endogenous Sharing Rules in Collective-Group Rent-Seeking," *Public Choice* 85, October 1995, 31–44.

Leffler, Keith B., "Physician Licensure: Competition and Monopoly in American Medicine," *Journal of Law and Economics* 21, April 1978, 165–86.

Lehner, Franz, "Pressure Politics and Economic Growth: Olson's Theory and the Swiss Experience," in D. C. Mueller, ed., 1983, 203–14.

Lehner, Franz, "The Political Economy of Distributive Conflict in the Welfare State," mimeo, Ruhr University, Bochum, 1985.

Leibenstein, Harvey, "Long-Run Welfare Criteria," in J. Margolis, ed., *The Public Economy of Urban Communities*, Baltimore: Johns Hopkins University Press, 1965, 539–57.

Leibenstein, Harvey, "Allocative Efficiency vs X-Efficiency," *American Economic Review* 56, June 1966, 392–415.

Leininger, Wolfgang, "More Efficient Rent-Seeking – A Münchhausen Solution," *Public Choice* 75, January 1993, 43–62.

Lerner, Abba P., *Economics of Control*, New York: Macmillan, 1944.

Leschke, Martin, "Constitutional Choice and Prosperity: A Factor Analysis," *Constitutional Political Economy* 11, September 2000, 265–79.

Levernier, William, "The Effect of Relative Economic Performance on the Outcome of Gubernatorial Elections," *Public Choice* 74, September 1992, 181–90.

Levine, M. E. and Charles R. Plott, "Agenda Influence and Its Implications," *Virginia Law Review* 63, May 1977, 561–604.

Levine, Ross and David Renelt, "A Sensitivity Analysis of Cross-Country Growth Regressions," *American Economic Review* 82, September 1992, 942–63.

Levitt, Steven D., "Using Repeat Challengers to Estimate the Effect of Campaign Spending on Election Outcomes in the U.S. House," *Journal of Political Economy* 102, August 1994, 777–98.

Levy, Brian and Pablo T. Spiller, "The Institutional Foundations of Regulatory Commitment: A Comparative Analysis of Telecommunications Regulation," *Journal of Law, Economics, and Organization* 10, October 1994, 201–46.

Levy, Frank, *Dollars and Dreams: The Changing American Income Distribution*, New York: Basic Books, 1987.

Lewin, L., *Self-Interest and Public Interest in Western Politics*, Oxford: Oxford University Press, 1991.

Lewis-Beck, Martin S., "Economic Conditions and Executive Popularity: The French Experience," *American Journal of Political Science* 24, May 1980, 306–23.

Lewis-Beck, Martin S., *Economics and Elections: The Major Western Democracies*, Ann Arbor: University of Michigan Press, 1988.

Libecap, Gary D., "The Rise of the Chicago Packers and the Origins of Meat Inspection and Antitrust," *Economic Inquiry* 30, April 1992, 242–62.

Lieserson, Michael, "Factions and Coalitions in One-Party Japan: An Interpretation Based on the Theory of Games," *American Political Science Review* 62, 1966, 70–87.

Lijphart, Arend, *Democracies*, New Haven: Yale University Press, 1984.

Lijphart, Arend, "Degrees of Proportionality of Proportional Representation Formulas," in B. Grofman and A. Lijphart, eds., 1986, 170–9.

Lijphart, Arend, "The Political Consequences of Electoral Laws, 1945–85," *American Political Science Review* 84, June 1990, 481–96.

Lijphart, Arend, *Electoral Systems and Party Systems: A Study of Twenty-Seven Democracies, 1945–90*, Oxford: Oxford University Press, 1994.

Lijphart, Arend, "Unequal Participation: Democracy's Unresolved Dilemma," *American Political Science Review* 91, March 1997, 1–14.

Lijphart, Arend, *Patterns of Democracy*, New Haven: Yale University Press, 1999.

Lijphart, Arend and Bernard Grofman, eds., *Choosing an Electoral System: Issues and Alternatives*, New York: Praeger, 1984.

Lijphart, Arend, Rafael Pintor Lopez, and Yasunori Sone, "The Limited Vote and the Single Nontransferable Vote: Lessons from the Japanese and Spanish Examples," in B. Grofman and A. Lijphart, eds., 1986, 154–69.

Lin, Tse-min, James M. Enelow, and Han Dorussen, "Equilibrium in Multicandidate Probabilistic Spatial Voting," *Public Choice* 98, January 1999, 59–82.

Lindahl, Erik, *Just Taxation – A Positive Solution*, Lund, first published in German, 1919; English translation in R. Musgrave and A. Peacock, 1967, 168–76.

Lindbeck, Assar, "Stabilization Policy in Open Economies with Endogenous Politicians," *American Economic Review* 66, May 1976, 1–19.

Lindbeck, Assar, "Redistribution Policy and the Expansion of the Public Sector, " *Journal of Public Economics* 28, December 1985, 309–28.

Lindbeck, Assar, "The Swedish Experiment," *Journal of Economic Literature* 35, September 1997, 1273–319.

Lindeen, J. W., "An Oligopoly Model of Political Market Structures," *Public Choice* 9, Fall 1970, 31–7.

Lindert, Peter H. and Geoffrey G. Williamson, "Growth, Equality and History," *Explorations in Economic History* 22, 1985, 341–77.

Lindsay, Cotton M., "A Theory of Government Enterprise," *Journal of Political Economy* 84(5), October 1976, 1061–77.

Little, I. M. D., "Social Choice and Individual Values," *Journal of Political Economics* 60, October 1952, 422–32.

Little, I. M. D., *A Critique of Welfare Economics*, 2nd ed., Oxford: Clarendon Press, 1957.

Locke, John, *An Essay Concerning the True Original Extent and End of Civil Government*; reprinted in *The English Philosophers*, New York: Modern Library, 1939.

Loeb, Martin, "Alternative Versions of the Demand-Revealing Process," *Public Choice* 29-2 (special supplement), Spring 1977, 15–26.

Lohmann, Susanne, "A Signaling Model of Informative and Manipulative Political Action," *American Political Science Review* 87, June 1993, 319–33.

Lohmann, Susanne, "The Poverty of Green and Shapiro," in J. Friedman, ed., 1996, 127–54.

Long, Ngo van and Neil Vousden, "Protectionist Responses and Declining Industries," *Journal of International Economics* 30, February 1991, 87–103.

Lopez, Rigoberto A. and Emilio Pagoulatos, "Rent Seeking and the Welfare Cost of Trade Barriers," *Public Choice* 79, April 1994, 149–60.

Lott, John R., Jr., "Political Cheating," *Public Choice* 52, March 1987, 169–87.

720   **References**

Lott, John R., Jr., "Attendance Rates, Political Shirking, and the Effect of Post-elective Office on Employment," *Economic Inquiry* 28, 1990, 133–50.

Lott, John R., Jr., "Does Additional Campaign Spending Really Hurt Incumbents?: The Theoretical Importance of Past Investments in Political Brand Name," *Public Choice* 72, October 1991, 87–92.

Lott, John R., Jr. and Stephen G. Bronars, "Time Series Evidence on Shirking in the U.S. House of Representatives," *Public Choice* 76, June 1993, 125–49.

Lott, John R., Jr. and Michael L. Davis, "A Critical Review and an Extension of the Political Shirking Literature," *Public Choice* 74, December 1992, 461–84.

Lott, John R., Jr. and Larry Kenny, "Did Women's Suffrage Change the Size and Scope of Government?" *Journal of Political Economy* 107, December 1999, 1163–98.

Lowery, David, "The Keynesian and Political Determinants of Unbalanced Budgets: U.S. Fiscal Policy from Eisenhower to Reagan," *American Journal of Political Science* 29, 1985, 429–60.

Lowery, David and Lee Sigelman, "Understanding the Tax Revolt: Eight Explanations," *American Political Science Review* 75, December 1981, 963–74.

Lowery, D. and W. O. Berry, "The Growth of Government in the United States: An Empirical Assessment of Competing Explanations," *American Journal of Political Science* 27, November 1983, 665–94.

Lowi, T. J., *The End of Liberalism*, New York: W.W. Norton, 1969.

Luce, R. Duncan and Howard Raiffa, *Games and Decisions*, New York: Wiley, 1957.

Lupia, Arthur and Mathew D. McCubbins, "Learning from Oversight: Fire Alarms and Police Patrol Reconstructed," *Journal of Law, Economics, and Organization* 10, April 1994, 96–125.

Lybeck, J. A. *The Growth of Government in Developed Countries*, Gower: Hants, 1986.

Lyons, David, "Nature and Soundness of the Contract and Coherence Arguments," in N. Daniels, ed., 1974, 141–67; based on material from "Rawls versus Utilitarianism," *Journal of Philosophy* 69, October 1972, 535–45, and "The Nature of the Contract Argument," *Cornell Law Review* 6, 1974, 59.

MacKay, Alfred F., *Arrow's Theorem: The Paradox of Social Choice*, New Haven: Yale University Press, 1980.

Mackay, Robert J., James C. Miller, III, and Bruce Yandle, *Public Choice and Regulation*, Stanford: Hoover Institution, 1987.

Mackay, Robert J. and Carolyn L. Weaver, "Agenda Control by Budget Maximizers in a Multi-Bureau Setting," *Public Choice* 37(3), 1981, 447–72.

MacRae, C. Duncan, "A Political Model of the Business Cycle," *Journal of Political Economy* 85, April 1977, 239–63.

Madsen, Henrick J., "Electoral Outcomes and Macro-Economic Policies: The Scandinavian Cases," in P. Whitely, ed., *Models of Political Economy*, London: Sage, 1980, 15–46.

Magee, Stephen P., "Protectionism in the United States," mimeo, University of Texas, Austin, 1982.

Magee, Stephen P., "Endogenous Protection: The Empirical Evidence," 1997, in D. C. Mueller, ed., 1997a, 526–61.

Magee, Stephen P., William A. Brock, and Leslie Young, *Black Hole Tariffs and Endogenous Policy Theory: Political Economy in General Equilibrium*, Cambridge: Cambridge University Press, 1989.

Majumdar, Sumit K., "Assessing Comparative Efficiency of the State-Owned, Mixed and Private Sectors in Indian Industry," *Public Choice* 96, July 1998, 1–24.

Malinvaud, E., "Procedures pour la Determination d'un Programme de Consommation Collective," *European Economic Review* 2(7), Winter 1970–71, 187–217.

Maloney, Kevin J. and Michael L. Smirlock, "Business Cycles and the Political Process," *Southern Economic Journal* 48(2), October 1982, 377–92.

Mann, H. Michael and Karen McCormick, "Firm Attributes and the Propensity to Influence the Political System," in J. J. Siegfried, ed., *The Economics of Firm Size, Market Structure and Social Performance*, Washington D.C.: FTC, 1980, 300–13.

Mann, Patrick C. and John L. Mikesell, "Ownership and Water Systems Operations," *Water Resources Bulletin* 12, 1976, 995–1004.

Mansbridge, Jane J., ed., *Beyond Self-Interest*, Chicago: University of Chicago Press, 1990.

Margolis, Howard, "Probability of a Tied Election," *Public Choice* 31, Fall 1977, 135–8.

Margolis, Howard, "A Thought Experiment on Demand-Revealing Mechanisms," *Public Choice* 38(1), 1982a, 87–91.

Margolis, Howard, *Selfishness, Altruism, and Rationality*, Cambridge: Cambridge University Press, 1982b.

Margolis, Howard, "A Note on Demand-Revealing," *Public Choice* 40(2), 1983, 217–25.

Marks, Stephen V., "Economic Interests and Voting on the Omnibus Trade Bill of 1987," *Public Choice* 75, January 1993, 21–42.

Markus, G. B., "The Impact of Personal and National Economic Conditions on the Presidential Vote: A Pooled Cross-sectional Analysis," *American Journal of Political Science* 32, 1988, 137–54.

Markus, G. B., "The Impact of Personal and National Economic Conditions on Presidential Voting: 1956–1968," *American Journal of Political Science* 36, 1990, 829–34.

Marlow, M. L., "Fiscal Decentralization and Government Size," *Public Choice* 56(3), March 1988, 259–69.

Marris, Robin, *The Economic Theory of Managerial Capitalism*, New York: Free Press, 1964.

Marsh, R. M., "Sociological Explanations of Economic Growth," *Studies in Comparative International Research* 23, 1988, 41–77.

Marvel, Howard P. and Edward J. Ray, "The Kennedy Round: Evidence on the Regulation of International Trade in the United States," *American Economic Review* 73, March 1983, 190–7.

Marwell, G. and R. E. Ames, "Economists Free Ride, Does Anyone Else?" *Journal of Public Economics* 15, June 1981, 295–310.

Mashaw, Jerry L., "Prodelegation: Why Administrators Should Make Political Decisions," *Journal of Law, Economics, and Organization* 1, Spring 1985, 81–100.

Mashaw, Jerry L., "Explaining Administrative Process: Normative, Positive, and Critical Studies of Legal Development," *Journal of Law, Economics, and Organization* 6, 1990, 267–98.

Matsusaka, John G., "Election Closeness and Voter Turnout: Evidence from California Ballot Propositions," *Public Choice* 76, August 1993, 313–34.

Matsusaka, John G., "Explaining Voter Turnout Patterns: An Information Theory," *Public Choice* 84, July 1995, 91–117.

Matsusaka, John G. and Filip Palda, "The Downsian Voter Meets the Ecological Fallacy," *Public Choice* 77, December 1993, 855–78.

Matsusaka, John G. and Filip Palda, "Voter Turnout: How Much Can We Explain?" *Public Choice* 98, March 1999, 431–46.

Mauro, Paolo, "Corruption and Growth," *Quarterly Journal of Economics* 110, August 1995, 681–712.

May, Kenneth O., "A Set of Independent, Necessary and Sufficient Conditions for Simple Majority Decision," *Econometrica* 20, October 1952, 680–4.

Mayer, L. S. and I. J. Good, "Is Minimax Regret Applicable to Voting Decisions?" *American Political Science Review* 69, September 1975, 916–17.

Mayer, Wolfgang, "Endogenous Tariff Formation," *American Economic Review* 74, December 1984, 970–85.

Mayhew, David R., *Party Loyalty among Congressmen: The Difference between Democrats and Republicans*, Cambridge, MA: Harvard University Press, 1966.

Mayhew, David R., *Congress: The Electoral Connection*, New Haven: Yale University Press, 1974.

McCallum, Bennett T., "The Political Business Cycle: An Empirical Test," *Southern Economic Journal* 44, 1978, 504–15.

McCallum, J. and André Blais, "Government, Special Interest Groups, and Economic Growth," *Public Choice* 54(1), 1987, 3–18.

McConnell, G., *Private Power and American Democracy*, New York: Alfred A. Knopf, 1966.

McCormick, Robert E. and Robert D. Tollison, *Politicians, Legislation, and the Economy*, Boston: Martinus Nijhoff, 1981.

McCubbins, Mathew D., Roger G. Noll, and Barry R. Weingast, "Administrative Procedures as Instruments of Political Control," *Journal of Law, Economics, and Organization* 3, 1987, 243–77.

McCubbins, Mathew D., Roger G. Noll, and Barry R. Weingast, "Structure and Process, Politics and Policy: Administrative Arrangements and the Political Control of Agencies," *Virginia Law Review* 75, 1989, 431–82.

McCubbins, Mathew D. and Thomas Schwartz, "Congressional Oversight Overlooked: Police Patrols versus Fire Alarms," *American Journal of Political Science* 28, 165–79.

McGann, A. J., "The Advantages of Ideological Cohesion: A Model of Constituency Representation and Electoral Competition in Multi-Party Democracies," mimeo, MBS 00-24, University of California, Irvine, 2000.

McGavin, B. H., "The Political Business Cycle: A Reexamination of Some Empirical Evidence," *Quarterly Journal of Business and Economics* 26, 1987, 36–49.

McGuire, M., "Private Good Clubs and Public Good Clubs: Economic Models of Group Formation," *Swedish Journal of Economics* 74, March 1972, 84–99.

McGuire, M., "Group Segregation and Optimal Jurisdictions," *Journal of Political Economy* 82, January/February 1974, 112–32.

McGuire, M. and H. Aaron, "Efficiency and Equity in the Optimal Supply of a Public Good," *Review of Economics and Statistics* 51, February 1969, 31–8.

McGuire, Martin C. and Mancur Olson, "The Economics of Autocracy and Majority Rule: The Invisible Hand and the Use of Force," *Journal of Economic Literature* 34, March 1996, 72–96.

McGuire, Robert A., "Constitution Making: A Rational Choice Model of the Federal Convention of 1787," *American Journal of Political Science* 32, 1988, 483–522.

McGuire, Robert A. and Robert L. Ohsfeldt, "An Economic Model of Voting Behavior Over Specific Issues at the Constitutional Convention of 1787," *Journal of Economic History* 46, 1986, 79–111.

McGuire, Robert A. and Robert L. Ohsfeldt, "Self-Interest, Agency Theory, and Political Voting Behavior: The Ratification of the United States Constitution," *American Economic Review* 79, March 1989, 219–34.

McGuire, Robert A. and T. Norman Van Cott, "Public versus Private Economic Activity: A New Look at School Bus Transportation," *Public Choice* 43(1), 1984, 25–43.

McGuire, Thomas, Michael Coiner, and Larry Spancake, "Budget-Maximizing Agencies and Efficiency in Government," *Public Choice* 34(3–4), 1979, 333–57.

McKelvey, Richard D., "Intransitivities in Multidimensional Voting Models and Some Implications for Agenda Control," *Journal of Economic Theory* 12, June 1976, 472–82.

McKelvey, Richard D., "Covering, Dominance, and Institution-Free Properties of Social Choice," *American Journal of Political Science* 30, May 1986, 283–314.

McKelvey, Richard D. and Peter C. Ordeshook, "A General Theory of the Calculus of Voting," in J. F. Herndon and J. L. Bernd, eds., *Mathematical Applications in Political Science*, Vol. 6, Charlottesville: University of Virginia Press, 1972.

McKelvey, Richard D. and Peter C. Ordeshook, "Symmetric Spatial Games without Majority Rule Equilibria," *American Political Science Review* 70, December 1976, 1172–84.

McKelvey, Richard D. and Peter C. Ordeshook, "Vote Trading: An Experimental Study," *Public Choice* 35(2), 1980, 151–84.

McKelvey, Richard D. and Peter C. Ordeshook, "An Experimental Study of the Effects of Procedural Rules on Committee Behavior," *Journal of Politics* 46, 1984, 182–205.

McKelvey, Richard D. and Peter C. Ordeshook, "Elections with Limited Information: A Multidimensional Model," *Mathematical Social Science* 14, 1987, 77–99.

McKelvey, Richard D. and Peter C. Ordeshook, "A Decade of Experimental Research on Spatial Models of Elections and Committees," in J. Enelow and M. J. Hinich, eds., *Advances in the Spatial Theory of Voting*, Cambridge: Cambridge University Press, 1990.

McKelvey, Richard D., Peter C. Ordeshook, and Mark D. Winer, "The Competitive Solutions for N-Person Games without Transferable Utility, with an Application to Committee Games," *American Political Science Review* 72, June 1978, 599–615.

McKeown, Timothy J., "Hegemonic Stability Theory and 19th Century Tariff Levels in Europe," *International Organization* 37, 1983, 73–91.

McMillan, M. L., "Toward the More Optimal Provision of Local Public Goods: Internalization of Benefits or Intergovernmental Grants?" *Public Finance Quarterly* 3, July 1975, 229–60.

Meade, James E., "External Economies and Diseconomies in a Competitive Situation," *Economic Journal* 62, March 1952, 54–67; reprinted in K. J. Arrow and T. Scitovsky, 1969, 185–98.

Meehl, P. E., "The Selfish Citizen Paradox and the Throw Away Vote Argument" *American Political Science Review* 71, March 1977, 11–30.

Meerman, Jacob, "Are Public Goods Public Goods?" *Public Choice* 35(1), 1980, 45–57.

Mehay, Stephen L., "The Effect of Governmental Structure on Special District Expenditures," *Public Choice* 44(2), 1984, 339–48.

Mehay, Stephen L. and Rodolfo A. Gonzalez, "Economic Incentives under Contract Supply of Local Governmental Services," *Public Choice* 46(1), 1985, 79–86.

Meltzer, Allan H. and Scott F. Richard, "Why Government Grows (and Grows) in a Democracy," *Public Interest* 52, Summer 1978, 111–18.

Meltzer, Allan H. and Scott F. Richard, "A Rational Theory of the Size of Government," *Journal of Political Economy* 89, October 1981, 914–27.

Meltzer, Allan H. and Scott F. Richard, "Tests of a Rational Theory of the Size of Government," *Public Choice* 41(3), 1983, 403–18.

Merrill, Samuel, III, "Strategic Decisions under One-Stage Multi-Candidate Voting Systems," *Public Choice* 36(1), 1981, 115–34.

Merrill, Samuel, III, "A Comparison of Efficiency of Multicandidate Electoral Systems," *American Journal of Political Science* 28, February 1984, 23–48.

Merrill, Samuel, III, "A Statistical Model for Condorcet Efficiency Based on Simulation under Spatial Model Assumptions," *Public Choice* 47(2), 1985, 389–403.

Merrill, Samuel, III and Bernard Grofman, *A Unified Theory of Voting*, Cambridge: Cambridge University Press, 1999.

Merville, Larry J. and Dale K. Osborne, "Constitutional Democracy and the Theory of Agency," *Constitutional Political Economy* 1, Fall 1990, 21–47.

Meyer, Robert A., "Publicly Owned versus Privately Owned Utilities: A Policy Choice," *Review of Economics and Statistics* 57, November 1975, 391–9.

Midlarsky, Manus I., "Political Stability of Two-Party and Multiparty Systems: Probabilistic Bases for the Comparison of Party Systems," *American Political Science Review* 78, December 1984, 929–51.

Mieszkowski, Peter, "Tax Incidence Theory," *Journal of Economic Literature* 7, December 1969, 1103–24.

Migué, Jean-Luc, "Public Choice in a Federal System," *Public Choice* 90, March 1997, 235–54.

Migué, Jean-Luc and Gerard Bélanger, "Towards a General Theory of Managerial Discretion," *Public Choice* 17, Spring 1974, 27–43.

Milbrath, L. W., *Political Participation*, Chicago: Rand McNally, 1965.

Milgrom, Paul and John Roberts, *Economics, Organization, and Management*, New York: Prentice-Hall, 1992.

Mill, John Stuart (1859), *On Liberty*, in *The English Philosophers*, New York: Modern Library, 1939, 949–1041.

Mill, John Stuart, *Considerations on Representative Government*, New York: Bobbs-Merrill, 1958 (first publication 1861).

Miller, Gary J., "Bureaucratic Compliance as a Game on the Unit Square," *Public Choice* 19, Spring 1977, 37–51.

Miller, Gary J., *Cities by Contract*, Cambridge, MA: MIT Press, 1981.

Miller, Gary J. and Terry M. Moe, "Bureaucrats, Legislators, and the Size of Government," *American Political Science Review* 77, June 1983, 297–322.

Miller, Nicholas R., "Logrolling, Vote Trading, and the Paradox of Voting: A Game Theoretical Overview," *Public Choice* 30, Summer 1977, 51–75.

Miller, Nicholas R., "A New Solution Set for Tournaments and Majority Voting: Further Graph-Theoretical Approaches to the Theory of Voting," *American Journal of Political Science* 24, February 1980, 68–96.

Miller, Nicholas R., "The Covering Relation in Tournaments: Two Corrections," *American Journal of Political Science* 27, May 1983, 382–5.

Milleron, J. C., "Theory of Value with Public Goods: A Survey Article," *Journal of Economic Theory* 5, December 1972, 419–77.

Minford, Patrick and David Peel, "The Political Theory of the Business Cycle," *European Economic Review* 17, February 1982, 253–70.

Mishan, E., "The Postwar Literature on Externalities: An Interpretative Essay," *Journal of Economic Literature* 9, March 1971, 1–28.

Mitchell, W. C., "Schumpeter and Public Choice, Part I: Precursor to Public Choice?" *Public Choice* 42(1), 1984a, 73–88.

Mitchell, W. C., "Schumpeter and Public Choice, Part II: Democracy and the Demise of Capitalism: The Missing Chapter in Schumpeter," *Public Choice* 42(2), 1984b, 161–74.

Moe, Terry M., "The Politics of Structural Choice: Toward a Theory of Public Bureaucracy," in O. E. Williamson, ed., *Organization Theory: From Chester Barnard to the Present and Beyond*, New York: Oxford University Press, 1990a.

Moe, Terry M., "Political Institutions: The Neglected Side of the Story," *Journal of Law, Economics, and Organization* 6, 1990b, 213–53.

Moe, Terry M., "The Positive Theory of Public Bureaucracy," 1997 in D. C. Mueller, ed., 1997a, 455–80.

Mohammad, Sharif and John Whalley, "Rent Seeking in India: Its Costs and Policy Significance," *Kyklos* 37, 1984, 387–413.

Moore, Thomas G., "The Effectiveness of Regulation of Electric Utility Prices," *Southern Economic Journal* 36, April 1970, 365–75.

Morgan, W. Douglas, "Investor Owned vs. Publicly Owned Water Agencies: An Evaluation of the Property Rights Theory of the Firm," *Water Resources Bulletin* 13, August 1977, 775–82.

Morris, Irwin and Michael Munger, "First Branch, or Root? The Congress, the President and the Federal Reserve," *Public Choice* 96, September 1998, 363–80.

Morton, Rebecca and Charles Cameron, "Elections and the Theory of Campaign Contributions: A Survey and Critical Analysis," *Economics and Politics* 4, 1992, 79–108.

Moser, Peter, *The Political Economy of Democratic Institutions*, Cheltenham: Edward Elgar, 2000.

Moulin, Hervé, "Dominance Solvable Voting Schemes," *Econometrica* 47, November 1979, 1337–51.

Moulin, Hervé, "The Proportional Veto Principle," *Review of Economic Studies* 48, July 1981a, 407–16.

Moulin, Hervé, "Prudence versus Sophistication in Voting Strategy," *Journal of Economic Theory* 24, June 1981b, 398–412.

Moulin, Hervé, "Voting with Proportional Veto Power," *Econometrica* 50, January 1982, 45–62.

Mouritzen, P. E., "City Size and Citizen Satisfaction: Two Competing Theories Revisited," *European Journal of Political Research* 17, 1989, 661–88.

Mudambi, Ram, Pietro Navarra, and G. Carmela Nicosia, "Plurality versus Proportional Representation: An Analysis of Sicilian Elections," *Public Choice* 86, March 1996, 341–57.

Müller, Christian, "The Veil of Uncertainty Unveiled," *Constitutional Political Economy* 9, March 1998, 5–17.

Mueller, Dennis C., "The Possibility of a Social Welfare Function: Comment," *American Economic Review* 57, December 1967, 1304–11.

Mueller, Dennis C., "Fiscal Federalism in a Constitutional Democracy," *Public Policy* 19, Fall 1971, 567–93.

Mueller, Dennis C., "Constitutional Democracy and Social Welfare," *Quarterly Journal of Economics* 87, February 1973, 60–80.

Mueller, Dennis C., "Allocation, Redistribution and Collective Choice," *Public Finance* 32(2), 1977, 225–44.

Mueller, Dennis C., "Voting by Veto," *Journal of Public Economics* 10(1), 1978, 57–75.

Mueller, Dennis C., *Public Choice*, Cambridge: Cambridge University Press, 1979.

Mueller, Dennis C., "Power and Profit in Hierarchical Organizations," *Statsvetenskaplig Tidskrift* (*The Swedish Journal of Political Science*), N. 5, 1980, 293–302; reprinted in Manfred J. Holler, ed., *Power, Voting and Voting Power*, Würzburg: Physica-Verlag, 1981, 65–77.

Mueller, Dennis C., "Redistribution, Growth, and Political Stability," *American Economic Review* 72, May 1982, 155–9.

Mueller, Dennis C., ed., *The Political Economy of Growth*, New Haven: Yale University Press, 1983.

Mueller, Dennis C., "Voting by Veto and Majority Rule," in H. Hanusch, ed., *Public Finance and the Quest for Efficiency*, Detroit: Wayne State University Press, 1984, 69–86.

Mueller, Dennis C., "Rational Egoism versus Adaptive Egoism as Fundamental Postulate for a Descriptive Theory of Human Behavior," *Public Choice* 51, 1986, 3–23.

Mueller, Dennis C., *Public Choice II*, Cambridge: Cambridge University Press, 1989.

Mueller, Dennis C., "Constitutional Rights," *Journal of Law, Economics, and Organization* 7, September 1991, 313–33.

Mueller, Dennis C., *Constitutional Democracy*, New York: Oxford University Press, 1996a.

Mueller, Dennis C., "Constitutional and Liberal Rights," *Analyse & Kritik* 18, September 1996b, 96–117.

Mueller, Dennis C., ed., *Perspectives on Public Choice*, Cambridge: Cambridge University Press, 1997a.

Mueller, Dennis C., "Public Choice in Perspective," 1997b, in D. C. Mueller, ed., 1997a, 1–17.

Mueller, Dennis C., "Constitutional Public Choice," 1997c, in D. C. Mueller, ed., 1997a, 124–46.

Mueller, Dennis C., "The Importance of Uncertainty in a Two-Stage Theory of Constitutions," *Public Choice* 108, September 2001, 223–58.

Mueller, Dennis C. and Peter Murrell, "Interest Groups and the Political Economy of Government Size," in Francesco Forte and Alan Peacock, eds., *Public Expenditure and Government Growth*, Oxford: Basil Blackwell, 1985, 13–36.

Mueller, Dennis C. and Peter Murrell, "Interest Groups and the Size of Government," *Public Choice* 48, 1986, 125–45.

Mueller, Dennis C., Geoffrey C. Philpotts, and Jaroslav Vanek, "The Social Gains from Exchanging Votes: A Simulation Approach," *Public Choice* 13, Fall 1972, 55–79.

Mueller, Dennis C. and Thomas Stratmann, "Informative and Persuasive Campaigning," *Public Choice* 81, 1994, 55–77.

Mueller, Dennis C. and Thomas Stratmann, "The Economic Effects of Voter Participation," *Journal of Public Economics*, 2002.

Mueller, Dennis C., Robert D. Tollison, and Thomas D. Willett, "Representative Democracy via Random Selection," *Public Choice* 12, Spring 1972, 57–68.

Mueller, Dennis C., Robert D. Tollison, and Thomas Willett, "The Utilitarian Contract: A Generalization of Rawls' Theory of Justice," *Theory and Decision* 4, February/April 1974a, 345–67.

Mueller, Dennis C., Robert D. Tollison, and Thomas D. Willett, "On Equalizing the Distribution of Political Income," *Journal of Political Economy* 82, March/April 1974b, 414–22.

Mueller, Dennis C., Robert D. Tollison, and Thomas D. Willett, "Solving the Intensity Problem in a Representative Democracy," in R. D. Leiter and G. Sirkin, eds., *Economics of Public Choice*, New York: Cyro Press, 1975, 54–94; reprinted in R. Amacher, R. D. Tollison, and T. Willett, *Political Economy and Public Policy*, Ithaca: Cornell University Press, 1976, 444–73.

Müller, Wolfgang C., "Decision for Opposition: The Austrian Socialist Party's Abandonment of Government Participation in 1966," in W. C. Müller and K. Strøm, 1999, 172–91.

Müller, Wolfgang C. and Kaare Strøm, eds., *Policy, Office, or Votes*, Cambridge: Cambridge University Press, 1999.

Müller, Wolfgang C. and Kaare Strøm, eds., *Coalition Governments in Western Europe*, Oxford: Oxford University Press, 2000a.

Müller, Wolfgang C. and Kaare Strøm, "Coalition Governance in Western Europe," 2000b, in W. C. Müller and K. Strøm, eds., 2000a, 559–92.

Munger, Michael C., "A Simple Test of the Thesis that Committee Jurisdictions Shape Corporate PAC Contributions," *Public Choice* 62, August 1989, 181–6.

Munley, Vincent G., "An Alternative Test of the Tiebout Hypothesis," *Public Choice* 38(2), 1982, 211–7.

Murrell, Peter, "The Comparative Structure of the Growth of the West German and British Manufacturing Industries," in D. C. Mueller, ed., 1983, 109–31.

Murrell, Peter, "An Examination of the Factors Affecting the Formation of Interest Groups in OECD Countries," *Public Choice* 43(2), 1984, 151–71.

Musgrave, Richard A., "The Voluntary Exchange Theory of Public Economy," *Quarterly Journal of Economics* 53, February 1939, 213–38.

Musgrave, Richard A., *The Theory of Public Finance*, New York: McGraw-Hill, 1959.

Musgrave, Richard A., "Approaches to a Fiscal Theory of Political Federalism," NBER, *Public Finances: Needs, Resources and Utilization*, Princeton: Princeton University Press, 1961, 97–122.

Musgrave, Richard A. and Peggy B. Musgrave, *Public Finance in Theory and Practice*, 3rd ed., New York: McGraw-Hill, 1980.

Musgrave, Richard A., "Leviathan Cometh – Or Dose He?" in H. F. Ladd and T. N. Tideman, eds., *Tax and Expenditure Limitations*, Washington D.C.: Urban Institute, 1981, 77–120.

Musgrave, Richard A. and Alan T. Peacock, eds., *Classics in the Theory of Public Finance*, New York: St. Martin's Press, 1967.

Muth, Richard F., *Public Housing: An Economic Evaluation*, Washington, D.C.: American Enterprise Institute for Public Policy Research, 1973.

Myerson, Roger B., "Theoretical Comparisons of Electoral Systems," *European Economic Review* 43, April 1999, 671–97.

Myerson, Roger B. and Robert J. Weber, "A Theory of Voting Equilibria," *American Political Science Review* 87, March 1993, 102–14.

Naert, Frank, "Pressure Politics and Government Spending in Belgium," *Public Choice* 67, October 1990, 49–63.

Nagel, Thomas, "Rawls on Justice," *Philosophical Review* 82, April 1973, 220–34; reprinted in N. Daniels, ed., 1974, 1–15.

Nagler, Jonathan and Jan Leighley, "Presidential Campaign Expenditures: Evidence on Allocations and Effects," *Public Choice* 73, April 1992, 319–33.

Nannestad, Peter and Martin Paldam, "The VP-Function. A Survey of the Literature on Vote and Popularity Functions," *Public Choice* 79, 1994, 213–45.

726   **References**

Nannestad, Peter and Martin Paldam, "It's the Government's Fault: A Cross-Section Study of Economic Voting in Denmark, 1990–93," *European Journal of Political Research* 28, 1996, 33–65.

Nannestad, Peter and Martin Paldam, "From the Pocketbook of the Welfare Man: A Pooled Cross-Section Study of Economic Voting in Denmark, 1986–92," *British Journal of Political Science* 27, 1997, 119–36.

Nardinelli, C., M. S. Wallace, and J. T. Warner, "Explaining Differences in State Growth," *Public Choice* 52(3), 1987, 201–13.

Nash, John F., "The Bargaining Problem," *Econometrica* 18, April 1950, 155–62.

Nath, S. K., "Liberalism, Pareto Principle and the Core of a Society," mimeo, University of Warwick, 1976.

Neck, R. and F. Schneider, "The Growth of the Public Sector in Austria," in J. A. Lybeck and M. Henrekson, eds., *Explaining the Growth of Government*, Amsterdam: North-Holland, 1988, 231–62.

Nelson, Douglas A., "Endogenous Tariff Theory: A Critical Survey," *American Journal of Political Science* 32, 1988, 796–837.

Nelson, Michael A., "An Empirical Analysis of State and Local Tax Structure in the Context of the Leviathan Model of Government," *Public Choice* 49(3), 1986, 283–94.

Nelson, Douglas and Eugene Silberberg, "Ideology and Legislator Shirking," *Economic Inquiry* 25, January 1987, 15–25.

Nelson, Michael A., "Searching for Leviathan: Comment and Extension," *American Economic Review*, 77, March 1987, 198–204.

Newman, P., *The Theory of Exchange*, Englewood Cliffs, NJ: Prentice-Hall, 1965.

Ng, Yew-Kwang, "The Economic Theory of Clubs: Optimal Tax/Subsidy," *Economica* 41, August 1974, 308–21.

Ng, Yew-Kwang, "Bentham or Bergson? Finite Sensibility, Utility Functions and Social Welfare Functions," *Review of Economic Studies* 42, October 1975, 545–69.

Ng, Yew-Kwang, *Welfare Economics*, New York: John Wiley & Sons, 1980.

Ng, Yew-Kwang, "Welfarism: A Defense against Sen's Attack," *Economic Journal* 91, June 1981a, 527–30.

Ng, Yew-Kwang, "Bentham or Nash? On the Acceptable Form of Social Welfare Functions," *Economic Record* 57, September 1981b, 238–50.

Ng, Yew-Kwang, "Beyond Pareto Optimality: The Necessity of Interpersonal Cardinal Utilities in Distributional Judgements and Social Choice," *Zeitschrift für Nationalökonomie* 42(3), 1982, 207–33.

Ng, Yew-Kwang, "Some Broader Issues of Social Choice," in P. K. Pattanaik and M. Salles, eds., *Social Choice and Welfare*, Amsterdam: North-Holland, 1983, 151–73.

Ng, Yew-Kwang, "Expected Subjective Utility: Is the Neumann-Morgenstern Utility the Same as the Neoclassical's?" *Social Choice and Welfare* 1, 1984a, 177–86.

Ng, Yew-Kwang, "Interpersonal Level Comparability Implies Comparability of Utility Differences," *Theory and Decision* 17, 1984b, 141–7.

Ng, Yew-Kwang, "Some Fundamental Issues in Social Welfare," in G. Feiwel, ed., *Issues in Contemporary Microeconomics and Welfare*, London: Macmillan, 1985a, 435–69.

Ng, Yew-Kwang, "Equity and Efficiency vs. Freedom and Fairness: An Inherent Conflict," *Kyklos* 38(4), 1985b, 495–516.

Ng, Yew-Kwang, *Efficiency, Equality and Public Policy*, London: Macmillan Press, 2000.

Nicols, Alfred, "Stock versus Mutual Savings and Loan Associations: Some Evidence of Differences in Behavior," *American Economic Review* 57, May 1967, 337–46.

Niemi, Richard G., "Majority Decisions-Making with Partial Unidimensionality," *American Political Science Review* 63, June 1969, 488–97.

Niemi, Richard G., "Why So Much Stability?: Another Opinion," *Public Choice* 41(2), 1983, 261–70.

Niemi, Richard G., "The Problem of Strategic Behavior under Approval Voting," *American Political Science Review* 78, December 1984, 952–8.

Niemi, Richard G. and Herbert F. Weisberg, "A Mathematical Solution for the Probability of the Paradox of Voting," *Behavioral Science* 13, July 1968, 317–23.

Niou, Emerson M. S. and Peter C. Ordeshook, "Universalism in Congress," *American Journal of Political Science* 29, 1985, 246–60.

Niskanen, William A., Jr., *Bureaucracy and Representative Government*, Chicago: Aldine-Atherton, 1971.

Niskanen, William A., Jr., "Bureaucrats and Politicians," *Journal of Law and Economics* 18, December 1975, 617–43.

Niskanen, William A., Jr., "Economic and Fiscal Effects on the Popular Vote for the President," in D. W. Rae and T. J. Eismeir, ed., *Public Policy and Public Choice*, London: Sage, 1979, 93–120.

Niskanen, William A., Jr., "The Case for a New Fiscal Constitution," *The Journal of Economic Perspectives* 6, Spring 1992, 13–24.

Nitzan, Shmuel, "Social Preference Ordering in a Probabilistic Voting Model," *Public Choice* 24, Winter 1975, 93–100.

Nitzan, Shmuel, "The Vulnerability of Point-Voting Schemes to Preference Variation and Strategic Manipulation," *Public Choice* 47, 1985, 349–70.

Nitzan, Shmuel, "Collective Rent Dissipation," *Economic Journal* 101, November 1991, 1522–34.

Nitzan, Shmuel, "More on More Efficient Rent Seeking and Strategic Behavior," *Public Choice* 79, June 1994a, 355–6.

Nitzan, Shmuel, "Modeling Rent-Seeking Contests," *European Journal of Political Economy* 10, 1994b, 41–60.

Nitzan, Shmuel, "Transfers or Public Good Provision? A Political Allocation Perspective," *Economic Letters* 45, August 1994c, 451–7.

Nitzan, Shmuel and Jacob Paroush, "Optimal Decision Rules in Uncertain Dichotomous Situations," *International Economic Review* 23, 1982, 289–97.

Nitzan, Shmuel, Jacob Paroush, and Shlomo I. Lampert, "Preference Expression and Misrepresentation in Point Voting Schemes," *Public Choice* 35(4), 1980, 421–36.

Nitzan, Shmuel and Ariel Rubinstein, "A Further Characterization of Borda Ranking Method," *Public Choice* 36, 1981, 153–8.

Nollen, Stanley D. and Harvey J. Iglarsh, "Explanations of Protectionism in International Trade Votes," *Public Choice* 66, August 1990, 137–53.

Nordhaus, William D., "The Political Business Cycle," *Review of Economic Studies* 42, April 1975, 169–90.

Nordhaus, William D., "Alternative Approaches to the Political Business Cycle," *Brookings Papers on Economic Activity* no. 2, 1989, 1–68.

North, Douglass C., *Structure and Change in Economic History*, New York: Norton, 1981.

North, Douglass C., "The Growth of Government in the United States: An Economic Historian's Perspective," *Journal of Public Economics* 28, December 1985, 383–99.

North, Douglass C. and John J. Wallis, "American Government Expenditures: A Historical Perspective," *American Economic Review* 72, May 1982, 336–40.

Notterman, J. M., *Behavior: A Systematic Approach*, New York: Random House, 1970.

Nozick, Robert, *Anarchy, State, and Utopia*, New York: Basic Books, 1974.

Oakland, William H., "Public Goods, Perfect Competition, and Underproduction," *Journal of Political Economy* 82, September/October 1974, 927–39.

Oates, Wallace E., "The Effects of Property Taxes and Local Public Spending on Property Values: An Empirical Study of Tax Capitalization and the Tiebout Hypothesis," *Journal of Political Economy* 77, November/December 1969, 957–71.

Oates, Wallace E., *Fiscal Federalism*, London: Harcourt Brace, 1972.

Oates, Wallace, "Lump-Sum Intergovernmental Grants Have Price Effects," in P. Mieszkowski and W. H. Oakland, eds., *Fiscal Federalism and Grants-in-Aid*, Washington, D.C.: Urban Institute, 1979, 23–30.

Oates, Wallace E., "Searching for Leviathan: An Empirical Study," *American Economic Review* 75, September 1985, 748–57.

Oates, Wallace E., "On the Measurement of Congestion in the Provision of Local Public Goods," *Journal of Urban Economics* 24, 1988a, 85–94.

Oates, Wallace E., "On the Nature and Measurement of Fiscal Illusion: A Survey, " in G. Brennan, et al., eds., *Taxation and Fiscal Federalism: Essays in Honour of Russell Mathews*, Canberra: Australian National University Press, 1988b, 65–82.

Oatley, Thomas, "Central Bank Independence and Inflation: Corporatism, Partisanship, and Alternative Indices of Central Bank Independence," *Public Choice* 98, March 1999, 399–413.

Oelert, W., "Reprivatisierung des öffentlichen Personalverkehrs," *Der Personenverkehr* 4, 1976, 108–14.

O'Halloran, Sharyn, *Politics, Process, and American Trade Policy*, Ann Arbor: University of Michigan Press, 1994.

Okun, Arthur M., *Prices and Quantities*, Washington D.C.: Brookings Institute, 1981.

Olson, Mancur, Jr., *The Logic of Collective Action*, Cambridge, MA: Harvard University Press, 1965.

Olson, Mancur, Jr., *The Rise and Decline of Nations: Economic Growth Stagflation and Social Rigidities*, New Haven: Yale University Press, 1982.

Olson, Mancur, Jr., "Why Some Welfare-State Redistribution to the Poor Is a Great Idea," in C. K. Rowley, ed., *Democracy and Public Choice*, Oxford: Basil Blackwell, 1987, 191–222.

Olson, Mancur, Jr., "Dictatorship, Democracy and Development," *American Political Science Review* 87, September 1993, 567–76.

Olson, Mancur, Jr., *Power and Prosperity: Outgrowing Communist and Capitalist Dictatorships*, New York: Basic Books, 2000.

Olson, Mancur, Jr., Naveen Sarna, and Anand V. Swamy, "Government and Growth: A Simple Hypothesis Explaining Cross-Country Differences in Productivity Growth," *Public Choice* 102, March 2000, 341–64.

Oppenheimer, Joe A., Relating Coalitions of Minorities to the Voters' Paradox, or Putting the Fly in the Democratic Pie, paper presented at the Southwest Political Science Association meeting, 1972.

Oppenheimer, Joe A., "Some Political Implications of 'Vote Trading and the Voting Paradox: A Proof of Logical Equivalence': A Comment," *American Political Science Review* 69, September 1975, 963–6.

Oppenheimer, Joe A., "The Democratic Politics of Distributive Justice: Theory and Practice," mimeo, College Park, MD, 1979.

Orbell, John M. and T. Uno, "A Theory of Neighborhood Problem Solving: Political Action vs. Residential Mobility," *American Political Science Review* 66, June 1972, 471–89.

Ordeshook, Peter C., *Game Theory and Political Theory*, Cambridge: Cambridge University Press, 1986.

Ordeshook, Peter C., "Constitutional Stability," *Constitutional Political Economy* 3, 1992, 137–75.

Ordeshook, Peter C., "Engineering or Science: What is the Study of Politics," in J. Friedman, ed., 1996, 175–88.

Ordeshook, Peter C., "The Spatial Analysis of Elections and Committees: Four Decades of Research," 1997, in D. C. Mueller, ed., 1997a, 247–70.

Ordeshook, Peter C. and Olga Shvetsova, "Ethnic Heterogeneity, District Magnitude, and the Number of Parties," *American Journal of Political Science* 38, 1994, 100–23.

Ordeshook, Peter C. and Langche Zeng, "Some Properties of Hare Voting with Strategic Voters," *Public Choice* 78, January 1994, 87–101.

Orzechowski, William, "Economic Models of Bureaucracy: Survey, Extensions, and Evidence," in T. E. Borcherding, ed., 1977, 229–59.

Osborne, Martin J. and Al Slivinski, "A Model of Political Competition with Citizen Candidates," *Quarterly Journal of Economics* 111, February 1996, 65–96.

Ostrom, Elinor, "A Public Service Industry Approach to Metropolitan Institutions: Structure and Performance," *Social Science Journal* 20, 1983, 79–96.

Ostrom, Elinor and James Walker, "Neither Markets nor States: Linking Transformation Processes in Collective Action Arenas," 1997, in D. C. Mueller, ed., 1997a, 35–72.

Ostrom, Vincent, *The Political Theory of a Compound Republic*, Blacksburg: Public Choice Society, 1971.

Overbye, Einar, "Making a Case for the Rational, Self-Regarding 'Ethical' Voter ... and Solving the 'Paradox of Not Voting' in the Process," *European Journal of Political Research* 27, 1995a, 369–96.

Overbye, Einar, "Explaining Welfare Spending," *Public Choice* 83, June 1995b, 313–35.

Overland, Jody, Kenneth L. Simons, and Michael Spagat, "Political Instability and Growth in Dictatorships," mimeo, Royal Holloway College, University of London, 2000.

Owen, G. and Bernard Grofman, "To Vote or Not to Vote: The Paradox of Nonvoting," *Public Choice* 42(3), 1984, 311–25.

Pack, Janet R., "The Political Policy Cycle: Presidential Effort vs. Presidential Control," *Public Choice* 54, 1987, 231–59.

Palda, Kristian S., "Does Advertising Influence Votes? An Analysis of the 1966 and 1970 Quebec Elections," *Canadian Journal of Political Science* 6, December 1973, 638–55.

Palda, Kristian S., "The Effect of Expenditure on Political Success," *Journal of Law and Economics* 18, December 1975, 745–71.

Palda, Filip and Kristian Palda, "Ceilings on Campaign Spending: Hypothesis and Partial Test with Canadian Data," *Public Choice* 45(3), 1985, 313–31.

Palda, Filip and Kristian Palda, "The Impact of Campaign Expenditures on Political Competition in French Legislative Elections," *Public Choice* 94, January 1998, 157–74.

Paldam, Martin, "Is There an Electional Cycle? A Comparative Study of National Accounts," *Scandinavian Journal of Economics* 81(2), 1979, 323–42.

Paldam, Martin, "A Preliminary Survey of the Theories and Findings on Vote and Popularity Functions," *European Journal of Political Research* 9, June 1981a, 181–99.

Paldam, Martin, "An Essay on the Rationality of Economic Policy: The Test-Case of the Electional Cycle," *Public Choice* 37(2), 1981b, 287–305.

Paldam, Martin, "Political Business Cycles," 1997, in D. C. Mueller, ed., 1997a, 342–70.

Paldam, Martin and Friedrich Schneider, "The Macro-Economic Aspects of Government and Opposition Popularity in Denmark, 1957–78," *Nationalkonomisk Tidsskrift* 118(2), 1980, 149–70.

Palfrey, Thomas R., "Spatial Equilibrium with Entry," *Review of Economic Studies* 51, January 1984, 139–56.

Palfrey, Thomas R. and Howard Rosenthal, "A Strategic Calculus of Voting," *Public Choice* 41(1), 1983, 7–53.

Palfrey, Thomas R. and Howard Rosenthal, "Participation and the Provision of Discrete Public Goods: A Strategic Analysis," *Journal of Public Economics* 24, 1984, 171–93.

Palfrey, Thomas R. and Howard Rosenthal, "Voter Participation and Strategic Uncertainty," *American Political Science Review* 79, March 1985, 62–78.

Paloheimo, Heikki, "Pluralism, Corporatism and the Distributive Conflict in Developed Capitalist Countries," *Scandinavian Political Studies* 7, 1984a, 17–38.

Paloheimo, Heikki, "Distributive Struggle and Economic Development in the 1970s in Developed Capitalist Countries," *European Journal of Political Research* 12(2), 1984b, 171–90.

Park, R. E., "The Possibility of a Social Welfare Function: Comment," *American Economic Review* 57, December 1967, 1300–4.

Parks, R. P., "An Impossibility Theorem for Fixed Preferences: A Dictatorial Bergson-Samuelson Welfare Function," *Review of Economic Studies* 43, October 1976, 447–50.

Parry, Geraint, George Moyser, and Neil Day, *Political Participation and Democracy in Britain*, Cambridge: Cambridge University Press, 1992.

Pashigian, B. Peter, "Consequences and Causes of Public Ownership of Urban Transit Facilities," *Journal of Political Economy* 84, December 1976, 1239–59.

Pateman, C. *Participation and Democratic Theory*, Cambridge: Cambridge University Press, 1970.

Pattanaik, Prasanta K., "Risk, Impersonality, and the Social Welfare Function," *Journal of Political Economy* 76, November 1968, 1152–69.

Pattanaik, Prasanta K., *Voting and Collective Choice*, Cambridge: Cambridge University Press, 1971.

Pattanaik, Prasanta K., "Stability of Sincere Voting under Some Classes of Non-Binary Group Decision Procedures," *Journal of Economic Theory* 8, June 1974, 206–24.

Pattanaik, Prasanta K., "The Liberal Paradox: Some Interpretations When Rights Are Represented as Game Forms," *Analyse & Kritik* 18, September 1996, 38–53.

Pattanaik, Prasanta K., "Some Paradoxes of Preference Aggregation," 1997, in D. C. Mueller, 1997a, 201–25.

Patterson, Samuel C. and Gregory A. Caldeira, "Getting Out the Vote: Participation in Gubernatorial Elections," *American Political Science Review* 77, September 1983, 675–89.

Paul, Chris W., II, "Competition in the Medical Profession: An Application of the Economic Theory of Regulation," *Southern Economic Journal* 48(3), January 1982, 559–69.

Paul, Chris and Niles Schoening, "Regulation and Rent Seeking: Prices, Profits, and Third-party Transfers," *Public Choice* 68, January 1991, 185–94.

Pauly, Mark V., "Clubs, Commonality, and the Core: An Integration of Game Theory and the Theory of Public Goods," *Economica* 35, August 1967, 314–24.

Pauly, Mark V., "Cores and Clubs," *Public Choice* 9, Fall 1970, 53–65.

Pauly, Mark V., "Overinsurance and Public Provision of Insurance: The Role of Moral Hazard and Adverse Selection," *Quarterly Journal of Economics* 88, February 1974, 44–62.

Pausch, R., *Möglichkeiten einer Privatisierung öffentlicher Unternehmen*, Göttingen, 1976.

Peacock, Alan T. and Jack Wiseman, *The Growth of Public Expenditure in the United Kingdom*, Princeton, NJ: Princeton University Press, 1961.

Peden, Edgar A., "Productivity in the United States and Its Relationship to Government Activity: An Analysis of 57 Years, 1929–86," *Public Choice* 86, December 1991, 153–73.

Peden, Edgar A. and Michael D. Bradley, "Government Size, Productivity, and Economic Growth: The Post-War Experience," *Public Choice* 61, June 1989, 229–45.

Peltzman, Sam, "Pricing in Public and Private Enterprises: Electric Utilities in the United States," *Journal of Law and Economics* 14, April 1971, 109–47.

Peltzman, Sam, "An Evaluation of Consumer Protection Legislation: The 1962 Drug Amendments," *Journal of Political Economy* 81, September 1973, 1049–91.

Peltzman, Sam, "Towards a More General Theory of Regulation?" *Journal of Law and Economics* 19, August 1976, 211–40.

Peltzman, Sam, "The Growth of Government," *Journal of Law and Economics* 23, October 1980, 209–88.

Peltzman, Sam, "Constituent Interest and Congressional Voting," *Journal of Law and Economics* 27, April 1984, 181–210.

Peltzman, Sam, "An Economic Interpretation of the History of Congressional Voting in the Twentieth Century," *American Economic Review* 75, September 1985, 656–75.

Peltzman, Sam, "How Efficient Is the Voting Market," *Journal of Law and Economics* 33, April 1990, 27–63.

Peltzman, Sam, "Voters as Fiscal Conservatives," *Quarterly Journal of Economics* 107, 1992, 327–61.

Pérez-Castrillo, J. David, and Thierry Verdier, "A General Analysis of Rent-Seeking Games," *Public Choice* 73, April 1992, 335–50.

Persson, Torsten and Guido Tabellini, *Macroeconomic Policy, Credibility and Politics*, Chur: Harwood Academic Publishers, 1990.

Persson, Torsten and Guido Tabellini, "Is Inequality Harmful for Growth?" *American Economic Review* 84, June 1994, 600–22.

Persson, Torsten and Guido Tabellini, "Comparative Politics and Public Finance," *Journal of Political Economy* 108, December 1998, 1121–61.

Persson, Torsten and Guido Tabellini, "The Size and Scope of Government: Comparative Politics with Rational Politicians," *European Economic Review* 43, 1999, 699–735.

Persson, Torsten and Guido Tabellini, *Political Economics – Explaining Economic Policy*, Cambridge, MA: MIT Press, 2000a.

Persson, Torsten and Guido Tabellini, "Political Institutions and Policy Outcomes: What are the Stylized Facts?" mimeo, Stockholm University, 2000b.

Persson, Torsten and Guido Tabellini, "Electoral Rules and Corruption," mimeo, Stockholm University, 2000c.

Pescatrice, Donn R. and John M. Trapani, III, "The Performance and Objectives of Public and Private Utilities Operating in the United States," *Journal of Public Economics* 13, April 1980, 259–76.

Pestieau, Pierre, "The Optimality Limits of the Tiebout Model," in W. E. Oates, ed., *The Political Economy of Fiscal Federalism*, Lexington: Lexington Books, 1977, 173–86.

Peters, Emory, "The Rational Voter Paradox Revisited," *Public Choice* 97, October 1998, 179–95.

Peterson, G. M., *The Demand for Public Schooling*, Washington D.C.: Urban Institute, 1973.

Peterson, G. M., "Voter Demand for School Expenditures," in J. E. Jackson, ed., *Public Needs and Private Behavior in Metropolitan Areas*, Cambridge, MA: Harvard University Press, 1975, 99–115.

Petrovic, W. M. and B. L. Jaffee, "Aspects of the Generation and Collection of Household Refuse in Urban Areas," mimeo, Indiana University, Bloomington, 1977.

Pfister, W., "Steigende Millionenverluste der Bayerischen Staatsforstverwaltung: Ein Dauerzustand?" *Mitteilungsblatt des Bayerischen Waldbesitzerverbandes* 26, 1976, 1–9.

Philipson, Tomas J. and James M. Snyder, Jr., "Equilibrium and Efficiency in an Organized Vote Market," *Public Choice* 89, December 1996, 245–65.

Phillips, Joseph D., "Estimating the Economic Surplus," in P. A. Baran and P. M. Sweezy, eds., *Monopoly Capital*, New York: Modern Reader, 1966, 369–91.

Philpotts, Geoffrey, "Vote Trading, Welfare, and Uncertainty," *Canadian Journal of Economics* 3, August 1972, 358–72.

Philpotts, Geoffrey, "A Note on the Representation of Preferences in the Lindahl-Johansen Diagram," *American Economic Review* 70, June 1980, 488–92.

Picot, Arnold and Thomas Kaulmann, "Comparative Performance of Government-owned and Privately-owned Industrial Corporations – Empirical Results from Six Countries," *Journal of Institutional and Theoretical Economics* 145, June 1989, 298–316.

Pier, William J., Robert B. Vernon, and John H. Wicks, "An Empirical Comparison of Government and Private Production Efficiency," *National Tax Journal* 27, December 1974, 653–56.

Pigou, Arthur, *The Economics of Welfare*, London: Macmillan, 1920; revised 1924, 1929, 1932.

Pincus, Jonathan, "Pressure Groups and the Pattern of Tariffs," *Journal of Political Economy* 83, August 1975, 757–78.

Pissarides, Christopher A., "British Government Popularity and Economic Performance," *Economic Journal* 90, September 1980, 569–81.

Pitkin, Hanna Fenichel, *The Concept of Representation*, Berkeley: University of California Press, 1967.

Pittman, Russell, "The Effects of Industry Concentration and Regulation on Contributions in Three U.S. Senate Campaigns," *Public Choice* 27, Fall 1976, 71–80.

Pittman, Russell, "Market Structure and Campaign Contributions," *Public Choice* 31, Fall 1977, 37–52.

Plott, Charles R., "A Notion of Equilibrium and Its Possibility under Majority Rule," *American Economic Review* 57, September 1967, 787–806.

Plott, Charles R., "Recent Results in the Theory of Voting," in M. Intriligator, ed., *Frontiers of Quantitative Economics*, Amsterdam: North-Holland, 1971, 109–27.

Plott, Charles R., "Ethics, Social Choice Theory and the Theory of Economic Policy," *Journal of Mathematical Sociology* 2, 1972, 181–208.

Plott, Charles R., "Path Independence, Rationality and Social Choice," *Econometrica* 41, November 1973, 1075–91.

Plott, Charles R., "Axiomatic Social Choice Theory: An Overview and Interpretation," *American Journal of Political Science* 20, August 1976, 511–96.

Poguntke, Thomas, "Winner Takes All: The FDP in 1982–1983: Maximizing, Votes, Office and Policy," in Müller and Strøm, eds., 1999, 216–36.

Pollack, Robert A., "Bergson-Samuelson Social Welfare Functions and the Theory of Social Choice," *Quarterly Journal of Economics* 93, February 1979, 73–90.

Pommerehne, Werner W., "Private versus Öffentliche Müllabfuhr; Ein Theoretischer und Empirischer Vergleich," *Finanzarchiv* 35, 1976, 272–94.

Pommerehne, Werner W., "Institutional Approaches to Public Expenditures: Empirical Evidence from Swiss Municipalities," *Journal of Public Economics* 9, April 1978, 163–201.

Pommerehne, Werner W. and Bruno S. Frey, "Two Approaches to Estimating Public Expenditures," *Public Finance Quarterly* 4, October 1976, 395–407.

Pommerehne, Werner W. and Friedrich Schneider, "Unbalanced Growth between Public and Private Sectors: An Empirical Examination," in R. H. Haveman, ed., *Public Finance and Public Employment*, Detroit MI: Wayne State University Press, 1982, 309–26.

Pommerehne, Werner W. and Friedrich Schneider, "Does Government in a Representative Democracy Follow a Majority of Voters' Preferences? – An Empirical Examination," in H. Hanusch, ed., *Anatomy of Government Deficiencies*, Berlin: Springer, 1983, 61–84.

Poole, Keith T. and Thomas Romer, "Patterns of Political Action Committee Contributions to the 1980 Campaigns for the United States House of Representatives," *Public Choice* 47(1), 1985, 63–111.

Poole, Keith T. and Thomas Romer, "Ideology, 'Shirking' and Representation," *Public Choice* 77, September 1993, 185–96.

Poole, Keith T., Thomas Romer, and Howard Rosenthal, "The Revealed Preferences of Political Action Committees," *American Economic Review* 77, 1987, 298–302.

Poole, Keith T. and Howard Rosenthal, "A Spatial Model for Legislative Roll Call Analysis," *American Journal of Political Science* 29, 1985, 357–84.

Poole, Keith T. and Howard Rosenthal, "Patterns of Congressional Voting," *American Journal of Political Science* 35, 1991, 228–78.

Poole, Keith T. and Howard Rosenthal, "The Enduring Nineteenth-Century Battle for Economic Regulation: The Interstate Commerce Act Revisited," *Journal of Law and Economics* 36, October 1993, 837–60.

Poole, Keith T. and Howard Rosenthal, *Congress: A Political-Economic History of Roll Call Voting*, Oxford: Oxford University Press, 1997.

Poole, Keith T. and Richard A. Smith, "A Spatial Analysis of Winning and Losing Motions in the U.S. Senate 1979–1981," *Public Choice* 78, January 1994, 23–41.

Porter, Richard D. and Amanda S. Bayer, "Monetary Perspective on Underground Economic Activity in the United States," in E. L. Feige, ed., 1989a, 129–57.

Posner, Richard A., "The Social Costs of Monopoly and Regulation," *Journal of Political Economy* 83, August 1975, 807–27; reprinted in J. M. Buchanan, R. D. Tollison, and G. Tullock, 1980, 71–94.

Posner, Richard A., "What Do Judges Maximize? (The Same Thing Everybody Else Does)," *Supreme Court Economic Review* 3, 1993, 1–41.

Potters, Jan, *Lobbying and Pressure: Theory and Experiments*, Amsterdam: Tinbergen Institute Research Monograph no. 36, 1992.

Potters, Jan and Randolph Sloof, "Interest Groups: A Survey of Empirical Models that Try to Assess Their Influence," *European Journal of Political Economy* 12, November 1996, 403–42.

Potters, Jan and Frans van Winden, "Lobbying and Asymmetric Information," *Public Choice* 74, 1992, 269–92.

Pourgerami, Abbas, "The Political Economy of Development: A Cross-National Causality Test of the Development-Democracy-Growth Hypothesis," *Public Choice* 58, 1988, 123–41.

Pourgerami, Abbas, "Authoritarian versus Nonauthoritarian Approaches to Economic Development: Update and Additional Evidence," *Public Choice* 74, October 1992, 365–77.

Powell, G. Bingham, Jr., "Party Systems and Political System Performance: Voting Participation, Government Stability and Mass Violence in Contemporary Democracies," *American Political Science Review* 75, December 1981, 861–79.

Powell, G. Bingham, *Contemporary Democracies: Participation, Stability, and Violence*, Cambridge, MA: Harvard University Press, 1982.

Powell, G. Bingham, Jr., *Elections as Instruments of Democracy*, New Haven: Yale University Press, 2000.

Price, Simon, "Political Business Cycles and Macroeconomic Credibility: A Survey," *Public Choice* 92, September 1997, 407–27.

Price, Simon and David Sanders, "Economic Competence, Rational Expectations and Government Popularity in Post-War Britain," *Manchester School of Economic and Social Studies*; 62(3), September 1994, 296–312.

Priest, George L., "The Common Law Practice and the Selection of Efficient Rules," *Journal of Legal Studies* 6, 1977, 65–82.

Primeaux, Walter J., John E. Filer, Robert S. Herren, and Daniel R. Hollas, "Determinants of Regulatory Policies toward Competition in the Electric Utility Industry," *Public Choice* 43(2), 1984, 173–86.

Pryor, Frederic L., "A Quasi-Test of Olson's Hypotheses," in D. C. Mueller, ed., 1983, 90–105.

Pryor, Frederic L., "Testing Olson: Some Statistical Problems," *Public Choice* 52(3), 1987, 223–6.

Przeworski, Adam and Fernando Limongi, "Political Regimes and Economic Growth," *Journal of Economic Perspectives* 7, 1993, 51–70.

Putnam, Robert D., *Bowling Alone: The Collapse and Revival of American Community*, New York: Simon and Schuster, 2000.

Puviani, Amilcare, *Teoria della illusione nelle netrate publiche*, Perugia, 1897.

Puviani, Amilcare, *Teoria della illusione Finanziaria*, Palermo, 1903.

Quiggin, John, "Testing the Implications of Olson's Hypothesis," *Economica* 55, August 1992, 261–77.

Rae, Douglas W., "Decision-Rules and Individual Values in Constitutional Choice," *American Political Science Review* 63, March 1969, 40–56.

Rae, Douglas W., *The Political Consequences of Electoral Laws*, rev. ed., New Haven: Yale University Press, 1971.

Rae, Douglas W., "The Limits of Consensual Decision," *American Political Science Review* 69, December 1975, 1270–94.

Rae, Douglas W., *Equalities*, Cambridge, MA: Harvard University Press, 1981.

Rae, Douglas W. and Eric Schickler, "Majority Rule," 1997, in D. C. Mueller, ed., 1997a, 163–80.

Ram, Rati, "Government Size and Economic Growth: A New Framework and Some Evidence from Cross-Section and Time-Series Data," *American Economic Review* 76, March 1986, 191–203.

Rama, Martin, "Endogenous Trade Policy: A Time-Series Approach," *Economics and Politics* 6, November 1994, 215–32.

Ramírez, Carlos D. and Christian Eigen-Zucchi, "Understanding the Clayton Act of 1914: An Analysis of the Interest Group Hypothesis," *Public Choice* 106, January 2001, 157–81.

Rapoport, Anatol and Albert Chammah, *Prisoner's Dilemma*, Ann Arbor: University of Michigan Press, 1974.

Rasch, Bjorn Erik and Rune Jorgen Sorensen, "Organizational Behavior and Economic Growth: A Norwegian Perspective," *Scandinavian Political Studies* 9, March 1986, 51–63.

Rattinger, Hans, "Unemployment and the 1976 Election in Germany: Some Findings at the Aggregate and the Individual Level of Analysis," in D. A. Hibbs, Jr. and H. Fassbinder, eds., 1981, 121–35.

Rawls, John A., *A Theory of Justice*, Cambridge, MA: Belknap Press, 1971.

Rawls, John A., "Some Reasons for the Maximin Criterion," *American Economic Review* 64, May 1974, 141–6.

Rawls, John A., *The Law of Peoples*, Cambridge, MA: Harvard University Press, 1999.

Ray, Edward J., "The Determinants of Tariff and Nontariff Trade Restrictions in the United States," *Journal of Political Economy* 89, 1981, 105–21.

Ray, Edward J., "Changing Patterns of Protectionism: The Fall in Tariffs and the Rise in Non-Tariff Barriers," *Northwestern Journal of International Law & Business* 8, 1987, 285–327.

Ray, Edward J., "Protection of Manufactures in the United States," in D. Greenway, ed., *Global Protectionism: Is the U.S. Playing on a Level Playing Field?* London: Macmillan, 1991.

Ray, P., "Independence of Irrelevant Alternatives," *Econometrica* 41, September 1973, 987–91.

Reid, Bradford G., "Endogenous Elections, Electoral Budget Cycles and Canadian Provincial Governments," *Public Choice* 97, October 1998, 35–48.

Reimer, M., "The Case for Bare Majority Rule," *Ethics* 62, October 1951, 16–32.

Renaud, Paul S. A. and Frans A. A. M. van Winden, "Political Accountability for Price Stability and Unemployment in a Multi-Party System with Coalition Governments," *Public Choice* 53(2), 1987a, 181–6.

Renaud, Paul S. A. and Frans A. A. M. van Winden, "Tax Rate and Government Expenditure," *Kyklos* 40, 1987b, 349–67.

Renaud, Paul S. A. and Frans A. A. M. van Winden, "Behavior and Budgetary Autonomy of Local Governments," *European Journal of Political Economy* 7, 1991, 547–77.

Reynolds, Morgan and Eugene Smolensky, *Public Expenditures, Taxes and the Distribution of Income*, New York: Academic Press, 1977.

Rheinland-Pfalz, Rechnungshof, *Jahresbericht über die Prüfung der Haushalts- und Wirtschaftsführung sowie der Landeshaushaltsrechnung 1971*, Drucksache 7/1750, 1972, 81–4.

Rhode, Paul W. and Koleman S. Strumpf, "A Historical Test of the Tiebout Hypothesis: Local Heterogeneity from 1850 to 1990," mimeo, University of North Carolina, Chapel Hill, 2000.

Rice, Tom W., "The Determinants of Western European Government Growth, 1950–1980," *Comparative Political Studies* 19, July 1986, 233–57.

Rich, M. J., "Distributive Politics and the Allocation of Federal Grants," *American Political Science Review* 83, 1989, 193–213.

Richards, Daniel J., "Unanticipated Money and the Political Business Cycle," *Journal of Money, Credit and Banking* 18, 1986, 447–57.

Richardson, Lilliard E., Jr. and Michael C. Munger, "Shirking, Representation, and Congressional Behavior: Voting on the 1983 Amendments to the Social Security Act," *Public Choice* 76, June 1993, 151–72.

Riker, William H., "Voting and the Summation of Preferences: An Interpretative Bibliographical Review of Selected Developments during the Last Decade," *American Political Science Review* 55, December 1961, 900–11.

Riker, William H., *The Theory of Political Coalitions*, New Haven: Yale University Press, 1962.

Riker, William H., *Federalism: Origins, Operation, Significance*, Boston: Little, Brown, 1964.

Riker, William H., "Is 'A New and Superior Process' Really Superior?" *Journal of Political Economy* 87, August 1979, 875–90.

Riker, William H., "The Two-Party System and Duverger's Law: An Essay on the History of Political Science," *American Political Science Review* 76, December 1982a, 753–66.

Riker, William H., *Liberalism against Populism*, San Francisco: W. H. Freeman, 1982b.

Riker, William H., "Political Science and Rational Choice," in J. E. Alt and K. A. Shepsle, eds., *Perspectives on Positive Political Economy*, Cambridge: Cambridge University Press, 1990.

Riker, William H. and S. Brams, "The Paradox of Vote Trading," *American Political Science Review* 67, December 1973, 1235–47.

Riker, William H. and Peter C. Ordeshook, "A Theory of the Calculus of Voting," *American Political Science Review* 62, March 1968, 25–42.

Riker, William H. and Peter Ordeshook, *Introduction to Positive Political Theory*, Englewood Cliffs, NJ: Prentice-Hall, 1973.

Riley, Jonathan, "On the Possibility of Liberal Democracy," *American Political Science Review* 79, December 1985, 1135–51.

Riley, Jonathan, "Constitutional Democracy as a Two-Stage Game," in J. Ferejohn, J. N. Rakove, and J. Riley, eds., 2001, 147–69.

Rob, Rafael, "Asymptotic Efficiency of the Demand Revealing Mechanism," *Journal of Economic Theory* 28, December 1982, 207–20.

Roberts, K. W. S., "Voting Over Income Tax Schedules," *Journal of Public Economics* 8, December 1977, 329–40.

Roberts, Kevin W. S., "Possibility Theorems with Interpersonally Comparable Welfare Levels," *Review of Economic Studies* 47, January 1980a, 409–20.

Roberts, Kevin W. S., "Interpersonal Comparability and Social Choice Theory," *Review of Economic Studies* 47, January 1980b, 421–39.

Roberts, Kevin W. S., "Social Choice Theory: The Single-Profile and Multi-Profile Approaches," *Review of Economic Studies* 47, January 1980c, 441–50.

Robinson, James A., "When is a State Predatory?" mimeo, University of California, Berkeley, 2000.

Rodgers, James D., "Explaining Income Redistribution," in H. M. Hochman and G. E. Peterson, eds., *Redistribution through Public Choice*, New York: Columbia University Press, 1974, 165–205.

Rodrik, Dani, "Political Economy of Trade Policy," in G. M. Grossman and K. Rogoff, eds., *Handbook of International Economics*, vol. III, Amsterdam: Elsevier, 1995, 1457–94.

Rodrik, Dani, "Why Do More Open Economies Have Bigger Governments?" *Journal of Political Economy* 106(5), October 1998, 997–1032.

Rogoff, Kenneth, "The Optimal Degree of Commitment to an Intermediate Target," *Quarterly Journal of Economics* 100, 1985, 1169–89.

Rogoff, Kenneth, "Equilibrium Political Budget Cycles," *American Economic Review* 80, 1990, 21–36.

Rogoff, Kenneth and Anne Sibert, "Elections and Macroeconomic Policy Cycles," *Review of Economic Studies* 55, 1988, 1–16.

Rogowski, Ronald, "Structure, Growth and Power: Three Rationalist Accounts," *International Organization* 37, Autumn 1983, 713–38.

Romer, Thomas and Howard Rosenthal, "Political Resource Allocation, Controlled Agendas, and the Status Quo," *Public Choice* 33(4), Winter 1978, 27–43.

Romer, Thomas and Howard Rosenthal, "The Elusive Median Voter," *Journal of Public Economics* 12, October 1979a, 143–70.

Romer, Thomas and Howard Rosenthal, "Bureaucrats versus Voters: On the Political Economy of Resource Allocation by Direct Democracy," *Quarterly Journal of Economics* 93, November 1979b, 563–87.

Romer, Thomas and Howard Rosenthal, "Median Voters or Budget Maximizers: Evidence from School Expenditure Referenda," *Economic Inquiry* 20, October 1982, 556–78.

Rosa, Jean J., "Economic Conditions and Elections in France," in P. Whitely, ed., *Models of Political Economy*, London: Sage, 1980, 101–20.

Rose, Richard, "Electoral Systems: A Question of Degree or of Principle?" in A. Lijphart and B. Grofman, eds., 1984, 73–81.

Rose-Ackerman, Susan, *Corruption*, New York: Academic Press, 1978.

Rose-Ackerman, Susan, *Corruption and Government*, Cambridge: Cambridge University Press, 1999.

Ross, J. P. and J. Burkhead, *Productivity in the Local Government Sector*, Lexington MA: Lexington Books, 1974.

Ross, V. B., *Rent-Seeking in LDC Import Regimes: The Case of Kenya*, Discussion paper in International Economics, No. 8408, Graduate Institute of International Studies, Geneva, 1984.

Roth, Alvin E., "Introduction to Experimental Economics," in J. H. Kagel and A. E. Roth, eds., 1995, 3–109.

Rothenberg, J., *The Measurement of Social Welfare*, Englewood Cliffs, NJ: Prentice-Hall, 1961.

Rothschild, Michael and Joseph E. Stiglitz, "Equilibrium in Competitive Insurance Markets: An Essay on the Economics of Imperfect Information," *Quarterly Journal of Economics* 90, November 1976, 630–49.

Roubini, Nuriel and Jeffrey Sachs, "Political and Economic Determinants of Budget Deficits in the Industrial Democracies," *European Economic Review* 33, May 1989, 903–38.

Rubin, Paul H., "Why is the Common Law Efficient?" *Journal of Legal Studies* 6, 1997, 51–64.

Runciman, W. and Amartya K. Sen, "Games, Justice and the General Will," *Mind*, October 1965, 554–62.

Rundquist, B. S., "On Testing a Military Industrial Complex Theory," *American Politics Quarterly* 6, 1978, 29–53.

Rundquist, B. S. and D. E. Griffith, "An Interrupted Time-Series Test of the Distributive Theory of Military Policy-Making," *Western Political Quarterly* 29, 1976, 620–6.

Rushing, William, "Differences in Profit and Nonprofit Organizations: A Study of Effectiveness and Efficiency in General Short-Stay Hospitals," *Administrative Science Quarterly* 19, December 1974, 474–84.

Russell, Bertrand, *Power*, New York: Morton, 1938.

Russell, K. P., "Political Participation and Income Level: An Exchange," *Public Choice* 13, Fall 1972, 113–14.

Russell, K. P., J. Fraser, and Bruno S. Frey, "Political Participation and Income Level: An Exchange," *Public Choice* 13, Fall 1972, 113–14.

Ruttan, Vernon W., "Bureaucratic Productivity: The Case of Agricultural Research," *Public Choice* 35(5), 1980, 529–47.

Saari, Donald G., "Susceptibility to Manipulation," *Public Choice* 64, January 1990, 21–41.

Saari, Donald G., *Geometry of Voting*, Berlin: Springer, 1994.

Salhofer, Klaus, Markus F. Hofreither, and Franz Sinabell, "Promotion of the Agricultural Sector and Political Power in Austria," *Public Choice* 102, March 2000, 229–46.

Samuelson, Larry, "Electoral Equilibria with Restricted Strategies," *Public Choice* 43(3), 1984, 307–27.

Samuelson, Paul A., *Foundations of Economic Analysis*, Cambridge, MA: Harvard University Press, 1947.

Samuelson, Paul A., "The Pure Theory of Public Expenditure," *Review of Economics and Statistics* 36, November 1954, 387–9; reprinted in K. J. Arrow and T. Scitovsky, 1969, 179–82.

Samuelson, Paul A., "Arrow's Mathematical Politics," in S. Hook, ed., *Human Values and Economic Policy*, New York: New York University Press, 1967.

Samuelson, Paul A., "Pure Theory of Public Expenditure and Taxation," in J. Margolis and H. Guitton, *Public Economics*, New York: St. Martin's Press, 1969, 98–123.

Samuelson, Paul A., "Reaffirming the Existence of 'Reasonable' Bergson-Samuelson Social Welfare Functions," *Economica* 44, February 1977, 81–8.

Samuelson, Paul A., "Bergsonian Welfare Economics," in S. Rosefielde, ed., *Economic Welfare and the Economics of Soviet Socialism*, Cambridge: Cambridge University Press, 1981, 223–66.

Sanderson, Fred H., ed., *Agricultural Protectionism in the Industrial World*, Washington, D.C.: Resources for the Future, 1990.

Sandler, Todd and John T. Tschirhart, "The Economic Theory of Clubs: An Evaluation Survey," *Journal of Economic Literature* 18, December 1980, 1481–521.

Sandler, Todd and John T. Tschirhart, "Mixed Clubs: Further Observations," *Journal of Public Economics* 23, April 1984, 381–9.

Sandler, Todd and John T. Tschirhart, "Club Theory: Thirty Years Later," *Public Choice* 93, December 1997, 335–55.

Santerre, Rexford E., "Representative Versus Direct Democracy: A Tiebout Test of Relative Performance," *Public Choice* 48, 1986, 55–63.

Santerre, Rexford E., "Representative Versus Direct Democracy: Are There Any Expenditure Differences," *Public Choice* 60, 1989, 145–54.

Santerre, Rexford E., "Representative Versus Direct Democracy: The Role of the Public Bureaucrats," *Public Choice* 76, July 1993, 189–98.

Sartori, Giovanni, *Parties & Party Systems*, vol. 1, Cambridge: Cambridge University Press, 1976.

Sass, Tim R., "Constitutional Choice in Representative Democracies," *Public Choice* 74, 1992, 405–24.

Satterthwaite, M. A., "Strategy-Proofness and Arrow's Conditions: Existence and Correspondence Theorems for Voting Procedures and Social Welfare Functions," *Journal of Economic Theory* 10, April 1975, 187–217.

Saunders, Peter, "*Explaining International Differences in Public Expenditure: An Empirical Study*," paper presented at Conference of Economists, Clayton, Victoria, 1986.

Saunders, Peter and Friedrich Klau, "The Role of the Public Sector: Causes and Consequences of the Growth of Government," *OECD Economic Studies*, Spring 1985, 5–239.

Saunders, R. S., "The Political Economy of Effective Protection in Canada's Manufacturing Sector," *Canadian Journal of Economics* 13, 1980, 340–8.

Savas, Emanuel S., "Municipal Monopolies versus Competition in Delivering Urban Services," in W. D. Hawley and D. Rogers, eds., *Improving the Quality of Urban Management*, Beverly Hills, CA: 1974, 473–500.

Savas, Emanuel S., *Evaluating the Organization and Efficiency of Solid Waste Collection*, Lexington: Lexington Books, 1977a.

Savas, Emanuel S., *The Organization and Efficiency of Solid Waste Collection*, Lexington: Lexington Books, 1977b.

Savas, Emanuel S., "Policy Analysis for Local Government: Public vs. Private Refuse Collection," *Policy Analysis* 3, Winter 1977c, 49–74.

Savas, Emanuel S., "Comparative Costs of Public and Private Enterprise in a Municipal Service," in W. J. Baumol, ed., *Public and Private Enterprise in a Mixed Economy*, New York: 1980, 234–94.

Scammon, Richard M., Alice V. Gillivary, and Rhodes Cook, *America Votes 22: A Handbook of Contemporary American Elections Statistics*, Washington, D.C.: Governmental Affairs Institute, 1998.

Scanlon, T. M., "Rawls' Theory of Justice," in N. Daniels, ed., 1974, 169–205; as adapted from "Rawls' Theory of Justice," *University of Pennsylvania Law Review* 121, May 1973, 1020–69.

Schattschneider, E. E., *Politics, Pressures and the Tariff*, Englewood Cliffs, NJ: Prentice-Hall, 1935.

Schelling, Thomas C., *The Strategy of Conflict*, Cambridge, MA: Harvard University Press, 1960.

Schelling, Thomas C., *Arms and Influence*, New Haven: Yale University Press, 1966.

Schneider, Friedrich, *Politisch-ökonomische Modelle: Theoretische und Empirische Ansätze*, Königstein: Athenaeum, 1978.

Schneider, Friedrich, "Politisch-ökonomische Modelle: Übersicht und Neuere Entwicklungen," *Jahrbuch für Neue Politische Ökonomie* 1, 1982, 57–88.

Schneider, Friedrich and Dominik H. Enste, "Increasing Shadow Economies all over the World – Fiction or Reality?" mimeo, Universtiy of Linz, 1998.

Schneider, Friedrich and Dominik H. Enste, "Shadow Economies: Size, Causes and Consequences," *Journal of Economic Literature* 38, March 2000, 77–114.

Schneider, Friedrich and Bruno S. Frey, "Politico-Economic Models of Macroeconomic Policy," in Thomas D. Willett, ed., *Political Business Cycle*, Durham: Duke University Press, 1988.

Schneider, Friedrich and Werner W. Pommerehne, "Politico-Economic Interactions in Australia: Some Empirical Evidence," *Economic Record* 56, June 1980, 113–31.

Schneider, H. K. and C. Schuppener, *Soziale Absicherung der Wohnungsmarktwirtschaft durch Individualsubventionen*, Göttingen, 1971.

Schneider, Mark, "Fragmentation and the Growth of Local Government," *Public Choice* 48(3), 1986, 255–63.

Schneider, Mark and Byung Moon Ji, "The Flypaper Effect and Competition in the Local Market for Public Goods," *Public Choice* 54, 1987, 27–39.

Schnytzer, Adi and Janez Šušteršič, "Why Join the Party in a One-Party System?: Popularity versus Political Exchange," *Public Choice* 94, January 1997, 117–34.

Schofield, Norman, "Instability of Simple Dynamic Games," *Review of Economic Studies* 45, October 1978, 575–94.

Schofield, Norman, "Coalitions in West European Democracies: 1945–1986," mimeo, St. Louis: Washington University, 1987.

Schofield, Norman, "Party Competition in a Spatial Model of Coalition Formation," in W. Barnett, M. J. Hinich, and N. Schofield, eds., *Political Economy: Institutions, Competition and Representation*, Cambridge: Cambridge University Press, 1993a, 135–74.

Schofield, Norman, "Political Competition in Multiparty Coalition Governments," *European Journal of Political Research* 23, 1993b, 1–33.

Schofield, Norman, "Coalition Politics: A Formal Model and Empirical Analysis," *Journal of Theoretical Politics* 7, 1995, 245–81.

Schofield, Norman, "The Heart of a Polity," in N. Schofield, ed., *Collective Decision Making: Social Choice and Political Economy*, Boston: Kluwer, 1996a, 183–200.

Schofield, Norman, "Rational Choice and Political Economy," in J. Friedman, ed., 1996b, 189–211.

Schofield, Norman, "Multiparty Electoral Politics," 1997, in D. C. Mueller, ed., 1997a, 271–95.

Schofield, Norman, Andrew D. Martin, Kevin M. Quinn, and Andrew B. Whitford, "Multiparty Electoral Competition in the Netherlands and Germany: A Model Based on Multinomial Probit," *Public Choice* 97, December 1998, 257–93.

Schotter, Andrew, *The Economic Theory of Social Institutions*, Cambridge: Cambridge University Press, 1981.

Schuck, Peter H., "The Politics of Economic Growth," *Yale Law and Policy Review* 2, Spring 1984, 359–81.

Schuknecht, Ludger, "The Political Economy of EC Protectionism: National Protectionism Based on Article 115, Treaty of Rome," *Public Choice* 72, October, 1991, 37–50.

Schuknecht, Ludger, "Fiscal Policy Cycles and Public Expenditure in Developing Countries," *Public Choice* 102, January 2000, 115–30.

Schultze, Charles, "The Distribution of Farm Subsidies," in K. E. Boulding and M. Pfaff, eds., *Redistribution to the Rich and the Poor*, Belmont, CA: Wadsworth, 1972, 94–116.

Schumpeter, Joseph A., *Capitalism, Socialism and Democracy*, 3rd ed., New York: Harper & Row, 1950.

Schwab, R. M. and E. M. Zampelli. "Disentangling the Demand Function from the Production Function for Local Public Services: The Case of Public Safety," *Journal of Public Economics* 33, July 1987, 245–60.

Schwartz, B. and H. Lacey, *Behaviorism, Science, and Human Nature*, New York: Norton, 1982.

Schwartz, Thomas, "Vote Trading and Pareto Efficiency," *Public Choice* 24, Winter 1975, 101–9.

Schwartz, Thomas, "The Universal-Instability Theorem," *Public Choice* 37(3), 1981, 487–501.

Schwartz, Thomas, *The Logic of Collective Choice*, New York: Columbia University Press, 1986.

Schwartz, Thomas, "Cyclic Tournaments and Cooperative Majority Voting," *Social Choice and Welfare* 7, 1990, 19–29.

Schwartz, Thomas, "Representation as Agency and the Pork Barrel Politics," *Public Choice* 78, January 1994, 3–21.

Schwert, G. William, "Public Regulation of National Securities Exchanges: A Test of the Capture Hypothesis," *Bell Journal of Economics* 8, Spring 1977, 128–50.

Scitovsky, Tibor, "Two Concepts of External Economies," *Journal of Political Economy* 17, April 1954, 143–51; reprinted in K. J. Arrow and T. Scitovsky, 1969, 242–52.

Scott, A. D., "A Note on Grants in Federal Countries," *Economica* 17, November 1950, 416–22.

Scott, A. D., "Evaluation of Federal Grants," *Economica* 19, November 1952a, 377–94.

Scott, A. D., "Federal Grants and Resource Allocation," *Journal of Political Economy* 60, December 1952b, 534–6.

Scully, Gerald W., "The Institutional Framework of Economic Development," *Journal of Political Economy* 96, 1988, 652–62.

Scully, Gerald W., "The Size of the State, Economic Growth and the Efficient Utilization of Natural Resources," *Public Choice* 63, November 1989, 149–64.

Scully, Gerald W., *Constitutional Environments and Economic Growth*, Princeton: Princeton University Press, 1992.

Scully, Gerald W. and Daniel J. Slottje, "Ranking Economic Liberty across Countries," *Public Choice* 69, February 1991, 121–52.

Sears, David O., Carl P. Hensler, and Leslie K. Speer, "Whites' Opposition to 'Busing': Self-Interest or Symbolic Politics?" *American Political Science Review* 73, June 1979, 369–84.

Sears, David O., R. R. Law, T. R. Tyler, and H. M. Allen, Jr., "Self-Interest vs. Symbolic Politics in Policy Attitudes and Presidential Voting," *American Political Science Review* 74, September 1980, 670–84.

Segal, Uzi and Avia Spivak, "On the Single Membership Constituency and the Law of Large Numbers: A Note," *Public Choice* 49(2), 1986, 183–90.

Seidl, Christian, "On Liberal Values," *Zeitschrift für Nationalökonomie* 35, 1975, 257–92.

Seidl, Christian, "On the Impossibility of a Generalization of the Libertarian Resolution of the Liberal Paradox," *Journal of Economics* 51, 1990, 71–88.

Selten, Reinhard, "Anwendungen der Spielthoerie auf die Politische Wissenschaft," in H. Maier, ed., *Politik und Wissenschaft*, München: Beck, 1971.

Sen, Amartya K., "A Possibility Theorem on Majority Decisions," *Econometrica* 34, April 1966, 491–9.

Sen, Amartya K., "Quasi-Transitivity, Rational Choice and Collective Decisions," *Review of Economic Studies* 36, July 1969, 381–94.

Sen, Amartya K., *Collective Choice and Social Welfare*, San Francisco: Holden-Day, 1970a.

Sen, Amartya K., "The Impossibility of a Paretian Liberal," *Journal of Political Economy* 78, January/February 1970b, 152–7.

Sen, Amartya K., "On Ignorance and Equal Distribution," *American Economic Review* 63, December 1973, 1022–4; reprinted in A. Sen, 1982, 222–5.

Sen, Amartya K., "Informational Basis of Alternative Welfare Approaches, Aggregation and Income Distribution," *Journal of Public Economics* 3, November 1974, 387–403.

Sen, Amartya K., "Liberty, Unanimity and Rights," *Economica* 43, August 1976, 217–45.

Sen, Amartya K., "Social Choice Theory: A Re-Examination," *Econometrica* 45, January 1977a, 53–89.

Sen, Amartya K., "On Weight and Measures: Informational Constraints in Social Welfare Analysis," *Econometrica* 45, October 1977b, 1539–72.

Sen, Amartya K., "Personal Utilities and Public Judgments: Or What's Wrong with Welfare Economics," *Economic Journal* 89, September 1979, 537–58.

Sen, Amartya K., *Choice, Welfare and Measurement*, Cambridge, MA: MIT Press, 1982.

Sen, Amartya K., "Foundations of Social Choice Theory: An Epilogue," in J. Elster and A. Hylland, 1986, 213–48.

Sen, Amartya K., "Minimal Liberty," *Economica* 59, May 1992, 139–59.

Sen, Amartya K., "Rationality and Social Choice," *American Economic Review* 85, March 1995, 1–24.

Sen, Amartya K., "Rights: Formulation and Consequences," *Analyse & Kritik* 18, September 1996, 153–70.

Sen, Amartya K., "The Possibility of Social Choice," *American Economic Review* 89, June 1999, 349–78.

Sen, Amartya K. and Prasanta Pattanaik, "Necessary and Sufficient Conditions for Rational Choice under Majority Decision," *Journal of Economic Theory* 1, August 1969, 178–202.

Sen, Manimay, "Strategy-Proofness of a Class of Borda Rules," *Public Choice* 43(3), 1984, 251–85.

Settle, R. F. and B. A. Abrams, "The Determinants of Voter Participation: A More General Model," *Public Choice* 27, Fall 1976, 81–9.

Shachar, Ron and Barry Nalebuff, "Follow the Leader: Theory and Evidence on Political Participation," *American Economic Review* 89, June 1999, 525–47.

Shapiro, Perry and J. Sonstelie, "Representative Voter or Bureaucratic Manipulation: An Examination of Public Finances in California Before and After Proposition 13," *Public Choice* 39(1), 1982, 113–42.

Shapley, Lloyd and Bernard Grofman, "Optimizing Group Judgmental Accuracy in the Presence of Interdependencies," *Public Choice* 43(3), 1984, 329–43.

Sheffrin, Steven M., "Evaluating Rational Partisan Business Cycle Theory," *Economics and Politics* 1, November 1989, 239–59.

Shepherd, Lawrence, "Licensing Restrictions and the Cost of Dental Care," *Journal of Law and Economics* 21, April 1978, 187–201.

Shepsle, Kenneth, A., "Institutional Arrangements and Equilibrium in Multidimensional Voting Models," *American Journal of Political Science* 23, February 1979, 27–59.

Shepsle, Kenneth A., "Statistical Political Philosophy and Positive Political Theory," in J. Friedman, ed., 1996, 213–22.

Shepsle, Kenneth A. and Barry R. Weingast, "Structure-Induced Equilibrium and Legislative Choice," *Public Choice* 37(3), 1981, 503–19.

Shepsle, Kenneth A. and Barry Weingast, "The Institutional Foundations of Committee Power," *American Political Science Review* 81, 1987, 86–108.

Sieg, Gernot, "A Federal Political Budget Cycle with States Governed by the Opposition," *Finanzarchiv* 55, 1998, 343–56.

Silberman, Jonathan I. and Garey C. Durden, "The Rational Behavior Theory of Voter Participation," *Public Choice* 23, Fall 1975, 101–8.

Silberman, Jonathan I. and Garey C. Durden, "Determining Legislative Preferences on the Minimum Approach," *Journal of Political Economy* 84, April 1976, 317–29.

References 739

Silver, Morris, "A Demand Analysis of Voting Costs and Voting Participation," *Social Science Research* 2, August 1973, 111–24.

Silver, Morris, "Political Revolution and Repression: An Economic Approach," *Public Choice* 17, Spring 1974, 63–71.

Simon, Herbert A., *Administrative Behavior*, New York: Macmillan, 1947.

Simon, Herbert A., "Notes on the Observation and Measurement of Power," *Journal of Politics* 15, 1953, 500–16; reprinted in R. Bell, D. V. Edwards, and R. H. Wagner, 1969, 69–78.

Simon, Herbert A., *Administrative Behavior*, 2nd ed., New York: Macmillan, 1961.

Simons, Henry, *Personal Income Taxation: The Definition of Income as a Problem of Fiscal Policy*, Chicago: University of Chicago Press, 1938.

Simpson, Paul B., "On Defining Areas of Voter Choice," *Quarterly Journal of Economics* 83, 1969, 478–90.

Sinn, Hans-Werner, "Pigou and Clarke Join Hands," *Public Choice* 75, January 1993, 79–91.

Skaperdas, Stergios, "Cooperation, Conflict, and Power in the Absence of Property Rights," *American Economic Review* 82, September 1992, 720–39.

Skaperdas, Stergios, "Contest Success Functions," *Economic Theory* 7, 1996, 283–90.

Skinner, B. F., *Walden II*, New York: Macmillan, 1948.

Slemrod, Joel, "What Do Cross-Country Studies Teach about Government Involvement, Prosperity, and Economic Growth?" *Brookings Papers on Economic Activity* 2, 1995, 373–415.

Sloan, J. and K. L. Tedin, "The Consequences of Regime Type for Public-Policy Outputs," *Comparative Political Studies* 20, 1987, 98–124.

Sloss, Judith, "Stable Outcomes in Majority Rule Voting Games," *Public Choice* 15, Summer 1973, 19–48.

Slutsky, Steven M., "Abstentions in Majority Rule Equilibrium," *Journal of Economic Theory* 53, 1975, 292–304.

Slutsky, Steven M., "A Characterization of Societies with Consistent Majority Decision," *Review of Economic Studies* 44, June 1977a, 211–25.

Slutsky, Steven M., "A Voting Model for the Allocation of Public Goods: Existence of an Equilibrium," *Journal of Economic Theory* 14, April 1977b, 299–325.

Slutsky, Steven M., "Equilibrium under α-Majority Voting," *Econometrica* 47, September 1979, 1113–25.

Smith, John H., "Aggregation of Preferences and Variable Electorate," *Econometrica* 41, November 1973, 1027–41.

Smith, Patricia K., "An Empirical Investigation of Interstate AFDC Benefit Competition," *Public Choice* 68, January 1991, 217–33.

Smith, Vernon L., "The Principal of Unanimity and Voluntary Consent in Social Choice," *Journal of Political Economy* 85, December 1977, 1125–39.

Smith, Vernon L., "An Experimental Comparison of Three Public Good Decision Mechanisms," *Scandinavian Journal of Economics* 81(2), 1979a, 198–215.

Smith, Vernon L., "Incentive Compatible Experimental Processes for the Provision of Public Goods," in V. L. Smith, ed., *Research in Experimental Economics*, Greenwich, CT: JAI Press, 1979b, 59–168.

Smith, Vernon L., "Experiments with a Decentralized Mechanism for Public Good Decisions," *American Economic Review* 70, September 1980, 584–99.

Smithies, Arthur, "Optimum Location in Spatial Competition," *Journal of Political Economy* 49, June 1941, 423–39.

Smyth, David J. and Pami Dua, "The Public's Indifference Map between Inflation and Unemployment: Empirical Evidence for the Nixon, Ford, Carter and Reagan Presidencies," *Public Choice* 60, January 1989, 71–85.

Smyth, David J., Pami Dua, and Susan Washburn Taylor, "Voters and Macroeconomics: Are They Forward Looking or Backward Looking?" *Public Choice* 78, March 1994, 283–93.

Smyth, David J. and Alan Woodfield, "Inflation, Unemployment and Macroeconomic Policy in New Zealand: A Public Choice Analysis," *Public Choice* 75, February 1993, 119–38.

Snyder, James M., Jr., "Election Goals and the Allocation of Campaign Resources," *Econometrica* 57, May 1989, 637–60.

Snyder, James M., Jr., "Campaign Contributions as Investments: The US House of Representatives 1980–86," *Journal of Political Economy* 98, 1990, 1195–227.

Snyder, James M., Jr., "Long-term Investing in Politicians; or Give Early, Give Often," *Journal of Law and Economics* 35, April 1992, 15–43.

Sorensen, R. J., "Macroeconomic Policy and Government Popularity in Norway, 1963–1986," *Scandinavian Political Studies* 10, 1987, 301–22.

Spann, Robert M., "Collective Consumption of Private Goods," *Public Choice* 20, Winter 1974, 63–81.

Spann, Robert M., "Public versus Private Provision of Governmental Services," in T. Borcherding, 1977, 71–89.

Stearns, Maxwell L., "The Misguided Renaissance of Social Choice," *Yale Law Journal* 103, 1994, 1219–93.

Stearns, Maxwell L., *Public Choice and Public Law: Readings and Commentary*, Cincinnati: Anderson Publishing, 1997.

Stein, R. M., "Tiebout's Sorting Hypothesis," *Urban Affairs Quarterly* 23, 1987, 140–66.

Steunenberg, Bernard, "Decision Making under Different Institutional Arrangements: Legislation by the European Community," *Journal of Institutional and Theoretical Economics* 150, 1994, 642–69.

Stevens, Barbara J., "Scale, Market Structure and the Cost of Refuse Collection," *Review of Economics and Statistics* 60, August 1978, 438–48.

Stevens, Barbara J. and Emanuel S. Savas, "The Cost of Residential Refuse Collection and the Effect Service Arrangements," *Municipal Year Book* 44, 1978, 200–5.

Stigler, George J., "The Theory of Economic Regulation," *Bell Journal of Economics and Management Science* 2, Spring 1971, 137–46.

Stigler, George J., "General Economic Conditions and Natural Elections," *American Economic Review* 63, May 1973, 160–7.

Stigler, George J., "The Sizes of Legislatures," *Journal of Legal Studies* 5, January 1976, 17–34.

Stigler, George J. and Gary S. Becker, "De Gustibus Non Est Disputandum," *American Economic Review* 67(2), March 1977, 76–90.

Stokes, Donald E., "Spatial Models of Party Competition," *American Political Science Review* 57, June 1963, 368–77.

Stratmann, Thomas, "What Do Campaign Contributions Buy? Causal Effects of Money and Votes," *Southern Economic Journal* 57, January 1991, 606–20.

Stratmann, Thomas, "Are Contributors Rational? Untangling Strategies of Political Action Committees," *Journal of Political Economy* 100(3), June 1992a, 647–64.

Stratmann, Thomas, "The Effects of Logrolling on Congressional Voting," *American Economic Review* 82(5), December 1992b, 1162–76.

Stratmann, Thomas, "Campaign Contributions and Congressional Voting: Does the Timing of Contributions Matter?" *Review of Economics and Statistics* 77, February 1995, 127–36.

Stratmann, Thomas, "Instability of Collective Choice Decisions? Testing for Cyclic Majorities," *Public Choice* 88, July 1996a, 15–28.

Stratmann, Thomas, "How Reelection Constituencies Matter: Evidence from Political Action Committees' Contributions and Congressional Voting," *Journal of Law and Economics* 39, October 1996b, 603–35.

Stratmann, Thomas, "Logrolling," 1997, in D. C. Mueller, ed., 1997a, 322–41.

Stratmann, Thomas, "The Market for Congressional Votes: Is Timing of Contributions Everything?" *Journal of Law and Economics* 41, April 1998, 85–113.

Strauch, Rolf A., "Information and Public Spending: An Empirical Study of Budget Processes in the US States," in R. A. Strauch and J. von Hagen, eds., 2000, 139–65.

Strauch, Rolf A. and Jürgen von Hagen, eds., *Institutions, Politics and Fiscal Policy*, Dordrecht: Kluwer Academic Publishers, 2000.

Strom, G., "Congressional Policy Making: A Test of a Theory," *Journal of Politics* 37, 1975, 711–35.

Strøm, Kaare, "Minority Governments in Parliamentary Democracies," *Comparative Political Studies* 17, 1984, 199–227.

Strøm, Kaare, "Party Goals and Government Performance in Parliamentary Democracies," *American Political Science Review* 79, 1985, 738–54.

Strøm, Kaare, *Minority Government and Majority Rule*, Cambridge: Cambridge University Press, 1990.

Strøm, Kaare and Wolfgang C. Müller, "Political Parties and Hard Choices," in W. C. Müller and K. Strøm, eds., 1999, 1–35.

Strumpf, Koleman S. and Felix Oberholzer-Gee, "Endogenous Policy Decentralization: Testing the Central Tenet of Economic Federalism," mimeo, University of North Carolina, Chapel Hill, 2000.

Stuart, Charles, "Welfare Costs per Dollar of Additional Tax Revenue in the United States," *American Economic Review* 74, June 1984, 352–62.

Sugden, Robert, *The Political Economy of Public Choice*, New York: Halsted Press, 1981.

Sugden, Robert, "Free Association and the Theory of Proportional Representation," *American Political Science Review* 78, March 1984, 31–43.

Sugden, Robert, "Liberty, Preference and Choice," *Economics and Philosophy* 1, 1985, 213–29.

Sugden, Robert, *The Evolution of Rights, Cooperation and Welfare*, New York: Basil Blackwell, 1986.

Sugden, Robert, "Welfare, Resources, and Capabilities: A Review of *Inequality Reexamined* by Amartya Sen," *Journal of Economic Literature* 31(4), December 1993, 1947–62.

Sugden, Robert and Albert Weale, "A Contractual Reformulation of Certain Aspects of Welfare Economics," *Economica* 46, May 1979, 111–23.

Sutter, Daniel, "Asymmetric Power Relations and Cooperation in Anarchy," *Southern Economic Journal* 61, January 1995, 602–13.

Suzuki, Motoshi, "Evolutionary Voter Sophistication and Political Business Cycles," *Public Choice* 81, December 1994, 241–61.

Suzumura, Kotaro, "On the Consistency of Liberal Claims," *Review of Economic Studies* 45, June 1978, 329–42.

Suzumura, Kotaro, *Rational Choice, Collective Decisions, and Social Welfare*, Cambridge: Cambridge University Press, 1983.

Suzumura, Kotaro, "On the Voluntary Exchange of Libertarian Rights," *Social Choice and Welfare* 8, 1991, 199–206.

Suzumura, Kotaro, "Welfare, Rights, and Social Choice Procedure: A Perspective," *Analyse & Kritik* 18, September 1996, 20–37.

Swank, Otto H., "Popularity Functions Based on the Partisan Theory," *Public Choice* 75, April 1993, 339–56.

Swank, Otto H. and R. Eisinga, "Economic Outcomes and Voting Behavior in a Multi-party System: An Application to the Netherlands," *Public Choice* 101, December 1999, 195–213.

Taagepera, Rein and Matthew S. Shugart, *Seats and Votes*, New Haven: Yale University Press, 1989.

Takacs, Wendy E., "Pressures for Protectionism: An Empirical Analysis," *Economic Inquiry* 19, October 1981, 687–93.

Tang, Eddie Wing Yin and R. Alan Hedley, "Distributional Coalitions, State Strength, and Economic Growth: Toward a Comprehensive Theory of Economic Development," *Public Choice* 96, September 1998, 295–323.

Tanzi, Vito, "Toward a Positive Theory of Public Sector Behavior: An Interpretation of Some Italian Contributions," Washington, D.C.: International Monetary Fund, 1980, mimeo.

Tanzi, Vito, "Public Expenditure and Public Debt: An International and Historical Perspective," in J. Bristow and D. McDonagh, eds., *Public Expenditure: The Key Issues*, Dublin: Institute of Public Administration, 1986, 6–41.

Tanzi, Vito and Ludger Schuknecht, *Public Spending in the 20th Century*, Cambridge: Cambridge University Press, 2000.

Tarr, David, *A General Equilibrium Analysis of the Welfare and Employment Effects of U.S. Quotas in Textiles, Autos and Steel*, Washington, D.C.: Federal Trade Commission, 1989.

Taylor, Michael J., "Proof of a Theorem on Majority Rule," *Behavioral Science* 14, May 1969, 228–31.

Taylor, Michael J., "Review Article: Mathematical Political Theory," *British Journal of Political Science* 1, July 1971, 339–82.

Taylor, Michael J., *Anarchy and Cooperation*, New York: Wiley, 1976.

Taylor, Michael J., *The Possibility of Cooperation*, Cambridge: Cambridge University Press, 1987.

Taylor, Michael J. and V. M. Herman, "Party Systems and Government Stability," *American Political Science Review* 65, March 1971, 28–37.

Taylor, Michael J. and Michael Laver, "Government Coalitions in Western Europe," *European Journal of Political Research* 1, September 1973, 205–48.

Taylor, Michael J. and Hugh Ward, "Chickens, Whales, and Lumpy Goods: Alternative Models of Public-Good Provision," *Political Studies* 30, September 1982, 350–70.

Teske, Paul E., "Rent Seeking in the Deregulatory Environment: State Telecommunications," *Public Choice* 68, January 1991, 235–43.

Thaler, Richard H., *Quasi Rational Economics*, New York: Russell Sage Foundation, 1991.

Thomas, James J., *Informal Economic Activity*, London: Harvester Wheatsheaf, 1992.

Thomas, S. J., "Do Incumbent Campaign Expenditures Matter," *Journal of Politics* 51, 1989, 965–76.

Thomas, S. J., "A Negative Advertising Theory of Campaign Expenditures," in W. C. Crain and R. D. Tollison, eds., *Predicting Politics: Essays in Empirical Public Choice*, Ann Arbor: University of Michigan Press, 1990.

Thompson, E. A., "A Pareto Optimal Group Decision Process," in G. Tullock, ed., *Papers on Non-Market Decision Making*, Charlottesville: University of Virginia, 1966, 133–40.

Thurner, Paul W. and Angelika Eymann, "Policy-Specific Alienation and Indifference in the Calculus of Voting: A Simultaneous Model of Party Choice and Abstention," *Public Choice* 102, January 2000, 51–77.

Tideman, T. Nicolaus, "Ethical Foundations of the Demand-Revealing Process," *Public Choice* 29-2 (special supplement), Spring 1977, 71–7.

Tideman, T. Nicolaus, "An Experiment in the Demand-Revealing Process," *Public Choice* 41(3), 1983, 387–401.

Tideman, T. Nicolaus and Gordon Tullock, "A New and Superior Process for Making Social Choices," *Journal of Political Economy* 84, December 1976, 1145–59.

Tideman, T. Nicolaus and Gordon Tullock, "Some Limitations of Demand Revealing Processes: Comment," *Public Choice* 29-2 (special supplement), Spring 1977, 125–8.

Tideman, T. Nicolaus and Gordon Tullock, "Coalitions under Demand Revealing," *Public Choice* 36(2), 1981, 323–8.

Tiebout, Charles M., "A Pure Theory of Local Expenditures," *Journal of Political Economics* 64, October 1956, 416–24.

Tien, Charles, "Representation, Voluntary Retirement, and Shirking in the Last Term," *Public Choice* 106, January 2001, 117–30.

Tollison, Robert D., "Rent Seeking: A Survey," *Kyklos* 35(4), 1982, 575–602.

Tollison, Robert D., "Superdissipation," *Public Choice* 61, April 1989, 97–8.

Tollison, Robert D., "Rent Seeking," 1997, in D. C. Mueller, ed., 1997a, 506–25.

Tollison, Robert D., Mark Crain, and P. Paulter, "Information and Voting: An Empirical Note," *Public Choice* 24, Winter 1975, 43–9.

Tollison, Robert D. and Thomas D. Willett, "Some Simple Economics of Voting and Not Voting," *Public Choice* 16, Fall 1973, 59–71.

Tosini, Suzanne C. and Edward Tower, "The Textile Bill of 1985: The Determinants of Congressional Voting Patterns," *Public Choice* 54(1), 1987, 19–25.

Trefler, Daniel, "Trade Liberalization and the Theory of Endogenous Protection: An Econometric Study of U.S. Import Policy," *Journal of Political Economy* 101, February 1993, 138–60.

Tsebelis, George, *Nested Games: Rational Choice in Comparative Politics*, Berkeley: University of California Press, 1990.

Tsebelis, George, "The Power of the European Parliament as a Conditional Agenda-Setter," *American Political Science Review* 88, 1994, 128–42.

Tsebelis, George, "Maastricht and the Democratic Deficit," *Außenwirtschaft* 52, June 1997, 29–56.

Tsebelis, George and Jeannette Money, *Bicameralism*, Cambridge: Cambridge University Press, 1997.

Tucker, Harvey J., "Contextual Models of Participation in U.S. State Legislative Elections," *Western Political Quarterly* 39, March 1986, 67–78.

Tuckman, Howard P. and Cyril F. Chang, "Cost Convergence between For-profit and Not-for-profit Nursing Homes: Does Competition Matter?" *Quarterly Review of Economics and Business* 28, Winter 1988, 50–65.

Tufte, Edward R., *Political Control of the Economy*, Princeton: Princeton University Press, 1978.

Tulkens, H., "Dynamic Processes for Allocating Public Goods: An Institution-Oriented Survey," *Journal of Public Economics* 9, April 1978, 163–201.

Tullock, Gordon, "Some Problems of Majority Voting," *Journal of Political Economy* 67, December 1959, 571–9; reprinted in K. J. Arrow and T. Scitovsky, 1969, 169–78.

Tullock, Gordon, *The Politics of Bureaucracy*, Washington, D.C.: Public Affairs Press, 1965.

Tullock, Gordon, *Toward a Mathematics of Politics*, Ann Arbor: University of Michigan Press, 1967a.

Tullock, Gordon, "The General Irrelevance of the General Impossibility Theorem," *Quarterly Journal of Economics* 81, May 1967b, 256–70.

Tullock, Gordon, "The Welfare Costs of Tariffs, Monopolies and Theft," *Western Economic Journal* 5, June 1967c, 224–32; reprinted in J. M. Buchanan, R. D. Tollison, and G. Tullock, 1980, 39–50.

Tullock, Gordon, "Federalism: Problems of Scale," *Public Choice* 6, Spring 1969, 19–30.

Tullock, Gordon, "The Paradox of Revolution," *Public Choice* 11, Fall 1971a, 89–100.

Tullock, Gordon, "The Charity of the Uncharitable," *Western Economic Journal* 9, December 1971b, 379–92.

Tullock, Gordon, *Logic of the Law*, New York: Basic Books, 1971c.

Tullock, Gordon, "The Cost of Transfers," *Kyklos* 4, December 1971d, 629–43; reprinted in J. M. Buchanan, R. D. Tollison, and G. Tullock, eds., 1980, 269–82.

Tullock, Gordon, *The Social Dilemma: Economics of War and Revolution*, Blacksburg: Center for Study of Public Choice, 1974.

Tullock, Gordon, "Comment on Rae," *American Political Science Review* 69, December 1975, 1295–7.

Tullock, Gordon, "Practical Problems and Practical Solutions," *Public Choice* 29-2 (special supplement), Spring 1977a, 27–35.

Tullock, Gordon, "The Demand-Revealing Process as a Welfare Indicator," *Public Choice* 29-2 (special supplement), Spring 1977b, 51–63.

Tullock, Gordon, "Demand-Revealing Process, Coalitions and Public Goods," *Public Choice* 29-2 (special supplement), Spring 1977c, 103–5.

Tullock, Gordon, "Revealing the Demand for Transfers," in R. Auster and B. Sears, eds., *American Re-Evolution*, Tucson: University of Arizona, 1977d, 107–23.

Tullock, Gordon, "Efficient Rent Seeking," in J. M. Buchanan, R. D. Tollison, and G. Tullock, eds., 1980, 97–112.

Tullock, Gordon, "Why So Much Stability," *Public Choice* 37(2), 1981, 189–202.

Tullock, Gordon, "More Thoughts about Demand Revealing," *Public Choice* 38(2), 1982, 167–70.

Tullock, Gordon, "Further Tests of a Rational Theory of the Size of Government," *Public Choice* 41, 1983, 419–21.

Tullock, Gordon, *Autocracy*, Dordrecht: Kluwer Academic Publishers, 1987.

Tullock, Gordon, "Future Directions for Rent Seeking Research," in C. K. Rowley, R. D. Tollison, and G. Tullock, eds., *The Political Economy of Rent Seeking*, Boston: Kluwer, 1988, 465–80.

Tullock, Gordon, *On Voting: A Public Choice Approach*, Cheltenham: Edward Elgar, 1998.

Tullock, Gordon and C. D. Campbell, "Computer Simulation of a Small Voting System," *Economic Journal* 80, March 1970, 97–104.

Turnbull, Geoffrey K. and Chinkun Chan, "The Median Voter According to GARP," *Southern Economic Journal* 64, April 1998, 1001–10.

Turnbull, Geoffrey K. and Salpie S. Djoundourian, "The Median Voter Hypothesis: Evidence from General Purpose Local Governments," *Public Choice* 81, December 1994, 223–40.

Turnbull, Geoffrey K. and Peter M. Mitias, "The Median Voter Model across Levels of Government," *Public Choice* 99, April 1999, 119–38.

Tussing, A. D. and J. A. Henning, "Long-Run Growth of Non-Defense and Government Expenditures," *Public Finance Quarterly* 2, 1974, 202–22.

Tyran, Jean-Robert and Rupert Sausgruber, "On Fiscal Illusion," mimeo, University of St. Gallen, Switzerland, 2000.

Uhlaner, Carole Jean, "Rational Turnout: The Neglected Role of Groups," *American Journal of Political Science* 33, 1989a, 390–422.

Uhlaner, Carole Jean, "'Relational Goods' and Participation: Incorporating Sociability into a Theory of Rational Action," *Public Choice* 62, September 1989b, 253–85.

Uhlaner, Carole Jean, "What the Downsian Voter Weighs: A Reassessment of the Costs and Benefits of Action," in B. Grofman, 1993a, 67–79.

Ulrich, Alvin, William H. Furtan, and Andrew Schmitz, "The Cost of a Licensing System Regulation: An Example from Canadian Prairie Agriculture," *Journal of Political Economy* 95, February 1987, 160–78.

Ursprung, Heiner W., "Macroeconomic Performance and Government Popularity in New Zealand," mimeo, Wellington: Victoria University, 1983.

Usher, Dan, *The Welfare Economics of Markets, Voting and Predation*, Ann Arbor: University of Michigan Press, 1992.

Usher, Dan, "The Significance of the Probabilistic Voting Theorem," *Canadian Journal of Economics* 27, May 1994, 433–45.

Usher, Dan, "The Coase Theorem is Tautological, Incoherent or Wrong," *Economic Letters* 61, October 1998, 3–11.

Vachris, M. Albert, "Federal Antitrust Enforcement: A Principal-Agent Perspective," *Public Choice* 88, September 1996, 223–38.

van Bastelaer, Thierry, "The Political Economy of Food Pricing: An Extended Test of the Interest Group Approach," *Public Choice* 96, July 1998, 43–60.

van Beek, James R., "Does the Decision to Retire Increase the Amount of Political Shirking?" *Public Choice* 19, October 1991, 444–56.

van Creveld, Martin, *The Rise and Decline of the State*, Cambridge: Cambridge University Press, 1999.

van Dalen, Hendrik P. and Otto H. Swank, "Government Spending Cycles: Ideological or Opportunistic?" *Public Choice* 89, October 1996, 183–200.

van Deemen, Ad M. A. and Noël P. Vergunst, "Empirical Evidence of Paradoxes of Voting in Dutch Elections," *Public Choice* 97, December 1998, 475–90.

van de Kragt, Alphons, John M. Orbell, and Robyn M. Dawes, "The Minimal Contributing Set as a Solution to Public Goods Problems," *American Political Science Review* 77, March 1983, 112–22.

van Roozendaal, Peter, "Centre Parties and Coalition Formations: A Game Theoretic Approach," *European Journal of Political Research* 18, 1990, 325–48.

van Roozendaal, Peter, "The Effect of Dominant and Central Parties on Cabinet Composition and Durability," *Legal Studies Quarterly* 17, 1992, 5–36.

van Roozendaal, Peter, "Cabinets in the Netherlands (1918–1990): The Importance of 'Dominant' and 'Central' Parties," *European Journal of Political Research* 23, 1993, 35–54.

van Winden, Frans, *On the Interaction between State and Private Sector*, Amsterdam: North-Holland, 1983.

van Winden, Frans, "On the Economic Theory of Interest Groups: Towards a Group Frame of Reference in Political Economics," *Public Choice* 100, July 1999, 1–29.

Varian, Hal R., "Equity, Envy, and Efficiency," *Journal of Economic Theory* 9, September 1974, 63–91.

Varian, Hal R., "Two Problems in the Theory of Fairness," *Journal of Public Economics* 5, April-May 1976, 249–60.

Vaubel, Roland, "The Political Economy of Centralization and the European Community," *Public Choice* 81, October 1994, 151–90.

Vaubel, Roland, "Constitutional Safeguards against Centralization in Federal States: An International Cross-Section Analysis," *Constitutional Political Economy* 7, 1996, 79–102.

Vedder, Richard and Lowell Gallaway, "Rent-seeking, Distributional Coalitions, Taxes, Relative Prices and Economic Growth," *Public Choice* 51(1), 1986, 93–100.

Verba, S. and N. H. Nie, *Participation in America*, New York: Harper & Row, 1972.

Vickrey, William, "Utility, Strategy, and Social Decision Rules," *Quarterly Journal of Economics* 74, November 1960, 507–35.

Vickrey, William, "Counterspeculation, Auctions, and Competitive Sealed Tenders," *Journal of Finance* 16, 1961, 8–37.

Vining, Aidan R. and Anthony E. Boardman, "Ownership versus Competition: Efficiency in Public Enterprise," *Public Choice* 73, March 1992, 205–39.

Voigt, Stefan, "Positive Constitutional Economics: A Survey," *Public Choice* 90, March 1997, 11–53.

Voigt, Stefan, *Explaining Constitutional Change*, Cheltenham: Edward Elgar, 1999.

Volckart, Oliver, "The Open Constitution and Its Enemies: Competition, Rent Seeking and the Rise of the Modern State," *Journal of Economic Behavior and Organization* 42, May 2000, 1–17.

von Neumann, John and Oskar Morgenstern, *The Theory of Games and Economic Behavior*, 3rd ed., Princeton: Princeton University Press, 1953.

Vousden, Neil, *The Economics of Trade Protection*, Cambridge: Cambridge University Press, 1990.

Wagner, R. H., "The Concept of Power and the Study of Politics," in R. Bell, D. V. Edwards, and R. H. Wagner, eds., 1969, 3–12.

Wallace, Richard L. and Paul E. Junk, "Economic Inefficiency of Small Municipal Electric Generating Systems," *Land Economics* 46, February 1970, 98–104.

Waller, Christopher J. and Carl E. Walsh, "Central Bank Independence, Economic Behavior, and Optimal Term Lengths," *American Economic Review* 86, 1996, 1139–53.

Wallis, John Joseph, "Laws and Legislatures," mimeo, University of Maryland, College Park, 1986.

Wallis, John J. and Wallace E. Oates, "Does Economic Sclerosis Set in with Age? An Empirical Study of the Olson Hypothesis," *Kyklos* 41, 1988, 397–417.

Walsh, Cliff, "Excludable Public Goods: On Their Nature and Significance," in R. Pethig, ed., *Public Goods and Exclusion*, Bern: Peter Lang Verlag, 1986.

Ward, Hugh, "The Risks of a Reputation for Toughness: Strategy in Public Goods Provision Problems Modelled by Chicken Supergames," *British Journal of Political Science* 17, January 1987, 23–52.

Warneryd, Karl, "Conventions," *Constitutional Political Economy* 1(3), Fall 1990, 83–107.

Warren, R. S., Jr., "Bureaucratic Performance and Budgetary Reward," *Public Choice* 24, Winter 1975, 51–7.

Warwick, Paul V., "The Durability of Coalition Governments in Parliamentary Democracies," *Comparative Political Studies* 11, January 1979, 465–98.

Warwick, Paul V., *Government Survival in Parliamentary Democracies*, Cambridge: Cambridge University Press, 1994.

Waters, Melissa and William J. Moore, "The Theory of Economic Regulation and Public Choice and the Determinants of Public Sector Bargaining Legislation," *Public Choice* 66, August 1990, 161–75.

Weatherby, J. L., Jr., "A Note on Administrative Behavior and Public Policy," *Public Choice* 11, Fall 1971, 107–10.

Weatherford, M. S., "Economic Conditions and Electoral Outcomes: Class Differences in the Political Response to Recession," *American Journal of Political Science* 22, November 1978, 917–38.

Webber, C. and A. Wildavsky, *A History of Taxation and Expenditure in the Western World*, New York: Simon and Schuster, 1986.

Weber, James S., "An Elementary Proof of the Conditions for a Generalized Condorcet Paradox," *Public Choice* 77, October 1993, 415–19.

Weber, Max, *The Theory of Social and Economic Organization*, in Talcott Parsons, ed., New York: Free Press, 1947.

Weede, Erich, "Democracy, Creeping Socialism, and Ideological Socialism in Rent-Seeking Societies," *Public Choice* 44(2), 1984, 349–66.

Weede, Erich, "Catch-up, Distributional Coalitions and Government as Determinants of Economic Growth or Decline in Industrialized Democracies," *British Journal of Sociology* 37, June 1986, 194–220.

Weede, Erich, "A Note on Pryor's Criticism of Olson's *Rise and Decline of Nations*," *Public Choice* 52(3), 1987, 215–22.

Weingast, Barry R., "A Rational Choice Perspective on Congressional Norms," *American Journal of Political Science* 23, 1979, 245–62.

Weingast, Barry R. and William Marshall, "The Industrial Organization of Congress; or, Why Legislatures, Like Firms, are not Organized as Markets," *Journal of Political Economy* 96, 1988, 132–63.

Weingast, Barry R. and Mark J. Moran, "Bureaucratic Discretion or Congressional Control? Regulatory Policymaking by the Federal Trade Commission," *Journal of Political Economy* 91, October 1983, 765–800.

Weingast, Barry R., Kenneth A. Shepsle, and Christopher Johnsen, "The Political Economy of Benefits and Costs: A Neoclassical Approach to Distribution Politics," *Journal of Political Economy* 89, August 1981, 642–64.

Welch, William P., "The Economics of Campaign Funds," *Public Choice* 20, 1974, 83–97.

Welch, William P., "The Effectiveness of Expenditures in State Legislative Races," *American Politics Quarterly* 4, July 1976, 333–56.

Welch, William P., "The Allocation of Political Monies: Economic Interest Groups," *Public Choice* 35(1), 1980, 97–120.

Welch, William P., "Money and Votes: A Simultaneous Equation Model," *Public Choice* 36(2), 1981, 209–34.

Whiteley, Paul F., "The Political Economy of Economic Growth," *European Journal of Political Research* 11, June 1983, 197–213.

Wicksell, Knut, *A New Principle of Just Taxation*, Finanztheoretische Untersuchungen, Jena, 1896; reprinted in R. A. Musgrave and A. Peacock, 1967, 72–118.

Wilde, James A., "The Expenditure Effects of Grants-in-Aid Programs," *National Tax Journal* 21, 1968, 340–8.

Wilde, James A., "Grants-in-Aid: The Analytics of Design and Response," *National Tax Journal* 24, 1971, 143–56.

Williams, J., "The Political Manipulation of Macroeconomic Policy," *American Political Science Review* 84, 1990, 767–95.

Williamson, Oliver E., *The Economics of Discretionary Behavior*, Englewood Cliffs, NJ: Prentice-Hall, 1964.

Williamson, Oliver E., *Markets and Hierarchies: Analysis and Antitrust Implications*, New York: Free Press, 1975.

Williamson, Oliver E. and Thomas J. Sargent, "Social Choice: A Probabilistic Approach," *Economic Journal* 77, December 1967, 797–813.

Wilson, G. W. and J. M. Jadlow, "Competition, Profit Incentives and Technical Efficiency in the Provision of Nuclear Medicine Services," *Bell Journal of Economics* 13, Autumn 1982, 472–82.

Wilson, James Q., "The Moral Sense," *American Political Science Review* 87, March 1993, 1–11.

Wilson, Robert, "An Axiomatic Model of Logrolling," *American Economic Review* 59, June 1969, 331–41.

Wilson, Robert, "A Game-Theoretic Analysis of Social Choice," in B. Liebermann, ed., *Social Choice*, New York: Gordon and Breach, 1971a.

Wilson, Robert, "Stable Coalition Proposals in Majority-Rule Voting," *Journal of Economic Theory* 3, September 1971b, 254–71.

Wintrobe, Ronald, "The Tinpot and the Totalitarian: An Economic Theory of Dictatorship," *American Political Science Review* 84, 1990, 849–72.

Wintrobe, Ronald, "Modern Bureaucratic Theory," 1997, in D. C. Mueller, ed., 1997a, 429–54.

Wintrobe, Ronald, *The Political Economy of Dictatorship*, Cambridge: Cambridge University Press, 1998.

Wise, Sherry Jo and Todd Sandler, "Rent Seeking and Pesticide Legislation," *Public Choice* 78, March 1994, 329–50.

Wittman, Donald A., "Parties as Utility Maximizers," *American Political Science Review* 67, June 1973, 490–8.

Wittman, Donald A., "Candidates with Policy Preferences: A Dynamic Model," *Journal of Economic Theory* 14, February 1977, 180–9.

Wittman, Donald A., "Multi-Candidate Equilibria," *Public Choice* 43(3), 1984, 287–91.

Wittman, Donald, *The Myth of Democratic Failure: Why Political Institutions are Efficient*, Chicago: University of Chicago Press, 1995.

Wolf, Charles, Jr., *Markets or Governments: Choosing between Imperfect Alternatives*, Cambridge, MA: MIT Press, 1988.

Worthington, Andrew C. and Brian E. Dellery, "Fiscal Illusion and the Australian Local Government Grants Process: How Sticky is the Flypaper Effect," *Public Choice* 99, April 1999, 1–13.

Wrede, Matthias, "Tragedy of the Fiscal Common? Fiscal Stock Externalities in a Leviathan Model of Federalism," *Public Choice* 101, December 1999, 177–93.

Wright, John R., "Contributions, Lobbying, and Committee Voting in the U.S. House of Representatives," *American Political Science Review* 84, June 1990, 417–38.

Wright, Matthew B., "Shirking and Political Support in the U.S. Senate, 1964–1984," *Public Choice* 76, June 1993, 103–23.

Wriglesworth, John L., *Libertarian Conflicts in Social Choice*, Cambridge: Cambridge University Press, 1985.

Wu, Wenbo and Otto A. Davis, "The Two Freedoms, Economic Growth and Development: An Empirical Study," *Public Choice* 100, July 1999, 39–64.

Wyckoff, Paul G., "A Bureaucratic Theory of Flypaper Effects," *Journal of Urban Economics* 23, 1988, 115–29.

Wyckoff, Paul G., "The Simple Analytics of Slack-Maximizing Bureaucracy," *Public Choice* 67, 1990, 35–47.

Wyckoff, Paul G., "The Elusive Flypaper Effect," *Journal of Urban Economics* 30, 1991, 310–28.

Yoo, Keum-Rok, "Intervention Analysis of Electoral Tax Cycle: The Case of Japan," *Public Choice* 96, September 1998, 241–58.

Young, H. Peyton, "An Axiomatization of Borda's Rule," *Journal of Economic Theory* 9, September 1974, 43–52.

Young, H. Peyton, "Condorcet's Theory of Voting," *American Political Science Review* 82, 1988, 1231–44.

Young, H. Peyton, "The Evolution of Conventions," *Econometrica* 61, January 1993, 57–84.

Young, H. Peyton, "Group Choice and Individual Judgments," 1997, in D. C. Mueller, ed., 1997a, 181–201.

Zardkoohi, Asghar, "On the Political Participation of the Firm in the Election Process," *Southern Economic Journal* 51, January 1985, 804–17.

Zax, Jeffrey S., "Initiatives and Government Expenditures," *Public Choice* 63, December 1989, 267–77.

Zupan, Mark A., "The Last Period Problem in Politics: Do Congressional Representatives Not Subject to Reelection Constraint Alter Their Voting Behavior," *Public Choice* 65, May 1990, 167–80.

Name index

Subject index